Labour & Employment Law in the Federal Public Service

SECOND EDITION

Labour & Employment Law in the Federal Public Service

SECOND EDITION

Christopher Rootham

IRWIN LAW

Labour and Employment Law in the Federal Public Service, second edition

Published in 2024 by
Irwin Law Inc
Suite 206, 14 Duncan Street
Toronto, Ontario
M5H 3G8
www.irwinlaw.com

ISBN 978-1-55221-711-5 (print) | 978-1-55221-712-2 (PDF)

Library and Archives Canada Cataloguing in Publication

Title: Labour & employment law in the federal public service / Christopher Rootham.
Other titles: Labour and employment law in the federal public service
Names: Rootham, Christopher, author.
Description: Second edition. | Previously published under title: Labour and employment law in the federal public service. | Includes bibliographical references and index.
Identifiers: Canadiana (print) 20230570917 | Canadiana (ebook) 20230570941 | ISBN 9781552217115 (softcover) | ISBN 9781552217122 (PDF)
Subjects: LCSH: Civil service—Canada. | LCSH: Labor laws and legislation—Canada.
Classification: LCC KE3240.F4 R66 2023 | LCC KF5365 .R66 2023 kfmod | DDC 342.71/068—dc23

Canada ONTARIO CREATES | ONTARIO CRÉATIF

Printed and bound by CPI Group (UK) Ltd, Croydon, CR0 4YY

1 2 3 4 5 28 27 26 25 24

For my family, whom I tell that this book is a murder mystery. My children are now old enough that they no longer believe me.

Summary Table of Contents

Detailed Table of Contents

CHAPTER FIVE

CHAPTER SIX

Collective Bargaining in the Federal Public Service 220

PART I

OVERVIEW

CHAPTER ONE

Introduction

A. INTRODUCTION

> The terms and conditions of employment of the federal government's quarter of a million current workers are set out in statutes, collective agreements, Treasury Board directives, regulations, ministerial orders, and other documents that consume bookshelves of looseleaf binders. Human resources personnel are recruited into the system, spend a career attempting to understand it and die out of it.[1]

With that somewhat macabre description, the Supreme Court of Canada introduced the topic of this book, *Labour and Employment Law in the Federal Public Service*. The title itself is anomalous because it refers to both "labour" and "employment" law. In the Canadian taxonomy of industrial relations, "labour" law refers to the laws that govern employees who are represented by trade unions and whose relationship with employers is consequently governed by collective agreements; "employment" law refers to the laws that govern employees who are not represented by trade unions and therefore have an individual, contractual relationship with their employer. Canadian textbooks typically address one topic or the other; those rare texts that address both topics still divide the work world into unionized and non-unionized workplaces.[2] "Employment" law is simply not relevant for unionized

1 *Vaughan v Canada*, 2005 SCC 11 at para 1, Binnie J.

2 Such as Labour Law Casebook Group, *Labour and Employment Law: Cases, Materials and Commentary*, 9th ed (Toronto: Irwin Law, 2018).

employees because they no longer have an individual relationship with their employer: the individual relationship has become subsumed by the collective relationship between their trade union and their employer.[3]

In the federal public service, however, labour and employment law remains relevant to all employees. Employees represented by a bargaining agent still have many of their terms and conditions of employment determined otherwise than by collective bargaining, and they have the right to pursue certain rights and recourses without their union's consent. Employees who are not represented by a bargaining agent must refer certain disputes to a grievance procedure and (in some cases) to determination by an independent third-party decision-maker—in other words, they are required to use a system of recourse that mirrors the arbitration system that is typically limited to unionized employees. Therefore, any book concerning the federal public service inevitably deals with some aspects of topics usually considered to be within the separate spheres of labour law and employment law.

The very title of this book, and the necessity of writing a book about the federal public service, speaks to one of the three theses of this book: exceptionalism. Federal public service labour and employment law is exceptional in that there are a number of significant differences between labour and employment law governing the federal public service and labour and employment law in other jurisdictions (whether the federally regulated private sector, provincial public services, or the provincially regulated private sector). This introduction will explain the three theses of this book. First, that federal public service labour and employment law is about the waxing and waning of two concepts: the merit principle and free collective bargaining. Second, that federal public service and employment law is "exceptional," and not always in a positive way. Third, that the role played by the judiciary and the concept of the "rule of law" should be more important in federal public service labour and employment law than in labour and employment law in the private sector. Before setting out these three theses in turn, this book will first explore the nature and characteristics of the federal public service.

3 *Isidore Garon ltée v Tremblay; Fillion et Frères (1976) inc v Syndicat national des employés de garage du Québec inc*, 2006 SCC 2 at para 13. Some statutory protections for individual employees remain in place, where those statutory provisions are capable of being incorporated into a collective agreement.

This book is not about basic concepts in labour or employment law. Rather, this book is about labour and employment law concepts as they apply to the federal public service. Some of those concepts are similar to those in the private sector or in other public sector legal regimes. In fact, many of the issues in this book are similar to the issues faced in other jurisdictions. Where that is the case, the law from other jurisdictions is noted and discussed, but not in detail. In most cases, this book focuses on the labour and employment law that applies to the federal public service. This book also does not contain a complete list of every judicial or administrative decision governing public service labour and employment law. Rather, it is meant to provide the leading cases and, where appropriate, a representative sample of decisions to explain or provide examples of particular points.

Finally, this book is about employment and labour law governing certain portions of the public sector. Specifically, it is about the employment and labour law governing most direct employees of government or government agencies. Some direct employees of government are not included in this book, particularly members of the Canadian armed forces, judges, and employees of Crown corporations.[4] This book instead describes the labour and employment law of direct employees of the government, employees of government agencies, members of the RCMP, and employees of Parliament. The scope of this book, as well as the scope of the various statutory regimes discussed in this book, is set out in Figure 1.

4 For a thorough treatment of the law governing judges, see K. Lysyk, L. Sossin & J. Hoskins, *Barristers & Solicitors in Practice* (Markham, ON: LexisNexis Canada, 2006) (loose-leaf), ch 11. The terms and conditions for armed forces personnel are found in *The King's Regulations and Orders for the Canadian Forces*. Employees of Crown corporations (except for those executives appointed by order in council) are covered by the *Canada Labour Code*, RSC 1985, c L-2.

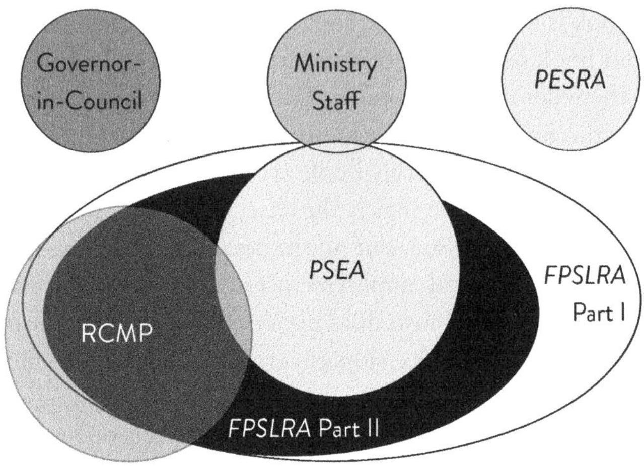

FIGURE 1.1. INTERACTION BETWEEN STATUTORY REGIMES AND CATEGORIES OF EMPLOYEES

Part I of this book provides an overview of federal public service labour and employment law. The remainder of this chapter discusses the various principles and themes animating federal public service labour and employment law, as well as the basic theses of this book. Chapter 2 is a short review of the history and evolution of labour and employment law as it relates to federal public servants. The historical evolution of federal public servants is canvassed from the time of the Stuart dynasty in England to the date of publication, with a particular emphasis on tracing the legal status of public servants, the merit principle, and "free" collective bargaining.

Part II of this book considers the normal "labour law" topics as they apply to direct employees of the government and employees of government agencies. Essentially, Part II of this book is about Part I of the *Federal Public Sector Labour Relations Act* (*FPSLRA*). Chapter 3 deals with the scope of labour law in the federal public service, with particular emphasis on the statutory and common law exclusions from the *FPSLRA*. The chapter also describes the process for becoming a "public servant." Chapter 4 examines the nature, functions, and jurisdiction of the Federal Public Sector Labour Relations and Employment Board. This chapter includes a description of the remedial jurisdiction of the Board, as well as its mandate to encourage mediation. Chapter 5 describes the process for certifying employee organizations as bargaining agents representing employees of the federal public service. This chapter includes the rules for initial certifications, successor applications, decertification, and the unique rules concerning the appropriate bargaining unit in the federal public service. Chapter 6 concerns industrial disputes—namely, the legal rules in place during the collective bargaining process. These rules include the obligation to bargain in good faith with a view to entering into a collective agreement, the scope of permitted bargaining in the federal public service, the conciliation process, strikes in the federal public service (including requirements and elements of essential services agreements), and the rules concerning binding interest arbitration for those bargaining agents who choose that process for dispute resolution. Chapter 7 deals with unfair labour practice complaints. This chapter deals with the unique procedural rules for unfair labour practice complaints in the federal public service, as well as the substantive law of statutory freezes and the other rights protected by the *FPSLRA*. Chapter 8 reviews the bargaining agents in the federal public service. It includes a brief history of the largest public service bargaining agents (the Public Service Alliance of Canada and the Professional Institute of the Public Service of Canada) and the two most significant legal rules governing bargaining agents: the duty of fair representation and the unfair labour practices committed by bargaining agents.

Part III of this book concerns the terms and conditions of employment for both unionized and non-unionized employees—essentially, Part II of the *FPSLRA*. Chapter 9 is a discussion of the terms and conditions of employment common to most or all federal public servants. This chapter includes a brief discussion of the terms and conditions of employment governing non-unionized employees (including Governor-in-Council appointees). It then moves on to consider the special duties of public servants (including political neutrality and conflict-of-interest guidelines), the terms and conditions as they relate to pay, the most common National Joint Council Directives, the importance of bilingualism in the federal public service, and other special terms and conditions for federal public servants. Chapter 10 describes the process for the resolution of rights disputes in the federal public service—in particular, the grievance and adjudication system in the federal public service. Both unionized and non-unionized employees (including managers) are entitled, and even obligated, to grieve their employment-related disputes.

Part IV of this book involves the legal regulation of the employment relationship in the federal public service—namely, the process for appointment to and within the federal public service. Again, these rules apply to both unionized and non-unionized employees (including managers). There are different rules and statutory regimes for direct employees of the federal government and for employees of those separate agencies whose constituting statutes give them the power to make appointments. Chapter 11 examines the *Public Service Employment Act* (*PSEA*), the statute governing appointments to and within the federal public service. It focuses on the evolution of the merit principle, as well as a consideration of the various statutory priorities for appointment to and within the federal public service. Chapter 12 then concludes this section of the book with a discussion of the classification of positions within the federal public service.

Part V of this book considers two groups of employees who have a different relationship to the Crown than other public servants: Chapter 13 discusses the legal regulation of RCMP members, and Chapter 14 focuses on parliamentary employees and the *Parliamentary Employment and Staff Relations Act* (*PESRA*).

Finally, Part VI of this book considers the role that courts play in the regulation of federal public service labour and employment law.

B. THE NATURE AND CHARACTERISTICS OF THE FEDERAL PUBLIC SERVICE

> [Public servants are the] guardians of a public trust underlying the exercise of all public authority.[5]

The Canadian Constitution is based on a separation of powers between the executive, legislative, and judicial branches of government. The executive branch[6] of government determines the policy of the Government of Canada, Parliament has the authority to enact legislation to implement that policy, and the judiciary ensures that the executive branch acts within the limits set by Parliament and that Parliament acts within the limits set by the Constitution. In Canada, the executive branch has (relative to the legislative branch) more power than in some other countries

5 Lorne Sossin, "Speaking Truth to Power? The Search for Bureaucratic Independence in Canada" (2005) 55 UTLJ 1 at 2.

6 Under the *Constitution Act, 1867* (UK), 30 & 31 Victoria, c 3, ss 11–12, the executive branch of government is composed of the King's Privy Council for Canada and the governor general. In practice, the executive branch in Canada is composed of the prime minister of Canada and the ministers responsible for the various departments and agencies of the federal government.

with constitutions based on a separation of powers, such as the United States. In part this is because the executive and legislative branches are fused (the prime minister and ministers sit in Parliament and so are members of both the legislative and executive branches) and in part because of the historical evolution of the royal prerogative:

> The royal prerogative derived from the ancient principle of the Queen-in-Parliament as sovereign helps to explain the remarkably broad de facto powers of Canadian executives, not only at the federal level but also in . . . several provinces. These powers contributed substantially to the development of the modern Canadian state, and their presence at both the federal and provincial levels contributed no less substantially to the endless tensions between these two levels, which have dominated Canadian politics since Confederation.[7]

The Supreme Court of Canada considers the public service to be part of the executive branch of government.[8] However, a more nuanced view of the public service is to treat it as subordinate to all three branches of government. The public service is *directly* subordinate to the executive branch in that ministers give the orders (or, more accurately, give direction to the public service) and public servants obey those orders. However, the public service is *indirectly* subordinate to the legislative and judicial branches: public servants must obey the laws and fulfill the duties set out by Parliament, and they must also follow the orders given to them by judges.[9] Lorne Sossin has also advocated for considering

7 John Rohr, *Civil Servants and Their Constitutions* (Lawrence, KS: University Press of Kansas, 2002) at 52.

8 *Fraser v Canada (Public Service Staff Relations Board)*, [1985] 2 SCR 455 at para 40. See also Benedict Sheehy & Donald Feaver, "Re-thinking Executive Control of and Accountability for the Agency" (2016) 54:1 Osgoode Hall LJ 175 at 193: "[Public sector] [a]gencies can be connected to any of the three branches of government, but are, for the most part, bodies of the executive branch."

9 See, for example, John Rohr, *Public Service, Ethics, & Constitutional Practice* (Lawrence, KS: University Press of Kansas, 1998). The public service may also be directly subordinate to Parliament through parliamentary oversight. The Public Service Commission, since 31 December 2005, reports directly to Parliament: *Public Service Employment Act*, SC 2003, c 22, s 23. The preamble to the *Public Service Employment Act* also states that the Public Service Commission should be accountable to Parliament, stating: "[T]hose to whom this appointment authority is delegated must exercise it within a framework that ensures that they are accountable for its proper use to the Commission, which in turn is accountable to Parliament."

the public service as a distinct constitutional entity, although he is not clear whether the public service should be considered a fourth arm of government distinct from the executive.[10] Other authors have also suggested that government officials (i.e., public servants) should be treated as a distinct constitutional branch of government.[11]

The public service is required to fulfill government policy by following the lawful orders of the executive branch and fulfilling the requirements set out for them by Parliament. The public service is also bound by a number of rules and guidelines concerning its role, some of which have developed to the point of becoming constitutional conventions. This portion of the introduction deals with the role of the public service in our constitutional scheme.

The first question that needs to be addressed is what is meant by the "public service" for constitutional purposes. There are two approaches to defining the public service: a "positivist" and a "classification" approach. The positivist approach involves defining public servants by listing a number of different government departments or agencies and decreeing that the employees working for those departments or agencies are the "public service." The classification approach examines the particular function of employees of the Crown to determine whether or not they should be considered part of the public service.

The federal statutes governing labour and employment law adopt a positivist approach to defining a public servant: they list a number of departments and agencies and decree that employees of those departments and agencies are employees of the public service.[12] However, for the purpose of identifying public servants bound by (or covered by) the various constitutional conventions and other rules setting out their constitutional role, Canadian courts have adopted the classification approach.[13] Sossin has advocated a definition of "public service" for constitutional purposes as follows:

---

10 Sossin, above note 5. See also his report to the Gomery Commission: *Defining Boundaries: The Constitutional Argument for Bureaucratic Independence and Its Implication for the Accountability of the Public Service* (2006), online (pdf): https://publications.gc.ca/collections/Collection/GomeryII/ResearchStudies2/CISPAA_Vol2_2.pdf.

11 See, for example, Janet McLean, "Between Sovereign and Subject: The Constitutional Position of the Official" (2020) 70 UTLJ 167.

12 See Chapter 3.

13 See *Osborne v Canada (Treasury Board)*, [1991] 2 SCR 69, where Sopinka J concluded that a complete ban on political activity by the federal public service

> The definition of a civil servant, in my view, ought to capture whosoever by reason of their discretionary or decision-making authority has a duty to discharge a public trust through conduct or action that political interference might undermine. In other words, a "civil servant" is an official of the Crown who must remain, to some degree and for some purposes, independent of the government of the day.[14]

This particular definition does not limit the public service (for constitutional purposes) to the most senior ranks (i.e., deputy ministers and assistant deputy ministers). Public servants at a "lower" level also make discretionary decisions that are of critical importance to citizens and therefore are part of the "public service" for constitutional purposes. As Kenneth Kernaghan put it:

> The exercise of discretionary powers is also pervasive in that these powers are dispersed to various levels of the hierarchy. Both the scope and importance of discretionary power increase, however, as one moves up the administrative pyramid into the upper echelons of the bureaucracy. It is therefore, among senior public servants that value problems and priorities are most crucial for the determination of public policy and the state of administrative responsibility. It is important, however, not to overestimate the value problems of the most senior bureaucrats and thereby to minimize the substantial, sometimes critical, significance of value choices made by professional, technical, and administrative personnel at lower levels of the hierarchy. The failure of such officials to act responsibly, particularly by making decisions that are efficient, effective, and responsive, may seriously jeopardize policies and programs determined at the top executive levels of the organization.[15]

---

was unconstitutional in part because the ban was overbroad. He stated that the objective of political neutrality in the public service did not require a ban on political activity by "all public servants" and that the legislation should have considered differentiating between public servants at different "levels."

14 Sossin, above note 5 at 18–19. Sossin refers to his definition as a third "purposive" definition and distinguishes it from the "classification" method of definition. However, his "purposive" method is so similar to the "classification" method that I doubt he has really created a third definition; he has just refined the classification approach.

15 Kenneth Kernaghan, "Power, Politics, and Bureaucracy" in R.S. Blair & J.T. McLeod, eds, *The Canadian Political Tradition: Basic Readings*, 2d ed (Scarborough, ON: Nelson Canada, 1993) at 454–55.

Using that definition of a public servant, what is the constitutional role of the public service? The Supreme Court of Canada has accepted that there is a constitutional convention of a non-partisan (or neutral) public service. The content of that convention, which also sets out nicely the role of the public service, is as follows:

> 1. Politics and policy are separated from administration; thus politicians make policy decisions and public servants execute those decisions.
> 2. Public servants are appointed and promoted on the basis of merit rather than of party affiliation or contributions.
> 3. Public servants do not engage in partisan political activities.
> 4. Public servants do not express publicly their personal views on government policies or administration.
> 5. Public servants provide forthright and objective advice to their political masters in private and in confidence; in return, political executives protect the anonymity of public servants by publicly accepting responsibility for departmental decisions.
> 6. Public servants execute policy decisions loyally, irrespective of the philosophy and programs of the party in power and regardless of their personal opinions; as a result, public servants enjoy security of tenure during good behaviour and satisfactory performance.[16]

Most of those provisions can be easily understood, and some of them—including appointment on the basis of merit, engaging in partisan political activities, and public criticism of the government—are dealt with in detail both in this chapter and throughout this book. However, the protection of the anonymity of public servants is not discussed elsewhere in this book, largely because it has fallen out of favour as an element of this constitutional convention. As two commentators put it:

> A fifth expectation—that [public servants] should remain anonymous—has been effectively abandoned in recent years. The expectation was not so much as to their conduct as that their anonymity would be preserved (by ministers) lest their ability to work for another

---

16 Sossin, above note 5 at 6–7. See also Ontario Law Reform Commission, *Report on Political Activity, Public Comment and Disclosure by Crown Employees* (Toronto: Ministry of the Attorney General, 1986) at 13–25, and Kenneth Kernaghan, "East Block and Westminster" in *The Handbook of Canadian Public Administration*, 3d ed (Toronto: Oxford University Press, 2018) at 99–100.

> government be impaired by reason of their identification with a particular policy or advice. The tradition of anonymity has been substantially eroded in recent years, however, without the fears expressed materializing.[17]

Donald Savoie has expressed the six elements of this constitutional convention as a "bargain" between federal public servants and their political masters:

> In the absence of formal rules, politicians and public servants some time ago struck a "bargain" or an understanding over their respective duties to guide mutual relations. This traditional bargain has over the years helped shape how power is distributed and controlled in modern society. Under the arrangement, public servants exchanged overt partisanship, some political rights, and a public profile in return for permanent careers, or at least indefinite tenure, anonymity, selection by merit, a regular work week, and the promise of being looked after at the end of a career that did not require paying close attention to their own material self-interest.[18]

Finally, before leaving the topic of the nature and characteristics of the public service, I would be remiss if I did not mention the stereotype of a public servant: a person who is process driven and punctilious to a fault. This stereotype has existed for as long as there has been a public service. Robert Dawson enumerated three characteristics of public servants back in 1929, or what he referred to as three "bureaucratic sins which appear with monotonous regularity in any large group of public officials":

- love of red tape ("each civil servant becomes so engrossed in his little job that he forgets he is only a small part of the whole");
- indifference and insolence toward the general public (intolerance of interference and criticism and a loss of contact with the "facts of life"); and
- lack of incentive.[19]

---

17 Terence Daintith & Alan Page, *The Executive in the Constitution* (Toronto: Oxford University Press, 1999) at 86–87.

18 Donald Savoie, *Breaking the Bargain: Public Servants, Ministers and Parliament* (Toronto: University of Toronto Press, 2003) at 5–6.

19 Robert MacGregor Dawson, *The Civil Service of Canada* (London: Oxford University Press, 1929) at 111–12.

While these sorts of considerations are not strictly relevant in a legal text, where the exceptionalism of public service labour and employment law is not explicitly explained, these stereotypes may be an unstated source of legislative intent behind that exceptionalism.

C. THE TWO THEMES OF PUBLIC SERVICE LABOUR AND EMPLOYMENT LAW: MERIT AND FREE COLLECTIVE BARGAINING

One of the central theses of this book is that the evolution of public service labour and employment law is largely about two themes: the development of the merit principle and access to free collective bargaining.

1) The Principle of Appointment According to Merit

As explained in Chapter 2 of this book, the principle of appointment to the public service according to merit has not always been considered the most appropriate principle for hiring civil servants. Political patronage was rampant in public service appointments in the nineteenth and early twentieth centuries.[20] This was not a by-product of an immature political system or reflective of some sort of "Dark Ages": it was by design. The Jacksonian[21] idea of public service appointment was a rotation system: Jackson believed that government duties could be so plain and simple that they should rotate between applicants. The rotation system evolved into a "spoils system," where the incoming political party would replace incumbent public servants with people who were more closely identified with the winning side. Even the "spoils system" was justified on theoretical grounds: it was a more democratic way of selecting public officials and ensured that the will of the people, instead of the rule of an unelected elite, was paramount.

Eventually, a second view took hold—that of the "science" of administration and the paramountcy of appointing public servants

---

20 Robert A. Vaison, "Collective Bargaining in the Federal Public Service: The Achievement of a Milestone in Personal Relations" in Barbara Carroll, David Siegel & Mark Sproule-Jones, eds, *Classic Readings in Canadian Public Administration* (Toronto: Oxford University Press, 2005) at 197.

21 Named for Andrew Jackson, president of the United States of America from 1828 to 1836.

according to merit. John Rohr explained this evolution in thinking (at least in the United States) as follows:

> The architects of the contemporary American bureaucracy were the civil service reformers of a century ago. Then, the Jacksonian principle of "rotation of office" had degenerated into a "spoils system," and public administration was all too "sensitive" to the political process. The need for reform was apparent, but a major obstacle was the theoretical argument that the spoils system, despite its abuses, was a more democratic way of selecting public officials. The merit system with its "good government" overtones was, nevertheless, an invitation to government by a ruling class.
>
> The reformers response to this argument was to structure a theory of a "science" of administration. This theory rested on a sharp dichotomy between politics and administration. Its leading proponent was Woodrow Wilson, then a professor of political science. . . . Wilson argued that administration was a science that could be learned by and entrusted to people who had the proper credentials and expertise. This dichotomy provided the theoretical justification for civil service reform. The people express their will through the electoral process; here, democracy reigns supreme. There can be no democratic administration, however, for the same reason that there can be no democratic chemistry. If public opinion enters the administrative process, it will only prove "meddlesome." Administrators must be freed from politics if they are to apply their politically neutral techniques to the problems involved in executing the policies determined by the people.[22]

Thus, there emerged a school of thought demanding that appointment to the public service be made on the basis of merit. Merit was also defined as appointing the best candidate for the job, as determined using objective criteria. Dawson put it this way:

> The problem of creating a good civil service may be stated in very simple terms: it is to secure the best possible men, to retain them, and to give them every encouragement to use their ability to advantage. All questions of selection, tenure, personnel, management, &c, must be determined by the manner in which they help or hinder the attainment of such ends. On this there is general agreement. . . .

---

22 Rohr, *Public Service, Ethics, & Constitutional Practice*, above note 9 at 4.

> Merit is secured by allowing any one to enter the contest (which is widely advertised) and by giving the prize to the victor.[23]

This justification of appointment according to merit has been criticized. First, appointment according to merit was based on the idea of a "science" of administration that should be immune from politics. This idea appears naïve today. Public servants have considerable discretionary powers that, in many cases, fall closer to "political" decisions than purely "administrative" decisions. When a public servant decides to fast-track an application for a work permit for foreign workers, for example, is that purely an administrative decision, or is it also a political decision? As Rohr put it:

> Their argument was that a civil service based on examination and merit rather than politics was not undemocratic because the civil service dealt with the "science" of administration, which was quite distinct from politics. Empirical evidence of the broad discretionary powers enjoyed by bureaucrats has demonstrated the inadequacy of the reformers' argument, but it leaves unsolved the problem they addressed—How can a democractic regime justify substantial political power in the hands of people who are exempt by law from the discipline of the ballot box?[24]

The requirement of appointment according to merit can be criticized as leading to a rules-oriented appointment system whose costs outweighed the benefits.[25] Do the administrative efficiencies of hiring the best-possible data entry clerk outweigh the costs of running a competitive examination with hundreds of candidates just to find that "best" data entry clerk?

Finally, Savoie has stated that appointment according to merit is part of the "bargain" between public servants and their political masters, with the merit principle being a benefit for public servants.[26] With respect, there is no particular reason why public servants would want appointment—particularly promotion—to be made according to

---

23 Dawson, above note 19 at 128–29.

24 Rohr, *Public Service, Ethics, & Constitutional Practice*, above note 9 at 6.

25 See, for example, Hon. Lucienne Robillard (President of the Treasury Board), testimony before the Standing Committee on Government Operations and Estimates, 27 February 2003, online: www.ourcommons.ca/DocumentViewer/en/37-2/OGGO/meeting-12/evidence, and the discussion in Chapter 11, below.

26 Savoie, above note 18 at 5–6.

merit. Instead, incumbent public servants have an interest in ensuring that *they* are promoted, not necessarily that the most meritorious candidate (who may be an outsider) is promoted or even appointed to the public service. As one author put it:

> [I]n theory, the aims of trade unions are clearly at variance with the professed rejection of any but merit considerations in employment. Trade unions do strive to promote the interests of their members, by way of attempts to facilitate their promotion in preference to outsiders, and through their attempts to gain a recognition for a union shop or closed shop, wherever possible....
>
> Once well entrenched, however, the union becomes interested, in turn, in the protection of its membership from outside competition, as well as in the betterment of their conditions. Two related aims will emerge: the imposition of restrictions on municipal hiring (closed shop, or a degree of union security) and the desire to gain participation in management functions. At this point a clash with the management side may occur.[27]

Savoie does not explain why public servants would want the merit principle as part of any bargain.[28]

I propose a different justification for a legislated merit principle: it is a replacement for the profit motive in private industry. Private employers are not obligated by law (and are rarely obligated by collective agreement) to hire the best or most qualified candidate for a position. If a private employer wants to hire the daughter of a friend of its human resource director's babysitter, then there are no legal impediments to this decision. The impediment to this decision is the discipline of the market: an employer will be at a competitive disadvantage if it hires anybody but the best available candidate. However, government is not a profit-maximizing entity: it is a political outcome–maximizing entity. The goal of the elected members of the executive is to continue to be elected. If the government does not hire the best available candidate,

27 M.Z. Prives, *Unionism and the Merit System in Municipal Labour Relations in Canada* (Montreal: 1958) at 4, 55.

28 That federal public servants are strong defenders of the merit principle speaks either to a civic-mindedness that cannot be explained using the contractual model adopted by Savoie or that the merit principle has become so entrenched that public servants defend it just as they would defend any aspect of the status quo. It is also possible that non-monetary benefits of the merit principle (pride, or esprit de corps) also lead public servants to support the merit principle.

then a particular public service will not be performed as well or as efficiently as it should. There are some situations where the nature of the service (or the extreme incompetence of the provider of that service) means that the failure to provide that particular service efficiently or effectively may have a political outcome; it is also possible that the cumulative effect of poor government services may have a political outcome. However, the political consequences of poor public services are difficult to predict. There is little incentive for the government to adhere to the merit principle voluntarily.

Therefore, it is necessary to legislate some reason for the government to hire the best candidates for positions. Citizens, however, have an interest in seeing government programs implemented effectively and efficiently. Parliament—as the representatives of citizens (and taxpayers)—can protect that interest by legislating the merit principle. The legislated merit principle is not necessary to protect the integrity of the "science" of administration per se, but it is necessary to replace the role of the private market to ensure that effective and efficient workers are hired to perform public services. In short, private employers apply the merit principle to avoid being disciplined by the market and their shareholders; public employers are not subject to market discipline nor to effective or predictable citizen/voter discipline. Therefore, the merit principle must be legislated as a replacement for market discipline.

In addition to criticisms of the existence of the merit principle, the definition of merit as the best-qualified candidate has also been criticized. The first criticism is this: qualified according to what criteria? In 1929, Dawson criticized the reliance on public service examinations that tested job-specific skills rather than more general skills that reflected the subjects being taught at universities. He was concerned that subject-specific examinations meant that "there is no deliberate effort to ascertain what the candidates are capable of doing in the future."[29] Another author studied unions' approaches to the merit principle in municipal governments in 1958 and concluded the following:

> The unions usually dispute the interpretation of the term "merit" which is used by management. While the latter see in the criterion a means of selection to be applied to the problem of finding the best suited candidate for the job or position, in relative disregard of personalities and in relative preoccupation with a theoretically detached,

29 Dawson, above note 19 at 140.

absolute "position," the unions take the opposite stand. Being interested in service to their members, they maintain two points:

a) disregard for seniority in pursuit of a theoretical advantage of a quest for the top candidate is self-defeating, for it jeopardizes the morale of the whole body of employees.
b) This quest for the top candidate is unrealistic, since the incentives offered, and foremost among them the pay are all predicated on the job, not on the caliber of its incumbent. Since management is not prepared to pay more for the services of the superior candidate, it has virtually declared that all it is interested in is a candidate who would be qualified to carry into execution the duties of the office in accordance with a fixed standard. Consequently there is no justification in refusing to appoint to the office the most meritorious—that is the most experienced and most senior—aspirant to the position if he is equal to the task. Any additional qualifications should be recognized as redundant and irrelevant. Thus the term merit acquires different meanings. In the sense used by management it means the highest qualifications among those displayed by the aspirants, while the unions ascribe to it a meaning of the most valid claim held among those who could qualify for the performance of the tasks involved.[30]

These ideas could be restated as follows. First, to what extent should "soft" people skills (such as the ability to get along with others) determine the most meritorious candidate? Second, should the morale of other employees be a relevant consideration in determining the qualifications of a candidate? Third, does the merit principle truly require the "best" candidate, or will a candidate who is "basically qualified" suffice? Fourth, should the merit principle be concerned with who the best candidate is today or who would be the best public service employee in several years' time?

The merit principle in the federal public service has evolved to reflect some of these concerns. For example, the morale of other employees used to be protected through a presumption that promotions would be made from within the federal public service instead of by hiring external candidates. The current legislation has removed that presumption. However, the current legislation has placed more emphasis on the future needs of the public service and has replaced the judicially

30 Prives, above note 27 at 55–56.

imposed requirement of the "best" candidate with a statutory definition of "merit" that accepts a basically qualified candidate in preference to the candidate who scores highest on a competitive examination.[31]

One of the theses of this book is that a legislated merit principle is a necessary replacement to the market forces that compel private sector employers to hire the best available candidate. Thus, I am suspicious of the decision to decrease the effectiveness of the merit principle by replacing the requirement to hire the best candidate with a candidate who is basically qualified. By watering down the merit principle, the federal government has made it more likely that appointments will be made on the basis of bureaucratic—and perhaps even political—patronage. If managers (up to and including a minister) are free to promote their personal favourites, this will lead to an emphasis on the value of cooperating with management instead of the value of critical discourse. The best public servants are often those people who are the least compliant by nature, and the merit principle needs to be strong enough to ensure the preservation of critical discourse within the federal public service.

The merit principle can also fit uncomfortably with broader goals of employment equity or ensuring a diverse public service with fair access to public service positions by members of equity-seeking groups. An assessment of the "best" candidate may simply be a reflection of the assessor's background and life experiences. Often "merit" and "diversity" have been treated as separate goals or, as one paper puts it, "[m]erit-based practices and diversity management have been developed through different historical contexts with distinct managerial emphases."[32] On the other hand, the Public Service Commission has stated that the idea that employment equity did not equate to merit is a "misconception,"[33] and the Organisation for Economic Co-operation and Development (OECD) has also concluded that the merit principle is a necessary requirement to ensure a diverse workplace, stating that "diversity cannot be achieved without first dealing with discrimination, and enhancing equality in

---

31 See Chapter 11 for a discussion of these changes to the *Public Service Employment Act*.

32 Sanghee Park & Jiaqi Liang, "Merit, Diversity, and Performance: Does Diversity Management Moderate the Effect of Merit Principles on Government Performance?" (2020) 49:1 Pub Personnel Mgmt 83 at 83.

33 Public Service Commission, "History of Employment Equity in the Public Service and the Public Service Commission of Canada" (October 2011) at 32, online (pdf): https://publications.gc.ca/collections/collection_2012/cfp-psc/SC3-159-2011-eng.pdf.

public employment, where merit should prevail."[34] The current legislative framework has not fully resolved whether employment equity is integrated within the merit principle or, conversely, is a separate policy goal pursued through different legal mechanisms.

2) The Principle of Free Collective Bargaining

Until 1967, free collective bargaining was foreign to the federal public service. When Parliament enacted the *Public Service Staff Relations Act*[35] in 1967, this Act opened the possibility of free collective bargaining in the federal public service. I use the word "possibility" because although the Act required free collective bargaining between the federal government and certified bargaining agents, the federal government always reserved the right to pass new (even temporary) legislation taking away the right to engage in free collective bargaining. The federal government has exercised this authority on a number of occasions: from 1975–78, 1982–83, 1991–97, and, to some extent, 2008–11, when the federal government suspended free collective bargaining and instead determined the terms and conditions of employment for unionized employees by legislation. In the private sector, free collective bargaining takes place in the shadow of the possibility of strike or lockout activity. However, in the federal public service, collective bargaining takes place in the shadow of legislative action: if the employer does not agree with a union's proposal, eventually it can just legislate its own point of view. This has had a chilling effect on free collective bargaining, as explained as follows:

> The findings from our various data sources suggest that in the first 10 to 15 years of public service collective bargaining, participants were generally positive about it. However, with the passage of time and an increase in the extent of unilateral government interventions such as pay freezes and the suspension of bargaining and arbitration, the parties have become more pessimistic about the bargaining system's ability to resolve problems. The lack of trust associated with long periods of unilateral government action was probably the single most serious concern of union and management representatives alike.
>
> . . .

34 OECD, "Fostering Diversity in the Public Service" (2009), online (pdf): www.oecd.org/gov/pem/paper-fostering-diversity-public-service.pdf.

35 *Public Service Staff Relations Act*, SC 1967, c 72.

> The concern most frequently cited—by both sides—is the degree of power the government possesses in its dual role as employer and legislator. This power, which is more than any private sector employer possesses, has been used on many occasions and has taken such varied forms as the suspension of bargaining and arbitration, pay freezes, and the passing of back-to-work legislation.[36]

Furthermore, collective bargaining—even when it is permitted to occur—does not permit bargaining on the same breadth of subjects as in the private sector. Seniority rights, pensions, and other subjects commonly bargained between employers and employees are not permitted in the federal public service.

Another central thesis of this book is that free collective bargaining is a fundamental right.[37] Therefore, this book examines the limitations on that right carefully and is critical of the federal government when the limitations on that right are not justified.

D. THE CASE FOR AND AGAINST EXCEPTIONALISM

As mentioned above, one of the themes of this book is the "exceptionalism" of federal public service labour and employment law. The laws governing federal public servants are different from those governing employees in the federally regulated private sector and are also different from the laws governing other public sector employees in many Canadian jurisdictions. At a fundamental level, federal public service labour law is substantially similar to labour law governing the private sector. Both public and private sector laws adopt the Wagner Act model of industrial relations: trade unions are certified by a tribunal to represent a defined group of employees, employers and trade unions are obligated to bargain in good faith with one other with a view to entering into a collective agreement, and disputes during the currency of a collective agreement must be dealt with by way of third-party arbitration instead of strike action. However, there are several differences between public sector and private sector laws. The most significant differences include the following:

---

36 First report of the Advisory Committee on Labour Management Relations in the Federal Public Service, *Identifying the Issues* (May 2000), online: www.tbs-sct.canada.ca/report/fryer/iti-ide01-eng.asp at 41–42 [Preliminary Fryer Report].

37 The Supreme Court of Canada has recognized it as such in *Health Services and Support—Facilities Subsector Bargaining Assn v British Columbia*, 2007 SCC 27.

- There is a reduced scope of topics that may be collectively bargained.
- Bargaining agents have the choice between resolving bargaining disputes by strike or binding arbitration.
- Employees do not always have the right to resolution of rights disputes by way of binding, third-party arbitration.
- Non-unionized employees have access to rights arbitration.
- A significant number of employees may not join trade unions or engage in collective bargaining (including a significant number of "managers" and all members of the RCMP).

The rest of this book describes these and other "exceptional" characteristics of federal public service labour and employment law. This chapter addresses the question: why should public service labour and employment law be "exceptional"? I will address various explanations for exceptionalism in turn and explain the extent to which they truly explain why exceptionalism is necessary in Canada.

First, the most common explanation for "exceptionalism" is the government's need to protect the public interest. As Jacob Finkelman and Shirley Goldenberg put it:

> It seems to have been widely accepted that certain fundamental differences between the private and public employer, in particular the public employer's overriding responsibility for the public interest, would have to be taken into account when granting bargaining rights to government employees.[38]

This concern for the public interest is usually expressed in terms of preventing strikes in essential services. The final Fryer Report makes that link clear:

> This is so because the public sector is in some ways qualitatively different from the private sector. Public service strikes can greatly inconvenience the public without imposing economic loss on the employer. The public interest must be protected and unique public-service-oriented legislation is the best way to achieve that end. The legislation must establish dispute resolution systems that preserve the rights of the

38 Jacob Finkelman & Shirley Goldenberg, *Collective Bargaining in the Public Service: The Federal Experience in Canada* (Ottawa: Institute for Research on Public Policy, 1983) at xxvii, 7.

> parties while, at the same time, protecting the public interest that citizens receive critical services from the state.[39]

However, fear of strikes is an unsatisfactory explanation for the exceptionalism of federal public service labour and employment law. First, most of the elements of exceptionalism are unrelated to strike action. If strike action were the reason for exceptionalism, then the legislation would simply limit or ban strikes. It does much more than that. Second, there are a number of employers governed by private sector labour law for whom strike action would be more detrimental to the public interest than strike action in the federal public service. A strike at Atomic Energy of Canada Limited or Canadian National Railway—both governed by the *Canada Labour Code*—could be more detrimental to the public interest than a strike by clerical workers in the Government of Canada. The *Canada Labour Code* has provisions dealing with essential services, and it is unclear why those provisions need to be different in the public service.

Second, differences in collective bargaining laws between countries usually reflect the history of industrial relations in those countries. Different historical patterns lead to different laws. In the public sector, collective bargaining laws must reflect the different forms of government in those countries:

> In each country, the constitutional form of government, political values and electoral systems and administrative traditions and cultures—each of which is subject to a unique pattern of legal regulation—impact on the structure and process of collective bargaining.[40]

In other words, the exceptionalism of the federal public service may simply be a reflection of historical and constitutional values.

However, our constitutional form of government and administrative traditions and cultures cannot entirely explain this exceptionalism. Our constitutional form of government is substantially similar to that

---

39 Final Report of the Advisory Committee on Labour Management Relations in the Federal Public Service, *Working Together in the Public Interest* (Ottawa: Treasury Board, 2001) at 14, online (pdf): https://publications.gc.ca/collections/collection_2011/sct-tbs/BT22-70-1-2001-eng.pdf.

40 Lorenzo Bordogna & David Winchester, "Collective Bargaining in Western Europe" in Carl Dell'Aringa, Giuseppe Della Rocca & Berndt Keller, eds, *Strategic Choices in Reforming Public Service Employment: An International Handbook* (New York: Palgrave, 2001) at 50.

of the United Kingdom and New Zealand, yet in those jurisdictions the legal relationship between the Crown and its employees is substantially similar to that between any other employer and employee. In New Zealand, "public sector pay-fixing and personnel matters are now largely determined under the same framework of rules as govern their conduct in the private sector."[41] One commentator has said about the United Kingdom's public service law that

> [t]he Crown, when looked at through the eyes of an employment lawyer, seems to be nothing more than an effective executive wielding no more than the authority it needs to fulfill its functions. Generally, there seems to be nothing to distinguish it from any other large employer save where its "employees" undertake special functions not found in other areas of life.[42]

Therefore, there is nothing in the Canadian constitutional form of government that necessitates exceptionalism.

Third, the locus of bargaining authority is more diffuse in the public sector than in the private sector. In the private sector, it is easier to get access to a single person who has the ultimate authority to bind the employer in a collective agreement or even in the settlement of an individual dispute. In the public sector, it is difficult to find a person with final authority because governments are, by their nature, consultative bodies where decisions are made after input from a number of different people. As one commentator put it:

> [There is] a fundamental difference between public and private sector collective bargaining: in the public services, the employers' side exhibits a considerable dispersion of power among government ministers, state officials, politicians and the managers of public services.... [N]egotiations should be viewed as a form of multilateral bargaining in

---

41 Pat Walsh, Raymond Hartbridge & Aaron Crawford, "Public Sector Industrial Relations in New Zealand" in *Strategic Choices in Reforming Public Service Employment*, *ibid* at 210.

42 Robert Watt, "The Crown and Its Employees" in Maurice Sunkin & Sebastian Payne, eds, *The Nature of the Crown: A Legal and Political Analysis* (Oxford: Oxford University Press, 1999) at 314. It should be noted that the Crown is not subject to the same rules as other employers: see, for example, *Employment Rights Act 1996*, 1996 c 18, s 191, which sets out the provisions of that statute that bind the Crown. However, as a general rule, more of the private law of employment governs Crown employees than it does in Canada.

> which the resolution of internal conflict on the employers' side complicates negotiations and invites political pressure from trade unions and professional associations. These pressures are most intense in public services that have the highest political profile in each country . . . and at the same time in the electoral cycle when politicians and government ministers are most sensitive to public opinion. Such pressures still exist, even if they have been partly attenuated by the increasing separation between political authorities and managerial functions and by the privatization process in some countries.
>
> . . . In any event, the application of this model to the public sector requires significant qualification. The idea of "responsible" trade union behavior in decentralized systems is based on the assumption that individual employers are financially responsible for their firms and for their capacity to compete with other firms, which gives rise to a more or less direct trade-off between real wage increases and employment levels where bargaining takes place. But this is rarely the case in public services—unless very radical structural reforms in the financing and provision of services have been carried out, making each unit responsible for its own budget. This partly explains why the decentralization of collective bargaining has been much less frequent and much more limited than is often suggested. It also explains why governments, anxious to reduce or contain public expenditures, often have found that they could control public sector wage costs more easily through a centralized system (at least in the short and medium term) even if, in principle, tight budget control is not incompatible with decentralized bargaining.[43]

This decentralization of bargaining authority (or, put another way, the inability to find somebody in government who has the authority to make a decision) exists in Canada. One of the findings of the first Fryer Report was that

> [b]oth sides are greatly concerned about the narrow mandate that the Treasury Board provides to government negotiators, and about the inability of particular departments to fashion settlements appropriate for their needs. It should be noted that dealing with the Treasury Board is a particularly serious problem for the separate agencies.[44]

43 Bordogna & Winchester, above note 40 at 51 and 58.

44 Preliminary Fryer Report, above note 36.

Canada has dispersed the legal centre of bargaining power (in particular to separate agencies) but still requires "multilateral bargaining" in that the designated "authority" in a particular department or separate agency still needs the approval of the Treasury Board to make final decisions or must consult with other elements in the government before making a final decision. However, the conflict between a government's desire to disperse bargaining power and centralize control over public expenditures does not explain, and appears unrelated to, many forms of exceptionalism.

Fourth, exceptionalism was historically justified on the basis of "sovereignty":

> Whether the issue raised by the appearance of staff associations is organization, or collective bargaining, or the possibility of strike action, official reaction tends to be rationalized in terms of the sovereign status of the state-employer.[45]

The "sovereignty" argument was basically that "[t]he Queen does not negotiate with her subjects." While the sovereignty argument was rejected back in 1967 when the federal government enacted legislation permitting some collective bargaining,[46] Parliament retained some residual level of "sovereignty" or limits on collective bargaining when necessary in the public interest. The president of Privy Council stated:

> [I]t is not necessary for me to remind hon. Members of the ultimate sovereignty of Parliament and its authority to protect and safeguard the public interest. It is, I believe, our duty in dealing with issues of this kind to legislate in such a way as to deny no man the ordinary rights and privileges of Canadian citizens unless in the public interest it is absolutely necessary to do so. On the other hand, no one should doubt the capacity or willingness of Parliament to qualify such rights and privileges where they are being used in gross disregard for the well-being of the community.[47]

---

45 Saul J. Frankel, *Staff Relations in the Civil Service: The Canadian Experience* (Montreal: McGill University Press 1962) at 11.

46 Jacob Finkelman, "When Bargaining Fails" in *Collective Bargaining in the Public Service: Theory and Practice* (Chicago: Public Personnel Association, 1967) at 121.

47 *House of Commons Debates*, 27-1 (31 May 1966) at 5787–88 (Hon E.J. Benson).

A more modern approach to this concern is that collective bargaining in the public sector "enables unions to distort democracy when they can combine political and economic pressures on employers."[48] This concern typically manifests itself with the view that public sector unions are able to combine this political and economic pressure to generate higher wages for public servants. The belief that public servants are overpaid is widespread; the empirical evidence for this belief is less clear.[49]

As can be seen above, this book argues against exceptionalism for labour law in the federal public service, except when it is truly necessary to reflect the constitutional role of the public service or the merit principle. Public servants should be treated differently to protect their constitutional role (including the constitutional convention of political neutrality) and to preserve the principle of appointment according to merit. Such differences would prevent (to take two examples) senior public servants from actively campaigning for election while they are employed and the negotiation of promotion solely according to seniority. However, these two forms of exceptionalism are justifiable by reference to the constitutional position of the public service. Other forms of exceptionalism—in particular, the ban on negotiating pensions and the refusal to refer all forms of rights disputes to binding third-party arbitration—are more difficult to justify. In short, "[t]he individual employment and collective bargaining regimes governing the public service should be the same regime in effect for other employees unless the difference is justifiable in the public interest."[50]

---

48 Mark Thompson & Sara Slinn, "Public Sector Industrial Relations in Canada: Does It Threaten or Sustain Democracy?" (2013) 34:2 Comp Lab L & Pol'y J 393 at 408.

49 For two sides of this debate, see Charles Lammam et al, "Comparing Government and Private Sector Compensation in Canada" (2015), online (pdf): www.fraserinstitute.org/sites/default/files/comparing-government-and-private-sector-compensation-in-canada.pdf (concluding that there is a wage differential), and Canadian Union of Public Employees, *Battle of the Wages: Who Gets Paid More, Public or Private Sector Workers?* (December 2011), online: https://cupe.ca/battle-wages-who-gets-paid-more-public-or-private-sector-workers.

50 Donald Carter, "Legal Regulation of Collective Bargaining in the Ontario Public Sector" (1974) 29 RI 776 at 778.

E. RULE OF LAW

The final thesis of this book is that the rule of law—or, more practically, judicial intervention—should be more prevalent and justifiable in public sector labour relations than in the private sector. I appreciate that this thesis is inconsistent with the Supreme Court of Canada's decisions that the legal relationship between the Crown and its servants is the same as between any employer and employee.[51] I also appreciate that this thesis contradicts my proposal above that public sector labour relations be treated no differently than private sector labour relations. I nevertheless justify this form of exceptionalism because of the necessity of restraining the power of the state to act arbitrarily in labour relations.

Private sector labour law is designed to protect employees from the arbitrary exercise of economic power. Employees are economically and legally subordinate to their employers and have joined together collectively to offset that economic power. The system of labour law in Canada has evolved to prevent the arbitrary exercise of the legal and economic power of employers. The state as employer, on the other hand, is not restrained by laws unless it so desires. The combination of the traditional common law immunities and privileges of the Crown as employer with the right of Parliament to exempt Crown employees—by legislation—from general labour law means that the state has almost unfettered authority to impose terms and conditions of employment on its servants.

The check on this virtually unfettered authority must come from the judiciary. From the time of the inception of the Crown servant, the judiciary has served as the guardian of the rights and liberties of Crown employees. Courts have often demanded that the Crown as employer act in accordance with the principles of natural justice when it dismisses its servants and (more recently) has carefully scrutinized government hiring decisions to ensure that they comply with the merit principle and to ensure that the "best" candidate is appointed to each position. At the same time as the executive branch of government demands to

51 *Dunsmuir v New Brunswick*, 2008 SCC 9 at para 102, and *Wells v Newfoundland*, [1999] 3 SCR 199 at paras 29–32. See also P.W. Hogg & P.J. Monahan, *Liability of the Crown*, 3d ed (Toronto: Carswell, 2000) at 240.

"let managers manage,"[52] the judiciary has the constitutional duty to remain vigilant to protect the rights and liberties of public servants. As Rohr put it:

> There is a natural and understandable tension between the courts, with their commitment to rights, and the managerial ethos of public administration that is deeply committed to utility. A normative theory of public administration that is grounded in constitutional principle must not collapse into managerial utilitarianism.[53]

The rule of law also has a direct impact on public servants by restraining the discretion they exercise during the course of their duties. Public servants themselves are bound by the rule of law. Sossin has advocated a constitutional convention of bureaucratic independence where public servants have the right to refuse orders that contravene the rule of law, stating:

> The . . . rule of law imperative applies to all civil servants. The rule of law doctrine imposes what might be characterized as a public trust obligation on civil servants to ensure that the rule of law is respected and that government directions that are inconsistent with the rule of law are not followed.[54]

I do not go so far as to advocate a constitutional convention of bureaucratic independence based on the rule of law. However, I do submit that the importance of the rule of law has led—and should lead—courts to intervene more in public sector labour relations than in private sector labour relations. This book is in large part a discussion of judicial limits on the powers of the executive acting as employer—and the consequences when the judiciary shirks its role in favour of "letting managers manage."

---

52 As Rohr put it: "More directly related to the NPM [new public management] is the impressive current literature criticizing it for its sometimes cavalier treatment of the rule of law, especially its free and easy slogans about eliminating red tape and letting managers manage." Rohr, *Civil Servants and Their Constitutions*, above note 7 at xi.

53 Rohr, *Public Service, Ethics, & Constitutional Practice*, above note 9 at 91.

54 Sossin, above note 5 at 23. See also Sossin, *Defining Boundaries*, above note 10 at 38.

CHAPTER TWO

History of Labour and Employment Law in the Federal Public Service

A. INTRODUCTION

Prior to examining the current state of federal public service labour and employment law, it is helpful to quickly review the history and evolution of labour and employment law that has governed federal public servants.

B. SITUATION IN BRITAIN UP TO THE NINETEENTH CENTURY: AN EVOLUTION TOWARD CROWN SERVANTS AND APPOINTMENT ON THE BASIS OF MERIT

The modern idea of a public servant—a person who serves their country as opposed to a particular person—evolved in Great Britain during the eighteenth and nineteenth centuries. Prior to that time, the workers we would now consider "civil servants" did not owe their loyalty to Great Britain but were instead considered to be the personal servants of the reigning monarch. Officials in the seventeenth century were "still his [the monarch's] servants, and not those of the Crown or the Public."[1] Even though the monarch was directly responsible for appointing their personal servants, these officials were not completely powerless in their dealings with the Crown. Officials were appointed by a letter patent. Therefore, the revocation of their appointments could be—and

1 G.E. Aylmer, *The King's Servants: The Civil Service of Charles I*, 2d ed (London: Routledge & Kegan Paul, 1971) at 464.

was—reviewed by the nascent court structure in place in England in the seventeenth century. Consequently, they "could choose to bargain with the Crown"[2] when the Crown sought to dismiss them, knowing that they could prevent—or at the very least delay—their dismissal through court proceedings.

During the eighteenth century, the concept of the civil service evolved so that public officials became servants of their particular ministers. Ministers appointed, promoted, and paid their civil servants out of the revenue generated within that particular ministry. Civil servants also collected fees from citizens who used the particular services offered by a ministry, and these fees were used to supplement their otherwise meagre salaries.

This obviously unsatisfactory situation began to modernize in the nineteenth century. In 1816, the British Parliament passed the first statute governing the civil service. That Act converted "those employed in the various departments from being servants of the Ministers in whose offices they served, to being servants of the Crown."[3] The 1816 Act was also the first time that Parliament dictated the pay for civil servants. Civil servants continued to collect fees and other sources of income by performing their duties, but they also received an annual salary set by Parliament.

In 1855, the British government established the Civil Service Commission by an order in council. The 1855 order in council gave the Civil Service Commission the authority to conduct the entry examinations for the British civil service:

> In effect, the Order transferred to the Commissioners the duties of conducting the examinations and inquiries which had been undertaken previously by the departments, thereby providing an impartial scrutiny of nominees.[4]

The reforms that occurred in the 1850s had several causes, two of which were more important than others. First, the British government had commissioned a report into its civil service. That report recommended, among other things, more rigorous scrutiny of incoming civil servants—not to completely eliminate patronage, but to ensure that patronage was only used to appoint candidates who had some basic qualifications for their positions. Second, the British military debacle

---

2 *Ibid.*

3 Emmeline W. Cohen, *The Growth of the British Civil Service 1780–1939*, 2d ed (London: Frank Cass & Co, 1965) at 20.

4 *Ibid* at 111.

in the Crimean War triggered a political outcry demanding significant improvement in British government administration. The maltreatment of British casualties led Florence Nightingale to help create a modern system of nursing and hospital care; the administrative malfeasance that caused many of those casualties in the first place forced the British government to re-evaluate who it was appointing as civil servants.

The Civil Service Commission was still no guarantee of appointment by merit: appointment still remained a political gift. However, if a candidate failed the Civil Service Commission examination, they were not appointed to a position. This was a guarantee that illiterate candidates would not become civil service clerks and that candidates who could not do basic sums would not be appointed as customs clerks or auditors.

In 1870, the British government went further and (again by order in council) instituted recruitment into the civil service by open competitive examination. As a political compromise, competitive examinations were not used in some departments whose ministers objected to open competitions as a matter of principle (most notably, the foreign secretary); however, the principle of appointment by merit had taken hold. By the end of the nineteenth century,

> certain basic principles had been agreed upon. It had been recognized that posts should be awarded on merit, and that merit should be objectively assessed, that the role of personal prejudice and political influence in recommending candidates for appointments should be eliminated as far as the Home Service was concerned.[5]

C. THE EARLY YEARS: THE INTRODUCTION OF APPOINTMENT ACCORDING TO MERIT IN CANADA

The first Canadian *Civil Service Act*[6] was enacted in 1857 in the United Province of Upper and Lower Canada. This early *Civil Service Act* did five things:

1) The people comprising the "staff" of each department of the Canadian civil service were divided into two classes: "officers" and "clerks." "Officers" were the deputy heads of each department,

---

5 *Ibid* at 166.

6 *An Act for improving the organization and increasing the efficiency of the Civil Service of Canada*, 20 Vict c 24 (1857).

along with some other senior public officials (such as the commissioner of customs and the deputy provincial register). "Clerks" were then divided into four classes (creatively named "first-class clerks," "second-class clerks," and so on). The fourth-class clerks were probationary employees.

2) Clerks of the civil service were only appointed after having attained a certain level of seniority. Thus, fourth-class clerks could be promoted after two years and third-class and second-class clerks after six years each.
3) Clerks' salaries were determined strictly according to their seniority in the civil service, at rates specified in the legislation. Fourth-class clerks were paid £125 a year; third-class clerks £150 a year, with an increase of £10 a year until they reached £200 a year; second-class clerks £225 a year, with annual increases of £10 until they reached a maximum of £275 a year; and first-class clerks £300 a year, with annual increases of £10 a year until they reached £350 a year.
4) Entrance into the civil service was preceded by an examination. The *Civil Service Act* established a board of examiners comprising twelve officers to conduct examinations of all candidates for the civil service. Only people who passed these examinations were eligible for appointment as clerks.
5) Finally, all vacancies for clerk positions were filled by way of promotion instead of external hire, where possible.

After Confederation, Parliament passed similar legislation, and most of the clerks and officials of the provinces of United Canada, as well as New Brunswick and Nova Scotia, became part of the federal civil service.

This is not to say that the principle of appointment and promotion according to merit had taken hold throughout the federal civil service. Patronage was still widespread, and appointments to the federal civil service still depended more on who you knew and which political party you supported than on merit or qualifications. In fact, the period from 1890 to 1918 has been referred to as "the most dismal period in civil service history."[7] The 1857 statute created entrance examinations, but the results of the examinations rarely mattered:

---

7 Robert A. Vaison, "Collective Bargaining in the Federal Public Service: The Achievement of a Milestone in Personal Relations" in Barbara Carroll, David

> [S]uccess in the basic entrance exam ... did not guarantee employment. The government would simply pick and choose those to be hired, as earlier, on the basis of partisan politics.[8]

In 1908, the federal government made its first attempt to legislate mandatory appointment according to merit. The *Civil Service Amendment Act*[9] of 1908 created the Civil Service Commission (the forerunner of today's Public Service Commission) in an effort to legislate the "principle of [an] Independent Commission in regards to appointments and promotions, or in other words, the Merit System."[10] The 1908 Act divided the civil service into two parts: the "Inside Service" (essentially civil servants in Ottawa) and the "Outside Service" (the rest of the civil service). The merit system applied only to the Inside Service. According to the 1908 Act, the Civil Service Commission was responsible for creating the list of successful candidates for any clerk-level positions. That list had to be made "in order of merit."[11] The commission was also responsible for administering examinations for the promotion of clerks from third-class to second-class positions.[12]

Despite the clear legislative intention to require appointment on the basis of merit,

> it quickly became evident that the desired state of affairs [appointment according to merit] had not yet been realized. Patronage remained less than a dead letter, in spite of overt opposition to it.[13]

The Right Honourable Robert Borden had promised that

> [p]ublic officials should be appointed upon considerations of capacity and personal character and not of party service alone. We boast of

---

Siegel & Mark Sproule-Jones, eds, *Classic Readings in Canadian Public Administration* (Toronto: Oxford University Press, 2005) at 197. Vaison's article was originally published in 1969.

8 Donald J. Savoie, *Breaking the Bargain: Public Servants, Ministers, and Parliament* (Toronto: University of Toronto Press, 2003) at 27.

9 *The Civil Service Amendment Act, 1908*, 7-8 Edward VII, c 15 (1908).

10 "The Civil Service of Canada," Special Issue, *The Civilian* (Ottawa: 1914) at 243.

11 *Civil Service Amendment Act, 1908*, s 17.

12 *Ibid* at s 26. Promotion from fourth class to third class was automatic after a six-month probationary period; promotion from second class to first class was made upon the recommendation of the deputy head and a certificate by the commission: ss 20 and 24.

13 Vaison, above note 7 at 198.

> our representative institutions, but these cannot be enduring if they develop a debased public service.[14]

Despite this promise, the aftermath of the election of 1911 saw an enormous number of "patronage" appointments to the public service, without much regard to the provisions of the 1908 Act or the merit principle. Essentially, the 1908 Act created the necessary legislative scheme, but "the machinery of implementation was absent."[15] During World War I, the size of the civil service doubled, and the Civil Service Commission was unable to check the rampant use of political patronage to fill those new positions.[16]

However, the Union government—in the election campaign of 1917—promised to limit the power of political patronage and followed through on their promise in the *Civil Service Act, 1918*.[17] The 1918 Act created a stronger Civil Service Commission: the commission was now responsible for the appointment and promotion of all positions in the civil service below the level of deputy head—it was no longer limited to the Inside Service.[18] Unlike in 1908, the commission was given real powers, and its powers were respected: appointment by reason of merit became the rule instead of the exception.

The other significant reform triggered by the 1918 Act was in the classification of the civil service. The Act provided for an elaborate classification scheme—or, to be more accurate, required the commission "as soon as may be practicable" to come up with "plans for the organization of the Inside Service and the Outside Service of each department."[19] In practice, the commission hired American consulting firms to determine a scheme of classification of the civil service.[20]

Although there were periodic pieces of legislation that concerned the civil service, the 1918 Act was the most significant legislative initiative concerning the public service until the reforms of 1967. The basic principle of the 1918 Act remains in place to this day: the idea of appointment according to merit, as determined by competitive examinations,

---

14 "The Civil Service of Canada," above note 10 at 1.

15 Vaison, above note 7 at 198.

16 *Ibid* at 198.

17 *The Civil Service Act, 1918*, 8–9 George V, c 12 (1918).

18 *Ibid* ss 16 and 38–39.

19 *Ibid*, s 9.

20 Vaison, above note 7; Saul J. Frankel, *Staff Relations in the Civil Service: The Canadian Experience* (Montreal: McGill University Press, 1962) at 23.

conducted by an impartial commission responsible for protecting the principle of appointment according to merit.

D. LABOUR RELATIONS IN THE FEDERAL PUBLIC SERVICE TO 1967

One of the two pillars of our current system of public service labour and employment law—appointment by merit—had been established by 1918. However, it would take until 1967 for the second pillar—free collective bargaining to be established.

The first public sector trade union formed in Canada was the Railway Mail Clerks' Association, established in 1889. It was followed shortly thereafter by a union of letter carriers in 1891. In 1907, the Civil Service Union was established—shortly thereafter renamed the Civil Service Association and then federated into the Civil Service Federation in 1914. The other main civil service association—the Professional Institute of the Public Service of Canada—was formed in 1920 as a reaction against concerns about the classification scheme, in particular hostility of higher civil servants to the American firms that had been hired to survey the organization and classification structure of the Canadian civil service.[21]

The 1918 *Civil Service Act* had given the Civil Service Commission the responsibility to recommend rates of pay. Parliament retained the final authority over the rates of pay in the federal public service. Therefore,

> [u]ntil 1944 virtually the only regular input that civil service organizations had in the determination of their terms and conditions of employment was by way of what has been called a "humble petition," albeit often expressed in vigorous language.[22]

Although public service associations wanted more input on terms and conditions of the employment of their members, they were always refused such input in the name of "sovereignty." As Saul Frankel has put it:

---

21 For a more detailed examination of the history of public service unions in Canada, see Chapter 8, below.

22 Jacob Finkelman & Shirley Goldenberg, *Collective Bargaining in the Public Service: The Federal Experience in Canada* (Ottawa: Institute for Research on Public Policy, 1983) at 9.

> Whether the issue raised by the appearance of staff associations is organization, or collective bargaining, or the possibility of strike action, official reaction tends to be rationalized in terms of the sovereign status of the state-employer.[23]

Sir George E Foster (then the acting prime minister) rejected the notion of negotiating with federal public service associations in 1920, stating:

> With regard to the right to organize, the Government stated that while this was already recognized as applying to industrial workers, the principle could not be applied to Government employees, who were obviously in a different category.[24]

Since there were already several staff associations in existence by 1920, Sir George's comments about "the right to organize" referred to the right to negotiate and strike rather than the simple right to belong to a staff association. Bargaining with public servants was seen as antithetical to preserving the sovereignty of the Crown. In support of the need for preserving sovereignty,

> it has been argued that it is necessary for the executive to have unfettered control over all or some of the employment relationship with the civil service in order to ensure that there is no impediment to fulfilling the democratic wishes of the citizens who elected the government. According to this argument, the government needs to have free control of public service human resources in order to protect the capacity to govern.[25]

Whenever public sector employee associations pressed for greater rights or a greater involvement in determining the terms and conditions of employment for public servants, they were inevitably—at least until the 1960s—met with some version of this response: "the Queen [or King] does not negotiate with her subjects."[26]

---

23 Frankel, above note 20 at 11.

24 Canada, *Labour Gazette*, XX (April 1920) at 372, cited in Frankel, above note 20 at 4.

25 Timothy Hadwen et al, *Ontario Public Service Employment & Labour Law* (Toronto: Irwin Law, 2005) at 20–21.

26 Or, in French, "La Reine ne negocie pas avec ses sujets," attributed to Premier Jean Lesage in the early 1960s, in different years depending on the source.

The government's arguments did not persuade public service associations to abandon their efforts to play a greater role in determining the terms and conditions of employment of their members. In 1924, the letter carriers went on strike—the first public sector strike in Canadian history. The more militant public service associations—such as the newly formed Associated Federal Employees of Ottawa—pressed for negotiation along the lines of the Whitley Council created in Great Britain. Under the Whitley Council system, public service associations bargained with the government about the full range of terms and conditions of employment and then referred any disputes to binding arbitration if a negotiated solution could not be found.

In Canada, public service associations were limited to lobbying the Civil Service Commission to recommend appropriate rates of pay or other changes to terms and conditions of employment or to lobbying Cabinet directly. The Civil Service Commission had, by 1928, become a somewhat discredited organization when it came to recommending pay rates. The postal strike of 1924 was to a large extent precipitated by the Civil Service Commission, which proposed a decrease in pay rates. The Commission's proposed pay rates were not only significantly lower than what postal workers had asked for, but also lower than what the Post Office Department had offered. When the government referred the matter back to the Commission to be redetermined after further submissions by both the associations and the department, the Commission returned its original proposals without change. The postal workers went on strike, and the government had to promise bonuses to postal workers (outside of the annual salaries) to top up their rates of pay to what they had been before the commission made its recommendations. Then, in 1928, the Commission "erred on the side of liberality rather than parsimony"[27] when it recommended significant increases for senior executives and professional and technical workers. This inconsistency discredited the Commission.

By 1930, the public service associations had convinced the government to create a Whitley-style council, which the government did by order in council; however, the Liberal government of Mackenzie King was soon defeated by the Conservative R.B. Bennett, and Prime Minister Bennett disavowed that order in council and refused to implement it.

---

27 J.E. Hodgetts et al, *The Biography of an Institution: The Civil Service Commission of Canada 1908–1967* (Ottawa: Public Service Commission of Canada, 1972).

The idea of a Whitley-style council still refused to go away. During World War II, public service associations finally convinced the government to create such a council. In 1944, the government created the National Joint Council by way of order in council.[28] The National Joint Council was a council of two sides: on one side were representatives of recognized public service staff associations; on the other side were representatives of the government, led by the chair of the Civil Service Commission. Although the official-side members were drawn from various government departments, the real power was concentrated at the Treasury Board:

> The NJC essentially operated by consensus, so that joint recommendations were then forwarded to the government for consideration. However, since most employment issues discussed had some fiscal dimension . . . in practice all recommendations ultimately had to be approved by the Treasury Board before they could subsequently be implemented by the Civil Service Commission, Treasury Board, or Governor General in Council—each of which had different administrative responsibilities. In effect, this made the Treasury Board the most powerful employer-side representative on the NJC.[29]

While the National Joint Council was obviously (from the perspective of the public service associations) an improvement on what had existed before, there were a number of problems with it.

First, the National Joint Council did not have any binding dispute-resolution mechanism. If the government and associations could not reach a consensus on a particular matter, then the "status quo continued."[30]

Second, even when the National Joint Council agreed on a particular issue, there was no guarantee that the agreement would be implemented by the government:

---

28 PC 3676, 16 May 1944.

29 Richard P. Chaykowski, "Advancing Public-Sector Labor-Management Relations Through Consultation: The Role of the National Joint Council of the Public Service of Canada" in Bruce Kaufman & Daphne Gottleib Taras, eds, *Nonunion Employee Representation* (New York: M.E. Sharpe, 2000) at 335.

30 Gene Swimmer, "Collective Bargaining in the Federal Public Service of Canada: The Last Twenty Years" in Gene Swimmer & Mark Thompson, eds, *Public Sector Collective Bargaining in Canada: Beginning of the End or End of the Beginning?* (Kingston, ON: IRC Press, 1995) at 369.

> The consensus, if any, arising out of deliberations could be accepted, rejected, or totally ignored by the administration and all three eventualities occurred. There was apparently no compulsion, even of a moral nature, for the government or Treasury Board to accept even unanimous decisions of the Council.[31]

Even when the government accepted the recommendations of the National Joint Council, implementation of those recommendations often took years.

Third, the National Joint Council had no mandate to deal with compensation systems. Thus, one of the most important items that staff associations wanted input on was foreclosed to them.

Fourth, the National Joint Council was plagued by what Chaykowski called "operational diversity."[32] Civil servants were represented by several different staff associations. Staff associations often came to the National Joint Council with different perspectives, reflecting different levels of militancy of their members or simply different concerns. On the employer side, the Treasury Board and Civil Service Commission had different mandates and often had different perspectives on issues. Therefore, it was difficult for the staff or the employer side to prepare a unified position on an issue let alone convince the other side to agree with that position.

Finally, public service associations were critical of the attitude of the employer-side negotiators at the National Joint Council:

> The paternalism long characteristic of management in the service flavoured whatever negotiating did occur and the staff-side representatives resented this more and more.[33]

These criticisms of the National Joint Council do not mean that it was completely ineffective. Through the National Joint Council, staff associations and the government were able to come to an agreement on many subjects, including health and safety issues, technological change, the establishment of medical plans, and even the introduction of cafeterias. Two of the most contentious issues before the National Joint Council were the attempt to move from a five-and-a-half-day workweek (of forty-four hours) to a five-day week (of forty hours) and the

31 Vaison, above note 7 at 202.

32 Chaykowski, above note 29 at 336.

33 Vaison, above note 7 at 202.

introduction of premiums for overtime pay; both issues were resolved satisfactorily in the 1950s. Finally, staff associations won a major concession in 1953 when, through the National Joint Council, they won the right to membership dues deduction, which in turn secured the financial strength of these organizations.[34]

One of the major complaints of the public service associations about the National Joint Council was that they were never provided with any data concerning public service pay. In 1957, the government finally addressed this concern in part by creating the Bureau of Pay Research. However, this bureau was a part of the Civil Service Commission and not a truly independent commission; therefore, while public service associations appreciated its existence, they did not entirely trust it to provide adequate or accurate information.

These problems with the National Joint Council in the 1950s coincided with a period of greater militancy among public servants. Civil servants had begun to lose "some of their docility."[35] In 1961, the Diefenbaker government attempted to address this concern with a new *Civil Service Act* that required "consultation" between the minister of finance (who effectively delegated this consultation to the Treasury Board) and public service associations on pay. The 1961 Act also contained provisions establishing a mechanism by which employees could appeal appointments to the public service to the Civil Service Commission. However, in 1963, the Diefenbaker government refused to implement a wage increase recommended after "consultation," destroying any trust that public service associations had in such a situation.[36] Before the election held that year, the Liberal Party promised to implement free collective bargaining for the public service, so the stage was set for significant reforms.

E. THE REFORMS OF 1967

The "bold experiment" of 1967 had its conception in the *Report of the Preparatory Committee on Collective Bargaining in the Public Service* (the Heeney Report).[37] The committee preparing that report was

34 Chaykowski, above note 29 at 336.

35 Vaison, above note 7 at 203.

36 Swimmer, above note 30 at 369.

37 *Report of the Preparatory Committee on Collective Bargaining in the Public Service* (Ottawa: Queen's Printer, 1965) [Heeney Report].

ordered to examine how to implement collective bargaining in the federal public service. It was *not* asked to consider whether to implement collective bargaining—in other words, concerns about sovereignty had been shelved for the time being. Instead, it had two main objectives: "ensuring an orderly introduction of collective bargaining, and establishing a satisfactory set of continuing relationships."[38] The Heeney Report recommended that the federal government adopt free collective bargaining along the Wagner Act model that had been adopted in the private sector in 1944.[39] Rather than dwell on the Heeney Report's recommendations, most of which were accepted, it is more interesting to comment on one recommendation that was not adopted: binding interest arbitration.

The Heeney Report recommended that public servants not have the right to strike. Instead, it recommended that all disputes be resolved by way of binding interest arbitration. Most public service associations accepted this recommendation, but the postal workers did not. Shortly after the report was issued, inside postal workers went on strike (supported by the Letter Carriers Union). Their strike was in part a response to the recommendation in the report that they not have the right to strike. After that particular strike was resolved, the postal unions announced that they would defy any collective bargaining legislation that denied them the right to strike. Their promise convinced the government that a statutory prohibition on the right to strike would be counterproductive: it would simply make strikes unlawful for groups (such as the postal workers) that were strong enough and determined enough to defy the law in any event. In other words, the only unions that would exercise the right to strike would go on strike even if it were illegal. Therefore, the government decided not to ban strikes in the new Act.[40]

In 1967, the government passed two pieces of legislation: the *Public Service Staff Relations Act* (*PSSRA*)[41] and the *Public Service Employment Act*[42] (replacing the *Civil Service Act*). The most important features of those statutes are summarized below.

---

38 Christopher Rootham, "Bargaining Unit Structure in the Federal Civil Service" (2002) 9 CLELJ 361 at 366.

39 PC 1003 (1944).

40 Finkelman & Goldenberg, above note 22 at 13.

41 *Public Service Staff Relations Act*, SC 1967, c 72.

42 *Public Service Employment Act*, SC 1967, c 71.

1) Scope of Coverage

The Heeney Report recommended that "steps should be taken to ensure that, with certain specified exceptions, all employees of the Federal Government . . . have access to a system of collective bargaining."[43] The *PSSRA* was drafted to permit "employees" to join bargaining agents and thus be covered by collective bargaining. An "employee" was anyone employed in the public service, with several exceptions:

- a person appointed by the Governor in Council under an Act of Parliament to a statutory position described in that Act;
- a person locally engaged outside Canada (typically locally engaged embassy staff abroad);
- part-time employees (defined as people who are not ordinarily required to work more than one-third of the normal period for persons doing similar work);
- RCMP officers and military officers;[44]
- casual or temporary employees (defined as someone employed for less than six months);
- a person employed by the Public Service Staff Relations Board; and
- a person employed in a "managerial or confidential capacity." These people included deputy heads, employees with "executive duties," employees who are "personnel administrators," employees involved in the grievance process, and any legal officers in the Department of Justice.

The new definition meant that the civil service, in its older and narrower sense, was enlarged to accommodate some 40,000 prevailing rate employees.[45]

2) Public Service Staff Relations Board

Under the provisions of industrial relations law applying generally in Canada at that time (and still applying today), responsibility for

43 Heeney Report, above note 37 at 27.

44 The Heeney Report recommended that those two groups be excluded "because of the nature of their duties and the fact that their conduct is subject to military or similar codes of law and discipline." Heeney Report, above note 37 at 27.

45 Trevor Bhupsingh & Peter Edwards, *Tracking the Role of the PSC in the Governance System of the Federal Public Service* (Ottawa: Public Service Commission of Canada, 1997).

administering labour law (such as the certification of bargaining agents and the provision of conciliation services) is normally divided between the minister of labour and a labour relations board. The Heeney Report concluded that while this division is appropriate in the private sector, "where a government can stand between an employer and a group of organized employees in a position of impartiality, such a division would be open to question in the Public Service system because the Government is the employer and the Minister of Labour is a member of the Government."[46] Therefore, the Heeney Report recommended that the administrative responsibility for labour law be concentrated in an independent body. The Heeney Report also considered using the Canada Labour Relations Board for this purpose; however, in the end it recommended the creation of a new board because of the "special character of the contemplated Public Service system."[47]

The *PSSRA* created the Public Service Staff Relations Board (PSSRB), a "tripartite"[48] board composed of a neutral chair and vice-chairs but also members recommended by bargaining agents and the employer. The PSSRB had primary responsibility for administering the *PSSRA*; however, one weakness of the board was that its orders are not enforceable through courts but instead by reporting on any non-compliance to the minister, who laid such reports before Parliament.

3) Industrial Dispute Resolution

Jacob Finkelman and Shirley Goldenberg considered the industrial dispute-resolution provisions of the *PSSRA* the "most original"[49] component of that Act. There were two dispute-resolution methods available under the Act: conciliation/strike and binding arbitration. The bargaining agent chose the method, without interference by the employer. Each bargaining agent made an initial choice that bound it during that bargaining round. However, the bargaining agent could change its election at any time, and that election was implemented the next time either party served a notice to bargain.

According to the 1967 version of the *PSSRA*, if the bargaining agent elected binding arbitration, then any disputes remaining after collective

46 Heeney Report, above note 37 at 25.

47 *Ibid.*

48 Finkelman & Goldenberg, above note 22 at 13.

49 *Ibid* at xxxv.

bargaining were referred to the Public Service Arbitration Tribunal for resolution. If the bargaining agent chose the conciliation/strike route, then, after bargaining in good faith, the parties referred their dispute to a conciliation board. The conciliation board would attempt to facilitate a settlement. If the conciliation board could not resolve the dispute, then the bargaining agent could begin a legal strike seven days after the conciliation board had prepared its report. The right to strike was limited by essential services provisions in the *PSSRA*.

Finally, the Pay Research Bureau was moved from the Civil Service Commission (now the Public Service Commission) to the PSSRB—ensuring the neutrality of the Pay Research Bureau.

4) Scope of Bargaining

Unlike in private sector collective bargaining legislation, the *PSSRA* curtailed the scope of bargaining in the federal public service. There was a specific exclusion of any term and condition of employment established by the *Public Service Employment Act*, *Public Service Superannuation Act*, *Government Employees Compensation Act*, and the *Government Vessels Discipline Act*. This meant, in effect, that bargaining agents could not negotiate about

- recruitment
- promotion
- transfer
- layoffs
- discharge for incompetence or incapacity (i.e., non-disciplinary discharge)
- rejection of employees during probation
- pensions

The *PSSRA* also contained a management-rights clause:

> Nothing in this Act shall be construed to affect the right or authority of the employer to determine the organization of the Public Service and to assign duties to and classify positions therein.[50]

Thus, bargaining agents could not negotiate about the classification of positions nor about the duties of a particular position.

50 *PSSRA*, s 7.

Finally, the *PSSRA* was even more restrictive about the topics that could be referred to binding arbitration. Section 70 of the *PSSRA* stated that an arbitral award *may* deal with

- rates of pay
- hours of work
- leave entitlements
- standards of discipline
- other terms and conditions of employment related directly to those items

The section then went on to state that an arbitral award *could not* deal with the following:

- appointment
- appraisal
- promotion
- demotion
- transfer
- layoff or release of employees
- any term or condition of employment that was not the subject of negotiation at the time before arbitration was requested

5) Bargaining Unit Determination

The *PSSRA* contained a statutory presumption that the bargaining unit established during the initial certification period[51] consisted of all employees of an occupational group. The Public Service Commission was required to define the occupational groups of the public service. These occupational groups were then placed within five occupational categories, each of which had a separate initial certification period. There were two exceptions to the occupational category bargaining unit. The first was a division between supervisory employees and non-supervisory employees. This exception was prompted by the suggestion of the Postal Workers Union, which had expelled all members who were supervisors (but who still may not have met the definition of

51 The initial certification period varied for each occupational category but generally ended by 1969.

"managerial" under the *PSSRA*).[52] In actual fact, this exception was only used once,[53] and even in that case the two groups eventually merged because they had the same bargaining agent and engaged in single-table bargaining. The second exception stipulated that an occupational group could be carved into different bargaining units if certification on an occupational basis would not permit "satisfactory representation of employees included therein."[54] This exception was advocated by the Confederation of National Trade Unions, which was in the midst of a campaign to sever Quebec unions from national union organization and wanted the ability to certify Quebec-only bargaining units. In actual fact, no Quebec-only bargaining unit was ever certified.[55] Concerning the bargaining unit structure, Finkelman and Goldenberg have stated:

> The guide-lines, based on occupational categories and groups, represent one of the more innovative features of the Act. They were designed, in part, to ensure some coincidence between the group of employees to which a particular pay scale or set of working conditions applied and the group of employees for which a particular bargaining agent would be certified to speak. They were also designed to pave the way for the orderly introduction of a collective bargaining regime by avoiding the inevitable arguments that would ensue if conflicting organizations were free to urge on the Board a variety of principles that would determine how bargaining units were to be constructed.[56]

6) Grievance Dispute Resolution

Prior to the *PSSRA*, individual employees had no avenue for recourse if a particular manager declined to follow the terms and conditions of employment established by the government, whether through the National Joint Council or otherwise. Courts also did not provide any relief at this time because Canada followed the British model whereby "the civil servant has no right to his salary which he could enforce in the

52 Jacob Finkelman, *The Rationale in Establishing Bargaining Units in the Federal Public Service of Canada* (Kingston, ON: Industrial Relations Centre, 1974) at 10.

53 *Hospital Services Case No 1* (1967), PSSRB Rep K6 at 13.

54 *PSSRA*, s 26(5).

55 Finkelman & Goldenberg, above note 22 at 17.

56 *Ibid* at xxxi.

ordinary courts of law" and also that "civil service regulations confer no legally enforceable rights upon the civil servant."[57]

The *PSSRA* established a system of grievances and adjudication of individual workplace complaints. Employees had a very broad right to file a "grievance" concerning any disciplinary action or a breach of the "terms and conditions" of their employment. These grievances were resolved by management. If an employee was dissatisfied with the resolution of their grievance, then they may have the right to refer the matter to adjudication depending on the subject matter of the grievance. Adjudication was conducted by members of the PSSRB. Employees could refer grievances about the following subjects to adjudication:

- collective agreement violations (only with the approval of and representation by the employee's bargaining agent)
- discipline resulting in a suspension, a termination, or a financial penalty

Employees could *not* grieve matters subject to a complaint mechanism under the *Public Service Employment Act* (such as termination for non-disciplinary reasons) or any other matter "in respect of which [an] administrative procedure for redress is provided in or under an Act of Parliament."[58]

7) Personnel Management

The *Public Service Employment Act*, along with a revised *Financial Administration Act*, reorganized the system of personnel management in the federal public service. The *Public Service Employment Act* abolished the Civil Service Commission and replaced it with a more limited Public Service Commission (PSC). The "employer," for the purposes of the *Public Service Employment Act*, was now the Treasury Board. One way to look at the changes was that "the Treasury Board was now recast as the *general manager* of the public service and the *employer* in the collective bargaining relationship."[59] Under the *Public Service Employment Act*, the PSC was responsible for "staffing," including

57 Leo Blair, "The Civil Servant—Political Reality and Legal Myth" (1958) Pub L 32 at 38 and 43.

58 For example, complaints that could be referred to the Canadian Human Rights Commission could not be grieved: *Boutilier v Canada*, [2000] 3 FC 27.

59 Bhupsingh & Edwards, above note 45.

recruitment, selection, and appointments. The PSC would no longer be responsible for the organization of departments, the classification of staff, and the determination of pay and conditions.

The *Public Service Employment Act* also continued the appeals mechanism established in the 1961 Act for employees or candidates dissatisfied with staffing actions, including appointments, promotion, layoff, or release for incompetence or incapacity. Those with staffing authority continued to have to select candidates on the basis of merit. The term "merit" was undefined in the *Public Service Employment Act*, and it fell to the PSC Appeal Board, and then the Federal Court, to breathe life into that concept over the next forty years. The *Public Service Employment Act* also established several "priorities" for appointment: for example, there was a statutory presumption that competitions would be open to current public servants before they would be opened up to the general public.

F. FEDERAL PUBLIC SERVICE 1967–2005

Within two years, over ninety-five percent of the eligible federal public servants had become unionized without any major work stoppages or disputes. In that sense, the *PSSRA* was a success. The essential structure of labour and employment relations in the federal public service established by the *PSSRA* and *Public Service Employment Act* in 1967 has remained in place until the present day. However, in the intervening years, there have been some modifications to those statutory regimes. For example, in 1975, the Public Service Arbitration Tribunal was abolished; henceforth, interest arbitration was conducted by the PSSRB. Several components of the federal public service became separate employers. In 1981, the *Canada Post Corporation Act*[60] removed postal employees from the federal public service; labour relations in the post office are governed by the *Canada Labour Code*.[61] The same thing happened to Nav Canada, the organization responsible for the safety and efficiency of the civil air navigation service.[62] In 1999, the Canada Customs and Revenue Agency also split off from the Treasury Board;[63]

60 *Canada Post Corporation Act*, RSC 1985, c C-10.

61 *Canada Labour Code*, RSC 1985, c L.2.

62 *Civil Air Navigation Services Commercialization Act*, 1996, c 20.

63 *Canada Customs and Revenue Agency Act*, SC 1999, c 17.

some 40,000 employees left the Treasury Board to be employed by this new "separate employer."

The most important legislative changes between 1967 and 2005, however, were the *Public Service Reform Act* (*PSRA*)[64] of 1992 and the various initiatives by the federal government to depart from the model set out in the *PSSRA* of a choice between strike and interest arbitration for the final determination of collective agreements.

1) *Public Service Reform Act*, 1992

In 1989, the federal government announced a public service renewal initiative: Public Service 2000. This initiative was intended to clarify the accountability relationships in human resources management, improve service to the public, and design and implement human resource policies to enable institutions and employees to meet what were seen as new challenges of a changing world. Public Service 2000 was a management-driven enterprise: it was led by the clerk of the Privy Council with assistance from the chair of the PSC and secretary of the Treasury Board. Ten task forces, composed mainly of senior public servants, were established to examine the issues of staffing, workforce adaptiveness, staff relations, classification and occupational group structures, remuneration, the executive group, compensation and benefits, staff training, resource management and budget controls, and service to the public. Eventually, the government produced a White Paper[65] in response to the task force's recommendations and then passed the *PSRA* in November 1992 to follow through on that White Paper.[66]

One of the more important changes in the 1992 Act was the creation of a staffing action termed "deployment." A deployment is a transfer of an employee from one position to another[67] that does not result in a promotion.[68] Deployments were not subject to the merit principle; instead, they only had to be voluntary and not constitute an

---

64 *Public Service Reform Act*, SC 1992, c 54 [*PSRA*].

65 *Public Service 2000: The Renewal of the Public Service of Canada* (Ottawa: Minister of Supply and Services, 1990).

66 For a more detailed discussion of Public Service 2000, see Swimmer, above note 30, or Jack Stilborn, *Federal Public Service Renewal—The La Relève Initiative* (Ottawa: Library of Parliament, 1998).

67 *PSRA*, s 2(2).

68 *Ibid*, s 22 (being s 34.2 of the amended *Public Service Employment Act*).

"abuse of authority."[69] An employee who was deployed or an employee in the work unit to which the deployment is made had the right to complain about the deployment, and that complaint would eventually be referred to the PSC for an investigation and determination of whether the deployment was proper.[70]

Another change to the *Public Service Employment Act* made by the 1992 Act was the creation of a class of appointments that were subject to a different conception of merit. Section 10(2) was added to the *Public Service Employment Act*, reading as follows:

> For the purposes of subsection (1), selection according to merit may, in the circumstances prescribed by the regulations of the Commission, be based on the competence of a person being considered for appointment as measured by such standard of competence as the Commission may establish, rather than as measured against the competence of other persons.

Prior to this amendment, it had become generally accepted that merit was to be assessed on a comparative basis: a candidate had to be the most meritorious candidate when assessed against the other candidates for the position.[71] Now, in limited circumstances, appointment could be made on the basis of individual, rather than comparative, merit. Those circumstances, which had been amended from time to time, included the following:

- when an employee is to be promoted within an apprenticeship or professional training program
- when an employee is to be appointed to a reclassified position
- when an employee who was a term employee was employed for a period of time and became an indefinite employee (three years from 2002 or five years from 1999)
- when a person who is a member of a disadvantaged group is to be appointed in accordance with an employment equity program
- in an emergency situation when a person is to be appointed for a specified period if the appointment cannot be made under the casual employment rules

---

69 *Ibid* (being s 34.3 of the amended *Public Service Employment Act*).

70 *Ibid* (being ss 34.4–34.5 of the amended *Public Service Employment Act*).

71 The merit principle will be discussed in depth in Chapter 11.

- when an employee is to be promoted within an occupational group in which positions are classified according to the qualifications of the incumbents (such as research scientists, who are appointed whenever they meet certain requirements instead of in a competitive process)

The 1992 Act also made some changes to the *PSSRA*. It added a definition of "managerial or confidential positions" as well as a procedure for determining whether those positions truly met the definition. The employer had to identify managerial or confidential positions and inform the board and the bargaining agent of the identification. The bargaining agent then had twenty days to object to that identification; if there was an objection, the board would determine whether the positions were truly managerial or confidential.[72] The 1992 Act also added a statutory duty of fair representation for bargaining agents.

The 1992 Act also made several changes concerning the process for industrial dispute resolution, both to the interest arbitration provisions and the conciliation provisions of the *PSSRA* and to the determination of essential services. First, the procedure for identifying essential services was changed. The parties were required to begin the process of designating essential positions six months before the contract expired. If they could not agree on a list, the matter was referred to an ad hoc tripartite board for a non-binding recommendation. If necessary, the matter could then be referred to the PSSRB for final determination. Second, the composition of arbitration panels was changed. Prior to 1992, arbitration boards comprised a "neutral" chair appointed by the PSSRB and two other members—also appointed by the PSSRB—to represent the interests of labour and management. However, those "side" members were not there to represent either side and could not publish minority decisions. The 1992 Act changed that method of appointment to the method used for conciliation boards: the PSSRB chose the neutral chair, but each party chose one "side" member.

Finally, the 1992 Act triggered an attempt at reorganizing the classification structure of the federal public service. Section 101 of the Act required the Treasury Board to specify new occupational groups within six years of that section coming into force (1999). As a result of that section, the Treasury Board entered into negotiations with the bargaining agents about consolidation of the occupational groups. Originally in

72 *PSRA*, s 33 (being ss 5.1–5.3 of the amended *PSSRA*).

1967, there were sixty-seven occupational groups—and hence, sixty-seven different bargaining units. By 1992, there were approximately seventy-two different occupational groups. In an effort to rationalize the collective bargaining set to resume in 1997,[73] the Treasury Board proposed reducing the number of bargaining units to a mere six. This proposal threatened the existence of a number of smaller bargaining agents. These smaller unions, which were supported by the larger ones, convinced the government that "there was tremendous potential for nasty inter-union fights across the public service as rival unions scrambled to win certification votes."[74] In the end, the Treasury Board and the bargaining agents agreed to a plan reducing the number of bargaining units to twenty-nine. As of 2000, there were twenty-five bargaining units in the Treasury Board: six represented by the Professional Institute of the Public Service of Canada, five by the Public Service Alliance of Canada, and the rest by other bargaining agents.[75]

2) Legislative Initiative Restricting Collective Bargaining or Interest Arbitration Initiatives

The bold initiative of the 1967 *PSSRA* was that the bargaining agent had the right to elect whether the final resolution of industrial disputes should be by way of arbitration or strike. Upon initial certification, 88 percent of bargaining units, representing 81 percent of employees, chose the arbitration route.[76] By 1984, most unions had elected the strike route: 56 percent of bargaining units, covering 75 percent of public servants, used the strike route. There are many explanations for this change, including evidence that wage increases were higher under the strike route, perceived unfairness with the arbitration procedures (in particular, the use—until 1992—of three relatively neutral arbitrators instead of a tripartite panel), the scope of arbitration,[77] and

73 See discussion below for why bargaining had been suspended.

74 Gene Swimmer, "Public-Sector Labour Relations in an Era of Restraint and Restructuring: An Overview" in Gene Swimmer, ed, *Public-Sector Labour Relations in an Era of Restraint and Restructuring* (Toronto: Oxford University Press, 2001) at 195.

75 Public Service Staff Relations Board, *33rd Annual Report 1999–2000* (Hull: Minister of Supply and Services, 2000) at 47.

76 Swimmer, above note 30 at 374.

77 The scope of arbitration was less than the scope of bargaining under the strike route.

philosophical changes within the bargaining agent, particularly in the Public Service Alliance of Canada.[78]

In any event, successive governments began to prohibit free collective bargaining. The first prohibition was the Anti-Inflation Program from 1975 to 1978. The Anti-Inflation Program required all collective agreements to conform to wage rate increases approved by the federal government. Since this program covered all public and private sector wages, it was not perceived as an attack on the right of federal public servants to engage in free collective bargaining, although it did limit the value of the strike route for federal public service unions. The second attempt was a wage control program instituted in 1982 called "six and five." This legislation extended all federal collective agreements for two years, with annual increases of 6 percent and 5 percent. As a result, collective bargaining over all issues (whether monetary or not) was suspended for two years. The government also froze all merit or increment increases during this period.[79]

Free collective bargaining returned after 1984, for a time. In 1991, the Public Service Alliance of Canada went on strike. The government legislated the union back to work after the strike had lasted a total of nine days (a week after 9 September 1991 and from 30 September–2 October 1991). The back-to-work legislation included a one-year pay freeze and an annual increase of 3 percent the following year.[80] Then, in 1992, the government legislated yet another wage freeze for two years.[81] The government also shut down the Pay Research Bureau that year.[82] In short, Public Service Alliance of Canada members—numbering over 150,000 at the time—received only a 3 percent wage increase over four years when collective bargaining was suspended.[83]

The Public Service Alliance of Canada denounced the Conservative government as "the worst employer they had ever had" and actively

78 Swimmer, above note 30 at 375–77.

79 *Ibid* at 382–84. Ironically, the 5 percent increase in year two was too high: private sector wage increases that year averaged only 2.8 percent.

80 *Public Sector Compensation Act*, SC 1991, c 30.

81 SC 1993, c 13.

82 Some commentators have suggested that the government was really trying to silence a messenger of "bad news" as the Pay Research Bureau had consistently supported the Public Service Alliance of Canada's arguments that administrative support employees were underpaid: Swimmer, above note 30 at 401.

83 *Ibid.*

worked to defeat it in the 1993 election.[84] However, the new Liberal government did not restore collective bargaining. In the 1994 budget, the government extended the public service wage freeze for another two years and also suspended increment increases.[85] When collective bargaining resumed in 1997, the government passed amendments to the *Public Sector Compensation Act* to ensure that compensation increases were restricted to approximately 2 percent, preventing employees from "making up" for the previous six years of restraint.[86] The government also suspended interest arbitration for three more years;[87] the suspension was eventually extended until 2001 (except for employee organizations representing employees of separate employers, who could elect interest arbitration earlier than employee organizations representing employees of the Treasury Board).

In short, one of the two main pillars of the public service labour and employment law system—free collective bargaining, with final resort to either interest arbitration or strike—was essentially suspended for the 1990s.

G. PUBLIC SERVICE MODERNIZATION: 2005

The *Public Service Modernization Act* involved a fairly substantial series of changes to federal public sector labour and employment law.[88] It was passed in 2003, but most of its provisions only came into effect in 2005. It repealed the *PSSRA* in its entirety and replaced it with the *Public Service Labour Relations Act* (*PSLRA*), later renamed the *Federal Public Sector Labour Relations Act* (*FPSLRA*).[89] It also repealed the *Public Service Employment Act* and replaced it with an entirely rewritten *Public Service Employment Act* and made some consequential amendments to the *Financial Administration Act*[90] and minor changes to some other statutes. Finally, it also created a new Canada School of Public Service.

84 First report of the Advisory Committee on Labour Management Relations in the Federal Public Service, *Identifying the Issues* (May 2000), online: www.tbs-sct.canada.ca/report/fryer/iti-ide01-eng.asp at 29.

85 SC 1994, c 18, s 4.

86 SC 1996, c 18, ss 12–13.

87 *Ibid* at 31.

88 *Public Service Modernization Act*, SC 2003, c 22

89 For the remainder of this book, references to the *FPSLRA* will include the *PSLRA* as it read prior to the change in the statute's name in 2017.

90 *Financial Administration Act*, RSC 1985, c F-11.

The *Public Service Modernization Act* was preceded by a report of an advisory committee on labour management relations entitled *Working Together in the Public Interest* (the Fryer Report).[91] The Fryer Report contained thirty-three core recommendations. The most far-reaching of those recommendations included the following:

- making public service labour law more consistent with private sector labour law, especially by
  - having the Canada Industrial Relations Board administer the Act,
  - using the more restrictive method of determining essential services contained in the *Canada Labour Code*, and
  - determining bargaining units using the private sector "community of interest" test
- allowing unions a greater scope for bargaining by making the staffing system, classification system, and pension plans the subject of co-determination at the National Joint Council
- creating a Public Interest Dispute Resolution Commission to assist the parties with resolving interest disputes
- creating a form of two-tier bargaining, with service-wide agreements providing the general outline of terms and conditions of employment but also scope for negotiation at the workplace or departmental level about how those provisions should be applied locally

The *Public Service Modernization Act* ignored or fell short of many of those recommendations. The bulk of the remainder of this book deals with the specifics of the new *FPSLRA* and *Public Service Employment Act*. However, what follows is a summary of the most significant changes made by that Act.

1) *Federal Public Sector Labour Relations Act*

The *FPSLRA* contains a preamble, as recommended by the Fryer Report. That preamble emphasizes effective, harmonious labour relations and the value of collective bargaining within a context where the protection of the public interest is the paramount consideration. The public interest consideration is, in fact, the first item mentioned in the preamble.

91 Second Report of the Advisory Committee on Labour-Management Relations in the Federal Public Service, *Working Together in the Public Interest* (Ottawa: Treasury Board, 2001).

The *FPSLRA* established a new board: the Public Service Labour Relations Board, replacing the old PSSRB. This new board was later renamed the Federal Public Sector Labour Relations and Employment Board (FPSLREB). The new board has three mandates: adjudication, mediation, and compensation and research services. The Board is also required to offer administrative support to the National Joint Council. Some other minor amendments have been made: for example, Board members serve for five years instead of ten.

The number of exclusions from collective bargaining has decreased: lawyers of the Department of Justice and the Canada Customs and Revenue Agency and employees of the Treasury Board Secretariat are no longer automatically considered to be managerial or confidential and thus excluded from collective bargaining.

The *FPSLRA* created an institutional structure for co-development between unions and employers known as "consultation committees." The deputy head must establish a consultation committee within each department. This committee may then negotiate "co-development of workplace improvements." Negotiation may take place under the auspices of the National Joint Council. This goes partway toward implementing the recommendation of the Fryer Report of two-tier bargaining.

The *FPSLRA* refined the determination of essential services to give greater discretion to the employer in determining which employees are not permitted to strike. The new Act also requires—for the first time—that unions conduct a secret ballot before going on strike, and it put in place a new timetable for strikes. Strikes may only occur

- more than thirty days after an essential services agreement is in place (or has been amended) and
- more than seven days after the Public Interest Commission (the conciliation body) has sent its report or more than seven days after the commission has given notice that it will not send a report

Finally, the *FPSLRA* also contained two main changes to the grievance procedure. First, human rights issues may now be grieved in some circumstances instead of referred to the Canadian Human Rights Commission. Second, the new Act contains provisions for group grievances and policy grievances.

2) *Public Service Employment Act*

One of the purposes of the new *Public Service Employment Act* is to devolve decision-making down from the PSC and deputy head and to place it in the hands of more junior managers. The preamble to the new *Public Service Employment Act* sets out this purpose:

> [D]elegation of staffing authority should be to as low a level as possible within the public service, and should afford public service managers the flexibility necessary to staff, to manage and to lead their personnel to achieve results for Canadians.

Staffing authority has thus been transferred downwards gradually since 1918, from the PSC to the Treasury Board and deputy heads in 1967 and now further down to managers in the public service.

The most significant change in the new *Public Service Employment Act* concerns the merit principle. The new *Public Service Employment Act* still requires appointments and promotions to be made on the basis of merit. However, the new *Public Service Employment Act* contains statutory definitions of merit that are different from those established by the Federal Court and the PSC under the old *Public Service Employment Act* and also limits the ability of candidates to argue that an appointment was not made on the basis of merit.

Section 30(1) of the new *Public Service Employment Act* states that appointments to or from within the public service must be based on merit and free of political influence. According to section 30(2), an appointment is based on merit when the person meets "the essential qualifications for the work to be performed, as established by the deputy head, including official language proficiency" and having regard to additional qualifications that the deputy head considers to be an asset, and current or future operational requirements and needs of the organization as identified by the deputy head.

Under this definition, deputy heads (not the PSC) establish the staffing requirements by defining

- the needs of their department or organization
- operational requirements
- essential qualifications
- qualifications that will be an asset to the job but that are not essential

The new *Public Service Employment Act* provides that it is not necessary to consider more than one person in order for an appointment to be based on merit. Moreover, advertised or non-advertised appointment processes can be used. Finally, the previous *Public Service Employment Act* stated that appointments must be made from within the public service where possible. Under the new *Public Service Employment Act*, there will no longer be a preference for hiring from within the public service.

The method of complaint about the merit principle has also been changed under the new *Public Service Employment Act*. Candidates for a position who allege that the position was not awarded on the basis of merit may bring a complaint to a new Public Service Staffing Tribunal (PSST). When a person brings a complaint to the PSST, it may be made on one of only three grounds:

- abuse of authority in the choice of person to appoint (this is only available on an internal appointment process)
- abuse of authority in choosing between an internal and an external process
- failure to assess the candidate in the language of their choice

Finally, the new *Public Service Employment Act* allows public servants to participate in a broader scope of political activities and establishes ground rules for public servants who want to participate in political activities.

H. THE POST-2005 ERA

Parliament continued to amend the *FPSLRA* after 2005. The most significant change to the *FPSLRA* came in 2017[92] as a result of the Supreme Court of Canada's decision in *Mounted Police Association of Ontario v Canada (Attorney General)*[93] that members of the RCMP had a constitutional right to collectively bargain their terms and conditions of employment and that their exclusion from the ambit of the *FPSLRA* was therefore unconstitutional. While the Supreme Court of Canada's decision left open the possibility that Parliament could enact a labour relations statute specifically for RCMP members, instead Parliament

92 *An Act to amend the Public Service Labour Relations Act, the Public Service Labour Relations and Employment Board Act and other Acts and to provide for certain other measures*, SC 2017, c 9.

93 2015 SCC 1.

amended the *FPSLRA* to comply with the Court's decision. The *FPSLRA* now permits RCMP members to join an employee organization and certify that organization as a bargaining agent. The *FPSLRA* also contains several rules specific to RCMP members, which are discussed in Chapter 13. Parliament also took advantage of this change to rename the Act and the Board. While the parliamentary record is silent on the reason for the change, the thought was that the new name would make it more clear what the legislation referred to (i.e., that it was federal and that it was the entire public sector).

In 2013, Parliament enacted separate legislation for what is now the FPSLREB, abolishing the PSST and, in essence, merging it with the existing Public Service Labour Relations Board, which deals with both labour and staffing issues.[94] Parliament later added two new members to the board in 2017 to deal with the increased workload, increasing the number of members from ten to twelve members in addition to the chair and two vice-chairs (along with part-time members).[95]

Parliament has also tinkered with the *Public Service Employment Act* since 2005 by, for example, enhancing the right of public service employees who are members of the reserve force to return to their position at the end of a leave of absence for that reserve service[96] and opening up hiring opportunities for serving and former members of the Canadian Forces.[97] Perhaps the most significant change to the *Public Service Employment Act* was amendments in 2021 that required that the establishment and review of qualification standards and the use of assessment measures include an evaluation of whether there are biases or barriers that disadvantage persons belonging to any equity-seeking group.[98] At the time of publication, it is too early to tell whether those changes will in fact improve employment equity in the federal public administration.

Parliament enacted substantial changes to the *FPSLRA* in 2013 that would have significantly impacted labour relations in the federal public

---

94 *Economic Action Plan 2013 Act, No 2*, SC 2013, c 40, Part III, Division 18.

95 *An Act to amend the Public Service Labour Relations Act, the Public Service Labour Relations and Employment Board Act and other Acts and to provide for certain other measures*, SC 2017, c 9, s 38.

96 *An Act to amend the Canada Labour Code, the Canada Student Financial Assistance Act, the Canada Student Loans Act and the Public Service Employment Act*, SC 2008, c 15.

97 *Veterans Hiring Act*, SC 2015, c 5.

98 *Budget Implementation Act, 2021, No 1*, SC 2021, c 23.

administration.[99] That legislation removed the choice of dispute resolution from bargaining agents and instead would have required all bargaining agents to use conciliation/strike unless 80 percent or more of the positions in that bargaining unit were necessary to provide an essential service. The legislation also granted the employer the exclusive right to determine what services are "essential" and the numbers of positions required to provide that service—in effect granting the employer virtually unlimited authority to set essential service levels (and then force bargaining units to try striking with large percentages of their workers still at work). For those rare bargaining agents who still had access to arbitration to resolve bargaining disputes, the criteria for arbitration boards (and for public interest commissions for those bargaining agents going on strike) were amended to create two "predominant" factors (recruitment and retention along with Canada's "fiscal circumstances relative to its stated budgetary policies") along with four other factors. Finally, arbitration awards were to be subject to review if the chair of the board (on their own or at the request of a party) requested the arbitration board to review its decision. In 2014, Parliament also passed legislation eliminating card-based certification for bargaining agents, instead requiring a vote whenever an employee organization obtained 40 percent support from the employees in the bargaining unit.[100] However, Parliament undid those changes in 2017 and 2018.[101]

The government anticipated this *volte-face* on arbitration by permitting bargaining agents to select "binding conciliation" during that round of bargaining—in essence replicating what would have happened had the bargaining agents retained their right to elect arbitration throughout[102] or through wage reopener clauses in collective agreements negotiated prior to that legislative change.[103]

---

99 *Economic Action Plan 2013 Act, No 2*, SC 2013, c 40, Part 3, Division 17.

100 *Employees' Voting Rights Act*, SC 2014, c 40.

101 *An Act to amend the Canada Labour Code, the Parliamentary Employment and Staff Relations Act, the Public Service Labour Relations Act and the Income Tax Act*, SC 2017, c 12 (restoring card-based certification), and *An Act to amend the Federal Public Sector Labour Relations Act and other Acts*, SC 2018, c 24 (restoring the right to select arbitration and the 2005 essential service regime).

102 See, for example, *Treasury Board v Association of Justice Counsel*, 2018 CanLII 119222.

103 See, for example, *Canada Revenue Agency v Public Service Alliance of Canada*, 2018 CanLII 12677.

The other significant legislative change in the period after 2005 was the enactment of the *Expenditure Restraint Act*.[104] The *Expenditure Restraint Act* was one response to the 2008 financial crisis. The Act fixed wage increases for the federal public sector and many Crown corporations for the period 2006–11 and prohibited any other increases to compensation.[105] Many bargaining agents reached agreements with the employer at the fixed rates that were announced ahead of the legislation coming into force; other bargaining agents did not reach agreement and therefore had these wage rates imposed on them. Courts upheld the constitutional validity of the *Expenditure Restraint Act* on the grounds that these rates were the "going rate" reached in those agreements, it was time limited, and the Act did not preclude consultation on other compensation-related issues.[106]

I. CONCLUSION

The history of labour and employment law in the federal public service demonstrates the evolution of the two key concepts enumerated in the opening chapter to this text: the merit principle and free collective bargaining. After an original period of skepticism about the merit principle, the federal government wholeheartedly adopted that principle in its 1918 reforms. However, over time the merit principle has been weakened by a countervailing pressure for administrative efficiency to become at least an equal priority with the merit principle.

Similarly, after an initial period of skepticism, the federal government recognized the right of its employees to embrace free collective bargaining in 1967. However, this right was never absolute as there have always been limitations on the scope of bargaining. Over time, the government's reluctance to engage in free collective bargaining has led it to legislate suspensions to collective bargaining during times that

104 *Expenditure Restraint Act*, SC 2009, c 2, s 393.

105 There was an exception for RCMP members, who could receive new allowances that were "critical to support transformation initiatives relating to the Royal Canadian Mounted Police": *Expenditure Restraint Act*, s 62.

106 *Meredith v Canada (Attorney General)*, 2015 SCC 2 at paras 28–29. See also *Gordon v Canada (Attorney General)*, 2016 ONCA 625, *Federal Government Dockyard Trades and Labour Council v Canada (Attorney General)*, 2016 BCCA 156, and *Association of Justice Counsel v Canada (Attorney General)*, 2012 ONCA 530, for other appellate courts that upheld the validity of the Act.

it considered itself to be suffering from fiscal distress. Free collective bargaining and appointment according to merit still exist in the federal public service, although not as absolute principles since a countervailing pressure for efficiency has limited the application of those two principles.

PART II

LABOUR LAW TOPICS

CHAPTER THREE

What Is the Federal Public Service?

A. OUTLINE OF THE FEDERAL PUBLIC ADMINISTRATION

This book is about labour and employment law in the federal public service. Therefore, the first question that must be answered is: what is the "federal public service"?

The answer to this question is found in the *Financial Administration Act* (*FAA*).[1] The *FAA*, as its name suggests, establishes the basic rules for financial administration in the federal public sector—rules that are far beyond the scope and subject matter of this book. The *FAA* serves a second purpose: it establishes rules for human resources administration in the federal public sector.

As a foundational legal principle, the employer of federal public servants is His Majesty the King in right of Canada. As a general rule, His Majesty does not exercise his functions of employer himself or through the Governor in Council;[2] instead, he delegates his functions as the employer to either the Treasury Board of Canada or to a separate agency. The *FAA* sets out the persons for whom the Treasury Board, on behalf of His Majesty, will be the employer and those for whom some separate agency will be the employer.[3] The Governor in Council

1 *Financial Administration Act*, RSC 1985, c F-11 [*FAA*].

2 The "Governor in Council" is the term for the "Governor General of Canada acting by and with the advice of, or by and with the advice and consent of, or in conjunction with the Queen's Privy Council for Canada"—that is, the federal Cabinet. *Interpretation Act*, RSC 1985, c I-21, s 35.

3 *Gingras v Canada*, [1994] 2 FC 734 at para 38 [*Gingras*].

has the ability to shift particular government units between the various schedules to the *FAA*.

The federal public service (or, to use its proper legal term, the "federal public administration") is best seen as a series of concentric circles, shown in Figure 3.1 with some examples of units within each ring.

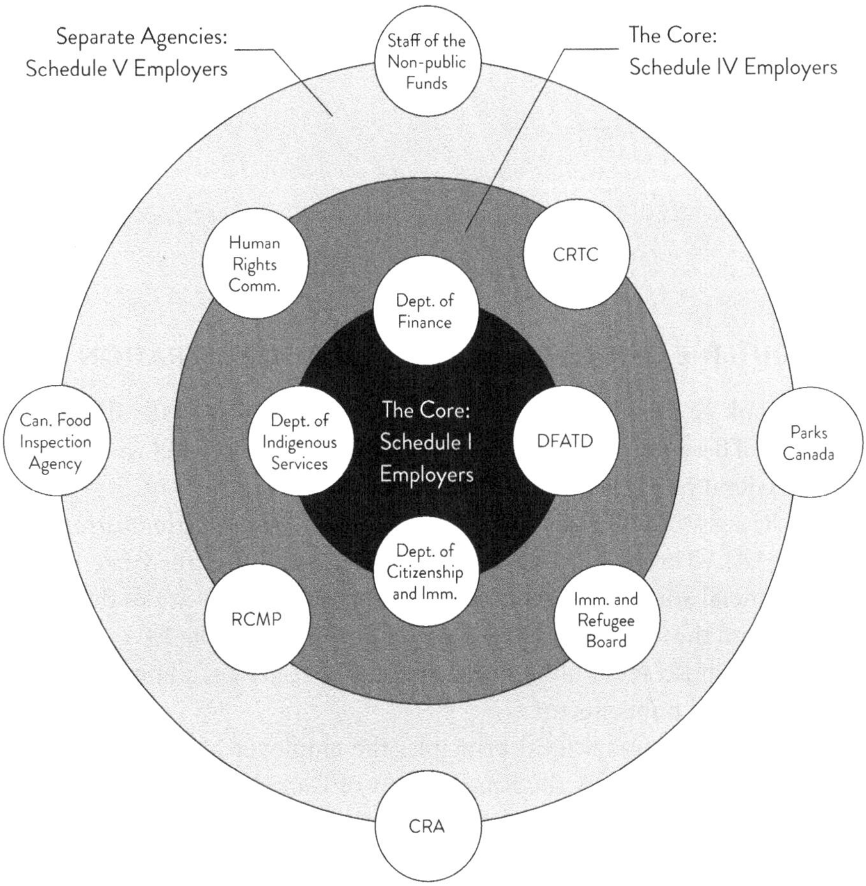

FIGURE 3.1. A CONCENTRIC CIRCLE MODEL OF THE FEDERAL PUBLIC ADMINISTRATION

The inner-most circle lists "departments" within the federal public service. A "department" is listed in Schedule I of the *FAA*. These departments include, for example, the Department of Foreign Affairs, Trade, and Development (DFATD; more commonly called Global Affairs Canada). As a practical matter, departments are responsible for designing and implementing government policy.

The second circle lists "portions" of the federal public administration. They are listed in Schedule IV of the *FAA*. As a practical matter, these portions, which are not departments, are more operational in nature: they provide a particular service to Canadians but are not responsible for designing government policy.

Together, the two inner circles comprise the "core public administration."

The third circle (in light grey) is composed of "separate agencies." Separate agencies are responsible for all aspects of the employment relationship; they are treated as separate employers for collective bargaining purposes and make their own decisions about appointing and dismissing employees.

This structure is further explained below.

1) The Core Public Administration and the Treasury Board

The core public administration refers to those departments and agencies listed in schedules I and IV of the *FAA*. More practically, public servants in the core public administration are employed by the Treasury Board instead of their particular department or agency. Most federal public servants are employed in the core public administration. As of 31 March 2019, for example, the core public administration had 220,310 employees (or 76.5 percent of the federal public service) compared to 67,668 (23.5 percent) in separate agencies.[4]

The core public administration comprises various departments of the federal public service, as well as certain agencies, boards, and commissions that are listed in Schedule IV and considered part of the core of the federal public service.

Employees in the core public administration are employed by the Treasury Board of Canada. The Treasury Board is a subcommittee of Cabinet established pursuant to section 5 of the *FAA* consisting of the president of the Treasury Board, the minister of finance, and four other Cabinet ministers. There are also a number of alternate members (other

---

4 Treasury Board of Canada Secretariat, "Population of the Federal Public Service" online: www.tbs-sct.gc.ca/psm-fpfm/modernizing-modernisation/stats/ssen-ane-eng.asp. In case you were wondering, this means that roughly 0.8 percent of Canadian citizens are employed in the federal public service, or 1.5 percent of Canadians in active employment.

Cabinet ministers) who form part of the Treasury Board in case of a conflict of interest.

The Treasury Board, broadly speaking, is responsible for overseeing the administration of the federal public sector. The specific responsibilities of the Treasury Board for human resources are set out in sections 7 and 11.1 of the *FAA* and include determining pay and allowances, determining the human resource requirements of the public service (i.e., how many employees there are), classifying positions, and preparing policies for departments to follow when implementing human resources decisions. The Treasury Board is also the employer for collective bargaining purposes in the core public administration.[5]

The Treasury Board is also responsible for financial management generally in the federal public service and for exercising powers under various other statutory instruments. The most notable of the Treasury Board's human resource powers outside of the *FAA* is its administration of the *Public Service Superannuation Act*[6] (the public service pension plan); one less notable power is that it is responsible for auditing the Office of the Auditor General.[7]

The actual work of the Treasury Board as employer is done by the Treasury Board Secretariat. The Treasury Board Secretariat is the administrative arm of the Treasury Board. According to the *Treasury Board of Canada Secretariat 2020–21 Departmental Plan*, the secretariat's four main areas of responsibility are spending oversight, administrative leadership, acting as the employer, and regulatory oversight.[8]

2) Separate Agencies

The second area of the public service comprises the "separate agencies" listed in Schedule V of the *FAA*. The Crown has delegated to each separate agency the power to act as the "employer" for employees within that agency. The Treasury Board is *not* considered the employer of employees of a separate agency. The separate agencies all have their

5 *Federal Public Sector Labour Relations Act*, SC 2003, c 22, ss 2 and 111 [*FPSLRA*].

6 *Public Service Superannuation Act*, RSC 1985, c P-36.

7 Answering the question "*Quis auditoret ipsos auditores?*" (Who audits the auditors?).

8 Treasury Board of Canada Secretariat, *Treasury Board of Canada Secretariat 2020–21 Departmental Plan* (30 April 2020), online: www.canada.ca/en/treasury-board-secretariat/corporate/reports/treasury-board-canada-secretariat-2020-21-departmental-plan.html.

own constituting statutes. Those constituting statutes establish—with greater or lesser degrees of particularity—that each separate agency has the power to appoint staff and fix their remuneration. The largest separate agencies are the Canada Revenue Agency (with almost 44,000 employees) and the Canadian Food Inspection Agency (with over 6,200 employees); the smallest is the Security Intelligence Review Committee (with only twenty-two employees).[9]

The Treasury Board still exercises some supervision over separate agencies. For example, a separate agency may only enter into a collective agreement "with the approval of the Governor in Council."[10] In 1967, the Governor in Council[11] issued a direction that separate employers could exercise the same power over their own employees as the Treasury Board exercised over employees in the core public administration. However, that authority was subject to two limits: (1) the separate employer had to consult with the Treasury Board before making or implementing new policies and (2) the separate employer had to obtain the "terms of reference" (or a "mandate") from the Treasury Board before entering into collective bargaining negotiations.[12] Therefore, the Treasury Board indirectly controls the collective bargaining for separate employers by controlling the "mandate" for negotiations.

When it comes to determining terms and conditions of employment outside of collective bargaining, some separate agencies are still subject to approval by the Governor in Council before they can fix remuneration,[13] while other separate agencies retain that power in their own right,[14] and still others retain that power but must consult with the Treasury Board before setting pay and allowances.[15]

---

9 Treasury Board of Canada Secretariat, "Population of the Federal Public Service by Department" (last modified 28 November 2022), online: www.canada.ca/en/treasury-board-secretariat/services/innovation/human-resources-statistics/population-federal-public-service-department.html.

10 *FPSLRA*, s 112.

11 Record of Cabinet Decision, 30 November 1967. This instrument is the delegation instrument contemplated by s 11.2 of the *FAA*.

12 This requirement to seek a Treasury Board "mandate" is also sometimes set out in statute: see *Canada Revenue Agency Act*, SC 1999, c 17, s 58.

13 See, for example, *National Research Council Act*, RSC 1985, c N-15, s 5(g), and the *National Capital Act*, RSC 1985, c N-4, s 8(3).

14 See, for example, the *Canadian Food Inspection Agency Act*, SC 1997, c 6, s 13(2).

15 *Canada Revenue Agency Act*, s 51(1)(d).

The Governor in Council may, at any time, move agencies, boards, or commissions to and from schedules IV and V—in other words, create and then disband separate agencies. Since separate agencies can be created (or abolished) by a decision of the Governor in Council, public servants have often been transferred en masse from the core public administration to a separate agency (or vice versa). When a new separate agency is created, the rules are set out in the statute creating that separate agency. When a group of employees are transferred from one portion of the public service (either a department or a separate agency) to another, the government need only enact a regulation to effect that transfer.[16]

3) Purpose Behind Dividing the Public Service

This approach—to divide the federal public service into the Treasury Board and separate employers—was recommended by the *Report of the Preparatory Committee on Collective Bargaining in the Public Service* (the Heeney Report).[17] The Preparatory Committee noted that employees in the public service are employed in over a hundred departments and agencies located throughout the country. Some of these departments and agencies had different levels of autonomy. Therefore, the difficulty was not in identifying who, legally, could be the employer (that would be the Crown) but in identifying the "focus of authority in which would be vested the jurisdiction to represent the employer for collective bargaining purposes."[18] The approach that the Preparatory Committee recommended was to

> divide agencies (other than the Crown corporations subject to the provisions of the *Industrial Relations and Disputes Investigation Act* [now the *Canada Labour Code*]) into two groups:
> (1) those subject to Government direction and control that may be appropriately treated as part of the 'central administration' in matters affecting rates of pay and conditions of employment, and

---

16 *Public Service Rearrangement and Transfer of Duties Act*, RSC 1985, c P-34. This is discussed in greater detail in Chapter 5.

17 *Report of the Preparatory Committee on Collective Bargaining in the Public Service* (Ottawa: Queen's Printer, 1965) [Heeney Report].

18 Jacob Finkelman & Shirley Goldenberg, *Collective Bargaining in the Public Service: The Federal Experience in Canada* (Ottawa: Institute for Research on Public Policy, 1983) at 72.

> (2) those subject in some degree to Government direction and control but having (by reason of statutory provision or administrative practice) or requiring (because of the nature of their function) a significant measure of independence in matters affecting rates of pay and conditions of employment.

> The Preparatory Committee eventually concluded that, for the purposes of the Public Service system of collective bargaining . . . all agencies in the first of these groups should be treated as parts of a single employer for which the Treasury Board would be recognized as the spokesman, and that each agency in the second group should be treated as a separate employer. Agencies granted "separate employer" status could have their own bargaining units and would have the capacity to enter into and administer their own collective agreements. However, their status in the collective bargaining system would in no way alter their relationship to the government.[19]

The *Federal Public Sector Labour Relations Act* (*FPSLRA*) (and its predecessor statutes) adopted this recommendation. Thus, section 111 of the *FPSLRA* gives the Treasury Board the authority to enter into a collective agreement for bargaining units other than those comprising employees in separate agencies,[20] and section 112 of the *FPSLRA* gives separate agencies the power to enter into collective agreements for bargaining units comprising employees of the separate agency.[21]

The *FPSLRA*, however, has created a statutory framework for bargaining at a departmental level in the core public administration, instead of solely between bargaining agents and the Treasury Board. This change was recommended by the Fryer Report, which stated:

> Under the current system, the employer and the unions negotiate the terms of service-wide collective agreements. This can mean that the financial terms and policies that are meant to provide flexibility to employees and managers do not respond fully to local needs. We reject the too rigid notion that service-wide determined terms and conditions of employment should apply in all circumstances and uniformly in all workplaces. We believe that the *process of bargaining should be more sensitive to individual workplace needs in order to provide the*

19 Heeney Report, above note 17 at 4–5.
20 *FPSLRA*, s 111.
21 *Ibid*, s 112.

> *flexibility the system requires.* We recognize that this concept of two tier negotiation is somewhat novel in the federal public service and believe that it should only be implemented on a voluntary basis.
>
> For example, a service-wide collective agreement for administrative employees might set the standard workweek at 37.5 hours. It can do this by stating that an employee with the base level of three weeks annual vacation must work a total of 1950 hours per year. In any one department, the managers and union representatives might agree that, to accommodate the requirements of certain work groups, the standard work week be defined as ranging from a minimum of 4 to a maximum of 8 days. Days off could be arranged in ways that appropriately compensate employees working longer or compressed workweeks. To respond to shift requirements in a specific work unit, the managers and union representatives might agree that the standard work day be defined as ranging from a set minimum to a set maximum, with correspondingly large blocks of time off for employees working longer days. Similarly, in work units with a seasonal component, they could also agree that the standard work year should be defined as ranging from nine to twelve months, which would give employees a solid block of time off in slack periods in return for working longer hours at peak periods.[22]

Thus, the Fryer Report recommended that collective agreements negotiated at the service-wide level provide the general outlines of the terms and conditions of employment and that the Act be amended to enable collective bargaining at the departmental or agency level. The *FPSLRA* permits just this result. Section 110 of the *FPSLRA* enables "two-tiered" bargaining. If the employer, bargaining agent, and deputy head of a department or agency[23] agree, then they may engage in collective bargaining respecting any terms and conditions of employment that apply in that department or agency.[24] Treasury Board guidelines concerning two-tier bargaining state that the parties should agree to a protocol for two-tier bargaining before it takes place. Despite being available for over fifteen years, at the time of publication these proto-

22 Final Report of the Advisory Committee on Labour Management Relations in the Federal Public Service, *Working Together in the Public Interest* (Ottawa: Treasury Board, 2001) , online (pdf): https://publications.gc.ca/collections/collection_2011/sct-tbs/BT22-70-1-2001-eng.pdf [Fryer Report] [emphasis added].

23 By "department or agency," I mean those entities listed in Schedule I or IV of the *FAA*.

24 *FPSLRA*, s 110(1).

cols have not yet been developed, and there are no two-tier agreements in the federal public service.[25] Two-tiered bargaining remains elusive.

4) Departmental Corporations and Crown Corporations

Before leaving this topic, there are two other entities that will be described: departmental corporations and Crown corporations.

The federal public sector includes a special type of corporation called a "departmental corporation." Departmental corporations are corporations created by Acts of Parliament and are listed in Schedule II of the *FAA*. They report to Parliament through a minister and are designed to function with greater autonomy than other departments. Their governing bodies (e.g., a board of directors) have roles specified in their constituting statutes. Identifying as a "departmental corporation" has no impact on labour or human resource jurisdiction: some departmental corporations are separate agencies; some are part of the core public administration; and some are completely outside of the federal public administration and considered a separate corporate entity.

A departmental corporation is treated as a department for the purposes of financial accounting and reporting required under the *FAA*.[26] This means that the Treasury Board is responsible for the financial management of departmental corporations, including "estimates, expenditures, financial commitments, accounts, fees or charges for the provision of services or the use of facilities, rentals, licences, leases, revenues from the disposition of property, and procedures by which departments manage, record and account for revenues received or receivable from any source whatever" as well as the review of annual or longer-term expenditure plans and programs.[27] This control over

---

25 The Union of Canadian Correctional Officers has entered into a "side agreement" with the Correctional Service of Canada on appointments and staffing issues, but this agreement is not a two-tier agreement as outlined in s 110 of the *FPSLRA*. See *Procureur général du Canada c Union of Canadian Correctional Officers—Syndicat des agents correctionnels du Canada—CSN (UCCO-SAAC-CSN)*, 2019 QCCA 979 at para 36. The Board in *Union of Canadian Correctional Officers—Syndicat des agents correctionnels du Canada—CSN v Treasury Board (Correctional Service of Canada)*, 2021 FPSLREB 22 referred to the 2018 version of this agreement as "a form of two-tier bargaining" under s 110 of the *FPSLRA*, but did not carefully consider whether the conditions set out in s 110 were met.

26 The *FAA* includes a departmental corporation in the definition of the term "department": s 2(1) "department," para (d).

27 *FAA*, s 7(1)(c) & (d).

financial management *does not* extend to control over human resources: in other words, a departmental corporation is not automatically subject to the Treasury Board on human resource issues. If the departmental corporation is also part of the core public administration, then it is subject to the Treasury Board; if not, it is not.

The funding of departmental corporations is supposed to be a combination of Parliamentary appropriations and revenues earned through services performed by the departmental corporation.

Crown corporations are further removed from the federal public service. A Crown corporation is a "corporation that is wholly owned directly by the Crown, but does not include a departmental corporation."[28] A corporation is wholly owned if all of the issued and outstanding shares of the corporation, other than shares necessary to qualify persons as directors, are held by the Crown (or in trust for the Crown), or if all the directors of the corporation, other than *ex officio* directors, are appointed by the Governor in Council or by a minister of the Crown with the approval of the Governor in Council.[29] Crown corporations can also be wholly owned subsidiaries of other Crown corporations.[30]

Crown corporations are managed and operated by a board of directors,[31] who in turn are appointed by the responsible minister with the approval of the Governor in Council.[32] The Treasury Board must approve the annual operating budget[33] and the capital budget of a Crown corporation.[34] The Treasury Board also sets some procedures for financial accounting (such as the types of forms used for audits of a Crown corporation).[35] Otherwise, Crown corporations are independent from the Treasury Board and, instead, accountable to Parliament and the Governor in Council through their minister. Some Crown corporations derive most or all of their revenue from commercial activities, while others are largely or almost completely dependent on parliamentary appropriations.

Employees of a Crown corporation are subject to the same labour and employment laws as employees in the federally regulated private

28 *FAA*, s 83.
29 *Ibid*, s 83(2).
30 *Ibid*, ss 83(1) and 83(4).
31 *Ibid*, s 109.
32 *Ibid*, s 105.
33 *Ibid*, s 123(1), (5). A small number of Crown corporations listed in Part II of Schedule III to the Act are exempt from this requirement.
34 *Ibid*, s 124(1), (8).
35 *Ibid*, s 132(3).

sector—in particular, the *Canada Labour Code*.[36] Crown corporations are therefore largely outside the scope of this book.

B. WHO IS AN EMPLOYEE?

1) Normal Test for "Employee"

At common law, and in most labour relations statutes in Canada, there is no single test for determining whether somebody is an "employee" or involved in some other legal relationship with the purported employer. In most cases, the need for such an assessment arises where it is necessary to determine whether a person is an "employee" or an "independent contractor." That dispute is resolved not by using a single definition or test but instead by examining the circumstances of the person's involvement with the purported employer and then deciding whether the relationship is more consistent with employer/employee or an independent contractor arrangement.

The leading case in Canada concerning this distinction is *McCormick v Fasken Martineau DuMoulin LLP*.[37] In that case, the issue was whether McCormick—an equity partner in the law firm Fasken Martineau DuMoulin—was an employee of the firm. Mr. McCormick was required to retire at age 65; he brought a complaint under British Columbia's *Human Rights Code*,[38] which only applied to employment relationships and not contractor relationships. Rather than adopt any of the competing "tests" that had been applied by previous courts or tribunals,[39] the Supreme Court of Canada stated that "[d]eciding who is in an employment relationship . . . means, in essence, examining how two synergistic aspects function in an employment relationship: control exercised by an employer over working conditions and remuneration, and corresponding dependency on the part of a worker."[40] Control and

---

36 *Canada Labour Code*, RSC 1985, c L-2.

37 *McCormick v Fasken Martineau DuMoulin LLP*, 2014 SCC 39 [*McCormick*].

38 *Human Rights Code*, RSBC 1996, c 210.

39 Those tests, broadly, were the "control" test focused on the level of control exercised over the worker, the "organization" test focused on the extent to which the worker is integrated into the workplace, and the "enterprise" test focused on who bears the ability to reduce or prevent risk of loss to third parties. For a summary of those tests, see *671122 Ontario Ltd v Sagaz Industries Canada Inc*, 2001 SCC 59.

40 *McCormick*, above note 37 at para 23.

dependency are not just about whether a worker receives instructions by a supervisor, but are also about the extent to which the worker has "the ability to influence decisions that critically affect his or her working life."[41] The Court concluded that Mr. McCormick, as a partner, exercised sufficient control and independence that he was not an employee.

2) Test for an Employee in the Federal Public Service: General Principles

Section 2 of the *FPSLRA* defines an employee as "a person employed in the public service." Therefore, the first inquiry that must be conducted is whether a person meets the common law test for an employee discussed above. However, it is not sufficient that a person meet the common law test for being an employee: they must also be an employee "in the public service." A person needs to be an employee at common law and also meet other statutory requirements to be an employee in the federal public service.

In *Canada (Attorney General) v Public Service Alliance of Canada* (*Econosult*),[42] the Supreme Court of Canada concluded that being an employee at common law was not sufficient to result in a person being employed "in the public service." In that case, the solicitor general had hired several teachers to provide educational programs for inmates of federal penitentiaries. In 1984, the solicitor general decided to privatize these educational programs by contracting these services out to the private sector. Accordingly, in May 1985, Supply and Services Canada contracted with Seradep Inc. to provide teachers for instruction at the Cowansville Penitentiary in Quebec. In 1987, the contract with Seradep expired, and the government entered a new contract with Econosult. Both contracts contained a clause specifically stating that the teachers were not hired as employees of the Crown.

While the first contract with Seradep was still in force, the Public Service Alliance of Canada (PSAC) filed an application with the Public Service Staff Relations Board seeking a declaration that the teachers at Cowansville Penitentiary were employees of the federal government and furthermore that they were members of the Educational Group bargaining unit for which PSAC was the certified bargaining agent. The

41 *Ibid* at para 27.

42 *Canada (Attorney General) v Public Service Alliance of Canada*, [1991] 1 SCR 614 [*Econosult*].

Board accepted PSAC's complaint and concluded that the government of Canada was the "true employer" of the teachers.

On eventual appeal to the Supreme Court of Canada, the Court quashed the Board's decision. The Court admitted that most labour boards in Canada (including the Canada Labour Relations Board) had the jurisdiction to determine who is an employee to prevent an employer from contracting out work in breach of a collective agreement. However, such was not the case in the federal public service. The statute specifically defines the term "employee" to include only people "employed in the public service." Therefore, the only people who are "employees" under the Act are those who have been appointed in accordance with the *Public Service Employment Act* (*PSEA*). The Court stated:

> The positions in the Public Service are determined by Treasury Board and appointments to the public service are within the exclusive right and authority of the Public Service Commission. Exceptions are carefully spelled out in the *Employment Act*. . . .
>
> In the scheme of labour relations which I have outlined above there is just no place for a species of *de facto* public servant who is neither fish nor fowl.[43]

The *Econosult* decision means that the common law test for determining who is an employee is not sufficient to make somebody an employee under the *FPSLRA*. A person's status as an employee is almost entirely dependent on whether they have been recognized as such by their employer (either the Treasury Board or the separate agency).

The process by which a position is created, and thereby a person becomes an employee of the Treasury Board, was set out by the Supreme Court of Canada in *Canada (Attorney General) v Brault*.[44] The process of becoming an employee is as follows:

> 1. The Minister or deputy head of a Department, in the exercise of his management authority, determines what positions are required in the Department and determines the qualifications for appointment to them; 2. Financial approval for a position must be obtained from the Treasury Board, which has authority under s. 7 of the *Financial Administration Act* . . . , to classify positions in the Public Service for

43 *Ibid* at paras 23 and 25.

44 *Canada (Attorney General) v Brault*, [1987] 2 SCR 489. This decision will be discussed in greater detail in Chapter 11, dealing with the merit principle.

> remuneration and other purposes; 3. The deputy head makes a request to the Public Service Commission to make the necessary appointment or makes the appointment himself under a delegation of authority; and 4. The appointment is made pursuant to the particular selection process required by the *Public Service Employment Act* and *Regulations*, the relevant provisions of which have been quoted above. The important point, for purposes of the issue in this appeal, is that it is the Minister or deputy head who creates a position and determines the qualifications for appointment to it, and that, subject to the necessary approval from the Treasury Board, this act does not call for any particular formality or expression. It is an administrative decision which identifies particular functions to be performed and defines the qualifications required for performing them.[45]

Although this case was decided in 1987, the process has not changed a great deal since then. The Public Service Commission retains the exclusive legal power to make appointments to the core public administration, unless there is authority to do so under any other Act of Parliament.[46] As discussed in Chapter 11, though, the power is in practice delegated to managers within each department or portion of the federal public administration.

Thus, a person may be paid by the Government of Canada, the tasks they perform may be dictated by the Government of Canada, the person may have no chance of profit or risk of loss—in other words, all of the relevant factors may point toward "employment" at common law—and yet a person is still not an employee of the public service until they are formally appointed by the Public Service Commission or its delegate.

For example, in *Professional Association of Foreign Service Officers v Canada*,[47] the Department of Foreign Affairs and International Trade established a Foreign Service Development Program. As part of this program, it recruited some sixty people into the foreign service, both from inside and outside the government. Successful candidates had to meet a certain level of proficiency in both official languages. Rather than turn away candidates for not being bilingual, the department asked successful candidates to undergo language training for up to twelve months.

---

45 *Ibid* at para 11.

46 *PSEA*, SC 2003, c 22, ss 12, 13, and 29(1).

47 *Professional Association of Foreign Service Officers v Canada*, [2001] CPSSRB No 103, aff'd [2003] FCJ No 483 (CA).

While they were on language training, the successful candidates were either paid their substantive rate (if recruited from within the public service) or 80 percent of their anticipated salary (if recruited from outside the public service). The candidates were also told they were part of the superannuation and dental plans (but in fact no money was deducted from their pay for those plans). In other words, successful candidates were controlled by the Government of Canada—they were told to attend language training, during the hours set, and paid accordingly.

The Professional Association of Foreign Service Officers brought an application before the Board alleging that the external candidates on language training were employees of the federal public service and that internal candidates on language training should be in the bargaining unit represented by that association. The Board rejected the association's application on the grounds that the candidates on language training had not received a formal offer of appointment from the department (using power delegated from the Public Service Commission). The Federal Court of Appeal agreed, stating:

> It was certainly open to the Board to consider that the "administrative and bureaucratic errors" which the applicant cites as evidence that *de facto* Ms. Qureshi [one of the candidates] and her colleagues were employees, could not have the effect of making these candidates "employees," because of the legal propositions I have mentioned above, and because of the letters which met the legal requirements and which indicated the contrary.[48]

Another example is found in *Gariépy v Canada*.[49] In that case, the plaintiff was first appointed in 1975 to the position of president and general manager of the Crown Asset Disposal Corporation, which she held until 1981. She was then appointed to the position of deputy executive director of Metric Commission Canada in the Department of Consumer and Corporate Affairs for a fixed term from 22 March 1982, to 22 March 1984. In January 1984, the plaintiff started to work in the Department of Transport in Montreal. In about February 1984, an agreement entitled "Secondment Agreement between Transport Canada and Corporate Affairs" was signed by the plaintiff, Consumer and Corporate Affairs, the Department of Transport, and the Public Service

48 *Ibid* at para 16.

49 *Gariépy v Canada*, [1998] FCJ No 698 (CA).

Commission. This agreement purported to extend her employment for two years. This agreement did not comply with the necessary requirements of the *PSEA* to constitute a valid appointment. When this two-year "secondment agreement" expired, Ms. Gariépy did not receive another job offer (contrary to the agreement) and brought suit as a result.

The Federal Court of Appeal dismissed the claim on the basis that no breach of the secondment agreement had occurred. However, the Court also concluded that the secondment agreement did not create an employment relationship, stating that the agreement

> could not create, in favour of the appellant, contractual rights of the nature of those attached to the indeterminate member of the public service, enforceable against the Queen. An employer-employee relationship between the Queen and an individual may not exist outside the parameters precisely established by the legislation.[50]

The rule in *Econosult* has led to the strange result that a worker is an "employee" for the purposes of some legislation, but not an "employee" under the *FPSLRA*. In *Estwick and Quintilio v Treasury Board (Correctional Service of Canada)*,[51] an adjudicator rejected a grievance because two "contractors" (who had worked full time for over two years and who had been declared to be employees for tax purposes and ordered to pay employment insurance and Canada Pension Plan premiums) had not been "given a formal instrument of appointment [under the *PSEA*] such as a letter of offer."[52] The adjudicator paid particular attention to the various procedures that the Public Service Commission is supposed to follow when making appointments, as well as the fact that the contracts were not offered by the person to whom the commission had delegated its hiring authority.

Another example is *Farrell v Canada*.[53] That case involved an alleged employment relationship between Mr. Farrell and the Canadian Security Intelligence Service (CSIS)—an agency that is not part of the core public service and that makes its own appointments independent from the Public Service Commission.[54] Mr. Farrell alleged that he was

---

50 *Ibid* at para 3.

51 *Estwick and Quintilio v Treasury Board (Correctional Service of Canada)*, 2006 PSLRB 14, aff'd 2007 FC 894 [*Estwick*].

52 *Ibid* at para 79.

53 *Farrell v Canada*, [2002] FCJ No 1723 [*Farrell*].

54 See discussion in *Gingras*, above note 3 at para 55.

offered a position with CSIS, provided that he did not tell anybody that he was working for the organization (his job was allegedly to spy on people's mail, so he was to tell people that he worked for Canada Post). He was allegedly offered this position by an officer of CSIS, accepted the offer, and worked for a short while before his employment was terminated. He brought a claim for wrongful dismissal, but the claim was dismissed on summary judgment by the Federal Court.

The *Canadian Security Intelligence Service Act*[55] gives the director of CSIS the exclusive authority to make appointments to CSIS. The best that Mr. Farrell could allege was that he was given an offer by some officer of CSIS other than the director. Therefore, the Federal Court concluded that he was never an "employee" of CSIS, stating:

> It is well settled that an individual cannot become an employee of Her Majesty in Right of Canada without a specific appointment made in accord with procedures established in accord with these statutes. In this case, since the Director of CSIS is expressly authorized by Parliament to make appointments to CSIS, employees in the public service employed by CSIS must be appointed by the process authorized by the Director.
>
> The principle that an appointment to employment in the public service is required to be made in accord with statutory authority is of long standing. Employment as a public servant does not arise by other means it may not be inferred from the facts alleged, unless those include facts alleging that the authorized process has been followed.[56]

Finally, a group of offenders incarcerated in a federal penitentiary who also work in that penitentiary attempted to certify a bargaining agent to represent them in collective bargaining. They argued that an employment relationship exists between offenders employed within the federal penitentiary system and the Treasury Board.[57] The Board dismissed their application because, while they may be employees in the

55 *Canadian Security Intelligence Service Act*, RSC 1985, c C-23, s 8.

56 *Farrell*, above note 53 at paras 9–10 [citations omitted].

57 Such an application is not as unusual as it sounds. The Ontario Labour Relations Board, for example, certified a bargaining agent representing inmates working in an abattoir as part of their rehabilitative activities: *Amalgamated Meat Cutters and Butcher Workmen of North America v Guelph Beef Centre Inc*, [1977] OLRB Rep March 184.

common sense of the word, they were not appointed in accordance with the *PSEA*. In other words, *Econosult* remains good law.[58]

These cases all stand for the proposition that to be "employed in the public service" requires that all of the necessary formalities under the *PSEA* (or other Acts governing separate agencies) must be followed before a person becomes an "employee." These "formalities" require that there be some documented appointment made by the proper authority: the Public Service Commission or its delegate or the person given the power of appointment to the separate agency.

There are some exceptions to this rule. The *PSEA* states that the Public Service Commission must make all appointments to the core public administration "unless there is authority to do so under any other Act of Parliament."[59] This exception became an issue in *Catlos and Treasury Board (Statistics Canada)*[60] when a census commissioner grieved the termination of his employment. Counsel for the Treasury Board alleged that Mr. Catlos was not an "employee" under the Act because he was not appointed to his position by the Public Service Commission. The Board disagreed. It was true that Mr. Catlos was not appointed to his position by the Public Service Commission: he was appointed to his position by virtue of section 5 of the *Statistics Act*.[61] The Board concluded that this triggered the exception in the *PSEA* normally requiring the Public Service Commission to appoint Mr. Catlos to his position. Therefore, the Board applied the normal test for an "employee at common law as opposed to an independent contractor."[62]

Thus, the common law test for an employee is, in rare cases, still sufficient to make one an employee in the federal public service. It is a necessary condition for being an "employee" under the *FPSLRA* that a person be an "employee" at common law as opposed to an independent contractor. Furthermore, there are some positions for which there are no formalities of appointment. The appointment under the *Statistics Act*

58 *Jolivet v Treasury Board (Correctional Service of Canada)*, 2013 PSLRB 1, aff'd 2014 FCA 1.

59 *PSEA*, s 29(1).

60 *Catlos and Treasury Board (Statistics Canada)*, [1998] CPSSRB No 58 [*Catlos*].

61 *Statistics Act*, RSC 1985, c S-19.

62 *Catlos*, above note 60 at para 50. The Board concluded that it did not have enough evidence to decide whether Mr. Catlos was an employee or an independent contractor. However, the Board dismissed the grievance because it was filed against the Treasury Board and concluded that Mr. Catlos's true employer was Statistics Survey Operations—a separate employer.

is one such position. Also, under the *National Film Act*,[63] the National Film Board may appoint employees, and there are no limits on the identity of the person making the appointment. Therefore, in *Syndicat Général du Cinéma et de la Télévision (SGCT) v The Queen*,[64] the applicant, Syndicat Général du Cinéma et de la Télévision, sought certification to represent "freelancers" working under personal contracts with the National Film Board. The Board refused the application on the basis that the "freelancers" were not employees within the meaning of the *Public Service Staff Relations Act* (*PSSRA*) because they were engaged under contracts for personal services under the *National Film Act* and did not occupy "positions" in the public service as defined in that Act and in sections 13 and 14 of the *National Film Act*. The Federal Court of Appeal quashed that decision and ordered the Board to instead determine whether the persons for whom certification was sought were employees rather than independent contractors, even though their services were engaged under a form of personal services contract.[65]

The specific wording of the legislation is important when considering whether an exception to the principles of *Econosult* applies. For example, workers at the Halifax Citadel National Historic Site who were paid through the Halifax Citadel Regimental Association were not employees of Parks Canada. The *Parks Canada Agency Act* states that the chief executive officer has exclusive authority to "appoint . . . employees of the Agency."[66] The Citadel workers were therefore not "employees" under the *FPSLRA* because they were not formally appointed by the chief executive officer. The Board pointed out that the statutory formalities at Parks Canada are not "onerous," but they "still must be met in order to be considered an employee."[67]

---

63 *National Film Act*, RSC 1985, c N-8.

64 *Syndicat Général du Cinéma et de la Télévision (SGCT) v The Queen*, [1978] 1 FC 346 (CA).

65 The Board eventually decided that persons engaged under contract pursuant to para 10(1)(d) of the *National Film Act* to direct specific projects, which they have initiated and which are subject both to the prior approval of the National Film Board, as well as approval at various stages of production, are independent contractors and not employees, but the other freelancers were employees: *Re Syndicat Général du Cinéma et de la Télévision*, [1979] CPSSRB No 3 at para 89.

66 *Parks Canada Agency Act*, SC 1998, c 31, s 13.

67 *Public Service Alliance of Canada v Parks Canada Agency*, 2009 PSLRB 176 at para 138, aff'd 2010 FCA 305 at para 6.

As seen above in the *Estwick* decision, a worker can be an "employee" for the purposes of some statutes and yet not an "employee" for the purposes of the *FPSLRA*. One area of recent development is whether the rule in *Econosult* applies to the *Public Service Superannuation Act*. For years, federal government contractors who would be "employees" at common law but who were not appointed formally under the *PSEA* were excluded from federal retirement pension benefits. In other words, *Econosult* applied to their position. For example, in *Cohen v Attorney General of Canada*, the Federal Court of Appeal upheld a decision denying access to pension benefits for an employee of the Law Reform Commission because that employee had not been formally appointed under the *PSEA*, specifically relying upon *Econosult* in doing so.[68] Similarly, in *Burley v Canada (Attorney General)*, the Federal Court relied upon *Econosult* in concluding that a worker was not an "employee" during a period of language training that occurred immediately before his formal appointment under the *PSEA* commenced.[69]

More recently, however, the Federal Court has taken a different view. In *Baribeau v Canada (Attorney General)*, the Federal Court set aside a decision denying superannuation service because the decision was made despite a finding by the Canada Revenue Agency that the worker was an employee for tax purposes and because the decision referred to common law principles, but the worker lived and worked in Quebec, where civil law principles would apply.[70] The Court did not refer to *Econosult* in its decision. The next year, in *Landriault v Canada (Attorney General)*, the Court again set aside a decision denying a worker superannuation service. This time, the Court acknowledged *Econosult* but noted that the pension centre making the decision did not rely exclusively upon *Econosult* and, instead, evaluated factors that were similar to the common law employment test. The Court concluded that, having listed these factors as relevant, the pension centre had to actually consider them.[71]

Finally, the Federal Court addressed *Econosult* in the superannuation context more directly in *Céré v Canada (Attorney General)*. Mr. Céré worked for approximately twelve years in the David Florida

68 *Cohen v Attorney General of Canada*, 2009 FCA 99 at para 3.

69 *Burley v Canada (Attorney General)*, 2008 FC 525.

70 *Baribeau v Canada (Attorney General)*, 2015 FC 615. The Court acknowledged that the result at civil law could have been the same as at common law at para 21.

71 *Landriault v Canada (Attorney General)*, 2016 FC 664 at para 67.

Laboratory, a spacecraft assembly and testing centre owned by the Government of Canada. Throughout this period, the Government of Canada contracted for Mr. Céré's services through third parties.[72] He was not appointed under the *PSEA* until he was later hired more formally in 1997. His application to count that period of service for superannuation purposes was denied, but the Federal Court set aside that decision. Dealing with *Econosult* specifically, the Court agreed with both parties in that case that "the principles stemming from *Econosult* should apply only in the context of labour relations and cannot be transposed into the field of pensions."[73]

In conclusion, *Econosult* continues to be applied in the context of labour and employment decisions under the *FPSLRA*. *Econosult* is limited to that context, however, and is not applied for other purposes, including tax and pension purposes. In those contexts, the more standard test for an employment relationship applies.

3) Exclusions Under the *FPSLRA*

Having defined an "employee" as somebody employed in the public service, the *FPSLRA* goes on to exclude several categories of workers from the application of all or part of that Act in the definition of "employee." These exclusions will be examined in turn.

a) Persons Appointed to Statutory Positions

> *a person appointed by the Governor in Council under an Act of Parliament to a statutory position described in that Act*

The *FPSLRA* excludes people appointed by the Governor in Council to statutory positions—in other words, it excludes statutory office holders. This exclusion has been in the legislation since 1967 and was designed to exclude "officers of parliament, statutory appointees, deputy heads of departments, and so forth."[74] This section has only been at issue before the Board on one occasion concerning ship inspectors appointed under

72 At common law, the existence of a corporation or contracting through a third party does not necessarily mean that the worker is not an employee: see *Braiden v La-Z-Boy Canada Limited*, 2008 ONCA 464 at para 30.

73 *Céré v Canada (Attorney General)*, 2019 FC 221 at para 35.

74 Statement of Dr. George Davidson, then secretary of the Treasury Board, to the Special Joint Committee of the Senate and the House of Commons on

the *Canada Shipping Act*,[75] and in that case the government passed an order in council declaring the affected inspectors to be employees.[76]

b) Locally Engaged People

a person locally engaged outside Canada

The *FPSLRA* excludes people locally engaged outside Canada. The reason for this exclusion—which has been in the legislation since 1967—is that such people fall within the jurisdiction of other sovereign states and Canada "cannot, by anything we do here, presume to establish employer-employee relations with respect to employees who may come under the jurisdiction of other legislation in other national jurisdictions."[77]

This exclusion was the subject of a dispute between the Alliance of Canadian Cinema, Television and Radio Artists (ACTRA) and the Treasury Board concerning employees of the Canadian Forces Network. In 1989, ACTRA submitted an application for certification to the Board seeking to represent a unit of announcers and reporters employed in the Canadian Forces Network of the Department of National Defence. A dispute arose concerning whether these people were "locally engaged outside Canada." Some of these broadcasters had been living in Canada when they were appointed and received their offer of employment in Canada before moving to Germany to take up their duties. ACTRA argued that these people were not "locally engaged" because they were Canadian citizens, hired in Canada, and not nationals of the host nation. The Treasury Board argued that these announcers and reporters were locally engaged outside Canada because they worked outside of Canada.

The Board originally dismissed ACTRA's application, concluding that the announcers and reporters were locally engaged outside Canada because they "were performing work exclusively at the CFN stations in Europe."[78] However, on judicial review, the Federal Court of Appeal

---

Employer-Employee Relations in the Public Service of Canada, *Minutes of Proceedings and Evidence* (Ottawa: Queen's Printer 1966) at 881 [*Proceedings 1966*].

75 *Canada Shipping Act*, RSC 1985, s 9.

76 *Public Service of Canada and Canada (Treasury Board)*, [1968] CPSSRB No 10.

77 *Proceedings 1966*, above note 74 at 881–82.

78 *Alliance of Canadian Cinema, Television and Radio Artists (ACTRA) and Treasury Board (Department of National Defence)*, [1990] CPSSRB No 18 at 10.

overturned that decision.[79] The Court referred to the French version of the Act, which excluded people who were "recrutées sur place à l'étranger" and concluded that the Board's decision "is patently wrong in law." The exclusion "can only apply to persons hired outside Canada to perform work outside of Canada."[80]

The matter was then remitted to the Board to determine which of the employees were hired outside Canada to perform work outside of Canada.[81] Five of the people covered by the application were living in Canada when they were hired. The Treasury Board argued that they were all hired outside Canada because the hiring authority (in this case, the base commander in Europe) was located outside of Canada. The Board rejected that argument for two reasons. First, it concluded that the hiring authority could just as easily be the deputy minister of national defence in Ottawa because the *Locally Engaged Staff Employment Regulations*[82] in force at that time provided that "the Deputy Minister of National Defence may employ persons locally at a post as civilian component employees." Second, and more importantly, the Board rejected the idea that the locus of the employing authority determines where an employee is hired. Instead, the Board applied the "postal rule" and the "closest connection" tests from the common law. The "postal rule" states that where an acceptance of an offer is posted, that is the location of the contract.[83] The "closest connection" test states that the locus of a contract is located in the place with the "closest and most real connection" to the parties.[84] Using those tests, the hiring took place in Canada.

The Treasury Board applied for judicial review of that decision, but the Federal Court upheld the decision, stating:

> The applicant admitted in this Court that the Board's conclusion was correct as a matter of contract law, but argued that the issue should be approached as one of statutory interpretation rather than of contract. The application was, however, understandably unable to show us that there was any general policy in the Act of encouraging exclusions from the unionized labour force.

---

79 *ACTRA v Canada (Public Service Staff Relations Board)*, [1990] FCJ No 902 (CA).

80 *Ibid* at 2.

81 *Alliance of Canadian Cinema, Television and Radio Artists (ACTRA) and Treasury Board (Department of National Defence)*, [1991] CPSSRB No 21 [*ACTRA*].

82 *Locally Engaged Staff Employment Regulations*, SOR/79-545, s 6(1).

83 *Adams v Lindsell* (1818), 1 B & Ald 681.

84 *Imperial Life Assurance Co v Colmenases*, [1967] SCR 443.

> Moreover, the words of the Act, as interpreted by this Court on the previous occasion, make it clear that the question of where the alleged "employees" had been engaged was determinative, and that the answer to it was to be determined by the Board as a matter of fact.[85]

Therefore, a person is "locally engaged outside of Canada" when they are both hired outside Canada and work outside of Canada. The location of hire is determined according to the normal laws of contract governing the locus of a contract.

c) Part-Time and Casual Employees

> *a person not ordinarily required to work more than one third of the normal period for persons doing similar work*
>
> *a person employed on a casual basis*
>
> *a person employed on a term basis, unless the term of employment is for a period of three months or more or the person has been so employed for a period of three months or more*

Casual and part-time employees were excluded in the 1967 version of the Act. The explanation given for these exclusions was that "the line had to be drawn somewhere"[86]—or more fulsomely:

> The real problem is how far you can go in recognizing the attachment of employees who are short term, casual or temporary employees as permanent employees who are potentially permanent members of a bargaining unit, whose votes may determine who is recognized and who is not recognized as the bargaining agent for the bargaining unit; whose votes may or may not determine whether or not the option is going to be for the arbitration or conciliation approach; whose votes may determine whether or not a proposal which is put forward on the negotiating table and agreed to is or is not going to be acceptable to the majority of the membership of the bargaining unit.[87]

The Board has also examined the purpose behind excluding casual employees and has justified it as follows:

---

85 *Canada (Attorney General) v ACTRA*, [1991] FCJ No 924 (CA) at 3.

86 Finkelman & Goldenberg, above note 18 at 29.

87 *Proceedings 1966*, above note 74 at 882.

> The purpose of paragraph (g) [now paragraph (f)] is to ensure that persons who have very little attachment to the bargaining unit and no community of interest with more permanent employees in that unit will not have an undue influence on the outcome of collective bargaining decisions.[88]

Despite these ostensibly fair purposes, the exclusion of part-time and casual employees from the *FPSLRA* may be of dubious constitutional validity.[89] Distinctions between part-time or casual employees and full-time employees are disproportionately harmful to women. In 1981, women made up 72 percent of all part-time workers that year.[90] By 2000, that figure had not changed a great deal: "among adult wage earners (age 25 to 54), women constitute the overwhelming majority of part-time workers, outnumbering men by a ratio of four to one."[91] In 2015, roughly three-quarters of adult wage earnings working part-time were women.[92]

The majority of people—especially people of prime working age—who suffer the adverse effects of being part-time or casual employees are women. Therefore, any deprivation of rights to part-time or casual employees constitutes adverse effect discrimination against women. Depriving part-time or casual employees of the right to associate with a bargaining agent under the *FPSLRA* could arguably violate the guarantee of equality in section 15 of the *Canadian Charter of Rights and Freedoms* (the *Charter*). The *FPSLRA* fails to take into account women's already disadvantaged position within Canadian society, resulting in substantively differential treatment between them and others on the basis of their gender, and that this differential treatment perpetuates

---

88 *ACTRA*, above note 81 at 8.

89 See Ronald Davis, *The OLRB Policy on Bargaining Units for Part-Time Workers* (Kingston, ON: IRC Press, 1991). Discrimination against part-time workers has been found to constitute discrimination against women under article 119 of the EEC Treaty: see *Bilka-Kaufhaus GmbH v Weber von Hartz*, [1986] ECR 1607 [*Bilka-Kaufhaus*]. See, more recently, *Fraser v Canada (Attorney General)*, 2020 SCC 28.

90 Joan Wallace, *Part-Time Work in Canada: Report of the Commission of Inquiry into Part-Time Work* (Ottawa: Supply and Services Canada, 1983) at 72.

91 Debra Parkes, *Employment Standards That Work for Women*, submission to the Manitoba Employment Standards Review (2008) at 8, citing Statistics Canada, *Women in Canada, 2000: A Gender-Based Statistical Report* (Ottawa: Department of Canadian Heritage, 2000) at 124.

92 Melissa Moyser, *Women and Paid Work* (Ottawa: Statistics Canada, 2017) at 16.

a pre-existing disadvantage of casual and part-time workers. Casual and part-time workers in Canada are paid less and have worse terms and conditions of employment than do other workers. Preventing them access to unionization perpetuates these disadvantages.[93]

Whether this discriminatory effect could be justified under section 1 of the *Charter* on the grounds that they have an insufficient "attachment to the bargaining unit" also has yet to be decided. In *Coles and Treasury Board (Agriculture Canada)*,[94] PSAC argued that excluding casual workers from the definition of "employee" violated section 15 of the *Charter*; however, the Board declined to answer that question, instead concluding that it did not have the jurisdiction to address the constitutional validity of its enabling statute.[95]

The exclusion of employees working not more than one-third of the normal period of a working period is assessed at a given point of time and not by considering the totality of the workers' period of service. In *Nemours v Deputy Head (Department of Veterans Affairs)*, the grievor worked as a nurse/team leader at Sainte Anne's Hospital beginning in 1992. She was dismissed in 2005 and grieved that dismissal. At the time of her dismissal, she was working under a contract as an "on-call" employee for less than one-third of the normal hours of work; however, during earlier parts of her careers, she sometimes worked more than one-third of the normal hours of work for similar employees. The adjudicator concluded that this past conduct was not relevant and, instead, assessed the grievor's situation at the time of her dismissal, stating:

> At the time of her dismissal, Ms. Nemours was not ordinarily required to work more than one-third of the normal period for persons doing similar work. The fact that, at certain times of the year preceding her dismissal, Ms. Nemours worked more than one-third of the normal period for persons doing similar work is not relevant here because

93 The European Court of Justice has concluded that rules disadvantaging part-time employees in general, and public servants in particular, are a form of adverse-effect discrimination on the basis of gender: *Bilka-Kaufhaus*, above note 89; *Magorrian v Eastern Health and Social Service Board*, [1998] ECR I-7153; and *Hill v Revenue Commissioners*, [1998] ECR I-3739.

94 *Coles and Treasury Board (Agriculture Canada)*, [1990] CPSSRB No 145.

95 This conclusion would not be valid today: see Chapter 4 concerning the jurisdiction of the Board to address constitutional issues.

> those hours were not worked during the period of employment immediately preceding her dismissal.[96]

This exclusion for working less than one-third of the normal hours is also based on the scheduled hours of work and does not include last-minute additional work provided to the worker. In *Bigdeli-Azari v Deputy Head (Department of Veterans Affairs)*, the grievor signed a contract to be an "on-call" employee. On-call employees informed their employer of their hours of availability at least one month in advance, and then the employer prepared a work schedule well in advance of that work. This grievor actually worked extra hours that he was called to voluntarily fill in, so his actual hours of work exceeded the one-third threshold four out of the six months he worked in the position. The adjudicator nevertheless concluded that this voluntary work did not make the grievor an "employee," stating that "the number of hours that a person is 'ordinarily required' to work is the number of hours planned on that person's normal work schedule."[97] In other words, voluntary work in excess of the usual hours does not count when assessing the one-third figure.[98]

The term "casual basis"—as that term was used in the now-defunct *PSSRA*—was the subject of some controversy—namely, did an employee have to serve ninety consecutive days before no longer being employed on a casual basis, or was a total of ninety days' employment within a given year sufficient? The controversy really revolved around the application of then section 21.2 of the old *PSEA*[99] to the definition of the term "casual." Section 21.2 of the *PSEA* stated that the Public Service Commission may appoint any person to the public service for a period not exceeding ninety days, so long as they do not work for greater than 125 days in any year. In *Marinos v Canada (Treasury Board)*,[100] Ms. Marinos was appointed pursuant to section 21.2 of the

---

96 *Nemours v Deputy Head (Department of Veterans Affairs)*, 2009 PSLRB 47 at para 50, aff'd *Nemours v Canada (Attorney General)*, 2010 FC 158.

97 *Bigdeli-Azari v Deputy Head (Department of Veterans Affairs)*, 2011 PSLRB 126 at para 20.

98 See also *Public Service Alliance of Canada v House of Commons*, 2017 FPSLREB 14, confirming that "voluntary overtime" does not count toward the minimum 700 hours of work needed to be an employee under the *Parliamentary Employment and Staff Relations Act*, RSC 1985, c 33 (2nd Supp), s 3.

99 Section 21.2 was added in the 1993 amendments to the *PSEA*.

100 *Marinos v Canada (Treasury Board)*, [2000] FCJ No 446 (CA) [*Marinos*].

PSEA. She worked "on call" for a total of 115 days between 5 January 1996 and 8 July 1996. She was terminated for disciplinary reasons on 17 July 1996 and attempted to grieve. The adjudicator accepted her grievance, stating that the term "on a casual basis" must be interpreted in its normal labour relations meaning, not simply by reference to section 21.2 of the *PSEA*. Ms. Marinos's services were needed on a regular basis: she worked an average of eighteen days a month for a continuous period of more than six months. Therefore, she was not a "casual" employee.

The Federal Court of Appeal overturned the adjudicator's decision and concluded that any person appointed pursuant to section 21.2 of the *PSEA* was a "casual" worker for the purposes of the *PSSRA*. The Court came to this conclusion notwithstanding that the text of section 21.2 of the *PSEA* never mentioned the term "casual." However, the heading above the English version of that section was "Casual Employment." In the French version, it was "Emploi tempraire"—a different term from that used in the French version of the *PSSRA* (which used the phrase "employees à titre occasionnel"). Despite the inconsistency in the French version of those statutes, the majority of the Court of Appeal concluded that an employee appointed pursuant to section 21.2 was, by definition, a "casual" employee under the *PSSRA*.[101]

The current versions of the *FPSLRA* and *PSEA* help resolve this particular problem. Section 2(4) of the *FPSLRA* helps define "casual" as follows:

> 2(4) For the purposes of paragraph (f) of the definition of "employee" in subsection (1), a person employed in the part of the public service to which the Public Service Commission has the exclusive right and authority to make appointments is employed on a casual basis if the person was appointed under section 50 of the *Public Service Employment Act*.

Section 50 of the *PSEA* then states that the commission may appoint casual employees so long as the period of employment does not exceed ninety working days in one calendar year in any particular department

101 Justice Rothstein, later of the Supreme Court of Canada, dissented. He concluded that section 21.2 did not define "a person employed on a casual basis" for the purposes of the *PSEA* let alone for the *PSSRA* as well.

or other organization. Section 50 also excludes casual workers from the provisions of the *PSEA*.

This statutory definition of "casual" only applies to the core public administration. Casual workers employed by separate employers are not appointed under section 50 of the *PSEA*. Therefore, the Board's decision in *Marinos*—even though it was overturned by the Federal Court of Appeal—is still valid to define "casual" for separate employers. This means that the term "casual" as it applies to workers in separate agencies will be interpreted in light of its normal labour relations meaning.

One final issue that has arisen before the Board about these provisions concerns the exception for term employees. It has been argued, on some occasions,[102] that employees whose term contracts are longer than the time period set out in the statute are not "employees" until they have actually worked the minimum period of time required under the Act. The term used to be six months; therefore, in those earlier cases, it was argued that a person on a temporary contract that was longer than six months was not an "employee" until they actually completed six months of work. The Board has consistently rejected that argument.

In the *University Teaching Group* case,[103] the union seeking certification argued that teachers who were engaged on an "academic year" basis were persons working on a temporary basis and that since the contracts started in July and the application was made in December, they had not been employed for a period of six months and were therefore not "employees" within the meaning of the Act. The Board rejected that submission. The Board rejected a similar submission by the Treasury Board in *ACTRA*[104] that two announcers hired on two-year contracts were not "employees" because they had not yet worked for six months and it could not be assumed that they would actually work for a period of six months or more.

d) Certain RCMP, CSIS, and FPSLREB Officers

a person who is an officer of the RCMP

a person employed in the Canadian Security Intelligence Service who does not perform duties of a clerical or secretarial nature

---

102 *ACTRA*, above note 81; *University Teaching Group* (PSSRB Decision No 142-2-92).
103 *Ibid.*
104 *ACTRA*, above note 81.

> *a person employed by the Administrative Tribunals Support Service of Canada who provides mediation, legal, or advisory services to the Board*

Police officers with the RCMP were excluded from the *FPSLRA* until a 2015 Supreme Court of Canada decision striking down that exclusion.[105] Officers of the RCMP—that is, RCMP members of the rank of Inspector and higher—remain excluded from the *FPSLRA*. Employees of CSIS are excluded from the collective bargaining provisions of the *FPSLRA* unless they perform clerical or secretarial duties. However, CSIS employees are still covered by Part II of the *FPSLRA*, meaning that they have the right to grieve and to refer those grievances to adjudication in certain circumstances.[106]

Among other consequences, the exclusion of these three classes of employees from Part I of the *FPSLRA* means that their staff associations are not governed by the statutory duty of fair representation. In *Palmer v Canadian Security Intelligence Service Employees' Association*,[107] Mr. Palmer alleged that the CSIS Employees Association failed in its duty of fair representation. Mr. Palmer was late in filing a grievance at the final level, and this grievance was dismissed. He relied upon the counsel of the CSIS employees' association in filing his grievance. The Board concluded that the CSIS employees' association was not subject to the *FPSLRA*'s duty of fair representation because it was not a bargaining agent—and could not be a bargaining agent for Mr. Palmer because he was not an "employee" under the *FPSLRA*. The Board concluded that it did not have the jurisdiction to "recognize a '*de facto*' bargaining agent"—aping the language of the Supreme Court of Canada in *Econosult* denying the Board the jurisdiction to recognize de facto employees.[108]

---

105 The exception for RCMP officers, as well as their staff relations system, will be discussed in Chapter 13.

106 *FPSLRA*, s 206(1), "employee."

107 *Palmer v Canadian Security Intelligence Service Employees' Association*, [2005] CPSLRB No 47.

108 It should be remembered that, despite the lack of a statutory duty of fair representation, an association may still owe legal obligations to its members, which may be enforceable at common law through the court system: see, for example, *De Silva v Toronto Police Assn*, [2004] OJ No 5038, for the existence of a common law duty of fair representation where no statutory duty exists.

e) Students

> *a person who is employed under a program designed by the employer as a student employment program*

The Board has indicated that it will examine the terms of any established "student employment program" carefully; if students hired in the public service do not meet the requirements of that program, then they will be considered employees for the purpose of the *FPSLRA*.

For example, in *Public Service Alliance of Canada and Treasury Board*,[109] Revenue Canada hired students full time during the summer and then offered some of them full- or part-time employment during the school year. PSAC brought an application seeking a determination that these students working during the school year were part of the Program Administration bargaining unit. At issue were the terms of the Federal Summer Student Employment Positions—the relevant "student employment program." The Board analyzed the program carefully and concluded that it only governed students who worked between 1 April and 30 September. Therefore, the students who worked for Revenue Canada during the rest of the school year were employees under the Act. The Board stated:

> In my view, even a cursory examination of that document makes it very clear that it was intended to provide special rules of the hiring of students during the traditional non-academic "summer" period, that is between April and September exclusively. The document permits no other possible interpretation.[110]

On reconsideration, the Board overturned its previous decision because the employer was able to explain that another memorandum of understanding between Revenue Canada and the Treasury Board specifically provided for a year-round student employment program.[111] However, the Board did not depart from its approach of closely examining the contents of the student program, nor did it indicate an unwillingness to consider students to be "employees" when they were not, strictly speaking, part of that program.

---

109 *Public Service Alliance of Canada and Treasury Board*, [1997] CPSSRB No 59.
110 *Ibid* at para 30.
111 *Public Service Alliance of Canada and Treasury Board*, [1997] CPSSRB No 138.

Finally, student employees are subject to a regulation excluding them from the operation of many provisions in the *PSEA*, except for the provisions dealing with citizenship.[112]

f) Managerial and Confidential Employees

a person who occupies a managerial or confidential position

The last group of exclusions listed in the definition of the term "employee" in the *FPSLRA* comprises persons employed in a managerial or confidential position. The exclusion of managerial employees only applies to Part I of the *FPSLRA*: managerial employees are still subject to Part II of the *FPSLRA* (namely, the grievance and adjudication procedure discussed in Chapter 10).[113]

Most labour relations statutes in Canada exclude from their ambit managers or employees who have access to confidential information about collective bargaining.[114] The British Columbia *Public Service Labour Relations Act* does not exclude managers from the Act per se, but states simply that collective agreements may exclude employees who

> (a) exercise the functions, and do exercise the functions, of a manager or superintendent in the direction or control of employees,
> (b) are in a confidential planning or advisory position in the development of management policy for the government, or
> (c) are in a confidential capacity in matters relating to labour relations or personnel.[115]

However, the *FPSLRA* goes further and excludes all employees who occupy a "managerial or confidential position." The *FPSLRA* then defines a "managerial or confidential position" as follows:

---

112 *Student Employment Programs Participants Exclusion Approval Order*, SI/2010-46.

113 *FPSLRA*, s 206(1), "employee."

114 See, for example, Ontario *Labour Relations Act*, SO 1995, c 1, Schedule A, s 1(3), which excludes employees "who, in the opinion of the Board, [exercise] managerial functions or [are] employed in a confidential capacity in matters relating to labour relations," or Ontario's *Crown Employees Collective Bargaining Act*, SO 1993, c 38, s 1.1(3), which also excludes "employees exercising managerial functions or employed in a confidential capacity in relation to labour relations."

115 *Public Service Labour Relations Act*, RSBC c 388, s 11(3).

> "[M]anagerial or confidential position" means a position declared to be a managerial or confidential position by an order made by the Board under subsection 62(1), section 63, subsection 74(1) or section 75.[116]

Thus, a position is "managerial or confidential" if the Board declares it to be so. In many circumstances, a position becomes "managerial or confidential" as the result of some unilateral action by the employer—for example, assigning particular duties or naming the employee as the first level of the grievance procedure. The Board has stated that "the employer is under the obligation, whenever possible, to arrange its affairs so as to minimize the need for exclusion."[117] However, as the cases below will reveal, the Board—as ordered by the Federal Court of Appeal on occasion—has not been overzealous in its scrutiny of the employer's actions. For example, the Board is not permitted to examine the necessity of naming an employee as the first-level grievance officer (thus excluding them), notwithstanding the employer's obligation.[118] Therefore, the managerial exclusion is a matter of some contention, and bargaining agents have accused employers of overzealous exclusions (sometimes with the effect of emasculating a bargaining unit).

Section 59 of the *FPSLRA* lists the eight circumstances in which an employer may apply to the Board for an order declaring a position to be "managerial or confidential." These eight circumstances will each be discussed in turn, but they are grouped into six headings.

i) *Persons Employed in a Confidential Capacity to a Number of Specified Officials*

> *59(1)(a) the position is confidential to the Governor General, a Minister of the Crown, a judge of the Supreme Court of Canada, the Federal Court or the Tax Court of Canada, or a deputy head*

> *59(1)(b) the occupant of the position has, in relation to labour relations matters, duties and responsibilities confidential to the occupant of a position described in paragraph (b), (c), (d), or (f)*

Both of these require a determination of whether a position is confidential. Before describing what constitutes a confidential position, it is

116 *FPSLRA*, s 2(1) "managerial or confidential position."

117 *Treasury Board and Association of Public Service Financial Administrators*, [1998] CPSSRB No 106 at para 68 [*Treasury Board and APSFA*].

118 See below notes 152 and following.

helpful to describe what is *not* included in the definition. In the 1960s and 1970s, the Board adopted the principle that there were two classes of confidential employees:

1. a person is confidential when their superior's duties are so onerous that the supervisor is compelled to delegate a significant portion of those duties that form the basis of the supervisor's exclusion, and where the duties so delegated require skill, judgment, trust, and confidence; or
2. a person is confidential where the services rendered by that person are of such a nature that the supervisor would normally have to rely to a substantial extent on the confidential person to perform them, having regard to modern technology and office organization.[119]

In 1979, the Federal Court of Appeal quashed a decision of the Board that applied these principles. The Court rejected those principles out of hand, stating that

> [t]he word "confidential" . . . is used in its usual sense which, contrary to what the Board assumed, does not imply any delegation of functions. An executive does not delegate any functions to his legal counsel; the counsel's position is nevertheless confidential to the executive.[120]

Therefore, a "confidential" position does not require any delegation of functions. In view of the Federal Court of Appeal's decision, the Board had to "reconsider its policy"[121] and redefine the criteria for a confidential position. In *Sisson*,[122] the Board did just that. It examined the much earlier decision of the Supreme Court of Canada in *British Columbia et al v Canada Safeway Ltd*,[123] which concerned the definition of "confidential" in the BC labour relations legislation. The Board concluded that in that case "Mr. Justice Rand concluded that the word 'confidential' must be given a narrow interpretation. If it were broadly interpreted, the majority of employees would be excluded

119 See, for example, *Cuddihy and Norton*, PSSR Reports K 745.

120 *The Queen in Right of Canada v Public Service Staff Relations Board*, [1979] 2 FC 60 (CA) at para 5.

121 Finkelman & Goldenberg, above note 18 at 39.

122 *Sisson*, [1979] CPSSRB No 9.

123 *British Columbia et al v Canada Safeway Ltd*, [1953] 2 SCR 46 [*Safeway*].

from collective bargaining, a result which Parliament clearly did not intend."[124] The Board drew the following rules from the *Safeway* decision and decisions of other labour relations boards in Canada:

> (1) The mere fact that an employee has access to confidential information does not, of itself, mean that he is employed in a confidential capacity.
>
> (2) To be considered a confidential exclusion, there must exist between the particular employee and the employer "a relation of a character that stands out from the generality of relations and bears a special quality of confidence." There is an element of personal trust which permits some degree of "thinking aloud" on special matters.
>
> (3) In many instances, it is of the essence of the confidence that the information not be disclosed to any member of any group or body of the generality of employees.[125]

Those principles became the basis of the Board's jurisprudence concerning whether an employee is in a "confidential" position.

In *Patry and Young*,[126] the Board added the qualification that such a confidential relationship cannot be "casual or fortuitous." Thus, it cannot be based on factors such as the personality or style of the particular supervisor to whom the employee is confidential, but it "must be inherent in the position occupied by the person identified by the employer."[127]

For positions identified in section 59(1)(a) of the *FPSLRA*, the position must simply be confidential to one of the named officeholders in any capacity. This determination depends heavily on the peculiarities of the position at issue. For example, in *Patry and Young*, the Board concluded that the position of law editor of the Supreme Court of Canada was confidential to a judge of the Supreme Court. Law editors were responsible for preparing summaries of judgments handed down by the Court. The Board concluded:

> In discussing the draft summary with a law editor a judge must have confidence that he can freely explain or elaborate his thinking so that important elements are not distorted or lost in the summary report.

---

124 *Sisson*, above note 122 at para 42.
125 *Ibid* at para 48.
126 *Patry and Young*, Board Decision No 172-2-296.
127 *Public Service Alliance and Treasury Board*, [1984] CPSSRB No 44 at para 16.

> For his part, the law editor must feel secure enough to make suggestions as to form and consistency. . . . The summary reports that are eventually published apparently represent, in many cases, a harmonization of the opinions of various judges and it would seem that the law editors play a significant role in this.[128]

On the other hand, registry officers of the Federal Court of Canada were not identified as confidential. The Board concluded that registry officers only discuss technical or procedural points with judges and that they participate in private conferences only as a recorder of minutes.[129]

In *Public Service Alliance of Canada and Canada (Treasury Board)*,[130] the Board concluded that a secretary of the minister of employment and immigration was not confidential in large part because Ms. Mercier did not have free access to the minster or regularly spend time with him; instead, her usual duties were to provide secretarial support to the minister's press secretary. While she had access to confidential and sensitive documents, this was not sufficient to make her position a "confidential" one. The Board pointed out that the Act does not bar all employees in a minister's office from being "employees"; therefore, the mere fact that an employee works in a minister's office where confidential information is bandied about and employees are expected to "enjoy the trust"[131] of the minister is not sufficient to exclude those employees from collective bargaining. Similarly, almost twenty years later, the Board also concluded that the head of the ministerial correspondence unit at Fisheries and Oceans Canada was not "confidential" on much the same reasoning.[132]

Legal counsel or legal advisors were generally considered in a confidential position considering the nature of their duties. In *PIPSC v Canada (AG)*, the Federal Court stated:

> When a portion of the government service has a legal advisor, in the nature of things, his services are provided on a confidential basis, and, when it has a legal branch, the responsibility of the director of that branch is to provide such services, and to discharge that responsibility

128 *Patry and Young*, above note 126 at para 13.

129 *Public Service Alliance and Treasury Board*, above note 127.

130 *Public Service Alliance of Canada and Canada (Treasury Board)*, [1981] CPSSRB No 8.

131 *Ibid* at para 35.

132 *Treasury Board v Public Service Alliance of Canada*, [2000] CPSSRB No 45.

> he must have the help of lawyers whose services must be provided to him or as directed by him on a confidential basis. If such a lawyer is not in a confidential position in relations to the director of his branch, or as the statute puts it, "confidential to" the director, I have difficulty to conceive, on the basis of my experience, of any person who is "confidential to" any other person in the Public Service.[133]

That case was relied on in determining that legal advisors to the Immigration and Refugee Board were in a confidential position.[134] However, the Federal Court also referred to the fact that, at the time, legal officers of the Department of Justice were excluded as a class. This is no longer the case: when the *FPSLRA* was enacted, Parliament removed that particular exclusion. Therefore, it is doubtful whether the Federal Court's decision that legal officers are always confidential is still determinative of all cases. Each case must be resolved on its particular facts.

The Board has more recently confirmed that the *Sisson* test applies to section 59(1)(h) of the *FPSLRA*. In *Treasury Board v Public Service Alliance of Canada*,[135] the employer applied for an order declaring a senior human resources assistant to be excluded from the bargaining unit. The position was largely clerical in nature: the occupant of the position entered data about grievances and updated systems and files. The Board declined to exclude the position under section 59(1)(h) because there was no element of "thinking aloud" with that position. The employer argued that the office configuration meant that the employee could overhear confidential discussions; the Board rejected that argument, stating instead that "the employer has a duty to organize its affairs so that its employees are not occasionally placed in a position of a potential conflict of interest if that result can readily be avoided."[136]

For positions identified in section 59(1)(h), it is not sufficient that they be confidential: they must be "in relation to labour relations matters." The term "labour relations" will be discussed further below regarding the exclusion in section 59(1)(c).

---

133 *PIPSC v Canada (AG)*, [1972] FC 1316 (CA) at 1322.

134 *PIPSC v Treasury Board*, [2000] CPSSRB No 8.

135 *Treasury Board v Public Service Alliance of Canada*, 2017 PSLREB 11.

136 *Ibid* at para 42.

ii) Executive Employees

> *59(1)(b) the position is classified by the employer as being in the executive group, by whatever name called*

Employees classified in the "EX" (executive) group are not eligible to engage in collective bargaining.

iii) Employees with Labour Relations Duties

> *59(1)(c) the occupant of the position provides advice on labour relations, staffing, or classification*

> *59(1)(f) the occupant of the position is directly involved in the process of collective bargaining on behalf of the employer*

Section 59(1)(c) is a new exclusion added to the *FPSLRA*. Under the old *PSSRA*, the Board concluded that a person who gave technical advice—as opposed to a person with actual decision-making authority—to policymakers in the field of personnel administration (in that case, compensation) was not excluded under that Act.[137] This is no longer the case: employees who give advice are excluded.

The main dispute in section 59(1)(c) concerns the interpretation of the term "labour relations." This interpretative issue was raised squarely in *Treasury Board v Association of Justice Counsel*.[138] That case involved three lawyers who provided advice to the Department of National Defence about human rights complaints, policy developments, possible amendments to legislation, workers' compensation complaints, and work refusals under occupational health and safety legislation. The case turned on the definition of the term "labour relations." The employer argued for an expansive interpretation of "labour relations" that included all labour and employment matters generally speaking, including anything affecting terms and conditions of employment. The Board concluded that this interpretation was too broad. Such a broad interpretation would run counter to the premise that the right to join an employee organization is both a statutory and a constitutional right. This broad interpretation was also contrary to the wording of section 59(1)(c) itself, which excluded "labour relations, staffing or classification," and also contrary to the

137 *Wing*, [1977] CPSSRB No 14 at para 21.

138 *Treasury Board v Association of Justice Counsel*, 2020 FPSLREB 3, aff'd *Attorney General of Canada v Association of Justice Counsel*, 2021 FCA 37.

wording of section 59(1)(e) excluding employees with responsibility for grievances. The employer's interpretation of "labour relations" would encompass "staffing or classification" and "grievances"—contrary to the rule that all words in legislation should have meaning. The Board therefore concluded that "labour relations" only encompassed matters that fall within the scope of Part I of the *FPSLRA*, such as collective bargaining and unfair labour practices. The Board, however, rejected the argument by the bargaining agent in that case that section 59(1)(c) only applied when the incumbent is giving advice about their own bargaining unit. The heart of the Board's decision reads:

> Accordingly, I find that to be considered a labour relations matter under ss. 59(1)(c) or (h), the advice or related duties and responsibilities at issue must be related to a matter that falls within the scope of Part 1 of the Act. As stated, I find that this interpretation of "labour relations" for the purposes of ss. 59(1)(c) and (h) follows its ordinary meaning, the context of s. 59(1), and the scheme and object of the Act.[139]

The Board confirmed this rule in *Treasury Board v Public Service Alliance of Canada*,[140] in that case concluding that health and safety issues were not "labour relations" because those issues concerned sections 124 to 125.5 of the *Canada Labour Code* and not the subjects set out in in Part I of the *FPSLRA*.

The Board has accepted that grievances fall within the ambit of "labour relations," despite the fact that grievances are covered in Part II of the Act and not Part I.[141] In that same case, the Board was rather more vague about whether discipline constituted "labour relations." The Board decided not to exclude certain employees under section 59(1)(c) of the Act because those employees only had the authority to issue an oral or written reprimand. While the Board in that case did not explain why that level of disciplinary authority was important, it may have

---

139 *Ibid* at para 47. The Federal Court of Appeal expressly cited this paragraph with approval: *ibid* at para 5.

140 *Treasury Board v Public Service Alliance of Canada*, 2021 FPSLREB 24. The Federal Court of Appeal set aside the Board's decision, but on the basis of the Board's assessment of s 59(1)(g) of the Act. The issue of "labour relations" was not argued before the Federal Court of Appeal: *Canada (Attorney General) v Public Service Alliance of Canada*, 2022 FCA 204.

141 *Canadian Energy Regulator v Professional Institute of the Public Service of Canada*, 2020 FPSLREB 120 at para 114 [*Canadian Energy Regulator*].

been noteworthy that reprimands may not be referred to adjudication under section 209(1)(b) of the Act so that the Board was suggesting that discipline that could be adjudicated constitutes "labour relations" but other forms of discipline do not.

An employee need only provide "advice" on labour relations, staffing, or classification matters to be excluded; however, they must be "directly involved" in collective bargaining to be so excluded. An employee is "directly involved" in collective bargaining if they are a member of the negotiating team, so long as that person's involvement is "real and not token, and it cannot be perfunctorily discharged."[142] However, direct participation in an arbitration or conciliation hearing is not a prerequisite for an employee to be directly involved in the collective bargaining process:

> In our view, the process of collective bargaining in the Federal Public Service encompasses a great deal more than the actual negotiation of terms and conditions of employment at the bargaining table. Without attempting to define the limits of the process it would certainly include the analysis and interpretation of relevant material necessary to the preparation of the employer's mandate and the analysis and preparation of a detailed employer response to proposals of the bargaining agent. If [an employee], in the conduct of his duties, performed only research and analysis that, although relevant to the bargaining process, was primarily developed for a variety of purposes and not directly to assist the employer representatives in the collective bargaining process, the Board would not consider that he would meet the requirements for designation. . . . This, however, is not the case. It is quite evident that Mr. Taylor prepares analysis and research that is fundamental to the negotiating position of the employer.[143]

iv) Employees Responsible for Government Policies or Programs

> *59(1)(d) The occupant of the position has substantial duties and responsibilities in the formulation and determination of any policy or program of the Government of Canada*

The Board has not dealt with this particular exception in any reported decision; therefore, there are no determinative cases concerning what

142 *Canada (Treasury Board) and PIPSC*, [1979] CPSSRB No 13 at paras 13–14.
143 *Taylor* (Board File No 172-2-339). See also *Ethier*, [1982] CPSSRB No 92.

constitutes the "formulation and determination of any policy or program of the government of Canada." However, the 1967 version of the *PSSRA* excluded employees who had "executive duties and responsibilities in relation to the development and administration of government programs." In defining the term "government programs" under the old *PSSRA*, the Board has stated:

> The fact that a particular plan of action towards some stated goal is developed and administered in the context of the operation of the government is not a sufficient reason for designating it as a government program. There must be hundreds of such plans of action within the various subdivisions of departments or agencies that are labeled as programs—vehicle maintenance, personnel training, consumer information, navigation aids, purchasing capital expenditures, animal inspection etc. etc. These cannot, however, be considered to be government programs within the meaning of [the Act].[144]

The Board in that case also made it clear that a "program" is not limited to programs that are directly established by statute or recognized in the Estimates as requiring a special vote.[145]

In *Paquin*,[146] the Board had to determine whether Mr. Paquin was excluded for being confidential to an employee (Mr. Leblanc) who was responsible for the development and administration of government programs. It was not contested that Mr. Leblanc had these duties, and in any event he was an EX-1 and so would have been excluded for other reasons after the 1993 amendments. However, the Board did explain why Mr. Leblanc was considered responsible for government policy as follows:

> The evidence shows, first, that Mr. J. Leblanc, EX-1, Director, Regional Secretariat and Economic Services, Quebec Region, Employment and Immigration Canada, indeed has executive duties and responsibilities in relation to the development and administration of government programs.... Mr. Leblanc's principal responsibilities, as described in his position analysis schedule, Exhibit 1, include (paragraph 19 of the

144 *Office of Auditor General of Canada and Public Service Alliance of Canada*, [1980] CPSSRB No 2 at para 12.

145 *Ibid.*

146 *Paquin*, [1991] CPSSRB No 119.

> Groulx Report) corporate controls, general planning, socio-economic studies, extradepartmental affairs and the library.[147]

Finally, there is a distinction between administering programs and formulating or developing them. The Board has stated that

> the term "developing" we take to include "the process of developing"—i.e. the ongoing process of amending, augmenting or diminishing—as well as the planning, creating or bringing into being of government programs. However, any "developmental" activity taking place after the planning or creating stage would need to be of such significance that it truly equated with "change" and not simply with ongoing operational activity.[148]

Under the old Act, the relevant section excluded employees who had

> executive duties and responsibilities in relation to the development and administration of government programs.[149]

Therefore, the Board concluded that the terms "development" and "administration" must be different. The *FPSLRA* does not mention "administration" of government programs because it does not contain the limitation that these employees must be performing "executive duties." However, it is still valid to distinguish between the administration of programs and the development or formulation of programs. Development or formulation requires the "design or planning" of government programs or the "establishment" of those programs.[150]

Concerning the term "policy," the Board in the *Wing* decision previously cited concerning the staff relations exception drew a distinction between advisors and those responsible for policy, stating that although the employees' advice is generally accepted, "they do not have the kind of decision making authority with respect to policy matters that would bring them within the concept of the 'management team.'"[151] The "policy matters" in question concerned personnel and staffing matters, such as the development of the disability insurance plan and other benefits. This

---

147 *Ibid.*

148 *Yano*, [1986] CPSSRB No 213.

149 *PSSRA*, SC 1967, c 72, s 2(1).

150 *Yano*, above note 148.

151 *Wing*, above note 137 at para 22.

implies that the term "policy" could include more than macro-level policies (such as drafting White Papers or legislative initiatives).

v) *Grievance Handling and Managerial Duties*

> *59(1)(e) the occupant of the position has substantial management duties, responsibilities and authority over employees or has duties and responsibilities dealing formally on behalf of the employer with grievances presented in accordance with the grievance process provided for under Part 2*

The exclusion in section 59(1)(e) has two parts: an exclusion for employees who deal with grievances and an exclusion for employees with generic "management" duties.

The exclusion for grievance officers appears, facially, to be the easier of the two concepts to determine, yet it remains a contentious exclusion. Any employee responsible for responding to grievances — from the first level on up — is excluded. The employee does not need to deal substantially with grievances, and the volume of grievances or the time spent dealing with grievances is not relevant.[152] Simply identifying the employee as the first step in the grievance procedure is sufficient: the Board may not examine the justification for naming those employees as grievance officers or decide whether it was truly necessary to designate those employees as grievance officers.[153] The employee must actually decide grievances; simply passing the grievance on to the first-level decision-maker does not trigger section 59(1)(e) of the Act.[154]

This almost unfettered power on the part of the employer has led to some abuses. For example, in 1994, the Treasury Board identified thirty-five correctional supervisors to be first-level grievance officers. This decision effectively destroyed the bargaining unit, leaving it with "only a handful of members." The Board concluded that this was not relevant in the absence of *mala fides* on the part of the employer.[155] There is very little that a bargaining agent can do in the face of such a

152 *Jobin*, [1998] CPSSRB No 61 at para 18.

153 *The Queen in Right of Canada v Public Service Alliance of Canada*, [1984] 2 FC 998 (CA).

154 *Canadian Energy Regulator*, above note 141.

155 *Public Service Alliance of Canada and Treasury Board*, [1995] CPSSRB No 41, aff'd *Public Service Alliance of Canada v Canada (Treasury Board)*, [1996] FCJ No 159 (CA).

designation by the employer. If the bargaining agent can demonstrate that the employer was motivated by *mala fides* or anti-union animus, then that can prevent the exclusion of those employees. Even in the case of the correctional supervisors, where a management witness admitted that it was "a probability" that union membership was a factor in management's decision to exclude those employees, the Board still concluded that there was no anti-union animus.[156] The Board has more recently confirmed that it does not have the authority to question the motives behind an employer's decision to designate an employee as a representative at a level of the grievance procedure.[157]

In *Canadian Food Inspection Agency v Professional Institute of the Public Service of Canada*,[158] the bargaining agent successfully used its collective agreement provisions governing the grievance procedure to defeat an employer's attempt to exclude two employees. In that case, the bargaining agent had proposed an amendment to its collective agreement (during bargaining) designating the regional director as the first level in the grievance process. The employer refused that demand but assured the bargaining agent that there would be no change in the person responsible for the first level of the grievance procedure (currently the regional director). After the collective agreement had been signed, the employer attempted to designate inspection managers as the first level of the grievance procedure. The bargaining agent successfully argued that the employer was estopped from identifying a new position as the first level in the grievance procedure because the bargaining agent had relied on the employer's representation during bargaining. This case means that a bargaining agent may negotiate the identity of the first-level grievance officers and thus deprive the employer of the ability to designate new officers and selectively remove employees from the bargaining unit. Aside from this creative solution, section 59(1)(e) applies rigidly.

The exclusion for "substantial management duties, responsibilities and authority over employees" is more difficult to define. The leading decision on this issue is *Treasury Board and APSFA*.[159] In that case, the

156 *Ibid* (CA) at para 13.

157 *Treasury Board v Professional Institute of the Public Service of Canada*, 2008 PSLRB 55 at para 20.

158 *Canadian Food Inspection Agency v Professional Institute of the Public Service of Canada*, [2001] CPSSRB No 76.

159 *Treasury Board and APSFA*, above note 117.

Board clearly distinguished between "supervisors" and "managers"—in other words, not all supervisors are managers. The employer proposed a definition of management that the Board considered overbroad:

> Planning, providing, coordinating, directing, evaluating and controlling all available efforts and resources of an organization for the accomplishment of the objectives and policies which are designated by and handed down from top executives of organizations.[160]

Although the Board rejected that definition, it did not attempt to provide a thorough definition of "management." Instead, its decision discloses some principles.

First, involvement in the disciplinary process is not a sufficient condition to conclude that the employee is a manager. Instead, the Board will examine the authority to discipline in the departmental context. For example, supervisors with the authority to reprimand employees are not managers.[161] Similarly, supervisors with the authority to suspend employees may not be managers depending on the extent of their discretion. Where the delegation of authority to suspend is associated with conditions (such as the mandatory involvement of a staff relations advisor), the employee is not a manager.[162]

Second, the notion of management duties involves the application of the earlier Board jurisprudence concerning the "management team."[163] The term "management team" is the group of employees who, together, are responsible for a particular operation. For example, in the Calgary International Airport, the "management team" comprised the general manager and three senior supervisors who met regularly each week to discuss all phases of airport operation.[164]

Third, it is important to remember that it is the position that is excluded, not the employee. Therefore, the fact that a particular employee performs management duties on an acting basis (e.g., to replace a manager while on leave) is not relevant, unless the position itself entails exercising the power of that manager as part of the regular

---

160 *Ibid* at para 66.

161 *Andres and Webb* (172-2-884 and -886); see also *Canadian Energy Regulator*, above note 141.

162 *Treasury Board and APSFA*, above note 117 at para 68.

163 The Board used the term "management team" in the context of the catch-all provision that existed in the 1967 version of the *PSSRA*.

164 *O'Connell et al* (174-2-157 & -158).

duties of that position.[165] For example, in *Lariviere and McQuade*, the positions required those employees to perform management duties whenever the senior manager went overseas, which was relatively frequent. They did not perform those duties as an acting manager but as part of their own position.[166] In *Sisson*, the employee was only a supervisor in the corrections service, except when he was called upon to be the head of institution. Again, this was not an acting position but part of his core duties, and it was frequently exercised.[167] This periodic responsibility for the entire institution made Mr. Sisson a manager as opposed to merely a supervisor.

These are obviously principles and guidelines instead of firm, fast rules. As the Board has put it:

> Although one may subscribe to the definitions quoted above there is not, in the view of the Board, any clear cut definition that will determine absolutely the role and function of a manager or a supervisor. In most large undertakings there is likely to be a long line of authority where managerial tasks are divided among a large number of people. It is difficult to determine the dividing line between management and supervision and there may well be input into the managerial process by any competent supervisor.[168]

The Board's determination of whether an employee is a supervisor or a manager is one of fact, and the distinction between managers and supervisors cannot be easily rendered into a rigid rule. The main concern is to ensure that employees do not find themselves with a "foot in both camps."[169]

The Board is also only concerned about employees with "substantial" managerial duties. For example, performance appraisal is a managerial duty; however, where the employee's performance assessments

165 *Treasury Board and APSFA*, above note 117 at para 78.

166 *Lariviere and McQuade* (172-2-178).

167 *Sisson*, above note 122.

168 *Ibid* at para 72. The Board also adopted a definition of "supervision" as follows: "The function and activity of making sure that the objectives of the organization are carried out according to plans and policies which are designated and handed down from management." This definition has been adopted by the Board more recently in *Saint-Marseille*, [2000] CPSSRB No 26.

169 *Treasury Board and APSFA*, above note 117 at para 88.

can be (and frequently are) overruled by a higher-level manager, that employee is not performing "substantial" managerial duties.[170]

vi) Residual Managerial Exclusion

> *59 (1)(g) the occupant of the position has duties and responsibilities not otherwise described in this subsection and should not be included in a bargaining unit for reasons of conflict of interest or by reason of the person's duties and responsibilities to the employer*

The exclusion in section 59(1)(g) is a form of residual exclusion for circumstances not contemplated or listed elsewhere in section 59 of the *FPSLRA*. In interpreting the scope of this paragraph, the Board has had to balance two contradictory principles: that "the section provides the Board with considerable discretion and that there is no clear definition of the range of circumstances under which that discretion may be exercise" and that the paragraph "should be used sparingly and applied only in unusual situations."[171] The Board has drawn on some of the other principles discussed above when interpreting the scope of section 59(1)(g), including the concept of the "management team"[172] and that access to information alone does not create a conflict of interest.[173]

Although the Board has not developed a definition of "conflict of interest," it has, on occasion, stated what a conflict of interest is *not*:

- It does not arise because of the opportunity to act in a higher position.
- It does not arise because of the possibility of a conflict of interest during a strike or because of duties related to planning management's response to a strike. Those concerns should be dealt with by the designation of positions under the essential services provisions in the *FPLSRA*.
- It does not arise as the result of responsibilities in dealing with employees in other bargaining units, including recommendations or actions concerning staffing.[174]

---

170 *Canadian Energy Regulator*, above note 141.

171 *Treasury Board v Public Service Alliance of Canada*, 2016 PSLREB 84 at para 11.

172 *Treasury Board v Public Service Alliance of Canada*, above note 135 at para 53.

173 *Treasury Board v Public Service Alliance of Canada*, above note 171 at para 33.

174 *Treasury Board and APSFA*, above note 117 at paras 88–89.

Four Board decisions provide examples of how the Board has balanced these competing principles.

In *Treasury Board (Correctional Service of Canada) v Public Service Alliance of Canada*,[175] the Board excluded the security intelligence officer (SIO) at a regional psychiatric centre run by the Correctional Service of Canada. The Board noted that the SIO did not bear many of the typical hallmarks for exclusion, such as the exercise of managerial functions, decision-making authority, and involvement in labour relations issues. However, the Board found that the SIO's job included "weighing and shaping" information about security risks to make recommendations "under demanding and time-sensitive conditions."[176] Therefore, it was a position with a unique level of mutual trust with management and, therefore, should be excluded under section 59(1)(g).[177]

In *Treasury Board v Public Service Alliance of Canada*,[178] the Board excluded five senior investigators under section 59(1)(g). The senior investigators investigated alleged employee wrongdoing, and their reports formed the basis for a decision by management about whether to discipline the employee being investigated. The senior investigators were often witnesses in discipline grievances. The bargaining agent pointed out that the incumbents of those positions had been working for as long as five years before the employer filed its application to exclude them from the bargaining unit, and during that time there were no problems with conflict of interest. The Board was critical of this delay but ultimately concluded that the delay did not affect the analysis under section 59(1)(g)—and found that investigating fellow employees for disciplinary purposes was a conflict of interest captured by that paragraph, and there was nothing the employer could do to reorganize its affairs to eliminate the conflict.

---

175 *Treasury Board (Correctional Service of Canada) v Public Service Alliance of Canada*, 2012 PSLRB 46.

176 *Ibid* at para 77.

177 One interesting result of this case is that a group of SIOs formed their own association and attempted to become a bargaining agent, arguing that the conflict of interest issue could be resolved by creating a bargaining unit comprised solely of SIOs. Their application was dismissed because they were not "employees" under the *FPSLRA*: *Union of Canadian Intelligence Officers v Treasury Board (Correctional Service of Canada)*, 2018 FPSLREB 33.

178 *Treasury Board v Public Service Alliance of Canada*, 2016 PSLREB 80.

In *Treasury Board v Public Service Alliance of Canada*,[179] the Board excluded twenty-seven positions working at the Canada Border Services Agency's (CBSA) National Border Operations Centre (BOC). The BOC is the single national control centre for all CBSA operations and is the conduit for all information flowing to and from the CBSA's various operations. The employer sought to exclude their positions based on three duties: incident reporting, participation in a daily issue management secretariat teleconference, and the transformation of the BOC into the CBSA's "strike/situation" centre during a strike or other labour relations situation. The Board would not have excluded the positions on the basis of the first two duties. Incident reporting would not have resulted in an exclusion because it was just preparing reports and did not involve the exercise of discretion; participating in the teleconference was not sufficient because while labour relations issues were sometimes discussed, the discussions were not substantial but instead more about assigning work to the various managers. The strike/situation centre, on the other hand, involved a critical labour relations role. The Board was clear that it was the quality of the work, not the quantity, that determined the result in that case, stating that "even a modest amount of labour relations work that is of critical importance . . . can justify granting an exclusion application."[180]

Finally, the case involving the senior human resources assistant discussed under section 59(1)(h) also addressed paragraph (g).[181] The Board refused to exclude the employee under paragraph (g) as well because the employer's concern came down to access to information alone—the assistant was not in any way part of the management team. If the employee was at risk of overhearing information, the employer had to reorganize its affairs (including the physical layout of the office) to address that problem: office location was not a reason to exclude the employee from the bargaining unit.[182]

These cases demonstrate the difficult balancing that the Board must undertake when assessing section 59(1)(g) of the Act and that the Board's decisions will typically be resolved on the basis of each case's unique facts instead of clear statements of principle.

---

179 *Treasury Board v Public Service Alliance of Canada*, above note 171.

180 *Ibid* at para 63.

181 *Treasury Board v Public Service Alliance of Canada*, above note 135.

182 *Ibid* at para 52.

g) Other Exclusions

Finally, there are some employees who are excluded yet not listed as such under the *FPSLRA*. For example, members of the Armed Forces of Canada are not covered by the *FPSLRA* or *PSEA*. The terms and relationships under which they serve are prescribed by the *National Defence Act*.[183] Also, employees of the House of Commons, Senate, and Library of Parliament are excluded from the *FPSLRA*.[184] They are covered instead by the *Parliamentary Employment and Staff Relations Act*.[185]

C. THE PROCESS FOR DETERMINING WHETHER PERSONS ARE "EMPLOYEES"

The issue of whether a person is an "employee" often arises incidentally during the course of another application or matter and is dealt with as part of that proceeding. For example, the employer could argue that a grievance should not be adjudicated because the grievor is not an "employee," or the employer could contest an application for certification on the grounds that the bargaining unit includes people who are not "employees" under the *FPSLRA*.

The situation is different for the exclusion for managerial and confidential employees. In the case of an application for certification, the employer may apply to the Board for an order declaring that a position in the proposed bargaining unit is a managerial or confidential position.[186] The employer's application must set out every position that the employer considers to be managerial or confidential,[187] specifically the position title, description, number, and classification; the department or agency to which the position belongs; the geographic location of the position; and the name of the occupant of the position.[188] An employer's failure to provide those specifics is not necessarily fatal to its application so long as the information provided to the bargaining agent is sufficient

---

183 *Bolling et al v Public Service Staff Relations Board*, [1978] 1 FC 85 (CA).

184 *House of Commons v Canada (Labour Relations Board)*, [1986] 2 FC 372 (CA) at para 7.

185 *Parliamentary Employment and Staff Relations Act*, RSC 1985, c 33 (2nd Supp). See Chapter 14 for a discussion of this Act.

186 *FPSLRA*, s 59(1).

187 *Ibid*, s 59(2).

188 *Federal Public Sector Labour Relations Regulations*, SOR/2005-79, s 33(1) [*FPSLR Regulations*].

for an informed decision to be made.[189] The bargaining agent must then file an objection to the application within twenty days.[190] If no objection is filed, then the Board makes an order declaring the position to be managerial or confidential.[191] This allows the parties to agree on a list of managerial and confidential positions and also effectively prevents the Board from reviewing an agreed-upon list.

In the case of a bargaining unit that has already been certified, the employer may also apply to the Board for an order declaring that a position in that bargaining unit is now a managerial or confidential position.[192] The procedure followed thereafter is identical to the procedure on an application prior to certification: the bargaining agent must file an objection, and if it does so, the Board hears the case in due course. If the bargaining agent objects, the employer must hold the membership dues paid by the employee in that position while the case is pending. If the application succeeds, the membership dues are remitted to the employee; if the application does not succeed, then the dues are remitted to the bargaining agent. According to the evidence before the Standing Committee on Government Operations and Estimates, this provision concerning dues was added to the *FPSLRA* because

> [w]hen we had the Canada-wide consultations with the employees, some of them told us they were frustrated when their manager proposed that their position be excluded, as they had to continue paying union dues for several months. And because both the employer and the union acted slowly, there was resistance and slowness in the system that resulted in the employee being penalized because he had to continue paying union dues. It is only after several months, often a year, that the Public Service Staff Relations Board makes its ruling, and the employee does not get reimbursed. So the employees themselves are very frustrated. It is in light of this consultation that we tried to put pressure on the two parties, the employer and the union, to resolve

---

189 *Department of National Defence (Communications Security Establishment) v PSAC*, [2001] CPSSRB No 22, where the Communications Security Establishment refused to include the job title and job description of the positions in question because the information was "classified." The Board concluded that the bargaining agent did not suffer prejudice and had enough information to address the application.

190 *FPSLR Regulations*, s 34(1).

191 *FPSLRA*, s 63.

192 *Ibid*, s 71(1).

> the exclusion problem and to ensure that agreements and bargaining proceed faster so that employees are not penalized financially.[193]

The *FPSLRA* also explicitly sets out the burden of proof in these applications, and that burden varies depending on the ground on which the employer is attempting to exclude a position. If the exclusion is based on paragraphs 59(1)(a) through (c), then the burden of proof is on the bargaining agent to demonstrate that the position is not referred to in those paragraphs.[194] If the exclusion is based on paragraphs 59(1)(d) through (h), then the burden of proof is on the employer.[195] This variable burden of proof was explained as follows:

> As far as I'm aware, other statutes in Canada go about it quite differently. What they purport to do is to exclude only managerial positions and not confidential positions. In classic shop-floor situations, the supervisor is part of the union as well, but the person above that supervisor is normally management.
>
> In the public service you have that model too for managers, but also you have the exclusion of confidential employees—executive assistants, for instance: people who are in daily, close proximity to the work and the activities of persons who are excluded. From that standpoint there are more exclusions in the federal public service because of this exclusion of confidential employees.
>
> With regard to the burden, specifically, all this statute does is recognize the present state of affairs. There's no such thing in the private sector, Mr. Stoffer, as being excluded if one is in the executive category. There's no such criterion. But in the public service, everyone who's an "EX," as we call them, is pretty high above that and would likely, if not all the time at least 99.9% of the time, be excluded under another head of the exclusions in this act.
>
> So it's very hard to make a parallel. But for those positions where the burden is on the union, they're quite clear; there's never much doubt at all. In the 35-odd years of jurisprudence in this area, there've been a handful of cases only where it wasn't as clear as day to both

193 House of Commons, Standing Committee on Government Operations and Estimates, *Evidence*, 37-2, No 36 (6 May 2003) at 9:45 (Monique Boudrias).

194 *FPSLRA*, s 62(2).

195 *Ibid*, s 62(3).

the employer and the union that someone fit under those particular descriptions—confidential to a judge, for instance.[196]

Another possible explanation for this statutory change in the burden of proof may be found in the decision of *The Queen v Professional Institute of the Public Service of Canada*.[197] In that case, the Treasury Board argued that the Board lacked the jurisdiction to inquire into whether an employee was confidential to a chief executive officer of the public service—an exclusion almost identical to the one currently found in section 59(1)(a). The Federal Court of Appeal disagreed and concluded that the Board had the jurisdiction to determine whether a person fell within that exclusion. The amendments to the *FPSLRA* do not deprive the Board of the jurisdiction to determine whether a person meets the criteria of sections 59(1)(a) through (c), but they do make it more difficult for a bargaining agent to challenge such an exclusion—which was the result sought by the government in that case.

Finally, the bargaining agent may also apply for an order revoking the order declaring that a position is managerial or confidential.[198] On such applications, the burden of proof is always on the bargaining agent to prove that the position is no longer a managerial or confidential position.[199]

196 House of Commons, Standing Committee on Government Operations and Estimates, Evidence, 37-2, No 34 (1 May 2003) at 10:25 (Michel LeFrançois).

197 *The Queen v Professional Institute of the Public Service of Canada*, [1980] 2 FC 295 (CA).

198 *FPSLRA*, s 77.

199 *Ibid*, s 78(2).

CHAPTER FOUR

The Federal Public Sector Labour Relations and Employment Board

A. INTRODUCTION

The Federal Public Sector Labour Relations and Employment Board (the Board) was created on 1 November 2014 with the coming into force of the *Federal Public Sector Labour Relations and Employment Board Act* (*FPSLREB Act*).[1] It is the successor to two tribunals: the Public Service Labour Relations Board (which itself was the successor to the Public Service Staff Relations Board) and the Public Service Staff Tribunal. The Board's primary mandate is to adjudicate disputes. The Board also provides mediation services related to this core adjudication mandate.

The Board's jurisdiction to hear disputes can be divided into four areas: industrial disputes (governed by Part I of the *Federal Public Sector Labour Relations Act* [*FPSLRA*][2]); grievances of rights disputes (governed by Part II of the *FPSLRA*); reprisal complaints relating to occupational health and safety (governed by Part III of the *FPSLRA*, which incorporates Part II of the *Canada Labour Code*); and complaints against certain categories of appointments under the *Public Service Employment Act*.[3]

The Board also administers the *Parliamentary Employment and Staff Relations Act*.[4] Finally, the Board, under an agreement with the

---

1 *Federal Public Sector Labour Relations and Employment Board Act*, SC 2013, c 40, s 365 [*FPSLREB Act*].

2 *Federal Public Sector Labour Relations Act*, SC 2003, c 22, s 2 [*FPSLRA*].

3 *Public Service Employment Act*, SC 2003, c 22, ss 12 & 13.

4 *Parliamentary Employment and Staff Relations Act*, RSC 1985, c 33 (2nd Supp).

Yukon government, administers the collective bargaining and grievance adjudication systems under the Yukon *Education Labour Relations Act*[5] and the Yukon *Public Service Labour Relations Act*.[6] When performing these functions funded by the Yukon government, the Board acts as the Yukon Teachers Labour Relations Board and the Yukon Public Service Labour Relations Board, respectively.

B. COMPOSITION OF THE BOARD

The Board is composed of a chair, up to two vice-chairs, up to twelve full-time members, and as many other part-time members as the Governor in Council may appoint.[7] There are no particular criteria for being a member of the Board, aside from being a Canadian citizen and not holding other office or employment in the public service or an employee organization that is a bargaining agent in the federal public service. The previous version of the legislation contained a statutory requirement that Board members have "knowledge of or experience in" labour relations. That provision was removed in 2014. In 2017, Parliament added a requirement that at least two members of the Board have "knowledge of police organizations"[8] when it also amended the *FPSLRA* to include members of the RCMP.

This absence of an express requirement for members to have labour relations knowledge or expertise is mitigated because members are appointed from a list prepared by the chair after consultation with the Treasury Board and the separate employers on the one hand and the bargaining agents on the other.[9] Members are then appointed so that, to the extent possible, an equal number are appointed from among the employers' recommendations and the bargaining agents' recommendations.[10] Members of the Board are appointed for terms not longer than five years and hold that office during "good behaviour"[11]—thus guaranteeing them security of tenure.

---

5 *Education Labour Relations Act*, RSY 2002, c 62.

6 *Public Service Labour Relations Act*, RSY 2002, c 185.

7 *FPSLREB Act*, s 4(2).

8 *Ibid*, s 6(1.1).

9 *Ibid*, ss 6(1) & (2).

10 *Ibid*, s 6(3).

11 *Ibid*, s 8(1).

In this way, the Board is — in some respects — a tripartite Board. However, this does not hold true in any particular hearing. As discussed below, most hearings are conducted before a single member. When hearings are conducted before three members, there is no obligation on the part of the chair to appoint one member from each of the employers' and bargaining agents' lists.[12] Furthermore, the *FPSLREB Act* specifically states that the Board is not a representative Board. Members recommended by employers or bargaining agents do not represent either the employer or employees and must act impartially.[13]

The chair has the authority to assign a panel of three members to hear a particular matter "when the complexity of a matter requires it."[14] For example, the Board has convened three-member panels to hear the first (and leading) case on what constitutes an essential service in the post-2005 legislation[15] and to hear competing applications for certification of a bargaining agent for members of the RCMP.[16] In virtually all cases, however, matters are heard by a single member of the Board.

Prior to the creation of the Board in 2014, grievances referred to adjudication were heard by an "adjudicator" who was also a member of the Board. This meant that, in practice, the Board heard adjudications but, legally, they were an "adjudicator" and not the Board. Parliament ended this charade in 2014 and amended the *FPSLRA* so that the Board is seized of a grievance unless the parties agree to refer the grievance to a different adjudicator.[17] The parties to an adjudication under Part II of the *FPSLRA* may specify their choice of adjudicator, either in the collective agreement or on a case-by-case basis.[18]

The parties may also elect to have the matter heard by a "board of adjudication" comprising one member of the Board appointed by the chair and two side members, each appointed by one of the parties.[19] According to the *FPSLRA*, the nominees may not have a "direct interest" in or connection with the grievance being referred, but otherwise there

12 *FPSLRA*, s 31.
13 *FPSLREB Act*, s 6(4).
14 *Ibid*, s 37(2).
15 *Public Service Alliance of Canada v Parks Canada Agency*, 2008 PSLRB 97.
16 *National Police Federation v Treasury Board*, 2019 FPSLREB 74.
17 *FPSLRA*, s 223(2.1).
18 *Ibid*, s 223(1)(a) & (b).
19 *Ibid*, s 224(1).

are no limits on the choice of side members.[20] Other arbitration panels have had to decide whether a particular nominee chosen by either side is disqualified from sitting on a panel because of their relationship to one of the parties.

There are, generally speaking, two schools of thought on the degree of impartiality required of a nominee. The "labour relations" school of thought recognizes that the parties should be free to choose their nominee. Each side is entitled to appoint to a Board a person who is not only well versed and briefed in the appointer's side of the argument but a person who would act as advocate of the appointer, and only the chair would be neutral. As one court has put it, a nominee must only "remain sufficiently detached from the parties and the issues in dispute so as to be able, in good faith, to bring their best judgment to bear on the matters in controversy."[21] Or, more bluntly, "a complete freedom of choice is recognized in the appointment of the two nominees or representative members of the Board."[22] The "judicial" school of thought requires that the nominees adhere to the same requirements as a court—namely, that they be free from a reasonable apprehension of bias.

Recently, both courts and arbitration panels have adopted the judicial school of thought for rights arbitrations and the more relaxed labour relations school for interest arbitration.[23] However, the rules of natural justice may be explicitly modified by statute;[24] therefore,

---

20 *Ibid*, s 224(2).

21 *Yorktown (City) v Yorktown Professional Fire Fighters Assn*, Local 1527 (2001), 207 DLR (4th) 651 (Sask CA) at para 33.

22 *Gypsumville District Teachers' Association, No 1612 of the Manitoba Teachers' Society v Consolidated School District of Gypsumville No 2461*, [1979] 6 WWR 616 (CA), aff'd without reasons *Manitoba Teachers' Society No 1612 v Gypsumville Consolidated School District No 2461*, [1980] 2 SCR 179.

23 See *Saskatoon Credit Union (2002) and UFCW, Loc 1400* (2005), 137 LAC (4th) 406 (Priel): "[I]t does still appear to be clear that the weight of judicial authority favours the requirement that the same degree of impartiality required of a court is required of all three members of a rights arbitration panel. Accordingly, it is our conclusion that the allegation that there is a reasonable apprehension of bias must be decided upon the principles of the judicial school of thought." See also *Abitibi Consolidated Inc and CEP, Loc 60(N)* (2004), 130 LAC (4th) 129 (Oakley), rev'd in part *Communication, Energy and Paperworkers Union of Canada Local 60N*, 2008 NLCA 4 [*Abitibi Consolidated*]. See also *NAPE v Newfoundland (Treasury Board)*, [1991] NJ No 57 [*NAPE*].

24 *Ocean Port Hotel Ltd v British Columbia (General Manager, Liquor Control and Licensing Branch)*, [2001] 2 SCR 781.

section 224(2) may arguably require the Board to adopt the labour relations school of thought when assessing whether a nominee should be rejected for bias; it depends on how the Board interprets the term "direct interest." The term is likely to exclude a solicitor for the party from acting as a nominee or an employee (either current or former) who was responsible for negotiating the language in the collective agreement being interpreted.[25] By contrast, previous employment with one of the parties (e.g., by a retiree) or involvement in negotiating previous collective agreements does not disqualify a nominee. As one arbitrator has put it, "[i]f a party's nominee could be challenged on the basis of previous employment or involvement in negotiations generally, it would be very difficult to find nominees who have the experience and knowledge necessary to sit on labour arbitration panels at all."[26]

C. JURISDICTION AND POWERS OF THE BOARD

The powers of the Board are set out in both the *FPSLRA* and the *FPSLREB Act*. The Board's main powers are described below.

1) Power to Accept Evidence

Section 20 of the *FPSLREB Act* sets out the Board's powers to accept and admit evidence and address pre-hearing production issues.

First, the Board has the power to summon witnesses "in the same manner as a superior court of record."[27] Sections 18 and 103 of the *Federal Public Sector Labour Relations Regulations* (*FPSLR Regulations*) provide that the Board may require that a summons contain "the name and address of the witness to be summoned and a statement of the evidence that the witness is expected to give at the hearing"[28] for Part I hearings and adjudications, respectively. Although the Board has the discretion not to require these elements, it is common practice for the Board to require these details to assess the need for a summons.

---

25 See *NAPE*, above note 23, and *Abitibi Consolidated*, above note 23. Both cases adopted the "judicial" school of thought, but both also considered that those two situations placed the nominee in a situation with a lack of independence.

26 *UNIFOR Canada, Local 594 v Consumer Co-operative Refineries Ltd*, [2016] SLAA No 18 (Hood) at para 20.

27 *FPSLREB Act*, s 20(a).

28 *Federal Public Sector Labour Relations Regulations*, SOR/2005-79, ss 18 and 103 [*FPSLR Regulations*].

The Board follows the usual practice of any tribunal and will provide a summons when the party seeking the summons provides a satisfactory explanation as to how those witnesses' evidence is related to the issue before the Board.[29] An application for a summons does not need to be provided to other parties.[30] A person who is summoned by the Board is entitled to the same witness fees as set out in the *Federal Courts Rules*.[31]

Second, the Board has the power to order the production of documents, either pre-hearing or during the hearing, that are arguably relevant to the proceeding.[32] To limit the number of pre-hearing motions to order the production of documents, the Board enacted a direction on 1 September 2018 that requires the parties to provide a document list to each other sixty days prior to the first day of a hearing. The document list is similar to an affidavit of documents in a civil court proceeding and lists all arguably relevant documents in the party's possession, no longer in the party's possession, not in the party's possession but in their power to obtain, and all privileged documents. If the opposing party requests a copy of any document on that list that is in the opposing party's control, then production must occur within seven days. The Board has also stated that it may refuse to accept a document into evidence if it is not listed or produced in accordance with this schedule.[33] The Board has not yet issued a decision on whether or when it will exclude evidence that was not provided through this pre-hearing process.

The decision of the Board in *Tipple v Deputy Head (Department of Public Works and Government Services)*[34] illustrates its power to order production of documents and some of the consequences of frustrating those orders. In that case, the grievor requested production of all relevant documents, specifying nineteen categories of relevant documents. The employer first objected on the basis that the production may interfere

---

29 *Okrent v Deputy Head (Department of Public Works and Government Services)*, 2013 PSLRB 65 at para 19.

30 *FPSLR Regulations*, s 7(3).

31 *FPSLRA*, s 248, and *FPSLREB Act*, s 41. The current witness fee is $20 per day plus reasonable travel expenses: *Federal Courts Rules*, SOR/98-106, s 43 and Tariff A.

32 *FPSLREB Act*, s 20(f). See *AB v Treasury Board (Royal Canadian Mounted Police)*, 2016 PSLREB 23 at para 62 [*AB*], for the "arguably relevant" test.

33 FPSLREB, "Pre-hearing Exchange of Document Lists (Labour Relations Matters)," online: https://pslreb-crtefp.gc.ca/en/resources/policies/prehearing-exchange.html.

34 *Tipple v Deputy Head (Department of Public Works and Government Services)*, 2010 PSLRB 83.

with the *Access to Information Act*[35] or *Privacy Act*;[36] the adjudicator concluded that "[t]he power to order disclosure is not subject to the *Access to Information* or *Privacy Acts*."[37] The employer next objected on the grounds that it also objected to the jurisdiction of the adjudicator to hear the grievance. The adjudicator rejected that objection and required production no later than 17 August 2007. The employer produced some documents. The adjudicator made three further and more specific production orders; the employer repeatedly underproduced or late-produced the required documents. In all, the first request for disclosure in May 2007 was not fully complied with until March 2009. The adjudicator, after ultimately allowing the grievance, awarded damages for "obstruction of process,"[38] later set at just over $45,000.[39]

The Board's power to order the production of documents does not extend to documents that are protected by privilege, including solicitor-client privilege. The Board has the authority to satisfy itself that a document is privileged. The Board must first satisfy itself that the documents sought to be produced are relevant. If that preliminary screening phase has been met, the Board may then order and review a detailed and descriptive affidavit describing the allegedly solicitor-client privileged document.[40] The Board will also not order production of documents protected by "labour relations privilege," although this form of privilege is not a "class" privilege but, instead, a case-by-case privilege. This means that the Board must consider the application of that privilege in each case in light of the "particularity of each case."[41]

Third, the Board has the power to admit evidence at a hearing. The Board's power to receive evidence is the same as other labour relations boards (or rights arbitrators) in Canada: it has the power to admit evidence, regardless of whether it would be admissible in a court of

---

35 *Access to Information Act*, RSC 1985, c A-1.

36 *Privacy Act*, RSC 1985, c P-21.

37 *Ibid* at para 13.

38 *Ibid* at para 356.

39 This award was upheld by the Federal Court of Appeal: *Tipple v Canada (Attorney General)*, 2012 FCA 158.

40 *Quadrini v Canada Revenue Agency and Hillier*, 2009 PSLRB 104 at paras 95–96. The Federal Court of Appeal overturned the Board's finding on the basis that the documents were not relevant but did not disturb the Board's jurisdiction to determine whether relevant documents are privileged: *Canada (Attorney General) v Quadrini*, 2011 FCA 115.

41 *Zhang v Treasury Board (Privy Council Office)*, 2010 PSLRB 46 at para 40.

law.[42] The Board is required to hear all relevant evidence, so long as doing so is consistent with the rules of procedural fairness and natural justice.[43] The Board therefore has the power to admit hearsay evidence. The Board will still give little or no weight to hearsay if it relates to "proof of critical facts that have not otherwise been established,"[44] but it can admit hearsay evidence when the surrounding circumstances and other evidence attests to the relevance and reliability of the hearsay document or oral evidence.[45]

2) Power to Control Its Own Proceedings

The Board has the power to dismiss summarily any application or complaint that is frivolous or vexatious.[46] This includes the power to summarily strike pleadings or a portion of them. For example, the Board struck part of a bargaining agent's reply to a duty of fair representation complaint when the reply set out various alleged misconducts of the complainant that were derogatory and not relevant to the complaint.[47] The Board has also interpreted that power as prospective in nature so that the Board could bar a vexatious litigant from commencing any further proceedings in the future, although the Board refrained from issuing such an order in that case.[48] The Board also has the power to go forward with a hearing and dispose of a matter if a party does not show up to that hearing or alternatively send a notice of status review and then deem the matter withdrawn if the parties do not respond.[49]

---

42 *FPSLREB Act*, s 20(e).

43 *Université du Québec à Trois-Rivières v Larocque*, [1993] 1 SCR 471 at paras 46–52.

44 *Lortie v Deputy Head (Canada Border Services Agency)*, 2016 PSLREB 108 at para 223.

45 *Williams v Treasury Board (Correctional Service of Canada)*, 2017 FPSLREB 39 at para 32.

46 *FPSLREB Act*, s 21.

47 *Lala v United Food and Commercial Workers Canada, Local 401*, 2017 PSLREB 23 at para 7.

48 *Pugh v Deputy Minister of Justice et al*, 2008 PSST 23 at paras 93–94. In fact, that same litigant did bring future complaints (but never successfully): *Pugh v Deputy Minister of Justice*, 2012 PSST 31. See also *Baker v Deputy Minister of Public Works and Government Services*, 2015 PSLREB 19, where the Board again stated that it had the power to make an order barring a vexatious litigant from future complaints.

49 *FPSLR Regulations*, ss 11.1 and 17(3).

Similarly, the Board has the power to dismiss a case where the case as pleaded does not show an "arguable case." This is similar to a court striking a pleading that does not disclose a cause of action.[50] The Board will only exercise this power when it concludes that the complaint has "no reasonable chance of success."[51] While the Board takes all of the facts alleged by the complainant as true, the Board may still consider the documents or facts provided by the respondent in the parties' exchange of particulars about the complaint when those facts are beyond doubt or not disputed.[52] The Board most commonly exercises this power for duty of fair representation complaints.[53]

The Board also has the authority to decide matters in writing without an oral hearing.[54] The Board has the discretion to decide when not to hold an oral hearing: it is the "master in its own house" and deserves the "greatest level of deference" when deciding whether to hold an oral hearing.[55] The Board is therefore free to conduct hearings in writing unless the circumstances dictate that the matter cannot be fairly decided without an oral hearing, such as when there are serious conflicts in the evidence that must be resolved through oral testimony.[56] The Board must put the parties on notice that it may decide a matter without an oral hearing to permit the parties to file sufficiently robust written submissions to address the key points in dispute.[57]

The Board has the power to convene pre-hearing conferences to resolve preliminary disputes and to effectively case-manage cases.[58] The Board is supposed to provide at least three days' notice of a pre-hearing conference,[59] but in practice the Board has waived that requirement

50 *Sganos v Association of Canadian Financial Officers*, 2022 FPSLREB 30 at paras 81–84.

51 *Corneau v Association of Justice Counsel*, 2023 FPSLREB 16 at para 93.

52 *Ibid* at paras 26–29.

53 See, for example, *Musolino v Professional Institute of the Public Service of Canada*, 2022 FPSLREB 46, and *Tohidy v Public Service Alliance of Canada*, 2022 FPSLREB 69.

54 *FPSLREB Act*, s 22.

55 *Professional Institute of the Public Service of Canada v Treasury Board*, [2006] FCJ No 806 (CA) at para 3.

56 *Boshra v Canadian Association of Professional Employees*, 2011 FCA 98 at paras 13–14.

57 *Canada (Attorney General) v Timson*, 2012 FC 719.

58 *FPSLREB Act*, 20(b).

59 *FPSLR Regulations*, s 16.

when the actual hearing is pending or the matter is urgent for some other reason.

The Board also has control over whether its proceedings are open to the public and whether documents will be subject to a sealing order. On both issues, as a starting point, "the Board adheres to the open court principle. Its hearings and files are public."[60] The Board will therefore only grant confidentiality orders or close a hearing to the public when such an order is necessary to prevent a serious risk to some important interest and the salutary effects of keeping the information confidential outweigh the deleterious effects on free expression and the open court principle.[61] This balancing test prevails over the *Privacy Act*.[62] The Board has granted orders to protect confidential settlement discussions;[63] anonymize decisions to protect the identity of the victims of sexual harassment;[64] protect the privacy interests of people who were not related to the grievance (such as, for instance, inmates and their personal issues,[65] individuals being investigated by the police,[66] and individuals in the witness protection program[67]); seal the details of harassment complaints when the allegations were found to be unsubstantiated;[68] seal portions of medical reports that had no bearing on the case being heard;[69] and seal investigative strategy case studies to train investigators of employment insurance fraud.[70] The Federal Court of

60 *Bell v Staff of the Non-Public Funds, Canadian Forces*, 2020 FPSLREB 14 at para 88.

61 *Basic v Canadian Association of Professional Employees*, 2012 PSLRB 120 at para 11 [*Basic*]; *Doe v Treasury Board (Canada Border Services Agency)*, 2018 FPSLREB 89 at para 16 [*Doe*].

62 *McMullen v Canada Revenue Agency*, 2013 PSLRB 64 at para 128.

63 *Basic*, above note 61; *Topping v Deputy Head (Department of Public Works and Government Services)*, 2014 PSLRB 74.

64 *Doe*, above note 61.

65 *Nadeau v Deputy Head (Correctional Service of Canada)*, 2017 PSLREB 31.

66 *Gill v Deputy Head (Correctional Service of Canada)*, 2019 FPSLREB 102 [*Gill*].

67 *AB*, above note 32. The Board refused a request by the employer to redact all references to the *Witness Protection Program Act*, SC 1996, c 15, as anonymizing the witnesses being protected and the names of other employees involved in that program was sufficient to protect the individuals who may be at risk.

68 *Boiko v National Research Council of Canada*, 2018 FPSLREB 11 at para 693.

69 *Herbert v Deputy Head (Parole Board of Canada)*, 2018 FPSLREB 76 at para 306.

70 *Therrien v Deputy Head (Department of Employment and Social Development)*, 2019 FPSLREB 82. The Board in that case refused to seal other documents, such as statistics of caseloads for employment insurance investigators and the chapter of a manual that dealt with performance indicators.

Appeal has also concluded that the Board must redact the names of witnesses who testified against a manager in a grievance against that manager's suspension out of concerns for those witnesses' privacy.[71] This list is meant to simply represent examples of circumstances when the Board has granted a sealing or confidentiality order; it is not meant to provide a list of categories when confidentiality orders will always be granted. The Board will always assess a request for a confidentiality order on a case-by-case basis.

3) Power to Grant an Extension of Time

Each form of proceeding before the Board comes with a deadline set out in statute or in a collective agreement. Those deadlines tend to be very short, such as forty days to refer a grievance to adjudication after it is dismissed at the final level[72] or ninety days to file an unfair labour practice complaint.[73] The Board has the power to extend the time limits that are set out by regulation[74] or under the *Public Service Employment Act* for staffing complaints.[75] As a matter of practice, a party seeking an extension of time must file an application with the Board. The Board may accept such an application made during the course of a hearing, but it is not obliged to do so.

The Board applies five factors when deciding whether to grant an extension of time: a clear, cogent, and compelling reason for the delay; the length of the delay; the due diligence of the party seeking the extension; balancing the injustice to the party if the extension is denied against the prejudice to the other party caused by the delay; and the chances of success of the grievance or other matter.[76] The criteria are not necessarily of equal importance, and the weight given to each criterion will depend on the facts of that case. While some earlier Board cases suggested that the first factor (a clear, cogent, and compelling reason for

---

71 *Canada (Attorney General) v Philps*, 2019 FCA 240.

72 *FPSLR Regulations*, s 90.

73 *FPSLRA*, s 190(2).

74 *FPSLR Regulations*, ss 12 and 61.

75 *Public Service Staffing Complaints Regulations*, SOR/2006-6, s 5(1).

76 *Schenkman v Treasury Board (Public Works and Government Services Canada)*, 2004 PSSRB 1. See *Popov v Canada (Attorney General)*, 2019 FCA 177 [*Popov*], as an example of the Federal Court of Appeal approving the "Schenkman factors." See also *Vidlak v Canada (Attorney General)*, 2007 FC 1182.

the delay) was always given the preponderance of weight, more recent Board decisions rejected that proposition and concluded that the weight given to each factor varies from case to case.[77]

The Board has accepted a variety of explanations, including that a grievor was living and working abroad when the deadline expired,[78] they had to care for a sick family member,[79] and they had a lack of knowledge of the nature of the issue raised in that case.[80] There are some Board decisions stating that a mistake by a bargaining agent or representative is not a compelling explanation for a delay,[81] but those decisions have been overtaken by more recent Board decisions that a union's negligence may be a compelling reason for an extension of time when the individual grievor or complainant was not also at fault and exercised due diligence.[82] This later line of authorities is undoubtedly correct given that the Board has the jurisdiction to remedy a union's breach of its duty of fair representation by extending the time period for a grievance or complaint.[83]

Board decisions have not been consistent about what constitutes a lengthy delay. In one case, for example, the Board stated that a delay of 137 days was "relatively long,"[84] but in another case referred to a delay of four to five months as "not excessive."[85] When assessing the fifth criterion (the chances of success), the Board only considers that criterion if the grievance or complaint has little to no chance of success.[86] The Board continues to state that extensions of time are exceptional and "should be allowed sparingly,"[87] although, in practice, extensions of time are not as rare as that dictum would suggest.

---

77 See, for example, *Apenteng v Treasury Board (Canada Border Services Agency)*, 2014 PSLRB 19 at paras 88–89.

78 *Prévost v Office of the Superintendent of Financial Institutions*, 2011 PSLRB 119.

79 *Gagné v Canadian Food Inspection Agency*, 2016 PSLREB 3

80 *Duncan v National Research Council of Canada*, 2016 PSLREB 75 [*Duncan*].

81 *Callegaro v Treasury Board (Correctional Service of Canada)*, 2012 PSLRB 110.

82 *D'Alessandro v Treasury Board (Department of Justice)*, 2019 FPSLREB 79.

83 *Prior v Canada Revenue Agency*, 2014 PSLRB 96 at para 127.

84 *Cowie v Deputy Head (Correctional Service of Canada)*, 2012 PSLRB 14 at para 36.

85 *Duncan*, above note 80 at para 147.

86 *Popov*, above note 76 at para 15.

87 *Ibid* at para 85.

The Board does not have the jurisdiction to extend the ninety-day time limit to commence a complaint under section 190 of the *FPSLRA*.[88]

4) Power to Add Intervenors

The Board has the power to permit persons to intervene in an ongoing proceeding so long as that person has a substantial interest in the proceeding.[89] The Board has stated that it has considerable latitude to add intervenors to a case and that this latitude should be exercised more flexibly than in a court.[90] The Board typically will not grant intervenor status because of a jurisprudential interest in the outcome of a case (as this is not a substantial interest in the proceeding).[91] While the Board has not expressly set out a list of factors it will consider in labour cases, the *Public Service Staffing Complaints Regulations* list four factors the Board must consider: whether the intervenor is directly affected by the proceeding; whether the intervenor's position is already represented in the proceeding; whether the public interest or the interests of justice would be served by allowing the intervention; and whether the input of the intervenor would assist the Board in deciding the matter.[92] An intervenor need not meet all of those criteria. Instead, the Board has characterized those factors as "to ensure that an intervenor is not there to simply restate the parties' positions, but will provide some added value for the consideration and ultimate disposition of the case."[93]

There are certain parties that may intervene in Board proceedings as of right. The Canadian Human Rights Commission has the right to receive notice of a proceeding and participate in hearings when the grievance or staffing complaint raises an issue involving the interpretation

---

88 *Castonguay v Public Service Alliance of Canada*, 2007 PSLRB 78; *Public Service Alliance of Canada v Treasury Board (Canada Border Services Agency)*, 2016 PSLREB 102.

89 *FPSLR Regulations*, ss 14 and 99; *Public Service Staffing Complaints Regulations*, s 19.

90 *Amos v Deputy Head (Department of Public Works and Government Services)*, 2008 PSLRB 74 at para 30.

91 *Federal Government Dockyard Trades and Labour Council (East) v Treasury Board (Department of National Defence)*, 2012 PSLRB 93.

92 *Public Service Staffing Complaints Regulations*, s 19(4).

93 *Wardlaw v President of the Public Service Human Resources Management Agency of Canada*, 2007 PSST 17 at para 19.

of the *Canadian Human Rights Act*.[94] Similarly, the accessibility commissioner has standing in cases that raise the *Accessible Canada Act*.[95] In staffing complaints, the Public Service Commission has the right to appear as a party in certain cases,[96] as does the successful candidate in a complaint against their appointment[97] and an employee in the part of an organization from which employees will be laid off in the context of a complaint against that layoff under the *PSEA*.[98]

5) Power to Address Constitutional Issues

Although the Board originally expressed the view that it did not have the jurisdiction to consider the *Canadian Charter of Rights and Freedoms* (the *Charter*),[99] it now clearly has the jurisdiction to address constitutional issues.[100] In *Nova Scotia (Workers' Compensation Board) v Martin*,[101] the Supreme Court of Canada set out the appropriate test for determining whether a tribunal has the power to deal with constitutional issues. It concluded that tribunals that have the jurisdiction to answer questions of law concerning the impugned provision can consider whether the Constitution affects the interpretation of that provision or other issues in the case. If the tribunal does not have an explicit grant of authority to determine questions of law, then

> it becomes necessary to consider whether the legislator intended to confer upon the tribunal implied jurisdiction to decide questions of law arising under the challenged provision. Implied jurisdiction must be discerned by looking at the statute as a whole. Relevant factors will include the statutory mandate of the tribunal in issue and whether

94 *FPSLRA*, ss 210, 217, and 222; *Public Service Staffing Complaints Regulations*, s 20.

95 *PSEA*, ss 65, 79, and 80.1; *FPSLRA*, s 210.1, 217.1, and 222.1.

96 *PSEA*, ss 65 (layoff), 75 (revocation of appointment), 79 (internal appointments), and 85 (failure to properly implement corrective action).

97 *PSEA*, s 79(1).

98 *Ibid*, s 65.

99 *Coles and Treasury Board (Agriculture Canada)*, [1990] CPSSRB No 145 at 6.

100 See, for example, *Public Service Alliance of Canada and Treasury Board*, [1986] CPSSRB No 74 at para 33, and *King v Treasury Board (Revenue Canada—Customs, Excise, and Taxation)*, [2000] CPSSRB No 23. In both cases, the Board rejected the *Charter* arguments but accepted that it had jurisdiction to address them.

101 *Nova Scotia (Workers' Compensation Board) v Martin; Nova Scotia (Workers' Compensation Board) v Laseur*, 2003 SCC 54.

> deciding questions of law is necessary to fulfilling this mandate effectively; the interaction of the tribunal in question with other elements of the administrative system; whether the tribunal is adjudicative in nature; and practical considerations, including the tribunal's capacity to consider questions of law. . . . As is the case for explicit jurisdiction, if the tribunal is found to have implied jurisdiction to decide questions of law arising under a legislative provision, this power will be presumed to include jurisdiction to determine the constitutional validity of that provision.[102]

The Board, in adjudicating grievances, has the explicit authority to interpret and apply the *Canadian Human Rights Act* and "any other Act of Parliament relating to employment matters"[103] and thereby has the explicit power to determine questions of law. The Board does not have the explicit power to determine questions of law under Part I of the *FPSLRA*, but it has the implied jurisdiction to do so: it is an adjudicative tribunal, and deciding questions of law is necessary to fulfilling its mandate of providing adjudication services in accordance with the *FPSLRA*.[104] The Ontario Superior Court of Justice has also stated that an adjudicator (which, today, includes the Board) "can dispense a remedy for a *Charter* breach."[105] The Board has decided a number of constitutional cases, including constitutional challenges to the *FPSLRA*,[106] arguments that particular legislative provisions should be interpreted consistently with the *Charter*,[107] and arguments that particular actions by the employer violated the *Charter*.[108]

---

102 *Ibid* at para 41.

103 *FPSLRA*, s 226(2)(a).

104 *Ibid*, s 13.

105 *Van Duyvenbode v Canada (Attorney General)*, [2007] OJ No 2716 at para 21, aff'd *Van Duyvenbode v Canada (Attorney General)*, 2009 ONCA 11.

106 *Association des membres de la Police Montée du Québec v Treasury Board*, 2019 FPSLREB 70.

107 *Association of Justice Counsel v Treasury Board*, 2009 PSLRB 20. The Board's approach to such arguments is that, in the absence of a direct challenge to the constitutionality of the legislation, the *Charter* is only necessary as an interpretive tool if the legislation is ambiguous.

108 *Association of Justice Counsel v Treasury Board (Department of Justice)*, 2015 PSLREB 31. The Supreme Court of Canada ultimately overturned the finding of a *Charter* breach in *Association of Justice Counsel v Canada (Attorney General)*, 2017 SCC 55, but there was no dispute that the Board had the jurisdiction to apply the *Charter*.

6) Remedial Power

The various remedies awarded by the Board in particular types of cases will be discussed in later chapters dealing with the various types of complaints and grievances. However, there are three threshold remedial issues that are generic to all types of complaints.

First, the Board does not have the jurisdiction to award legal costs. The Federal Court of Appeal has noted that the *FPSLRA* does not expressly provide the Board with the authority to award costs and concluded that the Board—like other tribunals—does not have the authority to award costs in the absence of an express grant of statutory jurisdiction.[109] As mentioned above, the Board has the power to award damages for obstruction of justice (in that case, repeated non-compliance with production orders), but it does not have the power to award legal costs to the winning party. The Board has otherwise followed the Court of Appeal's decision and refused to award costs.[110]

Second, the Board only has a limited authority to award interest. The *FPSLRA* gives the Board the express authority to award interest in grievances involving termination, demotion, suspension, or financial penalty.[111] In those cases, the Board typically awards interest on the Bank of Canada's established rate,[112] although the Board has awarded pre-judgment and post-judgment interest in accordance with the *Federal Courts Act*[113] in some cases instead.[114] The Board has sometimes awarded compound interest[115] but in most cases has awarded simple

---

109 *Tipple v Canada (Attorney General)*, 2012 FCA 158 at paras 20–32. The Federal Court of Appeal relied upon the Supreme Court of Canada's decision that the Canadian Human Rights Tribunal does not have the jurisdiction to award costs in the absence of an express grant of statutory authority to do so: *Canada (Attorney General) v Mowat*, 2011 SCC 53.

110 See, for example, *Grant v Deputy Head (Canada Border Services Agency)*, 2016 PSLREB 37 at para 167, and *Gill*, above note 66 at paras 236–40.

111 *FPSLRA*, s 226(2)(c).

112 *Hare v Treasury Board (Department of Indian Affairs and Northern Development)*, 2019 FPSLREB 59 at paras 329–30 [*Hare*]; *Union of Canadian Correctional Officers—Syndicat des agents correctionnels du Canada—CSN (UCCO-SACC-CSN) v Treasury Board (Correctional Service of Canada)*, 2019 FPSLREB 118 at para 50.

113 *Federal Courts Act*, RSC 1985, c F-7, ss 36–37.

114 *Bayani v Deputy Head (Correctional Service of Canada)*, 2019 FPSLREB 44 at paras 204–6.

115 *Ibid.*

interest[116]—again, without explanation as to why. In all other cases that are not grievances involving termination, demotion, suspension, or financial penalty, the Board does not have the jurisdiction to award interest. There is a common law rule that the Crown is not liable for interest on moneys due. Therefore, in the absence of a specific statutory provision, the Crown does not pay interest on judicial or tribunal awards against it. The *FPSLRA* only ousts that rule in the circumstances set out above; thus, Parliament chose to waive that common law rule in those circumstances but not in others. The Federal Court of Appeal has thus concluded that the Board does not have the jurisdiction to award interest except in the circumstances listed in section 226(2)(c) of the *FPSLRA*,[117] and the Board continues to apply that ruling.[118]

Finally, the remedial power of the Board is limited by the right to free speech of the parties.[119] Courts have found that labour boards or arbitrators may order an employer to provide a letter of reference or verbal recommendations for an employee who has been dismissed;[120] however, the Federal Court has concluded that the Canadian Human Rights Tribunal does not have the jurisdiction to order an employer to apologize in the absence of an express power to do so.[121] The Board has often been asked to order apologies[122] but has not yet ruled on whether it too does not have the jurisdiction to do so.[123]

---

116 *Hare*, above note 112.

117 *Nantel v Canada (Attorney General)*, 2008 FCA 351.

118 See, for example, *Federal Government Dockyard Chargehands Association v Treasury Board (Department of National Defence)*, 2013 PSLRB 139, where the Board did not award interest where the employer did not implement the collective agreement within ninety days as required by s 157 of the *FPSLRA*. The Board did, however, award general damages of $7,500 to the union for that breach.

119 This right is both guaranteed by s 2(b) of the *Charter* and by s 186(5) of the *FPSLRA*.

120 See *Slaight Communications Inc v Davidson*, [1989] 1 SCR 1038.

121 *Canada (Attorney General) v Stevenson*, 2003 FCJ No 491.

122 See, for example, *Chaves v Treasury Board (Correctional Service)*, [2005] CPSSRB No 46, where the Board declined to order an apology without addressing the jurisdiction issue.

123 See *McConnell v Professional Institute of the Public Service of Canada*, [2005] CPSSRB No 110, where the issue was placed before the Board but not answered.

7) Reconsideration of Board Orders

Section 43 of the *FPSLRA* gives the Board the power to "review, rescind or amend any of its orders or decisions."[124] This power of reconsideration is common in labour relations statutes. The power is commonly used on the consent of the employer and bargaining agent to vary certification orders, in particular bargaining unit definitions, to deal with the creation of new job classifications or other mechanical issues.[125]

In contentious cases, though, the Board is reluctant to reconsider earlier decisions. The Board has stated that reconsideration requests should be raised "at the earliest opportunity"—which means "a reasonable time after the applicant receives the evidence on which it intends to rely in supporting its reconsideration request."[126] The Board has also identified that a request for reconsideration must

1. not be a relitigation of the merits of the case;
2. be based on a material change in circumstances;
3. consider only new evidence or arguments that could not reasonably have been presented at the original hearing;
4. ensure that the new evidence or arguments have a material and determining effect on the outcome of the complaint;
5. ensure that there is a compelling reason for reconsideration; and
6. be used judiciously, infrequently, and carefully.[127]

In an older Board decision on this issue, it stated:

> In the Board's view, section 25 [now 43(1)] was not designed to enable an unsuccessful party to reargue the merits of its case. The purpose of section 25 was rather to enable the Board to reconsider a decision either in the light of changed circumstances or so as to permit a party to present new evidence or arguments that could not reasonably have been presented at the original hearing or where some other compelling reason for review exists. It would be not only inconsistent with the need for some finality to proceedings, but also unfair and burdensome

---

124 *FPSLRA*, s 43(1).

125 See, for example, *Treasury Board v Public Service Alliance of Canada*, 2019 FPSLREB 91, to amend the bargaining unit description to match changes to the occupational group definition made at the same time.

126 *Bernard v Canada (Revenue Agency)*, 2017 FCA 40 at para 12.

127 *Chaudhry v Treasury Board (Correctional Service of Canada)*, 2009 PSLRB 39 at para 29, aff'd *Chaudhry v Canada (Attorney General)*, 2009 FCA 376.

> to a successful party to allow the unsuccessful one to try to shore up or reformulate arguments that had already been considered and disposed of.[128]

The Board has consistently held that reconsideration is not meant to be an opportunity to reargue a case—that is best left to judicial review.

The "new evidence" required to trigger a reconsideration does not always mean that the evidence must have been completely unavailable or not in existence during the first hearing. In one case, the bargaining agent successfully argued that hiring university students during the school year was not part of a "student employment program" under the Act, and therefore those students working during the academic year were "employees." The employer applied for reconsideration based on new testimony that it wanted the Board to hear concerning another memorandum of understanding that indicated that the students were actually hired as part of a "student employment program." The memorandum of understanding was placed before the Board in the first hearing, and the Board concluded that it was not a "student employment program." However, the Board allowed reconsideration of its earlier decision on the ground that

> Mr. Lacombe's [the witness providing additional evidence] involvement in the Memorandum of Understanding, which dates back some ten years ago was not readily apparent until counsel had been permitted access to confidential Cabinet documents, as a consequence of the earlier decision. Accordingly, I also find that the new evidence presented at this hearing could not reasonably have been presented at the original hearing and therefore meets one of the criteria for review under section 27 as enunciated in the Board's decision of December 18, 1985.[129]

On the other hand, the "new evidence"—even if unavailable at the time of the original hearing—still needs to be relevant to the dispute. In *Czmola and Public Service Alliance of Canada*, the applicant applied for reconsideration two and a half years after the original decision based on new evidence that had just come to light. However, the Board still dismissed the application for reconsideration because the new evidence

128 *Public Service Alliance of Canada and Treasury Board*, [1985] CPSSRB No 25 at para 5.

129 *Public Service Alliance of Canada v Treasury Board*, [1997] CPSSRB No 138 at para 20.

would not have a "material and determining effect" on the Board's decision.[130]

The Board has never explicitly defined what it means by "special circumstances."[131] However, in one application for reconsideration, the Board agreed to review its previous decision because of the precedential value of the decision.[132]

The Board has also not defined what it means by "changed circumstances." However, one instance that it accepted an application for reconsideration on grounds that could be seen as "changed circumstances" was *PIPSC v Canadian Nuclear Safety Commission*.[133] In that case, the Professional Institute of the Public Service of Canada (PIPSC) asked the Board to review its earlier decision to order a representation vote for a particular bargaining unit. In the original Board decision, it ordered the creation of a bargaining unit that was broader than the one proposed by the PIPSC. Therefore, the PIPSC did not have membership evidence sufficient to convince the Board not to order a representation vote. The PIPSC applied for reconsideration and sought leave to introduce into evidence six membership cards signed by employees who were in the broader Board bargaining unit but not in the PIPSC's original proposed bargaining unit. Those six members would bring the PIPSC's membership in the bargaining unit above the 50 percent threshold. The Board granted the reconsideration application, stating:

> Given its decision to seek only the certification of a TS-SF bargaining unit (see original decision, paragraph 5), the applicant herein was justified in not submitting, with its original application, the six additional cards.
>
> It would therefore be inappropriate to exclude relevant acceptable memberships evidence that precedes the terminal date on the basis that it was available and could have been tendered earlier on. The PIPSC was not seeking certification for these employees and had no reason or obligation to file the cards in support of its original application.[134]

130 *Czmola and Public Service Alliance of Canada*, [1999] CPSSRB No 60 at paras 13–14.

131 The term was used in *Quigley and Treasury Board*, [1998] CPSSRB No 42 at para 17.

132 *Public Service Alliance of Canada v Treasury Board*, [1997] CPSSRB No 13 at para 8.

133 *PIPSC v Canadian Nuclear Safety Commission*, [2004] CPSSRB No 38.

134 *Ibid* at paras 12–13.

Although the Board's reasons could be read as allowing reconsideration on the basis of new evidence not available at the time of the original hearing, it is better viewed as a "changed circumstances" reconsideration, those changed circumstances being the larger bargaining unit ordered by the Board.

The Board in the 1985 *PSAC v Treasury Board*[135] case indicated that the Canada Industrial Relations Board's broader view of reconsideration resulted from the more limited right to judicial review in the *Canada Labour Code*. Since the Board is now also protected by a strong privative clause,[136] this justification no longer stands, and it might invite the Board to relax its rules concerning reconsideration and adopt an approach closer to that adopted by the Canada Industrial Relations Board.

Prior to the 2013 changes to the *FPSLRA*, there was no explicit power for a party to seek reconsideration of an adjudication of a grievance. With that 2013 amendment stating that the Board adjudicates grievance disputes (unless the parties agree otherwise), the reconsideration power in section 43 of the *FPSLRA* applies to adjudications by the Board in addition to its decisions in other matters.[137] However, even in the absence of that statutory power, adjudicators—like all tribunals—have the inherent power to reconsider their own decisions where there has been a mistake or "slip" in drawing up the order and where there was an error in expressing the manifest intention of the tribunal.[138] For example, in *Association of Justice Counsel v Canada (Attorney General)*, the association raised two issues in a policy grievance about performance pay. One of the two issues was conceded by the employer at the outset of the hearing. The Board went on to hear evidence and arguments on the second issue and found against the association on that second issue. The Board, though, issued an order dismissing the grievance in its entirety. When the association wrote to the Board to ask it to correct this mistake, the Board member concluded that he was *functus officio* and had no power to correct this mistake. The Federal Court of

135 *PSAC v Treasury Board*, above note 128.

136 *FPSLRA*, s 51.

137 *Canada (Attorney General) v Philps*, 2017 FCA 178.

138 *Chandler v Alberta Association of Architects*, [1989] 2 SCR 848.

Appeal quashed that decision, concluding that the Board member had the common law power to amend his decision to correct this mistake.[139]

D. ENFORCEMENT OF BOARD ORDERS

Under the old *Public Service Staff Relations Act*, there was no way to directly enforce an order of the Board. When a party refused to comply with an order of the Board, the Board was required to forward (through the minister) a report to Parliament, including a copy of its order. The matter then rested with Parliament to be resolved.[140]

The *FPSLRA*, unlike its predecessor, contains provisions to enforce Board orders. On the request of any party, the Board must file a certified copy of its order with the Federal Court unless there is no indication of failure or likelihood of failure to comply with the order, or there is another good reason why filing the order in Federal Court would serve no useful purpose.[141] Once the order of the Board is filed with the Federal Court, it becomes an order of that Court and is enforced as such.[142]

The Canada Industrial Relations Board has the identical power and has indicated in its jurisprudence that it is reluctant to exercise it. The Canada Industrial Relations Board has described the purpose behind this power as follows:

> The major intent of these provisions is to allow and equip the Board to use its officers, administrative processes and authority to adopt an accommodative approach to the resolution of labour relations problems and to give greater meaning and authority to Board decisions. All of this is intended to be in furtherance of the objectives of Part V expressed by the Preamble as they apply to the multitude of

---

139 *Association of Justice Counsel v Canada (Attorney General)*, 2016 FCA 56. The extent of the employer's concession was then disputed by the parties, and the employer asked the Board to clarify its initial decision; the Board refused to clarify its decision but, instead, set out what it understood the employer's concession to be and rendered an order on that basis: *Association of Justice Counsel v Treasury Board*, 2016 PSLREB 119.

140 *Public Service Staff Relations Act*, SC 1967, c 72, s 24.

141 *FPSLREB Act*, s 35(1), and *FPSLRA* s 234(1) (applied to adjudications).

142 *FPSLREB Act*, s 35(2), and *FPSLRA* s 234(2) (applied to adjudications).

circumstances and competing interests that arise in the dynamic circumstances of labour relations.[143]

Thus, the Canada Industrial Relations Board will not file a copy of its order with the Federal Court unless doing so would serve some labour relations purpose. For example, in *International Longshoremen's Association, Local 1846, and Maritime Employers' Association and Terminaux Portuaires du Québec*,[144] an employer was ordered to appoint a bargaining agent (the employer was part of an employer's association designated under the *Canada Labour Code*). The other members of the employer association had appointed a particular agent. However, this one employer, rather than cooperating and appointing the same agent, refused to comply with the Board's order and did not appoint any agent. The union and the agent of the rest of the employers asked the Canada Industrial Relations Board to file its order in Federal Court for enforcement. The Canada Industrial Relations Board dismissed that application. It agreed that the employer was not complying with its order and that there was no likelihood that the employer would comply with the order. However, it reviewed the history of this labour dispute (that had been ongoing, in some form or another, for over seven years) and stated that "[t]his is a very modest complaint when one considers the history of certification in the port of Bécancour."[145] The Canada Industrial Relations Board then concluded that filing the order could have only three results: the employer would appoint the same agent as the other employers in the area (which the Board concluded was unlikely), the employer could appoint a different agent, or the employer would be found in contempt of court. The Canada Industrial Relations Board concluded that the contempt option was not helpful because "this Board is not interested in sanctions for the sake of sanctions."[146] Therefore, instead of filing its earlier order, it granted a new order requiring the employer to appoint a particular agent as its bargaining agent—and then did not file that order with the Federal Court.

This case indicates that the Board—like the Canada Industrial Relations Board—has the jurisdiction to refuse to file its order when it

143 *Seafarers' International Union of Canada, and Seaspan International Ltd*, [1979] 2 Can LRBR 493.

144 *International Longshoremen's Association, Local 1846, and Maritime Employers' Association and Terminaux Portuaires du Québec*, 88 CLLC 16,007.

145 *Ibid.*

146 *Ibid.*

is convinced that doing so would not serve any labour relations purpose other than to punish the party that refuses to comply with the order, particularly where another labour relations solution is available.

The Board has not had many occasions to address its power to file a certified copy of an order in Federal Court. The Board in one case refused to exercise that power when the employer was complying with the strict meaning of the order. The bargaining agent believed that the order had broader implications than were clear on its face; the Board stated that a party could not "achieve something more" than what is on the face of an order through an application for the Board to file a certified copy of the order in Federal Court.[147]

The leading authority on this power, though, is *Bremsak v Professional Institute of the Public Service of Canada*.[148] That case was part of a seven-year legal battle that began when the Board of Directors of the PIPSC apologized on behalf of Ms. Bremsak (an elected official of the PIPSC) for comments she made about another member. Ms. Bremsak filed a complaint with the Board and was suspended from her elected and appointed positions shortly thereafter. The Board concluded that the suspension violated the *FPSLRA* and ordered the PIPSC to "restore the complainant's status as an elected official of the bargaining unit" and amend its internal policies. The PIPSC applied to Federal Court for judicial review and for a stay of that order; the Federal Court refused its application for a stay. The PIPSC then refused to restore Ms. Bremsak's status and, in fact, suspended her membership in the PIPSC because of further allegations of harassment against her. The Board reviewed the Canada Industrial Relations Board caselaw summarized above and decided that that caselaw should also apply to the Board. The Board stated that there are, in essence, two questions: has the respondent complied with the Board's decision, and if not, is there a good reason why filing the decision would serve no useful purpose? The Board concluded that the PIPSC had amended its policies to comply with the Board's order but that it had not restored Ms. Bremsak to her position. The subsequent suspension for alleged harassment did not justify the refusal to implement the Board's order. Therefore, the Board filed its order in Federal Court.

---

147 *Canadian Federal Pilots Association v Treasury Board*, 2011 PSLRB 84 at paras 95–97.

148 *Bremsak v Professional Institute of the Public Service of Canada*, 2009 PSLRB 159.

The Board applied this two-part test in *Weinstein v Deputy Head (Correctional Service of Canada)*,[149] stating that the Board must file a certified copy of its order with the Federal Court unless there is no indication or likelihood of a failure to comply with the order or there is some other good reason why filing it in the Federal Court would serve no useful purpose. In that case, the initial decision stated that the Board member would remain seized of any disputes over the implementation of his order for ninety days. The original order was the standard order for reinstatement with reimbursement of salary. The grievor was on workers' compensation benefits for part of the period covered by the order. The employer argued that it was not required to pay salary during that period. The Board was critical of the employer for not raising that issue during the ninety-day period in which the original Board member remained seized with the matter and concluded that these applications were not a forum to dispute or revisit the terms of a Board order.

The consequences of filing a Board order in Federal Court is that the order can be enforced through contempt proceedings in Federal Court. This is what happened in Ms. Bremsak's case. The PIPSC still refused to restore her to her elected position, in part because the term of those offices expired shortly before the Board referred its order to Federal Court. The Federal Court concluded that this refusal was contempt of court and the PIPSC did not have any lawful excuse for its failure to comply with the order; specifically, the order being enforced was the original Board order, not the later order referring the matter to Federal Court.[150] The Court then ordered that the PIPSC pay a fine of $400,000, later reduced to $250,000 by the Federal Court of Appeal.[151]

E. STANDING ON JUDICIAL REVIEW

Among the powers of the Board is the ability to intervene in judicial review applications concerning its own decision for the purpose of making submissions regarding the standard of review and the Board's jurisdiction, policies, and procedures.[152] The Canada Industrial Relations

149 *Weinstein v Deputy Head (Correctional Service of Canada)*, 2022 FPSLREB 35.

150 *Bremsak v Professionnal Institute of the Public Service of Canada*, 2012 FC 213, aff'd *Professional Institute of the Public Service of Canada v Bremsak*, 2012 FCA 147.

151 *Professional Institute of the Public Service of Canada v Bremsak*, 2013 FCA 214.

152 *FPSLREB Act*, s 34(2).

Board was given the same power and the same limitations in the 1998 amendments to the *Canada Labour Code*.[153] Despite that explicit grant of authority, the Federal Court of Appeal has continued to refer to the old common law cases concerning the limits of a tribunal to intervene in applications for judicial review of its own decisions. These common law rules permit tribunals to make submissions concerning their jurisdiction and procedures (including the standard of review), but they are not allowed to defend the merits of their own decisions.[154] However, courts have recently begun to relax the rules restricting tribunals when they intervene in judicial review applications and allow tribunals to defend the merits of their decisions in some cases.[155]

In *Canada (Attorney General) v Quadrini*,[156] the Federal Court of Appeal acknowledged this relaxing of the traditional rules of tribunal standing. At the same time, the Court of Appeal concluded that the common law restrictions on the scope of submissions a tribunal can make—including the obligation that an intervenor make useful submissions and not simply restate what others will be arguing—are "existing alongside" the express power set out in the Act. The issue raised in that appeal was whether the Board had the power to rule on the existence of solicitor-client privilege and order the disclosure of documents to test that existence. The Court of Appeal permitted the Board to intervene to "explore the implications associated with this Court granting the application for judicial review," but the Board was not permitted to "submit that it adopted the least intrusive means to investigate the existence of privilege without breaching it" because that submission came too close to an attempt to justify the merits of its decision. The Court of Appeal was influenced in that case by the fact that the respondent in the appeal was self-represented.

---

153 *Canada Labour Code*, RSC 1985, c L-2, s 22(1.1).

154 *Telus Communications Inc v Telecommunications Union*, [2005] FCJ No 1253 (CA) at para 108; *Northwestern Utilities Ltd v Edmonton (City)*, [1979] 1 SCR 684.

155 *Children's Lawyer for Ontario v Goodis, Senior Adjudicator, Information and Privacy Commissioner*, [2005] OJ No 1426 (CA).

156 *Canada (Attorney General) v Quadrini*, 2010 FCA 246.

F. MEDIATION

One of the Board's mandates is to provide mediation services to parties in a dispute.[157] These mediation services consist of assisting the parties with collective bargaining, assisting parties with "the management of the relations resulting from the implementation of collective agreements," and mediating grievances. There are several provisions in the *FPSLRA* that specifically require or enable the Board to mediate disputes. For example, the chair of the Board may, at any time (even on their own initiative), appoint a mediator to resolve collective bargaining disputes;[158] the Board may attempt to mediate or resolve unfair labour practice complaints;[159] the Board may mediate staffing complaints;[160] and the Board may mediate a resolution to a grievance with the consent of the parties without losing the ability to later resolve the complaint if mediation is unsuccessful.[161]

The Board has also established a service they call "preventative mediation." Parties to a conflict may call upon the mediation services of the Board even in the case of a file that has not officially been referred to adjudication or a complaint.

G. PAY RESEARCH

The Board used to have a mandate to provide compensation analysis and research services.[162] This includes compensation surveys, compiling information relating to compensation, analyzing that information and making it and the analysis available to the parties and to the public, and conducting any research relating to compensation that the chair of the Board may direct.[163] Parliament removed this mandate as part of the reforms in 2013, and this mandate has not been reinstated in the subsequent clawback of many of those reforms.

---

157 *FPSLRA*, s 14.

158 *Ibid*, s 108(1).

159 *Ibid*, s 191(1).

160 *PSEA*, s 97.

161 *FPSLREB Act*, s 23. It is, of course, common practice in the private sector for arbitrators to attempt to mediate disputes.

162 *FPSLRA*, s 13.

163 *Ibid*, s 16.

H. WORKLOAD

The Board sets out its workload in its annual reports. The annual report from 2017–18,[164] for example, set out its total caseload as follows:

Year	Labour Relations — Old	Staffing — Old	Labour Relations — New: Grievances	Labour Relations — New: Complaints	Labour Relations — New: Applications	Labour Relations Carried Forward (Total)	Staffing — New	Staffing Carried Forward
2014–15	4,537	206	1,365	73	387	4,897	602	204
2015–16	4,897	204	1,424	50	306	5,646	594	349
2016–17	5,646	349	1,633	47	299	6,522	736	417
2017–18	6,522	417	1,396	74	224	6,765	624	496

This chart does not reflect the actual number of cases heard by the Board. Sometimes a single hearing accounts for multiple grievances or complaints. Furthermore, the list includes cases that resolve at mediation—which accounted for 205 files in 2017–18, for example.[165]

The chart above hints at, but does not accurately record, the average delay in deciding cases. The Board does not publish statistics about the length of time it takes to render a decision. However, a random sample will serve to demonstrate the extent of the Board's delays. To pick the month of December 2019, the Board issued thirteen decisions that month. The delays in those cases were as follows:

164 Federal Public Sector Labour Relations and Employment Board, *2017–2018 Annual Report* (2018), online (pdf): www.fpslreb-crtespf.gc.ca/en/about-us/annual-reports/2017-2018/documents/FPSLREB_AR_E_2018.pdf.

165 *Ibid* at 23.

Case Name	Filed with Board	Board Hearing	Board Decision	Nature of Case
Valderrama v Deputy Head (Department of Foreign Affairs, Trade and Development), 2019 FPSLREB 115	Unknown, but discipline imposed between 2013 and 2015	23–25 October 2017	2 December 2019	Disciplinary suspension
Smith v Deputy Head (Department of National Defence), 2019 FPSLREB 116	Unknown, but discipline imposed 28 March 2014	7–9 August 2019	3 December 2019	Disciplinary suspension
Pelletier v Canada Revenue Agency, 2019 FPSLREB 117	1 April 2016	23–26 October 2018, 8–11 April and 28 May 2019	3 December 2019	Disciplinary dismissal
Union of Canadian Correctional Officers – Syndicat des agents correctionnels du Canada – CSN (UCCO-SACC-CSN) v Treasury Board (Correctional Service of Canada), 2019 FPSLREB 118	7 November 2014	Written submissions July and August 2019	5 December 2019	Policy grievance (severance pay)
Yeo v Deputy Head (Department of Employment and Social Development), 2019 FPSLREB 119	Unknown, but termination was 19 September 2014	12–15 February and 7–8 August 2019	6 December 2019	Dismissal for poor performance
Campeau v Treasury Board (Correctional Service of Canada), 2019 FPSLREB 120	23 September 2011	Written submissions ending 28 May 2019	9 December 2019	Collective agreement interpretation
Public Service Alliance of Canada v House of Commons, 2019 FPSLREB 121	3 May 2019	12 September 2019	20 December 2019	Interest arbitration
Campeau v Deputy Head (Canada Border Services Agency), 2019 FPSLREB 123	Unknown, but termination of employment was 27 September 2016	26–29 April 2019	17 December 2019	Disciplinary dismissal

Case Name	Filed with Board	Board Hearing	Board Decision	Nature of Case
Edwards v Treasury Board (Department of Health), 2019 FPSLREB 124	15 September 2015	5–6 March 2019	19 December 2019	Human rights complaint
Parent v Deputy Head (Department of National Defence), 2019 FPSLREB 125	Unknown, but suspension issued on 19 October 2015	13–15 August 2019	19 December 2019	Disciplinary suspension
Edwards v Deputy Head (Canada Border Services Agency), 2019 FPSLREB 126	17 May 2019	Written submissions ending 4 July 2019	19 December 2019	Extension of time
Chamberlain v Treasury Board (Human Resources and Skills Development), 2019 FPSLREB 127	15 February 2011	4 and 26 April 2019	19 December 2019	Issue estoppel in Part II *Canada Labour Code* complaint

When the first edition of this book was published, I could confidently advise employees that their grievances or complaints would be scheduled by the Board in approximately eight to nine months and then take several more months to decide. This is simply no longer the case. As can be seen from the random sample above, cases take years to be heard and then more months (or years) for a decision to be rendered.

Several explanations for this delay have been suggested. First, the workload of the Board is greater than what is reasonable for the number of decision-makers. The Board has often had vacancies that the government delays filling (or, in some cases, simply does not fill), which exacerbates this problem.

Second, the Board has experienced expanding jurisdiction. After the 2013 reforms, for example, staffing complaints fell under the jurisdiction of the Board. As discussed further in Chapter 10, the Board has jurisdiction over a number of human rights issues that, in earlier decades, would have gone to the Canadian Human Rights Commission.

Third, as discussed in Chapter 10, individual employees have the right to file grievances and complaints with the Board without being represented by their bargaining agent. This means that several Board hearings are conducted by self-represented litigants. These self-represented litigants are unfamiliar with the Board's processes and the process of litigation generally, which delays Board hearings and makes those hearings last longer.

Fourth, this delay is part of a larger trend in labour law generally. The average delay from the date the grievance was filed to the time an arbitral award was issued has grown from around 250 days in the early 1970s to approximately 420 days in the mid-1990s and almost 600 days by 2012.[166] This more general increase in delays has been attributed to the increasing "legalistic" nature of labour arbitrations in particular: unnecessary pre-hearing disclosure that used to be accomplished during the grievance procedure;[167] increases in preliminary objections;

166 Bruce Curran, "Event History Analysis of Grievance Arbitration in Ontario: Labour Justice Delayed?" (2017) 72:4 *Relations Industrielles* 621 at 632.

167 See in particular a lecture by Warren K. Winkler, CJ (Delivered at Queen's School of Policy Studies, Queen's University, 30 November 2010), online: www.ontariocourts.ca/coa/about-the-court/archives/2010-labour-arbitration-conflict-resolution.

increases in the number of witnesses (particularly expert witnesses); and more prolix credibility challenges.[168]

The Board has made some efforts toward reducing this delay. For example, the Board has introduced a process of expedited hearings for adjudications and staffing complaints. In both types of expedited hearings, though, the parties must agree that the decision of the Board may not be used as a precedent in other cases and, in adjudications, must also agree not to judicially review the Board's decision. The Board also issued a policy, effective 1 June 2019, that limited the ability of parties to request that a hearing be postponed. This new policy stated, among other things, that the parties' mutual desire for postponement would not be sufficient cause to grant a postponement.[169] Hopefully, these and other reforms will decrease the length of time that elapses between the onset of a dispute and a decision by the Board.

---

168 Curran, above note 166 at 642. See also Ronald A. Pink & David C. Wallbridge, "The Future of Labour Arbitration" (Paper delivered at the 2010 Administrative, Labour and Employment and Privacy and Access Law Conference, Ottawa, 26–27 November 2010) at 8, online (pdf): *Canadian Bar Association* www.cba.org/cba/cle/PDF/adm10_pink_paper.pdf: "In almost all circumstances, when a case gets unduly delayed it is the fault of the lawyers."

169 FPSLREB, "Policy on Postponements of Hearings," online: https://pslreb-crtefp.gc.ca/en/resources/policies/postponements-of-hearings.html.

CHAPTER FIVE

Acquisition of Bargaining Rights

A. INTRODUCTION

The prevailing pattern of labour relations legislation in Canada is that labour relations boards determine which organization has the exclusive right to represent a class or classes of employees in collective bargaining.[1] Labour boards allow employees to chose which organization will acquire this exclusive right of representation through a process known as "certification." This so-called Wagner Act model of labour relations—with the two principles of majoritarianism and exclusivity—is in force in most private sector and public sector workplaces.[2]

The *Federal Public Sector Labour Relations Act* (*FPSLRA*) is no different from other Canadian labour relations statutes in this respect. The only difference is that certification is the sole process by which an employee organization can earn the exclusive right to represent members in collective bargaining in the federal public service. In the private sector, some labour relations statutes permit "voluntary recognition" of bargaining agents. The *FPSLRA* does not permit voluntary recognition: the definition of a "bargaining agent" is "an employee organization that is certified by the Board" (at s 2(1)). As Finkelman and Goldenberg

1 Jacob Finkelman & Shirley Goldenberg, *Collective Bargaining in the Public Service: The Federal Experience in Canada* (Ottawa: Institute for Research on Public Policy, 1983) at 84.

2 *Mounted Police Association of Ontario v Canada (Attorney General)*, 2015 SCC 1 at para 94.

explained, "[B]y this means the employer (the government) thus relieves itself of any possible charge that it might be showing favouritism if it recognized one employee organization rather than another."[3]

This chapter explores the various issues that arise when employee organizations apply to be certified as the bargaining agent for a particular group of employees.

B. APPLICATIONS FOR INITIAL CERTIFICATION

1) The Applicant for Certification Must Be an "Employee Organization"

The *FPSLRA* defines an "employee organization" as an organization the purposes of which include the regulation of relations between the employer and its employees for the purposes of parts I and II of the *FPSLRA*.[4] The Board has seldom examined the bona fides of an employee organization applying for certification in great detail, and when the Board has done so, it has been rebuked by the Federal Court of Appeal.

The leading case concerning whether an organization is an employee organization remains the 1992 decision of the Federal Court of Appeal in *Canadian Association of Trades and Technicians v Canada (Treasury Board)*.[5] In that case, the Canadian Association of Trades and Technicians (CATT) applied to displace the Federal Government Dockyard Trades and Labour Council East as the bargaining agent for the Operational Category—East Coast bargaining unit. The incumbent bargaining agent argued that the constitution of CATT was "so flawed and invalid that CATT fails to meet the requirements of the definition of 'employee organization.'"[6] The Board agreed, stating that CATT "appears to be very autocratic and does not provide its members with some basic rights."[7] The Board then cited several specific deficiencies with CATT's constitution, including the failure to name an officer responsible for signing the collective agreement, the absence of

---

3 Finkelman & Goldenberg, above note 1 at 85.

4 *Federal Public Sector Labour Relations Act*, SC 2003, c 22, s 2, s 2(1), "employee organization" [*FPSLRA*]. The definition is unchanged from the old *Public Service Staff Relations Act* (*PSSRA*).

5 *Canadian Association of Trades and Technicians v Canada (Treasury Board)*, [1992] 2 FC 533 (CA) [*CATT v Treasury Board*].

6 *Board decision in Canadian Association of Trades and Technicians v Canada (Treasury Board)*, [1991] CPSSRB No 42 at 4.

7 *Ibid* at 5.

members' rights to ratify the collective agreement, and the absence of any right of members to be represented in grievances.

The Federal Court of Appeal quashed the Board's decision. The Court set out the three general criteria to be an "employee organization":

- it must be an organization of employees;
- it must be formed for labour relations purposes; and
- it must be a viable entity for collective bargaining purposes.[8]

The Board had also set out those three criteria and had refused to acknowledge CATT as an "employee organization" based on the third criterion. The Court took a much more narrow view of the circumstances in which an organization is not a viable entity for collective bargaining purposes. The Court stated that "some substantial ground must be shown to deprive an employee organization of its *prima facie* right to certification."[9] As a result:

> In order to decide if an organization is a viable union, therefore, the Board is not entitled to examine in minute detail each of the provisions of the constitution and pass judgment on their democratic flavour. These matters of detail are for the unions and their members to decide, not for the Board, unless it is given express statutory authority. The Board must limit itself to deciding if the organization has a written constitution, duly adopted by the members, which allows it to operate as a viable entity and to legally bind the organization and its members.[10]

The Court did not explain why it felt it necessary for an employee organization to have a written constitution, duly adopted by the members. In *Capital Coach Lines Ltd (Travelways) and Canadian Brotherhood of Railway, Transport and General Workers and Travelways Maple Leaf Garage Employees' Association*,[11] the Canada Labour Relations Board concluded that the existence of a written constitution gave an employee organization "sufficient status to operate as a viable entity and to legally bind the organization and its members." Since a trade union

---

8 *CATT v Treasury Board*, above note 5 at para 7.

9 *Ibid* at para 8, citing *New Brunswick Teachers' Federation v Province of New Brunswick* (1970), 3 NBR (2d) 189 (CA).

10 *Ibid* at para 11.

11 *Capital Coach Lines Ltd (Travelways) and Canadian Brotherhood of Railway, Transport and General Workers and Travelways Maple Leaf Garage Employees' Association*, (1980) 40 di 5.

is an entity governed by contract, and the terms of that contract are set out in the union constitution,[12] a union must have a constitution to be a viable organization. The *Trade Unions Act*[13] also requires unions registering under its provisions to file a copy of the "rules of the union," and this may have influenced earlier decisions of labour boards to require employee organizations to have a written constitution.

Another union that was denied status as an employee organization was the Canadian Air Line Pilots Association. When they applied in 1971, pilots employed in the federal public service were only entitled to "associate membership" in the association, by which they were not entitled to "general representation services," nor were they allowed any vote in the affairs of the association. The Board stated that the employees concerned must "play a role in the determination of their conditions of employment" and that the Board would not certify "what are commonly known as 'paper locals.'"[14]

In light of the Federal Court of Appeal's decision in the CATT case, it is doubtful that this is still good law. The real test is whether the limited rights of associate members make the union an unviable entity for collective bargaining.

The Board has generally accepted applications from new employee organizations without much debate or concerns expressed over their ability to function as a bargaining agent.[15]

Other earlier Board decisions raised a number of other issues concerning whether a union was an "employee organization" under the old *Public Service Staff Relations Act* (*PSSRA*). First, there was some dispute concerning the effective date the Board would use to determine

---

12 *Berry v Pulley*, [2002] 2 SCR 493.

13 *Trade Unions Act*, RSC 1985, c. T-14, s 6. Registering under the *Trades Union Act* is sufficient to guarantee immunity from prosecution for criminal conspiracy simply for being a trade union: s 29.

14 *Canadian Air Line Pilots Association and Canada (Treasury Board) (Aircraft Operations Group—Technical Category)*, [1971] CPSSRB No 2 at para 29 [*Canadian Air Line Pilots Association*].

15 See, for example, *Syndicat général du cinéma et de la télévision, Local 4835 (Canadian Union of Public Employees) v National Film Board*, 2007 PSLRB 117; *National Police Federation v Treasury Board*, 2018 FPSLREB 31; *Federal Government Dockyard Trades and Labour Council East v Treasury Board*, 2005 PSLRB 178; and *Federal Law Officers of the Crown v Treasury Board of Canada; Association of Justice Counsel v Treasury Board of Canada; Treasury Board of Canada v Professional Institute of the Public Service of Canada*, 2006 PSLRB 45.

whether an organization was an employee organization: the date of the application or the date of the hearing. In *Professional Institute of the Public Service of Canada and Canada (Treasury Board) (Home Economics Group—Scientific and Professional Category)*,[16] the Public Service Alliance of Canada (PSAC) argued that the Professional Institute of the Public Service of Canada was not an employee organization because the institute's constitution did not specifically refer to collective bargaining as one of its objects. The institute had passed a bylaw to change those objects, but the bylaw only had effect until the next annual general meeting of the institute—that is, it was not yet a permanent change to the constitution. The PSAC argued that the new bylaws could not be relied on as evidence that the institute was an employee organization. The Board disagreed. In essence, the Board concluded that it could take the bylaws as effective on the date of the application; a future change was not relevant in assessing current employee organization status.

Shortly thereafter, the Board confirmed that it must determine an organization's status as of the date of that organization's application. The constitutional defects in *Canadian Air Line Pilots Association and Canada (Treasury Board) (Aircraft Operations Group—Technical Category)* were explained above. The association sought to repair those defects by a constitutional amendment passed after it had applied for certification. The Board refused to consider those amendments, stating that "the entitlement of the Association to certification must therefore be determined on the basis of the situation as it was at the time of the making of the application."[17]

Second, when employee organizations were first being certified in 1967, some organizations (in particular, the PSAC) took the position that employee organizations needed to represent only employees of the federal public service. There is no provision in the *FPSLRA* (or in the earlier *PSSRA*) that expressly bars the acquisition of bargaining rights by an employee organization that includes as members people who are not federal public servants. However, since the definition of

16 *Professional Institute of the Public Service of Canada and Canada (Treasury Board) (Home Economics Group—Scientific and Professional Category)*, [1967] CPSSRB No 14.

17 *Canadian Air Line Pilots Association*, above note 14 at para 26. See also *Economists', Sociologists' and Statisticians' Assn (Operational Group—Scientific and Professional Category) and Canada (Treasury Board)*, [1974] CPSSRB No 17 at para 7 [*Economists', Sociologists' and Statisticians' Assn*].

"employee" includes only people employed in the "public service," some parties objected to employee organizations that included members not employed in the public service. The Board rejected that argument in *Council of Graphic Arts Unions of the Public Service of Canada and Canada (Treasury Board) (Printing Operations Group—Operational Category)*[18] because restricting the term "employee organization" to organizations that represent only public servants would unduly restrict those organizations when parts of the government are privatized—the organization would lose its right to represent public servants simply because the government privatized some entity (or at least turned it into a Crown corporation).[19]

The Board has, however, required that employee organizations provide some assurances that non-public servants will not influence the collective bargaining that takes place on behalf of public servants. The Board will not permit "extraneous influences" on the collective bargaining process: the Board will examine past practices of the organization, as well as undertakings from that organization that only members who are public servants will exercise control over the collective bargaining that takes place under the *FPSLRA*.[20] The Board has also stated that if it discovers that an employee organization has fallen under improper "extraneous influences," it could revoke the certification of that bargaining agent.[21]

The *FPSLRA* also permits certification of a "council of employee organizations"—defined simply as a council formed by two or more employee organizations.[22] The Board requires a degree of formality

18 *Council of Graphic Arts Unions of the Public Service of Canada and Canada (Treasury Board) (Printing Operations Group—Operational Category)*, [1967] CPSSRB No 13 at para 6 [*Graphic Arts Unions*]. See, to the same effect, *Public Service Alliance of Canada and Canada (Treasury Board) (Ships Crews Group—Operational Category)*, [1967] CPSSRB No 8 [*Ships Crews Group*], where the PSAC argued that the Canadian Brotherhood of Railway, Transport and General Workers did not have standing to intervene in the PSAC's application for certification because the brotherhood admitted members who were not public servants. The Board rejected that argument, more tersely than in the *Graphic Arts Unions* case.

19 *Graphic Arts Unions, ibid.*

20 *Retail Clerks Union and Canada (Staff of Non-Public Funds) (Canadian Forces Base—Cornwallis—Operational Category)*, [1980] CPSSRB No 4 at para 15.

21 *Ships Crews Group*, above note 18 at para 6. The process for revoking a certification is set out below.

22 *FPSLRA*, s 2(1), "council of employee organizations."

governing the relationship between the employee organizations before being willing to certify them as a council of employee organizations:

> A council of employee organizations is not a loosely knit collectivity of sovereign employee organizations. . . . It is, therefore, essential that the council establish to the satisfaction of the Board that the constitutional instrument which creates the council has been adopted with the approval of the members of the component organizations that make up the council.[23]

In the *Postal Operations Group* case, the Board set out some principles as to what is required to convince it to certify a council:

> an appropriate provision in the constitution of the employee organization adopted at a properly called convention or by referendum in accordance with the constitutional requirements of an employee organization or by the adoption of an appropriate resolution by the members of the employee organization.[24]

In a subsequent case, the Board made it clear that these are not firm rules: even when the employee organizations have not adhered entirely to their constitutions when deciding to form a council, they can still form a council, especially when they have already cooperated for a number of years "in a relationship with one another that was just a step removed" from being a council, and where the employee organizations have all designated (in one way or another) the council to act for it in collective bargaining matters.[25]

The fact that an employee organization is divided into several components, and that it involves the leaders of those components in the collective bargaining process when advisable, does not make the organization a council. In *Public Service Alliance of Canada and Canada (Treasury Board) (Hospital Services Group—Operational Category)*, the Confédération des syndicats nationaux argued that the PSAC was not an employee organization but really closer to a council. As discussed later in this book,[26] the PSAC is divided into a number of components, each of which assists with collective bargaining. However, this does not make the PSAC a council. The PSAC signs all of the collective agreements, and:

---

23 *Postal Operations Group* (Board File No 146-2-13).

24 *Ibid.*

25 *Graphic Arts Unions*, above note 18 at para 8.

26 See Chapter 8.

> [t]he fact that the Alliance must delegate its responsibility to negotiate agreements to a component . . . does not in any way derogate from its authority and capacity to act as the bargaining agent. There is nothing in the legislation that prevents a bargaining agent from acting through agents whether the agents constitute a committee, a component, a member of the legal profession or an industrial relations advisor, so long as the agent acts in the name of the bargaining agent.[27]

2) The Application for Certification Must Be Signed by a Duly Authorized Representative of the Employee Organization

Section 64(1)(b) of the *FPSLRA* requires the Board to certify an employee organization as a bargaining agent only if "the persons representing the employee organization in the making of the application [for certification] have been duly authorized to make the application." The Board will not inquire too closely into the status of who signs the application:

> Where an application is properly executed and attested by the duly elected officers of an employee organization which is authorized by its constitution to make such an application and no evidence is introduced by any party opposed in interest to show that they lack such authority, it is our opinion that the statement as to due authorization contained in the statutory declaration verifying the application should be accepted at face value.[28]

3) The Employee Organization Must Be Free from Employer Interference

Section 66(1) of the *FPSLRA* states that the Board may not certify an employee organization as a bargaining agent if the employer, or a person acting on behalf of the employer, has participated in the formation or administration of the employee organization in a manner that impairs its fitness to represent the interests of the employees in the bargaining unit for which it is proposed to be certified. Allegations of employer

---

27 *Public Service Alliance of Canada and Canada (Treasury Board) (Hospital Services Group—Operational Category)*, [1967] CPSSRB No 2 at 3 [*Hospital Services Group*].

28 *Ibid* at 4.

interference in the formation or administration of an employee organization—in the context of the certification of a bargaining agent—are rare in the federal public service.[29]

In *Czmola and Public Service Alliance of Canada*,[30] the Board explained that section 66(1) contains a two-part test. First, the employer or its agent must have participated in the administration or formation of the employee organization. Employees who occupy "managerial or confidential positions" are considered to be agents of the employer, and those who do not occupy those positions are not agents of the employer for the purposes of section 66(1).[31]

Second, the employer's participation would have to be of such a nature as to impair the bargaining agent's fitness to represent the interests of employees in the bargaining unit. The Board has not yet had the opportunity or cause to interpret this requirement. However, the Canada Industrial Relations Board, in interpreting a similar provision in the *Canada Labour Code*, has stated that the purpose of this provision is to ensure that the bargaining agent operates at "arm's length" from the employer. The expression "arm's length" relationship does not mean a permanent state of war but simply that the bargaining agent must truly represent the employees and not be so dominated by the employer that it cannot independently represent its members.[32] The Canada Industrial Relations Board has recognized that direct evidence of employer interference is rarely available or forthcoming. Therefore, it will look for the following:

> [E]xperience has shown that there are many signs which enable us to recognize a union that is dominated or influenced by an employer. Frequently, such a union will be an independent one [i.e., not affiliated with a national union], created when a unionization campaign is being conducted by another union. In general, this type of union is created in great haste and recruits a majority of the employees of the enterprise very quickly. This can often be explained by the more or less discreet support given the union by the employer or some of his

---

29 It is less rare to allege that the employer has committed an unfair labour practice by interfering with a bargaining agent; see Chapter 7.

30 *Czmola and Public Service Alliance of Canada*, [1999] CPSSRB No 60; application for judicial review dismissed [2000] FCJ No 382 (CA).

31 *Ibid* at para 12.

32 *Transport de l'Est Inc* (1993), 90 di 214.

representatives. Union meetings are held at the workplace and during the working hours of the employees, who are not penalized in any way. Recruitment is also done during working hours, often with the knowledge of the employer's representatives, if not their assistance. The emerging union has limited financial resources but can nevertheless afford all the professional or technical assistance it needs. Documents are typed or photocopied at the workplace by persons working in close collaboration with the employer or with his authorization. Management representatives attend or participate in union meetings or openly invite employees to attend. Needless to say, circumstances vary with each case. The fact remains, however, that a union which is dominated or influenced by an employer can seldom be set up without incidents of this nature occurring. Consequently, if there is evidence that such incidents have occurred, this must raise some doubt as to whether the union is genuinely independent of the employer.[33]

4) The Employee Organization Must Have Majority Support Within the Bargaining Unit

Section 64(1)(a) of the *FPSLRA* requires the Board to certify an employee organization as a bargaining agent if it is satisfied that a majority of employees in the bargaining unit for which the employee organization is seeking certification wish that employee organization to represent them as their bargaining agent. The *FPSLRA* then goes on to state that the Board may order that a representation vote be taken among the employees in the bargaining unit for the purpose of satisfying itself that the majority of them wish the employee organization to represent them as their bargaining agent.[34] Aside from these two provisions—the requirement of majority support among employees and the option to hold a vote—the *FPSLRA* does not contain any other explicit rules to determine whether or not a particular employee organization has enough support to become a bargaining agent.[35]

---

33 *CJRC Radio Capitale Ltée* (1977), 21 di 416; application for judicial review dismissed [1978] FCJ No 107 (CA).

34 *FPSLRA*, s 65(1).

35 As discussed in Chapter 2, there was a period between 2015 and 2017 when certification applications required a representation vote, and the Board could only order such a vote when the employee organization had the support of at least 40 percent of the employees in the unit who wished to have the employee

This absence of a more solid statutory framework stands in contrast to other labour relations statutes in Canada. For example, the *Canada Labour Code* is similar to the *FPSLRA* in that majority employee support is necessary. However, it goes on to specify a number of other rules, including that only employees who are employees in the bargaining unit at the date of filing the application are relevant;[36] the Board must order a vote if between 35 and 50 percent of the employees in the unit are members of the trade union;[37] the result of the representation vote is determined on the basis of the votes cast, not the total number of eligible voters, unless less than 35 percent of eligible voters actually cast a ballot;[38] and the Board must include "no union" as an option on the first ballot in a representation vote but not on a second ballot if no particular union won a majority of the votes cast.[39] The *Canada Industrial Relations Board Regulations* also specify the evidence necessary to establish that an employee is a member of a union: a signed application and at least $5 in membership dues.[40] The Ontario *Labour Relations Act*, on the other hand, requires representation votes in all cases[41] and also requires that an applicant trade union have signed up 40 percent of the employees in the bargaining unit as members.[42]

These various questions—when to order a vote, who is a member of a trade union, who is an employee in the bargaining unit, and what level of support is required to file an application—are left unanswered in the *FPSLRA*. Therefore, the answers to those issues must be found in the decisions of the Board.

Who is an employee in the bargaining unit? The Board had, in 1967, issued a policy statement in which they stated that the date for determining the number of employees in a bargaining unit and for identifying the employees who comprise the bargaining unit should be the last day of the month immediately preceding the month in which an application for

---

organization represent them as a bargaining agent. Two certification votes—both involving the RCMP—took place under that regime.

36 *Canada Labour Code*, RSC 1985, c L-2, s 29(1.1).

37 *Ibid*, s 29(2).

38 *Ibid*, s 31.

39 *Ibid*, ss 30(2) & 30(3).

40 *Canada Industrial Relations Board Regulations*, SOR/2001-520, s 31(1).

41 *Labour Relations Act*, SO 1995, c 1, Schedule A, s 10(2), unless the employer commits an unfair labour practice and the Ontario Labour Relations Board orders certification as a remedy under s 11(2)(c) of the Act.

42 *Ibid*, s 8(2).

certification is filed.[43] However, that policy statement was not binding on the Board and has lapsed into disuse in any event. The Board initially indicated that it would be comfortable with either the date of the application or the "closing date" specified by the executive director under the *Federal Public Sector Labour Relations Regulations*.[44] However, in a more recent case, the Board ordered that a representation vote include all employees who have a continuing interest in the bargaining unit, including employees who were laid off and subject to recall, employees on long-term disability, employees on authorized leave, and one part-time temporary employee who was a member of the bargaining unit on the date of the application for a revocation of certification.[45]

A more interesting situation occurs when a bargaining unit has a considerable number of part-time workers. Whether the part-time workers are employees depends on whether they are required to work at least one-third of the normal period.[46] In *Public Service Alliance of Canada v Statistics Survey Operations*,[47] the employer argued that part-time workers who met the definition of "employee" on the date of the application should be included in the bargaining unit for the purposes of determining employee support. The Board disagreed. It followed the practice of the Ontario Labour Relations Board and the Canada Industrial Relations Board and examined the hours worked by employees over a six-and-a-half month period prior to the application for certification. Those workers who met the definition of employee over that period (i.e., those who did not work less than one-third of the time[48]) were included in the pool of employees for the purpose of determining support for the employee organization. The parties had agreed to use six and a half months, but the Board indicated that this was the

43 Finkelman & Goldenberg, above note 1 at 91.

44 *Public Service Alliance of Canada v Statistics Survey Operations*, [2000] CPSSRB No 70 at para 13 [*PSAC v Statistics Survey Operations*]. The "closing date" is between fifteen and forty days from the date of application to allow sufficient time to inform employees about the application for certification: *Federal Public Sector Labour Relations Regulations* (*FPSLR Regulations*), SOR/2005-79, ss 23–24.

45 *Lala v United Food and Commercial Workers Canada, Local 401*, 2017 PSLREB 7 at paras 16 and 35 [*Lala*].

46 *FPSLRA*, s 2(1)(c).

47 *PSAC v Statistics Survey Operations*, above note 44.

48 *FPSLRA*, s 2(1), "employee," subparagraph (c).

minimum period of time it would consider as a representative period for determining if a worker is an "employee" in the bargaining unit.[49]

What evidence does an employee organization need to file to demonstrate majority support? The *FPSLRA* does not specifically require that support be demonstrated by evidence of membership, but section 39(1)(k) gives the Board the power to make regulations concerning the form in which, and the time as of which, evidence as to membership of employees in an employee organization is to be presented to the Board and the circumstances in which that evidence may be received. This is a strong indication that Parliament intended employee organizations to demonstrate support by signing up members. The Board's regulations, though, only state that the certification application must be accompanied by "the documentary evidence on which the applicant intends to rely to satisfy the Board that a majority of the employees in the proposed bargaining unit wish the applicant to represent them as their bargaining agent"[50] and also that the Board may require the employer to provide a list of employees along with "specimen signatures of the employees, the home addresses of the employees, or both."[51]

The *FPSLR Regulations* do not contain any provisions governing what constitutes evidence of membership in an employee organization—unlike the $5 rule in the *Canada Industrial Relations Board Regulations*.[52] In the *Hospital Services Group* case, the Board accepted evidence of dues check-off as evidence of membership in the PSAC. Prior to 1967, dues check-off was a matter determined through the National Joint Council. Employees from whom dues were deducted had to sign an authorization to that effect. The Board decided that employees whose dues were checked off were fully aware that they were considered to be members of the PSAC and that therefore everybody who was on the dues check-off list provided by the employer was a member of the PSAC.[53] The intervening union argued that some members of the PSAC only remained members because of favourable rates for group insurance available to members. The Board concluded that the reason an employee joins an employee organization is not relevant, unless there

49 *Lala*, above note 45 at para 15.

50 *FPSLR Regulations*, s 30.

51 *Ibid*, s 32.

52 *Canada Industrial Relations Board Regulations*, s 31(1)(b). A payment of $5 to a union is evidence that somebody has joined that trade union.

53 *Hospital Services Group*, above note 27 at 5–7.

is evidence that they have been induced to join by misrepresentation or other improper means.[54]

The Board's regulations do not set out any rules about electronic signatures or other electronic membership evidence. The Board did accept electronic membership evidence to certify the bargaining agent for members of the RCMP, but without commenting upon that evidence.[55] The Canada Industrial Relations Board has also accepted electronic membership evidence as a recognition that "requiring union officials to witness each signature on a membership card and witness the payment of a $5.00 fee would effectively prevent employees spread out across the country and overseas to exercise their right to join a union of their choice."[56]

Does an employee need to be a full member, or is some other category of membership sufficient? In *Graphics Arts Unions*, some of the affected employees were "provisional" members of the International Typographical Union. Provisional members did not have the right to vote in union affairs and paid a nominal sum as dues. However, the Board accepted them as members for the purpose of ascertaining employee support because provisional members could become full members at any time (and presumably would, once their council was certified as a bargaining agent), and it was a true matter of choice to accept the more limited rights of membership at that time.[57]

Probably the most important issue is how much support an employee organization needs to be certified, either with or without a vote. At the outset of certifications in the federal public service, the Board developed a policy of certifying employee organizations without a representation vote if they had signed up 52 percent of employees as members. The Board would order a vote if the employee organization had between 46 and 52 percent of the employees signed up as members and would dismiss the application for certification if the employee

---

54 *Ibid* at 6.

55 *National Police Federation v Treasury Board*, 2018 FPSLREB 31 at para 48. The Board ordered a vote in that case because the employee organization applied for certification prior to the 2017 amendments to the *FPSLRA* removing the automatic certification vote rule, discussed in Chapter 2.

56 *WestJet Professional Pilots Association v WestJet*, 2015 CIRB 785 at para 61—although the Board staff in that case did interview a sample of employees to satisfy the Board that the membership evidence was legitimate.

57 *Graphic Arts Unions*, above note 18 at para 24.

organization support fell below 46 percent.[58] The Board also refused to certify a bargaining agent (even after a representation vote) if it did not have a "clear" majority.[59]

The Board has subsequently recognized that requiring a "clear" majority was a "departure from the clear text of the Act" and now requires only "50 percent plus one" as majority support.[60] However, the Board was not clear that the "50 percent plus one" rule applied to membership support or the result of a representation vote. In *Professional Institute of the Public Service of Canada v Canadian Nuclear Safety Commission*, the Board concluded that the Professional Institute of the Public Service of Canada had membership cards showing "0.50145" support in the bargaining unit yet still ordered a representation vote without any other special circumstances.[61] That case could be explained as the Board requiring one clear vote in excess of 50 percent of the bargaining unit. There was evidence of 166 members filed in that case. Therefore, presumably the Board concluded that there were 331 employees in the bargaining unit.[62] Half of 331 employees is 165.5, so a clear support of "50 percent plus one" would require 167 members instead of 166. What the Board appears to have concluded in that case is that it requires evidence of "50 percent plus one" members, not just that the percentage of membership is greater than 50 percent.

There are still circumstances in which the Board will order a representation vote on an initial application for certification even where the bargaining agent has evidence of "50 percent plus one" membership in the bargaining unit. The Board has developed a policy of requiring a representation vote whenever it reconsiders the bargaining unit

---

58 *Research Council Employees' Association and (Canada) National Research Council (Communications Officers—Administrative and Foreign Service Category)*, [1973] CPSSRB No 3 at para 29 [*Research Council Employees' Association*].

59 See the discussion in *Professional Institute of the Public Service of Canada v Canadian Nuclear Safety Commission*, [2004] CPSSRB No 11 at para 60 [*Canadian Nuclear Safety Commission*].

60 *Ibid*.

61 *Ibid* at para 64. This decision was overturned on reconsideration when the institute filed evidence of six additional members in the larger bargaining unit ordered by the Board: [2004] CPSSRB No 38.

62 The institute submitted in its reconsideration application that the size of the Board's designated bargaining unit was only 324 employees, meaning that the institute actually had a great deal more than "50 percent plus one support." The Board did not address this problem in its reconsideration decision.

structure of an employer and amalgamates bargaining units.[63] The Board will order a representation vote even where there is only one employee organization listed on the ballot—that is, where the vote is not necessary to resolve a dispute as to which of two employee organizations will be certified.[64]

The Board will also order a representation vote when two different employee organizations are applying for certification and each has a majority of members (because some employees joined both unions) or both have a reasonable level of support.[65] However, evidence of employees holding "dual membership" does not automatically result in a vote.[66]

Finally, the Board will order a representation vote when the circumstances surrounding the membership evidence indicate that such a vote may be warranted. For example, in *Public Service Alliance of Canada and Canada (Social Sciences and Humanities Research Council) (Administrative Support Category)*,[67] one of the organizers of the certification campaign had told some employees (in ignorance) that there would be an automatic representation vote. The Board also received letters from some employees demanding a secret ballot, including one employee who also signed a membership card. In light of those facts, the Board ordered a representation vote despite approximately 53.5 percent support in the bargaining unit.[68]

It is unclear whether the required level of support is a majority of voters or a majority of all employees in the bargaining unit. In *United Food and Commercial Workers, Local 401 and Staff of the Non-Public Funds, Canadian Forces*,[69] the Board stated that it was prepared to consider the results of a representation vote on the basis of the number of votes cast. In that case, there were sixty-three employees in the

---

63 See, for example, *National Energy Board v Public Service Alliance of Canada*, 2003 PSSRB 79 [*National Energy Board*], and *Research Council Employees' Association*, above note 58.

64 See, for example, *Council of Graphic Arts Unions of the Public Service of Canada and Canada Communication Group*, [1994] CPSSRB No 46 [*Canada Communication Group*], and *Public Service Alliance of Canada and National Energy Board*, [1993] CPSSRB No 183.

65 Finkelman & Goldenberg, above note 1 at 96.

66 *Ibid.*

67 *Public Service Alliance of Canada and Canada (Social Sciences and Humanities Research Council) (Administrative Support Category)*, [1979] CPSSRB No 8.

68 *Ibid* at paras 28–29.

69 *United Food and Commercial Workers, Local 401 and Staff of the Non-Public Funds, Canadian Forces*, [1985] CPSSRB No 224.

bargaining unit; forty-nine of them voted, and there were thirty-one votes in favour of certification. Thus, roughly 63 percent of voters voted in favour of certification, but only 49 percent of all employees voted in favour. The Board concluded that, in light of the high turnout, it would consider the votes cast instead of the total number of employees. However, the Board left it open to future panels to refuse to certify an employee organization that won a majority of votes cast when there was a "small voter turnout."[70]

The Board's current practice in how to conduct a certification vote was described in *Lala v United Food and Commercial Workers Canada, Local 401*.[71] The Board in that case confirmed its decision to order a vote by electronic means. Voters received a voting package by registered mail explaining the details of the vote and how they could cast their ballots, including each individual's PIN. No proxy voting would be tolerated, and each elector had to cast an individual ballot. The vote itself took place over a period of time that varied according to the Board's discretion. The vote took place over five days in the *Lala* decision (involving employees who work at the Canadian Forces Base Edmonton), whereas the Board ordered a vote over thirty days for a national bargaining unit of RCMP members.[72]

5) There Must Be No Employer Interference with a Representation Campaign

It is an unfair labour practice for the employer to seek, by intimidation or coercion, to compel an employee to refrain from exercising any right under parts I and II of the *FPSLRA*.[73] The Board, applying a similar provision in the *PSSRA*, concluded that it was an unfair labour practice for the employer to interfere in a representation vote.[74] While the new *FPSLRA* contains a limited employer right of free speech, that right only defends against unfair labour practices listed in paragraphs 186(1)(a) and

70 *Ibid* at para 11. The Board has not had to elaborate on what constitutes a "small voter turnout," but the 35 percent threshold in s 31 of the *Canada Labour Code* may be instructive.

71 *Lala*, above note 45.

72 *National Police Federation v Treasury Board*, 2019 FPSLREB 74.

73 *FPSLRA*, s 189(1)(b).

74 *Public Service Alliance of Canada and National Capital Commission*, [1994] CPSSRB No 135 [*National Capital Commission*].

(b) of the *FPSLRA*.[75] Those paragraphs also prohibit the employer (or a manager) from interfering with the "formation or administration" of an employee organization.[76] Since interference with a representation vote is also a breach of section 189(1)(b), the right of free speech does not operate as a defence to an allegation of interference with a representation vote.

Regardless of the applicability of the statutory right to employer free speech, the Board concluded in *Public Service Alliance of Canada and National Capital Commission* that an employer was not precluded from making any statement during a representation vote. However, in that case, the employer did commit an unfair labour practice by sending out a letter to all employees with the following paragraphs:

> In the event that employees choose to be represented by PSAC, a period of collective bargaining would follow. Under the Public Sector Compensation Act, all matters related to compensation, administration of compensation, wages and benefits are frozen and non-negotiable until the end of the application of the Act in 1997-1998. A new collective agreement entered into by the parties would contain the provisions frozen by legislation and the non-monetary items negotiated by both parties.
>
> In the event that employees choose not to be represented by PSAC, the same legislated freeze applies. The terms and conditions of employees hired before May 1, 1994 would remain, as they are now, those of their former collective agreements. Employees hired on or after May 1, 1994 would remain subject to the Compendium of Terms and Conditions of Employment.
>
> If employees were to choose an alternative form of representation at a later date, negotiations could once again only address non-monetary items if they occurred under the freeze.[77]

The Board concluded that these paragraphs offended the Act by attempting to convey to employees that there is little point in voting in favour of certification of the PSAC because the legislation has frozen all compensation. The Board found the last paragraph suspicious and capable of many interpretations. The employer did not mention any of the benefits of certification outside of negotiation of compensation,

---

75 *FPSLRA*, s 186(5).

76 *Ibid*, s 186(1)(a).

77 *National Capital Commission*, above note 74 at 6–7.

including representation in the grievance procedure. Therefore, the Board allowed the complaint.[78]

As a remedy, the Board ordered that the ballots cast in that representation vote be destroyed and a new vote conducted. The PSAC applied for reconsideration of that decision, asking that the old votes be counted, and only if they were short of a majority should a new vote be conducted. The Board declined, stating that the voting process had been "tainted" by the employer's actions and that if the first vote had been counted and gone against PSAC, this would have had a "chilling effect" on any subsequent vote, thereby continuing the effects of the employer's unfair labour practice.[79]

The Board has also, on one occasion, heard a complaint that somebody outside of management interfered with a representation vote. In *Public Service Alliance of Canada and Canada (Fisheries Research Board—Technical Category—Ships Officers)*,[80] the captain of one of the vessels being canvassed wanted the Canadian Merchant Service Guild to be named the bargaining agent instead of the PSAC. The ballot, however, only listed the PSAC; therefore, he met with other officers (on his ship and others) to ask them to vote "no" so the guild could file its own application for certification. The PSAC complained, but the Board rejected their complaint, stating:

> In some jurisdictions in Canada, a direction for the taking of a representation vote is coupled with a prohibition against electioneering or propaganda during a fixed period immediately prior to the date of the taking of the vote and while the balloting is in progress. It is feasible to impose such a prohibition where what might be called a direct vote is conducted at a designated place or places and during a space of at most two or three days. No such prohibition has been imposed in any vote conducted under the Public Service Staff Relations Act. It would be a practical impossibility to police a mail vote conducted over a period of some four weeks or more to see if a "no propaganda" direction has

---

78 *Ibid* at 7. This is the extent of the Board's jurisprudence concerning employer interference in a representation vote, although there is a rich jurisprudence from the Canada Industrial Relations Board and other labour relations boards in Canada on this topic.

79 *Public Service Alliance of Canada and National Capital Commission*, [1994] CPSSRB No 139 at 3.

80 *Public Service Alliance of Canada and Canada (Fisheries Research Board—Technical Category—Ships Officers)*, [1969] CPSSRB No 6.

> been observed, Indeed, if we were to attempt to do so, few votes would pass unchallenged by an unsuccessful party in the hope that it might reap an advantage from bringing to the Board's attention instances of minor significance. Accordingly, we find that Walsh's activities in inducing the employees to become members of the Guild and in exhorting them to vote "no" during the voting period does not constitute any ground for nullifying the note. We wish to make it clear, however, that the freedom to campaign does not extend to improper pressure being exercised by a representative of any employee organization, whether it be an applicant seeking the support of the employees or an opposing employee organization seeking to defeat an applicant, or for that matter by anyone acting on behalf of management.[81]

The Board has, more recently in *Lala v United Food and Commercial Workers Canada, Local 401*, undertaken a thorough review of the principles underlying the prohibition against management interference with the certification process (or, in that case, the revocation process). The Board in that case adopted a two-stage analysis: first, whether the employer committed an unfair labour practice by interfering in the revocation application, and second, whether the circumstances surrounding that practice make it unlikely that the decertification vote would reflect the true wishes of the employees because the interference was both significant to and influential in the initiation of the revocation application or in the conduct of the vote.[82] For example, permitting the circulation of petitions during working hours may amount to improper employer involvement if, taken together with other factors, it demonstrates that the employer's conduct was both significant and influential—although in that case, the Board accepted that the employer put a stop to the campaigning during working hours when it found out about it.[83] The employer also did not interfere by providing the lead proponent of revocation with the number—but not the names—of employees in the bargaining unit.[84] Finally, the employer did commit an unfair labour practice by cancelling bargaining at the request of the employee who filed the revocation application, but this unfair labour practice would

---

81 *Ibid* at para 5.

82 *Lala v United Food and Commercial Workers Canada, Local 401*, 2017 FPSLREB 42 at para 188.

83 *Ibid* at paras 361 and 391.

84 *Ibid* at para 418.

not prevent the representation vote from disclosing the employee's true wishes.[85]

C. DISPLACEMENT OR REVOCATION APPLICATIONS

Applications for initial certification may be made at any time. Applications to displace one bargaining agent and either revoke the certification or replace the bargaining agent with another, however, may only be made during certain times, referred to as the "open period." Where there is a collective agreement in place, a displacement application may be made:

- in the case of a collective agreement with a term of two years or less, after the commencement of the last two months of its term;[86]
- in the case of a collective agreement with a term of more than two years, after the commencement of the twenty-third month and before the commencement of the twenty-fifth month, and then during the two-month period before the end of each year that the agreement continues to be in force, or after the commencement of the last two months of the agreement;[87] or
- if a collective agreement applies for a further term after its expiry if neither party serves a notice to bargain, then at any time as listed in the first two bullet points (whichever applies), or during the two-month period immediately before the end of each year that the agreement continues to operate after the term specified in the collective agreement.[88]

On several occasions, the federal government has extended the duration of collective agreements by legislation.[89] When this happens, the time period for filing a displacement application may be changed accordingly if the legislation extends a two-year agreement beyond its original term.[90]

85 *Ibid* at paras 835–45.

86 *FPSLRA*, s 55(1).

87 *Ibid*, s 55(2).

88 *Ibid*, s 55(3).

89 See Chapter 2.

90 See *Syndicat des employés de l'office national du film, CUPE Local 2656 and National Film Board*, [1984] CPSSRB No 19, where the Board declined to determine whether the *Public Sector Compensation Restraint Act*, SC 1991, c 30, operated to change the period in which to file a displacement application because the applicant missed the period for doing so regardless of how the period was calculated.

If a collective agreement has expired, and is not automatically renewed, then the displacement application may be brought at any time.[91]

An employee organization applying to displace a bargaining agent must file evidence with the Board indicating that they have majority support in the bargaining unit.[92] The Board has, with one exception, always ordered a representation vote where the employee organization applying to displace a bargaining unit has filed this evidence of majority support. In *Union of Canadian Correctional Officers — CSN v Treasury Board (Correctional Service Canada)*, the Board stated that it holds a representation vote in displacement applications "unless exceptional circumstances dictate otherwise."[93] The one exception was an application to revoke a bargaining certificate where the bargaining agent consented to the application.[94]

Finally, in a displacement application, while the Board has stated that "an employee organization seeking to displace a certified bargaining agent must take the bargaining unit as it finds it,"[95] there are ways for an employee organization (or the employer) to apply to change the scope of a bargaining unit. The Board, in making that comment, was referring to an attempt by an employee organization to argue that certain managerial exclusions were no longer valid. Section 77 of the *FPSLRA* states that a "bargaining agent" may apply for an order revoking the order that declared a position to be managerial or confidential. Since the applicant in a displacement application is not a "bargaining

91 *Professional Institute of the Public Service of Canada and Treasury Board*, [1988] CPSSRB No 361 at para 34.

92 In *Economists', Sociologists' and Statisticians' Assn*, above note 17, the employee organization presented evidence of 507 members. The Board noted that this may fall below 50 percent support depending on the exclusions sought by the employer; however, it allowed the employee organization to bring its application regardless because it fell within "the range of tolerance" of the Board. In all other cases, the Board has agreed to conduct a representation vote after the applicant provided evidence of "a majority of the employees in the bargaining unit": see *Professional Institute of the Public Service of Canada and Treasury Board*, [1992] CPSSRB No 100 at 8.

93 *Union of Canadian Correctional Officers — CSN v Treasury Board (Correctional Service Canada)*, [2000] CPSSRB No 69 at para 23.

94 *McCuaig v Public Service Alliance of Canada*, 2014 PSLRB 55. The bargaining unit comprised thirteen employees of the Canadian Institutes of Health Research.

95 *Treasury Board and Professional Institute of the Public Service of Canada*, [1993] CPSSRB No 40 at 3.

agent" yet, it has no standing to bring an application to revoke a designation of a position as managerial or confidential.

Notwithstanding the Board's comment, there is nothing preventing an employee organization that is not yet the bargaining agent from applying under section 70 of the *FPSLRA* to review the bargaining unit structure of the unit it is raiding. Furthermore, there is nothing preventing the employer from applying to change the bargaining unit structure or to vary the managerial exclusions at the same time as an employee organization is applying to displace a bargaining agent—subject, of course, to the more general prohibitions on anti-union conduct.

The *FPSLRA* contains no provisions setting out which union has carriage over grievances filed by the original union prior to the displacement application. Private sector arbitrators have concluded that the new bargaining agent does not have carriage over the grievance, and the displaced union has a vested right to the grievance. If the old bargaining agent withdraws the grievance, that withdrawal is valid.[96]

D. SUCCESSOR RIGHTS

Successor rights exist in all provincial labour acts and in the *Canada Labour Code*. While there are slight variations in the wording, the purpose attributed to successorship provisions is consistent. When an employer exercises its legal freedom to dispose of its business, this can have serious consequences for the situation of its employees. They may have struggled to become organized and achieve collective bargaining and then to arrive at a collective agreement. Once that agreement is finally settled, the employees naturally expect that its terms will be fulfilled in the conduct of the enterprise. These expectations could be set at naught by a simple change in corporate ownership. The employees may find themselves still working at the same plant, at the same machine, under the same working conditions, under the same supervision, doing exactly the same job as before, but for a different employer. The result of the sale of a business of which the employees may not even be aware is that the collective bargaining rights of the employees may have disappeared.

---

96 *Coca-Cola Bottling Co* (2004), 127 LAC (4th) 218 (Beck); *Middlesex County (Strathmere Lodge)* (2001), 96 LAC (4th) 197 (Lynk).

Realistically, one cannot expect these interests of the employees and their union to be at the forefront of the business negotiations in which employers are free to engage in. Accordingly, legislatures and Parliament have adopted a very straightforward protection: certification and other orders under labour relations legislation follow the business into the hands of the transferee. Legislatures went even further in private sector labour laws and imposed the collective agreement on a person who didn't sign it. It is up to the prospective purchaser to investigate the terms of the bargain its predecessor has made with the trade union and see that this is considered when setting the purchase price and other terms of the takeover before it steps into the shoes of the old employer.[97]

Thus, the primary purpose of successor rights provisions is to maintain and protect the collective bargaining rights of employees upon the sale or transfer of a business or an operation from one employer to another. Accordingly, what is generally of concern in successor rights applications is the continuity of existing collective bargaining relationships to ensure that employees affected by a change of employers are not thereby denied the previously acquired protections and benefits of collective bargaining.[98]

There are three categories of successor rights and obligations that apply to employees of the federal public service: the rights that apply upon a "conversion"; the rights that apply upon privatization of a part of the federal public service; and the rights that apply upon mergers, amalgamations, and transfers of jurisdiction among employee organizations.

1) Successor Provisions upon a Conversion

The main successor provisions in the *FPSLRA* concern the rights that accrue upon a conversion. The term "conversion" means the establishment of a separate agency, or the integration into an already existing separate agency, of any portion of the core public administration—in other words, when the Governor in Council moves employees from Schedule IV of the *Financial Administration Act* to Schedule V of the

97 *Lester (WW) (1978) Ltd v United Association of Journeymen and Apprentices of the Plumbing and Pipefitting Industry, Local 740*, [1990] 3 SCR 644.

98 *CCRA v Association of Public Service Financial Administrators*, [2000] CPSSRB No 49 at para 15.

same Act.[99] These provisions in the *FPSLRA* were introduced in the old *PSSRA* in 1996.[100] Prior to that amendment, whenever employees in the federal public service were transferred from the Treasury Board to a separate employer, or from one separate employer to a newly established separate employer, the move necessitated new applications for certification by the bargaining agent that represented the employees concerned.[101] The collective agreement governing these employees was also at an end and would need to be renegotiated after the employee organization was certified.[102] This absence of any successor rights upon the creation of a separate agency was considered unsatisfactory; therefore, the *FPSLRA* now contains provisions governing such transfers.

Section 81 of the *FPSLRA* states that, subject to the remaining successor provisions in the *FPSLRA*, a collective agreement that applies to employees in any portion of the core public administration before the conversion continues in force after the conversion and binds the new separate agency until its term expires.[103] By necessary implication, this also means that the bargaining agent certified for those employees in the core public administration continues to act as the bargaining agent after the conversion. This conclusion is evident from the wording of the *FPSLRA* (which, in section 82, refers to the "bargaining agent" being permitted to negotiate changes to the collective agreement notwithstanding section 81[104]) and also flows from the "scope" or "union recognition" clause common in public service collective agreements.[105] It is not necessary for any party to make an application to the Board to engage the successor rights provisions: they apply automatically.

When the successor rights provisions are triggered, the parties have a right to make an application to the Board to settle certain consequences flowing from the conversion. There are two situations governed by the *FPSLRA*: where the conversion takes place during the normal

99 *FPSLRA*, s 80, "conversion"; *Financial Administration Act*, RSC 1985, c F-11, s 11.
100 The amendments were introduced in SC 1996, c 18, s 18.
101 Finkelman & Goldenberg, above note 1 at 121.
102 *Public Service Alliance of Canada v CCRA*, [2001] CPSSRB No 24 at para 112.
103 *FPSLRA*, s 81.
104 *Ibid*, s 82.
105 These "union recognition" clauses state that the employer recognizes the bargaining agent as the exclusive representative and bargaining agent for the employees covered by the collective agreement. Since the collective agreement remains in force, so too does the union recognition clause.

currency of a collective agreement, and where the conversion takes place after one party has given the other notice to bargain.

Under normal circumstances, either party has a window (between 120 and 150 days after the conversion[106]) in which to make an application to determine new bargaining units; determine which employee organization is to be the bargaining agent for the employees; and if two or more bargaining units are merged, determine which collective agreements are to remain in force, and if so, for how long.[107] The Board has the power to shorten the term of a collective agreement so that if the Board decides to permit multiple collective agreements to remain in force for a particular bargaining unit, the Board may also ensure that there is a common expiry date for the collective units so that bargaining can commence at the same time.

The bargaining agent and the employer have the right to apply for permission to serve a notice to bargain after a conversion. If an application mentioned above is made, the new bargaining agent or the employer has a ninety-day window after the Board grants an order to apply for permission to serve a notice to bargain.[108] If no application is brought, they have a window between 151 and 240 days after the conversion (i.e., the ninety-day period after the deadline for filing an application has expired) to apply for permission to serve a notice to bargain.[109]

The *FPSLRA* contains separate provisions governing a situation where a bargaining agent served a notice to bargain prior to the conversion. The *PSSRA* did not contain these provisions. In *Public Service Alliance of Canada v CCRA*,[110] the PSAC served a notice to bargain prior to the conversion of Revenue Canada into the Canada Customs and Revenue Agency (CCRA).[111] The CCRA and the PSAC had already made applications for changes to the bargaining unit structure and other ancillary matters when the PSAC requested that the Board establish a conciliation board.[112] The Board recognized that the real issue behind this request was as follows: do the successor provisions

106 *FPSLRA*, s 84(2).

107 *Ibid*, s 84(1).

108 *Ibid*, s 85.

109 *Ibid*, s 86.

110 *PSAC v CCRA*, above note 102.

111 Now the Canada Revenue Agency.

112 Appointing a conciliation board (now called a public interest commission) was a step in collective bargaining that could lead to a legal strike. For a full discussion of conciliation, see Chapter 6.

contemplate the possibility of bargaining between a bargaining agent, whose certification has been continued, and the new separate employer prior to the Board making decisions concerning new bargaining units or other matters? The Board concluded that it had no authority to appoint a conciliation board because the *PSSRA* did "not contemplate bargaining between the PSAC and the CCRA for these employees until the Public Service Staff Relations Board has made its determinations"[113] concerning the appropriate bargaining unit and which bargaining agent will represent that unit. The Board indicated that any other conclusion would lead to "great instability in the workplace,"[114] particularly because the process could lead to a legal strike. The purpose behind the successor rights provisions is stability and the continuation of rights; this purpose is best served by not requiring the parties to bargain until after the Board has dealt with all of the consequences of the conversion.

The *FPSLRA* has essentially codified the Board's decision in that case. Section 87 of the *FPSLRA* states that a notice to bargain that was served before a conversion does not bind the new separate agency. Instead, the statutory freeze in place during the period after notice to bargain remains in place for 150 days.[115] During a window between the 120th and 150th days after the conversion, the parties may make an application to the Board to determine new bargaining units and the bargaining agents for those units.[116]

It should be noted that, to date, at least one of the parties has applied to the Board for a new bargaining unit structure in every instance where there has been a conversion.[117] Therefore, the rules that apply without such an application have never been tested. The usual course is for one (or, more commonly, both) of the parties to apply for a new bargaining unit structure and then for bargaining to commence some time after the Board has determined the appropriate bargaining unit structure.

The successor provisions in the *FPSLRA* cannot be used as a vehicle for a displacement application. In *CCRA v Association of Public Service Financial Administrators*,[118] the National Automobile, Aerospace, Transportation and General Workers Union of Canada (Canadian Auto

113 *PSAC v CCRA*, above note 102 at para 110.
114 *Ibid* at para 111.
115 *FPSLRA*, ss 88 and 107.
116 *Ibid*, s 89(a).
117 *PSAC v CCRA*, above note 102 at para 115.
118 *CCRA v Association of Public Service Administrators*, above note 98.

Workers (CAW)) applied to intervene in an application by the Professional Institute of the Public Service of Canada for the usual post-conversion remedies. The CAW had signed up some auditors in the CCRA as members. Auditors in the CCRA were represented by the institute prior to the conversion (and still are today). The CAW wanted to argue that it should be made the bargaining agent of the auditors bargaining unit proposed by the institute. Section 84(1)(b) of the *FPSLRA*[119] states that the Board must determine which "employee organization" is to be the bargaining agent representing each bargaining unit. The CAW argued that the use of the term "employee organization" meant that any organization could apply to be the bargaining agent, so long as it had a reasonable level of membership support. The Board disagreed, stating that "an employee organization which has not previously obtained established bargaining rights, and which seeks to represent employees of the new employer, must pursue that matter through an application for certification, and not merely seek to be an intervenor in a successor rights application."[120]

Section 83 of the *FPSLRA* specifically governs displacement applications after a conversion, and it states that a displacement application may be made during the usual two-month windows spelled out in section 55 of the *FPSLRA*.

The rules governing the determination of the appropriate bargaining unit after a conversion are the same as those that apply in all cases, which will be discussed below. However, one difference is that the new bargaining unit cannot contain any employees who were unrepresented prior to the conversion. In *Parks Canada Agency v Public Service Alliance of Canada*,[121] the Board created one bargaining unit comprising "all employees" of Parks Canada Agency and, after a representation vote, certified the PSAC as the bargaining agent. Prior to the conversion, some occupational groups in Parks Canada were unrepresented. The Parks Canada Agency applied to the Board for reconsideration of its bargaining unit description, asking the Board whether it intended for previously unrepresented employees to be in the bargaining unit (and hence to become represented by the PSAC). Section 84(1)(a) of the *FPSLRA* states that the Board may "determine whether the employees of the new separate agency *who are bound by any collective agreement*

119 Then s 48.1(4)(b) of the *PSSRA*.

120 *CCRA v Association of Public Service Financial Administrators*, above note 98 at para 20.

121 *Parks Canada Agency v Public Service Alliance of Canada*, [2001] CPSSRB No 94.

or arbitral award constitute one or more units appropriate for collective bargaining."[122] Therefore, the Board concluded that its description of the bargaining unit as "all employees" did not include employees classified in an occupational group that, at the time of the transfer, was not represented by a bargaining agent.[123]

The *FPSLRA* does not contain any provisions for the inverse situation of a group of employees being transferred from a separate agency to the core public administration. This transfer itself is conducted under the *Public Service Rearrangement and Transfer of Duties Act*[124] and regulations that are specific to that transfer. The transfer does not, however, have any collective labour relations implications: the employees being transferred simply roll into the appropriate bargaining unit in the core public administration. There have been several circumstances in which employees have been transferred from separate employers to the Treasury Board. In those circumstances, "few [labour relations] problems have arisen, since, in the vast majority of cases, the employees transferred continued to be represented by the same bargaining agent that had represented them when they were employees of a separate employer."[125] There are a number of cases involving disputes over the terms and conditions of employment for those employees—such as whether they are entitled to severance or other benefits from their former separate employer[126] or the appropriate salary protection rules for those employees[127]—but those issues are addressed by examining the relevant collective agreements in place at the former and the new employer, respectively.

2) Transfers to the Federally Regulated Private Sector

As stated above, without explicit statutory provisions to the contrary, a union's collective bargaining rights cease to operate upon the sale of a business. The same applies when a government privatizes a whole or part of its operations or when an operation moves from federal to provincial jurisdiction. Currently, the *Canada Labour Code* provides for

---

122 *FPSLRA*, s 84(1)(a) [emphasis added]. The predecessor *PSSRA* s 48.1(4)(a) was identical.

123 Above note 121 at para 15.

124 *Public Service Rearrangement and Transfer of Duties Act*, RSC 1985, c P-34.

125 Finkelman & Goldenberg, above note 1 at 121.

126 *Public Service Alliance of Canada v Canada Revenue Agency*, 2013 PSLRB 23.

127 *Public Service Alliance of Canada v Treasury Board*, 2016 PSLREB 61.

successor rights of bargaining agents when the federal government privatizes a portion of its operation and that portion remains under federal jurisdiction (i.e., under the jurisdiction of the *Canada Labour Code*).

Prior to amendments in 1996, the *Canada Labour Code* contained limited successor rights for bargaining agents representing employees in the federal public service. When those employees were transferred to a Crown corporation—that is, a corporation "established to perform any function or duty on behalf of the Government of Canada" that was not otherwise part of the federal public service—then successor rights provisions of the *Canada Labour Code* applied.[128] However, when the federal government transferred a portion of its operations to a truly private corporation or enterprise, then the successor provisions did not apply. For example, in 1993, the federal government transferred control over the Whitehorse General Hospital to the Yukon Hospital Corporation. Notwithstanding this transfer, the Canada Labour Relations Board refused to apply the successor provisions of the *Canada Labour Code* because the Yukon Hospital Corporation was not a Crown corporation in that it was not acting as a true agent of the Crown.[129]

In the report *Seeking a Balance*, the federal task force on Part I of the *Canada Labour Code* recognized that this absence of successor rights was unsatisfactory:

> Governments, at both federal and provincial levels, are pursuing "commercialization" of some of their activities in three different ways: (1) by privatization or by transferring government ownership of a crown corporation, corporate holding, or government service to the private sector; (2) by commercialization or by applying business-like approaches and using market forces, incentives or mechanisms in the delivery by the government of services; and (3) by contracting out or by entering into contractual agreements, which are not employment relationships, for securing the provision of goods and services to government or for the provision of government services to the public or to specific interests.
>
> To date, the federal government has completed at least twenty-four privatizations. The scope for further privatization of crown corporations or crown-owned corporations is now significantly diminished, largely because of the fact that there are relatively few left. The emphasis in the future is expected to be on commercialization, contracting

128 *Canada Labour Code*, s 5(1).

129 *Yukon Hospital Corporation*, (1995) 96 di 162.

> out, and on "partnership" arrangements in which the government and the private sector play a joint role in developing and delivering program activities.
>
> Section 47 does not apply to a transfer from the Public Service to the private sector. Such a privatization involves the severance of the former collective bargaining relationship and the termination of the existing collective agreements. In order to avoid any uncertainty as to the application of section 47, or to fill the gap in the Code, Parliament has sometimes enacted enabling legislation (*Museums Act, Airport Transfer (Miscellaneous Matters) Act for example*) which incorporates to some extent provisions similar to section 47 to deal with the bargaining rights of a specific group of employees.
>
> There are unique features to collective bargaining for those in the federal public service. Employees are covered not only by collective bargaining legislation, but by the *Public Service Employment Act* and by government pension arrangements. The resulting collective agreements, which cover a wide range of federal employees are sometimes quite inappropriate for a private sector employer, not just because of what they include, but also because of what they do not include, for example, matters dealt with by statute.[130]

Therefore, the task force recommended that the *Canada Labour Code* should be extended to cover sales from the public service to the private sector, as well as transfers to Crown corporations.

In 1996, Parliament amended the *Canada Labour Code* to adopt this recommendation. Section 47 of the *Canada Labour Code* now provides for successor rights upon the privatization of a portion of the federal public service.

As a general rule, bargaining rights will be continued and a trade union remains certified in either of two cases: where there is a deletion of the name of any portion of the specified public service that is established as or becomes part of a federally regulated business or corporation, or where there is a severance of a "portion of a portion" of the specified public service that is established as or becomes part of a federally regulated corporation or business. The provision for a "deletion" of a part of the federal public service covers the circumstances of the deletion

130 Canada, Task Force to Review Part I of the Canada Labour Code, *Seeking a Balance: Canada Labour Code, Part I, Review* (Ottawa, ON: Labour Canada, 1996) (Chairman: Andrew C.L. Sims).

of a government department from the federal public service, usually accompanied by the consequent creation of a Crown corporation.

The second circumstance—successor provisions upon a severance of a part of the public service—is designed to cover the situation of a piecemeal privatization of the federal public service, which does not involve the deletion of whole departments or large units of the public service. To qualify as a severance, four different elements are required:[131]

1) A "portion of a portion" of the public service must be involved. The "acceptable unit of measurement in determining a portion of the public service is 'positions.' In addition, there must be more than one employee."[132] This is because one employee cannot comprise a bargaining unit.
2) The portion must be specified in Part I, IV, or V of the *Financial Administration Act*—that is, be part of the public service.
3) There must be a "severance" of the portion of the public service. "The requirement is minimal: it involves the splitting-off of certain employees from a portion of the public service. This separation might occur in many different ways, including the letting-go, release or dropping of the employees from the public service."[133] A severance does not require a sale or transfer, but a sale of a portion of the public service may constitute a severance. For example, in *Public Service Alliance of Canada v Bombardier Inc*, the Canada Industrial Relations Board concluded that the severance of civilian support employees of the Department of National Defence was also a sale of a business. The Federal Court of Appeal quashed that decision, stating that "a section 47 severance is not the sale of a business.... However strange it might seem to the respondents, bargaining rights do indeed attach to the positions of the incumbent employees in a section 47 severance, for there is no business to which they may attach."[134]
4) The severed portion must become part of a corporation or business governed by the *Canada Labour Code* (i.e., a federal work or undertaking).

If these four conditions are met, the existing bargaining rights of the former public service employees automatically continue after the severance.

131 See *Public Service Alliance of Canada v Bombardier Inc*, [2001] 2 FCJ No 429 (CA).
132 *Ibid* at para 15(A).
133 *Ibid* at para 15(C).
134 *Ibid* at para 38.

Those rights are subject to variation by the Canada Industrial Relations Board: if a party brings an application in the window between the 120th and 150th day after the severance, the Board may vary the bargaining unit structure, determine which bargaining agent represents those new bargaining units, and decide which collective agreements apply to those units and whether the term of those agreements should be shortened—in short, the same relief as is available under section 84 of the *FPSLRA* and discussed above.

If one of the parties has served the other with a notice to bargain prior to the severance, then a slightly different regime applies. Section 47.1 freezes the existing terms and conditions of employment until either the right to strike or lockout has been obtained. Section 47.1 essentially continues the freeze that would have been in place under the *FPSLRA*. The parties again have the right to apply for a change in the bargaining unit structure; if they apply, they must serve a new notice to bargain after the Canada Industrial Relations Board determines the appropriate bargaining unit structure.[135]

These provisions of the *Canada Labour Code* only apply when the successor employer is governed by the *Canada Labour Code*—that is, they are a federal work or undertaking. There are no successor rights when a part of the federal public service is transferred to a provincial undertaking, except to the extent provided in provincial labour legislation.

When a dispute arises concerning the application of section 47 or 47.1 of the *Canada Labour Code*, then this dispute must be resolved by the Canada Industrial Relations Board, not the Federal Public Service Labour Relations Board.[136] However, the Board still has a residual role to play after section 47 or 47.1 of the *Canada Labour Code* is triggered. Sections 47(1)(b) and 47.1(b) state that the *FPSLRA* continues to apply in all respects to the interpretation and application of a collective agreement or the terms and conditions frozen in place by section 47.1(b). Therefore, the provisions of the *FPSLRA* continue to apply to any grievances that result after a severance of the public service—including the

---

135 *Canada Labour Code*, s 47.1(d).

136 *Public Service Alliance of Canada and Brookfield Lepage Johnson Controls*, [1999] CPSSRB No 45, where the Board concluded that the Canada Industrial Relations Board was the appropriate board to determine whether a business is governed by the *Canada Labour Code*.

obligation to refer those grievances to adjudication under the *FPSLRA* instead of an arbitrator appointed under the *Canada Labour Code*.[137] This situation continues to prevail until the parties have "bargained to an impasse under the Code"—in other words, are in a legal strike/lockout position or have negotiated a new collective agreement with an arbitration clause governed by the *Canada Labour Code*.[138]

Finally, section 47.2 of the Canada Labour Code gives the Governor in Council the authority to opt out of the successor rights provisions of sections 47 and 47.1 the *Canada Labour Code* where it is in the "public interest" to do so.[139]

3) Mergers, Amalgamations, and Transfers of Jurisdiction Among Employee Organizations

Under Canadian common law, an employee organization that merges or amalgamates with another organization is usually treated as having lost its right to represent the employee for whom it was the bargaining agent. Therefore, labour relations statutes in Canada contain provisions expressly continuing representation rights upon a merger or amalgamation of trade unions. The *FPSLRA* is no different. Section 79 of the *FPSLRA* states that if, "by reason of a merger or an amalgamation of employee organizations or a transfer of jurisdiction among employee organizations," one employee organization succeeds another that was a bargaining agent, then the successor employee organization becomes the bargaining agent and "is deemed to have acquired the rights, privileges, and duties of its predecessor."[140]

The circumstances triggering section 79 of the *FPSLRA* are a merger, an amalgamation, or a transfer of jurisdiction. The Board has defined those terms as follows:

> A merger involves the absorption of one union by another whereby the former ceases to exist while the latter continues. An amalgamation involves the combining of different unions so as to form a distinct, new body, and a transfer of jurisdiction involves the assignment by

137 *Jones v Frontec Corp*, [2000] CPSSRB No 14 at para 28.

138 *Ibid* at paras 28–30.

139 *Canada Labour Code*, s 47.2.

140 *FPSLRA*, s 79(1).

one parent union to another parent union of control over one of its subordinate branches or lodges.[141]

There have been a number of mergers and amalgamations involving bargaining agents in the federal public service. For example, the Canadian Air Traffic Control Association merged with the National Automobile, Aerospace, Transportation and General Workers Union of Canada (CAW) in 2001,[142] and the Marine Communications and Traffic Services Association also merged with the CAW in 2001.[143] In 2003, the Social Science Employees Association amalgamated with the Canadian Union of Professional and Technical Employees to form the Canadian Association of Professional Employees.[144] Finally, when the CAW and the Communications, Energy and Paperworkers Union of Canada merged in 2013 to form Unifor, the Board acknowledged that merger.[145] These mergers and amalgamations required the Board to make orders certifying the new employee organizations as successors to the old.

The Board has rejected successor rights applications where the application was not made by the official bargaining agent. For example, in *Syndicat canadien de la fonction publique*,[146] employees in the Operational Category bargaining unit of the National Film Board were represented by the Syndicat général du cinema et de la télévision (SGCT). Sometime after July 1977, the members of that bargaining unit purported to become an autonomous bargaining agent by virtue of changes to their constitution. Then, in 1982, the members of that bargaining unit voted to merge with the Canadian Union of Public Employees (CUPE) and brought a successor application before the

141 *Canadian Typographical Union and Treasury Board*, [1986] CPSSRB No 1 at para 16, adopting the definition found in Jeffrey Sack, Michael Mitchell & Sandy Price, *Ontario Labour Relations Board Law and Practice*, 3d ed (Toronto: LexisNexis, 1997).

142 *National Automobile, Aerospace, Transportation and General Workers of Canada v Treasury Board*, [2004] CPSSRB No 168. With the privatization of NavCan in 1996, there were only a small group of employees left in the federal public service when this merger occurred.

143 *Marine Communications and Traffic Services Assn v Treasury Board*, [2001] CPSSRB No 8.

144 *Canadian Union of Professional and Technical Employees v Treasury Board*, [2003] CPSSRB No 75.

145 *Unifor v National Automobile, Aerospace, Transportation and General Workers Union of Canada (CAW-Canada) and Treasury Board*, 2014 PSLRB 9.

146 *Syndicat canadien de la fonction publique*, [1983] CPSSRB No 69.

Board to that effect. The Board denied that application because neither the autonomous bargaining unit nor CUPE was a bargaining agent under the Act: the bargaining agent was still the SGCT, which was not a party to the application. Therefore, there is a condition precedent to a successor application under section 79 of the *FPSLRA*: at least one of the employee organizations that is involved in the merger, amalgamation, or transfer of jurisdiction must be a certified bargaining agent.[147] In other words, by not bringing a successor application when it became autonomous, the bargaining agent prejudiced its ability to merge or amalgamate in the future.

The jurisdiction of the Board under section 79 is very limited. For example, section 79 cannot be used to resolve internal disputes within a council of employee organizations. *Canadian Typographical Union and Treasury Board*[148] involved the Council of Graphic Arts Unions, a council of employee organizations composed of the International Typographical Union and two other employee organizations. The Canadian Typographical Union wanted to displace the International Typographical Union as a component of the Council of Graphic Arts Unions and had signed up members who also wanted that change to occur. Since the International Typographical Union was not a bargaining agent (the council was the bargaining agent), the Canadian Typographical Union could not bring a displacement application.[149] The Board also ruled that the successor provisions did not apply either: what had happened was a "transfer of allegiance," not a transfer of jurisdiction.[150]

Section 79 of the *FPSLRA* also does not apply to what are commonly referred to as "jurisdictional" disputes—disputes between trade unions about which particular tasks or jobs they represent. For example, the International Association of Machinists (IAM) Local 1723 historically exercised jurisdiction over ship repair mechanics on the Dartmouth side of the Halifax harbour, and the Ship Repair Machinists and Mechanics Union exercised jurisdiction over workers on the Halifax side. Both employee organizations were part of a council of employee organizations that was the bargaining agent for ship repair workers on the east coast of Canada. In 1995, the federal government moved its ship repair facilities from the Dartmouth side to the Halifax side. Therefore,

---

147 *Ibid* at para 26.

148 *Canadian Typographical Union and Treasury Board*, above note 141.

149 *Ibid* at para 14.

150 *Ibid* at para 16.

in *Ship Repair Machinists and Mechanics Union (Atlantic) and International Association of Machinists and Aircraft Workers, Local 1723,*[151] the Ship Repair Machinists and Mechanics Union asked the Board to amend the decision certifying the council of employee organizations to reflect the change in jurisdiction of those workers from IAM Local 1723 to the Ship Repair Machinists and Mechanics Union. The Board concluded that its reconsideration power was an inappropriate mechanism in which to deal with what was essentially a jurisdictional dispute within a council of employee organizations. The Board also concluded that the successor rights provisions of the Act do not apply to jurisdictional disputes, stating: "The Board believes that section 49 [now section 79] was not intended to confer on the Board authority to intervene in disputes between employee organizations as to their respective jurisdiction over union members."[152]

Finally, section 79 of the *FPSLRA* does not cover "contracting-in" situations. There have also been rare cases where the federal government has "contracted in" services that were formerly performed in the private sector (and therefore governed by the *Canada Labour Code* or provincial labour relations legislation). For example, in *Rostrust Investments Inc v Canadian Union of Public Employees,*[153] the cleaning services for L'Esplanade Laurier building complex in Ottawa, Ontario, were performed by Rostrust Investments Inc. Rostrust also owned the building and leased it to Public Works and Government Services Canada. As part of the lease agreement, Rostrust was responsible for cleaning the government offices in that building. Its cleaning staff were represented by CUPE, which was certified under the Ontario *Labour Relations Act.* In 2004, Public Works exercised its rights under the lease and decided to hire its own cleaning staff. It hired eight of ten Rostrust cleaners as public servants—and those new public servants became part of a bargaining unit represented by the PSAC. Rostrust brought an application under the successor rights provisions of the *PSSRA*, but the Board concluded that "this 'contracting-in' of maintenance services does not

151 *Ship Repair Machinists and Mechanics Union (Atlantic) and International Association of Machinists and Aircraft Workers, Local 1723*, [1996] CPSSRB No 32.

152 *Ibid* at para 18.

153 *Rostrust Investments Inc v Canadian Union of Public Employees*, [2005] CPSSRB No 1 [*Rostrust*]. See also the companion case of *Les Terrasses de la Chaudière v International Union of Operating Engineers (Stationary), Local 772*, [2005] CPSSRB No 149, involving the contracting-in of maintenance services at Les Terrasses de la Chaudière in Gatineau, Quebec.

constitute a transfer of jurisdiction."[154] The Board stated that "there are no provisions for successor rights when a formerly provincial activity becomes governed by the *PSSRA* regime (as there is under the *Canada Labour Code* in subsection 44(3))."[155] The effect of this contracting in was a termination of a contractual relationship and the subsequent hiring of former employees of Rostrust. The *FPSLRA* does not allow for any successor rights upon contracting-in to the federal public service.

E. APPROPRIATE BARGAINING UNIT

"No more important labor relations issue faces the public employer than the question of what the bargaining unit itself shall be—its size, composition, nature and scope."[156] A bargaining unit serves two distinct purposes. First, it is an electoral unit: it defines the group of workers who are asked whether they wish to be represented by the applicant union (or unions). Second, it serves to define the group of employees who are covered by a collective agreement negotiated by the employer and the union. Thus, labour relations boards must balance two different policy considerations when determining the appropriate bargaining unit: they must create a unit that is not so large or disparate as to make union organizing impossible, and they must ensure that the unit is not so small or specific as to make collective bargaining unfeasible.

In the federal public sector, the second policy consideration usually outweighs the first. The usual attitude of public sector employers in Canada was expressed in *Insurance Corp of British Columbia and CUPE, Local 1695*, where the public sector employer was said to be "not merely tolerant of collective bargaining, but rather anxious for it to get under way."[157] In the federal public sector, then, the question of the appropriate bargaining unit does not usually impact whether employees will have access to union representation at all.[158] Therefore,

---

154 *Rostrust*, above note 153 at para 10. The former employer was bringing the application in an effort to defeat a grievance filed by CUPE prior to the transfer asking for severance and termination pay for the transferred employees.

155 *Ibid* at para 27.

156 T.P. Gilroy & A.C. Russo, *Bargaining Unit Issues: Problems, Criteria, Tactics* (Chicago: International Personnel Management Association, 1973).

157 *Insurance Corp of British Columbia and CUPE, Local 1695* (1974), 1 Can LRBR 403 at 407 (BCLRB).

158 With some exceptions: see *Canadian Nuclear Safety Commission*, above note 59, discussed below in greater detail. Later, the bargaining unit was amended to

the second concern—successful industrial relations—is the paramount factor in determining the appropriate bargaining unit in the public sector in general and the federal public sector in particular. The importance of the determination of the appropriate public sector bargaining unit is therefore whether the union and the employer will be able to engage in successful collective bargaining. The size and composition of the bargaining unit impact the stability of the public employer's labour relations program as well as the cohesion of the union membership that represents a particular bargaining unit. It has also been argued that unit determinations have a direct impact on the eventual costs to the taxpayer for the delivery of public services and the continuance of such services without interruption.

The usual reasons employers give for preferring larger bargaining units (and arguing against "fragmenting" its workforce) are related to avoiding the following: wage leapfrogging between units; higher administration expenses; increase in work stoppages; and embroiling employers in jurisdictional disputes between unions.[159] There has been little empirical research on these claims. However, one such opportunity arose in 1989 when the National Labor Relations Board (NLRB) in the United States promulgated its first "rule" on the size of bargaining units: it designated eight potential bargaining units in each hospital.[160] This rule was created pursuant to the NLRB's rule-making power[161] and was applicable to acute care hospitals. This provided an opportunity to determine the effects of increasing the number of bargaining

---

include all classification levels when the employee organization obtained adequate support for unionization in those remaining pay bands: *Professional Institute of the Public Service of Canada v Canadian Nuclear Safety Commission*, 2010 PSLRB 108 [*PIPSC v CNSC*].

159 M. LeRoy, J. Schwarz & K. Koziara, "The Law and Economics of Collective Bargaining for Hospitals: An Empirical Public Policy Analysis of Bargaining Unit Determinations" (1992) 9 Yale J of Regulation 1 at 28–29.

160 29 CFR s 103.30 (1990). The rule created eight bargaining units: nurses; all professionals except nurses and physicians (roughly our paramedical professional unit); all technical employees (roughly our paramedical technical unit); all skilled maintenance employees; all business office clerical employees; all other non-professional employees; physicians; and security guards. The "rule" was subject to three exceptions: cases that present extraordinary circumstances (including when the eight-unit rule would produce a unit of five or fewer employees); cases in which non-conforming units already exist; and cases in which labour organizations seek to combine two or more of the eight specified units.

161 *National Labor Relations Act*, USC 151-169, s 6.

units in many hospitals that had to change their bargaining structures.[162] The evidence indicated that wage leapfrogging did not occur with an increase in bargaining units, but there was some evidence that strike activity increased with the number of bargaining units.[163] Other concerns raised about bargaining units in the public sector from the union side include its influence on the internal dynamics of the unit and of the bargaining agent and the ease with which the bargaining agent will be able to obtain, keep, and exercise its negotiating authority.

Before considering the rules for the determination of the appropriate bargaining unit under the *FPSLRA*, it is helpful to consider the context of bargaining unit determination in the private sector, as well as in other Canadian public sector jurisdictions and the public sector in the United States.

1) Private Sector Bargaining Unit Determination

The usual test for an appropriate bargaining unit is whether the employees in the unit share a "community of interest." The factors involved in this community of interest were set out by the Ontario Labour Relations Board in *Usarco Ltd*:

- nature of the work performed;
- conditions of employment;
- skills of employees;
- administration;
- geographic circumstances; and
- functional coherence and interdependence.[164]

In *Island Medical Laboratories Ltd*, the British Columbia Labour Relations Board recast the *Usarco* factors (changing them from six factors to four) and added two new factors that are appropriate to consider

162 Hospitals had lobbied the NLRB to limit the number of bargaining units to two: a professional unit and a non-professional unit. In certain individual cases prior to the rule being promulgated, hospitals were successful in their attempts to prevent a "registered nurses" bargaining unit from being formed instead of a broader "all-professional" bargaining unit: see *NLRB* v *Frederick Memorial Hospital*, 691 F (2d) 194 (4th Cir 1982).

163 *Ibid* at 29–31.

164 *Usarco Ltd*, [1967] OLRB Rep September 525. See also Sack, Mitchell & Price, above note 141 at paras 3.216–3.342.

when the unit determination is not taking place during an initial application for certification of an employer:

- similarity in skills, interests, duties, and working conditions;
- the physical and administrative structure of the employer;
- functional integration;
- geography;
- practice and history of the current collective bargaining scheme; and
- practice and history of collective bargaining in the industry and sector.[165]

The first factor, similarity of skills and working conditions, is fairly self-explanatory. The BC board in *Island Medical Laboratories*, however, pointed out that this factor is not accorded the same weight as in the past. This is a reflection of the change from a traditional view of community of interest that was concerned with separating white-collar from blue-collar workers. The BC board even stated that "these distinctions were no longer observed in the public sector."[166] Traditional boundaries have been erased in favour of more expansive bargaining units. The next three criteria concern the nature of the employer's organization. The second factor includes the organizational chart and physical layout of the employer. The third factor relates only to the functional integration of employees, not a functional integration between departments. Functional integration of employees is demonstrated by employee interchange and shared job duties. It must be continuous integration and not a one-off event such as holiday or sick relief. Geography refers to the degree of physical separation between employees. Finally, the history of collective bargaining is an important factor, especially where the history contradicts the other community of interest factors. For example, where there is a history of multiple bargaining units at an integrated workplace, the Board may still certify a bargaining unit that is not an all-employee unit, despite the functional integration of the workplace.

---

165 *Island Medical Laboratories Ltd* (1993), 19 Can LRBR (2d) 161 (BC). The Board has more usually quoted from the *Usarco* decision when it discusses the "community of interest" test.

166 *Ibid* at para 82. See discussion below about the Board's view on this point, which is that there can sometimes still be a distinction between "professional" and "non-professional" workers.

Labour boards will also define bargaining units in a way that improves access to collective bargaining. As the Canada Industrial Relations Board has recently put it:

> Factors considered by the Board in making its determination regarding the appropriateness of a bargaining unit include community of interest; viability of the unit; employee wishes; industry practice or pattern and the organizational structure of the employer. Although the Board has expressed a general preference for wider-based bargaining units, which it believes promote administrative efficiency, convenience in bargaining and industrial stability, the Board will often deviate from that expressed preference. For example, when seized with an application for certification of a newly organized bargaining unit, the Board will favour factors that increase access to collective bargaining and may certify units that consist of a subset of the occupations present in the workplace, even if such groupings are not optimal from the view point of the employer's organizational structure.[167]

The traditional community of interest test has led to private sector bargaining units being smaller than public sector ones. In Ontario, for example, the median size of a non-construction bargaining unit certified in fiscal year 2018–19 was between twenty and thirty-nine employees. The average size of a non-construction bargaining unit was thirty-two employees.[168] Thus, applying the traditional community of interest factors in the civil service would lead to a drastic increase in the number of bargaining units and shrinking of the size of those units.

2) Ontario Public Sector Model

The bargaining units in the core public sector in Ontario are determined by government fiat. The *Crown Employees Collective Bargaining Act* designates four bargaining units in the Ontario public service:

- Correctional bargaining unit
- Engineer bargaining unit

---

167 *International Association of Machinists and Aerospace Workers v Servisair Inc*, 2013 CIRB 692 at para 50.

168 Ontario Labour Relations Board, *Annual Report, 2018–2019* (2019), online (pdf): www.olrb.gov.on.ca/Publications/AnnualReports/OLRB-AnnualReport-2018-19-EN.pdf.

- Fourth bargaining unit
- Unified bargaining unit[169]

The Correctional and Unified bargaining units are represented by the Ontario Public Service Employees Union; the Fourth bargaining unit is represented by the Association of Administrative, Management and Professional Crown Employees of Ontario; and the Engineer bargaining unit is represented by the Professional Engineers Government of Ontario.[170] The Ontario Labour Relations Board (which administers the *Crown Employees Collective Bargaining Act*) does not have the jurisdiction to amend bargaining unit descriptions, meaning that the parties have to do so voluntarily,[171] and the *Crown Employees Collective Bargaining Act* also states that the parties cannot alter the bargaining unit definition either.[172]

Outside of the core Ontario public service, it was recognized in Ontario (before the Ontario Labour Relations Board became responsible for bargaining unit determinations in the broader public sector) that the determination of the appropriate bargaining unit would be different in the public sector than in the private sector. In *Ontario Housing Employees' Union*,[173] the union was organizing the Ontario Housing Corporation. There was already a bargaining unit established for the Metro Toronto area. The employer wanted the next bargaining unit to be an all-employee unit for outside of the Metro Toronto area, and the old board agreed. The old board stated:

> It would be a mistake to think that considerations relevant to the private sector are equally applicable to the public sector. The legislators by creating a separate legal structure for collective bargaining by Crown employees obviously considered that collective bargaining in the public sector of Ontario should not be treated in the same manner as private sector collective bargaining. Thus, in administrating this Act, this Tribunal must treat such decisions with caution and only use them when they appear appropriate for the public sector.[174]

169 *Crown Employees Collective Bargaining Act*, SO 1993, c 38, ss 22–23, and order in council 243/94.

170 *Ibid*, s 23.

171 *BA International Inc. v Ontario (Labour Relations Board)*, [2005] OJ No 5211 (Div Ct).

172 *Crown Employees Collective Bargaining Act*, s 25(5).

173 *Ontario Housing Employees' Union*, [1973] OPSLRT 762.

174 *Ibid*.

The old board in that case identified three relevant considerations: freedom of association and community of interest; the administrative costs of collective bargaining; and the public interest. When considering the community of interest, the Board applied the traditional considerations; however, when it came to the geographic factor, the Board opined that this is simply not as important in the public sector as in the private. Administrative costs are kept down by minimizing the number of bargaining units and by mirroring the existing organization of the public service. Finally, the Board considered it in the public interest for both parties to bargain on equal terms. Since there was no right for public employees to strike in 1974, "equal terms" meant that each side had more or less equal institutional resources for advocacy before binding interest arbitration.

3) US Public Sector Model

Labour relations in the US federal civil service are governed by the *Federal Service Labor-Management Relations Statute*.[175] That statute gave the Federal Labor Relations Authority (FLRA) the authority to determine the appropriate bargaining unit. The requirements of an appropriate bargaining unit are the same as in the 1969 Executive Order 11491 (which established government collective bargaining) and read:

> The Authority shall determine the appropriateness of any unit. The Authority shall determine in each case whether, in order to ensure employees the fullest freedom in exercising the rights guaranteed under this chapter, the appropriate unit should be established on an agency, plant, installation, functional, or other basis and shall determine any unit to be an appropriate unit only if the determination will ensure a clear and identifiable community of interest among the employees in the unit and will promote effective dealings with, and efficiency of the operations of the agency involved.[176]

Labour relations in the US government are a great deal more decentralized than in the Canadian government. The US executive is divided into agencies, such as the Department of Agriculture and the Department of Defense, plus a number of other independent agencies

175 *Federal Service Labor-Management Relations Statute*, 5 USC §7101 (1979).
176 *Ibid* at §7112.

and government-owned corporations. The definition of the formal bargaining unit is based in general terms on the agency division of the executive branch. Within each agency, there is room for further diversity in the number of bargaining units. Bargaining units in the US government may be certified at the national, regional, or installation level.[177] For the most part, bargaining units are smaller than in Canada and are established at a more local level than the national bargaining units prevailing in Canada. The US bargaining unit structure is not designed to generate pay equity throughout the civil service as it is in Canada: it is perfectly possible in the United States for employees who work for different agencies, but do the same job, to be paid differently. Although no statistics are available for the size of US government bargaining units, the cases demonstrate that bargaining units are very small, ranging from a few hundred employees down to ten or fewer.

Section 7112(a) of the *Federal Service Labor-Management Relations Statute* requires the FLRA to determine the appropriate bargaining unit based on three criteria: community of interest, effective industrial relations, and efficient operations of the agency involved. The FLRA has not specified an exhaustive list of factors needed to find a clear and identifiable community of interest. Some of the factors it has examined include whether the employees

- are part of the same organizational component of the agency;
- support the same mission;
- are subject to the same chain of command;
- have similar or related duties, job titles, and work assignments;
- are subject to the same general working conditions;
- are governed by the same personnel and labour relations policies;
- are geographically proximate;
- have distinct local concerns;
- compete against each other (and not outsiders) for promotion;
- interchange between other organizational components;
- are functionally or operationally separate; and
- have the same interests and concerns as the employee.[178]

177 R. Pegnetter, *Multiemployer Bargaining in the Public Sector: Purposes and Experiences* (Chicago: International Personnel Management Association, 1975).

178 See, for example, *United States Department of the Navy Fleet and Industrial Supply Center Norfold, Virginia and American Federation of Government Employees, Local 53 AFL-CIO*, 52 FLRA No 97 at 11–12 (1997) [*Norfold Supply Center*];

In assessing the effectiveness of industrial relations criteria, the FLRA examines the past bargaining experiences of the parties; the locus and scope of authority of the office responsible for personnel policies; the limitations, if any, on the negotiation of matters that may be of critical concern to employees; and the level at which labour relations policy is set at the agency.[179] Finally, the criterion of efficiency recognizes that "a unit that bears a rational relationship to an agency's operational and organizational structure could result in economic savings and increased productivity to the agency."[180] In other words, the bargaining unit must be designed with cost, productivity, and resources in mind.[181]

Section 7112(b) lists several statutory exclusions from bargaining units: managerial employees, confidential employees, personnel employees (unless clerical), intelligence or security employees, and employees in charge of investigations or audits of other employees in the bargaining unit. Also, like employees under the *National Labor Relations Act*, professional employees are not combined in bargaining units with non-professional employees unless they vote to be included.

Finally, section 7112(d) allows for accretion of bargaining units in the US civil service. It states:

> Two or more units which are in an agency and for which a labor organization is the exclusive representative may, upon petition by the agency or labor organization, be consolidated with or without an

---

Department of the Navy Naval Supply Center Puget Sound Bremerton, Washington and Bremerton Metal Trades Council, AFL-CIO, 53 FLRA No 23 at 7–8 (1997); *United States Department of Transportation Federal Aviation Administration and American Federation of State, County, and Municipal Employees Council 26, AFL-CIO*, 63 FLRA 118 at 359 (2009); *Department of the Navy, Portsmouth Naval Shipyard, Portsmouth, New Hampshire (Agency) and New England Regional Council of Carpenters, Local 3072 (Petitioner/Labor Organization) and Portsmouth Federal Employees Metal Trade Council, AFL-CIO (Incumbent/Labor Organization)*, 70 FLRA 197 (2018); and *Department of Commerce, National Oceanic and Atmospheric Administration, National Marine Fisheries Service, Southeast Fisheries Science Center (Agency) and American Federation of Government Employees, Local 2875, AFL-CIO (Petitioner/Labor Organization) and National Association of Independent Labor (Petitioner/Labor Organization)*, 73 FLRA 49 (2022).

179 *Norfold Supply Center*, above note 178 at 12; *United States Department of the Air Force, 82nd Training Wing 361st Training Squadron Aberdeen Proving Ground, Maryland and International Association of Machinists and Aerospace Workers, District Lodge 12* (2001), 57 FLRA No 39 [*District Lodge 12*].

180 *Norfold Supply Centre*, above note 178 at 12–13.

181 *District Lodge 12*, above note 179.

> election into a single larger unit if the Authority considers the larger unit to be appropriate. The Authority shall certify the labor organization as the exclusive representative of the larger unit.[182]

The FLRA has interpreted this section broadly to "facilitate consolidation of existing small units into more comprehensive ones, provided that the proposed consolidated unit is appropriate under the criteria of section 7112(a)(1)."[183] As one example, this provision has been used to consolidate non-professional support and hospital employees who worked at a submarine base.[184]

4) Bargaining Unit Determination Under the *FPSLRA*

a) Statutory Presumption of Following a Plan of Classification

The public sectors in Ontario and the United States demonstrate that there are different ways to determine the appropriate bargaining unit in the public sector. The appropriate bargaining unit could be specified in statute (as in the Ontario public service), or by reference to criteria similar to the "community of interest" test in the private sector (as in the US public service), or by reference to a modified "community of interest" test that takes into account the public interest.

The *FPSLRA* adopts its own path: a legislative presumption of the appropriate bargaining unit, which presumption does not apply in all cases. The *FPSLRA* requires the Board to "have regard to" the employer's classification scheme (including any occupational groups or subgroups established by the employer) and then requires the Board to establish bargaining units that are "co-extensive with the occupational groups or subgroups established by the employer unless doing so would not permit satisfactory representation of the employees to be included in a particular bargaining unit." Those presumptions apply in initial certifications,[185] bargaining unit review,[186] and successor applications.[187]

The *FPSLRA* specifically adopts that presumption in every situation where the Board is called upon to determine the appropriate bargaining

---

182 *Federal Service Labor-Management Relations Statute*, §7112(d).

183 *Department of Transportation, Washington, DC*, 5 FLRA 646, 652 (1981).

184 *Naval Submarine Base, New London*, 46 FLRA No 132 (1993). There used to be five bargaining units at the base, all represented by the same union.

185 *FPSLRA*, ss 57(2) & 57(3).

186 *Ibid*, ss 70(1) & (2).

187 *Ibid*, ss 91(1) & (2).

unit structure because of the Board's pre-*PSLRA* decision in *CCRA v Association of Public Service Financial Administrators*.[188] That case involved the determination of the appropriate bargaining unit in a successor situation (after the parties had served their notice to bargain). Prior to the 2005 amendments to the *FPSLRA*, the Act did not include the statutory presumption in the section dealing with determination of bargaining units after successor situations. The CCRA argued that it had created a new classification plan with a "management" occupation group and that the Board should respect its classification plan and certify a "management" bargaining unit. The Board disagreed, stating that the statutory presumptions had no application in a successor situation. It concluded that "the legal maxim *expressio unius est exclusio alterius* applies in these circumstances and, consequently, it is not open to the Board to presume that Parliament intended that subsection 33(2) [now section 57(2)] affect applications under section 48.1 [now section 87]."[189] Contrary to the Board's decision, Parliament obviously thought that the statutory presumption favouring bargaining unit determination along classification lines should apply in every situation, and the *FPSLRA* reflects that intention.[190]

This statutory presumption in favour of bargaining units that follow the employer's scheme of classification was proposed in 1965 by the *Report of the Preparatory Committee on Collective Bargaining in the Public Service* (the Preparatory Committee).[191] The Preparatory Committee was set up to examine whether and how to implement collective bargaining for the federal public service. It recommended a wholesale reorganization of the employment structure of the public service. The Preparatory Committee also examined how to determine bargaining units in the civil service. It essentially had to answer three questions: who the employer would be; what the bargaining units would be; and how disputes over the appropriate bargaining unit would be resolved.

---

188 *CCRA v Association of Public Service Financial Administrators*, [2001] CPSSRB No 98 [*CCRA v APSFA*].

189 *Ibid* at para 519.

190 The board in the *CCRA v APSFA* decision also concluded that the employer's proposed "management" bargaining unit was unviable and inappropriate, so it would not have designated that unit regardless of the statutory presumption.

191 *Report of the Preparatory Committee on Collective Bargaining in the Public Service* (Ottawa: Queen's Printer, 1965) [Heeney Report].

The Preparatory Committee considered treating each government department as a separate employer but concluded that

> [i]n the "central administration," the distribution of authority and responsibility dictated by Parliamentary control of funds and the collective responsibility of the Cabinet for expenditures would make it virtually impossible to establish an effective bargaining unit relationship on this basis.[192]

Therefore, the Preparatory Committee recommended that the civil service central administration have a single employer. It decided that the Treasury Board would act as the single employer for the entire civil service. As for the definition of the appropriate bargaining unit, the Preparatory Committee decided upon making each occupational group a single bargaining unit. For the first few years of collective bargaining, the bargaining units would be required to be identical to occupational groups; however, the Preparatory Committee recommended that eventually the rules for determining the appropriate bargaining unit would be more flexible. Finally, the Preparatory Committee recommended that the government continue its current practice of not allowing consensual certification; instead, the Board (created as a result of the Preparatory Committee's recommendations) would have sole jurisdiction over certification and bargaining unit issues. The Preparatory Committee proposed that, at first, the Board's jurisdiction would be limited to declaring each occupational group to be a bargaining unit and then determining the bargaining agent; however, after a period of strict limits on the definition of bargaining units, the Board would decide bargaining units on a case-by-case basis. This would give the Board the "flexibility needed to respond to changing pressures and conditions" in the civil service.[193]

The Preparatory Committee was largely concerned with two main purposes when it designed its approach: an orderly introduction of collective bargaining and a satisfactory set of continuing relationships. To facilitate the orderly introduction of collective bargaining, the Preparatory Committee recommended that during the initial period of certification the Public Service Staff Relations Board (PSSRB) be required to define bargaining units along occupational group lines. The Preparatory Committee was concerned that without statutory guidelines,

---

192 *Ibid* at 30.

193 *Ibid* at 31.

there would be a prolonged period of controversy and litigation over bargaining units proposed by different bargaining agents. As it stated:

> The history and existing pattern of employee representation was such as to make it inevitable that bargaining units based on a variety of conflicting principles would be proposed by organizations seeking certification as bargaining agents. The existing classification system, lacking order and a clear-cut set of underlying principles, would be of little or no help. The sheer size and organizational complexity of the Service would add its own complications. In the absence of statutory guide-lines, the Board could find itself faced with a prolonged period of controversy and litigation.[194]

Furthermore, if the government followed this recommendation, the thought was that "the collective bargaining system would bear fruit speedily."[195] Speed and certainty were foremost in the Preparatory Committee's mind when it made its recommendations.

However, the main rationale behind choosing occupational groups as the appropriate bargaining units was pay.[196] The Preparatory Committee considered it unfair that different public service employees, employed in the same occupational group and working side by side (but in different bargaining units), might earn different rates of pay. They stated that fragmenting bargaining units along lines different from occupational groups could result in "a patchwork of bargaining units offering little hope of a stable and productive set of relationships and serving in the long run to introduce serious inequities in rates of pay and conditions of employment."[197] These problems were stated even more explicitly by the committee set up in British Columbia in the 1970s to examine this same issue:

> Serious morale problems would inevitably arise, if employees working side by side within the same department of government, but being members of different bargaining units, found themselves subject to significantly different conditions of employment.[198]

---

194 *Ibid* at 30.

195 Finkelman & Goldenberg, above note 1 at 101.

196 Jacob Finkelman, *The Rationale in Establishing Bargaining Units in the Federal Public Service of Canada* (Kingston, ON: IRC, 1974) at 3.

197 Heeney Report, above note 191 at 30.

198 Commission of Inquiry into Employer-Employee Relationships in the Public Service of British Columbia, *Making Bargaining Work in the British Columbia Public Service* (1972) at 26.

The Preparatory Committee was concerned by what they called "equitable relativities,"[199] both within the civil service and between the public and the private sector generally. They were convinced that setting occupational groups as the basis of pay would assist the government and bargaining agents to relate rates of pay and conditions of employment in the civil service to those prevailing in the private sector. The Preparatory Committee therefore adopted a compromise between the statutory determination model and the community of interest model of bargaining units: it adopted an "initial statutory determination" model.[200]

Parliament more or less accepted the recommendations of the Preparatory Committee when it passed the *PSSRA* in 1966. During the initial certification period (a period that varied for each occupational category but was generally over by 1969), the only appropriate bargaining unit consisted of all employees of an occupational group.[201] Parliament did decide to include two exceptions to this rule. The first was at the suggestion of the secretary of the Treasury Board, Dr. George Davidson. In initial applications, the PSSRB could create two bargaining units in an occupational group: one for supervisory employees and one for regular employees. In large part, this suggestion was influenced by the Postal Workers' Union, which had expelled all members who were supervisors.[202] Supervisors are distinct from "management" as defined in the *PSSRA* and may join a union. The only example of this exception being used was in *Hospital Services Case No 1*;[203] however, in that case the two groups were eventually merged because they had the same bargaining agent and were engaged in single-table bargaining.

The second exception was the result of submissions made by the Confederation of National Trade Unions (CNTU). The exception stated that an occupational group could be carved into different bargaining units where such a bargaining unit would not permit "satisfactory representation of employees included therein."[204] The CNTU was in the middle of a campaign to sever Quebec unions from national union organizations. Its purpose, therefore, was to allow Quebec-only bargaining units to be

199 Heeney Report, above note 191 at 31.

200 G. Simmons & K. Swan, *Labour Relations Law in the Public Sector* (Kingston, ON: IRC, 1982).

201 *Public Service Staff Relations Act*, SC 1966-67, c 72, s 26(4).

202 Finkelman, above note 196 at 10.

203 *Hospital Services Case No 1* (1967), PSSR Rep K 6 at 13.

204 *PSSRA*, s 26(5).

certified in the civil service. In the end, this exception was never used to sever a Quebec-only bargaining unit and was rarely used by the PSSRB. Therefore, the Preparatory Committee's concerns were met:

> The rules of the game for the conduct of organizational campaigns were established and known at the very outset and employee organizations were able to devote their efforts to organizing the employees in pre-determined bargaining units rather than exhaust themselves in establishing footholds in fragments of an occupational group in the hope of having their claims to certification for a small bargaining unit ultimately recognized by the Board.[205]

After the initial period had expired, the PSSRB was free to choose different bargaining units so long as the units did not cross occupational category lines. In actual fact, long after the occupational category was no longer required to be the bargaining unit, the PSSRB continued to choose different bargaining units only in rare cases. One example of this policy was in *Le syndicat des controleurs aériens du Québec*.[206] In that case, a Quebec union wanted to break away from the Canadian Air Traffic Control Association and create a bargaining unit solely for Quebec air traffic controllers. The PSSRB refused to consider the language spoken by employees as an appropriate factor for determining a bargaining unit, stating:

> The Act's unmistakable thrust is in the direction of service-wide units based on occupational classifications. In our opinion, it is beyond the discretionary power of this Board—given the ramifications—to consider language designations, as such, to be a factor in determining the appropriateness of bargaining units.[207]

The PSSRB thus maintained a presumption in favour of occupational groups. It was "loath to split up existing service-wide units."[208]

The statute required the Public Service Commission to define the occupational groups within the public service.[209] The *PSSRA* specifically

205 Finkelman, above note 196 at 17.

206 *Le syndicat des controleurs aériens du Québec* (1978), PSSRB File No 143-2-164.

207 *Ibid* at 136.

208 Finkelman, above note 196 at 24.

209 *PSSRA*, s 26(1). The occupational groups are now defined by the Treasury Board by establishing a classification plan: *Financial Administration Act*, s 11(2)(c).

set out five occupational categories and then gave the PSSRB the discretion to create more categories.[210] Those five categories were:

- scientific and professional
- technical
- administrative and foreign service
- administrative support
- operational

A sixth occupational category of "management" was later adopted.

There were originally sixty-seven different occupational groups in the civil service. In the 1990s, the government became concerned about the large number of occupational groups and entered negotiations with unions about how to restructure collective bargaining in the civil service. The immediate spur for these negotiations was the fact that, after years of statutory wage freezes, collective bargaining was due to return in 1997. The government originally proposed having only six bargaining units. This would have threatened many smaller unions that only represent a few workers in the civil service in very small bargaining units. The smaller unions, supported by larger unions, convinced the government that "there was tremendous potential for nasty inter-union fights across the public service as rival unions scrambled to win certification votes"[211] and that it was in no one's interest to create chaos and worker anxiety while downsizing and restructuring was taking place. In the end, the parties agreed on a plan to reduce the number of bargaining units down to twenty-nine, guaranteeing all unions' existing jurisdiction. There are still twenty-nine bargaining units for which the Treasury Board is the employer (although their composition has changed since the *Public Service Reform Act* was implemented): six represented by the Professional Institute of the Public Service of Canada; five represented by the PSAC; and eighteen represented by other various smaller unions.[212]

---

210 The statutory definition of occupational category was repealed in 1992.

211 Gene Swimmer & Sandra Bach, "Restructuring Federal Public-Sector Human Resources" in Gene Swimmer, ed, *Public-Sector Labour Relations in an Era of Restraint and Restructuring* (Toronto: Oxford University Press, 2001) at 195.

212 Federal Public Sector Labour Relations and Employment Board, *2020–2021 Annual Report* (2021), online: www.fpslreb-crtespf.gc.ca/en/about-us/annual-reports/2020-2021/ar-202021.html.

b) Board's Preference for Large, All-Employee Bargaining Units

The Board has interpreted this legislative restriction on bargaining unit determination as a reason to "disapprove of fragmentation and multiplicity of bargaining units."[213] A review of some of the Board's leading decisions concerning bargaining unit structure demonstrates that, for the Board at least, "fewer is better." Furthermore, the Board—unlike other labour relations boards—will choose the *most* appropriate bargaining unit instead of simply *an* appropriate bargaining unit.

One of the most important bargaining unit decisions (or at least the one that probably affected the largest number of employees) was the Board's decision concerning the creation of the CCRA.[214] In that decision, the Board decided that the CCRA would consist of two bargaining units: the Program Delivery and Administrative Services unit (eventually represented by the PSAC) and the Audit, Financial and Scientific unit (eventually represented by the Professional Institute of the Public Service of Canada). Each party in that case proposed an additional bargaining unit: the employer proposed a separate management unit; the PSAC proposed a separate unit for customs officers; and the institute and the employer both proposed a separate unit for computer systems workers (the CS group). The Board rejected all three attempts to carve out smaller bargaining units. The Board reiterated its long-standing policy of promoting "broadly based bargaining units."[215] This is because

> [t]he fewer the bargaining units, the less likely the potential for impasses in negotiations, work disruptions and jurisdictional disputes. This is of particular concern in the context of public sector collective bargaining where the public interest is very much at stake.[216]

In rejecting the management bargaining unit, the Board did not agree with the employer's contention that management employees had not been satisfactorily represented. The Board recognized that management employees may have different bargaining objectives from other employees but also that even among the team leaders who would comprise the management bargaining units there was a diversity of bargaining objectives. Therefore, "there is no more likely to be a consensus

213 *Federal Law Officers of the Crown v Treasury Board*, [2006] CPSSRB No 40 at para 120 [*Federal Law Officers of the Crown*].

214 *CCRA v APSFA*, above note 188.

215 *Ibid* at para 514.

216 *Ibid* at para 521.

among this group than within a larger bargaining unit. It is inherent in the collective bargaining process that bargaining agents must address and reconcile divergent interests."[217] Therefore, creating a management bargaining unit would not solve any problems of representation.

In refusing to segregate CS workers, the Board refused to consider the market value of their work (which, at the time, was much higher than that of other CCRA employees). The Board held that market value is subject to fads and is hence neither a stable nor a reliable criterion for bargaining unit determinations. The fact that a group of workers finds themselves in demand at a particular point in time is no justification for fragmentation of a bargaining unit. The Board also did not find the fact that the employer and institute more or less agreed that the CS groups should be a separate bargaining unit compelling. Vice-chair Chodos dissented on this point. He would have created a separate bargaining unit for CS workers, in part because no party opposed such a group and in part because that group was unique in terms of its salary structure and its relationship to the broader marketplace.

Finally, the Board refused to carve out a unit of customs officers. The Board concluded that the views of the customs officers would be "heard within the larger bargaining unit" because of the high-profile nature of their responsibilities and the impact of their work on the well-being of Canadians.[218] The Board did not consider the impact on the rest of the employees in the bargaining unit if the customs officers were to achieve their collective bargaining objectives at the expense of the majority of employees simply because their jobs were more "high-profile."[219]

Another significant case where the Board adopted a policy of large bargaining units involved the Parks Canada Agency when it became a separate employer in 1998.[220] The Board decided that it must choose the *most* appropriate bargaining unit when considering several appropriate units. Other labour relations boards are required to choose *an* appropriate bargaining unit; therefore, when a union proposes a bargaining unit for certification, that bargaining unit will be accepted even if it is not the best bargaining unit so long as it is appropriate. The Board applied stricter criteria. The Board also confirmed its policy favouring large

---

217 *Ibid* at para 525.

218 *Ibid* at para 538.

219 Customs officers were eventually reintegrated into the core public administration.

220 *Parks Canada Agency v Professional Institute of the Public Service of Canada*, [2000] CPSSRB No 72.

bargaining units, stating that it "has always indicated and continues to believe that there should not be a fragmentation or multiplicity of bargaining units in the work place."[221] The reason for this belief is that "a bargaining unit that is too small in size will often have no real influence on the outcome of service wide issues and on the determination of the parameters for pay and benefits."[222]

In stating this belief, the Board confirmed a long line of cases that stated a "lack of uniformity in conditions of employment among various sections of the Public Service is more difficult to justify than it is in the private sector."[223] This policy choice, while echoed by the Preparatory Committee, has never been satisfactorily explained. Either uniformity is good or it is bad—the Board has not explained why uniformity, if good for the public sector, is not equally good for the private sector. Either people who do the same work should get the same pay or they should not. Whether someone works in the public or the private sector should not influence whether they are treated justly. If, in fact, the Board is advocating that the government act as a model employer by refusing to create artificial distinctions in pay based on criteria other than the work performed, then this runs contrary to one of the original purposes of the public bargaining unit structure as set out by the Preparatory Committee. The Preparatory Committee stated that one reason to impose bargaining units on the public service based on occupational classification was to make public sector pay comparable to the private sector. If this is the goal of public sector pay policy, then the government cannot at the same time be acting as a "model employer" with respect to pay rates. The two purposes contradict each other. Regardless of the absence of an explanation for this policy, the Board has maintained that policy throughout its existence.

The Board concentrated in *Parks Canada Agency v Professional Institute of the Public Service of Canada* on the employer's organizational structure and whether the bargaining unit would allow the parties to deal effectively with labour relations issues. In the end, the Board was influenced by the following factors:

221 *Ibid* at para 127.

222 *Ibid* at para 129.

223 *Heating, Power and Stationary Plant Operation Case No 2* (1970), PSSR Reports K 607 at 609.

- mobility, multitasking, and teamwork leading to a significant overlap of duties
- the specialized nature of the mandate and mission of the Parks Canada Agency, which leads to a community of interest[224]
- the need for a non-discriminatory classification system that applies across all occupational lines and the fact that the Parks Canada Agency was "well on its way" to developing a universal classification standard
- the fact that the different bargaining agents currently in place have consulted with each other in the past

The Board concluded that there should be one bargaining unit for the entire Parks Canada Agency, encompassing all employees.

The Board established a single bargaining unit for all lawyers employed by the Treasury Board.[225] The Federal Law Officers of the Crown wanted to create a separate bargaining unit for lawyers who report to the Ontario Regional Office, except for those lawyers employed in Ottawa.[226] The Board instead certified the Association of Justice Counsel as the bargaining agent for an all-lawyer bargaining unit, again demonstrating its policy in favour of large bargaining units.

The Board most recently confirmed this principle when establishing a bargaining unit for certain civilian members and employees of the RCMP. CUPE proposed two bargaining units for two different occupational subgroups (telecommunications operators and intercept monitors) within the broader Police Operations occupational group. The

---

224 This begs the question of whether there are any government agencies that do not have a specialized mandate and mission. The "band of brothers" mentality with the Communications Security Establishment is understandable, but with Parks Canada it is harder to accept without evidence.

225 *Federal Law Officers of the Crown*, above note 213. The *FPSLRA* established the right of lawyers to collectively bargain, so this was the first lawyer bargaining unit in the federal public service. Some employees who happened to be lawyers were members of other bargaining units (such as lawyers in the former LA classification group working outside of the Department of Justice represented by the Professional Institute of the Public Service of Canada).

226 The Federal Law Officers of the Crown essentially wanted to create a bargaining unit for which it could bargain different rates of pay for Toronto lawyers than for lawyers elsewhere in Canada. The Board rejected the "market forces" argument in favour of a distinct bargaining unit for Toronto lawyers, citing the *CCRA v APSFA* decision (above note 188). In any event, lawyers in Toronto were already paid more than their Ottawa counterparts.

Board rejected those two proposed bargaining units in favour of a single bargaining unit composed of the entire Police Operations occupational group (comprising both public service employees and civilian members of the RCMP). The Board relied upon its general approach that "there should not be fragmentation or a multiplicity of bargaining units in the workplace" to come to this conclusion.[227] The Board also repeated its rule that it will establish the most appropriate bargaining unit—unlike other labour boards that are satisfied whenever a union proposes an appropriate bargaining unit.

The Board provided some glimpse behind its preference for large, all-inclusive bargaining units when it dismissed an application to split apart one unit within the Canadian Food Inspection Agency. The Board considered an argument that the employees who wanted to break away to form their own bargaining unit did so because they did not share a community of interest with the rest of the bargaining unit. The Board, though, rejected that argument, finding instead that "[t]here is sufficient community of interest based on each cog in the 'machine' being essential to the machine's overall viability."[228]

c) Definition of a Plan of "Classification"

The *FPSLRA* requires the Board to consider the employer's plan of classification. The term "classification" is not defined in the *FPSLRA*; therefore, it fell to the Board to determine exactly what constituted a plan of classification. Similarly, the Board needed to define the terms "occupational groups or subgroups." The Board considered this issue in *Council of Graphic Arts Unions of the Public Service of Canada and Canada Communication Group*.[229] The Canada Communication Group was established as a separate employer in 1993, prior to the introduction of the successor rights provisions, so various employee organizations needed to apply for certification as bargaining agents for those employees they previously represented. The employer did not have a classification plan in place when the various employee organizations brought their applications; however, two months after those applications were

227 *Canadian Union of Public Employees v Treasury Board (Royal Canadian Mounted Police)*, 2017 FPSLREB 36 at para 79.

228 *Canadian Food Inspection Agency Financial Officer Association v Canadian Food Inspection Agency and Public Service Alliance of Canada*, 2015 PSLREB 68 at para 77 [*Canadian Food Inspection*].

229 *Canada Communication Group*, above note 64.

filed (and prior to the hearing before the Board), it established what purported to be a plan of classification.

The Board, however, rejected the employer's argument that it should consider this plan of classification, concluding instead that it was not a proper plan of "classification" as that term is meant in the Act. The employer hired a consultant to create a single classification plan covering all positions. The main concern of this plan was pay equity and not any other aspect of labour relations. This plan had four principles: it had to be simple to administer, it had to respect the principles of pay equity, it had to represent the values of the organization, and it had to be sufficiently flexible to enable it to adapt to changes in technology. However, according to the Board, the classification plan did not consider the duties and responsibilities of the positions. The Board concluded that "Parliament envisages that this plan of classification shall be formulated on the basis of the employees' occupations, that is, their duties and responsibilities" and that "to be a plan of classification for the purposes of section 33 [now section 57] . . . it must be based on the duties and responsibilities of the relevant employees."[230]

The Board also considered what constitutes a plan of classification in *Professional Institute of the Public Service of Canada v Canadian Nuclear Safety Commission*.[231] In that case, the employer had established one classification plan for all employees. However, within that classification plan there were separate pay bands for Science and Engineering (SE) and Technical Specialist (TS) groups. The SE and TS employees were all concentrated within the higher band of the employer's classification plan (positions classified at the RL-5 to RL-7 range: the total range was RL-1 to RL-7). The employer submitted that a single bargaining unit was most appropriate in light of its plan of classification. The Board disagreed: by establishing a separate pay plan or rate of pay for different positions, the Board concluded that the employer had created "groups or subgroups of the employer's plan of classification";[232] therefore, the statutory presumption did not compel the Board to create a single bargaining unit. The existence of a regional rate of pay, on the other hand, does not create an occupational subgroup.[233] To constitute a subgroup, there should be "pay bands," not simply different rates of pay.

230 *Ibid* at 25–26.

231 Above note 158.

232 *Ibid* at para 59.

233 *Federal Law Officers of the Crown*, above note 225 at para 117.

Without a plan of classification, the Board will determine the appropriate bargaining unit using the factors identified in the *Usarco* decision discussed earlier, as well as other factors that the Board has added from time to time. In *Canada Communication Group*,[234] the Board considered the following factors when deciding on two bargaining units instead of one all-employee unit:

- community of interest
  - » nature of the work performed
  - » conditions of employment (paid on hourly versus yearly basis, different hours of work)
  - » skills of employees (different educational backgrounds, only one group had an apprenticeship program)
  - » administration (uniforms and safety shoes only worn by one group of employees)
  - » geographic circumstances (one group of employees was physically separated from the other)
  - » functional coherence and interdependence (no contact and career mobility between the two groups)
- centralization of managerial authority
- economic factors
- source of work[235]
- history of certification and negotiations (the employees were divided into different bargaining units before the employer became a separate agency)
- wishes of employees (although the Board stated that this is not determinative, it was something the Board could take into account)

d) Circumstances in Which the Board Has Not Followed a Classification Plan

The statutory presumption in favour of determining a bargaining unit in accordance with a plan of classification (or occupational groups or subgroups) is just a presumption: it can be rebutted if following the classification "would not permit satisfactory representation of the employees to be included in the group."[236] The Board has, on occasion, decided to create bargaining units that did not conform to an

234 *Canada Communication Group*, above note 64.

235 These first four factors the board took from the *Usarco* decision.

236 *FPSLRA*, s 57(3).

employer's plan of classification. One of those circumstances is if an all-employee bargaining unit or a bargaining unit following the plan of classification would result in employees not being represented at all. In *Canadian Nuclear Safety Commission*, the Board adverted to that principle, stating:

> The employer's proposed all-inclusive bargaining unit cannot be accepted at this time. The employer's position might have been acceptable had there been before the Board a satisfactory indication of the desire of majority of employees at the [Canadian Nuclear Safety Commission] to participate in collective bargaining. The fact is that no employee at the RL-1 to RL-4 levels has shown an interest in being represented by the applicant. That fact is evidenced by the signed membership cards submitted by the PIPSC with its application. Accepting a single all-inclusive bargaining unit would therefore likely have the effect of preventing collective bargaining given the lower level APP's [Administration and Program Professional] clearly expressed opposition to unionization. The Board, in exercising its discretion on initial certification, must respect the purposes and objectives of the *PSSRA* which include the promotion and facilitation of collective bargaining within the federal public sector.[237]

The Board has also rejected an all-employee bargaining unit (in conformity with a plan of classification) where there was one category of employees who would be advantaged over another. In *Public Service Alliance of Canada and National Energy Board*,[238] the employer advocated a single all-employee bargaining unit. The Board noted that the employer treated professional and non-professional employees differently: "[T]he professionals are more likely to have the ear of [the National Energy Board], and their interests and concerns are different from the

237 *Canadian Nuclear Safety Commission*, above note 59 at para 62. The employees in the RL-1 through RL-4 later showed an interest in joining that same bargaining agent, and the Board expanded the bargaining unit to include all employees in classification RL-1 through RL-7 at that time: *PIPSC v CNSC*, above note 158.

238 *Public Service Alliance of Canada and National Energy Board*, [1993] CPSSRB No 183, aff'd on judicial review [1994] FCJ No 1894 (CA). Note that the Board reconsidered this choice of bargaining unit in 2003: above note 63. The employer's classification plan in this case had the same defects as the one in the *Canada Communication Group* case, above note 64, but the Board specifically declined to determine whether the employer's plan of classification was a true "classification" plan under the Act.

'non-professional' employees."[239] Since the professional employees outnumbered the non-professionals, the Board concluded that the concerns of non-professionals would not be satisfactorily represented if they were included in a bargaining unit with professionals. The Board ordered two bargaining units: one for professionals and one for non-professionals. The Board later changed its mind and consolidated the two bargaining units on the basis that "[r]ecent history has shown that the old divisions along professional and non-professional lines are not always easy to make nor are they necessarily useful."[240]

e) Review of Bargaining Units

The *FPSLRA* specifically gives the Board the power to review and amend bargaining units.[241] Parties have attempted to either break an existing bargaining unit into two or more units (a process known as "fragmentation") or to combine two or more bargaining units (a process known as "accretion"). On an application for review, the Board must consider the employer's plan of classification in the same manner as on an application for certification or a successor rights application. This is a change in the *FPSLRA*: under the predecessor *PSSRA*, there was no statutory obligation to consider classification plans on a review of bargaining units.

The Board has been cautious in reviewing bargaining unit structure, stating that "the threshold for review . . . must be significant change rendering an existing structure unsatisfactory."[242] However, the cases demonstrate that the Board is willing to change the bargaining unit structure in some circumstances. The cases also demonstrate that the Board is more favourably disposed toward accretion than fragmentation.

For example, the Board reconsidered its 1993 decision to create two separate bargaining units in the National Energy Board and merged them into one unit in 2003.[243] The Board concluded that there had been significant change since 1993, especially because the employer changed its method of service delivery and, consequently, created multidisciplinary teams for the delivery of those services. The employer's classification

---

239 *Ibid* at 12.

240 *National Energy Board*, above note 63.

241 *FPSLRA*, s 70.

242 *National Energy Board*, above note 63 at para 151. The Board rejected the stricter test of "evidence of real and demonstrable adverse labour relations" proposed by counsel for the PSAC.

243 *Ibid*.

plan had also been changed to better reflect the actual duties of positions, and that plan applied to all employees. In short, the divisions between professional and non-professional employees that concerned the Board in 1993 were no longer as easy to discern. Therefore, the Board amalgamated those two units into one all-employee bargaining unit. The Board also agreed to amalgamate two bargaining units at the Staff of the Non-Public Funds, on the consent of the bargaining agent and the employer, because the employees were represented by the same bargaining agent, covered by virtually identical terms of employment, and worked in the same city.[244]

Applications to fragment a bargaining unit, on the other hand, are harder to justify. In *Association of Marine Assessors, Inspectors and Investigators of the Public Service of Canada and Treasury Board*,[245] the Board referred to its "apprehensions about fragmenting existing bargaining units"[246] and its "predilection against the fragmentation of bargaining units."[247] The Board concluded that "there is a heavy onus on the part of the applicant to demonstrate that the current bargaining unit, which is coextensive with the Technical Inspection group definition, and has been in place for nearly thirty years, does not permit satisfactory representation in respect of those employees who are members of the Applicant."[248] The Board in that case decided not to fragment the Technical Inspection group by carving out a bargaining unit for Marine Inspectors and Investigators.

The Board came to a similar conclusion in *Canadian Food Inspection Agency Financial Officer Association v Canadian Food Inspection Agency and Public Service Alliance of Canada*.[249] In that case, a new employee organization attempted to carve out and then certify the financial officers from a larger all-employee group within the Canadian Food Inspection Agency. The Board repeated its principle that "there should not be a

244 *Public Service Alliance of Canada and Staff of the Non-Public Funds, Canadian Forces*, 2012 PSLRB 116. While geographic location is not usually a factor in federal public sector bargaining units, the Staff of the Non-Public Funds has several bargaining units based on geographic location—typically a particular Canadian Armed Forces base.

245 *Association of Marine Assessors, Inspectors and Investigators of the Public Service of Canada and Treasury Board*, [1998] CPSSRB No 47.

246 *Ibid* at para 62.

247 *Ibid* at para 63.

248 *Ibid* at para 64.

249 *Canadian Food Inspection*, above note 228.

fragmentation or multiplicity of bargaining units in the workplace"[250] in the absence of compelling evidence that the larger unit cannot effectively bargain on behalf of the smaller classification. The Board also refused to pull an occupational subgroup (the Ships Crews employees) out of the broader Occupational Services group, despite the fact that the Ships Crews employees would constitute a viable bargaining unit with a strong community of interest.[251]

This is not to say that the Board will never fragment a bargaining unit. In *Federal Government Dockyard Chargehands Association and Treasury Board*,[252] the Board fragmented an existing bargaining unit by carving out a new bargaining unit for 113 first-line supervisors known as chargehands. The Board concluded that the applicant met its "heavy burden" to convince the Board to fragment an existing bargaining unit because there was no community of interest between the chargehands and the rest of the bargaining unit: they had different qualifications, skills, and responsibilities; the nature of their duties was very different; and the chargehands were sometimes in conflict with other workers because they had to recommend discipline. The Board also considered the fact that relations between the chargehands and the council representing them "have become tense and have deteriorated."[253] However, in most cases the Board has no difficulty including supervisors in the same bargaining unit as the employees they supervise.[254]

f) Determination of Which Bargaining Unit a Position Belongs To

From time to time, disputes arise concerning the bargaining units to which particular positions belong. Section 58 of the *FPSLRA* requires the Board to determine every question that arises concerning whether any employee or class of employees is included in a bargaining unit. For the reasons discussed above, positions within the core public administration are assigned a bargaining unit according to their occupational

250 *Ibid* at para 79.

251 *Public Service Alliance of Canada v Treasury Board*, 2010 PSLRB 57.

252 *Federal Government Dockyard Chargehands Association and Treasury Board*, [1988] CPSSRB No 26.

253 *Ibid* at 8.

254 See, for example, *CCRA v APSFA*, above note 188, and *Canada Communication Group*, above note 64 at 29, where the Board stated: "We have included the supervisors in the first bargaining unit as we are satisfied that they have a greater community of interest with the people they supervise than with the other employees."

group. The definitions of these occupational groups are established by the Public Service Commission and set out in the *Canada Gazette*.

It has been well established in Board jurisprudence that the Board cannot involve itself in the classification process. As the Board has stated, "the purpose of an appropriate bargaining unit analysis pursuant to the *FPSLRA* is not to interfere with the employer's right to determine its organizational structure nor to second guess the classification of the positions."[255] That being said, a reclassification of positions does not automatically mean that the positions should also be placed in a new bargaining unit. The Board cannot review classification decisions, but it can—and does—ensure that employees are placed in the correct bargaining unit, regardless of the employer's view of their classification.

The Board has referred to its task as determining the "pith and substance" of employees' functions or their core duties and then comparing that "pith and substance" to the definition of the particular occupational group.[256] The Board's jurisprudence has also referred to the occupational category definition that is the "best fit" for the duties.[257]

The tensions between a "reclassification" and a "bargaining unit review" were demonstrated in *Federal Government Dockyards Trades and Labour Council (Esquimalt) v Treasury Board*.[258] In that instance, the employer reclassified two employees from the Ship Repair occupational group to the General Labour and Trades group. The Federal Government Dockyards Trades and Labour Council—the bargaining agent for the Ship Repair bargaining unit—argued that the two employees still belonged in that bargaining unit regardless of the reclassification. The employer argued that its reclassification was final and binding and that the Board did not have the jurisdiction to review its reclassification decision. The Board agreed that it could not review the reclassification but concluded that it could review whether the duties of those two employees' positions fell within the Ship Repair or General Labour and Trades bargaining unit. The Board reviewed the duties of those

255 *International Brotherhood of Electrical Workers Local 2228 v Treasury Board*, 2005 PSLRB 155 [*IBEW Local 2228*], aff'd on judicial review [2006] FCJ No 1405 (CA).

256 *International Brotherhood of Electrical Workers, Local 2228 v Treasury Board*, 2001 PSSRB 71.

257 *International Brotherhood of Electrical Workers, Local 2228 v Treasury Board*, 2000 PSSRB 52.

258 *Federal Government Dockyards Trades and Labour Council (Esquimalt) v Treasury Board*, [1984] CPSSRB No 74.

two positions and concluded that they belonged in the Ship Repair unit because their primary duties were the repair of RCMP vessels—something within the definition of the Ship Repair occupational group.

More recently, the Board affirmed that it is not bound by a position's classification when determining which bargaining unit the position belongs to. In *Canadian Federal Pilots Association v Treasury Board*,[259] three positions had been included in the Aircraft Operations bargaining unit. Their job descriptions were rewritten and their classifications altered accordingly. The essence of the change was that the requirement to hold a current pilot's licence and have experience as a pilot was deleted from their job description; the Aircraft Operations classification expressly excluded positions where a valid pilot's licence and experience as an aircraft pilot were not mandatory. The Board did not follow the classification decision and, instead, assigned these positions to the Aircraft Operations bargaining unit. The Board instead examined the primary purpose of the actual duties of the three jobs and concluded that they best fit within the Aircraft Operations bargaining unit in light of the statement within the classification group definition that certain tasks were included in that occupational group. The Board also concluded that the specific exclusion of employees without a requirement for a pilot's licence did not determine the outcome of the case, instead concluding that the "inclusions/exclusions dilemma can be resolved by applying the traditional 'best fit' approach."[260] On judicial review to the Federal Court of Appeal, the Court concluded that the Board's decision did not unreasonably override the presumption in favour of bargaining units along occupational group lines, stating:

> [A] decision made under section 58 is primarily focussed on whether an employee or class of employees is included in a bargaining unit, not on a comprehensive review of the appropriateness for collective bargaining purposes of an established unit. Hence, it would not seem unreasonable for the Board to decline to read into section 58 the statutory directions that the Board must follow when establishing or reviewing bargaining units under sections 57 and 70.[261]

---

259 *Canadian Federal Pilots Association v Treasury Board*, 2008 PSLRB 42 [*CFPA v Treasury Board*], aff'd *Public Service Alliance of Canada v Canadian Federal Pilots Assn*, 2009 FCA 223 [*PSAC v CFPA*].

260 *CFPA v Treasury Board*, above note 259 at para 20.

261 *PSAC v CFPA*, above note 259 at para 66.

The net result of this case is that a specific exclusion in an occupational group definition does not override the Board's jurisdiction to determine the proper composition of bargaining units in light of the best fit for that position.

As an interesting postscript to that case, the employer diverted union dues to the Canadian Federal Pilots Association and recognized their exclusive representation rights. However, the association understood that the effect of that decision was a "return to the status quo" — namely, that the three positions would be filled by persons having recent experience piloting aircraft. The Board disagreed, concluding that such a request would draw it into the realm of classification and staffing instead of bargaining unit determination. Having placed those three positions into the correct bargaining unit, the Board's task was complete — the question of staffing those positions remains with the employer.[262] Or, to put the point another way, "a bargaining certificate is intended to define the scope of the bargaining unit for the purpose of collective bargaining rather than to grant proprietary rights to the work of the unit."[263]

Finally, the Board is not always required to refer to the actual tasks performed by individual employees. Instead, it should have regard to the duties of the position. In a 2005 decision concerning the International Brotherhood of Electrical Workers (IBEW),[264] the Department of Foreign Affairs and International Trade had combined its various positions dealing with computer equipment into one position. To do so, it had merged positions from two different bargaining units (the Electrical group and the Computer Services group) and classified the new position in the Computer Services group. The IBEW, which represented the Electrical group, argued that the employees who used to be in that group should remain in that group because the actual tasks they performed had not changed with the creation of the new position. The evidence before the Board indicated that the reason their tasks had not changed was because they needed to be trained before completing all of the duties assigned to the position. Therefore, rather than consider the actual tasks performed by individual employees within a position, the

---

262 *Canadian Federal Pilots Association v Treasury Board*, 2011 PSLRB 84.

263 *Federal Government Dockyard Trades and Labour Council (East) v Treasury Board (Department of National Defence)*, 2014 PSLRB 51 at para 66.

264 *IBEW Local 2228*, above note 255.

Board considered the duties of the position as set out in the job description for that position. The Board refused to fragment the bargaining unit into two parts in light of this factual context and decided that the new position was a "better fit" in the Computer Services group than in the Electrical group.[265]

265 See also *Professional Institute of the Public Service of Canada v Treasury Board*, 2006 PSLRB 61, where the Board refused to declare that medical adjudicators within the Department of Social Development Canada should belong within the Health Services bargaining unit instead of the Program and Administrative Services bargaining unit. The Board refused to reallocate those positions because of the duties of the position: although medical adjudicators had to have medical qualifications to be appointed to the position, their primary duty was to determine eligibility for benefits under a specific government program and not to actually assess or treat patients.

CHAPTER SIX

Collective Bargaining in the Federal Public Service

A. INTRODUCTION

This chapter concerns the process of industrial dispute resolution in the federal public service—namely, collective bargaining, conciliation and strikes, and interest arbitration. Before beginning a discussion of the technical and legal details of industrial dispute resolution in the federal public service, it is worthwhile to examine the historical, political, and economic context of bargaining in the federal public service.

Collective bargaining in the public sector is qualitatively different than in the private sector. The most important factor distinguishing public sector collective bargaining from the private sector is politics. Collective bargaining in the public sector involves an effort to engage in political decision-making.[1] Governments, unlike private sector employers, focus primarily on public opinion and the likelihood of re-election rather than on profit maximization. This is particularly so at the federal level of government, where the tax base is broader and more flexible than at the provincial or municipal level; in addition, wages and salaries of the federal government account for a smaller share of the budget than in provincial or municipal governments.[2] Likewise, public service unions

1 See, for example, *British Columbia Teachers' Federation v British Columbia Public School Employers' Assn*, 2009 BCCA 39 at para 37: "Unlike the private sector, the primary target of the strike weapon is the government and public opinion; the strike is in that sense political."

2 Personnel expenses account for 40 percent of federal direct program spending, or $48.6 billion in 2016–17. This includes a combination of current and future

use the strike weapon to create public pressure on governments rather than to penalize their employer financially. Public service strikes do not cost governments revenue and, on the contrary, can actually assist their financial situation since they do not need to pay their employees who are on strike.[3] It has been suggested that political pressures on the public employer act as a substitute for the economic pressures to settle in the private sector bargaining model. There are, however, countervailing political pressures. The employer may be concerned about high wage settlements setting a precedent for private sector wage settlements or for other levels of government. This was one of the expressed purposes of the 1982 *Public Sector Compensation Restraint Act*[4] and the *Expenditure Restraint Act*.[5] While some public service unions have achieved higher-than-average settlements, a government cannot be expected to settle at any price.[6]

As a result, public sector labour relations outcomes are the product of both economics and politics. Because of this political dimension to collective bargaining in the public sector, some commentators have gone so far as to contend that public sector collective bargaining is inherently antidemocratic. As Malin stated, those critics "suggest that all issues discussed at the bargaining table are political issues that should be decided in the regular political process, and they consider it

---

expenditures: Office of the Parliamentary Budget Officer, *Federal Personnel Spending: Past and Future Trends* (20 March 2018) at 1, online (pdf): www.pbo-dpb.gc.ca/web/default/files/Documents/Reports/2018/Fed%20Personnel%20Spending/Fed_Personnel_Spending_EN.pdf. By contrast, and just to provide one example, Ontario's personnel expenses account for approximately 48 percent of direct program spending: Ontario, "Expenditure Estimates Volume 1 (2018–19)," Summary Table 3 (23 April 2018), online: www.ontario.ca/page/expenditure-estimates-volume-1-table-contents-2018-19. The City of Ottawa, to pick one municipal example, spends approximately 46 percent of its expenditures on compensation: "City of Ottawa 2019 Operating Budget," online: https://ottawa.ca/en/city-hall/budget/previous-budgets/budget-2019#2019-adopted-budget.

3 Jacob Finkelman & Shirley Goldenberg, *Collective Bargaining in the Public Service: The Federal Experience in Canada* (Ottawa: Institute for Research on Public Policy, 1983) at 256–58.

4 *Ibid*, discussing the *Public Sector Compensation Restraint Act*, SC 1980–81–82–83, c 122.

5 *Meredith v Canada (Attorney General)*, 2015 SCC 2 at para 64.

6 Gene Swimmer, "Public-Sector Labour Relations in an Era of Restraint and Restructuring: An Overview" in Gene Swimmer, ed, *Public-Sector Labour Relations in an Era of Restraint and Restructuring* (Toronto: Oxford University Press, 2001) at 2–3.

inappropriate to give unions, which they regard as one of many interest groups, an avenue of access to public decision makers that is not available to other interest groups."[7]

There are several rebuttals advanced against this argument. First, Malin herself argued that such concerns are misplaced because collective bargaining does not eliminate the influence of other interest groups, and collective bargaining helps even out a power imbalance that inherently favours interest groups other than trade unions:

> Concerns that public sector collective bargaining undermines democratic government are misplaced. When matters are not subject to collective bargaining, they are determined unilaterally by the employer after input from various interest groups. Labeling a matter a mandatory subject of collective bargaining does not eliminate the access of other interest groups to the public decision maker. The duty to bargain requires negotiation but does not compel the employer to reach agreement with the union. Public officials remain accountable to the public for the agreements they reach, or fail to reach, with their employees' unions.
>
> As users and consumers the public desires more and better services at lower costs. Labor costs are the largest part of most public-entity budgets. Consequently, unions seeking wage increases and other concessions that would raise labor costs are at a disadvantage vis-à-vis every other interest group in the budget-setting process. That disadvantage justifies providing them with collective bargaining as a special avenue of access.[8]

As Malin put it more bluntly in a later paper, "when employees' wages and working conditions are left to be decided in the political process, employees and their unions are inherently outnumbered by members of the public who as users and purchasers of the employees' services, desire greater and better services at the lowest possible cost."[9]

---

7 M. Malin, "Public Sector Labor Law Doctrine and Labor-Management Cooperation" in J. Brock & D. Lipsky, eds, *Going Public: The Role of Labor-Management Relations in Delivering Quality Government Services* (Champaign, IL: Industrial Relations Research Association Series, 2003) at 281. See also M. Malin, "The Paradox of Public Sector Labor Law" (2009) 84 Ind LJ 1369 at 1372.

8 *Ibid* at 282.

9 M. Malin, "The Motive Power in Public Sector Collective Bargaining" (2018) 36 Hofstra Lab & Empl LJ 123 at 156.

Second, some commentators have pointed out that the government retains the power—through legislation, if necessary—to ensure that the interests or preferences of unions and their members do not overwhelm the interests of the public.[10] Governments can use "an array of legislative and policy tools to control the parties' behaviors and bargaining outcomes,"[11] including legislation that limits the scope of bargaining, wage restraint legislation, and back-to-work legislation in the event of a strike.

Third, collective bargaining has also been justified as producing a better public service by encouraging cooperation or co-determinism between employees and management. A number of studies (admittedly, the studies focus on the private sector) show that when unions are strong they provide an independent employee voice that plays an important role in high-performance and high-productivity workplaces.[12] A related theory is that unions increase employment and economic efficiency by acting as a counterweight to employer monopsony power—and governments are certainly a monopsony on public sector employment.[13]

Fourth, public sector unions are themselves seen as instruments of democracy. Public sector unions enhance workplace democracy—and the Supreme Court of Canada has recognized workplace democracy as a core value protected by the *Canadian Charter of Rights and Freedoms* (the *Charter*).[14] Workplace democracy is, in this view, as important as other forms of democracy and therefore worthy of equal respect and protection.[15]

---

10 D. Rosenthal, "Public Sector Collective Bargaining, Majoritarianism and Reform" (2013) 91 Or L Rev 673 at 679.

11 Mark Thompson & Sara Slinn, "Public Sector Industrial Relations in Canada: Does It Threaten or Sustain Democracy?" (2013) 34 Comp Lab L & Pol'y J 393 at 411.

12 See, for example, Carol Gill, "Union Impact on the Effective Adoption of High Performance Work Practices" (2009) 19 Hum Resource Mgmt Rev 39; William N. Cooke, "Product Quality Improvement Through Employee Participation: The Effects of Union-Management Administration" (1992) 46 Indus & Lab Rel Rev 119; C. Doucouliagos & P. Laroche, "What Do Unions Do to Productivity? A Meta-Analysis" (2003) 42:4 Indus Rel 650. This argument was most famously set out in R. Freeman & J. Medoff, *What Do Unions Do?* (New York: Basic Books, 1984).

13 K. Dau-Schmidt & M. Khan, "Undermining or Promoting Democratic Government? An Economic and Empirical Analysis of the Two Views of Public Sector Collective Bargaining in American Law" (2014) 14 Nevada LJ 414 at 428.

14 *Health Services and Support—Facilities Subsector Bargaining Assn v British Columbia*, 2007 SCC 27 at para 85.

15 Thompson & Slinn, above note 11 at 412.

This author prefers a different justification of collective bargaining for employees of the federal public service: collective bargaining is a check on the arbitrary exercise of power. Collective bargaining in the private sector—and the associated statutory protections for trade unions and their members—acts as a check against the arbitrary exercise of economic power. The law of contract, with its emphasis on freedom of contract, does not take into account the inherent power imbalance between employers and employees: "[T]he relation between an employer and an isolated employee or worker is typically a relation between a bearer of power and one who is not a bearer of power. In its inception it is an act of submission, in its operation it is a condition of subordination."[16] Collective bargaining acts as a check on this arbitrary exercise of power.

Once we accept the premise that the arbitrary exercise of power is antithetical to our modern conception of employment relations, then it falls to the opponents of collective bargaining to demonstrate why it should not be available to federal public servants. Does the potential for bargaining agents to impact "political" issues justify subjecting public servants to the arbitrary exercise of authority by their employer? This author's view is that it does not. Collective bargaining is fundamentally a right to a process of good faith discussion and negotiation over terms and conditions of employment. Collective bargaining does not give unions free rein to establish terms and conditions of employment or determine government policy. It is difficult to find examples of any workplace or government that was improved by the exercise of arbitrary power instead of making decisions through a process of collaborative, good faith discussion, and negotiation.

Regardless of any person's individual views on the issue, in Parliament's view the question has been settled: its mandate to the Heeney Committee was to implement (rather than determine the usefulness of) collective bargaining, and its subsequent decision to enact the *Public Service Staff Relations Act* (*PSSRA*) in 1967 confirmed that intention.

By way of a caveat to future readers: the review of the law concerning industrial dispute resolution contained below sets out the state of the law as it stands at the date of publication. As of that date, the *Federal Public Sector Labour Relations Act* (*FPSLRA*)[17] actually

16 P. Davies & M. Freedland, *Kahn-Freund's Labour and the Law*, 3d ed (London, UK: Stevens and Sons, 1983) at 18. Cited with approval in *Wallace v United Grain Growers*, [1997] 3 SCR 701 at para 92.

17 *Federal Public Sector Labour Relations Act*, SC 2003, c 22, s 2.

governed collective bargaining in the federal public service. While the *FPSLRA* (and its predecessor, the *PSSRA*) contained the basic rules for bargaining, those rules have frequently been set aside by special legislation limiting the right to strike, arbitrate, or even collectively bargain.

Public sector bargaining has gone through at least three stages of development, and we may be in a fourth stage of development, the precise details of which are not yet known. The first stage, comprising the period up to 1967, prohibited collective bargaining in the public sector. Public service employees could combine for the purpose of advocating for improvements in working conditions through the federal National Joint Council or other Whitley Council forms of representation,[18] but real collective bargaining was prohibited.

The second stage reflects the "expansionary" years (1967 to 1976, or sometimes treated as lasting until 1982). During this period, there was a transformation in public sector labour relations. The period was marked by the adoption of the *PSSRA*, which enabled collective bargaining in the federal public service. Initially, this innovation spread collective bargaining to provincial government workers; subsequently, collective bargaining spread to employees in the broader provincial public sector (such as education and health care). There was a rapid expansion of public sector union membership in response to the *PSSRA*. The early stage of public sector bargaining was accompanied by high wage settlements as public employees attempted to "catch up" with the private sector. In some provinces, this was accompanied by relatively high strike activity, but not so in the federal public service. As the Preliminary Fryer Report stated:

> Between 1967 and 1976, public service bargaining worked reasonably well. In general, settlements were freely negotiated with little legislative intervention. Public service unions were able to gain not only good monetary settlements but improvements in benefits and working conditions as well.[19]

The third stage has gone by many names depending on the political inclinations of the authors involved—sometimes called the "restraint

18 See Chapter 1.

19 First report of the Advisory Committee on Labour Management Relations in the Federal Public Service, *Identifying the Issues* (May 2000) at 22 [Preliminary Fryer Report].

years,"[20] the "retrenchment years,"[21] or the "Bargaining as Budget Buster and Handcuff" years (for those who prefer florid language).[22] This author prefers the term "pendulum years." The period of 1975 through to the present has been characterized by swings of the pendulum away from and then back toward the rights of public servants to collectively bargain terms and conditions of employment. Throughout this period, the federal government has periodically enacted legislation that restricts collective bargaining, then reverted back to more fulsome collective bargaining, reacted by legislating limits to collective bargaining again, and so on. To summarize these lurches in public policy:

- **1975–78:** In October 1975, the federal government introduced a form of wage restraint through the Anti-Inflation Program. For a period of three years, collective bargaining continued, but all negotiated agreements had to be approved by the government-appointed Anti-Inflation Board.[23] The program was designed to cover all public and private sector wages (in this sense, it was not specifically targeted to public sector bargaining), it allowed exceptions, and it was designed to maintain real wages.
- **1979–82:** Back to normal.
- **1982–83:** Parliament enacted the *Public Sector Compensation Restraint Act* (known as the "6 and 5" Program). This initiative specifically targeted the federal public sector and imposed maximum wage increases of 6 and 5 percent in 1982 and 1983. The Act also extended collective agreements for two years, effectively suspending collective bargaining. This Act was followed in varying degrees by most of the provinces.

20 Joseph B. Rose, "Public Sector Bargaining: From Retrenchment to Consolidation" (2004) 59:2 RI 271 at 273. Professor Rose suggested that the retrenchment period ended in 1998 and was succeeded by a "consolidation" period thereafter; however, his own discussion of the period 2008–11 bears significant resemblance to the characteristics of the "retrenchment" period, including wage-rollback legislation and other difficulties in collective bargaining. See Joseph B. Rose, "Constraints on Public Sector Bargaining in Canada" (2016) 58:1 J Indus Rel 93.

21 *Ibid.*

22 Rosenthal, above note 10 at 689.

23 Gene Swimmer, "Collective Bargaining in the Federal Public Service of Canada: The Last Twenty Years" in Gene Swimmer & Mark Thompson, eds, *Public Sector Collective Bargaining in Canada: Beginning of the End or End of the Beginning?* (Kingston, ON: IRC Press, 1995) at 381.

- **1984–91:** Back to normal. During this period, collective bargaining continued. The government did enact back-to-work legislation for striking members of the Public Service Alliance of Canada in 1991, which started the next phase.
- **1992–99:** During this period, the government legislated pay freezes, first for one year as part of the back-to-work legislation in the 1991 strike, then a 3 percent increase the following year, followed by four years of wage freezes. When collective bargaining was restored in 1997, the *Public Sector Compensation Act*[24] still limited wage increases to approximately 2 percent a year to ensure there was no "catch-up" for the previous years of wage restraint.
- **2000–8:** Back to normal.
- **2009–11:** Parliament restricted wage increases through the *Expenditure Restraint Act*.[25] The wage limits were retroactive to the 2006–7 fiscal year and carried forward to the 2010–11 fiscal year.
- **2011–present:** Back to normal. The government did pass legislation in 2013 that limited collective bargaining on certain issues, including sick leave, but as discussed in Chapter 2, that legislation was never fully implemented and was repealed with the change in government.

It can be hard to know how to characterize this period. Is this "full collective bargaining with some exceptions," or is the existence of the exceptions the norm? In other words, is government interference with collective bargaining exceptional or structural? Does anyone care? Is anyone still reading?

The United States is entering a stage of significant reduction in public sector bargaining. One commentator has suggested that "public sector unions are under attacks unprecedented in modern times."[26] This is not just hyperbole. Collective bargaining is illegal for public sector workers in North Carolina, South Carolina, and Virginia. Other states do not make bargaining illegal but do not have any legal recognition of bargaining (such as West Virginia, Alabama, and Mississippi) or

---

24 *Public Sector Compensation Act*, SC 1991, c 30.

25 *Expenditure Restraint Act*, SC 2009, c 2, s 393.

26 Joseph E. Slater, "Public-Sector Labor in the Age of Obama" (2012) 87 Ind LJ 189 at 189.

permit bargaining but prohibit strikes and arbitration (such as Florida). Other states prohibit collective bargaining for specific categories of public servants (such as teachers and police officers in Georgia and firefighters and police officers in Tennessee). State governments in Ohio, Wisconsin, Iowa, and Indiana have enacted legislation since 2010 that restricts public sector unions.[27] Finally, the US Supreme Court's 2018 decision in *Janus v American Federation of State, County, and Municipal Employees, Council 31*[28] prohibiting union security agreements for public sector workers will also impede public sector unions from engaging in collective bargaining. So far, there seems to be little interest in importing these changes to Canada.

There is a significant concern that, notwithstanding legal protections in the *FPSLRA* protecting collective bargaining, the collective bargaining process in the federal public service is broken. The Preliminary Fryer Report indicated the problems as follows:

> The findings from our various data sources suggest that in the first 10 to 15 years of public service collective bargaining, participants were generally positive about it. However, with the passage of time and an increase in the extent of unilateral government interventions such as pay freezes and the suspension of bargaining and arbitration, the parties have become more pessimistic about the bargaining system's ability to resolve problems. The lack of trust associated with long periods of unilateral government action was probably the single most serious concern of union and management representatives alike.
>
> . . .
>
> The concern most frequently cited—by both sides—is the degree of power the government possesses in its dual role as employer and legislator. This power, which is more than any private sector employer possesses, has been used on many occasions and has taken such varied forms as the suspension of bargaining and arbitration, pay freezes, and the passing of back-to-work legislation.
>
> It is this imbalance of power which seems to be the root cause of much of the feeling of powerlessness and frustration described in

27 See Milla Sanes & John Schmitt, *Regulation of Public Sector Collective Bargaining in the States* (Washington, DC: Centre for Economic and Policy Research, 2014), online (pdf): https://cepr.net/documents/state-public-cb-2014-03.pdf, for a summary of the law as it stood in early 2014.

28 *Janus v American Federation of State, County, and Municipal Employees, Council 31*, 138 s Ct 2448 (2018).

> Chapter V. A related finding is that frequent legislative intervention has eroded confidence in the system and trust between the parties. Another, equally serious consequence is that the players in the public service labour-management system can become so used to government intervention that they lose the ability to work out problems for themselves. The imbalance of power also politicizes the system and has led some bargaining agents to attempt various types of direct political action.
>
> Frequent legislative intervention does have the positive consequence that politicians must take direct responsibility for the intervention themselves instead of handing it over to a labour relations board or some other form of administrative tribunal. But in our view, this potential benefit must be weighed against the many negative consequences of government intervention.[29]

The Preliminary Fryer Report was prepared in 2000. Since 2000, though, there have been a number of successful collective bargaining sessions, both with and without strike action. Collective bargaining—while not easy or without acrimony—has taken place. Collective agreements were also reached—with or without the influence of wage restraint legislation. Collective bargaining, in other words, is happening.

B. COMMENCEMENT OF COLLECTIVE BARGAINING: THE NOTICE TO BARGAIN AND ELECTION OF DISPUTE-RESOLUTION PROCESS

Collective bargaining commences after either party serves a "notice to bargain" on the other party.[30] The purpose of giving notice to bargain collectively is to trigger the statutory duty to bargain in good faith, or, as the Board has put it, "the commencement of collective bargaining must be viewed as the essential purpose of giving notice to bargain collectively."[31] There are no formal requirements concerning the form of the notice to bargain, although the Board has concluded that a letter asking to meet and discuss a wage rate issue was not a true notice to bargain (especially in light of a second, more formal notice to bargain

---

29 Preliminary Fryer Report, above note 19 at 41–42.

30 *FPSLRA*, s 105(1).

31 *Public Service Alliance of Canada and Staff of Non-Public Funds, Canadian Forces*, [1987] CPSSRB No 44 [*PSAC and Staff of Non-Public Funds*].

served a month later).[32] However, a party must meet three requirements before they can serve a notice to bargain.

The first requirement is that an employee organization must have been certified as the bargaining agent for the bargaining unit for whom the notice to bargain applies. The process for certification has already been canvassed in the previous chapter.

Second, the bargaining agent must have filed its process for dispute resolution (arbitration or conciliation/strike) with the Board, and the Board must have recorded that choice of dispute resolution.[33] This election is one of the more unique features of collective bargaining in the federal public service. Bargaining agents unilaterally decide whether bargaining disputes will ultimately be resolved by strike or by interest arbitration. As discussed in Chapter 2, the original intention was that bargaining disputes would be resolved by arbitration; strikes were seen as a necessary concession to postal unions, and it was expected that other bargaining agents would elect arbitration instead of strikes. This has not been the case. The largest bargaining agents have elected the strike method of dispute resolution instead of interest arbitration for most of their bargaining units. There are two main reasons for this decision. The first is ideological. Unions in Canada believe in the right to strike and have spent time, money, and effort in advocating for the right to strike in courts, at the International Labour Organization, and in public opinion. They did not do so just to decline to exercise that right. Second, as discussed below, there are limits on the subject matter of collective bargaining, but there are greater limits on the subject matter of arbitration awards. Bargaining agents that want to negotiate issues that cannot be arbitrated have little to no bargaining power when they do so; by contrast, a bargaining agent that can exercise a "strike weapon" has greater bargaining power over those issues.

All bargaining agents, once certified, must file their choice of process with the Board.[34] The Board has established a form for bargaining agents to fill out to establish their dispute-resolution process, and the form must be filed with the executive director of the Board.[35] Once

---

32 *Professional Institute of the Public Service of Canada and Canada (Treasury Board)*, [1978] CPSSRB No 2.

33 *FPSLRA*, s 105(1).

34 *Ibid*, s 103(1).

35 *Federal Public Sector Labour Relations Regulations*, SOR/2005-79, s 46 [*FPSLR Regulations*].

the Board has received the form, it records the process chosen by the bargaining unit. That process then governs the bargaining agent until it applies to change the process for dispute resolution. That change in process for dispute resolution becomes effective the next time a notice to bargain is given and then remains in force until changed again.[36]

Filing a form specifying the dispute-resolution system is a mandatory requirement before a bargaining agent can serve a notice to bargain. If the bargaining agent has not filed the form, then any purported notice to bargain has no legal effect—meaning in particular that the statutory freeze has not begun.[37]

There can be only one notice to bargain—served by either party—in each round of bargaining. Thus, if the employer serves a notice to bargain before the bargaining agent changes its election about the method of dispute resolution, then the parties will use the method in place at the time the employer served its notice to bargain.[38]

---

36 *FPSLRA*, s 104.

37 In *United Food and Commercial Workers Union and Staff of the Non-Public Funds, Canadian Forces (CFB Comox, British Columbia)*, [1986] CPSSRB No 18, the bargaining agent was certified on 24 July 1985, served a notice to bargain on 1 October 1985, and then filed its dispute-resolution election on 18 November 1985 (which was recorded by the Board two days later). On 30 November 1985, the employer terminated the employment of four employees. The bargaining agent alleged that these terminations were a violation of the statutory freeze in place once a notice to bargain has been served. The Board dismissed that complaint on the grounds that the statutory freeze had not yet begun because the notice to bargain was invalid. The Board concluded that filing the form specifying the dispute-resolution election was a "statutory precondition to the giving of written notice to bargain by either the bargaining agent or the employer." The fact that the bargaining agent had made its intention to commence bargaining clear on 1 October 1985 did not overcome this technical defect.

38 In *PSAC and Staff of Non-Public Funds,* above note 31, the bargaining agent had a collective agreement due to expire on 28 February 1987. It filed a form altering its dispute-resolution process from the conciliation to the arbitration route on 13 January 1987 and then served a notice to bargain on 14 January 1987. However, the employer had already served its notice to bargain on 31 December 1986—before the bargaining agent changed its method of dispute resolution. The bargaining agent argued that the change in dispute-resolution method was effective as soon as it filed its notice to bargain, so for this round of bargaining, the dispute-resolution method would be arbitration. The Board disagreed. The Board concluded that once either party had served a notice to bargain, both parties were under an obligation to meet and bargain in good faith, and, consequently, "a second notice is irrelevant." Therefore, the bargaining agent's change in dispute-resolution method would not become effective until the next round of bargaining: in this round of bargaining, it was stuck with conciliation.

All of the rules governing bargaining (under the dispute-resolution system in place) are also fixed when the notice to bargain is served. This rule became an issue when the government implemented a moratorium on arbitration as the method of dispute resolution in 1996. That moratorium was lifted for certain separate employers in 1999. In another case involving the Public Service Alliance of Canada (PSAC) and the Staff of the Public Funds of the Canadian Forces,[39] the bargaining agent served its notice to bargain during the moratorium on arbitration. Bargaining did not conclude quickly, and the moratorium was lifted while the parties were still bargaining. Therefore, the bargaining agent applied to have its bargaining dispute arbitrated, on the ground that it had never applied to the Board to have this dispute resolved by way of conciliation/strike. Since the statutory moratorium preventing arbitration had been lifted, the bargaining agent submitted that it was free to have the dispute referred to arbitration. The Board disagreed, stating that "the dispute resolution which is in effect, at the time notice to bargain is given, is the one applicable to parties for that round of bargaining."[40] Therefore, the bargaining agent had to follow the conciliation route because that was the route imposed on them when they served their notice to bargain.

Third, the parties must serve the notice to bargain during the appropriate time period. A party may serve a notice to bargain at any time if no collective agreement is in force and no request for arbitration has been made, or within four months before the expiry of a collective agreement or an arbitral award.[41] Thus, to guarantee that its dispute-

39 *Public Service Alliance of Canada v Canada (Canadian Forces—Staff of the Public Funds)*, [1999] CPSSRB No 130, application for judicial review dismissed [2000] FCJ No 419 (CA).

40 *Ibid* at para 18.

41 *FPSLRA*, s 105(2). This used to be three months under the *PSSRA*. One of the 2013 changes that was repealed in 2018 was to increase this period to twelve months.

resolution election will be valid for the next round of bargaining, a bargaining agent must file it at least four months prior to the scheduled expiry of a collective agreement.

As discussed previously, the government has—from time to time—enacted legislation creating a moratorium on collective bargaining. The *Public Sector Compensation Act*[42] (in place from 1991–98) extended the operation of "every compensation plan for employees."[43] Issues have arisen concerning the impact of that legislation on the ability of parties to serve notices to bargain. In *Canadian Association of Professional Radio Operators and Treasury Board*,[44] the bargaining agent attempted to serve a notice to bargain on 8 April 1992. When the employer changed its practice concerning holiday pay in 1995, the bargaining agent alleged that this change in practice constituted a violation of the statutory freeze in place after a notice to bargain has been served. The issue before the Board was whether the notice to bargain was ineffective because it was untimely. The bargaining agent argued that the *Public Sector Compensation Act* only extended the terms and conditions of employment, not the collective agreement itself; therefore, its notice to bargain was served within three months of the end of the collective agreement. The Board disagreed, concluding that the *Public Sector Compensation Act* extended the term of the collective agreement itself, not just the terms and conditions of employment. Therefore, the notice to bargain was untimely (as the collective agreement was not due to expire within three months when the notice was served), and the complaint about the statutory freeze was dismissed.[45]

When a bargaining agent has elected conciliation/strike as its method of dispute resolution, the parties are still free to agree to resolve their dispute without a strike. The parties may agree to have all or part of their collective agreement resolved by arbitration or other alternative dispute-resolution process;[46] the parties may also agree to be bound by

---

42 *Public Sector Compensation Act*, extended by the *Government Expenditures Restraint Act, 1993, No 2*, SC 1993, c 13, and the *Budget Implementation Act, 1994*, SC 1994, c 18.

43 *Public Sector Compensation Act*, s 5(1).

44 *Canadian Association of Professional Radio Operators and Treasury Board*, [1995] CPSSRB No 100.

45 The Board did mention that individual grievances filed about the employer's change in practice could proceed.

46 *FPSLRA*, s 182.

all or part of a public interest commission report (commonly referred to as "binding conciliation").[47]

C. OBLIGATION TO BARGAIN IN GOOD FAITH

Serving a notice to bargain triggers an obligation to bargain in good faith and make every reasonable effort to enter into a collective agreement.[48]

1) Basic Principles

The obligation in the *FPSLRA* to bargain in good faith and make every reasonable effort to enter into a collective agreement is similar for the Treasury Board, separate employers, and other employers in other jurisdictions in Canada.[49] Therefore, the Board has used jurisprudence from the private sector (in particular the Canada Industrial Relations Board and the Ontario Labour Relations Board) in establishing what does, and what does not, constitute good faith bargaining with a view to entering into a collective agreement.

The obligation to bargain has two facets. The parties must bargain in good faith, and they must also make every reasonable effort to enter into a collective agreement. Both components are equally important. The first is measured on a subjective standard, while the second is measured on an objective standard. This means that, in assessing the second component, the Board may look to comparable standards and practices followed by other employers. If the employer or bargaining agent makes proposals that are a significant departure from the accepted norms, then this indicates that they are not making every reasonable effort to enter into a collective agreement.[50]

---

47 *Ibid*, s 181. For a concise summary of the options available, see *Public Service Alliance of Canada v Canada (Attorney General)*, 2013 FC 918 at para 74.

48 *FPSLRA*, s 106.

49 *Public Service Alliance of Canada and Treasury Board*, [1991] CPSSRB No 230 at 5.

50 *Royal Oak Mines Inc v Canada (Labour Relations Board)*, [1996] 1 SCR 369 at paras 41–43 [*Royal Oak Mines*]. In that case, the employer's unwillingness to consider a clause permitting employees terminated for misconduct during a strike to have their dismissals heard by an arbitrator was so far from the established norm among Canadian employers that it was evidence that the employer was not making reasonable efforts to enter into a collective agreement.

The Ontario Labour Relations Board has stated the principle of good faith bargaining as follows:

> [B]oth parties are entitled to bargain hard for the agreement that they believe to be acceptable. This is so even if one of the parties has overwhelming strength at the bargaining table and is able to achieve most or all of its needs. The exercise of such raw bargaining power in good faith does not offend the bargaining duty imposed by the Act. . . .
>
> In order to make necessary but sensitive assessments of bargaining conduct the Board must assess the totality of a collective bargaining relationship. For example, the occurrence of flagrant employer unfair labour practices at the same time the parties are engaged in collective bargaining may belie an employer's claim that a negotiating position is merely hard bargaining with a trade union unwilling to accept its lack of negotiating "clout." Or patently unreasonable contract proposals lacking any semblance of business justification may suggest an employers' desire to embarrass the union and encourage its abandonment by the employees. The legislation requires the parties to make every reasonable effort to make a collective agreement, a duty which patently unreasonable proposals fly in the face of. On the other hand, this Board must exercise considerable restraint in intervening in negotiations between parties who are committed to reaching a collective agreement—a commitment which is more and more self-evident as parties proceed together beyond their first collective bargaining agreement. Too penetrating a review by this Board will only insert it as a third party in the bargaining arena to be tactically used by the negotiators, diverting their attention from the principal task at hand.[51]

Or, as the British Columbia Labour Relations Board has put it more bluntly:

> Collective bargaining is not a process carried on in accordance with the Marquess of Queensbury rules.[52]

When Jacob Finkelman and Shirley Goldenberg published their book on federal public service labour law in 1983, they could write that "so far there have been only three cases in which the [Public Service Staff

---

51 *United Steelworkers of America v Radio Shack*, 1979 CanLII 817 (ON LRB) at paras 66 and 69.

52 *Canadian Association of Industrial, Mechanical and Allied Workers and Noranda Metal Industries Limited* (1974), BCLRB Decision No 151/74.

Relations Board (PSSRB)] or its Chairperson expressed a view about the *nature* of the obligation to bargain in good faith."[53] Since that time, there have been several cases alleging a breach of that obligation. This has occurred notwithstanding that, for long periods of time since 1983, the federal government has imposed a statutory moratorium on collective bargaining and, by corollary, a moratorium on the obligation to bargain in good faith.[54] The Board has used these applications to enunciate a series of principles concerning the obligation to bargain in good faith and make every reasonable effort to enter into a collective agreement.

In those cases, the Board has adopted an approach to the general principles of the duty to bargain in good faith similar to that of other labour boards. In particular, in *Professional Institute of the Public Service of Canada v Treasury Board*,[55] the Board quoted from the decision in *Royal Oak Mines Inc v Canada (Labour Relations Board)* as well as other foundational good faith cases and applied those principles. The Board distinguished between "surface bargaining" and "hard bargaining." The Board also concluded that tabling a "take it or leave it" proposal is not bargaining in bad faith when negotiations were no longer fruitful and no further negotiations were scheduled, particularly when the employer's wage proposal was an increase from its earlier position and also corresponded with the employer dropping a number of its other objectives. The Board also recognized that an employer must explain its proposals—but that the employer had done so (in part by a public statement by the Treasury Board president). Finally, in the circumstances, giving the bargaining agent a "tight" timeline (roughly a week) to respond was not bad faith as it permitted the parties sufficient time for rational discussion. This case was unique in that the employer's wage proposal was about to be legislated into force. The employer was certainly engaging in "hard bargaining," but that is not necessarily bargaining in bad faith.

53 Finkelman & Goldenberg, above note 3 at 279 [emphasis in original].

54 See *Professional Institute of the Public Service of Canada and Treasury Board*, [1983] CPSSRB No 81, where the Board concluded that it lacked the jurisdiction to hear a complaint of bad faith bargaining during the currency of the *Public Sector Compensation Restraint Act*.

55 *Professional Institute of the Public Service of Canada v Treasury Board*, 2009 PSLRB 102, aff'd *Professional Institute of the Public Service of Canada v Canada (Attorney General)*, 2010 FCA 109.

Artificial Life and Artificial Immune Systems in Intelligent Computing

Special Session on Bio-oriented and Bio-inspired Information Systems

Special Session on Novel Applications of Knowledge Discovery on Bioinformatics

A Constrained Ant Colony Algorithm for Image Registration

Wen Peng, Ruofeng Tong, Guiping Qian, and Jinxiang Dong

State Key Laboratory of CAD & CG, Zhejiang University, Hangzhou 310027
pengwen@zju.edu.cn, trf@zju.edu.cn,
qianguiping@163.com, djx@zju.edu.cn

Abstract. Ant Colony optimization takes inspiration from the behavior of real ant colony to solve optimization problems. We attach some constraints to ant colony model and present a parallel constrained ant colony model to solve the image registration problem. The problem is represented by a directed graph so that the objective of the original problem becomes to find the shortest closed circuit on the graph under the problem-specific constraints. A number of artificial ants are distributed on the graph and communicate with one another through the pheromone trails which are a form of the long-term memory guiding the future exploration of the graph. The algorithm supports the parallel computation and facilitates quick convergence to the optimal solution. The performance of the proposed method as compared to those of the genetic-based approaches is very promising.

1 Introduction

Swarm intelligence research originates from work into the simulation of the emergence of collective intelligent behaviors of real ants. Ants are able to find good solutions to the shortest path problems between the nest and a food source by laying down, on their way back from the food source, a trail of an attracting substance – a pheromone. Based on the pheromone level communication, the shortest path is considered that with the greatest density of pheromone and the ants will tend to follow the path with more pheromone. Dorigo and his colleagues were the first to apply this idea to the traveling salesman problem [1]. This algorithm is referred to as ant colony algorithm (ACA). ACA has achieved widespread success in solving different optimization problems, such as the vehicle routing problem [2], the machine tool tardiness problem [3] and the multiple objective JIT sequencing problem [4].

Image registration is to find a correspondence function mapping coordinates from a source image to coordinates of homologous points in a target image. In clinical applications, it can be used to match images taken from the same patient over a period of time. Generally, image registration methods can be divided into intensity-based and landmark-based methods. Intensity-based methods [5, 6] find the deformation function by optimizing some criterion function that incorporates a measure of image similarity and can produce more precise registration results because of using the information of the whole images. Landmark-based methods [7, 8, 9, 10] involve extraction of landmarks that need to be matched. By interpolating discrete landmarks, a dense mapping for the whole image can be obtained quickly.

D.-S. Huang, K. Li, and G.W. Irwin (Eds.): ICIC 2006, LNBI 4115, pp. 1 – 11, 2006.

In this paper, a constrained ant colony model for solving the image registration problem is developed. Our image registration combines intensity and landmark information and exploits the advantages of both classes of information. Ant colony algorithm, which is constrained and modified to deal with image registration, can make algorithm amenable to parallel implementations, compared with other optimal approaches, for its distinct feature -- distributed computation. The proposed parallel algorithm can obtain the optimal solution in a reasonably shorter period of time.

2 The Constrained Ant Colony

2.1 Original Ant Colony

The ant colony algorithms have been introduced with Dorigo's Ph.D thesis. They are based on the principle that by using very simple communication mechanisms, an ant group is able to find the shortest path between any two points. During their trips a chemical trail (pheromone) is left on the ground. The role of this trail is to guide the other ants towards the target point. For one ant, the path is chosen according to the quantity of pheromone. Furthermore, this chemical substance has a decreasing action over time, and the quantity left by one ant depends on the amount of food found and the number of ants using this trail. As illustrated in Fig. 1, when facing an obstacle, there is an equal probability for every ant to choose the left or right path. As the left trail is shorter than the right one and so requires less travel time, it will end up with higher level of pheromone. More ants take the left path, higher pheromone trail is.

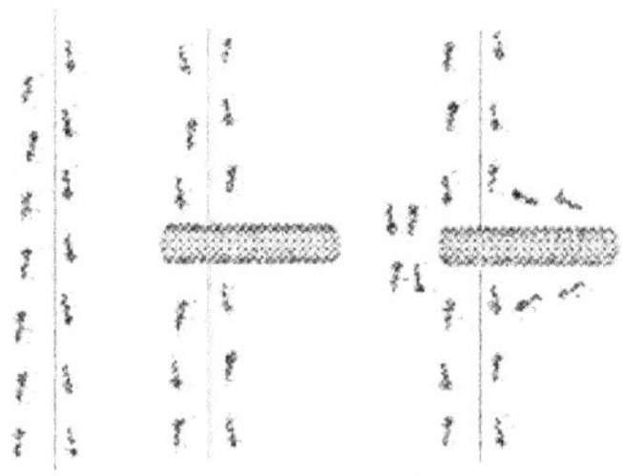

Fig. 1. Ants face an obstacle. When facing an obstacle, there is an equal probability for every ant to choose the left or right path. As the left trail is shorter than the right one and so requires less travel time, it will end up with higher level of pheromone. More ants take the left path, higher pheromone trail is.

The general principles for the ant colony simulation of real ant behavior are as follows.

(1) *Initialization.* The initialization of the AC includes two parts: the problem graph representation and the initial ant distribution. First, the underlying problem should be represented in terms of a graph, G = <N,E>, where N denotes the set of nodes, and E the set of edges. The graph is connected, but not necessarily complete,

such that the feasible solutions to the original problem correspond to paths on the graph which satisfy problem-domain constraints. Second, a number of ants are arbitrarily placed on the nodes chosen randomly. Then each of the distributed ants will perform a tour on the graph by constructing a path according to the node transition rule described next.

(2) *Node transition rule.* The ants move from node to node based on a node transition rule. According to the problem-domain constraints, some nodes could be marked as inaccessible for a walking ant. The node transition rule is probabilistic. For the kth ant on node i, the selection of the next node j to follow is according to the node transition probability:

$$p_{ij}^{k} = \begin{cases} \dfrac{(\tau_{ij})^{\alpha}(\eta_{ij})^{\beta}}{\sum\limits_{h \notin tabu_k} (\tau_{ih})^{\alpha}(\eta_{ih})^{\beta}} & if \;\; j \notin tabu_k \\ 0 & otherwise \end{cases} \tag{1}$$

where τ_{ij} is the intensity of pheromone laid on edge (i,j), η_{ij} is the value of visibility of edge (i,j), α and β are control parameters, and $tabu_k$ means the set of currently inaccessible nodes for the *k*th ant according to the problem-domain constraints. The intensity of pheromone laid on edge (i,j) reflecting the previous experience of the ants about this edge is shared memory which provides indirect communication between the ants.

(3) *Pheromone updating rule.* The ant keeps walking through edges to different nodes by iteratively applying the node transition rule until a solution to the original problem is constructed. We define that a cycle of the AC algorithm is completed when every ant has constructed a solution. At the end of each cycle, the intensity of pheromone trails on each edge is updated by the pheromone updating rule:

$$\tau_{ij} \leftarrow \rho\tau_{ij} + \sum_{k=1}^{m} \Delta\tau_{ij}^{k} \tag{2}$$

where $\rho \in (0,1)$ is the persistence rate of previous trails, $\Delta\tau_{ij}^{k}$ is the amount of pheromone laid edge (i,j) by the *k*th ant at the current cycle, and *m* is the number of distributed ants. In a real ant system, shorter paths will retain more quantities of pheromone; analogously, in the AC, the paths corresponding to fitter solutions should receive more pheromone quantities and become more attractive in the next cycle. Hence, if we define L_k, the total length of the *k*th ant in a cycle, as the fitness value of the solution, then $\Delta\tau_{ij}^{k}$ can be given by

$$\Delta\tau_{ij}^{k} = \begin{cases} \dfrac{Q}{L_k} & if \;\; edge\,(i,j)\; is\; traversed\; by \\ & the\; kth\; ant\; at\; this\; cycle \\ 0 & otherwise \end{cases} \tag{3}$$

where Q is a constant.

(4) *Stopping criterion.* The stopping criterion of the AC algorithm could be the maximal number of running cycles or the CPU time limit.

2.2 Constrained Ant Colony

For solving image registration, we modify and attach some constraints to the original ant colony model. In original ant colony model, the underlying problem should be represented in terms of a graph G = <N,E>, which is connected, but not necessarily complete, as shown in Fig. 2 (a). Now, following constraints are added to G for reducing the search space. 1) All the nodes construct a loop. 2) The adjacent node has no less than one edge. 3) The nonadjacent node has no edge. After applying these rules, an example of the graph with constraints is shown in Fig. 2 (b). When ant colony algorithm works on the graph with constraints, we call it constrained ant colony.

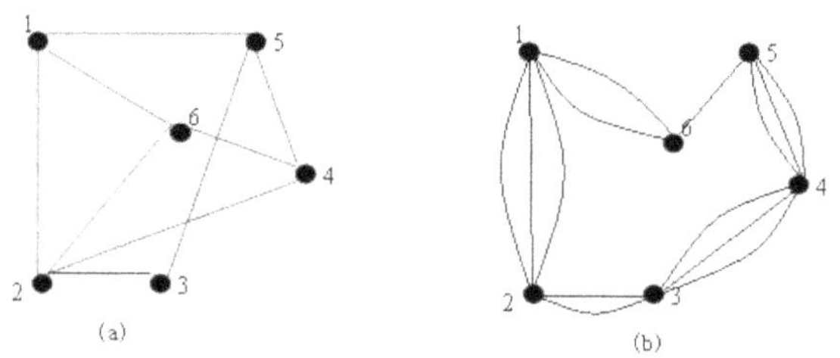

Fig. 2. The original graph and constrained graph. The constrained graph must satisfy following constraints. G. 1) All the nodes Ni construct a loop. 2) The joint node has no less than one edge. 3) The un-joined node has no edge.

3 Image Registration Problem

In this section, we introduce the structure of image registration problem and give some definitions of the notations. The goal of image registration algorithm is to determine a transformation function based on the landmarks from the source image $f_S(\mathbf{i})$ to the target image $f_T(\mathbf{i})$, where $\mathbf{i} \in \mathbf{I} \subset \mathbb{R}^2$, and $\mathbf{I}$ is a 2D discrete interval representing the set of all pixel coordinates in the image. We suppose that the source image is a geometrically deformed version of the target image. That is to say that the points with the same coordinate $\mathbf{x}$ in the target image $f_T(\mathbf{x})$ and in the warped source image $f_w(\mathbf{x})=f_S^c(\mathbf{g}(\mathbf{x}))$ should correspond. Here, f^c is a continuous version of the image and $\mathbf{g}(\mathbf{x}) : \mathbb{R}^2 \to \mathbb{R}^2$ is a deformation function to be identified.

3.1 Image Representation

To interpolate the images accurately, the image is represented as a continuous version using uniform B-splines [11]:

$$f^{c}(\mathbf{x}) = \sum_{\mathbf{i}\in\mathbf{I}\subset\mathbb{Z}^2} \mathbf{b}_{\mathrm{i}}\beta_3(\mathbf{x}-\mathbf{i}) \tag{4}$$

where β_3 is a tensor product of B-splines of degree 3, that is $\beta_3(\mathbf{x}) = \prod_{\mathbf{k}=1}^{2} \beta_3(\mathrm{x}_{\mathrm{k}})$, with $\mathbf{x} = (\mathrm{x}_1, \mathrm{x}_2)$.

3.2 Transformation Function

We choose the Locally Constrained Deformation (LCD) [12], shown in Eq. (5), as transformation function

$$\mathbf{g}(\mathbf{x}) = \mathbf{x} + \sum_{\mathrm{i}=1}^{\mathrm{N}} \alpha_{\mathrm{i}} \rho_{\mathrm{LCD}}\left(\frac{\| \mathbf{x}-\mathbf{p}_{\mathrm{i}} \|}{\mathbf{r}_{\mathrm{i}}}\right)$$
$$\rho_{\mathrm{LCD}}(\mathbf{r}) = \begin{cases} (1-\mathbf{r}^2)^3 & 0 \le \mathbf{r} \le 1 \\ 0 & 1 < \mathbf{r} \end{cases} \tag{5}$$

and it must fulfill the following constraints:

$$\mathbf{g}(\mathbf{p}_{\mathrm{i}}) = \mathbf{q}_{\mathrm{i}} \qquad \mathbf{i} = 1 \cdots \mathbf{N} \tag{6}$$

where α_{i} is the coefficients, $\mathrm{p}_{\mathrm{i}} \in \mathbb{R}^2$ $\mathrm{i} = 1\ldots\mathrm{N}$ constitute a given set of landmark points in the source image, $\mathrm{q}_{\mathrm{i}} \in \mathbb{R}^2$ $\mathrm{i} = 1\ldots\mathrm{N}$ are the corresponding landmark points in the target image and **N** is the number of the landmark points.

3.3 Cost Function

The two images f_T and f_W will not be identical because the assumption that there is a geometrical mapping between the two images is not necessarily correct. Therefore, we define the solution to our registration problem as the result of the minimization $\mathbf{g} = \arg\min_{\mathbf{g}\in\mathbf{G}} \mathbf{E}(\mathbf{g})$, where **G** is the space of all admissible deformation functions **g**. We choose the sum of squared difference (SSD) criterion as cost function because it is fast to evaluate and yields a smooth criterion surface. The form of SSD is

$$E = \sum_{i\in I} (f_{\mathrm{S}}^{c}(\mathbf{g}(\boldsymbol{i})) - f_{\mathrm{T}}^{c}(\boldsymbol{i}))^2 \tag{7}$$

3.4 Optimization Strategy

To minimize the criterion **E** in (7), some local iterative algorithms have been cast into the framework [13], but the computation of the derivate is required. Therefore, the constrained ant colony algorithm is introduced to minimize the criterion and the details are shown in section 4.

4 Constrained Ant Colony for Image Registration

Through the analysis of Eq. (5) and Eq. (6), the transformation function $\mathbf{g}(\mathbf{x})$ can be adjusted by varying the value of $\mathbf{r}_i$. Thus the optimal solution of $\mathbf{r}_i$ can be obtained to minimize the SSD of two images using constrained ant colony.

4.1 Graph Representation

To apply ant colony, the underlying problem should be represented in terms of a directed graph, G=<N,E>, which can avoid the ants walking backward. Apparently, for image registration problem, each landmark point p_i should be represented as a node of the graph, N=P. We represent the edge E as $\overrightarrow{(p_i, p_j, r_k)}$, where r is the action radius of landmark point p_j, as shown in Eq. (5). $ssd\overrightarrow{(p_i, p_j, r_k)}$ is the SSD of the edge $\overrightarrow{(p_i, p_j, r_k)}$ and is defined as E in Eq. (7) with only one landmark point p_j and action radius is r_k. In addition, there are many edges between two nodes in our graph, which differs from AC. Now, the problem of image registration is equivalent to finding a closed circuit, which satisfies the minimal SSD, on the directed graph.

4.2 Node Transition Rule

The node transition rule is a probabilistic one determined by the pheromone intensity τ_{ijk} and the visibility value η_{ijk} of the corresponding edge. In the proposed method, τ_{ijk} is equally initialized to any small constant positive value, and is gradually updated at the end of each cycle according to the average quality of the solution that involves this edge. On the other hand, the value of η_{ijk} is determined by a greedy heuristic method, which encourages the ants to walk to the minimal SSD edge. This can be accomplished by setting $\eta_{ijk} = 1/ssd\overrightarrow{(p_i, p_j, r_k)}$.

We now define the transition probability from node i to node j through directed edge $\overrightarrow{(p_i, p_j, r_k)}$ as

$$p_{ijk}(t) = \begin{cases} \dfrac{[\tau_{ijk}(t)]^{\alpha}[\eta_{ijk}]^{\beta}}{\sum\limits_{allowed\_list}[\tau_{ijk}(t)]^{\alpha}[\eta_{ijk}]^{\beta}} & if\ j \in allowed\_list \\ 0 & otherwise \end{cases} \tag{8}$$

where *allowed_list* are the accessible nodes by walking ants, and the means of other symbols are same to the Eq. (1).

4.3 Pheromone Updating Rule

The intensity of pheromone trails of an edge is updated at the end of each cycle by the average quality of the solutions that traverse along this edge. We simply apply and modify Eqs. (2) and (3) to update pheromone intensity.

$$\tau_{ijk} \leftarrow \rho . \tau_{ijk} + \sum_{s=1}^{m} \Delta \tau_{ijk}^{s} \tag{9}$$

$$\Delta \tau_{ijk}^{s} = \begin{cases} \dfrac{Q}{SSD_s} & \text{if the sth ant walks } \overrightarrow{(p_i, p_j, r_k)} \\ 0 & \text{otherwise} \end{cases} \tag{10}$$

where *SSDs* is the SSD of the *sth* ant's registration result at current cycle.

4.4 Constrained Ant Colony for Image Registration

According to the given definitions as above, the image registration based on constrained ant colony is described as following.

Input:
m: the number of ants.
MAX_CYCLE: the maximal number of running cycles.

1: *Construct the directed graph G=<N,E> as described in Section 4.1. Set NC=1 (NC is the cycles counter),* $\tau_{ijk}(t) = c$ *(* c *is constant),* $SSD_{global\_best} = \infty$ *(* SSD_{global_best} *saves the minimal SSD of the strip). Compute* η_{ijk} *on every edge* $\overrightarrow{(p_i, p_j, r_k)}$.

2: *For every ant do*
Select a starting node.
Repeat
Move to next node according to the node transition rule using Eq. (8).
until a closed tour is completed.
//a closed tours is completed when the ant arrives at the starting node again.

3: *Compute registration results and find out the minimal SSD among the m tours obtained at step2, say SSDcurrent_best.*

4: *If SSDcurrent_best < SSDglobal_best, then SSDglobal_best = SSDcurrent_best.*

5: *For every directed edge* $\overrightarrow{(p_i, p_j, r_k)}$ *do*
Update the pheromone intensity using Eqs. (9) and (10).

6: *If (NC = MAX_CYCLE), then output SSDglobal_best and strop;*
otherwise, NC = NC + 1 and goto step2.

5 Parallel Ant Colony

To solve efficiently large optimization problems, a parallel model of ant colony has been developed. The programming style used is a synchronous master/workers paradigm. The master initializes all kinds of data as stated in section 4.4 step1, and then sends the graph information including the trail density τ_{ijk} and the visibility η_{ijk} to workers. With the graph information, the worker takes charge of searching for a tour composed of the edge and completing image registration. The parallel algorithm works as follows Fig. 3. Each worker returns the SSD of registration result and the tour visited to the master, which later updates the intensity of trail on the edge and controls the flow of the algorithm. By this way all the workers can implement parallel packing by sharing the information from the master.

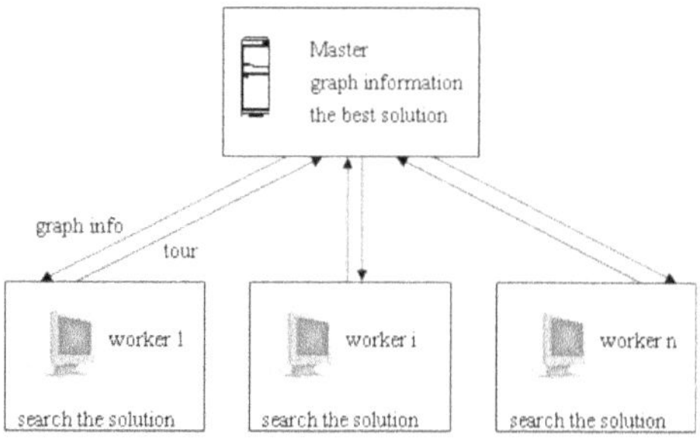

Fig. 3. Synchronous master/workers model for parallel ant colony. The master initializes all kinds of data and the worker takes charge of searching for a tour composed of the edge and completing image registration.

6 Experimental Results

The proposed algorithm has been programmed in VC++ language, and run in Windows 2000 Professional. According to Ref. [12], the action radius of the landmark point is constrained as:

$$r_i \geq 1.71 \| q_i - p_i \| \tag{11}$$

which should be satisfied in the constrained graph. Furthermore, every landmark point has limited action scope and it is constrained as $r_i \leq 15 \| q_i - p_i \|$. Thus between the node pi and pj, there are $NUM_j = \lfloor (15-1.71) * \| q_j - p_j \| / \Delta \rfloor$ edges, that is to say $\overrightarrow{(p_i, p_j, r_k)}$ $k = 1, 2, ..., NUM_j$, where Δ is used to control the accuracy of the algorithm and set $\Delta = 0.5$. In our implementation, $\alpha = 1.0$, $\beta = 2.0$, $\rho = 0.9$ and *MAX_CYCLE=200*.

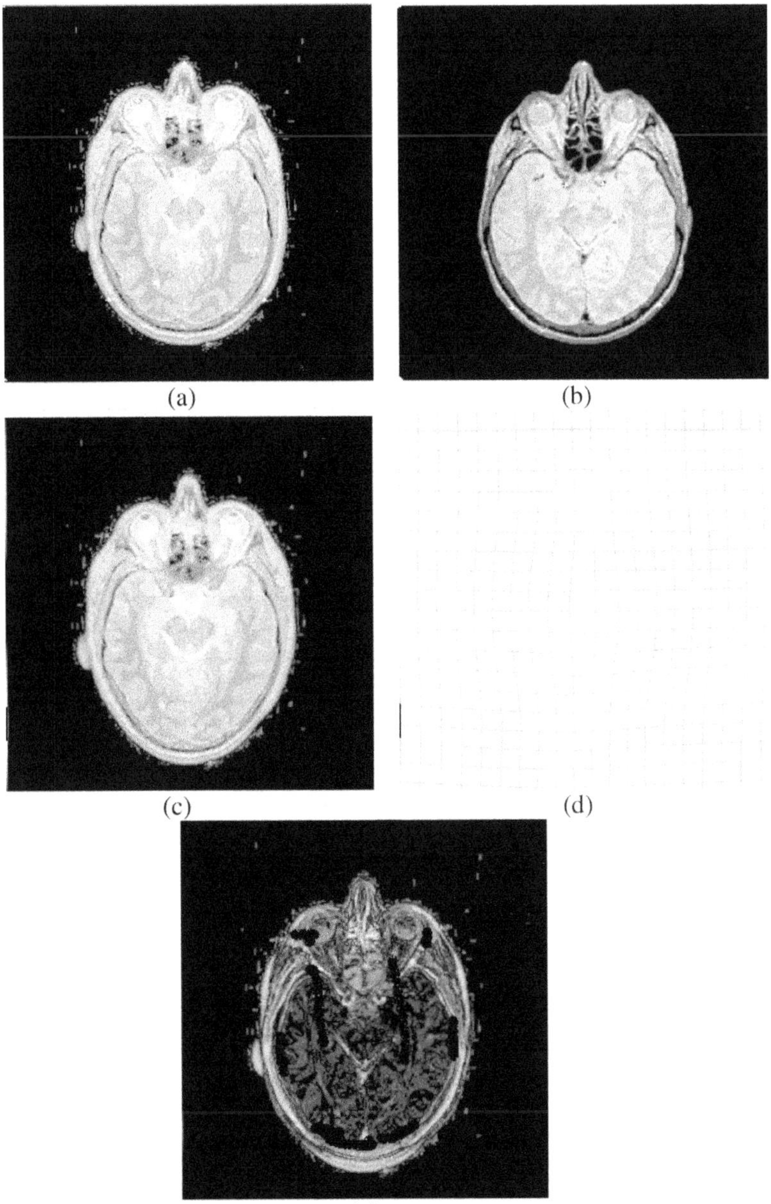

Fig. 4. Registration results. (a) source image; (b) target image; (c) registration result; (d) the underlying grid of (c); (e) difference between (b) and (c).

Fig. 4 shows an experimental result based on the presented algorithm. In the source image Fig. 4(a) and the target image Fig. 4(b), we interactively selected 10 pairs of point-landmarks. The registration result is shown in Fig. 4(c). To assess the form of the deformation, we have applied the algorithm to a regular grid and the result can be seen in Fig. 4(d). The obvious influence of the deformation is demonstrated in Fig. 4(e) where the reference image is subtracted from the registration result.

In addition, we compare the efficiency of our algorithm to the genetic algorithm. With variable number of the landmark points, we complete four examples whose results are listed in Table 1. In our algorithm, 10 workers are used to search the solutions. It is indicated from the results that our algorithm can converge more quickly to the better solutions because of the parallel implementation.

Table 1. Results from the different algorithms

Examples		Genetic algorithm	Ant colony algorithm
Example 1: 10 points	Time (minute)	10.0	2.9
Example 2: 15 points	Time (minute)	14.3	4.1
Example 3: 20 points	Time (minute)	17.6	6.0
Example 4: 25 points	Time (minute)	19.1	7.7

7 Conclusion

In this paper we have developed a powerful and robust algorithm for image registration, which bases on the constrained ant colony model. The proposed algorithm supports parallel computation and facilitates quick convergence to the optimal solution. The experimental result demonstrates that our algorithm can search the solution space more effectively and obtain the optimal solution in a reasonably shorter period of time.

Acknowledgements

The project is supported by the Natural Science Foundation (No.M603129) of Zhejiang Province, China.

References

1. Dorigo, M.: Optimization, Learning and Natural Algorithms. Ph.D. Thesis, Italy (1992)
2. Bullnheimer, B., Hartl, R. F., Strauss, C.: Applying the Ant System to the Vehicle Routing Problem. In the Second Metaheuristics International Conference, France (1997)
3. Bauer, A., Bullnheimer, B. Hartl, RF: An Ant Colony Optimization Approach for the Single Machine Tool Tardiness Problem. Proceeding of the Congress on Evolutionary Computation (1999) 1445-1450

4. McMullen, P.R.: An Ant Colony Optimization Approach to Addressing a JIT Sequencing Problem with Multiple Objectives. Artificial Intelligence (2001) 309-317
5. Kybic, J., Unser, M.: Fast Parametric Elastic Image Registration. IEEE Transaction on Image Processing, Volume 12, Issue 11, (2003) 1427-1442
6. Xie, Z., Farin, G. E.: Image Registration Using Hierarchical B-splines. IEEE Transaction on Visualization and Computer Graphics, Volume 10, Issue 1, (2004) 85-94
7. Hyunjin P., Peyton H. B., Kristy K. B., Charles R. M.: Adaptive Registration Using Local Information Measures. Medical Image Analysis, Volume 8, Issue 4, (2004) 465-473
8. Can, A., Stewart, C. V: A Feature-based, Robust, Hierarchical Algorithm for Registration Pairs of Images of the Curved Human Retina. IEEE Transaction on Pattern Analysis and Machine Intelligence, Volome 24, NO. 3 (2002)
9. Pennec X., Aysche N., Thirion J. P.: Landmark-based Registration Using Feature Identified Through Differential Geometry. Handbook of Medical Imaging, Academic Press (2000) 499-513
10. Chui, H., Anand, R.: A New Point Matching Algorithm for Non-rigid Registration. Computer Vision and Image Understanding, Volume 89, Issue 2-3, (2003) 114-141
11. Xie, Z., Farin G. E: Image Registration Using Hierarchical B-splines. IEEE Transaction on Visualization and Computer Graphics, Volume 10, Issue 1, (2004) 85-94
12. Pan J., Zheng J., Yang X.: Locally Constrained Deformation for Digital Images, Journal of Computer-Aided Design & Computer Graphics, Volume 14, NO. 5 (2002)
13. Kybic J., Thevenaz P., Nirkko A., Unser M.: Unwarping of Unidirectionally Distorted EPI images, IEEE Transaction on Medical Image, Volume 19, (2000) 80-93

A Novel ACO Algorithm with Adaptive Parameter

Han Huang[1], Xiaowei Yang[2], Zhifeng Hao[1,3], and Ruichu Cai[2]

[1] College of Computer Science and Engineering, South China University of Technology, Guangzhou 510640, P.R. China
bssthh@Springer.com
[2] College of Mathematical Science, South China University of Technology, Guangzhou 510640, P.R. China
[3] Nation Mobile Communications Research Laboratory Southeast University, Nanjing, 210096, China

Abstract. ACO has been proved to be one of the best performing algorithms for NP-hard problems as TSP. Many strategies for ACO have been studied, but little theoretical work has been done on ACO's parameters α and β, which control the relative weight of pheromone trail and heuristic value. This paper describes the importance and functioning of α and β, and draws a conclusion that a fixed β may not enable ACO to use both heuristic and pheromone information for solution when $\alpha = 1$. Later, following the analysis, an adaptive β strategy is designed for improvement. Finally, a new ACO called adaptive weight ant colony system (AWACS) with the adaptive β and $\alpha = 1$ is introduced, and proved to be more effective and steady than traditional ACS through the experiment based on TSPLIB test.

1 Introduction

ACO was first proposed by M. Dorigo and his colleagues as a multi-agent approach to deal with difficult combinatorial optimization problems such as TSP [1]. Since then, a number of applications to the NP-hard problems have shown the effectiveness of ACO [1]. Up till now, Ant Colony System (ACS) [2] and MAX-MIN Ant System (MMAS) [3] are so successful and classical that their strategies such as pheromone global-local update and Maximum-Minimum of pheromone are widely used in recent research [1].

At present, the study on the speed of convergence and the parameter selection is a hot topic [4].As for the ACO's convergence, W. J. Gutjahr [4-6], T. Stützle [7], M. Dorigo[7-9], A. Fahmy [10], and S. Fidanova [11, 12] have done a lot of work. For its parameter setting, M. Dorigo and L.M. Gambardella presented a formula for the optimal number of ants m based on the value of q_0 and ρ [2]. Watanabe and Matsui proposed an adaptive control mechanism of the parameter candidate sets based on the pheromone concentrations [13]. Pilat and White put forward the ACSGA-TSP algorithm [14] with an adaptive evolutionary parameters β, ρ, q_0 and gave the experimental values of these parameters for some TSP problems. A. C., Zecchin etc [15] applied their work of parametric study to water distribution system optimization.

D.-S. Huang, K. Li, and G.W. Irwin (Eds.): ICIC 2006, LNBI 4115, pp. 12–21, 2006.

The performance of ACS is mainly based on the cooperative work of artificial ants. According to pheromone trail and heuristic value, the ants choose components to form the solutions at each iteration. The value of parameters α and β , $\alpha > 0$ and $\beta > 0$, determines the relative importance of pheromone value and heuristic information [2, 9,15]. However, there is few theoretical research on the function of α and β . The experimental study of the various ACO algorithms for the TSP has identified parameter settings that result in good performance: α and β are set to 1 and [2, 5] respectively [8]. The values of α and β are usually set by experiment [3,16-18] in the interval [0, 5].

In this paper, firstly, the theoretical justification of α and β is explained. Secondly, following the justification, an adaptive β strategy is designed to optimize the searching process of ACO algorithm. Then, a new algorithm, called adaptive weight ant colony system (AWACS), is proposed with the adaptive β strategy to improve ACS and its convergence can be proved. In order to test its performance, the numerical experiments on TSPLIB [19] are given, and show AWACS can perform much better than ACS in TSP instances.

2 The Function of the Parameters α and β

In ACO algorithms, like AS [1], ACS [2], MMAS [3] and AS-AR [11], the state transition rule of the artificial ants is given as follows:

$$P_{gs}^{\ k}(t) = \begin{cases} \dfrac{[\tau_{gs}(t)]^{\alpha}[\eta_{gs}]^{\beta}}{\sum\limits_{r \in J_k(g)} [\tau_{gr}(t)]^{\alpha}[\eta_{gr}]^{\beta}} & if \quad s \in J_k(g) \\ 0 & otherwise \end{cases} . \tag{1}$$

Where:

$P^k_{\ gs}$ is the probability with which the ant k chooses to move from city g to city s in iteration t;

τ is the pheromone;

$\eta = 1/d$ is the reciprocal of distance d_{gs} ($\eta > 0$);

$J_k(g)$ is the set of cities not visited yet when ant k at city g;

α and β are the parameters that control the relative weight of pheromone trail and heuristic value.

Given $a, b \in J_k(g)$, if $P_{ga}^{\ k}(t) > P_{gb}^{\ k}(t)$, which means that city a may be chosen by the ant k as the next city to city g with higher probability than city b, then α and β satisfies the following formula:

$$P_{ga}^{\ k}(t) > P_{gb}^{\ k}(t) \Leftrightarrow [\tau_{ga}(t)]^{\alpha}[\eta_{ga}]^{\beta} > [\tau_{gb}(t)]^{\alpha}[\eta_{gb}]^{\beta}. \tag{2}$$

When $\tau_{ga}(t)=\tau_{gb}(t)$ or $\eta_{ga}=\eta_{gb}$, for $\forall\alpha,\beta>0$, the formula above holds, so we have: $P_{ga}^{\ k}(t)>P_{gb}^{\ k}(t)\Leftrightarrow\begin{cases}\eta_{ga}>\eta_{gb} & \tau_{ga}=\tau_{gb}\\ \tau_{ga}>\tau_{gb} & \eta_{ga}=\eta_{gb}\end{cases}$.

However, when
$\tau_{ga}(t)\neq\tau_{gb}(t), \tau_{ga}(t)>0, \tau_{gb}(t)>0$ and $\eta_{ga}\neq\eta_{gb}\,(\eta_{ga}(t)>0, \eta_{gb}(t)>0)$,
one has

$$P_{ga}^{\ k}(t) > P_{gb}^{\ k}(t) \Leftrightarrow [\tau_{ga}(t)]^{\alpha}[\eta_{ga}]^{\beta} > [\tau_{gb}(t)]^{\alpha}[\eta_{gb}]^{\beta}$$

$$\Leftrightarrow \alpha\log[\tau_{ga}(t)]+\beta\log[\eta_{ga}] > \alpha\log[\tau_{gb}(t)]+\beta\log[\eta_{gb}]$$

$$\Leftrightarrow \log\tau_{ga}(t)-\log\tau_{gb}(t) > \frac{\beta}{\alpha}(\log\eta_{gb}-\log\eta_{ga})$$

$$\Leftrightarrow\begin{cases}\dfrac{\beta}{\alpha}<\dfrac{\log\tau_{ga}(t)-\log\tau_{gb}(t)}{\log\eta_{gb}-\log\eta_{ga}} & \eta_{gb}>\eta_{ga}\\[2ex] \dfrac{\beta}{\alpha}>\dfrac{\log\tau_{ga}(t)-\log\tau_{gb}(t)}{\log\eta_{gb}-\log\eta_{ga}} & \eta_{gb}<\eta_{ga}\end{cases}.$$

Particularly, when $\alpha=1$, which exists in ACO algorithms like ACS, a conclusion can be drawn:

$$P_{ga}^{\ k}(t) > P_{gb}^{\ k}(t) \Leftrightarrow \begin{cases}\beta<\dfrac{\log\tau_{ga}(t)-\log\tau_{gb}(t)}{\log\eta_{gb}-\log\eta_{ga}} & \eta_{gb}>\eta_{ga}\\[2ex] \beta>\dfrac{\log\tau_{ga}(t)-\log\tau_{gb}(t)}{\log\eta_{gb}-\log\eta_{ga}} & \eta_{gb}<\eta_{ga}\end{cases}. \tag{3}$$

From the analysis above, one can see that the values of the parameters α and β can directly impact the path choosing process. They determine the probability order of the candidate paths, and make artificial ants select some paths with higher probability meeting rule (3). In ACS, β determines the relative importance of pheromone versus distance [2]. In ACO algorithms, a higher value of β directs the ants to the paths with the more optimistic heuristic values [17]. According to Formula (3), it can also hold that the higher β is, the more heuristic value $\eta=1/d$ is regarded. The relation between β ($\alpha=1$) and the state transition rule is used to design an ACO algorithm with adaptive β in the next section.

3 Adaptive Weight Colony Ant System

For the sake of convenience, some symbols about the pheromone trail are defined as follows:

$\tau_g^{\max}(t) = \max_{i\in J_k(g)}\{\tau_{gi}(t)\}$ is the highest pheromone trail among all the cities feasible to be selected as next stop to city g.

$\tau_g^{\min}(t) = \min_{i\in J_k(g)}\{\tau_{gi}(t)\}$ is the lowest one.

And $\tau_g^{ave}(t) = |J_k(g)|^{-1} \sum_{i\in J_k(g)} \tau_{gi}(t)$ is the average pheromone trail, where $|J_k(g)|$ is the number of elements in the set $J_k(g)$.

$\eta_g^{\max} = \max_{i\in J_k(g)}\{d_{gi}^{-1}\}$ is the highest heuristic value of elements in the set $J_k(g)$.

$\eta_g^{\min} = \min_{i\in J_k(g)}\{d_{gi}^{-1}\}$ stands for the lowest heuristic value.

And $\eta_g^{ave} = |J_k(g)|^{-1} \sum_{i\in J_k(g)} \eta_{gi} = |J_k(g)|^{-1} \sum_{i\in J_k(g)} d_{gi}^{-1}$ is the average heuristic value.

Let $\alpha = 1$, two cases are discussed in the following:

① $[\tau_g^{\max}(t)]^\alpha[\eta_g^{\min}]^\beta > [\tau_g^{ave}(t)]^\alpha[\eta_g^{\max}]^\beta$.

It means that the ants will select the paths with the maximum pheromone trail with a very high probability ACS.

According to Formula (3), one has $\beta < \dfrac{\log\tau_g^{\max}(t) - \log\tau_g^{ave}(t)}{\log\eta_g^{\max} - \log\eta_g^{\min}} = M_1(g,t)$, because it is obvious that $\eta_g^{\max} > \eta_g^{\min}$ holds in TSPLIB problems.

② $[\tau_g^{\min}(t)]^\alpha[\eta_g^{\max}]^\beta > [\tau_g^{\max}(t)]^\alpha[\eta_g^{ave}]^\beta$.

It means that the ants will select the paths with the maximum heuristic value with a very high probability in ACS.

It is obvious that $\beta > \dfrac{\log\tau_g^{\min}(t) - \log\tau_g^{\max}(t)}{\log\eta_g^{ave} - \log\eta_g^{\max}} = M_2(g,t)$ holds, when $\eta_g^{\max} > \eta_g^{ave}$ and $\tau_g^{\min}(t) > 0$.

According to the analysis of case ① and ②, ACO may work as a non-heuristic searching when $\beta < M_1(g,t)$, and as a greedy searching without using pheromone trail when $\beta > M_2(g,t)$.

Therefore, a fixed β may not enable ACO to find optimal solution by using both heuristic and pheromone information.

However, the process of ACO will not be in the extreme as non-heuristic or greedy searching when $M_1(g,t) \le \beta \le M_2(g,t)$.

So a new adaptive parameter β is designed as follows:

$$\alpha = 1,\ \beta(g,t) = \frac{\log \tau_g^{ave}(t) - \log \tau_g^{\max}(t)}{\log \eta_g^{ave} - \log \eta_g^{\max}} \ (\tau_g^{\min}(t) > 0). \tag{4}$$

where $M_1(g,t) \le \beta(g,t) \le M_2(g,t)$ can be proved.

Based on the adaptive parameter $\beta(g,t)$ strategy shown in Formula (4), a novel ACO algorithm, which is called adaptive weight ant colony system (AWACS) can be described as follows.

```
Initialize  /* β is chosen in [0, 5] randomly,
q0 = 0.6 */
Loop  /* at this level each loop is called iteration */
  Each ant is positioned on a starting node.
  Loop /* at this level each loop is called a step */
    Each ant applies a state transition rule to
    incrementally build a solution following Formula
(1)
    and a local pheromone updating rule in Ref [2]
  Until all ants have built a complete solution
  A global pheromone updating rule is applied in Ref
[2]
  β(g,t) is updated  ( g = 1,...,n ) following Formula (4)
Until End_condition
```

The proof of its convergence ($g = 1,...,n$) is the same as the one in Ref. [7]. According to the work of Ref. [7], it still holds that $\tau_g^{\min}(t) > 0$ and $\tau_g^{\max}(t) < +\infty$ ($g = 1,...,n$) when the adaptive parameter $\beta(g,t)$ strategy in Formula (4) is applied. Then, AWACS can be proved to find the optimal solution with probability one following the conclusion given by T. Stützle and M. Dorigo [7-8].

4 Numerical Result

In this section, a comparison of the performance of ACS and AWACS is given based on the experiments for some symmetric TSP instances. There is no local search strategy introduced to ACS and AWACS in the present experiment like

ACS-3-opt. In our experiments, the parameters are set as follows: $m=10$, $\alpha=\rho=0.1$, $\tau_0=(nL_{nn})^{-1}$. q_0 is set $q_0=0.9$ in ACS, and $q_0=0.6$ in AWACS , respectively. The initial value of β in AWACS is a random figure changing in the interval $[1,5]$. The initial feasible solutions of TSP are generated in the way from Ref [2].

The experiments on the first 10 TSP problems, where the distances between cities are measured by integer numbers, have been executed on a PC with an Intel Ceslon (r) III 1.0GHZ Processor and 256M DDR Memory, and the results are shown in Table 1. The experiments on the next 10 problems, where the distances between cities are measured by real numbers, are executed on another PC with an Intel Pentium III 333MHZ Processor and 256M SDR Memory, and the results are listed in Table 2. It should be noted that every instance is computed 10 times. The ACS and AWACS algorithms are both programmed in Visual C++6.0 for Windows System. They would stop when no better solution could be found in 500 iterations, which is considered as a virtual convergence of the algorithms. The datasets can be found in TSPLIB: http://www.iwr.uni-heidelberg.de/iwr/comopt/soft/TSPLIB95/TSPLIB.html.

Table 1. Comparison I of the results obtained by ACS and AWACS

Instance	Optimal	Best (ACS)	Best (AWACS)	Average (ACS)	Average (AWACS)	T_{avg}(s) (ACS)	T_{avg} (s) (AWACS)	Best β (ACS)
st70	654	657	657	675.9	675.5	16.9	27.4	4
rat99	unknown	1188	1188	1211.7	1199.4	53.2	59.7	3
pr107	unknown	44539	44398	44906.3	44783.9	39.5	55.4	4
pr124	unknown	59205	59067	59819.9	59646.6	59.2	42.3	4
eil101	612	614	613	634.6	631.4	22.4	76.3	5
rd100	7858	7909	7861	8100.4	8066.2	59.5	54.1	3
eil51	415	415	415	423.9	423.7	6.7	7.8	3
lin105	14345	14376	14354	14509.3	14465.6	73.7	50.8	4, 5
kroD100	21249	21486	21265	21893	21628.2	25.8	60	5
kroC100	20703	20703	20703	21165.3	20914.9	29.5	67.7	4

Table 2. Comparison II of the results obtained by ACS and AWACS

Instance	Optimal	Best (ACS)	Best (AWACS)	Average (ACS)	Average (AWACS)	T_{avg}(s) (ACS)	T_{avg} (s) (AWACS)	Best β (ACS)
kroA100	21282	21285.44	21285.44	21345.78	21286.33	51.3	51.8	2, 3
kroE100	22068	22078.66	22068.75	22206.62	22117.16	56.3	64.5	5
berlin52	7542	7544.36	7544.36	7544.36	7544.36	8.7	9.8	5
kroB150	26130	26127.35	26127.71	26332.75	26214.10	177.8	164.8	5
ch150	6528	6530.90	6530.90	6594.94	6559.66	373.6	118.1	2
kroB100	22141	22139.07	22139.07	22335.72	22177.47	55.5	68.6	4
kroA150	26524	26618.33	26524.86	26809.08	26685.73	204.5	242.9	5
u159	42080	42075.67	42075.67	42472.04	42168.54	356.7	80.2	1
pr76	108159	108159.4	108159.4	108610.6	108581.7	50.5	42.8	1
pr136	96772	96870.89	96785.86	97854.16	97236.61	344.3	158.9	1,4,5

Table 3. Comparison of standard deviations of the tour lengths obtained by AWACS and ACS

Instance \Standard deviation	AWACS	ACS $\beta=1$	ACS $\beta=2$	ACS $\beta=3$	ACS $\beta=4$	ACS $\beta=5$
kroA100	8.49	460.04	338.84	183.55	625.81	447.03
kroE100	123.82	327.01	467.75	529.73	330.12	366.49
berlin52	0.00	376.98	376.19	357.76	548.34	0.00
kroB150	221.98	447.98	652.57	821.48	664.54	486.91
ch150	54.50	114.76	153.71	109.36	171.66	54.81
kroB100	132.37	554.43	579.73	1091.25	558.86	233.01
kroA150	384.39	522.81	942.11	974.79	640.34	432.72
u159	623.16	726.99	3531.45	2458.43	1509.09	1661.63
pr76	1158.43	1180.56	5058.92	2088.68	1677.73	1411.15
pr136	1300.78	2386.53	5303.40	4572.69	3304.40	2173.27

As shown in the above tables, there might be something like precision and time cost in the result of our experiments different from those in the former research because of the different program tools, systems and computing machines. Another possible reason is that the distances between cities in the first 10 instances are measured by integer numbers. But ACS and AWACS are running in the same setting, so the result remains helpful to compare the performance of these two algorithms.

From Table 1-2, it could be seen that AWACS performs better than ACS with the fixed β. The shortest lengths and the average lengths obtained by AWACS are shorter than those found by ACS in all of the TSP instances. As Table 3 shows, it can be concluded that the standard deviations of the tour lengths obtained by AWACS are smaller than those of ACS with the fixed β. Therefore, we can conclude that AWACS is proved to be more effective and steady than ACS.

ACS has to change the best integer value of parameter β with respect to different instances in the experiments. AWACS can avoid the difficulty about how to choose the experimental value of β, because its adaptive strategy can be considered as a function trying to find the best setting for each path search via meeting the request of Formula 4. Though, the time cost t_{avg} of AWACS is more than ACS in some case, it is less than the sum of time ACS costs with $\beta = 1, 2, 3, 4, 5$ in all of the instances. As a result, the adaptive setting can save much time in choosing the experimental β. Item t_{avg} of AWACS is not less than ACS in all of the instances because it needs to compute the value of β n (number of cities) times in each iteration. However, the adaptive function of AWACS is feasible to use because of its acceptable time cost.

5 Discussions and Conclusion

In this paper, the function and relation of parameters α and β are discussed and proved to be able to influence the city selection in ACO directly. Following this analysis, a new algorithm (AWACS) with adaptive β and $\alpha = 1$ is proposed to improve the function of ACS. Its advantage that AWACS can keep using both heuristic and pheromone information for solution and avoid falling to the extremes as non-heuristic or greedy searching, is based on the adaptive β. Furthermore, AWACS can be proved to meet the precondition for convergence of ACO. In the test instances, AWACS also performs much better than ACS.

With the help of tuning methodologies, it is possible to find the best performing parameter settings in a very reasonable computational time. And the argument given in this paper that the adaptive setting can save time instead of choosing the β value experimentally is convincing as the numerical results show.

It is uncertain theoretically that the adaptive setting of AWACS is the best. Further study is suggested to explore the better management for the optimal setting of α β and other parameters, which will be very helpful in the application of ACO algorithms.

Acknowledgements

This work has been supported by the National Natural Science Foundation of China (60433020, 10471045), Social Science Research Foundation of MOE (2005-241), Natural Science Foundation of Guangdong Province (970472, 000463, 04020079), open foundation of Nation Mobile Communications Research Laboratory Southeast University (No.N200605), Excellent Young Teachers Program of Ministry of Education of China, Fok Ying Tong Education Foundation (91005), Guangdong Key Laboratory of Computer Network Foundation (CN200403), Key Technology Research and Development Program of Guangdong Province (2005B10101010), Key Technology Research and Development Program of Tianhe District (051G041) and Natural Science Foundation of South China University of Technology (E512199, D76010).

References

1. Dorigo, M., Caro, G.D., Gambardella, L.M.: Ant Algorithms for Discrete Optimization. Massachusetts Institute of Technology, Artificial Life 5 (1999) 137-172
2. Dorigo, M., Gambardella, L.M.: Ant Colony System: A Cooperative Learning Approah to the Travelling Salesman Problem. IEEE Transactions on Evolutionary Computation, 1 (1), (1997) 53-66
3. Stützle, T., Hoos, H.H.: MAX-MIN Ant System. Future Gener. Comput. Syst., Vol.16, No. 8, (2000) 889–914
4. Gutjahr, W.J.: Ageneralized Convergence Result for the Graph-Based Ant System Metaheuristic. Tech. Report 99-09, Department of Statistics and Decision Support Systems, University of Vienna, Austria (1999)
5. Gutjahr, W.J.: Agraph-Based Ant System and Its Convergence. Future Gen. Comput. Systems 16 (9) (2000) 873–888
6. Gutjahr, W.J.: ACO Algorithms with Guaranteed Convergence to the Optimal Solution. Information Processing Letters 82 (2002) 145–153
7. Stützle, T., Dorigo M.: A Short Convergence Proof for a Class of Ant Colony Optimization Algorithms. IEEE Transactions on Evolutionary Computation 6 (4) (2002) 358-365
8. Dorigo, M., Stützle, T.: Ant Colony Optimization. MIT Press, Cambridge, MA (2004)
9. Dorigo, M., Blum, C.: Ant colony optimization theory: A survey. Theoretical Computer Science 344 (2005) 243–278
10. Badr, A., Fahmy, A.: A Proof of Convergence for Ant Algorithms. Information Sciences 160 (2004) 267 –279
11. Fidanova, S.: ACO Algorithm with Additional Reinforcement. M. Dorigo et al. (Eds.): ANTS 2002, LNCS 2463 (2002) 292-293
12. Fidanova, S.: Convergence Proof for a Monte Carlo Method for Combinatorial Optimization Problems. M. Bubak et al. (Eds.):ICCS 2004, LNCS 3039 (2004) 523-530
13. Watanabe, I., Matsui, S.: Improving the Performance of ACO Algorithms by Adaptive Control of Candidate Set. Evolutionary Computation, 2003. CEC '03. The 2003 Congress on 2 (8-12) (2003) 1355-1362
14. Pilat, M.L., White, T.: Using Genetic Algorithms to Optimize ACS-TSP. M. Dorigo et al. (Eds.):ANTS 2002, LNCS 2463, (2002) 282-287

15. Zecchin, A.C., Simpson, A.R., Maier, H.R., Nixon, J.B.: Parametric Study for an Ant Algorithm Applied to Water Distribution System Optimization. IEEE Transactions on evolutionary computation, Vol. 9 No. 2 April (2005)
16. Dorigo, M., Gambardella L.M.: Ant Colonies for the Traveling Salesman Problem. BioSystems 43 (1997) 73-81
17. Sim, K.M., Sun, W.H.: Ant Colony Optimization for Routing and Load-Balancing: Survey and New Directions. IEEE Transactions on Systems, Man, and Cybernetics—Part A: Systems and Humans Vol. 33 No. 5 September (2003)
18. Blum, C., Dorigo, M.: Search Bias in Ant Colony Optimization: On the Role of Competition-Balanced Systems. IEEE Transactions on evolutionary computation, Vol. 9 No. 2 April (2005)
19. Reinelt, G.: TSPLIB. A Traveling Salesman Problem Library, ORSA Journal on Computing. 3(4) (1991) 376-384

Study of Parametric Relation in Ant Colony Optimization Approach to Traveling Salesman Problem

Xuyao Luo[1,3], Fang Yu[2], and Jun Zhang[1,3,*]

[1] Department of Computer Science, SUN Yat-sen University, P.R. China
[2] Department of Computer Science and Technology, Jinan University, P.R. China
[3] Guangdong Key Lab of Information Security
junzhang@ieee.org

Abstract. Presetting control parameters of algorithms are important to ant colony optimization (ACO). This paper presents an investigation into the relationship of algorithms performance and the different control parameter settings. Two tour building methods are used in this paper including the max probability selection and the roulette wheel selection. Four parameters are used, which are two control parameters of transition probability α and β, pheromone decrease factor ρ, and proportion factor q_0 in building methods. By simulated result analysis, the parameter selection rule will be given.

1 Introduction

The ant colony optimization emerged as a new heuristic algorithm in the early 1990s [1],[2] is based on the real acting of ant colony. The first ACO algorithm, which is called ant system, and many other ACO algorithms have been tested on combinatorial optimization problems. Like some heuristics derive form nature (HDNs) such as genetic algorithm (GA)[3],[4],[5] and neural network [6],[7],[8],[9], the ACO algorithm can reach state-of-the-art performance when approach to some combinatorial optimization problems (especially to discrete problems), for example, traveling salesman problem (TSP) [10],[11],[12], job shop scheduling problem(JSP)[13],[14], [15]and constraint satisfaction problem[16].

Despite its great performance, by now, the ACO algorithm still has some inherent problems which have not been solved properly. Like other HDNs, the performance of ACO lies on some preset control parameters of algorithms, so selecting the proper setting of control parameters is a crucial problem for the efficiency of ACO algorithm. Some effort had been made to the parametric study, for example, Marco Dorigo *et al* [17] had shown some proper value of a part of ACO parameters and A. C. Zecchin *et al* [18] had done parametric study of ACO when applied it to the water distribution system. However, our work is different from theirs. At first, two tour building methods are used in our algorithm, which are the max probability selection and the roulette wheel selection. And the proper setting of proportion factor of

* Corresponding author: This work was supported in part by NSF of China Project No.60573066; NSF of Guangdong Project No. 5003346 and Guangdong Key Lab of Information Security.

D.-S. Huang, K. Li, and G.W. Irwin (Eds.): ICIC 2006, LNBI 4115, pp. 22–32, 2006.

building methods which determines the probabilities of two tour building methods is researched in this paper. Second, the parameters in ACO are not investigated separately, they are assumed to be correlated. And after the results analysis, some deeper relationships of parameters will be shown.

By researching the relationship of parameters, we found an effective parameter setting rule to solve combination optimization problem and would develop new ACO algorithms which are more adaptive and competitive.

2 The Ant Colony Optimization Algorithm

2.1 Behavior of Real Ants

By use of pheromone, real ants in the nature can find the shortest path from their nest to the food source rather than use their vision. At the beginning, all ants explore the area around their nest randomly for food. As soon as a food source is found, the ant who finds the source will deposits chemical pheromone along the path as well as carries some food back when it returns to their nest. Ants not only deposit pheromone after them on the ground but also follow the pheromone which was previously deposited by other ants or itself. Depending on the quantity of pheromone on the path, ants choose different paths to go. In Fig.1, a process during which ants explore the shortest path between their nest and a food source is shown. In Fig.1, there are a colony nest (N), a food source (S), and an obstacle (X--Y). From N to S, two paths of unequal length are explored. It is assumed that the path NYS takes two time steps ($2\Delta t$) to traverse while the NXS only takes a single time step ($1\Delta t$) and there is no any other path from N to S except the two. At time t=0 (Fig.1 (a)), eight ants are setting out to find food (S) from their nest (N). Because they will select the two paths randomly, it is assumed that each path will be selected by four ants. At time t=$1\Delta t$ (Fig.1 (b)), the ants who select the path NXS have acquired the food and begin to return home while other four ants are still on their way to S. As there is some pheromone on path SXN, the probability of utilizing the path SXN by the ants that get the food is higher, three ants select SXN and one selects SYN. At time t=$2\Delta t$ (Fig.1 (c)), three ants that traverse SXN arrive at the nest and one ant that selects SYN is only half way along the path. Meanwhile, the four ants who traverse the NYS just reach the food source. At that time, the path NXS has more pheromone than NYS as the NXS has been traversed for seven times, while the NYS has been traversed for five times. So, there are three ants the path NXS and one ant selects the path NYS. At t=$3\Delta t$ (Fig.1 (d)), all ants return home. From Fig.1 (d), the shorter path NXS has more pheromone deposited than the longer path NYS (pheromone density of the path is represented by the darkness).

At last, the path NXS has a higher probability of being chosen by ants for it has more pheromone deposited than that of the path NYS.

In addition, the pheromone trails on every path will decay with time. If a path has not been added pheromone for a certain time, its pheromone density will reduce to zero. The decay of pheromone quality will also help ants to find the shorter path quicker for the pheromone on the longer paths receive less pheromone and their faster decay of pheromone will make it less attractive to ants.

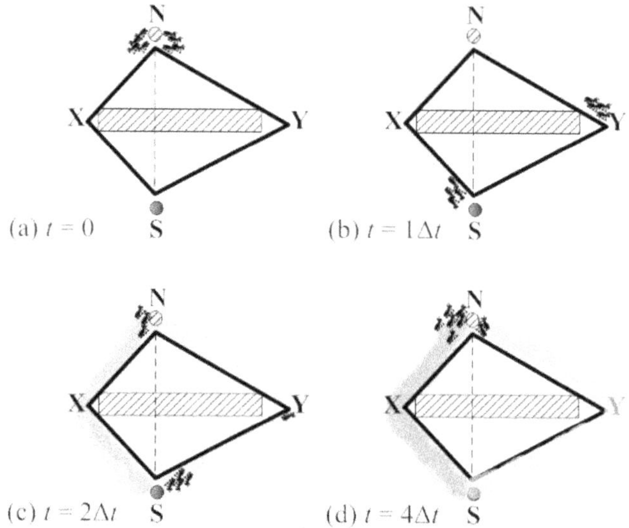

Fig. 1. Example of pheromone evolution in the nature. The real ants can find the shorter path.

2.2 ACO Algorithm Rules

In the past, there are many different ACO algorithms applied to TSP, the ACO algorithm used in this paper is the ant colony system (ACS). The rules of our ACO algorithm are shown in this section.

In our work, the parametric study is done on TSP, and a model of TSP is shown here: Let *Cites* = {*0, 1, 2..., n*} be a set of cities, *Edges* = {(*0, 1*), (*0, 2*),...,(*n, n-1*)} be the set of edges and to each edge (*f, t*)∈ *Edges*, there be a cost measure *C*(*f, t*) = *C*(*t, f*). The problem of TSP is to find a minimum cost closed tour which visits each city once.

Artificial ants are used in ACO to solve the TSP, they will select the edges to construct the TSP tour depending on the pheromone deposited on them, and meanwhile change the value of pheromone on the edges. In addition, the number of cities is denoted as m and the number of ants is denoted as n.

Random Proportion Rule. The transition probability (Pk (i, j)) with which the ant k in city i chooses to go to city j is given by the random proportion rule:

$$p^{k}_{(i,j)} = \begin{cases} \dfrac{[\tau_{ij}]^{\alpha} \cdot [\eta_{ij}]^{\beta}}{\sum\limits_{l \notin tabu[k]} [\tau_{il}]^{\alpha} \cdot [\eta_{il}]^{\beta}}, & if \quad j \notin tabu[k] \\ 0, & otherwise \end{cases} \tag{1}$$

where τ_{ij} is the pheromone of the edge between city i and city j, η_{ij} is ($1/D_{ij}$),the inverse of D_{ij} the distance between city i and city j. It is introduced that the artificial ants prefer the edges which are shorter and have more pheromone deposited.

State Transition Rule. In the ACO algorithm, each ant builds tour by repeatedly applying the state transition rule. An ant positioned on city i will choose next city j to move depending on the rule:

$$j = \begin{cases} \arg\max_{j \notin tabu[k]} \{[\tau_{ij}]^{\alpha} [\eta_{ij}]^{\beta}\}, & if \quad q < q_0 \\ J, & otherwise \end{cases} . \tag{2}$$

where the q_0 is a parameter, q is a random number uniformly distributed in [0, 1]. If $q \leq q_0$ the city with max value of transition probability will be selected to go, otherwise city J will be chosen. J is a random variable selected by applying roulette wheel method to transition probabilities distribution (1).

Local Update Rule. During the tour building process, ants visit edges and change the pheromone amount of them by using the local update rule:

$$\tau_{ij} \leftarrow (1-\rho)\cdot\tau_{ij} + \rho\cdot\tau_0, \qquad (\tau_0 = (n\cdot L_{nn})^{-1}) . \tag{3}$$

where ρ ($0<\rho<1$) is a parameter called pheromone decrease factor, τ_0 is the value of pheromone initialized to all edges at the beginning of algorithm. L_{nn} is the length of best tour obtained by Greedy algorithm.

*Global Update Rule.*After all ants have completed their tours, global update will be performed:

$$\tau_{ij} \leftarrow (1-\rho)\cdot\tau_{ij} + \rho\cdot\Delta\tau . \tag{4}$$

where

$$\Delta\tau_{(i,j)} = \begin{cases} (L_{T\_best})^{-1} & if \quad edge\ (i,j) \in T\_best \\ 0, & otherwise \end{cases} . \tag{5}$$

It is essential to note that the ρ ($0<\rho<1$) used in (3) and (4) is very the same algorithm parameter, say, pheromone decrease factor and L_{T_best} is the length of the global best tour *T*_best. Only the pheromone on edges belong to the global best tour is reinforced in the process.

2.3 ACO Algorithm Parameters

Here a summary of the ACO algorithm parameters which are tested in this paper is shown.

1) Decision Policy Control Parameters, α and β.
2) Pheromone Decay Factor, ρ.
3) Proportion Factor of Building Methods, q_0.

In addition, in this paper the number of artificial ants is not taken into account, in fact, we set m=10(m is the number of artificial ants) in all experiments according to the optimal number of ants in [10].

A rule of setting parameters will be proposed by researching the different performances in different parameter settings in next section.

3 An Analysis of Optimization Results

At the beginning of this section, it is necessary to reintroduce the two inherent questions of ACO which we intend to solve. First one, how to select the proper setting of parameters when using ACO algorithm? We only discuss the proper value of α, β, ρ which are used in the algorithm above. And the second, when two or more building tour methods are adopted, how to choose the best one? As two methods, say, max probability selection and roulette wheel selection are applied in our algorithm, and the value of factor q_0 and (1- q_0) indicates the probabilities of applying the two methods. The problem is researched by analyzing the performances of different values of factor q_0. In addition, 10 artificial ants are used in the algorithm.

3.1 Combination of α and β

Like some other heuristics, the parameter settings of ACO play a key role on the performance of algorithm. However, there always have so many parameters in the ACO algorithm to deal with. Naturally, we must choose which parameter should be managed first when an ACO algorithm is used. Four parameters are discussed in this

Table 1. Feasible set of combinations of α and β in Oliver_30 (a 30 cities TSP instance). ● : Good combinations. ◍ : Poor combinations. ○: Bad combinations. The algorithm runs 10 times for each set of parameters.

β \ α	0.0	0.5	1.0	1.5	2.0	2.5	3.0	3.5	4.0	4.5	5.0
0	○	◍	◍	◍	○	○	○	○	○	○	○
1	○	●	●	●	◍	◍	○	○	○	○	○
2	○	●	●	●	◍	◍	○	○	○	○	○
3	○	●	●	●	◍	◍	○	○	○	○	○
4	○	●	●	●	●	◍	◍	◍	○	○	○
5	○	●	●	●	●	●	◍	◍	◍	○	○

paper as known as α, β, ρ and q_0. As shown in section 2.2, α and β are used in the random proportion rule, q_0 is the factor of the state transition rule while parameter ρ is used in both the local update rule and the global update rule. In this paper, α and β are researched first for the random proportion rule has higher priority than other rules and must be treated first in the algorithm.

Table 2. Feasible set of combinations of α and β in eli51 (a 51 cities TSP instance). ● : Good combinations. ◍ : Poor combinations. ○: Bad combinations. The algorithm runs 10 times for each set of parameters.

β \ α	0.0	0.5	1.0	1.5	2.0	2.5	3.0	3.5	4.0
0	○	○	◍	◍	○	○	○	○	○
1	○	◍	●	●	◍	◍	○	○	○
2	○	◍	●	●	◍	◍	○	○	○
3	○	●	●	●	●	◍	◍	○	○
4	○	●	●	●	●	◍	◍	◍	○
5	○	●	●	●	●	●	◍	◍	◍

Table 3. Feasible set of combinations of α and β in korA100 (a 100 cities TSP problem). ● : Good combinations. ◎ : Poor combinations. ○: Bad combinations. The algorithm runs 10 times for each set of parameters.

β \ α	0.0	0.5	1.0	1.5	2.0	2.5	3.0	3.5	4.0
0	○	○	○	○	○	○	○	○	○
1	○	◎	●	●	●	◎	○	○	○
2	○	◎	●	●	●	◎	○	○	○
3	○	◎	●	●	●	◎	○	○	○
4	○	◎	●	●	●	◎	◎	◎	○
5	○	●	●	●	●	●	◎	◎	◎

As introduced previously, α and β determine the relative importance of pheromone intensity and desirability respectively, the two parameters are studied together. In our experiment, M_c means the max number of cycles in a single iteration. Different combinations of α and β are investigated with different values of ρ and q_0, M_c =1000 and the algorithm runs 10 times with each set of parameters. As the result is shown in Table.1, in Oliver_30 instance, the best solution can only be found in certain set of combinations of α and β. All combinations of α and β can be certified in three classes:

a) Good combinations: ACO algorithm finds the global best tour easily in most settings of parameter ρ and q_0. These combinations are therefore used in the following experiments and they are represented by the symbol ● in Table.1. In addition, the length of global best tour of Oliver_30 obtained by our algorithm is 424.87.

b) Poor combinations: Only in very small selection range of ρ and q_0, the algorithm can find the global best tour in 1000 cycles. In Table.1, these poor combinations are represented by the symbol: ◎.

c) Bad combinations: The global best solution can not find the very good solution in any setting of other parameters. It is shown in Table.1 that the algorithm has a very bad performance for high value of α.

And similar experiments were done in other TSP instances, and these results are presented in Table 2 and Table 3.

It is represented in the results of the experiments that a high value of α is harmful to obtain the optical solution and selecting proper combinations of α and β seems to be the first step to find the global best solution in the TSP.

3.2 Setting Rules of ρ

The pheromone decrease factor ρ controls the decay of the pheromone on edges. As it results in the graduate decrease of pheromone on paths which are not regularly traversed, the probability of choosing a better path will grow, and it allows the new, better information to guide the search as well. However, the selection to proper value of ρ is a hard work, for in different parameter settings, the proper value varies in a large scale. An example of the change is shown in Table 4. Different value of ρ results in different algorithm performance. Performance measures for each setting of parameters is averaged over 10 runs (α = *1.0*, β=*5.0 and* M_c= *1000*). The value of *H_n* indicates the number of runs in which the algorithm obtains the global optimization with the tour length of 424.87.

Table 4. Algorithm performance with different values of ρ in Oliver_30

ρ	*H_n* (*q0*=0.3)	*H_n* (*q0*=0.6)	*H_n* (*q0*=0.9)
0.05	9	10	8
0.10	10	10	8
0.20	8	5	7
0.50	1	0	0
0.99	0	0	0

A summary of $\rho(0<\rho<1)$ can derive from the results above and *Global/Local Update Rule*, when $\rho \to 1$, great amounts of pheromone are evaporated in each building step and meanwhile the algorithm can hardly get the global best tour, however, when $\rho \to 0$, the condition is the opposite, the speed of pheromone evaporation becomes slower, and the algorithm has more chance to obtain the global best tour. As shown in Table 4, lower value of ρ results in lower probability of being rolling in local optimization and in this case the algorithm always can find the optimal tour. However, algorithm performances with the same ρ setting are different when they have different value of q_0. At last, we must keep an eye on parameter q_0 during selecting proper value of ρ.

3.3 Setting Rules of q_0

Two building selection methods (max probability selection and roulette wheel selection) were adopted in the algorithm. It has been introduced previously that the value of factor q_0 and $(1- q_0)$ indicates the probabilities of applying the two methods in the ACO algorithm. The algorithm performance of an example with different value of q_0 is shown in Fig.2.

It is illustrated in Fig.2 that the performance of applying two methods is better when α=1.0, β=2.0 and ρ=0.10. In addition, the length of global best tour of Oliver_30 obtained by the algorithm is 424.87.

When q_0=0.0, the algorithm only uses the roulette wheel method to build tour. The tour length varies without tending toward a certain value (in other words, without a converging process) is shown in Fig.2 (a). The maximum probability method is the unique building tour method in Fig.2 (c), however, the global best tour is not obtained in this situation. In fact, the algorithm is rolling in local optimization. In Fig.2 (b), two building methods are applied at the same time, and the algorithm finds the best known tour during a convergence process. However, with different value of q_0, the transformations of tour length are different.

The similar experiments were done in other TSP instances, for example, the instance att48, a 48 cities TSP problem, and in Table 5 more detail about difference between algorithm performances with different values of q_0 is shown, where α=1.0, β=2.0 and ρ=0.10 and *M_g* is the min generation in which the algorithm gets the best tour of the iteration *T_iter* (not the global best).

As it is shown in Fig.2, and Table 5, the performance of applying single method in the algorithm is worse than applying both methods at the same time, and the selection of proper value of q_0 is significant to the performance of ACO.

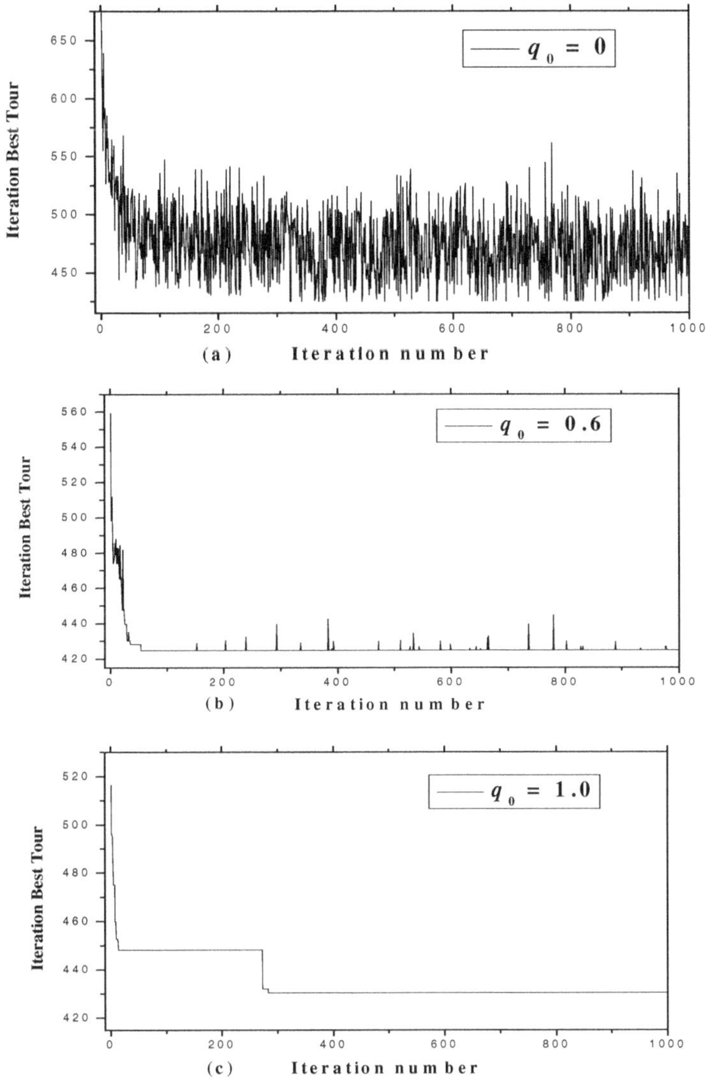

Fig. 2. The algorithm performance in Oliver_30 with different value of q0 when α=1.0, β=2.0 and ρ=0.10. Fig.2 (a) shows the optimization performance when the algorithm only used the roulette wheel method to build tour, Fig.2 (c) shows the performance when only the maximum probability method was used, while in Fig.2 (b) both method were used in the algorithm.

Assuming that there are some relations between q_0 and other parameters, we investigate the ACO behavior on Oliver_30 for different combinations of q_0 and other three parameters. Beside the episode to ρ, it is discovered that the β is more influential to the selection of q_0. Results are shown in Fig.3, which are obtained by running the algorithm 100 times with M_c=1000 for each setting of the parameters.

Table 5. Different performances with different values of q_0, when α=1.0, β=2.0 and ρ=0.10。The results are averaged over 10 runs

	Oliver_30			att48		
	q_0=0	q_0=0.6	q_0=1.0	q_0=0	q_0=0.6	q_0=1.0
Best tour length	424.87	424.87	428.32	33600.56	33538.34	33695.50
M_g	322	57	295	350	105	170

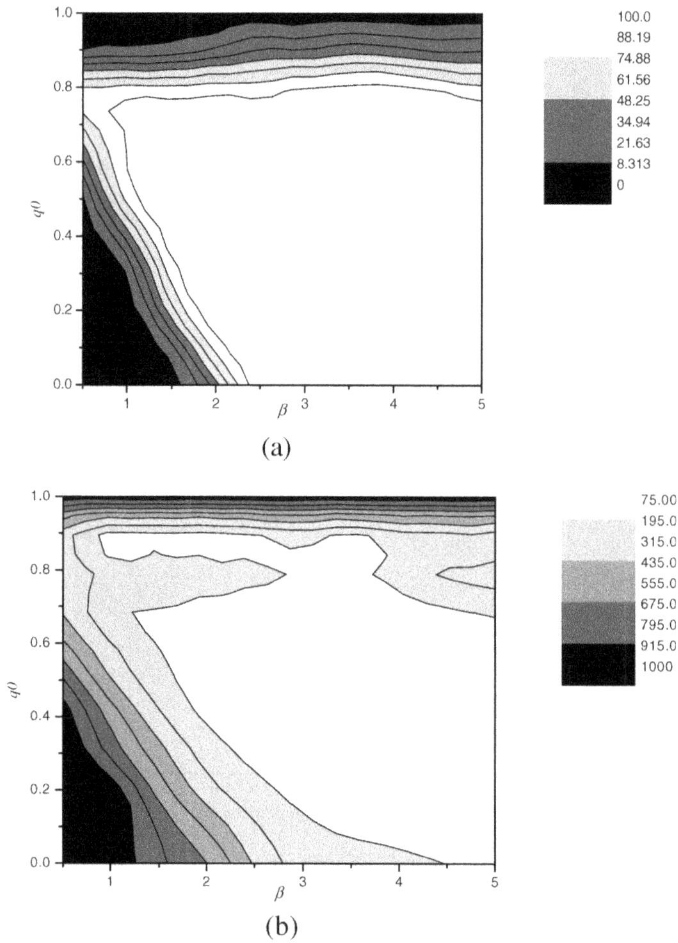

Fig. 3. Different values of *M_g* and *H_n* got with different combinations of β and q_0 in Oliver_30. Fig.3 (a) shows the different values of *M_g* got with different combinations of β and q_0. *M_g* is the min generation in which the algorithm gets the best tour of the iteration *T_iter*. Meanwhile, Fig.3 (b) shows Different values of *H_n* got with different combinations of β and q_0. *H_n* is the number of runs in which the algorithm obtains the global optimization.

M_g is the min generation in which the algorithm gets the best tour of the iteration *T_iter*. In Fig.3 (a), centered on the range $3 \leq \beta \leq 5$ and $0.3 \leq q_0 \leq 0.7$, the algorithm has a very well performance, for the global best tour can be obtained in less than 195 cycles. However, *M_g* increases from right to left as well as from bottom to top. It can be summarized that as the value of β grows, the feasible range of the value of q_0 outspread obviously. In the process, the probability of obtaining the global best tour when q_0 has a low value is growing. It means roulette wheel selection has a better performance in this condition.

In Fig.3 (b), it is shown that with the combinations of β and q_0 which locate in the white area, the ACO can obtain the global best solution for more than 88 times in 100 runs. *H_n* decreases from right to left as well as from bottom to top. The conclusion which is derived from Fig.3 (b) is as same as the one from Fig.3 (a). When $\beta \rightarrow 5$, the acceptable range of q_0 grows, and the algorithm performance for low value of q_0 becomes better indicating that the roulette selection method can perform more effectively in such condition.

4 Conclusion

The rule derived from the results of TSP instances can summarize as follows: First, select proper values of α and β at the beginning because some combinations of α and β are invalid to obtain the global best solution. In most experiments, the valid set of α is (1.0, 1.5).Second, the value of ρ can influence convergence rate. Don't select the value of ρ solely. For example, keeping an eye on the value of q_0 is necessary. Third, the performance of using two selection methods in the algorithm is better than using single one. And when $\beta \rightarrow 5$, the value of q_0 can be selected in a bigger range and it is shown that the roulette selection method is more effective during the process.

Future work will consider the parameters relation in other combination optimization problems, we also aim at extending our work to practical problems in the real world.

Finally, we aim to propose a universal rule of ACO depend on which can we select the proper value of parameters for other combinatorial optimization problems and to develop some ACO algorithms which can obtain better performance by modifying values of the parameters in the optimization process by themselves.

References

1. Alberto Colorni, Marco Dorigo, Vittorio Maniezzo: An Investigation of Some Properties of an 'Ant Algorith'. PPSN (1992)515-526
2. Marco Dorigo, Caro, G. Di, Gambardella, L M: Ant Algorithms for Distributed Discrete Optimization. Artificial Life, 5 (1995)137-172
3. Zhang, J., Henry S.H., Chung , W.L.LO.:Adaptive Genetic Algorithms using Clustering Technique. IEEE Trans. Evolutionary Computation (Accepted)
4. Zhang, J.: Chaotic Time Series Prediction using Lyapunov Exponents in Embedding Phase Space. Computer & Electrical Engineering, Elsevier Science, Volume 30, Issue 1, (2004)1-15

5. Zhang, J., Lo, W.L., Henry S.H. Chung: Design and Optimization of Power Electronics Regulators Using Pseudo-Coevolutionary Genetic Algorithms. IEEE Trans. Systems, Man, and Cybernetics, Part C. (In Press)
6. Huang, D.S., Horace H.S.Ip, Law Ken C K , Chi, Z. R.: Zeroing Polynomials Using Modified Constrained Neural Network Approach. IEEE Trans. On Neural Networks, Vol.16, No.3, (2005)721-732
7. Huang, D.S., Zhao, W. B.:Determining the Centers of Radial Basis Probabilities Neural Networks by Recursive Orthogonal Least Square Algorithms. Applied Mathematics and Computation, Vol.162, No.1, (2005)461-473
8. Huang, D.S.: A Constructive Approach for Finding Arbitrary Rroots of Polynomials by Neural Network.IEEE Transactions on Neural Network, Vol.15, No.2, (2004)477-491
9. Huang, D.S, Horace H.S.Ip, Chi, Z. R., Wong, H.S.: Dilation Method for Finding Close Roots of Polynomials Based on Constrained Learning Neural Networks. Physics Letters A, Vol.309, No.5-6, (2003)443-451
10. Dorigo, M., Gambardella, L. M.: Ant Colony System: A Cooperative Learning Approach toTSP.IEEE Trans. Evol. Comput, Vol. 1, (1997)53–66
11. Luca Maria Gambardella, Marco Dorigo: Ant-Q: A Reinforcement Learning Approach to theTraveling Salesman Problem. ICML (1995) 252-260
12. Marco Dorigo , Gianni Di Caro: Ant Colony Optimization: A New Meta-Heuristic. Evolutionary Computation, 1999. CEC 99. Proceedings of the 1999 Congress on, Volume: 2, 6-9 July 1999
13. Colorni, A, Dorigo, M., Maniezzo, V, Trubian, M: Ant System for Job-Shop Scheduling. Belgian Journal of Operations Research, Statistics and Computer Science, (1993)39-54
14. Zhang, J., Hu, X. M., Tan, X., Zhong, J.H., Huang, Q.: Implementation of an Ant Colony Optimization Technique for Job Shop Scheduling Problem.Transactions of the Institute of Measurement and Control 28, 1 (2006) 1-16
15. Blum, C., Dorigo, M.: Search Bias in Ant Colony Optimization: On the Role of Competition-Balanced Systems. IEEE Trans. Evol. Comput, Vol. 9, (2005) 159-174
16. Kannan, S., S. Mary Raja Slochanal, Narayana Prasad Padhy: Application and Comparison of Metaheuristic Techniques to Generation Expansion Planning Problem. IEEE Trans. Power systems. Vol. 20, (2005) 466-475
17. Marco Dorigo, Vittorio Maniezzo, Alberto Colorni: Ant System: Optimization by a Colony of Cooperating Agents. IEEE Trans, Systems, Man, and Cybernetics-Part B Cybernetics, Vol 26, February (1996) 19-41
18. Zecchin, A.C., Angus R. Simpson, Holger R. Maier, John B. Nixon: Parametric Study for an Ant Algorithm Applied to Water Distribution System Optimization. IEEE Trans. Evol. Comput, vol. 9, (2005)175-191

Ant Colony System for Optimizing Vehicle Routing Problem with Time Windows (VRPTW)

Xuan Tan[1,2], Xiaolan Zhuo[1], and Jun Zhang[1,2,*]

[1] Department of Computer Science, SUN Yat-sen University, P.R. China
[2] Guangdong Key Lab of Information Security
junzhang@ieee.org

Abstract. Research on the optimization of Vehicle Routing Problem with Time Windows (VRPTW) is a significant investigation area of ant colony system (ACS). This paper proposes an enhanced ACS, which embeds the sequential insertion heuristic method, to solve VRPTW. The main idea is to organize two respective ant colonies to successively achieve a multiple objective minimization. Experiments on a series of benchmark problems demonstrate the excellent performance of ACS when compared with other optimization methods.

1 Introduction

Vehicle Routing Problem with Time Windows is a well known combinatorial optimization problem related to many real-life applications, especially in the field of industry. In the past few years, great efforts have been put forward to solve this kind of problems. In 2001, Arbelaitz *et al* [1] proposed a parallelizable system based on simulated annealing to solve VRPTW. The combination of simulated annealing and parallelizable makes a fast and low cost parallel system and is able to reach 85% of the optimal solutions for the Solomon's benchmark problems [1]. In 2004, a multi-agent model based on dynamic generation coalition was proposed, which shows an encouraging performance [2]. Besides, A. Lim *et al* focused their research on an even more restricted VRPTW, with the number of vehicles being constrained. They design an improved Greedy Randomized Adaptive Search Procedure (GRASP) framework. This framework, which embeds a technique of a smoothed dynamic tabu search, proves to be an effective method that outperforms many published algorithms in accuracy [3]. However, the first paper to introduce ACS to the solving of VRPTW appeared earlier than all the above work. In 1999, L. M. Gambardella *et al* presented a multiple ant colony system called MACS-VRTPW [4]. They reduce the complex VRPTW problem to the optimization of a multiple objective function. MACS-VRPTW organizes a hierarchy of artificial ant colonies, each of which uses independent pheromone trails but collaborate each other by exchanging information. Inspired by the idea of MACS-VRPTW, this paper presents an enhanced ACS model, which makes use of two ant colonies with respective goals. The sequential insertion heuristic method is also added

* Corresponding author: This work was supported in part by NSF of China Project No.60573066; NSF of Guangdong Project No. 5003346 and Guangdong Key Lab of Information Security.

D.-S. Huang, K. Li, and G.W. Irwin (Eds.): ICIC 2006, LNBI 4115, pp. 33 – 38, 2006.

to improve its performance. In addition, we use the Nearest Neighbor Heuristic (NNH) to generate the initial solution so that ants can start from a favorable beginning. Experimental results show that this ACS outperforms many published methods in solving the benchmark problems.

2 Ant Colony System for VRPTW

Like the neural network [5][6], ACS is a heuristic method derived from natural behaviors. The main idea of ACS is to have a set of ants search in parallel for solutions and cooperate through pheromone-mediated indirect and global communication [7]. This section gives the detailed descriptions of the proposed ACS for VRPTW.

2.1 Definition of Vehicle Routing Problem with Time Windows (VRPTW)

VRPTW represents an important component of many distribution and transportation system services. Accurately, VRPTW refers to a class of problems in which a set of routes for a fleet of vehicles based at a depot must be determined for n geographically dispersed customers. Let $C=\{1,\ldots,n\}$ be a set of customers and 0 stands for the depot. Each customer c_i involves a service time S_i and asks for a quantity q_i of goods ($i=1,\ldots,n$). Moreover, there is a time window $[b_i, e_i]$ during which c_i has to be served (with b_0 be the earliest starting time and e_0 the latest returning time of each vehicle). $V=\{1,\ldots, t\}$ is a set of vehicles, each of which is associated with a capacity constraint Q. In addition, all the tours should begin at the depot and return to the depot.

2.2 Development of the ACS Model for VRPTW

The major goal of this elaborated ACS model is related to two objectives. We use two ant colonies to achieve this multiple objective minimization [4]. The first ant colony named ACS_vehicle is to minimize the vehicle number. The other one called ACS_time is to optimize the solution so that less traveling time is required.

2.3 Ants Search for Solutions in ACS_Vehicle

The ACS_vehicle colony, whose searching process is given in fig.1 (a), seeks for solutions by minimizing the vehicle number. It begins with an initial solution (possibly unfeasible), using one vehicle less than what the Nearest Neighbor Heuristic (NNH) requires. At the beginning, all ants set out from the depot. For ant k, it chooses the next customer according to the state transition rule (1).

$$\begin{cases} j = \arg\max_{j\in fea[k]}\left([\tau_{ij}][\eta_{ij}]^{\beta}\right), & if \quad q \le q_0 \\ p_{ij}^{k} = \dfrac{[\tau_{ij}][\eta_{ij}]^{\beta}}{\sum_{l\in fea[k]}[\tau_{il}][\eta_{il}]^{\beta}}, \quad j\in fea[k], & otherwise \end{cases} \tag{1}$$

τ_{ij} is the amount of pheromone on edge (i, j) and η_{ij} is defined by equation (2). In equation (2), *cur_time* refers to when the current vehicle will finish serving customer i. $\max(cur\_time+t_{ij},b_j)$ is the time to serve j and thus $(\max(cur\_time+t_{ij},b_j)-cur\_time)$

calculates the time span from now to when j begins to be served. (e_j-cur_time) is the measurement of the urgency of j to be served, indicating that those whose time window will expire soon will have the priority to be served first. IN_j is a variable to record the number of times that j fails to be inserted in each iteration [4].The set fea[k] records the current available customers.

$$\eta_{ij} = 1.0/\,((\max(cur\_time + t_{ij}, b_j) - cur\_time) * (e_j\text{-}cur\_time) - IN_j) \quad (2)$$

Once the current vehicle can not serve more customers, ant k starts a new route by adding another vehicle, unless the allowed vehicle number has been reached. By repeatedly applying (1), ant k constructs a solution Ψ_k. Considering the vehicle number constraint and other restrictions, it is possible that not all customers are included in Ψ_k. The sequential insertion heuristic method is then added to help serve as more customers as possible [8]. If Ψ_k is a feasible solution, the allowed vehicle number will decrease.

2.4 Pheromone Updating Rules in ACS_Vehicle

The Local Updating Rule. This rule (3) is used to update the pheromone on the edge which has just been selected by an ant. τ_0 is the initial pheromone amount.

$$\tau_{ij} \leftarrow (1-\rho)\cdot\tau_{ij} + \rho\cdot\tau_0 \qquad (0 < \rho < 1) \quad (3)$$

The Global Updating Rule. This rule (4) is applied twice: one for the solution with the maximum goods and the other for the global best feasible solution [4].

$$\tau_{ij} \leftarrow (1-\alpha)\cdot\tau_{ij} + \alpha\cdot\Delta\tau_{ij} \quad (4)$$

For the solution with the most goods, $\Delta\tau_{ij}$ is calculated by (5) where L_1 is the sum of distance of all the tours in the solution with the most goods.

$$\Delta\tau_{ij} = \begin{cases} (L_1)^{-1} & if\ (i, j) \in the\_most\_goods\_solution \\ 0 & \text{otherwise} \end{cases} \quad (5)$$

Likewise, for the global best feasible solution, $\Delta\tau_{ij}$ is calculated by (6) where L_{gb} is the sum of distance of this solution.

$$\Delta\tau_{ij} = \begin{cases} (L_{gb})^{-1} & if\ (i, j) \in global\_best\_solution \\ 0 & otherwise \end{cases} \quad (6)$$

2.5 Ants Search for Solutions in ACS_Time

The colony of ACS_time is designed in the purpose of minimizing the total transportation time. This process is described in fig.1 (b). Considering that the length of the distance in a solution is proportional to that of the transportation time, we take the total distance of a solution to evaluate its quality. In this way, the searching process of

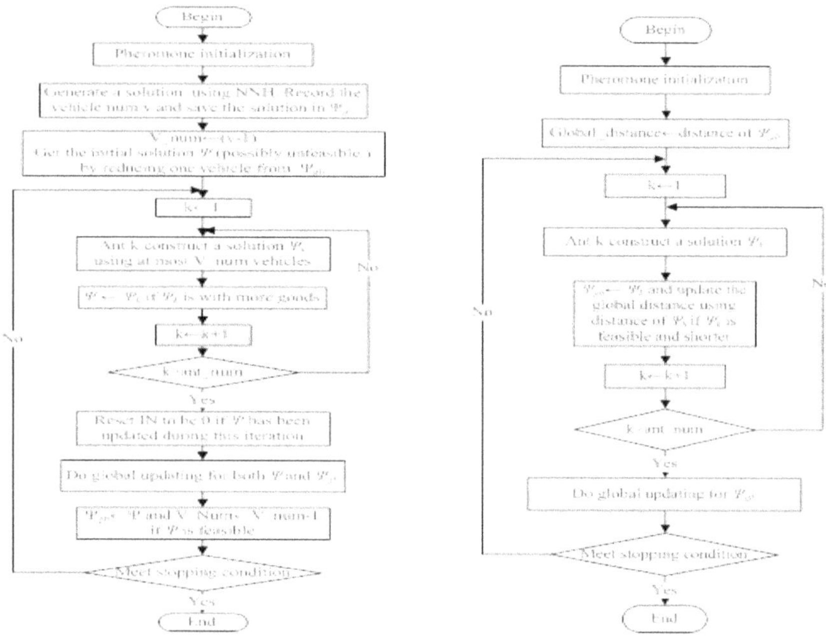

(a)ACS_vehicle (b)ACS_time

Fig. 1. Flow charts of the searching process for ACS_vehicle and ACS_time respectively

ACS_time is quite similar to that of the ant colony for solving the traveling salesman problem [7]. Therefore, ACS_time applies the same state transition rule and pheromone updating rules as those of the conventional ACS [7].

3 The Numerical Result of ACS for VRPTW

The proposed ACS for VRPTW has been tested on a set of benchmark problems, which are divided into three groups as *C, R* and *RC*. Group *C* consists of clustered customers whose time windows are generated based on a known solution. Group *R* have customers' location generated uniformly randomly over square. Group *RC* are combinations of randomly placed and clustered customers. The difference of these three types is the width of time windows for each customer.

3.1 Results on Benchmark Problems

Table.1 shows some satisfying experimental results. Each test is performed 10 times. We can see that for R103, R104 and RC102, ACS requires less vehicles than all the listed algorithms while for C101, C107, R106 and RC101, it can obtain solutions almost close to that of the other algorithms.

Fig.2 shows the computing process in the respective tests for R103 and RC102, from which we can see the process of the total distance of the optimal solution against the iteration count. As the iteration increases, the vehicle number decreases. Moreover, during those iterations with the same vehicle number, the total distance decreases.

Table 1. The experimental results of ACS for some benchmark problems

Problem	Optimal Solution by other algorithms			Optimal Solution by ACS	
	Number	Distance	Author	Number	Distance
C101	10	828.94	RT [9]	10	833
C107	10	827.3	KDMSS [10]	10	837
R103	13	1292.68	LLH[11]	12	1500
R104	11	971.5	IV[12]	10	1217
R106	13	1234.6	CR[13]+KLM [14]	13	1259
RC101	15	1619.8	KDMSS [10]	15	1623
RC102	14	1457.4	CR[13]+KLM [14]	13	1673

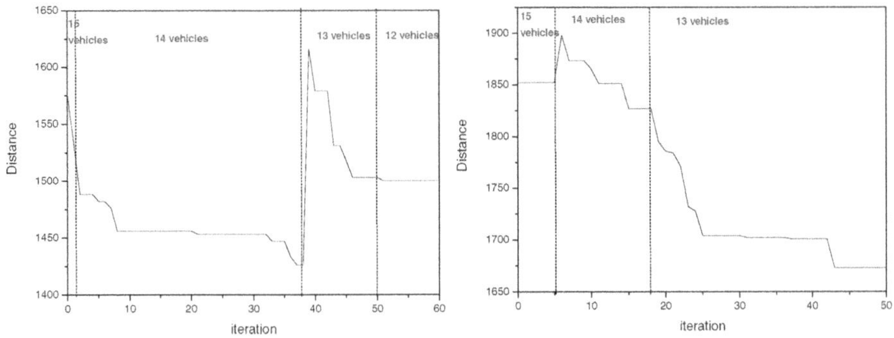

Fig. 2. Schematic illustrations of the computing process for R103 and RC102 respectively

4 Conclusion

In this paper, an enhanced ACS is presented to solve the VRPTW. This ACS model makes use of two respective ant colonies which are designed to obtain respective goals. With the initial solution generated by the Nearest Neighbor Heuristic, ACS is able to start from a favorable beginning. In addition, the sequential insertion heuristic method is embedded as an auxiliary skill. An extensive computational study on a set of benchmark problems has been conducted and the experimental results show that the proposed ACS is competitive when compared with other methods.

References

1. Arbelaitz, O., Rodriguez, C., Zamakola, I.: Low Cost Parallel Solutions for the VRPTW Optimization Problem. Parallel Processing Workshops (2001) 176 – 181
2. Boudali, I., Fki, W., Ghedira, K.: How to Deal with the VRPTW by Using Multi-Agent Coalitions. Hybrid Intelligent Systems. Proceedings (2004) 416 – 421
3. Lim, A., Wang, F.: A Smoothed Dynamic Tabu Search Embedded GRASP for m-VRPTW. Tools with Artificial Intelligence. ICTAI 2004.(2004) 704 –708

4. Gambardella .L.M, Taillard .E, Agazzi.G: MACS-VRPTW: A Multiple Ant Colony System for Vehicle Routing Problems with Time Windows. New Ideas in Optimization (1999) 63–76
5. Huang, D.S.: A Constructive Approach for Finding Arbitrary Roots of Polynomials by Neural Networks. IEEE Transactions on Neural Networks. 15(2004) 477–491
6. Huang, D.S., Horace, H.K., Chi, .Z.: Zeroing Polynomials Using Modified Constrained Neural Network Approach. IEEE Trans On Neural Networks, 16(2005) 721–732
7. Dorigo, M, Gambardella, L M: Ant Colony System: A Cooperative Learning Approach to the Traveling Salesman Problem. IEEE Trans on evolutionary computation. 1(1997) 53–66
8. Solomon, M.: Algorithms for the Vehicle Routing and Scheduling Problem with Time Window Constraints. Operations Research. 35 (1987) 254–265
9. Rochat, Y., Taillard, E.D.: Probabilistic Diversification and Intensification in Local Search for Vehicle Routing. Journal of Heuristics. 1 (1995) 147–167
10. Kohl, N., Desrosiers, J., Madsen, O. B. G., Solomon, M. M., Soumis, F.: 2-Path Cuts for the Vehicle Routing Problem with Time Windows, Transportation Science. (1999) 101–116
11. Li, H., Lim, A., Huang, J.: Local Search with Annealing-like Restarts to Solve the VRPTW. Working Paper, Department of Computer Science, National University of Singapore (2001)
12. Irnich, S., Villeneuve, D.: The Shortest Path Problem with K-cycle Elimination ($k \geq 3$): Improving a Branch-and-Price Algorithm for the VRPTW. INFORMS Journal of Computing.
13. Cook, W., Rich, J. L.: A Parallel Cutting Plane Algorithm for the VRPTW. Working Paper, Computational and Applied Mathematics, Rice University, Houston, TX (1999)
14. Kallehauge, B., Larsen, J., Madsen, O.B.G.: Lagrangean Duality and Non-Differentiable Optimization Applied on Routing with Time Windows - Experimental Results. Internal report IMM-REP-2000-8, Technical University of Denmark, Lyngby, Denmark (2000)

A Hybrid Particle Swarm Optimization for Binary CSPs

Qingyun Yang[1,2], Jigui Sun[1,2,3], Juyang Zhang[1,2], and Chunjie Wang[4]

[1] College of Computer Science and Technology, Jilin University,
Changchun, 130012, China
qyyang_jlu@yahoo.com.cn

[2] Key Laboratory for Symbolic Computation and Knowledge
Engineering of Ministry of Education, Jilin University,
Changchun, 130012, China

[3] Open Laboratory for Intelligence Information Processing, Fudan University,
Shanghai, 200433, China

[4] Basic Sciences of ChangChun University of Technology,
ChangChun University of Technology, Changchun, 130012, China

Abstract. The target of solving constraint satisfaction problems(CSP) is to satisfy all constraints simultaneously. The CSP model is transformed into a discrete optimization problem with boundary constraints and is solved by particle swarm optimization(PSO) in this paper. To improve the performance of the proposed PSO algorithm, ERA(Environment, Reactive rules, Agent) model is used to proceed with local search after the process of boundary constraints. Further improvement including nohope and tabu list are also combined with PSO. When particles can not explore more search space, nohope is introduced to improve the activities of particles. Tabu list is used to avoid cycling in the global best particle. We experiment with random constraint satisfaction problem instances based on phase transition theory. Experimental results indicate that the hybrid algorithm has advantages on the search capability and the iterative number.

1 Introduction

Particle Swarm Optimization (PSO) is a stochastic search technique developed by Kennedy and Eberhart[1] based on the simulation of social behavior metaphor, which is inspired by the behavior of bird flocking and fish schooling. PSO exploits a population of potential solutions to probe the search space. It initializes the population with random candidate solutions, called particles. Each particle is assigned a randomized velocity and is iteratively moved through the search space. It benefits from the experience of its own and that of the other members of the population.

PSO is widely used as optimizer for nonlinear functions, many experimental results show that PSO is a excellent stochastic search method on numeric optimization problems. Recently PSO is proposed to solve constrained optimization

D.-S. Huang, K. Li, and G.W. Irwin (Eds.): ICIC 2006, LNBI 4115, pp. 39–49, 2006.

problems[2],[3],[4] and integer programming[5]. Discrete PSO is a variant of the basic PSO and is proposed to solve binary constraint satisfaction problems[7]. Constraint satisfaction problems are usually discrete. In this paper constraint satisfaction problems are modeled as discrete constrained optimization problems and are solved by non-discrete PSO.

The remainder of this paper is organized as follows: Section 2 provides a short overview of constraint satisfaction problem, outlining the basic concept of CSP and how it can be adapted to be solved by PSO. The hybrid methods of particle swarm to solve binary CSPs are introduced in Section 3. The hybrid methods include: handling boundary constraints with *Periodic* mode, rounding real value position to integer value, combining ERA model to particle swarm as a local search technique, adding nohope to increase the opportunity for searching and adding tabu list to prevent cycle in the search procedure. Some experimental results are given in Section 4. All instances used in our test are generated by random CSP model under phase transition theory, which are the hardest to be solved and become the baseline to evaluate the efficiency of a algorithm. Section 5 is the conclusion and future work.

2 Constraint Satisfaction Problem

Constraint Satisfaction Problems (CSPs) are the most exciting research area of artificial intelligence over last decades. In real life, many problems such as timetabling, resource allocation, planning, configuration, vision etc. can be modeled as some certain type CSPs. It is a powerful tool to model and to solve many kinds of combinatorial problems, which has attracted widespread commercial interest as well. Most of those combinatorial problems are NP-Complete in general.

Researching into solving CSPs has been lasted for a long time and can be classified as complete and incomplete, depending on whether they can find all solutions or find a random solution. complete algorithms can detect infeasibility but the computational cost is expensive for large problem instances. There are no polynomial algorithms to solve CSPs so far. The dominating idea is backtracking that explores the search space in a systematic and complete way. Backtracking finds values for variables subject to a set of constraints, which selects an unlabelled variable to instantiate each time. When the instantiated variable doesn't meet with the constraints, the algorithm backtracks to a suitable search point. Backtracking algorithm traverses the entire solution space to get solutions. Different complete directions of solving CSPs have been approached: finding the CSPs' solutions from the possible solution space[9], reducing a CSP to a simpler or equivalent problem[10], and synthesizing the CSPs' solutions from partial solutions[11]. The desirable features of system and completeness in backtrack search become intractable on hard combinatorial problems for the exponential time complexity. This is particularly true when the problem is huge and system reduction cannot reduce the problem enough to make complete search feasible.

Hence, incomplete search approaches have been proposed that leave out combinatorial explosion. Incomplete methods are much faster, but can not guarantee finding solution within a limited amount of time or concluding the problem is infeasible. Incomplete methods in solving CSPs include: a number of local search approach, such as min-conflict heuristic[12], ERA model[13]; swarm intelligence based methods, such as ant colony optimization[6], discrete particle swarm optimization[7], genetic algorithm[8] etc.

A constraint network or Constraint Satisfaction Problem (CSP) is a triplet (X, D, C), here $X = \{x_1, x_2, \ldots, x_n\}$ is a set of Variables, which may take on values from a set of domains $D = \{D_1, D_2, \ldots, D_n\}$, and a set of constraints $C = \{C_1, C_2, \ldots, C_m\}$. A constraint C_i on the ordered set of variables $X(C_i) = (X_1, \ldots, X_n)$ is a subset of the Cartesian product $D(X_1) \times \ldots \times D(X_n)$ that denotes the compatible pairs of value for variable $X_1, \ldots, X_n$. A binary constraint C_{ij} on variable X_i and X_j is a set of pairs, C_{ij} allows for X_i to take the value v_i and X_j to take the value v_j iff $(v_i, v_j) \in C_{ij}$ and we say the binary constraint is *satisfied* otherwise it is *violated.* We call a CSP binary constraint satisfaction problem iff all the constraints in CSP are binary constraints. A solution of a constraint satisfaction problem is an assignment of values to the set of X such that all the constraints are satisfied simultaneously.

In this paper, we formulate a CSP as a discrete constrained optimization problem with a goal of minimizing $f(x)$ subject to a set of constraints.

$$f(x) = \sum_{i=1}^{|C|} g(C_i) \tag{1}$$

$$\text{s.t. } g(C_i) = 0 \quad \forall i \in 1, 2, \ldots, |C|$$

where $g(C_i) = 0$ if constraint C_i is satisfied, and $g(C_i) = 1$ if C_i is violated. if all constraints are satisfied, i.e. $f(x) = 0$, say a solution for the CSP is found. Now the main task is to solve the optimization problem, which is a more natural way for particle swarm optimization.

In the next section, particle swarm is adopted to solve the above CSP model and some additional techniques are combined with particle swarm to improve the performance.

3 Particle Swarm for Binary CSPs

Particle swarm is a general heuristic exploration technique which maintains a swarm of candidate solutions, referred to as *particle.* Particle swarm performs effective exploration through memory and feedback. Particles flow through hyper-dimensional search space, attracting towards the best position found by the neighborhood particle and the best historic position by themselves.

Assume that the search space is N-dimensional, i.e. the number of parameters the function being optimized, then the i-th particle in the swarm could be presented with a N-dimensional vector, $X_i = (x_{i1}, x_{i2}, \ldots, x_{iN})$. The velocity of this particle can be presented as $V_i = (v_{i1}, v_{i2}, \ldots, v_{iN})$. The best historic position visited by the i-th particle can be denoted as $P_i = (p_{i1}, p_{i2}, \ldots, p_{iN})$. g is defined as the index of the best neighborhood. For the popular PSO, the main manipulation according to the following two equations:

$$v_{ij}^{t+1} = \omega v_{ij}^{t} + c_1 r_{1j}(p_{ij} - x_{ij}^{t}) + c_2 r_{2j}(p_{gj} - x_{ij}^{t}) \tag{2}$$

$$x_{ij}^{t+1} = x_{ij}^{t} + v_{ij}^{t+1} \tag{3}$$

where i = 1, 2, ..., S, and S is the size of the swarm; j = 1, 2, ..., N; t = 1, 2, ..., is the number of iteration; ω is the inertia weight; c_1 and c_2 are acceleration coefficients; $r_{1j}^t, r_{2j}^t \sim U(0,1)$.

The optimization model of equation 1 transforms the constraints in CSP model into variables of the optimization model. The original variables in CSP are encoded into the positions of the particles, and the dimension of the particle now is $|X|$. The number of constraints satisfied denotes the partial solution's size of CSP. More constraints are satisfied, nearer approaching global solution. Thus the formulation of $f(x)$ is a straightforward method to compute fitness for particle. When calculating the fitness of a particle, first the consistencies of all constraints are checked with the values of the current positions presented by CSP model's variables, then $f(x)$ is computed by these consistency to determine fitness. Usually particle swarm is used to solve continuous optimization problems while the typical CSPs are discrete, thus we need discretize the values of positions. Rounding off the real value into the nearest integer value as [5] did is adopted in this paper.

3.1 Constraint Handling Technique

Constraint process is the key point in solving constrained optimization problems. While PSO is a computational procedure without constraint process. something else may be adopted to do this operation when a PSO algorithm is used to solve constrained optimization problems. [14] grouped the constraint handling methods into four categories: preserving feasibility of solutions; penalty functions; making a clear distinction between feasible and infeasible solutions; and other hybrid methods. There have two kinds of constraint in equation 1. One is the relations existing among the value pairs. Since the target is to satisfy all constraints in CSPs. We treat these relations as variables of equation 1 and the number of constraint violations as the fitness of particles. Thus constraints in CSPs need not process directly. The other is boundary constraint. CSPs are usually boundary but PSO does not discuss the bounds of particles' positions. Extra technique is needed to process boundary constraints. The simplest way is truncation. A value is less than the minimal bound then we set the minimal bound to it, and a value is greater than the maximal bound we set the maximal bound to it. [2] proposed a *Periodic* mode technique to handle boundary constraints. Experimental results denote its effectiveness and we adopt it in our hybrid algorithm. The formulations are as follows:

$$x_i = \begin{cases} u_i - (l_i - x_i)\% s_i & if \quad x_i < l_i \\ l_i + (x_i - u_i)\% s_i & if \quad x_i > u_i \\ x_i & if \quad x_i \in [l_i, u_i] \end{cases} \tag{4}$$

where % is the modulus operator, $s_i = u_i - l_i$ is the range of the ith dimension, l_i is the minimal bound, and u_i is the maximal bound.

After the process with *Periodic* mode, particles return to the feasible domain. Then ERA model can proceed with local search.

3.2 Velocity Transformation

The velocity of a particle is composed of three components: v^t, the velocity reserved last time; $p - x^t$ and $p_g - x^t$. The new velocity may a big value thus the result of the new position added by the old position and the new velocity may have large offset compares with the old position. The addition of a position and a new large velocity actually increases the chaos in the swarm and weaken the quality of the local search. To get more powerful global search capacity but not to decrease the solution quality reached by the local search, we transform the velocities into the interval [-1, 1]. The elements in a velocity is partitioned into two set, $Pos_v = \{v_{ij} | v_{ij} > 0, v_{ij} \in V_i, i = 1, 2, \ldots, S, j = 1, 2, \ldots, N\}$ and $Neg_v = \{v_{ij} | v_{ij} < 0, v_{ij} \in V_i, i = 1, 2, \ldots, S, j = 1, 2, \ldots, N\}$,where S is the population size and N is the dimension. Then the transformation formula is as follows:

$$v'_{ij} = \begin{cases} \dfrac{v_{ij}}{\sum\limits_{k=1, v_{ik} \in Pos_v}^{N} v_{ik}} & if \quad v_{ij} > 0 \\ \dfrac{v_{ij}}{\sum\limits_{k=1, v_{ik} \in Neg_v}^{N} |v_{ik}|} & if \quad v_{ij} < 0 \end{cases} \tag{5}$$

3.3 Hybrid ERA Model with Particle Swarm

ERA(Environment, Reactive rules, Agent) model[13] is similar to min-conflicts heuristic[12] though it is a distributed multi-agent system based on the theory of artificial life. Both of them are local search approach. Both of their search strategies are based on variables' conflicts. [13] compared ERA model with min-conflicts heuristic and pointed out the ERA model is superior to min-conflicts. In ERA, each agent represents a variable in CSP. Agents live in lattice environment, and sense the local and global information around them. The environment records agents' current state and computes the constraint violations for each value in the domains of all variables. each agent can only move within a row it located in and has predefined local reactive behaviors: *better_move*, *least_move* and *random_move*. Agents select them with some certain probability under the pressure of environment that based on constraint violations. *better_move* is to find a position with less violation number with a probability of *better_p*, *least_move* is to find the least violation number position with a probability of *least_p*, and *random_move* is to move randomly with a probability of *random_p*. *better_move* has less time complexity than *least_move* and may be more efficient at the early search stage. While obviously the *least_move* can accelerate convergence to local optima or global optima. *random_move* is a necessary technique to avoid getting stuck in local optima.

Three local behaviors have been analyzed in [13], and pointing out that maybe exist *random_p* < *better_p* < *least_p* for general purpose. Their experiments also indicate *least_p* / *random_p* = n (here n is the domain size of the specified problem) may be a good choice. We use this empirical setting for our test. From the algorithmic description of the ERA it can be concluded that there exists a approximate formulation, namely *better_p* + *random_p* + *least_p* = 1. Thus if *better_p* is specified, we can compute *random_p* and *least_p* with empirical approximate formulations:

$$random\_p = (1 - better\_p)/(d + 1) \quad (6)$$

$$least\_p = random\_p \times d \quad (7)$$

where d is the domain size of a constraint satisfaction problem(assuming all variables have the same domain size).

In this paper, ERA model is organized to carry out local search procedure after the update of particles' positions.

3.4 Further Improvement with Nohope and Tabu List

It is hard to find the solution when the particles wander about some local attractors. ERA model uses *random_move* to increase the opportunity to explore more search space. The similar mechanism is used in our algorithm by increasing the *random_p*. DPS redistributes all the particles in the search space while we only increase the probability of random selection on global best particle on consideration of performance. Thus it is a variant of nohope in our algorithm. Stochastic search algorithm may also repeatedly enter into the same state, i.e. particle swarm optimization find a position repeatedly. It is useless in the search procedure, especially after the nohope activity. We introduce a short tabu list to avoid cycling. Each time the global best position is recorded, and is compared with the elements in the tabu list after the specified times(we allow some repeat in searching procedure but a threshold is given). if the global best position already exists in the tabu list, nohope activates to increase the randomness. When the global best particle arrives at a new position(i.e. a less fitness it approaches) we add it into the tabu list. a fist-in-fist-out queue is used for tabu list in our algorithm and only global best particle uses nohope and tabu list.
The pseudocode of the entire hybrid algorithm is as follows:

```
main procedure
  initialize positions and velocities randomly with real number
  handle boundary constraints with equation 4
  ERA-LocalSearch with better move = 0.15
  evaluate fitness
  while(fitness != 0 and iteration < maxIteration) {
    update velocities with equation 2
    transform velocities
    update positions with equation 3
    handle boundary constraints with equation 4
    ERA-LocalSearch with better move = 0.15
    if(the gbest particle is stagnated for no-hope threshold times) {
      ERA-LocalSearch with better_move = 0.1
    }
    evaluate fitness
  }
```

4 Experimental Results

To compare the performance of hybrid PS algorithm with that of DPS proposed in [7] and ERA model (a multi-agent oriented stochastic search model), first we choose the Model E class with 15 variables and 15 domain elements as DPS did, and choose JavaCsp (JavaCsp is a random binary constraint satisfaction problem instance generator) [1] to generate instances. Model E has one parameter named p. The generation process is to select uniformly, independently and with repetition, $pd^2n(n-1)/2$ conflicts out of the $d^2n(n-1)/2$ possible, where d is the domain size and the n is the number of variables. In our observation, the phase transition point is approximately 0.31 in the development of JavaCsp. Thus we set parameter p at 11 values equals spaced between 0.21 and 0.31 instead of between 0.2 and 0.38. Random constraint satisfaction problem theories proved these values located in the *mushy region*, where interesting instances with few solutions can be sampled. Each value of p we sample 5 instances; each instance has at least one solution. In our test all algorithms stop when it has found a solution or when it has performed 10^6 evaluations in each case. 10^6 evaluations are considered no more solution can be found and are excluded from experimental results. 10 runs are performed for each instance. The experiments are made on PC(Intel Celeron CPU 1.8GHz, 512M RAM, Window XP SP2 and JDK 1.5).

Table 1. Comparison results with the success rate and the mean iteration of Model E class

p	ERA		DPS		HPS	
	succ.	mean iter.	succ.	mean iter.	succ.	mean iter.
0.21	50/50	5.7	50/50	102.84	50/50	**3.4**
0.22	50/50	13.7	50/50	2679.3	50/50	**3.5**
0.23	50/50	33.2	50/50	389.4	50/50	**4.1**
0.24	50/50	20.2	45/50	3344	50/50	**6.9**
0.25	50/50	41.8	45/50	8086.8	50/50	**14.5**
0.26	50/50	152.5	35/50	50057	50/50	**28.1**
0.27	50/50	183.8	35/50	42740.2	50/50	**44.5**
0.28	50/50	396.8	20/50	110818.6	50/50	**110.7**
0.29	50/50	564.1	15/50	77904.8	50/50	**43.9**
0.30	50/50	4377.4	0/50	–	50/50	**485.4**
0.31	50/50	53312.1	0/50	–	50/50	**3390**

The parameters of DPS in this test are set the quasi-optimal values described in [7]. Those values include: swarm size is 50, deflection = 2/n, where n is the number of variables, $\varphi_1 = \varphi_2 = 1$. The parameter setting for ERA model has only one value to be tuned for experimental convenience, given by our experience, where *better move* = 0.15. We adapt the c source code from book "Swarm

[1] http://www.xs4all.nl/~bcraenen/JavaCsp/resources/javacsp_1.0.2.jar.

Intelligence" to Java version in our test[2]. For our hybrid PSOs parameters, fixed values, consider as default, are used: $c_1 = c_2 = 2$; ω is gradually decreased from 0.9 but never below 0.4. V_{max}, to prevent the swarm from explosion, is still reserved in the newly developed algorithm. In our experiments V_{max} is always fixed, to the value of $V_{max} = 4$. the size of the swarm in our algorithm is set 10 instead of the DPS′s quasi-optimal parameter setting with 50. We also use the same parameter setting in ERA model to the hybrid particle swarm algorithm except for the nohope phase. In the nohope phase we give more random opportunity to the algorithm to get out of local optimum. The parameter change to *better move* = 0.1.

We test 11 instances with model E. All the 11 instances are solved by ERA and HPS but only 9 by DPS. When $p = 0.31$, i.e. p is near the phase transition point, the average iterations are increased with both ERA and HPS. But HPS reduces the iterations dramatically comparing with ERA both in the *mushy region* and at the phase transition point.

Table 2. Comparison results with the success rate and the mean iteration of partial instances generated by Model RB

instances	ERA		HPS	
	succ.	mean iter.	succ.	mean iter.
frb30-15-1.csp	3/10	265785	**6/10**	388744.7
frb30-15-2.csp	10/10	142236.6	10/10	**23619.4**
frb30-15-3.csp	0/10	–	**1/10**	**481845**
frb30-15-4.csp	10/10	77513	10/10	**8913**
frb30-15-5.csp	3/10	424908	**10/10**	**170257.6**
frb35-17-1.csp	0/10	–	**1/10**	**679207**
frb35-17-2.csp	0/10	–	**2/10**	**457798**
frb35-17-3.csp	1/10	797702	**3/10**	**745382**
frb35-17-4.csp	5/10	470313.2	**9/10**	**289837.2**
frb35-17-5.csp	1/10	534781	**3/10**	566332
frb40-19-1.csp	8/10	291275.4	**10/10**	**156683.1**
frb40-19-2.csp	2/10	496059	**5/10**	**349026.2**
frb40-19-3.csp	2/10	402676	**3/10**	552553.3
frb45-21-4.csp	0/10	–	**1/10**	**167119**

Further random constraint satisfaction problem theories are proved there exists exactly critical values at which the phase transitions occur. The hardest instances to solve are concentrated in the sharp transition region and become remarkable benchmark to evaluate the efficiency of the newly developed algorithms. These efforts result in the Model RB [15], the state of the art in random CSP Model theory, which is a revision to the standard Model B. Those studies also revise the drawback of Model E and produce in a simple model to generate

[2] http://www.swarmintelligence.org/SIBook/cdos.zip.

hard satisfiable instances[16] [3]. Now we use the benchmark problems generated from Model RB to test our algorithm [4]. In our experiments the repetitive constraint instances are omitted. The parameter setting unchange with the above setup. The DPS is completely defeated by these benchmarks and does not appear in the experimental results any longer.

In the test of 20 instances based on Model RB theory, ERA model can solve 10 instances while our hybrid particle swarm algorithm can tackle 14 instances. There are two instances with 40 variables and four instances with 45 variables are unsolved by the hybrid particle swarm algorithm. In the 14 instances, our hybrid particle swarm algorithm always has higher success rate on finding solutions and has less mean iterations for most instances comparing with ERA model.

5 Conclusion and Future Work

Backtracking is an ordinary way in solving constraint satisfaction problems, which selects an unlabelled variable to instantiate each time. When the instantiated variable doesn't meet with the constraints, the algorithm backtracks to a suitable search point. Backtracking algorithm traverses the entire solution space. The system and completeness in backtrack search become intractable on hard combinatorial problems for the exponential time complexity. This is especially true when the problem is huge and system reduction cannot reduce the problem enough to make complete search feasible. Particle swarm optimization is a global stochastic search technique and has excellent performance on continuous optimization problems. In this paper, CSPs are transformed into discrete constrained optimization problems and solved by PSO. Evidence denotes PSO for integer programming is superior to branch and bound but is not so good to discrete constrained problems in our experience. To improve the performance of pso for CSPs, ERA model is introduced as a local searcher in PSO. After the update of positions, ERA model is activated on rounded position to get better solution quality. Meanwhile nohope and tabu list are combined with PSO for avoiding sticking in the local optima and in the useless loop throughout the search procedure. Experimental results indicate the hybrid algorithm has advantages either on search capability or iterative number. The hybrid algorithm could reduce the iterative number dramatically on any instance generated by random constraint satisfaction problem generator developed based on phase transition theory and can find more solution on these instances. While we know some instances based on Model RB are not tackled yet and that is the effort in our further work.

---

[3] http://www.cril.univ-artois.fr/~lecoutre/research/tools/RBGenerator.jar.

[4] http://www.nlsde.buaa.edu.cn/~kexu/benchmarks/benchmarks.htm. or http://www.cril.univ-artois.fr/~lecoutre/research/benchmarks/benchmarks.html#instances. the former also includes the solved results comparison with CSP Solver Competition.

Acknowledgments

This work was supported in part by the National Natural Science Foundation of China under grant no. 60273080 and no. 60473003. This work also was supported in part by the Outstanding Youth Foundation of Jilin province of China under grant no. 20030107.

References

1. Kennedy, J, Eberhart, R. C: Particle Swarm Optimization. In: IEEE Int. Conf. on Neural Networks, Perth, Australia. (1995) 1942–1948
2. Wen–Jun Zhang, Xiao–Feng Xie, De–Chun Bi: Handling Boundary Constraints for Numerical Optimization by Particle Swarm Flying in Periodic Search Space. In: IEEE CEC, Oregon, USA. (2004) 2307–2311
3. K.E. Parsopoulos, M.N. Vrahatis: Particle Swarm Optimization Method for Constrained Optimization Problems. In P. Sincak, J. Vascak, V. Kvasnicka, and J. Pospichal, editors, Intelligent Technologies—-Theory and Application: New Trends in Intelligent Technologies, Frontiers in Artificial Intelligence and Applications, IOS Press. 76 (2002) 214–220
4. Hu, X., Eberhart, R. C: Solving Constrained Nonlinear Optimization Problems with Particle Swarm Optimization. In: Proc. of the Sixth World Multiconference on Systemics, Cybernetics and Informatics 2002 (SCI 2002), Orlando, USA. (2002) 203–206
5. Laskari, E. C., Parsopoulos, K. E., Vrahatis, M. N: Particle Swarm Optimization for Integer Programming. In: Proc. of the IEEE Congress on Evolutionary Computation (CEC 2002), Honolulu, Hawaii, USA. (2002) 1582–1587
6. Christine Solnon: Ants Can Solve Constraint Satisfaction Problems. In: Proc. of the IEEE Transactions on Evolutionary Computation (TEC 2002), 6 (2002) 347–357
7. L. Schoofs, B. Naudts: Swarm Intelligence on the Binary Constraint Satisfaction Problem. In: Proc. of the IEEE Congress on Evolutionary Computation (CEC 2002), Honolulu, Hawaii, USA. (2002) 1444–1449
8. Nicolas Barnier, Pascal Brisset: Optimization by Hybridization of a Genetic Algorithm with Constraint Satisfaction Techniques. In: Proc. of the IEEE Congress on Evolutionary Computation (CEC 1998), (1998)
9. E.C. Freuder: A Sufficient Condition for Backtrack-free Search. J. ACM, 29(1) (1982) 24–32
10. A. K. Mackworth, E. C. Freuder: The Complexity of Some Polynomial Consistency Algorithms for Constraint Satisfaction Problems. Artificial Intelligence, 25 (1985) 65–74
11. Wanlin Pang, Scott D. Goodwin: A Graph Based Synthesis Algorithm for Solving CSPs. In: Proc. of the 16th International Florida Artificial Intelligence Research Society Conference, Florida, USA. (2003) 197–201
12. S.Minton, M.D.Johnston, A.B.Philips,P.Laird: Minimizing Conflicts: A Heuristic Repair Method for Constraint–Satisfaction and Scheduling Problems. Artificial Intelligence, 58 (1992) 161–205
13. Jiming Liu, Han Jing, Y.Y.Tang: Multi-agent Oriented Constraint Satisfaction. Artificial Intelligence, 136 (2002) 101–104

14. Koziel,S., Michalewicz,Z.: Evolutionary Algorithms, Homomorphous Mappings, and Constrained Parameter Optimization. Evolutionary Computation, 7 (1999) 1944–1999
15. K. Xu, W. Li: Exact Phase Transitions in Random Constraint Satisfaction Problems. Journal of Artificial Intelligence Research, 12 (2000) 93–103
16. K. Xu, F. Boussemart, F. Hemery, C. Lecoutre: A Simple Model to Generate Hard Satisfiable Instances. In: Proc. of 19th International Joint Conference on Artificial Intelligence (IJCAI), Edinburgh, Scotland, (2005) 337–342

A New Hybrid Algorithm of Particle Swarm Optimization

Guangyou Yang[1,2], Dingfang Chen[2], and Guozhu Zhou[1]

[1] School of Mechanical Engineering, Hubei University of Technology, Wuhan, 430068, China
[2]Lab of intelligent manufacturing & control, Wuhan University of Technology, Wuhan, 430060, China
{canyang, dfchen, tzhou}@public.wh.hb.cn

Abstract. This paper presents a new hybrid algorithm of particle swarm optimization (PSO) called PSOSA, in which the mechanism of modified simulated annealing (SA) is embedded into standard PSO algorithm. The proposed algorithm not only keeps the characters of simple and easy to be implemented, but also enhances the ability of getting rid of local optimum and improves the speed and precision of convergence. The testing results of several benchmark functions with different dimensions show that the proposed algorithm is superior to standard PSO and the other PSO algorithms.

1 Introduction

Particle Swarm Optimization (PSO) was a swarm intelligence optimization which was proposed by Kennedy and Eberhan in 1995[1], [2], whose basic thinking was to find the optimal value through cooperation and sharing information among individuals of swarm. Compared with other optimizations, PSO is simple, high s peed, large scope and easy to be implemented by programs. However, it is outstanding that it was easy to be got into local optimum. When the particle swarm was got into the local optimum, the particle swarm lost the ability of finding other optimal value. In order to overcome shortcoming of standard PSO, the many improved methods had been proposed [3]-[13]. Both Eberhart and Angeline conclude that hybrid models of the standard GA and the PSO could lead to further advances. In this paper, we present such a new hybrid model called PSOSA. The PSOSA model merges the modified simulated annealing (SA) into PSO, whose basic concept includes two steps: First, the standard PSO algorithm was performed for particle swarm. Afterwards, individual's own best position was taken as initial state variables for modified SA. The paper describes the new hybrid particle swarm optimization algorithm and compares it with the standard PSO and other PSOs.

2 Standard Particle Swarm Optimization

PSO simulates the behaviors of bird flocking and used it to solve the optimization problems. PSO is initialized with a group of random particles (solutions) and then

D.-S. Huang, K. Li, and G.W. Irwin (Eds.): ICIC 2006, LNBI 4115, pp. 50 – 60, 2006.

searches for optima by updating generations. In every generation, each particle is updated by following two "best" values. The first one is the best solution (fitness) it has achieved so far. This value is called *pbest*. Another "best" value that is tracked by the particle swarm optimizer is the best value, obtained so far by any particle in the population. This best value is a global best and called *gbest*. The velocity and positions of each particle is updated according to their best encountered position and the best position encountered by any particle with following equation.

$$v_{i+1} = w * v_i + c_1 * rand * (pbest - p_i) + c_2 * rand * (gbest - p_i) \,. \tag{1}$$

$$p_{i+1} = p_i + v_{i+1} \,. \tag{2}$$

Where v_i is the particle velocity, p_i is the current particle position (solution), w is the inertia weight, the *pbest* and *gbest* are defined as stated before, rand is a random number between [0,1]. c1, c2 are learning factors, usually c1 = c2 = 2. If the velocity is higher than a certain limit called Vmax, this limit will be used as the new velocity for this particle in this dimension, thus keeping the particles within the search space.

3 Hybrid Algorithm of Particle Swarm Optimization (PSOSA)

When the optimal particle of particle swarm is got into local optimum, the particle swarm is very hard to jump out of the local optimum with standard PSO. The SA has the character of probability-sudden-jump so as to be able to jump out of the local optimum and approach the global minimum.

3.1 Simulated Annealing

Simulated Annealing (SA) was proposed by Metropolis in 1953 and Kirkpatrick successfully applied it in combined optimization in 1983 [13], which simulated the thermodynamics process of cooling of hot metal, that is, physical annealing process. It is able to jump out of the local optimum and approaches the global minimum whose essential reason is that it receives new state variable through probability judgment, which has been strictly proved in theory.

In order to find the optimal value, SA usually requires higher initial temperature, lower velocity of decreasing temperature, lower terminating temperature and enough samples in different temperature, so the process of SA is usually very long, which is the outstanding defect. In order to overcome this defect, the SA is modified below:

(1) The generator function of state variable take function express with Gaussian mutation as follows.

$$new\_pbest_d = pbest_d * (1 + \eta * \sigma) \tag{3}$$

where σ is a random number with Gaussian (0,1) distribution. Thus it could not only produce the lesser disturbance scope with the bigger probability to perform local searching, but also appropriately produce the bigger disturbance scope to jump out of local optima. The initial value of η is set 1.0, $\eta = \eta(1\text{-}interdec)$, *interdec* is a small constant.

(2) In order to decrease the iterative times, the sample stable principle is revised, that is, the process ends once the function value of new state variable is better than that of last generation individual.

3.2 PSOSA Optimization Strategy

Obviously, the modified SA disables the condition of global convergence so that it is hard to ensure the algorithm can converge to the global minimum. The concept of combining PSO with SA proposed in this paper merges the SA which has the ability to get rid of local minimum so as to avoid the premature convergence in the process of optimization; meanwhile, the parallel sample process can raise the time performance of optimization. The steps of PSOSA are described as follows:

Step 1: Set initial parameters of PSO: learning factor: c1, c2; swarm scale: m; maximum evolution generations: maxIter; SA: maxN1, maxN2;

Step 2: Generate m particle swarms randomly and determine the initial temperature of SA, temp=Temp0;

Step 3: updated velocity and position of the particle swarm according to formula (1) and (2);

Step 4: If it meets the convergence condition, be over; else operate the modified SA on particle swarm:

```
while TrailN < maxN1
    for j=1 to SwarmSize
        while AcceptN < maxN2
            Perform mutation on the optimal position pj of each
               individual of population according to formula (3).
            Calculating the fitness value new_fpbest of pj.
            if new_fpbest < fpbest
              Renew the corresponding individual's own the best fitness
                fpbest and position pbest, break;
            else if min{1, exp[-(fpbest - fbest)/temp]} > random[0, 1],
              Renew the corresponding individual's own current fitness
                fitnest and position pj , break;
            end if
            AcceptN = AcceptN + 1;
        end while
    end for
    temp = temp * TempRatio;
    TrailN = TrailN + 1;
end while
```

Step 5: If reach the maximum evolution generations or getting a satisfying value, end the optimization, else turn to step 3.

In the above algorithm, linearly decreasing weight was used. The initial temperature of SA is determined by formula (4) according to the maximum fitness(*fworse*) and minimum fitness(*fbest*) of initial swarm.

$$Temp0 = -(fworse - fbest)/ln(Pr) \tag{4}$$

where Pr is also small constant seeing reference [13] .

The PSOPA merges two different optimizations mechanisms into a whole which is in favor of enriching the search behavior during optimization process and enhancing the searching ability and efficiency in global and local. PSO enables SA to be parallel SA. Meanwhile, the SA enhances and complements the ability of PSO getting rid of local minimum, which avoid getting into local minimum and approach global minimum.

4 Experiments Setting and Results

For comparison, six benchmark functions that are commonly used in the evolutionary computation literature are used. All functions have same minimum value, which are equal to zero. The f0 and f3 are unimodal functions. The rest are multimodal functions.

The function f0 is the Sphere function:

$$f_0(x)=\sum_{i=1}^{n} x_i^2, x_i \in [-1000,1000]. \quad (5)$$

The function f1 is the Rastrigrin function:

$$f_1(x)=\sum_{i=1}^{n}(x_i^2-10\cos(2\pi x_i)+10), x_i \in [-5.12,5.12]. \quad (6)$$

The function f2 is the Griewank function:

$$f_2(x)=\frac{1}{4000}\bullet\sum_{i=1}^{n} x_i^{\,2}-\prod_{i=1}^{n}\cos(\frac{x_i}{\sqrt{i}})+1, x_i \in [-600,600]. \quad (7)$$

The function f3 is the Rosenbrock function:

$$f_3(x)=\sum_{i=1}^{n}(100(x_i^{\,2}-x_{i+1})^2+(1-x_1)^2), x_i \in [-30,30]. \quad (8)$$

The function f4 is the Ackley function:

$$f_4(x)=-20\times\exp\left(-0.2\sqrt{\frac{1}{n}\sum_{i=1}^{n} x_i^{\,2}}\right)-\exp\left(\frac{1}{n}\sum_{i=1}^{n}\cos(2\pi x_i)\right)+20+e, \quad x_i \in [-30,30] \quad (9)$$

The function f5 is the Schaffer function:

$$f_5(x)=0.5+\frac{(\sin\sqrt{x^2+y^2})^2 - 0.5}{(1.0+0.001(x^2+y^2))}, x, y \in [-5.12,5.12]. \quad (10)$$

For the purpose of comparison, we had 50 trial runs for benchmark functions above. The number of particle was set to 30. Three different dimensions of each function are used for comparison: 10, 20 and 30 (2 for Schaffer function). The goal value of Sphere, Rastrigrin, Griewank, Ackley and Schaffer functions were set to be 1.0e-10 and the goal value of Rosenbrock function was set to be 1.0e-6. For each algorithm, the maximum number of evaluations allowed was set to 300,000 (10,000 generations for PSO). Table 1 lists the Vmax values for all the functions, respectively. The acceleration constants were set as: c1=c2=2. The results for the benchmark functions are shown in table 2. In the table 2, the Avg/Std stands for average value and standard deviation of fitness value of 50 trail runs, the fevals stands for the average calculation times of function, Ras stands for the ratio of times of reaching goal value and the times of experiment. All results below 10e−10 were reported as ‘0’.

Figures 1–6 show typical convergence results of PSO and PSOSA. In each case it is seen that PSOSA performs better than PSO. On functions f0 and f4, there is almost a consistent performance pattern for both algorithm, they both converge

Table 1. Initial range of benchmark functions

Function	Vmax	Function	Vmax
f0	1000	f1	10
f2	600	f3	100
f4	30	f5	1

Table 2. The results of standard PSO and PSOSA

		StdPSO			PSOSA		
Fun	Dim	Avg/Std	fevals	Ras	Avg/Std	fevals	Ras
	10	0/0	140625.00	50/50	0/0	686.76	50/50
f0	20	0/0	188412.00	50/50	0/0	718.56	50/50
	30	0/0	221370.60	50/50	0/0	741.56	50/50
	10	1.433/1.067	276194.40	12/50	0/0	365.22	50/50
f1	20	11.860/4.644	300000	0/50	0/0	369.40	50/50
	30	26.824/6.587	300000	0/50	0/0	385.76	50/50
	10	0.062/0.024	300000	0/50	0/0	779.54	50/50
f2	20	0.035/0.030	284053.20	7/50	0/0	800.18	50/50
	30	0.016/0.018	269449.80	18/50	0/0	771.94	50/50
	10	6.609/16.563	300000	0/50	3.22E-07/3.02E-07	194891.70	50/50
f3	20	18.645/22.067	300000	0/50	3.29E-07/3.03E-07	354951.43	50/50
	30	44.687/72.424	300000	0/50	4.02E-07/3.22E-07	356490.00	50/50
	10	0/0	155889.00	50/50	0/0	612.34	50/50
f4	20	0/0	207005.40	50/50	0/0	621.48	50/50
	30	0/0	244439.00	50/50	0/0	621.80	50/50
f5	2	0.0001/0.002	857.58	47/50	0/0	491.10	50/50

exponentially toward the fitness optimum. However the convergence speed of PSOSA is much faster than that of PSO. In experiments with the f1, f2 functions the PSOSA clearly performs best and it finds the global optimum in all cases, and the PSO could not find the global optimum except several times when the test function is of low dimensionality for f1 and higher dimensionality for f2. For function f3

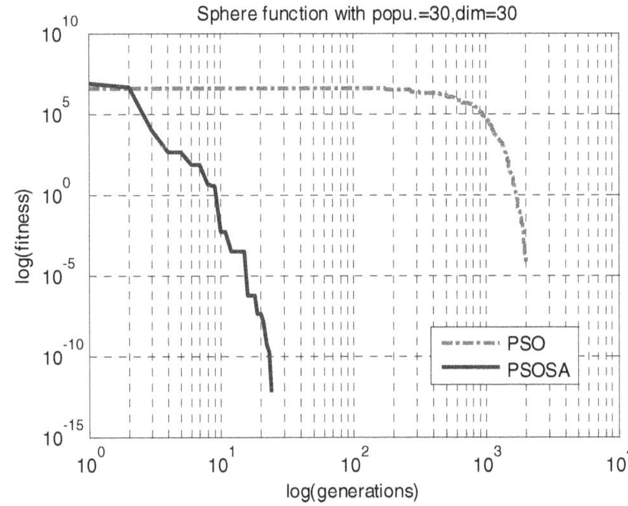

Fig. 1. Performance comparing of PSOSA and PSO on Sphere function

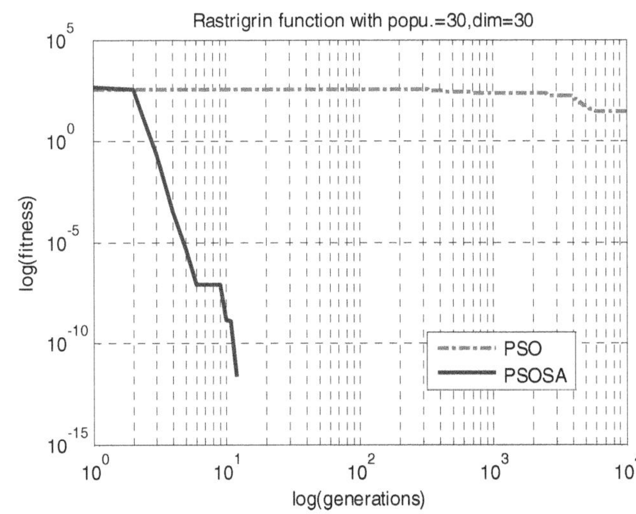

Fig. 2. Performance comparing of PSOSA and PSO on Rastrigrin function

PSOSA achieved the goal in any case, whereas PSO could not reach once. With function f5, PSO could not completely achieve the global optimum in all 50 runs. The stability of PSO is not good as PSOSA. By compare the results, it is easy to see that PSOSA have excellent performance. The performance of PSOSA is remarkably superior to PSO.

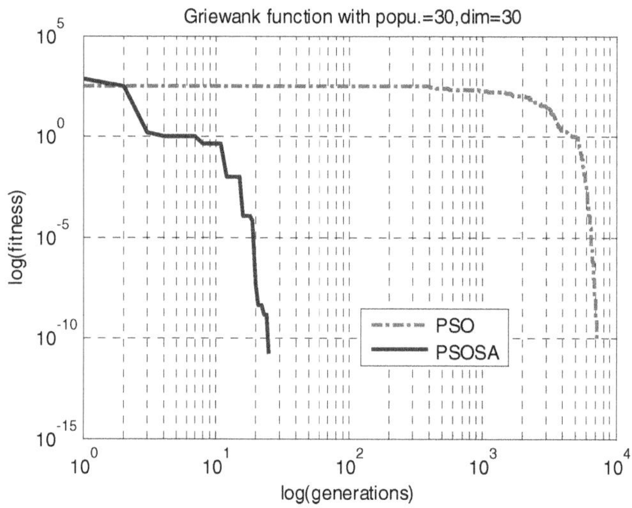

Fig. 3. Performance comparing of PSOSA and PSO on Griewank function

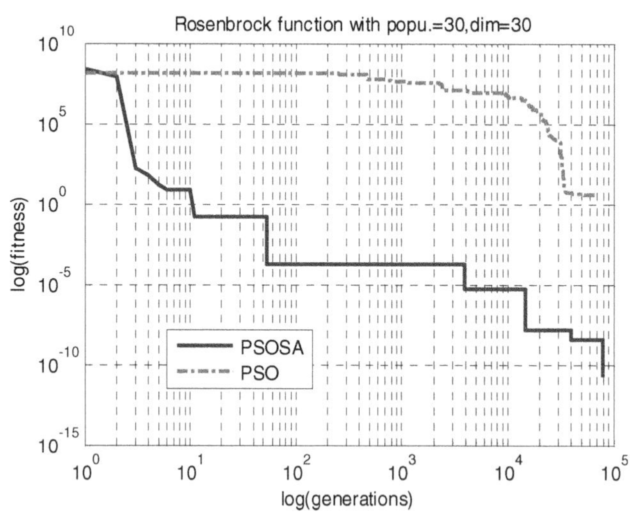

Fig. 4. Performance comparing of PSOSA and PSO on Rosenbrock function

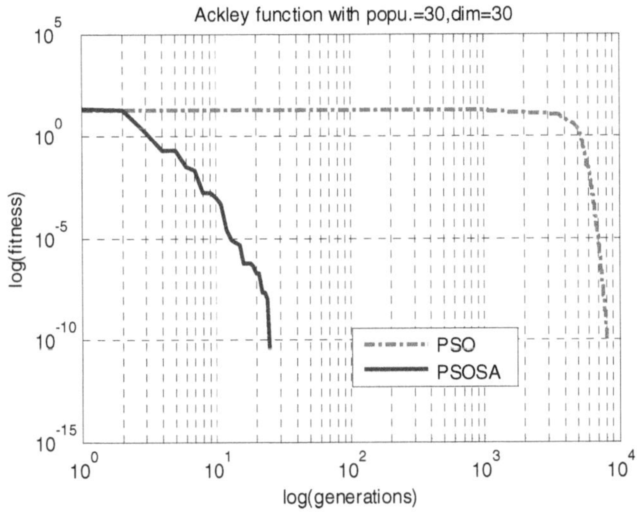

Fig. 5. Performance comparing of PSOSA and PSO on Ackley function

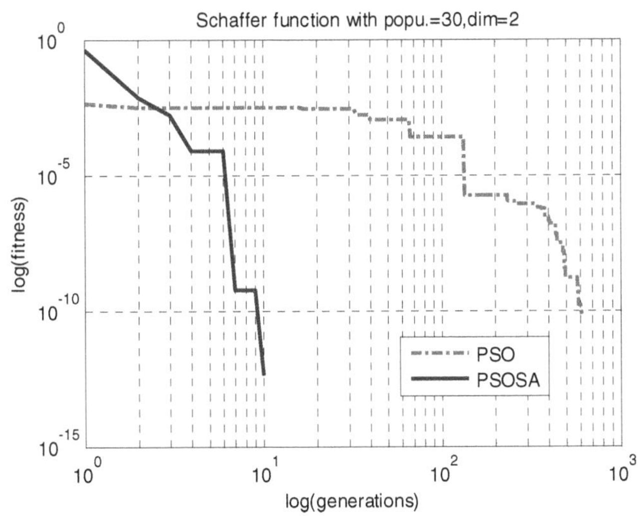

Fig. 6. Performance comparing of PSOSA and PSO on Schaffer function

5 Discussion

This paper has proposed a new particle swarm optimization algorithm called PSOSA. The implementation of this algorithm is simple based on SA. The new algorithm is shown to outperform PSO on all benchmark functions, being less susceptible to premature convergence, and less likely to be stuck in local optima. The many PSO algorithms about improvement of performance have recently been proposed by researchers. Lovbjerg, Rasmussen, and Krink also proposed hybridizing the algorithm borrowing the concepts from Genetic Algorithms [7]. Table 3 lists a representative set of results from [7]. The table also lists the corresponding average best fitness of the PSOSA and the standard GA. To make a fair comparison, the maximum number of evaluations allowed was set to 20,000, 30,000 and 40,000 for PSOSA algorithm when the number of particle is set to 20. Note that the numerical value 0 was obtained under Matlab. The number of the parenthesis in table 3 represents evaluations achieving the goal value.

In experiments with the Sphere function the PSOSA achieved the global minimum and had much faster convergence than both the standard GA and the Hybrid model. The GA and the Hybrid model found similar values. With the Rosenbrock function, the PSOSA had a better performance than both the GA and the Hybrid model. The Hybrid model only had a fitness value which is obviously better than standard GA when the test function was of low dimensionality. When the dimensionality of the test functions was higher, the GA accomplished almost the same results as the Hybrid model. In the experiments with the Griewank function, the GA failed to achieve a reasonable result compared to the other models. The PSOSA model had a faster convergence than the Hybrid model and standard GA. In experiments with the Rastrigin function, the PSOSA model was better than both the standard GA and the Hybrid.

Table 3. Performance comparison between PSOSA and Hybrid and GA for benchmark functions

function	Dim	Gen.	PSOSA	Std. GA	Hybrid
sphere	10	1000	0 ± 0(14902.77)	2.43E-04 ± 1.14E-05	2.42E-04 ± 2.17E-05
	20	1500	0 ± 0(14905.47)	0.00145 ± 6.22E-05	0.00212 ± 2.75E-04
	30	2000	0 ± 0(14866.37)	0.00442 ± 1.78E-04	0.01203 ± 6.33E-04
Rosenbrock	10	1000	0.17856 ± 1.25988	109.810 ± 6.212	43.521 ± 16.047
	20	1500	0.00043 ± 0.00111	146.912 ± 10.951	169.112 ± 21.535
	30	2000	0.57431 ± 4.05976	199.730 ± 16.285	187.033 ± 22.960
Griewank	10	1000	0 ± 0(651.57)	283.251 ± 1.812	0.09078 ± 0.03306
	20	1500	0 ± 0(699.57)	611.266 ± 3.572	0.00459 ± 0.01209
	30	2000	0 ± 0(703.90)	889.537 ± 3.939	0.09911 ± 0.00106
Rastrigin	10	1000	0 ± 0(702.73)	3.1667 ± 0.2237	3.0599 ± 0.1535
	20	1500	0 ± 0(777.10)	16.8732 ± 0.6007	11.6590 ± 0.3602
	30	2000	0 ± 0(728.57)	49.3212 ± 1.1204	27.8119 ± 0.8059

There are many modified versions of PSO algorithms at present besides the Hybrid algorithm. Table 4 shows a comparison of the performances in the PSOSA model, the DPSO modal [5], HPSO modal [9] and AEPSO modal [12] with regards to the optimum found. In all algorithms, the size of particle was set to 20, the dimension of test functions was set to 30, and the maximum number of evaluations allowed was 120,000. These comparisons suggest that PSOSA outperforms many of the recent improved PSO algorithms.

Table 4. Performance comparison between PSOSA and other PSOs for benchmark functions

Function	Algorithm	Min	Mean	Deviation	Max
Rosenbrock	DPSO	8.0e−02	34.02	35.10	1.4e+02
	HPSO	5.8e−02	1.1e+02	1.5e+02	7.2e+02
	AEPSO	2.8e−03	14.00	19.91	76.71
	PSOSA	7.6e-10	0.000031	0.000095	6.1e-004
Griewank	DPSO	4.4e−12	2.5e−02	3.0e−02	0.154
	HPSO	1.1e−16	1.5e−02	2.1e−02	8.5e−02
	AEPSO	0	1.2e−02	1.6e−02	6.6e−02
	PSOSA	0	0	0	0
Rastrigin	DPSO	7.2e−09	0.201	0.498	2.058
	HPSO	12.93	29.07	8.963	55.83
	AEPSO	0	0.577	1.084	3.980
	PSOSA	0	0	0	0

6 Conclusion

The paper proposes a new hybrid algorithm of PSO called PSOSA, which modify the SA and embedded it into the standard PSO so as to form a newly effective optimal algorithm. This algorithm not only keeps the characters of simple and easy to be implemented, but also strengthens the ability of getting rid of local optimum and raises the speed and accuracy of convergence. The testing results of typical benchmark functions with different dimensions demonstrate that the proposed algorithm is superior to particle standard PSO and other PSOs.

Acknowledgments

This work is supported by the NSF of Hubei Provincial Department of Education grant No. 2001Z02002.

References

1. Kennedy, J., Eberhart, R.C.: Particle Swarm Optimization. In: Proc. IEEE Int. Conf. on Neural Networks, Piscataway, NJ (1995) 1942-1948
2. Eberhart, R.C., Kennedy, J.: A New Optimizer Using Particle Swarm Theory. In: Proc. Sixth Int. Symposium on Micro Machine and Human Science, Nagoya, Japan (1995) 39-43
3. Shi, Y.H., Eberhart, R.C.: Fuzzy Adaptive Particle Swarm Optimization. In: Proc. of the IEEE Conference on Evolutionary Computation, Seoul, Korea (2001) 101-106
4. Thiemo, K., Jakob, S. V., Jacques, R.: Particle Swarm Optimization with Spatial Particle Extension. In: Proc. of the 2002 Congress on Evolutionary Computation, Honolulu, Hawaii (2002) 1474-1479
5. Xie, X.F., Zhang, W.J., Yang, Z.L.: Dissipative Particle Swarm Optimization. In: Proc. of the 2002 Congress on Evolutionary Computation. Honolulu, Hawaii (2002) 1456-1461

6. Angeline, P.J.: Evolutionary Optimization versus Particle Swarm Optimization: Philosophy and Performance Differences. In: Evolutionary programming VII: Proc. Of the Seventh Annual Conference on Evolutionary Programming (1998) 601-610
7. Morten, L., Thomas, K. R., Thiemo Krink: Hybrid Particle Swarm Optimization with Breeding and Subpopulations. In: Proc. of the third Genetic and Evolutionary Computation Conference, San Francisco Vol.1, (2001) 469-476
8. Natsuki H, Hitoshi I, Particle swarm optimization with Gaussian Mutation. In: Proc. of the Congress on Evolutionary Computation (2003) 72-79
9. Ratnaweera, A., Halgamuge, S.K., Watson HC.: Self-Organizing Hierarchical Particle Swarm Optimizer with Time-Varying Acceleration Coefficients. IEEE Trans. on Evolutionary Computation (2004) 240-255
10. 10.F van den, B.: An Analysis of Particle Swarm Optimizers. Ph.D. thesis, Department of Computer Science, University of Pretoria, South Africa (2002)
11. Thanmaya, P., Kalyan, V., Chilukuri, M.: Fitness-Distance Ratio Based Particle. Swarm Optimization. In: Proc. IEEE Swarm Intelligence Symposium, Indianapolis, Indiana (2003) 174-181
12. He, R., Wang, Y.J., Wang, Q., et al: An Improved Particle Swarm Optimization Based on Self-Adaptive Escape Velocity. Journal of Software, vol.16, (2005) 2036-2044
13. Wang, L.: Intelligent Optimization Algorithms with Applications. Tsinghua University Press, Beijing (2001)

A Novel Particle Swarm Optimizer Using Optimal Foraging Theory

Ben Niu[1,2], Yunlong Zhu[1], Kunyuan Hu[1], Sufen Li[1], and Xiaoxian He[1,2]

[1] Shenyang Institute of Automation, Chinese Academy of Sciences, Shenyang, 110016, China
[2] School of Graduate, Chinese Academy of Sciences, Beijing, 100039, China
{niuben, ylzhu}@sia.cn

Abstract. Based on the research of optimal foraging theory (OFT), we present a novel particle swarm optimizer (PSO) to improve the performance of standard PSO (SPSO). The resulting algorithm is known as PSOOFT that makes use of two mechanisms of OFT: a reproduction strategy to enhance the ability to converge rapidly to good solutions and a patch-choice based scheme to keep a right balance of exploration and exploitation. In the simulation studies, several benchmark functions are performed, and the performance of the proposed algorithm is compared to the standard PSO (SPSO). The experimental results show that the PSOOFT prevents premature convergence to a high degree, but still has a more rapid convergence rate than SPSO.

1 Introduction

In 1995, James Kennedy and Russell Eberhart applied Craig Reynolds's model to the problem of finding optima in a search space, which can be compared to a flock of birds looking for a food source, and created the PSO algorithm [1, 2]. Due to its simplicity in implementation and high computational efficiency in solving optimization problems, it has already come to be widely used in diverse scientific areas [3, 4].

However, it was pointed out that PSO usually suffers from premature convergence, tending to get stuck in local optima when strongly multi-modal problems are being optimized.

Various attempts have been made to improve the performance of basic PSO, which can be classified here as follows

i. tuning the parameters in the velocity and position update equations of PSO[5, 6, 7]
ii. designing different population topologies [8, 9, 10, 11]
iii. combining PSO with other search techniques [12, 13,14]
iv. incorporating bio-inspired mechanisms into the basic PSO[15, 16]
v. utilizing multi-population scheme instead of single population of the basic PSO [17, 18, 19, 20]

Nature always presents us with a wide variety of simple biological models which have the bonus effect of increasing our knowledge of how to design more powerful

D.-S. Huang, K. Li, and G.W. Irwin (Eds.): ICIC 2006, LNBI 4115, pp. 61 – 71, 2006.

intelligent algorithm. Because the underlying idea of PSO is to mirror the social behavior of a flock of birds during the search of food, it is natural to think that if some biological models in optimal foraging theory can be employed to improve the performance of SPSO.

Optimal foraging theory formulates the foraging problem as an optimization problem and via computational or analytical methods can provide an optimal foraging "policy" that specifies how foraging decisions are made [21]. Based on the research of OFT, we introduce two biological-inspired mechanisms as a first approach to enhance exploration without hurting the ability to converge rapidly to good solutions. The first mechanism is based on an analogy with reproduction in nature and aims to enhance the ability of convergence rate. The second mechanism is based on a patch choice scheme found in animal groups, where the particles (birds) are attracted to the position of the best particle with a predefined probability and simultaneously migrate to other palace in the searcher domain with another predefined probability.

We compare the performance of PSOOFT to that of the SPSO. In the next section the SPSO is reviewed. Description of the proposed algorithm PSOOFT is given in section 3. Next, experimental settings and experimental results are given in section 4. Finally, section 5 concludes the paper.

2 Review of Standard PSO (SPSO)

Similar to some evolutionary computation techniques such as genetic algorithms (GA) and evolutionary strategy (ES), PSO is a population-based stochastic optimization technique that belongs to the category of swarm intelligence [4] method. Although PSO bears some resemblances to evolutionary computation techniques, some evolution operators such as crossover, mutation and selection are not performed in PSO.

In PSO, the potential solutions, called particles, fly in a D-dimension search space with a velocity that is dynamically adjusted according to its own experience and that of its neighbors. The ith particle is represented as $\vec{x}_i = (x_{i1}, x_{i2}, ... x_{iD})$, where $x_{id} \in [l_d, u_d]$, $d \in [1, D]$, l_d, u_d are the lower and upper bounds for the dth dimension, respectively. The velocity for particle i is represented as $\vec{v}_i = (v_{i1}, v_{i2}, ..., v_{iD})$, which is clamped to a maximum velocity vector $\vec{v}_{\max}$. The best previous position of the ith particle is recorded and represented as $P_i = (P_{i1}, P_{i2}, ..., P_{iD})$, which is also called *pbest*. The index of the best particle among all the particles in the population is represented by the symbol g, and P_g is called *gbest*. At each iteration step t, the particles are manipulated according to the following equations:

$$v_i(t+1) = v_i(t) + R_1 c_1 (P_i - x_i(t)) + R_2 c_2 (P_g - x_i(t)). \quad (1)$$

$$x_{id} = x_{id} + v_{id}, \; i = 1, 2, \ldots S \text{ and } j = 1, 2, \ldots D. \quad (2)$$

where

S number of particles;
D number of dimensions in a particle;
w inertia weight;
c_1, c_2 acceleration constants;
R_1, R_2 random vectors with components uniformly distributed in [0, 1].

Shi and Eberhart [5] later introduced an inertia term w by modifying (1) to:

$$v_i(t+1) = w \times v_i(t) + R_1 c_1 (P_i - x_i(t)) + R_2 c_2 (P_g - x_i(t)). \quad (3)$$

They proposed that suitable selection of w will provide a balance between global and local explorations, thus requiring less iterations on average to find a sufficiently optimal solution. As originally developed, w often decreases linearly from about 0.9 to 0.4 during a run. In general, the inertia weight w is set according to the following equation:

$$w = w_{\max} - \frac{w_{\max} - w_{\min}}{iter_{\max}} \times iter. \quad (4)$$

where

$w_{\max}$ the initial weight;
$w_{\min}$ the final weight;
$iter$ the current iteration number;
$iter_{\max}$ the maximum number of allowable iterations.

3 A Novel PSO Based on Optimal Foraging Theory

3.1 Optimal Foraging Theory (OFT)

Animals as a group are what we call ingestive heterotrophs, which means they are unable to produce their own food and they must eat things to get nutrition. Obviously getting food is one of the most important and basic needs common to all animals, second only to reproduction. If successful reproduction is the ultimate destination of animals, then food is the fuel that allows the animal to reach its destination. Foraging behavior of animals has received much attention from behavioral biologists, on both empirical and theoretical grounds.

Foraging theory [21, 22] is based on the assumption that animals search for and obtain nutrients in a way that maximizes their energy intake E per unit time T spent foraging. Hence they try to maximize a function like E/T.

Maximization of such a function provides nutrient sources to survive and additional time for other import activities such as mating and reproducing. Successful foraging behaviors promote survival of foragers. On the other hand, animals that have poor foraging strategies will be eliminated by natural selection.

For many animals, nutrients are distributed among patches, e.g., a dike with rice paddies, a bush with berries and a group of trees with fruit. Foraging involves two essential decisions. The first is whether to enter a patch and search for food, and the second is to judge whether to continue searching for food in the current patch or to pursue alternative patches with more profitable nutrients than the current patch.

3.2 PSOOFT

Because the main concept of the PSO is to mimic the behavior of a swarm which search for food resources on a field, it is therefore natural to ask if optimal foraging theory can be employed to improve the performance of SPSO. Inspired the research discussed above, we found that two aspects of OFT is suitable to be incorporated into the SPSO model.

Table 1. Procedure for the implement of patch choice scheme

Step 1: Search within neighborhood of the birds' previous best positions with probability PC

Step 1.1: Select the original top SR individuals used for chaotic local search. Set $k=0$, and the maximum chaotic iteration K;

Step 1.2: For each individual, generate an initialized D-dimensional vector $z^0=[z_1^0, z_2^0, \ldots z_D^0]$, $z_d^0 \in (0,1)$ and that $z_d^0 \notin \{0.25, 0.5, 0.75\}$

Step 1.3: Determining the chaotic variables for the next iteration using: $z_i^{k+1}=uz_i^k(1-z_i^k)$ $(i=1,2,..SR, u=4)$.

Step 1.4: Do the local search within the neighborhood of the current best position of the birds according to $X_i^{k+1}=pbest_i+\alpha_i(2z_i^{k+1}-1)$. α_i is the radius of the local search and 0.1 that of the given value range of the corresponding variable.

Step 1.5: Evaluating the new solution with X_i^{k+1}

Step 1.6: For each bird, update $pbest$ when the new solution is better than it; let $k=k+1$ and go back to Step 1.1.

Step 1.7: Terminate if the maximum chaotic iteration is reached.

Step 2: Migrate to other palace in the searcher domain with probability $1-PC$ $X_i=rand(S,D)*(u_d-l_d)+l_d$.

Table 2. The pseudo code for PSOOFT

Initialize step: Set $S, D, u_d, l_d, c_1, c_2, w_{\max}, w_{\min}, NR, PC, K$. Random generate $X_0^d \in D$ in R^n, and $V_0^d \in [0, V_{\max}]$ $d = 1, 2, \ldots D$

Set $k := 0$

While (the termination conditions are not met)

FOR (each particle i in the swarm)

Calculate fitness: calculate the fitness value of current particle: $F(X_i)$

Update $pbest$ **and** $gbest$: compare the fitness value of $pbest$ with $F(X_i)$. If $F(X_i)$ is better than $pbest$, then set the $pbest$ to the current position X_i; Further more, if $F(X_i)$ is better that $gbest$, the reset $gbest$ to the current index in particle array

Update the velocity and positions: calculate velocities V_i and position X_i using Eq.1.and Eq.2, respectively

Limit the velocity: If $V_i > V_{\max}$ then $V_i = V_{\max}$. If $V_i < V_{\min}$ then $V_i = V_{\min}$

Reproduce particles: If $Mod(k, Nr) == 0$, sort particles fitness value in order. The SR particle with higher values die and the other SR particle with the best value split (and the copies that are made are placed at the same location as their parent).

Select Patch: **If** $rand < PC$, Step 1 is performed, Otherwise Step 2 is performed.

END FOR

Set $k := k + 1$

END WHILE

A. Reproduction

The birds incorporate some kind of pressure towards successful behavior, that is, birds that reach valleys must have some kind of reproductive reward, by generating more offspring-or by simply having a higher probability of generating offspring in each time step (suppose that the swarm is requested to find the lower values of one complex function).

After a given time step NR, a reproduction step is taken. Suppose that the population size is S. Let $SR = S/2$ be the number of population members who have had sufficient nutrients so that they will reproduce.

This reproduction procedure is performed as follow. The birds in the population are sorted in ascending order according to the value of the fitness function. Under this way, the population is divided into healthy part and unhealthy part, in which the SR birds with relatively lower fitness value are regarded as healthy one and possess the opportunity to reproduce, while the SR birds with higher fitness value indicated that they did not get as many nutrients during their lifetime of foraging and hence are unhealthy and thus unlikely to reproduce; then the SR unhealthy birds die and the other SR healthiest birds each split into two young birds, under this way the positions and velocities of the SR unhealthy birds is replaced by the SR healthy birds. It should be stressed that the personal best information associated with each of the birds is remained unchanged.

B. Patch Choice

To better understand how the patch choice model is incorporated in PSO, consider the following scenario: a group of birds are randomly searching food in an area. There are some pieces of food in the area being searched and only one piece of food is with more nutrients.

Suppose that X is the position of a bird and $F(X)$ $X \in R^D$ represents how much nutrients substances it get. Hence $pbest$ can be regarded as the previous position of the pieces of food searched by the birds and $gbest$ is the position where the best nutrients patch has been found. In each iteration time, the top SR healthy birds among the swarms search for the nearest resource within neighborhood of their previous best positions with probability PC, and migrate to other palace in the searcher domain with probability $1-PC$.

Because the underlying concept of chaotic local search [23] is similar to the bird's local search scheme, it was adopted to mimic the implement of the bird's local search around the neighborhood of the patches.

The procedure for the implement of patch choice model is described as Table 1. The overall procedure of PSOOFT is shown in Table 2.

4 Experiment and Result

In this section, six nonlinear benchmark functions that are commonly used in evolutionary computation literature [24, 25] are performed. The first two are unimodal while the latter three are multimodal with many local minima. They are listed in Table 3.

Table 3. Test functions

Sphere	$f_1(x) = \sum_{i=1}^{D} x_i^2$
Rosenbrock	$f_2(x) = \sum_{i=1}^{D} 100\times(x_{i+1} - x_i^2)^2 + (1-x_i)^2$
Rastrigrin	$f_3(x) = \sum_{i=1}^{D} (x_i^2 - 10\cos(2\pi x_i) + 10$
Griewank	$f_4(x) = \frac{1}{4000}\sum_{i=1}^{D} x_i^2 - \prod_{i=1}^{D}\cos(\frac{x_i}{\sqrt{i}}) + 1$
Ackley	$f_6(x) = -20\exp(-0.2\sqrt{\frac{1}{30}\sum_{i=1}^{D} x_i^2}) - \exp(\frac{1}{30}\sum_{i=1}^{D}\cos 2\pi x_i) + 20 + e$

For comparison, both the SPSO and PSOOFT were tested on those benchmark functions, when minimization was the focus.

The size of the population used for each problem as well as the initial hypercube into which the initial population was randomly taken, are presented in table 4.

The SPSO and PSOOFT parameters were set to the values $c_1 = c_2 = 2$, and a linearly inertia weight starting at 0.9 and ending at 0.4 was used. The maximum velocity of each particle was set to be half the length of the search space in one dimension. In addition, for PSOOFT the parameter NR, PC, K are set as 20, 0.8, 1000, respectively. A total of 50 runs for each experimental setting are conducted.

The experiment results (i.e. the best, worst, mean and standard deviation of the function values found in 50 runs) for each algorithm on each test function are listed in Table 5. From the values in table 5 we can conclude that the results obtained by PSOOFT are clearly better for all the test functions. Furthermore, with the PSOOFT concept, the standard deviation of the final solution for 50 trials was found to be significantly low for each function, which demonstrated the results generated by PSOSOT is more robust than that obtained by SPSO.

Table 4. Parameters of the test functions

Test Probem	Dim.	Popul. Size	Initial Hypercube
Sphere	30	40	$[50,100]^n$
Rosenbrock	30	40	$[15,30]^n$
Rastrigrin	30	40	$[2.56,5.12]^n$
Griewank	30	40	$[300,600]^n$
Ackley	30	40	$[16,32]^n$

Table 5. Comparison between PSOOFT and PSO

Algorithm	Mean	Worst	Best	Stddev
		Sphere		
SPSO	1.9909e-005	5.9520e-005	4.2271e-006	1.9601e-005
PSOOFT	1.0452e-049	1.0452e-048	6.3415e-089	1.0925e-049
		Rosenbrock		
SPSO	3.7921e+002	2.6053e+003	1.5444e+001	7.5566e+002
PSOOFT	2.8.428e+001	2.8820e+001	2.7832e+001	3.2630e-001
		Rastrigrin		
SPSO	5.0301e+001	8.5576e+001	2.5870e+001	1.2516e+001
PSOOFT	3.0516e+000	5.0148e+000	1.0102e+000	2.3450e-001
		Griwenk		
SPSO	2.1100e-002	1.713e-001	3.5229e-006	4.0300e-002
PSOOFT	1.7325e-005	6.7082e-004	1.3245e-006	9.8268e-005
		Ackley		
SPSO	1.98091e+001	2.1015e+001	8.600e-003	3.9017e+000
PSOOFT	1.8285e-008	8.2331e-007	1.5637e-10	1.1653e-007

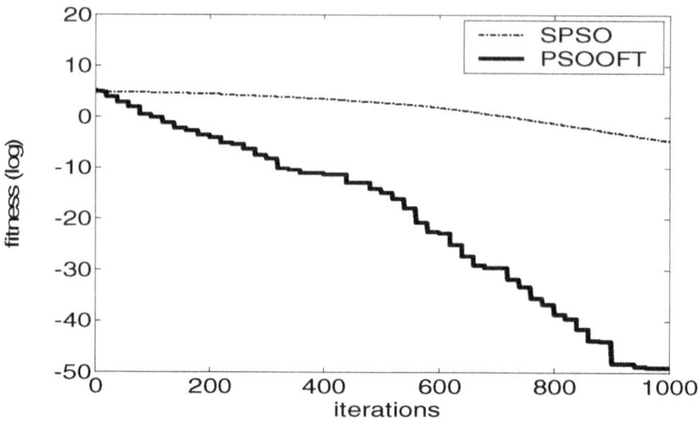

Fig. 1. Mean relative performance for Sphere function

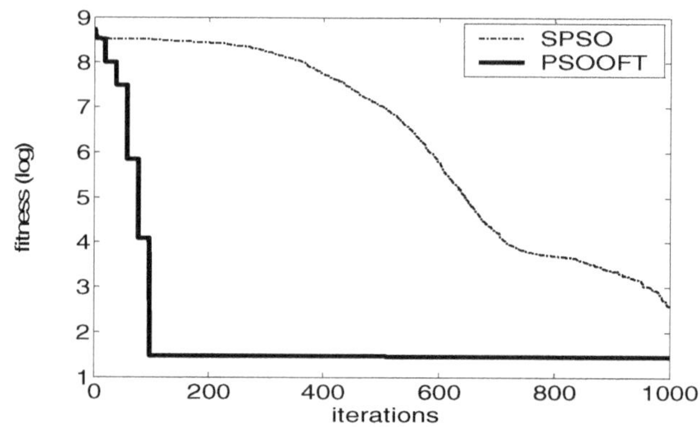

Fig. 2. Mean relative performance for Rosenbrock function

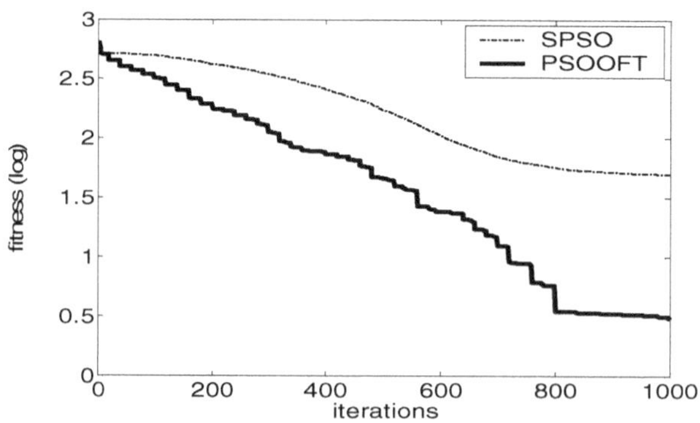

Fig. 3. Mean relative performance for Rastrigrin function

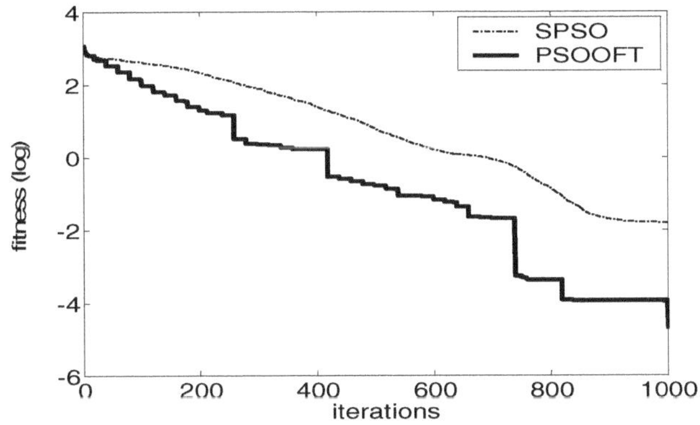

Fig. 4. Mean relative performance for Griewank function

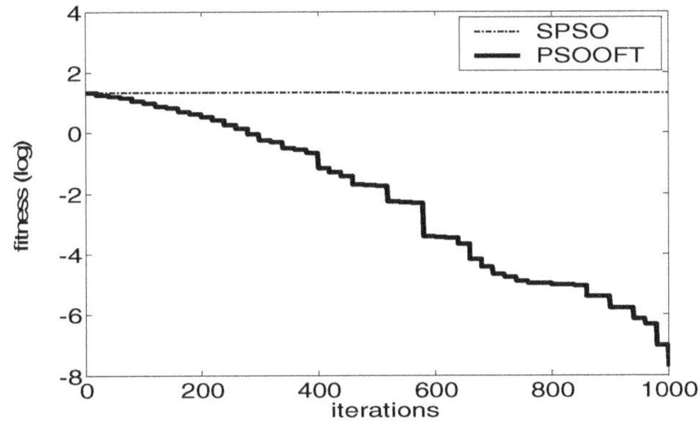

Fig. 5. Mean relative performance for Ackely function

The graphs presented in Figs.1-5 illustrated the evolution of best fitness for both algorithms, averaged for 50 runs of each algorithm. In a general analysis of the graphs in Figs.1-5 we can see it clearly PSOOFT converged faster and to a better value than the SPSO for all the test cases. The experiment with Ackley function illustrated this point very clearly. For SPSO there was almost no progression after the first 100 iterations, PSOOFT kept improving the best fitness in the swarm until the end of each run.

5 Conclusions and Future Work

Based on the research of Optimal Foraging Theory, two biological-inspired mechanisms (reproduction and patch choice) are introduced into SPSO and thus a novel particle swarm optimizer is presented. The resulting algorithm is referred to as PSOOFT, with the reproduction mechanism being the main responsible for the improvement of convergence rate, while the patch choice scheme clearly helped the algorithm escape local minima and yield promising results. A set of 5 benchmark functions has been used to test the performance of PSOOFT in comparison with SPSO. The performance comparisons indicate that PSOOFT is superior to SPSO in both solution quality and convergence rate.

PSO is a relatively new optimization technique and there is plenty of space for possible improvements. Our future work will continue to develop new PSO variants to improve its performance, in particular by incorporated some biological-inspired models into the basic PSO. In addition, some extensive application on more complicated practical optimization problems will be performed to illustrate those new PSO variants. The authors invite any comments on this paper to be sent to the first author.

Acknowledgements

This work is supported by the National Natural Science Foundation of China (Grant No. 70431003) and the National Basic Research Program of China (Grant No. 2002CB312200).

References

1. Eberchart, R. C., Kennedy, J.: A New Optimizer Using Particle Swarm Theory. In: Proceeding of the 6th International Symposium on Micromachine and Human Science, Nagoya, Japan (1995) 39-43
2. Kennedy, J., Eberhart, R. C.: Particle Swarm Optimization. In: Proceeding. of IEEE International Conference on Neural Networks, Piscataway, NJ (1995) 1942-1948
3. Eberchart, R.C., Shi, Y.: Particle Swarm Optimization: Developments, Applications and Resources. In: Proceedings of the IEEE Congress on Evolutionary Computation, Piscataway, NJ (2001) 81-86
4. Kennedy, J., Eberhart, R. C., Shi, Y.: Swarm Intelligence. Morgan Kaufmann Publishers, San Francisco CA (2001)
5. Shi, Y., Eberhart, R. C.: A Modified Particle Swarm Optimizer. In: Proceedings of IEEE International Conference on Evolutionary Computation, Piscataway, NJ(1998) 69-73
6. Chatterjee, A., Siarry P.: Nonlinear Inertia Weight Variation for Dynamic Adaptation in Particle Swarm Optimization. Computers & Operations Research 33 (2006) 859-871
7. Clerc, M., Kennedy, J.: The Particle Swarm: Explosion, Stability, and Convergence in A Multidimensional Complex Space. IEEE Trans. on Evolutionary Computation 6 (2002) 58 - 73
8. Kennedy, J.: Small Worlds and Mega-minds: Effects of Neighborhood Topology on Particle Swarm Performance. In: Proceedings of the Congress on Evolutionary Computation, Piscataway, NJ 1999 (1931-1938)
9. Kennedy, J., Mendes, R.: Population Structure and Particle Swarm Performance. In: Proceedings of the 2002 Congress on Evolutionary Computation. Piscataway, NJ (2002) 1671--1675
10. Suganthan, P.N.: Particle Swarm Optimizer with Neighborhood Operator. In: Proceedings of the Congress on Evolutionary Computation (CEC 1999), Piscataway, NJ (1999)1958-1962
11. Hu, X., Eberhart, R. C.: Multiobjective Optimization Using Dynamic Neighborhood Particle Swarm Optimization. In: Proceedings of the Congress on Evolutionary Computation, Honolulu, Hawaii, USA (2002)1677-1681

12. Zhang, W. J., Xie, X. F.: DEPSO: Hybrid Particle Swarm with Differential Evolution Operator. In: Proceedings of IEEE Int. Conf. on Systems, Man and Cybernetics, Washington DC, USA (2003) 3816-3821
13. Juang, C. F.: A Hybrid of Genetic Algorithm and Particle Swarm Optimization for Recurrent Network Design. IEEE Trans. Syst., Man, and Cyber., Part B: Cybernetics 34 (2)(2004) 997-1006
14. Shi, X. H., Liang, Y. C. Lee, H. P., Lu, C., Wang, L. M.: An Improved GA and A Novel PSO-GA-Based Hybrid Algorithm. Information Processing Letters 93 (2005) 255-261
15. He, S., Wu, Q. H., Wen, J. Y., Saunders, J.R., Paton, R.C.: A Particle Swarm Optimizer with Passive Congregation,. Biosystems 78 (2004) 135-147
16. Xie, X. F., Zhang, W., Yang, Z.: Hybird Particle Swarm Optimizer with Mass Extinction. In: Proceedings of the. International Conference on Communication, Circuits and Systems, Chengdu, China (2002)1170-1173
17. Niu, B., Zhu, Y. L., He, X. X.: Construction of Fuzzy Models for Dynamic Systems Using Multi-population Cooperative Particle Swarm Optimizer. In: Wang, L.P., Jin, Y.C. (eds.): Fuzzy Systems and Knowledge Discovery. LNCS, Vol. 3613. Springer-Verlag, Berlin Heidelberg New York (2005) 987–1000
18. Niu, B., Zhu, Y. L., He, X. X.: Multi-Population Cooperative Particle Swarm Optimization. In: Capcarrere, M., Freitas, A.A., Bentley, P.J., Johnson, C.G., Timmis, J. (eds.): Advances in Artificial Life. LNCS, Vol. 3630. Springer-Verlag, Berlin Heidelberg New York (2005) 874–883
19. Van den Bergh, F., Engelbrecht, A. P.: A Cooperative Approach to Particle Swarm Optimization. IEEE Trans. on Evol. Comput.,8(3) (2004) 225 - 239
20. Blackwell, T., Branke, J.: Multi-Swarm Optimization in Dynamic Environments. In: Raidl, GR (eds.): Applications of Evolutionary Computing. LNCS, Vol. 3005. Springer-Verlag, Berlin Heidelberg New York (2004) 489-500
21. Stephens, D. W., Krebs, J. R.: Foraging Theory. Princeton University Press, Princeton New Jersey (1986)
22. Giraldeau, L-A., Caraco. T.: Social Foraging Theory. Princeton University Press, Princeton, New Jersey (2000)
23. Choi C, Lee J.: Chaotic Local Search Algorithm. Artificial Life and Robotics 2(1) (1998) 41-47
24. Angeline, P. J.: Using Selection to Improve Particle Swarm Optimization. In: Proceedings of the 1998 IEEE Congress on Evolutionary Computation, Piscataway, NJ (1998) 84-89
25. Shi, Y., Eberhart, R. C.: Empirical Study of Particle Swarm Optimization. In: Proceedings of the 1999 IEEE Congress on Evolutionary Computation, Piscataway NJ (1999) 1945-1950

A Smart Particle Swarm Optimization Algorithm for Multi-objective Problems

Xiaohua Huo, Lincheng Shen, and Huayong Zhu

Mechatronics and Automation School, National University of Defense Technology, Changsha 410073, China
cindy.huo@gmail.com, lchshen@nudt.edu.cn, nethead@vip.sina.com

Abstract. Maintaining the diversity and convergence of Pareto optimal solutions is a desired task of optimization methods for multi-objective optimization problems(MOP). While accelerating the computing speed is important for algorithms to solve real-life MOP also. A Smart Particle Swarm Optimization algorithm for MOP(SMOPSO) is proposed. By setting the cooperative action of all the objective functions as the global best guide of swarm and selecting the closest or farthest archive member as the personal best guide of each particle, the SMOPSO method can find many Pareto optimal solutions in less iteration steps. Three well-known test functions have been used to validate our approach. Results show that the SMOPSO method is available and rapid.

1 Introduction

Problem with multiple objectives are present in a great variety of real-life optimization problems[1]. Since different objectives may be conflict with each other, multi-objective optimization problems(MOP) often have no unique optimal solution. Indeed the goal of MOP is to find a set of equilibrium solutions in one simulation run, which called Pareto-Optimal solutions, in stead of a single optimal solution. Evolutionary algorithms(EA) have proved very efficient in solving multi-objective optimization problems[2]. Different from evolutionary computation techniques, nowadays a new algorithm called Particle Swarm Optimization(PSO), is motivated from the simulation of insects and animals social behavior. A PSO consists of a population of particles, which on the contrary to evolutionary algorithms, survive up to the last generation[7]. Particles in the swarm search the variable space by moving with a special speed toward the best position using their experience from the past generations and communication among particles. PSO algorithm has proved very efficient in solving a number of problems in science and engineering.

Recently, investigators are paying more and more interest on PSO to solve MOP[1,2,3,4,?,6,7,8,9]. Change a PSO to a multi-objective PSO(MOPSO) requires a redefinition of what a guide is in order to obtain a front of optimal solutions[4]. Researchers proposed different strategies to find the best global guide for each particle, such as dynamic neighborhood[3], dominated tree[6], sigma dominance approach[7,8,9], a grid method[5], etc. , which will be discussed in section3. All of these methods focus on maintaining the diversity and

D.-S. Huang, K. Li, and G.W. Irwin (Eds.): ICIC 2006, LNBI 4115, pp. 72–80, 2006.

convergence of Pareto optimal solutions. Nevertheless computing speed of an algorithm is more important for solving many practical problems. Reducing the iteration step, population size and generation of algorithms can accelerate the computing speed. But it is difficult to keep the diversity and convergence of solutions at the same time. In this paper we present a new method to select the best global and personal guide for each particle in the swarm at each interval, which can find many Pareto optimal solutions rapidly.

The paper is organized as follows. In section 2, the basic concepts about MOP are defined. In section 3, the general PSO model is introduced firstly. Then researches on Multi-Objective PSO(MOPSO) in the literature are described briefly. In section 4, a smart MOPSO method is proposed, which can find more Pareto optimal solutions in less iteration step with small population size and generation, by redefining the global best and the personal best of particles. And the experiments and comparisons are given in section 5, which proved the conclusion. At last discussion conclusions and future works are describes in section 6.

2 Basic Concepts

The general Multi-Objective Optimization Problem can be defined as:

Definition 1. *Find a vector* $\overrightarrow{x} = [x_1, x_2, \ldots, x_n]^T \in \Omega$, *which minimizes the objective functions:* $F(\overrightarrow{x}) = (f_1(\overrightarrow{x}), f_2(\overrightarrow{x}), \ldots, f_k(\overrightarrow{x}))^T$, *and satisfies the constrains:* $G(\overrightarrow{x}) = (g_1(\overrightarrow{x}), g_2(\overrightarrow{x}), \ldots, g_l(\overrightarrow{x}))^T$, *where* $k, l \in N$, *indicate the number of objective functions and constrains,* $\Omega \in R^n$ *is the set of feasible solutions.*

Different objective functions restrict each other usually. The optimization of one objective may worsen others. A rather practical approach to deal with multi-objective problems is to find a Pareto Set, instead of a single aggregate objective-dependent global optimum. The concepts of Pareto optimal are defined as follows.

Definition 2. *(Pareto Dominance):A vector* $\overrightarrow{x} = [x_1, x_2, \ldots, x_n]^T$ *is said Pareto dominate, denoted by* $\overrightarrow{x} \prec \overrightarrow{y}$, *if* $\forall i \in \{1, 2, \ldots, k\} : f_i(\overrightarrow{x}) \leq f_i(\overrightarrow{y})$, *and at least one* i, $f_i(\overrightarrow{x}) < f_i(\overrightarrow{y})$. $\overrightarrow{x}$ *is weakly dominate* $\overrightarrow{y}$, *denoted by* $\overrightarrow{x} \preceq \overrightarrow{x}$, *if* $\forall i \in \{1, 2, \ldots, k\} : f_i(\overrightarrow{x}) \leq f_i(\overrightarrow{y})$.

Definition 3. *(Pareto Optimality):A vector* $\overrightarrow{x^*} = [x_1^*, x_2^*, \ldots, x_n^*]^T$ *is a Pareto optimal, if* $\forall \overrightarrow{x} \in \Omega$ *satisfies* $f_i(\overrightarrow{x^*}) \leq f_i(\overrightarrow{x}), \forall i \in \{1, 2, \ldots, k\}$, *and at least one* i *such that* $f_i(\overrightarrow{x^*}) < f_i(\overrightarrow{x})$.

Definition 4. *(Pareto Optimal Set):The non-dominated set of the entire feasible search space is the Pareto optimal set, which is defined as:*$P^* = \{\overrightarrow{x^*} \in \Omega | \overrightarrow{x^*} \prec \overrightarrow{x}, \forall \overrightarrow{x} \in \Omega\}$.

Definition 5. *(Pareto Optimal Front): The Pareto Optimal Set in the objective space is called Pareto Optimal Front, which can be defined as:* $F^* = \{F(\overrightarrow{x^*}) = (f_1(\overrightarrow{x^*}), f_2(\overrightarrow{x^*}), \ldots, f_k(\overrightarrow{x^*})) | \overrightarrow{x^*} \in P^*\}$.

3 Particle Swarm Optimization

3.1 General PSO

Particle swarm optimization(PSO) was first proposed by Kenedy and Elberhart in 1995[10], which was inspired by the choreography of a bird flock. PSO is a stochastic search algorithm that conducts searches using a population of particles. The status of a particle can be described by its position and velocity. The new velocity and position of a particle for the next interval are calculated using the following equations:

$$V_i^{k+1} = \omega * V_i^k + c_1 * rand1 * (pBest_i^k - P_i^k) + c_2 * rand2 * (gBest^k - P_i^k) \quad (1)$$

$$P_i^{k+1} = P_i^k + V_i^{k+1} \quad (2)$$

where V_i^k and P_i^k indicate for velocity and position of particle i at interval k. $pBest_i^k$ represents the best position of particle i in its past experience at interval k, and $gBest^k$ is the best position of the population.

The formulation includes three components. First is the particle present velocity, dedicating the particle current status, it can balance global and local searching capability. Second is cognition model, expressing the particles cognition ability, it can make particles have enough global searching capability avoiding local maximum. Last is social model, representing communication among particles. Particles land the best position effectively with three components acting together. Otherwise, as a particle adjusting its position according to velocity, it must keep the velocity in the range of min-velocity and max-velocity. $\omega, c_1, c_2 \geq 0$. ω is the inertia weight. c_1 and c_2 convey the weight information of cognition model and social model. $rand1$ and $rand2$ are two random values in the range $[0, 1]$. Shi and Eberhart[11] find that bigger inertia weight benefits particles search the problem space entirely, smaller inertia weight is in favor of local searching. They first introduced a linearly decreasing inertia weight to PSO. For more details about PSO algorithm, readers can be referred to [10,11,12].

Since PSO has few parameters to adjust and is easy to implement[12], it has been applied in a lot of areas. Multi-objective optimization problem is one of the most studied application areas of PSO algorithms[12].

3.2 Previous Research in Multi-objective PSO

During the past decade, several Multi-Objective Particle Swarm Optimization (MOPSO) methods have been proposed. In this section, we discussed briefly some of these methods.

Hu and Eberhart[3] use a dynamic neighborhood strategy to select the global best. In their method distances of a particle to other particles are calculated in terms of the first objective called *fixed objective*. Based on the calculated distances, local neighbors of each particle are found. Then the local best particle is selected in terms of the second objective values among the neighbors. Since the *fixed objective* must be selected firstly, a priori knowledge about the objective functions must be known.

Parsopoulos and Vrahatis[4] use a weighted aggregate approach and vector evaluated PSO dealing with on a number of two dimensional problems. The weighted aggregate algorithms need to be run several times, and get a single global best at each run. The vector evaluated PSO uses one swarm for each objective, and select the best particle of each swarm act as the global best particle guide each other. For example, the best particle of the second swarm is used determine the velocities of the first swarm. The main problem with [3] and [4] is their formulation purely for two-dimension problems.

Coello and Lechuga[5] proposed a grid method. The objective space is divided into many small hypercubes, and a fitness value is assigned to each hypercube depending on the number of elite particles that lie in it. The more elite particles the hypercube have, the less fitness value of it. Then select one of the hypercubes by roulette-wheel. Global best is a random particle selected from the selected hypercube. So, it is possible that a particle doesn't select a suitable guide as its local guide[7].

Fieldsend and Singh[6] used a dominated tree (D-Tree) for storing the particle, which consists of a list of composite points ordered by the weakly dominates relation. In this method the selection of the best global guide for a particle in the population is based on its closeness to a particle in the archive. The D-Tree method is said to be better than grid method proposed by Coello and Singn.

Bartz and Konstantinous[2] proposed a PSO using enhanced archiving techniques called DOPS. DOPS integrates well-known archiving techniques from evolutionary algorithms into PSO.

Cagnina and Esquivel[1] presented a hybrid PSO approach, including elitist policy, a mutation operator and a grid which is used as a geographical location over objective function space. This hybrid PSO method is an inspiration of multi-objective evolutionary algorithms also.

Mostaghim and Teich[7,8,9] proposed a sigma method for finding the suitable global best for each particle. Sigma values are calculated for each individual in the archive and new generation. Each particle selects the archive member with minimal sigma value to its sigma value as its social leader. And the sigma MOPSO method fixes the size of the archive to a certain amount using the idea of sigma dominance. Comparing to MOGA and D-Tree method, the Sigma MOPSO method has a better diversity and convergence.

4 Smart PSO for Multi-objective Problem

It is the cognition model and social model that guide a particle fly away its current position toward a better position in the search space, which we can find from the velocity and position updating formula(1) and (2). So, selection of the global best (*gBest*) and the personal best (*pBest*) is the key for PSO to solve multi-objective problems. The previous researches in MOPSO are focus on selection *gBest* from archive members. This paper, we present new selection methods of *gBest* and *pBest*, which can guide swarm members convergent rapidly and maintain the diversity of solutions.

In figure1, we can see how dose a particle fly in the two dimensional objectives space. For example, if there is only one objective function f_1 or f_2 , particle A will fly along v_1 or v_2. Since two objective functions affect on the particle at the same time, particle A will fly along $\overrightarrow{v}$ in stead of v_1 or v_2, until land the Pareto Front.

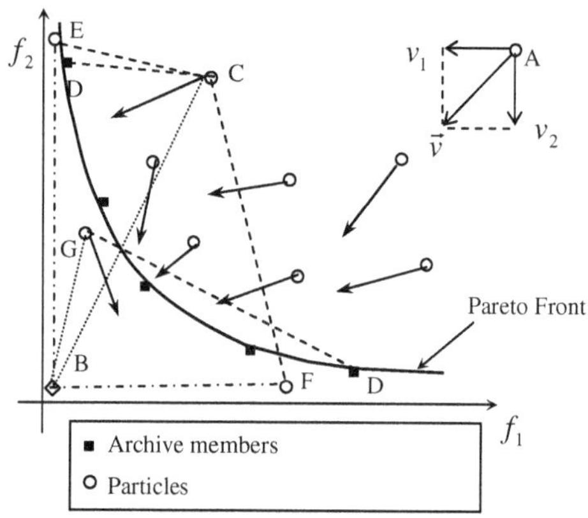

Fig. 1. Particles fly in the two-dimensional objective space

So the first important thing for MOPSO is how to guide particles fly along the direction incorporating all objective functions. The method we presented is to find the cooperative action of all objective functions as global best guide. Firstly, best particles for each objective function of MOP are selected by calculating the fitness values of every particles under each function. Secondly, the mean value of those particles is calculated. Then the mean value is set as *gBest* for particles of the swarm. As shown in figure 1, particle E is the best particle for objective f_1, particle F is the best particle for function f_2, point B indicates for the *gBest* of two dimensional problems. In fact, point B is not the true position of *gBest*, but a virtue position.

Particles directed by point B will fly across the Pareto Front and converge at a certain point. Then the next important problem is how to guide particles fly along the Pareto Front. Here we use archive members serve as the personal best to guide particles fly back to Pareto front. Firstly, the distances between each particle and non-dominate archive solutions are calculated. Then the archive member with minimal distance to one particle will be selected as *pBest* of a particle. For instance, the particle C in figure1 will fly toward Pareto front under the cooperative direction of point D, E and F. As iteration steps increasing, particles may fly slower and slower since they are too close to the Pareto front. Sometimes, those particles may gather together. So we add an additional strategy to disperse those clustering particles. That is guiding particles fly toward the remotest archive member with maximal distance to themselves. And set a *distance valve* as the boundary. While the distance between a particle and its closest archive member is less than the *distance valve*, its remotest archive member will be chosen as its *pBest*, otherwise its closest archive member will be chosen. The distance between particle p and archive member a can be calculated by formula:

$$Dis(p,a) = \|p - a\| = \{\sum_{i=1}^{n}(p_i - a_i)\}^{\frac{1}{2}} \quad (3)$$

The structure of SMOPSO for multi-objective optimization discussed above is shown in table1. First, particles are initialized randomly. In step 3, the non-dominated solutions are selected according to the Pareto optimal definitions. In step 4 and 5, *gBest* and *pBest* are selected using the strategies proposed in this paper. Generations are updated by formula (1) and (2) in step 6. Iterating step 2 to step7, the algorithm finds non-dominate solutions in the objective space, and updates archive with the new generations.

Table 1. Structure of SMOPSO Algorithm

	Begin
Step 1:	Set $k = 0$ and initialize particles.
Step 2:	Calculate fitness vale of particles under each objective.
Step 3:	Select the non-dominated solutions, keep in the archives and remove the dominated archive members.
Step 4:	Find the *gBest* of particle swarm.
Step 5:	Find the *pBest* of each particle.
Step 6:	Update generation.
Step 7:	$k = k + 1$. Go to step2 unless a termination criterion is met.
	End

5 Experiments

Following experiments have been performed on different test functions which selected from [13]and[7], shown in table 2. T_1 is a simple two-dimensional objective problem with only one parameter. T_2 is a composition of three functions f_1, f_2, g with thirty parameters, which g is the constrain function. And this two-dimensional objective problem has a discontinuous Pareto Front. T_3 is a typical three-dimensional objective problem, and always acts as a test function for multi-objective optimizing algorithms. Its Pareto Front satisfies the formula: $f_1(\overrightarrow{x}) + f_2(\overrightarrow{x}) + f_3(\overrightarrow{x}) = 1$.

Set ω, c_1, c_2 as: $\omega = 0.8 - (0.8 - 0.4)/k, c_1 = 0.4 + (0.8 - 0.4)/k, c_2 = 0.4 + (0.8 - 0.4)/k$, which k denotes the generation index. Tests are done for 200 particles, 10 generations and 100 particles, 3 generations on T_1 with 0 *distance valve* separately. Figure 2 (a) and (b) show the results of those tests. And set population size as 200 run for 10 generations on T_2 and T_3 with *distance valve* 0. 1 and 0. 35 separately. Tests are done for the Sigma MOPSO[4,5,6] method

Table 2. Test Functions:T_i

Test	Functions	Constrains
T_1	$f_1(x) = x^2$ $f_2(x) = (x-2)^2$	$x \in [-5, 7]$
T_2	$g(x_2, x_3, \dots, x_n) = 1 + 9 * (\sum_{i=2}^{n} x_i)/(n-1)$ $f_1(x_1) = x_1$ $f_2(\overrightarrow{x}) = 1 - {}^{f_1/g}\sqrt{-}(f_1/g) * \sin(10 * pi * f_1)$	$x_i \in [0, 1]$ $n = 30$ $i = 1, 2, \dots, n$
T_3	$f_1(\overrightarrow{x}) = (1 + x_3) * \cos(x_1 * pi/2) * cos(x_2 * pi/2)$ $f_2(\overrightarrow{x}) = (1 + x_3) * \cos(x_1 * pi/2) * \sin(x_2 * pi/2)$ $f_3(\overrightarrow{x}) = (1 + x_3) * \sin(x_1 * pi/2)$	$x_i \in [0, 1]$ $i = 1, 2, 3$

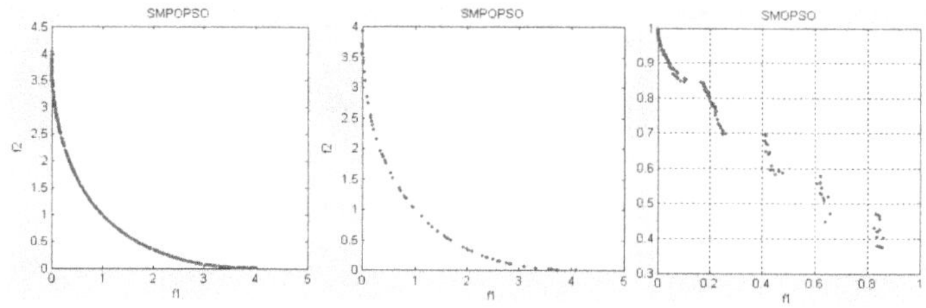

(a) (b) (c)

Fig. 2. Test results on function 1 and 2

on T_3 also. The parameters of the Sigma MOPSO method are: 200 particles, 10 generations with turbulence 0. 07.

Comparing figure 2 (b) with (a), we can see that the algorithm presented in this paper can cover the Pareto Front even the population size and generation are very small. This characteristic is very important to accelerate the computing speed. Figure 2 (c) shows the test result on test function 2. In fact several tests have been done on T_2. Increasing the populations size and generation, SMOPSO will find more solutions.

Figure 3 show the results on T_3. In those tests, we get 998 solutions by using the SMOPSO method and only 168 solutions by using the Sigma PSO method. Comparing the SMOPSO method with the Sigma method, the SMOPSO method can find more solutions on the front just in ten iteration steps, show in figure 3 (a-1) and (a-2). Sometimes the solutions may gather at some area of the Pareto Front. Some heuristic technique such as dynamic adaptive *distance value*, selective archiving, heuristic initialization, etc. , will be used to improve the algorithm for keeping diversity of solutions in future.

In order to evaluate the convergence of algorithms, we calculate the difference between archive member and Pareto optimal solution, which is defined as:

$$err = 1 - (f_1(\overrightarrow{x}) + f_2(\overrightarrow{x}) + f_3(\overrightarrow{x})), \ \forall i \in Archive. \tag{4}$$

Hence we can calculate the histogram which is the amount of points with a certain *err* and the trendline which is the line of archive members average

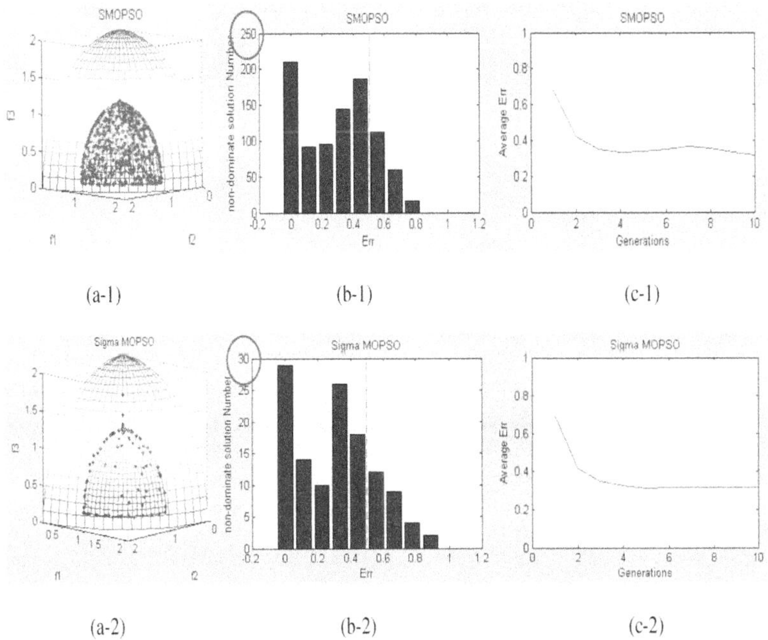

Fig. 3. Comparison of the SMOPSO and the Sigma MOPSO method applied on T_3

err value at each interval. Figure 3(b-1), (b-2), (c-1) and (c-2)show that both the SMOPSO method and the Sigma method can find solutions with $err < 0.5$, and both methods have a very rapid convergent speed. But the SMOPSO method can find more solutions with same population size and iteration step. This characteristic indicates that the SMOPSO method can find more Pareto-optimal solutions of the multi-objective problems in a very short time, and can maintain the diversity and convergence of solutions simultaneous.

6 Conclusion and Future Work

A new method called smart particle swarm optimization for multi-objective problems (SMOPSO) is described in this paper. By taking into account the actions of all objective functions, the global best is selected. By calculating the distance between the particles and archive members, personal best positions are chosen. Using these global best and personal best selection strategies, SMOPSO can find solutions with a good diversity and convergence, and can convergent on the Pareto Front with very little population size and generation, as our experiments on function 1, 2, and 3 shown. That is a very important character of the SMOPSO method proposed in this paper. Since smaller population and generation can accelerate computing speed, the SMOPSO method is fit for real-life multi-objective optimization problems which need to be solved in a very short time especially.

In the future, we would like to investigate and compare the influence of the different *distance valve* on the SMOPSO method, and apply the SMOPSO method for more test functions with higher number of objectives.

References

1. Cagnina L. , Esquivel S. : A Particle Swarm Optimizer for Multi-Objective Optimization. JCS and T. , **4** (2005) 204-210
2. Bartz-Bartz, T. , Limbourg, P. , Parsopoulos K. E. , Vrahatis M. N. : Particle Swarm Optimizers for Pareto Optimization with Enhanced Archiving Techniques. In Proc. Congress on Evolutionary Computation, Canberra, Australia, 3 (2003) 1780-1787
3. Hu, X. , Eberhart, R. : Multiobjective Optimization using Dynamic Neighborhood Particle Swarm Optimization. In Proc. IEEE World Congress on Computational Intelligence, Piscataway, IEEE Service Center. , NJ (2002) 1677-1681
4. Parsopoulos, K. E. , Vrahatis, M. M. : Particle Swarm Optimization Method in Multiobjective Problems. In Proc. Symposium on Applied Computing. (2002) 603-607
5. Coello, C. A. C. , Lechuga, M. S. : MOPSO: A Proposal for Multiple Objective Particle Swarm Optimization. In Proc. Congress on Evolutionary Computation, Piscataway, IEEE Service Center. , NJ, 2 (2002) 1051-1056
6. Fieldsend, J. E. , Singh, S. : A Multi-objective Algorithm Based upon Particle Swarm Optimization, An Efficient Data Structure and Turbulence. In Proc. Workshop on Computational Intelligence, Birmingham, UK. (2002) 34-44
7. Mostaghim, S. , Teich, J. : Strafegies for Finding Good Local Guides in Multi-objective Particle Swarm Optimization(MOPSO). In Proc. IEEE Swarm Intelligence Symposium, Indiana, USA (2003) 26-33
8. Mostaghim, S. , Teich, J. : The Role of ϵ Dominance in Multi-objective Particle Swarm Optimization Methods. In Proc. Congress on Evolutionary Computation, Canberra, Australia (2003) 1764-1771
9. Mostaghim, S. , Teich, J. : Covering Pareto-optimal Fronts by Subswarms in Multi-objective Particle Swarm Optimization. IEEE Press, New Youk (2004) 1404-1410
10. Kennedy, J. , Eberhart, R. C. : Particle Swarm Optimization. In Proc. IEEE International Conference on Neural Networks, Perth, Australia (1995) 1942-1948
11. Shi, Y. H. , Eberhart, R. C. A Modified Particle Swarm Optimizer. In Proc. IEEE International Conference on Evolutionary Computation, Piscataway (1998) 69-73
12. Shi, Y. H. : Particle Swarm Optimization. In Proc. IEEE Neural Networks Society, 4 (2004) 8-13
13. Deb, K. , Thiele, L. , Laumanns, M. , Zitzer, E. : Scalable Test Problems for Evolutionary Multi-objective Optimization. In Proc. IEEE World Congress on Evolutionary Computation, Honolulu (2002) 175-186

Adaptive Particle Swarm Optimization with Feedback Control of Diversity

Jing Jie[1,2], Jianchao Zeng[2], and Chongzhao Han[1]

[1] School of Electronic and Information Engineering, Xi'an Jiaotong University
710049, Xi'an City, China
Jjing277@sohu.com
[2] Division of System Simulation & Computer Application,
Taiyuan University of Science & Technology,
030024, Taiyuan City, China
zengjianchao@263.net

Abstract. Swarm-diversity is an important factor influencing the global convergence of particle swarm optimization (PSO). In order to overcome the premature convergence, the paper introduced a negative feedback mechanism into particle swarm optimization and developed an adaptive PSO. The improved method takes advantage of the swarm-diversity to control the tuning of the inertia weight (PSO-DCIW), which in turn can adjust the swarm-diversity adaptively and contribute to a successful global search. The proposed PSO-DCIW was applied to some well-known benchmarks and compared with the other notable improved methods for PSO. The relative experimental results show PSO-DCIW is a robust global optimization method for the complex multimodal functions, which can improve the performance of the standard PSO and alleviate the premature convergence validly.

1 Introduction

Particle swarm optimization (PSO) is a novel evolutionary algorithm that is inspired originally by the social and cognitive behavior lying in the bird flocking. Since the original version introduced in 1995 by Kennedy and Eberhart [1], PSO has attracted lots of attentions from researchers around the world and lots of research results have been reported in the literatures. As one of stochastic algorithms, PSO owns some attractive features such as simple model, few parameters, and easy implementation. Now, PSO has been applied successfully in many areas [2-6], including neural networks, multidimensional complex problems, multiobjective optimizations, and some project applications, etc.. However, like others stochastic algorithms, PSO also suffers from the premature convergence problem, especially in the large scale and complex problems.

As far as the premature convergence is concerned, a main reason is that a fast information interaction among particles in PSO leads to the swarm diversity declining and the particle clustering quickly. Some techniques have been proposed to avoid the premature convergence. Suganthan introduced the spatial neighborhood into PSO [7]; Li used species to choose the neighborhood adaptively [8]. Lovbjerg adopted the

D.-S. Huang, K. Li, and G.W. Irwin (Eds.): ICIC 2006, LNBI 4115, pp. 81 – 92, 2006.

concepts of "subpopulation" and "breeding" in Genetic Algorithms (GAs) to increase the diversity [9]; Riget developed an attractive and repulsive PSO(ARPSO) to adjust the diversity[10]; Shi and Eberhart modified the parameters to keep the balance between the exploration and the exploitation [11,12]., etc.. According to the relative literatures, those methods can improve the global convergence ability of PSO in certain degree but fewer can solve the premature convergence problem truly.

In order to overcome the premature problem, The paper introduced a negative feedback mechanism into particle swarm optimization and developed an adaptive PSO. The improved method takes advantage of the swarm diversity to control the tuning of the inertia weight (PSO-DCIW), which not only can vary the swarm diversity in turn, but also can manipulate the exploitation and the exploration adaptively. The proposed PSO-DCIW is used to some benchmark optimizations and compared with the other notable improvements for PSO, the results show PSO-DCIW can overcome the premature problem validly, and performs very well on the complex multimodal optimizations.

The remaining of the paper is organized as the follows. Section 2 provides some relative work on PSO. Section 3 describes the PSO-DCIW method in details. Section 4 presents the experiments and the relative results. Finally, Section 5 concludes with some remarks.

2 Some Relative Works

2.1 The Standard PSO (SPSO)

Since the original version of PSO proposed in 1995[1], lots of work has been done to develop it. In order to control the global exploration and the local exploitation validly, Shi and Eberhart [11] introduced a concept of inertia weight to the original PSO and developed a modified PSO. Compared with the original version, the modified PSO gets a notable improvement of the performance, so it is often referred to as the standard PSO version(SPSO) and adopted by many following researches. The SPSO version can be described by the following update equations:

$$v_{id}(t+1) = \omega v_{id}(t) + c_1 r_1 \left(P_{id}(t) - x_{id}(t)\right) + c_2 r_2 \left(P_{gd}(t) - x_{id}(t)\right) . \tag{1}$$

$$x_{id}(t+1) = x_{id}(t) + v_{id}(t+1) . \tag{2}$$

Supposed the particles flying through a d-dimensional space, X_i and V_i represent the position vector and velocity vector of the ith individual respectively, while P_i represents the personal best position of ith individual and P_g represents the global best position in the swarm; the inertia weigh ω is a scaling factor controlling the influence of the old velocity on the new one; c_1 and c_2 are constants known as "cognitive" and "social" coefficients which determine the weight of P_i and P_g respectively; r_1 and r_2 are two random numbers generated by the uniform distribution in the range [0,1] separated.

2.2 Some Improved SPSO Based on the Parameters

Many works have been done to study the parameters set of SPSO. Shi and Eberhart have analyzed the effect of the inertia weight through empirical experiments, and found that a larger ω can bring a better global convergent ability while a smaller ω can manipulate a better local search[12]. So, they manipulated SPSO with a linearly decreased ω over time (PSO-LDIW), where ω is given by the following equation:

$$\omega = (\omega_1 - \omega_2) \times \frac{(MAXITER - iter)}{MAXITER} + \omega_2 \ . \tag{3}$$

Here ω_1 and ω_2 are the initial and final values of the inertia weigh respectively, *iter* is the current iteration number and *MAXITER* is the maximum number of the iteration.

Moreover, Shi and Eberhart have proposed a random modification for the inertia weight (PSO-RDIW) to fit PSO with the dynamic problems effectively, where ω is modified randomly by the following equation:

$$\omega = 0.5 + rand(0,1)/2 \ . \tag{4}$$

According to the relative literatures, the two versions show rapid convergence, but often perform well in unimodal functions while are failure in multimodal functions. Later, Shi and Eberhart introduced a fuzzy controller to modify the inertia weight dynamically [13]. The adaptive fuzzy inertia weight controller is a promising technique for optimizing the parameter, but difficult for implementation.

Considering the two acceleration coefficients may have great influence on the performance of PSO, Ratnaweera et al. have developed SPSO with time-varying acceleration coefficients (PSO-TVAC)[15]. The method has the same motivation and the similar techniques as the PSO-LDIW, in which, the cognitive coefficient c_1 is decreased linearly and the social coefficient c_2 is increased linearly over time.

Though the methods with the time-varying parameters can make a good exploration in the early search and keep a fast convergence in the last search, they couldn't take advantage of any search information to modify the parameters and overcome the premature problem essentially. If the global solution just appears in the forepart search, the time-varying parameters can ensure the search converge to the global optimum with a rapid speed, or the time-varying parameters will lead to the search easily to be trapped in the local optimum.

3 PSO with Diversity-Controlled Inertia Weight (PSO-DCIW)

3.1 The Motivation of PSO-DCIW

As far as the premature convergence is concerned, the main reason is that a fast information interaction among particles in PSO leads to the swarm-diversity declining and the particle clustering quickly. In order to improve the global performance of SPSO, a more feasible idea is trying to maintain an appropriate swarm-diversity according to the current search state, and to modify the parameters under the guide of the search information.

Before the idea about the adaptive diversity-controlled PSO comes into being, let's go back to analyze the simulated behavior of PSO. How to do and what can prompt PSO to be a successful and robust optimization? Maybe, the answer just lies in its headstream----Swarm Intelligence. In general, Swarm intelligence can be defined as "the emergent complex intelligence inspired by the collective behavior of social insect colonies and other animal societies."[16]. Here, the swarm consists of some individuals that exhibit simple behaviors. In the swarm, no one is in charge, no one give out direct orders; but every individual can perceive and receive amount of information from different directions. The information interactions among individuals can be characterized as varieties of feedbacks lying in a self-organization system, which not only occur in the individual lever, but also take place between the individual lever and the swarm lever.

Based on the concept of Self-organization, the PSO system should be considered as a dynamic closed system, and its dynamic behaviors should be understood from two aspects: its low-lever ---the individual lever and its high-lever----the swarm lever, an emergence of a high-lever quality in such a system is mainly due to the internal interactions between the two levers. One aspect, the low-lever particles in the swarm continually interact the local information each other and try to get a collective output cooperatively; another aspect, each particle can perceive the swarm-lever state and make some decisions to modify its behavior intelligently. In other words, the swarm-lever outputs have an important influence on the behaviors of the particles, which just provide a guiding direction and prompt a higher-lever quality to emerge in the swarm.

According to the analysis above, we introduced a negative feedback mechinism into particle swarm optimization and developed an adaptive PSO. The improved method takes advantage of the swarm-diversity as the swarm-lever information to control the tuning of individual's parameter (inertia weight) that is referred to as PSO-DCIW here. Its architecture is discussed in details in the following part.

3.2 The Architecture of PSO-DCIW

According to Fig.1., PSO-DCIW can be regarded as a control system with a negative feedback. Here, the swarm is a dynamic component that consists of N particles modified by the PSO optimizer. Its dynamic properties can be described by the swarm-diversity Do and the best position Pgo. As far as the optimization problem is concerned, the swarm is anticipated to keep the swarm diversity with a relative steady variation to give a good output of Pgo. Obviously, the outputs of the system mainly

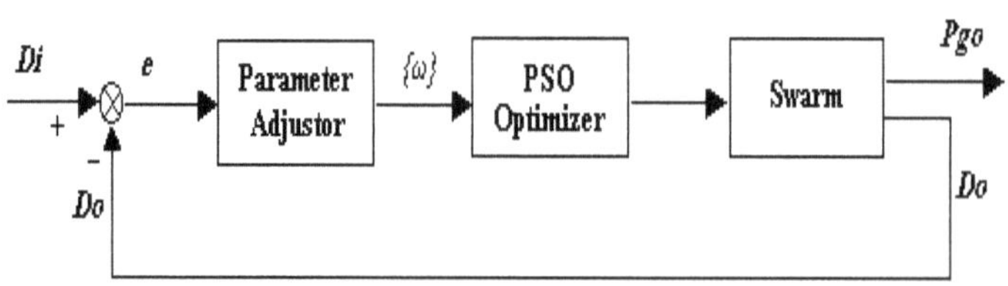

Fig. 1. The architecture of PSO-DCIW

depend on the appropriate parameters of the PSO optimizer, good parameters setting will lead to good outputs. So, how to design the parameter adjustor is the main consideration for PSO-DCIW

Here, we design the parameter adjustor into a ratio controller, whose ratio coefficient is denoted as Kp. During a search, the adjustor is expected to modify the inertia weight under the control of the swarm-diversity through the negative feedback, which can in turn adjust the swarm-diversity adaptively. Supposed $Di(t) = Do(t-1)$ in the tth iteration, the current input e of the parameter adjustor can be calculated by the following:

$$e(t) = \frac{Di(t) - Do(t)}{Di(t)} = \frac{Do(t-1) - Do(t)}{Do(t-1)} . \tag{5}$$

So, the output of the parameter adjustor ω is given by the follows:

$$\omega(t) = Kp \times e(t) = Kp(1 - \frac{Do(t)}{Do(t-1)}) . \tag{6}$$

Obviously, PSO-DCIW is different from PSO-LDIW essentially. PSO-DCIW modifies the tuning of the inertia weight adaptively under the control of the swarm diversity. During the search, if the swarm-diversity Do decreases quickly, a bigger ω will be offered to the following optimizer and lead to the exploration enhancing in the next iteration; if Do decreases very slowly, a smaller ω will be got to enhance the exploitation in the next iteration; if Do fluctuates with an increase in a special iteration, a negative value of ω will be provided to inverse the flying of the particles which in turn lead to the diversity decreasing . Through the negative feedback, PSO-DCIW can alleviate the acute fluctuation of diversity, especially in the forepart search, which contributes to the balance between the exploration and exploitation, and prevents the search from being trapped in the local optimum early.

Here, the swarm-diversity $D(\cdot)$ is computed according to the diversity–measure proposed by the literature [10]:

$$D(t) = \frac{1}{|S| \cdot |L|} \cdot \sum_{i=1}^{|S|} \sqrt{\sum_{j=1}^{N} (P_{ij}(t) - \bar{P}_j(t))^2} . \tag{7}$$

Where S is the swarm, $|S|$ means the size of the swarm, $|L|$ is the lenth of the longest diagonal in the search space, N is the dimension of the objective problem, P_{ij} is the jth value of the ith particle and $\bar{P}_j$ is the jth value of the average point $\bar{P}$.

During the iterations, the optimizer manipulates each particle flying through the different inertia weigh provided by the parameter adjustor. The update equation of the velocity for each particle is described as the follows:

$$v_{id}(t+1) = \omega(t)v_{id}(t) + c_1 r_1 \left(P_{id}(t) - x_{id}(t)\right) + c_2 r_2 \left(P_{gd}(t) - x_{id}(t)\right) . \tag{8}$$

3.3 The Pseudocode of PSO-DCIW

```
PSO-DCIW main {
  t=0;
  Initialize the swarm and Evaluate the swarm S(0)
  Get the best solution Pgo(0) and Calculate the swarm-diversity Do(0)
  while (not (Termination criteria)) {
  t=t+1
  Di(t)= Do(t-1)
  Calculate e(t)=( Di(t)-Do(t))/ Di(t)
  Calculate ω(t)=Kp* e(t)
  Update the swarm and Evaluate the swarm S(t)
  Update Pgo(t) and Do(t)
  }
}
```

Fig. 2. The pseudocode for PSO-DCIW

4 Experiments and Results

4.1 The Benchmark Functions

Four well-known benchmarks have been used to test the performances of PSO-DCIW in the experiments, which are widely adopted in the relative researches about PSO and evolutionary algorithms[10,12,15,17].

$$f_1 = \frac{1}{4000}\sum_{i=1}^{N} x_i^2 - \prod_{i=1}^{N}\cos\left(\frac{x_i}{\sqrt{i}}\right) + 1 \cdot \tag{9}$$

$$f_2 = 20 + e - 20\exp\left(-0.2\sqrt{\frac{1}{n}\sum_{i=1}^{n} x_i^2}\right) - \exp\left(\frac{1}{n}\sum_{i=1}^{n}\cos 2\pi x_i\right) \cdot \tag{10}$$

$$f_3 = \sum_{i=1}^{N}\left(x_i^2 - 10\cos(2\pi x_i) + 10\right) \cdot \tag{11}$$

$$f_4 = \frac{1}{N}\sum_{i=1}^{N}\left(x_i^4 - 16x_i^2 + 5x_i\right) \cdot \tag{12}$$

All of the above benchmarks are complex multimodal functions with many local optima. They are very difficult to solve for many optimization algorithms. The basic information of the test functions is listed in Table.1.

Table 1. Basic information about benchmarks

Benchmark	Solution space	Global minimum
f_1-Griewank	$[-600, 600]^N$	0
f_2-Ackley	$[-32, 32]^N$	0
f_3-Rastrigin	$[-5.12, 5.12]^N$	0
f_4-2^n minima	$[-5, 5]^N$	-78.3323

4.2 Experimental Results and Discussions

A series of experiments have been done to make some comparisons on the performance between PSO-LDIW, PSO-RDIW and PSO-DCIW. In PSO-DCIW, the inertia weight ω is controlled by *Kp*. Based on some preliminary experiments, a good range for the value of *Kp* is (0.9~1.6), here *Kp* =1.4 in the following experiments. The set of parameters in PSO-LDIW is same as the one adopted by the literature [12], where the inertia weight ω is linearly decreased from 0.9 to 0.4 over time, and the

Table 2. Comparison between PSO-DCIW and PSO-LDIW, PSO-RDIW. All results were averaged over 50 runs, where the max iteration is 100 times of the dimension in each run. The swarm size adopted by every algorithm is 100.

Function	Dimension	PSO-LDIW Mean Best (Std Dev)	PSO-RDIW Mean Best (Std Dev)	PSO-DCIW Mean Best (Std Dev)
F1	10	0.062731 (0.009796)	0.047974 (0.007509)	0.062245 (0.008452)
	20	0.031701 (0.006027)	0.020712 (0.004072)	0.030051 (0.007075)
	30	0.018148 (0.038629)	0.010826 (0.002191)	0.020908 (0.008824)
F2	10	2.11e-014 (1.69e-014)	6.38e-015 (2.93e-015)	5.98e-015 (2.87e-015)
	20	1.65e-011 (8.70e-012)	1.13e-014 (4.14e-015)	2.25e-014 (5.24e-015)
	30	1.48e-009 (3.94e-010)	1.96e-014 (3.04e-015)	1.36e-013 (7.56e-014)
F3	10	4.18881 (2.778225)	1.02595 (0.261539)	1.52714 (0.381425)
	20	15.7028 (8.53195)	11.9821 (2.41478)	10.1588 (2.11328)
	30	30.6257 (14.0846)	36.9387 (7.09514)	21.5464 (4.02996)
F4	10	-76.1303 (0.41612)	-78.3321 (6.36e-005)	-78.3323 (4.44e-006)
	20	-64.9035 (1.93951)	-77.6004 (0.138039)	-78.3123 (0.056546)
	30	-56.6634 (3.08283)	-73.5734 (0.727718)	-78.2758 (0.032646)

coefficients c1 = c2 =2.0; In PSO-RDIW, the inertia weight ω is produced randomly according to Equation (4) and c1 = c2 =1.49, which have proved a successful set of parameters [13]. In each experiment, the velocity is limited by the solution boundary of the objective function, that means $V_{max}=X_{max}$. Some important results are showed in the following table and figures.

In Table 2, PSO-DCIW is compared with PSO-LDIW and PSO-RDIW respectively. The final experimental results averaged over 50 runs are given, including the mean best function values and the standard deviation got by each algorithm. For f_1, PSO-DCIW performs worse than PSO-RDIW, but as well as PSO-LDIW. For f_2, the performance of PSO-DCIW is similar to the one of PSO-RDIW, and better than the one of PSO-LDIW. In the case of f_3, PSO-DCIW outperforms both two other methods a little. A notable difference in the performance between DCPSO and the other two methods occurs in the function f_4. f_4 is a multimodal function with 2^n minima and difficult to optimize, for its local minima increases exponentially with the dimension of the function increasing. Obviously, PSO-DCIW outperforms PSO-LDIW and PSO-RDIW a lot in f_4, which means PSO-DCIW is easy to escape from the local minima and converge to the global minimum robustly, while PSO-LDIW and PSO-RDIW seems easy to be trapped in local minima when facing to a very complex problem.

The results in Table 2 show PSO-DCIW performs better than or similar to PSO-LDIW and PSO-RDIW on the complex multimodal functions. The reason maybe lies in that PSO-DCIW takes advantage of the diversity feedback to guide the search. The following figures can make it clear.

Fig.3. and Fig.4. illustrate the dynamic processes of the swarm-diversity, the mean best value and the mean value of the swarm during the search, where PSO-DCIW, PSO-LDIW and PSO-RDIW were applied to f_2 and f_4 respectively. Compared with the other two methods, PSO-DCIW has a slower convergent speed with a higher swarm diversity in the forepart of the search, but it can converge to the global optimum with a smaller diversity in the end of the search. That maily owns to the negitive feedback of diversity to modify the parameters adaptively. Considering the optimization algorithm, the swarm diversity curve got by PSO-DCIW seems to be the best one, which keeps a higher swarm diversity in the early search and decreases slowly to a smaller value with the search going. In other words, such swarm diversity curve contributes to the improvement of PSO-DCIW in the global convergent performance.

For PSO-LDIW and PSO-RDIW, the function f_4 is more difficult to optimize. Though PSO-LDIW keeps the highest diversity in the most search, it fails to converge to the global optimum with a weak exploitation in the end. Compared with PSO-LDIW, PSO-RDIW has a notable improvement of the performance for f_4, but it still performs worse than PSO-DCIW a lot. According to Fig.4., it's easy to know that PSO-DCIW is the best method for f_4. Owning to the feedback control of the diversity, PSO-DCIW can modify the exploration and the exploitation adaptively, which leads to the search converge to the global optimum successfully. Its swarm diversity curve can prove the point. In other words, PSO-DCIW is easy to escape from the local minima and outperforms the other two methods with a rubust performance when faced to the complex optimization problems.

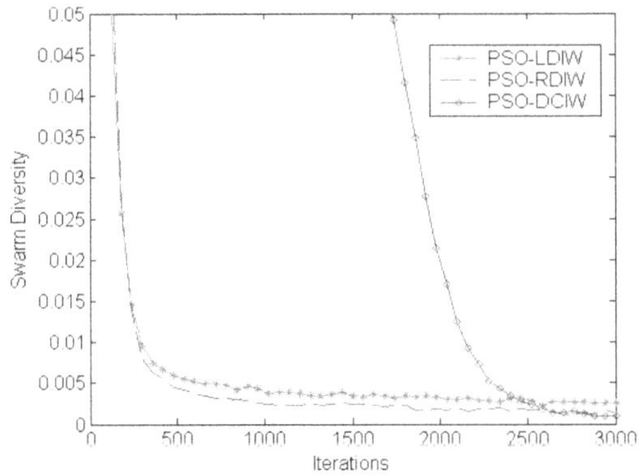

(a)

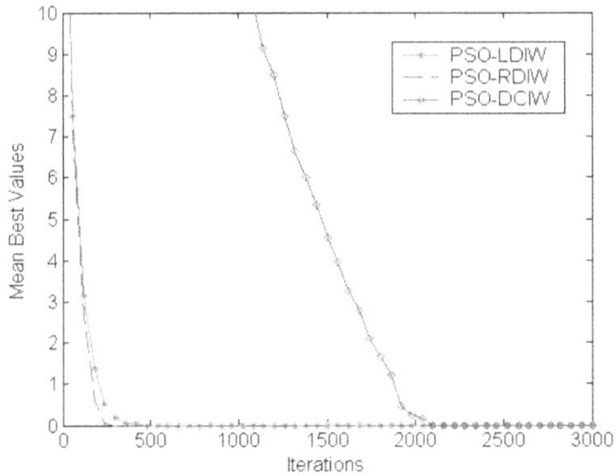

(b)

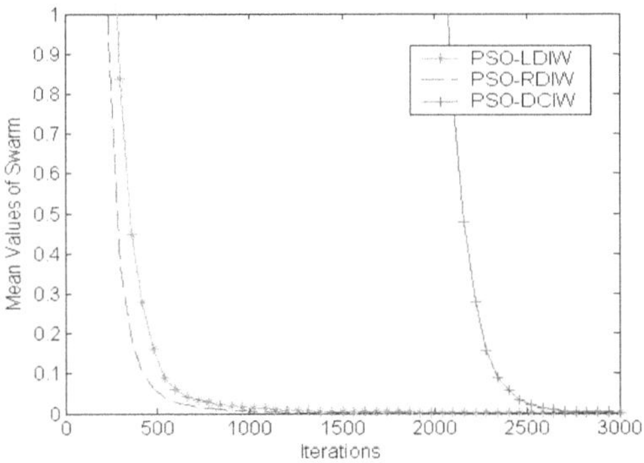

(c)

Fig. 3. Comparison among PSO- DCIW, PSO-LDIW and PSO-RDIW based on f_2. All results were averaged over 20 runs, where the dimension of f_2 is 30, the max iteration is 3000 and the swarm size is 100. (a) shows the swarm diversity, (b) shows the mean best values, and (c) illustrates the mean values of the swarm.

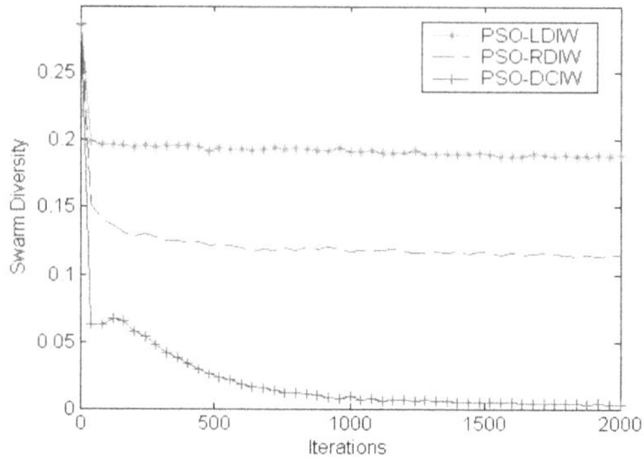

(a)

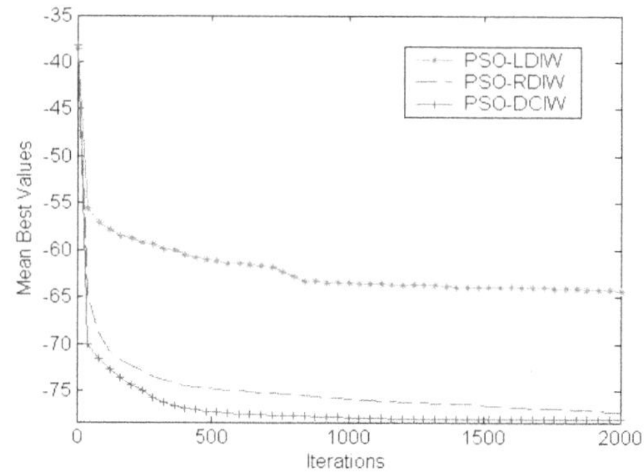

(b)

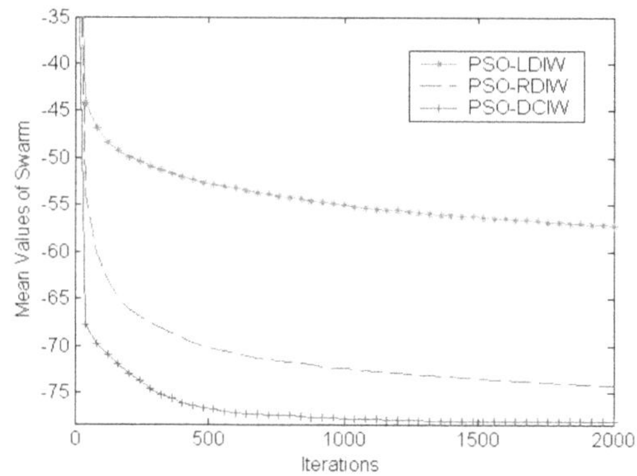

(c)

Fig. 4. Comparison among PSO- DCIW, PSO-LDIW and PSO-RDIW based on f_4. All results were averaged over 20 runs, where the dimension of f_4 is 20, the max iteration is 2000 and the swarm size is 100. (a) shows the swarm diversity, (b) shows the mean best values, and (c) illustrates the mean values of the swarm during a search.

5 Conclusions

The paper has introduced a negitive feedback mechanism into particle swarm optimization and developed an adaptive PSO. The improved method takes advantage of the swarm diversity to control the modification of the inertia weight (PSO-DCIW), which in turn can adjust the diversity and contribute to a successful global search. The proposed PSO-DCIW was applied to some well-known benchmarks and compared with two notable improved methods that are referred to as PSO-LDIW and PSO-RDIW. The relative experimental results show PSO-DCIW performs better than or similar to PSO-LDIW and PSO-RDIW on the complex multimodal functions. Owning to the feedback control of the diversity, PSO-DCIW can modify the exploration and the exploitation adaptively, which leads to the search converge to the global optimum successfully. When faced to more complex optimization with lots of local minima, PSO-DCIW is easy to escape from the local minima and converges to the global minimum robustly, while PSO-LDIW and PSO-RDIW seems easy to be trapped in local minima. All analysis and experimental results prove the method with the diversity feedback can improve the performance of the standard PSO validly, and PSO-DCIW is a robust global optimization method for complex multimodal optimizations.

Acknowledgments

This work is supported by the key science and technology fund project for national educational department under the grant No.204018, and the science and technology project for Shanxi educational department under the grant No.20051310.

References

1. Kennedy, J. , Eberhart, R.C.: Particle Swarm Optimization. In: Proc. IEEE Conference on Neural Networks, Perth, Australia: IEEE Service Center. 11(1995) 1942–1948
2. Bergh, F.V.D. , Engelbrecht, A.: Particle Swarm Weight Initialization in Multi-layer Perception Artificial Neural Networks. In: Development and Practice of Artificial Intelligence Techniques, Durban, South Africa. (1999) 41–45
3. Bergh, F.V.D., Engelbrecht, A.P.: Cooperative Learning in Neural Networks using Particle Swarm Optimizers. In: South African Computer Journal, vol.26.No.11.(2000) 84–90
4. Clerc, M., Kennedy, J.:The Particle Swarm--Explosion, Stability, and Convergence in a Multidimensional Complex Space. In: IEEE Transactions on Evolutionary Computation, Vol. 6. No.1. (2002) 58–73
5. Fukuyama, Y., Yoshida, H.:A Particle Swarm Optimization for Reactive Power and Voltage Control in Electric Power Systems. In: Proc. Congress on Evolutionary Computation, Seoul, Korea. Piscataway, NJ: IEEE Service Center. (2001) 87–93
6. Zeng, J.C., Jie, J., Cui, Z. H.: Particle Swarm Optimization. Beijing, Science Press, (2004)
7. Suganthan, P.N.:Particle Swarm Optimizer with Neighborhood Operator. In: Proc. Congress on Evolutionary Computation, Washington D.C, USA, July, Piscataway, NJ: IEEE Service Center, (1999) 1958–1961
8. Li, X.D.: Adaptively Choosing Neighborhood Using Species in a Particle Swarm Optimizer for Multimodal Function Optimization. In: Proceedings of the Genetic and Evolutionary Computation Conference. (2004)105–116

9. Lovbjerg, M., Rasmussen, T.K., Krink, T.: Hybrid Particle Swarm Optimiser with Breeding and Subpopulations. In: Proceedings of the Genetic and Evolutionary Computation Conference, San Francisco, USA, (2001)
10. Jacques, R., Jakob, S. V.: A Diversity-Guided Particle Swarm Optimizer –the ARPSO. http://citeseer.nj.nec.com/riget02diversityguided.html
11. Shi, Y. , Eberhart, R.C.: A Modified Particle Swarm Optimizer In: Proc. Conference on Evolutionary Computation: IEEE Press. Piscataway. (1998) 69–73
12. Shi, Y. , Eberhart, R. C.: Empirical Study of Particle Swarm Optimization. In: Proc. Congress on Evolutionary Computation, Piscataway, NJ: IEEE Service Center,.(1999) 1945–1950.
13. Eberhart, R. C., Shi, Y.H.: Tracking and Optimizing Dynamic Systems with Particle Swarms. In: Proc. Congress on Evolutionary Computation, Seoul, Kores: IEEE service Center. (2001) 94–97
14. Shi, Y. H., Eberhart, R. C.: Fuzzy Adaptive Particle Swarm Optimization. In: Proc. Congress on Evolutionary Computation, Seoul, Korea: IEEE service Center.(2001)101–106
15. Ratnaweera, A., Halgamuge, S.K. and Watson, H.C.: Self-Organizing Hierarchical Particle Swarm Optimizer With Time-Varying Acceleration Coefficients. IEEE Transactions on Evolutionary Computation. Vol.8. No.3. (2004) 240–255
16. Bonabeau, E., Dorigo, M., Theraulaz, G.: Swarm Intelligence From Natural to Artificial Systems. Oxford Univergity Press Inc. ISBN 0-19-513158-4; ISBN 0-19-513159-2, (1999) 1–22

An Improved Particle Swarm Algorithm and Its Application to Power System Transfer Capability Optimization

Si-jun Peng [1], Chang-hua Zhang[2], and Liang Tang[3]

[1] School of Science, Wuhan University of Technology, Wuhan 430070, Hubei Province, China
sjpeng@mail.whut.edu.cn
[2] Key Laboratory of Complex Systems and Intelligence Science, Institute of Automation, Chinese Academy of Sciences, Beijing, 100080. China
zchbashan@163.com
[3] Department of Automotive Engineering, Tsinghua University, Beijing 100084. China

Abstract. In this paper, an algorithm based on PSO (Particle Swarm Optimization) for power system transfer capability calculation is presented. A dual fitness scheme that takes both objective and constraint into account is adopted to evaluate the survival chance of any particle, thus avoid the drawbacks of traditional penalty method. In the evolution process, if the population best particle has no update during a prescribed number of consecutive generations, it is regarded as a local optimum solution and the searching space around this particle is locked to prevent other particles flying into it. And this particle is saved as one of the candidate solution. In the end, by comparing the fitness of all saved particles and the current population best particle the optimum value can be obtained. This improved particle swarm algorithm is then successfully applied to IEEE118 bus system optimization problem. Compared with a traditional well-known method, sequential quadratic programming, our proposal obtains better solutions for this problem.

1 Introduction

Available transfer capability (ATC) is the power transfer capability remaining in the physical transmission network for further commercial activity over and above already committed uses [1].

Under the development of power system, large amount of power are transferred from power plants to load center via transmission lines. It becomes a truth that the load centers stand far from the power plants. In power market circumstance, the electric power transfer is an important business for power company. So whether under the traditional electric circumstance or deregulated circumstance, to system operators, ATC calculation has a great significance.

Three main methods have been presented for ATC calculation: power transfer distribution factor method (PTDF) [2], continuous power flow method (CPFlow) [3] and optimization power flow method (OPF) [4].Because PTDF method needs no

D.-S. Huang, K. Li, and G.W. Irwin (Eds.): ICIC 2006, LNBI 4115, pp. 93 – 99, 2006.

iteration, ATC value can be acquired very quickly. But this method will lead to unacceptable error in heavy load power system with less reactive power supporting because its mathematical model is built on the direct flow model, and the affection of voltage and reactive power is ignored. CPFlow method bases on the homotopy theory. It solves the diffusion problem when system operation point is very close to addle-node in power calculation with common methods. But this method has to define the specified power transfer model firstly(this means that the selling power area defines the generation increasing pattern and buying power area defines the load increasing pattern). This will lead to conservative solution acquired. In OPF method, ATC problem is looked as an optimization problem. The objective function is the maximum transfer capability and equality constraints are power equations. Branch thermal constraints, bus voltage constraints and devices capability constraints are inequality constraints. On the basis of this mathematical model, kinds of optimization methods, such as sequence quadratic programming [4] ,primal-dual interior point method [5], Benders decomposition method [6] etc. are applied for ATC calculation. But OPF methods based on Newton criteria can only acquire the local optimization solution because the static feasible field of power system is always no convex.

In generally, optimization problem of power system is a nonlinear problem characterized by its feasible field no convex, discrete variants and continuous variants coexistence, and sometimes with a discontinuous objective function. So the traditional optimization methods based on Newton criteria always get the local optimization solution. And at the same time, with the enlargement of the size of power system analyzed, these methods will inherently bring out the "dimension disaster". As a new evolutionary computation tool, particle swarm optimization (PSO) is becoming a hot research point in these years. It has no special requirements for optimization object so it can be used to solve widely array of the optimization problems. In this paper, an improved Particle Swarm Optimization (IPSO) is introduced to solve the ATC calculation in power system.

2 PSO Introduction

2.1 PSO Definition

PSO is a population based optimization method first proposed by Eberhart and Kennedy in 1995 [8]. Just similar with Genetic Algorithm [9], PSO takes the concept of "population" and "evolution", and also operates basing on the fitness value. Here, it's assumed that the population consists of m particles and the search space is n dimension.

Every particle has the following three properties: a current position in search space, x_i ; a current velocity, v_i ; and the personal best position, p_i ,corresponds to the position in search space where particle i obtains the best fitness determined by the objective function and constraint condition. The best personal best position in the population is called the global best position, which denoted as p_g . In the first iteration, p_i is the initial position of each particle. In the following iteration, each particle new position is attracted by the position of p_i and p_g. This can be expressed as following equations:

$$v_{ij}(t+1) = wv_{ij}(t) + c_1 r_{1j}(t)(p_{ij}(t) - x_{ij}(t)) + c_2 r_{2j}(t)(p_{gj}(t) - x_{ij}(t)) \quad . \tag{1}$$

$$x_{ij}(t+1) = x_{ij}(t) + v_{ij}(t+1) \tag{2}$$

where, j denotes the search space dimension, $j = 1, 2, \ldots, n$; i denotes the number of particles, $i = 1, 2, \ldots, m$; t denotes the iteration times; w is the inertia weight; c_1 c_2 are acceleration coefficients; $r_{1j} \sim U(0,1)$ and $r_{2j} \sim U(0,1)$ are used to effect the stochastic nature of the algorithm. In order to reduce the likelihood of the particle leaving the search space, the value of each dimension of every particle velocity is clamped to the range $[-v_{j\max}, v_{j\max}]$. The value of $\mathbf{v}_{\max}$ is usually chosen to be $k\mathbf{x}_{\max}$, with $0.1 \le k \le 1$,where $\mathbf{x}_{\max}$ denoted the domain of search space.

2.2 Improved PSO Method

Paper [10] by *Boeringer et al.* investigated PSO and other evolutionary computation then he pointed out that PSO attractive features include the ease implementation and fast convergence, but it is also inclined to convergence at the local optimization solution. Yi-xiong Jin further analyzed this phenomenon then he concluded that with the process of evolution, the global best position is lack of self-evolution and whole population evolution halt lead to this [11]. To solve this problem, the author suggested an improved PSO method. If the global best position has not been changed for some generations, this position should be looked as a local optimum solution and the following searches around this point should be nonsense. So the searching space around this point within the specified radius should be locked to prevent other particles flying into. And the particles already locate in this space should die and be replaced with the new particles yielded randomly to keep the total number of the population unchanged. When the whole iteration finished, one or more of this kind local optimum position are acquired. The approximate global optimum solution can be determined after compare the fitness of these saved particles or making a deeply search around them.

When calculate the particles fitness, the traditional method always take penalty function to handle constraint conditions. It needs experience and patience to define the proper form of penalty function. The author of [12] suggested each particle has two fitness, objective fitness and constraint fitness and compare this two fitness to determine the particle quality. Paper [13] ranks the particle in the value of fitness and the constraint fitness has a priority than objective fitness. In this way, the feasible particle fitness is better than infeasible particle. So in the process of evolution, other particles are inclined to be attracted by feasible solution. This method can consolidate acquiring the optimum point and making particles enter into the feasible field and no need to set the proper weight of constraint fitness and objective fitness. 3 ATC Calculation With IPSO Method.

2.3 ATC Mathematical Model of Power System

For a power system operating with high reliability, it should satisfy three kinds of constraint, i.e., line thermal constraint, bus voltage magnitude constraint, and system stability constraints(which can be classified into static voltage stability, transient power & angle stability, dynamic power & angle stability). In ATC calculation, different constraints considered make up of different calculation model. In this paper, two hypotheses are assumed, that is each control variant changed slowly and system has enough damping to keep the dynamic stability. So the dynamic stability problem is not concerned here. As for transient problem, it can be checked up when ATC result acquired. So the ATC model built here just satisfies the first two constraints.

As an optimization problem, the objective function can be defined as the sum of the group of generators' outputs (these generators are denoted as set S) and the group load buss' load (these buss are denoted as set R) [4]. In this way, two kinds of variants: generator's output and the bus load, are optimized and the maximum ATC value between the areas can be acquired (of course, the initial value on the tie lines will be subtracted from the optimum power value on these lines when ATC value exported). This objective function can be expressed as following equation:

$$\max f(\bullet) = \sum_{k\in S} P_{Gk} + \sum_{d\in R} P_{Ld} \quad . \tag{3}$$

The equality constraints of this model are:

$$\begin{cases} P_i - V_i \sum_{j=1}^{N} V_j \left(G_{ij} \cos\theta_{ij} + B_{ij} \sin\theta_{ij} \right) = 0 \\ Q_i - V_i \sum_{j=1}^{N} V_j \left(G_{ij} \sin\theta_{ij} - B_{ij} \cos\theta_{ij} \right) = 0 \end{cases} \quad . \tag{4}$$

Where, P_i, Q_i are the net active power and reactive power injected into bus i; $V_i\angle\theta_i$ is the voltage on bus i; $\theta_{ij} = \theta_i - \theta_j$ is the phase difference between the voltages of bus i, j; $G_{ij} + jB_{ij}$ is the corresponding element in system admittance matrix and N is the total number of bus.

The net active power and reactive power injected in bus i is:

$$P_i = P_{Gi} - P_{Li}, \qquad Q_i = Q_{Gi} - Q_{Li} \qquad i = 1, 2, \ldots, N$$

Where, P_{Gi}, Q_{Gi} are the active power and reactive power outputs of generator on bus i; P_{Li}, Q_{Li} are the active power and reactive power of load on bus i; other terms, $P_{Gi}(i \notin S)$, $P_{Li}(i \notin R)$, $Q_{Li}(i \notin R)$ are constant; $P_{Gi}(i \in S)$, $P_{Li}(i \in R)$, $Q_{Li}(i \in R)$ are variants, corresponding to the each dimension of the particles; and the load power factors are assumed as constant here.

As discussed in the first part of this section, ATC calculation model here is a power system static model. So inequality constraints, that is, bus voltage magnitude limit, line thermal stable capacity and devices capacity limit, should be satisfied. All these inequality constraints can be expressed in mathematical form as:

$$\begin{cases} V_{j,\min} \le V_j \le V_{j,\max} & j = 1,2,..,N \\ 0 \le I_{ij} \le I_{ij}^{\max} & \\ P_{Gi,\min} \le P_{Gi} \le P_{Gi,\max} & i = 1,2,....N_g \\ Q_{iG,\min} \le Q_{iG} \le Q_{iG,\max} & \\ 0 \le P_{Lk} \le P_{Lk\max} & k = 1,2,...,N_l \\ Q_{Lk\min} \le Q_{Lk} \le Q_{Lk\max}. & \end{cases} \tag{5}$$

Where, N is the total number of buses; N_g is the total number of generators; N_l is the total number of loads; $V_{j,\min}, V_{j,\max}$ are the bus j voltage magnitude lower limit and upper limit; $P_{Gi\min}, P_{Gi\max}$ are active power lower limit and upper limit of generator i ; $Q_{Gi\min}, Q_{Gi\max}$ are reactive power lower limit and upper limit of generator i ; $P_{Lk\max}, Q_{Lk\min}, Q_{Lk\max}$ are the upper limit and lower limit of bus k , and this three variants are determined by the capacity of distribution devices attached with bus.

2.4 ATC Calculation Procedure Using IPSO

As discussed above, the procedure of ATC calculation with IPSO method is:

(1) Set the total number n of the particles in the population, acceleration coefficients $c_1 c_2$,inertia weight w , the maximum life $liter$ of global best position, the maximum iteration times $maxiter$ and the lock radius $radius$. Here, n =40, $liter$ =20, $radius$ =5, $c_1 = c_2$ =1.49618, w =0.7298, $maxiter$ =1000.

(2) Input the initial data, set maximum velocity and position range of particle's each dimension, define the selling and buying area, then evaluate the initial fitness of each particles. The personal best position of each particle is the particles' initial value itself.

(3) According to the position of each particle, calculate the solution of the power equation. If equation diverging or the slack generator's active output over its upper limit, a new particle should be yielded randomly to replace this particle and power equation should be calculated again until all particles satisfy the power equation.

(4)Basing the calculation result of power equation, calculate the object fitness and constraint fitness of each particle. According to fitness of particles update the global best position and personal best position of each particle.

(5)Basing the equation (1) (2) update the value of each particles. If some particles enter into the lock area, they die and should be replaced by new particles which are yielded randomly.

(6)Compared with the last generation, if the global best position has no change, its life adds 1. If it changed, to the new global best position, its life is set 1. If the global best position life is equal with variant $liter$, this global best position should be saved as a local optimization solution. And the searching space around this point within radius of $radius$ should be locked. All particles which fly into this locked space die and are replaced with the new particles yielded randomly to keep the total number of the

population unchanged. Then just like the method introduced above, define the new global best position in this new population and its life is set 1.
(7)Evaluate whether the iteration times equal *maxiter* or not. If not, go to (3).
(8)Acquire the global optimization solution. All saved best position values are compared and the best one is exported. Calculate the power equation corresponding to this best position and the power increment on the tie line between selling area and buying area is the ATC result in this case.

3 Case Study and Discussion

The proposed IPSO method has been test on IEEE 118 test system. The raw data of IEEE 118 test system has no line thermal capacity. Here, for the need of calculation, each line's thermal capacity is assumed. The whole area is divided into three areas. Doing this has no any bad effect on the test validity of IPSO. Here a comparison with traditional OPF method, sequence quadratic programming (SQP), was made. Use MATLAB 7.0 to write the program and run this program on pc computer with P4 2.9G processor. The result is showed in table 1:

Table 1. ATC value between areas of IEEE118 system and its contrast with SQP method

Area Pairs (Selling->Buying)	**ATC Result (MW)**		**Calculation CPU Time (s)**	
	IPSO	SQP	IPSO	SQP
1−>2	376.68	369.203	2485	1482.5
1−>3	768.23	467.68	2558	3008.49
2−>1	412.06	303.049	2471	3346.46
2−>3	1120.2	447.343	2581	2621.59
3−>1	441.64	239.27	2503	2159.83
3−>2	324.89	368.31	2495	2177.69

Table 1 shows that IPSO method can be used to solve ATC problem. Compared with SQP, IPSO can find the much better solution than the latter. And the number of the saved best particles shows that IPSO is inclined to converge at its local optimization point. The method presented in this paper can choose the best one of the all saved local optimization solution as the approximate global optimization solution. And the space around this local best point is locked to prevent other particles flying into it. In this way, the drawback of PSO method can be avoided.

But from the last field of the table 1, the time consumed in IPSO is also unbearable. This will limit the IPSO method application to ATC online calculation. But for some special case, this method can be used to get the maximum ATC value between areas and the result can be used as a signal to guide the system operators dispatching.

4 Conclusion

Different from the traditional OPF method basing on Newton criteria, IPSO method is introduced in this paper to solve the ATC problem in power system. Numerical simulation on IEEE 118 test system indicates that this method can solve the ATC problem and the much better solutions are acquired. This result can be used as a guidance signal to system operators dispatching.

References

1. Transmission Transfer Capability Task Force.: Available Transmission Capability Definitions and Determination. North American Electric Reliability Council. Princeton, New Jersey (1996)
2. North American Electric Reliability Council Available Transfer Capability Working Group.: Transmission Capability Margins and Their Use in ATC Determination White Paper. North American Electric Reliability Council, New York (1999)
3. Li, G.: Study On Transmission Transfer Capability Of Large Scale Interconnected Power System Based On Continuation Method. Doctorial thesis. Tianjing University, Tianjing, China (1998)
4. Diao, Q., Mohamed, S., Ni, Y.: Inter-area Total Transfer Capability Calculation Using Sequential Quadratic Programming Method in Power Market. Vol.24. Automation of Electric Power Systems (2000) 5-8
5. Wang, L., Wu, Z.: Calculation of Available Transfer Capability Taking Into Account Transient Stability Constraints Based on Interior-Point Solution In Electricity Market . Vol.14Proceeding of Electricity Power System Automation (2004)
6. Mohamed, S., Ni, Y., Wu, F.: Available Transfer Capability Evaluation by Decomposition. IEEE Power Engineering Society Summer Meeting, Vancouver (2001) 1122-1126
7. Wang, C., Li, H.: Calculation of Transfer Capability Taking into Account Voltage Stability Constraint. Vol.24. Electric Power Automation Equipment (2004)
8. Kennedy, J., Eberhart, R C.: Particle Swarm Optimization. IEEE International Conference on Neural Networks. Piscataway, NJ(1995) 1942-1948
9. Pan, Z., Kang, L.: Evolutionary Computation. Tsinghua University Press, Beijing, China (1998)
10. Boeringer, D. W., Werner, D. H.: A Comparison of Particle Swarm Optimization and Genetic Algorithms for A Phased Array Synthesis Problem. Antennas and Propagation Society International Symposium (2003) 181-184
11. Jin, Y., Cheng, H.: Local Best Embranchment Based Convergence Guarantee Particle Swarm Optimization And Its Use In Transmission Network Planning. Vol.25.Proceedings of the CSEE (2005)
12. Liu, H., Lin, Y.: A Modified Particle Swarm Optimization For Solving Constrained Optimization Problems. Vol.43.Proceedings of Jilin University (2005)
13. Dong, Y., Tang, J.: Application of Particle Swarm Optimization to Nonlinear Constrained Programming. Vol.24.Proceedings of Northeastern University (2003)

An Improved Particle Swarm Optimization Algorithm with Disturbance Term

Qingyuan He and Chuanjiu Han

Department of Communication and Information Engineering,
Guilin University of Electronic Technology, Guilin, Guangxi, 541004, China
cjhan@gliet.edu.cn
yuanq_h@163.com

Abstract. The standard particle swarm optimization (PSO) algorithm, existing improvements and their influence to the performance of standard PSO are introduced. The framework of PSO basic formula is analyzed. Implied by its three-term structure, the inherent shortcoming that trends to local optima is indicated. Then a modified velocity updating formula of particle swarm optimization algorithm is declared. The addition of the disturbance term based on existing structure effectively mends the defects. The convergence of the improved algorithm is analyzed. Simulation results demonstrated that the improved algorithm have a better performance than the standard one.

1 Introduction

The particle swarm optimization (PSO) is an optimization algorithm based on swarm intelligence theory, introduced by Kennedy and Eberhart[1], which developed out of work simulating the movement of flocks of birds. It guides optimization search through swarm intelligence produced by cooperation and competition of the particles. Compared to evolutionary computation techniques, PSO reserved global search strategy based on swarm, but its model implement more easily and avoid complicated genetic operation[2]. Its peculiar memory function gives it the ability to adjust its search strategy dynamically by tracing the current search condition. So it is a more efficiency parallel stochastic search algorithm than evolutionary algorithm.

PSO is initialized with a group of random solutions of the objective function. The individuals in the group are called as particles. Each particle has its own position x, transfer vector v, and its own p which represents the best position visited by the particle so far. All particles share pg, or the best position visited by all the particles so far. A particle forms a new transfer vector and position by tracing the two "best" values. The following equations characterized the particle's movement of PSO:

$$v_{id}^{k+1} = w \times v_{id}^{k} + c_1 \times r_1 \times (p_{id} - x_{id}^{k}) + c_2 \times r_2 \times (pg_d - x_{id}^{k}) . \quad (1)$$

$$x_{id}^{k+1} = x_{id}^{k} + v_{id}^{k+1} . \quad (2)$$

D.-S. Huang, K. Li, and G.W. Irwin (Eds.): ICIC 2006, LNBI 4115, pp. 100 – 108, 2006.

Where w is called the inertia weight in the (0,1) range, c_1 , c_2 are learning parameters, the most common setting is $c_1 = c_2 = 2$, r_1 , r_2 is a number chosen randomly from the uniform distribution in the (0,1) range. The value of v is clamped to the range $[-v_{max}, v_{max}]$ to reduce the likelihood that the particle might leave the search space.

The PSO algorithm is simple in concept, easy to implement and computational efficient. The pseudocode for a PSO procedure is as following:

```
Begin;
Generate random population of N solutions (particles);
       For each individual i∈N : calculate fitness (i);
       Initialize the value of the weight factor, w;
            For each particle;
                   Set pi as the best position of
particle i;
                   If fitness (i) is better than pi;
                   pi = fitness (i);
           End;
           Set pg as the best fitness of all particles;
           For each particle;
                   Calculate particle velocity
according to Eq. (1);
                   Update particle position according
to Eq. (2);
           End;
           Update the value of the weight factor, w;
Check if termination = true;
End
```

Like the other evolutionary algorithms, PSO is a population based search algorithm with random initialization, and there are interactions among population members. Unlike the other evolutionary algorithms, in PSO, each particle flies through the solution space, and has the ability to remember its previous best position, survives from generation to generation. Furthermore, compared with the other evolutionary algorithms, e.g. evolutionary programming, the original version of PSO is faster in initial convergence while slower in fine tuning[3],[4].

2 An Analysis to the Formula of Standard PSO

The new velocity v_{id}^{k+1} in equation can be seen as a sum of three terms. The first term $w \times v_{id}^{k}$ is just the current velocity of the particle and can be thought of as a momentum term. The second term $c_1 \times r_1 \times (p_{id} - x_{id}^{k})$, which is associated with a local search, is proportional to the vector $(p_{id} - x_{id}^{k})$ and points from the particle's current position back towards its personal best position. The third term $c_2 \times r_2 \times (pg_d - x_{id}^{k})$, which is associated with a global search, is proportional to $(pg_d - x_{id}^{k})$ and points towards the global best position. The cooperation of the three terms make particle change its own velocity and position stochastically when particle trace the individual best position and global best position, and then realize global and local search.

3 The Inherent Shortcoming of Standard PSO and Its Improvements

It is found from the velocity equation that the whole searching process of PSO is the process that particle depends on its "memory" ability and share information mechanism to trace the present best solution with some stochastic. In the early stage of the algorithm, because the individual best position p and global best position pg change frequently, the algorithm has strong global search ability and converges rapidly. But at the end stage of the algorithm, because of the relative stabilization of p and pg as well as the "compatibility" of particles, the velocity of particle will primarily determined by the first term and become smaller and smaller until drop down to zero. At this moment the position updating gets into stagnation state, and finally makes the algorithm only get local optima. More important the standard PSO algorithm can't drive particles get rid of that state. It is the main shortcoming of the standard PSO algorithm.

In order to improve this shortcoming and get better results, numerous improvements to the standard PSO have been proposed. These improvements probably can be separated into two types. The first type, such as inertia weight[5], fuzzy inertia weight[6], stochastic inertia weight, adaptive inertia weight[7] and so on, is to change the inertia weight w to make the algorithm has strong global searching ability in the early and also strong local searching ability in the evening. The second type tries to change the structure of the algorithm or associated with other optimization algorithms (e.g. genetic algorithm) such as Constriction factor [8], sequential niche technique[9], PSO with area of influence[10], Parallelizing PSO[11] and so on. Compared to the standard algorithm, these improved PSO always have better performance. But these improvements either can be applied in some aspects only or must design it's parameters in advance when used in practical problem. Especially these improvements didn't change the three terms composed structure of standard PSO, that's the reason that they can't solve the shortcoming of standard PSO thoroughly.

On account of the reason mentioned above, this paper presents a improved particle swarm optimization algorithm (PSO-DT) which add a disturbance term to the velocity updating equation based on the prototype of the standard PSO trying to improve (or avoid) the shortcoming of standard PSO. Of course, the PSO-DT doesn't exclude the improvement methods introduced above if they are indeed effective.

It must be pointed out that before our work several papers have used disturbance to improve the performance of Standard PSO. The typical papers are PSO with passive congregation[12] (PSOPC) and PSO with disturbance[13] (PSOD). In PSOD, it judge whether premature phenomenon occur and initialize the particle position entirely when it's true. Because this method throws over all former information of Particles, experiments show it can't get better performance. Compared to PSOPC, the method proposed by this paper realizes more easily and almost have the same effect to PSOPC.

4 The Improved PSO with Disturbance Term (PSO-DT)

Velocity updating equation:

$$v_{id}^{k+1} = w \times v_{id}^{k} + c_1 \times r_1 \times (p_{id} - x_{id}^{k}) + c_2 \times r_2 \times (pg_d - x_{id}^{k}) + a \times (r_3 - 0.5)\,. \tag{3}$$

We call $a \times (r_3 - 0.5)$ as disturbance term.

Position updating equation:

$$x_{id}^{k+1} = x_{id}^{k} + v_{id}^{k+1}\,. \tag{4}$$

Where a is a small constant, r_3 is a number randomly distribution in the (0, 1) range, the others parameters is the same as standard PSO.

In the early calculation, because a is very small compared to anterior three terms, and the mean value of $(r_3 - 0.5)$ equal to zero, the disturbance term even can be ignored since it exert little impact on the updating and searching capability of the whole optimization. While in the middle and later phases, when the velocity becomes slower and slower, the disturbance term ensures the searching velocity of particles will not drop down to zero, and as a result, the optimization will not stagnate, thus enabling the update to continue and overcoming the defects of easily falling into local optima of the standard PSO, therefore getting a more exact solution.

In order to testify what analyzed above, we take a simple simulation.

Given function:

$$f(x) = 3x^2 + 2x + x^2 \sin x \qquad\qquad x_i \in [-10, 10]\,.$$

Simulate particle velocity according to equation (1) and (3). Set parameter value $a = 0.04$, $c_1 = c_2 = 2$, $w_{max} = 0.9$, $w_{min} = 0.4$, generations=100. For the sake of watching conveniently, we set one particle only. Fig.1 and Fig.2 show the search curve of the standard PSO algorithm and PSO-DT algorithm respectively.

It is found from Fig.1 and Fig.2 that both standard PSO and PSO-DT have strong global search ability in the early stage of the algorithm. But the velocities of standard PSO algorithm decrease very quickly and equal to zero after 50 generations. However, because of the effect of the disturbance term, the velocity of PSO-DT decreases more reasonable. Even after 70 generations, the velocities of PSO-DT still not drop down to zero, as a result the searching processing continues.

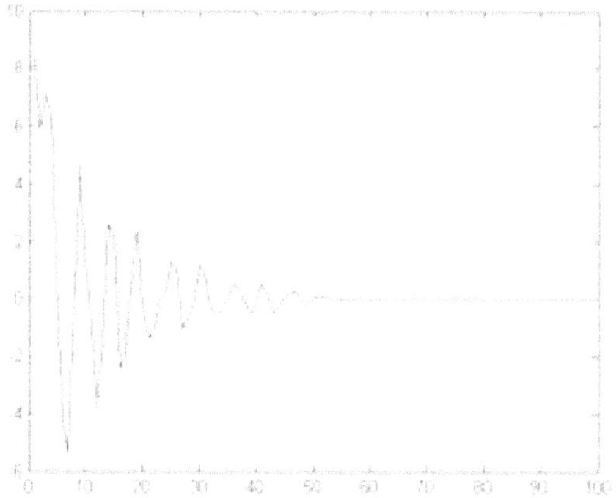

Fig. 1. Search curve of the standard PSO

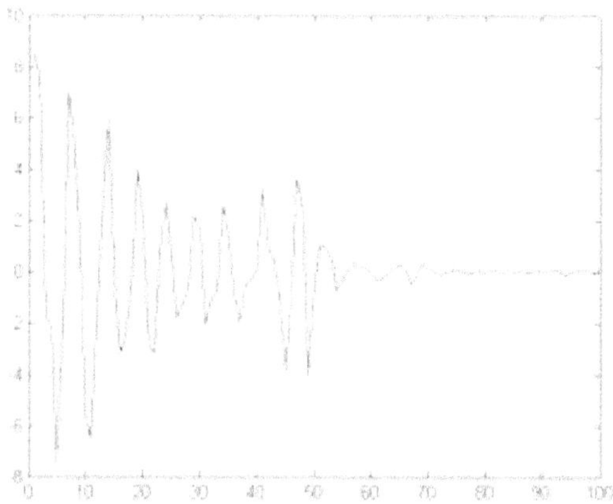

Fig. 2. Search curve of the PSO-DT

The inherent drive for searching in particle swarm optimization is its randomicity, so the participation of the disturbance term conforms to this principle. Experiments show that when the value of a is between 0 and 1, better performance than standard PSO can be realized.

5 Convergence Analysis of PSO-DT

Equations (3) and (4) which determine the behavior of particles are so complicated that we cannot analyze them as they are. Therefore we notice only one dimension of one particle, vector notation can be thrown out, and equations (3) can be transformed:

$$v^{k+1} = w \times v^k + (\Phi_1 + \Phi_2) \times (p - x^k) + c\,. \tag{5}$$

Where

$$c_1 \times r_1 = \Phi_1, c_2 \times r_2 = \Phi_2, \text{ and } a \times (r_3 - 1) = c$$

Then assume

$$\Phi_1 + \Phi_2 = \Phi\ ,\ p - x^k = y^k$$

Now equations (5) and (3) become:

$$v^{k+1} = w \times v^k + \Phi \times y^k + c\,. \tag{6}$$

$$y^{k+1} = -w \times v^k + (1 - \Phi) \times y^k\,. \tag{7}$$

Transform (6) and (7) to matrix form:

$$\begin{bmatrix} v^{k+1} \\ y^{k+1} \end{bmatrix} = \begin{bmatrix} w & \Phi \\ -w & 1-\Phi \end{bmatrix} \begin{bmatrix} v^k \\ y^k \end{bmatrix} + \begin{bmatrix} c \\ 0 \end{bmatrix} = M \begin{bmatrix} v^k \\ y^k \end{bmatrix}. \tag{8}$$

Moreover, by using matrix Q which is diagonalization matrix of M and λ which is an eigenvalue of M, this equation can be transformed as:

$$\begin{bmatrix} v^k \\ y^k \end{bmatrix} = Q \begin{bmatrix} \lambda_1^k & 0 \\ 0 & \lambda_2^k \end{bmatrix} Q^{-1} \begin{bmatrix} v^0 \\ y^0 \end{bmatrix} + \begin{bmatrix} c \\ 0 \end{bmatrix}. \tag{9}$$

Where

$$\lambda_{1,2} = \frac{w + 1 - \Phi \pm \sqrt{(w + 1 - \Phi)^2 - 4w}}{2}\,. \tag{10}$$

Equation (9) indicates that the condition in which a particle convergence is $|\lambda| < 1$. All of the above equations conclude that when equations (11) and (12) are satisfied, the dynamics of a particle become convergent, otherwise they becomes divergent.

$$0 < \Phi < 2 \times w + 2\,. \tag{11}$$

$$0 \le w < 1\,. \tag{12}$$

Analysis above indicates that the convergence condition of PSO-DT is the same to standard PSO, that's to say, the improved particle swarm optimization algorithm doesn't change the convergence condition of standard particle swarm optimization algorithm.

6 Simulation and Discussion

To test the performance of PSO-DT, some well-studied benchmark functions have been used. These benchmark functions stated as follows:

(1) Rosenbrock :

$$f_1(x)=\sum_{i=1}^{n-1}(100(x_{i+1}-x_i^2)^2+(x_i-1)^2) \quad x_i\in[-30,30]$$

(2) Rastrigrin :

$$f_2(x)=\sum_{i=1}^{n}(x_i^2-10\cos(2\pi x_i)+10) \quad x_i\in[-5.12,5.12]$$

(3) Griewank :

$$f_3(x)=\frac{1}{4000}\sum_{i=1}^{n}x_i^2-\prod_{i=1}^{n}\cos(\frac{x_i}{\sqrt{i}})+1 \quad x_i\in[-100,100]$$

(4) This function is proposed by paper [14], and has been studied by many papers:

$$\min_{x,y} f_4(x,y)=0.6224(0.0625y_1)x_1x_2+1.7781(0.0625y_2)x_1^2$$

$$+3.1661(0.0625y_1)^2x_2+19.84(0.0625y_1)^2x_1$$

s.t.

$$g_1(x,y)=0.0193x_1-0.0625y_1\le 0$$

$$g_2(x,y)=0.00954x_1-0.0625y_2\le 0$$

$$g_3(x,y)=750\times 1728-\pi x_1^2x_2-4\pi x_1^3/3\le 0$$

$$g_4(x,y)=x_2-240\le 0$$

In our tests the dimensions of function (1), (2) and (3) is 30. And swarm size of 30 is used in each experiment. The maximum numbers of iterations allowed is 5000. Both standard PSO and PSO-DT have used the inertia weights approach. Where $c_1=c_2=2$, $w_{max}=0.9$, $w_{min}=0.4$.

The following tables show the experiment results of the two version's PSO to benchmark functions listed above. Where ET (excellent times) express the times that simulation results is better than given value. The given value of function 1,2,3,4 respectively is: 100, 20, 0.02, and 6050. Each algorithm for each of the functions executed 20 times.

Table 1. Results for standard PSO

func	Best	Worst	Mean	ET	St Dev
f_1	48.32888	257.8889	143.654768	8	73.2364
f_2	14.92438	35.8185	24.475976	6	6.6187
f_3	0	0.083067	0.0175379	16	0.0230
f_4	5942.451	6487.137	6150.44682	8	157.8443

Table 2. Results for PSO with disturbance term

func	Best	Worst	Mean	ET	St Dev
f_1	25.18652	152.4703	75.169113	14	41.8212
f_2	10.99649	26.92238	19.415621	15	4.9320
f_3	0	0.039353	0.0114451	17	0.0115
f_4	5921.023	6266.626	6032.225161	15	102.9788

The tables show that PSO-DT has better performances in all problems compared to standard algorithm.

7 Conclusion

Based on the analysis of the standard PSO algorithm, the shortcoming of standard PSO has been introduced. To solve the shortcoming a disturbance term has been added to the basic velocity updating formula. Analysis indicates that the improved PSO has the same convergence conditions with standard PSO algorithm. Simulation experiments have been carried out and results show that the proposed algorithm have better performances on all benchmark functions. Then the feasibility and the advantage of the improved PSO are demonstrated.

References

1. Kennedy, J., Eberhart, R.: Particle Swarm Optimization. In IEEE International Conference on Neural Networks, Piscataway, NJ: IEEE Press, vol 4 (1995) 1942-1948
2. Kennedy, J., Spears, W M.: Matching Algorithms to Problems: An Experimental Test of the Particle Swarm and Some Genetic Algorithms on the Multimodal Problem Generator. Proc IEEE Int Conf on Evolutionary Computation. Anchorage(1998) 78-83
3. Angeline, P. J.: Using Selection to Improve Particle Swarm Optimization, Proceedings of the IEEE Congress on Evolutionary Computation (CEC 1998), Anchorage, Alaska, USA (1998)
4. Angeline, P. J.: Evolutionary Optimization Versus Particle Swarm Optimization: Philosophy and Performance Differences. Evolutionary Programming VII: Proceedings of the Seventh Annual Conference on Evolutionary Programming (1998)
5. Shi Y., Eberhart R C.: A Modified Particle Swarm Optimizer. IEEE International Conference of Evolutionary Computation, Anchorage, Alaska, May (1998)
6. Yuhui Shi, Eberhart R C.: Fuzzy Adaptive Particle Swarm Optimization. Proceeding of Congress on Evolutionary Computation. Seoul ,Korea(2001) 101-106
7. Keiichiro Yasuda.: Adaptive Particle Swarm Optimization using Velocity Information of Swarm. 2004 IEEE International Conference on Systems, Man and Cybernetics.Tokyo, NJ: IEEE Service Center (2004) 3475-3479
8. Clerc, M.: The Swarm and the Queen: Towards a Deterministic and Adaptive Particle Swarm Optimization. Proceedings of the IEEE Congress on Evolutionary Computation (CEC1999)(1999) 1951-1957
9. Beasley, D., Bull, D. T., Martin, R. R.: A Sequential Niche Technique for Multimodal Function Optimization. In Evolutionary Computation, volume 2, pages 101-125. MIT press(1993)
10. Kevin, J., Binkley, Masafumi Hagiwara.: Particle Swarm Optimization with Area of Influence: Increasing the Effectiveness of the Swarm. Swarm Intelligence Symposium. Proceedings 2005 IEEE June 8-10 (2005) 45-52
11. BoLi., Koichi Wada.: Parallelizing Particle Swarm Optimization. 2005 IEEE Pacific Rim Conference on Computers and Signal Processing] (2005) 288-291
12. He, S., Wu, Q.H. et al.: A Particle Swarm Optimizer with Passive Congregation, Bio-Systems 78 (2004) 135-147
13. Wei Jian, Yuncan Xue, Jixin Qian.: An Improved Particle Swarm Optimization Algorithm with Disturbance, Systems, Man and Cybernetics, 2004 IEEE International Conference on Volume 6, 10-13 Oct(2004) 5900 - 5904
14. Sabdgren, E .: Nonlinear Integer and Discrete Programming in Mechanical Design. ASME Journal Mechanical Design, 112(2) (1990) 223-229

Blending Scheduling Under Uncertainty Based on Particle Swarm Optimization with Hypothesis Test

Hui Pan and Ling Wang

Department of Automation, Tsinghua University, Beijing 100084, China
h-pan03@mails.tsinghua.edu.cn, wangling@mail.tsinghua.edu.cn

Abstract. Blending is an important unit operation in process industry. As a nonlinear optimization problem with constraints, it is difficult to obtain optimal solution for blending scheduling, especially under uncertainty. As a novel evolutionary computing technique, particle swarm optimization (PSO) has powerful ability to solve nonlinear optimization problems with both continuous and discrete variables. In this paper, the performance of PSO under uncertainty for blending scheduling problem is investigated, and a new hybrid approach (namely PSOHT) that combines PSO and hypothesis test (HT) is proposed. The simulation results based on an example of gasoline blending problem show that the proposed PSOHT algorithm is valid and effective for solving problem under uncertainty.

1 Introduction

Blending is a crucial step in process industry. The process involves the mixing of various stocks, which are the intermediate products from the refinery, along with some additives, such as antioxidants and corrosion inhibitors, to produce blends with certain qualities. It represents nonlinear programs with mass balance constraints, nonlinear blending properties and combinatorial aspects, etc. And the optimal scheduling is considered as an objective, which is very hard to achieve in process industry. In order to satisfy the economic objectives, blending scheduling is defined as the short-term manipulation of the maximization of the product profit, where the blended property is not a linear function of the inlet properties [1]. Moreover, for most optimization problems, uncertainties should be taken into account. As to scheduling problem, four types of uncertainty are mentioned: market uncertainty, process uncertainty, measurement uncertainty and model uncertainty [2].

In these days, linear programming (LP) strategies are often applied to deal with nonlinear problems, but they have some shortcomings in terms of robustness and convergence. Besides, non-linear programming (NLP) approaches do not provide a straightforward extension to handle discrete combinatorial elements in blending [2]. As a parallel search algorithm, genetic algorithm (GA) is applied to improve the fitness of a population and to discover the solution space related to a problem. It was applied to solve the task of gasoline fractions blending compounding keeping given conditions on octane numbers and amount of given types of commodity gasoline [3], but the problem of gasoline blending was simplified to linear relations.

D.-S. Huang, K. Li, and G.W. Irwin (Eds.): ICIC 2006, LNBI 4115, pp. 109–120, 2006.

Particle swarm optimization (PSO), as an alternative to GA, can be successfully applied in areas where GA can be applied. Compared with GA, PSO has memory, so knowledge of good solutions is retained by all particles. Whereas in GA, previous knowledge of the problem is destroyed, once the population changes. PSO has constructive cooperation between particles, particles in the swarm share information between them. Due to the simple concept, easy implementation and quick convergence, PSO algorithm shows good efficiency for many benchmark functions. And it also shows that PSO can deal with many kinds of optimization problems subject to constraints. In this paper, a hybrid PSO named PSOHT (Particle swarm optimization with hypothesis test) is proposed to solve the blending scheduling with uncertainty, where hypothesis test (HT) is used to compare solutions in uncertain environment, and to reserve good solutions for new swarm, and to maintain the diversity of the swarm.

The organization of the remaining content is as follows. In Section 2, we provide the mathematical formulation of blending scheduling problem. And in Section 3 we discuss the blending scheduling problem under uncertainty. In Section 4 we present the hybrid algorithm after briefly introducing PSO and hypothesis test. Then, in Section 5 we provide a blending scheduling problem for testing. Simulation results are provided in Section 6. Finally, we end with some conclusions.

2 Mathematical Formulation of Blending Scheduling

The blending scheduling problem is a nonlinear optimization problem, which can be generally formulated as follows:

$$\max_{x\in X} f(x), \quad s.t. \quad g(x) \le 0. \tag{1}$$

where $x=(x_c, x_d)\in R^{n_c}\times Z^{n_d}$ denotes decision variable, and $f: R^{n_c}\times Z^{n_d}\to R$ is objective function, and $X_c=\{x\in R^{n_c} \mid v^i \le x^i \le u^i, i\in\{1,2,...,n_c\}\}$ denotes continuous variable, and the constraint set $X_d=\{x\in Z^{n_d}\}$ contains the discrete non-zero integer variable, and $g: R^{n_c}\times Z^{n_d}\to R^m$ denotes inequality constraints. The aim is to find an optimal solution $x^*\in X$ that satisfies $g(x^*)\le 0$.

Usually, constraints are taken into account as penalty functions to the objective function, which are multiplied by a positive weighting factor μ that is monotonically increased. Penalty functions allow crossing the boundary of the feasible set and implementation of equality constraints. Penalty functions add a positive term to the objective function if a constraint is violated. To implement a penalty function for $g(x)\le 0$, the objective function can be modified as [4]:

$$\tilde{f}(x,\mu) = f(x) + \sum_{i=1}^{m} \mu_i \cdot \min(0, g^i(x))^2 . \tag{2}$$

3 Blending Scheduling Under Uncertainty

By adding a penalty term intended to minimize parametric sensitivity to the objective function, optimization problem of blending scheduling is developed. In addition, under uncertainty it needs to consider the feasibility of the constraints at an optimal solution for stochastic constraints. And a function penalizing violation of the constraints is enforced when constrains are not met. The penalty framework provides a mechanism for varying the feasibility requirements, ensuring operational flexibility with respect to the nonlinear constraints under uncertainty. The penalty parameter provides a trade-off between computational effort and accuracy of constraint satisfaction.

Based on Eq. (1), the optimization problem of blending scheduling under uncertainty can be formulated as follows:

$$\max_{u\in X} f(u,\theta), \quad s.t. \quad g(u,\theta)\le 0. \tag{3}$$

where $u\in R^n$ denotes a vector of decision variables, and θ denotes the uncertain information in the objective function, and f denotes an objective function, and g denotes a set of constraints.

Ideally, it expects that optimization algorithm works on the expected value f while not be misled by uncertainty. Since the expected value f cannot be estimated precisely with limited evaluations, in practice multiple samplings are used to calculate the following mean sum of a number of random samples $f(u,\theta)$ as a replacement for f.

$$J(u)=\frac{1}{n}\sum_{i=1}^{n} f(u,\theta_i)\,. \tag{4}$$

where n is sample size or evaluation number.

Thus, Eq. (3) can be transformed as follows:

$$\max_{u\in X} J(u)=E[f(u,\theta)], \quad s.t. \quad g(u,\theta)\le 0. \tag{5}$$

Taken into account the constraints by adding penalty functions as Eq. (2) under uncertainty, the problem can be described as follows:

$$\hat{J}(u,\mu,)=\frac{1}{n}\sum_{i=1}^{n}[f(u,\theta_i)+\sum_{j=1}^{m}\mu_j\cdot\min(0,g^j(u,\theta_i))^2]\,. \tag{6}$$

Taking $\hat{J}(u,\mu,)$ as a replacement for the objective function $J(u)$ under uncertainty, we can apply PSO to the uncertain optimization problem mentioned above. Obviously, it is worthy studying the optimization performance and robustness of PSO when uncertainty with different magnitude is present and limited sampling number is allowed. Next, a hybrid PSO-based approach will be proposed to for optimization under uncertainty.

4 Particle Swarm Optimization with Hypothesis Test

In this section, we will propose a hybrid PSO approach named PSOHT by combining PSO with hypothesis test (HT) optimization under uncertainty. Firstly, we briefly introduce PSO and HT.

4.1 Particle Swarm Optimization

The theoretical framework of PSO is very simple, and PSO is easy to be coded and implemented with computer [5]. Besides, it is computationally inexpensive in terms of memory requirements and CPU times. Thus, nowadays PSO has gained much attention and wide applications in various fields [5, 6].

PSO starts with the random initialization of a swarm of particles in the search space and works on the social behavior of the particles in the swarm. Therefore, it finds the global best solution by simply adjusting the trajectory of each individual towards its own best location and towards the best particle of the swarm at each time step. However, the trajectory of each individual in the search space is adjusted by dynamically altering the velocity of each particle, according to its own flying experience and the flying experience of the other particles in the search space.

The position and the velocity of the i th particle in the d-dimensional search space can be represented as $X_i = [x_{i,1}, x_{i,2}, ... x_{i,d}]$ and $V_i = [v_{i,1}, v_{i,2}, ... v_{i,d}]$ respectively. Each particle has its own best position ($pbest$) $p_i = (p_{i,1}, p_{i,2}, ... p_{i,d})$ corresponding to the personal best objective value obtained so far at time t. The global best particle ($gbest$) is denoted by $p_g = (p_{g,1}, p_{g,2}, ... p_{g,d})$, which represents the best particle found so far at time t in the entire swarm. The new velocity of each particle is calculated as follows:

$$v_{i,j}(t+1) = wv_{i,j}(t) + c_1 r_1 (p_{i,j} - x_{i,j}(t)) + c_2 r_2 (p_{g,j} - x_{i,j}(t)), \; j = 1,2...,d. \tag{7}$$

where c_1 and c_2 are constants called acceleration coefficients, w is called the inertia factor, r_1 and r_2 are two independent random numbers uniformly distributed in the range of [0, 1].

The inertial weight factor w provides the necessary diversity to the swarm by changing the momentum of particles and hence avoids the stagnation of particles at local optima. Usually, it needs to define a maximum velocity for each modulus of velocity vector, which is often set as the upper limit of the each modulus of position vector. This helps to control the unnecessary excessive roaming of particles outside the predefined search space. Thus, the position of each particle is updated in each generation according to the following equation:

$$x_{i,j}(t+1) = x_{i,j}(t) + v_{i,j}(t+1), \quad j = 1,2,...,d\,. \tag{8}$$

The procedure of standard PSO can be summarized as follows:

Step 1: Initialize a population of particles with random positions and velocities, where each particle contains d variables.

Step 2: Evaluate the objective values of all particles, let *pbest* of each particle and its objective value equal to its current position and objective value, and let *gbest* and its objective value equal to the position and objective value of the best initial particle.

Step 3: Update the velocity and position of each particle according to Eqs. (7) and (8).

Step 4: Evaluate the objective values of all particles.

Step 5: For each particle, compare its current objective value with the objective value of its *pbest* . If current value is better, then update *pbest* and its objective value with the current position and objective value. Furthermore, determine the best particle of current swarm with the best objective value. If the objective value is better than the objective value of *gbest* , then update *gbest* and its objective value with the position and objective value of the current best particle.

Step 6: If a predefined stopping criterion is met, then output *gbest* and its objective value; otherwise go back to Step 3.

4.2 Hypothesis Test

Hypothesis test (HT) is an important statistical technique used to make test for predefined hypothesis using experiment data [7, 8]. To perform HT for two different decision solutions when solving uncertain optimization problems, it often needs multiple independent evaluations to provide suitable performance estimations. If n_i independent simulations are carried out for solution X_i, then its unbiased estimated mean value $\bar{J}_i$ and variance s_i^2 can be calculated as follows:

$$\bar{J}_i = \bar{L}(X_i) = \sum_{j=1}^{n_i} L(X_i, \xi_j) / n_i \,. \tag{9}$$

$$s_i^2 = \sum_{j=1}^{n_i} [L(X_i, \xi_j) - \bar{J}_i]^2 / (n_i - 1) \,. \tag{10}$$

Considering two different solutions X_1 and X_2 , whose estimated performances $\hat{J}(X_1)$ and $\hat{J}(X_2)$ are two independent random variables. According to the law of large number and central limit theorem, the estimation $\hat{J}(X_i)$ subjects to $N(\bar{J}_i, s_i^2 / n_i)$ when n_i approaches to ∞ . Suppose $\hat{J}(X_1) \sim N(\mu_1, \sigma_1^2)$ and $\hat{J}(X_2) \sim N(\mu_2, \sigma_2^2)$, where the unbiased estimations of μ_1 , μ_2 and s_1^2 , s_2^2 are given by Eqs. (9) and (10), and let the null hypothesis H_0 be "$\mu_1 = \mu_2$" and the alternative hypothesis H_1 be "$\mu_1 \neq \mu_2$". If $\sigma_1^2 = \sigma_2^2 = \sigma^2$ and σ^2 is unknown, then the critical region of H_0 is described as follows:

$$\left|\bar{J}_1 - \bar{J}_2\right| \geq t_{\alpha/2}(n_1 + n_2 - 2) \cdot \sqrt{\frac{n_1 + n_2}{n_1 n_2}} \cdot \sqrt{\frac{(n_1 - 1)s_1^2 + (n_2 - 1)s_2^2}{n_1 + n_2 - 2}} = \tau . \qquad (11)$$

Thus, if $\left|\bar{J}_1 - \bar{J}_2\right| < \tau$, i.e., the null hypothesis holds, then it can be regarded that the performances of those two solutions have no significant difference in statistical sense, otherwise they are significantly different. Furthermore, for uncertain minimization problem it is assumed that X_2 is better than X_1 if $\bar{J}_1 - \bar{J}_2 \geq \tau$, while X_1 is better than X_2 if $\bar{J}_1 - \bar{J}_2 \leq -\tau$. In addition, for a specific problem it often supposes that the theoretical performance variances of all solutions are the same [7,8], so the hypothesis test can be made according to Eq. (11). For a multi-modal stochastic optimization problem, repeated search can be avoided to some extent by applying HT to search process, but pure blind search with comparison under hypothesis test can often be trapped into local optima. Since PSO is of good performances for continuous deterministic optimization problems, it motivates us to investigate the performance of PSO by combining HT for uncertain optimization.

4.3 The Framework of PSOHT for Optimization Under Uncertainty

Based on the above description, we know that the population-based search mechanism of PSO can be applied for well exploration and exploitation among solution space, and HT can be used to reserve good particles for new swarm and to reduce repeated search, so as to maintain the quality and diversity of the new swarm. Thus, we propose a hybrid PSO approach named PSOHT for optimization under uncertainty, whose optimization procedure is described as follows:

Step 1: Initialize a population of N particles with random positions and velocities.

Step 2: Estimate the objective values of all particles for sampling n times. Then, determine the *pbest* of each particle and the *gbest* of the swarm.

Step 3: Update the velocity and position of each particle according to Eqs. (7) and (8).

Step 4: Estimate the objective values of new positions for sampling n times. Then, update the *pbest* of each particle.

Step 5: Use HT to form the new swarm:

- *Step 5.1:* Order all particles both with the old positions and with the new positions from the best to the worst, and denote them sequentially by $\theta_1, \theta_2, \cdots, \theta_{2N}$. Let $m = 1$, $j = 2$, and put θ_1 into the next swarm and denote it as θ_m.
- *Step 5.2:* Perform hypothesis test for θ_j with θ_m which is in the next swarm. If the null hypothesis holds, i.e. Eq. (9) does not hold, then θ_j is discarded; otherwise, θ_j is put into the next swarm denoted as θ_{m+1} and let $m = m + 1$.
- *Step 5.3:* If $m < N$ and $j < 2N$, then let $j = j + 1$ and go to Step 5.2; otherwise go to Step 5.4.

Step 5.4: If $m = N$, it means that the new swarm has been formed; otherwise, generate $N - m$ new particles randomly and evaluate them n times to form the new swarm.

Step 5.5: Update the *gbest* of the swarm if necessary.

Step 6: If a predefined stopping criterion is met, then output the *gbest* and its estimated objective value and the expected objective value by large number of simulations; otherwise go back to Step 3 to perform the PSO-based search.

It can be seen from the above procedure that, the PSOHT inherits the fundamental population-based searching framework of PSO. Secondly, HT can reserve the best solutions and maintain the diversity of the next swarm by deleting some particles with similar performances, which is also useful to reduce repeated search to some extent. In a word, both the search element and the evaluation element are simultaneously considered in PSOHT for optimization problem under uncertainty.

5 Formulation of Blending Using PSO

Blending applications can also be found in several variations throughout all branches of process industry. One notable example is the important application of the gasoline blending. Gasoline is one of the most important refinery products as it can yield 60%—70% of total revenue of a typical refinery's [9]. Gasoline blending is the process of combining a number of components, produced by other refinery process units, together with small amounts of additives to make a mixture meeting certain

Table 1. Component data

Component	Reformate	LSR naphtha	n-Butane	Catalytic gas	Alkyl ate
RON	94.1	70.7	93.8	92.9	95.0
MON	80.5	68.7	90.0	80.8	91.7
olefin, %	1.0	1.8	0	48.8	0
aromatics, %	58.0	2.7	0	22.8	0
RVP, psi	3.8	12.0	138.0	5.3	6.6
Available, $bbl \cdot d^{-1}$	12000	6500	3000	4500	7000
cost, $\$ \cdot bbl^{-1}$	34.0	26.0	10.3	31.3	37.0

Table 2. Production Requirements

	regular	premium
value, $\$ \cdot bbl^{-1}$	33.00	37.00
Max, $bbl \cdot d^{-1}$	8000	10000
Min, $bbl \cdot d^{-1}$	7000	10000
Min *RON*	88.5	91.5
Min *MON*	77.0	80.0
Max *RVP*	10.8	10.8

quality specifications. The flow sheet of gasoline blending is shown in [4]. And the component data and production requirements are extracted from the published results of gasoline blending in [10], as shown in Table 1 and Table 2.

The objective function of the blending scheduling is formulated as follows:

$$
\begin{aligned}
f(x) = {} & 33.0y_1 + 37.0y_2 - 34.0(x_1 + x_6) - 26.0(x_2 + x_7) \\
& - 10.3(x_3 + x_8) - 31.3(x_4 + x_9) - 37.0(x_5 + x_{10}), \\
s.t.\ & y_1 = x_1 + x_2 + x_3 + x_4 + x_5, \\
& y_2 = x_6 + x_7 + x_8 + x_9 + x_{10}, \\
& 7000 \le y_1 \le 8000, y_2 = 10000, x_i \ge 0, \\
& RON_1 \ge 88.5, MON_1 \ge 77, RVP_1 \ge 10.8, \\
& RON_2 \ge 91.5, MON_2 \ge 80, RVP_2 \ge 10.8.
\end{aligned} \tag{12}
$$

Specifications on gasoline qualities include Octane Number, Volatility, Sulphur Content, Aromatics Content, Reid Vapor Pressure (*RVP*) and Viscosity etc. As the most important quality index of gasoline products, Research Octane Number (*RON*), Motor Octane Number (*MON*) and *RVP* are constraints with nonlinear property correlations in the process of blending scheduling. By contrast with predictive components octane properties of other methods, the ethyl RT-70 models have higher prediction accuracy [11]. They are found to exhibit the best combination of predictive accuracy and parsimony for Octane Numbers, and therefore adopted to represent the mixing rules for Octane Numbers, namely,

$$RON_{blend} = \bar{r} + a_1(\overline{rs} - \bar{r} \cdot \bar{s}) + a_2(\overline{O^2} - \bar{O}^2) + a_3(\overline{A^2} - \bar{A}^2). \tag{13}$$

$$MON_{blend} = \bar{m} + a_4(\overline{ms} - \bar{m} \cdot \bar{s}) + a_5(\overline{O^2} - \bar{O}^2) + a_6[(\overline{A^2} - \bar{A}^2)/100]^2. \tag{14}$$

The *RVP* model adopted to represent the blending process is the blending index approach that has the following form:

$$
\begin{aligned}
& RVPBI = (RVP)^{1.25}, \\
& (RVPBI)_{blend} = \sum_{i=1}^{n} (RVPBI)_i.
\end{aligned} \tag{15}
$$

where r denotes *RON*, m denotes *MON*, s=r-m, O denotes the olefin content, A denotes the aromatics content. Moreover, $a_1 = 0.03224$, $a_2 = 0.00101$, $a_3 = 0$, $a_4 = 0.04450$, $a_5 = 0.00081$, $a_6 = -0.0645$. $\bar{r} = \sum x_i RON_i / \sum x_i$, $\bar{m} = \sum x_i MON_i / \sum x_i$, $\bar{s} = \sum x_i s_i / \sum x_i$, $\overline{rs} = \sum x_i s_i RON_i / \sum x_i$, $\overline{ms} = \sum x_i s_i MON_i / \sum x_i$, $\bar{O} = \sum x_i O_i / \sum x_i$, $\overline{O^2} = \sum x_i \cdot O_i^2 / \sum x_i$, $\bar{A} = \sum x_i A_i / \sum x_i$, $\overline{A^2} = \sum x_i \cdot A_i^2 / \sum x_i$.

6 Simulation Results Under Uncertainty

Since there are many parameters could be uncertain in blending scheduling, we only consider measurement uncertainty for representative. Suppose the *RVP*, *RON* or *MON* of n-Butane component is an uncertainty parameter. Then Eqs. (13), (14) and (15) are nonlinear constraints with uncertain parameters. Their uncertainty is taken as 5% of their normal distribution of expectation.

For PSOHT, PSO and GA, the parameters are all set as follows: population size is 20, the maximum generation is 500, evaluation number for each particle 10. Then Eqs. (12)-(15) and other constraints are displaced in Eqs. (6). The simulation results of gasoline blending scheduling are listed in Table 3 through Table 12.

(1) Table 3 and Table 4 show the results of gasoline blending scheduling when only *RVP* of n-butane component has 5% of their normal distribution of expectation.
(2) Table 5 and Table 6 show the results of gasoline blending scheduling when only *RON* of n-butane component has 5% of their normal distribution of expectation.
(3) Table 7 and Table 8 show the results of gasoline blending scheduling when only *MON* of n-butane component has 5% of their normal distribution of expectation.
(4) Table 9 and Table 10 show the results of gasoline blending scheduling when *RVP* and *RON* of n-butane component both have 5% of their normal distribution of expectation.
(5) Table 11 and Table 12 show the results of gasoline blending scheduling when *RVP*, *RON* and *MON* of n-butane component all have 5% of their normal distribution of expectation. For such a case, the sample times of each particle changes to 20.

Table 3. Results when *RVP* of n-butane component is uncertain

Algorithm	Reformate	LSR naphtha	n-Butane	Catalytic gas	Alkyl ate
PSOHT					
regular	6011.43	1938.20	155.43	0	0
premium	4200.43	875.94	207.35	4500	216.28
PSO					
regular	6085.47	1914.53	0.01	0	0
premium	4216.48	883.54	237.65	4500	162.32
GA					
regular	6062.48	1924.23	13.29	0	0
premium	4236.57	882.30	32.71	4500	348.42

Table 4. Results under uncertain *RVP*

	PSOHT			PSO			GA		
	RON	*MON*	*RVP*	*RON*	*MON*	*RVP*	*RON*	*MON*	*RVP*
regular	90.0	77.0	10.3	88.5	77.7	6.0	88.5	78.1	6.7
premium	92.0	80.0	10.0	91.5	80.0	10.65	91.6	80.2	10.5
profit		64507			61680			57418	

Table 5. Results when *RON* of n-butane component is uncertain

Algorithm	Reformate	LSR naphtha	n-Butane	Catalytic gas	Alkyl ate
PSOHT					
regular	5915.34	1930.85	153.81	0	0
premium	4336.36	879.64	197.47	4500	220.34
PSO					
regular	6740.21	1246.21	13.58	0	0
premium	3716.16	1230.88	254.60	4500	298.36
GA					
regular	6012.38	1981.64	5.98	0	0
premium	4221.75	905.73	18.44	4500	354.08

Table 6. Results under uncertain *RON*

	PSOHT			PSO			GA		
	RON	*MON*	*RVP*	*RON*	*MON*	*RVP*	*RON*	*MON*	*RVP*
regular	90.0	77.0	10.3	91.6	77.4	5.7	88.9	78.6	6.2
premium	92.7	80.0	9.7	92.0	80.0	10.8	92.6	80.2	5.9
profit		64700			59428			56765	

Table 7. Results when *MON* of n-butane component is uncertain

Algorithm	Reformate	LSR naphtha	n-Butane	Catalytic gas	Alkyl ate
PSOHT					
regular	6266.18	1502.33	231.49	0	0
premium	3995.49	938.75	195.26	4500	370.50
PSO					
regular	6093.91	1895.30	10.79	0	0
premium	4203.96	892.05	228.14	4500	175.85
GA					
regular	5971.01	2011.35	17.64	0	0
premium	4254.27	802.69	45.82	4500	397.22

Table 8. Results under uncertainty *MON*

	PSOHT			PSO			GA		
	RON	*MON*	*RVP*	*RON*	*MON*	*RVP*	*RON*	*MON*	*RVP*
regular	91.0	77.5	10.5	90.1	77.0	6.3	89.8	77.1	6.6
premium	92.6	80.0	9.9	92.7	80.0	10.5	92.8	80.0	6.4
profit		62681			61584			56975	

Table 9. Results when *RVP* and *RON* of n-butane component are uncertain

Algorithm	Reformate	LSR naphtha	n-Butane	Catalytic gas	Alkyl ate
PSOHT					
regular	6402.23	1487.32	110.45	0	0
premium	4121.27	882.66	238.92	4500	257.15
PSO					
regular	6257.07	1711.85	31.08	0	0
premium	4063.03	988.54	120.39	4500	328.04
GA					
regular	6432.31	1574.32	2.37	0	0
premium	3789.17	1085.44	38.04	4500	587.35

Table 10. Results under uncertain *RVP* and *RON*

	PSOHT			PSO			GA		
	RON	*MON*	*RVP*	*RON*	*MON*	*RVP*	*RON*	*MON*	*RVP*
regular	91.0	77.3	8.7	90.5	77.2	6.7	90.9	77.6	5.7
premium	92.7	80.1	10.5	92.5	80.0	8.3	92.3	80.0	6.5
profit		60618			58359			54615	

Table 11. Results when *RVP*, *RON* and *MON* of n-butane component are uncertain

Algorithm	Reformate	LSR naphtha	n-Butane	Catalytic gas	Alkyl ate
PSOHT					
regular	6127.91	1857.33	14.76	0	0
premium	3953.19	893.42	220.84	4500	432.55
PSO					
regular	6588.95	1408.37	2.68	0	0
premium	4005.85	785.36	221.59	4500	487.20
GA					
regular	6704.55	1289.63	5.82	0	0
premium	3963.78	1013.80	9.68	4500	512.74

Table 12. Results under three uncertainty parameters

	PSOHT			PSO			GA		
	RON	*MON*	*RVP*	*RON*	*MON*	*RVP*	*RON*	*MON*	*RVP*
regular	90.2	77.0	6.4	91.2	78.0	5.5	91.5	78.3	5.5
premium	92.7	80.1	10.4	92.9	80.0	10.3	92.5	80.2	5.8
profit		60442			55553			51407	

From the above Tables, it can be seen that PSOHT is of better performance than PSO and GA. In addition, it can also be seen from the Tables that PSO is of better performance than GA for the blending scheduling under uncertainty. The merits of PSOHT lie in two aspects: it applies the population-based searching framework of PSO for exploration and exploitation in solution space; and it applies HT to reserve the best solutions and maintain the diversity of the next swarm by deleting some particles with similar performances and to reduce repeated search to some extent. Thus, PSOHT is of good searching quality and robustness. So, the proposed PSOHT is an effective approach for function optimization under uncertainty.

7 Conclusion

In this paper, a new hybrid approach (namely PSOHT) combining PSO and hypothesis test (HT) was proposed and applied to blending scheduling problem under uncertainty. The simulation results based on an example of gasoline blending problem demonstrated the effectiveness of the proposed method. The future work is to study some adaptive mechanism to further improve the performance of the algorithm.

Acknowledgements

This work is supported by NSF of China (Grant No. 60374060, 60574072) and National 973 Program (Grant No. 2002CB312200).

References

1. Chang, D.M., Yu, C.C., Chien, I.L.: Coordinated Control of Blending Systems. IEEE Trans. Contr. Sys. Tech. 6 (4) (1998) 495-506
2. Zhang, Y., Nadler, D., Forbes, J.F.: Results Analysis for Trust Constrained Real-time Optimization. J. Process Contr. 11 (2001) 329-341
3. Litvinenko, V.I., Burgher, J.A., Vyshemirskij, V.S., Sokolova, N.A.: Application of Genetic Algorithm for Optimization Gasoline Fractions Blending Compounding. In: Proceedings of The IEEE International Conference on Artificial Intelligences Systems (ICAIS'02), Divnomorskoe, Russia (2002)
4. Zhao, X.Q., Rong, G.: Blending Scheduling under Uncertainty Based on Particle Swarm Optimization Algorithm. Chinese J. Chem. Eng., 13 (4) (2005) 535-541
5. Liu, B., Wang, L., Jin, Y.H., Huang, D.X.: Advances in Particle Swarm Optimization Algorithm. Control Instrum Chem Ind 32(3) (2005) 1-6
6. Liu, B., Wang, L., Jin, Y.H., Huang, D.X.: Designing Neural Networks Using Hybrid Particle Swarm Optimization. Lecture Notes in Computer Science 3496 (2005), 391-397
7. Pugachev, V.S.: Probability Theory and Mathematical Statistics for Engineers. Pergamon Press, NY, 1984
8. Wang, L., Zhang, L., Zheng, D.Z.: A Class of Hypothesis-test Based Genetic Algorithm for Flow Shop Scheduling with Stochastic Processing Time. International Journal of Advanced Manufacturing Technology 25(11-12) (2005) 1157-1163
9. Glismann, K., Gruhn, G.: Short-term Scheduling And Recipe Optimization of Blending Process. Comput. Chem. Eng. 25 (2001) 627-634
10. Singh, A., Forbes, J.F., Vermeer, P.J., Woo, S.S.: Model-based Real-time Optimization of Automotive Gasoline Blending Operations. J. Process Contr., 10 (2000) 43-58
11. Zhang, Y., Monder, D., Forbes, J.F.: Real-time Optimization under Parametric Uncertainty: A Probability Constrained Approach. J. Process Contr. 12 (2002) 373-389

Fixed Parameter Estimation Method Using Gaussian Particle Filter

Lixin Wang

School of Communication Egineering, Hangzhou Dianzi University,
No.2 Street, Xia Sha, Hangzhou, Zhejiang Province, China
wgydfd@vip.sina.com

Abstract. The degeneracy problems of general particle filtering frequently occur. Although this kind of problems can be mitigated by resampling, but the diversity characteristic between particles may be lost because the higher weighted particles will be replicated and the lower weighted particles will be discarded. For parameter-fixed application cases, the standard particle filter is invalid as no importance density function can be sampled for new particles required by the predictive distribution, and particles will quickly be exhausted. This paper proposes a new method for the parameter-fixed estimation by use of Gaussian particle filter, which can avoid making particles exhausted and can improve the estimation performance. Refer to a practical example of Direction of Arrived (DOA) estimation for coherent signals propagated in space with multi-path fading, the computer simulation has been performed. The simulation results have indicated that the performance of the new method is rather than general particle filtering.

1 Introduction

In the modern signal processing field, non-linear state estimation is widely applied in many cases, including robot control, computer vision, target tracking, etc.. The Extended Kalman Filter (EKF) is the classical estimation technique for non-linear state space model, which performs linear approximation by Talor-Expansion, but it required derivative for non-linear transform and Gaussian noise assumption in system model, and the algorithm used often become to divergence in case of impropriety of initial state estimation. In highly non-linear and non-Gaussian situations, it is invalid to gain a precise solution in analytical form. With the computation cost reduction, it is possible to develop a new sequential Monte Carlo particle filter based Bayesian principle. Particle filter technique can be used in any non-linear system which can be presented as state space model, and performance of asymptotic closed to MMSE can be achieved [1], [2], [3].

The iterative process of general particle filters involves three procedures, first of all, drawing particles from importance density function, next, calculating weight values related to these particles based on the system model, finally, replicating higher weighted particles and discarding lower weighted particles to obtain filtering distribution. Nevertheless, the degeneracy phenomena could frequently be encountered in general

D.-S. Huang, K. Li, and G.W. Irwin (Eds.): ICIC 2006, LNBI 4115, pp. 121 – 129, 2006.

particle filter, i.e. after some iterative processes, weights of many particles become lower and a large number of particles will be ignored in algorithm besides a few with higher weight value.

For the estimation of parameter-fixed system model, the standard particle filter algorithm will become invalid because of no importance density function to be drawn in predictive distribution and particles exhausted quickly [4]. Unfortunately, there are many applications for the estimation of fixed parameter in non-linear system, for example, the Direction Of Arrived (DOA) estimation for signals propagated in space can be expressed as basic non-linear model, and , the non-linear model becomes more complex in muti-path propagation. It is difficult to obtain satisfied result through use of analytical method, such as EKF, UKF etc.. The paper addresses problems of fixed parameter estimation based Gaussian particle filter, has overcome the drawback of degeneracy existed in the conventional particle filter, and the performance improvement are given out in simulation.

The remainder of this paper is organized as follows: the standard particle filter approach and the problems for fixed parameter estimation are simply described, in section 2. The Gaussian particle filter technique is introduced in section 3. The applications of fixed parameter model and example of DOA estimation based Gaussian particle filter for coherent signals propagated in space through muti-path is described in section 4, and simulation results present in section 5. Finally, conclusion is given in section 6.

2 General Particle Filter

In principle, particle filter is a posterior probabilistic density estimation approach based on Monte Carlo sample method, it is an innovation by contrast with traditional technology [5], [6], [7]. In general situation, according to Bayesian principle,

$$p(\mathbf{x} \mid \mathbf{z}) = \frac{p(\mathbf{z} \mid \mathbf{x})p(\mathbf{x})}{\int p(\mathbf{z} \mid \mathbf{x})p(\mathbf{x})d\mathbf{x}} . \tag{1}$$

where, $p(\mathbf{x} \mid \mathbf{z})$ is the posterior probabilistic density function, $p(\mathbf{z} \mid \mathbf{x})$ is the likelihood function, and $p(\mathbf{x})$ is the prior probabilistic density function. When a set of observation are obtained, the posterior distribution of state can be computed, the expectation of arbitrary function for $\mathbf{x}$ can be expressed as

$$E[g(\mathbf{x})] = \int g(\mathbf{x})p(\mathbf{x} \mid \mathbf{z})d\mathbf{x} . \tag{2}$$

If there is a large number of particles drawn from $p(\mathbf{x} \mid \mathbf{z})$, equation (2) can be approximated as

$$E[g(\mathbf{x})] \approx \frac{1}{N}\sum_{i=1}^{N} g(\mathbf{x}^i) .$$

where, $\{\mathbf{x}^i, i=1,\cdots N\}$ denotes N particles drawn independently from $p(\mathbf{x}|\mathbf{z})$, and when $N \rightarrow \infty$, the above equation is accurately equal. It can be seen that the posterior probabilistic density can be expressed approximately as a set of discrete particles, the approximation replies on the value of N.

Bayesian importance sampling approach is used to estimate the posterior distribution. The detailed process is as follows, selecting an importance density function first, and then drawing particles from this distribution and obtaining a set of particles, $\{\mathbf{x}^i, i=1,\cdots N\}$. To approximate the posterior density $p(\mathbf{x}\,|\,\mathbf{z})$ as weighted particles that drawn from importance density function, equation (2) can be rewritten as

$$E[g(\mathbf{x})] \approx \sum_{i=1}^{N} g(\mathbf{x}^i)\tilde{w}^i \quad . \tag{3}$$

where, $$\tilde{w}^i = \frac{w^i}{\sum_{j=1}^{N} w^j}, \quad w^i = \frac{p(\mathbf{z}\,|\,\mathbf{x})p(\mathbf{x})}{q(\mathbf{x}\,|\,\mathbf{z})} \quad .$$

In order to estimate the posterior distribution sequentially, the sequential importance sampling could be considered as the transformation of the above mathematics. This new idea is described as follows. Let $\{\mathbf{x}_{0:k}^i, i=1,2,\cdots N\}$ denotes a set of sample particles which drawn from the importance density function, $\mathbf{x}_{0:k} = \{\mathbf{x}_j, j=0,1,\cdots,k\}$ denotes the state set which up to time k, thus, the posterior distribution at time k can be expressed approximately as

$$p(\mathbf{x}_{0:k}\,|\,\mathbf{z}_{1:k}) \approx \sum_{i=1}^{N} w_k^i \delta(\mathbf{x}_{0:k} - \mathbf{x}_{0:k}^i) \quad . \tag{4}$$

Weighting value is recursively presented as

$$w_k^i = w_{k-1}^i \cdot \frac{p(\mathbf{z}_k\,|\,\mathbf{x}_k^i)p(\mathbf{x}_k^i\,|\,\mathbf{x}_{k-1}^i)}{q(\mathbf{x}_k^i\,|\,\mathbf{x}_{k-1}^i, \mathbf{z}_k)} \quad . \tag{5}$$

For general dynamic system model,

$$\mathbf{x}_k = f(\mathbf{x}_{k-1}, \mathbf{v}_{k-1}) \quad . \tag{6}$$

$$\mathbf{z}_k = h(\mathbf{x}_k, \mathbf{w}_k) \quad . \tag{7}$$

To implement particle filtering, it is required to sequentially perform following steps.

1) According to initial probabilistic density $p(\mathbf{x}_0)$, draw N discrete particles from this distribution based on the Monte Carlo method, and denote the result as

$$\{\mathbf{x}_{0|0}^1, \mathbf{x}_{0|0}^2 \cdots \mathbf{x}_{0|0}^N\} .$$

2) *Predictive distribution*: With respect to filtering particles at last time k-1, particles predicted in one step is obtained from system process equation (6), denote as

$$\mathbf{x}^i_{k|k-1} = f(\mathbf{x}^i_{k-1|k-1}, v_{k-1}),\ i = 1,\cdots,N \ . \tag{8}$$

3) *Filtering update*: For the acceptation of a new observation, calculate the weighting value for each predictive particle, denote as,

$$b_i = \frac{p(\mathbf{z}_k \mid \mathbf{x}^i_{k|k-1})}{\sum_{j=1}^{N} p(\mathbf{z}_k \mid \mathbf{x}^j_{k|k-1})} \ . \tag{9}$$

Afterwards, in order to obtain filtering particles, it is required to performing N times resampling against the predictive particles set according to the above weighted value, this behavior can be formulated as

$$\Pr[\mathbf{x}^n_{k|k} = \mathbf{x}^i_{k|k-1}] = b_i \ ,\ i,n = 1,2,\cdots,N \ .$$

where, $\Pr[\cdot]$ denotes probability.

4) repeat step 2 and step 3 recursively.

It can obviously be shown that there is no importance density to be drawn for particles obtained in step2 when system state evolution is in fixed form, e.g. the state is a constant parameter (notice $\mathbf{x}_k = \mathbf{x}_{k-1}$), therefore, the algorithm will be invalid because of particles exhausted quickly.

3 Gaussian Particle Filter

Gaussian particle filter (GPF) is used to approximate the predictive distribution and filtering distribution as Gaussian [8], i.e.

$$p(\mathbf{x}_k \mid \mathbf{z}_{1:k-1}) \approx \mathcal{N}(\mathbf{x}_k ; \bar{\boldsymbol{\mu}}_k, \bar{\Sigma}_k) \ .$$

$$p(\mathbf{x}_k \mid \mathbf{z}_{1:k}) \approx \mathcal{N}(\mathbf{x}_k ; \boldsymbol{\mu}_k, \Sigma_k) \ .$$

where, $\mathcal{N}(\ )$ denotes normal distribution, $\boldsymbol{\mu}_k, \Sigma_k, \bar{\boldsymbol{\mu}}_k, \bar{\Sigma}_k$ is filtering mean, variance and predictive mean, variance respectively. But $\boldsymbol{\mu}_k, \Sigma_k, \bar{\boldsymbol{\mu}}_k, \bar{\Sigma}_k$ can not analytically be presented, and these parameters must be estimated from particles using Monte Carlo method.

Detailed procedures are described as follows,

1) Draw N particles from initial probabilistic density $p(\mathbf{x}_0)$ based on Monte Carlo method. The result obtained can be denoted as,

$$\left\{\mathbf{x}^1_{0|0}, \mathbf{x}^2_{0|0} \cdots \mathbf{x}^N_{0|0}\right\} .$$

2) *Predictive distribution*: From system process equation (6), a particle distribution predicted in one step is obtained

$$\mathbf{x}^{*i}_{k|k-1} = f(\mathbf{x}^{i}_{k-1|k-1}, v_{k-1}), i = 1, \cdots, N .$$

Then, calculate
$$\begin{cases} \bar{\boldsymbol{\mu}} = \dfrac{1}{N}\sum_{i=1}^{N} \mathbf{x}^{*i}_{k|k-1} \\ \bar{\Sigma}_k = \dfrac{1}{N}\sum_{i=1}^{N} (\mathbf{x}^{*i}_{k|k-1} - \bar{\boldsymbol{\mu}}_k)(\mathbf{x}^{*i}_{k|k-1} - \bar{\boldsymbol{\mu}}_k)^T \end{cases} . \tag{10}$$

And redraw particles from $\mathcal{N}(\mathbf{x}_k; \bar{\boldsymbol{\mu}}_k, \bar{\Sigma}_k)$, then, we obtain

$$\left\{\mathbf{x}^{1}_{k|k-1}, \mathbf{x}^{2}_{k|k-1} \cdots \mathbf{x}^{N}_{k|k-1}\right\}.$$

3) *Filtering distribution*: For the acceptation of a new observation, calculate the weighting value for each predictive particle according to (9), and then calculate

$$\begin{cases} \boldsymbol{\mu}_k = \dfrac{1}{N}\sum_{i=1}^{N} b_i \mathbf{x}^{i}_{k|k-1} \\ \Sigma_k = \dfrac{1}{N}\sum_{i=1}^{N} b_i (\mathbf{x}^{i}_{k|k-1} - \boldsymbol{\mu}_k)(x^{i}_{k|k-1} - \boldsymbol{\mu}_k)^T \end{cases} . \tag{11}$$

and redraw particles from $\mathcal{N}(\mathbf{x}_k; \boldsymbol{\mu}_k, \Sigma_k)$, then, we obtain

$$\left\{\mathbf{x}^{1}_{k}, \mathbf{x}^{2}_{k} \cdots \mathbf{x}^{N}_{k}\right\}.$$

4) repeat step 2 and step 3 recursively.

Gaussian distribution is depend on first two moment, i.e. mean and variance, so it is easy to redraw particles in each iteration for avoiding particles degeneracy.

4 Fixed Parameter Estimation

For parameter-fixed problems, system can be modeled in general form as

$$\begin{cases} \mathbf{x}_k = \mathbf{x}_{k-1} \\ \mathbf{z}_k = h(\mathbf{x}_k) + \mathbf{w}_k \end{cases} \tag{12}$$

where, $\mathbf{w}_k$ is an additive Gaussian noise, $\mathbf{x}$ is the unobserved parameter vector, $\mathbf{z}_k$ is measurement vector at time k, $h(\cdot)$ is the non-linear transform. Equation (12) is significant in general wireless telecommunication and other radio system, it has been demonstrated that Bayesian posterior estimation of parameters is a Gaussian variant. In other cases if $\mathbf{w}_k$ is not a Gaussian, it is also a favorite idea that the posterior estimation of the state is assumed to approximate to Gaussian, so that the computation complexity is reduced. DOA estimation is one of many practical examples, where it is very difficult for coherent signals propagated in space with multi-path fading. This is one of non-linear problems with highly complexity often appeared in array signal processing field, and it is very difficult to find correction solution by use of the conventional analytical method.

For an instance, let one plane wave impact to circle array sensors with N elements in figure 1, the signal arrived at the center of circle is

$$s_0(t) = A \cdot \cos[\omega_0 t + \varphi_0] \ .$$

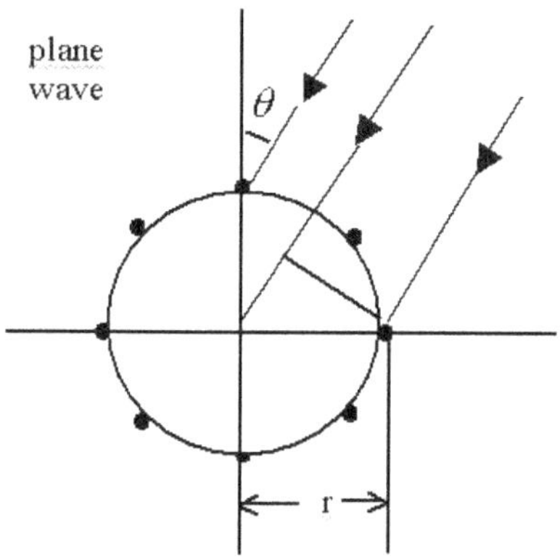

Fig. 1. Circle array sensors

The signal arrived i-th sensor can be expressed as

$$s_i(t) = A \cdot \cos[\ \omega_0 (t + \tau_i) + \varphi_0\ ] \ .$$

$$\tau_i = \frac{r}{c} \cdot \cos(\frac{2\pi \cdot i}{N} - \theta) \ .$$

Where, r is the radius of the circle, θ is the incident angle, τ_i is the time delay (or prior to) that arrived at i-th element, ω_0 is the signal frequency of incident wave, φ_0 is the initial phase, c is the velocity of light. When there are M coherent waves which are incident to the array, the equation above can be rewritten as

$$s_i(t) = \sum_{l=1}^{M} A_l \cdot \cos\left\{\omega_0[t + \frac{r}{c} \cdot \cos(\frac{2\pi \cdot i}{N} - \theta_l)] + \varphi_0\right\} . \qquad (13)$$

For the array output, it can be expressed as

$$\mathbf{z}(t) = \mathbf{s}(t) + \mathbf{w}(t) \ . \tag{14}$$

Where, $\mathbf{w}(t) \sim \mathcal{N}(0, \sigma^2 \mathbf{I})$ is the noise vector, $\mathbf{z}(t) = [z_1(t), z_2(t), \cdots z_N(t)]^T$ is the observation vector, $\mathbf{s}(t) = [s_1(t), s_2(t), \cdots s_N(t)]^T$ is the array signal vector. The likelihood function is

$$p(\mathbf{z}|\boldsymbol{\theta}) = \frac{1}{(2\pi)^{N/2} |\mathbf{R}_n|^{1/2}} \exp\left[-\frac{(\mathbf{z}-\mathbf{s})^T \mathbf{R}_n^{-1} (\mathbf{z}-\mathbf{s})}{2} \right] .$$

Here, $\mathbf{R}_n$ is the covariance matrix of the array noise. Suppose that the posterior distribution $p(\boldsymbol{\theta} | \mathbf{z})$ can be estimated, so according to Bayesian principle, the DOA parameter $\boldsymbol{\theta}$ can be estimated as

$$\hat{\boldsymbol{\theta}} = E(\boldsymbol{\theta} | \mathbf{z}) = \int \boldsymbol{\theta} p(\boldsymbol{\theta} | \mathbf{z}) d\boldsymbol{\theta} \ .$$

and the performance is asymptotic to MMSE. Rewrite the signal model in discrete time to the state space form of the equation (12), where,

$$\mathbf{x}(k) = [A_1(k), \cdots, A_M(k); \theta_1, \cdots, \theta_M; \varphi_0]^T \ .$$

is state vector involving amplitude, DOA, and initial phase parameters related to the coherent signals , at time k respectively, and the array output signals at time k can be denoted as

$$\mathbf{z}(k) = [z_1(k), \cdots, z_N(k)]^T \ .$$

We have used Gaussian particle filter to estimate DOA for coherent signals, it is believed that the performance is asymptotic optimal when number of particles is sufficient large.

5 Simulation Results

The array with 9 elements uniformly spaced in a circle of 2m diameter is used, the signal frequency is 150MHz, the number of particles equals to 1000, computer simulation is performed under some conditions, and the posterior distribution of DOA parameter $\boldsymbol{\theta}$ is given in histogram form of particle number vs. azimuth. (Notes that the θ_1, θ_2 characteristics are indicated in solid and dash line respectively.)

Figure 2 illustrates the DOA estimation results for coherent signals by use of the general particle filter, in these cases, there are two coherent signals to incident to the array, with azimuth of 50°,150°, respectively, and the signal to noise ratio (SNR) is 10dB at array output. It can be observed that the particles degeneracy phenomena occurs, and the estimation is invalid.

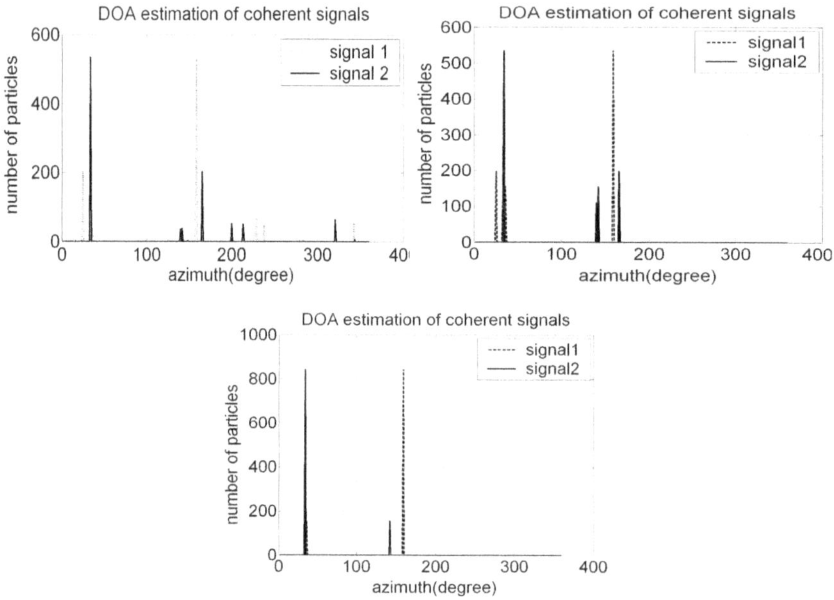

Fig. 2. DOA estimation of coherent signals by use of the general particle filter with 1 iteration (*left upper case*) and 2 iterations (*right upper case*) and >3 iterations (*left bottom case*), where azimuth=50°,150°, SNR=10dB

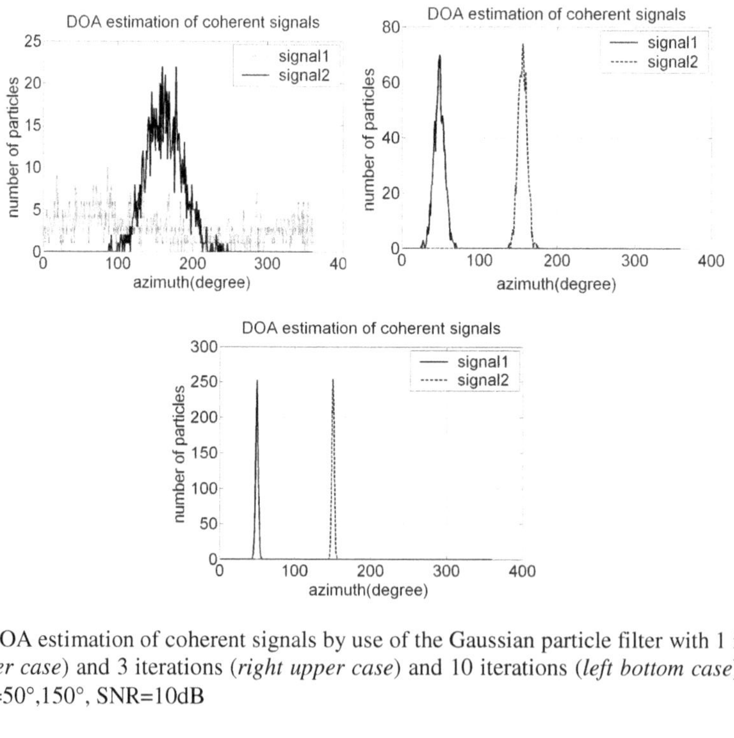

Fig. 3. DOA estimation of coherent signals by use of the Gaussian particle filter with 1 iteration (*left upper case*) and 3 iterations (*right upper case*) and 10 iterations (*left bottom case*), where azimuth=50°,150°, SNR=10dB

Figure 3 illustrates the DOA estimation results for coherent signals by use of Gaussian particle filter with the same conditions indicated in figure 2, but results are convergence to true parameter. It is obviously shown that, after a few iterations, the estimation is utilized in practice only with a few observations, and this approach is successful to be applied.

6 Conclusion

There are many issues for unknown parameter-fixed estimation in highly non-linear system. The conventional analytical methods such as EKF and etc. are inefficient to process these issues. The sequential Bayesian method involves predictive and filtering distribution estimation recursively, but due to degeneracy and exhaustion of particles in iterations, the standard particle filter cannot handle above problems.

Gaussian particle filter can avoid to exhausting of particles, and thus has much-improved estimation performance. This approach overcomes the drawback inherently occurred in the traditional particle filters. It is believed that the new Gaussian particle filter method will be widely applied in practice.

References

1. Jian K., Si X.C., Rui G.S.: Particle Filtering Techniques Based on Bayesian Theorem. Modern Radar. 26 (2004) 34-36
2. Carpenter, J., Clifford, P., Fearnhead, P.: Improved Particle Filter for Nonlinear Problems. IEE Proc. Radar Sonar Navig, (1999) 146
3. Sanjeev, M., Maskell, S., Gordon, N., Clapp, T.: A Tutorial on Particle Filters for Online Nonlinear/Non-Gaussian Bayesian Tracking. IEEE Trans. on Signal Processing. 50 (2002) 174-188
4. Miguez, J., Bugallo, F., Djuric, M.: Novel Particle Filtering Algorithm for Fixed Parameter Estimation in Dynamic Systems. Proceedings of The 4th International Symposium on Image and Signal Processing and Analysis, (2005) 46-51
5. Herman, S., Moulin, P.: A Particle Filtering Approach to FM-Band Passive Radar Tracking and Automatic Target Recognition. IEEE Aerospace Conference Proceedings, (2002) 1789 -1808
6. Karlsson, R., Gustafsson, F.: Particle Filter for Underwater Terrain Navigation. IEEE Workshop on Statistical Signal Processing, (2003) 526 - 529
7. Karlsson, R., Gusfafsson, F., Karlsson, T.: Particle Filtering and Cramer-Rao Lower Bound for Underwater Navigation. IEEE International Conference on Acoustics, Speech, and Signal Processing, (2003) VI - 65-8
8. Kotecha, H., Djuric, M.: Gaussian Particle Filtering. IEEE Trans. on Signal Processing, 51 (2003) 2592-2601

Improving Quantum-Behaved Particle Swarm Optimization by Simulated Annealing

Jing Liu, Jun Sun, and Wenbo Xu

School of Information Technology, Southern Yangtze University, Wuxi, Jiangsu, 214122, China
{liujing_novem, sunjun_wx, xwb_sytu}@hotmail.com

Abstract. Quantum-behaved Particle Swarm Optimization (QPSO) is a global convergence guaranteed search method, which introduced quantum theory into original Particle Swarm Optimization (PSO). While Simulated Annealing (SA) is another important stochastic optimization with the ability of probabilistic hill-climbing. In this paper, the mechanism of Simulated Annealing is introduced into the weak selection implicit in our QPSO algorithm, which effectively employs both the ability to jump out of the local minima in Simulated Annealing and the capacity of searching the global optimum in QPSO algorithm. The experimental results show that the proposed hybrid algorithm increases the diversity of the population in the search process and improves its precision in the latter period of the search.

1 Introduction

Particle Swarm Optimization (PSO) [1], inspired by the collective behaviors of birds, is a population based stochastic optimization technique proposed by Kennedy and Eberhart. As an emerging intelligent technology, simple and easy to realize, particle swarm has gained a lot of attention in recent years and has been investigated from various perspective. However, there are still many issues in particle swarm, such as slow convergence during the latter search, poor precision and being easy to trap in local minima. To overcome the above problems, a lot of revised PSO have emerged.

The improvement emphases of PSO algorithm mainly concentrate on combing PSO with the concepts of evolutionary computation, such as selection, recombination, breeding and so on. As articles written by Angeline [2] in 1999, the operators of selection and cross in Evolutionary computation are introduced into PSO algorithm to guarantee the convergence. And in view of breeding and cross, Lovbjerg etc. [3] further apply evolutionary mechanism into PSO algorithm to present a concrete form and the experimental results based on benchmark functions show the validity of algorithm. On the other hand, to improve the global convergence, the diversity maintenance is vital to PSO algorithm. To overcome the problem of premature convergence, the diversity measure, attractive and repulsive PSO algorithm, is applied to control the swarm by Jacques Riget [11]. In 2004, from the point of view of probability statistics, Kennedy [4] eliminated the velocity formula and sample from the Gaussian

D.-S. Huang, K. Li, and G.W. Irwin (Eds.): ICIC 2006, LNBI 4115, pp. 130 – 136, 2006.

distribution, using a random number generator and experimental results show that some remarkable degree of success can be achieved through simple collaborative probabilistic search within regions defined by particles' success. In 2004, we proposed Quantum-behaved Particle Swarm Optimization (QPSO) [5][8], which is kept to the philosophy of PSO. QPSO algorithm is depicted only with the position vector without velocity vector, which is a simpler algorithm. And the results show that QPSO performs better than standard PSO on several benchmark test functions and is a promising algorithm due to its global convergence guaranteed characteristic.

Simulated Annealing is another important stochastic optimization method based on the Monte Carlo importance-sampling, but it is very slow [9]. It starts from an initial point and takes a single point iterative strategy. And it accept not only the evolved but also the degenerated solutions with the Metropolis acceptance criterion during its annealing procedure, which makes the SA be of the potentially to find the global minimum instead of falling to local minima.

In this paper, based on our proposed Quantum-behaved Particle Swarm Optimization, Simulated Annealing, as selection operator, is introduced to improve the capacity of fine-tuning solution in the latter period of the search, which effectively employs the ability to jump from the local minima in Simulated Annealing algorithm and the capacity of global search in QPSO algorithm.

The rest of this paper is organized as follows. Section 2 briefly describes PSO and Quantum-behaved PSO algorithm. Then the mechanism of Simulated Annealing introduced into QPSO is presented in Section 3. Section 4 shows the experimental settings and the comparative results of hybrid algorithm on test functions. Finally, conclusions are made.

2 PSO and Quantum-Behaved PSO

2.1 Dynamics of Classical PSO

In a classical PSO system proposed by Kennedy and Eberhart[1], each particle flies in a D-dimensional space S according to its own historical experience and others. The velocity and location for the ith particle is represented as $\vec{v}_i = (v_{i1},\dots,v_{id},\dots,v_{iD})$ and $\vec{x}_i = (x_{i1},\dots,x_{id},\dots,x_{iD})$, respectively. The particles are manipulated according to the following equation:

$$v_{id} = w \cdot v_{id} + c_1 \cdot rand() \cdot (p_{id} - x_{id}) + c_2 \cdot rand() \cdot (p_{gd} - x_{id}) \tag{1a}$$

$$x_{id} = x_{id} + v_{id} \tag{1b}$$

where c1 and c2 are acceleration constants, rand ( ) are random values between 0 and 1.In (1a),the vector p_i is the best position (the position giving the best fitness value) of the particle i, vector p_g is the position of the best particle among all the particles in the population. Parameter w is the inertia weight [6], which does not appear in the original version of PSO [1]. In [7], M. Clerc and J. Kennedy analyze the trajectory and prove that, whichever model is employed in the PSO algorithm, each particle in the PSO system converges to its local point p, whose coordinates are $p_d = (\varphi_{1d} p_{id} + \varphi_{2d} p_{gd}) / (\varphi_{1d} + \varphi_{2d})$ so that the best previous position of all particles will converge to an exclusive global position with $t \to \infty$, where φ_{1d}, φ_{2d} are random numbers distributed uniformly on [0,1].

2.2 Dynamics of Quantum-Behaved PSO

Keeping to the philosophy of PSO algorithm, we introduced the quantum theory into PSO algorithm and proposed a Quantum-behaved PSO algorithm [5][8]. In the quantum model of a PSO, the state of a particle is depicted by wave function $\Psi(\vec{x},t)$, instead of position and velocity. The dynamic behavior of the particle is widely divergent from that of the particle in traditional PSO systems in that the exact values of x and v cannot be determined simultaneously. We can only learn the probability of the particle's appearing in position x from probability density function $|\psi(X,t)|^2$, the form of which depends on the potential field the particle lies in.

The particles move according to the following iterative equation [5][8]:

$$x(t+1) = p \pm \beta * |mbest - x(t)| * \ln(1/u) \tag{2a}$$

Where

$$mbest = \frac{1}{M}\sum_{i=1}^{M} P_i = \left(\frac{1}{M}\sum_{i=1}^{M} P_{i1}, \ \frac{1}{M}\sum_{i=1}^{M} P_{i2}, \ \cdots, \ \frac{1}{M}\sum_{i=1}^{M} P_{id}\right) \tag{2b}$$

$$p_{id} = \varphi * p_{id} + (1-\varphi) * p_{gd}, \varphi = rand() \tag{2c}$$

mbest (Mean Best Position) is defined as the mean value of all particles' the best position, φ and u are random number distributed uniformly on [0,1] respectively, β, called Contraction-Expansion Coefficient, is the only parameter in QPSO algorithm.

3 The Proposed Hybrid Algorithm

3.1 Simulated Annealing

Simulated annealing was essentially introduced as a Monte Carlo importance-sampling technique for doing large-dimension path integrals arising in statistical physics problem, which exploits an analogy between the way in which a metal cools and freezes into a minimum energy crystalline structure (the annealing process) and the search for a minimum in a more general system [10]. The method consists of three functions, i.e., (1) *f(x)*: probability density of state-space of D parameters $x = \{x^i; i = 1, D\}$; (2) *p(x)*: probability density for acceptance of new cost-function given the just previous value; (3)*T(k)*: schedule of annealing the temperature T in annealing-time steps *k*, i.e. of changing the volatility or fluctuation of the two previous probability densities.

SA's major advantage over other methods is an ability to avoid becoming trapped at local minima. The algorithm starts from an initial point and takes a single point iterative strategy, which not only accepts changes that decreases objective function f, but also some changes that increase it. The latter are accepted with a probability *p=exp(-delta(f)/T)*, Where *delta(f)* is the increase in f and T is a control parameter, varied with the objective function involved. This allows the SA algorithm to escape from local extrema at the early stages of the search and to efficiently hill-climb as the temperature approaches zero.

3.2 Improving Quantum-Behaved Particle Swarm Optimization by Simulated Annealing

Although QPSO is a global convergence guaranteed optimization, there are still many inevitable issues in Quantum-behaved particle swarm algorithm as other Evolutionary Algorithm, such as poor fine-tuning solutions and premature convergence during the latter search. And it seems that QPSO lacks a hill-climbing capability to close the goal. However, SA has a stochastic hill-climbing capability and the solution state cannot stay at a fixed point for a long time. Therefore, the idea on hybridizing the QPSO with SA for performance improvement is proposed. Based on the QPSO algorithm, Simulated Annealing, as selection operator, is introduced to select those degenerated particles with Metropolis acceptance criterion in QPSO algorithm.

In QPSO algorithm, the mechanism of weak selection implicit in the search process is to select the best position of the individual particle, comparing the current fitness value of particle with its historical personal best. The selection method serves to redirect the search towards those positions in the search space that have shown a relative advantage over others recently visited. Thus, the particles with low fitness were discarded. However, those particles with low fitness may have potentially preferable evolutionary tendency and then decelerate the degeneration of the whole swarm. Therefore in our proposed hybrid algorithm, introduction the concept of Simulated Annealing into the mechanism of selection in QPSO algorithm, the particles with low fitness were also accepted with the probability to further increase the search space. Thus the particles with low fitness value but a preferable evolutionary tendency seem to be a certain probability of continuing to fly in the search space, which effectively avoid being trapped at local minima and then increase the diversity of population. Meanwhile, the proposed selection operator from SA offers QPSO a hill-climbing capability to close the optimum.

In the proposed algorithm, the probability of accepting the particles with low fitness is defined as: $p_k = \exp(-\Delta f / T_k)$, where k=1,2,3,...and $\Delta f = f(x^{'}) - f(x)$ is the change in the objective function. The annealing operation is defined as: $T_{k+1} = T_0 \cdot CR^{T_k}, k \leftarrow k+1$, where k corresponds to the number of generation.

The simulation of the proposed hybrid algorithm begins with the initial population and initial temperature. The particles then randomly search according to evolutionary equations of QPSO algorithm to generate a new population. And the new population will be compared with their best position and those particles with worse fitness will be accepted with the probability from SA. Then the results obtained will become the individuals of the next generation. The simulation is repeated until the terminal crite rion is met. And the terminal criterion is always set to the maximum generations of search.

Procedure of algorithm is stated below:

Step1: Initialize of population and temperature.
Step2: Evaluate of initial population.
Step3: Annealing operation $T_{k+1} = T_0 \cdot CR^{T_k}, k \leftarrow k+1$
Step4: Update position of particles according to evolutionary equation Eq(2a).
Step5: If the position of particle is better than *pbest*, then replace *pbest*;
Else accept the position of particle with probability of $p_k = \exp(-\Delta f / T_k)$
Step6: find the global best position *gbest*
Step7: If the stop criterion is met, then algorithm ends; else go to Step3.

3.3 Discussions

In theory, both QPSO algorithm and SA algorithm are optimization techniques based on probability distribution. However, SA is an optimization with the probability of which is varied with generations and finally converges to zero during the process of search, which can effectively jump out of local minima and converge to global optimum. While QPSO is a global convergence guaranteed population-based optimization algorithm, which imitates the cooperation and competition behavior of flocks. The combination of the two different optimization mechanism algorithms will enrich the search behavior greatly during the search process and increase its search capacity and efficiency in global and local area. Moreover, the redundancy and history search information in the SA algorithm is so scarce because the only solution was retained at each generation. But in QPSO algorithm, the history information of individual and the whole swarm are kept to direct the search process through cooperation and competition among the particles. The combination of these two operations with different functions improves the search structure and search space. In addition, SA, as selection mechanism with adaptive probability, increases and compliments the evolutionary capacity of QPSO. And finally, the premature is evitable in the process of search due to the loss of diversity in QPSO algorithm. The incorporation of SA is able to control the premature convergence and degeneration and then increase the diversity to jump out of the local minima. In a word, the proposed hybrid algorithm has the merits of both QPSO with mutation operator algorithm and Simulated Annealing by introducing an annealing selection operator, which ensures both search space and good solution quality.

4 Experimental Setting and Results

In the proposed hybrid algorithm, the only parameter β decreases linearly from 1.0 to 0.5.The initial parameters of algorithm are described as follows: the initial annealing temperature $T_0 = 2$, the annealing operation is set to $T_{k+1} = T_0 \cdot CR^{T_k}, k \leftarrow k+1$, where CR=0.95. To evaluate the performance of algorithm, mean optimum and standard deviation of test functions obtained from 50 runs experiments will be recorded.

Table 1 gives the test functions: Rastrigrin, Rosenbrock and Griewank, mathematics expression, its initialization range and the corresponding limits to the search space and its function value.

Table 1. Test Functions

F	Mathematic expression	Initial range	f_{min}	X_{max}
F_1	$\sum_{i=1}^{n}(100(x_{i+1}-x_i^2)^2+(x_i-1)^2)$	(15,30)	0	100
F_2	$f(x)_3=\sum_{i=1}^{n}(x_i^2-10\cos(2\pi x_i)+10)$	(2.56, 5.12)	0	10
F_3	$f(x)_4=\frac{1}{4000}\sum_{i=1}^{n}(x_i-100)^2-\prod_{i=1}^{n}\cos(\frac{(x_i-100)}{\sqrt{i}})+1$	(300,600)	0	600

Table 2. Experimental Values for Rosenbrock Functions

			SPSO		QPSO		QPSO-SA	
P	D	G	Mean	St. Dev	Mean	St. Dev	Mean	St. Dev
	10	1000	94.1276	194.3648	59.4764	153.0842	25.5521	58.8202
20	20	1500	204.336	293.4544	110.664	149.5483	98.9765	122.2852
	30	2000	313.734	547.2635	147.609	210.3262	112.0748	54.0904
	10	1000	71.0239	174.1108	10.4238	14.4799	10.7750	12.5061
40	20	1500	179.291	377.4305	46.5957	39.5360	38.1721	33.4951
	30	2000	289.593	478.6273	59.0291	63.4940	47.9188	39.2296
	10	1000	37.3747	57.4734	8.63638	16.6746	6.7566	6.7435
80	20	1500	83.6931	137.2637	35.8947	36.4702	59.2269	99.7291
	30	2000	202.672	289.9728	51.5479	40.8490	41.6666	29.9889

Table 3. Experimental Values for Rastrigrin Functions

			SPSO		QPSO		QPSO-SA	
P	D	G	Mean	St.Dev	Mean	St.Dev	Mean	St.Dev
	10	1000	5.5382	3.0477	5.2543	2.8952	4.9388	2.6520
20	20	1500	23.1544	10.4739	16.2673	5.9771	13.6808	4.6682
	30	2000	47.4168	17.1595	31.4576	7.6882	29.5396	7.6264
	10	1000	3.5778	2.1384	3.5685	2.0678	2.7779	1.3363
40	20	1500	16.4337	5.4811	11.1351	3.6046	10.8366	4.5036
	30	2000	37.2796	14.2838	22.9594	7.2455	21.1007	5.0758
	10	1000	2.5646	1.5728	2.1245	1.1772	2.1476	1.3866
80	20	1500	13.3826	8.5137	10.2759	6.6244	8.5381	6.4073
	30	2000	28.6293	10.3431	16.7768	4.4858	15.1721	3.9442

Table 4. Experimental Values for Griewank Function

P			SPSO		QPSO		QPSO-SA	
	D	G	Mean	St.Dev	Mean	St.Dev	Mean	St.Dev
	10	1000	0.09217	0.08330	0.08331	0.06805	0.0858	0.0660
20	20	1500	0.03002	0.03225	0.02033	0.02257	0.0255	0.0257
	30	2000	0.01811	0.02477	0.01119	0.01462	0.0110	0.0140
	10	1000	0.08496	0.07260	0.06912	0.05093	0.0571	0.0464
40	20	1500	0.02719	0.02517	0.01666	0.01755	0.0246	0.0431
	30	2000	0.01267	0.01479	0.01161	0.01246	0.0095	0.0104
	10	1000	0.07484	0.07107	0.03508	0.02086	0.0311	0.0268
80	20	1500	0.02854	0.02680	0.01460	0.01279	0.0166	0.0124
	30	2000	0.01258	0.01396	0.01136	0.01139	0.0092	0.0123

As in [2], for each function, three different dimension sizes, 10,20 and 30 are tested. The corresponding maximum generations are 1000, 1500 and 2000 respectively. And the population size is set to 20, 40 and 80. A total of 50 runs for each experimental setting are conducted.

Table 2-Table 4 show the mean fitness value of the best point found by the end of the trial for the 50 trials along with the standard deviation for each set of trials in the experiment. The tests showed for all functions the mean best point found by the hybrid algorithm to be statistically significantly better than pure QPSO algorithm.

5 Conclusions

An efficient hybrid algorithm has been proposed in this paper. As the results above demonstrate, the introduction mechanism of Simulated Annealing into the Quantum-behaved Particle Swarm Optimization improves the performance of QPSO significantly on three benchmark functions in this study. The proposed hybrid algorithm incorporates effectively the characteristics of both QPSO algorithm and SA to improve the capacity of escaping from the local minima and the ability to global search.

With the development of algorithm theory study and the spread of application field, global search algorithm have a nice prospect of research and application. And the main further research will focus on the study of hybrid algorithm.

References

1. Kennedy, J., Eberhart, R.: Particle Swarm Optimization. Proc. IEEE Conf. On Neural Network (1995) 1942-1948
2. Angeline, P.J.: Using Selection to Improve Particle Swarm Optimization. Proceedings of the IEEE Conference on Evolutionary Computation, ICEC (1998) 84-89
3. Rasussen, M.T.K., Krink., T.: Hybrid Particle Swarm Optimiser with Breeding and Subpopulations. Proc. the third Genetic and Evolutionary Computation Conferences (2001)
4. Kennedy, J.: Bare Bones Particle Swarms. IEEE Swarm Intelligence Symposium (2003) 80-87
5. Sun, J., Feng, B., Xu, W.: Particle Swarm Optimization with Particles Having Quantum Behavior. IEEE Proc.Congress on Evolutionary Computation (2004) 325-331
6. Shi, Y., Eberhart, R..: Empirical Study of Particle Swarm Optimization. Proc. Congress on Evolutionary Computation (1999) 1945-1950
7. Clerc, M., Kennedy K.: The Particle Swarm: Explosion, Stability and Convergence in a Multi-Dimensional Complex Space. IEEE Transaction on Evolutionary Computation vol.6 (2002) 58-73
8. Sun, J. *et al.*: A Global Search Strategy of Quantum-behaved Particle Swarm Optimization. IEEE conference on Cybernetics and Intelligent Systems (2004) 111-116
9. Metropolis, N. et al.: Equations of State Calculations by Fast Computing Machines. J. Chem. Phys (1958) 1087-1092
10. Davis, L.: Genetic Algorithms and Simulated Annealing. Pitman Publishing, London (1987)
11. Riget, Vesterstrom J. S.: A Diversity-Guided Particle Swarm Optimizer-ARPSO. Denmark (2002)

Optimization of a Child Restraint System by Using a Particle Swarm Algorithm

Liang Tang, Meng Luo, and Qing Zhou

State Key Laboratory of Automotive Safety and Energy
Tsinghua University, 100084 Beijing, China
{Tang-L04, Luo-M04}@mails.tsinghua.edu.cn,
zhouqing@tsinghua.edu.cn

Abstract. Child restraint system (CRS) is a system in automotive vehicles for the protection of child occupants in traffic accidents. Design of appropriate CRS has been one of the major subjects for both the research community and the automotive industry. In this paper, a CRS, which includes a child booster and an adult seatbelt with load limiting function, is optimized for a ten-year child dummy. The model is built and simulated using MADYMO. Several key parameters of the system are optimized to minimize the injury to child passengers under the crash test circumstance in accordance with the ECE Regulation 44 by using a recently emerged optimization scheme, particle swarm algorithm. In order to validate this optimization approach, another optimization method, AutoDOE, a built-in subroutine of MADYMO, is also utilized for comparison. The results indicate that the particle swarm algorithm has certain advantages over the AutoDOE method in terms of the solution quality. Moreover, regarding the computational efficiency, for this particular problem the particle swarm algorithm outperforms AutoDOE.

1 Introduction

Child injuries occurred in road traffic accidents are gaining more and more attentions from consumers, the industry, the research community and governments. According to a census of World Health Organization in 2002 [1], in every 10 traffic accidents around the world, there is one involving the injury of child passengers. In 2002, 49,736 infants between 0~4 years old and 130,835 children between 5~14 were injured or killed while traveling as occupants in motor vehicles. The injury to children caused by traffic accidents has ranked the second place in significance among all kinds of injuries. In the recent years, the research communities and the car manufactories have conducted extensive studies on the safety of child passengers. The child safety related regulations have been in place in the most developed countries, and most require that children using child assistant seat while traveling in ground vehicles. For child passengers between 7 to 12 years age, the existing protection means is using booster seat and 3-ponit adult seatbelt, aiming to make the seatbelt better fit with the child. However, the belt system is usually designed for an average sized male occupant, and therefore, in a collision accident, the belt load could reach a harmful level to

D.-S. Huang, K. Li, and G.W. Irwin (Eds.): ICIC 2006, LNBI 4115, pp. 137 – 144, 2006.

the child passenger. The safety regulations specify certain injury parameters for different body regions of the crash dummy and give maximum values for the parameters. These parameters and their values have been correlated with the severity of child injuries under crash loading. So the goal for car manufacturers and CRS producers is to design and optimize the CRS parameters such as the height of the child booster and the stiffness of the belt for the injury parameters of the dummy to meet the requirements in the standard crash tests.

Using physical tests alone to develop the CRS is costly. Therefore, computer modeling and simulation are utilized as one of the primary tools in the process. In this study, MADYMO software is selected as the simulation tool. It has shown excellence in simulating multi-body dynamics in many problems [2] [3]. A CRS model is first built in MADYMO for a concerned age group of children. The model and the parameters in the system are then converted to an optimization problem, aiming at obtaining a valid CRS scheme in the early design stage and yielding some useful guidelines for the later stages.

An AutoDOE scheme has been developed specifically for the optimization coupling with MADYMO. Its mathematical foundation refers to the principle of *design of experiments* (DOE) [4]. In [5], a genetic algorithm is implemented within MADYMO to optimize the front shape of a car in order to minimize the injury to pedestrians in collision with the car. However, due to the highly nonlinear and complex nature of vehicle collisions, it is hardly to claim that any particular optimization method is perfect, or even good enough, for all problems related to passenger safety in vehicle collisions. In this paper, a novel global optimization algorithm, particle swarm algorithm (PSA), is introduced for a CRS analysis.

2 CRS Model in MADYMO

MADYMO (MAthematical DYnamic MOdel) is a program developed by TNO that simulates the dynamic behavior of physical systems emphasizing the analysis of vehicle collisions and assessing injuries sustained by passengers. It is fit for the modeling of conceptual designs in the early development phase of products. Compared with other multi-body dynamics simulators, MADYMO has its distinct properties such as easy modeling, fast computation, effective and reliable results, to list a few. These properties make it possible for designers to conduct optimization by comparing a large number of design schemes.

2.1 CRS Model

The CRS model is shown in Figure 1, which includes a TNO P10 child dummy that represents a 10-year-old passenger, a child booster, and a 3-point adult seatbelt. The child dummy is restrained by both the seatbelt and the booster. The booster makes the child dummy sitting in a higher position for its body to better fit with the route of the lap/shoulder belt designed for an adult passenger.

The child dummy and the seatbelt are selected from the MADYMO library, and both are modeled as a set of multiple rigid bodies. For simplicity, the booster is also modeled as a rigid body. A main reason of not modeling the booster as a deformable body is to avoid large computation load, which would result in prohibitive computing time consumption in the optimization process.

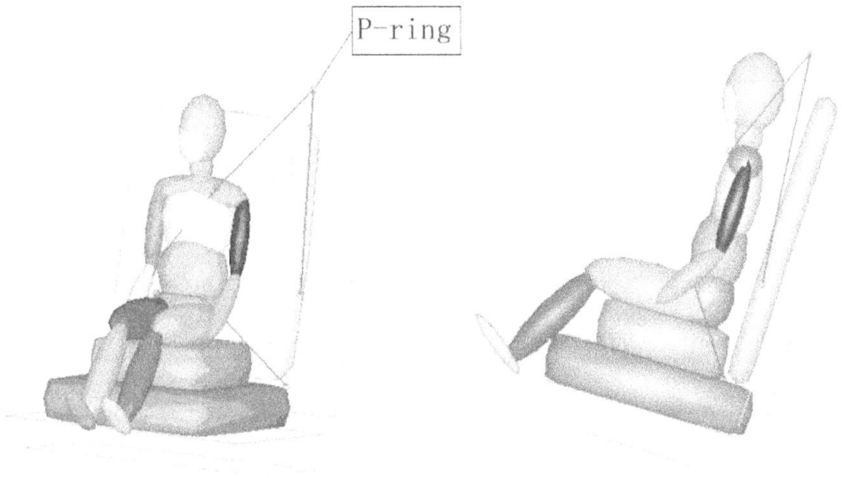

Fig. 1. Madymo model of child restraint system

A frontal impact test simulation is conducted in accordance with ECE regulation 44. As in the actual test, the model shown in Figure 1 is set on a sled that has an initial velocity of 50 km/h and then experiences the impact deceleration pulse specified in the regulation.

2.2 Optimization Model of CRS

The CRS system shown in Fig. 1 has five major parameters determining its characteristics in terms of child safety (see Table 1). All of the five parameters are selected as the design variables. In crash related optimization occupant injury parameters are usually selected as the objective and the constraints. In this case, Head Injury Criteria (HIC) of the dummy, a head injury parameter calculated from the head deceleration time history, is selected as the objective to be minimized with the maximum head displacement as the constraint. According to ECE Regulation 44, the maximum head displacement of the child should not exceed 550mm during the impact test. This value is used as the upper limit of the head displacement.

It should be noted that neither the objective nor the constraint can be expressed as an explicit function of the design variables. This is a common nature for most simulation based optimization problems. As a result, those traditional optimization techniques requiring gradient information are excluded from the set of choices. Moreover, due to the high complexity of impact and the nonlinearity of the occupant-vehicle system, the (implicit) objective function might possess multiple local optima. Fig. 2 shows the 3-D contour of HIC with two design variables, the belt load limit and the friction coefficient between the dummy and the booster. Clearly, the surface contains several local minima. Since most traditional optimization techniques only guarantee to find local optima, in such cases, it is likely to get trapped in local optima and fail to find the global one. Optimization of such a complicated occupant protection system is challenging and calls for efficient global optimization techniques.

Table 1. Design variables of CRS

Subsytsem	Optimization variable	Bounds	Initial value
Child booster	Stiffness Factor	0.5-3.0	1.0
Seatbelt	Stiffness Factor	0.5-0.9	0.7
Load limiter [a)]	Load limit (N)	2000-6000	4000
P-ring [b)]	Height (mm)	900-1200	1100
Dummy and booster	Friction coefficient	0.1-0.6	0.3

a) P-ring is labeled in Fig.1.

b) A load limiting seatbelt provides a limited belt force level (called load limiter) to the occupant in severe impact as opposed to increasing the force without any limit in traditional belt and thus inflicts injury.

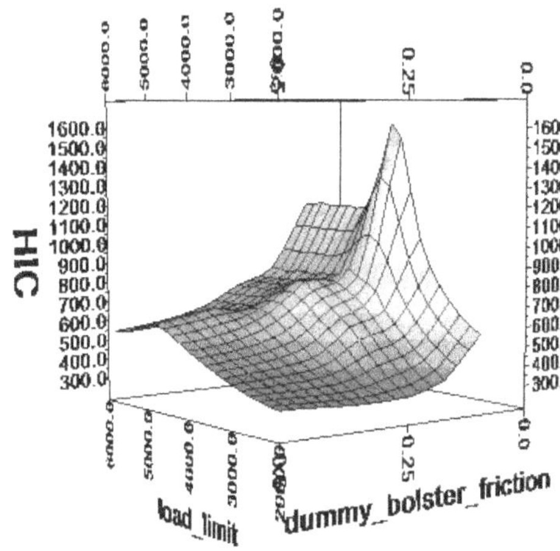

Fig. 2. Response surface of HIC with respect to the belt load limit and the friction coefficient between the dummy and the booster

3 Coupling of MADYMO and Particle Swarm Optimization

3.1 Particle Swarm Optimization

In 1995, Kennedy and Eberhart proposed the concept of Particle Swarm Optimization (PSO), which originated from the study of social behavior of bird flocks and fish schools [6]. It is related to genetic algorithms and falls into the framework of evolutionary optimization algorithms. In general, PSO has a very loose requirement on the optimization problem. For instance, the design variables can be either continuous or discrete, the objective function can be either explicit or implicit, and the feasible region can be either convex or concave. Due to its distinct characteristics from traditional optimization schemes and other evolutionary schemes, PSO has attracted much attention from the computational intelligence community to a wide variety of disciplines. The study of the algorithm itself as well as its application is booming in the literature.

The original PSO for unconstrained optimization can be briefly described as follows [6]. Assume the design variable is n-dimensional. At first, a set of random solutions (called particles) $\mathbf{x}_i \in R^n$, i=1,..., m, are generated in the design space, where m denotes the population size (the number of particles). Each particle is assigned a random velocity $\mathbf{v}_i \in R^n$, which represents the displacement of the corresponding particle in the design space at current iteration. By evaluating the fitness (usually the objective value) of the particles, one can determine each particle's best location that it has ever visited so far, denoted by $\mathbf{p}_i \in R^n$; and the entire population's best location that all the particles have ever visited so far, denoted by $\mathbf{p}_g \in R^n$. Then the velocity and position of each particle for the next iteration is updated as

$$\begin{aligned} v_{ij}(t+1) &= wv_{ij} + c_1 r_{1j}(t)(p_{ij}(t) - x_{ij}(t)) + c_2 r_{2j}(t)(p_{gj}(t) - x_{ij}(t)) \\ x_{ij}(t+1) &= x_{ij}(t) + v_{ij}(t+1) \end{aligned} \quad . \qquad (1)$$

where i=1,...,m, j=1,...,n, t stands for the current iteration number, w, c_1, c_2 are coefficients that can be adjusted by the user. r_{1j} and r_{2j} are two independent random functions whose values are between (0,1).

To handle constrained optimization, one usually converts the problem into an unconstrained one by adding a penalty for the violation of the constraints to the original objective function. However, the selection of an appropriate penalty function together with a set of related parameters for a particular problem requires a lot of experience and patience. Another technique is adopted in this study to handle the constraints. For each particle, its objective function value and the total violation of constraints are calculated and stored as its two properties. In assigning fitness to the entire population of particles, the following principle is adopted (assuming that the goal is to minimize the objective function, and higher fitness means better).

- Feasible particles always have higher fitness than infeasible particles.
- For feasible particles, those with smaller objectives have higher fitness than those with greater objectives.
- For infeasible particles, those with less violation of the constraints have higher fitness than those with more violation of the constraints.

3.2 Interface Between MADYMO and Particle Swarm Algorithm (PSA)

In addition to the GUI execution mode, MADYMO is able to run in a batch mode by defining its input file. In either mode, MADYMO produces several output files in the end. These files provide a possibility for other programs or third-party software to interact with MADYMO. Fig. 3 shows a brief flow chart regarding solving the MADYMO simulation based optimization problems by using PSA. It is observed that except the MADYMO module all tasks of the modules in Fig. 3 should be accomplished by the program that codes PSA. In other words, MADYMO can be viewed as a black-box in the process.

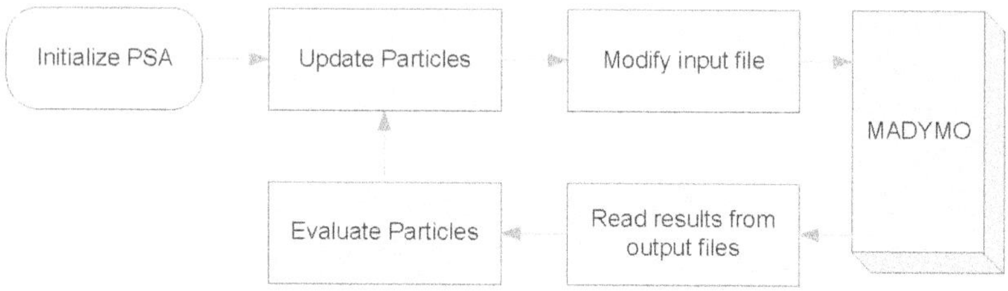

Fig. 3. MADYMO based optimization process by using PSA

4 Optimization Results

The population size is set to 30, and the algorithm terminates after 20 iterations. So the total number of function evaluations (MADYMO callings) is 600. In the update formula (1), set $c_1 = c_2$ =1.9, and w =0.7. Ten runs have been conducted and the statistical data are summarized in Table 2. The discrepancy of the ten HIC results is acceptable, with a standard deviation of 10.5(±4.9%) , and all output solutions satisfy the head displacement constraint. The best solution found by PSA among the 10 runs is shown in Table 3. Compared with the initial design scheme, the optimal scheme has much lower HIC value without sacrifice of much head displacement. Fig. 4 shows the CRS at different time stages in the ECE Regulation 44 frontal impact test.

Table 2. Statistical data for 10 runs of the PSA

	Best	**Worst**	**Average**	**Standard deviation**	**Tolerance**
Optimization objective: HIC	192	228	213	10.5	±4.9%
optimization constraint : Head displacement<550 mm					

Table 3. Optimization results of CRS

	Load Limit (N)	**Friction Coefficient**	**Belt Stiffness**	**Bolster Stiffness**	**P-ring Height (mm)**	**HIC**	**Head displacement (mm)**
Initial	4000	0.3	0.7	1	1100	711	399
PSA	2123	0.46	0.89	2.43	937	192	442
AutoDOE	2000	0.5	0.9	2	900	213	435

The last row of Table 3 lists the optimal results from AutoDOE, the scheme specifically developed for MADYMO based optimization [4]. Before the optimization, one has to discretize each variable into several levels. These discrete values of variables constitute a set of combinations of all variables. AutoDOE evaluates each

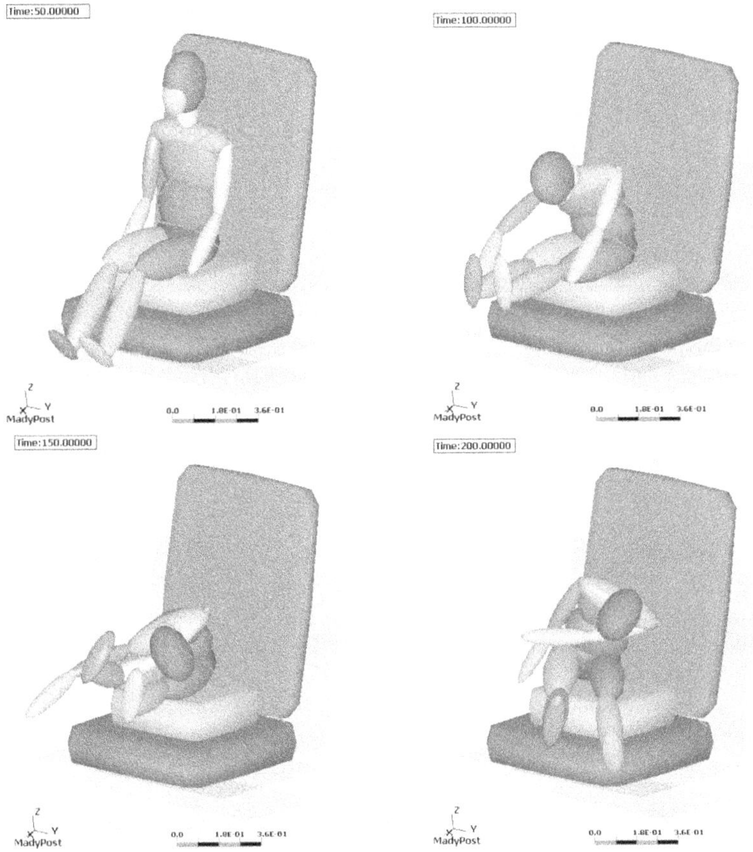

Fig. 4. Simulation of CRS in the frontal impact test. The corresponding times in millisecond are displayed in the top-left corner on each picture.

Table 4. Levels of variables for AutoDOE optimization

Level	1	2	3	4	5	6
Load Limit (N)	2000	3000	4000	5000	6000	--
Friction Coefficient	0.1	0.2	0.3	0.4	0.5	0.6
Belt Stiffness	0.5	0.6	0.7	0.8	0.9	--
Bolster Stiffness	0.5	0.75	1.0	2.0	3.0	--
P-ring Height (mm)	900	1000	1100	1200	--	--

combination of variables by calculating the corresponding objective and constraint values, and then chooses the best one as *optimum*. For this problem, the levels of variables shown in Table 4 are selected. Based on these levels AutoDOE evaluates 3000 solutions in total. The optimum is listed in Table 3.

The results listed in Tables 2 and 3 indicate that the PSA achieves the same quality solutions as AutoDOE does. But PSA calculates much fewer times of objective functions than AutoDOE. For both methods, most of execution time is spent on the evaluation of the objective function, i.e., MADYMO executions, and each evaluation takes about 12 seconds on a 1.8 GHz personal computer. Hence, 2400 fewer evaluations result in significantly less computing time and is favored by users.

5 Conclusions

In this paper, the design of a child restraint system is modeled and optimized based on the multi-body dynamics simulator MADYMO. A particle swarm algorithm that adopts a novel technique for handling constraints is used to solve the problem. Compared with AutoDOE, a built-in optimization method of MADYMO that can only handle low dimensional problems, the PSA does not have this limitation, and hence is suitable for simulation based complex optimization problems. Moreover, the comparison between the proposed PSA and AutoDOE shows that the former is more computational efficient than the latter for achieving same quality solutions.

Acknowledgement

We appreciate that TNO provides us with the educational license of MADYMO. The first author also thanks Mr. Zhang Changhua from Institute of Automation, Chinese Academy of Sciences for his help in coding PSA.

References

1. Peden, M., Scurfield, R., Sleet, D., *et al.*: World Report on Road Traffic Injury Prevention. World Health Organization, Geneva (2004)
2. Pipkorn, B., Eriksson, M.: A Method to Evaluate the Validity of Mathematical Models. In: Proc. 4th European MADYMO User's Meeting (2003)
3. Berlioz, E., Breda, F.: Frontal Impact Using MADYMO/RADIOSS Coupling. In: Proc. 5th European MADYMO User's Conference, Cambridge, Sept. (2005) 9-12
4. Olivares, G., Hampson, D.: System Development using DOE Techniques. In: Proc. 10th International MADYMO User's Meeting, Oct. (2004)
5. Carter, E., Ebdon, S., Neal-Sturgess, C.: Optimization of Passenger Car Design for the Mitigation of Pedestrian Head Injury Using a Genetic Algorithm. In: Proc. Conference on Genetic and Evolutionary Computation, June (2005) 2113-2120
6. Kennedy, J., Eberhart, R.C.: Particle Swarm Optimization. In: Proc. IEEE International Conference on Neural Networks, IEEE Service Center, NJ (1995) 1942-1948

Predicted-Velocity Particle Swarm Optimization Using Game-Theoretic Approach

Zhihua Cui[1,2], Xingjuan Cai[2], Jianchao Zeng[2], and Guoji Sun[1]

[1] State Key Laboratory for Manufacturing Systems Engineering
Xi'an Jiaotong University, Xi'an, 710049, P.R. China
[2] Division of System Simulation and Computer Application
Taiyuan University of Science and Technology, 030024, P.R. China
cui_zhi_hua_7645@sohu.com,
cxj19801006@sohu.com,
zengjianchao@263.net,
gjsun@sei.xjtu.edu.cn

Abstract. In standard particle swarm optimization, velocity information only provides a moving direction of each particle of the swarm, though it also can be considered as one point if there is no limitation restriction. Predicted-velocity particle swarm optimization is a new modified version using velocity and position to search the domain space equality. In some cases, velocity information may be effectively, but fails in others. This paper presents a game-theoretic approach for designing particle swarm optimization with a mixed strategy. The approach is applied to design a mixed strategy using velocity and position vectors. The experimental results show the mixed strategy can obtain the better performance than the best of pure strategy.

1 Introduction

Inspired by the bird flocking and fish schooling, particle swarm optimization (PSO)[1][2] is propsed to simulate animal social behaviors, and has been applied many areas successfully[3][4][5][6][7][8].

Though many techniques have been proposed to enhance the computational efficiency, there still exists work to do by providing a proportional search direction selection principle. In PSO, each particle maintains two different information: position and velocity. Usually, position vector limited by constant v_{max} is used to search the optima as well as velocity provides a direction to guide the search. The empirical results[9] performed by Shi and Eberhart show that the limitation of velocity does not necessary. Furthermore, Z.H.Cui proposed a new version of PSO[10] which is using velocity and position vectors to search without any differences, and the corresponding theoretical analysis without velocity limitation v_{max} is illustrated in [11]. Since velocity information is considered as a predictor,while position information as one corrector, the algorithm is called predicted-velocity PSO (PVPSO). Though the velocity vector is used as one operator similar with position vector to making global search during the search

D.-S. Huang, K. Li, and G.W. Irwin (Eds.): ICIC 2006, LNBI 4115, pp. 145–154, 2006.

process. One main problem relating with effectiveness is how to select the historical best position found by each particle?

One simple way is to compute the velocity and position vectors respectively, determining the historical best position related with velocity and position vectors. There are few researches towards this direction[10][12].

In this paper, we propose a different way to design a mixed strategy. It mixed position and velocity vectors. In this way, each particle chooses one of these strategies to generate its new historical best position to a mixed distribution.

The paper is organized as follows. Section 2 gives a brief survey of particle swarm optimization. The hybrid modal using game theory is introduced in section 3. Seven benchmark functions are used to testify the new algorithm's efficiency in section 4. Finally, the useful conclusions are made.

2 Brief Survey of Particle Swarm Optimization

Particle swarm optimization is based on the sociological behavior associated with bird flocking[13]. Each *'bird'*(called particle) flies within search space, owning two characters: position and velocity, while position vector is used to determine the situation, and velocity vector to provide a displacement value. The position and velocity update equations of standard PSO at time $t+1$ are presented in equation (1) and (2):

$$v_{jk}(t+1) = wv_{jk}(t) + c_1r_1(p_{jk}(t) - x_{jk}(t)) + c_2r_2(p_{gk}(t) - x_{jk}(t)) \quad (1)$$

$$x_{jk}(t+1) = x_{jk}(t) + v_{jk}(t+1) \quad (2)$$

where the kth dimensional variable $v_{jk}(t+1)$ of velocity vector $V_j(t+1) = (v_{j1}(t+1), v_{j2}(t+1), ..., v_{jn}(t+1))$ (n denotes the dimension of problem space) limited by

$$|v_{jk}(t+1)| < v_{max} \quad (3)$$

where $v_{jk}(t)$ and $x_{jk}(t)$ are the kth dimensional variables of velocity and position vectors of particle j at time t, $p_{jk}(t)$ and $p_{gk}(t)$ are the kth dimensional variables of historical positions found by particle j and the whole swarm at time t respectively. w is an inertia weight between 0 and 1, c_1 and c_2 are both constants known as accelerator coefficients, and r_1 and r_2 are two random numbers generated with uniform distribution within $(0, 1)$.

PVPSO[10][11] is a new version using velocity and position to search optima, while the difference between PVPSO and PSO is only the selection principle of historical best position. It is defined as follows for particle j:

$$p_{jk}(t+1) = \begin{cases} p_{jk}(t), \text{if} f(p_j(t)) = \min\{f(p_j(t)), f(x_j(t+1)), f(v_j(t+1))\} \\ x_{jk}(t+1), \text{if} f(x_j(t+1)) = \min\{f(p_j(t)), f(x_j(t+1)), f(v_j(t+1))\} \\ v_{jk}(t+1), \text{otherwise} \end{cases} \quad (4)$$

3 Predicted-Velocity PSO Using Game-Theoretic Approach

In this paper, particles are regarded as players in an artificial evolutionary game, who apply different strategies (position and velocity vectors) to generate the historical best position at arbitrary time, and the distribution is adaptive adjusted.

Position vector or velocity vector of each particle can be considered as a *pure strategy* in the terms of game theory, and a *pure strategy profile* is reward of pure strategies used by particles.

At beginning, the selection probabilities of position and velocity vectors are both set to 0.5. If one pure strategy is selected and the historical best position is updated by it, suppose $\rho_j(t)$ denotes the selection probability of this strategy of particle j at time t, then its selection probability is changed as follows.

$$\begin{cases} \rho_j(t+1) = \rho_j(t) + (1 - \rho_j(t))\gamma \\ \rho_k(t+1) = \rho_k(t) - \rho_k(t)\gamma, if(k \neq j) \end{cases} \tag{5}$$

On the contrary, if one pure strategy is selected and the historical best position is not updated by it, its selection probability is changed with

$$\begin{cases} \rho_j(t+1) = \rho_j(t) - \rho_j(t))\gamma \\ \rho_k(t+1) = \rho_k(t) + \rho_k(t)\gamma, if(k \neq j) \end{cases} \tag{6}$$

In this paper, γ is set to 0.3. The pseudocode of predicted-velocity particle swarm optimization using game-theoretic approach(PVGPSO) is as follows:

- Step1. Initiazing the coefficients c_1,c_2,w, the position and velocity vectors of each particles, t:=0;
- Step2. Updating the position and velocity vectors of each particle at time $t+1$;
- Step3. Determining one pure strategy to update the historical best position of each particle;
- Step4. Modifying selection probability of corresponding pure strategy with formula (5) and (6);
- Step5. Updating the historical best positions of the swarm, t=t+1;
- Step6. If stop criteria is satisfied, the fitness value of historical best position of swarm is given. Otherwise, go to step 2.

4 Simulation Results

The benchmark functions in this section provide a balance of unimodal and multi-modal with many local minima as well as easy and difficult functions.

Sphere Modal:

$$f_1(x) = \sum_{j=1}^{n} x_j^2$$

where $\min f_1(x) = f_1(0,0,...,0) = 0.0$.

Schwefel Problme 1.2:

$$f_2(x) = \sum_{j=1}^{n}(\sum_{i=1}^{j} x_i)^2$$

where $\min f_2(x) = f_3(0,0,...,0) = 0.0$.

Schwefel Problem 2.21:

$$f_3(x) = max_j\{|x_j|, 1 \leq j \leq n\}$$

where $\min f_3(x) = f_4(0,0,...,0) = 0.0$.

Schwefel Problem 2.26:

$$f_4(x) = -\sum_{j=1}^{n}(x_j sin(\sqrt{|x_j|}))$$

where $\min f_4(x) = f_6(420.9687, 420.9687, ..., 420.9687)$.

Rastrigin Function:

$$f_5(x) = \sum_{j=1}^{n}[x_j^2 - 10cos(2\pi x_j) + 10]$$

where $\min f_5(x) = f_8(0,0,...,0) = 0.0$.

Ackley Function:

$$f_6(x) = -20exp(-0.2\sqrt{\frac{1}{n}\sum_{j=1}^{n} x_j^2}) - exp(\frac{1}{n}\sum_{j=1}^{n} cos 2\pi x_j) + 20 + e$$

where $\min f_6(x) = f_9(0,0,...,0) = 0.0$.

Griewank Function:

$$f_7(x) = \frac{1}{4000}\sum_{j=1}^{n} x_j^2 - \prod_{j=1}^{n} cos(\frac{x_j}{\sqrt{j}}) + 1$$

where $\min f_7(x) = f_{10}(0,0,...,0) = 0.0$.

Table 1. Comparison Results of Sphere

Algorithm	Mean Value	Standard Deviation
SPSO	7.215190e-008	7.450365e-008
PVPSO	4.172490e-011	1.046000e-010
PVGPSO	2.660275e-013	5.973800e-013

Table 2. Comparison Results of Schwefel Problem 1.2

Algorithm	Mean Value	Standard Deviation
SPSO	1.975425e+001	8.721134e+000
PVPSO	6.489995e-016	2.114932e-015
PVGPSO	5.932653e-018	1.614740e-017

Table 3. Comparison Results of Schwefel Problem 2.21

Algorithm	Mean Value	Standard Deviation
SPSO	6.415644e-001	1.876893e-001
PVPSO	8.403330e-007	1.709603e-006
PVGPSO	4.311013e-007	1.101034e-006

Table 4. Comparison Results of Schwefel Problem 2.26

Algorithm	Mean Value	Standard Deviation
SPSO	-6.456704e+003	6.567289e+002
PVPSO	-9.037158e+003	4.029658e+002
PVGPSO	-8.435084e+003	4.392656e+002

Table 5. Comparison Results of Rastrigin

Algorithm	Mean Value	Standard Deviation
SPSO	3.039597e+001	9.654424e+000
PVPSO	1.050993e-010	2.228909e-010
PVGPSO	2.762235e-014	7.448329e-014

Table 6. Comparison Results of Ackley

Algorithm	Mean Value	Standard Deviation
SPSO	4.384384e-005	2.229432e-005
PVPSO	2.832723e-006	6.603540e-006
PVGPSO	1.463668e-007	3.216559e-007

Table 7. Comparison Results of Griewank

Algorithm	Mean Value	Standard Deviation
SPSO	9.106786e-003	1.321899e-002
PVPSO	2.533268e-010	9.538407e-010
PVGPSO	2.291722e-012	4.545413e-012

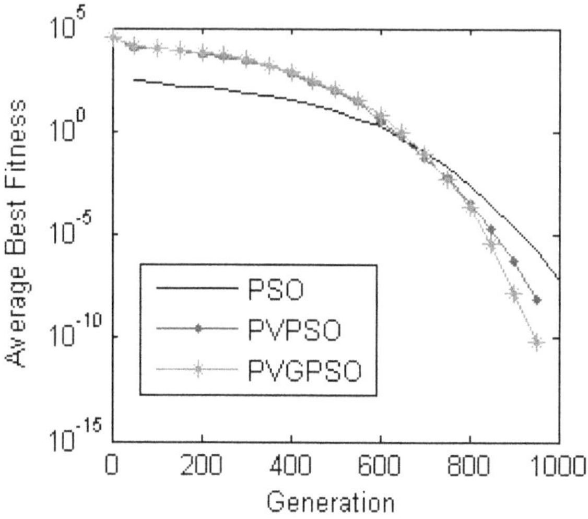

Fig. 1. Comparison Results of Sphere

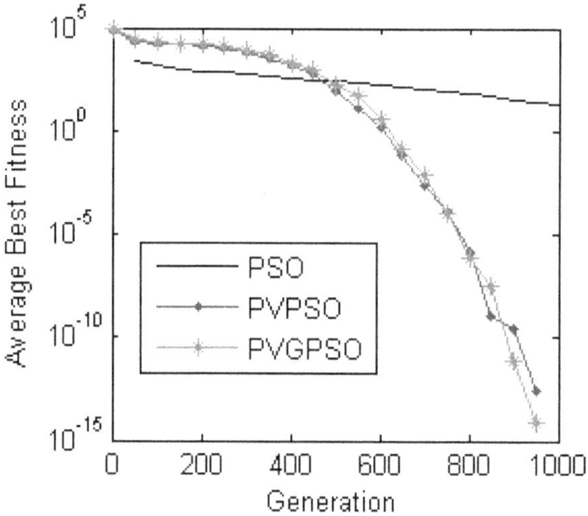

Fig. 2. Comparison Results of Schwefel Problem 1.2

Sphere, Schwefel problem 1.2 and 2.21 are n-dimensional unimodal functions while Schwefel problem 2.26, Rastrigin, Ackley and Griewank are n-dimensional multimodal functions with many local minima.

To give a more detail comparison, two different versions of PSO are used to compare: standard PSO (SPSO) and predicted-velocity PSO (PVPSO). For each experiment the simulation records the mean value and standard deviation value over all the runs. The coefficients of SPSO,PVPSO, and PVGPSO are set as

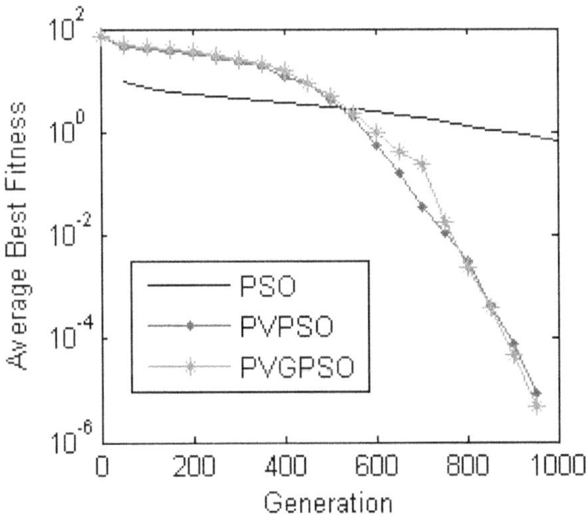

Fig. 3. Comparison Results of Schwefel Problem 2.21

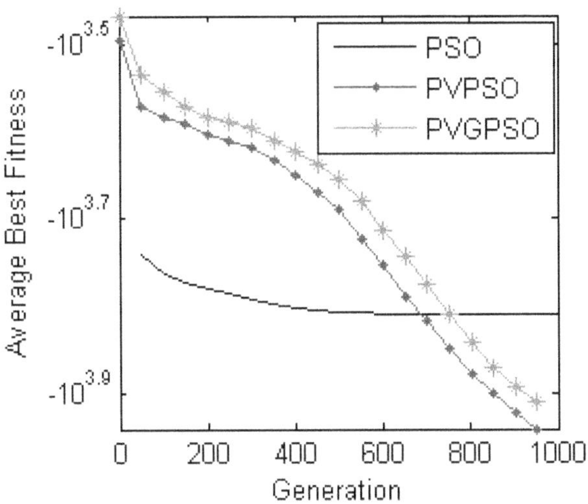

Fig. 4. Comparison Results of Schwefel Problem 2.26

follows. The inertia weight w is decreased linearly from 0.9 to 0.4 during the course, and two accelerator coefficients are set to 2.0. The dimension of each problem is 30. Total particles are 100, and v_{max} is set to 10% of the upper bound of domain in SPSO. Each experiment the simulation run 20 times while each time the largest evolutionary generation is 1000.

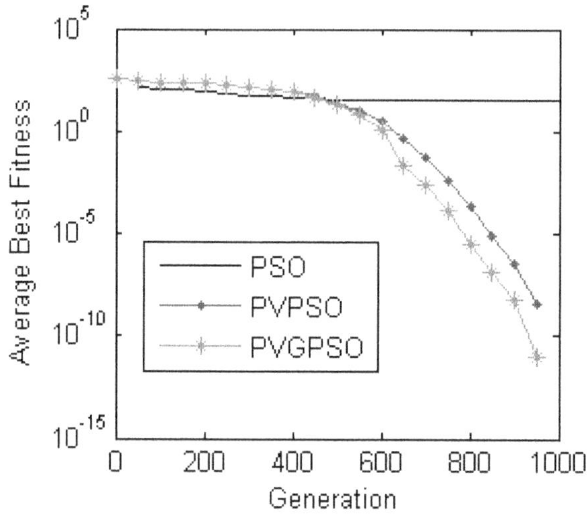

Fig. 5. Comparison Results of Rastrigin

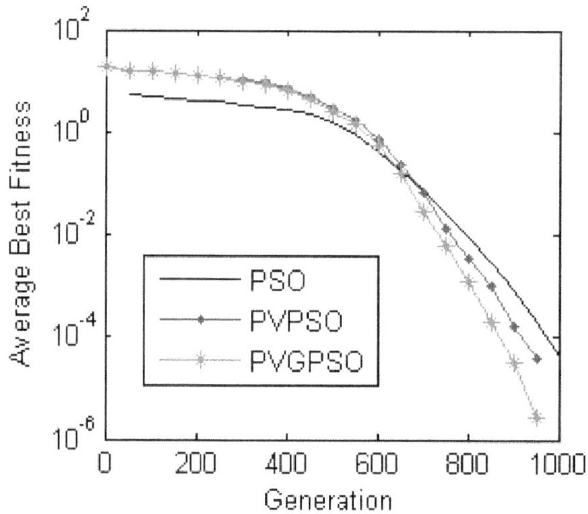

Fig. 6. Comparison Results of Ackley

Table 1 to 3 (see also Fig.1 to 3) are the comparison results of unimodal function. PVGPSO surpasses the PVPSO and SPSO in the final strategy while the SPSO is superior than PVPSO and PVGPSO at the first period.

Table 4 to 7 (see also Fig.4 to 7) are the comparison results of multi-modal functions with many local optima. PVGPSO can always find better quantity solution than PVPSO and SPSO except for Schwefel problem 2.26. In one word, PVGPSO is a better hybrid method based on game theory than single version of PVPSO and SPSO.

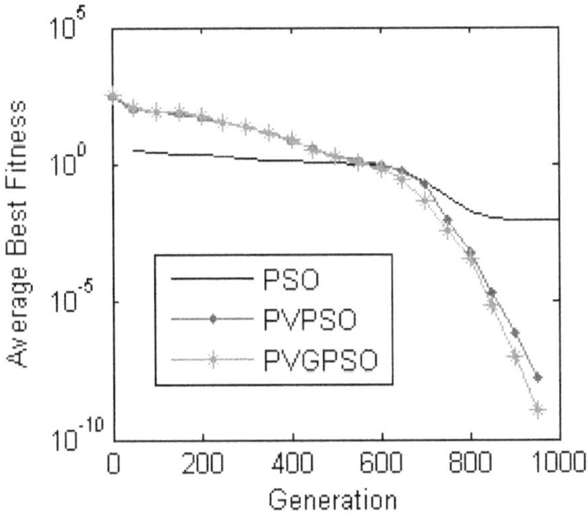

Fig. 7. Comparison Results of Griewank

5 Conclusion

This paper introduces a new hybrid version of particle swarm optimization using game theory. The results show that the proposed algorithm has a good performance of computational efficiency. The further research is the hybrid strategy about n-players game theory.

Acknowledgement

This work is supported by Educational Department Key Project Science and Technology Funds under Grant No.204018, and Shanxi Educational Department Science and Technology Funds under Grant No.20051310.

References

1. Eberhart, R. C., Kennedy, J. : A New Optimizer Using Particle Swarm Theory, *Proceedings of the Sixth International Symposium on Micro Machine and Human Science*, Nagoya, Japan, (1995) 39-43
2. Kennedy, J. , Eberhart, R. C.: Particle Swarm Optimization, *Proceedings of IEEE International Conference on Neural Networks*, IV,(1995) 1942-1948
3. Zhang,C., Shao,H.: An ANN's Evolved by A New Evolutionary System and Its Application, *Proceedings of the* 39th *IEEE Conference on Decision and Control*, (2000) 3562-3563
4. Salerno,J.: Using The Particle Swarm Optimization Technique to Train A Recurrent Neural Modal, *Proceedings of the* 9th *IEEE International Conference on Tools with Artificial Intelligence*, (1997)45-49

5. Chen, C.Y., Ye,He.: Particle Swarm Optimization Algorithm and Its Application to Clustering Analysis, *Proceedings of IEEE International Conference on Networking, Sencing and Control*, (2004) 789-794
6. Sousa,T., Silua,A., Neves,A.: Particle Swarm Based Data Mining Algorithms for Classification Tasks, *Parallel Computing*, vol.30, no.5, (2004) 767-783
7. Li,X.: Better Spread and Convergence: Particle Swarm Multi-Objective Optimization Using The Maximum Fitness Function, *Proceedings of the Genetic and Evolutionary Computation Conference*, (2004) 117-128
8. Juang, C.F.: A Hybrid of Genetic Algorithm and Particle Swarm Optimization for Recurrent Network Design, *IEEE Transactions on System, Man and Cybernetics-Part B: Cybernetic*, vol.34, no.2, (2004) 997-1006
9. Shi,Y., Eberhart,R.C.: Empirical Study of Particle Swarm Optimization, *Proceedings of IEEE Congress on Evolutionary Computation*, USA, (1999) 1945-1949
10. Cui,Z.H., Zeng,J.C.: A Modified Particle Swarm Optimization Predicted by Velocity, *Proceedings of Genetic and Evolutionary Computation Conference*, (2005) 277-280,
11. Cui,Z.H., Zeng,J.C.: Modified Particle Swarm Optimization Based on Differential Modal, *Journal of Computer Research and Development*, vol.43,no.4,(2006) 646-653
12. Cui,Z.H., Zeng,J.C., Sun, G.J.: Predicted Particle Swarm Optimization, *Proceedings of IEEE 2006 International Conference on Cognitive Information*, Accepted, (2006)
13. Reynolds,C.W.: Flocks,Ferds, and Schools: A Distributed Behavioral Model, *Computer Graphics*,vol.21, no.4,(1987) 25-34

Solving the Hard Knapsack Problems with a Binary Particle Swarm Approach

Bin Ye[1], Jun Sun[1], and Wen-Bo Xu[1]

School of Information Technology, Southern Yangtze University,
No.1800, Lihu Dadao, Wuxi, Jiangsu 214122, P.R. China
yebinxie@yahoo.com.cn,
sunjun_wx@hotmail.com,
xwb@sytu.edu.cn

Abstract. Knapsack problems are important NP-Complete combinatorial optimization problems. Although nearly all the classical instances can be solved in pseudo-polynomial time nowadays, yet there are a variety of test problems which are hard to solve for the existing algorithms. In this paper we propose a new approach based upon binary particle swarm optimization algorithm (BPSO) to find solutions of these hard knapsack problems. The standard PSO iteration equations are modified to operate in discrete space. Furthermore, a heuristic operator based on the total-value greedy algorithm is employed into the BPSO approach to deal with constrains. Numerical experiments show that the proposed algorithm outperforms both the existing exact approaches and recent state-of-the-art search heuristics on most of the hard knapsack problems.

1 Introduction

The well-known NP-complete knapsack problem (KP) is defined as: given a set of items with corresponding unit profits p_j and unit weights w_j, along with a knapsack capacity limit c, selects a subset of the items such that the total profit is maximized with the total weight not exceeding c. It can be assumed, without lose of generality, that all profits and weights are positive, that all weights are smaller than the knapsack capacity c and that the total weight exceeds the capacity. By introducing the binary decision variable x_j, with $x_j = 1$ if item j is selected, and $x_j = 0$ otherwise, the classical 0/1 knapsack problem can be formulated as:

$$\text{maximize} \quad \sum_{j=1}^{n} p_j x_j$$

$$\text{subject to} \quad \sum_{j=1}^{n} w_j x_j \le c \qquad \text{with} \quad x_j \in \{0,1\},\ j = 1,\ldots,n\ .$$

In the last few decades, many exact or heuristic techniques have been proposed to solve the knapsack problems. The exact algorithms include dynamic

D.-S. Huang, K. Li, and G.W. Irwin (Eds.): ICIC 2006, LNBI 4115, pp. 155–163, 2006.

programming [1,2] and branch-and-bound [3,4], while the heuristic search procedures focusing on solving the problem approximately include tabu search [5], genetic algorithm (GA) [6,7] and other randomized methods. A good overview of all recent exact approaches can be seen in [8]. It is shown that although the existing algorithms are capable of solving nearly all the KP instances cited in the existing literature within reasonable time, there are two groups of new test KP problems which are hard to solve. For the first group of difficult instances with large coefficients the running times of the dynamic programming algorithms are unacceptably high, while for the other group containing six categories of structurally instances with small coefficients the branch-and-bound algorithms perform badly.

In this paper a novel BPSO algorithm is developed to solve the hard knapsack problems. A heuristic operator converting infeasible solutions into feasible solutions is applied to deal with the knapsack constrains. The procedure of the operator is based on the total-value heuristic which picks the item that contributes the highest total profit given the remaining knapsack capacity at each stage. In order to test the BPSO algorithm thoroughly, we adopt the technique in [8] to construct test instances. The experimental results of three different types of algorithms are compared with ours.

The rest of the paper is organized as follows. In Section 2, a brief introduction of PSO is given. Then a binary particle swarm algorithm for knapsack problems are proposed in Section 3. Section 4 presents the generation of the two groups of difficult instances and the performance comparison of our algorithm and the most recent algorithms on the instances. A set of conclusions are given in Section 5.

2 Particle Swarm Optimization

The particle swarm optimization was originally invented for the function optimization in continuous real-number spaces by Kennedy and Eberhart [9]. A review of its recent approaches to global optimization problems is presented in [10]. In a PSO model, a potential solution is represented as a particle with position X_{id} and velocity V_{id} in a D-dimensional space. Each particle maintains a record of the position with best fitness value the particle experienced so far, called personal best position or *Pbest*. Each particle share its *Pbest* with its neighborhoods, so there is a global best solution *Gbest*. At each search iteration, the ith particle moves according to the following equations:

$$V_{id} = V_{id} + \alpha \cdot (Pbest_{id} - X_{id}) + \beta \cdot (Gbest_{d} - X_{id}) \tag{1}$$

$$X_{id} = X_{id} + V_{id} \tag{2}$$

where α and β are random numbers whose upperbounds determine the influence of *Pbest* and *Gbest*.

In order to improve the performance of the original PSO algorithm, some revised versions of PSO algorithm are proposed. One of the approaches is to introduce inertia weight ω into (1), so (1) is substituted by

$$V_{id} = \omega \cdot V_{id} + \alpha \cdot (Pbest_{id} - X_{id}) + \beta \cdot (Gbest_{d} - X_{id}) \ . \tag{3}$$

A BPSO algorithm which operates in discrete space has been developed in [11]. But this BPSO algorithm is susceptible to function saturations, which occur when velocity values are either too large or too small. A technique using angle modulation to reduce the complexity of binary problems is proposed in [12]. Though efficient it leaves the discrete constraint satisfaction problems untouched. We will present our BPSO algorithm based on the inertia weight PSO model in the next section.

3 A BPSO Algorithm for KP

3.1 Representation

Like GA, the first step in implementing a BPSO algorithm is to design a scheme to denote individuals. Since the decision variable x_j is binary, it is an obvious choice to represent a solution using an n-bit binary string, where n is the number of items in the KP. Thus each particle's position and velocity in our algorithm are initialized as n-bit binary-coded random vectors.

3.2 Iteration Equations

Before presenting the iteration equations, we begin with introducing some new operators to be applied in our proposed BPSO.

In a binary space, a particle moves to nearer or farther corners of the hypercube (searching space) by flipping bits in its position vector. So the distance between a particle's current position and its previous best position (in (3) denoted as "$Pbest_{id} - X_{id}$" of the dth dimension) can be stated by a vector whose bit is 1 if the alleles of X_i and $Pbest_i$ are different and sets to 0 otherwise. For example, a particle's current position and its previous best position are:

$$\begin{aligned} X &: (10011) \\ Pbest &: (00011) \end{aligned}$$

so the distance will be (10000) since the first bits in the two vectors are different. From this simple example, it can be observed that the distance is the output of the binary XOR function which takes X and $Pbest$ as its two inputs. In this way, the operation "$Pbest_{id} - X_{id}$" in (3) will be substituted with "$Pbest_{id} \oplus X_{id}$". Similarly, the distance between a particle's current position and the global best position will be evaluated by "$Gbest \oplus X_i$".

From (3), it can be seen that a particle's velocity at iteration $t+1$ is primarily determined by three elements: the velocity at iteration t, the distance between X_i and $Pbest$ and the distance between X_i and $Gbest$. Since the functions of the three elements (also vectors) are to reverse the corresponding bits in the position vector consistently, they can be united into one vector. Consequently, this procedure is implemented using the OR operation. Here is an example: supposing the three elements are

$$\begin{aligned} A &: (10001) \\ B &: (01000) \\ C &: (00100) \end{aligned}$$

respectively, then the velocity will be $V = A + B + C = (11101)$.

A particle's position vector will be updated at the next step using the velocity vector. If any bit in the velocity vector is 1, the allele in the position vector will be reversed. And this operation is a equivalence of binary XOR function. This can be illustrated by going on with the previous example. With a arbitrary position vector being (10000), the updated position vector will be (01101) at next iteration.

As a result, a particle in a binary space moves according to the following equations:

$$V_{id} = \omega \cdot V_{id} + \alpha \cdot (Pbest_{id} \oplus X_{id}) + \beta \cdot (Gbest_d \oplus X_{id}) \tag{4}$$

$$X_{id} = X_{id} \oplus V_{id} \tag{5}$$

where inertia weight ω is generally set to less than 1.0. α and β are called acceleration coefficients used to control the convergence speed of the algorithm. Based on the previous work in [13], we have set the typical parameters for a population of 50, the inertia weight ω of 0.729, α of 1.49 and β of 1.49.

3.3 Constraints Handling

Obviously, the solutions generated by (4) may not be feasible because one of the knapsack constraints may be violated. To deal with constraints, a number of standard ways are proposed. Comparing their performance through preliminary experiments, we adopt in our BPSO the approach of using a heuristic operator to convert an infeasible solution to a feasible one.

The heuristic operator is traditionally based on a density-ordered greedy algorithm which picks the item with the highest unit profit to unit weight ratio at each stage. Instead of using the density-ordered greedy algorithm, our heuristic operator is based on a total-value greedy algorithm in which the item with highest profit will be selected if its weight does not exceed the remaining knapsack capacity at each stage. It has been shown that the total-value greedy heuristic dominates the density-ordered greedy algorithm with regard to both the worst-case performance and the average-case performance [14].

Our heuristic operator is constituted of two phases: the drop phase and the add phase. The drop phase is implemented as follows. Once a solution $X_i = (x_1, x_2, \ldots, x_n)$ generated by BPSO is infeasible, first calculate its redundancy weight $\sum_{j=1}^{n}(w_j x_j - c)$ (bigger than zero obviously). Then, among the items picked in the infeasible solution, find out the subset of items with the weight of each item is smaller than the redundancy weight. Throw out the items one by one in the subset with ascent order in weight until the solution becomes feasible.

The add phase aim to improve the fitness of a feasible solution. Given the remaining knapsack capacity, the add phase continue to add the item with the largest profit among the items that are not included in the solution and whose weights are smaller than the remaining knapsack capacity until feasibility is violated.

3.4 Algorithm Outline

The general steps in our algorithm are described as follows:

```
initialize each particle with a random position and velocity;
initialize t_max;
while t<t_max {
    for i=1:population size {
        if a solution is infeasible {
            make the solution feasible;
        }
        calculate fitness value;
    }
    find Pbest and Gbest;
    updating each particle's position according to (4,5);
}
```

4 Computational Experiments

In order to test our algorithm for the knapsack problem more thoroughly, we will analyze its performance in terms of both efficiency and accuracy. Efficiency is a measure of the time required to complete the search and accuracy is what evaluates the quality of the solutions obtained. The test instances we use for measurements are some of the instances from [8], which contains a large variety of instances types. The performance for different instance types and data ranges of our approach is compared with that of the GA [6] and two well-known exact approaches, namely Expknap [4] and Minknap [1].

Two groups of difficult instances are considered in our experiments. One group consists of the traditional instances with larger coefficients; and the other group includes instances with small coefficients, but where present algorithms perform badly. The first group make the dynamic programming algorithm run slower while the second group mainly challenge the branch-and-bound algorithms.

4.1 Difficult Instances with Large Coefficients

Six types of traditional data instances are briefly described below. Because the traditional test instances with small data range are too easy to draw any meaningful conclusions, we choose each type with data range R=10^6 and 10^7 for different problem sizes (i.e. n=100, 500, 1000, 5000 and 10000) for testing.
Uncorrelated instances (uncorr.): The weights w_j and the profits p_j are chosen randomly in $[1, R]$.

Weakly correlated instances (weak corr.): The weights w_j are distributed in $[1, R]$ and the profits p_j in $[w_j - R/10, w_j + R/10]$ such that $p_j \geq 1$.
Strongly correlated instances (str. corr.): The weights are chosen in $[1, R]$ and the profits are set to $p_j = w_j + R/10$.
Inverse strongly correlated instances (inv. str. corr.): The profits p_j are chosen in $[1, R]$ and $w_j = p_j + R/10$.
Almost strongly correlated instances (al. st. corr.): The weights w_j are distributed in $[1, R]$ and the profits in $[w_j + R/10 - R/500, w_j + R/10 + R/500]$.
Subset-sum instances (sub.sum): The weights w_j are distributed in $[1, R]$ and $p_j = w_j$.

In order to eliminate the capacity-dependency of the performances, we choose the capacity in each instance as

$$c = \frac{h}{1000 + 1} \sum_{j=1}^{n} w_j$$

for instance number $h = 1, 2, \ldots, 1000$. We test all the instances on an Intel Pentium 4, 2.9GHz with 256M RAM. The average execution time for each instance type, which is also the average time the BPSO takes for all the 1000 instances, is calculated. Table 1-3 gives the results for the three algorithms. For each instance type, if not all instances are solved in a time limit of 30 minutes or space limit, it is marked with a "–" in the table. "Best-so-far" values searched in 50 runs by our algorithm and GA during the same time period are compared in Table 4. A typical run for GA is set for a probability of crossover of 0.8; a probability of mutation of 0.01; and a population of 50 (same as the population in our BPSO algorithm). In each run we choose the time limit of 10 minutes as the stopping conditions for GA and our BPSO.

It is clear that our BPSO algorithm has a stable performance on all the instance types whereas the exact algorithm Expknap can solve only a few instances within the given time or space limit. For the dynamic programming algorithm Minknap, the average execution time for the strongly correlated and the inverse strongly correlated instances grow to run out of the time limit due to the rapid increasing of the computational complexity. From the results in Table 4, it can be observed that the near-optimal solutions obtained by our BPSO algorithm are more closer to the optimal solution than those obtained by GA for a majority of instances.

4.2 Difficult Instances with Small Coefficients

The following are some difficult instances with small coefficients. The capacity is chosen as in the previous section. The outcomes are summarized in Table 5-7.
Spanner instances(v,m): The weights w_k of a set of v items (the spanner set) are chosen in [1,R] randomly and the profits according to the three distributions (uncorrelated, weakly correlated and strongly correlated respectively). Then the v items are normalized by setting p_k=$[2p_k/m]$ and w_k=$[2w_k/m]$. The n items are constructed by repeatedly multiplying a random number in the interval

Table 1. Average execution times (ms) for instances with large coefficients, Expknap

	uncorr.		*weakcorr.*		*str.corr.*		*inv.str.corr.*		*al.str.corr.*		*sub.sum*	
$n \backslash R$	10^6	10^7	10^6	10^7	10^6	10^7	10^6	10^7	10^6	10^7	10^6	10^7
100	0.1	-	-	-	-	-	-	-	627.1	-	13.1	187.4
500	0.1	0.1	-	-	-	-	-	-	-	-	18.9	-
1000	0.3	-	-	-	-	-	-	-	-	-	27.6	-
5000	1.1	1.3	-	-	-	-	-	-	-	-	-	-
10000	2.4	-	-	-	-	-	-	-	-	-	-	-

Table 2. Average execution times (ms) for instances with large coefficients, Minknap

	uncorr.		*weakcorr.*		*str.corr.*		*inv.str.corr.*		*al.str.corr.*		*sub.sum*	
$n \backslash R$	10^6	10^7	10^6	10^7	10^6	10^7	10^6	10^7	10^6	10^7	10^6	10^7
100	0.2	0.2	0.6	0.5	755.1	-	442.3	-	12.4	8.9	553.6	-
500	0.2	0.3	0.5	0.6	-	-	-	-	256.1	247.3	512.6	-
1000	0.4	0.4	0.9	0.9	-	-	-	-	636.8	897.1	681.7	-
5000	1.4	1.4	7.3	4.8	-	-	-	-	8634.7	-	736.3	-
10000	2.6	3.3	18.3	20.7	-	-	-	-	-	-	841.8	-

Table 3. Average execution times (ms) for instances with large coefficients, BPSO

	uncorr.		*weakcorr.*		*str.corr.*		*inv.str.corr.*		*al.str.corr.*		*sub.sum*	
$n \backslash R$	10^6	10^7	10^6	10^7	10^6	10^7	10^6	10^7	10^6	10^7	10^6	10^7
100	7.3	8.7	7.1	7.1	6.7	7.2	7.3	6.8	6.9	8.1	7.3	9.8
500	37.9	20.9	38.4	31.4	31.2	25.6	38.5	46.2	35.4	36.3	51.4	21.2
1000	77.1	42.4	59.4	53.7	41.0	40.6	79.7	87.5	41.6	40.9	52.8	32.8
5000	318.3	411.2	309.0	305.5	304.1	303.6	312.8	344.6	303.6	411.1	308.6	325.3
10000	976.2	963.6	879.4	1160.1	935.6	1267.3	1577.6	1960.7	881.9	923.1	919.5	939.2

Table 4. Optimal values found by GA and our BPSO, $R = 10^6$, $c = \frac{1}{2}\sum_{j=1}^{n} w_j$ for all the instances

	uncorr.		*str.corr.*	
n	GA	BPSO	GA	BPSO
100	39465410	39465410	32995624	33048651
500	201957104	202661372	157736230	157803943
1000	400917743	403053093	315650918	315789002
5000	2436292167	2446654061	1593860725	1597840513
10000	3751841203	3759039860	2800845121	2801430527

$[1, m]$ and any item from the spanner set. Here, we will consider uncorrelated span(2,10), weakly correlated span(2,10) and strongly correlated span(2,10).
Multiply strongly correlated instances mstr(k_1,k_2,d): The weights are chosen in [1,R] randomly. If the weight can divide exactly by d, then the profit $p_j = w_j + k_1$, otherwise $p_j = w_j + k_2$. The parameters are $k_1 = 3R/10$, $k_2 = 2R/10$, $d = 6$.

Table 5. Average execution times (ms) for instances with small coefficients, Expknap

	span(2, 10)			$mstr(\frac{3R}{10}, \frac{2R}{10}, 6)$	*pceil*(3)	$circle(\frac{2}{3})$
n	uncorr.	weak. corr.	str. corr.			
100	-	-	-	52.1	-	24.7
500	-	-	-	-	-	-
1000	-	-	-	-	-	-
5000	-	-	-	-	-	-
10000	-	-	-	-	-	-

Table 6. Average execution times (ms) for instances with small coefficients, Minknap

	span(2, 10)			$mstr(\frac{3R}{10}, \frac{2R}{10}, 6)$	*pceil*(3)	$circle(\frac{2}{3})$
n	uncorr.	weak. corr.	str. corr.			
100	0.1	0.1	0.1	1.0	0.5	0.8
500	1.2	1.3	2.1	12.4	5.4	37.4
1000	15.6	23.9	17.9	40.0	39.3	54.9
5000	363.2	817.4	803.1	465.0	1133.5	613.9
10000	1142.9	1600.4	3720.4	1350.8	3661.2	1109.5

Table 7. Average execution times (ms) for instances with small coefficients, BPSO

	span(2, 10)			$mstr(\frac{3R}{10}, \frac{2R}{10}, 6)$	*pceil*(3)	$circle(\frac{2}{3})$
n	uncorr.	weak. corr.	str. corr.			
100	7.9	5.7	7.2	7.3	3.9	3.5
500	34.4	28.4	28.1	32.2	36.5	21.4
1000	65.6	73.9	65.9	87.0	74.3	77.3
5000	667.1	690.9	633.1	912.0	764.0	868.7
10000	2595.0	1967.3	2136.6	1974.5	2003.1	1084.3

Table 8. Optimal values found by GA and BPSO, for three types of difficult instances, R=1000

	str.corr.span(2, 10)		$mstr(\frac{3R}{10}, \frac{2R}{10}, 6)$		*pceil*(3)	
n	GA	BPSO	GA	BPSO	GA	BPSO
100	13488	13497	39613	39710	24210	24210
500	53016	53035	199662	199673	126543	126501
1000	366142	366061	405512	405547	244767	244776
5000	1069621	1070096	2025096	2030286	1255665	1255665
10000	2233409	2233650	4055139	4050196	2515947	2516037

Profit ceiling instances(d): The weights are randomly distributed in [1,R] and profits p_j=$d\lceil w_j/d\rceil$. The parameter d is chosen as d=3.
Circle instances(d): The weights are randomly distributed in [1,R] and $p = d\sqrt{4R^2 - (w-2R)^2}$. We choose $d = \frac{2}{3}$.

From these results, it is clear that Expknap has the worst performance than any other algorithms. Although Minknap is a bit faster than our algorithm for smaller problem size n, the solution times for both algorithm are very stable. Here again, Table 8 shows that our BPSO algorithm performs better than GA.

5 Conclusion

In this paper, we proposed a novel binary particle swarm approach and apply it to the hard knapsack problems. Based on the total-value greedy algorithm, a heuristic operator is designed to handle the knapsack constrains. The approach has been thoroughly evaluated with different instance types and problem sizes. The evaluation is made by comparing our algorithm with some of the best known approaches in the existing literatures. As the obtained results show, our approach exhibits an excellent level of accuracy and efficiency to the hard knapsack problems.

References

1. Pisinger, D.: A Minimal Algorithm for the 0-1 Knapsack Problem. Operations Research, 45 (1997) 758–767
2. Martello, S., Pisinger, D., Toth, P.: Dynamic Programming and Strong Bounds for the 0-1 Knapsack Problem. Management Science, 45 (1999) 414–424
3. Martello, S., Toth, P.: A New Algorithm for the 0-1 Knapsack Problem. Management Science, 34 (1988) 633–644
4. Pisinger D.: An Expanding-Core Algorithm for the Exact 0-1 Knapsack Problem. European Journal of Operational Research, 87 (1995) 175–187
5. Gandibleux, X., Freville, A.: Tabu Search Based Procedure for Solving the 0-1 Multiobjective Knapsack Problem: The two Objectives Case. Journal of Heuristics, **6** (2000) 361–383
6. Chu, P.C., Beasley, J. E.: A Genetic Algorithm for the Multidimensional Knapsack Problem. Journal of Heuristics, 4 (1998) 63–86
7. Thiel, J., Voss, S.: Some Experiences on Solving Multiconstraint Zero-One Knapsack Problems with Genetic Algorithms. INFOR, Canada, 32 (1994) 226–242
8. Pisinger, D.: Where are the Hard Knapsack Problems? Computers & Operations Research, 32 (2005) 2271–2284
9. Kennedy, J., Eberhart, R. C.: Particle Swarm Optimization. IEEE int. Conf. on Neural Networks, Perth Australia, 325 (1995) 1942–1948
10. Parsopoulos, K. E., Vrahatis, M. N.: Recent Approaches to Global Optimization Problems through Particle Swarm Optimization. Natural Computing: An International Journal, 1 (2002) 235–306
11. Kennedy, J., Eberhart, R. C.: A Discrete Binary Version of the Particle Swarm Algorithm. In Proceedings of the World Multiconference on Systemics, Cybernetics and Informatics, IEEE Press, (1997) 4104–4109
12. Pampara, G., Franken, N.,Engelbrecht, A. P.: Combining Particle Swarm Optimization with Angle Modulation to Solve Binary Problems. IEEE Congress on Evolutionary Computation, 1 (2005) 89–96
13. Van Den Bergh, F.: An Analysis of Particle Swarm Optimizers. PhD thesis, Department of Computer Science, University of Pretoria, South Africa (2002)
14. Kohli, R., Krishnamurti, R., Mirchandani. P.: Average Performance of Greedy Heuristics for the Integer Knapsack Problem. European Journal of Operational Research 154 (2004) 36–45

Collective Behavior of an Anisotropic Swarm Model Based on Unbounded Repulsion in Social Potential Fields

Liang Chen and Li Xu

College of Electrical Engineering, Zhejiang University
Hangzhou 310027, P.R. China
leonchanzju@sohu.com, xupower@zju.edu.cn

Abstract. Swarm system with flexible structures adapts well to variable environment. In this article, we propose an anisotropic swarm model based on unbounded repulsion and social potential fields. The unbounded repulsion ensures the independence among autonomous agents in social potential fields, which consist of obstacles to avoid and targets to move towards. Simulation results show that the aggregating swarm can construct various formations by changing its anisotropy coefficient, and the collective behavior of mass individuals emerges from combination of the inter-individual interactions and the interaction of the individual with outer circumstances.

1 Introduction

In nature there are many biological swarms with collective behavior, such as colonies of bees and ants, schools of fish, flocks of birds, and herds of mammals. Living as aggregations, such swarms have more chances to avoid predators and to find food [1]. Operational principles from these systems can be applied to engineering for developing coordinated control and distributed control of multi-agent systems such as unmanned air vehicles [2] and multiple autonomous robots [3,4,5,6]. Modeling and exploring the collective dynamics has become an important issue and many investigations have been carried out [7,8,9,10,11]. The general understanding now is that the swarming behavior of mass animals is a result of an interplay between a long range attraction and a short range repulsion among individuals [12]. According to this conclusion, Gazi and Passino proposed a swarm model of engineering multi-agent systems that consists of a number of individuals with identical interaction strength and studied its cohesion stability [13]. However, the complex environment and various interaction of a practical swarm system are of importance for modeling in a common framework. The purpose of this article is to provide some results on this topic.

2 Anisotropic Swarm Model

Swarm model with anisotropic property can adapt well to environment by changing its structures. To achieve the variation of swarm aggregation and the

D.-S. Huang, K. Li, and G.W. Irwin (Eds.): ICIC 2006, LNBI 4115, pp. 164–173, 2006.

individual independence, we consider an anisotropic swarm including N individuals (members) in an n-dimensional Euclidean space, and model the individuals as points and ignore their dimensions. It is assumed that all of them move simultaneously and know the exact positions of others. The equation of motion for individual i is given by

$$\dot{x}^i = h_{x^i} + \sum_{j=1, j\neq i}^{M} \varepsilon_{ij} g(x^i - x^j), i = 1, \ldots, M. \tag{1}$$

where $x^i \in \mathbb{R}^n$ represents the position of member i. The equation (1) is composed of three main factors: 1) h_{x^i} stands for the effect in heading direction resting with social potential fields around individual i, 2) ε_{ij} expresses the anisotropic factor affected by the positions of individual i and j , 3) $g(\cdot)$ is the attraction/repulsion function that governs the inter-individual original interactions. Note that the direction and magnitude of motion of each member are determined as a weighted sum of the attraction and repulsion of all the other members on this one.

In general, the form of attraction/repulsion function that we consider is

$$g(y) = -y[g_a(\|y\|) - g_r(\|y\|)]. \tag{2}$$

where $g_a : \mathbb{R}^+ \to \mathbb{R}^+$ represents the magnitude of the attraction term, whereas $g_r : \mathbb{R}^+ \to \mathbb{R}^+$ represents the magnitude of the repulsion term. According to the study results on smarming behavior, the effect of function $g(\cdot)$ should be attractive for large distances and repulsive for short distances. By equating $g(y) = 0$, one can easily get the constant distance δ where attraction and repulsion balance. In other words, there exists δ such that $g_a(\delta) = g_r(\delta)$, and for $\|y\| > \delta$, $g_a(\|y\|) > g_r(\|y\|)$ means attraction dominates, and for $\|y\| < \delta$, $g_a(\|y\|) < g_r(\|y\|)$ means repulsion dominates.

In [13], Gazi and Passino presented an inter-individual interaction function with linear attraction and bounded repulsion

$$g(y) = -y\Big[a - b\exp\Big(-\frac{\|y\|^2}{c}\Big)\Big]. \tag{3}$$

Simulation experiments show that the bounded repulsion may cause overlap of the individual positions [14]. To ensure the independence among autonomous agents in collective motion, the anisotropic swarm model that we consider in this article is based on unbounded repulsion interaction $g_r(\|y\|) = \frac{b}{\|y\|^2}$, and linear attraction $g_a(\|y\|) = a$. The attraction/repulsion function $g(\cdot)$ can take the form

$$g(y) = -y\Big(a - \frac{b}{\|y\|^2}\Big). \tag{4}$$

The $\|y\| = \sqrt{y^\top y}$ in (4) is the Euclidean norm, and for $\|y\| \to 0$, we have $g(y) \to \infty$, which prevents individuals from collision completely. For $y \in \mathbb{R}^1$ case and $a = 1$ $b = 1$, this function is shown in Fig. 1. By equating $g(y) = 0$, we can

Fig. 1. Linear attraction/Unbouded repulsion function $g(\cdot)$

get the balance distance $\delta = \sqrt{\frac{b}{a}} = 1$. It can be proved that the boundary of swarm aggregation is $\varepsilon = \sqrt{(M-1)\frac{b}{2a}}$, which is different from [13].

The anisotropy coefficient ε_{ij} in (1) is the main factor that affect the structures of swarm systems. Based on simple rules, many kinds of collective behavior such as swarm aggregating and formation transforming emerge from variable interactions among mass individuals. To achieve the variety of swarming structures, we present

$$\varepsilon_{ij} = \alpha \left[\frac{h_{x^i}}{\|h_{x^i}\|} \cdot \frac{x^j - x^i}{\|x^j - x^i\|} \right], \ \alpha > 0. \tag{5}$$

where α represents the anisotropy weight of aggregation, and $\frac{x^j - x^i}{\|x^j - x^i\|}$ is the unit direction from individual i to j. The cartesian product of $\frac{h_{x^i}}{\|h_{x^i}\|}$ and $\frac{x^j - x^i}{\|x^j - x^i\|}$ expresses the direction sensitivity with environment of all members in the swarm model. For $\varepsilon_{ij} = 1$, the swarm will converge to a hyperball with isotropic property, and for other cases, the anisotropic factor will affect the collective behavior of swarm members in the heading direction. We can also amplify the degree of anisotropy weight artificially to change swarming formation and collective motion. With this property, this swarm model can adapt well to various environment.

Note that the anisotropic interaction here is different from the interactive efficiency presented in [15], which introducing a concept of coupling matrix to reflect the interaction strength between individuals. The anisotropic interplay presented in (5) inherits from the physics researches on swarming behavior and assumes that the anisotropy originates from the effect of interaction with the environment and relative positions of individuals.

3 Motion in Social Potential Fields

The interactions with environment in this model are based on artificial potential functions, a concept that has been used extensively for robot navigation and control [16,17]. The environment model is built with the combination of social potential fields, in which one can take the obstacle as a high potential region and the destination as a low potential region.

The social potential fields were defined by $\sigma(\cdot)$ which consist of artificial potential functions that model the environment containing obstacles to avoid and targets to moved toward. The negative gradient $-\nabla\sigma(x^i)$ expresses the motion of the individuals toward regions with lower potential (analogous to destination) and away from regions with higher potential (analogous to obstacles). So the heading factor in (1) equate to $h_{x^i} = -\nabla\sigma(x^i)$. The artificial potential functions which are the modeling of social potential fields constructing reference circumstances [18] can take the following forms:

(1) Plane potential function

$$\sigma(x) = a_\sigma^\top x + b_\sigma,\ a_\sigma \in \mathbb{R}^n, b_\sigma \in \mathbb{R}. \tag{6}$$

One can see that the gradient of this potential field is given by $\nabla\sigma(x) = a_\sigma$. This function describes an environment with constant gradient in which individuals can move along the reverse of the gradient direction.

(2) Quadratic potential function

$$\sigma(x) = \frac{A_\sigma}{2}\left\|x - c_\sigma\right\|^2 + b_\sigma,\ A_\sigma \in \mathbb{R}, b_\sigma \in \mathbb{R}, c_\sigma \in \mathbb{R}^n. \tag{7}$$

Note that this potential field has a global extremum at $x = c_\sigma$. Its gradient at point $x \in \mathbb{R}^n$ is given by $\nabla\sigma(x) = A_\sigma(x - c_\sigma)$. For the case $A_\sigma > 0$ the swarm will converge to the minimum of the potential field, and for the case $A_\sigma < 0$ the swarm will diverge from the maximum of the around region, which make swarms move forward to destination and far away from obstacles.

(3) Gaussian potential function

$$\sigma(x) = -\frac{A_\sigma}{2}\exp\left(-\frac{\left\|x - c_\sigma\right\|^2}{l_\sigma}\right) + b_\sigma,\ A_\sigma \in \mathbb{R}, b_\sigma \in \mathbb{R}, l_\sigma \in \mathbb{R}^+, c_\sigma \in \mathbb{R}^n. \tag{8}$$

This potential field also has an extremum at $x = c_\sigma$. The l_σ and A_σ are coefficients which affect the scope and intensity of the potential field around the individual. The gradient of this smooth environment can be obtained by $\nabla\sigma(x) = \frac{A_\sigma}{l_\sigma}(x - c_\sigma)\exp(-\frac{\|x-c_\sigma\|^2}{l_\sigma})$.

(4) Multimodal Gaussian potential function

$$\sigma(x) = -\sum_{i=1}^{N}\frac{A_\sigma^i}{2}\exp\left(-\frac{\left\|x - c_\sigma^i\right\|^2}{l_\sigma^i}\right) + b_\sigma,\ A_\sigma \in \mathbb{R}, b_\sigma \in \mathbb{R}, l_\sigma \in \mathbb{R}^+, c_\sigma \in \mathbb{R}^n. \tag{9}$$

It is a combination of Gaussian potential functions. Each of them has its own extremum at c_σ^i for individual i. Note that since the A_σ^i can be positive or negative, there can be both hills and valleys leading to a complex environment. The gradient of the environment is $\nabla\sigma(x) = \sum_{i=1}^{N} \frac{A_\sigma^i}{l_\sigma^i}(x - c_\sigma^i)\exp(-\frac{\|x-c_\sigma^i\|^2}{l_\sigma^i})$.

These artificial potential functions discussed above can compose social potential fields with which multi-agent systems interact. The combination of them can model reference environments for collective motion of swarms.

4 Simulation Results

As to the anisotropic swarm model based on unbounded repulsion, we chose an $n = 2$ dimensional space to visualize the results and used the region $[-5, 5] \times [-5, 5]$ of the space. In following simulation results the swarm has $M = 20$ members, and parameters of the attraction/repulsion function (4) are $a = 1$ and $b = 1$. We performed simulations for all the social potential fields and anisotropic property discussed above.

Fig. 2 shows the paths of all the members of a swarm moving in a plane potential field with parameter $a_\sigma = [1, 1.2]^\top$. The circles dispersed on the top right corner represent initial random locations of individuals, and the circles arrived at the left corner are the positions of all the members in steady state. The paths composed of blank dots denote the trajectories of individuals. One can easily see that in this social potential field, as expected, the swarm moves along the negative gradient direction $-\nabla\sigma(x) = -a_\sigma$ and congregates to an aggregation. Note that initially for this example some of the individuals move in the direction opposite the negative gradient. It is because the inter-individual attraction is stronger than the intensity of this potential field. If the potential intensity is high enough to dominate the individual motion, the convergence of swarms will need more steps to be observed.

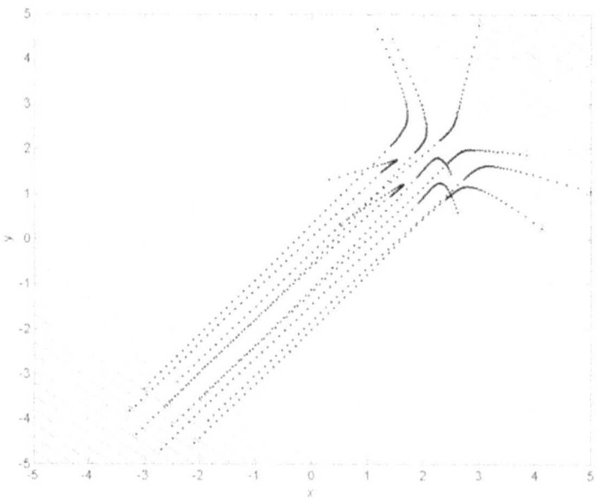

Fig. 2. Collective behavior of swarm in plane social potential field

For the quadratic potential field as shown in Fig. 3, we appointed the environment with minimum at $c_\sigma = [2, 2]^\top$ and its magnitude $A_\sigma = 1$. As discussed above, for $A_\sigma > 0$, the swarm will converge to the minimum of the potential field, and for $A_\sigma < 0$, the swarm will diverge from the maximum of around environment. In Fig. 3, circles dispersed on the left corner represent initial random positions of these individuals, and the circles on the top right are the positions of all the members in steady state. The individual trajectories are denoted by blank dots. This simulation result shows that swarm move towards the minimum of social potential field as aggregating at the same time for the case $A_\sigma > 0$. Note that the swarm size would be affected by potential environment, which can be understand easily if we consider the effect in negative gradient direction as an attraction comes from outside.

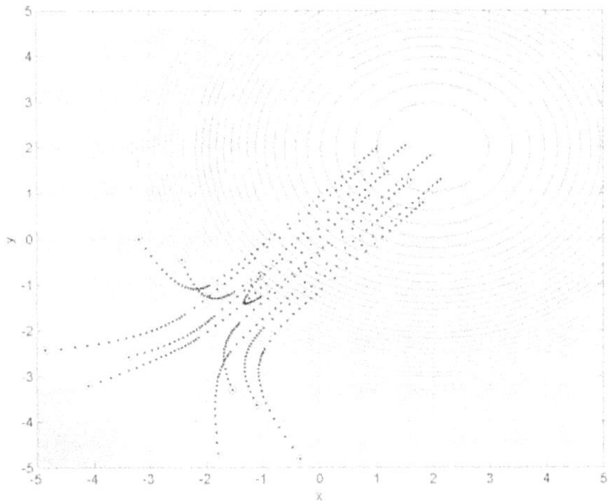

Fig. 3. Collective behavior of swarm in quadratic social potential field

Result from a similar nature was obtained also for the Gaussian potential field as shown in Fig. 4 and Fig. 5, in which we assumed $c_\sigma = [1, 1]^\top$ as the minimum of the environment. The other parameters of this artificial potential function were chosen to be $A_\sigma = 2$ and $l_\sigma = 10$. Fig. 4 shows the social potential field that is analogous to smooth environment for swarms. The collective behavior of individuals in this swarm is shown in Fig. 5. Note that for the case $A_\sigma > 0$, the swarm will converge to the minimum of the potential field along negative gradient direction as expected. This situation exists in all the simulations that we performed.

In the simulation results for the multimodal Gaussian potential field we chose the artificial environment shown in Fig. 6, which has several minima and maxima. As is shown in Fig. 6, we appointed the positions $[2, 2]^\top, [4, 3]^\top, [8, 1]^\top$ as the minima and $[7, 8]^\top, [5, 6]^\top, [2, 7]^\top$ as the maxima. The intensity of potential field is affected by l_σ and A_σ, which are [1,3,2,2,1,2] and [-2,6,3,-8,2,-4] respectively. Note that the region of this simulation example was chosen to be $[0, 10] \times [0, 10]$.

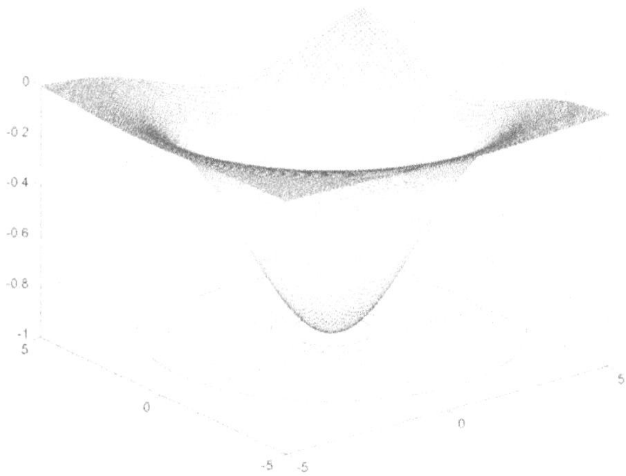

Fig. 4. Gaussian social potential field

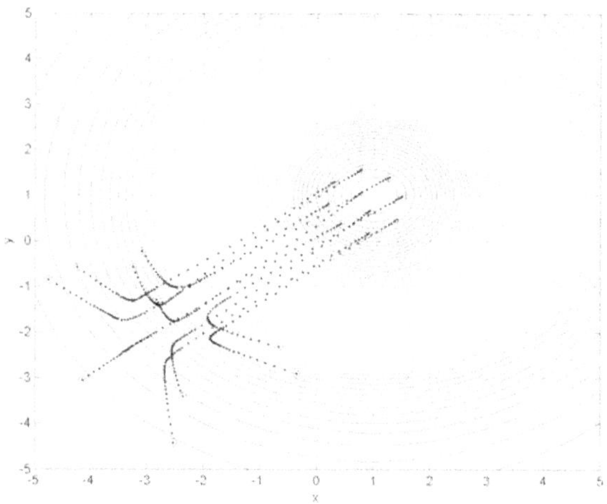

Fig. 5. Collective behavior of swarm in Gaussian social potential field

The global minimum is located at $[4, 3]^{\top}$, with the magnitude $A_{\sigma} = 6$ and the spread $l_{\sigma} = 3$. The plots in Fig. 7 show swarm members congregate to an aggregation and converge to the minimum of the whole region.

Due to the unbounded repulsion, the members will form a cohesive swarm without overlapping of individual positions. And the attrahen/repellent interplays between individuals ensure swarms to aggregate, with this property members will not trap into local extremum and move forward destination. Swarm will converge at the lowest potential region of the whole environment along negative gradient direction.

To observe the results of anisotropic property proposed in this model, we changed the parameter α of anisotropy coefficient ε_{ij} and chose a swarm in

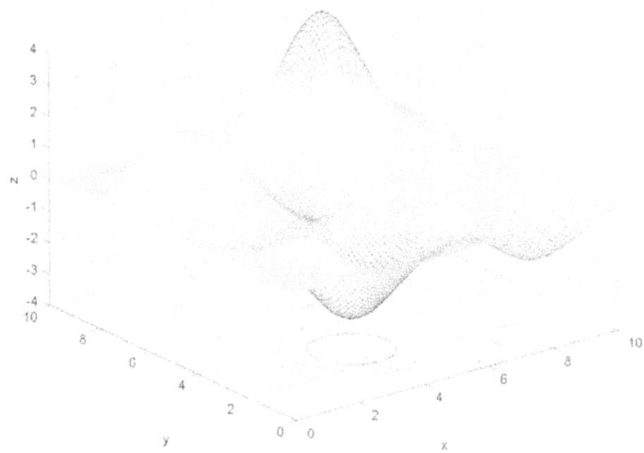

Fig. 6. Multimodal Gaussian social potential field

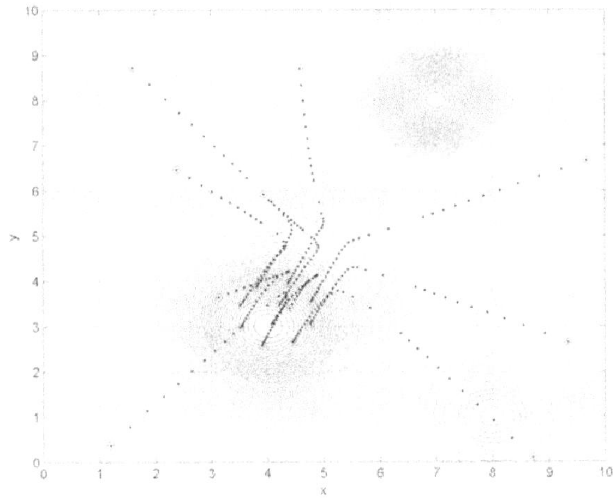

Fig. 7. Collective behavior of swarm in Multimodal Gaussian social potential field

which there are $M = 20$ members. As is shown in Fig 8, the swarm can aggregate as a cluster at broad place and form line formation at narrow place. Accordingly, this swarm with variable structures adapts well to external environment. In a plane potential field with parameter $a_\sigma = [1.1, 1]^\top$, individuals based on inter-individual attraction/repulsion can keep certain formation and move towards the target. The collective behavior of transforming formations and avoiding obstacles emerge from the interactions among mass individuals and interplay with environment, which can be seen as a reference approach for the coordinated control of multi-agent systems in engineering.

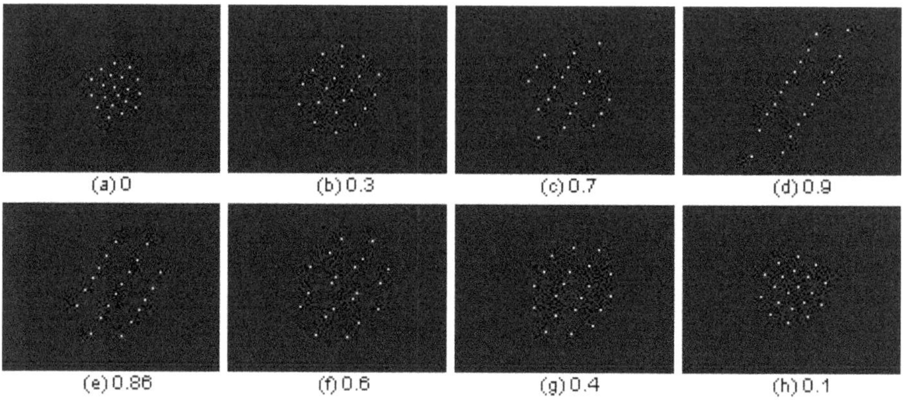

Fig. 8. Formation variety of anisotropic swarm as changing parameter α continually

5 Conclusions

In this article, we propose an anisotropic swarm model based on unbounded repulsion in social potential fields, and analyze its collective behavior. To avoid overlapping of individual positions, the unbounded repulsion is introduced to constitute attraction/repulsion function $g(\cdot)$. The circumstances modeled by social potential fields taking the form of artificial potential functions consist of obstacles to avoid and targets to move towards in various conditions. The simulation results prove that the multi-agent system based on proposed swarm model can eventually form an aggregation of finite size around swarm center, and converge to advantaged region of the environment. By changing the parameters of anisotropy coefficient ε_{ij}, swarm can transform its formation to adapt to various environments. Based on these simple rules, many kinds of collective behavior emerge from variable interactions among mass individuals and the interaction with outer circumstances. The results obtained in this article may provide an extension to the collective motion of autonomous multi-agent systems, and the trajectories generated by this model can be used as reference trajectories for the agents to follow or track.

References

1. Grünbaum, D.: Schooling as A Strategy for Taxis in A Noisy Environment. Evolutionary Ecol. **12** (1998) 503–522
2. Giulietti, F., Pollini, L., Innocenti, M.: Autonomous Formation Flight. IEEE Control System Magazine. **20** (2000) 34–44
3. Balch, T., Arkin, R.C.: Behavior-Based Formation Control for Multirobot Teams. IEEE Trans. Robot Automat. **14** (1998) 926–939
4. Desai, J.P., Ostrowski, J., Kumar, V.: Controlling Formations of Multiple Mobile Robots. Proc. of IEEE Int. Conf. Robotics Automation. (1998) 2864–2869
5. Suzuki, I., Yamashita, M.: Distributed Anonymous Mobile Robots: Formation of Geometric Patterns. SIAM J. Comput. **28**(4) (1998) 1347–1363

6. Egerstedt, M., Hu, X.: Formation Constrained Multi-Agent Control. IEEE Trans. Robot. Automat. **17** (2001) 947–951
7. Grünbaum, D., Okubo, A.: Modeling Social Animal Aggregations. In: Frontiers in Theoretical Biology. Volume 100., New York, Springer-Verlag (1994) 296–325
8. Reynolds, C.: Flocks, Herds, and Schools: A Distributed Behavioral Model. Computer Graphics. **21**(4) (1987) 25–34
9. Mogilner, A., Edelstein-Keshet, L.: A Non-Local Model for A Swarm. Journal of Mathematical Biology. **38** (1999) 534–570
10. Czirok, A., Vicsek, T.: Collective Behavior of Interacting Self-Propelled Particles. Physica. A. **281** (2000) 17–29
11. Shimoyama, N., Sugawa, K., Mizuguchi, T., Hayakawa, Y., Sano, M.: Collective Motion in A System of Motile Elements. Phys. Rev. Lett. **76**(20) (1996) 3870–3873
12. K, W., Lazarus, J.: Tendency-Distance Models of Social Cohesion in Animal Groups. Journal of Theoretical Biology. **150** (1991) 473–488
13. Gazi, V., Passino, K.M.: Stability Analysis of Swarms. IEEE Trans. Automat. Contr. **48** (2003) 692–697
14. CHEN, L., XU, L.: An Aggregating Swarm Model Based on Unbounded Repulsion. Journal of Zhejiang University ENGINEERING SCIENCE. **accepted to appear** (2006)
15. Chu, T., Wang, L., Mu, S.: Collective Behavior Analysis of An Anisotropic Swarm Model. In: Proc. of the 16th International Symposium on Mathematical Theory of Networks and Systems. (2004)
16. Reif, J.H., Wang, H.: Social Potential Fields: A Distributed Behavioral Control for Autonomous Robots. Robot. Auton. Syst. **27** (1999) 171–194
17. Rimon, E., Koditschek, D.E.: Exact Robot Navigation Using Artificial Potential Functions. IEEE Trans. Robot. Automat. **8** (1992) 501–518
18. Gazi, V., Passino, K.M.: Stability Analysis of Social Foraging Swarms. IEEE Trans. Systems, Man, and Cybernetics. **34**(1) (2004) 539–557

Combining Particle Swarm Optimization and Neural Network for Diagnosis of Unexplained Syncope*

Liang Gao, Chi Zhou, Hai-Bing Gao, and Yong-Ren Shi

Department of Industrial & Manufacturing System Engineering
Huazhong Univ.of Sci. & Tech., Wuhan, 430074, China
gaoliang@mail.hust.edu.cn

Abstract. Given the relative limitations of BP and GA based leaning algorithms, Particle Swarm Optimization (PSO) is proposed to train Artificial Neural Networks (ANN) for the diagnosis of unexplained syncope. Compared with BP and GA based training techniques, PSO based learning method improves the diagnosis accuracy and speeds up the convergence process. Experimental results show that PSO is a robust training algorithm and should be extended to other real-world pattern classification applications.

1 Introduction

In industry, economic and medicine, many real world problems such as quality control, bankruptcy prediction, pattern reorganization, and medical diagnosis can be treated as pattern classification problems. Many industrial processes exhibit nonlinear and dynamic behavior, thus nonlinear model should be developed accordingly. With the characteristics of strong self-learning, self-organization, robust error toleration and accurate nonlinear relation approximation, artificial neural network (ANN) is an appropriate tool to deal with the above-mentioned complex pattern classification problems.

Multi-layer ANN with sigmoid activation function has been shown to be able to approximate any continuous nonlinear functions [1] and is an attractive technique that can be applied to nonlinear process modeling. However, the realization of the above capability is based on sufficient training. Therefore, training techniques have much influence on the performance of the ANN for pattern classification problems.

Back-propagation (BP) training algorithm is probably the most frequently used one in practical application. However, it proved that gradient-descent based method is slow, easy to be trapped in local optimum, short of generalization and rather sensitive to initial weights [2]. Due to these drawbacks especially the local optima characteristics, ANN trained by BP cannot guarantee consistency and prediction, which will eventually reduce the reliability of its pattern classification performance.

Compared with BP, Genetic Algorithm (GA) has parallel search strategy and global optimization characteristics, which make the trained neural network have

* This paper is supported by the National Basic Research Program of China (973 Program), No.2004CB719405 and the National Natural Science Foundation of China, No. 50305008.

D.-S. Huang, K. Li, and G.W. Irwin (Eds.): ICIC 2006, LNBI 4115, pp. 174 – 181, 2006.

higher classification accuracy and faster convergence speed [3]. As a population based heuristic, GA encodes ANN architecture (weights) as chromosome and randomly generates a group of individuals. The population evolves by the "survival of fitness" principle and repeats the genetic procedure such as selection, production, crossover and mutation to explore the solution space until the terminal condition is satisfied. The best individual is decoded to correspond to the desired ANN architecture. However, the complex genetic operators make the computational expense exponentially increase with the problem scale [4]. In addition, due to the lack of effective local search mechanism, GA converged slowly and even stagnated when approaching the optimum [5].

Particle Swarm Optimization (PSO) algorithm is based on the theory of swarm intelligence. This algorithm can provide efficient solutions for optimization problems through intelligence generated from complex activities such as cooperation and competition among individuals in the biologic colony. Compared with evolutionary computation, PSO still maintains the population based global search strategy, but its velocity-displacement search model is simple and easy to implement. Also this algorithm avoids the design of complex genetic operators such as crossover and mutation. This algorithm has been applied successfully to complex nonlinear function optimization [6], task assignment [7], reactive power and voltage control [8] and so on.

The syncope is an abrupt and transient state of unconsciousness. This disease is various in pathogenesis and almost 60~70% are unexplained. Equivalently, this disease is called unexplained syncope. Due to its tremendous harm to the human health, unexplained syncope is always posing as a difficult but meaningful research topic in the medical field. However, till now, no effective methods are available to solve this compelling problem.

This paper employed PSO to train ANN and applied it to the diagnosis of unexplained syncope. Compared with BP and GA, PSO based learning algorithm can improve the diagnosis accuracy as well as accelerate the convergence process. The simulated results show that PSO is an effective ANN training method and it should be extended to other pattern classification problems.

2 Particle Swarm Optimization

The investigation and analysis on the biologic colony demonstrated that intelligence generated from complex activities such as cooperation and competition among individuals can provide efficient solutions for specific optimization problems [9]. Inspired by the social behavior of animals such as fish schooling and bird flocking, Kennedy and Eberhart designed the Particle Swarm Optimization (PSO) in 1995 [10]. This method is a kind of evolutionary computing technology based on swarm intelligence. The basic idea of bird flocking can be depicted as follows: In a bird colony, each bird looks for its own food and in the meantime they cooperate with each other by sharing information between them. Therefore, each bird will explore next promising area by its own experience and experience from the others. Due to these attractive characteristics, i.e. memory and cooperation, PSO is widely applied in many research area and real-world engineering fields as a powerful optimization tool.

The basic PSO model consists of a swarm of particles moving in a d-dimensional search space. The direction and distance of each particle in the hyper-dimensional space is determined by its fitness and velocity. In general, the fitness is primarily related with the optimization objective and the velocity is updated according to a sophisticated rule.

In PSO, it starts with the random initialization of a population of individuals (candidate solutions) in the search space and then simulates the social behavior of the particles in the swarm till achieves the optimum solution by iterative exploration. The position and velocity of the ith particle is denoted as $x_i = (x_{i1}, x_{i2}, \cdots x_{id})$ and $v_i = (v_{i1}, v_{i2}, \cdots v_{id})$ respectively. At each iteration step the velocity is updated and the particle is moved to a new position. The best previously visited position of the ith particle is denoted as its personal best position $p_i = (p_{i1}, p_{i2}, \cdots p_{id})$. Define g as the index of the best particle of the whole swarm, the position of the best individual of the whole swarm is denoted as the global best position p_g, and the new velocity of each particle is calculated as follows:

$$v_i = w \times v_i + c_1 \times Rand() \times (p_i - x_i) + c_2 \times rand() \times (p_g - x_i) \tag{1}$$

$$x_i = x_i + v_i \tag{2}$$

where *Rand*() and *rand*() are two independent random numbers uniformly distributed in the range of [0, 1]. c_1, c_2 are two constants called learning factors usually $c_1=c_2=2$ [11]. w is called the inertia factor to deliver a balance between global exploration and local exploitation.

It is noticeable that three components typically contribute to the new velocity. The first part is proportional to the old velocity and is the tendency of the particle to continue in the same direction it has been traveling [12]. It can be thought of as a momentum term. The second component, which is associated with a local search, is considered as the cognitive part representing the private thinking. The third term, which is associated with a global search, is considered as the social part representing the social-psychological adaptation of knowledge. In addition, studies of inertia weight w yield the conclusion that starting with a high value and lowering it throughout the iterations will help enhance the possibility of converging globally and save the computational expense in the local search procedure.

3 PSO for Neural Networks

An artificial neural network is composed of a series of interconnected nodes and the corresponding weights between them. It aims at simulating the complex mapping between the input and output. A 3-layer feed-forward ANN basically consists of input units, hidden units and output units. Let w_{ih} denotes the weight between the input node and the hidden one. Likewise, w_{ho} denotes the weight between the hidden node and output one. ANN is characterized by the ability of self-learning and error toleration. With the appropriate activation functions and trained weights, ANN can approximate any smooth, nonlinear function or relationship between the input and output. The training process is carried out on a set of data including input and output parameters. Usually, the data are split into two parts namely training samples and testing samples. The learning procedure is based on the training samples and the testing samples are used to verify the performance of the trained network. During the training, the weights in the network are adjusted iteratively till a desired error depicted as equation (3) is obtained.

$$E = \sum_{i=1}^{m} \sum_{k=1}^{n_o} (t_i^k - y_i^k)^2 / 2 \tag{3}$$

where, t_i^k and y_i^k represents the actual and the predicted function values respectively, m is the number of training samples, and n_o is the number of output nodes.

The neural network is trained by minimizing the above error function in a search space based on weights. PSO generates possible solutions and measure their quality by using a forward propagation through the neural network to obtain the value of the error function. This error value is used as the particle's fitness function to direct it toward the more promising solution. The global best particle is corresponded to the desired trained network after adequate iterations.

PSO based training algorithm can be summarized in the following steps:

Step1. Define the network structure, parameters of PSO and the fitness function.

Step2. Encode the candidate weight solution as $x = \{w_{ih}, w_{ho}\}$.

Step3. Initialize the position (weights) and velocity of each particle (change of weights in a single iteration) randomly in the predefined range. Evaluate the fitness of each particle according to the previously defined error function.

Step4. Identify the personal best fitness value and update the corresponding position for each particle; Identify the global best fitness value and update its position.

Step5. Update the velocity and the position for the whole particle swarm according to equation (1) and (2).

Step6. If the stopping condition is not satisfied, go to step 4. Otherwise, terminate the iteration and obtain the best weight setting from the global best solution.

4 Experimental Results and Analysis

The upright tilt table test is a commonly used diagnostic technique for unexplained syncope [13]. Basic upright tilt table test, as well as isoproterenol tilt table test, is a quite effective diagnostic technique for unexplained syncope. The diagnostic parameters used in the test can be listed and classified as follows:

1. General diagnostic parameters: sex and age.
2. Subjective diagnostic parameters: nausea, fatigue, swelling in the legs, dizziness, sweating, pallor, palpitations, chest pain, shortness of breath, muscle cramps, numbness, fainting, unconsciousness.
3. Auxiliary diagnostic parameters: heart rate (HR) and blood pressure (BP).

The diagnostic results yielded by the above parameters approximately fall into two categories: negative response and positive response. The latter can be further classified into three categories: heart restraint class, blood vessels restraint class and the syndrome class.

The data of unexplained syncope are obtained from the Biomedical Department at Wuhan University. From the total samples, 177 samples are specified as training set, while the remaining 59 are specified as testing set. The input nodes represent the diagnostic parameters in the upright tilt table test. The output nodes mean the classes of the diagnostic results. All the source data should be preprocessed and normalized as follows:

1. Sex: male (1), female (0).
2. Age: 15-30 (0), 30-40 (0.5), and 40-70 (1).
3. Symptoms: presence (1), absence (0).
4. BP/HR: presence (1), absence (0).
5. Diagnostic results: negative (1000), heart restraint (0100), blood vessels restraint (0010), and syndrome (0001).

The data before the bracket present the practical diagnostic data and the inside present the normalized ones which will be served as actual parameters for the input nodes of the neural network.

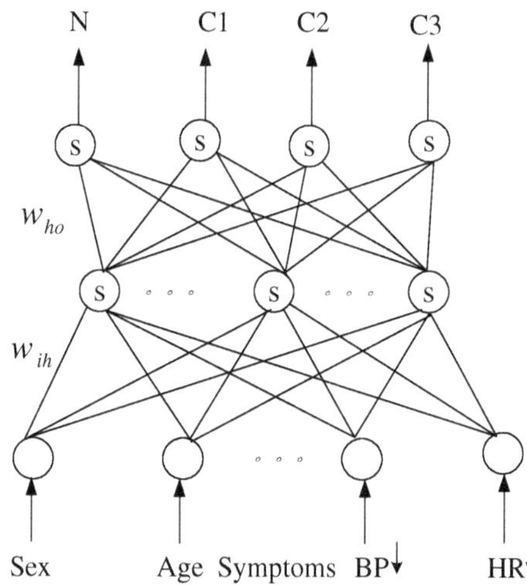

Fig. 1. The ANN model for diagnosis of unexplained syncope

The structure of the neutral network model for the diagnosis of unexplained syncope is constructed as Figure 1. The 18 input nodes of the 3-layer feed-forward ANN represent the diagnostic parameters. The 4 output nodes represent the diagnostic results. The number of the hidden nodes is specified by the empirical equation. Sigmoid function is selected as activation function.

Before the training process, we should set the parameters of the training algorithm. In this paper, for PSO, we set population size n=80, w=0.5, c_1=c_2=2. The inertial weight decreases from 0.9 to 0.4 linearly. The initial weights are randomly generated between [0, 1]. The termination condition is defined as follows: (1) The predefined maximum iteration number *Itermax* is reached or (2) the training error is smaller than the threshold *e*. To validate the performance of PSO, BP and GA were also adopted as the training algorithms. In BP, the learning rate is 0.3 and momentum factor is 0.8. In GA, the crossover probability P_c is 0.9 and the mutation probability Pm is 0.1. Also, roulette wheel selection, binary encoding scheme and elite strategy are used. The population size is the same as that in PSO. It should be pointed out that each experiment was randomly carried out for 20 times, the typical results (medium performance) were recorded in the tables and figures.

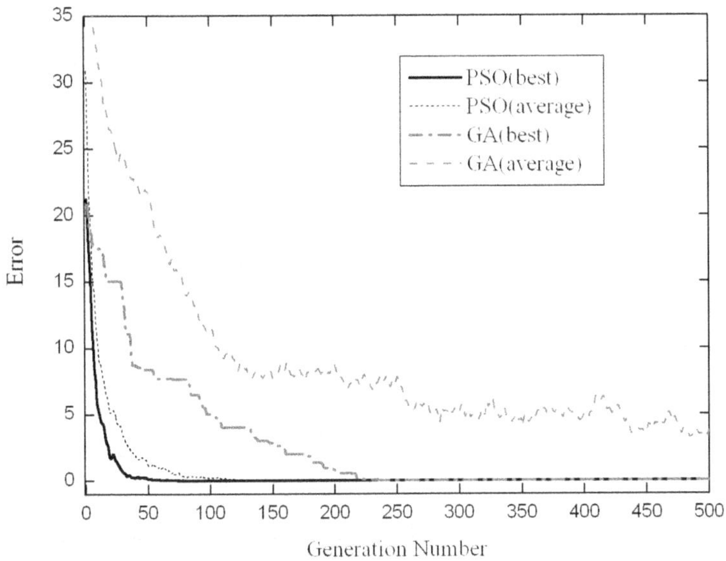

Fig. 2. Training error curves of PSO and GA

The simulation experiment is carried out in two steps:

Firstly, set *Itermax*=500, 1000 as the termination condition (1) to compare the training error and diagnosis accuracy of neural network trained by PSO, GA and BP. The experimental results are presented in Table 1 and Table 2. The comparison of convergence between the two population based algorithms is illustrated in Figure 2. Several conclusions can be drawn from the results: (a) When the maximum iteration is reached, all the particles in PSO converged to the optimum region whereas the individuals in GA distributed more diversely, which demonstrated that PSO is obviously superior in terms of convergence consistency. (b) Compared with BP and GA, PSO not only guaranteed high diagnostic accuracy but also performed better regarding error precision, which in turn improved the diagnostic reliability. (c) GA suffered from the intrinsic slow convergence flaw although it could also get promising weight solution. (d) With the relative small iteration scale, BP converged much faster and the training performance was even better than GA to some extent, but it would trap into local optimum with the increasing of the iteration scale.

Table 1. Comparison of different performance (Itermax=500)

Training algorithms	Error			Diagnostic accuracy
	Worst	Average	Best	
PSO	7.2E-20	7.2E-20	7.2E-20	98.6 %
GA	16.5	1.6	1.0E-10	89.4 %
BP	–	7.4E-03	–	98.4 %

Table 2. Comparison of different performance (Itermax=1000)

Training algorithms	Error			Diagnostic accuracy
	Worst	Average	Best	
PSO	5.3E-30	5.3E-30	5.3E-30	99.2 %
GA	11.2	0.7	2.1E-18	97.6 %
BP	–	3.6E-03	–	98.6 %

Table 3. Comparison of different computational expense (e=0.001)

Training algorithm	Iteration number	CPU time (s)
PSO	76	8.2
GA	522	42.1
BP	3538	169.2

Table 4. Comparison of different computational expense (e=0.0001)

Training algorithm	Iteration number	CPU time (s)
PSO	144	15.762
GA	702	56.476
BP	32798	845.824

Secondly, set training error less or equal to 0.001, 0.0001 as the termination condition. This trial aimed at comparing the computational expense between BP, GA and PSO with equivalent training precision. As can be seen from Table 3 and Table 4, although GA can obtain the desired convergence, PSO performed much better in terms of computational expense without the loss of convergence quality. In addition, BP suffered severe stagnation in achieving the desired precision.

5 Conclusion

PSO is an optimization algorithm based on swarm intelligence. It directs the search through the intelligence generated from cooperation and competition among the individuals. The merits of this novel algorithm can be summarized as follows: Firstly, with the parallel search strategy, it can locate the global optimum consistently.

Secondly, its velocity-displacement search model is simple and easy to implement. Thirdly, few parameters should be considered and set up. Moreover, the information flow with single direction can absolutely speed up the convergence process. Finally, variable inertial weight can effectively guarantee the compromise between global search and local search.

In this paper, a neural network based on PSO is proposed for the diagnosis of unexplained syncope. Compared with BP and GA, PSO can improve the diagnosis accuracy and speed up the convergence simultaneously. The experimental results reveal that PSO is a promising training algorithm and we should explore its potential in other optimization areas.

Further research could to be done in the future. In the algorithm itself, several predefined parameters such as the inertial weight and learning factors can be adjusted dynamically by tracking the current process. Also analysis on the trained network can generate different patterns of input parameters, which could be used to conduct the rule acquisition. In addition, improved model is desired for other real-world problems with larger amount of source data and more complicated mapping relationship.

References

1. Hornik, K., Stinchcombe, M., White, H.: Multilayer Feed-forward Networks Are Universal Approximators. Neural Networks. 2 (1989) 359–366
2. Rumelhart, D.E., Hinton, G.E., Williams, R.J.: Learning Representations by Back Propagating Errors. Nature. 323 (1986) 533-536
3. Sexton, R.S., Dorsey, R.E.: Reliable Classification Using Neural Networks: A Genetic Algorithm and Back Propagation Comparison. Decision Support Systems. 30 (2000) 11-22
4. Yang, J.M., Kao, C.Y.: A Robust Evolutionary Algorithm for Training Neural Networks. Neural Computing and Application. 10 (2001) 214-230
5. Franchini, M.: Use of A Genetic Algorithm Combined with A Local Search Method for the Automatic Calibration of Conceptual Rainfall-runoff Models. Hydrological Science Journal. 41 (1996) 21-39
6. Shi, Y.H., Eberhart, R.C.: Empirical Study of Particle Swarm Optimization. IEEE Congress on Evolutionary Computation (1999)
7. Salman, A., Ahmad, I.: Particle Swarm Optimization for Task Assignment Problem. Microprocessors and Microsystems. 26 (2002) 363-371
8. Yoshida, H., Kawata, K., Yoshikazu F.: A Particle Swarm Optimization for Reactive Power and Voltage Control Considering Voltage Security Assessment. IEEE transaction on power system. 15 (2000) 1232-1239
9. Kennedy, J., Eberhart, R.C., Shi, Y.: Swarm Intelligence. Morgan Kaufman, San Francisco (2001)
10. Kennedy, J., Eberhart, R.C.: Particle Swarm Optimization. Proceedings of IEEE International Conference on Neutral Networks, Perth, Australia (1995) 1942-1948
11. Shi, Y.H., Eberhart, R.C.: Parameter Selection in Particle Swarm Optimization. The 7th Annual Conference on Evolutionary Programming, San Diego, USA (1998)
12. Shi, Y.H., Eberhart, R.C.: A Modified Particle Swarm Optimizer. IEEE International Conference on Evolutionary Computation, Anchorage, Alaska (1998)
13. Yao Y.J., Sun X.Q., Wu X.Y, Wu Y.: Upright Tilt Table Testing and Syncope Evaluation. Space Medicine & Medical Engineering 15(2002) 136-139

Parameter Estimation Approach in Groundwater Hydrology Using Hybrid Ant Colony System

Shouju Li, Yingxi Liu, and He Yu

State Key Laboratory of Structural Analysis for Industrial Equipment, Dalian University of Technology, Dalian, 116024, China
{Lishouju, Yxliu}@dlut.edu.cn

Abstract. A new approach to parameter estimation in groundwater hydrology is developed using hybrid ant colony system with simulated annealing. Based on the information from the observed water heads and calculated water heads, an objective function for inverse problem is proposed. The inverse problem of parameter identification is formulated as an optimization problem. Simulated annealing has the ability of probabilistic hill-climbing and is combined with ant colony system to produce an adaptive algorithm. A hybrid ant colony optimization is presented to identify the transmissivity and storage coefficient for a two-dimensional, unsteady state groundwater flow model. The ill-posedness of the inverse problem as characterized by instability and non-uniqueness is overcome by using computational intelligence. Compared with gradient-based optimization methods, hybrid ant colony system is a global search algorithm and can find parameter set in a stable manner. A numerical example is used to demonstrate the efficiency of hybrid ant colony system.

1 Introduction

Parameter identification, or model calibration, is a critical step in the application of mathematical models in hydrologic sciences. Unfortunately, parameter identification is an inherently difficult process and, as an inverse problem, it is plagued by the well-documented problems of nonumiquenes, nonidentifiability and instability [1]. Numerous optimization techniques have been used to solve groundwater remediation design and parameter identification problems. In a parameter identification problem, the objective function can be the weighted difference between the observed and calculated values at certain observation points in the aquifer. The identified parameters can be hydraulic conductivity or other aquifer parameters, such as storage coefficient[2]. In recent years, global optimization methods are being increasingly used to solve groundwater remediation design and parameter identification problems. These methods include simulated annealing, genetic algorithm, tabu search and ant colony system. Compared with gradient based local search methods, global optimization methods do not require the objective function to be continuous, convex, or differentiable. They have also shown other attractive features such as robustness, ease of implementation, and the ability to solve many types of highly complex, nonlinear problems. One common drawback of these global optimization methods is

D.-S. Huang, K. Li, and G.W. Irwin (Eds.): ICIC 2006, LNBI 4115, pp. 182 – 191, 2006.

that many objective function evaluations are typically required to obtain optimal or near-optimal solutions [3]. The ant colony system is a kind of natural algorithm inspired by behavior or processes presented in nature. Ant colony system has been widely used in the traveling salesman problem, job-shop scheduling problem and quadratic assignment problem. When compared with traditional first-order methods, the ant colony system is recognized to have a better capability to find the global optimum solution. The objective of this paper is to present a new method based on hybrid ant colony system for obtaining the parameters of a linear groundwater flow model.

2 Classical Ant Colony System

Ant colonies have always fascinated human beings. Social insects, such as ants, bees, termites and wasps, often exhibit a collective problem-solving ability[4].The ant colony system is first applied to the traveling salesman problem. In Ant System, the traveling salesman problem is expressed as a graph (N, E), where N is the set of towns and E is the set of edges between towns. The objective of the traveling salesman problem is to find the minimal length closed tour that visits each town once. Each ant is a simple agent to fulfill the task. It obeys the following rules: 1) It chooses the next town with a probability which is a function of the town distance and of the amount of trail present on the connecting edge; 2) before a tour is completed, it can not choose the already visited towns; 3) when it completes a tour, it lays a substance called trail on each edge (i, j) visited; 4) it lives in an environment where time is discrete. It must choose the next town at time t, and be there at time t+1. Let m, n be the total number of ants and towns. An iteration of the Ant system is called, as the m ants all carry their next moves during time interval (t, t+1). The n iterations constitute a cycle. In one cycle, each ant has completed a tour. Let $\tau_{ij}(t)$ denote the intensity of trail on edge (i, j). After a cycle, the trail intensity is updated as[5]:

$$\tau_{ij}(t+1) = \rho\tau_{ij}(t) + \Delta\tau_{ij} \tag{1}$$

Where ρ is a coefficient, and (1-ρ) represents the evaporation of trail between times t and t+1

$$\Delta\tau_{ij} = \sum_{k=1}^{Z} \Delta\tau_{ij}^{k} \tag{2}$$

Where $\Delta\tau_{ij}$ is the quantity per unit of length of trail substance placed on path(i,j) by the kth ant between times t and t+1[6]

$$\Delta\tau_{ij}^{k} = \begin{cases} Q/J_k & path(i,j) \quad is \quad selected \\ 0 & otherwise \end{cases} \tag{3}$$

Where Q is a constant related to the quantity of trail laid by ants. Ants build solutions using a probabilistic transition rule. The probability $p_{ij}^{k}(t)$ with which ant k in town i at iteration t chooses the next town j to move to is a function of the heuristic function of the desirability η_{ij} and the artificial pheromone trail $\tau_{ij}(t)$:

$$p_{ij}^{k}(t) = \frac{[\tau_{ij}]^{\alpha}[\eta_{ij}]^{\beta}}{\sum_{l=1}^{L}[\tau_{ij}]^{\alpha}[\eta_{ij}]^{\beta}} \tag{4}$$

Where α, β are adjustable constants, which can weigh the relative importance of pheromone trail and of objective function, L is the number of states that will be visited. A reasonable heuristic function is written as follows:

$$\eta_{ij} = \frac{1}{J_k} \tag{5}$$

Where J_k is the objective function of kth ant path. Ant colony system could not perform well without pheromone evaporation. From Eq. (4), it is obvious that the transition probability is proportional to the visibility and the trail intensity at time t. The visibility shows that the closer towns have a higher probability of being chosen. The mechanism behind this is a greedy constructive heuristic. While the trail intensity shows that the more trail on edge (i, j), the more attractive it is. The process can be characterized by a positive feedback loop, in which an ant chooses a path thus reinforces it. In order to constrain the ants not to visit a previous visited town, a data structure called the tabu list is associated with each ant. All the visited towns are saved in it. When an ant finishes a cycle, the tabu list is then emptied and the ant is free again to choose. Let tabu_k denote the tabu list of the kth ant.

3 Parameter Estimation Approach in Groundwater Hydrology Using Hybrid Ant Colony System

3.1 Solution Definition of Inverse Problem and Its Ill-Posedness

The parameter identification problem can be formulated to find the model parameters by adjusting m until the measured data match the corresponding data computed from the parameter set in a least-squares fashion. The objective function is defined as follows [7]

$$J(m) = (h_m - h_c(m))^T w(h_m - h_c(m)) \tag{6}$$

Where h_m is the measured displacement vector; h_c is the computing displacement vector, which is related to the identified parameter vector m. $\boldsymbol{w}$ is weighting matrix in order to take into account the different observed equipments for the water head measurements [8,9]. This objective function clearly depends on the measured data and the parameters of model.

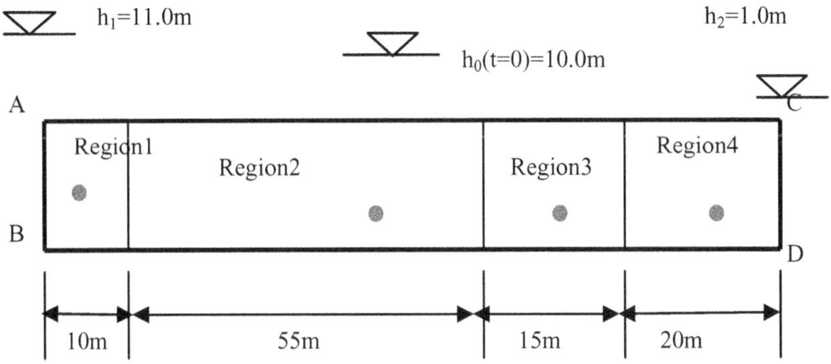

Fig. 1. Configuration of the two-dimensional groundwater flow model

Fig. 1 shows the groundwater flow model, in which the four observing points for water heads are set in order to get measurement data and to identify the aquifer parameters. The objective function can become complex as shown as Fig.2, such as non-convex, or even multi-modal if errors contained in the model equation or /and errors in the measurement data are large. The multi local minima can be found from Fig.2. In such a case, the solution may vibrate or diverge when conventional gradient-based optimization methods are used, which gives rise to the necessary for a robust optimization method such that a stable convergence is always achieved.

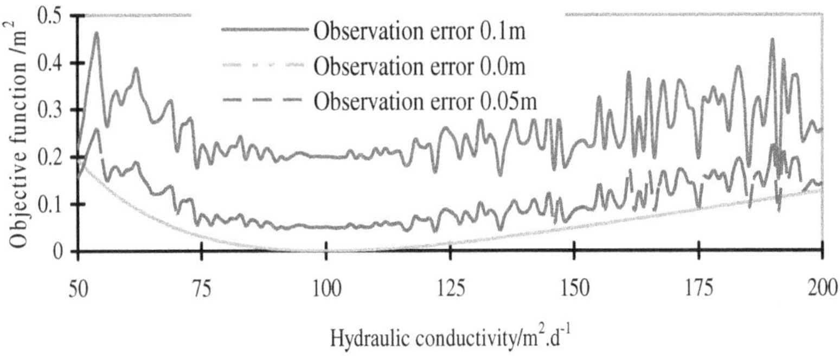

Fig. 2. Objective functions of the different measurement errors

3.2 Simulated Annealing Algorithm for Neighborhood Search

Simulated annealing is another important algorithm which is powerful in optimization and high-order problems. It uses random processes to help guide the form of its search for minimal energy states. Simulated annealing is a generalization of a Monte Carlo method for examining the equations of state and frozen states of n-body systems. The concept is based on the manner in which liquids freeze or metals recrystalize in the process of annealing[10]. In an annealing process a melt, initially at high temperature and disordered, is slowly cooled so that the system at any time is approximately in thermodynamic equilibrium. As cooling proceeds, the system becomes more ordered and approaches a "frozen" ground state at T=0. Hence the process can be thought of as an adiabatic approach to the lowest energy state. If the initial temperature of the system is too low or cooling is done insufficiently slowly the system may become quenched forming defects or freezing out in meta-stable states, that is, trapped in a local minimum energy state. Simulated annealing is a very general optimization method which stochastically simulates the slow cooling of a physical system. The idea is that there is a objective function *F*, which associates a objective function with a state of the system, a temperature T, and various ways to change the state of the system. The algorithm works by iteratively proposing change and either accepting or rejecting each change. Having proposed a change we may evaluate the change δF in *F*. The proposed change may be accepted or rejected by the Metropolis criterion; if the objective function decreases ($\delta J<0$), the change is accepted unconditionally; otherwise it is accepted but only with probability $exp(-\delta J/T)$. For given old solution, a new solution can be created as following [11]:

$$m_{new} = m_{old} + \Delta m \tag{7}$$

Where Δm is a random perturbation of solution. The accepted probability of the new solution, p_{new}, will be expressed:

$$p_{new} = \begin{cases} 1 & J_{old} \geq J_{new} \\ \exp[-\delta J / T_k] & J_{old} < J_{new} \end{cases} \tag{8}$$

Where $\delta J=J_{new}-J_{old}$. Three parameters essential for implementation of the simulated annealing algorithm are as follows:1)initial value of the control parameter, T_i, 2)the number of perturbations generated at each *T*, and 3)the decrement of the control parameter *T*. These parameters affect the speed of the algorithm and the quality of the final solution. A simple approach is to choose a value for T_i that allows a large percentage of non-improving solutions to be accepted [10]. The number of solutions generated at each *T* is selected to allow equilibrium to take place before decreasing *T*. The decrement of *T* is chosen such that it allows only small changes in the value of *T*. The equation used for decreasing *T* is expressed as follows:

$$T_{k+1} = \xi T_k \tag{9}$$

Where ξ=0.9 is a typical selection. A crucial requirement for the proposed changes is reachability or ergodicity-that there be a sufficient variety of possible changes that one can always find a sequence of changes so that any system state may be reached from any other. When the temperature is zero, changes are accepted only if *F* decreases, an algorithm also known as hill-climbing, or more generally, the greedy algorithm. The initial temperature can be determined as [12]

$$T_i = \frac{-1}{\ln p_i} \tag{10}$$

Where p_i is the desired initial acceptable probability. It is usually between 0.7and 0.9. similarly, the final temperature can be determined as

$$T_f = \frac{-1}{\ln p_f} \tag{11}$$

Where p_f is the desired final acceptable probability. It is usually very close to zero. The system soon reaches a state in which none of the proposed changes can decrease the objective function, but this is usually a poor optimum. In real life, we might be trying to achieve the highest point of a mountain range by simply walking upwards; we soon arrive at the peak of a small foothill and can go no further. On the contrary, if the temperature is very large, all changes are accepted, and we simply move at random ignoring the cost function. Because of the reachability property of the set of changes, we explore all states of the system, including the global optimum. The system evolves until a stop criterion is reached. Very fast simulated annealing scheme proposed by Ingber is applied to produce new solution [13]

$$\Delta m_i = \eta_i (m_{i\max} - m_{i\min}) \tag{12}$$

$$\eta_i = sign(u_i - 0.5)T_i[(1 + \frac{1}{T_i})^{|2u_i - 1|} - 1] \tag{13}$$

Where m_{max} and m_{min} represent up and down bounds for parameters□respectively; u_i is a random value in [-1,1]domain, the value of η_i is just located in [-1,1]. The whole process for parameter identification using simulated annealing is shown as follows: Step 1: Initial parameters (initial T and temperature descent rate α) are fixed. Step 2: Initial solution is generated and the corresponding J is calculated. Step 3: The system solution is updated according to the mechanism designed. Step 4: Parameter T is modified according to the descent rate established. Step 5:One comes back to the step 3 to calculate the next solution from the current one up to T or ε reaches a value fixed beforehand. Step 6: The best solution visited is written as last solution of inverse problem.

3.3 Hybrid Ant Colony System for Parameter Identification

Ant colony system is global search techniques for optimization. However, it is poor at hill-climbing. Simulated annealing has the ability of probabilistic hill-climbing. Therefore, the two techniques are combined here to produce a new algorithm that has the merits of both ant colony system and simulated annealing, by introducing a local search. A new hybridization of ant colony system with simulated annealing is proposed. Fig 3 shows the fundamental structure of hybrid ant colony system with simulated annealing.

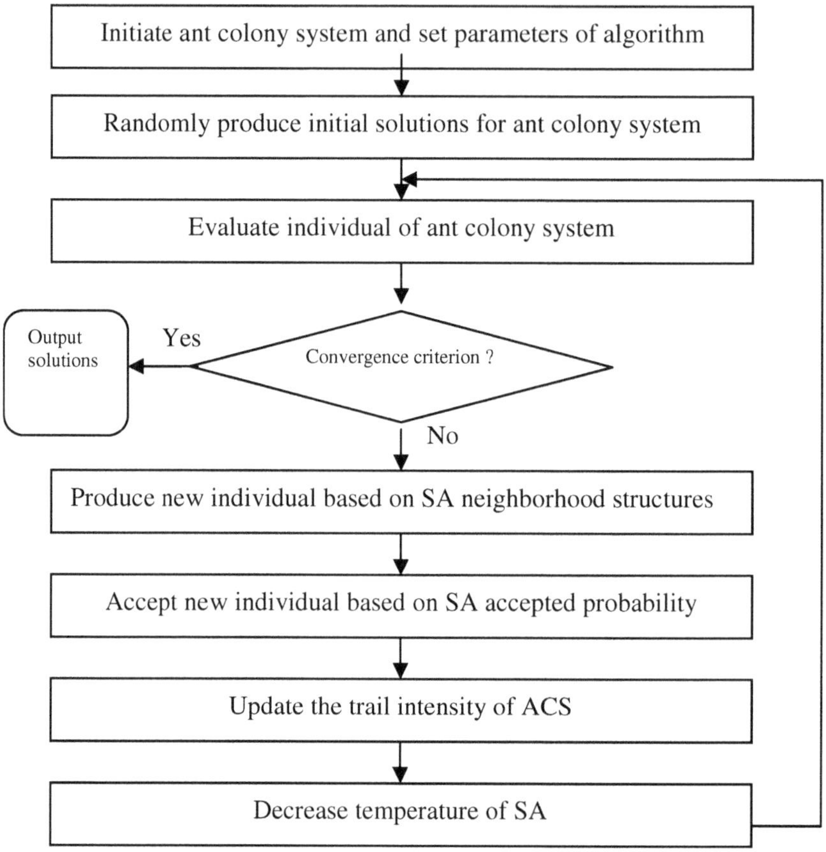

Fig. 3. Fundamental structure of hybrid ant colony system with simulated annealing

The main concept of inverse problem of parameter identification with the hybrid ant colony system can be summarized in the following steps: Step 1: depict each unknown parameter by an interval based on available prior information; Step 2: discretize each interval into a number of strata, let the middle of each stratum represent that stratum; Step 3: run the simulation model of choice for all, or a randomly selected subset of all the possible parameter combinations; Step 4: evaluate each stratum on the bases of the smallest of the value of the objective function in such a way that small values of the objective function receive higher scores; Step 5: Produce new individual based on SA neighborhood structures; Step 6: Accept new individual based on SA accepted probability. Step 7: on the basis of the value of the objective function, place a certain amount of trail(pheromone in the case of real ants) on each stratum visited along its pathway. Step 8: Decrease temperature of SA according to decreasing scheme; Step 9: repeat step 4 to step 8 until the some convergence criterion is satisfied.

4 Experiment

To test the applicability and efficiency of the hybrid ant colony system, a two dimensional flow problem is considered, as shown as Fig.1. The aquifer is bound by two constant-head boundaries with the initial heads both at 11m at t>0, the head at right boundary is instantaneously lowered to 10m. The transient head distribution is simulated using finite element method with a time step of 0.1 day. Hydraulic conductivity and specific storage coefficient are listed in Table 1. Table 2 records measured water head data at different points at different times.

Table 1. Hydraulic conductivity and specific storage coefficient

Parameters	k_1 / $m^2 \cdot d^{-1}$	k_2 / $m^2 \cdot d^{-1}$	k_3 / $m^2 \cdot d^{-1}$	k_4 / $m^2 \cdot d^{-1}$	S_s
Values	2000.0	100.0	10.0	1000.0	0.02

Table 2. Measured water head data at different points at different times

Observation time/d	Observation point 1# /m	Observation point 2#/m	Observation point 3#/m	Observation point 4#/m
0.1	10.68716	9.979836	9.170668	3.640028
0.2	10.72888	9.807406	8.396107	3.374715
0.3	10.69714	9.537611	7.756343	3.121658
0.4	10.63557	9.198385	7.028817	1.584894
0.5	10.56086	8.835012	6.398876	1.423336

According to the flow mathematical model with finite element method and measured water-head data, the aquifer parameters are identified with hybrid ant colony system with simulated annealing. Fig. 4 shows the influence of initial temperature of simulated annealing algorithm to convergence process.

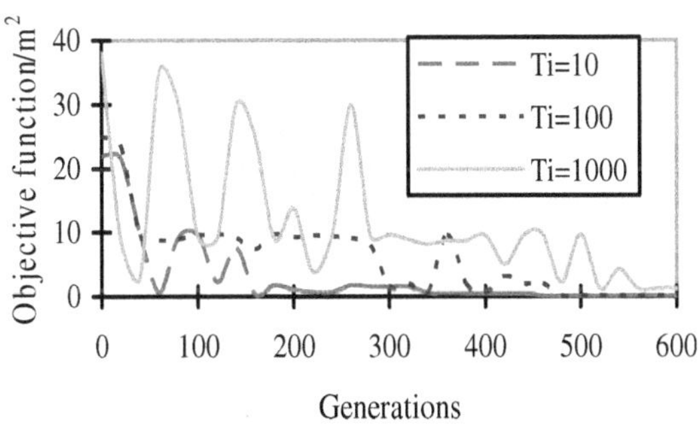

Fig. 4. Influence of initial temperatures to convergence process

In order to simulate observation errors, the measured water heads can be simulated by adding a random error to the theoretical values

$$h_{\mathrm{m}}^{*} = h_{\mathrm{m}} + sign(R-0.5)\times\Delta h \tag{14}$$

Where h_{m}^{*} are the measured data with observation errors, h_m are the measured data without observation errors. *Sign* is the sign function, and R is a random variable in the interval [0,1], Δh is observation error. Comparison of identified hydraulic conductivity and specific storage coefficient with theoretical values is listed in Table 3. Fig. 5 shows the convergence process of objective function with classical ant colony system and hybrid ant colony system.

Table 3. Comparison of identified hydraulic conductivity and specific storage coefficient with theoretical values

Model parameters	k_1 / m^2·d^{-1}	k_2 / m^2·d^{-1}	k_3 / m^2·d^{-1}	k_4 / m^2·d^{-1}	S_s
Theoretical Values	2000.0	100.0	10.0	1000.0	0.02
Identified values by HACS	2010.3	99.7	10.2	1009.0	0.018
Identified values by ACS	2022.7	110.2	9.95	1012.5	0.025

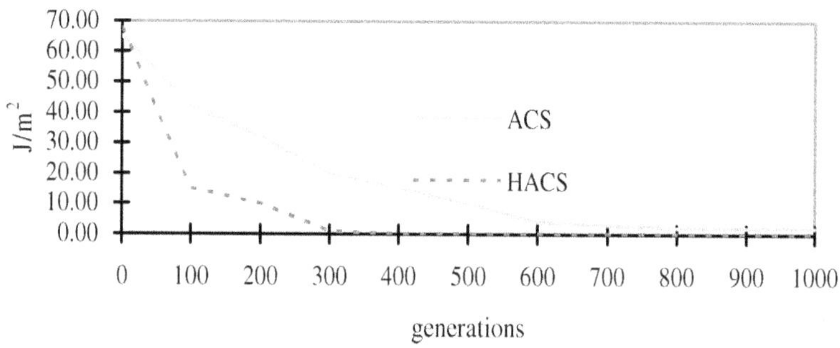

Fig. 5. Convergence process of objective function with different searching method

5 Conclusion

Hybrid ant colony system for solving the parameter identification problem is proposed. The three characteristics of the ant colony system, such as positive feedback process, greedy constructive heuristic and distributed computation, work together to find the solution to the inverse problems fast and efficiently. However, classical ant colony system is poor at hill-climbing. Simulated annealing has the ability of probabilistic hill-climbing. Therefore, the two techniques are combined here to produce a new algorithm that has the merits of both ant colony system and simulated annealing, by introducing a local search. A new hybridization of ant colony system with simulated annealing is proposed.. Modern heuristic search techniques, such as genetic algorithm, simulated annealing and ant colony system, are well suited for solving the parameter identification problem in groundwater flow model. The gradient based methods are not applicable for this type of inverse problem because of the difficulty in evaluating the function derivatives and the presence of many local minimum points in the objective function. One of the advantages of ant colony system over other optimization methods is that it is easy to implement complex inverse problem.

Acknowledgements

This research is funded by the National Natural Science Foundation of China (No. 10472025).

References

1. Zheng. C.: Parameter Structure Identification Using Tabu Search and Simulated Annealing. Advances in Water Resources. 129 (996) 215-224
2. Kool, J.B.: Parameter Estimation for Unsaturated Flow and Transport Models- A Review. J. Hydrol. 91 (1987) 255-293
3. Wang. P.P.: An Efficient Approach for Successively Perturbed Groundwater Models. Advances in Water Resources. 21 (1998) 499-508
4. Chang, C.S.: A New Approach to Fault Section Estimation in Power Systems Using Ant System. Electric Power Research. 49 (1999) 63-70
5. Dorigo, M.: Ant Colonies for the Travelling Salesman Problem. BioSystem. 43 (1997) 73-81
6. Dorigo, M.: Ant Algorithms and Stigmergy. Future Generation Computer Systems. 16 (2000) 851-871
7. Abbaspour, K.C.: Estimating Unsaturated Soil Hydraulic Parameters Using Ant Colony Optimization. Advances in Water Resources. 24 (2001) 827-841
8. Simoni, L.: An Accelerated Algorithm for Parameter Identification in a Hierarchical Plasticity Model Accounting For Material Constraints. Int. J. for Numerical and Analysis Methods in Geomechanics. 25 (2001) 263-272
9. Mattsson, H.: Optimization Routine for Identification of Model Parameters in Soil Plasticity. Int. J. for Numerical and Analysis Methods in Geomechanics. 25 (2001) 435-472
10. Alkhanmis, T.M.: Simulated Annealing For Discrete Optimization With Estimation. European Journal of Operational Research. 116 (1999) 530-544
11. Jeong, I.K.: Adaptive Simulated Annealing Genetic Algorithm for System Identification. Engineering Applications of Artificial Intelligence. 9 (1996) 523-532
12. Chen, T. Y.: Efficiency Improvement of Simulated Annealing In Optimal Structural Designs. Advances in Engineering Software. 33 (2002) 675-680
13. Rosen, I.I.: Comparison of Simulated Annealing Algorithms for Conformal Therapy Treatment Planning. Int. J. Radiation Oncology Biol. Phys. 33 (1995) 1091-1099

Route-Exchange Algorithm for Combinatorial Optimization Based on Swarm Intelligence*

Xiaoxian He[1,2], Yunlong Zhu[1], Kunyuan Hu[1], and Ben Niu[1,2]

[1] Shenyang Institute of Automation, Chinese Academy of Sciences, Shenyang
[2]Graduate school of the Chinese Academy of Sciences, Beijing
{hexiaoxian, ylzhu}@sia.cn

Abstract. Inspired by the information interaction of individuals in swarm intelligence, a new algorithm for combinatorial optimization is proposed, which is called as Route-Exchange Algorithm (REA). This is a heuristic approach, in which the individuals of the swarm search the state space independently and simultaneously. When one encounters another in the process, they would interact with each other, exchange the information of routes toured, and utilize the more valuable experiences to improve their own search efficiency. An elite strategy is designed to avoid vibrations. The algorithm has been applied to Traveling Salesman Problem (TSP) and assignment problem in this paper. Some benchmark functions are tested in the experiments. The results indicate the algorithm can quickly converge to the optimal solution with quite low cost.

1 Introduction

Since the social insects have evolved to fit the ever-changing environments for millions of years, it is believed that their behaviors are most effective in the collective way. Therefore, scientists have been returning to social insects for heuristics recently, such as ants, bees etc. In 1991, Marco Dorigo was inspired by the forage behaviors of ants, and proposed Ant Colony Optimizer (ACO) [1] for distributed optimization problems. After that, J. Kennedy and R. C. Eberhart were inspired by the forage behaviors of birds and fish, and proposed Particle Swarm Optimizer (PSO) [2] for continuous optimization problems. These methods have been applied to many problems and proved successful. Since then, there have been many analogous methods [3], [4], [5] reported.

Social insects are usually characterized by self-organization. Complex collective behavior emerges from the interactions of individuals who exhibit simple behaviors by themselves. In social insects, central control is not necessarily needed. Every individual is self-autonomous. They can only obtain local information, and interact with their geographical neighbors. They can also change the local environment or mark in the local environment to interact with the remote individuals indirectly, namely stigmergy. These features all characterize swarm intelligence. Swarm intelligence is

* This work is supported by the National Natural Science Foundation, China (No. 70431003) and the National Basic Research Program, China (2002CB312204).

D.-S. Huang, K. Li, and G.W. Irwin (Eds.): ICIC 2006, LNBI 4115, pp. 192–200, 2006.

defined as any attempt to design algorithms or distributed problem-solving devices inspired by the collective behaviors of the social insect colonies and other animal societies [6]. Generally speaking, swarm intelligence denotes that more complex intelligence emerges from the interactions of individuals who behave as a swarm [1], [6].

In the swarm systems, environment, individual and behavior rule are all sufficiently considered by researchers as three elementary factors [7]. Based on them, however, systematical and general theory still cannot be established. In fact, the information interaction of the individuals is very important. All methods mentioned above imply the information interactions, and it plays a key role for solving problems. In this paper we focused on the information interactions, and proposed a novel algorithm for combinatorial optimization. It is called as Route-Exchange Algorithm (REA), in which each individual put the better experiences in its memory by interacting with others, and behaves according to the best experiences in the next repetition.

The new approach is applied to solve traveling salesman problem (TSP) and assignment problem firstly. Since they are classical combinatorial optimization problems, various approaches for them have been reported [8], [9], [10]. Though REA is just a new computational method, it has shown its efficiency in the solving process. This paper is organized as follows. Section 2 describes REA. It is applied to TSP in section 3 and assignment problem in section 4. Section 5 gives some conclusions and remarks.

2 Route-Exchange Algorithm

Assuming a finite state space of a problem, each state can be denoted by a node. If individual can transits between state c_i and state c_j, then node c_i and c_j is connected. Meanwhile, the cost of the transition is denoted by d_{ij}. Solving the problem implies finding the shortest route to the given state with some constraint conditions.

The REA is a heuristic approach inspired by the information interactions of population, in which every individual searches the state space independently and simultaneously. As far as people are concerned, if a number of them are asked to fulfill the same task independently, they would interact with each other, and learn from each other to improve their own performances. This mechanism is applied in the route-exchange algorithm.

2.1 Search Process of Individuals

Given a complete graph of n nodes, m individuals are required to find the shortest Hamiltonian cycle independently from different starting nodes with the same velocity v, where $m \leq n$. They could encounter the fellows somewhere in the process, which enable them to interact information. Each individual has two storages: one is for the permutation of nodes $(c_{\pi(1)}, c_{\pi(2)}, \cdots, c_{\pi(r)})$ visited by itself in the current iteration, another is for the best permutation $(c_{\pi^*(1)}, c_{\pi^*(2)}, \cdots, c_{\pi^*(q)})$ visited by itself or others ever encountered in the current repetition. For the convenience of depiction, we denote the former with *route-storage-A, RS_A* for short, and the latter with *RS_B*. When two individuals encounter, they would compare the quality of the two routes visited in the current repetition with each other, put the better one into *RS_B*, and continue to tour. In the next repetition, the individual would prefer *RS_B* of previous repetition and follow it first, then previous *RS_A*.

2.2 State Transition Function

As for the *k*th individual, if he is at node i sometime, then the probability that he selects the node j as his next node is as follows:

$$p_{ij}^{k}=\begin{cases}\dfrac{(\eta_{ij})^{\alpha}\cdot\rho_{B}}{\sum\limits_{r\in allowed_k}(\eta_{ir})^{\alpha}}, l_{ij}\in RS\_B_{k}\\ \dfrac{(\eta_{ij})^{\alpha}\cdot\rho_{A}}{\sum\limits_{r\in allowed_k}(\eta_{ir})^{\alpha}}, (l_{ij}\in RS\_A_{k})\wedge(l_{ij}\notin RS\_B_{k})\\ \dfrac{(\eta_{ij})^{\alpha}\cdot\rho_{C}}{\sum\limits_{r\in allowed_k}(\eta_{ir})^{\alpha}}, else\end{cases} \tag{1}$$

where $\eta_{ij}=1/d_{ij}$, l_{ij} denotes the edge (i,j), $allowed_k$ denotes the set of all candidate nodes when the *k*th individual is at node *i*, ρ_A, ρ_B and ρ_C are selection parameters, $\rho_C<\rho_A<\rho_B$, and α is a control parameter.

2.3 Encounter Operation

Given that the *k*th individual reaches the node i at time T_k, and the *l*th individual reaches the same node at time T_l. If the inequality (2) is satisfied, then the two individuals are judged encountered.

$$|T_k-T_l|\leq\frac{\bar{d}_{ij}}{\beta v},\ j\in Neighbor_i \tag{2}$$

where $Neighbor_i$ is the set of nodes connected directly with node i, and β is a control parameter.

In order to evaluate the quality of the route $(c_{\pi(1)},\cdots,c_{\pi(q)})$, we have G that

$$G = \left(\frac{1}{q}\right)^{\delta} \cdot \frac{\sum_{i=1}^{q-1} d_{i,i+1}}{q} \tag{3}$$

where δ is a control parameter. The smaller the value of G is, the better the quality of the route is.

2.4 Elite Strategy

We have designed an elite strategy to avoid vibrations. After each repetition, the individual who has the best results in the current repetition is required to save his experience, and take the same tour in the next repetition. In this way, the best individual can keep his capability of influence on others, and accelerate others to improve their fitness.

2.5 Step by Step Procedure of REA

```
Step1: Initialize

Put all individuals on different nodes randomly, NC=1.

Step 2: Search the State Space

For each individual, tour the nodes by Formula (1) with
velocity v.

Step 3: Encounter Judgment and Operations

For each node, calculate the time T that every individ-
ual reaches it, determine whether two individuals en-
counter with each other according to Equality (2). If
yes, compare their routes with G in Formula (3) and put
the better routes into RS_B.

Step 4: Elite Strategy

Find the individual who has the best results in the
current repetition, put the route of RS_A into RS_B.

Step 5: Stop Criterion

If NC=NC_max, stop the program and return the results,
otherwise, NC=NC+1, select the first node of RS_B as
the starting node and return to the next repetition. If
RS_B is empty, take the first node of RS_A instead.
```

3 REA for TSP

Traveling salesman problem (TSP) is probably the most well-known NP-hard combinatorial optimization problem. The task of the traveling salesman problem is to find the shortest route for a traveling salesman to visit all the cities once and only once, and return to the starting city, which is also known as a Hamiltonian cycle. The problem can be described as follows.

Given a set of cities $C=\{c_1,c_2,\cdots,c_n\}$, for each pair (c_i,c_j), $i\neq j$, let $d(c_i,c_j)$ be the distance between city c_i and c_j. Solving the TSP entails finding a permutation π^* of the cities $(c_{\pi^*(1)},\cdots,c_{\pi^*(n)})$, such that

$$\sum_{i=1}^{n} d(c_{\pi^*(i)},c_{\pi^*(i+1)}) \leq \sum_{i=1}^{n} d(c_{\pi(i)},c_{\pi(i+1)}), \forall \pi \neq \pi^*, (n+1)\equiv 1 \quad (4)$$

In the symmetric TSP $d(c_i,c_j)=d(c_j,c_i), \forall i,j$, while in the asymmetric TSP this condition is not satisfied. In this work we consider the symmetric TSP.

REA is designed for TSP. It can be easily coded into program. We tested it on some TSP instances defined in the TSPLIB [11]. The experiments were conducted on several Windows XP Pentium IV 1.60 GHz PCs with 256 Mbytes of memory. The results of the instances are summarized in Table 1. The first column stands for the names of the test instances, the second for exact optimal tour length for each problem given in the TSPLIB. The third column stands for the best results we have obtained, the fourth to the sixth for the results in each run time, the seventh for the average results, and the eighth for the relative error (Err), respectively, where the relative error is calculated as

$$Err=\frac{Ave-Opt}{Opt}\times 100\% \quad (5)$$

The ninth column denotes the repetition times required, and the last denotes the number of individuals employed in the program.

Table 1 indicates that the proposed route-exchange algorithm can be used to solve symmetric TSP effectively. It can be seen that among 8 test problems, the maximum relative error is 6.81% (of the test problem Eil51) and the average relative error of all is easily calculated to be 3.23%. While the number of nodes increases, the repetition times required doesn't increase remarkably. In other words, the results can converge quickly to good solutions, and the complexity of the computation can be kept quite low. Fortunately, we have obtained better solutions than that given in the TSPLIB for

Table 1. Summary of the experiment results

Problem	Opt	Best Result	Run1	Run2	Run3	Ave.	Err(%)	NC_{max}	Ind
Burma14	33.23	31.88	33.23	31.88	33.21	32.77	-1.38	10	10
Ulys-ses22	75.67	75.67	76.06	76.63	75.67	76.12	0.59	30	20
Bayg29	9074	9336	9399	9336	9433	9389	3.47	30	20
Bays29	2020	2097	2097	2097	2107	2067	2.33	30	28
Swiss42	1273	1303	1325	1329	1303	1319	3.61	30	30
Att48	33524	34707	35073	34707	36458	35413	5.63	30	40
Eil51	426	451	451	454	459	455	6.81	30	40
Berlin52	7542	7870	7870	7918	7931	7900	4.75	30	40

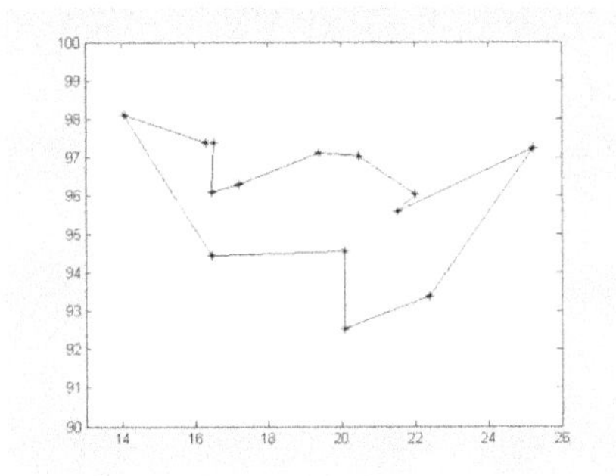

(a) Burma14, length=31.88

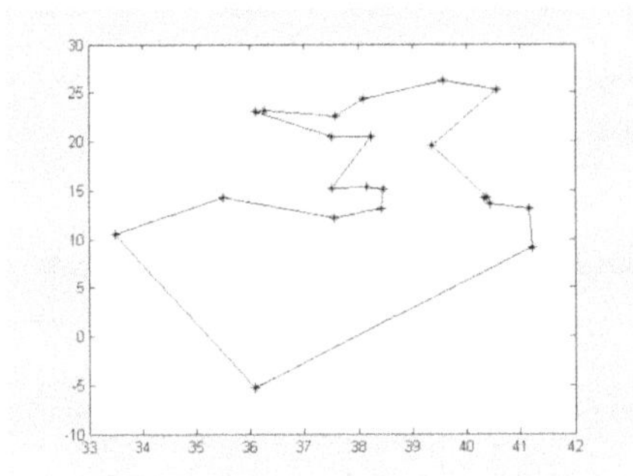

(b) Ulysses22, length=75.67

Fig. 1. The best tours we obtained in the experiments

Burma14. Fig. 1 illustrates the best tours of two instances we tested. Obviously the results are very well.

4 REA for Assignment Problem

There are n jobs can be done by n workers. The cost of job i done by worker j is c_{ij}. Assuming one worker can only do one job, the objective is to assign jobs to right workers to minimize the total cost.

Since the famous Hungarian method for the assignment problem was proposed in 1955 [12], various approaches for assignment, quadratic assignment have been proposed in past five decades. Although there are many special topics in this area [13], such as multi-dimensional assignment, dynamic assignment and constrained assignment [14], the foundation of all assignment problems is the basic assignment problem and Quadratic Assignment Problem (QAP).

We denote the jobs and workers as two types of node sets J and W. The distance of node c_i ($c_i \in J$) and c_j ($c_j \in W$) is denoted with d_{ij}, which is the cost of job

i done by worker j. When applying REA to the assignment, individuals cannot select more than one node in the same type of node set continuously. In addition, if there are u nodes in the individual's *RS_A*, we set η_{ij} that

$$\eta_{ij} = \begin{cases} d_{ij}, (u+1)/2 = 0 \\ 1/d_{ij}, else \end{cases} \tag{6}$$

If the length of the route in *RS_A* is denoted with len, and the individual will go to node c_j from c_i, then the increase of length is

$$len_{u+1} = \begin{cases} len_u, (u+1)/2 = 0 \\ len_u + d_{ij}, else \end{cases} \tag{7}$$

Table 2. The cost matrix of 10 jobs and 10 workers

i\j	1	2	3	4	5	6	7	8	9	10
1	7	33	91	96	5	7	73	46	20	79
2	19	57	4	4	80	66	53	24	91	23
3	40	47	16	73	81	40	65	35	84	16
4	87	76	40	99	1	90	76	51	47	24
5	98	47	67	56	88	49	63	34	86	42
6	44	7	35	50	46	57	89	50	83	30
7	63	44	76	37	15	80	17	42	77	85
8	41	34	88	90	39	60	52	52	93	1
9	56	85	46	53	37	10	73	14	16	93
10	91	55	95	68	44	13	78	31	50	77

Table 3. The best solution for the assignment problem

Job i	1	2	3	4	5	6	7	8	9	10
Worker j	1	4	3	5	8	2	7	10	9	6
Cost C_{ij}	7	4	16	1	34	7	17	1	16	13

Table 4. The performance of REA for examples of different size

Example	1	2	3	4	5
Size	20	30	40	50	60
Best Val.	154	189	191	174	169
Mean Val.	154	189	192.45	174	173.33
Max Val.	154	189	198	174	182
Best Rate	1	1	0.64	1	0.84

For an example of 10 jobs, its cost matrix was generated via a random number generator as shown in Table 2. After 20 repetitions, the best solution achieved is shown in Table 3.

The optimal value is 116. By Hungarian method, we can confirm that the achieved solution is optimal.

To test the performance of REA, we run it on several randomly generated examples of different size. For each example, we run the program of REA for 50 times by starting from different random nodes. The achieved best values, maximum values, mean values and the rate to achieve the best solution are shown in Table 4.

From Table 4 we can see that REA can be applied to solving assignment problem successfully. We noticed that the lowest "best rate" occurred in problem 3 instead of problem 4 and problem 5 with larger size, because the best rate depends not only on the size but also on the structure of cost matrix of the problem.

5 Conclusions

In REA, individuals achieve their goals by exchanging information with each other. In this way, the better routes have more chances to be taken. Because the exchange of route information is the most important idea in the algorithm, it is called as route-exchange algorithm. As can be seen in the experiments and results, this algorithm can converge quickly to a good solution with quite low computing complexity. The stagnancy in local optimum, which is generally existent as a defect in the analogous other algorithms, can be effectively avoided. Also, the elite strategy we designed plays a very important role in this algorithm, which helps to attract other individuals to the global optimum step by step.

On the other hand, it can be seen that the information interaction based on swarm intelligence is worth well exploring in the context of solving optimization problems. Interaction rule is the most important rule in a swarm system, which has showed its great powers. There may be a lot of algorithms inspired by it emerging in the near future.

References

1. Bonabeau, E., Dorigo, M., Theraulaz, G.: Swarm Intelligence-from Natural to Artificial System. Oxford University Press, New York (1999)
2. Kennedy, J., Eberhart, R. C.: Particle Swarm Optimization, Proceedings of IEEE International Conference on Neural Networks, Piscataway, NJ,(1995) 1942-1948
3. Zhong, W.C., Liu, J., Xue, M.Z., Jiao, L.C.: "A Multiagent Genetic Algorithm for Global Numerical Optimization", IEEE Trans. on System, Man, and Cybernetics-Part B, 34(2), (2004)1128-1141
4. Liu. J., Zhong, W.C., Liu. F., Jiao. L.C.: Organizational Coevolutionary Classification Algorithm for Radar Target Recognition, Journal of Infrared and Millimeter Waves, 23 (3), (2004) 208-212
5. Du, H.F., Jiao, L.C.: Clonal Operator Antibody Clone Algorithms. In: Proceedings of 2002 International Conference on Machine Learning and Cybernetics, Beijing, China (2002) 506-510

6. Kennedy, J., R. C. Eberhart., Y. Shi.: Swarm Iintelligence. Morgan Kaufmann Publishers, San Francisco (2001)
7. Han, J., Cai, Q.S.: Emergent Intelligence in AER Model, Chinese Journal of Pattern Recognition and Artificial Intelligence, 15(2), (2002)134-142
8. Kirkpatrick, S., Gelatt, C. D., Vecchi, M. P.: Optimization by Simulated Annealing, Science, No.220 (1983) 671-680
9. Grefenstette, J., Gopal, R., Rosimaita, B., Gucht, D. Van.: Genetic Aalgorithms for the Traveling Ssalesman Problem, Proceedings of the International Conference on Genetics Algorithms and their Applications, (1985) 160-168
10. Croes, G. A.: A Method for Solving Traveling Salesman Problems, Operations Research, No. 6 (1958)791-812
11. http:// www.iwr.uni-heideberg.de/groups/comopt/software/TSPLIB95
12. Kuhn, H. W.: The Hungarian Method for the Assignment Problem, Naval Research Logistics Quart, No.2 (1955) 83-97
13. Burkard, R. E.: Selected Topics on Assignment Problems, Discrete Applied Mathematics, 123 (2002)257-302
14. Caron, G., Hansen, P., Jaumard,B.: The Assignment Problem with Seniority and Job Priority Constraints, Operations Research, Vol. 47, No. 3 (1999) 449-453

Stability Analysis of Swarm Based on Double Integrator Model*

Dan Jin and Lixin Gao

Institute of Operations Research and Control Sciences,
Wenzhou University, Zhejiang 325000, China
jindan0702@163.com, lxgao@wzu.edu.cn

Abstract. In this paper, we consider an M-member individual-based continuous-time double integrator swarm model in an n-dimensional space. The swarm model based on the Newton's law is more suitable to describe the swarm aggregation and has wide practical applications. We present stability analysis for the case of linear attraction and bounded repulsion to characterize swarm cohesiveness, size and ultimate motions while in a cohesive group. Finally, some numerical examples and simulation results are presented to illustrate the effectiveness of the swarm model.

1 Introduction

In recent years, the problem of coordination and control of multiple agents is becoming one of the hotspots. This is partly due to broad applications of multi-agent systems in many areas including cooperative control of unmanned air vehicles, flocking of birds, schooling for underwater vehicles, distributed sensor networks, etc. Although the application backgrounds are different, the fundamental principles are very similar, that is, coordinating multiple agents to achieve a goal of the whole system.

Aggregating behavior of multi-member, such as flocks of birds, schools of fish, herds of animals, and colonies of bacteria [4,7,8,9], draws many scientists' attention, which mainly lines in the researching value of the swarms' inner operational mechanism of self-organization. From the principle we can use it to the areas of unmanned air vehicles, attitude alignment for cluster of satellites, formation control of multi-robot teams [2,12,13]. The aggregating model used to simulate flock behavior has been presented in [3]. That paper explored an approach based on simulation as an alternative to scripting the paths of each bird individually. The aggregate motion of the simulated flock is created by a distributed behavioral birds choose their own course.

In the early days biologists worked on understanding and modeling of swarming behavior, they brought forward swarm models supposed of attractin/repulsion functions [5,6]. Recently [1,10,11] continued the topic, authors all had

* This work was partly supported by China Postdoctoral Science Foundation of China under Grant 200537121. L. Gao is also a post-doctor of Institute of Systems Science, Chinese Academy of Sciences, Beijing 100080, China.

D.-S. Huang, K. Li, and G.W. Irwin (Eds.): ICIC 2006, LNBI 4115, pp. 201–210, 2006.

proved the swarm could converge to a bounded region, and used the Lyapunov method to show their stability. [11] extended the results in [1] by specifying a class of general attraction/repulsion functions. It is very significant to introduce the "safety area "to the engineering, for example, it can decrease the friction between machines, increase the safe coefficient of operation and so on. The drawback is that the center of the model is stillness, which is inconsistent with biology since any creature is moving. In this paper, we establish a double integrator swarm model which considers the motion of the swarm.

The paper is organized as follows. In section 2, we establish a double integrator model of the swarm. The swarm size after aggregating is discussed in section 3, and the stability analysis of swarm is given in section 4. We also provide numerical simulations to reify our theories in section 5.

2 Model of an Aggregation Swarm

As is known to us, the derivative of position is velocity, and the second derivative of position is acceleration. So if the model is an integrator such as ones in [1,10,11], it is equal to use force to control velocity, but we know the change of velocity needs a process, during the period the acceleration plays an important part, so it is quite necessary to consider the double integrator model, meanwhile it expresses the relation between the force and the acceleration. [11] pointed out that the swarm model should be generalized to a double integrator model based on the Newton's law $F = ma$. The double integrator model is more practical and has more applications. When a swarm arrives to the state of balance, it requires not only the member of the swarm not scattered, but also velocity matching. Thus, we assume the expectant velocity of the swarm member is v_d.

Consider a swarm of M individuals (members) in an n-dimensional Euclidean space. We assume synchronous motion and no time delays, i.e., all the members move simultaneously and know the exact positions of all the other members. Thus, we propose a swarm model in which each agent is expressed in the form of a double integrator:

$$\begin{cases} \dot{x}_i = v_i \\ \dot{v}_i = \sum\limits_{j=1, j\neq i}^{M} g(x_i - x_j) - k(v_i - v_d), \end{cases} \qquad i = 1, 2, ..., M \tag{1}$$

where $x_i \in \mathcal{R}^n$ represents the position of individual i, $v_i \in \mathcal{R}^n$ represents the velocity of individual i, $g : \mathcal{R}^n \to \mathcal{R}^n$ represents the function of attraction and repulsion between individuals, $k \in \mathcal{R}^+$ is a constant.

Consider functions $g(\cdot)$of type

$$g(y) = -y[g_a(\| y \|) - g_r(\| y \|)]$$

where $g_a : \mathcal{R}^+ \to \mathcal{R}^+$ represents the magnitude of the attraction term, whereas $g_r : \mathcal{R}^+ \to \mathcal{R}^+$ represents the magnitude of the repulsion term, the vector y determines the alignment, so the actual attraction and repulsion are $-yg_a(\| y \|)$, and $yg_r(\| y \|)$ respectively, where $\| y \|= \sqrt{y^T y}$ is the Euclidean norm. Assume that $g(\cdot)$ satisfies the following Assumptions.

(A1) $g(\cdot)$ is an odd function that have terms for attraction and repulsion acting in opposite direction, i.e., $g(y) = -g(-y)$.

(A2) There exists a unique distance δ at which we have $g_a(\delta) = g_r(\delta)$. Moreover, we have $g_a(\| y \|) > g_r(\| y \|)$ for $\| y \|> \delta$ and $g_r(\| y \|) > g_a(\| y \|)$ for $\| y \|< \delta$.

(A3) There exist corresponding functions $J_a : \mathcal{R}^+ \rightarrow \mathcal{R}^+$ and $J_r : \mathcal{R}^+ \rightarrow \mathcal{R}^+$ such that

$$\nabla_y J_a(\| y \|) = y g_a(\| y \|) \quad \textit{and} \quad \nabla_y J_r(\| y \|) = y g_r(\| y \|) \ .$$

$J_a(\cdot)$, $J_r(\cdot)$ are the *artificial social potential functions* of the attraction and repulsion between the individuals, respectively.

Assumptions (A1),(A2) and (A3) were introduced by [11]. We denote $\mathcal{G}(\cdot)$ as the set of $g(\cdot)$ which satisfies (A1-A3).

The inter-individual attraction/repulsion is based on an interplay between attraction and repulsion forces with the attraction dominating on large distances, and the repulsion dominating on short distances, and there is a unique constant distance where attraction and repulsion balance. It has been observed that the individuals in swarms desire neither too close (avoiding crowding) nor too far (avoiding dispersion) from other individuals. Too close the distance between two individuals is, they will disperse; too far the distance between two individuals is, they will close. Therefore, the dependence on this kind of functions makes intuitive sense, the size of the swarm is finite.

For simplicity, we use a variable substitution $x_i^{'} = x_i - v_d t$, $v_i^{'} = v_i - v_d$ to the model (1). Then, we can rewrite the model (1) as follows

$$\begin{cases} \dot{x}_i^{'} = \dot{x}_i - v_d = v_i - v_d = v_i^{'} \\ \dot{v}_i^{'} = \dot{v}_i = \sum\limits_{j=1, j\neq i}^{M} g(x_i - x_j) - k(v_i - v_d) \\ \quad\;\; = \sum\limits_{j=1, j\neq i}^{M} g(x_i^{'} - x_j^{'}) - k v_i^{'}, \quad i = 1, 2, ..., M \end{cases} \tag{2}$$

Using x_i, v_i instead of $x_i^{'}, v_i^{'}$ for convenience, the model (2) can be rewritten as

$$\begin{cases} \dot{x}_i = v_i \\ \dot{v}_i = \sum\limits_{j=1, j\neq i}^{M} g(x_i - x_j) - k v_i, \end{cases} \qquad i = 1, 2, ..., M \tag{3}$$

The properties of the swarm model (1) can be obtained by analyzing the swarm model (3). So we analyze the model (3) in this paper for convenience.

It is clear that the center of the swarm should be defined as $\bar{x} = \frac{1}{M} \sum\limits_{i=1}^{M} x_i$.

Thus, the velocity of the center is obtained as $\bar{v} = \dot{\bar{x}} = \frac{1}{M} \sum\limits_{i=1}^{M} \dot{x}_i = \frac{1}{M} \sum\limits_{i=1}^{M} v_i$.

Theorem 1. *The center $\bar{x}$ of the swarm described by model (3) with an attraction/repulsion function $g(\cdot) \in \mathcal{G}(\cdot)$ converges to a fixed point.*

Proof. Consider the model (3), the time derivative of center is given by

$$\begin{aligned}
\dot{\bar{x}} &= \tfrac{1}{M}\sum_{i=1}^{M}\dot{x}_i = \tfrac{1}{M}\sum_{i=1}^{M} v_i = \bar{v} \\
\dot{\bar{v}} &= \tfrac{1}{M}\sum_{i=1}^{M}\dot{v}_i = \tfrac{1}{M}\sum_{i=1}^{M}\left[\sum_{j=1,j\neq i}^{M} g(x_i - x_j) - kv_i\right] \\
&= \tfrac{1}{M}\sum_{i=1}^{M}\left\{\sum_{j=1,j\neq i}^{M} -\left[g_a(\| x_i - x_j \|) - g_r(\| x_i - x_j \|)\right](x_i - x_j) - kv_i\right\} \\
&= -\tfrac{1}{M}\sum_{i=1}^{M-1}\sum_{j=i+1}^{M}\{\left[g_a(\| x_i - x_j \|) - g_r(\| x_i - x_j \|)\right](x_i - x_j) + \\
&\quad \left[g_a(\| x_j - x_i \|) - g_r(\| x_j - x_i \|)\right](x_j - x_i)\} - \tfrac{1}{M}\sum_{i=1}^{M} kv_i \\
&= -k\bar{v}
\end{aligned}$$

So the center of the swarm satisfies

$$\begin{cases} \dot{\bar{x}} = \bar{v} \\ \dot{\bar{v}} = -k\bar{v} \end{cases} \tag{4}$$

From (4), we can get $\bar{v} = \bar{v}(0)e^{-kt}$, $\bar{x} = \bar{x}(0) + \frac{\bar{v}(0)}{k} - \frac{\bar{v}(0)}{k}e^{-kt}$ which means that as $t \to \infty, \bar{v} \to 0$, and $\bar{x} \to \bar{x}(0) + \frac{\bar{v}(0)}{k} \triangleq \xi$(a constant). ∎

Thus, it is clear that as $t \to \infty$, the velocity of the center of the swarm model (1) will tend to v_d, and the center will tend to $v_d t + \xi$, i.e., the center will begin with the initial position and move at the expectant speed v_d.

3 Analysis of Swarm Cohesion

The position difference between the individual i and the center of the swarm is defined as $e_i = x_i - \bar{x}$, and the velocity difference between the individual i and the center of the swarm is defined as $p_i = v_i - \bar{v}$.

In [1,10], the following attraction/repulsion function is considered

$$g(y) = -y\left[a - b\exp\left(-\frac{\| y \|^2}{c}\right)\right] \tag{5}$$

The attraction term is linear and the repulsion term is bounded for (5). In this paper, we extend the function to a kind of $g(\cdot)(\in \mathcal{G}(\cdot))$ which is composed of linear attraction terms and bounded repulsion terms, i.e.,

$$\begin{cases} g_a(\| y \|) = a \\ g_r(\| y \|) \| y \| \leq b \end{cases} \tag{6}$$

where $a > 0, b > 0$ are finite positive constants. The swarm model (1) or (3) using more general attraction/repulsion functions $g(\cdot)(\in \mathcal{G}(\cdot))$ can also be analyzed similarly by using the method given in this paper. $g_a(\| y \|) = a$ means that $g_a(\| y \|)$ is invariant, but it is compatible with the Assumption A2 because $g_r(\| y \|)$ has relation with the distance $\| y \|$.

From (2), we have

$$\dot{e}_i = \dot{x}_i - \dot{\bar{x}} = v_i - \bar{v} = p_i \tag{7}$$

and

$$\begin{aligned} \dot{p}_i &= \dot{v}_i - \dot{\bar{v}} \\ &= \sum_{j=1, j\neq i}^{M} - \left[g_a(\|x_i - x_j\|) - g_r(\|x_i - x_j\|)\right](x_i - x_j) - kv_i + k\bar{v} \\ &= -aMe_i + \sum_{j=1, j\neq i}^{M} g_r(\|x_i - x_j\|)(x_i - x_j) - kp_i \end{aligned} \tag{8}$$

Let $\epsilon_i = col(e_i, p_i), i = 1, ..., M$. Then we have

$$\dot{\epsilon_i} = \begin{pmatrix} \dot{e}_i \\ \dot{p}_i \end{pmatrix} = \left[\begin{pmatrix} 0 & 1 \\ -aM & -k \end{pmatrix} \otimes I_n\right] \epsilon_i + \begin{pmatrix} 0 \\ \sum_{j=1, j\neq i}^{M} g_r(\| x_i - x_j \|)(x_i - x_j) \end{pmatrix}.$$

Let $F = \begin{pmatrix} 0 & 1 \\ -aM & -k \end{pmatrix}$ and $f = \begin{pmatrix} 0 \\ \sum_{j=1, j\neq i}^{M} g_r(\| x_i - x_j \|)(x_i - x_j) \end{pmatrix}$. Then we can obtain eigenvalues of the matrix F as follows

$$\lambda(F) = \frac{-k \pm \sqrt{k^2 - 4aM}}{2}$$

if $\sqrt{k^2 - 4aM} \geq 0$ then $\lambda(F) < 0$, which implies that F is a stable matrix; if $\sqrt{k^2 - 4aM} < 0$, then the real part of $\lambda(F)$ is negative, which also implies that F is a stable matrix. Thus, for any given symmetric positive definite matrix Q, the Lyapunov equation $F^T P + PF = -Q$ has a symmetric positive definite solution matrix P.

The maximum and minimum eigenvalues of any symmetric positive definite matrix S are denoted as $\lambda_{max}(S)$ and $\lambda_{min}(S)$ respectively. Note that for any symmetric positive definite matrix S with fit dimensions the following inequalities are satisfied

$$\lambda_{min}(S) \| \epsilon_i \|^2 \leq \epsilon_i^T S \epsilon_i \leq \lambda_{max}(S) \| \epsilon_i \|^2 . \tag{9}$$

Then we establish the following theorem.

Theorem 2. *Consider the swarm described by model (3) with an attraction/repulsion function $g(\cdot)(\in \mathcal{G}(\cdot))$ given in (6) . As time progresses, all the members of the swarm will converge to a hyperball*

$$B(\bar{x}) = \left\{x : \|x - \bar{x}\| \leq \frac{2\lambda_{max}(P)[(M-1)b]}{\lambda_{min}(Q)}\right\}.$$

Proof. Choose the Lyapunov function $V_i = \epsilon_i^T(P \otimes I_n)\epsilon_i$ for each individual. Then, we have

$$\begin{aligned} \dot{V}_i &= \dot{\epsilon_i}^T(P \otimes I_n)\epsilon_i + \epsilon_i^T(P \otimes I_n)\dot{\epsilon_i} \\ &= ((F \otimes I_n)\epsilon_i + f)^T(P \otimes I_n)\epsilon_i + \epsilon_i^T(P \otimes I_n)((F \otimes I_n)\epsilon_i + f) \\ &= -\epsilon_i^T(Q \otimes I_n)\epsilon_i + 2\epsilon_i^T(P \otimes I_n)f, \end{aligned} \tag{10}$$

from which we can obtain

$$\begin{aligned} \dot{V}_i &\leq -\epsilon_i^T(Q \otimes I_n)\epsilon_i + 2 \parallel \epsilon_i \parallel \lambda_{max}(P)(M-1)b \\ &= -\lambda_{min}(Q) \parallel \epsilon_i \parallel^2 + 2 \parallel \epsilon_i \parallel \lambda_{max}(P)(M-1)b \\ &= - \parallel \epsilon_i \parallel (\lambda_{min}(Q) \parallel \epsilon_i \parallel - 2\lambda_{max}(P)(M-1)b). \end{aligned} \tag{11}$$

If $\parallel \epsilon_i \parallel > \frac{2\lambda_{max}(P)}{\lambda_{min}(Q)}(M-1)b$, then $\dot{V}_i < 0$. This implies that as $t \to \infty$, ϵ_i will converge into the ball around $col(\bar{x}, \bar{v})$ defined by $\parallel \epsilon_i \parallel \leq \frac{2\lambda_{max}(P)}{\lambda_{min}(Q)}(M-1)b$, and $\parallel x_i - \bar{x} \parallel \leq \parallel \epsilon_i \parallel \leq \frac{2\lambda_{max}(P)}{\lambda_{min}(Q)}(M-1)b, i = 1, 2, ..., M$. This proves the theorem. ∎

Remark 1. Note that $\parallel v_i - \bar{v} \parallel \leq \parallel \epsilon_i \parallel \leq \frac{2\lambda_{max}(P)}{\lambda_{min}(Q)}(M-1)b$, it expresses that the velocity of agent i can not exceed $\frac{2\lambda_{max}(P)}{\lambda_{min}(Q)}(M-1)b$ relative to the velocity of the center; once $\parallel v_i - \bar{v} \parallel$ or $\parallel x_i - \bar{x} \parallel$ exceeds the bound, the agent will run towards to minimize its potential. Finally, the distance and speed relative to the center will not exceed $\frac{2\lambda_{max}(P)}{\lambda_{min}(Q)}(M-1)b$.

Remark 2. The above result is an asymptotic result, i.e., $x_i(t) \to B(\bar{x})$ as $t \to \infty$. However, from stability theory we can show that the swarm of any size a little larger than $\frac{2\lambda_{max}(P)}{\lambda_{min}(Q)}(M-1)b$ will be formed in a finite time.

From (9),(10) and $g_r(\parallel y \parallel) \parallel y \parallel \leq b$, we have

$$\dot{V}_i \leq -\frac{\lambda_{min}(Q)}{\lambda_{max}(P)}V_i + 2\frac{1}{\sqrt{\lambda_{min}(P)}}\sqrt{V_i}\lambda_{max}(P)(M-1)b \tag{12}$$

Set $\beta = \frac{\lambda_{min}(Q)}{2\lambda_{max}(P)}$. From (12) we have

$$\begin{aligned} \dot{V}_i &\leq -2\beta V_i + 2\frac{1}{\sqrt{\lambda_{min}(P)}}\sqrt{V_i}\lambda_{max}(P)(M-1)b \\ &= -\beta V_i - \left[\sqrt{\beta V_i} - \frac{\lambda_{max}(P)(M-1)b}{\sqrt{\lambda_{min}(P)\beta}}\right]^2 + \frac{[\lambda_{max}(P)(M-1)b]^2}{\lambda_{min}(P)\beta} \\ &\leq -\beta V_i + \frac{[\lambda_{max}(P)(M-1)b]^2}{\lambda_{min}(P)\beta} \end{aligned} \tag{13}$$

Then we obtain

$$V_i \leq V_i(0)e^{-\beta t} + \frac{[\lambda_{max}(P)(M-1)b]^2}{\lambda_{min}(P)\beta^2}(1 - e^{-\beta t}) \tag{14}$$

where $V_i(0)$ is the value when the time $t = 0$, the above function implies that the swarm will congregate with a convergence exponent no less than β.

Remark 3. The right hand of Equation (14) will tend to $\frac{[\lambda_{max}(P)(M-1)b]^2}{\lambda_{min}(P)\beta^2}$ as t tends to infinity, then $V_i \leq \frac{[\lambda_{max}(P)(M-1)b]^2}{\lambda_{min}(P)\beta^2}$. From (9) $\| \epsilon_i \| \leq \frac{1}{\sqrt{\lambda_{min}(P)}}\sqrt{V_i} \leq \frac{\lambda_{max}(P)(M-1)b}{\lambda_{min}(P)\beta} = \frac{\lambda_{max}(P)}{\lambda_{min}(P)}\frac{2\lambda_{max}(P)(M-1)b}{\lambda_{min}(Q)}$, the bound is $\frac{\lambda_{max}(P)}{\lambda_{min}(P)}$ times bigger than the primary bound, the reason consists in Equation (12) which magnifies relative to Equation (11). Comparatively, the former bound is better than the latter, but from the latter we can get the boundary about the convergent rate of swarm.

4 Stability Analysis of a Cohesive Swarm

Section 3 shows the swarm members described with model (3) will converge into a bounded region. It does not mention anything about how the swarm members move. This issue is investigated in this section. We first define the state $x = col(x_1, x_2, \cdots, x_M)$ as the vector of the swarm members' positions and the state $v = col(v_1, v_2, \cdots, v_M)$ as the vector of their velocities. We will prove that $v(t) \to 0$ as $t \to \infty$ in the next theorem for swarm model (3), which means that the swarm will converge to a constant configuration. Moreover, we conclude that the configuration to which the swarm members converge move at the velocity of v_d for model (1).

Theorem 3. *Consider the swarm described by model (3) with an attraction/repulsion function $g(\cdot)(\in \mathcal{G}(\cdot))$ given in (6). As $t \to \infty$, $v(t) \to 0$.*

Proof. Choose the (generalized) Lyapunov function $J : \mathcal{R}^{nM} \times \mathcal{R}^{nM} \to \mathcal{R}$ defined as

$$J(x,v) = \sum_{i=1}^{M-1}\sum_{j=i+1}^{M}[J_a(\| x_i - x_j \|) - J_r(\| x_i - x_j \|)] + \frac{1}{2}v_i^T v_i$$

Calculating the gradient of $J(x,v)$ with respect of x_i yields

$$\begin{aligned}\nabla_{x_i}J(x,v) &= \sum_{j=1,j\neq i}^{M}[\nabla_{x_i}J_a(\| x_i - x_j \|) - \nabla_{x_i}J_r(\| x_i - x_j \|)] \\ &= \sum_{j=1,j\neq i}^{M}[(x_i - x_j)g_a(\| x_i - x_j \|) - (x_i - x_j)g_r(\| x_i - x_j \|)] \\ &= -\dot{v}_i - kv_i\end{aligned} \tag{15}$$

Now, taking the time derivative of the Lyapunov function along the motion of the system we obtain

$$\begin{aligned}\dot{J}(x,v) &= [\nabla_x J(x,v)]^T\dot{x} + \sum_{i=1}^{M}\dot{v_i}^T v_i = \sum_{i=1}^{M}[\nabla_{x_i}J(x,v)]^T\dot{x}_i + \sum_{i=1}^{M}\dot{v_i}^T v_i \\ &= \sum_{i=1}^{M}(-\dot{v_i} - kv_i)^T v_i + \sum_{i=1}^{M}\dot{v_i}^T v_i = -k\sum_{i=1}^{M}\| v_i \|^2 \leq 0\end{aligned} \tag{16}$$

for all $t \geq 0$. From theorem 2, the swarm members move in a bounded region. Then, using the LaSalle's Invariance Principle we conclude that as $t \to \infty$, the swarm will converge to the largest invariant subset of the set defined as

$$\Omega = \{(x,v) : \dot{J}(x,v) = 0\} = \{(x,v) : \dot{v} = 0\}$$

which implies that as $t \to \infty$, $v(t) \to 0$. ∎

Note that $v(t) \to 0$ implies $x(t) \to C$(a constant), meanwhile it implies the distance between any two individuals is fixed, i.e., the configuration of the swarm is fixed. Relative to model (1), the results above provides us information that the swarm with a fixed configuration runs with a constant velocity v_d as $v(t) \to 0$.

5 Simulation Examples

In this section we will provide some simulation examples in order to illustrate the results of this paper. We choose $n = 3$ for the simulation for easy visualization. However, note that the results hold for any n. The swarm model considered in this section is model (3), and the attraction/repulsion function $g(\cdot)(\in \mathcal{G}(\cdot))$ is given in (6) with the parameters $a = b = 0.2$.

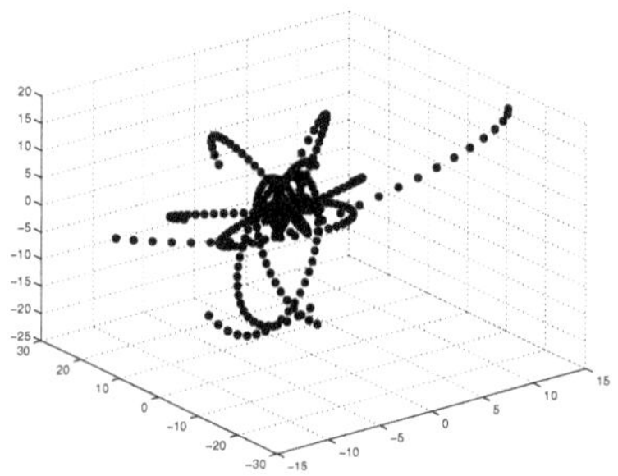

Fig. 1. The paths of swarm members

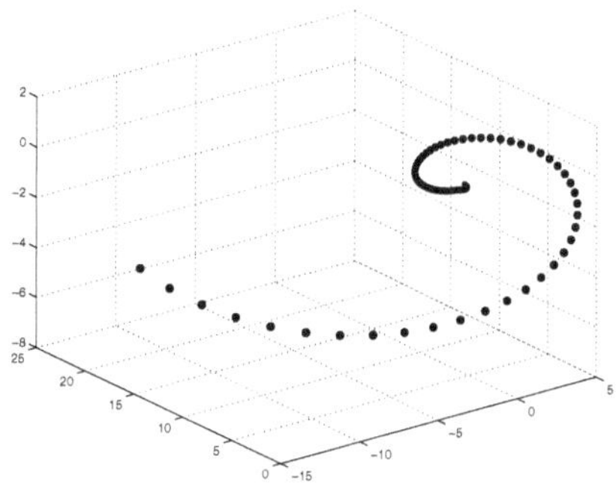

Fig. 2. The path of a member

The plot in Fig. 1 shows the behavior of $M = 10$ swarm members with initial positions and velocities brought at random. As one can see, the individuals form a cohesive cluster as predicted by the theory. The center of the swarm will be fixed, in fact, it will run with a constant velocity v_d in model (1). One member's path is depicted in Fig. 2. As the figure depicts, the member's path is gyroidal, which accords with practicality, all the swarm's members can not aggregate in a direct way since every member has its initial velocity, besides, the direction of its velocity is stochastic.

As to the velocity, see Fig. 3 and Fig. 4. Here all the figures are simulated with the model (3), so the velocity will tend to zero. Of course the velocity will tend to v_d if we use the model (1).

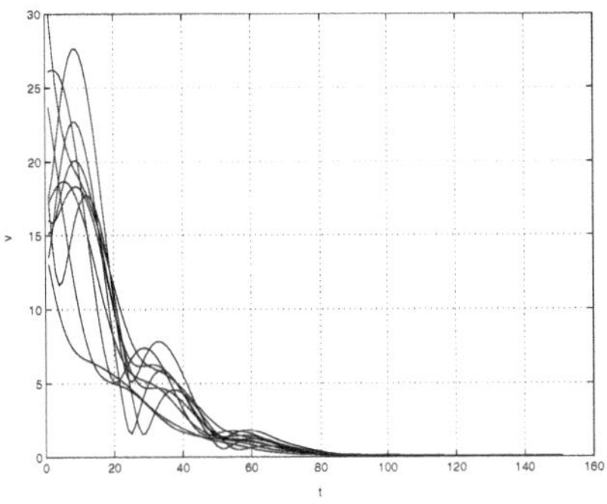

Fig. 3. The speed of swarm members

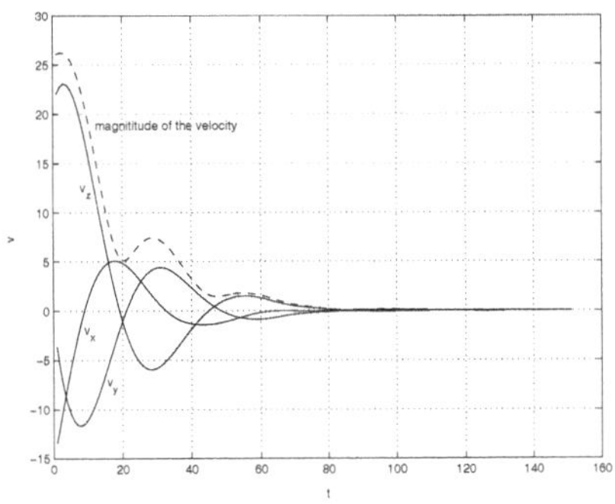

Fig. 4. The speed of a member, v_x, v_y, v_z are the components of the velocity

6 Conclusion

In this paper we consider a double integrator model of aggregating for multi-agent system, using Lyapunov function to analyze swarms' stability. Actually, the swarm model discussed here can be viewed as performing distributed optimization using a distributed gradient method. The attraction/repulsion functions considered here are not limited to only the swarm model, they can be used to describe anisotropic swarms with reciprocal and nonreciprocal interactions [10] (one integrator model), or swarms moving in a noisy environment [15]. We get our inspiration from biology, otherwise, aggregating has important relations to control and automation. we believe that our work is helpful to the multi-agent coordination and control literature.

Our model is a kinematic model, it is fit for individuals which move basing on the Newton's law in an environment. In our model the initial positions and initial velocities are known, and all the individuals know the exact relative positions of all the other individuals, it is a model's advantage. In biological swarms, the ranges of individuals' senses are limited, i.e., each individual usually can see (or sense) only the individuals in its neighborhood. Therefore, the final behavior of the swarms described by our model may not be in harmony with real biological swarms very well. Nevertheless, the analysis about the swarm's behavior is a first step toward developing the stability theory for aggregating of swarms. Moreover, in engineering applications the sensing limitations of the agents can be overcome with technologies such as global positioning system (GPS).

By observing the model, we know that the model is global basing on the definition of the attraction/repulsion function over the entire domain, and holds for any dimension n . In the future, we can extend the work to the local information problem, communication or sensing delay problem, time varying attraction/repulsion problem and so on.

References

1. Gazi, V., Passino, K. M.: Stability Analysis of Swarms. IEEE Transactions on Automatic Control **48** (2003) 692–697
2. Jadbabaie, A., Lin, J., Morse, A. S.: Coordination of Groups of Mobile Autonomous Agents Using Nearest Neighbor Rules. IEEE Transaction on Automatic Control **48** (2003) 988–1001
3. Reynolds, C. W.: Flocks, Herds, and Schools: A Distributed Behavioral Model. Computer Graphics, ACM SIGGRAPH '87 Conference Proceedings **21** (1987) 25–34
4. Mogilner, A., Edelstein-Keshet, L., Bent, L., Spiros, A.: Mutual Interactions, Potentials, and Individual Distance in a Social Aggregation. J. Math. Boil. **47** (2003) 353–389
5. Breder, C. M.: Equations Descriptive of Fish Schools and Other Animal Aggregations. Ecology **35** (1954) 361–370
6. Bender, J., Fenton, R.: On the Flow Capacity of Automated Highways. Transport. Sci. **4** (1970) 52–63
7. H.-S. Niwa, Mathematical Model for the Size Distribution of Fish Schools. Computers Math. Applic. **32** (1996) 79–88
8. Niwa, H.-S.: Self-organizing approach to fish schooling. J.Theor. Biol. **171** (1996) 123–136
9. Warbuton, K., Lazarus, J.: Tendency-distance Models of Social Cohesion in Animal Groups. J.Theoret. Biolo. **150** (1991) 473–488
10. Chu, T., Wang, L., Mu, S.: Collective Behavior of an Anisotropic Swarm Model. The 16th International Symposium on Mathematical Theory of Networks and Systems, Leuven, Belgium, 2004
11. Gazi, V., Passino, K. M.: A Class of Attractions/Repulsion Functions for Stable Swarm Aggregations. Int. J. Control **77** (2004) 1567–1579
12. Fax, A., Murray, R. M.: Information Flow and Cooperative Control of Vehicle Formation. IEEE Transactions on Automatic Control **49** (2004) 1453–1464
13. Hong, Y., Hu, J., Gao, L.: Tracking Control for Multi-agent Consensus with an Active Leader and Variable Topology, Automatica (to appear)
14. Gazi, V., Passino, K. M.: Stability Analysis of Social Foraging Swarms. IEEE Transactions on Systems, Man, and Cybernetics-part B: Cybernetics **34** (2004)
15. Liu, Y., Passino, K. M.: Stable Social Foraging Swarms in a Noisy Environment. IEEE Transactions on Automatic Control **49** (2004) 1453–1464

Interest Based Negotiation Automation

Xuehong Tao[1], Yuan Miao[2], ZhiQi Shen[3], ChunYan Miao[4], and Nicola Yelland[5]

[1] School of Education, Victoria University, P.O. Box 14428, Melbourne, VIC 8001, Australia
xuehongTao@gmail.com
[2] School of Computer Science and Mathematics, Victoria University, P.O. Box 14428, Melbourne, VIC 8001, Australia
yuan.Miao@vu.edu.au
[3] Information Communication Institute of Singapore, Nanyang Technological University, Nanyang Ave, Singapore 639798
zqshen@ntu.edu.sg
[4] School of Computer Engineering, Nanyang Technological University, Nanyang Ave, Singapore 639798
ascymiao@ntu.edu.sg
[5] School of Education, Victoria University, P.O. Box 14428, Melbourne, VIC 8001, Australia
nicola.Yelland@vu.edu.au

Abstract. The negotiation in general sense, as one of the most fundamental and powerful interaction of human beings, represents the dynamic process of exchanging information and perspectives towards mutual understanding and agreements. Interest based negotiation allows negotiators to discuss the concerns behind the negotiation issues so that a mutually acceptable win-win solution is more likely to be reached. This paper, for the first time, proposes a computational model for interest based negotiation automation which enables the automation of the fundamental elements of negotiation. Based on the model, algorithms are designated to automate the fundamental elements with practical computational complexity. This model provides not only a theoretical foundation for software agent based negotiation automation, but also a practical approach.

1 Interest Based Negotiation

Negotiation, as one of the most fundamental and powerful interaction, represents comprehensive human interactive activities, varying from simple information interchanges, to cooperation and coordination, in wide areas including education, business process, entertainment and other social activities. Similar as Information Systems which free people from the repeated or routine works, negotiation automation is able to free people from tedious interactions including both trivial actions, e.g. selection of a new laptop computer for purchase, and complex tasks, e.g. supply chain management, learning path selection and composition of interactive movies.

The traditional negotiation is Position Based Negotiation (PBN). In a PBN, the involved parties are firmly committed to their bargaining positions. They exchange proposals and counter proposals in the anticipation that one or more parties will compromise to achieve a settlement of the dispute. It is also know as win-lose negotiation. A position of a negotiation party tells others what he/she wants, and reflects his/her

D.-S. Huang, K. Li, and G.W. Irwin (Eds.): ICIC 2006, LNBI 4115, pp. 211 – 222, 2006.

point of view on a certain issue. It does not tell others about the complex decision making process that lead to the position; nor does it provide others the opportunity to take his/her interests into account. In position based negotiation, the involved parties argue only their positions. Their underlying interests may never be explicitly mentioned. If no agreement on the positions, the negotiation fails.

Interest Based Negotiation (IBN) [1] is a process that seeks to discover and satisfy the underlying interests of parties rather than to meet the stated positions or demands that they bring to negotiation. It is also known as win-win negotiation. Interests of a negotiation party tell others why he/she wants something. They reflect his/her underlying concern, needs or desire behind an issue. In interest based negotiation, the interests of participants are identified and explored, which helps them to understand the others' perspectives instead of simply reacting to the positions. By discussing the reasons behind the positions, mutually acceptable agreement is more likely to be reached. Interest based negotiation is therefore not only a much more powerful tool for conflict resolution, but also a good tool for coordination and cooperation.

For example, both party A and party B want to buy a same land. The position of each party is to have the land. There is no settlement in PBN unless one party gives in. Though, the underlying reason for having the land could be that, party A, as an international company, wants to have a local office in that location, and party B, as a real estate developer, wants to generate income by building something on the land for sale. Using IBN, the agreement could be that, B builds an office block and sells to A.

Software (intelligent) agent, as a new type of autonomous components for construction of open, complex and dynamic systems, is one of the most suitable software entities to carry out negotiation automation. In fact, software agent based negotiation automation has gained increasing prominence. On the other hand, agent community also takes negotiation as a core part of agent interactions. Some negotiation definitions are even presented in software agent context. For example, Jennings et al.[2] defined negotiation as the process by which a group of agents try to come to a mutually acceptable agreement on some matter. Negotiation underpins attempts to cooperate and coordinate and is required both when the agents are self interested and when they are cooperative. However, these pioneer work limits at introducing negotiation into computer science or software agent literature. They remain at a high level of abstraction, which lack of theoretical foundation for turning this opportunity into reality.

The research of negotiation automation in software agent community can be categorized into three main approaches: game theoretic approach [3][4], heuristic approach [5][6] and argumentation-based approach [7][8]. The game theoretic approach models a negotiation situation as a game, and attempts to find dominant strategies for each participant by applying game theory techniques. The heuristic-based approach models agents' decision making heuristically during the course of the negotiation. In both of the approaches, negotiators are not allowed to exchange additional information other than the proposal. This is a restriction on supporting general negotiations especially when the participants have limited information about the environment, or when their decisions depend on those of the others.

The Argumentation-Based approach allows agents to exchange additional information such as justifications, critiques, and other forms of persuasive information within the interactions. It enables agents to gain a wider understanding of their counterparts, thereby make it easier to resolve certain conflicts, for an instance, conflicts due to incomplete knowledge. This approach has been advocated as a promising means of resolving conflicts within agent societies. For example, Rahwan et al [9] tried to equip intelligent agents with the ability to conduct interest based negotiation using argumentation based approach. They studied the relationships between agent's goals and the types of arguments that may influence other agents' decision, as well as defined a set of locutions that can be used in the negotiation procedure.

Overall, the existing literature in argumentation based negotiation automation remains at a high level discussion. Theoretical foundation has not yet been reported towards the realization of negotiation automation. For example, there is no research to automatically generate the arguments for the process of interest based negotiation. This paper proposes a general computational model for negotiation automation, based on which, algorithms are proposed to automate the process. The rest of the paper is organized as the follows. Section 2 proposes the general computational model for interest based negotiation automation. Section 3 are the algorithms to automate the negotiation. Section 4 illustrates the approach with a case study and Section 5 concludes the paper.

2 Computational Model of Interest Based Negotiation

The Computational Model of Interest Based Negotiation (CMIBN) proposed in this section is a generic conceptual model representing the core parts of negotiation in a form that can be feasibly realized by computing techniques. It includes belief base, plan base, reasoning engine and negotiation engine. The CMIBN is defined as

$$CMIBN = <B_b, P_b, R_e, N_e>,$$

$$N_e = <PJG, CD, R, A>,$$

where B_b is the belief base, P_b is the plan base, R_e is the reasoning engine and N_e is the negotiation engine.

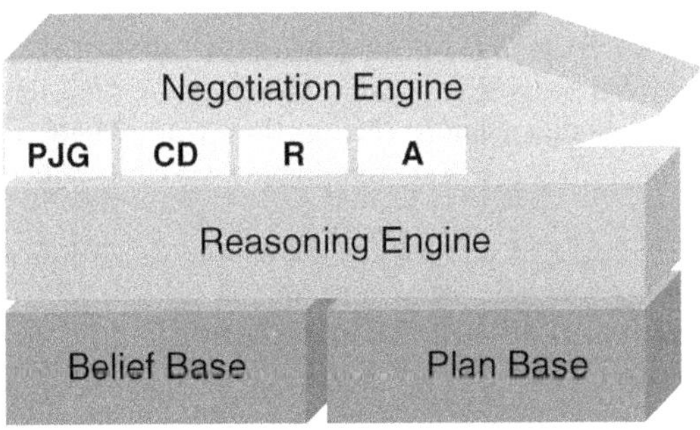

Fig. 2.1. Computational model of interest based negotiation

In the CMIBN, each party negotiates according to the reasoning over his/her belief and plan. Fig. 2.1 illustrates the architecture of the CMIBN, followed by details.

Belief base is the knowledge base of the negotiator. It can be defined by a set of rules.

Plan Base keeps the knowledge about how to achieve each position. In the Plan Base, each plan is defined by a set of organized actions to be performed towards a position. Plan base and the corresponding negotiation will be covered by a separate paper.

Reasoning Engine, based on the needs of the negotiation and the Belief Base, generates negotiation positions and makes selections among different positions to pursue.

Negotiation Engine, with the support of the Reasoning Engine, manages the negotiation process and generates the negotiation related arguments automatically. It has four components, namely, PJG – Proposal and Justification Generation; CD- Conflict Discovery; R – Recommendation; A – Adjustment.

<1> PJG, *proposal and justification generation*: To make proposal and provide justifications (reasons) for the proposal.

<2> CD, *conflict discovery*: To find the conflicts between the participants. By questioning the justifications behind the proposal (such as giving proof of incorrect information used), one party can persuade the other party to change the decision.

<3> R, *recommendation*: To recommend alternative solutions and provide justifications for a new solution. If the alternative option is more attractive to the counterparties, the counterparties may change the original decision.

<4> A, *adjustment*: To revise its knowledge base to incorporate new information obtained from the counterparties during the negotiation process. The negotiation process is also the process for the participants to gain more complete information about the environment.

For example, the PJG of a personal agent (A1) can make a proposal "Book a next Monday ticket of Air China from Melbourne to Shanghai" to a travel agency's agent (A2), with the justification "I would travel to Shanghai on Monday. Air China has directly flight from Melbourne to Shanghai". The CD of A2, for an instance, provides information that "Air China does not have direct flight from Melbourne to Shanghai on next Monday". This can persuade A1 to change proposal. Alternatively, component R of A2, for an instance, makes recommendation "Book a ticket of Qantas Airline from Melbourne to Shanghai on next Monday" with the justification "Qantas Airline flies from Melbourne to Shanghai on Monday". In the negotiation process, A1 acquires new information that Qantas Airline flies from Melbourne to Shanghai on Monday while Air China does not. The component A of A1 may adjust its belief base accordingly.

3 Interest Based Negotiation Automation

Interest based negotiation is to solve conflicts by discussing the underlying reasons behind the positions and seek alternative solutions. The conflicts may be due to some conflicting belief or contention on the resources while perusing the position. It can be therefore categorized into two types of negotiation: belief negotiation and plan negotiation, to address the different types of conflicts. For example, the father of a kid believes that the happiness of his child relies on the success of his career, which leads to a high requirement on the kid's school performance. The mother of the kid however, believes that the happiness of her child comes from the freely growth with little pressure. This is a belief conflict. On the other hand, if there is no belief conflict. Both of the father and mother believe that they should spend a good amount of time with their kid. They can still have conflicts for example how to arrange their time. This becomes a plan conflict. This paper focuses on the belief negotiation and leaves plan negotiation to another report.

The belief conflicts are normally due to the incomplete or incorrect knowledge of the environment. Through argumentation, negotiation parties may form a more complete and accurate understanding of the environment. Agreement between negotiators could be possibly reached through the decision making on the new belief.

To automate interest based negotiation, a key issue is to automate the arguments generation for the basic components of the negotiation engine, namely, proposal generation, conflict discovery, recommendation and adjustment.

The rest of the paper considers belief base as a set of rules in propositional logic. Namely, given a language L of propositional logic with finite variable set U, a belief base is a finite set of propositional formulas in L. Every $u \in$ U is an atom, and any atom or negated atom is a literal. We use "~" to denote negation. We consider the case that all formulas are disjunction of two literals, i.e. in the form of $x \vee y$ (or $\sim x \rightarrow y$), where x, y are literals (If a formula is a fact x, it can be represented in the form of $x \vee x$ for consistency). Usually the belief of negotiators can be represented as the "IF … THEN …" format. For example, a young man believes that to become a software engineer, he needs to have a software engineering degree, hence he should enter a university. His belief can be modeled as: become a software engineer → have a software engineering degree, have a software engineering degree → enter a university.

3.1 Conflict Discovery

In the interest based negotiation process, if the participants have conflicts in their positions, they may exchange the justifications (set of rules used in the reasoning process) leading to the position. One party may start the conflict discovery process, trying to break the logic flow in other parties' justifications. Obviously, a computational model of conflict discovery is fundamental to automate interest based negotiation.

Identifying the apparent conflict, e.g. party A believes "Pre-school children can study math" while party B believes "pre-school children cannot study math", is easy. However, it is not easy to discover the implied conflicts caused by steps of deduction over a large amount of rules among the negotiation parties. This sub-section presents the Conflict Discovery Algorithm, as a fundamental enabling component, to discover conflicts of two parties automatically.

The Conflict Discovery Algorithm of a negotiation party takes one rule from the opposing party's justification, generates a *proof* (knowledge subset) of the negation of that rule automatically. If such a proof exists, the arguments of proof can be passed to the counterpart as a challenge to its justification.

Definition 3.1. Graph Representation of a Formula Set: For a formula set S={$x_1 \vee y_1$, $x_2 \vee y_2$, …, $x_n \vee y_n$}, let U={ u_1, u_2, …, u_m} be the atom set of S. A graph G=(V, E) is defined as the graph representation of S, where

$$V=\{ u_i, \sim u_i \mid 1 \le i \le m\},$$

$$E=\{(\sim x_i , y_i), (\sim y_i , x_i) \mid x_i \vee y_i \in S, 1 \le i \le n\}.$$

Algorithm 3.1. Conflict Discovery Algorithm (CDA)

Input: Formula $p=x_0 \vee y_0$ *// a rule from the opposing party*

Formula set S={ $x_1 \vee y_1$, $x_2 \vee y_2$, …, $x_n \vee y_n$}

// belief base of the negotiator, or the subset of the belief base relevant to p.

Let U={ u_1, u_2, …, u_m} be the atom set of S$\cup\{p\}$

Output: If there is formula subset S'$\subset$S such that S' $\Rightarrow \sim p$, output S'.

Otherwise output "no proof".

(1) Construct a graph G=(V, E) corresponding to S$\cup\{p\}$, where,

$V=\{ u_i, \sim u_i \mid 1 \le i \le m\}$

$E=\{(\sim x_i , y_i), (\sim y_i , x_i) \mid x_i \vee y_i \in S\cup\{p\}, 0 \le i \le n\}$

(2) If there is no $u_i \in$ U such that there are directed paths from u_i to $\sim u_i$ and from $\sim u_i$ to u_i (directed closed walks containing u_i and $\sim u_i$), return "no proof".

(3) Let E' be the directed closed walk containing u_i and $\sim u_i$ found in (2)

Let S'={$(x \vee y) \mid (\sim x, y) \in$E'}-{ $x_0 \vee y_0$ }, return S' // the proof for $\sim p$

Computational Complexity Analysis of Conflict Discovery Algorithm

In the CDA algorithm, step (1) has complexity of O(m+n). In step (2), the directed path from one vertex to another can be found using DFS algorithm in time O(m+n). At most m atoms in U are tested, which gives the complexity of O(m(m+n)). Step (3) has complexity of O (n). So the algorithm can be implemented in an order of O(m(m+n)).

Theorem 3.1 *There are conflicts between a rule and a belief base if and only if the algorithm CDA presents a proof for the negation of the rule.*

Proof

According to CDA, if the u_i exists, there are directed paths from u_i to $\sim u_i$ and vice versa, each of these directed closed walks provides evidence that S$\cup\{p\}$ is unsaitisfiable[10], which is a resolution refutation for S$\cup\{p\}$[11]. If S is consistent and there is a resolution refutation for S$\cup\{p\}$, S $\Rightarrow \sim p$ [12]. In other words, S' $\Rightarrow \sim p$, S' is the proof for $\sim p$. If there is no such u_i exists, S$\cup\{p\}$is consistent[10] and no proof for $\sim p$. ■

3.2 Recommendation

The belief bases regulate the behavior of the involved parties in an automated negotiation process. Based on the belief base, each party makes proposals to others. If they cannot reach an agreement, one party may try to persuade the other parties to change their minds by recommending alternative solutions. If the alternative solution is more attractive, the opposing party may change the original position. This process is a fundamental component of interest based negotiation: recommendation. The following result is to enable the automation of recommendation.

Definition 3.2.1. Transitive Closure: Let G be a directed graph with n vertices. The transitive closure of the adjacency matrix of G is an $n \times n$ matrix A, where

$$A[i,j] = \begin{cases} 1, & i = j \text{ or there exists a directed path from vertex } i \text{ to } j \\ 0, & \text{otherwise} \end{cases}$$

Definition 3.2.2. Matrix Representation of a Formula Set: Suppose G is the graph representation of a formula set S, A is the transitive closure of the adjacency matrix of graph G. A is called the Matrix Representation of S.

The computational model of recommendation automation proposed in this paper is called Belief Base Matrix (BBM). The idea behind BBM is as follows. If A[i, j] =1, there exists a path from i to j. That is, j can be derived from i by applying the formulas following the order they appear in the path. So the matrix representation can be used as a model for the reasoning process of recommendation. It can be stored and reused until the belief base is revised.

In the follows, the Belief Base Matrix Algorithm is to compute the matrix representation of a belief base. The recommendation automation is then modeled by the Recommendation Algorithm. Given one interest from the other party, the algorithm will automatically generate the recommendation and the justification based on its knowledge (the belief base matrix).

Algorithm 3.2.1. Belief Base Matrix Algorithm (BBMA)

Input: Formula set S={ $x_1 \vee y_1$, $x_2 \vee y_2$, …, $x_n \vee y_n$} // S is consistent
Let U={ u_1, u_2, …, u_m} be the atom set of S
Output: The matrix representation of S.
(1) Construct a graph G=(V, E) corresponding to S, where,
V={ u_i, ~ u_i | $1 \le i \le m$} also noted as V={v_1, v_2, …v_{2m}}
E={(~ x_i , y_i), (~y_i , x_i)| $x_i \vee y_i \in$ S , $1 \le i \le n$}
(2) *// Construct the transitive closure of the adjacency matrix of graph G.*
For each v_i , $v_j \in$ V do
If (v_i , v_j)$\in$E or $v_i = v_j$ then $A_0[v_i, v_j]$=1
Else $A_0[v_i, v_j]$=0
End For
For $k \leftarrow 1$ to $2m$ do
For each v_i , $v_j \in$ V do
$A_k[v_i, v_j] = A_{k-1}[v_i, v_j] + A_{k-1}[v_i, v_k] \cdot A_{k-1}[v_k, v_j]$
// "·" and "+" are logic multiplication and logic addition
End For
End For
Return A_{2m} // A_{2m} is the matrix representation of S.

Computational Complexity Analysis of BBMA

In the algorithm BBMA, step (1) can be finished in O(m+n) time and the complexity order of step (2) is O(m^3). So the complexity of the algorithm is O(m^3+n).

Algorithm 3.2.2. Recommendation Algorithm (RA)

Input: Literal v *// interest of the opposing party*

Formula set S={ $x_1 \vee y_1, x_2 \vee y_2, \ldots, x_n \vee y_n$} *// belief base, consistent*

Let U={ $u_1, u_2, \ldots, u_m$} be the atom set of S

Matrix A *// matrix representation of S*

Graph G *// graph representation of S*

Output: Recommendation v_r, formula set S'⊂S if S'∪{v}⇒ v_r and v_r is preferable for itself. Otherwise output "no recommendation".

(1) If $v \notin$ U and $\sim v \notin$ U Then return "no recommendation".
// no relevant information about v according to its knowledge

(2) Let R={ v' | A [v, v'] =1, $v' \neq v$ }
If R= { } then return "no recommendation" .

(3) Select $v_r \in$ R as recommendation
// R is the set of results can be derived from v, i.e. the set of recommendation
// the designation of selection strategy is not a focus of this paper
Find a path E' from v to v_r in G
Let J={($\sim v_i \vee v_j$)| (v_i , v_j) ∈E'} , *// J is the justification of v_r*
Return "recommendation:"+ v_r + ", its justification: " + J

Computational Complexity Analysis of RA

In the algorithm, step (1) and step (2) can be finished in O(m) time. In step (3) the path can be found using DFS algorithm in O(m+n) time, J can be constructed in O(n) time, thus step (3) can be finished in O(m+n) time. So the complexity of the algorithm is O(m+n).

3.3 Proposal and Justification Generation

As proposal generation is a similar process as recommendation, it is omitted in this paper.

3.4 Adjustment

Upon receiving the new knowledge from other parties (for example, new knowledge comes from the proof of a conflict, or the justification of a recommendation), a negotiator will exam the new knowledge and adjust its belief, i.e revise its belief base to incorporate the new knowledge. From the adjusted belief base, he/she may make new decision (new positions).

To revise the belief base, the negotiator needs to add new knowledge, remove or modify the old knowledge in the belief base, and keep the consistency at the same time. The relationship among knowledge could be very complicated, which makes the detecting and eliminating inconsistency difficult. Similar to conflict discovery, all the apparent and *implied* inconsistency are to be addressed. In general, revising a knowledge base to incorporate new knowledge is not tractable [13].

Most of the time, different rules in a knowledge base are of different importance. For instance, if the new formula is more certain than others, the least certain inconsistent knowledge can be dropped. Alternatively, formulas may also be ordered according to their arrival time in the knowledge base. Then the oldest inconsistent knowledge might be rejected in order to restore consistency.

Based on prioritized knowledge base, it is possible to automate the adjustment process with polynomial complexity algorithms [14]. The detailed result will be reported separately.

4 Case Study

Suppose X is a company in the manufacturing industry. It has strong intention to improve its competency in the global market. X believes that developing new products and increasing productivity are the steps to improve competency. To increase productivity, X believes it needs to extend working hours, thus needs to update product line hardware. The belief base of company X can be represented as:

$B_b^{(X)}=\{a_1, a_1\rightarrow a_2, a_1\rightarrow a_3, a_3\rightarrow a_4, a_4\rightarrow a_5, a_6\rightarrow a_7\}$, where

a_1: improve competency
a_2: develop new products
a_3: increase productivity
a_4: extend working hours
a_5: update product line hardware
a_6: improve efficiency
a_7: update product line software

The belief base can also be represented as

$B_b^{(X)}=\{a_1\vee a_1, \sim a_1\vee a_2, \sim a_1\vee a_3, \sim a_3\vee a_4, \sim a_4\vee a_5, \sim a_6\vee a_7\}$,

which is a rule set where negotiation automation algorithms proposed in Section 3 apply.

Suppose Y is a computer company specialized in manufacturing software. Y believes that encouraging organizational learning through knowledge management systems is an excellent way to improve the competency of an organisation. It is currently promoting its knowledge management products. The belief base of Y can be represented as:

$B_b^{(Y)}=\{a_1, a_1\rightarrow a_2, a_1\rightarrow a_3, a_1\rightarrow a_8, a_8\rightarrow a_9, a_3\rightarrow a_6, a_4\rightarrow \sim a_6\}$.

Or

$B_b^{(Y)}=\{a_1\vee a_1, \sim a_1\vee a_2, \sim a_1\vee a_3, \sim a_1\vee a_8, \sim a_8\vee a_9, \sim a_3\vee a_6, \sim a_4\vee \sim a_6\}$,

where

a_8: encourage organizational learning
a_9: adopt knowledge management systems

4.1 Making Proposal

X wants to improve the competency, based on its belief $\{a_1, a_1\rightarrow a_3, a_3\rightarrow a_4, a_4\rightarrow a_5\}$, it makes a proposal a_5, that is to buy new product line hardware. Proposal generation is similar to recommendation generation, the detailed procedure is omitted here.

4.2 Conflict Discovery

Company Y does not have the product line hardware X wants. No agreement can be reached upon this position. After knowing the reason behind X's position, Y can generate recommendation to X, or provide proof to challenge X's justification. The automation of generating a proof to challenge $a_3 \rightarrow a_4$ in $B_b^{(X)}$ is illustrated here. The recommendation will be covered in Section 4.3.

The graph representation of $B_b^{(Y)} \cup \{a_3 \rightarrow a_4\}$ is

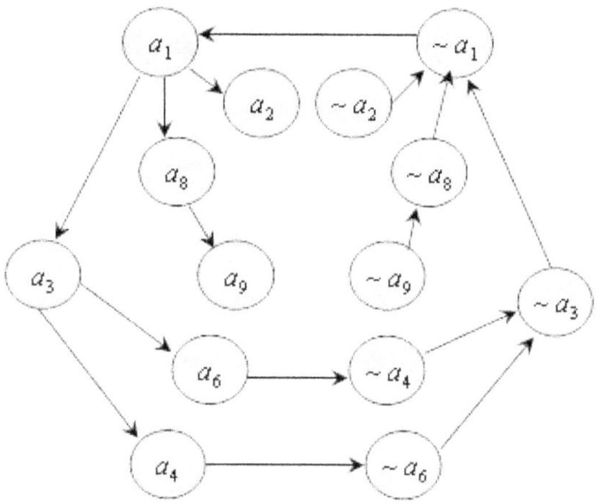

Fig. 4.2.1. Graph representation of $B_b^{(Y)} \cup \{a_3 \rightarrow a_4\}$

There is a directed closed walk containing a_3 and $\sim a_3$:

$$a_3 \rightarrow a_4 \rightarrow \sim a_6 \rightarrow \sim a_3 \rightarrow \sim a_1 \rightarrow a_1 \rightarrow a_3$$

The logic proof for $\sim (a_3 \rightarrow a_4)$ is $\{a_4 \rightarrow \sim a_6, a_3 \rightarrow a_6, a_1 \rightarrow a_3, a_1\}$. The interpretation is that:

increase productivity → improve efficiency ($a_3 \rightarrow a_6$) ,

improve efficiency → ~ extend working hours ($a_4 \rightarrow \sim a_6$ i.e. $a_6 \rightarrow \sim a_4$) ,

It tells that productivity can not be increased by extending working hours. This provides a proof to challenge X's justification $a_3 \rightarrow a_4$ for the position to purchase product line hardware.

4.3 Recommendation

Algorithm BBMA automatically creates the matrix representation of Y's belief base. The matrix is omitted here due to the restriction of length. Based on the matrix, algorithm RA finds all the results that can be derived from the interest a_1 (to improve competency). Among them a_9 (adopt knowledge management system) is what Y is promoting.

The path $a_1 \rightarrow a_8 \rightarrow a_9$ tells that adopting knowledge management systems can also improve the competency, so Y recommends X to buy the knowledge management system products. If X is satisfied with the recommendation and persuaded by the justification, it will accept the recommendation. Then agreement is reached.

4.4 Adjustment

X receives the new knowledge during the recommendation or conflict discovery process from Y, for example, $a_1 \rightarrow a_8$, $a_8 \rightarrow a_9$, $a_3 \rightarrow a_6$, $a_4 \rightarrow\sim a_6$. It may store them in a temporary place. If some knowledge appears repeatedly or come from a trust party, X may initiate the adjustment process. Suppose X is going to add $\{a_3 \rightarrow a_6, a_4 \rightarrow\sim a_6\}$ to its belief base, and give them the highest priority. The challenged knowledge $a_3 \rightarrow a_4$ is given the lowest priority. After the adjustment the belief base becomes[1]:

$$B_b^{(X)}=\{a_3 \rightarrow a_6, a_4 \rightarrow\sim a_6, a_1, a_1 \rightarrow a_2, a_1 \rightarrow a_3, a_4 \rightarrow a_5, a_6 \rightarrow a_7 \}$$

In a later stage, if X wants to improve its competency, probably it will make a new proposal a_7 (update product line software) based on the belief $\{ a_1, a_1 \rightarrow a_3, a_3 \rightarrow a_6, a_6 \rightarrow a_7 \}$.

5 Conclusion and Future Work

This paper proposed a computational model for interest based negotiation automation. The negotiation studied in this paper is in general sense, which includes general processes of exchanging information and perspectives towards mutual understanding and agreements. It represents wide range of activities in most areas that involves dynamic interactions, including education, organisation management, cooperation, commerce and business.

As interest based negotiation allows involved parties to dig into the reasons behind their positions, it is much more powerful and constructive than position based negotiation. It therefore has raised significant attention in various communities including researchers. However, the existing literature is largely limited at high level discussions. This paper addresses the challenge by proposing a computational model of interest based negotiation, including algorithms for the main negotiation automation elements, namely proposal generation, conflict discovery and recommendation for belief negotiation. A case study has illustrated how interest based negotiation automation can be feasibly carried out by computational entities, e.g. software agents. Due to the limitation of length, plan negotiation will be reported in a separate paper.

References

1. Fisher, R., Ury, W.: Getting to Yes: Negotiating Agreement without giving in. Penguin boks, new york (1983)
2. Jennings, N.R., Faratin, P., Lomuscio, A. R., Parsons, S., Sierra, C., Wooldridge, M.: Automated Negotiation: Prospects, Methods and Challenges. Int. Journal of Group Decision and Negotiation, Vol. 10, No. 2 (2001) 199–215
3. Hu, W. B., Wang, S. M.: Research on the Negotiation Mechanism of Multi-agent System Based on Game Theory. Proceedings of the Ninth International Conference on Computer Supported Cooperative Work in Design, Vol. 1 (2005) 396 – 400

[1] The justification automation will be covered by a separate report.

4. Chen, J. H., Chao, K. M., Godwin, N., Reeves, C., Smith, P.: An Automated Negotiation Mechanism Based on Co-evolution and Game Theory. Proceedings of the 2002 ACM symposium on Applied computing (2002) 63 - 67
5. Faratin, P., Sierra, C., Jennings, N.R.: Using Similarity Criteria to Make Issue Trade-offs in Automated Negotiations. Journal of Artificial Intelligence, Vol. 142, No. 2 (2002) 205-237
6. Jonker, C., Robu, V.: Automated Multi-Attribute Negotiation with Efficient Use of Incomplete Preference Information. Proceedings of the Third International Joint Conference on Autonomous Agents and Multiagent Systems (2004) 1054-1061
7. Karunatillake, N.C., Jennings, N.R., Rahwan, I., Norman, T.J.: Argument-based Negotiation in a Social Context. Proceedings of the fourth international joint conference on Autonomous agents and multiagent systems (2005) 1331-1332
8. Rahwan, I., Ramchurn, S.D., Jennings, N.R., McBurney, P., Parsons, S., Sonenberg, L.: Argumentation-based Negotiation. The Knowledge Engineering Review, Vol.18, No.4 (2004) 343-375
9. Rahwan, I., Sonenberg, L., Dignum, F.: On Interest Based Negotiation. Lecture Notes in Computer Science, Springer-Verlag, Vol. 2922 (2004) 383-401
10. Aspvall, B., Plass, M., Tarjan, R.: A Linear-time Algorithm for Testing the Truth of Certain Quantified Boolean Formulas. Information Processing Letters (1979) 121-123
11. Subramani, K.: Optimal Length Tree-Like Resolution Refutations for 2SAT Formulas. ACM Transactions on Computational Logic, Vol.5, No.2 (2004) 316-320
12. Robinson, J.A.: A Machine-oriented Logic Based on the Resolution Principle. Journal of the ACM, Vol. 12 (1965) 23-41
13. Eiter, T., Gottlob, G.: On the Complexity of Propositional Knowledge Base Revision, Updates, and Counterfactuals. Artificial Intelligence, Vol. 57, No. 2-3 (1992) 227-270
14. Tao, X. H., Sun, W., Ma, S. H.: A Practical Propositional Knowledge Base Revision Algorithm. Journal of Computer Science and Technology, Vol.12, No.2 (1997) 154-159

Phase Transition of a Skeleton Model for Surfaces

Hiroshi Koibuchi

Ibaraki National College of Technology,
Nakane 866, Hitachinaka, Ibaraki 312-8508, Japan

Abstract. A spherical model of skeleton with junctions is investigated by Monte Carlo simulations. The model is governed by one-dimensional bending energy. The results indicate that the model undergoes a first-order transition, which separates the smooth phase from the crumpled phase. The existence of phase transition indicates that junctions play a non-trivial role in the transition.

1 Introduction

Surface model of Helfrich, Polyakov and Kleinert (HPK) [1,2,3] has long been investigated for a model of biological membranes [4,5,6,7,8,9]. A curvature energy called the bending energy is assumed in the Hamiltonian, which is discretized on triangulated surfaces in numerical studies [10]. It was reported that the model undergoes a first-order transition between the smooth phase and a crumpled (or wrinkled) phase [11,12,13]. Experimentally, a similar transition was recently observed in an artificial membrane [14].

The curvature energy in HPK model is a two-dimensional one, and it reflects a homogeneous structure of membranes as a two-dimensional surface. In fact, the conventional picture of biological membranes is connected to such homogeneity, and moreover many artificial membranes are known as homogeneous.

However, membrane skeleton, called the cytoskeleton in biological membranes, has been considered to play a crucial role in maintaining shape and motion. Recent experimental studies reveal that free diffusion of lipids suffers from the existence of cytoskeletons: the so-called hop-diffusion was actually observed [15]. The artificial membrane, in the above-mentioned experimental study, is considered not to be a homogeneous surface, because it is partly polymerized [14].

Therefore, it is interesting to study whether the phase transition occurs in a skeleton model, which is obviously different from the conventional surface model such as HPK model. The skeleton model is significantly simplified as a model for surfaces; it contains only skeletons and the junctions. Consequently, we consider that the simplified model enable us to focus on whether skeletons play a crucial role on the phase transition in biological and artificial membranes.

In this paper, we report numerical evidence that a phase transition occurs in a skeleton model, which is governed by one-dimensional bending energy. This result is remarkable, because no phase transition can be observed in one-dimensional object described by Hamiltonian of local interactions.

D.-S. Huang, K. Li, and G.W. Irwin (Eds.): ICIC 2006, LNBI 4115, pp. 223–229, 2006.

2 Model and Monte Carlo Technique

By dividing every edge of the icosahedron into some pieces of the uniform length, we have a triangulated surface. The compartment structure is built on the surface by eliminating the vertices inside the compartment. The boundary of the compartment forms the skeletons with junctions. We denote by (N, N_S, N_J, L) the total number of vertices (including those in the junctions and their neighboring vertices), the total number of vertices in the skeletons (excluding both vertices in the junctions and their neighboring vertices), the total number of junctions, and the number of bonds between two neighboring junctions in a compartment, respectively. Note that $L-1$ is the number of vertices in the skeleton between the junctions.

A starting configuration of Monte Carlo (MC) simulation is shown in Fig. 1(a), 1(b), where $(N, N_S, N_J, L) = (2562, 1440, 162, 4)$ and $(N, N_S, N_J, L) = (19362, 10890, 1212, 4)$. The dots are clearly seen in (a) and unclear in (b) because the size of (b) is relatively large. The surface of the sphere is shown in the snapshot for clarity. The hexagon and the pentagon (which are clearly seen in (a)) correspond to the junctions. Total number of the pentagon is 12, and the remaining junctions are hexagonal.

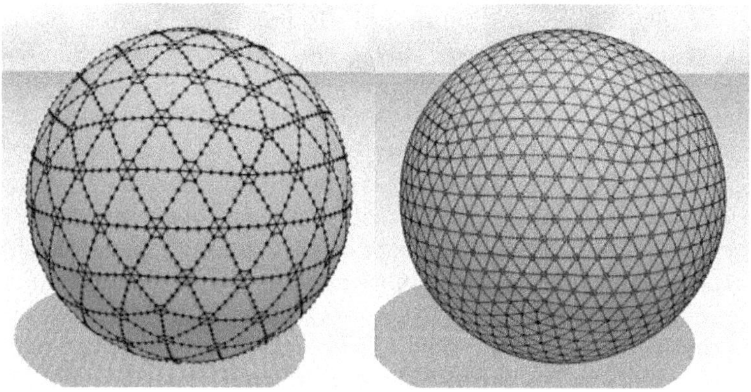

(a) $(2562, 1440, 162, 4)$ (b) $(19362, 10890, 1212, 4)$

Fig. 1. Starting configuration of surfaces of (a) $(N, N_S, N_J, L) = (2562, 1440, 162, 4)$ and (b) $(N, N_S, N_J, L) = (19362, 10890, 1212, 4)$. Thick lines denote the skeletons and the junctions, and small dots the vertices. The dots are clearly seen in (a) and unclear in (b) because the surface size is relatively large. The surface of the sphere is shown for clarity in both (a) and (b).

Henceforth, we use terminology *junction* for the hexagonal (or pentagonal) objects or for the central vertices of these objects, *skeleton* for linear object between junctions, and *surface* for junction + skeleton.

The Gaussian bond potential S_1, the one-dimensional bending energy $S_2^{(1)}$ for skeletons, and the two-dimensional bending energy $S_2^{(2)}$ for junctions, are given by

$$S_1 = \sum_{(ij)} (X_i - X_j)^2, \quad S_2^{(1)} = \sum_{[ij]} (1 - \mathbf{t}_i \cdot \mathbf{t}_j), \quad S_2^{(2)} = \sum_{\langle ij \rangle} (1 - \mathbf{n}_i \cdot \mathbf{n}_j), \quad (1)$$

where $\sum_{(ij)}$ in S_1 is the sum over bonds (ij) connecting all the vertices i and j (including those at the junctions and their neighboring vertices), $\sum_{[ij]}$ in $S_2^{(1)}$ is the sum over nearest neighbor bonds i and j on the skeletons between junctions, $\sum_{\langle ij \rangle}$ in $S_2^{(2)}$ is the sum over bonds $\langle ij \rangle$ connecting the central point of the junction i and the nearest neighbor vertex j. The symbol $\mathbf{t}_i$ in $S_2^{(1)}$ is the unit tangential vector of the bond i. The symbol $\mathbf{n}_i$ in $S_2^{(2)}$ is the unit normal vector of the triangle i.

$S_2^{(2)}$ is defined only at the junctions. Note also that the bond $[ij]$ in $S_2^{(1)}$ includes the bonds connected to the central point of the junction. S_1 includes bonds that connect the vertices nearest neighbor to the junctions. The reason of this is for the sake of the in-plane elasticity at the junctions. When S_1 excludes such bonds, skeletons at the junctions freely move into the in-plane directions. The potential S_1 describes a one-dimensional interaction between vertices in the skeletons and a two-dimensional interaction only at the junctions.

The partition function of the model is defined by

$$Z = \int^{\prime} \prod_{i=1}^{N} dX_i \exp(-S), \quad S = S_1 + b_1 S_2^{(1)} + b_2 S_2^{(2)}, \quad (2)$$

where b_1, b_2 are the one-dimensional bending rigidity and the two-dimensional bending rigidity. In this paper, b_2 is fixed to $b_2 = 5$, and b_1 is varied in the MC simulations. The center of the surface is fixed in the MC simulations, and this is denoted by $\prime$ in $\int^{\prime} \prod_{i=1}^{N} dX_i$.

The canonical Metropolice MC technique is used to obtain the mean value of physical quantities. The vertices X of the skeleton are sequentially shifted so that $X' = X + \delta X$, where δX is randomly chosen in a small sphere. The new position X' is accepted with the probability $\mathrm{Min}[1, \exp(-\Delta S)]$, where $\Delta S = S(\mathrm{new}) - S(\mathrm{old})$. The vertices of junctions (hexagons and pentagons) are shifted in two steps. Firstly 7 (or 6) vertices at one junction are shifted simultaneously at random, and the second step is a random translation and a random rotation of the hexagon (or the pentagon) as a rigid object. Those shifts are controlled by small numbers given at the beginning of the simulations to maintain about 50% acceptance rates.

Four different sizes are assumed for surfaces in the MC simulations. The surface size (N, N_S, N_J, L) are $(19362, 10890, 1212, 4)$, $(10242, 5760, 642, 4)$, $(5762,$

3240, 362, 4), and (2562, 1440, 162, 4). In the simulations, two parameters are fixed: the total number of vertices L in the skeleton between junctions and the two-dimensional bending rigidity b_2 are fixed to

$$L = 5, \quad b_2 = 5. \tag{3}$$

3 Results

First, we show snapshots of surface obtained at $b_1 = 2.9$ (crumpled phase) and $b_1 = 2.93$ (smooth phase) in Figs.2(a) and 2(b), respectively. The size of surface is $(N, N_S, N_J, L) = (19362, 10890, 1212, 4)$. The surface sections are shown in Figs.2(c),2(d). We clearly find that the surface is crumpled (smooth) at $b_1 = 2.9$ ($b_1 = 2.93$).

Figure 3(a) is plots of S_1/N against b_1 obtained on the surfaces of size (19362, 10890, 1212, 4), (5762, 3240, 362, 4), and (2562, 1440, 162, 4). Because of the scale invariant property of the partition function Z in Eq.(2), S_1/N is predicted to be $S_1/N = 3N/2(N-1) \simeq 1.5$. We find from the figure that the predicted relation for S_1/N is satisfied. The line connecting the data was obtained by multi-histogram reweighting technique.

(a) $b_1 = 2.9$, crumped (b) $b_1 = 2.93$, smooth

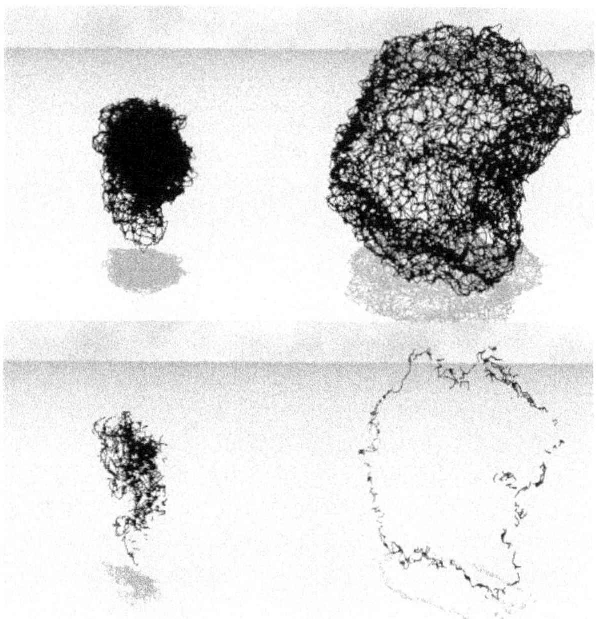

(c) the surface section of (a) (d) the surface section of (b)

Fig. 2. Snapshots of surfaces of size $(N, N_S, N_J, L) = (19362, 10890, 1212, 4)$obtained at (a) $b_1 = 2.9$ (crumpled) and (b) $b_1 = 2.93$ (smooth). (c) The surface section of (a), and (d) the surface section of (b).

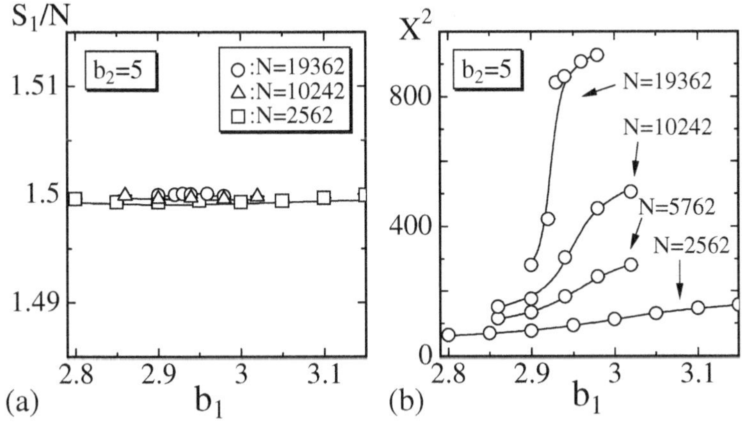

Fig. 3. (a) S_1/N against b_1, and (b) X^2 against b_1. b_2 is fixed to $b_2 = 5$. The curves are drawn by multi-histogram reweighting technique.

Figure 3(b) is the mean square size X^2 defined by

$$X^2 = \frac{1}{N}\sum_i \left(X_i - \bar{X}\right)^2, \quad \bar{X} = \frac{1}{N}\sum_i X_i, \tag{4}$$

where $\bar{X}$ is the center of the surface. The size X^2 of surfaces increases with increasing b_1 and varies rapidly at intermediate b_1 on the surface of $(19362, 10890, 1212, 4)$. This indicates the existence of the crumpling transition.

The bending energy $S_2^{(1)}/N_V$ against b_1 is plotted in Fig. 4(a), where $N_V = N - N_J$ is the total number of vetices where $S_2^{(1)}$ is defined. We find again a rapid varying of $S_2^{(1)}/N_V$ against b_1 as the surface size increases.

Figure 4(b) shows the specific heat $C_{S_2^{(1)}}$ defined by

$$C_{S_2^{(1)}} = \frac{b^2}{N_V}\langle \left(S_2^{(1)} - \langle S_2^{(1)}\rangle\right)^2 \rangle. \tag{5}$$

The curves drawn by multi-histogram reweighting technique indicate an anomalous behavior of $C_{S_2^{(1)}}$. This can be considered as a sign of the phase transition. We expect that the transition is of first-order because of the sharp peak in $C_{S_2^{(1)}}$ at the surface of $(N, N_S, N_J, L) = (19362, 10890, 1212, 4)$. The junctions play a nontrivial role in the phase transition, because we know that one-dimensional linear skeleton such as an elastic circle has no phase transition. The finite-size scaling analysis can be done with more extensive MC simulations including larger surfaces rather than those in this paper, and the first-order transition will be confirmed.

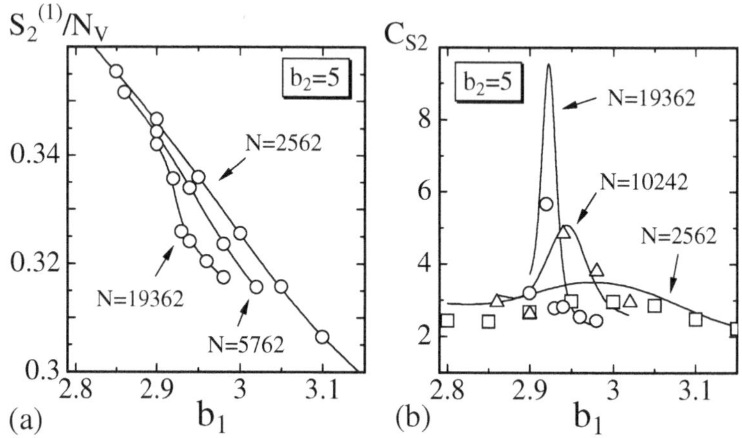

Fig. 4. (a) $S_2^{(1)}/N_V$ against b_1, and (b) $C_{S_2^{(1)}}$ against b_1. $N_V = N - N_J$ is the total number of vetices where $S_2^{(1)}$ is defined. b_2 is fixed to $b_2 = 5$. The curves are drawn by multi-histogram reweighting technique.

4 Summary and Conclusion

We have investigated the phase structure of a skeleton model for membranes by using Monte Carlo simulation technique. Linear skeletons are joined with junctions and form a surface, which covers a sphere. Hamiltonian is a linear combination of the Gaussian bond potential, one-dimensional bending energy $S_2^{(1)}$, and the two-dimensional bending energy $S_2^{(2)}$, which is defined only at the junctions. Four different sized surfaces were used in the simulation. The length L of skeleton between junctions was fixed to $L = 5$ in those surfaces, and the two-dimensional bending rigidity b_2 was also fixed to $b_2 = 5$.

We found that there are two distinct phases in the model; the smooth phase and the crumpled phase, which are characterized by small $S_2^{(1)}$ and large $S_2^{(1)}$, respectively, and also by small X^2 and large X^2. Moreover, these two phases are separated by a phase transition, which was predicted to be of first-order on account of the anomalous behavior of the specific heat for $S_2^{(1)}$.

Although we have obtained a sign of first-order transition in the skeleton model, more extensive MC simulations are necessary to confirm the result. The junctions are expected to play a non-trivial role in the phase transition, because we know that one-dimensional linear skeleton such as an elastic circle has no phase transition. Then, it is interesting to study the dependence of junction elasticity on the phase transition. A rigid junction model is also interesting. Rigid junction has an infinite in-plane and bending resistance against force, while the junction in this paper has finite elastic resistance. Phase structure of skeleton models can be clarified by further numerical studies.

Acknowledgement

This work is supported in part by a Grant-in-Aid for Scientific Research, No. 15560160.

References

1. Helfrich, W.: Elastic Properties of Lipid Bilayers: Theory and Possible Experiments. Z. Naturforsch, 28c (1973) 693 - 703
2. Polyakov, A.M.: Fine Structure of Strings. Nucl. Phys. B 268 (1986) 406 - 412
3. Kleinert, H.: The Membrane Properties of Condensing Strings. Phys. Lett. B 174 (1986) 335 - 338
4. Nelson, D.: The Statistical Mechanics of Membranes and Interfaces. In: Nelson, D., Piran, T., Weinberg, S. (eds.): Statistical Mechanics of Membranes and Surfaces. 2nd edn. World Scientific (2004) 1 - 16
5. Gompper, G., Schick M.: Self-assembling Amphiphilic Systems. In: Domb, C. and Lebowitz, J.L. (eds.): Phase Transitions and Critical Phenomena 16. Academic Press (1994) 1 - 176
6. Bowick, M., Travesset, A.: The Statistical Mechanics of Membranes. Phys. Rep. 344 (2001) 255 - 308
7. Peliti, L., Leibler, S.: Effects of Thermal Fluctuations on Systems with Small Surface Tension. Phys. Rev. Lett. 54 (15) (1985) 1690 - 1693
8. David, F., Guitter, E.: Crumpling Transition in Elastic Membranes: Renormalization Group Treatment. Europhys. Lett. 5 (8) (1988) 709 - 713
9. Paczuski, M., Kardar, M., Nelson, D.R.: Landau Theory of the Crumpling Transition. Phys. Rev. Lett. 60 (1988) 2638 - 2640
10. Kantor, Y., Nelson, D.R.: Phase Transitions in Flexible Polymeric Surfaces. Phys. Rev. A 36 (1987) 4020 - 4032
11. Kownacki, J-P., Diep, H.T.: First-order Transition of Tethered Membranes in Three-dimensional Space. Phys. Rev. E 66 (2002) 066105(1 - 5)
12. Koibuchi, H., Kuwahata, T.: First-order Phase Transition in the Tethered Surface Model on a Sphere. Phys. Rev. E 72 (2005) 026124(1 - 6)
13. Endo, I., Koibuchi, H.: First-order Phase Transition of the Tethered Membrane Model on Spherical Surfaces. Nucl. Phys. B 732 [FS] (2006) 426 - 443
14. Chaieb, S., Natrajan, V.K., El-rahman, A.A.: Glassy Conformation in Wrinkled Membranes. Phys. Rev. Lett. 96 (2006) 078101(1 - 4)
15. Murase, K., Fujiwara, T., Umehara, Y., Suzuki, K., Iino, R., Yamashita, H., Saito, M., Murakoshi, H., Ritohie, K., Kusumi, A.: Ultrafine Membrane Compartments for Molecular Diffusion as Revealed by Single Molecule Techniques. Biol. J. 86 (2004) 4075 - 4093

A Novel Approach Model for Chinese Postman Problem

Jiang Bo[1], Shi Xiaoying[2], and Xu Zhibang[2]

[1] Wuhan Second Ship Design and Research Institute, Wuhan 430064, China
jb_263@263.net
[2] School of Electronics and Electric Engineering, East China Jiaotong University, Nanchang 330013, P.R. China

Abstract. Molecular programming(MP) has been proposed as an evolutionary computation algorithm at the molecular level. MP is different from other evolutionary algorithms in its representation of solutions using DNA molecular structures and its use of bio-lab techniques for recombination of partial solution. In this paper, Chinese Postman Problem(CPP) has been solved by means of molecular programming. We make use of the encoding scheme of S.Y.Shin for encoding real values. The new method is biologically plausible and has a fixed code length.

1 Introduction

Aldeman who showed the potential of using biomolecules for solving computational problem pioneered the field of DNA computing [1]. He solved the hamiltonian path problem using DNA molecules, and Lipton came up with a method to solve the satisfiability(SAT) problem [2]. In 1997, Q.ouyan et al presented a molecular biology based experimental solution to the maximal clique problem [3]. In 2000, liu et al designed DNA model system, a multi-based encoding strategy is used in a one word approach to surface-based DNA computation [4]. In 2001, wu analyzed and improved their surface-based method [5]. In 2005, Shi et al proposed a scheme of 3-states programmable automaton by DNA computing [6]. All their works use the tools of molecular biology and all demonstrate the feasibility of carrying out computations at the molecular level. One of the formal frameworks for molecular computations is Tom Head's splicing system, which gives a theoretical foundation for computing based on DNA recombination [7]. DNA computing represents the problem with DNA molecules and solves them by biological laboratory techniques.

DNA is a double-helix structure, the main characteristics of which are: (1) DNA molecule are convoluted by two single parallel deoxynucleotide chain; (2) the deoxyribose and phosphoric, which link to each other alternately, array in outer side; (3) the base group of two single chain can complement under the process that A complements T and C complements G, which is called base-pairing. After found the structure of DNA, many experimental methods have been invented including hybridization, annealing, amplifying, melting, separating, cutting, ligation, polymerase chain reaction(PCR), affinity column, gel electrophoresis and so on, which conduce to solving the information output and information storage. One advantage of DNA computing is

D.-S. Huang, K. Li, and G.W. Irwin (Eds.): ICIC 2006, LNBI 4115, pp. 230–237, 2006.

massive parallelism. Another benefit is its enormous information storage capacity. 1umol DNA contains approximately 1020 molecules which allow a big problem space can be searched in almost constant time. Despite significant progress, several problems remain and need to be resolved. Firstly, for a complex issue, a large amount of DNA is need in coding, which is hard to be achieved. Secondly, DNA computing is inaccurate, which can be caused by inaccurate hybridization, the effect of secondary structure of DNA molecule, the inaccuracy of experiment and large cost for biological lab experiments, all of these affecting the result of DNA computing. These problems can be alleviated by a software tool, which simulates DNA computing in advance to optimize DNA codes and experimental conditions [8]. Molecular programming (MP) has been proposed for this purpose. MP is a tool for programming DNA computers by means of artificial evolution [9]. On the other hand, MP can be regarded as a new evolutionary computation method that represents problem in DNA double strands and uses bio-lab techniques as search operators. In 2002, Yin et al. solved the Chinese postman problem with DNA computing, but this method is based on the fact that all weights are integer [10]. In that paper, we used molecular programming to solve Chinese Postman Problem. Most of the problems solved by DNA computing are non-weighted graph, such as Hamilton path problem [1] and maximal clique problem [2]. In contrast, the Chinese Postman Problem has weight (usually real valued) associated with edges. Shine proposed a method to represent weights in DNA codes to solve travelling salesman problem [9]. This method is based on the fact that hybridization between G/C pairs occurs more frequently those those between A/T pairs. It is because there are 3 hydrogen bonds between G and C, whereas 2 hydrogen bonds between A and T. Similar to the method, we can solve Chinese Postman Problem. For terminologies and notations not defined in this paper, the readers are referred to Ref. [12], [13].

2 Chinese Postman Problem

All graphs considered in the paper are finite, undirected and connected graphs. Let G be a connected graph and eij a edge of G. Let wij be a weight of eij . We call a sequence constructed from vertex and edge with alternating is closed walk, if its Starting vertex is the same as finishing vertex; Call a tour is generalized Euler tour if it contains all of the edges of graph G at least once. Let G be a connected weighted graph, Chinese Postman Problem is to find a generalized Euler tour that satisfy the sum of weight of all edges is minimum and starting vertex is fixed. We designed the following algorithm to solve it:

Step 1: Generate random closed walk through the graph.
Step 2: Keep only those closed walk that begin with fixed vertex and end with fixed vertex (keep only all closed walk passing through the fixed vertex).
Step 3: Keep only those closed walk that enter all of the edge of the graph at least once. (namely, keep only those generalized Euler tour).
Step 4: Find the shortest closed walk, it will be our solution.
Step 5: Determine postman path.

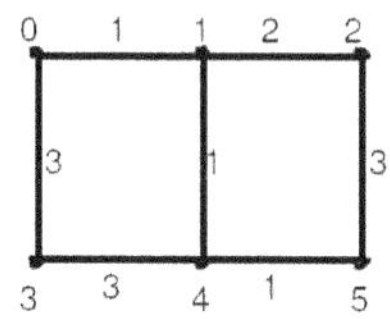

Fig. 1. Shows an instance of a graph that has 6 vertices. Let the fix vertex be 0, then the generalized Euler tour is 0-1-2-3-4-1-4-5-0 and the sum of weight is 14.

3 Coding Scheme on Chinese Postman Problem

Most existing DNA computing methods follow the Adleman's coding scheme to solve NP-complete problems. Here, the vertex codes are generated at random and then the edge codes, which link the vertices, are produced using the vertex codes.

Ouyang et al proposed a new coding scheme in which the edges have binary values coded in sequences. Recently, Zhang et al proposed an improved DNA algorithm to solve travelling salesman problem [9], coding scheme of the method can overcome the difficult brought by real valued weights. According to the coding scheme, we represent edge sequences in two components: link sequences and weight sequences, represent the weight of edges by varying the amount of A/T pairs and G/C pairs in weight sequences. Generally, DNA length and the G/C contents influence the ligation among DNA sequences. The longer the sequences the more often they get hybridized, thus leading to longer sequences of ligations. Similarly, the more G/C pairs the sequences have, the more probable they get hybridized. The reason is that the hybridizations between the G/C pairs are preferred to those between A/T pairs, since there are 2 hydrogen bonds formed between A and T and 3 hydrogen bonds between G and C. We encode the vertex with 4 components: 10bp weight sequence (W2), 10bp position sequence (P1), 10bp position sequence (P2), and 10bp weight sequence (W1), where the vertex position sequence for all the randomly generated.

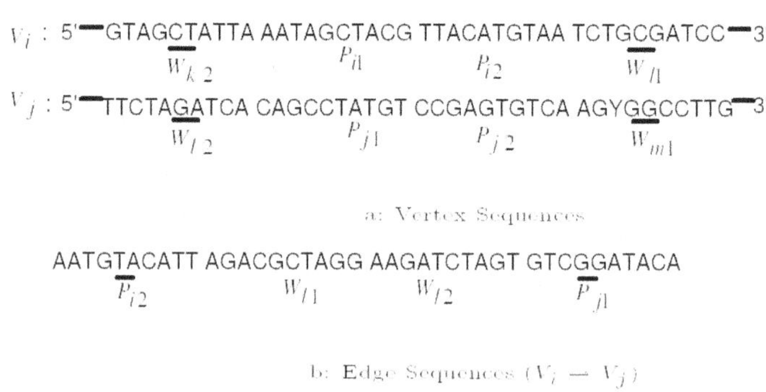

Fig. 2. The fixed length coding scheme. Vertex sequence Vi, Vj, with their the edge sequence (Vi →Vj).

We also encode edge sequences with 4 components: 10-bp link sequence (Pi2), 10-bp weight sequence (W1), 10-bp weight sequence (W2), and 10-bp link sequence (Pj1) (see Fig.2 and Fig.3).The polarity of edge codes is the opposite (3'-5') to vertex codes. The position sequences represent a specific vertex; the weight sequence denotes a weight value in an edge. The weight sequences describe the proportion of edge weights, so the coding scheme can express the real value weights. The way to describe the edge weights is explained in the fitness function [9].

We use Fig1 detailed to illustrate the coding scheme. In step 1, the vertex position sequences Pi1 and Pi2 for all i is randomly generated. In step 2 and 3, the whole edge sequences are designed. For the case of Vi-Vj , We design link sequences Pi2, Pj1 , weight sequence W =(W1,W2) and then they are combined. In Step 4, the vertex weight sequence is designed in a similar way; vertex weight sequences are generated by the edge weight sequences, and then are combined position sequences and weight sequences. In Step 5, the amount of G/C contents in edge sequences is optimized by a genetic algorithm [9]. This is done so that the edges with smaller weights have more G/C contents and thus have higher probability of being contained in the final solution. Encode to Fig.1 is presented Table 1.

Table 1. Coding scheme of Fig.1

(a). Vertex sequence: weight and position sequence

1 →0 → 1: 5'-CTAATGACTGCAACCCAAAACCTGGTAGAGATCTATGATA-3'

1 →0 → 5: 5'-CTAATGACTGCAACCCAAAACCTGGTAGAGGCACGTGCAT-3'

5 → 0 → 1: 5'-CGACTACCGTCAACCCAAAACCTGGTAGAGATCTATGATA-3'

5 → 1 → 5: 5'-CGACTACCGTCAACCCAAAACCTGGTAGAGGCACGTGCAT-3'

0 → 1 → 2: 5'-CTAATGACTGATATCGCGGGTTCAACGTGCCACATGCGTC-3'

2 → 1 → 0: 5'-CGAGTACCGTATATCGCGGGTTCAACGTGCATCTATGATA-3'

0 → 1 → 0: 5'-CTAATGACTGATATCGCGGGTTCAACGTGCATCTATGATA-3'

2 → 1 → 2: 5'-CGAGTACCGTATATCGCGGGTTCAACGTGCCACATGCGTC-3'

0 → 1 → 4: 5'-CTAATGACTGATATCGCGGGTTCAACGTGCTATACATGAT-3'

4 → 1 → 4: 5'-CTAGAACTTGATATCGCGGGTTCAACGTGCTATACATGAT-3'

4→ 1 → 0: 5'-CTAGAACTTGATATCGCGGGTTCAACGTGCTCTATGATA-3'

4 → 1 → 2: 5'-CTAGAACTTGATATCGCGGGTTCAACGTGCCACATGCGTC-3'

2 → 2 → 4: 5'-CGAGTACCGATATCGCGGGTTCAACGTGCTATACATGAT-3'

1 → 2 → 3: 5'-CGAGTACCGTCAGTTGACATGCAGGATCGAGCCGGCCGCG-3'

1 → 2 → 1: 5'-CGAGTACCGTCAGTTGACATGCAGGATCGACACATGCGTC-3'

3 → 2 → 3: 5'-GGCCGCGCCGCAGTTGACATGCAGGATCGAGCCGGCCGCG-3'

3 → 3 → 1: 5'-GGCCGCGCCGCAGTTGACATGCAGGATCGACACATGCGTC-3'

2 → 3 → 2: 5'-GGCCGCGCCGAACCTGGTACCAAGCTTGACGCCGGCCGCG-3'

4 → 3 → 4: 5'-GTATACTACAAACCTGGTACCAAGCTTGACGAATTCATCT-3'

2 → 3 → 4: 5'-GGCCGCGCCGAACCTGGTACCAAGCTTGACGAATTCATCT-3'

4 → 4 → 2: 5'-GTATACTACAAACCTGGTACCAAGCTTGACGCCGGCCGCG-3'

3 → 4 → 5: 5'-GTATACTACATGGTTTGGACTGGTCAAGTTGGCCCGGCGC-3'

5 → 4 → 3: 5'-GGCCCGGCCGTGGTTTGGACTGGTCAAGTTGAATTCATCT-3'

3 → 4 → 3: 5'-GTATACTACATGGTTTGGACTGGTCAAGTTGAATTCATCT-3'

5 → 4 → 5: 5'-GGCCCGGCCGTGGTTTGGACTGGTCAAGTTGGCCCGGCGC-3'

1 → 4 → 1: 5'-CTAGAACTTGTGGTTTGGACTGGTCAAGTTTATACATGAT-3'

3 → 4 → 1: 5'-GTATACTACATGGTTTGGACTGGTCAAGTTTATACATGAT-3'

1 → 4 → 3: 5'-CTAGAACTTGTGGTTTGGACTGGTCAAGTTGAATTCATCT-3'

1 → 4 → 5: 5'-CTAGAACTTGTGGTTTGGACTGGTCAAGTTGGCCCGGCGC-3'

5 → 5 → 1: 5'-GGCCCGGCCGTGGTTTGGACTGGTCAAGTTTATACATGAT-3'

0 → 5 → 0: 5'-CGTAGCTCGATATAGCGCATGCAGGATCGAGCACGTGCAT-3'

4 → 5 → 4: 5'-GGCCCGGCCGTATAGCGCATGCAGGATCGAGGCCCGGCGC-3'

4 → 5 → 0: 5'-GGCCCGGCCGTATAGCGCATGCAGGATCGAGCACGTGCAT-3'

0 → 5 → 4: 5'-CGTAGCTCGATATAGCGCATGCAGGATCGAGGCCCGGCGC-3'

(b). Edge sequence: Link and weight sequence

0 → 1: 3'-GGACCATCTCTAGATACTATGATTACTGACTATAGCGCCC-5'

1 → 0: 3'-AAGTTGCACGTAGATACTATGATTACTGACGTTGGGTTTT-5'

1 → 2: 3'-AAGTTGCACCGTGTACGCAGGCTCATGGCAGTCAACTGTA-5'

2 → 1: 3'-CGTCCTAGCTGTGTACGCAGGCTCATGGCATATAGCGCCC-5'

2 → 3: 3'-CGTCCTAGCTCGGCCGGCGCCCGGCGCGGCTTGGACCATC-5'

3 → 2: 3'-GTTCGAACTGCGGCCGGCGCCCGGCGCGGCGTCAACTGTA-5'

3 → 4: 3'-GTTCGAACTGCTTAAGTAGACATATGATGTACCAAACCTG-5'

4 → 3: 3'-ACCAGTTCAACTTAAGTAGACATATGATGTTTGGACCATG-5'

4 → 5: 3'-ACCAGTTCAACCGGGCCGCGCCGGGCCGGCATATCGCGTA-5'

5 → 4: 3'-CGTCCTAGCTCCGGGCCGCGCCGGGCCGGCACCAAACCTG-5'

5 → 0: 3'-CGTCCTAGCTCGTGCACGTAGCATCGAGCTGTTGGGTTTT-5'

0 → 5: 3'-GGACCATCTCCGTGCACGTAGCATCGAGCTATATCGCGTA-5'

1 → 4: 3'-AAGTTGCACCATATGTACTAGATCTTGAACACCAAACCTG-5'

4 → 1: 3'-ACCAGTTCAAATATGTACTAGATCTTGAACTATAGCGCCC-5'

The notation 0 → 1 → 2 in Table1(a) means that vertex 1 has in-edge from vertex 0 (0 → 1) and out-edge to vertex 2 (0 → 2). Note that the edge sequences with high weights have more G/C pairs than A/T pairs. Similarly, the edge sequences with low weights have more A/T pairs than A/T pairs. The link sequences contain the same number of A/T pairs and G/C. Thus, the weight sequences control the edge weight, and the link sequences have little effect on representing weight values.

4 Molecular Algorithm on Chinese Postman Problem

To implement Step 1 of algorithm, for each vertex i in the graph and for each edge i → j in the graph, 50pmol of oligoncleotide strand "i" and 50pmol of oligoncleotide strand "i → j" , respectively, were mixed together in a single ligation reaction, the oligoncleotides "i → j" served as splints to bring oligoncleotides associated with compatible edges together for ligation (Fig.3).

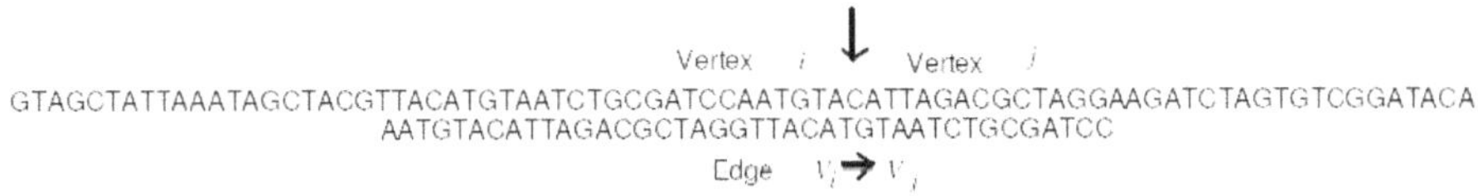

Fig. 3. Ligation procedure

Hence the ligation reaction resulted in the formation of DNA molecules encoding random closed walk through the graph. The scale of this ligation reaction far exceeded what was necessary for the graph under consideration. For each edge in the graph, approximately 6×10^{13} copies of the associated oligonucleotide were added to the ligation reaction. Hence it is likely that many DNA molecules encoding the closed walk were created. In fact, the creation of a single such molecule would be sufficient. As a result, for this graph quantities of oligonucleotides less than an attomle would be sufficient. Alternatively, a much larger graph could have been processed with the picmole quantities used here. To implement Step 2 of the algorithm, the product of Step 1 was amplified by polymerase chain reaction(PCR) using rear 10bp of position sequence oligonucleotide "0" and former 10bp of position sequence oligonucletide "0" as primer. Thus only those molecules encoding generalized Euler tour that begin with vertex 0 and end with vertex 0 were amplified. To implement Step 3 of the algorithm, the produce of Step 2 was affinity-purified with a biotin-avidin magnetic beads system. First generating single-stranded DNA from the double-stranded DNA produce of Step 2 and then incubating the single-sranded DNA with corresponding complement sequence of TAGATACTATGATTACTGAC conjugated to magnetic beads accomplished this. Only those single-standed DNA molecules that contained the sequence TAGATACTATGATTACTGAC and hence encoded closed walk that through edge 0 → 1 or 1 → 0 edge at least once, denaturalize to the bound complement sequence of ATGTCGTCTG and were retained.

This process was repeated successively with corresponding complement sequence of GTGTACGCAGGCTCATGGCA, CGGCCGGCGCCCGGCGCGGC, CTTAAGTAGACATATGATGT, CCGGGCCGCGCCGGGCCGGC, CGTGCACGTAGCATCGAGCT and ATATGTACTAGATCTTGAAC. Only those single-stranded DNA molecules that contained the sequences GTGTACGCAGGCTCATGGCA, CGGCCGGCGCCCGGCGCGGC, CTTAAGTAGACATATGATGT, CCGGGCCGCGCCGGGCCGGC, CGTGCACGTAGCATCGAGCT and ATATGTACTAGATCTTGAAC.

Hence encoded closed walk that through edge $0 \to 1$ or edge $1 \to 0$, edge $1 \to 2$ or edge $2 \to 1$, edge $2 \to 3$ or edge $3 \to 2$, edge $3 \to 4$ or edge $4 \to 3$, edge $4 \to 5$ or edge $5 \to 4$, edge $5 \to 0$ or edge $0 \to 5$, edge $1 \to 4$ or edge $4 \to 1$ at least once. Namely, we can find out all generalized Euler tour of Fig 1. To implement Step 4 of algorithm, we observed the number of hydrogen bonds 0f products of Step 3. It is for us to find the shortest DNA strand (for the graph Fig 1, the number of hydrogen bonds 0f the shortest DNA sequences must be Minimum). Extract the DNA stand, afterwards, this product was PCR-amplified and gelpurified several times to enhance its purity. To implement Step 5 of algorithm, we carry through sequencing to products of Step 4. Thereby, we can find out the solution of Chinese Postman Problem. Similarly S.Y.Shin's experimentation, we can all accomplish bio-experiment Step 1, Step 2, Step 3 and Step 4. Moreover, sequencing to implement Step 5, we must purified products after each operation, it brings us convenience to sequencing by Sanger's method, we can also use the method of SBH(sequencing by hybridization) [13]. Consequently, we may read out postman paths of Chinese Postman Problem.

5 Conclusion

The potential of molecular computation is impressive, what is not clear is whether such massive numbers of inexpensive operation can be productively used to solve real computational problems. We presented a weight encode scheme for molecular programming and demonstrated its performance on Chinese postman problem. In this encoding, the relative values of G/C contents against A/T contents are taken into account to represent real-valued weight of the edge in the graph. Since G/C pairs have 3 hydrogen bonds and A/T pairs 2, we can represent real-valued x by according to G/C contents. We have shown that the method is effective for reliable DNA computing applied to Chinese postman problem. The method can easily be modified to use in other graph problem in which edges are associated with real-valued costs. Nonetheless, for certain intrinsically complex problem, such as Chinese Postman Problem where existing electronic computers are very inefficient and where massively parallel searches can be organized to take advantage of the operations that molecular biology currently provides, it is conceivable that molecular computation might compete with electronic computation to our problem. We encode a graph with n vertices, only encode position sequences of the n vertices and weight sequences of all edges oligoncleotide sequences of all vertices and edge will be determined. Thus, difficulty of encoding will be debased. Approach in the paper may be solving Chinese Postman problem and it is very convenience. We can also solve the shortest path problem, TSP problem with the method in the paper.

Acknowledgments

This work is supported by the National Scientific Foundation of China (Grant numbers: 60533010, 60373089 and 30370356).

References

1. Adleman, L. M.: Molecular Computation of Solutions to Combinatorial Problems. Science. 266 (1994) 1021-1023
2. Lipton, R. J.: DNA Solution of Hard Computational Problems. Science. 268 (1995) 542-545
3. Ouyang,Q., Kaplan,P.D., Liu,S. M.: DNA Solution of the Maximal Clique Problem. Science. 278 (1997) 446-449
4. Liu, Q.: DNA Computing on Surfaces. Nature. 403 (2000) 175-179
5. Wu, H.: An Improved Surface-based Method for DNA Computation. Biosystems. 59 (2001) 1-5
6. Shi, XL, Li, X., Zhang, Z., et al.: Improve Capability of DNA Automaton: DNA Automaton with Three Internal States and Tape Head Move in Two Directions. LECT NOTES COMPUT SC 3645 (2005) 71-79
7. Yin, Z., Zhang, F., Xu, J., et al.: A General 0-1 Programming Problem Based on DNA Computing, Biosystems. 70 (2003) 73-79
8. Head, T.: Formal Language Theory and DNA: an Analysis of the Generative Capacity of Specific Recombinant Behaviors. Bull. Math. Biol, 49 (1987) 737-759
9. Shine S. Y.: Solving Travelling Problems using Molecular Programming. IEEE. 35 (1999) 994-1000
10. Zhang, B. T., Shin,S. Y.: Code Optimization for DNA Computing of Maximal Cliques. Advances in Soft Computing-Engineering Design and Manufacturing, Springer-Verlag. (1998)
11. Yin, Z., Zhang, F., Xu, J.: A Chinese Postman Problem Based on DNA Computing. Journal of Chemical Information and Computing Science. 42 (2002) 222-224
12. Bondy, J. A., Murty, U. S. R.: Graph Theory with Applications. The Macmillan Press LTD. (1976)
13. Yin, Z.: DNA computing in Graph and combinatorial optimization. Science Press, BeiJin, China. (2004)
14. Mirzabekov, A. D.: DNA sequencing by hybridization a megasequencing method and adiagnostic tool. TIBTECH. 12 (1994) 27-32

DNA Computing Model of the Integer Linear Programming Problem Based on Molecular Beacon

Zhi-xiang Yin[1,2], Jian-zhong Cui[1], Jin Yang[1], and Jin Xu

[1] Department of Mathematics and Physics
Anhui University of Science and Technology. Anhui Huainan (232001) China
[2] Department of Control Science and Engineering
Huazhong University of Science and Technology Huibei Wuhan (430074) China
zxyin66@163.com

Abstract. Biological chip technology and DNA computing are new research areas in biology science and information science separately. The essential characteristic of both is the massive parallel of obtaining and managing information. The integer linear programming problem is an important problem in opsearch and it is an NP-complete problem. But up to now, there does not exist any good algorithm yet. A new DNA computing model is provided to solve a integer linear programming problem based on Molecular Beacon chip. In the method, the integer linear programming problem is solved with molecular beacon by fluorescing upon hybridization to their complementary DNA targets. The method has some significant advantages such as simple encoding, excellent sensitivity, high selectivity, low cost, low error, short operating time, reusable surface and simple experimental steps. The result suggest s the potential of Molecular Beacon used as a DNA computer chip.

1 Introduction

In 1961, Feynman gave a visionary talk describing the possibility of building computers that were sub-microscopic [1]. Despite remarkable progress in computer miniaturization, this goal has yet to be achieved. Computer scientists rank computational problems in three classes: easy, hard and incomputable [2]. About thirty years ago there was developed a conception designating a hierarchy of complexity classes for problems on finite sets. And so long as we use digital computers with finite memory storing discrete objects to resolve computational problems, it is relevant for any non-trivial algorithm designing. With the current state-of-the-art the most important complexity classes are P (problems solvable in polynomial time) and NP (problems whose solution certificate can be verified in polynomial time). The most fruitful result of the conception is that complexity classes have so-called complete problems. A problem of a class is complete if you can solve any other problem of this class in polynomial time having a polynomial time algorithm for the first one. Hence complete problems are hardest in their own classes and as they exist we may choose any of them to advance solving techniques for the entire class. The concept of complete problems for a class is generalized to hard problems for the class by inclusion of all other problems, whose polynomial time algorithm gives polynomial time solvability for the class. So, there are NP-complete

D.-S. Huang, K. Li, and G.W. Irwin (Eds.): ICIC 2006, LNBI 4115, pp. 238 – 247, 2006.

and NP-hard problems [3,4]. One of the major achievements of computer science in the last two decades in the understanding that many important computational search problems are NP-complete and thus are unlikely to have efficient algorithms that solve the problem exactly. Adleman (1994) showed that DNA can be used to solve a computationally hard problem, the directed hamiltonian path problem (DHPP), and demonstrated the potential power of parallel, high-density computation by molecules in solution [5]. This parallelism allows DNA computers to solve larger hard problems such as NP-complete problems in linearly increasing time, in contrast to the exponentially increasing time required by an electronically computer. After Adleman initiated the field of DNA computing, Lipton (1995) proposed DNA experiments to solve the satisfiability (SAT) problem [6]. In 1997, Ouyang et al presented a molccular biology based experimental solution to the "maximal clique" problem [2]. In 2000, Liu et al designed DNA model system; a multi-based encoding strategy is used in a one-word approach to surface-based DNA computation [7]. In 2001, Wu analyzed and improved their surface-based method [8]. In 2002, Yin et al gave a Chinese postman problem based on DNA computing [9]. All of these efforts made use of molecular biology and demonstrated the feasibility of carrying out computation at the molecular level. One of the formal frameworks for molecular computations is Tom Head's splicing system, which gives a theoretical foundation for computing based on DNA recombination [10]. 0-1 programming problem and the satisfiability problem are closely related, and 0-1 programming problem is a generalization of the satisfiability problem. Up to now, there have been many results for solving the satisfiability problem [6,7,11,12]. In 2002, Braich et al solved a 20-variable instance of the NP-Complete three-satisfiability problem on a simple DNA computer, and proposed this computational problem may be largest yet solved by non-electronic means [13]. A molecular beacon (MB) is a synthetic short hairpin oligonucleotide molecule that consists of a loop and a stem structure. The loop portion of a MB is a probe sequence complementary to a target molecule. In the absence of target, the self-complementary domains anneal to form a stem-loop hairpin structure in a uni-molecular reaction that serves to bring the fluorescence reporter group into close proximity with the quencher group and results in quenching of the reporter. In the presence of target, the central loop domain will hybridize with the complementary target DNA in a bimolecular reaction, forcing the molecule to unfold: reporter and quencher are now physically separated and the fluorescence of the reporter dye will be restored upon excitation. In 2004, Yin et al proposed DNA computing model for 0-1 programming problem [14]. In 2005, Wang et al proposed DNA algorithm for integer linear programming problem [15]. It is regret biological operation method hasn't given in their paper. In the paper, we solved the integer linear programming problem with molecular beacon by fluorescing upon hybridization to their complementary DNA targets, and presented detail biological operation method.

For terminologies and notations not defied in this paper, the readers are referred to Ref. [16].

2 Basic Theory of Integer Linear Programming Problem

Let us consider the integer linear programming problem (ILP):

$$\begin{gathered} max(min)\ C^T x \\ Ax = b \\ x \geq 0,\ x \text{ is integer} \end{gathered} \tag{1}$$

Where the entries of $A=\{a_{ij}\}_{m\times n}$, $b=\{b_i\}_{m\times 1}$ and $c=\{c_i\}_{n\times 1}$ are integer. Let $a_1 = max_{i,j}\{|a_{ij}|\}$, $a_2 = max_i\{|b_i|\}$ and $a_3 = max(\{a_1, a_2\} \cup \{|c_j| : j=1,2,\cdots,n\})$.

Theorem 1[17]. If the above ILP has a finite optimum, then it has an optimal solution x such that $|x_j| \leq n^3[(m+2)a_3]^{4m+2}$, $j=1,2,\cdots,n$.

Theorem 2[15]. Every ILP is equivalent to a 0-1 linear programming (ZOLP).

Theorem 3[17]. ILP is NP-complete problem.
By Theorem 2 and 3, we have the following theorem:

Theorem 4[15]. ZOLP is NP-complete problem.

Let $a_j = max_i\{a_{ij}, c_j\}$. We replace each term $a_{ij}x_j$ of the ZOLP by $\sum_{k=1}^{a_j} a_{ij}^k x_{jk}$ and each term $c_j x_j$ by $\sum_{k=1}^{a_j} c_j^k x_{jk}$, where:

(1) x_{jk} are 0-1 variables;

(2) $a_{ij}^k = 1\ (1 \leq k \leq a_{ij}),\ a_{ij}^k = 0\ (a_{ij} \leq k \leq a_j)$ when $a_{ij} > 0$;

(3) $a_{ij}^k = -1\ (1 \leq k \leq |a_{ij}|),\ a_{ij}^k = 0\ (|a_{ij}| \leq k \leq a_j)$ when $a_{ij} < 0$;

(4) $a_{ij}^k = 0\ (1 \leq k \leq a_j)$, when $a_{ij} = 0$;

(5) $c_j^k = 1(1 \leq k \leq c_j),\ c_j^k = 0(c_j < k \leq a_j)$, when $c_j > 0$;

(6) $c_j^k = -1(1 \leq k \leq |c_j|),\ c_j^k = 0(|c_j| < k \leq a_j)$, when $c_j < 0$;

(7) $c_j^k = 0(1 \leq k \leq a_j)$ when $c_j = 0$;

(8) $\sum_{k=1}^{a_j} x_{jk} = a_j$ or $0\ (1 \leq j \leq n)$.

The resulting ZOLP is denoted by ZZOLP.

Theorem 5[15]. Every ZOLP is equivalent to a ZZOLP, and their optimums are the same.
By Theorem 4 and 5, we have the following.

Theorem 6. ZZOLP is NP-complete problem.

3 The Model System of ZZOLP

Let $\{A_i \mid i \in I\}$ be a family of sets indexed by a nonempty set I. The Cartesian product of the sets A_i is the set of all functions $f: I \to \bigcup_{i\in I} A_i$ such that $f(i) \in A_i$ for all $i \in I$, It is denoted $\prod_{i\in I} A_i$. If $I = \{1,2,\cdots,t\}$, the product $\prod_{i\in I} A_i$ is often denoted by $A_1 \times A_2 \times \cdots \times A_t$ and is identified with the set of all ordered t-tuples $(a_1, a_2, \cdots, a_t)$, where $a_i \in A_i$ for $i = 1,2,\cdots,t$. Let m be a minimum integer such that $4^m \geq n$, set $<n>= 0,1,2,\cdots,2^n - 1$ and $A_i = \{A, G, C, T\}$.

3.1 DNA Algorithm of ZZOLP

Let us consider the ZZOLP

$$\begin{aligned} &max\, C^T x \\ &Ax = b \\ &x = 0 or 1 \end{aligned} \quad (2)$$

where the entries of $b = \{b_i\}_{m\times 1}$ are integer and the entries of $A = \{a_{ij}\}_{m\times n}$ and $c = \{c_i\}_{n\times 1}$ are -1, 0, 1. We will use the set $x = (x_1, x_2, \cdots, x_n)^T$ instead of $<n>$. Then there exists and injection f from x to $\coprod_{i=1}^m A_i$. For example, $f: x_1 \to$ AACCTGGTTGGT when $x_1 = 1$, $x_1 \to$ AGGCCTGACTGA when $x_1 = 0$; $x_2 \to$ ACCATAGCTAGC when $x_2 = 1$, $x_2 \to$ ACCGATTCATTC when $x_2 = 0$; $x_3 \to$ AGAGTCTCAGAG when $x_3 = 1$, $x_3 \to$ AAGGCCTGCCTG when $x_3 = 0$. where $x = (x_1, x_2, x_3)^T$ = (AACCTGGTTGGT, ACCATAGCTAGC), AGAGTCTCAGAG)T instead of 7, $x = (x_1, x_2, x_3)^T$ = (AGGCCTGACTGA, ACCATAGCTAGC, AGAGTCTCAGAG)T instead of 3.

Set $X = (M(f(x_1)), M(f(x_2)), \cdots, M(f(x_n)))^T$, where $M(f(x_i))$ is a molecular beacon with loop $f(x_i)$, $\overline{X} = (\overline{f(x_1)}, \overline{f(x_2)}, \cdots, \overline{f(x_n)})$ and $\overline{X}^* = (\overline{f(x_1)}^*, \overline{f(x_2)}^*, \cdots, \overline{f(x_n)}^*)$, where $\overline{f(x_i)}$ is complementary stands of $f(x_i)$ and $*$ is a color fluorescent tag. Immobilize the 2^n same columns $\xi = (X, X, \cdots, X)$ on the surface.

We designed the following algorithm to solve ZZOLP:

Step 1. i:=1

Step 2. If i=m+1, then return step 7.

Step 3. Cover every $\overline{f(x_i)}$ when the coefficients of x_i are -1 and every $\overline{f(x_2)}^*$ when the coefficients of x_i are 1 in the ith equality constraint.

Step 4. Hybridizing, choose the columns whose $S^+ - S^- = b_i$ (where S^+ is the number of the components which have two color fluorescents tags and S^- is number which only have one color fluorescent tags in the column vector).

Step 5. Delete the above surplus columns and uncover the covered $\overline{f(x_i)}$ and $\overline{f(x_2)}^*$.

Step 6. Let i:=i+1 and return step 2

Step 7. Cover every $\overline{f(x_i)}$ when the coefficients of x_i are -1 and every $\overline{f(x_2)}^*$ when the coefficients of x_i are 1 in the object function.

Step 8. Hybridizing, choose the columns whose $S^+ - S^-$ is Maximum.

Step 9. Record the above columns and $S^+ - S^-$

Step 10. End

3.2 Biological Operation for DNA Algorithm of ZZOLP

For a system of equations that contains n variables $x_1, x_2, \cdots, x_n$ and m equations, in order to implement biological operation of algorithm mentioned above, the progress can be separated into the following steps.

Step1: Synthesis $3n$ oligonucleotides divided into 3 groups, which include n oligonucleotides in each group. The oligonucleotides in the first group represent variable $x_1, x_2, \cdots, x_n$ respectively and written as $x_1, x_2, \cdots, x_n$; the second represent variable $\bar{x}_1, \bar{x}_2, \cdots, \bar{x}_n$ respectively ($x_i = 1$ if and only if $\overline{x_i} = 0$ and written as $\bar{x}_1, \bar{x}_2, \cdots, \bar{x}_n$; the third group represent complementary strands of the first group respectively, individual written as $x'_1, x'_2, \cdots, x'_n$. (pay attention to oligonucleotide x_i represents variable $x_i = 1$ and oligonucleotide $\bar{x}_i$ represents variable $\bar{x}_i = 0$, $i = 1,2,\cdots,n$).

Step2: Constructing 2^n molecular beacons with loop $x_1, x_2, \cdots, x_n, \bar{x}_1, \bar{x}_2, \cdots, \bar{x}_n$ as probes and tagging oligonucleotides $x'_1, x'_2, \cdots, x'_n$ with fluorescent green ABI, written their as $x_1^*, x_2^*, \cdots, x_n^*$. Our molecular beacon has total of 22 bases, of which 12 bases corresponding to $x_1, x_2, \cdots, x_n, \bar{x}_1, \bar{x}_2, \cdots, \bar{x}_n$ are the sequence of interest and 5 base pairs form stem, Texas Red is used as fluorophore and DABCYL as the quencher. Fix the 2^n molecular beacons on the surface and where the molecular beacons are arranged in 2^n rows representing all variables of the given computational problem (fixed method can be seen [18]).

Step3: Add x'_i to the surface when the coefficients of x_i are -1 and add x_i^* to the surface when the coefficients of x_i are 1 in the ith equality constraint. Any solution that satisfies this equality will be the columns whose $S^{+} - S^{-} = b_i$ (where S^{+} is the number of the components which have two color fluorescents tags and S^{-} is number which only have one color fluorescent tags in the column vector). Further, we can determine the solution for satisfying (dissatisfying) the constraint equation by a method of fluorescence image, and observe their color and record.

Step4: The temperature is raised to separate all double-stranded DNA into single-strands by thermal denaturation. After washing with the certain buffer, the surface is returned to the initial state.

Step5: we can remove all infeasible solution and obtain feasible solution of the problem by repeating step3 and step4. Add x'_i to the surface when the coefficients of x_i are -1 and add x_i^* to the surface when the coefficients of x_i are 1 in the object function and choose the satisfied constraint equation columns whose $S^{+} - S^{-}$ is Maximum, the variable value of the columns are optimum solutions.

4 The Discussion of the Simple ZZOLP

We discuss in detail simple 0-1 programming problem as below:

$$\max u = x - y + z$$

$$\begin{cases} x + y - z = 1 \\ x + y + z = 1 \\ x, y, z = 0,1 \end{cases} \tag{3}$$

To discuss the 0-1 programming problem, the progress was separated into six steps:

Step1: Synthesis 9 oligonucleotides divided into 3 groups, which include 3 oligonucleotides in each group. The oligonucleotides in the first group represent variable x, y, z respectively and written as x, y, z ; the second represent variable $\overline{x}, \overline{y}, \overline{z}$ respectively ($x = 1$ if and only if $\overline{x} = 0$, such as y, z) and written as $\overline{x}, \overline{y}, \overline{z}$; the third group represent complementary strands of the first group respectively and written as x', y', z' (see Fig.1). (pay attention to oligonucleotide x represents variable $x = 1$ and oligonucleotide $\overline{x}$ represents variable $\overline{x} = 0$, y and z are also so).

x : 5'-AACCTGGTTGAC-3' y : 5'-ACCATAGCACTG-3'

z : 5'-AGAGTCTCATGC-3' $\overline{x}$: 5'-CCAAGTTGCCGT-3'

$\overline{y}$: 5'-GTTGGGTTCGGT-3' $\overline{z}$: 5'-AGCTTGCATACG-3'

x' : 5'-TTGGACCATGAC-3' y' : 5'-TGGTATCGGTCA-3'

z' : 5'- TCTCAGAGGCTG-3'

Fig. 1. Detailed encoding of all variables

Step2: Constructing 6 molecular beacons with loop $x, y, z, \overline{x}, \overline{y}, \overline{z}$ as probes and tagging oligonucleotides x', y', z' with fluorescent green ABI, written their as x^*, y^*, z^*. Our molecular beacon has total of 22 bases, of which 12 bases corresponding to $x, y, z, \overline{x}, \overline{y}, \overline{z}$ are the sequence of interest and 5 base pairs form stem, Texas Red is used as fluorophore and DABCYL as the quencher. Fix the 6 molecular beacons on the surface and where the molecular beacons are arranged in 8 rows representing all variables of the given computational problem (see Fig.2).

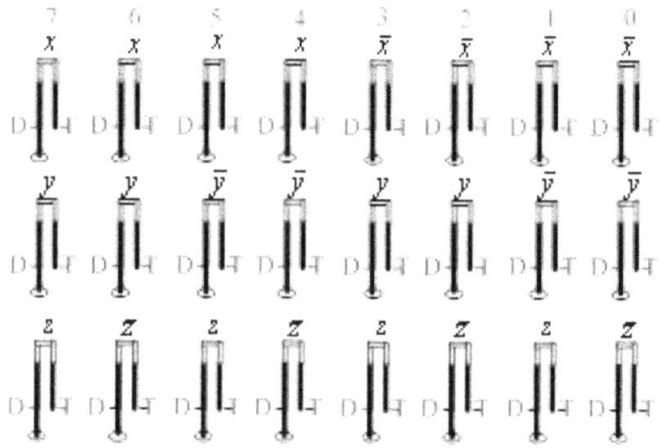

Fig. 2. Fixed molecular beacons on the surface

Step3: For the first constraint equation, we add the complementary strands tagged fluorescent green ABI x^*, y^* and complementary strands untagged fluorescent green ABI z' to the surface. Any solution that satisfies this equality will be the columns whose $S^+ - S^- = 1$ (where S^+ is the number of the components which have two color fluorescents tags and S^- is number which only have one color fluorescent tags in the column vector). Further, we can determine the solution for satisfying (dissatisfying) the constraint equation by a method of fluorescence image, and observe their color and record. (the feasible solution of the problem is "2,4,7", see Fig.3).

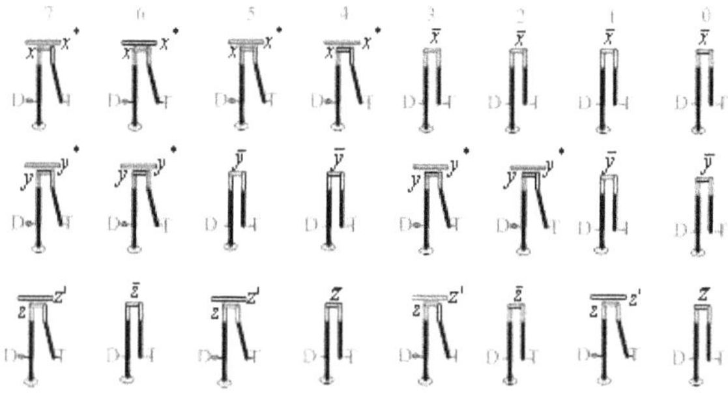

Fig. 3. Hybridize figure of the first constraint equation

Step4: The temperature is raised to separate all double-stranded DNA into single-strands by thermal denaturation. The surface is returned to the initial state by washing in buffer (without regard for infeasible solution determined above). For the second constraint equation, similar to step3 above by adding the complementary strands tagged fluorescent green ABI x^*, y^*, z^* to the surface, we can determine the solution of satisfying constraint equation by a method of fluorescence-image, and observe their color and record, Any solution satisfied this equality will be will be the columns whose $S^+ - S^- = 1$ (the feasible solution of the problem is "1,2,4", see Fig.4).

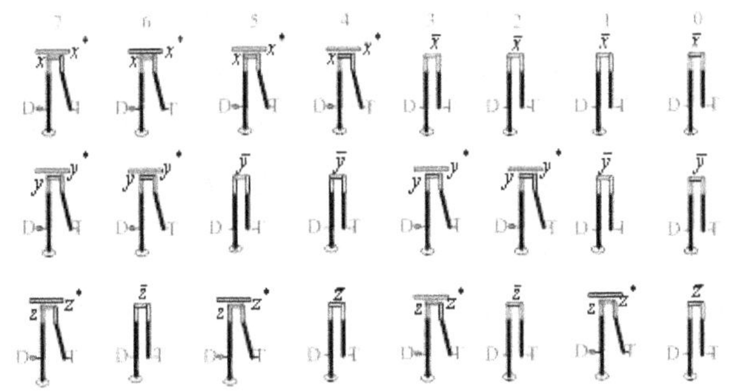

Fig. 4. Hybridize figure of the second constraint equation

Step5: For the object function, we add the complementary strands tagged fluorescent green ABI x^*, z^* and complementary strands untagged fluorescent green ABI y' to the surface and choose the satisfied constraint equation columns whose $S^+ - S^-$ is Maximum, the variable value of the columns are optimum solutions (we only care the two columns of "2", "4", the optimum solution is "4", it shows that variable value is (1,0,0), see Fig.5). We can obtain optimum solution (1,0,0), and the maximum value of objective function is 1 .

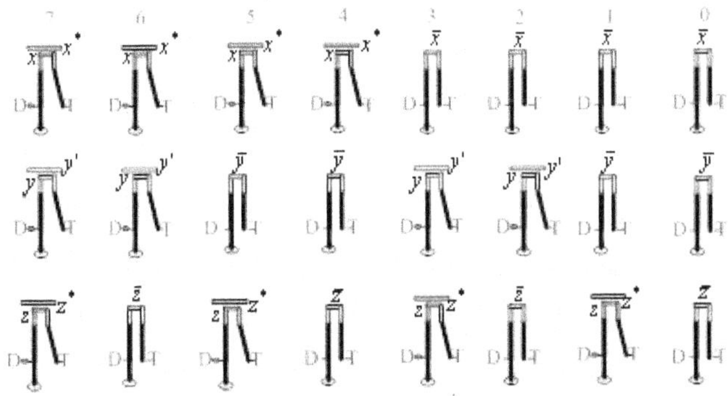

Fig. 5. Hybridize figure of the objective function

The experiment is not complicated and we can accomplish a result that is similar to the experiment performed by Fang [19].

5 Analysis Conclusions

Because computers have obvious limits in storage, speed, intelligence and miniaturization, recently, concerns regarding the methods of DNA computation have arisen, especially their efficient parallelism. In order to solve a practical issue, there are still some problems that need a farther study in biologic technology. In this article, we highlight a DNA computing model to solve an integer linear programming problem based molecular beacon. The model we proposed has a potential to solve linear programming problem, which is an important issue in operational research. With the advance of the biologic technology and the molecule biology, the general linear programming problem will be solved. In our method, we adopt fluorescence marking technique, laser focus technique and molecular beacon technique, and read solution by viewing fluorescence, the method of which has some significant advantages such as simple encoding, excellent sensitivity, high selectivity, low cost, low error, short operating time, reusable surface and simple experimental steps. The result suggest s the potential of Molecular Beacon used as a DNA computer chip.

Acknowledgment

The authors sincerely appreciate the encouraging comments of the Editor of the journal on this paper. They also wish to thank an anonymous referee of this paper who provided many useful and constructive suggestions for the improvement of this paper. Finally, thanks to all the authors that appear in the references. This project is supported by CNSF (Grant 60274026,30570431,60373089); China Postdoctoral Science Foundation Grant 2004035176; New Century Excellent Talents in University; Science Foundation of Educational government of Anhui Province of China(2006kj068A); Excellent Youth Science and Technology Foundation of Anhui Province of China (06042088); Huazhong University of Science and Technology Postdoctoral Foundation Grant, AnHui University of Science and Technology Doctoral Foundation Grant.

References

1. Feynmam, R.P. In: Gilbart, D.H. (eds): Minaturization. Reinhold, New York (1961) 282-296
2. Ouyang, Q.P., Kaplan, D.S., Liu, M. AND libchaber, A.: DNA Solution of the Maximal Clique Problem. Science, 278 (1997) 446-449
3. Christos, H. AND Papadimitriou. In: Combinatorial Optimization: Algorithms and Complexity. Prentice-Hall, Inc., Englewood Cliffs, New Jersey (1989)
4. Cox, J.C.: The Complexities of DNA Computation. TIBTECH, 17 (1996) 151-154
5. Adleman, L.M.: Molecular Computation of Solutions to Combinatorial Problems. Science, 266 (1994) 1021-1023

6. Lipton, R.J.: DNA Solution of Hard Computational Problems. Science, 268 (1995) 542-545
7. Liu, Q.: DNA Computing on Surfaces. Nature, 403 (2000) 175-179
8. Wu, H.Y.: An Improved Surface-based Method for DNA Computation. Biosystem, 59 (2001) 1-5
9. Yin, Z.X., Zhang, F.Y. AND Xu, J.: A Chinese Postman Problem Based on DNA Computing. Journal of Chemical Information and Computing Science, 42 (2002) 222-224
10. Head, T.: Formal Language Theory and DNA: an Analysis of the Generative Capacity of Specific Recombinant Behaviors. Bull. Math. Biol, 49 (1997) 737-759
11. Liu, Q.: Progress Toward Demonstration of a Surface Based DNA Computation: a One Word Approach to Solve a Model Satisfiability Problem. Biosystems, 52 (1999) 25-33
12. Sakamoto, K.G. AND Hidetaka, et al.: Molecular Computation by DNA Hairpin Formation. Science, 288 (2000) 1223-1226
13. Braich, R.S.: Solution of a 20-Variable 3-SAT Problem on a DNA Computer. Science, 296 (2002) 499-502
14. Yin, Z.X., Zhang, F.Y. AND Xu, J.: The General Form of 0-1 Programming Problem Based on DNA Computing. Biosystems, 70 (2003) 73-78
15. Wang, S.Y. AND Yang, A.M.: DNA Solution of Integer Linear Programming. Applied Mathematics and Computation. 17 (2005) 626-632
16. 1Bondy, J.A. AND Murty, U.S.R.: Graph Theory with Applications. The Macmillan Press LTD. New York (1976)
17. Gass, S. L.: Linear Programming Methods and Applications. 5th edn. Mc Graw Hill Book company (1988)
18. Wang, Y.J., Wang, H. AND Lie, L.B., et al.: The Molecular Beacon Technology. Hua xue tong bao, 67(12) (2004) 912-918
19. Fang, X.H., Liu, X.J. AND Schuster, S., et al.: Designing a Novel Molecular Beacon for Surface Immobilized DNA Hybridization Studies. J. Am. Chem. Soc. 121 (1999) 2921-2922

DNA Computing Processor: An Integrated Scheme Based on Biochip Technology for Performing DNA Computing

Yan-Feng Wang[1,2], Guang-Zhao Cui[1,2], Bu-Yi Huang[2], Lin-Qiang Pan[1], and Xun-Cai Zhang[1]

[1] Research Institute of Biomolecular Computer, Huazhong University of Science and Technology, 430074, Wuhan, Hubei, China
wangyf@mail.hust.edu.cn

[2] College of Electrical and Electronic Engineering, Zhengzhou University of Light Industry, 450002, Zhengzhou, Henan, China
cgzh@zzuli.edu.cn

Abstract. An integrated scheme based on biochip technology for performing DNA computing is proposed here. This work is motivated by the goal of integrating all the steps of DNA computing into one machine called DNA computing processor. The basic structure of processor consists of making DNA micro-arrays unit, encoding DNA sequences unit, micro-reaction unit, solution extraction unit and micro-control unit. The functions of each unit are discussed in detail, especially for the solution extraction unit, where the optimal solution spaces are extracted. Finally, conclusions are drawn and future studies are discussed.

1 Introduction

Since Adleman's seminal publication [1], there have already been many interesting and exciting results about DNA computing. These works have led to hope of a DNA computer that can outperform the fastest realizable super computers at NP-complete combinatorial problems. Although the models, algorithms and biological operations of each successful instance may be different, the fundamental ideas of DNA computing are same. Namely, first, the extra complex structure of organism is resulted from a series of simple manipulations of the original information expressed by DNA strands. Second, the computable function can be obtained by a series of elementary and simple computing. DNA computing is just based on the both similarities, [2].

Three kinds of approaches for performing DNA computing, which are test tube-based, surface-based and biochip-based, respectively. Test tube-based model is the primary grade of DNA computing, and always used to verify whether the algorithm is feasible or not. Surface-based model is the bridge between test tube-based and biochip-based. Biochip-based model is the only way to realize the real DNA computer.

In this paper, we propose an integrated scheme based on biochip technology for performing DNA computing to try integrating all the steps of DNA computing into one machine called DNA computing processor, and making DNA computing is

D.-S. Huang, K. Li, and G.W. Irwin (Eds.): ICIC 2006, LNBI 4115, pp. 248–257, 2006.

hands-free and reliable. The rest of this contribution is organized as follows. In section 2, we present a simple description of DNA computing principle and biochip technologies. In section 3, we then propose the integrated scheme based on biochip technologies for performing DNA computing. Section 4 introduces the functions of each unit in detail. Finally, we conclude in section 5 by present some problems to be further considered in the future.

2 Backgrounds

2.1 The Steps of DNA Computing

In general, DNA computing may be considered as consisting of a concatenation of three major stages:

Encoding DNA Sequences Stage. This stage can be considered as mapping the instances of an algorithmic problem in a systematic manner onto DNA molecules;

Biological Reactions Stage. Intrinsic molecular interactions of DNA molecules are exploited and generate a very large space of solution candidates;

Solution Extraction Stage. All the generated molecules representing solution candidates are subjected to a series of mechanical manipulations and other physical processes to identify and extract specify molecules, if available, that are regarded as the exact encodings of the optimal solutions of the original computational problem.

Thus, the steps of DNA computing can be illustrated in Figure 1. The double-lines are data lines.

Fig. 1. The steps of DNA computing

2.2 Biochip Technology

Biochip is a small solid platform made of plastic materials, membrane, or glass, upon which biological information can be stored, retracted, and analyzed. Biochip technology incorporates elements of micro-fluidics, micromachining, synthetic chemistry, separation technology, and detection technology of biological molecules. Biochip technology is moving towards the following directions, [3]:

Miniaturization. Tiny apparatus to handle tiny amount of samples;

Integration. A small apparatus to perform multiple functions;

Parallelism. Biological reactions and information are analyzed in parallel.

With the rapid progress in biochip technologies, it is possible that lab-on-a-chip will come true. Thus, the ideas discussed here may realize in the future.

3 DNA Computing Processor

As discussed above, the basic structure of DNA computing processor may consist of making DNA micro-arrays unit, encoding DNA sequences unit, micro-reaction unit, solution extraction unit and micro-control unit. The structure of DNA computing processor is shown in Figure 2. The real lines, broken lines and double-lines represent control lines, feedback lines and data lines, respectively.

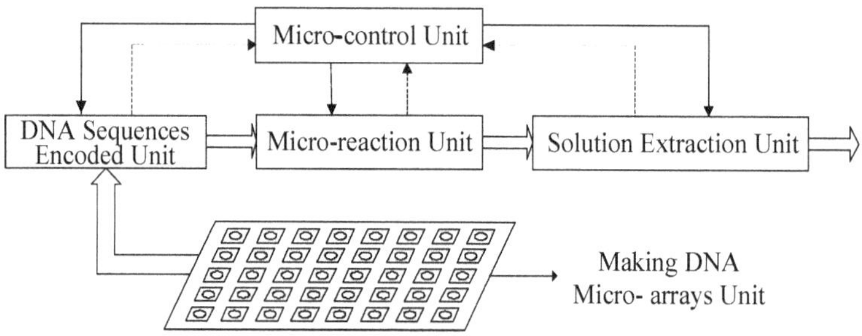

Fig. 2. DNA computing processor organization

The functions of each unit are as follows.

4 The Functions of Each Unit

4.1 Making DNA Micro-arrays Unit

This unit performs DNA micro-arrays preparation from original micro-structure and micro-systems under the control of micro-control unit. There exist two variants of the chips: cDNA micro-arrays and oligonucleotide arrays. Two commonly used types of chips differ in the size of the arrayed nucleic acids. In cDNA micro-arrays, relatively long DNA molecules (longer than 100nt) are immobilized by high-speed robots on a solid surface. The oligonucleotide arrays, relatively short nucleic acids are fabricated either in-situ light-directed chemical synthesis or by conventional synthesis followed by immobilization on a glass substrate. Since nucleic acid sequences utilized in DNA computing are always short, here, we only introduce in-situ synthesis.

Usually oligos are built up base-by-base on the surface of the array. This takes place by covalent reaction between the 5' hydroxyl group of the sugar of the last nucleotide to be attached and the phosphate group of the next nucleotide. Each nucleotide added to the oligonucleotide on the glass has a protective group on its 5' position to prevent the addition of more than one base during each round of synthesis. The protective group is then converted to a hydroxyl group either with acid or with light before the next round of synthesis. The different methods for deprotection lead to the three main technologies for making in-situ synthesized arrays: photodeprotection using masks, photodeprotection without masks and chemical deprotection with synthesis via inkjet technology. For knowing more, see [4] please.

4.2 Encoding DNA Sequences Unit

This unit is mainly made up of making DNA micro-arrays biochips. In this unit, the design and selection of encoding DNA sequences set is crucial. The encoding design problem for DNA computing consists of mapping the instances of an algorithmic problem in a systematic manner onto specific molecules so that the underlying chemical reactions avoid all these sources of error, and the resulting products contain, with a high degree of reliability, enough molecules encoding the answers to the problem's instances to enable a successful extraction, [5].

In fact, for each successful instance of DNA computing, in any case, how ingenious the designing algorithms are, the basic biological manipulations are absolutely necessarily, which are separating, fusing, lengthening, shortening, cutting, linking, modifying, and multiplying etc. all the manipulations on DNA sequences can be regarded as operators of DNA computing and must ensure these manipulations have no errors. Thus, encoding problem come down to DNA sequences design at last. That is to say, encoding problem can be regarded as DNA sequences design for making sure the underlying chemical reactions controllable.

To ensure biological reactions controllable, some constraints should be considered according to the definition of encoding problem, thus, many approaches for encoding problem have been proposed in the last decade, [6-19]. All of which focus on the design of DNA sequences to reduce the possibility for undesirable reactions.

4.3 Micro-reaction Unit

In this unit, intrinsic molecular interactions of DNA molecules are exploited in parallel and generate a very large space of solution candidates. To extract few desirable solutions, the polymer chain reaction (PCR) is absolutely necessarily before solution extraction stage. PCR allows the production of more than 10 million copies of a target DNA sequence from only a few molecules. The sensitivity of this technique means that the sample should not be contaminated with any other DNA or previously amplified products that may reside on chip. The efficiency and specificity of amplification in PCR is always highly dependent on the nature of the template DNA and primers. Therefore optimization of reaction conditions is often necessary. The common method is to design a Kit to simplify optimization and contains ready-to-use reaction buffers covering a wide range of possible values for all components, [20].

4.4 Solution Extraction Unit

Based on the several successful applications have been demonstrated in the last decade, [21-24], we can draw the following conclusion: In DNA computing, solutions either are separated by electrophoresis, then extracted by biological detection device, or extraction followed reactions tightly. On the other hand, it is considered that there does not exit a universal detection method due to the variety and complexity of samples, in addition, in order to control and transfer special analysis software stored in memory unit more easily, here we give a modularized design method for detection. Besides, bus topology is utilized for data transfer to extend and maintain modules.

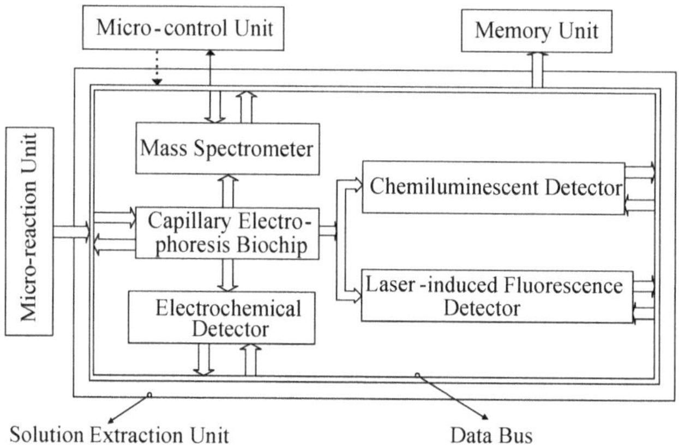

Fig. 3. The modularized scheme for solution extraction

The functions of each module are as follows.

Microchip Capillary Electrophoresis. Microchip capillary electrophoresis that integrates sequential method process steps such as sample handling, staining, destaining, detection and analysis into a single process that creates a complete laboratory on a chip, has been demonstrated that it can significantly improves the quality of data for nucleic acid fragment analysis when compared to classical gel techniques. Specifically, the new technology provides enhanced resolution and better reproducibility. The main operations of this technology are as follows.

i) Samples are loaded into the chip's micro-channels and are connected with electrodes when placed in the instrument. Voltage drives the sample from the sample well through the micro-channels and into the separation channel, where a polymer sieves the DNA fragments by size.
ii) Intercalating dye binds to DNA fragments, which fluoresce when excited by a laser.
iii) Software plots fluorescence intensity versus time and produces an electropherogram for each sample. The data can also be displayed in tabular format or in a gel-like image, simulating traditional gel electrophoresis.
iv) The Bioanalyzer software quantitates approximate concentration and accurately sizes each protein or DNA/RNA fragment in a digital format, [25].

Chemiluminescent Detector. Chemiluminescent detector has become a competitive device due to no light required and smaller volume. The interface between capillary electrophoresis units and chemiluminescent detector is complex. Besides, dead volume and overfall phenomena may be introduced, and then reduce separation efficiency. Making zero-dead volume column reactor using micro processing technique can solve these problems.

Electronic systems based on charge-coupled device (CCD) detectors are a way of visualizing various types of gel media, the systems generate digital images that can be archived, reproduced, and analyzed. Chemiluminescent samples emit light at extremely low levels, and the inherent electronic noise of CCD chips and limitations of much of the associated hardware have resulted in the majority of so called chemiluminescent-ready systems being incapable of producing accurate, reproducible results.

The requirement is for a system that combines high levels of accuracy and automation, leaving the user to concentrate on applications and results. The second requirement for high-quality chemiluminescent imaging is automation, [26].

Laser-induced Fluorescence Detector. Laser-induced fluorescence (LIF) is a spectroscopic method. The preferred specie is excited with help of a laser. The wavelength is often selected to be the one at which the specie has its largest cross section. The excited specie will after some time, usually in the order of few nanoseconds to microseconds, deexcite and emit light at a wavelength larger than the excitation wavelength. This light, fluorescence, is measured.

Two different kinds of spectra exists, LIF-spectra and excitation scans. The LIF-spectra are performed with a fixed lasing wavelength, as above and the fluorescence spectrum is analyzed. Excitation scans on the other hand collects all fluorescent light, without measuring the wavelength.

Instead the lasing wavelength is changed. The advantage over absorption spectroscopy is that it is possible to get two- and three-dimensional images since fluorescence takes place in all directions. The signal-to-noise ratio of fluorescence signals to very high, providing a good sensitivity to the process. It is also possible to distinguish between more species, since both the lasing wavelength can be tuned to a particular excitation of given specie, [27].

Mass Spectrometer. Mass spectrometers use the difference in mass-to-charge ratio of molecules to separate them from each other. Mass spectrometry is therefore useful for quantization of molecules and also for determining chemical and structural information about molecules. Molecules have distinctive fragmentation patterns that provide structural information to identify structural components.

The general operation of a mass spectrometer is:

i) Create gas-phase ions;
ii) Separate the ions in space or time based on their mass-to-charge ratio;
iii) Measure the quantity of ions of each mass-to-charge ratio.

In general a mass spectrometer consists of an ion source, a mass-selective analyzer, and an ion detector. Since mass spectrometers create and manipulate gas-phase ions, they operate in a high-vacuum system. The magnetic-sector, quadrupole, and time-of-flight designs also require extraction and acceleration ion optics to transfer ions from the source region into the mass analyzer. The details of mass analyzer designs are discussed in the individual documents listed below. Basic descriptions of sample introduction/ionization and ion detection are discussed in separate documents on ionization methods and ion detectors, respectively, [28].

Electrochemical Detector. The Electrochemical Detector can operate in three different detection modes:

i) In the Conductivity mode, current conducted by ions in solution in an electric field is measured;
ii) In DC Amperometry, a constant voltage is applied to the working electrode in the amperometry cell and the resulting current is the detector output;
iii) Integrated Amperometry is similar to DC Amperometry in that the same cell and associated circuitry are used. After the initial stages of signal processing, the cell current is integrated and the resulting charge is the detector output reported for each integration period. A user-programmed waveform, or repetitive series of potentials, is applied to the cell, and the same waveform program sets the start and finish of the integration period. The program is entered from the waveform screen.

An important distinction between conductivity and amperometric detection is that no electron transfer reactions occur during conductivity detection. During DC and integrated amperometric detection, electrons are actually transferred between the electrode and the analyte molecules. Although, in theory, all three detection modes could employ the same detector cell, a cell optimized for conductivity is not appropriate for amperometry, and vice versa, [29].

4.5 Micro-control Unit

The main functions of micro-control unit are to control and direct the above four units to perform the physical and biological operations in order. The main control steps are as follows.

As making DNA micro-arrays unit, micro-control unit mainly performs building the oligonucleotides on the glass array one base at a time, at each step, adding the base via the reaction between the hydroxyl group 5' of the terminal base and the phosphate group of the next base. Note, there is a protective group on the 5' of the base being added, which prevents the addition of more than one base at each step. Following addition, there is a deprotection step at which the protective group is converted to a hydroxyl group to allow addition of the next base.

As encoding DNA sequences unit, micro-control unit mainly performs extracting DNA polymerase chain and controlling its length in terms of the need of micro-reactions. Besides, combining DNA and the correlative enzymes automatically, labeling the digestion sites, and making it available for the following micro-reactions and biological detection.

As micro-reaction unit, micro-control unit mainly performs controlling the PCR conditions, the main controls parameters are as follows.

Initial Denaturation Stage. The initial denaturation should be performed over an interval of 1-3min at 95°C if the GC content is 50% or less. For GC-rich templates the denaturation interval should be prolonged up to 10min.

Denaturation Stage. Usually denaturation for 0.5-2min at 94-95°C is sufficient. The GC content should be taken into consideration. Denaturation time can be optimized empirically.

Primer Annealing Stage. Usually the optimal annealing temperature is 5°C lower than the melting temperature of primer-template DNA duplex. Incubation for 0.5-2min is usually sufficient. However, if non-specific PCR products are obtained in addition to the expected product, the annealing temperature should be optimized by increasing it stepwise by 1-2°C.

Extending Stage. Usually the extending step is performed at 70-75°C.
Number of Cycles. The number of PCR cycles depends on the amount of template DNA in the reaction mix and on the expected yield of the PCR product. In most cases, 25-35 cycles are sufficient.

Final Extending Stage. After the last cycle, the samples are incubated at 72°C for 5-15min to fill-in the protruding ends of newly synthesized PCR products, [30].

As solution extraction results unit, micro-control unit mainly performs controlling the following operations, such as exciting and controlling applicator, transforming optical signal into digital signal (using image manipulation technology), transforming related data into relevant digital signal, and sending it to memory subsystem, then using special analysis software to analyze data quantificationally, at last, the digital computer performs processing data and readout results.

5 Discussion

In the previous sections, we show the DNA computing processor which integrates all the steps of DNA computing into one machine. Besides, the functions of each unit also are discussed in detail, especially for the detection and analysis unit, where the optimal solution spaces are extracted.

It should be mentioned that the DNA computing processor proposed here is only a virtual machine. To realize real DNA computer, At least, the following research subjects should be emphasized: designing DNA computing model and arithmetic, organizing biochemical units, data storage technology, interface and communication, micro flow control, performance tuning etc. The technical problems need to be solved are as follows. How to realize the operation automatically? How to realize the communication between processor or EMS memory and computer interior? How to evaluate its performance?

Acknowledgements

The work of this paper is supported by the National Scientific Foundation of China under grants 30370356, 60573190, 30570431, 60403002, Scientific Foundation of Zhejiang Province of China (Y106654), Excellent Youth Science and Technology Foundation of Anhui Province of China (06042088), and Program for New Century Excellent Talents in University.

References

1. Adleman, L.M.: Molecular Computation of Solutions to Combinatorial Problems. Science. 11 (1994) 1021-1023
2. Meng, D. Z., Cao, H.P.: DNA Computing and Biological Mathematics. Acta Biophysica Sinica (in Chinese). 2 (2002) 163-174
3. Charlot, B., et al.: Research Activities, http://tima.imag.fr/research/files/gr-04/mns.pdf
4. Gabig, M., Wegrzyn, G.: An Introduction to DNA Chips: Principles, Technology, Applications and Analysis. Acta Biochimica Polonica. 3 (2001) 615-622
5. Garzon, M.H., Deaton, R.J.: Codeword Design and Information Encoding in DNA Ensembles. Natural Computing. 3 (2004) 253–292
6. Tanaka, F., Nakatsugawa, M., Yamamoto, M., Shiba, T., Ohuchi, A.: Developing Support System for Sequence Design in DNA Computing. In: Proc. 7th Int. Workshop DNA Based Comput. (2001) 340–349
7. Frutos, A.G., et al.: Demonstration of a Word Design Strategy for DNA Computing on Surfaces. Nucleic Acids Res. 23 (1997) 4748–4757
8. Faulhammer, D., Cukras, A.R., Lipton, R.J., Landweber, L.F.: Molecular Computation: RNA Solutions to Chess Problems. In: Proc. Natl. Acad. Sci. U.S.A. 97 (2000) 1385–1389
9. Arita, M., Kobayashi, S.: DNA Sequence Design Using Templates. New Generation Comput. 20 (2002) 263–277
10. Arita, M., et al.: Improving Sequence Design for DNA Computing. In: Proc. Genetic Evol. Comput. (2000) 875–882
11. Tuplan, D.C., Hoose, H., Condon, A.: Stochastic Local Search Algorithms for DNA Word Design. In: Proc. 8th Int. Workshop DNA Based Comput. (2002) 229–241
12. Andronescu, M., et al.: Algorithms for Testing that DNA Word Designs Avoid Unwanted Secondary Structure. In: Proc. 8th Int. Workshop DNA Based Comput. (2002) 182–195
13. Zhang, B.T., Shin, S.Y.: Molecular Algorithms for Efficient and Reliable DNA Computing. In: Proc. Genetic Program. (GP). (1998) 735–742
14. Feldkamp, U., Saghafi, S., Banzhaf, W., Rauhe, H.: DNA Sequence Generator–A Program for the Construction of DNA Sequences. In: Proc.7th Int. Workshop DNA Based Comput. (2001) 179–188
15. Hartemink, A. J., Gifford, D. K., Khodor, J.: Automated Constraint Based Nucleotide Sequence Selection for DNA Computation. In: Proc. 4th DIMACS Workshop DNA Based Comput. (1998) 227–235
16. Deaton, R., Chen, J., Bi, H., Rose, J. A.: A Software Tool for Generating Noncrosshybridization Libraries of DNA Oligonucleotides. In: Proc. 8th Int. Workshop DNA Based Comput. (2002) 252–261
17. Deaton, R., et al.: A PCR-Based Protocol for in Vitro Selection of Noncrosshybridizing Olgionucleotides. In: Proc. 8th Int. Workshop DNA Based Comput. (2002) 196–204
18. Tanaka, F., Kameda, A., Yamamoto, M., Ohuchi, A.: Design of Nucleic Acid Sequences for DNA Computing Based on a Thermodynamic Approach. Nucleic Acids Res. 3 (2005) 903-911
19. Shin, S.Y., Lee, I. H., Kim, D., Zhang, B.T.: Multi-Objective Evolutionary Optimization of DNA Sequences for Reliable DNA Computing. IEEE Trans. Evol. Comput. 2 (2005) 143-158
20. Taylor, T. B., Emily, S., et al.: Optimization of the Performance of the Polymerase Chain Reaction in Silicon-Based Microstructures. Nucleic Acids Res. 15 (1997) 3164-3168
21. Braich, R.S., Chelyapov, N., et al.: Solution of a 20-Variable 3-SAT Problem on a DNA Computer. Science. 19 (2002) 499-502

22. Liu, Q.H., Wang, L., et al.: DNA Computing on Surfaces. Nature. 13 (2000) 175-178
23. Zhang, F.Y., Yin Z.X., et al.: DNA Computation Model to Solve 0-1 Programming Problem. Biosystems. 74 (2004) 9-14
24. Shi, X.L., Li, X., Zhang, Z., et al.: Improce Capability of DNA Automaton: DNA Automaton with three Internal States and Tape Head Move in Two Directions. Lecture Notes in Computer Science, Vol. 3645. Springer-Verlag, Berlin Heidelberg New York (2005) 71-79
25. Wang, H., Lin B.C.: Capillary Electrophoresis on Microchip and its Application in Life Science. Journal of Analytical Chemistry (in Chinese). 3 (2002) 359-364
26. Thompson, S.: Chemiluminescent Detection of Nucleic Acids. International Biotechnology Laboratory. 10 (2000) 14
27. Momoko, K., Tamao, O., et al.: Laser-Induced Fluorescence Microscopic System Using an Optical Parametric Oscillator for Tunable Detection in Microchip Analysis. Analytical and Bioanalytical Chemistry. 4 (2005) 992 – 995
28. Scott, E., Van, B.: An Introduction to Mass Spectrometry, http://science.widener.edu/svb/massspec/massspec.pdf
29. Walter, R., Vandaveer, S.A., et al.: Recent Developments in Electrochemical Detection for Microchip Capillary Electrophoresis. Electrophoresis. 25 (2004) 3528–3549
30. Ennis, M.A., Gelfand, D.H., et al.: PCR Protocols: a Guide to Methods and Applications, Academic Press, Inc. (1990)

General DNA Automaton Model with R/W Tape

Shi Xiaolong, Pan linqiang, and Xu Jin

Department of Control Science and Engineering Huazhong University of Science and Technology, 430074 Wuhan, P.R. China
shixiaolong@mail.hust.edu.cn

Abstract. Since Turing machine is consisted of R/W Tape head and Turing Tape, that means a DNA based Turing machine must realize the read and write processes on Turing Tape with DNA molecules, and make the head move in two directions either. Based on our previous works on DNA computing, especially on DNA automaton and the relationship between enzymes and their computation ability with DNA automaton model. We combined different enzymes together to modify the cut and recognition sites with a programmable Tape head to embody the read and write symbol procedure on Turing tape. And this article will describe how the programmable Tape head moves in two direction and read/write procedure of Turing Tape in details.

1 Introduction

One of the main goals of the research on DNA Computing is to realize a Turing machine by DNA molecules. A Turing machine is a kind of state machine. At any time the machine is in any one of a finite number of states. Instructions for a Turing machine consist in specified conditions under which the machine will transition between one state and another. A Turing machine has an infinite one-dimensional tape divided into cells. Traditionally we think of the tape as being horizontal with the cells arranged in a left-right orientation. The tape has one end, at the left say, and stretches infinitely far to the right. Each cell is able to contain one symbol. The machine has a read-write head, which at any time scanning a single cell on the tape. This read-write head can move left and right along the tape to scan successive cells.

Some schemes of realization Turing computations through DNA computing have been proposed. The pioneer conceiving of DNA automaton is the DNA Turing model proposed by C. Bennett [1] in 1973, but a feasible model of DNA automaton is constructed by Rothemund [2] using restriction enzymes in 1995. In this DNA computing model, the Turing tape is encoded by DNA sequence, the restriction enzyme recognizes the specific sequence of DNA sequence which acts as the tape head of automaton, cuts correspondence sites to make the tape head move forward and therefore the transition of automaton status achieved. This model is quite perfect in theory, and makes a great contribution to the research of DNA automatons. In fact, the succeed models of DNA automatons are based on this model in which DNA sequence encoded tape symbols and restriction enzyme trigger the automaton. The drawback of this model is that it is too idealized to realize by experiment. Therefore, Smith and Scheweitzer [3] make effort to use DNA and standard laboratory technique to realize the DNA Turing model. Whereafter, Beaver [4] proposed a DNA Turing machine to operate single molecule. In 1995, winfree [5] proposed a cellular automata model of

D.-S. Huang, K. Li, and G.W. Irwin (Eds.): ICIC 2006, LNBI 4115, pp. 258 – 266, 2006.

DNA computing, and realize a programmable self-assembly DNA model in 1998 by experiment [6].

In order to explore the feasibility of autonomous molecular computing, kensaku sakamoto [7] proposed a DNA computing model use the hairpin formation by single-stranded DNA molecules to solve a famous NP problem, the so-called satisfiability problem (SAT) in 2000. The problem is elaborately encoded with DNA hairpin structure, and the selected DNA hairpin structure is well-designed to contain a recognition site of given restriction enzyme to cut off them. This model approves the feasibility of DNA automatons, but it is so well-designed to extend.

Till 2001, Yaakov benenson[8] proposed a programmable molecule automaton model based on DNA computing, and the restriction enzyme in this DNA automaton is *FokI*. The main merit of this DNA automaton model is that it is programmable. In this model, the distribution between states and symbols depends on the length of the spacer between the recognition site and the restriction site of the particular restriction enzyme employed. Benensons automaton realized the basic features and processes of a finite automaton with two internal states using enzyme *FokI* with DNA computing. This automaton has an alphabet comprising two input symbols therefore can have eight possible transition rules, 255 possible transition-rule selections and 3 possible selections of accepting states, resulting in 765 syntactically distinct programs. In 2004 Yaakov benenson applied his DNA automaton in cancer diagnosing [9].

We have some DNA based automaton models already. In formal works on DNA automaton, we have studied the computation ability of finite DNA automaton with different enzymes and gives out the formula to calculate probable maximum states directly from the features of restriction enzyme. With further discussions, we proposed a DNA finite automaton with three internal states which is more powerful than the finite automaton [10].

In this paper, we give out the scheme of DNA automaton model with its tape head moves in two directions, and how symbols can be read from and write into the tape, which will surly lead to the realization of DNA Turing machine.

Since Turing machine is consisted of R/W Tape head and Turing Tape, that means a DNA based Turing machine must realize read and write processes on Turing Tape by DNA molecules, and make the head move in two directions either. Based on our previous works on DNA computing, especially on DNA automaton and the relationship between enzyme and its computation ability, we combined different enzymes together to modify the cut and recognition sites with a programmable Tape head to embody the read and write symbol procedure on Turing tape. And this article will describe the programmable Tape head move in two direction and read/write procedure of Turing Tape in details.

2 Programmable Tape Head Move in Two Directions

The symbol-read procedure of a finite DNA automaton using *Fok I* is implement by the stick process of the sticky ends of the Turing tape and the state-transfer molecular, so that the virtual Tape head of a finite DNA automaton is located on the sticky end of the Turing tape made by *Fok I*. From the state change procedure of finite state DNA automaton we can see, whatever two states or three states finite DNA automaton of

Benenson type using *Fok I*, the length of the encoded DNA Tape will become shorter by the state change procedure, thus the position of the virtual Tape head will move forward to the next symbol correspondingly and the move direction of the virtual head can move only in one direction in the same way. If we can make the Turing tape longer after state changed, likewise we can make the virtual Tape head move backward, that is to say, the manner of state-change procedure should be changed.

Typically a DNA automaton is consists with three molecular units: software unit, double-stranded DNA encodes input and output information with programming amounts; regulation unit, which regulate software molecule concentrations, and hence make automaton transit according to a definite procedure; Hardware unit, Restriction Enzyme which provide state change method. The key point of a DNA automaton is Restriction Enzyme that makes automaton transition possible, while the cutting site and recognizing site of Restriction Enzyme determined the computation ability of a DNA automaton. In order to make the virtual Tape head move in two directions as program, new state-change method should be added into the scheme of DNA automaton. Since the state-change procedure is determined by Restriction Enzyme the hard ware unit of DNA automaton, new enzyme must be introduced and combined with previous enzyme to make possible a programmable virtual tape head move in two directions.

Let's compare the two kinds of enzymes with different features: one is cut site beside the only recognition site and the other is cut site between two recognition sites. Restriction enzymes with a recognition site and a cut site beside have some wonderful features, and have been successfully used in DAN computing. These enzymes act on DNA sequence as follows *(FokI in this example)*:

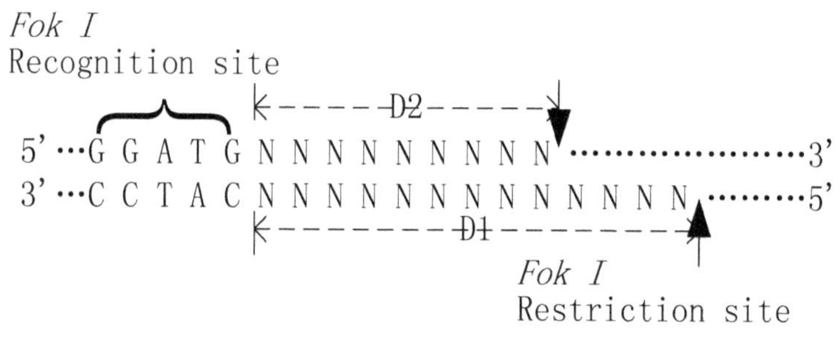

Fig. 1. N denotes any base that can be encoded. The distance between recognition site and restriction site of the restriction enzyme provides the encoding space for states and symbols. D1 and D2 determine the state transition mode the restriction enzyme can provide for DNA automaton. The restriction enzyme used in programmable DNA automaton model is of this kind[1].

Given a restriction enzyme with one recognition site and a cut site beside, the distances between recognition site and restriction site are D1 and D2 (Fig. 2.), and D1 > D2. We can calculate probable maximum states directly from the features of this kind of restriction enzyme.

Because the cut site of this kind of enzyme is located on the right side of recognition site, the Turing tape will become shorter as state changes. And using this type of enzyme the virtual tape head of DNA automaton can only move forward.

As to the Restriction enzyme with two recognition sites and a cut site between them, the situation became different. This kind of restriction enzyme has two recognition sites, thus gives more restriction to encoding process of DNA automaton, the action of these restriction enzymes can be demonstrate as *(BstXI in this example)*:

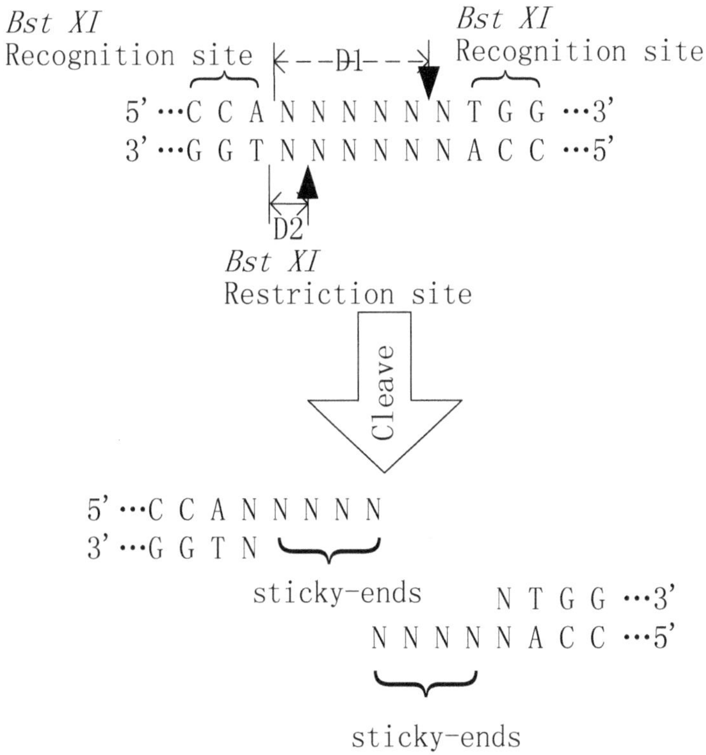

Fig. 2. *Bst XI* has two recognition site, D1 and D2 provide the encoding space for DNA automaton. Since D1 > D2, the separated pieces have single stranded "sticky-ends," which allow the complementary pieces to combine. Therefore, this kind of restriction enzyme can also provide several state transition modes due to D1 + D2 is not zero. In fact, *Bst XI* has been successfully applied in DNA automaton of hairpin model to solve SAT problem[10].

A restriction enzyme with two recognition sites and a cut site between them can provide some new state transition scheme for DNA automaton. With this feature, we can make tape head moves not only forward but also backward, which should be cooperate with a felicitous coding scheme of DNA sequence.

2.1 Forward to Backward Transition

We introduce restriction enzyme *BstXI* to provide a forward to backward procedure, the transition unit for change the direction of Turing tape from Forward to backward is as follows:

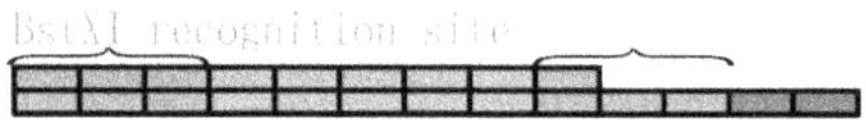

Fig. 3. Tape head direction Transition unit, forward to backward. Orange cells represent the recognition sites of *Bst XI*, green cells represent the encoding DNA sequence that will add to the Turing tape, purple cells represent the encoding sticky end.

This transition unit can change the move direction of current Turing tape from forward to backward, the direction changing procedure of the virtual tape head is demonstrated as follows:

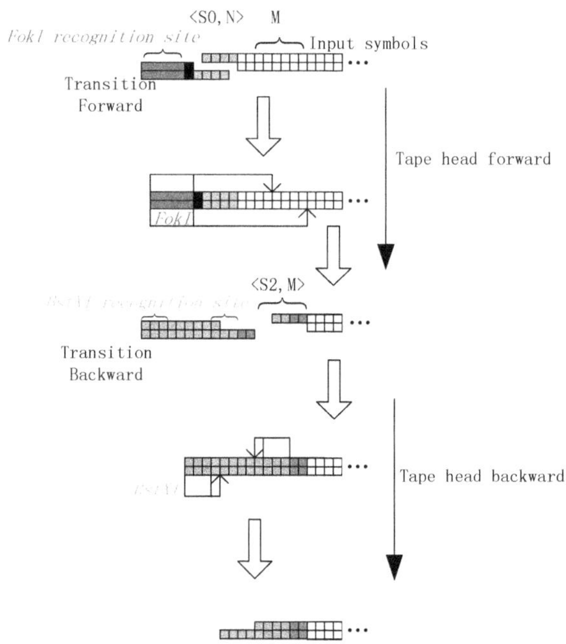

Fig. 4. Tape head direction changing procedure from forward to backward. Red cells represent the recognition sites of *FokI*, Orange cells represent the recognition sites of *Bst XI*, green cells represent the encoding DNA sequence, purple cells represent the encoding sticky end. M is the programmed command symbol indication the direction changing procedure from forward to backward, when the virtual tape head read symbol M, with correspond direction transition unit from forward to backward present, the exposure sticky end of Turing tape with stick with the direction transition unit, the offspring sequence contains the recognition site of *Bst XI*, after cleave action by *Bst XI*, the sticky end of Turing tape is upside down when virtual tape head change its direction, and the move direction of virtual Tape head changed.

The length of DNA sequence encoded input symbols increased as *Bst XI* cleaves it, thus makes the tape head move backward. Since the sticky end is upside down when tape head change its direction, the state transition molecule must change accordingly.

2.2 Backward Transition Procedure

After the direction of virtual Turing tape head changed, the exposure sticky end of Turing tape changed upside down as fig. 4, therefore absolutely forbid the Turing tape to react with any forward transition unit as previous finite state DNA automaton, which will reduce the constraint condition of encoding of DNA automaton. In order to make the two direction virtual Turing tape really sound, the tape head should be able to continue the backward movement after direction changes, that is to say, a new type of transition unit so called backward transition unit should make the continue backward movement possible. The backward transition unit is designed as follows, which is based on the feature of restriction enzyme *BstXI*:

Fig. 5. Backward transition unit. Orange cells represent the recognition sites of *Bst XI*, green cells represent the encoding DNA sequence that will add to the Turing tape, purple cells represent the encoding sticky end.

The backward transition unit enables the virtual tape head to continue the backward movement. And the backward transition procedure is demonstrated as follows:

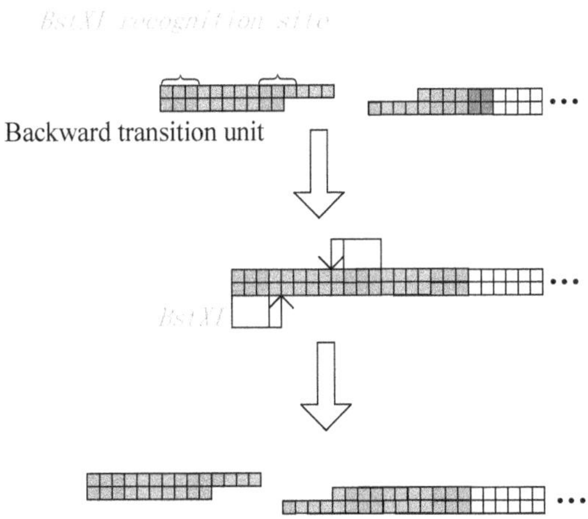

Fig. 6. Backward transition procedure. Orange cells represent the recognition sites of *Bst XI*, green cells represent the encoding DNA sequence that will add to the Turing tape, purple cells represent the encoding sticky end.

Each time a transition procedure finished, the Turing tape increase in 7bp(Bp is the unit of the Count of the cells which represent oligonucleotides), in which 3bp is the recognition site that can not be coded, 4bp is encoding DNA sequence.

The move speed of virtual tape head(in bp per transition bp/T) is programmable, which is determined by the scheme of backward transition unit. With enzyme *Bst XI*, we can provide three mode of backward transition with different speed 7bp/T, 6bp/T and 5bp/T.

2.3 Backward to Forward Transition

Consider the automaton is running in a backward transition mode, if the automaton could not return back to a forward transition mode in some condition, we can't say this automaton has a free programmable tape head.

We used the feature of enzyme *FokI* to realize the backward to forward transition unit. The scheme of this unit is designed as follows:

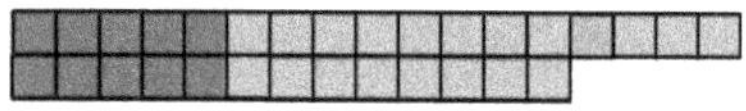

Fig. 7. Backward to forward transition unit. Red cells represent the recognition sites of *FokI*, Orange cells represent the recognition sites of *Bst XI*, green cells represent the free coding space of DNA sequence.

With the backward to forward transition unit, the backward to forward transition procedure is as follows:

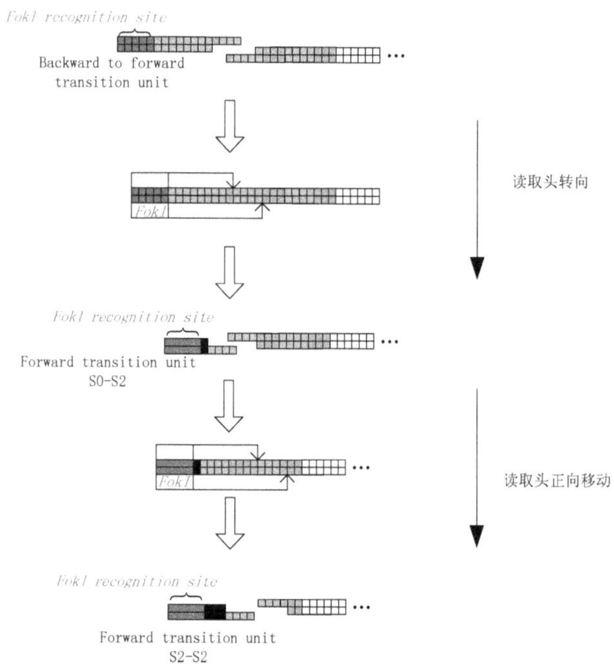

Fig. 8. Backward to forward transition procedure. Red cells represent the recognition sites of *FokI*, Orange cells represent the recognition sites of *Bst XI*, green cells represent the free coding space of DNA sequence.

As the tape head of DNA automaton moves backward, we can give a command to change it direction to forward movement. When the exposed sticky end of backward movement Turing tape matches the sticky end of backward to forward transition unit, the DNA automaton enters the backward to forward transition procedure.

The offspring of backward to forward transition unit and Turing tape contains recognition site of enzyme *FokI*, after cleaves by *FokI*, the exposed sticky end is same as its forward movement sticky end as formal finite DNA automaton, thus accomplish the backward to forward transition procedure. After the procedure, the virtual tape head of DNA automaton can continue its forward movement with programmed transition units and enzyme *FokI*.

3 Symbol Write Procedure of DNA Automaton

Another problem from finite automaton to the Turing machine is that a tape head of Turing machine can write symbols to Turing tape.

Write symbol procedure can be realized by add new symbols to current tape, but add new symbol encoded DNA sequences directly to current tape is not a feasible way, because the new symbols that will directly add to the tape couldn't contain any more sticky end that can react with any other transition unit, or else the new symbols sequence will be destroyed by with the transition unit presents, thus the offspring of the new symbols and tape couldn't keep the sticky end of formal tape, and the DNA automaton can't react with any other transition units, that is to say the DNA automaton will stop if any new symbols is added to its tape directly.

In fact, we can use the backward transition procedure as Fig. 6 to write symbols to the Turing tape. Since the tape of DNA automaton increase with backward transition procedure, and the added sequence contain free coding space (green cells in Fig. 6), together with the forward to backward transition procedure in Fig. 4, backward to forward transition procedure in Fig. 8, the entire programmable symbol read and write procedure is totally settled.

4 Conclusion

Based on the previous works on finite state DNA automaton, by combined two enzymes Fok and Bst together, we provide a feasible way to realize a DNA automaton with programmable free virtual tape head, which can read and write symbols. These works will lead to the prospective realization of a DNA Turing machine will further experimentation and application validation.

Acknowledgments

This work is supported by the National Scientific Foundation of China (Grant No.s: 60533010, 60373089 and 30370356), and Program for New Century Excellent Talents in University.

References

1. Bennett, C. H.: On Constructing a Molecular Computer. IBM Journal of Research and Development, 17 (1973) 525~532
2. Paul Wilhelm, Karl Rothemund.: A DNA and Restriction Enzyme Implementation of Turing Machine. http://www.ugcs.caltech.edu.~pwkr /oett.html
3. Smith W., Scheweitzer A.: DNA Computer in Vitro and Vivo. DIMACS Workshop on DNA based Computing. Princeton, (1995)
4. Beaver D.: Computing with DNA. Journal of computation biology, 3 (1996) 254~ 257
5. Erik Winfree: On the Computational Power of DNA Annealing and Ligation, Technical Report, California Institute of Technology, USA, May (1995)
6. Erik Winfree, et al.: Design and Self-Assembly of Two-Dimensional DNA Crystals, Nature, 394 (1998) 539-544
7. Kensaku Sakamoto, et al.: Molecular Computation by DNA Hairpin Formation, Science, 19 (2000) 1223-1226
8. Yaakov Benenson, Paz-Elizur T., Adar R., Keinan E., Livneh Z., Shapiro E.: Programmable and Autonomous Computing Machine Made of Biomolecules. Nature, 22 (2001) 430~434
9. Yaakov Benenson, Binyamin Gil, Uri Ben-Dor1, Adar R., Shapiro E.: An Autonomous Molecular Computer for Logical Control of Gene Expression. Nature, 27 (2004) 423~429
10. Shi, X. L., Li, X., Zhang, Z., et al.: Improve Capability of DNA Automaton: DNA Automaton with Three Internal States and Tape Head Move in Two Directions. LECT NOTES COMPUT SC 3645 (2005) 71-79

Interpolated Hidden Markov Models Estimated Using Conditional ML for Eukaryotic Gene Annotation

Hongmei Zhu, Jiaxin Wang, Zehong Yang, and Yixu Song

State Key Laboratory of Intelligent Technology and Systems,
Department of Computer Science and Technology, Tsinghua University,
Beijing, 100084, China
zhuhongmei00@mails.tsinghua.edu.cn

Abstract. To improve the performance of computational gene annotation programs, we introduced the well known interpolated Markov Chain (IMC) technology to the class Hidden Markov models (CHMM). CHMM was applied in one of the best eukaryotic gene prediction systems: HMMgene. The conditional Maximum Likelihood estimation (CMLE) algorithm was educed to estimate the interpolation parameters. The resulting gene prediction program improves exon level sensitivity by 3% and specificity by about 1% compared to HMMgene as trained and tested on some standard human DNA sequence dataset.

1 Introduction

In the field of computational biology, eukaryotic gene annotation methods are used to annotate the exon-intron structures of genes scattered in genome sequence. Although methods based on the comparison of two or more genomes have greater accuracy, there are still several good reasons to develop improved single-genome predictors [1].

Rogic et al. did a comprehensive evaluation of popular gene annotation programs based on single-genome using the human, mouse and rat genome sequences as test dataset, among which HMMgene [2] had the highest prediction accuracy [3]. The model of HMMgene is totally a class hidden Markov model (CHMM) [4] and it can be estimated in one go from scratch by using conditional maximum likelihood estimation (CMLE). We introduced the well known Interpolated Markov chain (IMC) technology to this CHMM, and estimated the interpolation parameters by CMLE. The interpolation scheme has been successfully applied in microbial gene identification [5] and gene annotation for small eukaryotes [6]. But it hasn't been applied in any class hidden Markov models for high eukaryotic gene annotation yet. And no estimation algorithms were devised to estimate the interpolation parameters under this model. Our gene prediction program improves exon level sensitivity by 3% and specificity by about 1% compared to HMMgene as trained and tested on standard human DNA sequence dataset.

D.-S. Huang, K. Li, and G.W. Irwin (Eds.): ICIC 2006, LNBI 4115, pp. 267–274, 2006.

In the following we first give a brief description of HMMgene and interpolated Markov models. And then we describe our interpolated class hidden Markov models (ICHMM) and estimation methods. Finally the performance of this ICHMM gene predictor is presented and compared with that of HMMgene.

2 HMMgene and IMC

2.1 CHMM, CMLE and HMMgene

According to [2], the gene annotation problem is part of a general class of problems which has a class label associated with each observation. In gene annotation the observations are nucleotides and the classes are for instance coding, intron or intergenic. Fig. 1 is taken from [2] to illustrate this situation. The observation sequence is associated with a label sequence of the same length.

Gene annotation problem described above can fit in the HMM framework neatly if the states are also labeled. Such a model was called a class HMM. Here each state emits an observation symbol and a class label which is associated with the observation. A discriminative estimation approach and an effective decoding algorithm were designed by Krogh, A. for this application [2][4].

First some notations are defined as following. Let θ be the model parameters. A DNA sequence is denoted by $s = s_1, \cdots, s_L$ and the label sequence $c = c_1, \cdots, c_L$. For the training procedure, we have the DNA sequences and their corresponding label sequences, and estimate the model parameters. For the gene prediction procedure, we have the DNA sequences and the model parameters, and decode the label sequences. To estimate the model parameters by standard ML, the likelihood of the sequences with their corresponding labels is maximized:

$$\theta^{ML} = \arg\max_{\theta} P(s, c|\theta) \tag{1}$$

Probability $P(s, c|\theta)$ can be obtained by trivial modification of the forward algorithm, which makes each observation go with model states with the same label.

```
AGCGGATCCCCCGGTGGCCTCATGTCGCGCAGTGGAACCGATCCTCAGCAACGCCAGCAGGCGT
000000000000000000000CCCCCCCCCCCCCCCCCCCCCCCCCCCCCCCCCCCCCCCCCCC

CAGAGGCGGACGCCGCAGCAGCAACCTTCCGGCAAACGGTAACTGCACCGCGGCAGGGACTCG
CCCCCCCCCCCCCCCCCCCCCCCCCCCCCCCCCCCCCCIIIIIIIIIIIIIIIIIIIIIIIII

...GAGCTTGGGCCTGCTGGTGGGTGAGACCCAGGAGAGAGGGAGCTAGAGGGGGGAGCTCTGA
...IIIIIIIIIIIIIIIIIIIIIIIIIIIIIIIIIIIIIIIIIIIIIIIIIIIIIIIIIIIII

GGACTGATCTTGACTGTCTGCCCCCAGACCATCAGCATATCCGCTACAACCCGCTGCAGGATGA
IIIIIIIIIIIIIIIIIIIIIIIIIIICCCCCCCCCCCCCCCCCCCCCCCCCCCCCCCCCCCCC

GTGGGTGCTGGTGTCAGCTCACCGCATGAAGCGGCCCTGGTAGGGTCAAGTGGAGCCCCAG...
CCCCCCCCCCCCCCCCCCCCCCCCCCCCCCCCCCCCCCCCCCC000000000000000000...
```

Fig. 1. Annotation of A DNA sequence containing a gene (Taken from [2]) . For each nucleotide its label is written below. The coding regions are labeled 'C', the introns 'I', and the intergenic regions '0'. The shaded areas are the coding regions. To annotate a gene is to find the labels.

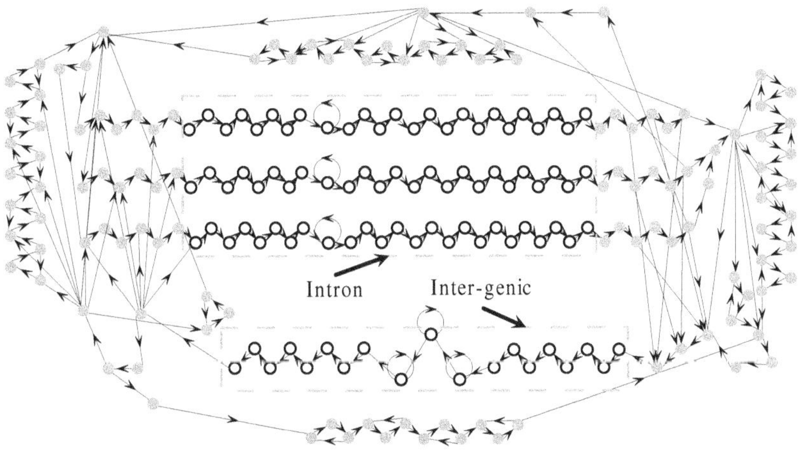

Fig. 2. The CHMM structure of HMMgene. The circles denote the states in CHMM. "Gray" states emit nucleotides in the coding regions, and "white" states in the intron region or inter-genic region as showed by the boxes with dashed frames. This picture was produced with the Java software BioLayout [7].

Krogh, A. used a discriminative approach, conditional ML:

$$\theta^{CML} = \arg\max_{\theta} P(c|s, \theta) \tag{2}$$

This probability can be rewritten as

$$P(c|s, \theta) = P(s, c|\theta)/P(s|\theta) \tag{3}$$

Probability $P(s|\theta)$ was calculated by the forward algorithm disregarding labels.

To be able to discover genes, we need a Markov model that satisfies the grammar of genes. The structure of HMMgene was shown in Fig. 2. For both model training and gene predicting, we align observation sequences with the model. Each observation symbol corresponds to a state. So the observation sequence leads to some state sequences after the alignment, and every state sequence produce a label sequence which gives annotation for the observation sequence.

2.2 Interpolated Markov Chains (IMC)

Nth order Markov chain is also called an $(N + 1)$-mer sequence model. In order to fully exploit the information represented in the lower order models, we can use a linear interpolation scheme:

$$P(s_t|s_{t-2}s_{t-1}) = \lambda_1 \tilde{P}(s_t) + \lambda_2 \tilde{P}(s_t|s_{t-1}) + \lambda_3 \tilde{P}(s_t|s_{t-2}s_{t-1}) \tag{4}$$

In this example, the model order is 2.

To facilitate the following description, we rewritten (4) as:

$$\bar{\theta}_t^2 = \lambda_0 \cdot \tilde{\theta}_t^0 + \lambda_1 \cdot \tilde{\theta}_t^1 + \lambda_2 \cdot \tilde{\theta}_t^2 \tag{5}$$

Here λ_k denotes the interpolation parameters, $\tilde{\theta}_t^k$ denotes the conditional probability of seeing s_t given k previous symbols in a fixed order model of order k, and $\bar{\theta}_t^k$ denotes the conditional probability of seeing s_t given k previous symbols in an interpolated model with order k.

So far interpolation scheme hasn't been applied in any class hidden Markov models for eukaryotic gene annotation. And no estimation algorithms were devised to estimate the interpolation parameters under this model.

3 ICHMM and Parameter Estimation

3.1 Interpolated Class Hidden Markov Models (ICHMM)

In a standard HMM, each state is with fixed order. And there're two kinds parameters: the probability of going from one state to another (transition parameter) and the conditional probability of seeing a base in a state (emission parameter). After the interpolation technology is introduced to HMM, some or all of the states are not with fixed order. The transition parameters remain the same and the emission parameters of interpolated states take the form of (5).

In principle, using higher order is always preferable to using lower order, but only if sufficient data is available to produce reliable probability estimates. By using the interpolation scheme we try to take advantage of multiple fixed order models and give precise and reliable estimation.

3.2 Parameter Estimation for ICHMM by Using CMLE

CMLE was used to estimate ICHMM parameters: transition, emission and interpolation parameters. After interpolation is used, we re-separate transition and emission into two groups: emission parameters associated with interpolated states (denoted by $\bar{\theta}$), and the other emission and transition parameters (denoted by $\hat{\theta}$). $\bar{\theta}$ has the form of (5). In the following θ is still used to denote both groups sometimes for concision. And (2) is rewritten as

$$\theta^{CML} = \arg\max_{\hat{\theta}, \tilde{\theta}, \lambda} P(c, s|\hat{\theta}, \tilde{\theta}, \lambda) / P(c|s, \hat{\theta}, \tilde{\theta}, \lambda) \tag{6}$$

To do the optimization in (6), first it is converted to logarithms. Define

$$L_f = -\log P(s|\theta) \tag{7}$$

$$L_c = -\log P(c, s|\theta) \tag{8}$$

Then to estimate $\hat{\theta}$, $\tilde{\theta}$ and λ, we need to maximize

$$L = \log P(c, s|\theta)/P(s|\theta) = L_f - L_c \tag{9}$$

Here the maximization approach is based on the gradient of L.

Calculation of the Gradient. First we give two more denotations. Since a fixed order conditional probability $\tilde{\theta}^k$ (k is the order) may contribute to more than one interpolated conditional probabilities $\bar{\theta}$ with order $K \geq k$. We use Θ to denote an interpolated probability set, in which all the probabilities are associated with certain $\tilde{\theta}^k$. And we use π to denote a path by which a sequence goes through the model.

The probability $P(s|\theta)$ is written as a sum over all possible paths through the model,

$$P(s|\theta) = \sum_{\pi} P(s, \pi|\theta) \tag{10}$$

And the probability for a given path is

$$P(s, \pi|\theta) = \prod_{i=1}^{N} \theta_i^{n_i(s,\pi)} \tag{11}$$

where $n_i(s, \pi)$ is the number of times the parameter θ_i is used in the path π for sequence s. The derivative calculation of (7) with respect to parameter θ_j can be found in [4] :

$$\partial L_f/\partial\theta_j = -n_j(s)/\theta_j \tag{12}$$

Here $n_j(s)$ is the expected number of times θ_j is used by the sequence s, *i.e.*, the average of $n_j(s, \pi)$ over all possible paths, and is calculated by standard forward-backward algorithm.

Now we calculate the gradient of the log likelihood L_f with respect to $\hat{\theta}$, $\tilde{\theta}$ and λ. The gradient with respect to $\hat{\theta}$ is the same as (12). The gradient of the log likelihood L_f with respect to $\tilde{\theta}$ is written as

$$\frac{\partial L_f}{\partial\tilde{\theta}_q^k} = \sum_{\bar{\theta}_j \in \Theta} \frac{\partial L_f}{\partial\bar{\theta}_j} \frac{\partial\bar{\theta}_j}{\partial\tilde{\theta}_q^k} = -\sum_{\bar{\theta}_j \in \Theta} \lambda_{j,k} \cdot \frac{n_j(s)}{\bar{\theta}_j} \tag{13}$$

Here $\lambda_{j,k}$ is the $(k+1)$th interpolation parameter of $\bar{\theta}_j$ (see (5)), and q and j denote index of probability parameters in the model. And the gradient of the log likelihood L_f with respect to λ is written as

$$\frac{\partial L_f}{\partial\lambda_{j,k}} = \frac{\partial L_f}{\partial\bar{\theta}_j} \frac{\partial\bar{\theta}_j}{\partial\lambda_{j,k}} = -\tilde{\theta}_q^k \cdot \frac{n_j(s)}{\bar{\theta}_j} \tag{14}$$

where $\tilde{\theta}_q^k$ contributes to $\bar{\theta}_j$ as a kth order member.

The gradients of the other log likelihood L_c can be calculated in a similar manner. For example the gradient of L_c respect to λ is

$$\partial L_c/\partial\lambda_{j,k} = -\tilde{\theta}_q^k \cdot m_j(c, s)/\bar{\theta}_j \tag{15}$$

Here $m_j(c,s)$ is the expected number of times θ_j is used by the sequence s and giving the correct labeling c. This number can be calculated by a trivial modification of the standard forward-backward algorithm, which makes each observation only go with the model states with the same label.

Parameter Updating Algorithm. Here the extended Baum-Welch algorithm (EBW) [8] is used. First we define another kind of set Ω: all values in this set sum up 1. EBW re-estimates parameters for each iteration. The updating formula is given as following using λ as an example:

$$\overset{*}{\lambda}_{i,j} = \frac{\lambda_{i,j}(\frac{\partial L}{\partial \lambda_{i,j}} + D)}{\sum\limits_{\lambda_{i,k} \in \Omega} \lambda_{i,k}(\frac{\partial L}{\partial \lambda_{i,k}} + D)} \tag{16}$$

After some iterations, L will converge to a local optimum for a sufficiently large value of the constant D.

4 Application and Discussion

4.1 Training and Testing Datasets

Both HMMgene and our ICHMM program are trained on Genie96 dataset collected by Martin Reese (http://www.fruitfly.org/seq_tools/datasets/Human). The dataset HMR195 by Sanja Rogic [3] is used as test dataset. It contains 195 human, mouse and rate sequences entering GenBank after Genie96 was produced.

4.2 Application of ICHMM for Gene Annotation

Order of States. In HMMgene, the coding regions were modeled by 2th order states, the inter-genic and the internal intron regions by 3th order states and the splice signal regions mostly by 1th order states. These orders gave the best estimation and generalization ability with this model structure. The structure of our ICHMM is the same as that of HMMgene. In our ICHMM, 3th order interpolated states were used for coding regions, 4th order for inter-genic and internal intron regions, and 1th order for most of exon part of splice signal regions. All the other states remain the same as fixed order states in HMMgene.

Parameter Initiation. First we set part of the interpolation parameters to zero so that the ICHMM was actually CHMM just the same as HMMgene. The standard Baum-Welch algorithm was used to do the optimization in (1).

After this ML estimation, we used the ad-hoc weighting approach based on χ^2 test [5] to initiate the interpolation parameters. Then interpolated states with these interpolation parameters were used to replace fixed order states in this ML trained model, which was used as our initial model for CML training.

Procedure of CML Iteration. During the iteration of the extended Baum-Welch algorithm the model accuracy on the test set was monitored and after

20 iterations, the model with the highest accuracy was chosen. After both our ICHMM program and the re-implemented HMMgene were trained like this, we compared their highest accuracy.

Accuracy Comparison. At the exon level, predicted exons (PE) are compared to annotated exons (AE). True exons (TE) is the number of predicted exons which are exactly identical to an annotated exon (i.e. both endpoints correct). Three numbers were calculated:

1. Exon sensitivity: $Sn = TE/AE$.
2. Exon specificity: $Sp = TE/PE$.
3. Average of exon sensitivity and specificity.

Table 1 shows the highest predicting accuracy on the test set of both programs. We can see our ICHMM program improves exon level sensitivity by 3% and specificity by about 1% compared to HMMgene as trained/tested on human DNA sequence dataset described above.

Table 1. Gene annotation accuracy comparison

Program	Exon sensitivity	Exon specificity
ICHMM	79.9%(757/948)	81.5%(757/929)
HMMgene	77.0%(730/948)	80.7%(730/905)

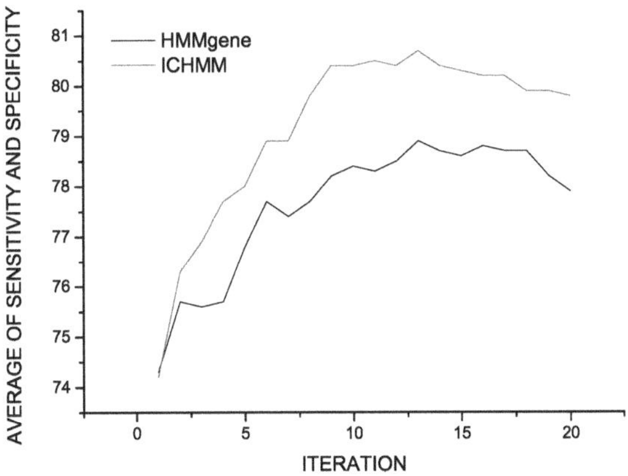

Fig. 3. The average of exon sensitivity and specificity on test set during training

The performance of HMMgene here was comparative to that presented in [3], which indicates our re-implementation of HMMgene was successful. Since HMMgene had the highest prediction accuracy from Rogic's evaluation using the same test dataset as in this work . Since then no comprehensive evaluation of ab initio gene prediction programs for human genome was published, we didn't elaborate the comparison between ICHMM and other popular predictors.

To achieve a more comprehensive comparison between the predicting ability of these two programs, we plotted the average of exon sensitivity and specificity as a function of training iterations (Fig. 3). Fig. 3 indicates that both performance lines are mono-modal during the first 20 iterations. After the performance reaches the peak value, it drops gradually because the models are getting over-fitting to the training data. In general ICHMM outperforms HMMgene in a reliable way.

4.3 Discussion

From the design and application detail of ICHMM, we can see the interpolation scheme here was not used to smooth the "specific probabilities" with the "general probabilities", but to make the "good probabilities" contribute more to the interpolated probabilities. The "good probabilities" are both reliable and precise. The CMLE algorithm estimated the interpolation parameters automatically.

5 Conclusion

The linear interpolation scheme was introduced to the class hidden Markov models, which resulted in our interpolated class hidden Markov models. The CHMM was used in one of the best eukaryotic gene annotation systems: HMMgene. The conditional Maximum Likelihood estimation algorithm was educed to estimate the interpolation parameters. Finally we applied this ICHMM for gene annotation, the final program compares favorably to HMMgene as trained and tested on Human DNA sequences. Exon level sensitivity was improved by 3% and specificity by about 1%.

References

1. Michael, B.R., Roderic, G.: Recent advances in gene structure prediction. Current Opinion in Structural Biology **14** (2004) 264–272
2. Krogh, A.: Two methods for improving performance of an hmm and their application for gene-finding. In: proceedings of the 5th international Conference on Intelligent Systems for Molecular Biology, Menlo Park, CA, AAAI Press (1997) 179–186
3. Rogic, S., Mackworth, A., Ouellette, B.: Evaluation of gene finding programs on mammalian sequences. Genome Research **11** (2001) 817–832
4. Krogh, A.: Hidden markov models for labeled sequences. In: proceedings of the 12th IAPR international Conference on Pattern Recognition, Los Alamitos, California, IEEE Computer Society Press (1994) 140–144
5. Salzberg, L.S., Delcher, A., Kasif, S., White, O.: Microbial gene identification using interpolated markov models. Nucleic Acids Research **26**(2) (1998) 544–548
6. Salzberg, L.S., Pertea, M., Arthur, L.D., Malcolm, J.G., Tettelin, H.: Interpolated markov models for eukaryotic gene finding. Genomics **59**(1) (1999) 24–31
7. Enright, A., Ouzounis, C.: an automatic graph layout algorithm for similarity visualization. Bioinformatics **17**(9) (2001) 853–854
8. Woodland, P., Povey, D.: Large scale discriminative training for speech recognition. In: Proceedings of the Workshop on Automatic Speech Recognition, Paris, France (2000)

Predicting Melting Temperature (Tm) of DNA Duplex Based on Neural Network

Xiangrong Liu[1], Wenbin Liu[2], Juan Liu[3], Linqiang Pan[1], and Jin Xu[1]

[1] Research Institute of biomolecular Computer, Huazhong University of Science and Technology, Wuhan City 430074, China
[2] School of Computer Science and Engineering, Wenzhou Normal College, Wenzhou City 325027, China
[3] The Department of Electronic Science and Technology, Huazhong University of Science and Technology, Wuhan City 430074, China
xrliu@mail.hust.edu.cn

Abstract. In DNA computing, similar thermodynamic stability of the encoding DNA sequences is conduced to improve the reliability and precision of the computing process. The melting temperature is a suitable parameter used to evaluating the stability of DNA duplex. Traditional method to predict Tm in biological engineering may exist lager error for a few sequences. Thus it misfits the lager amount of DNA sequences in DNA computing. In this paper, we introduced artificial neural network to predict the Tm based on Next-Nearest-Neighbor model. Our result shows that the methods have a higher precision than TP methods based on nearest-neighbor model.

1 Introduction

The concept of DNA computing first proposed by Adleman in 1994[1]. The potential power of massive parallelism and high information density of bio-molecules offers a novel method to solve complex computational problems. Subsequently, many scientists devoted themselves to this new research area, and presented a lot of DNA computing models about combinatorial NP-complete problems.

In DNA computing, information is encoded in DNA sequences, its processing is accomplished through a series of biochemical reactions, and the retrieval of information is mainly implemented through specific hybridization between DNA sequences. Therefore, the result of DNA computing heavily depends on the biochemical reactions, which will be greatly influenced by the thermodynamic stability of DNA duplex. And melting temperature (Tm) determination is the easiest and fastest method to evaluate the stability of a DNA duplex. So accurate prediction of DNA melting temperature is important for DNA computing.

With the primary aim of predicting DNA stability from sequence alone, one widely used method for predicting nucleic acid duplex stability uses a Nearest-Neighbor model. Several nearest-neighbor parameter sets for predicting DNA duplex stability are available in literature [2-7]. These methods can work while the number of sequences is less. According to the augment of problem scale, the number of DNA code increased

D.-S. Huang, K. Li, and G.W. Irwin (Eds.): ICIC 2006, LNBI 4115, pp. 275 – 285, 2006.

rapidly. Artificial neural network have been widely applied in performing function approximation, pattern association, and pattern classification. A study of prediction of the Tm of RNA/DNA duplexes using neural networks based on the nearest-neighbor model has been reported [8]. In order to improve the predicting precision of Tm, we established a neural network model to predict the Tm of DNA duplex based on the Next-Nearest-Neighbor parameter. And a method to obtain the eigenvector of the DNA sequences have been developed, which will be regarded as the input of neural networks.

2 Materials and Methods

2.1 Melting Temperature (Tm)

Generally, Tm is the temperature at which half of the heated DNA molecules have denatured. It is affected by the purification of DNA, the concentration of buffer solutions and the pH. Tm can be calculated according to

$$Tm = \Delta H^\circ /(\Delta S^\circ + R \ln C_t) . \tag{1}$$

In which △H°and △S°is the changes enthalpy and entropy, and R is the gas constant [1.987cal/(K mol)]. C_t is the mol concentration of DNA, which is replaced by C_t /4 for non-self-complementary molecules.

2.2 Nearest-Neighbor (N-N) Model

The Nearest-Neighbor model pioneered by Borer et al in 1974[2]. In the Nearest-Neighbor model, the thermodynamic stability of a base pair is dependent on the identity of the adjacent base pairs. In duplex DNA there are 10 such unique doublets.. Table 1 listed the Nearest-Neighbor thermodynamic parameters [7].

To illustrate the calculation procedure for 5 ' —GCTAGC—3 ' next. C_t is 01.mM.

AA	AT	TA	CA	GT	CT	GA	CG	GC	GG
TT	TA	AT	GT	CA	GA	CT	GC	CG	CC
0	0	1	0	0	2	0	0	2	0

Fig. 1. The number of base pairs

$$\begin{aligned}\Delta H^\circ(predicted) &= \Delta H^\circ(gc/cg) + 2\Delta H^\circ(ct/ga) + \Delta H^\circ(ta/at) \\ &+ \Delta H^\circ(Init) + \Delta H^\circ(Sym) = -40.7 kcal/mol\end{aligned} \tag{2}$$

$$\begin{aligned}\Delta S^\circ(predict) &= 2\Delta S^\circ(gc/cg) + 2\Delta S^\circ(ct/ga) + \Delta S^\circ(ta/at) \\ &+ \Delta S^\circ(Init) + \Delta S^\circ(Sym) = 114.8 eu\end{aligned} \tag{3}$$

$$Tm = \Delta H^\circ /(\Delta S^\circ + R \ln C_t) = 305.8K \tag{4}$$

Table 1. Thermodynamic Parameters for DNA ([Na+]=1M,pH=7) [7]

Propagation sequence	△H(kcal/mol)	△S(eu)
AA/TT	-8.4 ± 0.7	-23.6 ± 1.8
AT/TA	-6.5 ± 0.8	-18.8 ± 2.3
TA/AT	-6.3 ± 1.0	-18.5 ± 2.6
CA/GT	-7.4 ± 1.1	-19.3 ± 2.9
GT/CA	-8.6 ± 0.7	-23.0 ± 2.0
CT/GA	-6.1 ± 1.2	-16.1 ± 3.3
GA/CT	-7.7 ± 0.7	-20.3 ± 1.9
CG/GC	-10.1 ± 0.9	-25.5 ± 2.3
GC/CG	-11.1 ± 1.0	-28.4 ± 2.6
GG/CC	-6.7 ± 0.6	-15.6 ± 1.5
Initiation at G·C	0	-5.9 ± 0.8
Initiation at A·T	0	-9.0± 3.2)
Symmetry correction	0	-1.4
5\`-terminal T·A bp	0.4	0

2.3 Next-Nearest-Neighbor (N-N-N) Model

The different duplex sequences containing the same number of nearest-neighbors have differences in Tm's up to 5.3℃. For instance, the DNA duplexes TCTATAGA and TAGATCTA (the number of nearest-neighbors all is 0120022000,based on Scheme 1) in 1 M Na^+ have melting temperatures of 28.1 and 33.4℃, respectively, at the same total single strand concentration of C_T=0.1 mM. Thermodynamic properties of such duplexes are not distinguishable in the N-N model, because the calculation procedure of the N-N model is based solely on the numbers of nearest-neighbors. Thus, the N-N model predicts the same Tm for such duplexes and more accurate prediction cannot be obtained with the N-N model. Logical extension to possibly account for these observations would be to formulate a Next-Nearest-Neighbor model that also takes into account interactions in next-nearest-neighbor base pairs (triplets) [10].

Actually the consecutive next-nearest-neighbor subunits partially overlay each other and share the same doublet. This treatment is possible because the shorter range. Because each triplet consists of two successive N-N doublets, the N-N-N interactions are evaluated as a deviation from the average N-N interactions. For instance, triplet 5′-CGC-3′ can be considered as the combination of 5′-CG-3′ and 5′-GC-3′ stacks. Thus, the N-N-N interaction in 5\`-CGC-3\` is a deviation from the average of the 5′-CG-3′ and 5′-GC-3′ N-N interactions. This approach to the N-N-N model is an extension of the single formalism of the N-N model.

In the N-N-N model, there are 32 possible triplets in DNA duplex. The calculating procedure for N-N-N model is illustrated at Fig.2. The DNA is 18 base pairs long. The first four triplets from the left side are marked, CGC/GCG, GCG/CGC, CGT/GCA, GTA/CAT.

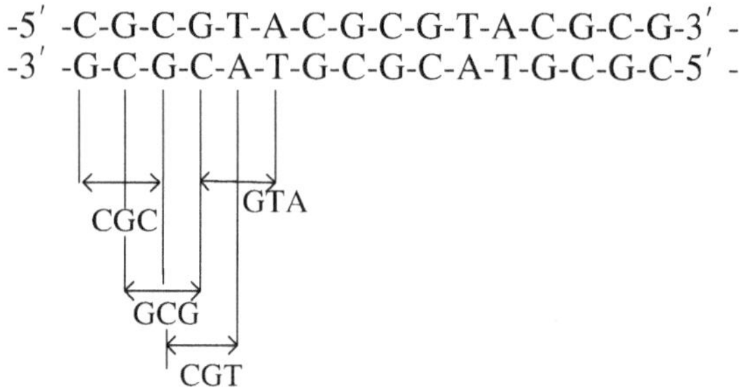

Fig. 2. Structure and central sequences of the DNA duplex used in evaluation of next-nearest-neighbor parameters

If F denotes the times of triplet, the numbers of the 32 possible triplets in the DNA are,

$F_{AAA/TTT} = 0$	$F_{AAG/CTT} = 0$	$F_{AAT/ATT} = 0$	$F_{AAC/GTT} = 0$
$F_{AGA/TCT} = 0$	$F_{AGG/CCT} = 0$	$F_{AGT/ACT} = 0$	$F_{AGC/GCT} = 0$
$F_{ATA/TAT} = 0$	$F_{ATG/CAT} = 0$	$F_{ATC/GAT} = 0$	$F_{ACA/TGT} = 0$
$F_{ACG/CGT} = 4$	$F_{ACC/GGT} = 0$	$F_{GAA/TTC} = 0$	$F_{GAG/CTC} = 0$
$F_{GAC/GTC} = 0$	$F_{GGA/TCC} = 0$	$F_{GGG/CCC} = 0$	$F_{GGC/GCC} = 0$
$F_{GTA/TAC} = 4$	$F_{GTG/CAC} = 0$	$F_{GCA/TGC} = 0$	$F_{GCG/CGC} = 6$
$F_{TAA/TTA} = 0$	$F_{TAG/CTA} = 0$	$F_{TGA/TCA} = 0$	$F_{TGG/CCA} = 0$
$F_{TTG/CAA} = 0$	$F_{TCG/CGA} = 0$	$F_{CAG/CTG} = 0$	$F_{CGG/CCG} = 0$

The frequencies of next-nearest-neighbor triplet for a given sequence were used as the input data of the network. In order to reduce the size of the input vectors and improve the generalization of the neural network, we presented a method to obtain the eigenvector of the DNA sequences.

When sequences are synthetic and melt in a single cooperative transition, the melting temperature Tm is calculated simply as $\triangle H°/\triangle S°$[9]. Base on the N-N model, we calculated the $\triangle H°$, $\triangle S°$ and $\triangle H°/\triangle S°$ of 32 possible next-nearest-neighbor triplets. It is showed in Table 2. The data is sorted by the values of $\triangle H°/\triangle S°$ in ascending order.

The dimension of the input vector is large to the problem. Therefore, we united the approximately data. If the difference of $\triangle H°/\triangle S°$ between two adjacent triplets is less than 2, we think they should belong in one. So we divided the possible 32 triplets into 16 groups. The composition in each group is listed in Table 2.

Table 2. The enthalpy (△H°) and entropy (△S°), △H°/△S° of 30 possible next-nearest-neighbor triplets [7]*

G	Triplet	△H° (kcal/ mol)	△S° (eu)	△H°/△ S° (k)	G	Triplet	△H° (kcal/ mol)	△S° (eu)	△H°/△ S°(k)
C1	ATA/TA	-12.8	-0.0373	343.2	C8	AGA/TCT	-13.8	-0.0364	379.1
C2	TAA/TT	-14.7	-0.0421	349.2	C8	GAG/CTC	-13.8	-0.0364	379.1
C3	AAT/AT	-14.9	-0.0424	351.4	C9	TGA/TCA	-15.1	-0.0396	381.3
C4	AAA/TT	-16.8	-0.0472	355.9	C9	CAG/CTG	-13.5	-0.0354	381.4
C5	TAG/CT	-12.4	-0.0346	358.4	C10	ACG/CGT	-18.7	-0.0485	385.6
C5	GTA/TA	-14.9	-0.0415	359	C10	AGC/GCT	-17.2	-0.0445	386.5
C6	ATC/GA	-14.2	-0.0391	363.2	C10	GCA/TGC	-18.5	-0.0477	387.8
C6	AAC/GT	-17	-0.0466	364.8	C10	TCG/CGA	-17.8	-0.0458	388.6
C6	ATG/CA	-13.9	-0.0381	364.8	C11	GCG/CGC	-21.2	-0.0539	393.3
C6	AAG/CT	-14.5	-0.0397	365.2	C12	ACC/GGT	-15.3	-0.0386	396.4
C6	GAA/TT	-16.1	-0.0439	366.7	C13	GGA/TCC	-14.4	-0.0359	401.1
C7	TTG/CA	-15.8	-0.0429	368.3	C14	AGG/CCT	-12.8	-0.0317	403.8
C8	AGT/AC	-14.7	-0.0391	375.9	C14	TGG/CCA	-14.1	-0.0349	404
C8	GAC/GT	-16.3	-0.0433	376.4	C14	GGC/GCC	-17.8	-0.044	404.5
C8	ACA/TG	-16	-0.0423	378.3	C15	CGG/CCG	-16.8	-0.0411	408.8
C8	GTG/CA	-16	-0.0423	378.3	C16	GGG/CCC	-13.4	-0.0312	429.5

*Solutions are 1 M NaCl sodium cacodylate, and 0.5 mM Na_2EDTA, pH 7. The units for △S°(eu) are cal/K per mol of interaction. TAA/TTA means 5′-TAA-3′Watson-Crick base paired with 5′-TTA- 3′.

The 16 patters in Fig.3 correspond to the 16 groups of triplets. Then we calculated the frequencies of 16 patters to a DNA duplex. In this calculation, each base pair in the middle of the sequence is used three times, but each base pair at the end is used only once and each base pair next to the end is used twice. Therefore we propose the

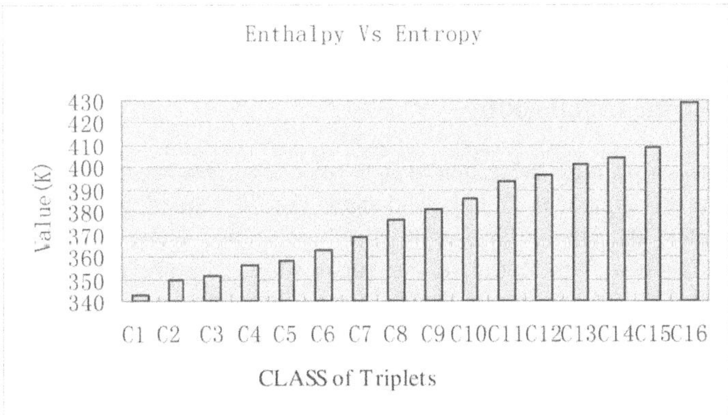

Fig. 3. Class of possible triplets based on enthalpy VS entropy

two end parameters initiation C • G and initiation A • T as a correction. InitiationA • T parameter for duplexes that contain only A·T base pairs [7], then C17=1,C18=0. Initiation G • C parameter for duplexes contain at least one G • C base pair, then C17=0 and C18=1. In the Fig.3 the frequencies of the end parameters are C17=0 and C18=1. In our method the symmetry effect and the 3ˋ-terminal phosphate present on some oligomers are ignored.

2.4 Back-Propagation (BP) Method

The back-propagation algorithm [11] is a generalization of the least mean squares algorithm that modifies network weights to minimize the mean square error between the desired and actual outputs of the network. The input and target vectors are used to train a network until it can approximate a function, associate input vectors with specific output vectors, or classify input vectors in an appropriate way as defined by you. Networks with biases, a sigmoid layer, and a linear output layer are capable of approximating any function with a finite number of discontinuities. The appropriate notation used in the two-layer logsig/purelin network is showed next.

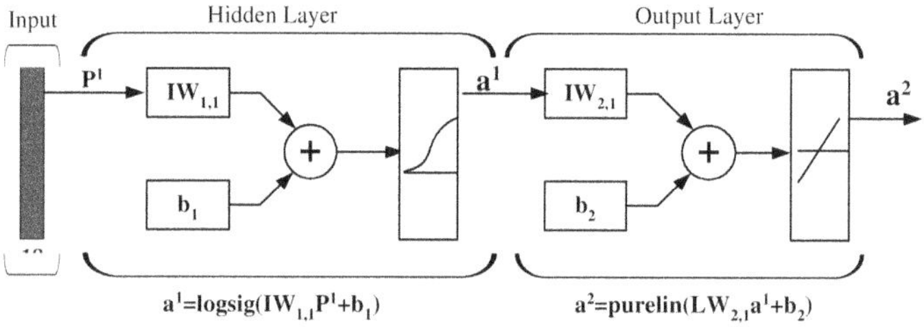

Fig. 4. Three-layer network

We constructed three-layer traditional BP neural networks with 18 neurons in the input layer, one neuron in the output layer. And we have tried six, five, four or three neurons in the hidden layer. But we found the network with four neurons in the hidden layer have the best result.

3 Results and Discussion

In the process of training these neural networks, the train set and test set are set as random from 84 sequences [7,12]. And there are 72 sequences in train set and 12 sequences in test set. The initial weight values are set as random real numbers and the BP method is utilized to optimize the final weights, while the supervisor is the measured Tm data. We predicted the Tm based on nearest-neighbor thermodynamic parameter (TP) [7] for comparison. To test the repeatability of neural network, we repeated the learning and testing processes using different random real numbers as initial weights and obtained very similar results.

The predicted results based on neural networks (NN) and nearest-neighbor thermodynamic parameter (TP) for the training and test sets are listed in Table 3 respectively. And the comparison of NN and TP methods is also illustrated in Fig. 5 and Fig.6.

Table 3. Predictions of Tm (K) by NN and TP methods for training and test set*

No.	Sequences	Experiment Tm (k)	Predicted Tm by NN (k)	Error of NN (k)	Predicted Tm by TP (k)**	Error of TP (K)
Train Set						
1	ccgg	289.75	290.30	-0.55	285.54	4.21
2	tgatca	294.05	295.35	-1.30	289.66	4.39
3	tcatga	295.95	295.35	0.60	289.66	6.29
4	gcgc	300.65	301.51	-0.86	299.35	1.3
5	tctataga	301.25	300.42	0.83	296.88	4.37
6	cgtgc	303.25	304.57	-1.32	308.97	-5.72
7	aataccg	303.45	303.69	-0.24	312.33	-8.88
8	ggattga	303.55	303.88	-0.33	312.46	-8.91
9	aaaaaaaa	304.35	304.53	-0.18	305.45	-1.1
10	caaaaag	304.65	304.25	0.40	305.84	-1.19
11	agccg	304.75	305.48	-0.73	309.65	-4.9
12	gcgagc	306.35	313.05	-6.70	322.6	-16.25
13	gtgaac	306.35	302.80	3.55	305.1	1.25
14	tagatcta	306.55	304.88	1.67	296.88	9.67
15	agcttca	306.95	310.60	-3.65	309.73	-2.78
16	cgatcg	307.45	308.59	-1.14	309.56	-2.11
17	cgtacg	308.15	308.59	-0.44	309.71	-1.56
18	ggtatacc	309.15	307.54	1.61	313.37	-4.22
19	gacgtc	309.25	310.40	-1.15	310.09	-0.84
20	ttttataataaa	309.45	309.29	0.16	314.12	-4.67
21	caaaaaag	310.05	310.89	-0.84	312.5	-2.45
22	acctagtc	310.45	312.38	-1.93	319.52	-9.07
23	accgca	311.15	310.03	1.12	315.6	-4.45
24	aatccagt	311.55	311.88	-0.33	313.41	-1.86
25	cggtgc	312.55	313.55	-1.00	322.79	-10.24
26	ctagtgga	313.45	314.01	-0.56	319.4	-5.95
27	caaataaag	314.55	312.44	2.11	313.12	1.43
28	agcgtaag	315.55	314.92	0.63	323.26	-7.71
29	agtcctga	315.85	316.56	-0.71	318.35	-2.5
30	cccggg	316.15	315.01	1.14	325.11	-8.96
31	cgctgtaa	316.35	313.37	2.98	324.75	-8.4
32	ggaattcc	316.95	316.73	0.22	318.85	-1.9
33	cgatatcg	317.25	314.77	2.48	316.79	0.46
34	caaaaaaag	317.35	317.01	0.34	317.59	-0.24
35	caagcttg	317.75	318.22	-0.47	319.19	-1.44
36	gggacc	318.05	317.34	0.71	318.46	-0.41

Table 3. (*continued*)

37	gtagctac	318.05	318.46	-0.41	313.83	4.22
38	gaagcttc	318.35	319.30	-0.95	318.97	-0.62
39	caaagaaag	318.35	320.79	-2.44	319.85	-1.5
40	gccagtta	318.65	319.17	-0.52	323.65	-5
41	gtcgaaca	319.35	320.67	-1.32	326.45	-7.1
42	gatgcatc	319.65	319.30	0.35	317.92	1.73
43	caaacaaag	320.45	319.89	0.56	321.45	-1
44	gccagttaa	320.55	320.56	-0.01	327.61	-7.06
45	gatcgatc	320.75	319.30	1.45	317.25	3.5
46	gttgcaac	320.85	318.22	2.63	322.39	-1.54
47	agccgtg	320.85	320.93	-0.08	328.73	-7.88
48	atctatccg	321.15	323.23	-2.08	323.41	-2.26
49	acgacctc	321.35	321.63	-0.28	330.36	-9.01
50	gccagttat	322.55	323.21	-0.66	325.87	-3.32
51	ctcacggc	325.65	325.19	0.46	334.67	-9.02
52	ggcgcc	327.05	325.91	1.14	328.54	-1.49
53	ggagctcc	327.55	327.09	0.46	329.75	-2.2
54	ggacgtcc	328.25	327.09	1.16	332.15	-3.9
55	ccgcgg	328.35	329.65	-1.30	328.19	0.16
56	cgcgcg	328.85	328.53	0.32	330.4	-1.55
57	gcgcgc	329.25	328.53	0.72	330.66	-1.41
58	gccggc	330.85	331.60	-0.75	328.54	2.31
59	atgagctcat	331.25	329.35	1.90	322.66	8.59
60	cacggctc	331.65	326.55	5.10	334.69	-3.04
61	caacttgatattatta	331.95	334.17	-2.22	332.42	-0.47
62	cggccg	332.75	331.60	1.15	328.19	4.56
63	gtataccggtatac	335.35	335.36	-0.01	336.13	-0.78
64	gcgaaaagcg	338.35	339.52	-1.17	340.3	-1.95
65	catatggccatatg	338.45	338.14	0.31	337.58	0.87
66	catattggccaatatg	339.05	339.87	-0.82	340.27	-1.22
67	gtataaccggttatac	339.45	340.50	-1.05	338.94	0.51
68	cgcatgggtacgc	339.65	344.12	-4.47	352.86	-13.21
69	ccatcgctacc	340.75	336.88	3.87	342.65	-1.9
70	gcgaattcgc	341.05	338.28	2.77	337.92	3.13
71	cgcgaattcgcg	348.55	349.72	-1.17	348.11	0.44
72	cgcgtacgcgtacgcg	364.15	361.86	2.29	358.71	5.44
	AME			1.30		3.59
	RMSE			1.80		4.81
	ρ		0.99		0.94	

Table 3. *(continued)*

Test Set						
1	cgcg	296.85	301.51	-4.66	298.1	-1.25
2	ggatcc	303.95	305.95	-2.00	303.79	0.16
3	gctagc	307.45	309.01	-1.56	305.79	1.66
4	gcatgc	309.65	309.01	0.64	311.16	-1.51
5	cacggc	313.15	311.77	1.38	322.79	-9.64
6	gtacgtac	318.25	318.46	-0.21	317.05	1.2
7	catcgatg	320.55	319.30	1.25	317.45	3.1
8	cccaggg	321.25	319.36	1.89	330.33	-9.08
9	gcataatacgt	328.65	328.74	-0.09	330.3	-1.65
10	cgtcgacg	331.45	329.54	1.91	333.33	-1.88
11	ccattgctacc	336.65	335.38	1.27	338.13	-1.48
12	ctgacaagtgtc	338.85	338.88	-0.03	339.39	-0.54
	AME			1.41		2.56
	RMSE			1.85		3.71
	ρ		0.99		0.96	

* AME, absolute mean error; ρ, relation coefficient; The sequences for train and test are from [7] and [12]; RMSE, root mean square error, $RMSE = [\sum_{i=1}^{N}(Xi - Yi)^2 / (N-1)]^{1/2}$;

**The Tm was predicted based on nearest-neighbor thermodynamic parameter (TP) [7].

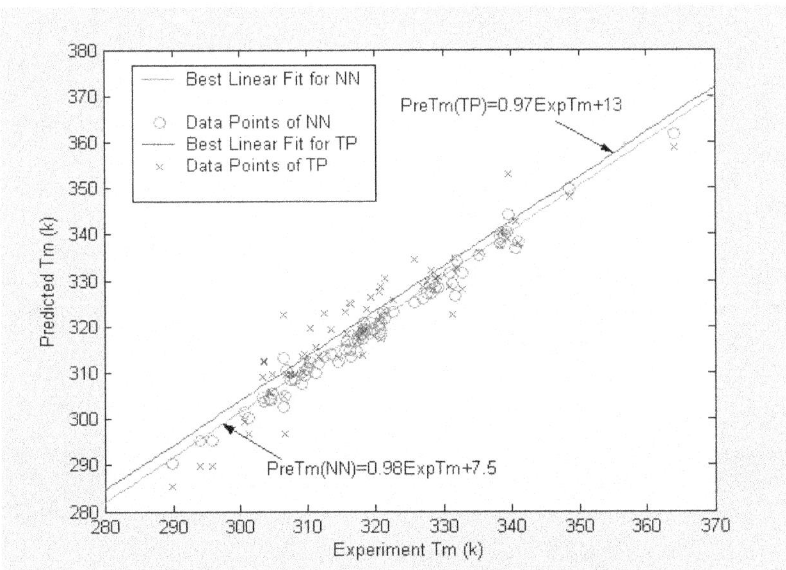

Fig. 5. Comparison of NN and TP methods for training set

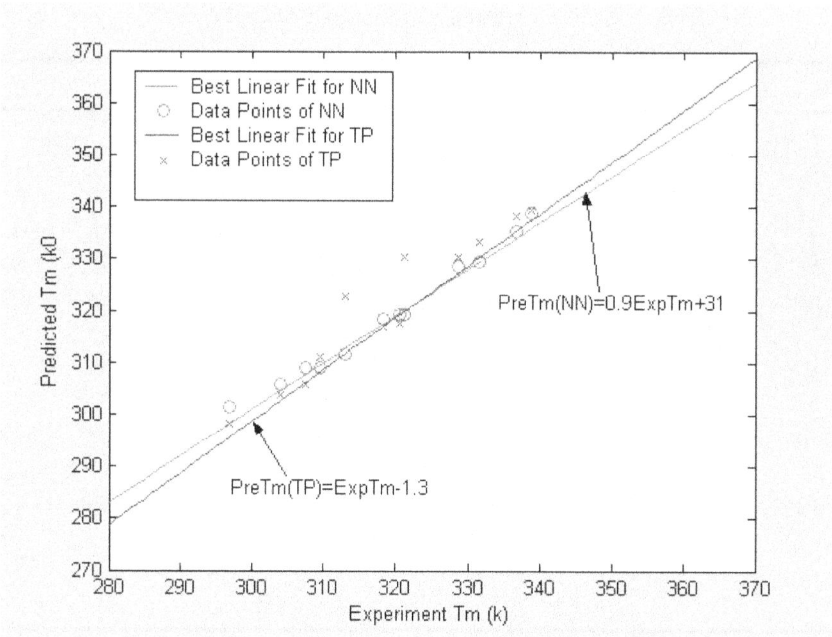

Fig. 6. Comparison of NN and TP methods for test set

As seen above, the predicted Tm of the train and test sets by NN methods (AME=1.3K, RMSE=1.8K, ρ=0.99 for Train Set and AME=1.41K, RMSE=1.85K, ρ=0.99 for Test Set) agree with the experimental data better than TP method (AME=3.59K, RMSE=4.81K, ρ=0.94 for Train Set and AME=2.56K, RMSE=3.71K, ρ=0.96 for Test Set). The best linear fit for NN is better than TP. The RMSE and best linear fit results of NN illuminated that most predicting Tm approached the experiment Tm well. It is possible for us to apply the methods into predicting Tm of a number of coding sequences in DNA computing.

From the sequences TCTATAGA (ExpTm=301.25k, PreTm(NN) =300.42k, PreTm(TP)=296.88k) and TAGATCTA (ExpTm=306.55k, PreTm(NN)=304.88k, PreTm(TP)=296.88k), it is showed that the methods based on next-nearest-neighbor model and neural networks distinguish the sequences have the same number of nearest-neighbors well. It can not be distinguish in the nearest-neighbor thermodynamic parameter methods (the two sequences have the same Tm 296.88K).

4 Conclusion

Thus we can conclude that the neural network method is a reliable way to predict melting temperatures of DNA duplexes. The interactions in next-nearest-neighbor base pairs (triplets) being taken into account, we obtain higher precision in predicting the Tm than nearest-neighbor TP methods. It can be applied in the complex code designing of DNA computing, such as designing the code scheme of DNA automaton

[13]. And certainly it can be used to predict Tm of DNA duplex in commonly experiment designing.

However, the methods didn't solve the problem that the sequences have the same number of nearest-neighbors but different Tm completely, which is only great reduced. We hope we can discuss it in the next work.

Acknowledgments

This paper supported by the National Scientific Foundation of China under grants 60533010,60403002 and 60373089. The authors are gratefully acknowledged to the authors who appeared in the references.

References

1. Alderman, L.:Molecular Computations to Combinatorial Problems. Science, Vol. 266 (1994) 1021-1024
2. Borer, P. N., Dengler, B., Tinoco, I. Jr., Uhlenbeck, O. C.: Stability of Ribonucleic Acid Double-Stranded Helices. J. Mol. Biol., Vol. 86 (1974) 843-853
3. Gotoh, O., Tagashira, Y.: Stabilities of Nearest-Neighbor Doublets in Double-Helical DNA Determined by Fitting Calculated Melting Profiles to Observed Profiles. Biopolymers, Vol.20 (1981) 1033-1042
4. Breslauer, K. J., Frank, R., Blöcker, H., Marky, L.: A. Predicting DNA Duplex Stability From the Base Sequence. Proc. Natl. Acad. Sci., Vol. 83 (1986) 3746-3750
5. Delcourt, S. G., Blake, R. D.: Stacking Energies in DNA. J. Biol. Chem, Vol. 266 (1991) 15160-15169
6. Gray, D. M: Derivation of Nearest-Neighbor Properties from Data on Nucleic Acid Oligomers.□. Thermodynamic Parameters of DNA•RNA Hybrids and DNA Duplexes. Biopolymers ,Vol. 42 (1997b) 795-810
7. Santalucia, J. Jr., Allawi, H., Seneviratne, P.: A. Improved Nearest-Neighbor Parameters for Predicting DNA Duplex Stability. Biochemistry, Vol.35 (1996) 3555-3562
8. Lixin, M., Changmei, C., Xiaohong, L., Yufen, Z., Anlin, W., Piet, H.; A Neural Network for Predicting the Stability of RNA/DNA Hybrid Duplexes. Chemometrics and intelligent laboratory systems, (2004) 123-128
9. Owczarzy, R., Vallone, P. M., Gallo, F. J., Paner, T. M., Lane, M. J., Benight, A. S.: Predicting Sequence-Dependent Melting Stability of Short Duplex DNA Oligomers. Biopolymers, Vol. 44 (1997) 217-239
10. Santalucia, J. Jr.: "A Unified View of Polymer, Dumbbell, and Oligonucleotide DNA Nearest-Neighbor Thermodynamics,' in Proc. of Natl. Acad. Sci. USA, Vol.95 (1998) 1460-1465
11. Rumelhart, D. E., Hinton, G. E., Williams, R. J.: Learning Representations by Back-Propagating Errors. Nature, Vol 323 (1986) 533-536
12. Wu, P., Nakano, S., Sugimoto. N.: Temperature Dependence of Thermodynamic Properties for DNA/DNA and RNA/DNA Duplex Formation. Eur. J. Biochem, Vol. 269 (2002) 2821-2830`1
13. Shi, XL, Li, X., Zhang, Z., et al. :Improve Capability of DNA Automaton: DNA Automaton with Three Internal States and Tape Head Move in Two Directions. LECT NOTES COMPUT SC, Vol. 3645 (2005) 71-79

Programmable Pushdown Store Base on DNA Computing

Zheng Zhang[1], Jin Xu[1], Jie Liu[2], and Linqiang Pan[1]

[1] Department of Control Science and Engineering,
Huazhong Univ of Sci&Tech,
[2] Institute of Material Science and Engineering, Huazhong Univ of Sci&Tech,
Wuhan 430074, China
leaf@hust.edu.cn

Abstract. DNA computing aims at using nucleic acids for computing. Micromolar DNA solutions can act as billions of parallel nanoprocessors with few consume. Finite automation is a general compute model. Now, A programmable finite automation based on DNA computing is available[1]. It's act as a basic features and processes of a finite automaton with two internal states and an alphabet comprising two input symbols. Here we describe a new finite automata made of biomolecules, which can be used as a programmable pushdown store.

1 Introduction

DNA computing aims at using nucleic acids for computing. The concept of the DNA computing was given by T.Head in 1987[2], Adleman's successful solution of a seven-vertex instance of the NP-complete Hamiltonian directed path problem by a DNA algorithm initiated the field of biomolecule computing in 1994[3]. In the past ten years, Both the theory and the experiment method of DNA computing was improved greatly [4-9]. The DNA computing model include: sticker system[10], splicing system[11-12] etc, the hairpin formation[13] and the plasmids[14] can be used for DNA computing too.

A DNA solution can act as billions of parallel nanoprocessors with few consume. But a particular method must be given to solve a special problem by the original DNA computing model (such as splicing system, stick model). There is no generally way to dispose all of them now. In the other hand, electronic computer can solve problem in a universal way (base Turing machine), although it's need vast time and consume. An automata made of biomolecules can combine the strongpoint of the two ways for computation.

A finite automaton A over Σ, where å $= \{s_1, s_2, L, s_n\}$, is a finite directed graph in which every vertex has n arrows leading out from it, with each arrow labeled by a distinct s_i (1 £ i £ n). There is one vertex, labeled by a '-'sign, called the initial vertex, and a (possibly empty) set of vertices, labeled by a '+' sigh, called the final vertices. Fig 1. shows a graph which describe a certain finite automaton.

D.-S. Huang, K. Li, and G.W. Irwin (Eds.): ICIC 2006, LNBI 4115, pp. 286 – 293, 2006.

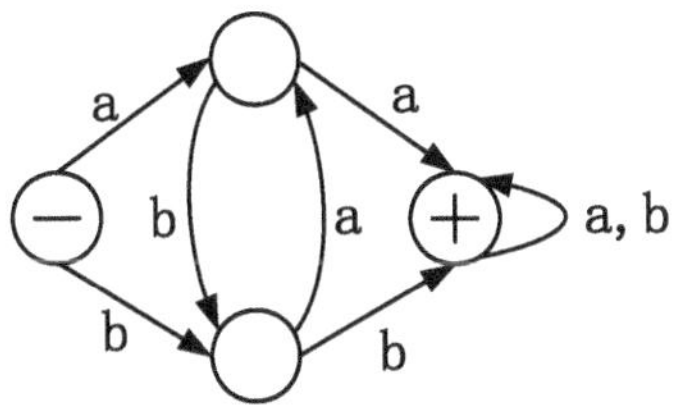

Fig. 1. All words over ∑containing two consecutive a's or two consecutive b's

Now, the realization of computing devices operating autonomously on the molecular scale is available [15]. It's a programmable finite automaton comprising DNA and DNA-manipulating enzymes that solves computational problems autonomously. The automaton's hardware consists of a restriction nuclease and ligase, the software and input are encoded by double-stranded DNA, and programming amounts to choosing appropriate software molecules. Upon mixing solutions containing these components, the automaton processes the input molecule via a cascade of restriction, hybridization and ligation cycles, producing a detectable output molecule that encodes the automaton's final state, and thus the computational result. It's act as a basic features and processes of a finite automaton with two internal states and an alphabet comprising two input symbols.

Here we describe a new finite automata made of biomolecules, which can be used as a programmable pushdown store. A new kind of restriction nuclease is used as hardware to manipulate it.

2 A Simple Pushdown Store

DNA chain is combined with four kinds of base, which is A, G, C and T. If the bases were coded compatibly, then the DNA chain can considered as a data chain which can store some information.

A biomolecule pushdown store have two actions, the one is "push" (write the data) and the other is "pop" (read the data). The data can be read/write by straightly get/set the DNA sequence, but this way not suitable for automata because of some extra electric instruments is needed. A new way should be find to realize the two actions of the pushdown store.

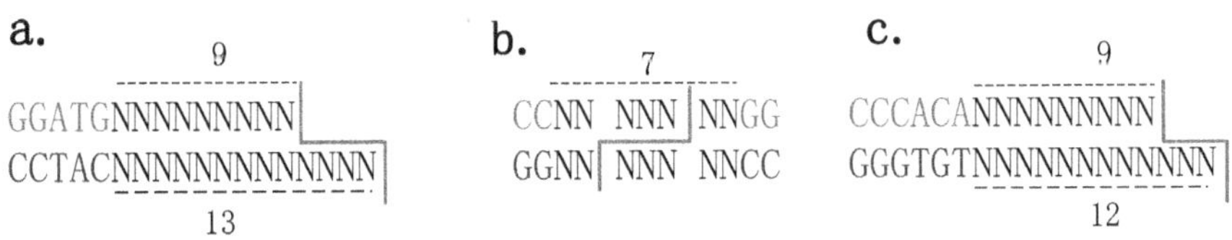

Fig. 2. Show the enzyme's recognition site. N for any type of base. a for FokI, b for BslI and c for RleAI.

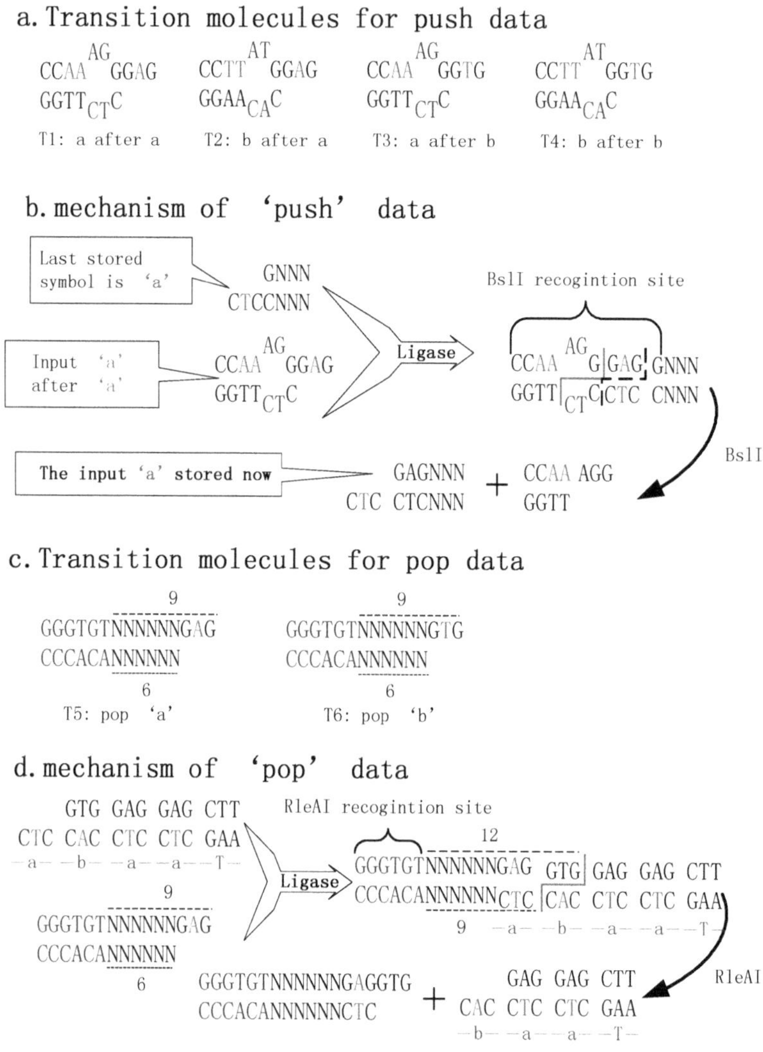

Fig. 3. a, the encode of the transition molecules for input, each for input an 'a' after an 'a', a 'b' after an 'a', an 'a' after a 'b' and a 'b' after a 'b'. Each of the four transition molecules is encoded with two bp mismatch (the blue part), which can't prevent the two terminal product ligate again. **b,** an example to illustrate the mechanism for 'push' data action of the pushdown store. One of the two terminal product of one transition is the lengthened pushdown store molecular (the left one of the '+'), and the other is useless now (the right one of the '+'). **c,** the encode of the transition molecules for pop data. T5 for pop an 'a' from the pushdown store, while T6 for pop a 'b'. **d,** an example fro illustrate the mechanism for 'pop' data, the Terminal state is encoded with 'GAA'(the last three bp). The data pop will not stop till the ruin of the transition data or the terminal state of pushdown is exposed.

In fact, each action of the pushdown store is similar to the state transition of a programmable automation. A model of programmable and autonomous computing machine made of biomolecules was proposed in 2001[1]. Because of the input/output DNA was cut when this computing machine complete a state transition, the input/output DNA will be shorter and shorter when the machine running. So the path of the state transition can't be save under this mechanics, neither any information can be stored.

In Benenson's automata, the restriction nuclease FokI was used to cut the DNA strain as a part of the hardware. It recognition site can be pictured by the Fig. 2a. We can see it's hardly to increase the length of the DNA strain.

BslI (recognition site show in Fig. 2b) will be used as the part of the hardware of the new type of automata to push the data, and RleAI (recognition site show in Fig. 2c) will be used to pop the data instead of FokI.

A simple pushdown store can be constructing now. Its hardware consists of a mixture of the restriction nucleases BslI and RleAI, T4 DNA ligase and ATP.

2.1 Push the Data to the Store

For push the data to the pushdown store, the 'transition molecules' should be designed properly (One of the schemes show in Fig.3a), which encode the four possible transition rules and the input.

An example was given to illustrate the "push" (write the data) mechanism of the pushdown store in Fig.3b. First, add some input to the solution, in this example the input symbol is 'a'. The sticky end of the inputted transition molecule ligates to the pushdown store molecule. The product will be cleaved by BslI inside the current symbol encoding, the pushdown store molecule get a new sticky end, coded as current symbol. To prevent the leftover of the transition molecules and the store molecules ligates together again, the transition molecules is encoded with two bp mismatch. More transition molecular can be put into the solution to save the data to the pushdown store.

2.2 Pop the Data from the Store

To pop the data from the pushdown store, two extra 'transition molecules' are needed (Fig.3c). The "pop" action of the pushdown store is illustrated in Fig.3d. When pop the data. First add transition molecules (T5 and T6) to the solution, one type of the transition molecules (in the example is T5) will ligates to the pushdown store molecule. The product will be cleaved by RleAI, and the cleave position between the current data's and the next data's encoding, exposing a new three-nucleotide sticky end. The "pop" action will continuous till the pushdown store reach its 'Terminal State', if the 'transition molecules are enough.

3 Programmable Finite Automata Based on the Pushdown Store

The simple pushdown store aforementioned can also be treated as a finite automaton. It act as a finite automaton with two internal states and an alphabet comprising for

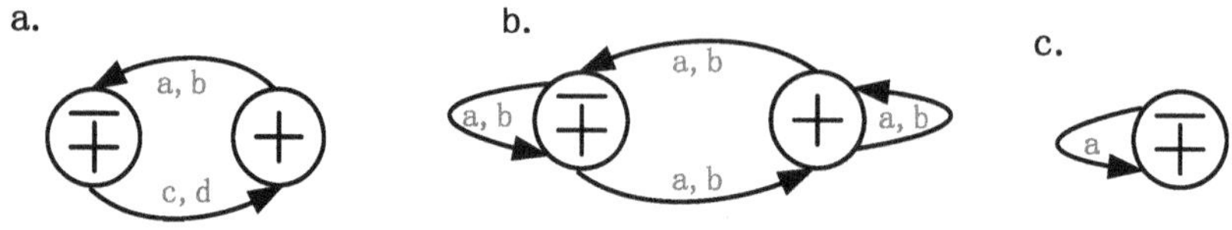

Fig. 4. The states transition graph for pushdown store. **a.** the states transition graph for pushdown store when pushing data, **b.** the stats transition graph for pushdown store when popping data. **c.** The stats transition graph for pushdown store when popping data if use only one state transition molecular.

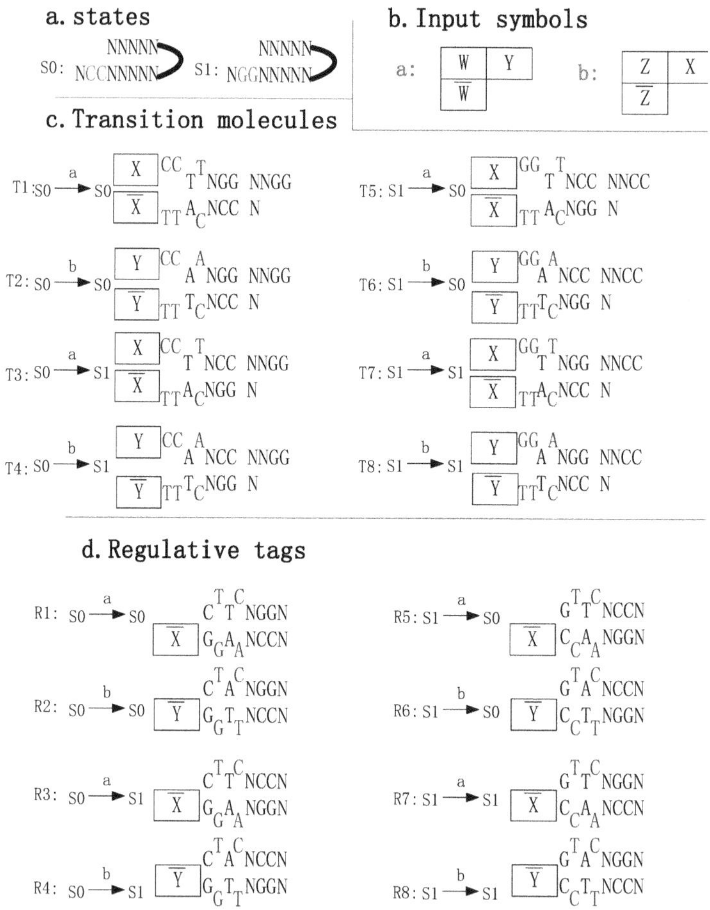

Fig. 5. Design detail of the molecular finite automaton. **a.** the two states of the automaton:S0 and S1. These hairpin formations are the computing molecules too. **b.** Two symbols of the input. The sticky end of one symbol can match the sticky end of the Regulative tags (Fig.5d) for another input symbol. In simple words, a match with the R2, 4, 6, 8 and b match the R1, 3, 5, 7. **c.** Eight transition molecules. The blue bp is mismatched to prevent the transition before the adding of the input symbol. Each of them will match with its Regulative tags (T1 v R1, T2 v R2…T8 v R8) and the states of the automaton. (T1, 2, 3, and 4 matched with S0, T5, 6, 7 and 8 matched with S1). **d.** Eight regulative tags.

input symbols when pushing data (Fig4.a); On the other hand, it process as a finite automaton with two internal states and an alphabet comprising two input symbols when popping data (Fig4.b). Both of the finite automatons can't be programmed.

The pushdown store described before can be improve to a programmable finite automata which has two internal stats (Fig. 5a) and an alphabet comprising two input symbols(Fig. 5b). Its hardware consists of a mixture of the restriction nuclease BslI, T4 DNA ligase, ATP and the computing molecules (Fig. 5a); while the software comprises eight transition molecular (Fig. 5d) and eight regulative tags (Fig.5e). The computation starts when the hardware, software and input are mixed together, one and only one type of the input molecular needed be put into the solution for one state transition.

This automaton is programmable obviously. It can be programmed by use different software, in another word choose different transition molecules and regulative tags. A selection of such programs is shown in Fig. 6a

The automaton process the input as shown in Fig. 6c. First, put one type of the input molecules into the solution ('a' in this example). Then let the double strained software molecular to be single strained. The input molecules will regulate the tags, in this example, the input molecules will match all regulative tags for 'b', only the

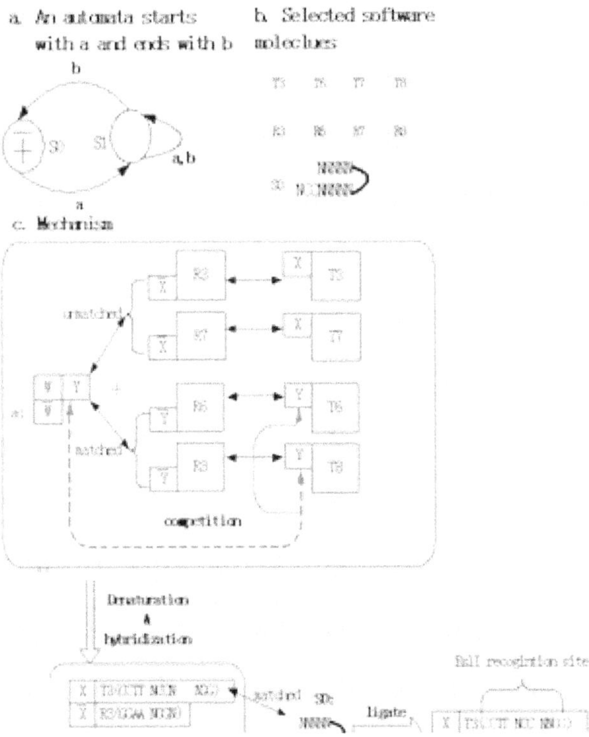

Fig. 6. Mechanism of the Molecular Automata

regulative tags for 'a' are active now. These tags will match with exist transition molecules, and the transition molecules match the initial states will ligate to the computing molecules. The product will be cleaved by BslI, and exposed a new sticky end which can express the new states of the automaton. The computation proceeds until no transition molecule matches the input and the states. To prevent the transition start before the input molecules adding, some base pair of the transition molecules are mismatched. (Especially the recognition site of the BslI).

The computing molecules will be lengthen when the automaton processing, and the transition history is stored in it. In this sense this automaton is a pushdown store too

4 Conclusion and Discussion

A simple pushdown store was described first, which can push(write, lengthen the sequence) and pop(read, shorten the sequence) data by two kinds of nucleases and exact environment. But this pushdown store can't be programmable. An improved pushdown store was given as a finite automaton which has two internal stats (S0,S1) and an alphabet comprising two input symbols(a,b). It can not only store the transition history in the automaton computing molecules, but also be programmed by change the selection of its software molecules base on the transition map, which can used in more complex computing.

The Programmable finite automaton can be improved further. The 'N' in the software molecules can coded for store more information, then the Programmable finite automaton can be improved to a more powerful programmable Biomolecule pushdown store. For this, sixteen transition molecules and the corresponding regulation tags must be encoded for sixteen situations as shown in Table 1. This programmable pushdown store can be treated as a finite automation too, which have 4 internal states and 4 input symbols. For it too inconvenient to describe, this automaton will not illustrate here, and will be studied in future.

Table 1. The columns classify the software molecules by states transition, and the row classify it by input symbol

	S0 to S0	S0 to S1	S1 to S0	S1 to S1
a after a	T1	T5	T9	T13
b after b	T2	T6	T10	T14
b after a	T3	T7	T11	T15
b after b	T4	T8	T12	T16

The sequence of the new automata is not shorter and shorter but longer and longer in the processing, which is the most import difference between the new automata and the Benenson's. The added sequence can use too store some information, it can be read it one by one through the reverse procession or using some special tools. A general DNA computing model is useful for solve routine problems. And a finite automaton was realized now. But it less power than the Turing computer model. More powerful increase the state of the automaton [16]. It's can be shown that the class of finite machines with two pushdown stores has exactly the same power as the class of Turing machines and more pushdown stores can't strength its power. Then a pushdown stores should be designed for construct a finite automaton which as powerful as Turing machines.

Of course, all of the automation described below is more complex than before and more difficult too get a perfect result. New technical should be used in the experiment such as molecular beacon etc.

Acknowledgment

This paper supported by the National Scientific Foundation of China under grants 60533010, 60373089. The authors are gratefully acknowledged to the authors who appeared in the references.

References

1. Benenson, Y., Paz-Elizur, T., Adar, R.,.: Programmable and Autonomous Computing Machine Made of Biomoleculars, Nature Vol 414(6862) (2001) 430-434
2. Head., T.: Formal Language Theory and DNA: An Analysis of the Generative Capacity of Specific Recombinant Behaviors, Bulletin of Mathematical Biology, Vol 49 (1987) 737--759
3. Adleman, L.M.: Molecular Computation of Solutions to Combinatorial Problems， Science, Vol 266(11) (1994) 1021-1023
4. Lipton, R.J.: DNA Solution of Hard Computational Problem. Science, Vol 268 (1995) 542-545
5. Ouyang, Q., Kaplan, P.D., Liu, S.: DNA Solution of the Maximal Clique Problem. Science, Vol 278 (1997) 446-449
6. Landweber, L.F., Lipton, R.J., Rabin, M.O.: DNA Based Computers III: DIMACS Workshop, June 23-27, University of Pennsylvania (eds Rubin, H. & Wood, D. H.) (1997) 161-172
7. Liu, Q.: DNA Computing on Surfaces. Nature , Vol 403 (2000) 175-179
8. Faulhammer, D., Cukras, A. R., Lipton, R.J., Landweber, L.F.: Molecular Computation: RNA Solutions to Chess Problems. Proc. Natl Acad. Sci. USA Vol 97 (2000) 1385-1389
9. Ruben, A.J., Landweber, L.F.: The Past, Present and Future of Molecular Computing. Nature Rev. Mol.Cell Biol. Vol 1 (2000) 69-72
10. Roweis, S., Winfree, E., Burgoyne, R., Goodman, M., Rothemund, P., Adleman L A .: Sticker Based Model for DNA Computation，2nd DIMACS Workshop on DNA Based Computers，Princeton，DIMACS Series，(1999) 1-29
11. Kari, L.: DNA Computing: Arrival of Biological Mathematics. Math. Intelligencer, Vol 19(2) (9997) 9-22
12. Praun, G., Rozenberg, G., Salomaa, A.: DNA Computing—New Computing Paradigms. Springer, Berlin(1998)
13. Sakamoto, K., Gouzu, H., Komiya, K.: Molecular Computation by DNA Hairpin Formation. Science, Vol 288 (2000) 1223-1226
14. Head, T., Rozenberg, G.，Bladergroen, R.B., Breek, C.K.D., Lommerse, P.H.M., Spaink, H.P.: Computing with DNA by Operating on Plasmids. BioSystems，Vol 57 (2000) 87-93
15. Benenson, Y., Paz-Elizur, T.，Adar, R.: Programmable and Autonomous Computing Machine Made of Biomoleculars, Nature, Vol 414(6862) (2001) 430-434
16. Shi, X.L., Li, X., Zhang, Z., et al. Improve Capability of DNA Automaton: DNA Automaton with Three Internal States and Tape Head Move in Two Directions. LECT NOTES COMPUT SC Vol 3645 (2005) 71-79

Research on the Counting Problem Based on Linear Constructions for DNA Coding

Xiangou Zhu[1], Chuan Sun[2], Wenbing Liu[1], and Wenguo Wu[1]

[1] College of Computer Science and Engineering, Wenzhou University, Wenzhou, Zhejiang, 325027, China
zhuxo@wz.zj.cn, wbliu@mail.hust.edu.cn, jsj_wwg@wzu.edu.cn
[2] Dept. of Mechanic and electronic Engineering, HuangShi Institute of Technology, Huangshi, Hubei, 435003, China
sunch5985@yahoo.com.cn

Abstract. This article advances linear coding construction method for DNA codes based on three-letter alphabets. Further more it also advances the new conception of Constrain Strength and algorithm of Construction and Search. We use the former to evaluate the coding amount of combinatorial constraints and use the latter to validate the evaluated results. Experiments show that experiment result accords with the theoretically evaluated value very well.

1 Introduction

In 1994, Adleman introduced a feasible way to solve Hamiltonian Path Problem (HPP)[1] by utilizing the biochemical experiments underlying DNA recombination and separation, thus inaugurated a new era of DNA computation. Up to this day, the encoding still is an important and difficult problem in DNA computation, because the errors of biochemical response are beyond control in DNA computation. For this reason, people hope to make up for them through appropriate DNA sequences codes. When DNA strands incompletely match, the hybridization (annealing) which performs the basic core processing may happen, thereby DNA strands form unwanted secondary structure. This is a very problematic source of errors.

In order to reduce the possibility that DNA strands form unwanted secondary structure, many researchers put forward various kinds of encoding method for DNA computing. Garzon defines DNA coding problem in computation [2]. Baum proposes a hypothesis to reduce degree of similarity with sequences of DNA [3]. Feldkamp advance another method to define similarity of DNA sequences [4]. Suyama present DNA coding number based on gene expression and analysis[5]. Frutos gives a strategy for DNA sequence designing using template [6]. Arita give another single template method for DNA computing encode[7,8]. Wenbin Liu describes a constructing method that produces more coding sequences based on template strategy[9]. Braich presents constraints for DNA sequence designing over three-letter alphabets, which is already applied in DNA computing experiment and got satisfactory result [10].

Two important factors in the DNA computing encoding are coding quality and coding amount. The higher coding quality, the more stringent the coding constraints,

D.-S. Huang, K. Li, and G.W. Irwin (Eds.): ICIC 2006, LNBI 4115, pp. 294 – 302, 2006.

and the less coding amount. In order to increase the reliability of DNA computing, we must set the strictest constraint according to codes amount, so codes amount is a very important problem in DNA sequence designing. Now articles in this aspect are very scarce, what's more, most of them only focus on single-constraint counting problem which mainly deals with the Hamming distance constraint and the length of minimal subsequences constraint[3,4]. The literature[2,11,12,13] presents codes counting expressions about the minimal Hamming distance constraint. But there are few articles about codes counting that satisfy combinatorial constraints for DNA computing.

Based on the three-letter alphabets coding strategy and linear coding theory[14], this paper successfully solve the coding counting problem for the combinatorial constraints which are the Hamming constraint for a minimal distance d, the length of minimal subsequences constraint and the fixed GC-content constraint.

2 DNA Codes Construction Method Based on Linear Codes

2.1 DNA Coding Problem

The three-letter alphabets strategy which was introduced by Braich is simple and effective. Its codes sequences contain only three bases of nucleotide$\{A,T,C\}$ without base G, and its advantages are following. Fristly the secondary structures of DNA molecule that only contain three bases are far less than contain four bases, so it can improve biological specificity of DNA molecule very much. In the second it can decreases difficulty of biological operation, because the base G is most difficult in composed DNA molecule. But the disadvantage is that the amount of fundamental codes decrease drastically.

The DNA codes problem over three-letter alphabets may be formulated as following. For an alphabet $\Sigma=\{A,T,C\}$, there exists a fundamental set Z of codewords length of which is l, $Z=\Sigma^l=\{<b_1,b_2,\ldots,b_l>|b_i\in\Sigma,\ i=1,2,\ldots,l\}$, obviously $|Z|=3^l$. Seeking a subset W of Z, which satisfy

$$\forall x_i,x_j\in W \quad \tau(x_i,x_j)\geq k$$

Where k is a positive integer, τ is evaluation criterion of DNA codewords, such as the minimal Hamming distance, the fixed GC-content and the length of minimal subsequences. On one hand, we have to consider the size of set W(e.g. $|W|$) in the DNA coding problem.

In [2,6,3,4,13], three different constraints on DNA codes are considered: the minimal Hamming distance constraint, the length of minimal subsequences constraint and the fixed GC-content constraint. The purpose of the first two constraints is to make nondesirable hybridizations between different DNA strands less likely to happen, they influence the change in the Gibb's free-energy[15] when DNA molecules hybridize, so they are important indication among biological specificity of encoded DNA molecules. The fixed GC-content constraint is used to obtain similar melting temperatures.

2.2 Constraints on DNA Coding

2.2.1 Fixed *GC*-Content Constraint

The *GC*-content constraint is that for each codewords $x \in W$ there is the same *GC*-weight when the l length of codewords is fixed. In the fundamental codewords, eq(1) is *C*-weight i distribution over three-letter alphabets.

$$P_c(i) = C_l^i \times 2^{(l-i)} / 3^l \ , \ i=0,1,2,\ldots,l \tag{1}$$

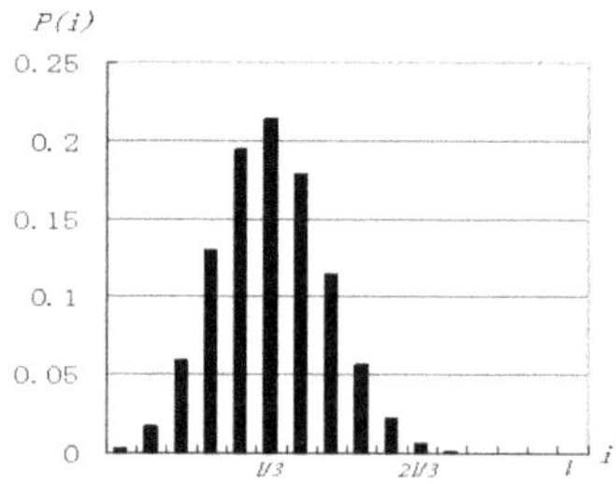

Fig. 1. This is *GC*-content distribution over three-letter alphabets when l=15, vlaues of codewords at 4,5,6 base *C* are largest. Without effort, the *GC*-content constraint is about 1/3, it can preserve fundamental codewords to greatest degree.

2.2.2 Minimal Hamming Distance Constraint

The Hamming distance is the number of digits by which two blocks of the same length differ, the distance of words x_1 and x_2 marked as $H(x_1,x_2)$. The Minimal Hamming distance d for a DNA code W is that $H(x_1,x_2) \geq d$ for all $x_1,x_2 \in W$ with $x_1 \neq x_2$. This constraint will be enforced in all of the codes we consider, it has been proposed as a necessary criterion for reliable DNA-based computation, in a general way $d \geq l/2$. The bigger value of d, the more reliable computation is.

Now the questios is how to construct codewords that satisfy the minimal Hamming distance constraint. We might as well denote three bases *A*,*T*,*C* with number 0,1,2, so that DNA codes sequences is turned into ternary number sequences. Experiment shows that constructing DNA codes using linear system codes is a excellent method.

$$H = \begin{bmatrix} p_{11} & p_{12} & \cdots & p_{1k} & 1 & 0 & \cdots & 0 \\ p_{21} & p_{22} & \cdots & p_{2k} & 0 & 1 & \cdots & 0 \\ \vdots & \vdots & \ddots & \vdots & \cdots & \cdots & \ddots & \vdots \\ p_{r1} & p_{r2} & \cdots & p_{rk} & 0 & 0 & \cdots & 1 \end{bmatrix}, \ p_{ij}=0,1,2 \ (i=1,2,\ldots,d, \ j=1,2,\ldots,k)$$

According to linear coding theory[14], we first search a check matrix H of l-k row and l column, H is canonical form:$H=[P\ I]$, let $r=l-k$, where P is a r row k column matrix, I is a r rank identity matrix, so as to get any d-1 column of H, whose d-1 column column vector is linearly independence. Second, check matrix H is turned to generator matrix G using $G=[I\ -P^T]$, where I is k rank identity matrix, $-P^T$ is negative transpose of matrix P. Then, $M=\{0,1,2\}^K$, $W=M \times G$, we get codewords matrix W, each row vector of matrix W is a codeword, the minimal Hamming distance is exactly d. We call these codewords as linear codes marked as $[l, k, d]$.

$$|W|=3^k \tag{2}$$

If we construct codewords which satisfy the minimal Hamming distance constraint in this way, amount of codewords generated is fixed(3^k), and easy to be operated. The key part of this method is searching for check matrix H with (d-1) linearly independence columns. To construct [l, k, d] linear codes, this paper use optimum searching method to get check matrix for linear codes that have [20,15,4], [14,8,5], [14,7,6] and [11,3,7].

2.2.3 The Length of Minimal Subsequence Constraint

In all subsequences of sequences, there always exists a subsequence whose minimal length is s+1 and which causes the subsequence appear only in all codewords. We call such subsequence as minimal subsequences. For example: {*ATCCAATTCC*} and {*ACTACTATCC*}, {*ATCC*} is maximal repeated subsequence and s=4.

Due to overlength of minimal subsequences may bring on baneful shift hybridization, the shorter the length of minimal subsequences, the better encoding performance for DNA computing is. In general the length of minimal subsequences is less than or equals half of codewords length, e.g $s \le l/2$.

The minimal subsequences with length s+1 have total 3^{s+1} permutations for three-letter alphabets, and each sequences of codewords contain l-s minimal subsequences. So from the upper limit of amount of codewords sequences $|W|$, we get eq(3).

$$|W| \le 3^{s+1}/(l-s) \quad (s<l) \tag{3}$$

The algorithmic experiment shows that through the random algorithm the amount of codewords that satisfy the length of minimal subsequences constraint may attain 90%±5% of eq(3) with W taking the maxium value[16]. This shows that it is a feasible way to evaluate amount of codewords which must satisfy constraint of minimal subsequences length. It also shows that random algorithm can efficiently find codewords that satisfy the constraint of minimal subsequences length.

2.3 Algorithm of Construction and Search

Through analysis of counting problem of codewords under single constraint we find that the length of minimal subsequences constraint and the minimal Hamming distance constraint are most stringent in DNA computation. They all come down to interrelation between any two codewords in encoding space, their computational complexity is high in algorithm realization and amount of desired codewords sometimes is very scarce. Other constraints is less stringent, they only restrict single codewords, their algorithms are easy to realize and their computational complexity is not high too.

To avoid searching codewords that satisfy constraints in fundamental space that will greatly decreases size of search space, we introduce a coding design algorithm called Construction and Search. This algorithm is: first constructing primary codewords that satisfy the minimal Hamming distance constraint; then sequencely filtrating primary codewords using other constraints, using less stringnet constraint first and then more stringent constraints, and finally get consequential codewords. For example, given d as the minimal Hamming distance and s+1 as the length of minimal subsequences and the fixed GC-content on three-letter alphabets as 1/3, the steps of this algorithmis will be:

1. Seek for linearly independence any d-1columns of check matrix H in GF(3).
2. Generate homologous linear codes with H, construct codewords that satisfy the minimal Hamming distance is d on three-letter alphabets, get primary codewords.
3. Filtrate primary codewords using feeble constraint that is GC-content≈1/3, get secondary codewords.
4. Finally, filtrate secondary codewords using random algorithm that solve the problem of minimal subsequences length $s+1$, get resulted codewords.

As to $[l, k, d]$ linear, there exists the relation of l-k≥d+1[14](not getting equal sign when codewords designed for DNA computation), so search space of wordcodes is only 3^{-d} of fundamental space, thereby decrease computational complexity for search by leaps and bounds.

3 Counting Problem of Codewords Under Combinatorial Constraints

To effectively solve problem of codewords quality and amount, our purpose is to reward high quality of codewords and not blindly intensify constraint so that amount of codewords decreases very much. So we need to research on counting problem of codewords for DNA computation, to get expressions between amount of codewords and parameters of combinatorial constraints for counting, thus to find optimum parameters of constraints when amount of codewords is fixed.

3.1 Constrain Strength

This paper introduces a new concept--Constrain Strength in order to solve counting problem of codewords that satisfy combinatorial constraints. Given $|W|$ as maximum amount of codewords that satisfy a constraint τ , then the Constrain Strength of constraint τ marked as $A(\tau)$. The definition of $A(\tau)$ is

$$A(\tau)=(|Z|-|W|)/|W|\text{, } |Z| \text{ is size of fundamental space of codewords} \tag{4}$$

The more stringent the constraint, the smaller the $|W|$, and the bigger $A(\tau)$. When $|W|=|Z|$, constraint τ is nothing, here $A(\tau)=0$; when $|W|=0$, constraint τ is so stringent that no codewords can satisfy it, $A(\tau)=\infty$.

The length of minimal subsequences $s+1$ marked as constraint τ_s , according to definition we substitute eq(3) into eq(4) and get $A(\tau_s)$. Using τ_d as the minimal Hamming distance constraint, we get the Constrain Strength $A(\tau_d)$ by substitute eq(2) into eq(4) for construct $[l, k, d]$ linear codes. The τ_{sd} is combinatorial constraints that satisfy constraint both τ_s and τ_d . How to get the Constrain Strength $A(\tau_{sd})$? Through a great deal of computing experiment, we have found that

$$A(\tau_{sd})=A(\tau_s)+A(\tau_d) \tag{5}$$

Over three-letter alphabets for DNA computation, if n_s is maximal amount of codewords that satisfy constraint τ_s , n_d is maximal amount of codewords that satisfy constraint τ_d and n_{sd} is maximal amount of codewords that satisfy combinatorial constraints τ_{sd} , by eq(5) and eq(4) we get

$$n_{sd} = \lfloor n_s n_d / ((n_s + n_d) - n_s n_d / |Z|) \rfloor \quad (6)$$

So eq(5) is true only when eq(6) is true, the evaluated result n_{sd} from eq(6) can be validated by result of construction and search algorithm. After the random algorithm is run time after time independently, we select maximal amount of resultant codewords, we get the experimental result as in table 1. The formula of evaluated result n_{sd} may be substituted using the approximate formula eq(7) in verification, see evaluated value in table 1.

$$n_{sd} \approx \lfloor n_s n_d / (n_s + n_d) \rfloor \quad (7)$$

From eq(2) we get $n_d = 3^k$ in eq(7). From eq(3) and search efficiency (90%±5%) of random algorithm we get n_s as

$$n_s = \lfloor (\lfloor 3^{s+1} / (l - s) \rfloor) \times (90\,\% \pm 5\%) \rfloor \quad (8)$$

Table 1. Here lists all sorts of combinatorial constraints τ_{sd} with d=5~6, s=4~7, to compare maximum value of n_{sd} for evaluate and experiment. Here, we get the minimal Hamming distance d using linear codes [10,5,5], [11,5,6], [11,6,5], [12,6,6], [13,6,6] and [14,7,6].

l, k, d	s=4		s=5		s=6		s=7	
	evaluated	experiment	evaluated	experiment	evaluated	experiment	evaluated	experiment
10,5,5	31±2	31	84±3	87	162±3	163	216±2	220
11,5,6	26±2	26	74±3	74	150±4	150	208±2	210
11,6,5	28±2	27	94±5	97	255±10	270	487±9	481
12,6,6	26±2	24	82±4	79	225±9	219	450±10	456
13,6,6	23±2	23	72±4	75	202±8	203	418±10	414
14,7,6	20±1	21	69±4	70	220±11	222	608±25	609

If we compare the values for evaluated and experiment in tab2, we find they are in accord with each other in error range. This has not only validated correctness of eq(5), but also enriched connotation of Constrain Strength. With the Constrain Strength we can solve codewords counting problem under combinatorial constraints in DNA computation.

3.2 Evaluated Amount of Codewords Under Three-Combination Constraints

In DNA codewords designing for computing, besides taking into account the length of minimal subsequences and the minimal Hamming distance, we also have to consider the other important factor that is the fixed GC-content. As to three-letter alphabets, from eq(1) and figure 1 we find that GC-content distribution density of fundamental codes is maximal when the GC-content locate at 1/3.

Following is the algorithm evaluated for amount of codewords that includes the fixed GC-content constraint.

1. Through linear codes[l, k, d] the amount of codewords is $n_d=3^k$.
2. Integraal of eq(1) is $\sum_i C_l^i \times 2^{(l-i)}/3^l$, from which we get amount percentage of codewords that satisfy the fixed GC-content i/l (i is weight of a codewords for base C), then amount of linear codes that satisfy the fixed GC-content, $n_d=\left\lfloor 3^{k-l} \times \sum_i (C_l^i \times 2^{(l-i)}) \right\rfloor$ (presume the GC-content distribution is identical in linear and in fundamental codes).
3. According to the length of minimal subsequence constraint and search efficiency of random algorithm,we get n_s from eq(8).
4. Finally, from eq(6) or eq(7), we evaluate amount of codewords under three-combination constraints.

Table 2. The values of counting codewords for evaluated and experiment compare under three-combination constraints (The value of evaluation in the table is calculated according as before-mentioned evaluational approach for amount of codewords, the experimental value is result of algorithm of Construction and Search in section 2.3, the algorithm run time after time independently on various instances, we select maximal amount of resultant codewords.)

l, k, d	$w_C(W)$	$s=4$		$s=5$		$s=6$		$s=7$	
		evaluated	experiment	evaluated	experiment	evaluated	experiment	Evaluated	experiment
10,5,5	3	22±1	22	42±1	41	55±1	55	61±1	61
	3,4	27±1	26	61±2	60	95±1	91	111±1	111
11,5,6	4	19±1	18	37±1	36	49±1	48	54±1	56
	3,4	23±2	22	55±2	51	88±2	85	106±1	106
11,6,5	4	25±2	22	66±2	64	120±3	115	154±1	156
	3,4	27±2	25	82±4	75	184±5	173	280±3	273
12,6,6	4	23±2	21	60±2	55	113±3	108	150±1	149
	4,5	24±2	22	71±3	66	159±4	144	246±3	228
	3,4,5	25±2	23	77±4	70	192±7	178	334±5	310
13,6,6	4	20±1	18	54±2	47	104±2	94	142±1	135
	4,5	22±2	19	64±3	55	148±5	129	240±4	226
14,7,6	5	20±1	18	62±3	54	160±6	139	300±6	267
	4,5	20±1	18	66±4	55	194±9	157	443±13	384

Comparing the evaluated result and experiment result in table 2, we know that the calculated value of evaluational approach accord with the result of algorithmic experiment by and large. When k increases, and amount of linear increases at exponential speed, computational quantity of filtration in algorithm increase speedly, so that the times of the algorithm running independently decrease, such causing discrepance between evaluated result and experinent increase, but range of error still is 10% inside.

So that, we can evaluate the code amount using above evulational method. Given the amount of codewords, we can select select high quality (high reliability) codewords basic parameters (code length l, GC-content, length of minimal subsequence s+1 and minimal Hamming distance d) for practical computation model. For instance, to solve three-coloring for graph of 20 vertex in DNA computation, we need 60 codewords for all color vertexs, so we may select (l, d, s, $w_C(W)$)=(12, 6, 5, (4,5)) from evaluated values in table2. Also we may select (11, 5, 5, 4) or (10, 5, 5, (3,4)). Amount of codewords for small-scale DNA computation need is not bigger than 20, then we can select l=11, s=4, d=6.

4 Conclusion

This paper research on codewords for DNA computing based on linear encoding method over three-letter alphabets. In it we present a new conception of Constrain Strength and evaluational approach for coding amount of combinatorial constraints. Through result of Construction and Search algorithm, we validate evaluational approach, it is useful in selecting appropriate parameters for codewords designing, it has guiding significance for DNA computing coding. The above method can also be applied to four-letter alphabets coding counting problem which satistfies some of four-letter alphabets contraints because it has much more constraints.

Acknowledgements

The authors would like to acknowledge the financial support from the National Science Foundation of China under Grant No.60403002, the Natural Science Foundation of Zhejiang Province of China under Grant Y106654, and the Postdoctor Science Foundation of China under Grant 2004036130.

References

1. Adleman, L.: Molecular Computation of Solution to Combinatorial problems. Science, Vol.266 (1994)1021-1024
2. Garzon, M. et al.: A New Metric for DNA Computing. Proc. of the 2nd Annual Genetic Programming Conference (1997) 472-487
3. Baum, E. B.: DNA Sequences Useful for Computation. Proc. of 2nd DIMACS Workshop on DNA Based Computers (1996)
4. Feldkamp et al.: A DNA Sequence Compile. Proc. of 6th DIMACS Workshop on DNA Based Computers (2000)
5. Suyama, B. et al.: DNA Chips- Intergrated Chemical Circuits for DNA Diagnosis and DNA computers. Proc. 3rd International Micromachine Symp(1997) 7-12
6. Frutos, B. G. et al.: Demonstration of a Word Design Strategy for DNA Computing on Surface. Nucleic Acids Research, Vol.25 (1997) 4748-4757
7. Arita, M. et al.; The Power of Sequence Desire in DNA Computing. 4th International Conference on Computational Intelligence and Multimedia Applications (2001)
8. Arita, M. et al.: DNA Sequence Design Using Template. New Generation Comput. Vol.20(3): (2002) 263-277
9. Wenbin, Liu et al.: DNA Sequence Design Based on Template Strategy, J. Chem. Inf. Comput. Sci. Vol.43 (2003)2014 – 2018
10. Braich, R S. et al.: Solution of a Satisfiability Problem on a Gel-Based DNA Computer. DNA 2000, LCNS 2054, (2001)27-42
11. Deaton, R. et al.: Genetic Search of Reliable Encodings for DNA-Based Computation. 1st Genetic Programming Conference, 1996
12. Deaton, R. et al.: Good encodings for DNA-based Solutions to Combinatorial Problems, In Proc. of 2nd DIMACS Workshop on DNA Based Computers (1996)
13. Marathe, B. et al.: On Combinatorial DNA Word Design, J. Comput. Biol. 8 (2001) 201–220

14. MacWilliams, F.J. et al.: The Theory of Error Correcting Codes, North-Holland (1977)
15. John SantaLucia et al. Improved Nearest-Neighbor Parameters for Predicting DNA Duplex Stability. Biochemistry, Vol.35, (1996)3555-3562
16. Zhu, Xiangou., Liu wenbing., Sun Chuan.: Research on the DNA Words and Algorithm. Acta Electronica Sinica, (2006)

The Board picked up the broader point linking good faith bargaining to the willingness to discuss issues in *Canadian Federal Pilots Association v Department of Transport, Transportation Safety Board, and Treasury Board Secretariat*.[56] The bargaining agent in that case complained that the employer was unwilling to discuss one of its proposals. The Board began by summarizing the nature of the duty to bargain in good faith with a series of principles:

- The duty reinforces the employer's obligation to recognize the bargaining agent.
- The duty is intended to recognize rational, informed discussion, thus minimizing the potential for unnecessary conflict.
- Both parties have the duty to share the intent of entering into a collective agreement.
- The negotiation process should be looked at as a whole.
- The duty depends on how negotiations are conducted and not on the content of the proposals brought to the bargaining table.
- The important factor is the quality of the discussion.
- The parties have a duty to communicate with each other.
- Hard bargaining, albeit ruthless, is not bad faith bargaining.
- The test is open and rational discussion.
- The parties must be prepared to explain the rationales for their positions.
- The complainant bears the burden of proving its allegations.[57]

On the facts of the case, the bargaining agent wanted to negotiate a Professional Aviation Currency Program with a view to incorporating that program into the collective agreement. The employer opposed that objective and proposed that the parties agree to a mediated discussion of the underlying issues. The Board concluded that this was a form of rational discussion sufficient to meet the duty to bargain in good faith. The Federal Court of Appeal also confirmed that the mediation sessions are part of the bargaining process, stating that "it is not unusual for parties in complex negotiations to hive off particularly contentious issues and

56 *Canadian Federal Pilots Association v Department of Transport, Transportation Safety Board, and Treasury Board Secretariat*, 2018 FPSLREB 91, aff'd *Canadian Federal Pilots Association v Canada (Attorney General)*, 2020 FCA 52.

57 *Ibid* (FPSLREB) at para 125.

send them to mediation or to discuss them in a setting smaller than at the main bargaining table in an effort to explore resolution possibilities."[58]

The Board has applied the law established by other labour boards when considering whether changes to bargaining positions are a form of bad faith bargaining. The Board has stated that it is not bad faith bargaining to withdraw previous offers. The employer's final offer in that case was (according to the bargaining agent) worse than its previous offers. The Board stated that withdrawing previous offers is not bad faith: "collective bargaining is not a static process; in the absence of an acceptance of an offer, no party is obliged to keep an offer open indefinitely for consideration and acceptance by the other party at its leisure and at its convenience."[59] The key determination is whether the change in bargaining stance is motivated by a desire to discourage or prevent the negotiation of a collective agreement.

In *Public Service Alliance of Canada v Senate of Canada*,[60] the parties were discussing a collective agreement clause setting out paid leave for bargaining preparation. The clause set out that the bargaining agent would reimburse the employer for the salary and benefit costs of that leave. The employer made a proposal to increase the benefit costs. The bargaining agent opposed any increase in the benefit costs. The employer responded to that position by proposing to delete the clauses altogether. The bargaining agent alleged that this was a form of "receding-horizon" bargaining and therefore in bad faith. The Board agreed that receding-horizon bargaining is often an indication of bad faith bargaining; however, the Board decided that the change in position in that case was a reaction to the bargaining agent's own "rigid position." The Board concluded that, put in context, the employer's change of position "was not of such a magnitude to allow [it] to conclude that receding-horizon bargaining took place."[61]

Finally, the Board has also applied general labour principles to assessing the specific proposals advanced by each party. In almost all cases, the Board will not assess the reasonableness of a party's proposal.[62] However, the Board has concluded that a "poison pill" pro-

58 *Ibid* (CA) at para 10.

59 *Professional Institute of the Public Service of Canada and Treasury Board*, [1991] CPSSRB No 104 at 16 [*PIPSC and Treasury Board*].

60 *Public Service Alliance of Canada v Senate of Canada*, 2008 PSLRB 100.

61 *Ibid* at para 57.

62 See, for example, *ibid* at para 58.

posal can indicate that a party has not bargained in good faith. In *Professional Association of Foreign Service Officers v Treasury Board*,[63] the bargaining agent began to engage in a legal strike. The bargaining agent proposed to resolve the dispute through voluntary arbitration. The employer responded by accepting binding arbitration subject to certain conditions that would require the arbitrator not to consider certain classifications (that formed the basis of the bargaining agent's main position in bargaining) as a valid comparison for the purpose of determining compensation and, instead, to base their decision on other factors dictated by the employer. The Board concluded that this proposal went beyond hard bargaining, stating, "[P]roposing conditions that the respondent knew could not be accepted by the complainant and that would prevent them from putting forward any argument on behalf of the bargaining unit goes beyond hard bargaining and crosses into surface bargaining."[64] The Board did not go so far as to order the parties to participate in fair voluntary arbitration but simply declared that the employer had violated its duty to bargain in good faith.[65]

2) Timing

The *FPSLRA* requires parties to meet within twenty days after the notice is served.[66] In most cases, serious collective bargaining does not begin that early, and it usually takes months, if not years, to negotiate a collective agreement.

That said, the parties may not unduly delay the negotiation process. The Board, for example, concluded that the employer did not make every reasonable effort to enter into a collective agreement when it delayed providing the necessary payroll data to the bargaining agent, taking seventy-seven days to provide partial data and an additional eighty-one days to provide the rest. This failure to provide the necessary data meant that three days of scheduled bargaining were cancelled. The Board also concluded that the employer's overall delays constituted

63 *Professional Association of Foreign Service Officers v Treasury Board*, 2013 PSLRB 110.

64 *Ibid* at para 63.

65 The parties reached a collective agreement roughly two weeks after this decision, after a strike that lasted for a total of five months and twenty-four days—the longest strike in federal public service history.

66 *FPSLRA*, s 106(a).

bargaining in bad faith. As a result of postponements, cancellations, time to allegedly study the bargaining agent's proposals, time to bring a new negotiator on board, and that negotiator's decision to use scheduled bargaining days to meet with his own negotiating team instead of the other side, the parties met face to face for a total of four days over a period of eight months after notice to bargain was served. The Board concluded that this delay violated the duty to bargain in good faith.[67]

One issue that the Board has had to address is the impact of referring a dispute to arbitration on the duty to bargain in good faith. This issue led to two Board decisions issued within three months of each other that are difficult to reconcile. In the first decision,[68] the bargaining agent filed a complaint after referring the dispute to arbitration. As discussed further below, the *FPSLRA* requires that the parties bargain in good faith prior to referring a dispute to arbitration. The Board therefore reasoned that, by referring its dispute to arbitration, the bargaining agent had essentially admitted that there had been bargaining in good faith. The Board therefore concluded that it did not have jurisdiction to decide that complaint.

In the second decision, the same bargaining agent (negotiating on behalf of a different bargaining unit) filed a bad faith bargaining complaint against the same employer. In that case, the bargaining agent filed its complaint and then, before the complaint was heard, referred the dispute to arbitration six months later. The Board decided that this situation was different as it was called upon to "look at the situation as it was"[69] when the complaint was filed. The Board reasoned that bad faith could have existed when the complaint was filed,[70] but there could have been good faith negotiations afterwards that led to the request for arbitration.

---

67 *Professional Institute of the Public Service of Canada v Canadian Food Inspection Agency*, 2008 PSLRB 78 [*PIPSC v CFIA*].

68 *Professional Institute of the Public Service of Canada v Canadian Food Inspection Agency*, 2008 PSLRB 50.

69 *PIPSC v CFIA*, above note 67 at para 20.

70 The complaint was later amended, and the Board reasoned that bad faith could have existed on the date of the amendment as well.

The Federal Court of Appeal heard an application for judicial review from the first decision. The Court dismissed that application and concluded that the two decisions could both be correct.[71]

The controversy in those two decisions is partly about a larger issue: the nature of a complaint of bargaining in good faith. On the one hand, the duty to bargain in good faith is continuous and lasts until a collective agreement is concluded or an arbitral award is imposed on the parties. On the other hand, a complaint of bad faith bargaining is usually based on particular events that occur at particular points in time. The Board is therefore concerned with a continuous obligation but also concerned with events at particular points in time. The Board has articulated these contradictory principles as follows:

> The duty to bargain in good faith is a continuous and ongoing duty. Therefore, the Board can examine the entire collective bargaining process and consider all the relevant facts to determine whether the ongoing duty to bargain in good faith has been respected. That does not mean that the complaint is an open-ended one. The focus of the examination by the Board will still be on the grounds for the complaint set out by the [Professional Institute of the Public Service of Canada (PIPSC)] in its complaint (at paragraph 2 of this decision). The PIPSC has filed a complaint against the tabling of a final offer by the employer. The bargaining that took place after that final offer is relevant to an assessment of whether the final offer met the requirement of bargaining in good faith.[72]

It can be difficult to discern the difference between the "focus of the examination" (i.e., things that happened before the complaint was filed) and the evidence that is "relevant to an assessment" of the complaint (i.e., things that happened after the complaint was filed).

The Board further addressed this issue in a later decision. In that case, the bargaining agent filed a bad faith bargaining complaint before the first bargaining proposals were exchanged. When the hearing commenced, a dispute arose with respect to the evidentiary scope of the complaint—namely, whether statements made at the bargaining table post-complaint could be received in evidence. The Board ruled that the complaint crystallized the date it was filed, before first proposals were

---

71 *Professional Institute of the Public Service of Canada v Canada (Attorney General)*, 2009 FCA 184.

72 *Professional Institute of the Public Service of Canada v Treasury Board*, 2009 PSLRB 102 at para 79.

exchanged. The bargaining agent then brought a motion to amend its complaint to add additional facts that arose subsequent to filing the complaint, specifically statements made during a bargaining session. The Board permitted the amendment by applying the usual test for amending an existing proceeding (whether the amendment fundamentally alters the nature of the dispute, whether the other party is taken by surprise by the amendment, and whether the amendment should be dealt with in a separate proceeding).[73]

This approach by the Board demonstrates a view by the Board, in that case at least, that the duty to bargain in good faith comprises a series of discrete events. With respect, this view is mistaken. The proper approach is set out in the Board's earlier decision cited above—namely, to recognize that the duty to bargain in good faith is a continuous and ongoing duty. The Federal Court of Appeal concluded in a 1983 decision that what was then the Canada Labour Relations Board should address post-complaint evidence in a bad faith bargaining complaint, stating that the "intention to develop good relations between labour and management would not be served by limiting the Board, once seized of a complaint, to consideration of incidents recited in the complaint or antedating it when its subject-matter is, by its nature, ongoing, as here."[74] The Board schedules bad faith bargaining complaints months or even years after they have been filed. During that period, the parties should—and are required to—continue bargaining. The parties should not have to serially amend a complaint to reflect every instance of bad faith bargaining that occurs after the initial complaint is filed. Rather, so long as notice of the nature of the evidence that will be relied on during the hearing is provided to the other party, the Board should consider all of the evidence to determine whether the parties have met their obligation to bargain in good faith. Hopefully, the Board reverts to the approach in its 2009 decision quoted at length above and examines the conduct of the parties throughout the bargaining process rather than specific slices of time identified prior to a complaint being filed.

73 *Public Service Alliance of Canada v Treasury Board of Canada*, 2015 PSLREB 46.

74 *Eastern Provincial Airways Ltd v Canada (Labour Relations Board)*, [1984] 1 FC 732 (CA) at para 12. The Federal Court of Appeal set aside the CLRB's decision for other reasons.

3) No Preconditions

The Board has stated that it is a breach of the obligation to bargain in good faith to insist on the other party agreeing to preconditions prior to entering into bargaining. In *Public Service Alliance of Canada and Treasury Board*,[75] the employer was trying to negotiate a wage restraint program of a 0 percent increase in the first year and 3 percent in the second year. The employer insisted that the bargaining agent agree to this wage proposal before negotiating any other terms of the collective agreement (such as pay equity and national rates of pay). The Board stated simply that insisting upon preconditions to bargaining was a breach of the obligation to bargain in good faith and incompatible with the requirement to make every reasonable effort to negotiate a collective agreement.[76]

The context of this board decision is worthy of note. The federal government had announced in its February 1991 budget that it wanted a one-year freeze on global payroll, and annual increases in subsequent years would not exceed 3 percent. The PSAC went on strike on 9 September 1991 and filed the complaint mentioned above on 10 September. The Board heard the case on 14 September and rendered its decision on 16 September; however, the government passed a law that same day extending all unsettled collective agreements for two years with 0 and 3 percent increases for those two years (effectively making the strike illegal). The employer argued that the Board should decline to hear the case in light of the then-pending legislation, but the Board rendered its decision regardless.

At least one commentator has stated that this Board ruling "effectively blamed the government for the strike it was preparing to outlaw."[77] The context behind that case does illustrate a weakness of the obligation to bargain in good faith in the *FPSLRA*—namely, that the obligation is subject to being overridden by Parliament in favour of the unilateral imposition of terms and conditions of employment by way of legislation. At the end of the day, the obligation to bargain in good faith is only really binding on the employer when the employer agrees to be bound by it: where the employer feels strongly enough that it does not

---

75 *Public Service Alliance of Canada and Treasury Board*, [1991] CPSSRB No 230.

76 *Ibid* at 5.

77 Swimmer, above note 23 at 400. The Board's decision does not make this sort of value-laden judgment explicitly.

want to bargain, it simply legislates the outcome. In the private sector, violations of the obligation to bargain in good faith lead to significant repercussions against the employer, up to and including the imposition of a collective agreement.[78] No such remedies are available against the government when it chooses to legislate collective bargaining solutions in the federal public service, absent a constitutional challenge.

More recently, the Board has concluded that an employer did not fulfill its duty to bargain in good faith when it refused to schedule negotiation sessions until an application by an employee to revoke the bargaining unit's certification had been decided.[79] This is another example of a party not being permitted to place preconditions on bargaining.

4) Bargaining Structure

There are two main issues that arise in the federal public service concerning the structure of bargaining.

The first issue arises with separate agencies. As discussed in Chapter 3, a separate agency is the "employer" for the purposes of collective bargaining. However, the separate agency is also required to obtain a mandate from the Treasury Board to negotiate a collective agreement. This leads to the difficult situation where negotiations take place with an employer who does not have a mandate to freely agree to a bargaining agent's proposals; instead, the separate agency must go back to the Treasury Board for permission or a "mandate" to agree to a particular proposal or make a counterproposal. In *Professional Institute of the Public Service of Canada v Canadian Food Inspection Agency*,[80] notice to bargain was served on 12 April 2005, but the Treasury Board did not provide a mandate to negotiate wages until 11 or 12 January 2007. The bargaining agent named the Treasury Board as a respondent to its complaint of bad faith bargaining. The Board concluded that the Treasury Board must be removed as a party because it was not the legal employer. While the Board dismissed the complaint against the separate agency as well because the complaint was filed after the dispute was

78 *Royal Oak Mines*, above note 50. This remedy is awarded only in the rarest of cases.

79 *United Food and Commercial Workers Union, Local 401 v Staff of the Non-Public Funds, Canadian Forces*, 2016 PSLREB 57.

80 *Professional Institute of the Public Service of Canada v Canadian Food Inspection Agency*, 2008 PSLRB 50.

referred to arbitration, the Board did state in *obiter* that an undue delay in obtaining a clear mandate to respond to a wage demand is bargaining in bad faith.[81] It is not clear what practical effect a declaration of bad faith would have: assuming that the employer has diligently pressed the Treasury Board for a mandate (and it is not clear that it did so in that case), there is little the employer can do to ensure that it bargains in good faith. This requirement of a Treasury Board mandate, while ensuring central control over compensation expenditures in the federal public service, frustrates the collective bargaining process and leads to unnecessary delays in reaching collective agreements.

The second issue arises with the appropriate structure or mechanics of collective bargaining when a bargaining agent represents more than one bargaining unit with the employer. The Board has concluded that the duty to bargain in good faith applies to bargaining at the bargaining unit level and that the parties are under no obligation to agree to a structure to govern bargaining for multiple bargaining units. For example, in the 1980s, the PSAC represented twenty-seven bargaining units for whom the Treasury Board was the employer. One of the PSAC's goals (along with other bargaining agents) was to rationalize bargaining with the Treasury Board. In the 1985 round of bargaining, the PSAC and the Treasury Board agreed to two sets of bargaining: a "Master Agreement" determining issues such as leave entitlements and the grievance procedure and agreements with individual bargaining units to deal with wages, hours, allowances, and other similar issues. When the 1988 round of bargaining rolled around, the PSAC wanted further consolidation of bargaining at one table for all bargaining units that had elected the right to strike. The PSAC eventually moderated its demands to seven "tables" for bargaining, but the Treasury Board refused, insisting on a process similar to the 1985 round of one Master Agreement and individual agreements for each bargaining unit. Collective bargaining broke down over this issue of the appropriate bargaining structure. Both the PSAC and the Treasury Board alleged that the other was refusing to bargain in good faith. The Board dismissed both their applications. Both the Treasury Board and the PSAC told the Board that they were willing to negotiate for any given bargaining unit; therefore, the Board dismissed both complaints, stating:

81 *Ibid* at para 44.

> The Board appreciates the frustrations of both parties caused by the failure to reach agreement on the renewal of the Master Agreement. The Master Agreement had been an historic and important step for both parties. However, a year later they found themselves unable to renew it. We are, therefore, unable to condemn either party for their interpretation of the facts and their views on each other's actions. We also find that the two applications under section 18 were premature since the parties did not give bargaining a chance even though they honestly were ready and willing to meet and bargain in good faith with respect to individual bargaining units.[82]

Thus, the obligation to bargain in good faith does not require either party to agree to the other's proposed structure for bargaining. The duty is owed at a bargaining unit level, unless the parties voluntarily agree to use a different structure, in which case the duty is owed at the level at which bargaining takes place within that structure.

As discussed in Chapter 3, the *FPSLRA* allows the parties to engage in collective bargaining at the departmental or agency level (so-called "two-tier" bargaining). Bargaining that occurs at this level must also be conducted in good faith,[83] but there is no statutory obligation on the part of the employer or bargaining agent to act in "good faith" when deciding whether to consent to engage in two-tiered bargaining at all. It was suggested that since acquiescence to more bargaining may be contrary to the interests of a government committed to practising fiscal restraint, two-tiered bargaining may not be widely used;[84] indeed, this is what has happened and there have been no two-tiered bargaining agreements in the period since 2005.

---

82 *Public Service Alliance of Canada and Treasury Board*, [1988] CPSSRB No 55 at para 38. Eventually, with the help of the chair of the Board acting as a mediator, the Treasury Board and the PSAC agreed on a bargaining structure composed of seven "tables" that would bargain all issues simultaneously. Currently, there are five "tables" with the PSAC and the Treasury Board: Program and Administrative Services, Operational Services, Technical Services, Education and Library Science, and Border Services. The first four of those tables commonly negotiate at the same time to address common issues shared by those tables.

83 *FPSLRA*, s 110(3).

84 J. Illingworth, "Collective Bargaining, Dispute Resolution and Strike Action: New Procedures, New Challenges" (Paper presented at the conference for the "Public Service Modernization Act," Canadian Institute, 31 May 2004) at 5.

5) Disclosure

The Board has confirmed that the duty to bargain in good faith requires the parties to disclose certain information to each other. The duty to bargain in good faith requires the employer to share basic information with the union, such as the current terms and conditions of employees (in a first-contract situation) and, on occasion, economic or financial data about the cost of any proposals. The Board set out a general principle about sharing information, stating:

> The Board is of the opinion that, in order to ensure a "rational, informed discussion," the parties must disclose to each other the grounds upon which they are relying on the issues in dispute.[85]

In other words, the parties must have enough information to be able to explain their positions to each other fully, thereby permitting the other party to correct any errors or provide a rebuttal. In respect of economic and financial data in particular, the Board has commented that

> [i]n collective bargaining, it is essential for a bargaining agent to have extensive payroll data. A bargaining agent is not in a position to cost its monetary proposals without that data. It cannot estimate the financial impact of each of those proposals. In a nutshell, it cannot bargain intelligently.[86]

The Board has also addressed the more interesting and related issue of when the employer has to inform a bargaining agent about its future plans. In *Professional Institute of the Public Service of Canada and Treasury Board*,[87] the union alleged that the employer violated the duty to bargain in good faith by failing to inform the bargaining team about a pending wage control policy (announced in the 1991 budget). The Board followed the same test as labour relations boards in the private sector and stated that

> [i]n those cases which have dealt with the question of whether impending decisions (as opposed to hard information) must be disclosed, labour relations boards have required such disclosure where failure to do so was "tantamount to a misrepresentation."

---

85 *Public Service Alliance of Canada and Canada (Treasury Board)*, [1977] CPSSRB No 16.

86 *PIPSC v CFIA*, above note 67.

87 *PIPSC and Treasury Board*, above note 59.

The Board then cited from a Saskatchewan decision, listing four types of information that must be disclosed:

> 1. information with respect to existing terms and conditions of employment, particularly during negotiations for a first collective agreement;
> 2. information needed by a union to adequately comprehend a proposal or employer response at the bargaining table;
> 3. decisions already made that will be implemented during the term of a proposed agreement and that may have a significant impact on the bargaining unit; and
> 4. honest answers to whether it will probably implement changes during the term of a proposed agreement that may significantly impact the bargaining unit. This obligation is limited to plans likely to be implemented so that the employer maintains a degree of confidentiality in planning, because premature disclosure of plans that may not materialize could have an adverse effect on the employer, the union, and employees.[88]

The Board concluded that plans for wage control in the budget did not fall into any of these four categories. The wage control policy in the budget was just a reflection of the employer bargaining team's mandate, and the duty to bargain in good faith does not require a party to disclose its bargaining mandate.

The Board applied that rule more recently in *Canadian Federal Pilots Association v Treasury Board (Department of Transport)*.[89] In that case, eight months after a collective agreement was negotiated, the employer announced that it was selling a substantial percentage of its aircraft. This meant that Ottawa-based flying inspectors could not undertake a regular flying program to keep up their qualifications and would, instead, have to use flight simulators and other means. The bargaining agent argued that the employer's failure to disclose this plan during bargaining was a breach of the duty to bargain in good faith. The Board disagreed, concluding that the obligation to provide unsolicited disclosure was exceptional and only applied in extreme cases where the information concerned an issue of fundamental importance (such as a plant closure).

---

88 *Ibid* at 19, citing *Government of Saskatchewan and Saskatchewan Government Employees' Union* (1990), 5 CLRBR (2d) 254.

89 *Canadian Federal Pilots Association v Treasury Board (Department of Transport)*, 2014 PSLRB 64.

In this case, the collective agreement did not require the employer to provide aircraft: there was a contractual right to maintain currency, not to fly aircraft to do so. Therefore, the employer did not have a duty to disclose its decision to sell a substantial percentage of the department's aircraft and to reduce the number of aircraft based in Ottawa.

Finally, the employer has a duty to disclose personal contact information of employees to their bargaining agents.[90] The prolix litigation that has taken place about this issue will be addressed in Chapter 8 in the context of the rights and obligations of employee organizations.

6) Ratification

Finally, the Board has addressed the issue of whether a bargaining agent must recommend ratification of an agreement reached between its negotiating team and the employer's negotiating team. The Board appears to have concluded that the existence of this obligation depends on the wording of the agreement signed by the bargaining agent's negotiating team, but its decisions are not easy to follow. In *Treasury Board and Public Service of Canada*,[91] the bargaining team signed an agreement stating:

> The representatives of the Public Service Alliance of Canada and the Treasury Board have accepted and have unanimously agreed to recommend to their respective principals for ratification, terms of settlement as follows.

The bargaining agent did not recommend that its members ratify the agreement, and the members in fact voted down the agreement.

The Board noted that

> good faith is a crucial and important element in collective negotiations. The parties must trust each other and when a tentative agreement is reached, they must have faith in each other and respect what they have agreed upon. Once the parties agree to the terms of settlement, they must respect them and act in good faith with a view to the conclusion of a collective agreement. To do otherwise would undermine the meaning and purpose of collective bargaining.[92]

---

90 For example, *Professional Institute of the Public Service of Canada v Treasury Board and Canada Revenue Agency*, 2008 PSLRB 13.

91 *Treasury Board and Public Service of Canada*, [1988] CPSSRB No 141.

92 *Ibid* at para 57.

The Board concluded that the agreement quoted above meant that the bargaining agent promised to recommend that its members ratify the agreement, and its recommendation to the contrary was a breach of the obligation to bargain in good faith.[93]

On the other hand, in *Treasury Board v Professional Association of Foreign Service Officers*,[94] the Board concluded that an almost identical agreement did not bind the bargaining agent to recommend that its members ratify the agreement. That agreement also required the bargaining team to recommend ratification to its "principals." The bargaining agent's negotiator indicated to the employer that the agreement would have to be "brought" to the union executive because the tentative agreement was beyond the mandate of the bargaining team. In light of this evidence, the Board concluded that the employer and bargaining agent negotiating teams had "a clear misunderstanding"[95] about what they had agreed upon: the bargaining agent's team thought they simply had to recommend acceptance to the union executive, which would make up its own mind. Therefore, when the union executive recommended that the members not ratify the agreement, the union did not breach the obligation to bargain in good faith. There is very little to distinguish between these two board decisions or to explain why one panel of the Board found a breach of the duty to bargain in good faith while the other did not.

D. SCOPE OF BARGAINING

It is one of the defining features of federal public service labour law that bargaining agents are limited in the scope of their bargaining. The general rule in Canada in the private sector is that all issues surrounding terms and conditions of employment may be bargained (save for clauses that are "illegal"—in that they are barred by the general law of Canada); neither party has an ironclad right to keep an issue out of a collective agreement. Bargaining on all issues is permitted, and it is up to the parties to decide whether an issue will find its way into the collective

93 The Board did not order any particular remedy in that case. The employer asked for a new vote with a positive recommendation from the bargaining agent, but the Board decided that such a remedy would not serve any useful purpose.

94 *Treasury Board v Professional Association of Foreign Service Officers*, [2000] CPSSRB No 20.

95 *Ibid* at para 29.

agreement, subject to the duty to bargain in good faith. There is a category of bargaining demands that, while not illegal in themselves, are inconsistent with the scheme of their labour statutes or are destructive of the system of collective representation that the statute creates. These demands may be made and may be bargained by the parties but constitute bad faith bargaining if pressed to the point of industrial conflict. This category of issues includes demands to overbargain or underbargain a certificate (i.e., to have a collective agreement cover more or fewer employees than listed in a certificate); a demand by the employer for union amnesty for employees who crossed the picket line; and an employer demand for a ratification vote among employees where such a vote is not mandatory—in short, those demands that are inconsistent with the scheme of the labour relations statute or destructive of the system of collective representation and collective bargaining.[96]

In the United States, the scope of bargaining is more restrictive. The National Labor Relations Board has stated that wages, hours, and other conditions of employment may be bargained to impasse but that bargaining about other issues is purely voluntary—that is, neither party may strike or lock out over the voluntary issues. Public sector labour relations statutes in the United States take diverse approaches to defining what subjects must be negotiated by a public employer with its employees' exclusive bargaining representative—but none of those statutes permit bargaining on the wide scope of issues available in the Canadian private sector. At best, some statutes copy the language of the *National Labor Relations Act* (*NLRA*) and thus require bargaining on wages, hours, and terms and conditions of employment. Others expressly define those subjects over which collective bargaining is required by listing a range of topics that is narrower than the *NLRA*'s. Statutes of both types often contain broadly worded management rights provisions not found in the *NLRA*, further limiting the scope of bargaining. Even where a statute lacks express management rights language, courts in the United States have implied their own concept of inherent managerial prerogatives.[97]

The *FPSLRA* does not permit the broad scope of permissible bargaining available to parties in the Canadian private sector. Instead, it

---

96 See, for example, *Global Lethbridge, a division of CanWest Global Communications Corp*, [2002] CIRB No 187, and the cases cited therein.

97 Malin, "Public Sector Labor Law Doctrine," above note 7 at 268.

imposes several limits on the scope of collective bargaining, closer to the model in the US public sector. There are limits on what the parties may bargain; there are additional limits on what the parties may refer to a public interest commission for conciliation; and then there are yet further limits on what the parties may refer to an arbitration board if they have chosen that method of final dispute resolution.

1) Limits to Collective Bargaining Under Section 113

First, section 113 of the *FPSLRA* limits the scope of bargaining. That section states that a collective agreement may not, directly or indirectly, alter or eliminate any existing term or condition of employment if doing so would require the enactment or amendment of any legislation by Parliament or if the term or condition is one established under the *Public Service Employment Act* (*PSEA*; i.e., dealing with appointments, promotions, and layoffs), the *Public Service Superannuation Act* (*PSSA*; i.e., dealing with pensions), or the *Government Employees Compensation Act* (*GECA*; i.e., dealing with workers' compensation for injuries arising out of employment).[98]

The main practical implications of this provision is that bargaining agents cannot collectively bargain the terms of the pension plan and staffing issues for those employers whose staffing is governed by the *PSEA*.[99] The Union of Canadian Correctional Officers challenged those two exclusions on the grounds that they interfered with the constitutional protection afforded to collective bargaining. The Quebec Court of Appeal agreed that those exclusions violated that right but concluded that the violations were justified under section 1 of the *Charter*.[100] In so doing, the Quebec Court of Appeal also identified the purposes behind excluding those topics from collective bargaining. The objectives behind excluding the pension plan from collective bargaining are threefold: to promote the mobility of employees from one part of the public service to another, to ensure pension predictability (including spreading

98 *FPSLRA*, s 113.

99 As described in Chapter 11, the core public administration (i.e., the Treasury Board) and some separate agencies are governed by the *PSEA*, while other separate agencies are not included.

100 *Procureur général du Canada c Union of Canadian Correctional Officers—Syndicat des agents correctionnels du Canada—CSN (UCCO-SACC-CSN)*, 2019 QCCA 979.

the cost of the pension plan over many employees), and to permit the government to maintain control over its financial obligations since it draws on public money to fund the pension plan. The objective behind excluding staffing from collective bargaining is to ensure the survival of the merit system (discussed more fully in Chapter 11).[101]

There can sometimes be a fine line between negotiating a term or condition that impermissibly implicates those statutes and a term or condition that concerns some permissible topic that may have some consequence to those statutes. To provide an obvious example, salaries implicate pension rights, but obviously bargaining agents can negotiate salaries without implicating a term or condition that is established under the *PSSA*. The Board's decision in *Association of Justice Counsel v Treasury Board* addressed a number of these "fine line" issues. In that case, the bargaining agent wanted to refer several issues to arbitration. The Board therefore had to consider whether it could refer those issues to arbitration under section 150 of the *FPSLRA*. Paragraphs 150(1)(a) and (b) of the *FPSLRA* are identical to section 113 of the Act, so the Board had to address some of those proposed terms and conditions in the same way as they would be assessed using section 113 of the Act. The Board's conclusion on those specific bargaining proposals is as follows:

Proposal	**Conclusion**
President of the Association of Justice Counsel (AJC) and up to two additional officers will be on leave, and their period of leave will be counted for pension purposes. There was a similar proposal that all lawyers on leave would count their leave toward pensionable service. The proposal also stated that it was "subject to any applicable legislation."	This proposal, as it related to pensionable service or benefits, was impermissible. Adding the phrase "subject to any applicable legislation" did not save the proposal.

101 *Ibid* at para 44.

Proposal	Conclusion
The employer agrees that, upon request, it will provide all documentation relating to the grievance available to the person or persons making the decision being grieved. The bargaining agent proposed an amended version that stated that disclosure was subject to the *Access to Information Act* and *Privacy Act*.	The initial proposal was not permitted, but the Board accepted the alternative proposal.
The employer will consult with the bargaining agent over the rules governing the filling of vacancies.	The *PSEA* contains a provision stating that the Public Service Commission shall consult with an employee organization with respect to certain policies, including appointments. Therefore, this term was not permitted as it would establish a new term or condition that had already been established in the *PSEA*.
Performance pay will become part of base salary, and lawyers whose performance increase will take them above the maximum of the salary range will receive a lump-sum payment of the excess, which payment will be pensionable.	The part of the proposal that refers to the lump sum being pensionable is not permissible as pensionable service is governed by the *PSSA*.

There is also an important difference between paragraphs 113(a) and (b) of the *FPSLRA*. Section 113(a) prohibits terms that would "require the enactment or amendment of any legislation by Parliament," whereas section 113(b) prohibits any term that "has been or may be established" under the *PSEA*, *PSSA*, or *GECA*. This means that parties may negotiate terms that provide greater rights than those set out in statutes other than the three listed in section 113(b). This became an issue in *Professional Association of Foreign Service Officers v Treasury Board*[102] when the bargaining agent proposed a term that an employee "may refuse to work in an environment that would endanger their health or life." The employer objected to this term on the grounds that it may provide greater rights than under Part II of the *Canada Labour Code* dealing with the right to refuse work. The Board rejected that argument, concluding that a clause providing greater protection than the *Canada Labour Code* does not require an amendment to that legislation. The

102 *Professional Association of Foreign Service Officers v Treasury Board*, 2018 FPSLREB 16.

Board did reject a clause that accidental death and dismemberment coverage would be a "non-taxable benefit" on the grounds that this would require an amendment to the *Income Tax Act*.

The other limitation on the scope of bargaining is found in the definition of the term "collective agreement," which is defined as "an agreement . . . containing provisions respecting terms and conditions of employment."[103] The *FPSLRA* does not define what is a "term and condition of employment." The Supreme Court of Canada, in addressing different labour relations statutes, has stated that a provision may be "characterized as a condition of employment on the basis that it had a real connection with the contract of employment."[104] Thus, a union security clause is a term and condition of employment, regardless of the fact that it does not result in any compensation or other rights for employees against their employer.[105] In one instance, the Treasury Board argued that a voluntary medical plan in place only for Ontario employees was not a term or condition of employment and thus could not be enforced during a statutory freeze. The Board concluded that a group surgical and medical plan that applied to all employees was obviously a term or condition of employment and that making it voluntary and applicable only to a particular group of employees did not make it any less a term or condition of employment.[106] These broad interpretations of what constitutes a term or condition of employment mean that the definition of "collective agreement" in the *FPSLRA* does not severely limit the scope of bargaining; however, it is conceivable that certain bargaining demands by either party could be rejected as having no real connection with the contract of employment.

2) Limits to Public Interest Commissions

Second, section 161 of the *FPSLRA* states that a party may request conciliation in respect of "any term or condition of employment that may be included in a collective agreement."[107] Therefore, the request for

---

103 *FPSLRA*, s 2(1), "collective agreement."

104 *Isidore Garon Ltee v Tremblay*, [2006] SCJ No 3 at para 26.

105 *Syndicat Catholique des Employés des Magasins de Québec Inc v Cie Paquet Ltée*, [1959] SCR 206.

106 *Public Service Alliance of Canada and Canada (Treasury Board)*, [1970] CPSSRB No 6 at para 14.

107 *FPSLRA*, s 161.

conciliation may not contain issues listed in section 113 of the *FPSLRA*. It may also not address any issues that were not bargained by the parties prior to conciliation.

Section 177 of the *FPSLRA* further limits the report of the public interest commission that results from conciliation. The public interest commission may not recommend a collective agreement that impacts the issues listed in section 113 and also may not make recommendations that affect a term or condition that relates to standards, procedures, or processes governing the appointment, appraisal, promotion, deployment, rejection on probation, or layoff of employees. In the case of separate agencies, the public interest commission recommendation may not concern terms or conditions relating to termination of employment other than termination for a breach of discipline.[108] This last limitation for separate agencies also exists for the Treasury Board as these topics are covered in the *PSEA* and thus cannot be contained in a collective agreement, as stated above.

The intention of the extra limitation on public interest commissions was discussed in *Professional Association of Foreign Service Officers v Treasury Board*.[109] In that case, the bargaining agent wanted to refer an issue concerning performance appraisals to conciliation. The proposals generally related to the procedure involved in making performance appraisals (including a right to review your own performance appraisals) and did not create any standards for appraisal. The Board stated that the purpose behind the exclusion now found in section 177(1)(c) of the *FPSLRA* was "to keep within the employer's sole purview the power or ability to appraise its employees. In other words, the intent of this section is to grant the employer exclusive domain over the official or formal assessment of an employee's strength and weaknesses."[110]

This main new prohibition can also involve a fine line between appointments and appraisals on the one hand and rates of pay on the other. Returning to the *Association of Justice Counsel* decision referred to above, the Board had to address a number of proposals skirting that line. The Board's conclusions on those specific proposals are as follows:

108 *Ibid*, s 177(1).

109 *Professional Association of Foreign Service Officers v Treasury Board*, [2004] CPSLRB No 172.

110 *Ibid* at para 25.

Proposal	Conclusion
For the purposes of determining their salary upon return to work following the leave, lawyers on full- or part-time leave for union positions will, in the case of [lawyers with the classification level] LA-2s and above, be deemed to have received performance pay at the "meets expectations" level, and in the case of LA-1s, to have moved through the LA-1 increment steps and promotion from LA-1 to LA-2 during the period of the leave.	The clause promoting lawyers from LA-1 to LA-2 was impermissible as it requires the promotion of an employee and, therefore, concerns appointments. The rest of the proposal was a pay-related proposal and, therefore, permitted.
Employees will not be disciplined or negatively evaluated for raising concerns about professional obligations or refusing to act in a manner contrary to their professional obligations.	The Board struck out the portion of the proposal that referred to evaluations as it impermissibly governed the "appraisal" of employees.
Each employee is entitled to reasonable notice of, and to apply to, any competition respecting a bargaining unit employee position.	The requirement related to the processes and procedures governing staffing (appointment, promotions, and deployments) and therefore could not be included.
If, during the term of this agreement, a new classification standard for a group is established and implemented by the employer, the employer shall, before applying rates of pay to new levels resulting from the application of the standard, negotiate the rates of pay and the rules affecting the pay of employees on their movement to the new levels.	This term was about pay, not classification, and therefore could be included.
Any timekeeping will be consistently administered (including methodology and targets). Timekeeping data will not be used for the purpose of adversely evaluating an employee, nor in an arbitrary, discriminatory, or bad faith manner. The employer will consult with the AJC over work and activities to be included in timekeeping and in meeting any timekeeping targets, including time spent on AJC business. Both managers and lawyers will receive training in the proper use and implementation of timekeeping.	The portion of the proposal that limited the use of timekeeping data for evaluation was related to appraisals and therefore not permitted. The Board accepted an alternative proposal deleting "adversely evaluated" and substituting "disciplined."

Proposal	Conclusion
Those lawyers in the LA-1 pay scale with more than four years will be promoted to the minimum of the new LA-2A scale.	This relates to the appointment of employees. The Board accepted an alternative proposal to pay LA-1 lawyers a prorated pay increment every six months.
A minimum of 30 percent of lawyers in the AJC bargaining unit will be classified as LA-2B or above.	This proposal relates to both classification and appointments, and the Board did not accept it.
The effective date for pay purposes for former Professional Institute of the Public Service of Canada lawyers will be 28 February 2006.	The Board agreed with the bargaining agent that this proposal was about pay, not classification.
Effective with the PREA [Performance Review and Employee Appraisal] performance increase payable 1 April 2006, the performance increase for LA-2s will be 5 percent for those who "meet expectations" and 8 percent for those who "exceed expectations." The "exceeds expectations" category will not be less than 20 percent of the complement of LA-2 lawyers in the bargaining unit (or such other groupings as are agreed between AJC and the employer) and no more than 2 percent of lawyers in the bargaining unit (or such other groupings as are agreed between AJC and the employer) may receive a performance increase of less than 5 percent. For LA-3s, the performance rating levels and applicable percentages in the existing PMP [Performance Management Program] will continue in effect.	The Board pointed out that performance pay is a pay-related matter that also indirectly relates to the appraisal or evaluation of employees. The portion of the proposal that states the percentage of lawyers who will receive specified appraisal ratings is excluded; the provision that seeks to limit the percentage of employees who receive a performance increase of less than 5 percent is also excluded.
The existing "Performance Review and Employee Appraisal Policy" will apply to lawyers covered by this collective agreement and is hereby incorporated into this collective agreement.	The Board rejected this proposal as it concerned appraisals.

As mentioned in the chart above, performance appraisals may not be included in a public interest commission, but terms and conditions relating to discipline may be included. In *Canadian Federal Pilots*

Association v Treasury Board,[111] the Board had to consider whether a term removing a "letter of expectation" from a personnel file within two years was about discipline or appraisals. The Board concluded that letters of expectation are performance based and not disciplinary in nature and, therefore, outside the scope of a public interest commission or an arbitral award. The Board in that same case concluded that clauses stating the employees have the right to conduct themselves in a manner consistent with the *Values and Ethics Code for the Public Sector* and their statutory duties did not limit the employer's ability to appraise employees' performance.

The public interest commission is also prohibited from dealing with terms and conditions that were not negotiated: that restriction also applies to arbitral awards and is discussed below.

3) Limits to Arbitral Awards

Finally, section 150 of the *FPSLRA* further limits the scope of an arbitral award. Section 150(1) contains five limits:

a) Requiring the enactment of amendment of legislation by Parliament (the same as section 113(a)).
b) The term or condition is one that has been or may be established under the *PSEA*, *PSSA*, or *GECA* (the same as section 113(b)).
c) The term or condition is one that relates to standards, procedures, or processes governing the appointment, appraisal, promotion, deployment, rejection on probation, or layoff of employees (the same as section 177(1)(c)).
d) In the case of a separate agency, the term or condition relates to termination of employment other than for breach of discipline or misconduct (the same as section 117(1)(d)).
e) The term or condition would affect the organization of the public service or the assignment of duties to, and the classification of, positions and persons employed in the public service (new).[112]

By way of background, the old *PSSRA* used to restrict arbitral awards to "rates of pay, hours of work, leave entitlements, standards

111 *Canadian Federal Pilots Association v Treasury Board*, 2019 FPSLREB 41 [*Canadian Federal Pilots Association*].
112 *FPSLRA*, s 150.

of discipline and other terms and conditions of employment related directly thereto."[113] There is a rich body of jurisprudence concerning whether issues are "related directly" to the permitted items in the old *PSSRA*.[114] However, Parliament removed that particular restriction in the *Public Service Reform Act* of 1992.[115] Therefore, arbitral awards may now deal with a broader range of subjects than before.

The restriction on arbitral awards that is expressly stated in the *FPSLRA* was only added by the *Public Service Reform Act* in 1992. Prior to that time, assignment of duties and classification were still beyond the scope of an arbitral award because of the management rights provision in section 7 of the *FPSLRA*. Section 7 reads as follows:

> 7. Nothing in this Act is to be construed as affecting the right or authority of the Treasury Board or a separate agency to determine the organization of those portions of the federal public administration for which it represents Her Majesty in right of Canada as employer or to assign duties to and to classify positions and persons employed in those portions of the federal public administration.

The Federal Court of Appeal in *Public Service Alliance of Canada v Canada (Treasury Board)* stated that "to determine that a proposal is arbitrable, it must be established . . . that its effect would leave intact the untouchable prerogatives of Government defined in section 7."[116]

In other words, section 7 of the *FPSLRA* prohibits an arbitral award that would touch those prerogatives; however, parties may still voluntarily enter into collective agreements that impact the management rights preserved in section 7.[117] The older line of cases applying this principle under the *PSSRA* continue to govern section 7 of the *FPSLRA* as well.[118]

Section 7 restricts the scope of binding dispute resolution when the parities are engaged in arbitration or when the parties refer issues to conciliation by a public interest commission and then agree to be

113 *PSSRA* (1967), s 70(1).
114 See Finkelman & Goldenberg, above note 3 at 164–94.
115 SC 1992, c 54.
116 *Public Service Alliance of Canada v Canada (Treasury Board)*, [1987] 2 FC 471 (CA) at 2.
117 *Ibid* at para 5; *PSAC v Canada (Treasury Board)*, [1987] FCJ No 240 (CA) at 8.
118 *Professional Institute of the Public Service of Canada v National Research Council of Canada*, 2014 PSLRB 57 at para 62.

bound by the conciliation report (a process known as "binding conciliation").[119] On two occasions, the Federal Court has stated that when the parties refer issues for binding conciliation those issues may not limit the management rights preserved in section 7 of the *FPSLRA*. In *Canada (Attorney General) v Canada (Public Service Staff Relations Board)*,[120] the Federal Court quashed a decision to refer matters that both the bargaining agent and the employer admitted fell within the scope of section 7 of the Act to binding conciliation. Matters that fall within section 7 of the Act may be bargained but only "voluntarily" by the employer; however, the employer must "first agree to be bound by a matter that would fall within the parameter of section 7. It, the Applicant (Employer) can, if it wishes, give up some of its rights under Section 7. But the Applicant (Employer) must do so voluntarily."[121] Whether the dispute resolution is arbitration or binding conciliation, the rule is the same: the employer cannot be compelled to give up rights that are preserved by section 7.[122]

A bargaining proposal must clearly fall outside of the prohibited grounds to be arbitrated (or referred to binding conciliation). In *Professional Institute of the Public Service of Canada v Canada (Attorney General)*,[123] the institute made a bargaining proposal to establish a committee to investigate the "classification and pay problems" affecting biologists and proposed that the committee would prepare a final and binding report to resolve such problems that "does not deal with the classification of these employees." Biologists had a long-standing complaint that they were paid approximately 35 percent less than medical doctors doing essentially identical work; therefore, the institute made that bargaining proposal to rectify the complaint. The Federal Court recognized that the proposal was designed to deal with pay, which is distinct from classification; however, the proposal was "sufficiently ambiguous"[124] that it could result in a binding report that would impact management rights other than classification (such as the duties of biologists). Therefore, a proposal must not only deal with issues outside

119 *FPSLRA*, s 181.

120 *Canada (Attorney General) v Canada (Public Service Staff Relations Board)*, [1988] FCJ No 633.

121 *Ibid* at 8.

122 The Federal Court confirmed this rule in *Professional Institute of the Public Service of Canada v Canada (Attorney General)*, [1988] FCJ No 948.

123 *Ibid*.

124 *Ibid* at 5.

of management rights preserved by section 7 of the *FPSLRA*; it must unambiguously fall outside of the rights preserved by section 7. It would be fair to state that, following the same logic, bargaining proposals must unambiguously fall outside of the list of issues that are ineligible for bargaining, conciliation, or arbitration under sections 113, 177, and 150 of the *FPSLRA*, respectively.

The Board and Federal Court have dealt with whether particular bargaining proposals fall within section 7 of the *FPSLRA* a number of times. For example:

- A proposal that overtime must be offered first to employees who normally perform the duties involved was *not* an infringement on management rights. Section 7 speaks of assigning duties to "positions," not employees; therefore, an obligation to offer overtime to the incumbents of the corresponding positions does not affect management's freedom to organize the public service or assign duties to the positions it has created.[125]
- A proposal limiting the daily classroom hours of teachers is an infringement on management rights as an integral part of the assignment of duties to positions.[126]
- A proposal concerning the employer's job evaluation plan that included a review of job descriptions and organization charts was sufficiently linked to "classification" to be outside the scope of an arbitral award.[127]
- A proposal limiting "contracting out" dealt with the organization of the employer and was therefore not eligible to be referred to arbitration.[128]
- A proposal for creating new procedures governing performance reviews was *not* excluded from conciliation as it did not relate to the employer's power to appraise employees but only to procedural elements to be followed after such appraisals.
- A proposal that the time period for being employed in an entry-level position be reduced was *not* excluded from conciliation.[129]

125 *Public Service Alliance of Canada v Treasury Board*, above note 116.

126 *Ibid.*

127 *Public Service Alliance of Canada v National Capital Commission*, [1997] FCJ No 1418.

128 *Ibid.*

129 *Ibid.*

- A proposal that the competencies necessary for the successful completion of the entry-level position "need to be discussed to reflect a more realistic approach" was excluded from conciliation because it concerned the standards of appraisal of employees.[130]
- A proposal governing the rate of pay of employees whose positions are reclassified downward was *not* excluded from arbitration because the proposal concerned pay rates and did not affect the employer's right to reclassify.[131]
- A proposal for an article on "Professional Ethics" was *not* excluded.[132]
- A proposal that term employees be made indeterminate after a cumulative working period of three years without a break in service longer than sixty days was excluded from conciliation as concerning the appointment of employees.[133]
- A proposal seeking to give retroactive application to rates of pay attached to a new classification plan that the employer had not yet declared to be of full force and effect was excluded from an arbitration panel because it was tantamount to imposing an effective date of the plan and relates directly to the employer's authority over classification.[134]
- A proposal requiring the employer to assign a certain amount of duty time to employees aboard different types of aircraft and flight simulators as part of allowing employees to maintain their pilot's licence was excluded because it encroached on managerial prerogative to assign duties.[135]
- A proposal that the parties undertake a study of the employer's pay plan to identify problems does not interfere with the employer's power to make performance appraisals even though the pay plan included classification and performance issues.[136]

---

130 *Ibid.*

131 *Economists', Sociologists' and Statisticians' Association v Public Service Staff Relations Board*, [1983] 1 FC 407 (CA).

132 *Canadian Food Inspection Agency*, [2005] CPSSRB No 22.

133 *Statistics Survey Operations*, [2003] CPSSRB No 66.

134 *Public Service Alliance of Canada v Communications Security Establishment, Department of National Defence*, [2004] CPSSRB No 5.

135 *Canadian Federal Pilots Association*, above note 111.

136 *Professional Institute of the Public Service of Canada v Treasury Board*, 2008 PSLRB 72.

- Proposals that provided that hours of work are to be assigned by seniority, that the employer may only hire new employees if there are no sufficient available employees to do the work, that would require the employer to offer hours of work based on geography, and that the employer would offer work to indeterminate employees before term employees restricted the employer's ability to assign duties, contrary to section 150(e) of the Act.[137]

Despite the common overlap between them, sections 7 and 150(1)(e) of the *FPSLRA* are not completely identical. This means that a particular proposal may not infringe the prerogatives set out in section 7 of the *FPSLRA* but still infringe section 150(1)(e) of the Act.[138]

In addition to the limits on arbitral awards set out in sections 7 and 150(1) of the *FPSLRA*, section 150(2) of the Act prohibits an arbitral award from dealing with a term or condition of employment that was not the subject of negotiation between the parties prior to arbitration. Interest arbitrators in other jurisdictions commonly have to determine whether a particular argument in arbitration is a "late proposal"; section 150(2) of the Act assigns that responsibility to the Board instead of the arbitrator. The Board has explained the policy behind this provision as follows:

> [P]reventing an award from dealing with a matter not raised in negotiations is an integral part of the policy of the Act to the effect that the parties must bargain to an impasse before either may request arbitration ... It would be undermining that policy to allow a party to request arbitration on a matter that the other had not had a reasonable opportunity to consider and respond to in the course of bargaining.[139]

While the jurisprudence commonly refers to these issues as involving a "late proposal," both the Act and the jurisprudence are clear that the focus is on whether the "term or condition of employment" was the subject matter of negotiation, not whether the precise proposal was negotiated. For example, in *Association of Justice Counsel v Treasury*

137 *Public Service Alliance of Canada v Statistics Survey Operations*, 2013 PSLRB 98 and 2013 PSLRB 99, aff'd *Public Service Alliance of Canada v Canada (Attorney General)*, 2015 FC 55.

138 *Public Service Alliance of Canada v Canada (Attorney General)*, 2015 FC 55.

139 *Treasury Board v Economists, Sociologists and Statisticians Association (ESSA)*, PSSRB File No 185-02-281 (19841221) (unreported).

Board,[140] the Board accepted a late proposal by the bargaining agent that amended its initial proposal for a closed office for employees to add that those offices should have exterior windows. The Board concluded that the term or condition of employment (office space) was negotiated prior to arbitration. Similarly, in *Professional Institute of the Public Service of Canada (Computer Systems Administration Group) v Treasury Board*,[141] the Board accepted a late proposal from the bargaining agent to add to the "Standards of Discipline" clause a provision obliging the employer to supply employees with a copy of the standards. The "Standards of Discipline" clause was negotiated prior to arbitration, so the Board concluded that the term or condition of employment had been negotiated.

By contrast, simply raising an issue for discussion is not sufficient to meet the requirement of negotiating a term or condition of employment. For example, in *Professional Institute of the Public Service of Canada (Engineering Group) v Treasury Board*,[142] the employer had raised and discussed recruitment and retention problems for engineers. After the bargaining agent requested arbitration, the employer submitted a proposal to put in place a terminable allowance for those engineers. The Board concluded that the term or condition of employment was the terminable allowance and, therefore, it was late. In *Research Council Employees' Association v National Research Council of Canada*,[143] the employer discussed the issue of severance pay during negotiations. After the bargaining agent referred the dispute to arbitration, the employer proposed a term that would include certain payments made in exchange for giving up severance pay toward the maximum layoff benefits available for employees. The Board concluded that while the general topic (severance pay) was discussed, the proposal to change this specific term or condition of employment was not negotiated prior to arbitration. The Board stated that

> the term and condition of employment, as per subsection 150(2) of the *Act*, is not severance pay. It is rather each substantial benefit under

140 *Association of Justice Counsel v Treasury Board*, 2009 PSLRB 20.

141 *Professional Institute of the Public Service of Canada (Computer Systems Administration Group) v Treasury Board*, PSSRB File No 185-02-28 (19710629).

142 *Professional Institute of the Public Service of Canada (Engineering Group) v Treasury Board*, PSSRB File No 185-02-227 (19800812).

143 *Research Council Employees' Association v National Research Council of Canada*, 2012 PSLRB 115.

> that heading, such as the entitlement to severance pay, the conditions to receive it, the applicable quantum or formula, whether it is payable to surplus employees, under what conditions, etc. Each of those benefits is a separate term and conditions of employment under severance pay.[144]

Therefore, the proposal was prohibited. Finally, in *Treasury Board v Association of Justice Counsel*,[145] the employer raised some general principles concerning performance pay during bargaining but did not present any particular solution or proposal to deal with those principles. The employer attempted to turn those principles into collective agreement language after the dispute had been referred to a binding conciliation panel. The binding conciliation panel concluded that it would not entertain this "late proposal" as the terms or conditions attached to the proposal had never been negotiated. The employer attempted to argue that it was prevented from doing so because the bargaining agent moved to binding conciliation too quickly; the parties had in fact been negotiating for three years by that point, and the binding conciliation panel concluded that "there was nothing to prevent it from sending a proposal to the AJC well before the matter was referred to conciliation."[146]

E. THE CONCILIATION/STRIKE ROUTE

1) Essential Services Agreements

There are, broadly speaking, three models for dealing with strikes and essential services:

1) The "no strike" model, where strikes and lockouts are illegal and disputes are usually resolved by way of compulsory arbitration.
2) The "unfettered strike" model, where the standard strike/lockout regime is applied to a sector where essential services are performed, meaning that the only restrictions on strikes and lockouts are the standard procedural constraints set out in the applicable labour relations statute.
3) The "designation" model, standing between the first two models, which permits strikes but creates an enclave to shelter essential

144 *Ibid* at para 27.

145 *Treasury Board v Association of Justice Counsel*, 2018 CanLII 119222 (CA LA).

146 *Ibid* at para 78.

> services and ensure that enough workers remain at work during strikes and lockouts to ensure the provision of essential services.[147]

The *FPSLRA* is the Canadian "prototype" of the designation model.[148] Although employees in the federal public service have the right to go on strike, it is widely accepted that unrestrained work stoppages in essential service sectors may impose too much risk and too much hardship on the public at large. Therefore, the *FPSLRA*—like most other Canadian labour relations statutes, particularly those governing public servants—contain provisions to ensure that essential services continue to be performed in the event of a strike.

The idea that essential services must be maintained even when employees go on strike is an internationally recognized principle of labour law. The International Labour Organization (ILO) has developed extensive jurisprudence on the concept of "essentiality" and how it may be used to restrict the right to strike. While no ILO convention explicitly recognizes the right to strike, "that right has long been treated as an intrinsic part of the right to association and bargain collectively by bodies within the ILO which oversee compliance with its conventions and constitutional principles."[149] The ILO has further refined its position so that the right to strike is not absolute. One of the restrictions on the right to strike is the obligation or necessity of maintaining essential services. The ILO has, however, insisted that such restrictions be drawn narrowly:

> [The Committee of Experts] considers that essential services are only those the interruption of which would endanger the life, personal safety or health of the whole or part of the population. Furthermore, it is of the opinion that it would not be desirable—or even possible—to attempt to draw up a complete and fixed list of services which can be considered as essential.[150]

---

147 Bernard Adell, Michel Grant & Allen Ponak, *Strikes in Essential Services* (Kingston, ON: IRC Press, 2001) at 14; Timothy Hadwen & David Strang, *Ontario Public Service Employment & Labour Law*, 2d ed (Toronto: Irwin Law, 2024) at 467.

148 Adell et al, above note 147 at 28.

149 *Ibid* at 11.

150 International Labour Conference, Committee of Experts on the Application of Conventions and Recommendations, *Freedom of Association and Collective Bargaining* (Geneva: International Labour Office, 1994), online: www.ilo.org/public/libdoc/ilo/P/09661/09661(1994-81-4B).pdf at 70.

a) Analytic Path to an Essential Service Agreement

Since federal public servants were given the statutory right to strike in 1967, there have always been limits on the right to strike to preserve services that are necessary in the interest of the safety or security of the public. These limits were, until 2005, set out in the *PSSRA*. That Act made it a condition precedent to a strike that employees (or, after amendments made in 1992, positions) be designated as either performing or not performing duties that were necessary to preserve during a strike in the interest of the safety or security of the public.

The *FPSLRA* set out a significantly different approach to essential services. Under the *FPSLRA*, the employer and the bargaining agent are responsible for negotiating an essential services agreement. An essential services agreement must set out three things: the types of positions, number of positions, and specific positions in the bargaining unit that are necessary for the employer to provide essential services.[151] If the parties are unable to negotiate an essential services agreement, then the Board is responsible for determining matters that have not been agreed upon that may be included in an essential services agreement other than the level of service.

In *Public Service Alliance of Canada and Parks Canada Agency*,[152] the Board heard its first essential services dispute under the new Act. It recognized that the labour relations community required guidance on the appropriate approach to essential services disputes in light of the statutory changes. Therefore, the Board took the uncommon step of assigning three members in a panel to hear an initial "test case" in an essential services dispute, stating explicitly that its intention was to set out the appropriate analytic path to follow in future essential services disputes. The Board set out a three-part analytic path to the process leading to an essential service:

- What services are necessary for public safety or security in the event of a strike?
- What is the level of service to be performed during a strike?
- What are the type of positions, number of positions, and specific positions necessary to provide essential services at the determined level of service?

151 *FPSLRA*, s 4(1), "essential services agreement."

152 *Public Service Alliance of Canada and Parks Canada Agency*, 2008 PSLRB 97 at para 113 [*Parks Canada*].

i) What Services Are Necessary for Public Safety or Security in the Event of a Strike?

The first stage of the analytic path is to determine what comprises the essential services performed by employees in a bargaining unit. The Board reasoned that this was a necessary first step before being able to set out the type, number, and specific positions that are necessary to provide essential services.[153] In later cases, both the Board and the Federal Court of Appeal characterized the nature of this regime as "service-based," to distinguish it from the pre-2005 "position-based" regime.[154] This focus on the essential service, instead of the actual positions, led the Board to conclude that it had the jurisdiction to deem a definition of essential services to be part of an essential services agreement.[155] Finally, the burden of proof is on the employer to convince the Board that "there is a reasonable and sufficient basis for finding that a service is essential."[156]

While the Board concluded that the *FPSLRA* is substantially different from the *PSSRA*, the Board did note that the concept of "safety or security of the public" was common between the old and new Acts. Therefore, decisions under the old Act on whether a particular service was essential for the "safety or security of the public" remain good law.[157]

The first issue for the Board (or, during negotiation of an essential services agreement, the parties) to determine is whether the duties of a position are "necessary for the safety or security of the public." This determination involves a careful balancing of the interests of the public against the ability of employees in the public service to exercise their lawful right to strike. As the Fryer Report put it:

> While it is essential that certain government services continue in the event of a strike—and all public sector labour legislation provides for essential services to be provided in such cases—not all government

---

153 *Ibid* at para 186.

154 *Treasury Board v Professional Institute of the Public Service of Canada*, 2010 PSLRB 60 at para 102, aff'd *Canada (Attorney General) v Professional Institute of the Public Service of Canada*, 2011 FCA 20 [*Professional Institute 2011*]; *Professional Institute of the Public Service of Canada v Canada (Attorney General)*, 2011 FCA 143 at para 32.

155 *Treasury Board v Professional Institute of the Public Service of Canada*, above note 154.

156 *Parks Canada*, above note 152 at para 180.

157 *Ibid* at para 177.

> jobs are essential to the safety and well being of the public. . . . While public service strikes may be undesirable, the solution is not to disallow them in basic labour legislation but to avoid them by introducing dispute resolution strategies that help the parties work out their differences.[158]

Even that preliminary decision has two components: what is related to "safety or security," and who is the "public"?

Concerning the first component of "safety or security," the Board has tread a fine line between a too-limited and a too-robust view of "safety or security." In one case, the bargaining agent argued that the phrase "safety or security of the public" must be interpreted as meaning only circumstances of imminent physical danger or possible infringement of national security. The Board rejected that definition as too narrow.[159] Similarly, in the same case, the employer argued that the term "safety or security" encompassed the emotional as well as the physical security of the public. The Board rejected that definition as too broad.[160]

Instead, the Board has taken the position that "safety or security" means more than simple economic inconvenience but less than imminent national danger. The Board has stated:

> As noted by the bargaining agent's representative, a common theme throughout the Board's decisions on safety and security designations has been the importance of distinguishing between inconvenience to the public on the one hand, and safety and security on the other. The designation process represents an attempt to balance the rights of employees who are members of a bargaining unit to participate with their fellow employees in what is otherwise a lawful strike, against the need to protect the vital interests of the public. In determining the proper balance, the Board has said that inconvenience is a natural result of a withdrawal of services (otherwise what purpose did those services serve in the fist place).[161]

---

158 Final Report of the Advisory Committee on Labour Management Relations in the Federal Public Service, *Working Together in the Public Interest* (Ottawa: Treasury Board, 2001) [Final Fryer Report].

159 *Public Service Alliance of Canada and Canada (Treasury Board) (Data Processing Group—Administrative Support Category)*, [1980] CPSSRB No 5 at para 24 [*Data Processing Group*].

160 *Ibid* at para 25.

161 *Treasury Board and Public Service Alliance of Canada*, [1997] CPSSRB No 21 at para 25 [*Treasury Board and PSAC*].

Similarly, the term "safety or security" does not cover loss or damage to property.[162] The employer is not entitled to designate certain positions as essential for the sole purpose of minimizing the inconvenience to the public or the economic hardship that some members of the public might suffer by reason of a strike.[163] Stated more fully:

> We do not propose to attempt to provide a definitive answer as to the meaning to be attached to the words in question, if indeed a single meaning can be given which would fit all circumstances. The nature of the duties that are required to be performed in the interest of the safety or security of the public obviously will vary, depending on the services that are performed by the employees in the bargaining unit. The concluding words of subsection 79(1) lend themselves more readily to definition in the negative than in the positive. We have no hesitation in saying that duties, the performance of which are necessary in the interest of the safety or security of the public, do not encompass such duties as would serve only to permit the Employer to carry on business as usual; nor do they encompass such duties as would serve only to protect the Employer or the public from economic hardship; nor do they encompass such duties as would serve only to prevent inconvenience to the public.
>
> Expressed more positively, in our view, duties that are necessary to be performed in the interest of the safety or security of the public do encompass those that, in any given set of circumstances, would reasonably be required to prevent or guard against the probability or even the rational possibility of harm or injury to the health or physical well-being of individuals. To encompass, as well, within the words "safety or security" the mental, psychological or emotional state of individuals strains the ordinary meaning of those words and this is particularly so in the context in which they are used. Even the more limited ambit of what we perceive as being encompassed by the words "safety or security" is fraught with difficulties when one comes to the actual identification of those duties and the employees who are required to perform them, in the event of the withdrawal of the services of the employees in any particular bargaining unit. Indeed, in the Electronics Designated Employees Case No. 1 (File 181-2-8), the

162 *CSL Group Inc v Canada*, [1996] FCJ No 1618 (TD), aff'd [1998] FCJ No 989 (CA) [*CSL Group*].

163 *Ibid* at para 65.

> Board described the obligation placed upon it to determine who are to be designated employees under section 79 of the Act, in the absence of an agreement by the parties, as being an "awesome responsibility." The Board correctly observed that, in the final analysis, it was called upon to speculate as to what conditions might arise in the course of a strike that might endanger the safety or security of the public. It further went on to say that in these circumstances the Board ought to err, if err it does, on the side of caution. We do not quarrel with this dictum.[164]

There are two cases worth mentioning by way of example. In the first, the Board concluded that three librarians at the Federal Court were not engaged in duties necessary for the "safety or security" of the public. The Board agreed that the proper functioning of the court system was related to "safety or security" and that a law library was an "indispensable tool in the administration of justice and the performance of judicial responsibilities"; however, the withdrawal of services by these three librarians would do no more than "inconvenience" users of the library, so the positions were not essential services.[165]

In the second case, the Board had to determine whether data processors who provided support services for certain welfare programs were providing an essential service. The Board set out the following principle in that case:

> [O]nly the payment provided to that segment of recipients who had such a degree of income dependency that there might be a risk or hazard to their health, if they were deprived of the opportunity to receive the payment to which they were entitled and on which they relied as the only reasonable and reliable source to meet their minimum needs for sustenance could be deemed to fall within the contemplation of section 79 [now section 4(1)] of the Act as being necessary for the safety or security of the recipients.[166]

In its first decision involving this bargaining unit, the Board decided that in the event of a strike, entitlement to payment under most of the programs should be income tested so that only those recipients who are dependent on payments under each program would continue to receive

164 *Canada (Treasury Board) and Public Service Alliance of Canada (Radio Operation Group—Technical Category)*, [1979] CPSSRB No 7.

165 *Treasury Board and PSAC*, above note 161 at paras 28–31.

166 *Data Processing Group*, above note 159 at para 30.

them. The Board had in mind that the government would send an application to each recipient asking them if they were dependent upon that particular source of income. Two years later, the Board decided that this approach was unworkable (because a number of recipients did not complete the application) and instead assessed each welfare program to determine whether its withdrawal was likely to create a risk or hazard to the health of the recipient.[167]

More recently, the Board has considered the scope of essential services under the new Act. In the *Parks Canada* decision, the Board had to determine the essential services performed by workers in Pukaskwa National Park of Canada. The bargaining agent started with the premise that the national park was almost entirely for recreational use and, therefore, the park could simply be closed during a strike. The Board concluded that it did not have the authority to close national parks. Furthermore, even if the park was closed, as a practical matter members of the public (including, but not limited to, members of First Nations who had treaty rights to enter the park) would enter the park anyway. The Board identified four main risks to public safety: forest fires, a member of the public becoming lost or injured, contamination of the water supply, and the risk associated with animal–human conflicts. The Board, however, was not satisfied with this level of generality and, instead, listed the specific essential services:

- monitoring forest fire hazards for the purpose of identifying situations that require a response and coordinating that response;
- coordinating and implementing search and rescue efforts where a member of the public in the park or in the waters proximate to the park becomes lost, sustains an injury, encounters a dangerous bear, or requires other urgent assistance;
- piloting and maintaining the search and rescue vessel;
- ensuring the integrity of the water supply in the park's public facilities; and

167 The Board eventually concluded that the Indian Welfare Program, Canada Pension Plan, Canada Pension Commission, Old Age Security, War Veterans Allowance, Public Service Superannuation, RCMP Superannuation, Canadian Forces Superannuation, MPs' Retiring Allowance, Family Allowances, Indian Allowances for Foster Children, and Unemployment Insurance were essential and that the Canadian Government Annuities, Indian Eskimo Tuition, and Canada Manpower Training payments were not essential. *Ibid* at paras 37–38.

- ensuring the proper handling and storage of garbage to reduce the risk of dangerous animal–human conflict.[168]

In the period after *Parks Canada*, the Board issued a series of decisions defining essential services. In *Public Service Alliance of Canada v Canada (Treasury Board)*,[169] the Board had to determine the essential services performed by the Program Administration group; more specifically, in that case it considered the services delivered by citizen service officers at Service Canada. These positions dealt with the Employment Insurance (EI), Canada Pension Plan (CPP), and Old Age Security/Guaranteed Income Supplement (OAS/GIS) programs. The Board concluded that it could not declare the EI, CPP, and OAS/GIS programs in their entirety to be an essential service. The Board reviewed some of the older social welfare decisions cited in this chapter above and concluded that while benefit payments must continue in the event of a strike, there was still a dispute about what specific functions are performed to ensure the processing of applications and the payment of benefits. The Board rejected any attempts to impose a means test on recipients of these benefits and, instead, concluded that the essential service was providing assistance to members of the public to enable them to submit applications and receive the benefits of EI, CPP, and OAS/GIS.

In *Canada Revenue Agency v Public Service Alliance of Canada*,[170] the Board was asked to determine the essential services performed by call centres dealing with inquiries for GST and HST credits. The Board reviewed the social welfare program decisions discussed above (particularly the EI, CPP, and OAS/GIS case) and considered whether low-income Canadians were dependent on GST and HST credits. The Board reviewed the evidence and then pointed out that it is impossible to determine the importance of the credit to an individual taxpayer and that, while most people do not depend on the credit, "the Board must err on the side of caution when determining economic security."[171] The Board concluded that "comfort calls" from people checking on the status of a payment were not essential. However, the Board concluded

168 *Parks Canada*, above note 152 at para 208.

169 *Public Service Alliance of Canada v Canada (Treasury Board)*, 2009 PSLRB 55 [*PSAC v Canada (Treasury Board)*].

170 *Canada Revenue Agency v Public Service Alliance of Canada*, 2010 PSLRB 101.

171 *Ibid* at para 85.

that responding to telephone inquiries for address changes and reports of credit payments not received was an essential service.

The Board had to decide three cases involving the essential services performed by computer services (CS) employees at Elections Canada,[172] the Canada Border Services Agency,[173] and the Government Operations Centre of Public Safety Canada.[174]

In the *CS Elections* case, the main issue was whether preparing for and conducting federal "electoral events" (which the Board read down to mean a general federal election) are an essential service. The Board concluded that preparing for and conducting an election are not necessary to protect the safety and security of the public. Rather, the Governor in Council could simply postpone the election until the strike is over.[175] Essentially, the Board concluded that "Canadians are not prone to violent manifestations"[176] over the delay of an election.[177] The Board therefore declared that the essential services agreement for the CS group would not include a provision that identifies an essential service performed by Elections Canada.

In the *CS CBSA* case, the main dispute was over the degree of precision necessary when setting out the essential services. The employer and the bargaining agent agreed that ensuring that persons or goods of risk do not enter or leave Canada is an essential service. The Board concluded that the essential service did not include activities related to customs, excise, or trade agreements since those matters are not related to the safety and security of the public. The Board, however, simply defined the essential service as "[t]he provision of computer systems and

172 *Treasury Board v Professional Institute of the Public Service of Canada*, 2009 PSLRB 120 [*CS Elections*].

173 *Treasury Board v Professional Institute of the Public Service of Canada*, 2009 PSLRB 128 [*CS CBSA*], quashed on judicial review, *Professional Institute of the Public Service of Canada v Canada (Attorney General)*, 2011 FCA 143.

174 *Treasury Board v Professional Institute of the Public Service of Canada*, 2010 PSLRB 15 [*CS GOC*], additional reasons and order *Treasury Board v Professional Institute of the Public Service of Canada*, 2010 PSLRB 60, aff'd *Professional Institute 2011*, above note 154.

175 *CS Elections*, above note 172 at para 209.

176 *Ibid* at para 217.

177 The employer argued that rioting during the Stanley Cup playoffs demonstrated Canadians' propensity toward civil unrest. The Board was unpersuaded. The author notes, parenthetically, that at the time of publication the Toronto Maple Leafs have not advanced to the Stanley Cup final since the 2005 enactment of the *FPSLRA*.

services related to securing the border by managing the access of people and goods (including food, plants and animals) to and from Canada for the purpose of protecting the safety or security of the public."[178] The Board rejected an argument by the bargaining agent that the essential services performed by CS employees were to support thirty-eight listed computer systems that deal with persons or goods of risk. The Federal Court of Appeal, however, set aside the Board's description of the essential service because it was too vague. The Board's definition did not capture its intention to limit the services so that they exclude customs and tariff issues. Furthermore, the phrase "provision of computer systems and services" was of little assistance in identifying the type, number, and specific positions necessary to provide the essential service—in other words, the definition of the service must feed into the content of the essential services agreement. The Federal Court of Appeal noted that "nothing in principle prevents the Board from incorporating into the definition of essential services the systems, which the parties agree, are required for the provision of essential services, if this should assist."[179]

In the EI, CPP, and OAS/GIS case discussed above, the Board had concluded that an essential service agreement did not need to be cast at the same level of detail as a job description.[180] A simplified statement of essential service is possible so long as it is sufficiently precise to allow the creation of an essential services agreement.

Finally, in the *CS GOC* case the parties agreed that some computer service positions within the Government Operations Centre perform essential services because threats to public safety require a coordinated emergency response. The parties again disputed whether the essential services should be linked to the specific equipment serviced by these employees. The Board again decided not to define the essential services by reference to specific equipment.[181] Unlike in the *CS CBSA* case, though, the Board defined the essential services more explicitly. The Board's actual definition applied to the Government Operations Centre was as follows:

---

178 *CS CBSA*, above note 173.

179 *Ibid* at para 44.

180 *PSAC v Canada (Treasury Board)*, above note 169 at para 106.

181 The Board rendered this decision without the benefit of the Federal Court of Appeal's decision in the *CS CBSA* case.

> For the Government Operations Centre, including the Canadian Cyber Incident Response Centre, the following services are essential:
> (a) installing, testing, maintaining and repairing,
> (b) identifying, investigating and resolving compatibility issues and malfunctions for, and
> (c) providing direct technical assistance for
>
> the software, systems, applications and devices used *directly* to identify and analyze risks or threats that may require a response coordinated by the GOC, to communicate information to partners about those risks and threats, and to take actions and provide for the immediate expenditure of emergency funds to prevent, mitigate, prepare for, respond to and recover from those risks and threats.[182]

The Board has also concluded that services performed by veterinarian medicine workers (who typically work in abattoirs to diagnose potentially diseased meat samples) perform essential services. These essential services include not only meat hygiene at abattoirs but also issuing import and export licences and the care of animals within laboratories.[183] Interestingly, provincial meat inspectors in the province of Ontario do not perform an essential service.[184] The difference is partly one of scale. Most meat is federally inspected because it crosses provincial borders; provincial meat inspection is therefore only a fraction of federal meat inspection. Largely, though, the Board decided that Canadians cannot last without meat, concluding that "[n]ot having meat on hand for any prolonged period would be disastrous."[185]

The second component of the preliminary issue is whether the services are for the "public." Some statutes, such as the British Columbia *Labour Relations Code*,[186] specifically limit the scope of the word

---

182 *CS GOC*, above note 174 at para 101 [emphasis in original]. The Board also spelled out some specific essential services for the Canadian Cyber Incident Response Centre.

183 *Professional Institute of the Public Service of Canada v Canadian Food Inspection Agency*, 2011 PSLRB 16 [*PIPSC v CFIA*], aff'd *Professional Institute of the Public Service of Canada v Canada (Canadian Food Inspection Agency)*, 2012 FCA 228.

184 *The Crown in Right of Ontario, as represented by Management Board of Cabinet v The Ontario Public Service Employees Union*, 1996 OLRD No 914.

185 *PIPSC v CFIA*, above note 183 at para 129. Vegetarians everywhere despaired at this ruling.

186 *Labour Relations Code*, RSBC 1996, c 244.

"public" to the residents of British Columbia. The *FPSLRA*, however, does not define the term "public."

Like federal legislation, Quebec's statute governing essential services does not define the word "public." In *Hydro-Québec et Syndicat des employées de métiers d'Hydro-Québec*,[187] the Conseil des services essentiels ordered that essential services be maintained not only for those who were clients of Hydro-Québec in Quebec but also those outside the province. The *Canada Labour Code* likewise does not contain a definition of the term "public." However, the Canada Industrial Relations Board has held that the term should be given its "usual" meaning. Thus, in *Aéroports de Montréal*,[188] the Canada Industrial Relations Board concluded that the term "public" in the context of a dispute about firefighting services at an airport should be defined as follows:

> Since the Code does not provide any special definition for interpretation purposes, the term should be given its usual meaning. The Concise Oxford Dictionary defines the "public" as "the community in general, or members of the community." Since that definition fits in unequivocally with the interpretation of the Code, the Board sees no reason to limit its scope solely because the right to strike is involved. For the purposes of section 87.4, the "public" therefore means the community using airport services.[189]

The Board has also stated that the term "public" must be interpreted broadly. In *Public Service Alliance of Canada and Treasury Board*,[190] the Board concluded that all building maintenance staff were essential because they were responsible for ventilation and sewage treatment in government buildings and without their services the "public" could suffer health risks when in those buildings. The Board took an expansive view of the term "public," stating:

> According to the dictionary definitions cited to the Board, the word "public" does not necessarily mean everybody in the community and can refer to a particular section, group or portion of the community. It can be argued that had it been intended by subsection 79(1) to

187 *Hydro-Québec et Syndicat des employé(e)s de métiers d'Hydro-Québec*, 24 August 1999 (CSEPQ).

188 *Aéroports de Montréal*, [1999] CIRB No 23.

189 *Ibid* at para 19.

190 *Public Service Alliance of Canada and Treasury Board*, [1985] CPSSRB No 83.

> extend the protection afforded by the designation process to everyone, including federal public servants, that result could have been accomplished by using the words "any person" instead of the word "public." It can also be argued that since the function of the Public Service is to implement the policies and programmes of the federal government, the word "public" in subsection 79(1) must refer only to that portion of the community at large which public servants are employed to service.
>
> Be the foregoing as it may, the Board is of the opinion that where the issue is one of safety or security the word "public" must be given the broader interpretation in the absence of any clear indication that the more restrictive meaning was intended. Accordingly, we accept the position advanced by both counsel for the Employer and the representative of the Bargaining Agent that the "public" in subsection 79(1) means the people as a whole which includes federal public servants. Incidentally, we agree with counsel for the Employer that inmates of penal institutions are members of the public within the meaning of subsection 79(1).[191]

ii) What Is the Level of Service to Be Performed During a Strike?

The issue of the level of service to be performed during a strike has been contentious for over forty years. In the years immediately following the introduction of the *PSSRA*, it was generally assumed that the Board had the ultimate authority to decide which services, and what levels of those services, would have to be maintained to protect public safety or security. Using the data processors case as an example, after determining that only some of the welfare programs were truly essential, the Board stated that the designated employees need only perform those duties that are in the chain of functions culminating in the issuance of regular income payment cheques under those programs.[192]

However, in a 1982 decision the Supreme Court of Canada held that the employer has the unilateral authority to determine the level of service to be performed in the event of a strike.[193] That case involved air traffic controllers. When air traffic controllers threatened to strike in 1980, the federal government wished to ensure that commercial airlines

---

191 *Ibid* at paras 53–54.

192 *Data Processing Group*, above note 159 at para 39.

193 *Canadian Air Traffic Control Association v Canada (Treasury Board)*, [1982] 1 SCR 696 [*CATCA*].

maintained normal operations. Therefore, the minister of transport made a decision that the commercial air system must be maintained in the event of a strike. The Treasury Board, acting on this decision, filed with the Board a notice designating all 1,782 operational controllers in the Air Traffic Control group. The bargaining agent objected on the basis that these numbers were excessive to simply maintain sufficient services for emergency purposes. Their fears grew, naturally, from the possibility that they would not be able to put enough pressure on their employer without a strike.

The Board arrived at its decision by concluding that its role was to designate only the number of air traffic controllers required for essential air services in the event of a strike. It took note that in the past, the parties had assumed that regular commercial air services would not be maintained.

The Federal Court of Appeal heard the Crown's appeal and held that the employer was not restricted to maintaining essential-type air service at anytime, even in the event of a strike, and could choose whether to maintain full commercial air service or not. The Court noted that the Board's authority was to determine the employees or classes of employees in the bargaining unit that were necessary for the safety and security of the public. The legislation was not found to require a determination only for what was necessary in a strike situation.

The Supreme Court of Canada upheld the Federal Court of Appeal's interpretation of the *PSSRA*, setting a precedent that it was the employer who set the level of public service to be maintained at anytime, including a strike situation. The Board therefore did not have the power to decide that certain services could safely be suspended in the event of a strike and to designate only enough employees to provide the remaining services safely. The Board was instead limited to deciding how many employees were needed to safely maintain the level of service decided on by the employer, leaving it to the government to decide which essential services (if any) would be cut back if a strike occurred.[194] The Supreme Court stated:

> As I see it, the task of the Board ... is to consider those employees and classes of employees in the bargaining unit who have been designated by the employer, and to decide whether the performance of their stipulated duties as employees is necessary for public safety or security.

194 Adell et al, above note 147 at 31.

> ... I can find nothing in the section to indicate that the function of the Board is to determine, if conciliation should fail, what services normally provided by employees in the bargaining unit are, in the event of strike action, necessary to be continued in the interest of public security or safety, and the section contains no reference to any power in the Board to designate the duties of employees necessary in the interest of the safety or security of the public during a strike.[195]

Thus, the Supreme Court's decision means that the government has the unilateral right to determine the level of service and also that employees must perform all of their "stipulated duties," not just those duties that are essential.[196] This conclusion also flows from the fact that *positions* are essential under the *FPSLRA*, not *employees*. The Board may determine the number of positions that are needed to perform an essential service, but the Board cannot order employees in positions declared essential to stop performing their entire job during a strike.

The decision in *Canadian Air Traffic Control Association v Canada (Treasury Board)* (*CATCA*) significantly curtailed the ability of public service unions to engage in strike action. After the *CATCA* decision, 60 percent of public service bargaining units had over half of their members designated, and 35 percent had all or virtually all of their members designated—a significant increase in the number of essential services designations.[197]

The *CATCA* decision has been codified in the *FPSLRA*. Section 120 of the Act states:

> The employer has the exclusive right to determine the level at which an essential service is to be provided to the public, or a segment of the public, at any time, including the extent to which and the frequency with which the service is to be provided. Nothing in this Division is to be construed as limiting that right.

Notwithstanding this "exclusive right," the employer's determination of the level of service can still be reviewed. In *Public Service Alliance of Canada v Treasury Board (Program and Administrative Services*

195 *CATCA*, above note 193 at 8.
196 Hadwen, above note 147 at 489.
197 Swimmer, above note 23 at 379–81.

Group),[198] the employer advised the bargaining agent that citizen service officers spent 77 percent of their working time on the delivery of the essential services defined by the Board (described above) and that these essential services would be provided at 100 percent during a strike. The bargaining agent queried the 77 percent figure and also asked for documentation relating the employer's decision to set the level of service at 100 percent and the process by which the decision was made. The employer refused that request, so the bargaining agent applied to the Board for an order of production. The Board decided that this required it to determine whether it had jurisdiction to consider whether the employer complied with the *FPSLRA* when it determined the level of service. The Board concluded that section 36 of the *FPSLRA*—which gives the Board the jurisdiction to exercise powers incidental to the attainment of the objects of the Act—granted it the jurisdiction to review the employer's decision for "abuse of discretion." While the Board did not provide firm limits on what would constitute an abuse of discretion, it concluded that one example would be if the employer unreasonably delayed in making a decision about the level of service to frustrate the completion of an essential services agreement (and thus frustrate the right to strike).[199] The Board also concluded that it had the power to consider an allegation that the employer has violated a principle of administrative law, such as acting in a manner that is arbitrary, capricious, or in bad faith.[200]

iii) *What Are the Type of Positions, Number of Positions, and Specific Positions Necessary to Provide Essential Services at the Determined Level of Service?*

The Board has not yet had to rule on this third stage of the analytic path. However, the wording of the statute itself coupled with various decisions on similar issues provides some guidelines.

In determining the number of essential positions in a bargaining unit, the Board is permitted to take into account that some employees may be required by the employer to perform those of their duties that relate to the provision of essential services in a greater proportion during

198 *Public Service Alliance of Canada v Treasury Board (Program and Administrative Services Group)*, 2010 PSLRB 88, aff'd *Canada (Attorney General) v Public Service Alliance of Canada*, 2011 FCA 257.

199 *Ibid* (PSLRB) at para 165.

200 *Ibid* at para 167.

a strike than they do normally.[201] However, the number of employees necessary to provide the essential service must be determined without regard to the availability of other persons to provide the essential service during a strike and on the basis that the employer is not required to change the manner of its normal operation (including hours of work, use of overtime, and the equipment used).[202] Therefore, the bargaining agent cannot argue that managers or other excluded employees should be used to provide the essential service.

The *FPSLRA* also states that if the essential services application relates to a specific position to be identified in the essential services agreement (as opposed to simply the number of positions), the employer's proposal is to prevail unless the position is not of the type necessary to provide essential services.[203] The Board had placed the onus of proof in essential services cases with the employer: the mere assertion by the employer that a position is essential is not proof, and the primary onus rests with the employer, although there is an obligation on both parties to provide convincing evidence and arguments in support of their respective positions.[204] Section 123(7) of the *FPSLRA* reverses that onus of proof when the application relates to whether a particular position is essential, as opposed to the number of positions that should be essential.

Positions that are necessary to support the work done by other positions that are essential are themselves essential positions. For example, the Board has designated employees required to provide adequate supervision for other designated employees[205] and employees who were responsible for maintaining buildings worked in by essential employees.[206] This principle is standard throughout Canada when dealing with essential services.[207]

---

201 *FPSLRA*, s 123(5).

202 *Ibid*, s 123(6).

203 *Ibid*, s 123(7).

204 *Parks Canada*, above note 152 at para 180, and *PSAC v Canada (Treasury Board)*, above note 169 at para 70.

205 *Air Traffic Control Case No 4* (1972), PSSR Reports K 839.

206 *Heating, Power and Stationary Plant Operations Designated Employees Case No 1* (1972), PSSR Reports K 900.

207 See, for example, *Ontario (Management Board Secretariat)*, [1999] OLRB Rep January/February 21, where the OLRB concluded that overhauling the computer system for "Y2K" was essential because the primary service itself was essential, the computer component involved in that service was essential, and the Y2K preparation service was essential to allow the computer component to proceed.

On occasion, bargaining agents have asked the Board to designate a larger number of positions than the employer requested. They have done so for unspecified strategic reasons. The Board, under the *PSSRA*, ruled that it did not have the jurisdiction to designate more positions than requested by the employer.[208] However, those decisions were based on the wording of the *PSSRA*, which stated that it was the employer who referred positions in dispute to the Board if the parties continue to disagree after considering the recommendations of a designation review panel. There was no legislative provision permitting a bargaining agent to refer disputed positions to the Board. The *FPSLRA*, on the other hand, requires the parties to negotiate and allows either party to apply to the Board to determine whether a position is essential.[209] Therefore, it is likely that the Board may now entertain applications by bargaining agents to designate a larger number of employees as essential.

The issue of whether an employer may hire replacement workers to perform essential or non-essential duties during a strike has not arisen in the federal public service. However, the issue has arisen in British Columbia and Ontario, with different results. In British Columbia, the BC board ruled that an employer cannot require essential services workers to attend work while at the same time hiring replacement workers to perform non-essential work. The Board essentially relied on "labour relations reasons":

> Rather than exercising its discretion in a neutral way with a view to maximizing the economic pressure on both sides to advance the public interest by shortening a labour dispute affecting an essential service, while at the same time ensuring that the labour dispute does not interfere with the provision of that level of services necessary or essential to prevent immediate or serious danger to life, health or safety, the employer would have the Board act in a manner which directly and powerfully advances the employer's interests. A Board order directing members of the HEU [Health Employees' Union] to work alongside hired paid replacements would have the certain result of removing any impact of the lawful strike on the employer. This result does not operate in the long term interest of the public, simply because without

208 *Treasury Board and Professional Institute of the Public Service of Canada*, [1999] CPSSRB No 53, and *Canadian Food Inspection Agency and Professional Institute of the Public Service of Canada*, [2000] CPSSRB No 10.

209 *FPSLRA*, s 123(1).

> any economic pressure on the employer's side of the equation of the labour dispute, the dispute is likely to endure for a much longer time and to result in a much longer disruption to the public's access to that essential service. That is not the result contemplated by Section 73.[210]

The Ontario Labour Relations Board, while agreeing with that labour relations principle, concluded that it did not have the jurisdiction to grant such an order, stating:

> While the analysis and conclusion of the B.C. Board in BEACON HILL LODGE makes labour relations sense and addresses the fundamental and underlying issues inherent in the balancing of interests in public sector labour disputes, the Ontario Labour Relations Board is not subject to the same statutory framework. The CECBA [*Crown Employees Collective Bargaining Act*] only mandates the Board to address certain matters arising out of that statute, and makes no reference to the Board's general remedial powers under the LABOUR RELATIONS ACT, 1995. The thrust of Part IV of the CECBA, dealing with essential services, envisions the Crown employer and the trade union identifying the services which will be essential and then working out the number and identity of the bargaining unit employees needed to provide those essential services. It is only if and when one of the parties to the negotiations applies to the Board for assistance in resolving an issue that the Board is engaged in the essential services agreement process.[211]

In other words, the Board's role in Ontario concerning essential services was too narrow to encompass a remedy preventing the employer from hiring replacement workers. While the BC model certainly makes good labour relations sense, the *FPSLRA* is closer to the Ontario statute than the BC statute, and therefore the Board will likely follow the Ontario board's decision in preference to the BC board's.

Similarly, the issue of the bargaining agent's obligations should an employee in an essential position not show up for work has not been addressed by the Board.[212] The Ontario Labour Relations Board has addressed this issue and has required the employer to use an employee

---

210 *Beacon Hill Lodge v BCNU and HEU* (1986), No 2/86 (BCLRB), aff'd *Beacon Hill Lodge v British Columbia*, [1987] BCCA, No 713.

211 *Ontario (Management Board Secretariat)*, [1998] OLRD No 3050 at para 22.

212 The consequences for that employee are discussed below.

from the bargaining agent (as opposed to a manager or outside contractor) but also required the bargaining agent and the employer to negotiate a protocol to deal with such situations quickly; however, the Ontario board has not yet rendered a clear decision on whether the government can use its own non-essential workers (managers or employees who cross the picket line) to do essential services work.[213]

If negotiations break down, the parties proceed to the Board and the Board determines which positions should be designated in an essential services agreement. The incumbents of designated positions may not go out on strike. Both the procedure and the substance of the law of essential services are of fundamental importance to determining—or, more accurately, limiting—the right of federal public servants to strike.

b) Negotiating an Essential Services Agreement and Other Procedural Issues

The negotiation of an essential services agreement is triggered by the employer giving the bargaining agent a notice in writing that the employer considers that employees in the bargaining unit occupy positions that are necessary to provide essential services.[214] The employer must give this notice no later than twenty days after notice to bargain has been served.[215] This twenty-day deadline used to be very significant as the Board only had limited jurisdiction to extend that deadline if the employer missed it. In 1987, the Treasury Board missed the twenty-day deadline for at least nine bargaining units represented by the PSAC. Under the legislation in force at that time, the parties did not have to negotiate an essential services agreement: instead, the employer "designated" certain employees as performing essential services, and then it was up to the Board to resolve any dispute concerning whether the employer had designated too many employees. The Board allowed the Treasury Board to designate those employees even though the Treasury Board had missed the deadline for doing so. However, on judicial review, the Federal Court of Appeal quashed the Board's decision. The Court concluded that the time limit was mandatory, stating:

> It seems to me to be far more reasonable to read section 79 as allowing the employer to submit a list within the time prescribed and implying

213 See Hadwen, above note 147 at 497–98.

214 *FPSLRA*, s 122(1).

215 *Ibid*, s 122(2).

> that, in the absence of a timely submission, the parties are presumed to have agreed that there are to be no designated employees within the relevant bargaining unit. Such a reading seems to me to be more in keeping with the scheme of the Act as a whole and with the general context of labour relations law and practice in Canada today.[216]

The Court did indicate that there could be rare exceptions where "the Board could, in a proper case and for good cause shown, relieve the government from the consequences of its default."[217]

Therefore, the Treasury Board proceeded back to the Board and argued that the late filing should be permitted because the duties performed by the employees it wanted to designate were very important, and this justified relief from the time limits for filing the designation. The Board rejected that argument, and the Federal Court of Appeal agreed. The Court clarified what it meant by "good cause," stating:

> [G]ood cause relates to explaining the delay in late filing not to why relief should be given to the government from the consequences of its late filing. . . . [A]lthough specific time limits should as a general matter be taken seriously, I do not think it does harm to statutory interpretation or Parliament's intent to acknowledge that such time limits can be treated as being legally met where an event or happening akin to an accident, *force majeure* or Act of God has intervened to prevent literal compliance with the time limit. It takes little imagination in our modern complex life to think of circumstances where, through no fault or shortcoming of the employer, the filing of the list was delayed. . . . Accordingly I believe the PSSRB does have an implied but very limited jurisdiction to relieve the government—employer—of its default if it is persuaded by the reasons for the delay in what would likely be most unusual or extraordinary circumstances.[218]

There was significant fallout from these decisions. Three of the bargaining units affected —Ships Crews, Welfare Programs, and Hospital Services—had previously been 100 percent designated (meaning that none of the members of those bargaining units had the right to strike). Those three bargaining units rejected the Treasury Board's last offer and

216 *Public Service Alliance of Canada v Canada (Treasury Board)*, [1989] 2 FC 445 (CA) at 4.

217 *Ibid.*

218 *Canada (Attorney General) v PSAC*, [1989] 3 FC 585 at 590–91 (CA).

went on strike from 11 November to 15 December 1989. The government of the day had to pass legislation to end the strikes.[219]

Finally, as a result of the strike by Ships Crews (many of whom worked on coast guard vessels), the government had to shut down the St. Lawrence River between Quebec City and Les Escouminis for two days in December 1989. There were other delays in transportation during that period. One major shipping company sued the federal government for over $4 million, alleging that the government negligently failed to designate employees in a timely manner. The Federal Court dismissed the claim on the grounds that the Treasury Board did not have a legal duty to designate employees under the *PSSRA*.[220]

The Board has granted relief to the employer from late filing of the list of designated positions[221] when the delay resulted from a computer error. The employer had prepared a list of designated positions on a diskette that it had given to the bargaining agent in an attempt to convince the bargaining agent to consent to the list of designated positions; however, when copying that list to the diskette eventually given to the Board, it inadvertently (and mysteriously) left 142 positions off that list. The Board allowed the employer to add those 142 positions to its list, notwithstanding that the twenty-day deadline had elapsed.[222]

The *FPSLRA* has given the Board the jurisdiction to extend the period of time for the employer to serve the designation notice, along with any other period of time relating to essential services.[223] In light of this statutory change, the Board has not yet addressed whether it will continue to follow the Federal Court decisions discussed above and only allow such extensions in the case of an accident or other *force majeure*. The Federal Court's admonishment to employers to take deadlines seriously should continue to be relevant to the Board, and the interpretation of the Board's new statutory authority that is most consistent with prior jurisprudence is that the Board's ability to extend time limits should be exercised rarely and also that the importance of the duties of the positions at issue should not be a relevant factor in deciding whether

219 *Government Services Resumption Act*, SC 1989, c 24.

220 *CSL Group*, above note 162.

221 In 1992, the *PSSRA* was amended so that positions, and not employees, were designated. That remains the situation under the *FPSLRA*.

222 *Treasury Board and Professional Institute of the Public Service of Canada*, [1997] CPSSRB No 60.

223 *FPSLRA*, s 133.

to extend the time for serving a notice. The new wording of the *FPSLRA* may, however, give the Board the jurisdiction to address allegations of estoppel or waiver.

Finally, the employer must give the notice, in writing, to the bargaining agent.[224] Giving a notice to the Board is now obviously insufficient, and the Board concluded that even under the old designation procedure in the *PSSRA* giving notice to the Board only was insufficient.[225]

Assuming that the employer has given notice in a timely fashion, the parties must begin negotiating an essential services agreement and must "make every reasonable effort to enter into an essential services agreement as soon as possible."[226] This obligation is akin to the obligation to bargain in good faith discussed above, and there is no reason to suspect that the rules concerning this obligation are different from the general rules concerning the obligation to bargain in good faith. The only difference in the wording of the obligation is the additional requirement that the parties complete their negotiations "as soon as possible."

It is doubtful that this obligation to make every reasonable effort to enter into an essential services agreement is of any practical relevance. If the parties are unable to complete an essential services agreement, then they may apply to the Board to determine any unresolved matter. In the event that one of the parties does not comply with the obligation to make every reasonable effort to enter into an essential services agreement, it is likely that the other party will simply ask the Board to resolve the issue rather than ask the Board to declare that the offending party has not negotiated in good faith.[227] The Board has the right to delay dealing with such a request until it is satisfied that the parties have made every reasonable effort to enter into an essential services agreement,[228] so perhaps the Board will use that power to force parties to negotiate in good faith; at the time of publication, the Board had not yet addressed this issue.

That being said, negotiating essential services agreements is an improvement on simply having the Board rule on whether the employer's

---

224 *Ibid*, s 122.

225 *Aircraft Operations Group Association and Treasury Board*, [1989] CPSSRB No 305.

226 *FPSLRA*, s 122(1).

227 Hadwen, above note 147 at 474.

228 *FPSLRA*, s 123(2).

list of positions is too broad. For example, as the result of the Treasury Board agreeing to have departmental managers confer directly with local union officials of the PSAC to designate essential employees in 1991, the overall percentage of designated positions dropped from 40 percent to 29 percent.[229]

As just mentioned, if the parties are unable to enter into an essential services agreement, either party may apply to the Board for a determination of any unresolved issue.[230] They must do so no later than fifteen days after a request for conciliation is made by either party, or fifteen days after the parties have been informed that the chair of the Board is going to establish a public interest commission on their own recommendation.[231] The Board may then make an order deciding which positions are essential services; at that point, the Board's order may be deemed to be part of an essential services agreement, and the parties may be deemed to have entered into an essential services agreement.[232]

Once the parties have entered into an essential services agreement (or are deemed to have entered into one pursuant to a board order), that agreement remains binding on them until there are no employees in the bargaining unit who occupy the essential services positions.[233] The parties have the right to give notice that they wish to negotiate an amendment to the essential services agreement only when a collective agreement is still in force and no later than sixty days following a notice to bargain.[234] Therefore, once the collective agreement has expired, or sixty days after notice to bargain has been served, the parties are bound by the essential services agreement they previously negotiated.[235]

The *FPSLRA* permits the parties to apply to the Board at any time for a "temporary" amendment to an essential services agreement because of an "emergency."[236]

---

229 Swimmer, above note 23 at 392.

230 *FPSLRA*, s 123(1).

231 *FPSLRA*, s 123(1).

232 *Ibid*, s 123(3).

233 *Ibid*, s 125.

234 *Ibid*, s 125(2).

235 This is a change from the *PSSRA*, where an application to amend an existing designation could be made at any time prior to a request for conciliation: see *Professional Institute of the Public Service of Canada v Canadian Food Inspection Agency*, [2004] CPSSRB No 64.

236 *FPSLRA*, s 131.

The Board has not addressed the issue of whether third parties should be permitted to intervene in essential services applications. The Ontario Labour Relations Board and Ontario Divisional Court, however, have denied third parties the right to intervene in essential services applications. In one case, the Ontario Labour Relations Board dismissed a request by the Ontario Provincial Police Association to make submissions on the level of essential services provided by civilian employees working as communication dispatchers for the Ontario Provincial Police.[237] The Ontario board stated that the police association could pursue its arguments in "other avenues or forums," without explaining those other avenues or forums.[238] The Divisional Court also rejected a request by meat packers to be given notice of Ontario board hearings concerning whether meat slaughter inspection workers were providing an essential service, stating that the Ontario board is not obliged to give notice to third parties simply because its proceedings may have financial implications for those third parties.[239]

Once positions have been declared essential in an essential services agreement, the employer must notify every employee who occupies such a position that their position is essential. The *FPSLRA* and *FPSLR Regulations* do not specify the timing of this notice, but the Board concluded that (at the request of the parties) it would permit the employer to provide this notice up to thirty days from the date of request for conciliation.[240]

Finally, essential services agreements may be filed with the Board and then enforced in the same manner as any other board order.[241]

2) The Conciliation Process

The conciliation process under the *FPSLRA* is triggered by a request for conciliation, filed by either party to the chair of the Board.[242] Prior

237 *Ontario v OPSEU (Institutional and Health Care Bargaining Unit)*, [1995] OLRD No 4443.

238 *Ibid* at para 2.

239 *Weston Abattoir Ltd v Ontario Public Service Union*, [1996] OJ No 5379.

240 *Public Service Alliance of Canada and Treasury Board*, [1997] CPSSRB No 13. The old regulations appeared to require notice to the employee within thirty days of the decision designating their position.

241 *FPSLRA*, s 134.

242 *Ibid*, s 161.

to requesting conciliation, the parties must have bargained to an impasse,[243] and the chair of the Board has the right to delay appointing a public interest commission to conduct the conciliation until they are satisfied that the party making the request has bargained "sufficiently and seriously" with respect to the matters referred to conciliation.[244] Once the chair has received a request for conciliation, they must either recommend that the minister appoint a public interest commission or declare that a public interest commission will not be appointed.[245]

The party requesting conciliation must list the issues they want dealt with by the public interest commission, and the other party then has seven days to add issues to that list.[246]

Conciliation is conducted by a public interest commission. The creation of a public interest commission is a new development in the *FPSLRA* and is a more limited version of the recommendations presented in the Fryer Report. That report recommended the creation of a permanent public interest commission, as well as several other reforms to the conciliation process.[247]

The *FPSLRA* did not create a permanent public interest commission that addresses all aspects of the collective bargaining process. However, the public interest commission in the *FPSLRA* does encompass some of the recommendations in the Fryer Report. In particular, it is a representative body. The chair of the Board must prepare a list of people who are eligible to serve on the public interest commission. That list contains people recommended by both the bargaining agent and the employer, or people recommended by the chair if they feel that the parties have not jointly recommended enough people.[248] The public interest commission may be a single member chosen from that list prepared by the chair of the Board.[249] While the minister chooses from the list, the chair of the Board may recommend a particular person from that list.[250] The public interest commission may also be composed of three people

243 *Ibid*, s 160(b).

244 *Ibid*, s 162(2).

245 *Ibid*, s 162(3).

246 *FPSLRA*, ss 160(2)(a) and 160(4). The issues that may be dealt with on conciliation have been discussed above.

247 Final Fryer Report, above note 158.

248 *FPSLRA*, s 165(2).

249 *Ibid*, s 166(1).

250 *Ibid*.

if either party elects a tripartite process: a nominee of the bargaining agent, a nominee of the employer, and a neutral chair chosen by the two nominees.[251] If the nominees cannot choose a chair of the public interest commission, then the minister chooses the chair using the list mentioned above.[252]

Once established, the public interest commission must endeavour to assist the parties in entering into a new collective agreement.[253] The public interest commission may determine its own procedure but must allow both parties a full opportunity to present evidence and make representations.[254] Then, within thirty days after being established (unless the parties or the chair of the Board extends that period of time), the public interest commission must prepare a report. In preparing a report, the public interest commission must consider the same factors as an arbitration panel.[255] The report is presented to the chair of the Board, who must then send a copy to the parties and also publish the report "in any manner that he or she considers appropriate."[256] This requirement to publish the report was one of the recommendations of the Fryer Report:

> Within two weeks of issuing its report to the parties, the Commission should make it available to the public. In this way, if either party chose to reject the report's recommendations, there would be pressure to demonstrate why the Resolution Commission's Report was unacceptable when compared to their own positions.
>
> For these reasons, and because the availability of an array of dispute resolution strategies would likely make a freely negotiated settlement seem relatively more attractive, we expect the Public Interest Dispute Resolution Commission to reduce public service strikes as well as the government's use of ad hoc legislation to end those strikes or impose settlements. These options, we believe, would be unattractive to the parties after the Commission issued its report.[257]

---

251 *Ibid*, s 167(1)–(3).
252 *Ibid*, s 167(4).
253 *Ibid*, s 172.
254 *Ibid*, s 173(1).
255 *Ibid*, s 175. See further discussion below.
256 *Ibid*, s 180.
257 Final Fryer Report, above note 158.

The Fryer Report also recommended that a bargaining agent have the right to unilaterally apply to have the public interest commission's report imposed as a resolution to collective bargaining if the employer rejected it. The Fryer Report did not consider it necessary to give the employer this power because the employer could simply request that the government legislate the terms and conditions of employment—either to enforce the public interest commission's report or to nullify it after the bargaining agent applied to have that report enforced.[258]

The *FPSLRA* sets out some limits on public interest commissions that were discussed above when discussing the scope of bargaining: it may not, for example, recommend the alteration or elimination of any term governing appraisals.[259]

The *FPSLRA* does not contain any provision for the parties to apply to have the public interest commission's report enforced; however, the parties may agree—prior to the report being issued—to be bound by that report—a process commonly referred to as binding conciliation.[260]

3) Strikes

If after bargaining and conciliation the parties have still not agreed on a collective agreement, the last resort is a strike. Aside from the obvious condition that strikes are not permitted when the bargaining agent has elected arbitration as its dispute-resolution mechanism, there are several other conditions that have to be met before an employee organization can call a legal strike.

First, the employee organization must have been certified as a bargaining agent.[261]

Second, the collective agreement must not be in force.[262] An automatic renewal clause in a collective agreement (or a clause stipulating that the collective agreement remains in force until a new agreement has been negotiated) does not have the effect of removing or limiting the right to strike.[263]

---

258 *Ibid.*

259 *FPSLRA*, s 177(1).

260 *Ibid*, s 181.

261 *Ibid*, s 194(1)(a).

262 *Ibid*, s 194(1)(b).

263 *Bradburn v Wentworth Arms Hotel Ltd*, [1979] 1 SCR 846.

Third, the parties must have served a notice to bargain and then proceeded through the conciliation process (or had the chair of the Board decide that there would be no public interest commission appointed). The bargaining agent must wait seven days after the conciliation report was sent by the chair of the Board before calling a strike.[264]

Fourth, the essential services agreement process must have been completed. This means that if the employer gave notice to negotiate or amend an essential services agreement, that agreement must have been completed (either through negotiation or through the Board imposing an agreement).[265] The bargaining agent must wait at least thirty days after an essential services agreement comes into force before calling a strike.[266] If the Board has suspended an essential services agreement because of an emergency, then the bargaining agent may not call a strike and the strike must end.[267]

Fifth, the bargaining agent must have conducted a strike vote within sixty days of beginning the strike (unless that time limit has been extended with the consent of the employer).[268] The requirement of a strike vote is new in the *FPSLRA*; however, secret ballot strike votes are mandatory in all Canadian jurisdictions.[269] The *FPSLRA* requires the bargaining agent to allow all employees in the bargaining unit to participate in the strike vote,[270] which is also consistent with every province except Quebec (where the law allows unions to limit strike votes to members only).[271]

Since the requirement of a strike vote is new, the Board has not had the opportunity to refine some of the requirements of that vote. For example, there is a difference of opinion among labour relations boards in Canada about whether a strike vote may be combined with a ratification vote. Often a ratification vote will include only two options: accept the employer's last offer or go on strike. The Ontario Labour Relations

---

264 *FPSLRA*, ss 194(1)(k)–(m).

265 *Ibid*, ss 194(1)(f)–(i).

266 *Ibid*, s 194(1)(i).

267 *Ibid*, ss 131 and 194(1)(j).

268 *FP Ibid SLRA*, ss 184 and 194(1)(r).

269 Canada, Task Force to Review Part I of the Canada Labour Code, *Seeking a Balance: Canada Labour Code, Part I, Review* (Ottawa, ON: Labour Canada, 1996) (Chairman: Andrew C.L. Sims) [Sims Report].

270 *FPSLRA*, s 184(1).

271 Sims Report, above note 269.

Board[272] has concluded that these types of votes are valid "strike votes" and that the union does not need to include a third option of rejecting the employer's offer but ordering the union to return to the bargaining table. However, the Saskatchewan Labour Relations Board has rejected the Ontario approach.[273] The Canada Industrial Relations Board has sided more closely with the Ontario approach and stated that a union may combine a ratification vote with a strike vote. However, the ballot must clearly state that the consequence of rejecting the employer's final offer is a strike. In *Canada Steamship Lines*,[274] the bargaining agent conducted a ballot that only had two options: accept or reject the employer's last offer. The Canada Industrial Relations Board concluded that it

> does not object to options that present, as an alternative to ratifying a final contract offer, a vote in favour of strike action, it does not find, in this case, that those options were, in fact, presented to the membership. Although section 87.3(1) of the Code does not specify the form of the strike ballot nor the way that the options on the ballot should appear, the section is, nonetheless, clear that it must be a strike vote.[275]

While the Board has not ruled on this issue directly, one decision indicates that it may not permit strike and ratification votes to be combined. In *Sturkenboom v Professional Institute of the Public Service of Canada*,[276] an employee alleged that the bargaining agent breached its duty of fair representation when it limited ratification votes to members. The employee was a "Rand formula" employee: he paid dues but was not a member of the union. The Board concluded that Rand formula employees do not have the right to participate in a ratification vote. The Board did point out, however, that section 184 of the *FPSLRA* permits all employees—regardless of whether they are union members—to participate in a strike vote. The Board concluded that since Parliament specifically provided that all employees may participate in a strike vote

272 *Wal-Mart Canada Inc*, [1998] OLRB Rep Nov/Dec 1037, aff'd *Wal-Mart Canada v United Steelworkers of America (Retail, Wholesale Canada, Canadian Services Sector)*, [1999] OJ No 2855.

273 *Saskatchewan Telecommunications*, [1987] May Sask Labour Rep 55.

274 *Canada Steamship Lines*, [2002] CIRB No 201.

275 *Ibid* at para 81.

276 *Sturkenboom v Professional Institute of the Public Service of Canada*, 2012 PSLRB 81 [*Sturkenboom*]. On this point, see more recently *Bernard v Professional Institute of the Public Service of Canada*, 2020 FPSLREB 11, confirming the result in *Sturkenboom*.

and the Act is silent on ratification votes (except when ordered by the minister, as discussed below), then this silence meant that there is no right to vote in a ratification vote. This ruling does mean in practice that a bargaining agent that limits ratification votes to members only—and they all do—cannot hold both a strike vote (open to all employees) and a ratification vote (open only to members) at the same time.

The English version of section 184(1) of the *FPSLRA* requires employees to be given a "reasonable opportunity" to participate in the vote, whereas the French version requires the bargaining agent to provide all employees with the opportunity to participate in a vote, without any further qualification. The Board has concluded that the French version is more consistent with the purpose of the *FPSLRA*.[277] Bargaining unit members may apply to the Board to have a vote declared invalid when there are irregularities.[278] The Board may summarily dismiss such an application when the irregularities would have made no difference to the outcome of the vote,[279] which means, effectively, that "[s]ome minor errors and irregularities may occur"[280] so long as a different outcome was a "sufficiently remote possibility"[281] that the Board will not intervene.

Sixth and finally, the *FPSLRA* allows the Governor in Council to prohibit strikes when Parliament has been dissolved for a general election. The Governor in Council may delay the strike until twenty-one days after the election has taken place.[282] This provision is designed to ensure that Parliament is available to pass back-to-work legislation if a strike is having a considerable and detrimental impact on the national interest.

Unlike the *Canada Labour Code*, the *FPSLRA* does not require bargaining agents to give notice to the employer of a pending strike, nor does the *FPSLRA* require the bargaining agent to inform the employer of the results of a strike vote. The *FPSLR Regulations* do require the bargaining agent to file the results of a strike vote with the Board within one day of the results of the vote being announced.[283]

277 *Paterson v Public Service Alliance of Canada*, 2023 FPSLREB 44 [*Paterson*].
278 *FPSLRA*, s 184(2).
279 *Ibid*, s 184(3).
280 *Paterson*, above note 277 at para 37.
281 *Ibid* at para 64.
282 *FPSLRA*, s 197.
283 *FPSLR Regulations*, s 54.

Section 183 of the *FPSLRA* permits the minister responsible for the Act[284] to order a vote on the employer's last offer.[285] This "final offer vote" does not prevent or delay a strike,[286] but if the majority of employees vote in favour of the final offer, then the strike must cease, and the final offer becomes the collective agreement.[287] This power is rarely exercised. In fact, the only time the minister ever exercised this power, the Federal Court struck down the minister's decision because the minister owed the bargaining agent a duty of procedural fairness, including "the right to be informed of the reasons the Employer invoked in support of its request for a ministerial-ordered vote; the opportunity to make submissions on the issue; and the right to have them considered by the minister in making the decision as to whether a vote . . . is in the public interest."[288]

The *FPSLRA* also contains some limitations on picketing. The *FPSLRA* prohibits any person from impeding or attempting to impede an employee entering a workplace if that employee occupies an essential services position.[289] Any "person" (not just an employee) who contravenes that prohibition is guilty of an offence and liable on summary conviction to a fine of up to $1,000. The *FPSLRA* does not require that the person intend to impede an essential employee, nor does it provide a definition of "impede."

The absence of any element of intent means that the offence is a "strict liability" offence.[290] Thus, the Crown is required to prove beyond a reasonable doubt that the essential employee was impeded; then the accused has the opportunity to prove due diligence or the absence of negligence on a balance of probabilities.[291] The person who impeded the essential worker cannot avoid conviction simply by proving that

---

284 The specific minister is not set out in the Act and rotates from government to government. *FPSLRA*, s 2(1), "minister."

285 *FPSLRA*, s 183(1).

286 *Ibid*, s 183(2).

287 *Ibid*, s 183(3).

288 *Public Service Alliance of Canada v Canada (Attorney General)*, 2013 FC 918 at para 60.

289 *FPSLRA*, s 199.

290 The court will presume that the offence is "strict liability" as opposed to "absolute liability" in the absence of statutory language making it clear that guilt would follow on mere proof of the prescribed act. Since the *FPSLRA* does not explicitly state that interfering with an essential employee is an absolute liability offence, it is *prima facie* a strict liability offence: *R v Sault Ste Marie (City)*, [1978] 2 SCR 1299 [*Sault Ste Marie*]. See also *Strasser v Roberge*, [1979] 2 SCR 953 [*Strasser*].

291 *Sault Ste Marie*, above note 290.

they did not know that the person impeded was an essential employee; however, if they acted with due diligence to ascertain if the person was an essential employee, then the conviction should be avoided.

The absence of any definition of "impede" raises some interesting issues. The Supreme Court of Canada has held that picketing—no matter how peaceful—inevitably impedes access to the location being picketed. In affirming an injunction preventing any picketing at BC courthouses during a strike by the BC Government Employees' Union, the Supreme Court stated:

> [B]oth courts below have found that the picketing would inevitably have had the effect of impeding and restricting access to the courts. There surely can be little doubt as to the correctness of that conclusion. The very purpose and intent of the picket line in a labour dispute is to discourage and dissuade individuals from entering the premises which are being picketed.... One of the great strengths of the trade union movement is the spirit of solidarity. By standing together as a collective whole, trade unionists are able to aspire to improved wages and working conditions unattainable if each individual member were left to his or her own devices.... Picketing sends a strong and automatic signal: do not cross the line lest you undermine our struggle....
>
> A picket line both in intention and in effect, is a barrier.[292]

The Ontario Court of Appeal has recently concluded that, notwithstanding more recent Supreme Court of Canada decisions more sympathetic toward picketing,[293] the decision in *British Columbia Government Employees' Union v British Columbia (Attorney General)* is still valid law: a picket line automatically impedes.[294]

If all picket lines impede, then section 199 of the *FPSLRA*—on its face—prohibits traditional picketing at all workplaces where essential employees may attend work. I have used the term "traditional" picketing because the Supreme Court of Canada has also concluded that

292 *British Columbia Government Employees' Union v British Columbia (Attorney General)*, [1988] 2 SCR 214 at 230–31.

293 *Retail, Wholesale and Department Store Union, Local 558 v Pepsi-Cola Canada Beverages (West) Ltd*, 2002 SCC 8 [*RWDSU, Local 588*], and *United Food and Commercial Workers, Local 1518 (UFCW) v KMart Canada Ltd*, [1999] 2 SCR 1083 [*UFCW, Local 1518*].

294 *Ontario Public Service Employees Union v Ontario (Attorney General)* (2002), 58 OR (3d) 577 (CA).

"leafleting" is different from traditional picketing and does not impede access to a facility so long as the leafleting is not coercive or intimidating, does not involve a large number of people, and is not unduly disruptive to people trying to enter the location being leafleted.[295] Since essential employees are present in almost all government offices, section 199—on its face—constitutes an almost complete bar to picketing workplaces during strikes. This leads to the bizarre conclusion that secondary picketing is now the only lawful form of picketing permitted under the *FPSLRA*.[296]

Since the right to strike is preserved in the *FPSLRA*, and presuming that picketing is an inherent part of the right to strike,[297] a broad interpretation of "impede" would frustrate the preservation of that right. Therefore, it is likely that the definition of "impede" in the *FPSLRA* will be interpreted in a less restrictive manner to permit primary picketing at government workplaces. For example, in Ontario a judicial convention has been established sanctioning a ten-minute delay in the entry into government buildings that are being picketed.[298] However, there were exceptions to the ten-minute rule for essential services such as transporting inmates to and from prison, emergency services, and time-tested samples for testing at public health laboratories.[299] Therefore, if the Ontario example is followed, a picket line could exist at a government building without impeding essential services if essential employees and equipment are allowed entry into the building with no or minimal delay.

The *FPSLRA* prohibits employees occupying essential positions and non-employees from striking.[300] The employer is also entitled to discipline employees who occupy essential positions yet do not attend work or perform their duties during a strike, including imposing fines[301] or suspensions.[302] The employer may also discipline employees for other

---

295 *UFCW, Local 1518*, above note 293.

296 The Supreme Court of Canada has concluded that the common law bar on secondary picketing is unconstitutional; therefore, unions may lawfully engage in secondary picketing: *RWDSU, Local 588*, above note 293.

297 See, for example, *Potash Corp of Saskatchewan Mining v Todd*, [1987] SJ No 10 (CA), about the importance of picketing to the success of a strike.

298 Hadwen, above note 147 at 542–46.

299 *Ibid* at 546–49.

300 *FPSLRA*, s 196(j).

301 *Caron v Treasury Board*, [2000] CPSSRB No 55, aff'd *Caron v Canada (Treasury Board)*, [2001] FCJ No 1565.

302 *Justice and Treasury Board (Solicitor General Canada)*, [1984] CPSSRB No 101.

"illegal strike" activity—in other words, the employer is not limited to applying to the Board for relief under the Act and may, instead, discipline and even terminate employees for counselling or procuring an illegal work stoppage.[303]

Situations have arisen where employees occupying essential positions have applied for sick leave when their colleagues were on strike. The Board has been skeptical of medical notes provided in support of those applications unless the employees have informed their doctors that they work in an essential position.[304] This is consistent with the Board's more general proposition that the onus of proof shifts to the employee who missed work to demonstrate that they did so for medical reasons as opposed to acting as part of the strike.[305] The Supreme Court of Canada has commented on the onus of proof against an employee alleged to have engaged in an illegal strike as follows:

> If the prohibition is to be effective—and it must be assumed that the Act intends it to be—the only method is to reverse the burden of proof and impose on the accused the obligation of showing that he did not have the required intent and took reasonable steps to avoid committing the offence. This burden, on the other hand, will not weigh unduly on an accused who really has a defence; it should not be too difficult for him to prove, for example, that he had good reasons for not knowing there was a strike, that he had just been injured and could not go to work, or that he took all reasonable steps to go to work but was prevented from doing so by an unbreachable blockade: leaving aside the defence of impossibility, which the Court does not have to decide upon, such evidence could show that, although the accused refrained from providing his services, he did not do so with the intent of participating in the strike.[306]

The Board has the jurisdiction to enforce the prohibitions against illegal strikes, including the prohibition against picketing that "impedes" essential services. The Board also has the power to order the bargaining agent to revoke the declaration or authorization of the strike, requiring

---

303 *King v Deputy Head (Canada Border Services Agency)*, 2010 PSLRB 125, aff'd *King v Canada (Attorney General)*, 2013 FCA 131.

304 *Storey and Treasury Board (Department of Transport)*, [1983] CPSSRB No 7.

305 *Perry and Treasury Board (Employment and Immigration Canada)*, [1994] CPSSRB No 54.

306 *Strasser*, above note 290.

an employee from ceasing their participation in the strike and requiring an employee organization to give notice of the Board's notice.[307]

F. THE ARBITRATION ROUTE

1) Procedure Establishing an Arbitration Board

If the bargaining agent has elected the arbitration route for dispute resolution, then either party may request arbitration of any terms remaining in dispute after they have completed bargaining. They may make the request at any time prior to entering into a collective agreement, but not later than seven days after having entered into a collective agreement (containing the rest of the terms agreed upon).[308] The other party then has seven days to request adding additional issues for arbitration.[309] The request for arbitration is made to the chair of the Board, who must then establish an arbitration board.[310] The chair of the Board may delay establishing the arbitration board if they think that the party requesting arbitration has not bargained "sufficiently and seriously."[311]

An arbitration panel may comprise a single person or three people. If it comprises a single person, the parties must jointly recommend that arbitrator.[312] If it comprises a three-person panel, then the parties each choose a nominee, and the nominees choose the neutral chair of the panel.[313] The chair of the Board is also responsible for referring the "matters in dispute" to the arbitration board.[314] This means that the chair of the Board has the exclusive jurisdiction to determine what matters may be included in an arbitral award—that is, to determine the scope of issues that may be referred to arbitration. The arbitration panel itself does not have the jurisdiction to add or remove issues from consideration.[315]

---

307 *FPSLRA*, s 198(2).
308 *Ibid*, s 136(2).
309 *Ibid*, s 136(5).
310 *Ibid*, s 137(1).
311 *Ibid*, s 137(2).
312 *Ibid*, s 139.
313 *Ibid*, s 140.
314 *Ibid*, s 144(1).
315 *Public Service Alliance of Canada v National Capital Commission*, [1997] FCJ No 1418 at para 10.

The parties do not have unfettered discretion in choosing their nominee. Section 141 of the *FPSLRA* states:

> 141. No person may act as a member of an arbitration board in respect of a matter referred to arbitration if the person has, at any time during the six months before the person's date of appointment, acted in respect of any matter concerning employer-employee relations as counsel or agent of the employer or of any employee organization that has an interest in the matter referred to arbitration.

This reflects the normal view that nominees to an interest arbitration panel are not required to be completely unbiased but must not have a direct interest in the outcome. The Saskatchewan Court of Appeal has put the point thus:

> Customarily, the representative members of these boards of arbitration do not pretend to neutrality, not in any rigorous sense. The reality is that neither party nominates indifferent persons. They nominate persons who, at the very least, bear no institutional antipathy toward them. Further, they nominate persons who, by reason of their particular experience, are apt to be generally pre-disposed in their favour. Indeed they go even further, nominating persons who, to some extent, are expected to advocate their interests in a fair hearing and an acceptable outcome. Not only is this the reality, it appears unobjectionable in light of what the legislature intended in relation to the representative members. . . .
>
> As for the outermost limits, neither nominee may be so pre-disposed to a particular result, or so closed-minded in respect of particular issues, as to reduce the role of arbitrator to a sham. Thus persons with a direct or intense interest in the outcome—as, for example, the city manager and the president of the fire fighters association or their respective negotiators—are unable to serve as arbitrators. So are other employees of the city or other members of the association. That would not only offend the spirit of the statute and make a mockery of the oath, it would distort the mechanism adopted by the legislature for resolving collective bargaining impasses.[316]

---

316 *Yorkton Professional Fire Fighters Association, Local 1527 v Yorkton (City)*, [2001] SJ No 711 (CA) at paras 39 and 41.

2) Substance of Arbitration: Guidelines for Decisions

The *FPSLRA* requires arbitration boards to consider five factors, set out in section 148 as follows:

> 148. In the conduct of its proceedings and in making an arbitral award, the arbitration board must take into account the following factors, in addition to any other factors that it considers relevant:
> (a) the necessity of attracting competent persons to, and retaining them in, the public service in order to meet the needs of Canadians;
> (b) the necessity of offering compensation and other terms and conditions of employment in the public service that are comparable to those of employees in similar occupations in the private and public sectors, including any geographic, industrial or other variations that the arbitration board considers relevant;
> (c) the need to maintain appropriate relationships with respect to compensation and other terms and conditions of employment as between different classification levels within an occupation and as between occupations in the public service;
> (d) the need to establish compensation and other terms and conditions of employment that are fair and reasonable in relation to the qualifications required, the work performed, the responsibility assumed and the nature of the services rendered; and
> (e) the state of the Canadian economy and the Government of Canada's fiscal circumstances.[317]

One arbitration board tersely summarized section 148 as follows:

> Without restating the legislation word for word, the factors outlined in section 148 can be summarized under these headings: Recruitment and Retention, External Comparability, Internal Relativity, Fair and Reasonable Terms and Conditions of Employment and, finally, the Canadian Economy and Fiscal Considerations.[318]

Arbitrators under the *FPSLRA* (or, formerly, the Board itself) have not stated whether any of these factors has priority over the others. The Board in one case indicated that they were a helpful guideline only:

---

317 These are the same factors as for conciliation.

318 *Public Service Alliance of Canada v Social Sciences and Humanities Research Council*, [2008] CPSLRB No 253.

> It is obvious that they are couched in broad general terms. They are akin to isometric lines from an observance of which an informed forecast may be made by the Tribunal. Despite what might be considered by some as imprecisions, they do provide some terms of reference for the Arbitration Tribunal to observe.[319]

One more recent arbitration decision states that the statutory criteria do not limit the discretion of an arbitration panel to consider all relevant factors:

> Before considering the application of these criteria to the issues before us, it is important to observe that their application, as with the criteria found in other interest arbitration statutes, is not intended to cause a predetermined result. While requiring a board to put its mind to various factors that might be relevant to its ultimate determination, they do not abridge the broad discretion of an interest board of arbitration to consider and weigh all the relevant factors in any given case in coming to a freely determined result that is fair and reasonable in all the circumstances. The discretion given to an interest board of arbitration in this regard is fundamental to the functioning of an interest arbitration process that serves as an alternative to free collective bargaining under which the parties are able to resort to economic sanctions in the form of strike or lockout in support of their respective positions. Where the legislature, in its wisdom, decides that in the interest of the greater public good the right to free collective bargaining must be restricted to the extent that economic sanctions are not permitted, i.e. police, fire and health services, the alternative must be fair, impartial and transparent. This is why statutory criteria, as found in the various interest arbitration statutes, including the *Fire Protection and Prevention Act*, do not remove the ultimate discretion of a board of interest arbitration to make a fair and impartial award that takes into account all relevant considerations.[320]

FPSLRA arbitrations do not often contain detailed reasons behind their decisions, or, if they do, then they do not contain prolix

319 *Professional Institute of the Public Service of Canada v Canada (Treasury Board)*, [1973] CPSSRB No 6.

320 *Toronto (City) v Toronto Professional Fire Fighters Association, Local 3888*, 2013 CanLII 62276.

explanations of the principles applied.[321] Therefore, it is helpful to refer to arbitration decisions in the broader public sector to consider these factors, as well as discover other important principles in interest arbitration.

a) Replication Principle

The leading interest arbitration principle is "replication": "to replicate what conventional bargaining would have produced."[322] The job of an interest arbitrator is not to apply "an abstract notion of social justice"[323] but instead to replicate the result of collective bargaining. The term replication "refers to the objective of fashioning an award that, to the extent possible, replicates the settlement the parties would have reached had the dispute been allowed to run its full course."[324] Replication does not mean that the arbitrator should simply speculate as to how the issues would have played out in collective bargaining had the parties been able to exercise the right to strike: "the interest arbitrator is required to 'act adjudicatively' and base the final result on rational objective criteria."[325] Some of the objective factors that act as predictors of the results of free collective bargaining are as follows:

> (a) The terms and conditions of employment freely negotiated by other employers and unions in the same industry within the relevant community.

---

321 Arbitration boards are required to provide reasons for their decisions that "reflect" the factors in s 148 of the Act: *Canada (Attorney General) v Association of Justice Counsel*, 2011 FC 530 at para 81 [*Canada v Association of Justice Counsel*]. Some commentators have advocated that interest arbitration boards should provide more prolix and detailed reasons for their decisions, explaining how they consider each statutory factor: see, for example, Richard P. Chaykowski, *Time to Tweak or Re-boot? Assessing the Interest Arbitration Process in Canadian Industrial Relations* (4 April 2019), C.D. Howe Institute, Commentary No 539, online (pdf): www.cdhowe.org/sites/default/files/2021-11/Commentary_539.pdf.

322 *Construction Labour Relations Assn of British Columbia v Operative Plasterers' and Cement Masons' International Assn, Local 919*, [2006] BCCA No 11 at para 7 [*Construction Labour Relations Assn of British Columbia*].

323 *Vernon (City) v CUPE, Local 626*, [2004] BCCA No 17 at para 8.

324 *Air Canada v CAW-Canada, Local 2002*, [2011] CLAD No 362 (Burkett) at para 66 [*Air Canada v CAW-Canada*].

325 *Ibid* at para 12.

(b) The terms and conditions of employment freely negotiated by other employers and unions generally within the relevant community.
(c) The terms and conditions of employment contained in the expired collective agreement.
(d) The bargaining history between the parties.
(e) The economic situation in which each party finds itself.[326]

These predictors obviously include some of the factors explicitly listed in the *FPSLRA*, including the "comparability" principle (found in factors (b) and (c)[327] in the *FPSLRA*) and the "economic position" principle (found in factor (e) in the *FPSLRA*). Therefore, in a very real sense, the other principles discussed below are subsumed within the fundamental guiding principle of replication.

b) Conservatism or Gradualism Principle

Another feature or principle of interest arbitration is that it is an inherently conservative exercise: "as a general rule, neither party should look for a major breakthrough from a third party neutral; that is reserved for negotiations."[328] Often this conservative approach by interest arbitrators has been criticized. One arbitrator noted that

> [w]here, as in some parts of the public sector, interest arbitration is always the means of settling the collective agreement, this conservative approach, can, if carried too far, stifle desirable development and renewal in collectively bargained relationships. In those contexts replication may have to be largely submerged in reasonableness.[329]

Instead, interest arbitrators prefer a gradual approach that "reflects the reality that collective bargaining between mature bargaining parties, as these are, is a continuum that most often accomplishes gradual change as distinct from drastic change."[330] Therefore, absent some

---

326 *Ibid* at para 14, citing *Westmin Resources Ltd and CAW-Canada, Local 3019*, [1994] BCCAAA No 302.

327 One arbitrator in another jurisdiction has suggested that the statutory requirement to consider "internal comparators" (e.g., section 148(c) of the *FPSLRA*) is just a codification of the replication theory: *Kentville (Town) v Kentville Police Association, Local 107 of the Atlantic Police Assn*, [2017] NSLAA No 2 at para 58.

328 *Construction Labour Relations Assn of British Columbia*, above note 322 at para 8.

329 *Northumberland Ferries Ltd v Canadian Merchant Service Guild*, [2004] CLAD No 75 at para 34.

330 *Air Canada v CAW-Canada*, above note 324 at para 67.

strong evidence showing a demonstrated need for change, interest arbitral awards favour incremental changes over more drastic ones. Interest arbitrators can award a "breakthrough" item, but only when a party convincingly establishes the need for such a change—arbitrators refer to this as a "demonstrated need."[331]

Since the *FPSLRA* gives bargaining agents the choice between arbitration and conciliation/strike to resolve bargaining disputes, this criticism is less warranted in the federal public service: if arbitration is stifling development, then the bargaining agent can simply opt for conciliation and go on strike.

c) Necessity Principle (Statutory Factors (a) and (b))

The first two statutory factors in the *FPSLRA* concern attracting and retaining competent public servants and maintaining comparability between public sector and private sector wages. The Board has recently examined those two statutory factors and determined that they are part of a principle of "necessity." The Board stated:

> The primary element of s.148 (a) and (b) of the new Act seems to be the concept of necessity, in operational terms. S.148 (a) refers broadly to the issue of recruitment and retention. S.148 (b) speaks more narrowly to the market conditions of compensation and terms and conditions packages with regard to comparable employees to any given group in the public service. This board reads both of these subsections (refined from the more ambiguous language utilized in s.67 (a) and (b) of the old Public Service Staff Relations Act) as directing a board of arbitration to consider whether the public service is able to attract and retain competent persons. In other words, the central issue is whether the public service is experiencing recruitment and retention difficulties. Therefore, this board is not persuaded by the Local's contention that s.148 (b) stands quite apart from s.148 (a) and is "about equities and fairness; ensuring that the public sector is not looked upon as 'cheap labour' vis-à-vis the private sector." Rather, in light of all five considerations set down for a board of arbitration by s.148, in the absence of demonstrated necessity, in operational terms, what is warranted are

331 *Ibid.*

> economic increases in line with those that now prevail, over the course of the relevant three years, in most of the public service.[332]

The Federal Court agreed that the Board's decision was reasonable, stating:

> In my view, it was reasonably open to the Board to interpret subsections 148(a) and (b) as encompassing the concept of operational necessity with the broader inquiry under subsection 148(a) being directed at recruitment and retention and the more narrow inquiry under subsection 148(b) at market conditions in relation to terms and conditions of employment.
>
> . . . [S]ubsection 148(a) is directed at the goal of ensuring that competent people are attracted to and will remain in the public service. Where there are difficulties in the area of recruitment and retention, subsection 148(b) requires a board to consider the necessity of offering terms and conditions of employment in the public sector that are comparable to those of employees in similar occupations to overcome the difficulties and to address the goal articulated in subsection 148(a).[333]

The Board's decision (affirmed by the Federal Court) is inconsistent with its own previous jurisprudence and interest arbitration decisions in the rest of the public sector concerning the relevance of private sector wage rates and other terms when determining the appropriate wages and terms in the public sector. As discussed more thoroughly below, public sector wages are supposed to be comparable to those in the private sector—as expressly stated by the *FPSLRA* in section 148(b).

The *FPSLRA* refers to the "necessity" of maintaining comparability between the public and the private sector in section 148(b). In *Canadian Air Traffic Control Assn (CATCA CAW Local 5454) v Treasury Board*, just quoted, the Board refused to apply comparability between the public and the private sector unless the bargaining agent could demonstrate that such comparability was "necessary" to ensure that the public service did not have recruitment and retention difficulties. This interpretation of section 148(b) is not compelling. Rather, the term "necessity" in section 148(b) means that the *FPSLRA* deems it necessary to maintain comparability between the public and private sectors. An arbitration

332 *Canadian Air Traffic Control Assn (CATCA CAW Local 5454) v Treasury Board*, [2005] CPSLRB No 109, aff'd on judicial review [2006] FCJ No 1470.

333 *Ibid* at paras 24–25.

board is not required to examine whether comparability between the public and the private sector is necessary: the *FPSLRA* deems it necessary. The only question is *how* to achieve comparability, not *whether* comparability is necessary.

Similarly, section 148(a) refers to the "necessity of attracting competent persons to, and retaining them in, the public service." The wording of section 148(a) is also clear that recruitment and retention of competent people are necessary: the issue for the arbitration board is then whether there needs to be a wage increase or other adjustment of the terms and conditions of employment to ensure that this "necessity" is met. Interest arbitrators often examine objective evidence to determine whether the employer is having a retention or recruitment problem and will increase wages (or offer retention or recruitment bonuses) to meet that problem. If, however, there is no evidence of a retention or recruitment problem, then this is a factor indicating that wage increases or bonuses may not be necessary.[334]

d) Comparability Principle (Statutory Factors (b) and (c))

The second factor also relates to the principle of comparability: pay should be comparable to the private sector and the broader public sector. The third factor relates to another aspect of the comparability principle, that pay should be comparable to other similarly situated positions within the federal public service. These two aspects of comparability are sometimes referred to as external and internal comparability, respectively. The Board has affirmed that where pay rates are "out of line" with the private sector, it will increase or decrease those pay rates to something more comparable, stating in one case:

> The Board agrees with the employer that pay comparability is not the only factor relevant to the establishment of rates of pay for this bargaining unit, and it has not relied on it to the exclusion of other factors. However, where, as here, the evidence indicates unequivocally that bargaining unit rates of pay are significantly out of line with

---

334 See, for example, *Peel Halton Acquired Brain Injury Services and OPSEU, Loc 587* (2005), 144 LAC (4th) 398, where the arbitrator reviewed the evidence and concluded that there was a recruitment and retention problem, and consequently that "wage increases that are normative relative to the broader social service and health care sectors are critical to the recruitment and retention of qualified and committed staff" (at para 21).

> outside sector rates, the Board feels obliged to move in the direction of eliminating or reducing the disparity.[335]

Arbitration boards are also concerned about internal comparability. In a 2005 arbitration decision concerning employees of the Social Sciences and Humanities Research Council (SSHRC), the Board emphasized internal comparability.[336] In that case, unionized employees of that employer worked side by side with non-unionized employees of the Natural Sciences and Engineering Research Council. Those two employers jointly prepared a new classification plan to comply with their pay equity obligations under the *Canadian Human Rights Act*, and the non-unionized employer implemented that plan, including higher maximum and minimum rates of pay for employees. The unionized employer, however, refused to implement those higher rates of pay. The Board awarded the higher rates of pay in arbitration, applying the principle of comparability, stating:

> An interest board under the Public Service Staff Relations Act has to respond to the evidence of appropriate comparator groups, at least where that evidence is compelling. It is difficult to imagine a more compelling case of "comparability" than the present one. The employees of SSHRC and the employees of NSERC perform similar jobs, under a common administration, with a history of exact parity on wage rates. In the Common Directorate many of the employees notionally employed by one or the other of the Councils in fact perform the same duties. Simply put, when NSERC decided to move ahead and establish the rates under the new Classification Plan for its own employees, the die was cast for the SSHRC employees.[337]

Concerning comparability, other decisions of public sector arbitrators commonly rely on information about occupations performing the same or similar work. Arbitrator Mitchnick emphasized the importance of internal comparability in a decision in the Ontario university sector:

---

335 *Public Service Alliance of Canada and Treasury Board (Financial Administration Group—Administrative and Foreign Service Category)*, [1986] CPSSRB No 74 at para 46.

336 *Public Service Alliance of Canada v Canada (Social Sciences and Humanities Research Council)*, [2005] CPSSRB No 8.

337 *Ibid* at para 5.

> The first, and principal one, is the question raised by the Association of private sector comparability (not in terms of level of increases, but in absolute terms). Arbitrators, no less than the parties in this sector, have long accepted the primacy of maintaining relative parity within the University sector in the determination of appropriate compensation levels.[338]

Along a similar vein, the Board rejected an attempt to create a bargaining unit for lawyers in Ontario (outside of Ottawa) where the main motivation behind the creation of such a unit was to allow Toronto-based lawyers to earn more money than their national counterparts.[339] The Board held that regionally based market forces do not justify creating a separate bargaining unit. While it should be noted that there are regional rates of pay for lawyers employed by the Department of Justice, the Board's decision still indicates a reluctance to treat employees differently simply because of their location.

e) Economic Factors (Statutory Factor (e))

There is some dispute concerning how economic or financial considerations should impact interest arbitration in the public sector. The use of "ability to pay" as a factor in public sector interest arbitration is a matter of considerable controversy. The federal government has the power to determine its own ability to pay through its ability to increase taxes, borrow, or alter its spending priorities. By limiting grants or transfer payments, the government (or, more accurately, the Treasury Board) may also control the ability to pay of publicly funded institutions. Where the federal government (or Treasury Board) is the direct employer, it may set its budget to leave only a limited amount, if any at all, available for wage or benefit improvements. At the end of the day, this unilateral authority may infringe on the public sector employee's right to fair and reasonable remuneration.

Interest arbitrators traditionally have refused to consider "ability to pay" as a relevant criterion in the public sector. Arbitrator Christie has stated:

---

338 *Queens University Faculty Association and Queens University*, [2000] OLAA No 395 (Mitchnick). See also *McMaster University and McMaster University Faculty Association* (1990), 13 LAC (4th) 199 (Shime), and *Winnipeg Police Services Board and the Winnipeg Police Association*, [2002] MGAD No 3.

339 *Federal Law Officers of the Crown v Treasury Board*, [2006] CPSSRB No 40 at para 121.

> Interest arbitrators in the Canadian public sector have, apparently, universally rejected the legitimacy of an "ability to pay" argument. They have not allowed governments as employers to hide behind their own skirts in their role as the source of funds, to escape pay increases indicated by the other criteria. This has been so even where, as in the Ontario hospital sector, the employing body and the funding body are legally and formally different.[340]

Arbitrator Teplitsky has also voiced a similar reluctance to accept "ability to pay" as a principle of interest arbitration, stating that "[t]he reality is that it is not a question of ability to pay. It is a question of unwillingness to pay.... [I]t has long been recognized that public sector employees do not have to subsidize the community by accepting sub-standard wages and benefits.[341] Other arbitrators have been concerned that "ability to pay" robs them of their independence.[342]

In response to these views, the Government of Ontario has explicitly required arbitrators to consider the government's "ability to pay" in rendering interest arbitral awards in certain public sectors.[343] Those statutes contain separate provisions requiring arbitrators to consider both "ability to pay" and the "economic situation."[344] Thus, the reference to the state of the Canadian economy in section 148(e) of the *FPSLRA* is not an invitation for the arbitration boards to consider "ability to pay" as a relevant criterion for an interest arbitral award. However—perhaps influenced by those statutory changes in Ontario—some arbitrators have been willing to consider "ability to pay" in a limited fashion.[345]

Section 148(e) is a new addition to the *FPSLRA*,[346] so arbitration boards now must consider general economic conditions and the state of the Government of Canada's fiscal condition in determining their awards. However, even where "ability to pay" is relevant, arbitrators

340 *University of Toronto*, unreported, 13 February 1981 (Christie) at 8.

341 M. Teplitsky, Speech to the Ontario Bar Association—Ontario Labour Law Section (30 January 1996) [unpublished].

342 *Newfoundland (Treasury Board) and NAPE* (1995), 52 LAC (4th) 250.

343 See, for example, *Ambulance Services Collective Bargaining Act*, SO 2001 c 10, s 21(2); *Fire Protection and Prevention Act*, SO 1997, c 4, s 50.5(2).

344 *Ibid.*

345 See, for example, *Yarmouth (Town) v Yarmouth Fire Fighters' Assn*, [2003] NSLAA No 7 at para 36.

346 The *PSSRA* did not contain any factor concerning economic conditions.

do not blithely accept that difficulties in government finance justify lower-than-normal wage rates. Instead, arbitrators have stated that the test is what a fair-minded, well-informed taxpayer would accept:

> The test, then, is the arbitration board's view of what a majority of fair-minded, well-informed taxpayers would consider to be a fair and reasonable award, even if it meant tax increases. The greater the tax increase required to support the arbitration award, the more confident the Board must be that that award is a reasonable and credible one, one that a majority of fair-minded, well-informed taxpayers would see as reasonable and fair. This squares precisely with another of the new criteria, "the extent to which services may have to be reduced, if the current funding levels are not increased." If services are to be reduced, then that is an operational and political decision which the employer, not the arbitration board, must make. On the other hand, the greater the probability of that happening, the greater the onus on the arbitration board to be confident that its award is a fair and reasonable one, one that would be understood and supported by a majority of the informed, fair-minded public.[347]

Put another way,

> While a Government has considerable scope in the political choices it can make in determining what to fund and to what extent it will be funded, it must be seen to exercise those choices responsibility, fairly and on the basis of some rationally based criteria. One must not accept the Employer's "ability to pay" argument without careful scrutiny, but it is a factor which, like the other factors, must be considered and given the appropriate weight in the circumstances.[348]

The wording of section 148(e) of the *FPSLRA* permits both sides to rely on the reality of the general financial situation rather than relying merely on a surface review of the employer's fiscal situation.

---

347 *Niagara (Regional Municipality) Police Services Board and Niagara Police Association* (1997), 78 LAC (4th) 42 at 58–59.

348 *Yarmouth (Town) v Yarmouth Fire Fighters' Assn*, [2003] NSLAA No 7 at para 36.

3) Is the Arbitration Process Fundamentally Flawed? The Corrosive and Narcotic Effect of Interest Arbitration

A number of people have argued that the arbitration process is antithetical to free collective bargaining. Those commentators usually criticize the "corrosive and narcotic" effect on bargaining: corrosive in that it decreases the number of real collectively bargained settlements, and narcotic in that it is addictive or habit forming. Joseph Rose, for one, has engaged in an extensive review of interest arbitration in the Ontario public sector and has concluded that interest arbitration has had a "corrosive and narcotic effect" on bargaining: the settlement rate for employees without binding arbitration was 95 percent between 1980 and 1992 versus only 60 percent during the same period for employees with binding arbitration.[349]

While interest arbitration may have a corrosive and narcotic effect in some sectors, it does not appear to have the same effect in the federal public service—or at least has not had a narcotic effect.[350] At the outset of collective bargaining in the federal public service, most bargaining units opted for arbitration.[351] However, as time has gone on, most bargaining units have opted for the conciliation route. By the mid-1980s, "the arbitration route was largely the domain of professionals, who found the possibility of a strike abhorrent or ineffective, or of groups who had almost all members classified as essential."[352] Even the Association of Canadian Financial Officers (the bargaining agent representing accountants in the federal public service) elected the conciliation/strike route for its 2006 collective bargaining round.

There may be many explanations for this, including dissatisfaction with arbitration results, concerns about the narrow scope of issues that

---

349 Joseph Rose, "The Leech, the Tortoise and the Owl: The World of Interest Arbitration in Ontario" (1994–95) Labour Arbitration Yearkbook 387 at 393.

350 This is not to say that arbitration has not had a corrosive or narcotic effect in the past or in particular bargaining units. In *Treasury Board and Economics, Sociologists and Statisticians Association—Scientific and Professional Category*, [1984] CPSSRB No 215, the Board expressed concern that in all seven bargaining rounds since the bargaining agent had been certified, the bargaining disputes were resolved by interest arbitration. The Board therefore decided to exercise "considerable restraint in amending existing terms and conditions of employment for this bargaining unit" in an effort to get the parties to negotiate changes to the collective agreement rather than rely on arbitration to resolve their differences.

351 With the notable exception of bargaining units represented by postal unions.

352 Swimmer, above note 23 at 180.

may be referred to binding arbitration, or that bargaining agents were "weaned" off arbitration by the statutory freeze on arbitration from 1992 to 2001. Whatever the reason, arbitration in the federal public service appears not to have had the same corrosive or narcotic effect as in other public sectors.

4) Duration of an Arbitral Award

The *FPSLRA* provides that an arbitral award may not be for a term of less than one year or more than two years from the day on which it becomes binding on the parties unless the arbitration board decides otherwise based on the terms of previous collective agreements or other relevant collective agreements.[353] The arbitration board's ability to depart from the one- to two-year period is only adopted when there is an "exceptional situation that would justify a term of less than one year."[354] The purpose behind the minimum one-year rule is to ensure that the collective agreement does not expire shortly after the issuance of the award, so the parties have the chance to see how the new collective agreement works before immediately returning to bargaining.[355] Arbitration panels will, however, exercise their jurisdiction to line up the terms of the collective agreement with the "bargaining cycles" of collective agreements elsewhere in the public service where previous collective agreements have lined up with those cycles. In *Canadian Federal Pilots Association and Treasury Board*, this meant that the arbitration panel ordered an arbitral award lasting from 2015 to 2023 inclusive because complying with the timelines in section 156(3) of the Act "would therefore place the collective agreement behind the current bargaining cycle and necessitate the immediate start of collective bargaining for these parties."[356] Arbitral panels will also move outside the time periods in section 156(3) of the Act when both parties agree and

353 *FPSLRA*, s 156(3).

354 *Research Council Employees' Association and National Research Council of Canada*, PSLRB 585-09-60 (3 June 2014) at para 59.

355 *Ibid* at para 59. See also *PIPSC v National Energy Board*, PSLRB File No 585-26-21 (2008).

356 *Arbitral Award (Canadian Federal Pilots Association and Treasury Board)*, 2019 CanLII 129003 at para 31.

the agreed duration corresponds with the usual "bargaining cycle" in the public service.[357]

The *FPSLRA* also states that an employer must implement an arbitral award within ninety days after the award is issued unless the arbitral panel orders otherwise. The arbitration board has no jurisdiction to extend this period—but the Board may do so. An arbitration board may order that certain provisions in its award come into force more than ninety days after the award itself is issued—for example, an arbitration board ordered that new overtime provisions came into force 120 days from the date of the award.[358]

G. CONSULTATION AND CO-DEVELOPMENT

Among its other proposed reforms, the Final Fryer Report recommended that the federal public service begin a process whereby some subjects would be the subject of consultation or co-development. The Final Fryer Report discussed consultation and co-development as follows:

> Union-management consultation should be a regular aspect of the development of policies and practices in all workplaces and departments across the public service. Consultation has to be real. It has to be done before the fact, before ideas are set in individuals' minds, before implementation plans are started, even before some of the inevitable trade-offs are fully identified. Both parties need to feel that they are truly part of the planning, that they are partners in developing options and in analyzing the situation, assessing advantages and disadvantages and recommending specific actions.
>
> . . .
>
> In the public service to date, a form of co-development has been largely the creation of the National Joint Council. We believe that now is the time to formalize this process of co-development and, at the same time, extend it to such important employment related matters as the classification and staffing systems within government. Co-development involves both parties undertaking research and presenting background information to feed into the process of developing policies. It involves real give and take, with neither party expecting to achieve

357 *Public Service Alliance of Canada v Statistical Survey Operations*, 2019 CanLII 14632 at para 24.

358 *Canada v Association of Justice Counsel*, above note 321 at para 99.

> all its goals on the subject. It is a process that helps to build trust and that relies on trust to be effective. It can play a major role in ensuring that employees' voices and their preferences are heard and reflected in internal government policies. At the service-wide level, co-development has already resulted in such major achievements as the creation of the Public Service Health Care Plan Trust and the modernization of the National Joint Council mandate and its by-laws. It is an important building block in the framework for improved labour management relations in the public service.[359]

The Final Fryer Report recommended that staffing, classification, pensions, and other subjects that cannot be collectively bargained should be subject to co-development and that any disputes about this co-development should be resolved through the National Joint Council.

The *FPSLRA* adopted these recommendations in part. Section 8 of the *FPSLRA* requires each deputy head (either the deputy minister of a department or the chief executive officer or equivalent of a government agency) to establish a consultation committee composed of management and bargaining agent representatives. This consultation committee must discuss "issues relating to the workplace." Although the *FPSLRA* does not define "issues relating to the workplace," it gives two examples: harassment and whistle-blowing.[360] The *FPSLRA* also permits the employer and a bargaining agent, or a deputy head and a bargaining agent, to engage in co-development of "workplace improvements"[361]—defined as consultation on workplace issues—with a view to adopting mutually agreed upon solutions.[362] This co-development may take place under the auspices of the National Joint Council.[363] In practice, almost all departments and agencies have set up labour–management consultation committees with its bargaining agents.

---

359 Final Fryer Report, above note 158.

360 *FPSLRA*, s 8.

361 *Ibid*, s 10.

362 *Ibid*, s 9.

363 *Ibid*, s 11.

CHAPTER SEVEN

Complaints Against Employers

A. INTRODUCTION

This chapter is about complaints against the employer brought pursuant to section 190 of the *Federal Public Sector Labour Relations Act* (*FPSLRA*). Section 190 requires the Board to examine and inquire into any complaint made to it that the employer has failed to bargain in good faith, failed to observe certain terms and conditions during a statutory freeze, committed an unfair labour practice, or failed to implement a collective agreement or an arbitral award. As the requirements of the duty to bargain in good faith have already been addressed in detail,[1] this chapter will focus on the other three requirements a breach of which may result in a complaint under section 190 of the *FPSLRA*.

B. STATUTORY FREEZE

A statutory freeze refers to provisions of the *FPSLRA* (like other labour relations statutes) that continue the terms and conditions of employment applicable to employees in the bargaining unit that is subject to the statutory freeze. There are four freeze periods under the *FPSLRA*:

1) **During certification.** The statutory freeze is in place from the date the employer is notified of an application for certification until the application is withdrawn, or thirty days from the date on which the

1 See Chapter 6.

Board certifies an employee organization as the bargaining agent for the unit.[2]

2) **During bargaining.** The statutory freeze is in place after notice to bargain is given (by either party) until a collective agreement is entered into, or an arbitral award is rendered, or a legal strike can be declared or authorized.[3]
3) **When the bargaining agent is in a legal strike position, for essential services employees only.** The statutory freeze for essential services employees in place during a strike lasts until a collective agreement is entered into.[4]
4) **After a conversion** (i.e., the creation of a new separate agency). If a bargaining agent had served notice to bargain prior to the conversion, then the second statutory freeze remains in effect for at least 150 days.[5]

The fourth freeze may not be a complete freeze. Section 88 of the *FPSLRA* continues the statutory freeze for 150 days or, if an application to change the bargaining units or bargaining agents is made, until the date the Board completes that application. Section 87 of the *FPSLRA* states that a notice to bargain that was given prior to the conversion does not bind the new separate agency and that "a new notice may be given only in the circumstances described in paragraph 89(b)." Paragraph 89(b) only applies "if the Board makes by determination under paragraph (a)" that new bargaining units are necessary. Therefore, if neither the employer nor the bargaining agent makes an application for new bargaining units, section 87 of the *FPSLRA* could be read as preventing the bargaining agent from filing a new notice to bargain, thus also preventing it from triggering a new freeze period. The better view is that section 105(2)—giving the bargaining agent the right to file a notice to bargain when no collective agreement is in effect—applies from 150 days after the conversion (if no successor rights application has been filed), therefore permitting the bargaining agent to serve a new notice to bargain and restart the statutory freeze period. However, section 87 could actually be a way to force bargaining agents to file successor rights applications to ensure that they have the right to serve

2 *FPSLRA*, SC 2003, c 22, s 2, s 56.
3 *Ibid*, s 107.
4 *Ibid*, s 132.
5 *Ibid*, s 88.

a new notice to bargain at the end of such applications. The Board has not yet been faced with such a problem because the new employer has always brought a successor rights application after a conversion in order to consolidate bargaining units.

The statutory freeze in the *FPSLRA* is similar to the various statutory freezes that exist in private sector labour relations legislation.

The wording of the first statutory freeze is different from the last three because there is no collective agreement in force. The first statutory freeze continues the "terms and conditions of employment that are applicable to the employees in the proposed bargaining unit."[6] The last three statutory freezes apply to "each term and condition of employment applicable to the employees in the bargaining unit to which the notice relates *that may be included in a collective agreement* and that is *in force* on the day the notice is given."[7]

The two main statutory freezes—the freeze during certification and the freeze during bargaining—serve somewhat different purposes. The statutory freeze during certification was added in the 2005 legislative overhaul, whereas the freeze during bargaining has been in place since the inception of collective bargaining in the public service in 1967.

The purpose behind the second statutory freeze during bargaining is to provide a stable platform for collective bargaining. As the Board has explained, the purpose is to

> maintain the status quo of the employer relationship so that the union is given an opportunity to enter negotiations and bargain for a collective agreement from a fixed point of departure and in an atmosphere of industrial relations security that is undisturbed by alterations in conditions of employment.[8]

This statutory freeze is therefore "designed to promote orderly and fair collective bargaining [because] [t]here must be some firm and stable reference from which bargaining can proceed."[9]

---

6 *Ibid*, s 56.

7 *Ibid*, ss 107 and 132 [emphasis added].

8 *Federal Government Dockyard Chargehands Association v Treasury Board (Department of National Defence)*, 2016 PSLREB 26 at para 47 [*Dockyard Chargehands*], citing *Canadian Union of Public Employees v Scarborough Centenary Hospital Association*, [1978] OLRB Rep July 679.

9 *The Queen in Right of Canada as Represented by the Treasury Board v Canadian Air Traffic Control Association*, [1982] 2 FC 80 (CA) at para 24 [*CATCA*]. See also *PSAC v Canada (Treasury Board)*, [1987] FCJ No 240 (CA) at 8, and

The purpose behind the first statutory freeze during certification is slightly different. As the Board has put it:

> The post-application-for-certification freeze is also meant to keep a fixed point of departure in place for collective bargaining, but first and foremost, its purpose is to foster the exercise of the right of association, to facilitate the certification itself. It limits employer influence and eases the concerns of employees who actively exercise their rights by limiting the employer's power to manage during a critical period.[10]

While the two statutory freezes are applied virtually identically, one difference between the two is that the employer may apply to the Board for consent to change a term or condition of employment during a certification freeze.[11] In the only decision in which the Board had to rule on this issue, it declined to grant consent for the portion of the employer's request that was opposed by the employee organization seeking certification and implied that consent of the employee organization is a necessary condition for the Board to consent to a change to a term or condition of employment—or, at the very least, that the employee organization expresses no interest in negotiating the term or condition when it is certified.[12]

1) Stage One of the Statutory Freeze Analysis

In deciding statutory freeze cases, the Board conducts a two-stage analysis. The first stage is whether the bargaining agent or employee organization has met its burden to demonstrate four things:

1) that a notice to bargain or application for certification was filed;
2) that the employer changed a term or condition of employment that was in force the day notice to bargain or the application for certification was filed (i.e., that the change took place during the "freeze period");

Professional Institute of the Public Service of Canada v Canada (Treasury Board), [2005] CPSLRB No 31, aff'd [2006] FCJ No 806 (CA).

10 *National Police Federation v Treasury Board*, 2020 FPSLREB 44 at para 44, aff'd *Canada (Attorney General) v National Police Federation*, 2022 FCA 80 [*National Police Federation*].

11 *FPSLRA*, s 56.

12 *Canadian Union of Public Employees v Treasury Board (Royal Canadian Mounted Police)*, 2018 FPSLREB 3.

3) that the term or condition might have been included in a collective agreement; and
4) that the Board (in the case of a precertification freeze) or bargaining agent (in the case of a bargaining freeze) did not consent to the change.[13]

In considering the third element, in early cases there was some dispute concerning the scope of topics that could be subject to the statutory freeze—namely, whether the term had to be in a collective agreement and that the collective agreement be legally enforceable. The Federal Court of Appeal settled this dispute in two cases, which concluded as follows:

- The term "may be included" means that the term or condition of employment is capable of being included in a collective agreement, not necessarily a term that is already in the collective agreement.[14]

---

13 *Public Service Alliance of Canada v Canada Revenue Agency*, 2019 FPSLREB 110 at 137 [*Sudbury Taxation Centre*].

14 *CATCA*, above note 9. In that case, the Canadian Air Traffic Control Association alleged that the Treasury Board violated the statutory freeze when it implemented a compulsory overtime policy, in place of a voluntary overtime policy, after notice to bargain had been served. The Board upheld the complaint, and the Federal Court of Appeal concurred. The employer argued that its voluntary overtime policy was just a policy and that the collective agreement only set some maximum overtime limits and required the employer to endeavour to keep overtime work to a minimum. Therefore, the collective agreement's silence meant that the employer retained the power to implement voluntary or compulsory overtime policies as it saw fit. The Federal Court of Appeal disagreed, stating:

> I take it that the words "may be embodied" as they appear in section 51 [now "may be included" in section 107] mean that the term or condition of employment is "capable of being embodied" in the agreement. There is equally no question, as I see it, that the policy, so long as it subsisted, constituted, or resulted in, a term or condition of employment....
>
> I am, moreover, unable to adopt the narrow view that the words "in force" in the context of the wording of section 51 mean "enforceable in law." They mean, in my opinion, "in place," "existing," "operating" or some word or words of similar import.... While [the overtime policy] might not have been a right or privilege which could have been enforced as part of the collective agreement it certainly was one which existed or, in the words of the section, was "in force" when the freeze imposed by section 51 came into play.

See also *Public Service Alliance of Canada v Treasury Board (Correctional Service of Canada)*, 2017 FPSLREB 11 at para 102: "I do not find that there is

To put this another way, the statutory freeze protects a "privilege"[15] as well as a term or condition already contained in a collective agreement.

- The terms capable of being included are not limited to those terms capable of being arbitrated but include all terms capable of being negotiated into a collective agreement. Thus, terms that impact management's rights under section 7 of the *FPSLRA* are still subject to the statutory freeze.[16]

---

any difference in the way labour boards determine freeze complaints depending on whether the term or condition of employment involved is found in a collective agreement or may be included in one but was not when notice to bargain was given" [*PSAC v Treasury Board (CSC)*]; aff'd *Canada (Attorney General) v Public Service Alliance of Canada*, 2019 FCA 41 [*Canada (Attorney General) v PSAC*].

15 *Dockyards Chargehands*, above note 8 at para 49. See also *Canadian Association of Professional Employees v Treasury Board (Department of Public Works and Government Services)*, 2016 PSLREB 68 at para 134 (a practice of giving parliamentary translators the choice of working days during an intersessional period was protected by the freeze) [*CAPE v Treasury Board*]; *Public Service Alliance of Canada v Treasury Board*, 2016 PSLREB 107 at paras 21 and 25; and *Public Service Alliance of Canada v Canada Revenue Agency*, 2017 FPSLREB 16 (a practice of permitting compressed work schedules) [*PSAC v CRA*]. See, however, *Canadian Federal Pilots Association v Department of Transport, Transportation Safety Board, and Treasury Board Secretariat*, 2018 FPSLREB 91 at para 338 [*Canadian Federal Pilots*] (aff'd *Canadian Federal Pilots Association v Canada (Attorney General)*, 2020 FCA 52), where the Board stated, in *obiter*, that the statutory freeze in the *FPSLRA* did not protect "privileges" but only terms and conditions of employment. That Board decision is an outlier and has not been followed, nor should it be. It is also contradicted by that same Board member's earlier decision that "[t]he jurisprudence establishes that a term or condition of employment referred to in section 107 can take the form of an agreement or unilateral exercise of management authority": *Public Service Alliance of Canada v Treasury Board (Canada Border Services Agency)*, 2013 PSLRB 46 at para 186 [*PSAC v Treasury Board (CBSA)*].

16 *PSAC v Canada (Treasury Board)*, above note 9. In that case, the collective agreement in place at the time that the notice to bargain was served contained a cap on teaching hours. The employer refused to negotiate an extension of that term into the new collective agreement, and as the bargaining agent elected arbitration as its dispute-resolution mechanism, the new collective agreement would not contain a provision placing a cap on teaching hours because such a cap would be a limitation on management rights preserved in section 7 of the *FPSLRA*. However, the Federal Court of Appeal concluded that this limitation on management rights would continue during the statutory freeze period because the employer was free to negotiate limitations on its management rights. The cap on hours was capable of being embodied in a collective agreement and was therefore subject to the statutory freeze. In *Professional Institute of the Public Service of Canada v*

- The term "in force" means in place or existing, not "enforceable in law."[17]

The Board has more recently confirmed that the existence of a statutory right to establish terms and conditions of employment (in that case, the right to modify hours of work in the *Financial Administration Act*[18]) does not limit the statutory freeze. The Board pointed out in that case that if a statutory authority could make a term or condition of employment that overrode the freeze, "there could never be a violation of the freeze provided for under the Act by virtue of the very existence of the employer's residual powers."[19] The Board has applied the same logic to the preservation of management rights in section 7 of the *FPSLRA*, concluding that section 7 does not override the statutory freeze or constitute an exception to the statutory freeze.[20]

The terms or conditions of employment do not need to apply to the entire bargaining unit or even a substantial size of the bargaining unit. The statutory freeze applies to terms and conditions that "may apply to a small group of employees in the bargaining unit."[21]

If the employer commits a breach of an expired collective agreement during the freeze period, then that breach may be referred to adjudication instead of the Board by way of a complaint.[22] This is undoubtedly necessary in light of the lengthy period during which collective agreements are negotiated in the federal public service. The sad fact is that most collective agreements expire shortly after they are ratified and signed so

---

National Research Council of Canada, 2014 PSLRB 57 at para 62, the employer argued that changes to the legislation in 2005 meant that this 1987 Federal Court of Appeal decision was no longer good law, but the Board rejected that argument. See also *Library of Parliament v Canadian Association of Professional Employees*, 2013 FCA 237 at paras 28–32, where the Federal Court of Appeal rejected the employer's argument under the similarly worded *Parliamentary Employment and Staff Relations Act*, RSC 1985, c 33 (2nd Supp).

17 *CATCA*, above note 9.

18 *Financial Administration Act*, RSC 1985, c F-7, s 11.1(1)(c).

19 *CAPE v Treasury Board*, above note 15 at para 137. See also *PSAC v CRA*, above note 15 at para 82.

20 *National Police Federation v Treasury Board (Royal Canadian Mounted Police)*, 2021 FPSLREB 77, aff'd *Attorney General of Canada v National Police Federation*, 2023 FCA 75.

21 *PSAC v Treasury Board (CBSA)*, above note 15 at para 187.

22 See, for example, *RP Lariviere and Treasury Board (Transport Canada)*, [1984] CPSSRB No 9.

that the parties are in the freeze period more often than not. If collective agreement breaches were addressed through the statutory freeze instead of the grievance procedure, there would be very few collective agreement grievances. Therefore, most of the Board's decisions about the statutory freeze do not involve actions by the employer that breach the collective agreement. Instead, most statutory freeze cases concern those terms and conditions of employment that may be contained in a collective agreement but for whatever reason have not been so included.[23]

2) Stage Two of the Statutory Freeze Analysis

The second stage of a statutory freeze is to consider the employer's justification or response once the complainant has met its burden in the first stage. The Board has followed the same approach as that of other labour relations boards across Canada and recognized that the statutory freeze is not static. The employer may make changes if those changes fall "within an established pattern in the employment relationship."[24] This concept is most commonly expressed as "business as before" or "business as usual."

Labour relations boards across Canada have expressed the flexible nature of the freeze by using the aphorism "business as before"—the idea being that employers should be permitted to act in the same fashion before and after the statutory freeze. Labour relations boards have also used a similar, but not identical, concept of "reasonable expectations"—the idea being that employers should be permitted to make changes during a statutory freeze so long as employees could anticipate or expect those changes. The Board has explained that these two concepts are similar—so similar, in fact, that there is no meaningful difference between them. The Board explained that "the 'business as before test' . . . would not be contradicted by the 'reasonable expectations test,"[25] or

> [t]he concept of employees' expectations is an inherently logical aspect of a business-as-usual analysis. If employees have a reasonable expectation that something will happen, in the absence of evidence to the

23 See, for example, *PSAC v Treasury Board (CSC)*, above note 14, where the collective agreement arguably permitted the change in hours of work that was the subject matter of the complaint, but the change was still a breach of the statutory freeze.

24 *Ibid* at para 61, aff'd *Canada (Attorney General) v PSAC*, above note 14.

25 *Public Service Alliance of Canada v Treasury Board (Canada Border Services Agency)*, 2016 PSLREB 19 at para 76 [*PSAC v Treasury Board (CBSA)* (2016)].

> contrary, one can assume that they have that expectation because it happened before, because it usually happens, or because they were told it would happen. Their expectations are not made out of whole cloth but are based on their workplace experiences or on what they have been told. It is a simple matter of logic and probability.[26]

The Board, when applying the business as before approach, has had to address a number of issues in how to apply that approach.

a) Reserved Discretion

One issue that the Board has addressed is about the scope of management's right to exercise its discretion in managing the workplace. Specifically, when management has enacted a particular policy but has reserved to itself (either in the collective agreement or in the terms of the policy itself) the discretion to change that policy, may management change that policy during the statutory freeze? There are two lines of authority on this issue, one permitting the exercise of management discretion and the other preventing it.

The line of authorities permitting the exercise of management discretion in changing policies or practices begins with a decision by the Federal Court of Appeal concerning shift schedules. The Treasury Board changed the shift schedule for firefighters at Thunder Bay Airport from a sixteen-hour shift schedule to a nine-hour shift schedule after it had been served with notice to bargain. The collective agreement stated that the employer was free to change the shift schedule after consultation with the bargaining agent (which took place prior to the schedule change). The Court concluded that changing the shift schedule did not violate the statutory freeze because the overriding or governing term or condition of employment in the present case is one providing that a shift schedule may be changed by the employer.[27]

The Board has applied this same theory—that a collective agreement term granting management discretion permits management to change its policies or practices during the statutory freeze—in several other cases, discussed below.

In *PIPSC and Treasury Board*,[28] the employer introduced a self-funded leave plan during the statutory freeze period. The collective

26 *National Police Federation*, above note 10 at para 70.

27 *PSAC v Canada (Treasury Board)*, [1983] FCJ No 700 (CA) at 3–4.

28 *PIPSC and Treasury Board*, [1989] CPSSRB No 4.

agreement gave the employer the power to grant leave without pay for any purpose "at its discretion." The Board concluded that implementing the self-funded leave plan was an exercise of the discretion retained under the collective agreement and was therefore permitted during the freeze period.

In another case involving the Canadian Air Traffic Control Association (CATCA) and overtime,[29] the Treasury Board changed its overtime practice from "call-in" overtime to "scheduled" overtime. It was common ground between the parties that, under the collective agreement, the employer retained the right to assign overtime either by call-in or by scheduling. The Board concluded that the employer did not violate the statutory freeze because it never gave up the right to schedule overtime, despite the fact that it never exercised that right during the life of the collective agreement. The Board distinguished the earlier Federal Court of Appeal decision concerning overtime on the grounds that, in that case, the overtime practice was the product of consultation between the employer and the bargaining agent.

In *UCCO-SACC-CSN v Treasury Board*,[30] the employer changed the shift schedule by, in essence, ceasing to pay employees for their half-hour lunch break. The collective agreement did not require the employer to pay employees for their lunch break, but that had been the practice for eighteen years. The Board concluded that this was not a breach of the statutory freeze because "before notice to bargain was filed, the employer had the right to amend shift schedules and this right had to continue after notice was filed."[31]

The Board has applied a similar principle when management's policies or practices are expressed in writing and explicitly reserve for management the right to amend or cancel those policies. In yet another case involving CATCA and overtime,[32] the employer had implemented an overtime policy whereby overtime could be used to cover off-leave for one shift per day; however, this policy was contingent on the availability of funds. The employer argued that it stopped permitting overtime to cover off-leave because of a scarcity of funds. The Board concluded that

---

29 *Canadian Air Traffic Control Association and Treasury Board (Transport Canada)*, [1989] CPSSRB No 8.

30 *UCCO-SACC-CSN v Treasury Board*, [2004] CPSSRB No 35.

31 *Ibid* at para 32.

32 *Canadian Air Traffic Control Association and Treasury Board*, [1991] CPSSRB No 185.

the employer's decision to cancel its overtime policy did not violate the statutory freeze because the employer was simply exercising its right under its stated proviso and that the proviso "must be considered part of the terms and conditions of employment."[33] The Board came to a similar conclusion when assessing the change of a parking policy.[34] The Treasury Board had announced a change to the parking policy prior to bargaining (requiring employees to pay for parking), but had not implemented the policy change for computer workers at a particular Ottawa location. It then implemented the policy during a statutory freeze period. The Board concluded that this implementation did not violate the statutory freeze:

> The policy, as it exists, was a term or condition of employment before the statutory freeze period and remained so thereafter. What the bargaining agent is attempting to argue is that even though the policy has not changed, management's "choice" to implement the policy has changed and therefore the terms and conditions have changed.
>
> This argument can be rejected. . . . Firstly, it is the policy itself which is the term or condition of employment, not the form of implementation which is the term or condition. In the present case the policy was not changed one iota.[35]

In another case, the Canada Revenue Agency attempted to cancel telework arrangements for certain employees during the statutory freeze period.[36] The telework policy was not part of the collective agreement, and it explicitly stated that management reserved the right to cancel telework arrangements on reasonable notice. Therefore, the Board concluded that management retained the right to cancel telework arrangements during the freeze period.

In *Canadian Federal Pilots Association v Department of Transport, Transportation Safety Board, and Treasury Board Secretariat*,[37] the bargaining agent argued that the sale of certain aircraft flown by employees was a breach of the statutory freeze. The Board rejected the claim because the relevant policy that was the product of negotiation between the parties (which governed the assignment of flying) stated specifically that it was subject to change. In other words, the language

---

33 *Ibid* at 8.

34 *PIPSC and Treasury Board*, [1991] CPSSRB No 23.

35 *Ibid* at 9.

36 *PIPSC v Canada Revenue Agency*, [2006] CPSLRB No 29.

37 *Canadian Federal Pilots*, above note 15.

used by the parties gave the employer discretion not to assign flying because of the non-availability of aircraft; therefore, the employer's exercise of discretion expressly reserved was consistent with its business as usual approach.

On the other hand, the Board has sometimes upheld complaints where the employer changed its practices in a way that may not have breached the collective agreement. The 1982 decision in *The Queen in Right of Canada as Represented by the Treasury Board v Canadian Air Traffic Control Association* is an example of that: the collective agreement did not limit management's right to assign overtime, yet a change in practice from voluntary to compulsory overtime was a breach of the statutory freeze. The principle that an employer's practices must continue during the statutory freeze period—regardless of whether the employer retained the right to change those practices under the collective agreement—is consistent with the business as usual approach to the statutory freeze applied in the private sector. The Board has explicitly adopted that approach and characterizes it as follows:

> [T]he Board will review the employer's normal business practices and will attempt to determine, through the evidence, whether the changes complained of are part of the employer's normal practices, or whether they do not conform to those practiced previously.[38]

Thus, the "business as usual" test does not consider whether the employer has retained its discretionary management rights under the collective agreement or in whatever written document created the policy or practice but instead considers the employer's actual practices and requires the employer to maintain those practices during the statutory freeze period. The employer must "maintain the employees' reasonable expectations as to the employer's conduct, in other words 'normal business practice' or 'business as usual.'"[39]

---

38 *Public Service Alliance of Canada and National Capital Commission*, [1995] CPSSRB No 101, aff'd [1995] FCJ No 57 (CA). The Federal Court of Appeal, on judicial review of that case, expressed some concern about whether the "business as usual" test was appropriate because it "goes further than this Court found it necessary to go in *CATCA* and includes in the statutory freeze not only express and implied terms of employment, informal agreements and established employer policies . . . but also the employees' reasonable expectations as to the employer's conduct."

39 *Professional Association of Foreign Service Officers v Treasury Board*, [2003] CPSSRB No 4.

For example, in yet another CATCA case about overtime,[40] the employer changed its overtime practice from a standard 8.92-hour overtime shift to an 8-hour overtime shift. The collective agreement did not limit management discretion about overtime, and the last written policy stated that "[o]vertime shifts will normally be the same as a regular schedule shift. At the discretion of the Supervisor/Acting Supervisor, these hours may be increased or decreased, as operational circumstances dictate." Despite this express retention of discretion, the Board concluded that management breached the statutory freeze when it changed its overtime shift length, concluding that the concept of an 8.92-hour overtime shift was a term or condition of employment and was capable of being embodied in a collective agreement.

In two other cases, the Board concluded that the employer violated the statutory freeze by ending a practice of permitting employees to work compressed or flexible hours of work in one case or reducing hours of work in the other, despite the fact that there was nothing in the collective agreement or an existing policy that would restrict the employer's discretion to set hours of work.[41]

It appears as if the two lines of cases can only be reconciled by a careful consideration of the facts underlying each case.

b) Implementing Previous Decisions

The employer has often responded to an allegation of a breach of the statutory freeze by arguing that it was implementing a decision that had been made prior to the onset of the freeze period. This response is a rational corollary to the reasonable expectations doctrine: employees can reasonably expect an employer to implement something it announced.

For example, in one case the employer changed employees' shift schedules on a Navy vessel because it had decided to decommission the vessel and, therefore, it reduced the overall hours the ship was operated (which changed the employees' shift schedules when conducting security rounds). While the actual change in shift schedule was made during the freeze period, the employer had conducted a review a year earlier, after which it announced that it would recommend decommissioning the vessel and changing the vessel's operating hours. The Board

40 *CATCA and Treasury Board*, [1991] CPSSRB No 102.

41 *PSAC v CRA*, above note 15, and *PSAC v Treasury Board (CSC)*, above note 14.

therefore concluded that employees knew that their shift schedule had "destabilized and could not be counted on to continue."[42]

In another case, the employer changed its parking practices from a free of charge, first-come, first-served model to charging employees $45 each month. While the change itself was implemented during the freeze period, the employer had made several announcements and decisions in the years leading up to the onset of the statutory freeze requiring paid parking for certain employees and announcing that the free parking for these employees was not a sustainable option and that it was considering implementing full-pay parking. In light of these announcements, the employees could not reasonably have expected free parking to remain in place during the freeze period.[43]

To take advantage of this approach, an employer must announce its decision (or at least announce the possibility of a decision) to employees in the bargaining unit. It is not sufficient that management was working on the solution prior to the statutory freeze period: an employer must communicate its intention to the employees or bargaining agent; otherwise, the internal decision cannot create an expectation on the part of employees that a change was coming.[44] For example, in one case the employer drafted a policy that would impose changes to normal scheduled hours of work but then decided not to implement the policy because of objections by the bargaining agent. After notice to bargain was served, the employer went ahead and changed the scheduled hours of work. The Board concluded that even though the employer would have normally had the discretion to change hours of work, having led the bargaining agent to believe that it would not do so, the employer could not change those hours of work during the statutory freeze period.[45]

In another example, the senior executive committee of the RCMP decided to change its promotions policy so that RCMP regular members could only be promoted after taking certain courses. The senior executive committee met and made this decision prior to the onset of the freeze but changed how it would implement this policy several times before and after the onset of the statutory freeze and did not inform RCMP members about the change until after the statutory freeze had commenced. The Board concluded that this change violated the

---

42 *PSAC v Treasury Board*, above note 15 at para 52.

43 *Dockyard Chargehands*, above note 8.

44 *Ibid* at para 50.

45 *Canadian Federal Pilots Association v Treasury Board*, 2006 PSLRB 86.

statutory freeze, stating that "[t]o have any credence, the concept of 'wheels in motion' has to mean work being done to implement a firm decision that employees know about. Wheels turning silently on an exclusively inside track mean nothing."[46]

c) Reasonable Employer Practices

More recently, employers have responded to statutory freeze complaints by arguing that changes to terms and conditions of employment do not violate the statutory freeze because those changes are reasonable or consistent with how a reasonable employer would act in the absence of an application for certification or notice to bargain. This argument has its genesis in some remarks by the Supreme Court of Canada in a 2014 decision in *United Food and Commercial Workers, Local 503 v Wal-Mart Canada Corp*, where the arbitrator concluded that the employer violated the statutory freeze by closing a facility in part because this was not consistent with what a reasonable employer in the same position would have done.[47] The Board has rejected this argument, but in three different ways or for three different reasons.

In the *Dockyard Chargehands* decision, the bargaining agent led evidence that attempted to demonstrate that the employer's decision to implement paid parking was unreasonable or unsound. The Board concluded that this evidence was irrelevant because "[t]he issue before me is not whether the employer's decision to alter its parking policy and to charge a monthly parking fee was well motivated, legitimate, or sound."[48]

In *Sudbury Taxation Centre*[49] the Board concluded that the "reasonable employer" defence was only available when a previous practice (either supporting or denying the change) cannot be identified. The

46 *National Police Federation*, above note 10 at para 82. For most of the federal public administration, a policy about promotions would be outside the scope of the statutory freeze because it would be a term or condition of employment subject to the *Public Service Employment Act*, SC 2003, c 22, ss 12 & 13, and, therefore, outside the scope of collective bargaining. As discussed in Chapter 13, RCMP members are not appointed under the *Public Service Employment Act*, and there is no prohibition on their negotiating terms and conditions relevant to promotions or appointments.

47 *United Food and Commercial Workers, Local 503 v Wal-Mart Canada Corp*, 2014 SCC 45 at paras 56–57.

48 *Dockyard Chargehands*, above note 8 at para 55.

49 *Sudbury Taxation Centre*, above note 13 at para 156.

Board referred to this as a "precondition" for that particular response by an employer. The Board in that case concluded that the precondition was not met. However, even if the precondition did exist, the Board concluded that the employer did not act reasonably because the change to hours of work in that case was only implemented in one tax office out of many affected by the broader policy changes that the employer used to attempt to justify the change. Furthermore, the Board explained that this argument would rarely succeed, pointing out that "once more, [that] a reasonable employer might have exercised its powers in a certain way in counterfactual circumstances should not be a sufficient defence in most circumstances."[50]

In the *National Police Federation*[51] decision about the change in promotions policy, the Board distinguished between two parts of this argument: that the change was consistent with how a reasonable employer would act and that the employer would have acted the same even without the application for certification or notice to bargain. The employer in that case did not expressly rely on the first part of that test. Nevertheless, the Board went on to assess the reasonableness of the employer's actions. The Board concluded that the change to criteria for promotions was unreasonable for two reasons: there was no urgency to the change, so the employer could have waited for the freeze period to expire, and the employer did not discuss the proposed changes with the employee organization that had applied for certification or seek the consent of the Board to make those changes.

When moving to the second part of the argument, the Board concluded that an employer cannot respond to a statutory freeze complaint by arguing that it would have made the same change in the absence of an application for certification or notice to bargain. The Board pointed out that anti-union animus is not part of the test for a statutory freeze; however, allowing the employer to respond to a complaint in this way "would be tantamount to importing some suggestion of a requirement of anti-union animus."[52]

Of these three approaches (reasonableness is irrelevant, reasonableness only if the past practice cannot be discerned, or reasonableness

---

50 *Ibid* at para 171. The Board repeated this assessment of the *Sudbury Taxation Centre* decision in *National Police Federation*, above note 19 at para 67, although in *obiter* as the employer was not relying upon that argument in that case.

51 *National Police Federation*, above note 19.

52 *Ibid* at para 110.

requires urgency and consultation with the employee organization or bargaining agent), the first approach is preferred. The Supreme Court of Canada's offhand reference to reasonable employers must be understood in the factual context of that case and the arbitrator's findings that the employer acted outside the bounds of how any reasonable employer would act. The arbitrator and the Supreme Court of Canada drew comfort from the fact that the employer's unreasonableness buttressed the conclusion that the employer's actions were inconsistent with the reasonable expectations of employees—because employees never (or perhaps should not have to) expect their employer to act unreasonably. The first approach is also consistent with other court decisions discouraging legal principles that are "overly intrusive" in the workplace.[53] Courts and labour boards should not be in the business of assessing the reasonableness of management decisions. Labour boards can assess whether there has been a change and whether the change is consistent with business as usual: labour boards should not have to assess whether the change was necessary or reasonable.

C. OTHER UNFAIR LABOUR PRACTICES BY EMPLOYERS

The *FPSLRA* prohibits three unfair labour practices by employers and managers:

1) participating in or interfering with the formation or administration of an employee organization[54]
2) discriminating against an employee organization[55]
3) taking some action that prevents an employee from participating in an employee organization or exercising a right under parts 1, 2, and 2.1 of the *FPLSRA*[56]

These prohibitions are common in labour legislation across Canada in both the public and private sectors. Rather than articulate the unfair labour practice principles that are common across jurisdictions, this

53 *Wallace v United Grain Growers Ltd*, [1997] 3 SCR 701 at para 76. See also *Piresferreira v Ayotte*, 2010 ONCA 384 at para 62: "[I]t is unnecessary and undesirable to expand the court's involvement in [work performance] questions."
54 *FPSLRA*, s 186(1)(a).
55 *Ibid*, s 186(1)(b).
56 *Ibid*, s 186(2).

chapter will discuss some of the issues that have arisen in the particular context of the federal public service.

1) Identity of the Respondent

The *Public Service Staff Relations Act* (*PSSRA*) contained some eccentricities concerning the unfair labour practices that have been removed in the *FPSLRA*. Under the *PSSRA*, no "person who occupies a managerial or confidential position" could interfere with an employee organization or discriminate against employees for exercising rights under the Act. The Board and Federal Court of Appeal both concluded that the term "person who occupies a managerial or confidential position" did not include the employer itself.[57] Therefore, employees who complained about unfair labour practices under the *PSSRA* had to name as a respondent the individual manager or managers who they allege committed the unfair labour practice.

This peculiar requirement to name the manager personally as opposed to the employer was explained by the Board as a matter of procedural fairness: "[W]ithout having before it specific allegations against such identified persons the employer is not in a position to prepare a defence."[58] The Board did not explain why a simple request for particulars (if the complaint form does not contain sufficient detail about the allegations) would not be sufficient to solve this problem; however, in the one case where the Board attempted to address the problem through particulars, the Federal Court of Appeal quashed that decision and the Board ultimately had to dismiss the complaint.[59] Furthermore, it is of questionable worth—from a labour relations perspective—to have to name specific managers against whom complaints are directed rather than name the employer and have it take ultimate responsibility for the actions of its managers.

The *FPSLRA* has eliminated this eccentricity. Section 186 of the *FPSLRA* states that neither "the employer nor a person who occupies a managerial or confidential position" may interfere with an employee

57 See *Union of Canadian Correctional Officers v Conseil du Tresor*, 2005 FCA 331 [*Union of Canadian Correctional Officers*].

58 *Economists' Sociologists' and Statisticians Association and Canada (Treasury Board)*, [1978] CPSSRB No 6 at para 14.

59 *Union of Canadian Correctional Officers*, above note 57, and *UCCO-SACC-CSN v Treasury Board (Correctional Service of Canada)*, 2006 PSLRB 1.

organization nor discriminate against employee organizations or employees who exercise rights under the Act. Therefore, complaints may now be brought against the employer instead of naming the particular manager involved. Notwithstanding this change, individual managers or even a department may be named as the respondent in an unfair labour practice complaint.[60]

2) Identity of the Complainant

One difference between complaints under sections 186(1) (i.e., the first two types of unfair labour practices set out above) and 186(2) (i.e., the third type of unfair labour practice) is the identity of the complainant. Section 186(1) relates to the rights of employee organizations, while section 186(2) concerns the rights of individuals to participate in employee organizations or exercise other rights under the *FPSLRA*. The *PSSRA* contained a similar division: sections 8(1) and 9(1) of the *PSSRA* concerned interference with or discrimination against employee organizations, while section 8(2) concerned discrimination against or intimidation of members of employee organizations. Essentially, sections 8(1) and 9(1) of the *PSSRA* became section 186(1) of the *FPSLRA*, and section 8(2) of the *PSSRA* became section 186(2) of the *FPSLRA*.[61]

The Board held that only an employee organization may complain of a violation of sections 8(1) and 9(1) of the *PSSRA* because those prohibitions clearly affect the rights that belong to employee organizations.[62] The Board did not go so far as to require that only employee organizations could be named as the complainants in such cases. However, to have standing to bring such a complaint, a person must be acting on behalf of an employee organization.[63] For example, in *Rioux v LeClair*, the complainant used to be a representative of the Public Service Alliance of Canada (PSAC). However, by the time she filed her complaint, she had lost her status as representative for two reasons: she did not run in

60 *Choinière Lapointe v Correctional Service of Canada*, 2019 FPSLREB 68 at paras 4–7 [*Lapointe*].

61 Section 186 of the *FPSLRA* is broader than ss 8 and 9 of the *PSSRA* in some ways, but in terms of the organization of the Acts, the provisions are similar enough for the purposes of this discussion.

62 *Rioux v LeClair*, [2006] CPSLRB No 10 at para 143 [*Rioux*]; *Reekie v Thomson*, [1998] CPSSRB No 120 at paras 13–14.

63 *Feldsted v Treasury Board*, [1999] CPSSRB No 57 at para 8.

the local's elections, and the local had been placed under trusteeship by the PSAC, which named a different representative. The collective agreement between the PSAC and the Treasury Board contained a provision permitting the PSAC to name its representatives and requiring the PSAC to do so in writing. Since Ms. Rioux was not named as a representative pursuant to her collective agreement (because she did not run for election and her local was under trusteeship), she did not have the requisite standing to bring a complaint under section 8(1) of the *PSSRA*.

The Board has confirmed that its approach remains unchanged under the *FPSLRA*—namely, that individual employees do not have standing to file unfair labour practice complaints under section 186(1) of the Act. As the Board has put it succinctly:

> [W]hen Parliament enacted subsections 186(1) and (2) of the new Act, it had in mind two different and distinct statutory protections against potential unfair labour practices by employers. One was to protect the interests of employee organizations, and the other was to protect the interests of individual employees.[64]

Individual employees therefore do not have standing to file unfair labour practice complaints under section 186(1) of the *FPSLRA*.

3) Burden of Proof

There are two parts to the prohibitions in section 186: those in subsection 186(1) and those in subsection 186(2). Broadly speaking, section 186(1) prohibits interference with or discrimination against an employee organization, and section 186(2) prohibits actions taken against a person as a result of their membership in or involvement with an employee organization. The burden of proof on a complaint based on section 186(1) is on the complainant. However, section 191(3) of the *FPSLRA* states that a written complaint concerning section 186(2) "is itself evidence that the failure actually occurred" and that if the respondent disputes that allegation, "the burden of proving that it did not is on that party."[65] Therefore, for complaints based on section 186(2), the burden of proof has shifted to the respondent (typically the employer).

64 *Bialy v Heavens and Treasury Board*, 2011 PSLRB 101 at para 18 [*Bialy*]. See also *Verwold v Treasury Board (Correctional Service of Canada)*, 2015 PSLREB 66.

65 *FPSLRA*, s 191(3).

This shift in the burden of proof means that the Board must take the existence of the complaint as proof that the employer failed to observe an identified statutory prohibition.[66] However, the complainant still bears an initial burden to demonstrate a *prima facie* or arguable case before the burden shifts to the respondent. The Board has described this threshold as whether, taking all of the facts alleged in the complaint as true, there is an arguable case that the respondent has contravened the applicable provision in the *FPSLRA*.[67] The Board has also decided that even a "tenuous" possibility of an arguable case is sufficient to trigger reverse onus.[68] This reverse onus means that the respondent must refute the presumption on the balance of probabilities.[69] The reverse onus does not mean that, where two versions of events exist, the Board must accept the complainant's version; instead, the Board still assesses which version is more credible and may deny a complaint if it concludes that the respondent's version is more credible.[70]

The burden of proof for allegations in section 186(1) remains on the complainant.[71]

4) Interaction Between Adjudication and Complaints

Several (if not all) collective agreements in the federal public service contain provisions protecting certain rights of employees and employee organizations that are also protected by sections 186(1) and (2) of the *FPSLRA*. For example, collective agreements generally contain provisions permitting employees who are about to be disciplined to have a union representative present during meetings with management. This right is also protected under section 186(2)(c)(i) of the *FPSLRA*.[72] Therefore, employees — in a way — have a choice between filing a grievance and filing an unfair labour practice complaint with the Board.

---

66 *Quadrini v Canada Revenue Agency and Hillier*, 2008 PSLRB 37 at para 28.

67 *Ibid* at para 32.

68 *Hager et al v Statistics Survey Operations and the Minister Responsible for Statistics Canada*, 2009 PSLRB 80 at para 41.

69 *Lapointe*, above note 60 at para 194.

70 *Gal v Chouinard and St Amand*, 2014 PSLRB 92, aff'd *Gal v Canada (Revenue Agency)*, 2015 FCA 188.

71 *Bialy*, above note 64 at para 22.

72 See, for example, *Rioux*, above note 62 (where the complaint was dismissed but addressed under the former section 8(2) of the *PSSRA*).

The wording of the *FPSLRA* limits this choice but does so in a way that is not entirely straightforward, and the Board's decisions are unhelpful in delineating this choice. In summary, however:

- An adjudicator does not have the jurisdiction to hear a grievance that could also constitute an unfair labour practice complaint unless the Board has already exercised its jurisdiction under section 191(2) of the *FPSLRA*.
- A grievance officer does not have the jurisdiction to hear a grievance that may also constitute an unfair labour practice complaint unless the grievance may be referred to adjudication and the Board has already exercised its jurisdiction under section 191(2) of the *FPSLRA*.
- If a final-level grievance officer does hear and deny a grievance that could constitute an unfair labour practice complaint, and the grievor subsequently files an unfair labour practice complaint with the Board, then the Board may decline to hear the merits of the complaint in those rare circumstances where hearing the complaint would constitute an abuse of process.

A more detailed discussion of this issue follows.

Section 208 of the *FPSLRA* prevents an employee from filing a grievance "in respect of which an administrative procedure for redress is provided under any Act of Parliament."[73] The Board has concluded that administrative procedures in "any Act of Parliament" include the complaints procedure in what is now section 190 of the *FPSLRA*.[74] More recently, the Federal Court has also agreed that section 208 of the *FPSLRA* (then section 91 of the *PSSRA*) referred to "an Act of Parliament" and not "another Act of Parliament." Thus, the grievor in that case could not grieve an allegation of intimidation for exercising his right to engage in union activity and instead had to proceed by way of an unfair labour practice complaint.[75]

Section 214 states that a decision taken at the final level of the grievance procedure is "final and binding for all purposes of this Act and no further action under this Act may be taken on it."[76] The *FPSLRA* also

73 *FPSLRA*, s 208. For a more detailed discussion of this limitation on grievances, see Chapter 10.

74 *Steer and Canada (Treasury Board)*, [1977] CPSSRB No 12 [*Steer*].

75 *Ryan v Canada (Attorney General)*, [2005] FCJ No 110.

76 *FPSLRA*, s 214.

states that decisions by adjudicators are final.[77] The Board attempted to reconcile the finality of the grievance procedure and the requirement that grievances not deal with matters with alternative methods of administrative redress in a situation where an employee presented a grievance concerning certain events, was unsuccessful at the final level of the grievance procedure, and then filed a complaint alleging an unfair labour practice. The Board concluded that the grievance decision was final and binding on the complainant and that the Board therefore had no jurisdiction to hear his complaint.[78]

However, the Board did not address the issue of how the matter proceeded to the final level of the grievance procedure in the first place. Section 208 of the *FPSLRA* means that the final level of the grievance procedure does not have the jurisdiction to address unfair labour practices—if a grievance could have been construed as a section 190 complaint, it is outside the scope of the grievance procedure.

To this jurisdictional morass Parliament has added another contradictory provision of the *FPSLRA*. Section 191(2) of the *FPSLRA* states:

> 191(2) The Board may refuse to determine a complaint made under subsection 190(1) in respect of a matter that, in the Board's opinion, could be referred to adjudication under Part 2 by the complainant.

The Board has decided to take a practical, rather than an overly technical, approach to section 191(2) of the *FPSLRA*, relying on its discretion granted through the word "may" in section 191(2). The Board has therefore concluded that earlier grievances that were not referred to adjudication did not bar an unfair labour practice complaint because "a third party has not had an opportunity to rule on the claims of unfair labour practice."[79] The Board has also ruled that it will exercise its discretion under section 191(2) to hear statutory freeze complaints even though the subject matter of those same complaints may form the basis of a grievance.[80]

---

77 *Ibid*, s 233.

78 *Steer*, above note 74.

79 *Gignac v Fradette*, 2009 PSLRB 18 at para 30.

80 *PSAC v CRA*, above note 15; *PSAC v Treasury Board (CSC)*, above note 14.

5) No Requirement of Intent

Under the former *PSSRA*, there was some dispute concerning whether the complainant needed to prove that the respondent intentionally committed an unfair labour practice—that is, whether the respondent's actions were tainted by "anti-union animus." Some Board decisions indicated that intention was a necessary element of an offence of unfair labour practice,[81] while others did not.[82] However, the Federal Court of Appeal resolved this issue in *Social Science Employees Assn v Canada (Attorney General)*[83] and concluded that intention or an anti-union animus was a necessary element of an unfair labour practice under the *PSSRA*. In that case, the Social Science Employees Association alleged that the employer was discriminating against its members because it used a different method of salary computation on promotion for unionized and non-unionized employees.[84] The Board agreed that this was discriminatory and an unfair labour practice, but the Federal Court of Appeal reversed that decision. Concerning the issue of intent, the Court stated:

> At paragraph 94 of its decision, the Board correctly, in my view, states that discrimination contrary to sections 8 and 9 of the Act "requires intent or anti-union animus." . . .
>
> It is clear from the Board's decision that there was no proof adduced before it which could support a conclusion of anti-union animus on the part of Treasury Board. Consequently, the only possible conclusion that the Board could have reached, on the evidence, was that the respondents had not met their burden of proof.[85]

As mentioned before, the *FPSLRA* has reversed the burden of proof for unfair labour practice complaints concerning section 186(2). This reverse burden of proof rests uneasily next to a requirement on the part of a complainant to show intent or anti-union animus. The Board has addressed this aspect of the unfair labour practice test by stating that the burden rests with the respondent to show that it was not motivated by the complainant's membership in an employee organization,

---

81 *Jackson and Seguin*, [1988] CPSSRB No 14 at para 37.

82 *Union of Canadian Correctional Officers and Treasury Board*, 2004 PSSRB 71.

83 *Social Science Employees Assn v Canada (Attorney General)*, [2004] FCJ No 741 (CA) [*Social Science Employees*].

84 For more details concerning these rules, see Chapter 9.

85 *Social Science Employees*, above note 83 at paras 53–54.

participation in a hearing under the *FPSLRA*, or whatever other action forms the basis of the complaint.[86] In other words, while intent or anti-union animus is still a condition of that unfair labour practice, the onus is on the respondent to demonstrate that they did not act intentionally or with anti-union animus.

This reverse onus does not apply to complaints concerning section 186(1); therefore, the requirement of intent still exists under that section. As the Board has stated, that provision "should be interpreted with the aim of determining whether an employer expresses an anti-union animus through the different treatment" on a prohibited ground.[87]

6) Scope of Activities Protected: What Are the "Rights" That May Be Exercised Under the *FPSLRA*?

Section 186(2) prohibits discrimination against or intimidation of employees who exercise "any right under this Part or Part 2" of the *FPSLRA*. The most important statement of those "rights" is contained in section 5 of the *FPSLRA*, which reads as follows:

> 5. Every employee is free to join the employee organization of his or her choice and to participate in its lawful activities.

The Board considers that section to be of fundamental importance when assessing an unfair labour practice complaint. The Board has stated that

> [t]he words contained in section 6 [now section 5] are fundamental to the object of the Act. They are the statutory Magna Carta of the rights conferred on every employee within the jurisdiction of the P.S.S.R. Act. In simple, concise language, it provides that every employee may be a member of an employee organization and may participate in the lawful activities thereof. They are rights to be exercised by any and every employee without any fear or restraint whatsoever from or by any person. In the absence of these rights, the balance of the provisions of the P.S.S.R. Act regarding certification of a bargaining

---

86 *Lapointe*, above note 60 at para 199.

87 *International Association of Machinists and Aerospace Workers and District Lodge 147, National Association of Federal Corrections Officers and Correctional Service of Canada*, 2006 PSLRB 76 at para 97 [*District Lodge 147*].

> agent, collective bargaining, mediation, and resolution of disputes and grievances would be a mere mockery.[88]

Therefore, employees may not be disciplined or otherwise discriminated against because of their participation on the lawful activities of their chosen employee organization. For example, in *Public Service Alliance of Canada and Canada Customs and Revenue Agency*,[89] the Canada Customs and Revenue Agency (CCRA) disciplined eleven PSAC members for picketing the home of a manager who was on the CCRA board of management. The PSAC was negotiating a collective agreement at the time and was frustrated by management's proposals. Therefore, the PSAC organized a peaceful picket. The CCRA disapproved of the picket and disciplined eleven employees who participated. The Board overturned the discipline on an unfair labour practices complaint. Secondary picketing being per se lawful, the picket was lawful unless there were torts or other unlawful acts committed during the demonstration. Therefore, "the 11 demonstrators were involved in the lawful activities of an employee organization away from the workplace ... [and] such activities are protected by section 6 of the *PSSRA*."[90]

Similarly, the Board has concluded that wearing union pins or hats is *prima facie* lawful unless they contain statements that are derogatory or damaging to the employer's reputation or detrimental to its operations.[91] Therefore, an order for employees not to wear the union pins or hats of an employee organization that was seeking to displace the current bargaining agent was interference with the lawful activities of an employee organization.[92] In one case that is probably more amusing in hindsight than at the time, a union gave its members bright orange shoelaces that read, "I support my bargaining team." A number of employees used the shoelaces as bracelets or to tie their hair. The

---

88 *Stonehouse and Canada (Treasury Board)*, [1977] CPSSRB No 11.

89 *Public Service Alliance of Canada and Canada Customs and Revenue Agency*, 2001 PSSRB 105.

90 *Ibid* at para 57. There is considerable debate concerning the appropriateness of picketing somebody's home. See *Telus v TWU et al*, 2005 BCSC 1236, where the BC Supreme Court concluded that employees may not picket managers' homes, and *Telus Communications Inc v Telecommunications Workers Union*, 2005 ABQB 719, where the Alberta Court of Queen's Bench concluded that picketing somebody's home is *prima facie* lawful.

91 *Quan v Canada*, [1990] 2 FC 191 (CA).

92 *International Association of Machinists and Aerospace Workers v Correctional Service Canada*, [2005] CPSLRB No 56.

employer tried to ban the use of shoelaces for anything other than tying shoes, but the Board concluded that this prohibition was an unfair labour practice.[93]

One issue that has become more prevalent concerns a union's right to access the workplace or use the employer's communication facilities to communicate with members. The current jurisprudence does not consider a union's right to represent its members to extend to require the employer to permit the use of its communication facilities or physical access to the workplace. For example, the Board has dismissed complaints against employers who prohibited a corrections employee from using the employer's telephone during his off-hours to make any personal calls, including to his union,[94] and who prohibited a union member from delivering information about bargaining by way of a "desk drop."[95] The Board did conclude, however, that blocking physical mail from an employee organization during a certification campaign interfered with the formation of that employee organization.[96]

In terms of email correspondence, the Board has concluded that a bargaining agent has no absolute right to send emails to employees' work email addresses; however, the employer in that case committed an unfair labour practice by blocking the bargaining agent's emails without first discussing the matter and providing notice. The Board also concluded that the employer committed an unfair labour practice by reviewing the content of the bargaining agent's emails. The employer did not, however, commit an unfair labour practice by prohibiting an out-of-office auto reply that stated that there may be a delay in responding because the union was in a legal strike position. The Board in that case stated that "generally, an employee organization does not have the right to use the employer's property to communicate with its

93 *Bartlett v Treasury Board (Canada Border Services Agency)*, 2018 FPSLREB 66. Curiously, the employer had no objection to employees wearing a bright orange sticker with the same message. Despite this, the Board accepted that it was the message that the employer objected to, not the fashion faux pas of using shoelaces as a hair tie.

94 *Merriman and Union of Canadian Correctional Officers—Syndicat des agents correctionnels du Canada (UCCO-SACC-CSN) v MacNeil and Justason*, 2011 PSLRB 87.

95 *Public Service Alliance of Canada v Treasury Board (Canada Border Services Agency)*, 2013 PSLRB 138.

96 *District Lodge 147*, above note 87. As discussed below, the complaint was dismissed on other grounds.

members and where that right exists it is usually the result of collective bargaining."[97]

This line of authorities about email is unfortunate and does not fully capture the nature of electronic communication at work. Employees receive hundreds, if not thousands, of emails each day, many of them unsolicited or advertising services or "cold" emails as a result of the publication of many email addresses on the Government Electronic Directory Services website. It is not entirely clear why the employer suffers prejudice by a bargaining agent sending an email to its members when those members receive emails asking them to, for example, buy new suits by a tailor in town.

The Board has concluded that a bargaining agent's representative has the right to enter a workplace and meet with employees (during breaks) to discuss collective bargaining issues.[98] The Board then extended that right to a bargaining agent's representative to conduct "walkthroughs and on-site meetings"; however, the Federal Court of Appeal overturned that decision on the grounds that the walkthroughs were not necessary to ensure that the union was on an equal footing with the employer during collective bargaining and that the Board's decision contradicted the parties' own collective agreement clause setting out a more limited right of union access to the workplace.[99] The Federal Court of Appeal referred to the earlier Board decision permitting access for collective bargaining preparation but neither relied upon it nor distinguished it when making its decision. The Board has not yet been asked to reconsider that earlier decision in light of the more recent Federal Court of Appeal's ruling. The two decisions may be reconcilable as the first has to do explicitly with collective bargaining and the second has to do with standard representation—although one of the walkthroughs was denied specifically because the Department of National Defence did not permit any activity related to collective bargaining on its premises. The result in any future cases will likely depend on the purpose behind the access to the workplace and whether the access is necessary to place the bargaining agent on an "equal footing" with the employer in collective bargaining.

---

97 *Professional Association of Foreign Service Officers v Treasury Board (Department of Foreign Affairs, Trade and Development)*, 2013 PSLRB 111.

98 *Public Service Alliance of Canada v Treasury Board (Canada Border Services Agency)*, 2012 PSLRB 58.

99 *Canada (Attorney General) v Canada (Public Service Alliance)*, 2017 FCA 208.

Many collective agreements contain provisions guaranteeing the right of a bargaining agent representative to attend disciplinary meetings. There is a rich body of arbitral jurisprudence about when an investigation meeting has become disciplinary in a way that triggers that right that this book will not reproduce. However, absent a collective agreement provision, there is no right to union representation in an investigation meeting.[100] This means that, in one case, the employer did not commit an unfair labour practice by permitting "observers" in an investigation meeting but prohibiting those observers (who were also union representatives) from taking notes during the investigation meeting.[101]

Finally, a bargaining agent has the right to obtain home contact information for all employees—both members and "Rand" employees (i.e., non-union members who are in the bargaining unit and pay union dues)—from the employer. This right exists precisely because the employer can block union communication at the workplace and "[t]he tripartite nature of the employment relationship means that information disclosed to the employer that is necessary for the union to carry out its representational duties should be disclosed to the union in order to ensure that the union and employer are on an equal footing with respect to information relevant to the collective bargaining relationship."[102] Therefore, bargaining agents in the federal public service

---

100 *Naidu v Canada Customs and Revenue Agency*, 2001 PSSRB 124.

101 *PSAC v Treasury Board (CBSA)* (2016), above note 25. On the facts of this case, though, this was a breach of the statutory freeze as the new "no notes" policy was implemented during the freeze period without consultation with the bargaining agent.

102 *Bernard v Canada (Attorney General)*, 2014 SCC 13 at para 29. This decision was the culmination of three board hearings and two rounds of judicial review to the Federal Court of Appeal. The Board granted the order the first time (*Professional Institute of the Public Service of Canada v Canada Revenue Agency*, 2008 PSLRB 58). Ms. Bernard was not present at that hearing. She applied for judicial review to the Federal Court of Appeal, which ordered the Board to reconsider the matter in light of the privacy rights of employees (*Bernard v Canada (Attorney General)*, 2010 FCA 40). The Board did so and maintained the order (*PIPSC v CRA*, 2011 PSLRB 34) with some amendments to require greater protection of personal information. The Federal Court of Appeal affirmed that order (*Bernard v Canada (Attorney General)*, 2012 FCA 92), and the Supreme Court of Canada did likewise. The complainant did not drop the matter there: she brought a motion requesting that the Supreme Court of Canada rehear her appeal, which was denied. She filed a reconsideration application with the Board, which was denied (*Bernard v PIPSC, Treasure Board and CRA*, 2015 PSLREB 59). She applied for judicial review of that decision, which was denied (*Bernard v Canada*

routinely obtain orders from the Board requiring the employer to disclose home contact information for all employees. These orders, after the Supreme Court of Canada's decision, are on consent; nevertheless, board orders are obtained (rather than simply handing over the information) to ensure that the personal contact information is safeguarded in a manner consistent with the *Privacy Act*.[103]

7) Limitations on Unfair Labour Practice Complaints: The Employer's Rights

The *FPSLRA* contains several limitations on unfair labour practice complaints. Some of these limitations act to the benefit of both employee organizations and the employer. For example, section 186(3) of the *FPSLRA* states that it is not an unfair labour practice for the employer to pay employees during the time that they are conferring with the employer on behalf of their employee organization and that employers may permit bargaining agents to use the employer's premises for union business.[104]

Other provisions of the *FPSLRA* protect the employer against unfair labour practice complaints. Section 186(5) states that the employer or a person does not commit an unfair labour practice "by reason only that the employer or person expresses their point of view, so long as they do not use coercion, intimidation, threats, promises or undue influence." This employer free speech provision was added to the *FPSLRA*.

The difficulty with these "employer free speech" clauses is where to draw the line between free speech on the one hand and an unfair labour practice on the other. The Board has adopted the approach from the Canada Industrial Relations Board interpreting a similar provision in the *Canada Labour Code*.[105] That approach is summarized as follows:

(Revenue Agency), 2017 FCA 40). She filed another request for reconsideration with the Board, which was also denied (*Bernard v CRA*, 2017 PSLREB 46)—and this time, the Board issued an order prohibiting her from filing any further complaints or proceedings about home contact information.

103 Dozens of these orders have been made. See, for example, *International Brotherhood of Electrical Workers, Local 2228 v Treasury Board*, 2014 PSLRB 20, for some standard terms of these orders.

104 As discussed above, however, the employer has the ability to limit that access as well depending on the circumstances.

105 *Canada Labour Code*, RSC 1985, c L-2, s 94(2)(c).

- An employer is entitled to express its views and is not confined to mere platitudes. There is a middle ground between mere platitudes and interference and undue influence in which an employer is free to express its views.
- In evaluating employer conduct, the Board should seek to establish whether the employer's conduct has detrimentally affected the employees' ability to express their true wishes. In other words, has the employer's conduct deprived the employees of the ability to express their true wishes in exercising their decision to associate or not?
- The definition of intimidation, coercion, and undue influence in a labour relations context contains this basic element: the invocation of some form of force, threat, undue pressure, or compulsion for the purpose of controlling or influencing an employee's freedom of association.
- The fact that an employer does not want a union and expresses its opinion to that effect is not necessarily a violation of the *Canada Labour Code*; a factual analysis must be conducted to determine whether the manner in which this opinion is expressed contains an element of coercion, intimidation, threats, promises, or undue influence.
- The Board should consider the context in which the statements are made and the probable effect on a reasonable employee of the means used. Circulation of written material is the preferable mode as the choice of written text is less intrusive than captive audience meetings or private discussions with employees.[106]

For example, an employer representative did not commit an unfair labour practice when he made comments that could have been seen as supportive of an employee leading an application for decertification.[107] An employer also did not commit an unfair labour practice by communicating directly with bargaining agent members through surveys and meetings with employees because there was no threat to or pressure put on employees through those surveys and meetings.[108]

---

106 *Lala v United Food and Commercial Workers Canada, Local 401*, 2017 FPSLREB 42.

107 *Ibid.*

108 *Canadian Federal Pilots*, above note 15.

Section 188 of the *FPSLRA* contains a series of limitations on the rights of employee organizations, one of which benefits the employer on unfair labour practice complaints. Section 188(a) of the *FPSLRA* prevents an employee organization from organizing at an employee's place of employment during the employee's working hours. The Canada Labour Relations Board has referred to a similar provision in the *Canada Labour Code* as a shield, not a sword,[109] indicating that it is meant as a defence to an unfair labour practice complaint.

The Board has addressed this provision in detail in a case involving the International Association of Machinists and Aerospace Workers (IAM).[110] The IAM was involved in a campaign to replace another union for correctional officers. As part of that campaign, it sent a letter to every corrections officer. It sent those letters to their home addresses when possible; however, it did not have the home address of every employee, so it sent the letter to some employees through their work address. The employer allowed employees to receive personal mail at work but refused to deliver any letter from the IAM. The IAM alleged that this interfered with the formation of an employee organization contrary to section 186(1) of the *FPSLRA*. The Board concluded that this rule did interfere with the formation of an employee organization contrary to section 186(1)[111] but dismissed the complaint because it found that section 188(a) provided a complete defence for the employer.

The Board explicitly adopted two principles set out by the Canada Labour Relations Board in the *Time Air* decision:

1) No-solicitation or no-distribution rules that prohibit union solicitation on company property by employees during their non-working time are presumptively an unreasonable impediment to self-organization and are therefore invalid; however, such rules may be validated by evidence that special circumstances make the rule necessary to maintain production or discipline.
2) No-solicitation or no-distribution rules that prohibit union solicitation by employees during working time are presumptively valid as to their promulgation in the absence of evidence that the rule was adopted for a discriminatory purpose or applied unfairly.

---

109 *Time Air Inc*, (1989) 77 di 55.

110 *District Lodge 147*, above note 87.

111 As discussed above.

This distinction between working and non-working hours is mirrored in the text of section 188(a) of the *FPSLRA*. Therefore, the issue before the Board was whether a letter sent to a work address that could be opened at any time constituted solicitation "during the employee's working hours." The Board stated that the onus of proof was on the employer to demonstrate that the solicitation did occur during working hours but that the employer met that burden of proof despite providing no evidence that any corrections officer would have opened the letter during working hours had it been delivered. The Board stated:

> Consider the clear example of a union organizer approaching an employee during working hours to persuade him or her to sign a card. While the employee in these circumstances might indeed demonstrate "good judgment" and walk away from the solicitation, the action of the organizer still constitutes a violation of paragraph 188(a) of the *FPSLRA*. And so it is in this case. The employer could have concluded that the complainants' mailing opened the possibility of membership solicitation in the workplace during working hours, an activity prohibited by paragraph 188(a) of the *FPSLRA*. The employer was neither obliged to leave it to the good judgment of employees to walk away from the solicitation until working hours were over nor to advise employees in advance not to read the mailing during working hours. The employer, in short, did not need to weigh the probability that the act of contacting employees could be temporally separated from the act of soliciting employees. The reasonable probability of solicitation during working hours was sufficient to justify the employer's response.[112]

The Board made special mention of the fact that correctional facilities operate at all hours, making it difficult to separate between working and non-working hours:

> In an operation that runs on a "24/7" basis with rotating shift schedules, finding that the concept of "the employee's working hours" operates strictly on an individual employee-by-employee basis could result in a situation where two employees undertake the same activity side-by-side at the same time, one lawfully because it is outside his/her personal work hours, the other unlawfully because it is within his/her schedule. I am concerned that this interpretation does not reflect the intent of paragraph 188*(a)* of the *FPSLRA*. At minimum, it does

112 *District Lodge 147*, above note 87 at para 117.

> suggest that care is needed to apply the expression "employee's working hours" in a reasonable and practical fashion according to the context of the workplace and the situation of employees.[113]

Therefore, in a government workplace that does not operate "24/7," the Board may take a more liberal view of the right of an employee organization to solicit at the workplace. However, at present, employee organizations may not solicit an employee during that employee's working hours, and this extends to sending that employee mail that the Board reasonably expects may be opened during working hours.

8) Failure to Implement an Arbitral Award or a Collective Agreement

Both parties are required to implement a collective agreement within ninety days from either the date agreed to in the agreement or the date it is signed unless they agree on a longer period of time,[114] or within ninety days from the date an arbitral award becomes binding on them.[115] Complaints that the employer has not implemented an arbitral award or a collective agreement are dealt with through section 190 of the *FPSLRA*. Most collective agreements contain a term that they will be implemented within a certain period of time after the execution of the agreement. This means, in practice, that "the minimum time to actually implement the provisions of the agreement is the 90 days plus whatever period occurs between the date of the successful negotiation and the agreements' execution."[116]

The employer has the ability to apply to the Board for an extension of time to implement a collective agreement or arbitral award. Under the former *PSSRA*, the Board stated that the employer has a "heavy onus" to show that the problems causing the implementation delays could not have been foreseen[117] and admonished the employer when it requests an extension without having raised possible implementation problems at the bargaining table.[118] However, the *FPSLRA* starts the

---

113 *Ibid* at para 109.

114 *FPSLRA*, s 117.

115 *Ibid*, s 157.

116 *Treasury Board v Federal Government Dockyard Trades and Labour Council East*, 2014 PSLRB 13 at para 70 [*Dockyard Trades*].

117 *Treasury Board and Public Service Alliance of Canada*, [1999] CPSSRB No 119; *Treasury Board and Public Service Alliance of Canada*, [2000] CPSSRB No 66.

118 *Ibid*.

ninety-day period from the date the agreement is signed, whereas the *PSSRA* started the ninety-day period from the date the agreement was executed. The Board has therefore extended the period of time when the employer could, in good faith, plead that the complexity of the changes led to the compensation services being "overwhelmed with work."[119]

The Board has also concluded that an employer is required to make an application for an extension of time at the earliest opportunity and certainly must do so within the ninety-day period for implementation. An employer may not, for example, respond to a complaint that it has violated this time period by filing an application for an extension of time.[120]

When an employer does not implement a collective agreement or an arbitral award within the statutory deadlines, that failure "goes to the heart of the relationship between the parties, and failing to rectify it in a meaningful way could give rise to cynicism about labour-management relations and could undermine the ability of the union to represent its members effectively."[121] As a result, the Board has concluded that it may award damages for that breach. The Board has done so on only a single occasion to date—and awarded $7,500 to the bargaining agent (or roughly $100 per member of the bargaining unit). The Board made it clear that this award was meant to serve as a deterrent, but without being punitive.[122] In several collective agreements completed in 2019, the bargaining agents agreed to extend the time period for implementation to 120 days for the non-pay portions of the agreement and 180 days for the pay provisions in exchange for a $400 payment to each employee. The bargaining agents also agreed that the employer may extend the 180-day period, but for each ninety-day period it took to implement the pay provisions, employees would be paid an additional $50.

There can be a fine line between alleging that the employer has not implemented a collective agreement and alleging that the employer has simply not complied with the collective agreement. An individual does have standing to bring a complaint alleging that the employer has failed

---

119 *Dockyard Trades*, above note 116 at para 78.

120 *Public Service Alliance of Canada v Parliamentary Protective Service*, 2020 FPSLREB 1 (applying the identical provisions of *Parliamentary Employment and Staff Relations Act*).

121 *Dockyard Chargehands*, above note 8 at para 41.

122 *Ibid*.

to implement a collective agreement or an arbitral award;[123] however, the dispute must be about actual implementation and not a dispute over the interpretation of the collective agreement (and such grievances require the support of the bargaining agent).[124]

---

123 *Sousa-Dias v Public Service Alliance of Canada*, 2018 FPSLREB 46.

124 See Chapter 10.

CHAPTER EIGHT

Employee Organizations in the Federal Public Service

A. INTRODUCTION

This chapter provides a brief overview of the history, duties, and rights of the main employee organizations in the federal public service.

B. THE BARGAINING AGENTS IN THE FEDERAL PUBLIC SERVICE

There are currently twenty employee organizations[1] certified as bargaining agents under the *Federal Public Sector Labour Relations Act* (*FPSLRA*)[2] in eighty-two different bargaining units in both the Treasury Board and separate employers. Those employee organizations represent over 242,000 employees employed in the federal public service.

By far the largest employee organization in the federal public service is the Public Service Alliance of Canada (PSAC). The PSAC was formed in 1966 as the result of a merger between most members of the Civil Service Federation of Canada and the Civil Service Association of Canada. The PSAC's predecessors were organized in the early part of the twentieth century. The Civil Service Association of Ottawa was founded in 1907. This employee organization was open to all civil servants in the national capital area. In 1909, a number of employee

1 This includes employee organizations with several locals representing separate bargaining units.

2 *Federal Public Sector Labour Relations Act*, SC 2003, c 22, s 2 [*FPSLRA*].

organizations formed the Civil Service Federation of Canada. The Civil Service Federation of Canada was composed of smaller organizations of civil servants organized along departmental lines. The Civil Service Association of Ottawa decided to join the Civil Service Federation of Canada at that time and (along with the "outside" organizations) retained a fair degree of autonomy within the federation.

By the 1950s, tensions had arisen between the geographically based Civil Service Association of Ottawa and the other departmentally based organizations that composed the Civil Service Federation of Canada. The two organizations split in 1954 after a dispute over whether departmentally based employee organizations would be allowed to recruit members who worked in Ottawa. However, both organizations recognized the need for unity among public servants, and merger talks of various forms continued throughout the 1950s and early 1960s. In 1957, the Civil Service Association of Ottawa merged with the Amalgamated Civil Servants of Canada (an employee organization founded in 1920, largely composed of postal workers based in Western Canada) to form the Civil Service Association of Canada. Eventually, the Civil Service Association of Canada merged with the Civil Service Federation of Canada (less the postal workers organization that was a part of the federation) to form the Public Service Alliance of Canada in 1966.

The PSAC has retained some features of a federation of unions and other features of a centrally organized union. The PSAC itself has been certified as the bargaining agent,[3] and the central body of the PSAC is responsible for collective agreement negotiation.[4] However, the PSAC is still divided into a number of "components" that used to roughly reflect departmental lines, although departmental reorganizations in the past fifty years have made it more difficult to track components exclusively in various departments.[5] The components are responsible for enforcing the collective agreements applicable to its members, including

3 See *Public Service Alliance of Canada and Canada (Treasury Board) (Hospital Services Group—Operational Category)*, [1967] CPSSRB No 2 at 3.

4 *Constitution of the Public Service Alliance of Canada* (November 2018), s 7(2), online: https://psacunion.ca/our-constitution.

5 Aside from the components that exist along departmental lines, there are three components that represent employees in territorial governments and the public sector in those territories. The PSAC also has what it refers to as "directly chartered locals" who represent employees outside of the federal and territorial public services.

processing grievances and appeals based on the merit principle up to (but not including) adjudication.[6]

The current structure of the PSAC represents a compromise between the centrally organized structure of the Civil Service Association of Canada and the decentralized, departmentally organized Civil Service Federation of Canada. It also reflects the requirement in the *Public Service Staff Relations Act* (*PSSRA*), recommended by the Heeney Committee prior to the merger that formed the PSAC, that bargaining units be organized across departmental lines. As one author explained:

> One of the major explanations for the emergence of the Alliance structure is the Public Service Staff Relations Act and, of course, the government which sponsored it. With statutory bargaining units and centralized bargaining directed by the Treasury Board, the Alliance has to be centralized at least with regard to collective bargaining and related functions.
>
> The PSAC structure is also influenced by the structure of the employer. The government is administered through departments which have some autonomy, so it is logical that the Alliance has similar divisions with corresponding autonomy.
>
> Finally, the Alliance structure is explained by its history. Since the PSAC emerged from the merger of the Civil Service Association of Canada and the Civil Service Federation, its founders borrowed parts of both structures (which were initially determined in part by the structure of the employer). We have thus a central administration to deal with the Treasury Board and the Government, and components to deal with the departments.[7]

The second largest bargaining agent in the federal public service is the Professional Institute of the Public Service of Canada (PIPSC). The PIPSC was founded in 1920 in response to concerns about classification reform as an organization for scientific and professional employees. As the lines between professionals and non-professionals have become blurred—particularly in the federal public service—the PIPSC has evolved into an employee organization similar to the others representing employees in the federal public service.

---

6 *Constitution of the Public Service Alliance of Canada*, above note 4, s 9(5).

7 Maurice Lemelin, *Public Service Alliance of Canada* (Los Angeles: Institute of Industrial Relations, 1978) at 88–89.

C. STATUTORY DUTIES OF EMPLOYEE ORGANIZATIONS

1) Duty of Fair Representation

Section 187 of the *FPSLRA* forbids bargaining agents from acting in a manner that is arbitrary, discriminatory, or in bad faith in the representation of any employee in the bargaining unit. This statutory duty of fair representation is common in most labour relations legislation in Canada, and there is a rich jurisprudence concerning the scope and limits of a union's duty of fair representation. The Board has adopted the general principles of the duty of fair representation that apply in other jurisdictions, in particular the Supreme Court of Canada's summary of the duty of fair representation as follows:

> 1. The exclusive power conferred on a union to act as spokesman for the employees in a bargaining unit entails a corresponding obligation on the union to fairly represent all employees comprised in the unit.
> 2. When, as is true here and is generally the case, the right to take a grievance to arbitration is reserved to the union, the employee does not have an absolute right to arbitration and the union enjoys considerable discretion.
> 3. This discretion must be exercised in good faith, objectively and honestly, after a thorough study of the grievance and the case, taking into account the significance of the grievance and of its consequences for the employee on the one hand and the legitimate interests of the union on the other.
> 4. The union's decision must not be arbitrary, capricious, discriminatory or wrongful.
> 5. The representation by the union must be fair, genuine and not merely apparent, undertaken with integrity and competence, without serious or major negligence, and without hostility towards the employee.[8]

Thus, a bargaining agent does not have to provide representation in every case. Instead, the *gravamen* of the duty of fair representation is the prohibition against bad faith or arbitrary and discriminatory treatment. A bargaining agent is permitted to consider the implications of a

---

8 *Canadian Merchant Service Guild v Gagnon*, [1984] 1 SCR 509. The Board has cited this test approval in, *inter alia*, *Bialy v Gordon*, 2016 PSLREB 87 [*Bialy*].

grievance or case on the workplace as a whole and decline to represent an individual grievor accordingly. As the Board has stated: "It is the role of a bargaining agent to determine what grievances to proceed with and what grievances not to proceed with. This determination can be made on the basis of the resources and requirements of the employee organization as a whole."[9] This means, for example, that a bargaining agent can settle a collective agreement grievance without the employee's approval or decline to represent an employee further if the employee refuses to sign a settlement when the settlement serves the interests of the broader membership as a whole, so long as the settlement does not deliberately ignore the employee's interests.[10]

Finally, the burden of proof rests with the complainant to demonstrate arbitrary, discriminatory, or bad faith behaviour.[11]

One particular problem that arises in the federal public service is the scope of subject matters captured by the duty of fair representation. The theoretical foundation of the duty of fair representation is the exclusive right of a bargaining agent to represent its members. Since in most jurisdictions, the collective agreement encompasses all of an employee's rights in the workplace and the union has carriage of all grievances concerning a breach of the collective agreement, a union must fairly represent its members because they would otherwise have no ability to enforce their rights against their employer. In the federal public service, however, individual employees have several rights that may be exercised without the involvement of the bargaining agent. Therefore, the issue arises as to whether the duty of fair representation applies to cases where an employee has an individual right to proceed with a particular matter.

The Board has resolved this issue by distinguishing between issues that arise under the *FPSLRA* or the collective agreement on the one hand and issues that arise outside of those two areas on the other. This dispute comes up most frequently in staffing disputes. The Board has concluded that it does not have jurisdiction over the duty of fair representation when faced with an employee who is complaining about representation relating to a staffing matter unless that staffing matter

9 *Mangat v Public Service Alliance of Canada*, 2010 PSLRB 52 at para 44.

10 *Ross v Public Service Alliance of Canada*, 2017 FPSLREB 13; *Sayeed v Professional Institute of the Public Service of Canada*, 2010 PSLRB 44; *Bialy*, above note 8.

11 See, for example, *Ouellet v Luce St-Georges and Public Service Alliance of Canada*, 2009 PSLRB 107.

arises out of the *FPSLRA* or the collective agreement.[12] The Board also does not have jurisdiction over complaints about representation relating to a compensation claim under workers' compensation legislation.[13] This is the case even if the bargaining agent at one point voluntarily offered to represent the employee in matters that fall outside the scope of the duty of fair representation.[14]

The Board has concluded that the duty of fair representation applies to disciplinary grievances notwithstanding that employees have an individual right to grieve disciplinary decisions without bargaining agent approval or support.[15] However, a bargaining agent does not breach its duty of fair representation if it refuses to refer a matter to adjudication after it made a careful analysis and determined, in good faith, that the matter cannot be referred to adjudication. As the Board has stated, "The duty of fair representation is not the equivalent of an insurance against error and omissions."[16]

Human rights complaints are another, similar area where the Board has not yet addressed the scope of the duty of fair representation. In *Despres v Public Service Alliance of Canada*,[17] the Board heard a duty of fair representation complaint alleging that the bargaining agent discriminated against him by entering into a pay equity agreement with the Treasury Board that did not protect certain pay rights upon promotion. The Board dismissed the complaint but did not address the bargaining agent's argument that it was without jurisdiction to hear the complaint because it concerned a human rights matter, and the member should therefore have proceeded to the human rights commission. Since the *FPSLRA* includes the right to have human rights complaints proceed by way of grievance, the duty of fair representation probably extends to human rights complaints. Section 69 of the *Federal Public Sector*

---

12 *Abeysuriya v Professional Institute of the Public Service of Canada*, 2015 PSLREB 26 at para 38; *Tran v Professional Institute of the Public Service of Canada*, 2014 PSLRB 71.

13 *Elliott v Canadian Merchant Service Guild*, 2008 PSLRB 3.

14 *Gabon v Public Service Alliance of Canada*, 2022 FPSLREB 2 (staffing matters); *Millar v Public Service Alliance of Canada*, 2021 FPSLREB 68 (workers' compensation matters).

15 *Taylor v Public Service Alliance of Canada*, 2015 PSLREB 35 at para 81 [*Taylor*].

16 *Jakutavicius v Public Service Alliance of Canada*, 2005 PSLRB 70 at para 125 [*Jakutavicius*].

17 *Despres v Public Service Alliance of Canada*, [2003] CPSSRB No 72.

Labour Relations Regulations[18] requires individuals seeking to grieve the interpretation or application of a collective agreement to have the authorization of their bargaining agent. The Supreme Court of Canada in *Parry Sound (District) Social Services Administration Board v OPSEU, Local 324*, concluded that the Ontario *Human Rights Code* was incorporated into collective agreements in that province:

> [T]he substantive rights and obligations of the Human Rights Code are incorporated into each collective agreement over which an arbitrator has jurisdiction. Because of this interpretation, an alleged violation of the Human Rights Code constitutes an alleged violation of the collective agreement, and falls squarely within the Board's jurisdiction.[19]

If *Parry Sound* means that the *Canadian Human Rights Act* is also incorporated into federal collective agreements, then arguably any human rights complaint concerns the interpretation or application of a collective agreement. This in turn means that the bargaining agent has the exclusive right of representation in human rights proceedings that are addressed by way of a grievance and a corresponding duty of fair representation—at the very least when a collective agreement contains a "no discrimination" clause, as is standard in the federal public administration. The bargaining agent, by contrast, would not have a duty of fair representation in a complaint to the Canadian Human Rights Commission because that complaint falls outside the scope of the collective agreement and the *FPSLRA*.

Finally, the Board has occasionally addressed the duty of fair representation in an application for judicial review. The duty of fair representation extends to a decision to assist a member in an application for judicial review from a final decision (whether of an adjudicator or a final-level grievance officer), and the same considerations apply: a bargaining agent may refuse to bring an application for judicial review if they have carefully considered the case and come to the conclusion (in good faith) that the application is unlikely to be successful. However, in many situations, the member themself would have standing to apply for judicial review. In such a case, the Board has concluded that the bargaining agent owes a duty to inform the member of their right to proceed by way of

---

18 *Federal Public Sector Labour Relations Regulations*, SOR/2005-79.

19 *Parry Sound (District) Social Services Administration Board v OPSEU, Local 324*, 2003 SCC 42 at para 55 [*Parry Sound*].

judicial review in a timely manner,[20] in particular where the member has expressed an interest in contesting an unfavourable response at the final level of the grievance procedure or at adjudication.[21]

Another issue that arises in most workplaces but appears to come up with particular intensity in the federal public service is how to deal with allegations of workplace harassment. The PSAC had a policy that it would not represent an employee to dispute a harassment finding; it would only represent that employee with respect to the quantum of the ensuing penalty. The Board concluded that this policy was arbitrary because it could lead to a decision to deny representation to an employee falsely accused of harassment.[22]

2) Unfair Labour Practices by Employee Organizations

Section 188 of the *FPSLRA* was added as part of the broader amendments that came into force on 1 April 2005. The pre-2005 *PSSRA* had no provisions that governed the internal affairs of employee organizations aside from the duty of fair representation. The Board followed the approach by other labour boards across Canada that the duty of fair representation does not confer on the Board the power to regulate the internal affairs of a bargaining agent.[23] Disputes over internal union affairs were left to the courts.

Section 188 of the *FPSLRA* lists five "unfair labour practices" that employee organizations are prohibited from engaging in. The first such practice is a prohibition against recruiting members at the workplace during working hours,[24] and that practice has already been discussed in Chapter 7. The other four unfair labour practices all concern the treatment of members (or potential members) by an employee organization.

Section 188(b) of the *FPSLRA* prohibits an employee organization from expelling from, suspending from, or denying membership to an employee "in a discriminatory manner." Paragraph (c) similarly

20 Since the *Federal Courts Act*, RSC 1985, c F-7, requires an application for judicial review to be filed within thirty days, a "timely manner" would appear to be almost immediately.

21 *Jakutavicius*, above note 16.

22 *Taylor*, above note 15 at para 94.

23 *Hibbard v Public Service Alliance of Canada*, [1976] CPSSRB No 11 at para 16; *St-James and Canada Employment and Immigration Union Component (PSAC)*, [1992] CPSSRB No 44 at 5–6.

24 *FPSLRA*, s 188(a).

prohibits an employee organization from taking disciplinary action against a member "in a discriminatory manner." The crucial phrase in both paragraphs is the phrase "in a discriminatory manner."

The Board has stated some *dicta* that, taken on its face, would limit the application of paragraphs 188(b) and (c). The Board has, for example, stated that the existence of those provisions does not make the Board a "final appeal for the internal decisions made by a bargaining agent"[25] and that these provisions "raise specific issues under the [*FPSLRA*] and they do not authorize the Board to act as the final arbitrator of all internal disputes within a bargaining agent. They do not, for example, authorize the Board to decide the scope of offences that may be the subject of discipline within the bargaining agent." Notwithstanding this *dicta*, the Board has interpreted the phrase "discriminatory" so broadly that it has, in effect, turned the Board into an appeals body for internal union affairs.

The Board's decisions in *Veillette v Professional Institute of the Public Service of Canada* spell out this expanded jurisdiction. In the first board decision involving these parties,[26] the complainant was suspended from his duties as a steward for two years after getting into a physical altercation with another member. The employee organization followed its policy for internal discipline: it hired an investigator, who interviewed the protagonists and other witnesses; the investigator made a recommendation that the complainant had acted inappropriately, and the board of directors of the employee organization ultimately agreed and suspended the complainant. The employee organization followed this policy in lieu of an older bylaw providing a different process, which the employee organization believed only applied to actions taken that were prejudicial to the employee organization as bargaining agent, not to an intra-union fight. The Board concluded that the phrase "in a discriminatory manner" meant a decision-making process free from discrimination. The Board went on to conclude that the term "free from discrimination" did not mean discrimination in a human rights sense but, instead, was "a concept of administrative justice."[27] From this interpretation, the Board then concluded that the phrase "free from

---

25 *Bremsak v Professional Institute of the Public Service of Canada*, 2009 PSLRB 103 at para 61 [*Bremsak #1*].

26 *Veillette v Professional Institute of the Public Service of Canada*, 2009 PSLRB 58 [*Veillette*].

27 *Ibid* at para 28.

discrimination" was broad enough to require an assessment of two things: whether the employee organization acted within the framework of its constitution and bylaws and whether it followed the rules of procedural fairness.[28] On the facts of that case, the Board concluded that the employee organization did not follow its bylaws (but followed the policy instead). Finally, the Board concluded that since the bylaw mentioned a progressive scale of disciplinary measures, the employee organization's decision was also "discriminatory" because it did not apply progressive discipline.[29] An application for judicial review from this decision was commenced but ultimately discontinued.

In a decision rendered shortly after *Veillette*, the Board issued another decision on the meaning of the phrase "in a discriminatory manner." In *Bremsak v Professional Institute of the Public Service of Canada*, the complainant was accused of harassing another member. The employee organization ultimately agreed with the accusation and asked the complainant to apologize. When she refused, they apologized on her behalf. She alleged that this was a penalty imposed in a discriminatory manner. The Board dismissed this aspect of her complaint but, in doing so, applied a test that is frankly difficult to fully understand:

> In the context of administrative justice and labour relations, a broad interpretation of discrimination within the bounds of the legislation is appropriate, and the Board must consider not only the "... result of the application of disciplinary standards but also the basis for their application and the manner in which they have been applied." ...
>
> The goal of preventing discrimination under that provision is inclusive and is achieved by preventing bargaining agents from excluding employees from the activities of an employee organization based on attributed rather than actual abilities. The essence of the protection is to prevent illegal, arbitrary or unreasonable barriers. On the other hand, barriers or distinctions that are legally valid and genuinely based on a rule or policy that has a fair and rational relationship to the decision being made may be valid and defensible. In some cases, the treatment of an employee will be based on a valid distinction rather than prohibited discrimination, even though the distinction has a negative impact on the employee: "[n]ot every distinction is discriminatory."[30]

28 *Ibid* at para 30.

29 *Ibid* at para 49.

30 *Bremsak #1*, above note 25 at para 87.

The difficulty with the Board's logic is that every act of discipline draws a distinction between the member who has been disciplined on the one hand and every non-disciplined member on the other. The effect of the Board's decision is that it is required to rule on whether every disciplinary decision by an employee organization is "illegal, arbitrary or unreasonable" — which requires it to perform the very appellate function that it disavowed earlier in the same decision. This problem was demonstrated again in another case involving Ms. Bremsak, this time involving a five-year suspension from membership flowing from a finding of harassment. While the Board upheld the suspension, it nevertheless did so on the basis that "there was a rational reason for the five-year suspension from membership."[31]

Fortunately, subsequent board decisions have not adopted this broad of an approach. In *Gilkinson v Professional Institute of the Public Service of Canada*, the Board stated that in respect of "discriminatory" behaviour, the Board has concluded that "not every distinction is discriminatory." Instead, the term refers to an "illegitimate distinction based on irrelevant grounds."[32] In *Pronovost v Professional Institute of the Public Service of Canada*, the Board departed even further from *Veillette*, stating that "[t]he purpose of a complaint under s. 188(c) of the *Act* is not to determine whether the decision was unreasonable, arbitrary, or made in bad faith or whether it violated the rules of procedural fairness. Once again, the only way for the Board to analyze the complaint is to determine whether the disciplinary standards might have been applied discriminatorily"[33] — implying that a decision that was unreasonable or contrary to procedural fairness is not necessarily discriminatory. The Board in the second *Bremsak* case concluded that there was no breach of procedural fairness on bias grounds because the

31 *Bremsak v Professional Institute of the Public Service of Canada*, 2013 PSLRB 22 at para 497 [*Bremsak #2*], aff'd *Bremsak v Professional Institute of the Public Service of Canada*, 2014 FCA 11 [*Bremsak FCA*].

32 *Gilkinson v Professional Institute of the Public Service of Canada*, 2018 FPSLREB 62 at para 19. See also *Leach v Fortin*, 2018 FPSLREB 67 at para 35: "The essence of the complainant's allegations is simply that the respondents applied the CIU's [Customs and Immigration Union] by-laws and the PSAC's constitution incorrectly and arbitrarily. Without more, there is no arguable case that disciplinary action was taken against him or a penalty was imposed on him in a *discriminatory* manner within the scope of s. 188(c)" [emphasis in original].

33 *Pronovost v Professional Institute of the Public Service of Canada*, 2020 FPSLREB 24 at para 41 [*Pronovost*].

executive committee did not "lacked [*sic*] the will to reach an honest conclusion about the facts of her case"—which is a fairly low standard for procedural fairness.[34] This more restrictive approach by the Board is surely preferable to the *Veillette* approach, which had the effect (even if avowedly not the intention) of turning the Board into an appellate body from disciplinary decisions of employee organizations.

The Board's new approach brings it closer into line with the Canada Industrial Relations Board. The Canada Industrial Relations Board has only required unions to follow a minimal degree of natural justice while exercising their disciplinary powers, stating that "[i]n convening trial boards and conducting trials in disciplinary matters, unions will not be held under sections 95(f) and (g) to the same standards of natural justice as a statutory tribunal. They must nonetheless observe the fundamental tenets of natural justice."[35] The Canada Industrial Relations Board has not been clear on whether this is a free-standing obligation or whether adherence to the rules of natural justice is required because most union constitutions contain some provision guaranteeing a fair and impartial trial, and a breach of the rules of natural justice is also a breach of the union's constitution and thus presumptively discriminatory treatment.[36] The Canada Industrial Relations Board has also stated that section 95 of the *Canada Labour Code* does not require unions to follow their constitutions (so long as they breach their constitutions in a non-discriminatory manner) but that a breach of the constitution may corroborate evidence of discrimination.[37] Therefore, the better view is that a breach of natural justice (even on a relaxed standard) is evidence of arbitrary treatment, which is itself discriminatory.

Despite this expansive definition of "discriminatory," in most cases the Canada Industrial Relations Board is reluctant to interfere with disciplinary decisions unless the union imposes different penalties on different members without cause. In *Angelo Mangatal*,[38] for example, the Board dismissed a complaint against expulsion for three years

---

34 *Bremsak #2*, above note 31 at paras 394 and 473, aff'd *Bremsak FCA*, above note 31 at paras 19–22.

35 *Donna Beaven et al* (1996), 100 di 96 at para 59.

36 See, for example, *ValUdvarhely and Canadian Air Line Flight Attendants Association* (1979), 35 di 87.

37 *Mark Conlin* (1994), 95 di 145. See also *Canada Labour Code*, RSC 1985, c L-2, s 95.

38 *Angelo Mangatal*, (1997) 105 di 1.

because that discipline was neither disproportionate nor different than the discipline imposed on other members for crossing a picket line, stating: "[T]he discipline imposed on Mangatal was consistent with, and equal to, that given to each and every other member across Canada who was 'convicted' by Hargrove of the offenses in question. Furthermore, it cannot be said that in the circumstances the penalty imposed, for crossing a picket line, was unfair or discriminatory."[39]

As mentioned above, section 188(c) restricts "disciplinary" actions that result in a "penalty." Again, the Board took an expansive view of "disciplinary" in *Veillette*, but it has been taking a more restrictive view in subsequent cases. On the facts of *Veillette*, the member was suspended as a steward—clearly, a disciplinary decision in any meaning of the word. In a second *Veillette*[40] decision (heard shortly after the first *Veillette* decision), the employee organization refused to reinstate the complainant to his position of shop steward while the dispute was still before the Board. The employee organization characterized this as a purely administrative matter, relying on board jurisprudence distinguishing between administrative and disciplinary actions against employees. The Board pointed out, though, that the wording of section 188(c) is different from the equivalent provision governing employees (section 209) because section 188(c) refers to "any penalty." Accordingly, section 188(c) regulates any sanction imposed on a member, whether disciplinary or not.[41]

The Board has recently taken a more restrictive view on what constitutes a "penalty." For example, the Board has concluded that the refusal to appoint an employee as a shop steward (at first because the employee was engaged in a serious dispute with the employer that would distract her from representing other employees and later because the employee settled the dispute on the condition that she no longer appear at the workplace) was not a "penalty" for the purposes of section 188(c).[42] The Board has also ruled that being subject to an investigation process,[43] a decision not to reinstate a member (roughly nine years after being expelled in the first place),[44] a decision not to renew a

39 *Ibid* at para 20.

40 *Veillette v Professional Institute of the Public Service of Canada*, 2009 PSLRB 64.

41 *Ibid* at para 32.

42 *Pronovost*, above note 33.

43 *Corbett v Professional Institute of the Public Service of Canada*, 2016 PSLREB 82.

44 *Hunter v Union of Canadian Correctional Officers—Syndicat des agents correctionnels du Canada—CSN*, 2017 FPSLREB 4 [*Hunter*].

member as a steward,[45] and a decision not to allow the complainant to participate in a disciplinary appeal process (where he was the original complainant against the person being disciplined) are not penalties.[46]

Sections 188(d) and (e) of the *FPSLRA* prohibit an employee organization from expelling or suspending from membership in the employee organization, taking disciplinary action against, or imposing any penalty against a member for exercising a right under Part 1, 2, or 2.1 of the *FPSLRA*. Paragraph (e) goes further and prohibits an employee organization from intimidating or coercing a member because that person has testified or participated in a proceeding under Part 1, 2, or 2.1 of the *FPSLRA* or filed a complaint under those parts.

Prior to the introduction of this provision, many employee organizations had policies that prohibited elected officials from proceeding to "outside" bodies for relief against the employee organization. In the first *Bremsak* decision discussed above, in addition to the harassment and apology issue, the employee organization suspended the complainant from all of her elected positions because she filed her initial complaint with the Board. The employee organization argued that such a policy was necessary to protect against the conflict of interest inherent in serving as an elected official in an organization at the same time as pursuing legal action against the organization. The Board accepted the logic of that argument but concluded that it did not mean that elected officials must, in all cases, automatically be expelled from their office during the life of a complaint. Instead, the Board found as follows:

> I am nonetheless unable to accept that all situations involving an application to an outside body require a suspension from elected office or that all duties of such a position are properly the subject of a suspension. In my view, some proportionality is required to balance the various factors at play so that the legitimate interests of the bargaining agent are protected and harmful actions of an elected person do not threaten those interests.[47]

The Board found, for example, that it would be legitimate to require an elected official to recuse themselves from discussions relating to their own complaint, and if they refuse, they may be expelled from that meeting.

45 *Myles v Professional Institute of the Public Service of Canada*, 2017 FPSLREB 30.

46 *Nolet v Public Service Alliance of Canada*, 2019 FPSLREB 38.

47 *Bremsak #1*, above note 25 at para 117.

The Board stated, though, that a certain amount of disruption is inherent in union politics. This particular complainant did attend meetings after being suspended and was disruptive, but the Board found that it did not create real harm to the employee organization. The Board therefore allowed the complaint and ordered the employee organization to amend its policy and restore the complainant's status as an elected official.[48]

Finally, section 190(3) of the *FPSLRA* contains a defence against an allegation of discriminatory treatment by an employee organization under sections 188(b) and (c): a complainant may not bring a complaint to the Board unless they have first used the internal appeal or grievance mechanisms available within the employee organization,[49] unless the complaint is such that it should be dealt with by the Board without delay or the employee organization has not given the complainant ready access to the appeal procedure.[50] If a union delays its response for more than six months, then the defence is also unavailable.[51]

The Board has not had an opportunity to consider this provision in detail. In one case, the Board rejected an argument based on section 190(3) on the basis that the appeal clause was unclear and could be read so that the particular issue involved was not capable of being appealed; however, the Board dismissed the complaint as untimely and because it did not fit into any category of unfair labour practice.[52]

The Canada Industrial Relations Board has stated that the purpose of the equivalent section in the *Canada Labour Code* is "to ensure that certain complaints against trade unions, such as complaints alleging that a trade union applied membership rules to an employee in a discriminatory manner, be made as a last resort—that is, after the aggrieved party has made reasonable attempts to exhaust all internal avenues of appeal."[53] The complainant is expected to have at least attempted to use the union's internal remedies before turning to the Board for relief, unless the complainant does not have ready access to those remedies.

---

48 Ultimately, the employee organization did not reinstate her to her position. The Board agreed to file the order in Federal Court (*Bremsak v Professional Institute of the Public Service of Canada*, 2009 PSLRB 159), and the employee organization was found in contempt of that order and fined $250,000 for its contempt (*Professional Institute of the Public Service of Canada v Bremsak*, 2013 FCA 214).

49 *FPSLRA*, s 190(3).

50 *Ibid*, s 190(4).

51 *Ibid*, s 190(3)(b)(ii).

52 *Hunter*, above note 44.

53 *Hollingsworth* (1998), 106 di 96 at para 59.

For example, where the available appeal is to a national convention of the union held every two or three years, this is not "ready access" to a grievance or appeal procedure, and the complainant need not exercise this right prior to filing a complaint.[54] Finally, using an employee organization's internal appeal route extends the deadline for filing a complaint under section 190 of the *FPSLRA*: the complaint needs to be filed within ninety days of receiving the union's final response (or within ninety days of the expiry of the union's six-month window in which to respond to such a complaint).

3) Legal Status of Employee Organizations (at Common Law)

Notwithstanding the Board's expanded jurisdiction to regulate internal union affairs, many questions concerning an employee organization's interpretation of its own constitution are a matter for the courts.

A union constitution is a contractual instrument between the members and the union itself. While union membership used to be seen as a "web of contracts" between the members,[55] the Supreme Court of Canada considered this analysis to be outdated and instead adopted a model whereby unions have independent legal status as organizations that enter into contracts with their members:

> [T]he time has come to recognize formally that when a member joins a union, a relationship in the nature of a contract arises between the member and the trade union *as a legal entity*. By the act of membership, both the union and the member agree to be bound by the terms of the union constitution, and an action may be brought by a member against the union for its breach; however, since the union itself is the contracting party, the liability of the union is limited to the assets of the union and cannot extend to its members personally. I say that this relationship is in the *nature* of a contract because it is unlike a typical commercial contract. Although the relationship includes at least some of the indicia of a common law contract (for example offer and acceptance), the terms of the contractual relationship between the union and the member will be greatly determined by the statutory

---

54 *Ibid* at para 62, where the ultimate review was a convention held every three years; see also *Wheadon (Ronald) et al* (1983), 54 di 134, where the ultimate review was a convention held in Miami, Florida, every two years.

55 *Orchard v Tunney*, [1957] SCR 436.

> regime affecting unions generally as well as the labour law principles that courts have fashioned over the years. With this in mind, for ease of reference I will refer to the membership agreement between the individual member and the union as a contract.[56]

Therefore, questions about union membership and union discipline also fall within the preserve of the civil courts, with only exceptional cases being within the jurisdiction of the Board. This includes disputes between unions and their members, as well as disputes between components of the PSAC.[57] Furthermore, locals of a union are also legal entities in their own right, and a national or parent union is not legally responsible for the actions of a local simply because they are affiliated.[58]

This contractual model of union/member relations means that the courts retain jurisdiction to resolve disputes between members and the union about the terms of the constitution and, specifically, whether those terms are unconscionable. In *Birch v Union of Taxation Employees, Local 70030*,[59] the constitution of the Union of Taxation Employees (a component of the PSAC) contained a provision stating that a member in a legal strike position who crossed a picket line is guilty of an offence punishable by a fine equal to the amount of daily remuneration earned by the member for each day the member crosses the picket line. During a legal strike, several employees crossed the picket line and were fined. They refused to pay their fines, so the union commenced a court proceeding to collect them. The Ontario Court of Appeal ultimately concluded that the union had standing to commence that claim but that the particular provision in the union constitution was unconscionable and, therefore, could not be enforced. The Court of Appeal concluded that there is an inequality of bargaining power on the part of individual union members and that the fines themselves were unfair, in part because they reflected gross wages instead of the member's actual take-home pay (net of taxes). The implication of the Ontario Court of Appeal's decision, though, is that a more modest fine under a union constitution may be enforceable. The court also rejected the union's argument that the members should have exhausted the union's appeal mechanisms and

56 *Berry v Pulley*, 2002 SCC 40 at para 48 [emphasis in original].

57 See *National Health and Welfare Union v Public Service Alliance of Canada*, [2006] OJ No 2744 [*National Health and Welfare Union*].

58 *Fullowka v Pinkerton's of Canada Ltd*, 2010 SCC 5 at paras 127–30.

59 *Birch v Union of Taxation Employees, Local 70030*, 2008 ONCA 809.

the ability to complain to the Board rather than simply refusing to pay the fine.[60]

The recognition by the Supreme Court of Canada that trade unions are a legal entity has had an impact on the legal right of federal public service unions in Ontario to commence civil claims. Prior to *Berry v Pulley*, it was doubtful whether trade unions had the legal status to assert rights in court, including common law rights. The Ontario *Rights of Labour Act* confirmed this approach by stating: "A trade union shall not be made a party to any action in any court unless it may be so made a party irrespective of this Act or of the Labour Relations Act."[61] However, federal public service unions do not have any rights created by the Ontario *Labour Relations Act*: their rights and duties are set out either at common law or by the *FPSLRA*. In *Public Service Alliance of Canada v Attorney General of Canada*,[62] the PSAC and other employee organizations brought a civil action in its own name against the Government of Canada concerning changes to pension legislation. On motion by the government, the PSAC was struck out as a party because of the *Rights of Labour Act*. However, the Ontario Court of Appeal allowed an appeal and reinstated the PSAC and the other unions as a party. The court concluded that the *PSSRA* gave the PSAC the legal status to sue in their own names, "at least for the purpose of discharging their functions in performing their roles in the field of labour relations."[63] Since the

60 The court in a later case did uphold a motion judge's decision that three union members seeking a declaration that a provision in a union constitution was unconscionable had standing to do so but that the application for a declaration should be stayed while the three members exhausted their rights under the union constitution to challenge or modify the offending rule: *Brown v Hanley*, 2019 ONCA 395.

61 *Rights of Labour Act*, RSO 1990, c R-33, s 3(2).

62 *Public Service Alliance of Canada v Attorney General of Canada* (2002), 62 OR (3d) 682 (CA).

63 *Ibid* at para 31. In the *National Health and Welfare Union* case, above note 57, there was no issue raised about the status of the National Health and Welfare Union (NHWU) to bring an action in civil court. The NHWU, as a PSAC component, has no legal status under the *FPSLRA*, and it is not incorporated either. Since *Berry v Pulley*, above note 56, recognized the legal status of trade unions because of the various duties imposed by statutory regimes, and since the components have no status under the *FPSLRA*, I question whether a component is a proper party to a civil suit against other components or the PSAC itself. The matter may be different if it involves a claim made by or against a member because the contract of membership is with the component as well as the PSAC.

PSAC derived its status from the *PSSRA* (and not the Ontario *Labour Relations Act*), their action was not barred by the *Rights of Labour Act*. The other three unions were permitted as parties because they had all incorporated themselves (as corporations, they have the right to bring legal actions regardless of the topic of the claim).

PART III

TERMS AND CONDITIONS OF EMPLOYMENT

CHAPTER NINE

Terms and Conditions of Employment of Federal Public Servants

A. INTRODUCTION

This chapter concerns some of the terms and conditions of employment for employees in the federal public service. It is beyond the scope of this book, or probably any book, to prepare a complete description of all the terms and conditions of employment of federal public servants. For one thing, many of these terms and conditions are contained in collective agreements and so will obviously differ from bargaining unit to bargaining unit. For another, there are simply too many terms and conditions to list. As the Supreme Court of Canada has put it:

> The terms and conditions of employment of the federal government's quarter of a million current workers are set out in statutes, collective agreements, Treasury Board directives, regulations, ministerial orders, and other documents that consume bookshelves of loose-leaf binders. Human resources personnel are recruited into the system, spend a career attempting to understand it and die out of it.[1]

Rather than devalue the efforts of human resource personnel, who "spend a career" learning to understand the terms and conditions of employment, by attempting to summarize these terms and conditions in a single chapter, this book will focus on some of the service-wide conditions, as well as those that are, if not unique, then at least particularly relevant to the public service. This book will also mention, in summary

1 *Vaughan v Canada (Attorney General)*, 2005 SCC 11 at para 1 [*Vaughan*].

only, some of the most frequently litigated terms and conditions applicable in the core public administration.

B. LEGAL NATURE OF TERMS AND CONDITIONS FOR UNREPRESENTED EMPLOYEES

Approximately 10 percent of employees in the federal public service are not represented by a bargaining agent.[2] For represented employees, their terms and conditions of employment are set out in various collective agreements. Unrepresented employees obviously do not have their terms and conditions set out in collective agreements and must have those terms and conditions set out elsewhere.

As explained in Chapter 2 of this book, the legal status of public servants has been a matter of some dispute. The Supreme Court of Canada in a 1980 decision stated that a junior non-unionized employee could sue the Government of Quebec for an employment-related debt in small claims court. In so doing, the Supreme Court stated that this casual employee was a "contract employee" and that it did not see "anything preventing application of the ordinary law of contract" to that case.[3] Even after that case, the nature of the relationship between the Crown and public servants was still in doubt as it was not clear whether the decision in *Attorney General of Quebec v Labrecque* applied outside of junior, casual employees.

This doubt was meant to be resolved by the Supreme Court of Canada in a 1999 decision, *Wells v Newfoundland*.[4] In that case, Mr. Wells was dismissed from his position as a member of the Public Utilities

---

2 According to internal statistics, there were 262,696 employees in the federal public service in 2017 (excluding a handful of separate agencies for whom statistics were not available), of whom 237,580 were represented by a bargaining agent: Treasury Board of Canada Secretariat, "Population of the Federal Public Service," online: www.canada.ca/en/treasury-board-secretariat/services/innovation/human-resources-statistics/population-federal-public-service.html, and Federal Public Sector Labour Relations and Employment Board, *2018–2019 Annual Report* (2019) at 35, online (pdf): https://pslreb-crtefp.gc.ca/en/about-us/annual-reports/2018-2019/documents/FPSLREB-AR_2019.pdf. By way of comparison, the union density rate for the public sector (including Crown corporations and government-funded establishments such as schools, universities, and hospitals) is a little over 75 percent (precisely 75.5 percent in 2017): Statistics Canada, "Union Status by Industry," online: www150.statcan.gc.ca/t1/tbl1/en/tv.action?pid=1410013201.

3 *Attorney General of Quebec v Labrecque*, [1980] 2 SCR 1057 at 1083.

4 *Wells v Newfoundland*, [1999] 3 SCR 199 [*Wells*].

Board when the Newfoundland legislature reconstituted the board with fewer members. Mr. Wells was appointed to hold office during good behaviour until the age of seventy—in fact, he was dismissed well before his seventieth birthday. Therefore, he claimed damages for unjust dismissal. The Supreme Court of Canada upheld his claim for damages and in so doing confirmed that senior public servants and public officeholders have a contractual relationship with their employer. The Court stated:

> In my opinion, it is time to remove uncertainty and confirm that the law regarding senior civil servants accords with the contemporary understanding of the state's role and obligations in its dealings with employees. Employment in the civil service is not feudal servitude. The respondent's position was not a form of monarchical patronage. He was employed to carry out an important function on behalf of the citizens of Newfoundland. The government offered him the position, terms were negotiated, and an agreement reached. It was a contract.
>
> As Beetz J. clearly observed in *Labrecque, supra*, the common law views mutually agreed employment relationships through the lens of contract. This undeniably is the way virtually everyone dealing with the Crown sees it. While the terms and conditions of the contract may be dictated, in whole or in part, by statute, the employment relationship remains a contract in substance and the general law of contract will apply unless specifically superceded by explicit terms in the statute or agreement.[5]

There are exceptions to this rule: judges, ministers of the Crown, and other people who fill constitutionally defined state roles do not have their terms and conditions dictated by contract but by "the terms and conventions of the Constitution."[6] For example, the appointment of an ambassador remains an appointment purely at pleasure and, therefore, an ambassador has no claim for breach of contract when their term of office is terminated prematurely.[7]

The Supreme Court of Canada confirmed this result in its 2008 decision in *Dunsmuir v New Brunswick*.[8] In that case, a public servant was dismissed from his employment on a "without cause" basis as a

---

5 *Ibid* at paras 29–30.

6 *Ibid* at para 31.

7 *Gagliano c Canada (Procureur général)*, 2009 QCCS 3001, aff'd 2011 QCCA 894.

8 *Dunsmuir v New Brunswick*, 2008 SCC 9 [*Dunsmuir*].

result of some performance concerns. The public servant grieved on several bases, including that he was not provided with procedural fairness in the employer's decision to terminate his employment. Upon eventual appeal to the Supreme Court of Canada, the Court confirmed that public servants "have a contractual employment relationship."[9] The Court also concluded that the principles of procedural fairness—absent some statutory requirement—do not apply to public servants, stating that "where a dismissal decision is properly within the public authority's powers and is taken pursuant to a contract of employment, there is no compelling public law purpose for imposing a duty of fairness"[10] and, therefore, "disputes relating to dismissal should be resolved according to the express or implied terms of the contract of employment and any applicable statutes and regulations."[11] On the facts of that case, the Court concluded that the public servant was entitled to damages for failure to provide him with reasonable notice of his dismissal, but he was not entitled to procedural fairness or any right of reinstatement.

Having established that public servants are in a contractual relationship with the Crown, what then are the terms and conditions of that contract? In *Wells*, the Supreme Court stated that these terms are found in "the written and verbal manifestations of the agreement [in that case, on hiring], applicable statutes and regulations, and the common law." In the passage from *Vaughan* cited above, the Supreme Court mentioned "statutes, collective agreements, Treasury Board directives, regulations, ministerial orders, and other documents."

The answer to this question depends first on the relevant legislation. For employees in the core public administration, the *Financial Administration Act* states that the Treasury Board has the authority to determine the terms and conditions of employment of persons employed in the federal public administration,[12] including, more specifically, the power to determine rates of pay.[13] This statutory power to determine the terms and conditions of employment does not, however, oust all basic contract principles. For employees in separate agencies, the respective constituting legislation of the separate agency will set out the power of that particular agency.

9 *Ibid* at para 97.

10 *Ibid* at para 106.

11 *Ibid* at para 113.

12 *Financial Administration Act*, RSC 1985, c F-11, s 7(1)(e).

13 *Ibid*, s 11.1(1).

One term or condition of employment is that the Treasury Board must inform employees before changing terms and conditions of employment. This notice must be provided broadly when the change involves a change in a term or condition that applies to a group of unrepresented employees and must also be made to individual employees when the change only applies to those individuals. The first category is exemplified by *Appleby-Ostroff v Canada (Attorney General)*. In that case, the employee was dismissed from her employment as a result of a discontinuance of her function. Long prior to her dismissal, the Treasury Board had enacted a policy called the Executive Employment Transition Policy. The Treasury Board later repealed that policy shortly before dismissing the employee and enacted various policy documents stating explicitly that this policy was no longer in effect. The Treasury Board argued, however, that it adopted a measure by which this policy was made to apply to the employee (and a broader group of employees)—but it never informed those employees that the policy remained in effect. The Federal Court of Appeal concluded that this secret clause was not enforceable and the policy did not apply to this employee, stating,

> In the absence of specific legislation to the contrary, because these terms and conditions of employment established by the Treasury Board become part of the employee's contract of employment, it would be inconsistent with principles of fairness and good faith to empower the Treasury Board to determine these terms and conditions without disclosing them to the concerned employee, particularly in the event of a dispute as to the scope of their application.[14]

Therefore, the Treasury Board's power to amend terms and conditions of employment for groups of employees does not extend to the power to amend those terms in secret.

The second category involving individual terms and conditions of employment is demonstrated in *Plumadore v Canada (Attorney General)*. That case involved pay for overtime. The employee's position was initially in a bargaining unit, but, unbeknownst to him, the employer obtained an order designating his position for exclusion. The employer never informed the employee. One important distinction between unionized and excluded positions is that unionized employees were entitled to overtime and excluded employees were not. The employee worked

14 *Appleby-Ostroff v Canada (Attorney General)*, 2011 FCA 84 at para 30 [*Appleby-Ostroff*].

1,785.5 hours of overtime over a forty-one-month period before the employer noticed its mistake and insisted that the employee pay back $145,477.88 in overtime payments. The Federal Court set aside the order to pay back that money because it breached the terms of the employee's contract since the employer had never informed the employee of the change from unionized to excluded position. As the Court put it:

> In private employment contracts both parties must to [*sic*] agree to a change of the terms. This contract is somewhat different as Treasury Board has the unilateral right to make changes under the [*Financial Administration Act*]. That, however, does not mean the changes, in this particular case, were effective without being communicated to the Applicant.[15]

Another issue is whether the Treasury Board may change terms and conditions of employment without consideration. Under the general law of contract, changes to a contract must be supported by new or additional consideration (some benefit flowing to each side as part of the change). This principle applies in employment law as well: changes to an employment contract (typically some change that limits an employee's entitlement upon dismissal) must be supported by consideration[16] unless the employer makes a promise to the employee to forbear from exercising its right to terminate the employee for a reasonable period, thus enhancing the employee's security of employment as the "consideration."[17] In the federal public service, the Treasury Board policies and instruments that govern the terms and conditions of employment are amended from time to time. To date, however, courts have not required that changes to those policies and instruments be supported by consideration to be effective—or, put another way, it is a term of the contract of employment of public servants that the employer is permitted to change its policies and instruments that govern employees without providing additional consideration. In *Babcock v Canada (Attorney General)*, unrepresented lawyers in Vancouver brought an action claiming that the Treasury Board breached a term of their employment contract by using a differential pay scale resulting in higher salaries for lawyers employed in the Ontario region. The court concluded that the Salary Administration Plan (SAP) enacted by the Treasury Board was a contractual instrument:

---

15 *Plumadore v Canada (Attorney General)*, 2016 FC 553 at para 49.

16 *Francis v Canadian Imperial Bank of Commerce* (1994), 21 OR (3d) 75 (CA).

17 *Hobbs v TDI Canada Ltd.*, [2004] OJ No 4876 (CA).

> It is an express term of the plaintiffs' employment contracts that they are to be paid according to the SAP. The defendant's offers of employment expressly stated that the terms and conditions of their employment would be the Regulations and the SAP.[18]

Despite this, the Court concluded that the Treasury Board could change the SAP without consideration:

> [T]he specific contents of the SAP are not a set of obligations binding on the defendant for two reasons. First, the [*Financial Administration Act*] clearly permits the [Treasury Board of Canada (TBC)] to unilat erally alter the SAP. This authority is inconsistent with the notion that the contents of the SAP are a set of legally binding obligations. Second, the SAP is rife with language evidencing an intention that the contents of the document are not meant to create legally binding obligations. Many of the key sections defining the SAP are in Appendix B, Annex 1, which refers to them as "guidelines" not obligations. . . .
>
> Therefore, while I find that it is an express term of the plaintiffs' employment contracts that they are to be paid according to the SAP, the contents of the SAP are not binding legal obligations between the parties. They are guidelines that are subject to TBC's discretion to change or modify. The plaintiffs must be paid in accordance with the classification system and performance pay plan created by the SAP. Not to do so would be a breach of an express term of their contracts. However, the contents of the SAP may be changed or modified by the TBC without constituting a breach of the plaintiffs' employment contracts.[19]

Another issue is whether the duty of good faith and fair dealing in the manner of dismissal applies to federal public servants. To date, courts and the Board have concluded that this duty does apply. The leading authority on this point is *Tipple v Canada (Attorney General)*. In that case, a senior executive was dismissed, purportedly as a result of a discontinuance of his function. The Board concluded that this reason was a sham or contrivance and that the deputy head was not justified in terminating his employment. In addition to the usual award of

---

18 *Babcock v Canada (Attorney General)*, [2005] BCJ No 880 (SC) at para 177. The Court also cited *Granger v Canada (Treasury Board)*, [2000] FCJ No 836 (CA), where the Federal Court of Appeal stated (at para 6) that the SAP "constitutes the essence of [their] employment contract."

19 *Ibid* at paras 178 and 180.

lost salary, the Board awarded damages of $125,000 for psychological injury and $250,000 for loss of reputation. Ultimately, the Federal Court of Appeal concluded that the duty of good faith in the manner of dismissal applies to federal public servants. The Court affirmed the award of $250,000 for loss of reputation, concluding that "[w]hen [the Department of Public Works and Government Services of Canada (PWGSC)] decided to terminate Mr. Tipple's employment in the midst of press reports impugning his integrity on the basis of information leaked from PWGSC which senior officials of PWGSC knew to be false, the duty of good faith included the duty to take reasonable steps to ensure that the termination did not cause undue and unjustified harm to Mr. Tipple's reputation."[20] The Federal Court had earlier affirmed that the Board could award damages for psychological injury, but set aside the amount of the award as being too high.[21]

There is also some indication that public servants may have a claim for damages for "bad faith" even in the absence of a dismissal. In *Canada (Attorney General) v Gatien*,[22] a manager was suspended for ten days as a result of how she dealt with a difficult employee.[23] She grieved, and the Board set aside her suspension. The manager ended up being diagnosed with post-traumatic stress disorder. She claimed damages for mental distress in her grievance. The Board denied her claim, and the Federal Court of Appeal ultimately upheld that denial. However, the Court of Appeal concluded that the Board's decision was reasonable because the employer's conduct was not so egregious as to warrant an award of aggravated damages for mental distress. Importantly, the Court of Appeal did not conclude that damages for mental distress are only available when there has been a termination of employment—the Board and the Court of Appeal were both prepared to award damages for mental distress in a suspension case, just not on the facts of this particular case.

As discussed in *Dunsmuir*, employees in the private sector can be dismissed on a without-cause basis and are then entitled to notice either in accordance with the express terms of their contract of employment or,

---

20 *Tipple v Canada (Attorney General)*, 2012 FCA 158 at para 19.

21 *Canada (Attorney General) v Tipple*, 2011 FC 762, varied above note 20. The Board did not, in the end, resolve the quantum of damages for psychological injury.

22 *Canada (Attorney General) v Gatien*, 2016 FCA 3.

23 Characterizing the employee as "difficult" is probably an understatement: among other things, the employee assaulted her manager and bullied her co-workers.

alternatively, the implied term of reasonable notice. For non-unionized employees in the federal public service, the approach is not so simple.

The *Financial Administration Act* states that the termination of employment for public servants—both employed by the Treasury Board and by a separate agency—may only be "for cause."[24] However, the *Public Service Employment Act* (*PSEA*) permits a deputy head in the core public administration (i.e., departments for whom the Treasury Board is the employer) and those separate agencies without the express authority to appoint employees[25] to lay off an employee who is "no longer required by reason of lack of work, the discontinuance of a function or the transfer of work or a function outside those portions of the federal public administration."[26] The definition of a layoff will be discussed in greater detail in Chapter 10 as it plays an important role in determining whether an employee who has been laid off may challenge that layoff through adjudication. For this chapter, it is sufficient to note that employees may not challenge a bona fide layoff through adjudication but that all other terminations of employment may be referred to adjudication.

As a practical matter, non-unionized employees in the core public administration are either entitled to reinstatement as a remedy or, if properly laid off, to the terms and conditions set out in the Treasury Board's policies governing payments to employees who are laid off. Those terms and conditions for executives and some other excluded positions are, as of the date of publication, set out in the *Directive on Terms and Conditions of Employment for Executives* (hereinafter *Executive Directive*). The *Work Force Adjustment Directive*, discussed below, does not apply to executives in the core public administration. The *Executive Directive* requires either that the executive obtain other work in the federal public administration or be paid a lump sum payment. The lump sum payment is normally between twenty-six and thirty-two weeks' base pay plus a percentage of base salary to compensate for the loss of various non-salary elements of an executive's compensation, but the *Executive Directive* permits the deputy head to pay up to fifty-two weeks' salary in all cases and then pay in excess of fifty-two weeks' salary in "exceptional" cases.

---

24 *Financial Administration Act*, s 12(3).

25 *Public Service Employment Act*, SC 2003, c 22, ss 12, 13, 29 (*PSEA*).

26 *Ibid*, ss 29 (defining the scope of the Act as it pertains to appointments and layoffs) and 62 (right to lay off).

As discussed in greater detail in Chapter 10, employees in separate agencies who are dismissed for reasons other than misconduct may proceed to court with a civil claim against their employer. Those employees are entitled to damages in lieu of the implied term of reasonable notice.[27] Implied terms can, of course, be replaced by a specific term governing an employee's entitlements upon dismissal. In *Klassen v Canada*,[28] a former commissioner of the Canadian Wheat Board had a contract with the following clause:

> LOSS OF OFFICE PAYMENT
> - Two (2) years' salary after three (3) years of continuous Board service.
> - This benefit is paid upon termination, voluntary resignation or retirement.
> - A Commissioner is prohibited from accepting employment in a commercial grain marketing organization for up to two (2) years after leaving the Board.[29]

The commissioner claimed damages for failure to provide reasonable notice of termination. The Federal Court of Appeal concurred with the trial judge and summarized the trial judge's reasoning as follows:

> There could be no doubt that the Terms and Conditions, having been fully negotiated, were binding on the appellant and that the most reasonable interpretation thereof and, in particular, of clause 7, was that upon termination of his office, the appellant would become entitled to two years of salary in lieu of damages.[30]

The plaintiff had argued that the two years' pay required upon dismissal was compensation for the undertaking not to accept a position in a commercial grain marketing organization for two years, and that he was therefore entitled to his salary until his mandatory retirement at age seventy. Therefore, neither party in that case argued for reasonable notice: the plaintiff argued that his was a fixed-term contract until age seventy, and the Crown argued that the fixed-term contract could be terminated in accordance with the express terms of that contract. However,

---

27 *Gelinas v Financial Transactions and Reports Analysis Centre of Canada*, 2004 FC 1755.

28 *Klassen v Canada*, [2005] FCJ No 1162 (CA).

29 *Ibid* at para 9.

30 *Ibid* at para 10.

both arguments were still consistent with a contractual view of the plaintiff's employment and only differed on the terms of that contract.

Aside from the normal common law terms of employment contracts, there are several terms that are set out explicitly (typically to do with pay or the requirements of the position). In the federal public service, those terms are set out in a number of policies, directives, or other non-statutory instruments published by the employer. The Supreme Court of Canada in *Vaughan* indicated that those instruments are contractually binding; however, lower courts have not been as consistent in treating them as such. The Federal Court, instead, has determined on a case-by-case basis whether a particular policy has the "force of law." For example, the Federal Court and Federal Court of Appeal have concluded that the Treasury Board Bilingualism Bonus Plan,[31] a post-employment and conflict of interest guideline,[32] the Government Security Policy and Personnel Security Standard,[33] the Deployment Policy and Deployment Guidelines of the Treasury Board,[34] and the Canadian Security Intelligence Agency's policy with respect to abandonment of position[35] have the "force of law" and could be legally enforced against the employer. By contrast, the Federal Court has refused to enforce a policy stating that probationary employees should be warned about their performance deficiencies,[36] a policy setting out when new employees may negotiate higher rates of pay than the minimum upon appointment,[37] a policy requiring prior notice before ending a term of employment,[38] and a Treasury Board policy about negotiating claims and *ex gratia* payments.[39] While there is no single legal test for the dividing line between a policy with the force of law and one without, the Federal Court has considered whether the enabling statute requires the

---

31 *Gingras v Canada*, [1994] 2 FC 734

32 *Peet v Canada (Attorney General)*, [1994] 3 FC 128 [*Peet*].

33 *Myers v Canada (Attorney General)*, 2007 FC 947 [*Myers*], although see *Hughes v Canada (Attorney General)*, 2008 FC 832, where the Court refused to enforce a draft version of a similar policy.

34 *Nieboer v Canada* [1996] FCJ No 1299, and *Vavrecka v Canada*, [1996] FCJ No 328.

35 *Gilmour v Canada,* [2000] FCJ No 1880.

36 *Kagimbi v Canada (Attorney General)*, 2014 FC 400, aff'd 2015 FCA 74.

37 *Glowinski v Canada (Treasury Board)*, 2006 FC 78 [*Glowinski*].

38 *Endicott v Canada (Treasury Board)*, 2005 FC 253.

39 *Sandiford v Canada (Attorney General)*, 2009 FC 862; *Byer v Canada*, 2002 FCT 518; and *Stemmler v Canada (Attorney General)*, 2016 FC 1299.

department to issue the policy, whether the policy is precise, whether it confers a concrete benefit, and whether the policy leaves discretion to government departments.

C. GOVERNOR-IN-COUNCIL APPOINTMENTS

A Governor-in-Council appointment is an appointment made by the governor general on the advice of the King's Privy Council of Canada represented by Cabinet. There are approximately 4,000 Governor-in-Council appointments made by the federal government: approximately 1,000 of those appointments are judges, and the rest are some 100 heads of mission, including ambassadors and high commissioners, as well as some 1,500 part-time appointees in a wide array of agencies, boards, commissions, Crown corporations, and government departments. These appointees include deputy ministers, heads of agencies and members, CEOs and directors of Crown corporations, and returning officers.

Any formal, legal requirements in the appointment process of Governor-in-Council appointments are set out in the statute governing the positions to which they are appointed. In most cases, there are few if any requirements for the appointment. For example, the chair of the board of directors of the Canada Post Corporation "shall be appointed by the Governor in Council to hold office during pleasure for such term as the governor in council considers appropriate."[40] There are no requirements concerning the chair's prior experience or abilities. Challenges to Governor-in-Council appointments are difficult to sustain because such appointments are "discretionary and made on the basis of broad public policy grounds which can only be set aside on the basis of the abuse of discretion including acting in bad faith."[41] For example, Democracy Watch has challenged the appointment of the commissioner of lobbying, alleging that the Governor in Council did not properly consult with the leader of every recognized party in the Senate and House of Commons as required in the *Lobbying Act*.[42] The Federal Court concluded that Democracy Watch could not challenge an appointment on the basis of inadequate consultation as any challenge to that consultation rested solely with the party leaders—who did not

40 *Canada Post Corporation Act*, RSC 1985, c C-10, s 7(1).

41 *Griffin v Canada*, [1997] FCJ No 322 at para 21.

42 *Lobbying Act*, RSC 1985, c 44 (4th Supp), s 4.1.

challenge the appointment and, in fact, voted in favour of a motion to appoint the nominated candidate.[43]

This statutory obligation to consult prior to the appointment by the Governor in Council does not impose a corresponding obligation to consult prior to terminating the appointment. In *Pelletier v Canada (Attorney General)*,[44] the chair of the board of directors of VIA Rail was terminated from his position. That initial termination was set aside on judicial review for a lack of procedural fairness, so he was immediately terminated a second time. Section 105 of the *Financial Administration Act* requires the appropriate minister to consult with the board of directors of a Crown corporation before appointing officer-directors such as the chair of VIA Rail. The Federal Court of Appeal concluded that the obligation to consult prior to appointment does not mean that there is an obligation to consult prior to termination.

An argument could be made that appointments may also be overturned if they are patently unreasonable. For example, under the Ontario *Hospital Labour Disputes Arbitration Act*, the minister of labour appoints, as chairs of ad hoc boards of interest arbitration, people who are "in the opinion of the minister, qualified to act."[45] In 1998, the minister appointed retired judges to chair those interest arbitration boards without informing unions or consulting with them about the suitability or acceptability of using retired judges as interest arbitrations. In *CUPE v Ontario (Minister of Labour)*,[46] the Supreme Court of Canada ruled that the appointment of retired judges was patently unreasonable because the minister did not properly evaluate whether retired judges had labour relations expertise and broad acceptability to the parties. Although those appointments were not Governor-in-Council appointments, the *CUPE* case is an indication that appointments may still be overturned if they are patently unreasonable.

Governor-in-Council appointments are often politically motivated—or, more generously, involve a political judgment. As the Ontario Court of Appeal has pointed out, "[I]t would be intellectually naive not to recognize that elected governments must have room to make political decisions and to conduct themselves in a manner to assure that their

---

43 *Democracy Watch v Canada (Attorney General)*, 2018 FC 1291 at paras 96 and 99.

44 *Pelletier v Canada (Attorney General)*, 2008 FCA 1 [*Pelletier*].

45 *Hospital Labour Disputes Arbitration Act*, RSO 1990, c H.14, s 6(5).

46 *CUPE v Ontario (Minister of Labour)*, 2003 SCC 29 [*CUPE*].

political policies are implemented."[47] Allowing political considerations to influence the appointment process is permitted. The Saskatchewan Court of Queen's Bench has stated this principle as follows:

> Order in Council appointments to the public service frequently are politically motivated. The members of political parties who are elected to govern this province face an enormous task. To aid them in this task they must rely upon persons within the public service whose employment falls within the purview of the Public Service Commission. However, in addition to the permanent, non-political, professional staff of the civil service elected representatives frequently must also rely upon a small group of persons who share their political views and who in a broad way wish to mold our society in particular fashion. The views of this group of persons of necessity must coincide with those of their political masters, since if they do not, the will of the electors as expressed by those representatives may be thwarted.[48]

Therefore, working on the election campaign of the minister responsible for recommending the appointment[49] or making donations to the governing political party does not prevent a person from being appointed to an administrative tribunal pursuant to a Governor-in-Council appointment.

In 2016, the federal government introduced a new process for making these appointments that it called an "open, transparent, and merit-based selection process."[50] While there is no legal requirement to follow any particular process, let alone a process that is "open, transparent, and merit-based," anecdotally there have been accounts of a more robust review of candidates for Governor-in-Council positions. Legally, however, there is no obligation to follow the policy or practice of a more merit-based appointment process. Governments have previously resisted attempts to legally curtail their discretion in making Governor-in-

47 *Hewat v Ontario* (1998), 37 OR (3d) 161 at para 21 (CA) [*Hewat*].

48 *Ken Neil v Government of Saskatchewan and George McLean* (13 April 1984) [unreported], cited in *Muscillo Transport v Ontario (Licence Suspension Appeal Board)* (1997), 149 DLR (4th) 545 (Ont Div Ct).

49 *Ibid.*

50 Prime Minister of Canada, News Release, "Prime Minister Announces New Governor in Council Appointment Process (25 February 2016), online: https://pm.gc.ca/en/news/news-releases/2016/02/25/prime-minister-announces-new-governor-council-appointment-process.

Council appointments. In 2006, Parliament amended the *Salaries Act*[51] to permit the Governor in Council to create a Public Appointments Commission to review Governor-in-Council appointments. This Public Appointments Commission would have overseen, monitored, reviewed, and reported on the selection process for appointments by the Governor in Council and ensured that every such process was widely made public and conducted in a fair, open, and transparent manner and that the appointments are based on merit. It would also have provided a code of practice to ensure that this occurs, and then monitored and audited compliance with that code of practice. However, the first proposed chair of that commission was rejected by the Government Operations Committee of Parliament, and the government reacted by declining to nominate another chair. The commission was eventually abolished in 2012. *Sic semper auditoris.*

At present, the standing orders of the House of Commons provide that standing committees of the House of Commons, which have members from all political parties in the House, have the authority to review all non-judicial appointments made by the Government of Canada.[52] Shortly after an appointment is made, a copy of the appointing order in council is tabled in the House of Commons for consideration by one of the standing committees of the House for a period of not greater than thirty days.[53] The members of the standing committee can then choose whether they will request an appointee to appear before the committee.[54] The committee must complete its review of the appointee within ten sitting days.[55] The order in council comes into effect when it is signed, and appointees need not wait until the order is tabled and reviewed before assuming their duties within the organization to which they have been appointed. Standing committees do not have the power to veto appointments, but a negative recommendation by a committee has resulted in an appointee resigning his position.[56]

---

51 *Salaries Act*, RSC 1985, c S-3.

52 *Standing Orders of the House of Commons*, as amended as of 20 April 2020, s 110.

53 *Ibid.*

54 *Ibid*, s 111(1).

55 *Ibid*, s 111(4).

56 For example, Gwen Morgan was appointed to be the first chair of the Public Appointments Commission but eventually stepped aside because of a motion by the Government Operations Committee of the House of Commons declaring him "unsuitable" for the post.

Governor-in-Council appointments are usually made for a fixed term. For example, the *Financial Administration Act* requires officer-directors of Crown corporations to hold their offices for terms of no more than four years.[57] Where an appointment is for a fixed term, it ends on the date fixed without any further action being taken. Appointments are also made either on "good behaviour" or "at pleasure." An appointment during good behaviour means that an incumbent may only be removed from office for cause or incapacity. These causes may include both conduct in the performance of the appointee's office and conduct outside of the appointment. For example, in *Wedge v Canada (Attorney General)*, an appointee to the Veterans Appeal Board was removed from office because of irregularities he committed during the Prince Edward Island provincial election. The appointee argued that his conduct outside of the Veterans Appeal Board was not relevant to his "good behaviour." The Federal Court disagreed:

> In order to determine whether a holder of public office meets the standard of good behaviour necessary to remain in office, Cabinet, that is, the Governor in Council, must examine the conduct of that individual to assess whether it is consistent with the measure of integrity the Governor in Council deems necessary to maintain public confidence in federal institutions and the federal appointment process. . . .
>
> In my view, given the position of trust and influence conferred upon appointees to federal office, including the Veterans Appeal Board, and their influence as representatives of that office on the public's perception, it is not for this Court to limit the scope of discretion vested by Parliament in the Governor in Council. In my view, whether in a given case it is appropriate to assess the conduct of appointees only with regard to activities which transpire in the discharge of functions of an office is a matter within the discretion of the Governor in Council.[58]

Good behaviour also includes an obligation to be fit to perform the duties of the position: an appointee who is permanently disabled so as to be incapable of performing their functions may be found to be in breach of good behaviour.[59] By contrast, if an officeholder is appointed "at pleasure," the appointment may be ended whenever the Governor in

57 *Financial Administration Act*, s 105 (as amended by the *Federal Accountability Act*, SC 2006, s 9). Prior to the *Federal Accountability Act*, the limit was three years.

58 *Wedge v Canada (Attorney General)*, [1997] FCJ No 872 at paras 30 and 33 [*Wedge*].

59 *Gratton v Canadian Judicial Council*, [1994] 2 FC 769.

Council chooses, in good faith, to end the appointment. As the Federal Court of Appeal stated in *Pelletier*, officeholders at pleasure have an "intrinsically precarious status."[60]

Some officeholders can be appointed both at pleasure and on good behaviour. For example, in *Keen v Canada (Attorney General)*,[61] the president of the Canadian Nuclear Safety Commission was removed from her designation as president but remained a member of the commission. Members of the commission were appointed on good behaviour, but the legislation was silent about the nature of the appointment as president. The Federal Court concluded that this silence means that section 23 of the *Interpretation Act*[62]—which deems all appointments to be at pleasure—governed the appointment to the position of president. In other words, she could be removed as president at pleasure, but was entitled to remain as a member of the commission so long as she continued to act in good behaviour.

Regardless of whether the appointment is on good behaviour[63] or at pleasure,[64] the appointee is entitled to procedural fairness prior to their dismissal. The content of this procedural fairness is subject to a variable standard and will be decided by taking all of the circumstances into account. Procedural fairness does not necessarily require an oral hearing.[65] It does, however, require that the appointee be provided with the reasons for the Governor in Council's dissatisfaction and an opportunity to respond.[66] In most cases, an appointee also needs to be informed that disciplinary action against them is being considered; however, in some circumstances, it should be obvious to the appointee that disciplinary action is being considered, so express notice is not required. In the first decision involving *Pelletier v Canada (Attorney General)*,[67] the Crown argued that the appointee should have known that disciplinary action was being

60 *Pelletier*, above note 44 at para 33. See also *Shoan v Canada (Attorney General)*, 2018 FC 476 at para 20, and *Keen v Canada (Attorney General)*, 2009 FC 353 at para 48.

61 *Ibid*. See also on this point *Houle v Canada*, [1987] 2 FC 493, aff'd (1988), 86 NR 38.

62 *Interpretation Act*, RSC 1985, c I-21, s 23.

63 *Nicholson v Haldiman-Norfolk Regional Board of Commissioners of Police*, [1979] 1 SCR 311.

64 *Knight v Indian Head School Division*, [1990] 1 SCR 653.

65 *Wedge*, above note 58.

66 *Pelletier v Canada (Attorney General)*, [2005] FCJ No 1891, aff'd above note 44.

67 *Ibid*.

contemplated because of his "professional and political experience." The Federal Court disagreed, in part because of the short time frame of the events that the Crown argued should have given notice to Mr. Pelletier and in part because experience can compensate for "minor shortcomings in procedural fairness," and the shortcomings in that case were more substantial. As mentioned above, Mr. Pelletier was terminated a second time after being given the opportunity to provide reasons why he should not be terminated, both in writing and in an in-person meeting with the minister of transport. The Federal Court of Appeal ultimately upheld the dismissal. Mr. Pelletier argued that the minister was biased against him because of statements made in Parliament that he was taking steps to terminate him a second time. The Federal Court of Appeal concluded that in light of the "political and discretionary" nature of the decision, the normal rules of bias did not apply, and, instead, the lower standard of requiring the decision-maker not to have a "closed mind" applied.[68]

In *Vennat v Canada (Attorney General)*,[69] the Federal Court stated that an appointee appointed "during good behaviour" deserves greater procedural protection than an appointee appointed "during pleasure." Most Governor-in-Council appointees are appointed "during pleasure": only three heads of Crown corporations are appointed during "good behaviour,"[70] and therefore this implies greater procedural protection for those appointees.[71] In that case, the Court concluded that the appointee was entitled to a "personalized inquiry" before being dismissed. A "personalized inquiry" is an inquiry with some degree of autonomy in researching information that contemplates the person facing removal from office.[72] In that case, the Governor in Council failed to hold a "personalized inquiry" and also violated the rules of procedural fairness because

- the meeting attended by Mr. Vennat was only two hours long;
- Mr. Vennat only had eight days to provide his oral and written submissions;

---

68 *Pelletier*, above note 44 at paras 48 and 57.

69 *Vennat v Canada (Attorney General)*, 2006 FC 1008 [*Vennat*].

70 The heads of the Canadian Broadcasting Corporation (*Broadcasting Act*, 1991, c 11, s 36(3)), the Bank of Canada (*Bank of Canada Act*, RSC 1985, c B-2, s 6(3)), and the Business Development Corporation (*Business Development Bank of Canada Act*, SC 1995, c 28 s 6(2)).

71 *Vennat*, above note 69 at para 112.

72 *Ibid* at paras 177–79.

- Mr. Ritchie (the chair of the Business Development Corporation's board of directors) did not attend the meeting and Mr. Vennat requested his presence; and
- the Governor in Council applied a standard of proof that was too onerous.[73]

Finally, the Court put some limits on the rules of procedural fairness that the Governor in Council needed to follow. For example, the Governor in Council was permitted to be "somewhat predisposed" to dismissing Mr. Vennat—in that case, by suspending him without pay pending the completion of the investigation.[74] The Governor in Council only had a duty to "play fair, of transparency."[75]

Even if a dismissal is quashed by a court on judicial review (for procedural unfairness or because there was no cause for the dismissal of an appointee appointed during good behaviour), that does not necessarily mean that courts will reinstate the appointee. In *Shoan v Canada (Attorney General)*,[76] the Federal Court did quash a decision to dismiss a "good behaviour" appointee of the Canadian Radio-television and Telecommunications Commission (CRTC) for cause because of, among other things, *ex parte* communications with parties and alleged harassment of staff. A previous Federal Court decision had set aside the finding of harassment because of procedural unfairness.[77] The Federal Court concluded that the applicant's ultimate dismissal also violated the rules of procedural fairness because it could not tell, from the record before it, why the applicant was denied an in-person meeting and also why the Governor in Council relied on the harassment report that had been set aside as one of the bases of its decision. More importantly for the purposes of remedy, the Court simply granted the application without any direction for the Governor in Council. The Governor in Council then terminated the applicant's appointment a second time without an in-person

73 Their standard of proof was the same as that necessary to avoid an issue estoppel argument—namely, that the decisions of Denis J were fatally incorrect, tainted by fraud or dishonesty, or that Mr. Vennat had new evidence not previously available to the judge. Justice Noel held that this standard was too high a burden.

74 *Vennat*, above note 69 at paras 183–84.

75 *Ibid* at para 185.

76 *Shoan v Canada (Attorney General)*, 2017 FC 426 [*Shoan*, 2017].

77 *Shoan v Canada (Attorney General)*, 2016 FC 1003 [*Shoan*, 2016]. The Court also concluded that aspects of the harassment finding were unreasonable but did not have to set aside the decision on that ground because of the procedural unfairness.

meeting and without obtaining any further submissions from the applicant—but this time not referring to the harassment investigation. The Federal Court upheld the second termination. The Court concluded that an in-person meeting was not required given that the harassment investigation was not considered and the other issues were not of a nature where an in-person meeting would have assisted the applicant. The Court also concluded that the Governor in Council's decision was reasonable and that it had cause to terminate the applicant for having publicly and privately criticized the CRTC chair and for having had *ex parte* contact with stakeholders who were appearing before the CRTC.[78]

Other courts have awarded damages for lost wages and other monetary items that the appointee would have received during their period in office rather than reinstatement.[79] Furthermore, because the claim for damages is essentially a contract claim, the normal rules of mitigation apply.[80]

The terms and conditions of employment of Governor-in-Council appointments are set out in the order in council appointing them. Most orders in council do nothing more than set out the salary range of the position. The other terms and conditions of employment (including the various salary ranges) are set out in the Terms and Conditions of Employment for Full-Time Governor in Council Appointees policy prepared by the management priorities and senior personnel secretariat of the Privy Council Office,[81] as well as various salary grids prepared from time to time by the Privy Council Office on the advice of the Advisory Committee on Senior Level Retention and Compensation. Finally, while the Governor in Council has the right to appoint (and revoke) appointments, the working conditions of Governor-in-Council appointees are subject to management by people other than the Governor in Council so long as those managerial actions do not materially impair the ability of the appointee to perform their mandated duties and responsibilities.[82]

---

78 *Shoan*, 2017, above note 76.

79 See, for example, *Hewat*, above note 47, and *Preston v British Columbia* (1994), 116 DLR (4th) 258.

80 *Wells*, above note 4 at para 65.

81 Privy Council Office, "Terms and Conditions of Employment for Full-Time Governor in Council Employees," online: www.canada.ca/en/privy-council/programs/appointments/governor-council-appointments/compensation-terms-conditions-employment/terms-conditions.html.

82 *Shoan*, 2016, above note 77 at para 27.

Governor-in-Council appointees are also subject to different conflict of interest laws than public servants. The *Conflict of Interest Act*[83] applies to most Governor-in-Council appointees, as well as ministers and members of ministerial staff.[84] The Act defines a conflict of interest as follows:

> [A] public office holder is in a conflict of interest when he or she exercises an official power, duty or function that provides an opportunity to further his or her private interests or those of his or her relatives or friends or to improperly further another person's private interests.[85]

The Act goes on to specify certain examples of conflict of interest, including preferential treatment, the use of insider information, contracting with public sector entities, or accepting gifts or other advantages.[86] The conflict of interest rules are enforced by the conflict of interest and ethics commissioner appointed under the *Parliament of Canada Act*[87] with the power to investigate complaints and impose penalties of up to $500 for certain offences.[88] Despite these significant conditions, decisions of the commissioner are not subject to judicial review by the Federal Court as members of the public have no right to have their complaint investigated[89]—meaning that there is no judicial oversight of the commissioner's decision to choose not to investigate an alleged conflict of interest. Furthermore, even when the commissioner chooses to investigate and make a decision, the Federal Court of Appeal has refused to declare that such a decision is amenable to judicial review.[90]

D. THE SPECIAL DUTIES OF PUBLIC SERVANTS

There are a number of special or particular duties that attach to public servants. Those duties will be discussed in turn.

---

83 *Conflict of Interest Act*, SC 2006, c 9, s 2.
84 *Ibid*, s 2(1), "public office holder."
85 *Ibid*, s 4(1).
86 *Ibid*, ss 6–19.
87 *Ibid*, s 2(1), "commissioner," and ss 43–62.
88 *Ibid*, ss 52–62.
89 *Democracy Watch v Conflict of Interest and Ethics Commissioner*, 2009 FCA 15.
90 *Democracy Watch v Canada (Attorney General)*, 2018 FCA 194: the Federal Court of Appeal concluded that the commissioner's decision was reasonable and, therefore, it did not have to decide whether it was capable of being judicially reviewed.

1) Duties Related to a Public Servant's Duty of Fidelity and Loyalty

All employees owe their employer a duty of fidelity and loyalty. In the private sector, disputes over this duty usually concern an employee's obligation not to compete against their employer during the course of their employment and also any restrictions that persist after the end of the employment relationship.[91]

In the public sector, the duty of loyalty is less about the duty not to harm the economic interests of the employer and, instead, about the duty of a public servant to act in the public interest. One way to conceptualize the public servant's duty of loyalty is the "East Block Convention" articulated by Kenneth Kernaghan as comprising six principles:

1. Politics and policy are separated from administration; thus, politicians make policy decisions and public servants execute these decisions.
2. Public servants are appointed and promoted on the basis of merit instead of political party affiliation.
3. Public servants do not engage in partisan political activities.
4. Public servants do not express publicly their personal views on government policies or administration.
5. Public servants provide forthright and objective advice to their political masters in private and in confidence; in return, political executives protect the anonymity of public servants by publicly accepting responsibility for departmental decisions.
6. Public servants execute policy decisions loyally, irrespective of the philosophy and programs of the party in power and regardless of their personal opinions; as a result, public servants enjoy security of tenure during good behaviour and satisfactory performance.[92]

Several aspects of this "East Block Convention" will be addressed in other chapters, such as appointment according to merit (which will be addressed in Chapter 11). One of the aspects of a public servant's duty of loyalty, though, is that the duty is owed to the Crown and not to the particular political party that has been elected. To put this another way: politicians decide policy, and public servants implement

---

91 See, for example, *Zoic Studios BC Inc v Gannon*, 2015 BCCA 334.

92 Kenneth Kernaghan, "East Block and Westminster Conventions, Values, and Public Service" in *The Handbook of Canadian Public Administration*, 3d ed (Toronto: Oxford University Press, 2018) at 99–100.

policy. The Supreme Court of Canada has articulated the nature of this duty as follows:

> The federal public service in Canada is part of the executive branch of Government. As such, its fundamental task is to administer and implement policy. In order to do this well, the public service must employ people with certain important characteristics. Knowledge is one, fairness another, integrity a third.
>
> As the Adjudicator indicated, a further characteristic is loyalty. As a general rule, federal public servants should be loyal to their employer, the Government of Canada. The loyalty owed is to the Government of Canada, not the political party in power at any one time.[93]

This duty of loyalty and fidelity is confirmed in the *PSEA*, which requires employees to swear an oath of loyalty as follows:

> I, ______, swear (or solemnly affirm) that I will faithfully and honestly fulfil the duties that devolve on me by reason of my employment in the public service of Canada and that I will not, without due authority, disclose or make known any matter that comes to my knowledge by reason of such employment. (*Add, in the case where an oath is taken,* "So help me God" (*or name of deity*).)[94]

This portion of this chapter will consider the duty of fidelity and loyalty of public servants in four respects:

1) the relationship between the duty of fidelity and loyalty and free speech
2) statutory whistle-blowing protections for public servants
3) the obligation of political neutrality and the extent to which a public servant may participate in political activity
4) conflicts of interest

---

93 *Fraser v PSSRB*, [1985] 2 SCR 455 at paras 40–41 [*Fraser*].

94 *PSEA*, s 54. The federal public service oath of loyalty does not expressly require the public servant to swear loyalty to the King. An oath to the reigning monarch, however, is still a part of the oath sworn by new citizens and also for members of the Canadian Armed Forces. There have been several unsuccessful *Charter* challenges to referring to the (then) Queen in the oath, on the grounds that such an oath violates freedom of expression in favour of republicanism: see *Giolla Chainnigh v Canada (Attorney General)*, 2008 FC 69, and *Roach v Canada (Minister of State for Multiculturalism and Citizenship)*, [1994] 2 FC 406.

a) The Relationship Between the Duty of Loyalty and Free Speech

Federal public servants owe the Crown a duty of fidelity and loyalty. This duty can, depending on the context, override the right of public servants to free speech concerning political issues. There are limits on the right of public servants to criticize government programs and policies regardless of whether they swear the oath. These limits exist because of the public interest in both the actual and the apparent impartiality of the public service. The Canadian tradition of the public service emphasizes the characteristics of impartiality, neutrality, fairness, and integrity.[95]

The leading case on this issue remains *Fraser v PSSRB*.[96] In that case, an employee of Revenue Canada was adamantly opposed to the metric system. He criticized the government of the day for implementing the metric system in Canada.[97] Despite being warned to stop his public criticism, he escalated his criticisms and extended them to the repatriation of the Constitution and comparing the current government to the communist regime in Poland. He was eventually dismissed because of his criticisms, and his dismissal was upheld by an adjudicator and, eventually, the Supreme Court of Canada.

As a general principle, public servants have the right to criticize the government, just as every citizen has a right of free speech. However, such criticism is subject to the limits imposed by the duty of loyalty and fidelity, and a public servant should exercise caution when it comes to making criticisms of the government. The degree of restraint depends on the position and visibility of the public servant, as well as the nature of the criticism. As the Supreme Court of Canada stated:

> A public servant need not vote for the governing party. Nor need he or she publicly espouse its policies. And indeed, in some circumstances a public servant may actively and publicly express opposition to the policies of a government. This would be appropriate if, for example, the Government were engaged in illegal acts, or if its policies jeopardized the life, health or safety of the public servant or others, or if the public servant's criticism had no impact on his or her ability to perform effectively the duties of a public servant or on the public perception of that ability. But, having stated these qualifications (and

95 *Fraser*, above note 93 at paras 42 & 43.

96 *Ibid*.

97 His opposition included wearing a placard stating, "Your freedom to measure is a measure of your freedom."

> there may be others), it is my view that a public servant must not engage, as the appellant did in the present case, in sustained and highly visible attacks on major Government policies.[98]

In *Fraser*, the employee's criticisms of the government "went much too far."[99] Although there was no actual evidence that the employee's ability to do his job was impaired by his criticisms, impairment could be implied from the circumstances: the criticism was prolonged, it was increasingly derogatory in tone, it questioned the integrity of the government, and it occurred on a national and an international basis.

Fraser was decided before the *Canadian Charter of Rights and Freedoms* (the *Charter*) came into force. In a later case, the Federal Court decided that the limits on free expression established by the duty of loyalty and fidelity expressed in *Fraser* were consistent with the *Charter*. In *Haydon v Canada*,[100] two drug evaluators working for Health Canada's Health Protection Branch were reprimanded for breaching their duty of loyalty following certain public comments they made during an appearance on a national television program about the drug review process in Health Canada. The two employees argued that the restrictions on free expression inherent in the duty of loyalty contravened their *Charter* right to free speech. The Federal Court agreed that those limits violated section 2(b) of the *Charter* but decided that those limits were justified under section 1 of the *Charter*. The objective of the common law duty of loyalty is to promote an impartial and effective public service, and the duty is rationally connected to that objective. The duty also minimally impairs a public servant's right to freedom of expression because it "does not demand absolute silence from public servants."[101] Finally, the infringement of free speech is proportional to the impairment of free speech given that it only has modest and tailored effects on a public servant's freedom of expression.

Even though the duty of loyalty survived *Charter* scrutiny in that case, the reprimands were still overturned on judicial review. The Court concluded that the disclosures involved policies that jeopardized the life, health, or safety of the public and that the grievors had attempted to resolve those issues through internal mechanisms before going public

98 *Fraser*, above note 93 at para 41.

99 *Ibid* at para 50.

100 *Haydon v Canada*, [2000] FCJ No 1368.

101 *Ibid* at para 82.

with their concerns. Therefore, the Crown had not met its onus of proving that the grievors' free speech did not fall within one of the *Fraser* exceptions.

There is some issue about whether the decision in that case means that an employee must attempt to resolve their concerns internally before going public. In another case titled *Haydon v Canada* (2002), an adjudicator concluded that a grievor did need to exhaust internal review mechanisms before going public;[102] however, on judicial review, the Federal Court did not address that issue.[103] Instead, the Federal Court upheld the discipline because the public comments were unrelated to issues of public health or safety.[104] In *Read v Canada (Attorney General)*, the Federal Court appears to have confirmed that an employee must exhaust internal avenues of redress, stating, "[The grievor] was precluded from [going public] because he had not exhausted internal recourses."[105] However, in another application for judicial review, the Federal Court upheld an adjudicator's decision but stated that the failure to seek internal resolution of differences was not a necessary condition to public disclosure.[106] These contradictory cases were decided within a little over a month of one another, and the Federal Court of Appeal has not yet resolved which decision is correct. However, the Supreme Court of Canada—in *obiter*—did approve of the "up the ladder" approach and cited the *Read* decision in support of that approach.[107]

There is also some dispute over whether an employee needs to prove the truth or accuracy of their public comments. In *Read*, the employee alleged that it was sufficient that he honestly believed in the truth of his public comments. The Federal Court stated that "[h]onesty is not

---

102 *Haydon v Canada*, 2002 PSSRB 10.

103 *Haydon v Canada (Treasury Board)*, [2005] 1 FC 511, aff'd [2005] FCJ No 1146 (CA) [*Haydon*, 2005].

104 The grievor in that case stated that the Canadian government's ban on Brazilian beef was politically motivated and that there was no health risk in Brazilian beef. The Court concluded that since the employee herself stated that there was no health risk, her disclosure did not concern public health and safety.

105 *Read v Canada (Attorney General)*, [2005] FCJ No 990 at para 123, aff'd [2006] FCJ No 1257 (CA) [*Read*]. The Court of Appeal did not comment on this requirement, instead focusing on the fact that the "whistle-blower" had no evidence to support his allegation that members of the RCMP were corrupt.

106 *Chopra v Canada (Treasury Board)*, [2005] FCJ No 1189 at para 34, aff'd [2006] FCJ No 1349 (CA) [*Chopra*].

107 *Merk v International Association of Bridge, Structural, Ornamental and Reinforcing Iron Workers, Local 771*, 2005 SCC 70 at para 24 [*Merk*].

enough. There must be some rational basis to the allegations."[108] However, the Court in *Chopra* stated that an employee does not need to provide evidence of the truth of all public comments to avoid disciplinary action.[109] In an older case, the Federal Court of Appeal concluded that an employee breached his duty of loyalty by publicly criticizing his employer (alleging that his superiors were guilty of tolerating frauds on unemployment insurance and breaching the *Privacy Act*) without being able to prove that his criticisms were true, stating:

> The fact remains, however, that having chosen the drastic course of publicly accusing his superiors of illegalities, it was up to the applicant to prove his allegations if he wished to avoid the otherwise natural consequences of his actions. As the applicant himself admitted at the hearing before us, the record is devoid of such proof. The applicant's own unsubstantiated allegations are certainly not enough.[110]

The requirement that an employee prove (presumably on the balance of probabilities) that their public statements are true cannot be a necessary condition to avoiding discipline for a breach of the duty of loyalty. The exceptions in *Fraser* are meant to protect the freedom to criticize the government, which must include the freedom to express opinions on issues that are not subject to proof on any standard. Stating that the government is not, for example, providing sufficient funding to support those with a physical disability is not a matter that can be proven (or disproven) empirically. Requiring an employee to provide proof before speaking publicly would not be consistent with protecting the freedom of expression.

In *Haydon v Canada* (2005), the trial division of the Federal Court rejected Haydon's argument that she should not have been disciplined for her remarks about the Brazilian beef ban in part because "the evidence reveals that the applicant did not check her facts or address her concerns internally before she spoke to *The Globe and Mail*."[111] Rather than require the employee to prove or disprove their allegations, the Court decided that the employee should simply be required to check the

---

108 *Read*, above note 105 at para 100. The Court of Appeal decided not to deal with the question of standard of proof because "Corporal Read did not even come close to proving his allegations on a balance of probabilities."

109 *Chopra*, above note 106.

110 *Grahn v Canada (Treasury Board)*, [1987] FCJ No 36.

111 *Haydon*, 2005, above note 103 at para 69.

facts before going public. Such a requirement would constitute a more appropriate balance between the duty of loyalty and employees' right to criticize the government.[112]

The Federal Court of Appeal's decision in *Read* also made it clear that the common law whistle-blowing defence is the exception, not the rule, and that it is limited to the narrow issues involving life, health, or safety of the public. The whistle-blowing defence is not available simply because the issue is a matter of public interest or importance:

> The exceptions formulated in *Fraser*, i.e. where the government is engaged in illegal activity or where its policies jeopardize the life, health or safety of the public or members of the public, are no doubt matters of legitimate public concern. It is clear, however, from the words used by Dickson C.J. in *Fraser*, that he did not intend to create an exception so as to allow public servants to voice all of their concerns or disagreements with government policies and departmental activities. I have no doubt that had that been his intention, the exceptions would have been articulated in a very different manner. Thus, I am in agreement with Harrington J. when he says, at paragraph 109 of his reasons, that "[h]owever, I do not find that legitimate public interest at large is an exception to the duty of loyalty owed by an employee to his or her employer."[113]

The Board came to a similar conclusion in *Therrien v Deputy Head (Department of Employment and Social Development)*.[114] In that case, a public servant leaked internal information about the Employment

---

112 Dr. Haydon's complete story is set out in *Haydon v Deputy Head (Department of Health)*, 2019 FPSLREB 26. Dr. Haydon was suspended in 2004 for a series of public statements in 2002 and 2003 and later dismissed in 2004 for insubordination. Her dismissal was originally upheld, but the Federal Court set aside her 2004 suspension for being made too late after the public statements. The Court remitted that issue back to the Board, who set aside the suspension. The Board then concluded that since Dr. Haydon had a clean disciplinary record, her dismissal was not warranted. The Board reinstated her to her position but limited the amount of compensation owing as a result of her failure to mitigate. Dr. Haydon was one of a group of three scientists who were fired at the same time in part for speaking out publicly about Health Canada's drug approval process. Of those three, Dr. Chopra was the only one not reinstated when the Federal Court of Appeal upheld his dismissal in *Chopra v Canada (Attorney General)*, 2017 FCA 176.

113 *Read*, above note 105 at para 120.

114 *Therrien v Deputy Head (Department of Employment and Social Development)*, 2019 FPSLREB 82.

Insurance program—specifically, that public servants' performance was measured on the basis of Employment Insurance savings, the implication being that public servants were pressured to turn down meritorious Employment Insurance claims. The Board concluded that this type of information did not fall within the scope of the common law whistle-blowing defence as it was unrelated to health or public safety. The Board also criticized the grievor for not raising her concerns internally first (providing another example of an employee being expected to go "up the chain" before going to the media) and also for alleging that her concerns amounted to gross mismanagement without providing "a scintilla of evi dence to support her allegations of gross mismanagement"[115] (implying that she did not need to prove her claim on the balance of probability but needed to demonstrate a reasonable basis for her belief).

In *Labadie v Deputy Head (Correctional Service of Canada)*,[116] a corrections officer wrote a book stating that the management of a particular correctional institution was engaged in criminal acts including smuggling drugs into the institution to gain an inmate's cooperation, perjury, falsification of evidence, and making death threats. The Board upheld the corrections officer's dismissal. The Board concluded that there was no rational basis for the claims made in the book as they were based either on the information provided by an inmate or on general rumours at the institution.[117] The Board also concluded that he did not use the internal disclosure mechanisms available to him and that this use of an internal mechanism was a necessary condition to the whistle-blowing defence.[118]

The Board has also upheld a five-day suspension for an employee who published an "advertorial" in the *National Post* that personally criticized both his minister and several senior officials in his department.[119] The Board summarized the jurisprudence into several factors to assess whether this advertorial was a permissible exercise of free speech:

- the working level of the employee within the government;
- the nature and content of the expression;

---

115 *Ibid* at para 134.

116 *Labadie v Deputy Head (Correctional Service of Canada)*, 2008 PSLRB 85.

117 *Ibid* at paras 226–32.

118 *Ibid* at para 208.

119 *MacLean v Treasury Board (Department of Public Works and Government Services)*, 2011 PSLRB 40.

- the visibility of the expression;
- the sensitivity of the issue discussed;
- the truth of the statement made;
- the steps taken by the employee to determine the facts before speaking;
- the efforts made by the employee to raise the concerns with the employer;
- the extent to which the employer's reputation was damaged; and
- the impact on the employer's ability to conduct business.[120]

In summary, the common law whistle-blower defence has rarely been effective in shielding public servants from discipline. The foregoing cases disclose that the whistle-blowing defence has the following elements:

1) A public servant's right to freedom of expression does not permit the public servant to disclose information or criticize the government in all cases. Public criticism, particularly "leaking" information to the media, is permitted only to the extent that it is protected by the common law whistle-blowing defence.
2) The subject matter of the disclosure must relate to the life, health, or security of the public or the public servant. Issues of significant public importance or interest do not necessarily meet this threshold.
3) The public servant must disclose their concerns internally before going public.
4) The public servant must have at least a rational basis for their concerns. This does not require the public servant to prove the truth of their allegations, but it does require some credible and reasonable basis for their allegations.

b) The Obligation of Political Neutrality

Closely linked to the duty of loyalty and fidelity is the obligation of some federal public servants to remain politically neutral. The political neutrality of the public service is a fundamental feature of British democratic government and as such was imported to Canada as part of our democratic tradition. The political neutrality of public servants has become a constitutional convention, requiring "political neutrality

120 *Ibid* at para 118.

and impartial service to whichever political party is in power."[121] There are traditionally five arguments given in favour of prohibiting public servants from engaging in partisan political activity (or, at least, limiting their involvement):

1. It preserves trust in government so that members of the public are assured that political affiliation is not a consideration when dealing with public servants.
2. It ensures that public servants retain the trust of political superiors regardless of the results of an election.
3. It ensures that there is no politically motivated turnover of public servants with a change in government.
4. It discourages patronage-based appointments and encourages merit-based appointments instead.
5. It protects public servants against financial or other forms of exploitation by political or administrative superiors who are affiliated with a particular party or candidate.[122]

These reasons for a non-partisan public service must be balanced against the constitutional rights of public servants to participate fully in partisan political activity. A complete ban on political activity by public servants also deprives both the general public and political parties of a well-educated and well-informed pool from which to draw both volunteers and candidates.[123] In *Osborne v Canada (Treasury Board)*,[124] several federal public servants challenged the bars on political activity then in place in the *PSEA*. The *PSEA* at that time prevented employees from engaging in work for a candidate or political party, or being a candidate for election, subject to the right of employees below the level of deputy head to apply to the Public Service Commission (PSC) for the right to be granted a leave of absence to be a candidate in an election.

The Supreme Court of Canada struck down the law because it violated the right of public servants to free speech and did not minimally impair that right. The Court concluded that the restrictions applied to too many public servants whose duties were apolitical and also restricted too broad a class of activities:

---

121 *Ontario (Attorney General) v OPSEU*, [1987] 2 SCR 2.

122 Kernaghan, above note 92 at 102.

123 Several senior politicians began their careers as public servants, including prime ministers William Lyon Mackenzie King and Lester B. Pearson.

124 *Osborne v Canada (Treasury Board)*, [1991] 2 SCR 69.

> The result of this broad general language is that the restrictions apply to a great number of public servants who in modern government are employed in carrying out clerical, technical or industrial duties that are completely divorced from the exercise of any discretion that could be in any manner affected by political considerations. The need for impartiality and indeed the appearance thereof does not remain constant throughout the civil service hierarchy.... To apply the same standard to a deputy minister and a cafeteria worker appears to me to involve considerable overkill and does not meet the test of constituting a measure that is carefully designed to impair freedom of expression as little as reasonably possible.
>
> ...
>
> With respect to the nature of the political activity, the situation is similar. While a public servant may attend a political meeting and contribute money to a candidate or a political party, he or she may not take part in the discussion at the meeting or make a public statement of support for the party which he or she supports financially. Activity such as volunteer work in making telephone calls or stuffing envelopes for a candidate or partisan questioning of candidates at a political meeting are all included in the section's general language.[125]

The Court declared the legislation to be of no force and effect, except as it applied to deputy heads. Therefore, there was—for a period—effectively no legislative restriction on political activity by federal public servants.

The history of public servants' ability to engage in political activity has been varied. For a short period of time immediately after Confederation in 1867, there were no restrictions on the political activities of public servants. Parliament remedied this obviously unsatisfactory state of affairs in 1878 with the enactment of *An Act further securing the Independence of Parliament*.[126] That 1878 statute prohibited a person who held "any office, commission or employment ... in the service of the Government of Canada"[127]—that is, any federal public servant—from becoming a member of Parliament. This statute effectively barred any federal public servant from running for federal elected office. The public servant would have to resign before campaigning for

125 *Ibid* at paras 61 and 63.

126 *An Act further securing the Independence of Parliament*, SC 1878, c 5, s 1.

127 *Ibid*, s 1(a).

public office. If they failed to do so, their election would be void;[128] if, for whatever reason, they were not caught immediately, they risked a $200 fine for each day they sat as a member of Parliament while holding office as a federal public servant.[129]

In 1908, Parliament enacted the first *Civil Service Amendment Act*.[130] The 1908 Act declared that public servants were permitted to vote in federal and provincial elections but were otherwise prohibited from engaging in "partisan work in connection with any such election."[131] When the 1908 Act was repealed and replaced in 1918, the new Act also prohibited contributing to or dealing in any way with money for a political party.[132]

This prohibition against partisan electoral political activity was extended to non-electoral activity in the 1967 *PSEA*.[133] The *PSEA* contained a blanket prohibition against engaging in any work for or on behalf of a political party regardless of whether that work related to electoral activity.[134] This prohibition had two exceptions. First, federal public servants were permitted to donate money to political parties or candidates for office.[135] Second, federal public servants were allowed to run for political office if they first obtained an unpaid leave of absence from the PSC.[136] If the public servant was elected, they immediately ceased to be a public servant;[137] if they were not elected, they returned to their job. These two exceptions were not available to deputy heads.[138] The prohibition in the 1878 statute referred to above was also modified in the 1970 *Canada Elections Act*[139] to permit public servants to run for office if they first obtained a leave of absence from the PSC—essentially bringing the *Canada Elections Act* in line with the *PSEA*.

As discussed above, the Supreme Court of Canada struck down this total prohibition against partisan political activity in its 1991 decision

128 *Ibid*, s 3.
129 *Ibid*, s 5.
130 *Civil Service Amendment Act*, 1908, 7–8 Edward VII, c 15.
131 *Ibid*, s 43.
132 *Civil Service Act*, 8-9 George V, c 12 (1918), s 55.
133 *Public Service Employment Act*, SC 1966–67, c 71 [*PSEA*] .
134 *Ibid*, s 32(1).
135 *Ibid*, s 32(2).
136 *Ibid*, s 32(3).
137 *Ibid*, s 32(5).
138 *Ibid*, s 32(1).
139 *Canada Elections Act*, RSC 1970 (1st Supp), c 14, ss 21(1)(e) and 21(2)(g).

in *Osborne*. The majority of the Court in *Osborne* struck down the prohibition against general political activity but did not touch the requirement that a candidate for office obtain permission from the PSC.

The majority of the Court suggested that Parliament could redraft the section to address any lingering concerns about political neutrality. For whatever reason, Parliament did not choose to do so until 2005; therefore, from 1991 and until those amendments to the *PSEA* came into force, there was no statutory prohibition against partisan political activity by public servants. Public servants still needed permission from the PSC to run for Parliament or a provincial legislature, but that was the extent of legislated limits for public servants.[140]

The new *PSEA* sets out Parliament's response to the *Osborne* decision. The Act starts out by setting out the purpose of restrictions on political activity by stating:

> The purpose of this Part is to recognize the right of employees to engage in political activities while maintaining the principle of political neutrality in the public service.[141]

The Act then distinguishes between general political activity and running as a candidate in an election. Public servants below the rank of deputy head may engage in political activity and run for office in accordance with certain rules and principles set out in the Act, which are described below.

The rules governing political activities set out in the *PSEA* apply to employees in the core public administration. The rules also apply to some separate agencies where provided in the statute establishing the separate agency. For example, the *Canada Revenue Agency Act*[142] states that the political activity rules in the *PSEA* apply to employees of the Canada Revenue Agency.

These rules do not apply to all public servants. Most separate agencies, however, do not have any statutory rules concerning political activities. They rely instead on values and ethics codes. Furthermore, there

---

140 Parliament also amended the *Canada Elections Act* in 2000 to repeal the prohibition against public servants being candidates in a federal election: see *Canada Elections Act*, SC 2000, c 9, s 65(d). This prohibition had earlier been made redundant by the 1967 changes discussed above (which side-stepped the *Canada Elections Act* by requiring a leave of absence).

141 *PSEA*, s 112.

142 *Canada Revenue Agency Act*, SC 1999, c 17, s 57.

are different rules for RCMP members[143] and members of the Canadian Armed Forces.[144]

i) Being a Candidate for Political Office

The *PSEA* sets out a regime for public servants who wish to stand as a candidate for a federal, provincial, or territorial election. A public servant who wishes to be a candidate or seek nomination to be a candidate on behalf of a political party must obtain permission from the PSC.[145] This permission must be sought *before* the public servant announces their candidacy on social media or otherwise.[146] During the federal, provincial, or territorial election period, a public servant must take an unpaid leave of absence;[147] the PSC may also order that the public servant take a leave of absence prior to the election period.[148] The Act does not expressly set out when that leave of absence will end. There are also regulations setting out how an employee must apply for permission to run as a candidate and, if necessary, a leave of absence. If the public servant is elected in a federal, provincial, or territorial election, they immediately cease to be an employee on the day they are declared elected.[149] Finally, the PSC must publish the names of all employees granted leave to run as a candidate in the *Canada Gazette*.[150]

The Act states that the PSC may only grant permission for a public servant to run for office if it is satisfied that "the employee's ability to perform his or her duties in a politically impartial manner will not be

143 The current RCMP Code of Conduct (*Royal Canadian Mounted Police Regulations*, 2014, SOR/2014-281) requires members to abide by applicable RCMP policies dealing with political activity. Those policies are similar to the pre-2014 regulations (*Royal Canadian Mounted Police Regulations, 1988*, SOR/88-361), which required candidates to obtain a leave of absence and prohibited campaigning while wearing a uniform.

144 Members of the Canadian Armed Forces are not allowed to take an active part in political parties or run for federal or provincial office. They may run for municipal office with the permission of the chief of defence staff: *Queen's Regulations and Orders for the Canadian Forces*, ch 19.44, online (pdf): www.canada.ca/content/dam/dnd-mdn/migration/assets/FORCES_Internet/docs/en/about-policies-standards-queens-regulations-orders-vol-01/Volume-1_Final.pdf.

145 *PSEA*, s 114(1).

146 PSC investigation file 17-18-01.

147 *PSEA*, s 114(3).

148 *Ibid*, s 114(7).

149 *Ibid*, s 114(8).

150 *Ibid*, s 116.

impaired or perceived to be impaired."[151] These are the crucial provisions of this legal regime: actual or perceived impairment of the ability of a public servant to perform their duties in a politically impartial manner. The regime is future-looking: "The Commission is not asked to decide if seeking elected office has impaired a public official's ability to perform their duties in a politically impartial manner in a given case, but rather if seeking elected office will impair a public official's ability to do so in the future."[152] The Act sets out a list of non-exhaustive factors the PSC may consider: (1) the nature of the election, (2) the nature of the employee's duties, and (3) the level and visibility of the employee's position.[153]

There are very few decided cases concerning this regime. The leading case involved a federal prosecutor who applied for a leave of absence to run for elected office in the 2015 federal election. The PSC declined the prosecutor (Ms. Taman) permission to do so, but the Federal Court of Appeal ultimately set aside that decision. In so doing, the Court of Appeal provided some principles that are useful in assessing the ability of federal public servants to run for political office.

The most important of those principles is that the PSC must assess each application for leave to run for political office carefully. It is not sufficient for the PSC to simply list the public servants' duties and level: it must assess whether those duties mean that the public servant will be impaired or perceived to be impaired in their ability to perform those duties in the event of an unsuccessful campaign. The Federal Court of Appeal pointed out that all public servants owe a duty of loyalty to the Crown while they remain employed and reasoned that the PSC cannot presume that a public servant would breach that duty of loyalty. Therefore, the PSC must "ask how autonomy and discretion in a given official's duties are indicative of how that official will behave (or be perceived to behave) following an unsuccessful attempt to be elected to office."[154]

In Ms. Taman's case, the PSC refused to grant her permission to run for office because her position as prosecutor came with a significant degree of autonomy about the conduct of prosecutions and was highly visible (particularly in a courtroom). The Court of Appeal concluded

151 *Ibid*, s 114(4).

152 *Taman v Canada (Attorney General)*, 2017 FCA 1 at para 21 [*Taman*].

153 *PSEA*, s 114(6).

154 *Taman*, above note 152 at para 26.

that these factors alone did not justify the decision to refuse her permission to run for office, stating:

> Ms Taman's autonomy, discretion and visibility would have been the same before and after the election. If they did not contribute to the impairment of her ability (as opposed to a perception of her ability) to discharge her duties before the election, why would they have done so after the election? The opportunity to act in a partisan manner would have been the same before and after the election. If Ms Taman's political opinions did not colour the exercise of her discretion before the election, why would they do so after the election?[155]

The Court of Appeal concluded that there may be answers to those questions, but the PSC had not provided those answers and, therefore, its decision could not stand. Those questions, however, were likely unanswerable in Ms. Taman's case—these questions would be challenging for the PSC to answer in almost any case. The Court of Appeal's decision has shifted away from a functional analysis based on the nature of the position toward a more individualized analysis based on the actions of the particular public servant applying for permission to run for office. By starting with the premise that public servants will remain loyal, the Court of Appeal has effectively rendered those questions unanswerable in the abstract. The PSC's inquiry therefore must become focused on the actions of the individual public servant applying for permission to run for office. Essentially, the PSC must assess whether that public servant has done anything to demonstrate that they would act (or be reasonably perceived as acting) in a politically partial manner after an unsuccessful election campaign.

This individually focused inquiry is consistent with earlier Federal Court jurisprudence on this subject. In a 2004 decision involving another federal prosecutor, the Federal Court addressed a PSC decision refusing that prosecutor permission to run as a candidate in the 2004 federal election. While the Court dismissed the application as moot because it was heard well after the 2004 election, the Court went on to conclude that it would have set the PSC's decision aside. The Court was critical of the PSC's decision because it focused on hypothetical conflicts of interest that may arise post-election instead of likely outcomes. The PSC relied too heavily on a statement by the candidate's supervisor to

155 *Ibid* at para 38.

the effect that the candidate could be asked to run a politically sensitive prosecution; instead, the PSC should have "conducted a more comprehensive inquiry to determine whether it was likely that the applicant would be responsible for cases of that nature in the near future."[156]

In respect of the perception of impartiality, the Court of Appeal also made it more difficult for the PSC to refuse permission for public servants to run for elected office. The Court of Appeal concluded that any perception of political partiality must be held in good faith and not be motivated by partisan political interests, stating:

> Politics is a partisan activity; activists of other political parties might well attack Ms Taman's performance of her duties for purely partisan reasons, unrelated to any actual or perceived partiality. This may or may not come within the notion of perception of impairment of her ability to perform her duties in a politically impartial manner. That is a matter for the Commission to decide but there is an argument to be made that Ms Taman's right to participate fully in the electoral process should not be curtailed by the possibility of bad faith attacks on her impartiality.[157]

In that case, the director of public prosecution opposed her candidacy in part because the prosecution service had to defend a motion brought by an accused who alleged that a different prosecutor was biased against him as a result of being a candidate for political office some twenty years prior. The Court of Appeal concluded that the department's "sensitivity"[158] to this motion was not, by itself, a sufficient reason to deny Ms. Taman permission to run for political office.

It is worth noting that Ms. Taman's case was unusual in that the PSC actually refused her permission to stand as a candidate. In fact, she was the only public servant whom the PSC refused permission to run as a candidate in a federal, provincial, territorial, or municipal office from 2014 to 2018. During that same period, 317 public servants received permission to run for political office. Not every public servant who receives permission actually runs for office. For example, forty-six public servants received permission to run in the 2015 federal election,

---

156 *Harquail v Canada (Public Service Commission)*, 2004 FC 1549 at para 36.

157 *Taman*, above note 152 at para 42.

158 *Ibid* at para 46.

but only seventeen actually did (and of those seventeen candidates, only two were elected).[159]

The PSC has the discretion to impose terms on public servants who are granted permission to run for political office. The terms range from an unpaid leave of absence prior to the election period to an admonishment against canvassing co-workers during working hours.

In conclusion, the PSC has the discretion to decide whether a particular public servant may run for political office. The PSC's role is to assess whether there will be actual or perceived political partiality in the event that the public servant is not elected and returns to duty. The PSC may consider the nature of the election, the nature of the public servant's duties, the level or visibility of the public servant, and any other factors it considers relevant. The PSC, however, must assess how those factors would actually lead to political partiality in light of the presumption that a public servant will comply with their duty of loyalty to the Crown. The PSC cannot simply assume that a public servant will abuse their autonomy or discretion after returning from an unsuccessful campaign.

ii) Other Electoral Activities

The *PSEA* contains a general provision permitting public servants to engage in any "political activity"—defined as activity taken in support of or in opposition to a political party or in support of or in opposition to an election candidate[160]—so long as the political activity does not impair or is not perceived as impairing the employee's ability to perform their duties in a politically impartial manner.

Unlike when running for elected office, public servants do not require permission from the PSC before engaging in political activity. Instead, this provision is enforced in one of two ways. First, each department and agency subject to the political activities' provisions of the *PSEA* has designated a "political activities representative" to handle inquiries about political activity. Public servants commonly inform their departmental representative about their intended political activity. The department can then assess whether the particular activity should be permitted; if the department forbids such activity, then the public

159 Public Service Commission of Canada, *2015–2016 Annual Report* (2016) at 15, online (pdf): www.canada.ca/en/public-service-commission/services/publications/public-service-commission-canada-2015-2016-annual-report.html.

160 *PSEA*, s 111(1).

servant is expected to obey that directive or face disciplinary consequences for insubordination. The public servant can challenge the direction through the grievance procedure.

This was the situation faced by another prosecutor, Kristen Mohr, who wanted to be a canvasser in the 2015 federal election. Her department concluded that this would impair (or be perceived to impair) her ability to serve as a prosecutor. While Ms. Mohr obeyed that instruction, she did grieve the decision. In 2018, the Board allowed her grievance and set aside the department's decision (on the consent of all parties).[161] This decision was obviously too late to permit Ms. Mohr to canvass in the 2015 election, but it serves as a salutary lesson that a department's instruction not to volunteer during an election faces scrutiny and must be supported.

Second, public servants do not need to obtain permission from their department to engage in political activity. If they do so without permission, however, they risk an investigation by the PSC after the fact. If the PSC concludes that the public servant engaged in political activity that impaired (or was perceived as impairing) their ability to perform their duties in a politically impartial fashion, then the PSC may take corrective action against the employee—up to and including dismissal.[162]

These investigations are relatively infrequent. One example, dating from 2013, involved a director who was also the secretary of a riding association of a political party. The director used their work computer to revise and translate the minutes of the riding association meeting. The PSC concluded that these activities at the least created a perception of a lack of partisan impartiality. The director retired shortly before the PSC completed its report, so the consequences were limited to having to obtain permission from the PSC if the director applied for new employment for the next three years.[163] The PSC does have the discretion to take corrective action against an employee, including dismissal.[164]

c) Conflict of Interest

The Crown is entitled to enjoin public servants from putting themselves in a position of a conflict of interest, both actual and apparent. The

161 *Mohr v Treasury Board (Office of the Director of Public Prosecutions)*, 2018 FPSLREB 45.

162 *PSEA*, s 118.

163 PSC File Number 2013-DEPT-00067.16874 (2013).

164 *PSEA*, s 118.

existence of an apparent conflict of interest must be determined by an informed person in an objective and rational manner. The Federal Court of Appeal has put that requirement thus:

> Would an informed person, viewing the matter realistically and practically and having thought the matter through, think it more likely than not that the public servant, whether consciously or unconsciously, will be influenced in the performance of his official duties by considerations having to do with his private interests?[165]

Pursuant to its power to prevent conflicts of interest, the Treasury Board has enacted a set of guidelines governing its employees. The most recent of those guidelines is the *Directive on Conflict of Interest*, effective 1 April 2020.[166] The *Directive on Conflict of Interest* sets out a number of conflict of interest measures that apply both during and (for designated employees) for a one-year period after employment in the public service. Broadly speaking, the directive addresses outside employment, contracting with the government, accepting hospitality or gifts, prohibition on the use of government property for personal gain, and political activity other than the activities set out in the *PSEA* that require PSC approval.

Public servants are permitted to accept outside employment, but if that employment is likely to give rise to a conflict of interest or in any way undermine the neutrality, then the public servant must prepare a confidential report, and their deputy head may then require that those outside activities be curtailed, modified, or even terminated. For example, in *Canada (Treasury Board) v Spinks*,[167] two employees were dismissed from their employment for owning and operating a business (called "Mystl") that proposed to put on a seminar entitled "How to Maximize Your Opportunities for Selling to the Federal Government." The seminar—despite its title—would not have divulged insider information but only information that was already in the public domain. The adjudicator overturned their dismissals (and the Federal Court of Appeal affirmed that ruling). The adjudicator ruled that operating that seminar was not a conflict of interest because the grievors would not provide any inside information, only advice and information on

165 *Threader v Canada (Treasury Board)*, [1986] FCJ No 411 at para 23.

166 Treasury Board of Canada Secretariat, *Directive on Conflict of Interest* (1 April 2020), online: www.tbs-sct.gc.ca/pol/doc-eng.aspx?id=32627.

167 *Canada (Treasury Board) v Spinks*, [1987] FCJ No 1141 (CA).

contracting that was already in the public domain but not covered by other seminars offered by the federal government. The adjudicator also noted that the grievors had disclosed their ownership of Mystl, including a general outline of Mystl's activities (putting on seminars for the business community), and that the lack of specificity in this disclosure statement did not indicate an intention to deceive their employer. On the other hand, in *Oliver v Canada (Customs and Revenue Agency)*,[168] an employee of Canada Customs and Revenue Agency was dismissed for preparing income tax returns for remuneration while still employed by the agency and refusing to stop when requested.

The Board has also upheld orders by employers not to engage in outside employment when those orders have been grieved. For example, in *Campione v Canada Revenue Agency*,[169] the Board upheld the Canada Revenue Agency's order that an international tax auditor not operate a consulting business that provided advice on financial issues, accounting issues, business reorganizations, and the preparation of business and marketing plans and valuations. The Board agreed with the employer that this business could have tax implications for the employee's clients and, therefore, the outside business gave rise to an appearance of a conflict of interest. In *Duske v Canadian Food Inspection Agency*,[170] the Board decided that an employee of the Canadian Food Inspection Agency (CFIA) was in a conflict of interest by working for an outside company that operated a muskox harvest that the CFIA regulated. Although the grievor's duties were not related to the work that he did for the outside company, the CFIA found that he was in a conflict of interest because he was working in an industry that it regulated and used his specialized knowledge gained from working for the CFIA in interpreting CFIA regulations. The Board also noted that it would be difficult to reconcile the grievor's employment with the CFIA with his involvement with a company it regulated in the event of media attention resulting from some activity of the outside company.

Public servants are not supposed to accept gifts, hospitality, or other benefits that have a real, apparent, or potential influence on the

---

168 *Oliver v Canada (Customs and Revenue Agency)*, [2004] FCJ No 1769.

169 *Campione v Canada Revenue Agency*, 2013 PSLRB 161. The Board came to a similar decision in *Cavanagh v Canada Revenue Agency*, 2015 PSLREB 7, aff'd 2016 FCA 27, involving a director of the Toronto Centre Tax Services Office whose side business performed business valuations.

170 *Duske v Canadian Food Inspection Agency*, 2007 PSLRB 94.

objectivity of the person employed in carrying out their official duties and responsibilities or may place the person employed under obligation to the donor.[171] Public servants are allowed to accept gifts that are infrequent and of minimal value; are within the normal standards of courtesy or protocol; arise out of activities or events related to the official duties and responsibilities of the person employed; and do not compromise or appear to compromise the integrity of the person employed or the organization.[172]

In *Assh v Canada (Attorney General)*,[173] a pension advocate was left a bequest of $5,000 in the will of a former client whom he had not seen in five years. He reported the bequest to his supervisor, who ordered him to return it. He returned the bequest but grieved the decision. His grievance was denied. The Federal Court quashed that decision and concluded that he could keep the bequest, but the Court of Appeal overturned that decision and reinstated the denial of Mr. Assh's grievance.

The Federal Court concluded that the bequest could not influence Mr. Assh in the performance of his duties and responsibilities (because the testatrix would not have any more dealings with the government, being dead), and the bequest was within the bounds of propriety because the amount was not large in light of the size of the estate and the amounts given to the testatrix's dependents and other beneficiaries.

The Court of Appeal disagreed. That Court stated that the legal test is whether a reasonable person, who was informed of the facts of a given case and had thought the matter through in a practical manner, would think that the acceptance of this particular benefit could influence the employee in the performance of their official duties. In this particular case, the question was whether a reasonable, fully informed person would think that accepting the legacy *could* influence a pension advocate to give preferential treatment to clients whom they believed might leave a legacy as a reward for professional services rendered.[174] The question is not whether the benefit *would* influence the employee but whether it *could* influence the employee.[175] The majority of the Court of Appeal concluded that a reasonable person would think that

171 *Directive on Conflict of Interest*, above note 166, art 4.2.13.

172 *Ibid*, art 4.2.14.

173 *Assh v Canada (Attorney General)*, [2005] FCJ No 1714 (FC), overturned on appeal [2006] FCJ No 1656 (CA) [*Assh*].

174 *Assh* (CA), *ibid* at paras 64 and 73.

175 *Ibid* at paras 75–76.

there was a realistic possibility that a pension advocate's acceptance of a $5,000 legacy could influence the performance of their duties to other clients.[176]

Typically, the issue of soliciting or accepting gifts is more straightforward than a bequest from a former client. For example, the Board upheld a two-week suspension of an employee who solicited and accepted free concert tickets when clearing Elton John's plane for entry into Canada.[177]

Conflict of interest rules can also apply to certain political activities. For example, in *Gauthier v Canada (Attorney General)*,[178] an Employment Insurance investigator was also a municipal counsellor in the city of Saint-Jean-sur-Richelieu. The Federal Court of Appeal set aside a decision by his assistant deputy minister that his position as a municipal counsellor created a conflict of interest on the grounds that the assistant deputy minister misunderstood whether his municipal district overlapped with the geographic area in which he was responsible for conducting investigations. The Court of Appeal confirmed that being a municipal counsellor could constitute a conflict of interest but that the actual decision had to balance the political rights of a public servant on the one hand against the public interest in an honest, impartial, and effective public service on the other.

As another example, in *Gendron v Treasury Board (Department of Canadian Heritage)*,[179] the Treasury Board dismissed an employee for a political conflict of interest. Ms. Gendron worked for the Department of Canadian Heritage in the part of the department responsible for promoting French language rights outside of Quebec. Ms. Gendron also became president of "Le Quebec, un pays!," an organization whose main objective was to promote Quebec sovereignty. The Treasury Board argued that her presidency in that organization was a conflict

176 One judge dissented in the result: he agreed with the majority of the Court about the proper legal test but concluded that a reasonable person, fully informed, would not conclude that accepting a legacy could influence Mr. Assh in the performance of his duties. This demonstrates how difficult it is to apply this particular test: three judges, fully informed, came to different conclusions about whether a reasonable person would think that this legacy could influence Mr. Assh's performance of his duties.

177 *Stewart v Deputy Head (Canada Border Services Agency)*, 2016 PSLREB 106.

178 *Gauthier v Canada (Attorney General)*, 2008 FCA 75.

179 *Gendron v Treasury Board (Department of Canadian Heritage)*, [2006] CPSLRB No 15.

of interest with her position with the government because one of the purposes of her government position was to promote national unity through protecting French language rights outside of Quebec. The issue, therefore, was whether this "indirect criticism" of government policy placed Ms. Gendron in a conflict of interest with her employer. The adjudicator concluded that this did create a conflict of interest and, after examining the nature and field of activities concerned, her visibility and role, and her level of power and influence, stated:

> Accordingly, from the perspective of any reasonable person, a conflict of interest can be perceived between, on the one hand, the grievor's personal activities as president of a sovereigntist organization, given the symbolism and visibility of that office and, on the other hand, her duties as a representative of the Department with the mandate of promoting Canadian unity, despite the fact that the level of her position and her decision-making power were not significant.[180]

The adjudicator concluded that dismissal was an excessive penalty for this conflict of interest and instead ordered the employer to find Ms. Gendron a job that would not place her in a position of conflict of interest.

Finally, public servants must avoid giving preferential treatment to friends and family in the staffing process or when making decisions that will result in a financial award to an external party.[181] Preferential treatment does not include giving family members information that is easily accessible to the public. The term "friends and family" may be given a wide interpretation under the right circumstances.[182]

---

180 *Ibid* at para 174.

181 See, for example, *McEwan v Deputy Head (Immigration and Refugee Board)*, 2015 PSLREB 53 [*McEwan*], where a senior employee was dismissed because of her involvement in the staffing process for her son and a friend. See also *Mercer v Deputy Head (Department of Human Resources and Skills Development)*, 2016 PSLREB 11, where the Board upheld a two-day suspension of an employee who accessed his family members' records at their request to assist them with their Employment Insurance claims.

182 In *Bellavance v Canada (Human Resources Development)*, [2000] FCJ No 1784, for example, an employee was dismissed because he processed the unemployment insurance files of his former employees in a grocery business he owned. The adjudicator concluded that this was a conflict of interest, but that dismissal was an excessive penalty in the circumstances (although the adjudicator also decided not to reinstate the employee). The Federal Court upheld that result. See also *Brazeau v Deputy Head (Department of Public Works and Government*

The Federal Court has been inconsistent in deciding whether conflict of interest policies are legally binding. In *Peet v Canada (Attorney General)*,[183] the Court stated that the conflict of interest code had sufficient legal force that a deputy head's decision made under the Code was subject to judicial review, even going so far as stating that the Code was "implied or quasi-legislation."[184] In *Assh*, the Federal Court came to the opposite conclusion and stated that the Code should not be treated as law, although the Court went on to interpret Mr. Assh's entitlement to a bequest based on the Code.[185] However, the Court of Appeal disagreed, stating:

> The legal status of the Conflict of Interest Code is not clear-cut. It lacks the quality of "law" in that it is neither contained in legislation, issued pursuant to a discrete statutory power, nor promulgated as an order in council. On the other hand, many of its provisions impose quite specific obligations on employees and compliance is a condition of their employment.[186]

The Court of Appeal concluded that the Code should be treated as "law" for the purposes of determining the appropriate standard of review of the grievance officer's decision concerning the Code.

d) Statutory Whistle-Blower Protection

Many of the cases discussed above concerning the duty of fidelity and loyalty involved employees who relied on a so-called whistle-blower defence: they were disclosing information necessary to protect the health and welfare of Canadians and therefore did not breach their duty of loyalty by disclosing information to the public. Whistle-blowing (or disclosing wrongdoing by fellow employees, supervisors, or more senior management) is a contentious issue in the public service; however,

---

Services), 2008 PSLRB 62, where an employee was dismissed for being involved in awarding a contract to a company owned by the cousin of his mother; *Pagé v Deputy Head (Service Canada)*, 2009 PSLRB 26, where the employee was dismissed for granting Canada Pension Plan benefits to her stepsister; and *El-Menini v Canadian Food Inspection Agency*, 2018 FPSLREB 40, where the grievor was dismissed in part for being involved in the hiring of his brother-in-law.

183 *Peet*, above note 32.

184 *Ibid* at para 13.

185 *Assh* (FC), above note 173 at para 19.

186 *Assh* (CA), above note 173 at para 38.

in recent years, there appears to have evolved a consensus that whistle-blowing is appropriate behaviour for federal public servants and that whistle-blowers should be protected against reprisals. As put in the "Report of the Working Group on Disclosure of Wrongdoing":

> An effective regime for the identification, disclosure and correction of wrongdoing is a necessary component of any overall approach to strengthening public sector management and creating more ethical government. Such a regime provides public servants with the tools and support they need to reveal and correct instances where conduct and decision-making fall short of the high standards expected in public institutions. In addition, a trusted disclosure regime can make a significant contribution to public service morale and conduct, and to public confidence in government. In this context it is imperative that the Government of Canada move quickly to introduce the changes necessary to improve the existing regime.[187]

In a 2005 decision,[188] the Supreme Court of Canada endorsed the importance of laws protecting employees making good faith disclosures of wrongdoing by their employers. Although the facts of the case were about an employee's disclosure of wrongdoing by her private sector employer (who happened to be a trade union), the Court's comments about the purpose of "whistle-blower" legislation apply to public sector employees as well:

> Whistle-blower laws create an exception to the usual duty of loyalty owed by employees to their employer. When applied in government, of course, the purpose is to avoid the waste of public funds or other abuse of state-conferred privileges or authority. In relation to the private sector (as here), the purpose still has a public interest focus because it aims to prevent wrongdoing "that is or is likely to result in an offence." (It is the "offence" requirement that gives the whistle-blower law a public aspect and filters out more general workplace complaints.) The underlying idea is to recruit employees to assist the state in the suppression of unlawful conduct. This is done by providing employees with a measure of immunity against employer retaliation. "[R]eports

187 Public Service Human Resources Management Agency, "Report of the Working Group on Disclosure of Wrongdoing" (2003).

188 *Merk*, above note 107.

from insiders allow for early detection and reduction of harm, reduce the necessity for and expense of public oversight and investigation, and may ultimately deter malfeasance."[189]

These concerns about the necessity of protecting employees who, in good faith, disclose wrongdoing by their employer led to the enactment of the *Public Servants Disclosure Protection Act*.[190] That Act is responsible for protecting whistle-blowers in the federal public service.

i) *Purpose of the* Public Servants Disclosure Protection Act

The *Public Servants Disclosure Protection Act* contains a preamble setting out the purposes of that Act. The preamble recognizes that the public service of Canada is an important national institution that is part of the essential framework of Canadian parliamentary democracy. Among other things, the preamble notes that public servants owe a duty of loyalty to their employer and enjoy the right to freedom of expression as guaranteed by the *Charter* and that the Act strives to achieve an appropriate balance between those two important principles. The Act also requires the Treasury Board and other separate employers to establish their own codes of conduct:[191] the *Charter* mentioned in the preamble is in addition to and separate from those codes. In addition to the preamble, section 4 of the Act requires the minister responsible for the Public Service Human Resources Management Agency of Canada to promote ethical practices in the public sector and a positive environment for disclosing wrongdoings by disseminating knowledge about the Act and its purposes and processes.[192] Courts have summarized the purpose behind the Act as "establishing effective procedures for the disclosure of wrongdoings and for protecting public servants who disclose wrongdoings." The purpose is thus twofold: to denounce and punish wrongdoing in the public sector and ultimately build public confidence in the integrity of public servants and to protect whistle-blowers and other people taking part in an investigation from reprisals.[193]

---

189 *Ibid* at para 14, citing E.S. Callahan, T.M. Dworkin & D. Lewis, "Whistle-blowing: Australian, UK, and US Approaches to Disclosure in the Public Interest" (2004) 44 Va J Intl L 879 at 882.

190 *Public Servants Disclosure Protection Act*, SC 2005, c 46 [*PSDPA*].

191 *Ibid*, ss 5–7.

192 *Ibid*, s 4.

193 *Agnaou v Canada (Attorney General)*, 2015 FCA 29 at paras 60 and 62 [*Agnaou*]. See also *Biles v Canada (Attorney General)*, 2017 FC 1159 at para 41 [*Biles*].

ii) Scope of the Public Servants Disclosure Protection Act

The *Public Servants Disclosure Protection Act* applies not only to the "public service" as that term is defined in the *Federal Public Sector Labour Relations Act* (*FPSLRA*)[194] but to the broader "public sector," including federal Crown corporations. The Canadian Forces, Canadian Security Intelligence Service, and Communications Security Establishment are exempt from the Act.[195] Certain sections of the *Public Servants Disclosure Protection Act* restrict the ability of RCMP members to file complaints relating to investigations into disciplinary measures under the RCMP Code of Conduct unless the specific RCMP processes have been exhausted.[196]

iii) Disclosing Wrongdoing Under the Public Servants Disclosure Protection Act

The *Public Servants Disclosure Protection Act* protects public servants who make a "protected disclosure" of "wrongdoing." A "protected disclosure" must be made in good faith in one of four circumstances: in accordance with the Act, in the course of a Parliamentary proceeding, in the course of a proceeding established by another Act of Parliament, or when lawfully required.[197]

The Act does not define when disclosure is in "good faith." It is also not clear why this requirement exists. A 2017 parliamentary report resulting from a statutory review of the Act recommended eliminating this requirement. In hearings before the relevant standing committee, the public sector integrity commissioner at the time stated that he had never rejected a disclosure of wrongdoing on the basis of "bad faith" and that he found it an unnecessary disincentive to disclosure, going so far as to state that "[m]otivation is not relevant. What is relevant is whether a wrongdoing or reprisal took place."[198]

The Act also only applies to the following categories of "wrongdoings":

---

194 *Federal Public Sector Labour Relations Act*, SC 2003, c 22, s 2 [*FPSLRA*].

195 *PSDPA*, s 2, "public sector."

196 *Ibid*, s 19.1(5).

197 *Ibid*, s 2, "protected disclosure."

198 Standing Committee on Government Operations and Estimates, *Strengthening the Protection of the Public Interest within the* Public Servants Disclosure Protection Act, 42-1 (June 2017) (Chair: Tom Lukiwski) at 30, online (pdf): www.ourcommons.ca/DocumentViewer/en/42-1/OGGO/report-9.

(a) a contravention of any Act of Parliament or of the legislature of a province, or of any regulations made under any such Act;
(b) a misuse of public funds or a public asset;
(c) a gross mismanagement in the public sector;
(d) an act or omission that creates a substantial and specific danger to the life, health or safety of persons, or to the environment, other than a danger that is inherent in the performance of the duties or functions of a public servant;
(e) a serious breach of a code of conduct established under section 5 or 6 of the Act; and
(f) knowingly directing or counselling a person to commit a wrongdoing set out in any of paragraphs (a) to (e).[199]

These terms are not defined specifically and are capable of many definitions. The Federal Court of Appeal has pointed out, for example, that "[t]he phrase 'gross mismanagement' used in section 8 of the Act is not defined and depends, of course, on the organization involved."[200] The Office of the Public Sector Integrity Commissioner has published guidelines about how it will interpret "gross mismanagement," "misuse of public funds," and "serious breach of a code of conduct." While these guidelines are not legally binding, they are helpful guides nonetheless. They stipulate that gross mismanagement involves something that is "more than trivial wrongdoing or negligence" or something involving "serious errors that are not debatable among reasonable people."[201] Similarly, a "serious breach of a code of conduct" requires a "significant departure" from the norm or a "systemic or endemic" problem.[202] Misuse of public funds involves a more objective test: it includes "expenditures made without proper authorization" as well as spending money in a way that is "wastefully unnecessary."[203]

---

199 *PSDPA*, s 8.

200 *Agnaou*, above note 193 at para 88.

201 Office of the Public Sector Integrity Commissioner of Canada, "Gross Mismanagement," online (pdf): https://psic-ispc.gc.ca/en/faqs#gross.

202 Office of the Public Sector Integrity Commissioner of Canada, "Serious Breach of a Code of Conduct," online (pdf): https://psic-ispc.gc.ca/en/serious-breach-code-conduct.

203 Office of the Public Sector Integrity Commissioner of Canada, "Misuse of Public Funds or a Public Asset," online (pdf): https://psic-ispc.gc.ca/en/misuse-public-funds-or-public-asset.

The Act sets out three stages of disclosure. The first stage of disclosure is through the internal disclosure procedures established by the employer. Those internal procedures must establish a "senior officer" to be responsible for receiving disclosure.[204]

The next level of disclosure is to the public service integrity commissioner. Under the Act as originally passed, a public servant could only disclose information to the commissioner in three circumstances: if the public servant believed on reasonable grounds that it would not be appropriate to disclose information to their supervisor, if the public servant already disclosed the information to their supervisor and was of the opinion that the matter was not appropriately dealt with, or if the public servant was in a designated portion of the public sector. However, the *Federal Accountability Act*[205] amended the *Public Servants Disclosure Protection Act* to permit unconditional disclosure to the commissioner.[206]

The commissioner may not deal with a disclosure if "a person or body acting under another Act of Parliament is dealing with the subject-matter of the disclosure."[207] The Federal Court has interpreted this phrase narrowly. In *Canada (Attorney General) v Canada (Public Sector Integrity Commissioner)*,[208] the commissioner investigated and reported that RCMP pilots had made false entries in their aircraft journey log-books. Transport Canada was also investigating the same issue. The RCMP therefore argued that the commissioner should not report on the wrongdoing he discovered. The Federal Court concluded that the commissioner retained the jurisdiction to report on this wrongdoing despite Transport Canada's investigation. The Court pointed out that the two investigations served different purposes: the commissioner's investigation was designed to "addresses wrongdoings of an order of magnitude that could shake public confidence if not reported and corrected"[209] and to "uncover past wrongs, bring them to light in public and put in place corrections to prevent recurrence."[210] The Transport

204 *PSDPA*, s 10(2).

205 *Federal Accountability Act*, SC 2006, c 9.

206 *PSDPA*, s 13.

207 *Ibid*, s 23(1).

208 *Canada (Attorney General) v Canada (Public Sector Integrity Commissioner)*, 2016 FC 886.

209 *Ibid* at para 106.

210 *Ibid* at para 107.

Canada investigation, by contrast, was designed to "find gaps in existing procedures and provide advice with respect to future regulations."[211] Transport Canada was also reporting its findings to the RCMP (the wrongdoer), with no obligation to make its recommendations public. The Court concluded that in light of the different nature and purposes of the two investigations, the Transport Canada investigation did not prevent the commissioner from proceeding.

Additionally, the commissioner may refuse to deal with a disclosure or commence an investigation in six circumstances: (1) the subject matter of the disclosure or the investigation has been adequately dealt with, or could more appropriately be dealt with, according to a procedure provided for under another Act of Parliament; (2) the subject matter of the disclosure or the investigation is not sufficiently important; (3) the disclosure was not made in good faith or the information that led to the investigation was not provided in good faith; (4) the length of time that has elapsed since the date when the subject matter of the disclosure or the investigation arose is such that dealing with it would serve no useful purpose; (5) the subject matter of the disclosure or the investigation relates to a matter that results from a balanced and informed decision-making process on a public policy issue; or (6) there is a valid reason for not dealing with the subject matter of the disclosure or the investigation.[212] For example, the commissioner has refused to investigate disclosures of harassment against an employee on the grounds that the harassment complaint procedure was a proper alternative.[213]

The final level of disclosure is public disclosure. Disclosure to the public is permitted only when there is not sufficient time to make internal disclosure (to the commissioner or the employee's supervisor), and the public servant believes on reasonable grounds that the subject matter of the disclosure is an act or omission that constitutes a serious offence under an Act of Parliament or the legislature of a province, or constitutes an imminent risk of a substantial and specific danger to the life, health, and safety of persons or to the environment.[214]

Subsection 16(2) of the Act specifically states that the Act does not affect the right of a public servant to make disclosure to the public under any other law; therefore, the limitation on public disclosure in

211 *Ibid* at para 107.
212 *PSDPA*, s 24(1).
213 *Gupta v Canada (Attorney General)*, 2016 FC 1416, aff'd 2017 FCA 211.
214 *PSDPA*, s 16(1).

section 16(1) of the Act does not limit the common law defence set out in *Fraser*.[215]

Finally, if the employee is alleging wrongdoing by the commissioner, then disclosure may be made to the auditor general instead of the commissioner.[216]

iv) Reprisals

The *Public Servants Disclosure Protection Act* protects public sector employees against "reprisal" for having made a protected disclosure. The public servant complaining of the reprisal does not need to prove that their protected disclosure was ultimately found to constitute wrongdoing, but instead only that their attempt to disclose what they perceived as wrongdoing was made in good faith. Furthermore, the public servant does not need to refer expressly to the Act or mention the definition of "wrongdoing" to permit a finding that they have made a protected disclosure.[217]

A reprisal is a disciplinary measure, a demotion, a termination, a measure that adversely affects the employment or working conditions of the public sector employee, or a threat to do any of those four things.[218] The Act originally required complaints about reprisals to be made to the Canada Industrial Relations Board or the Public Service Labour Relations Board; however, after the *Federal Accountability Act*, complaints about reprisals are made to the commissioner instead.

Reprisal complaints may be filed by "any public servant who has reasonable grounds for believing that a reprisal has been taken against him or her."[219] Complaints about reprisals must be made within sixty days that the public servant knew or ought to have known of the reprisal.[220] This sixty-day time limit requires that the particular act of reprisal be committed within the sixty-day period prior to the complaint—an ongoing chain of reprisals does not extend the time period to complain about the reprisal measures that occurred more than sixty days before the complaint. A complainant may rely on relevant facts taking place outside of the sixty-day period to support a timely complaint (as earlier

215 *Fraser*, above note 93.

216 *PSDPA*, s 14.

217 *Agnaou*, above note 193 at paras 73–76.

218 *PSDPA*, s 2(1), "reprisal."

219 *Ibid*, s 19.1(1).

220 *Ibid*, s 19.1(2).

events may demonstrate a desire to punish the public servant), but a complaint may not be based on a reprisal committed prior to the sixty-day time limit.[221] The commissioner has the discretion to extend that sixty-day period in appropriate circumstances.[222]

Within fifteen days from the complaint being filed, the commissioner must decide whether to deal with the complaint.[223] There are two separate provisions setting out the power of the commissioner to refuse to deal with a complaint. First, section 19.3(1) of the Act states that the commissioner may refuse to deal with the complaint where they are of the opinion that (1) the complaint's subject matter has been—or could be—adequately dealt with according to a procedure provided for under any other Act of Parliament or a collective agreement; (2) if the complainant is a member or former member of the RCMP, the subject matter of the complaint has been adequately dealt with by the procedures in the *RCMP Act* relating to discipline; (3) the complaint is beyond the jurisdiction of the commissioner; or (4) the complaint was not made in good faith.[224] Second, section 19.3(2) of the Act states that the commissioner may not deal with a complaint if a person or body acting under another Act of Parliament or a collective agreement is dealing with the subject matter of the complaint other than as a law enforcement authority.

The grounds in sections 19.3(1)(a) and 19.3(2) appear similar, but there are two important differences. First, the ground in section 19.3(1)(a) is permissive, whereas section 19.3(2) is mandatory. Second, the ground in section 19.3(2) may be temporary. That provision requires that the commissioner examine the grievance and determine whether the grievance will in fact include an assessment of the reprisals. This may, in many cases, require the commissioner to wait for a final decision in the grievance to ensure that the reprisal measures were considered. Merely filing the grievance is not enough to meet that requirement.[225]

If a public servant files a reprisal complaint, they may not commence any other procedure in respect of the measure alleged to constitute the reprisal; however, if the commissioner decides not to deal with the complaint, the public servant may commence some other process,

---

221 *Gupta v Canada (Attorney General)*, 2016 FCA 50.

222 *PSDPA*, s 19.1(2).

223 *Ibid*, s 19.4(1).

224 *Ibid*, s 19.3(1).

225 *Therrien v Canada (Attorney General)*, 2017 FCA 14 at para 9.

such as a grievance.[226] In effect, this means that a public servant can choose between a reprisal complaint and a grievance but, having made that choice, cannot switch later unless one or the other is dismissed for lack of jurisdiction or without having addressed the reprisal aspect of the case.[227]

Once the commissioner decides to investigate an allegation or reprisal (or, more accurately, appoint an investigator), then the employer may not enact any discipline against the complainant until the complaint has been resolved,[228] and any discipline already enacted must be suspended until the complaint has been resolved.[229] The investigator may recommend that a conciliator be appointed to attempt to resolve the complaint.[230] Any settlement must be agreed to by the complainant, a person with authority to implement the remedy, and the commissioner.[231] When the investigation is complete, the investigator must prepare a report for the commissioner.[232] The commissioner may then either dismiss the complaint[233] or refer the complaint to the Public Servants Disclosure Protection Tribunal.[234]

The commissioner's role in this process is similar to the screening function played by the Canadian Human Rights Commission under the *Canadian Human Rights Act*. This means that, like the Canadian Human Rights Commission, the commissioner's investigation must be neutral, fair, unbiased, and thorough.[235] Like the Canadian Human Rights Commission, the commissioner may only dismiss a complaint at the initial, admissibility stage if it is "plain and obvious" that it cannot be dealt with for one of the reasons described in section 19.1(3) of the Act.[236] Furthermore, the commissioner's role is not to determine the credibility of the persons involved or to rule on the legal issues raised in

---

226 *PSDPA*, s 19.1(4). The original wording of the Act prohibited employees from referring any complaint about reprisal to an arbitrator or adjudication.

227 This ability to file a grievance is specifically protected by s 51 of the *PSDPA*. See *Wilson v Atomic Energy of Canada Limited*, 2017 CanLII 81327, on this point.

228 *PSDPA*, s 19.5.

229 *Ibid*, s 19.6.

230 *Ibid*, s 20.

231 *Ibid*, ss 20.1 & 20.2.

232 *Ibid*, s 20.3.

233 *Ibid*, s 20.5.

234 *Ibid*, s 20.4.

235 *Biles*, above note 193 at para 54.

236 *Agnaou*, above note 193 at para 66.

a complaint but instead "to decide whether there is an objective basis for justifying that the reprisal complaint be investigated on its merits by the Tribunal."[237] In other words, the threshold is whether the commissioner has reasonable grounds for believing that a reprisal was taken against the complainant—and, if so, the complaint must be referred to the tribunal.[238]

The Public Servants Disclosure Protection Tribunal is composed of superior court judges.[239] It is a quasi-judicial tribunal with significant powers similar to those of the Canadian Human Rights Tribunal or other federal tribunals.[240]

The tribunal may also require the employer to discipline the person who made the reprisal.[241] Employees disciplined under this provision may not grieve that discipline.[242] The employee responsible for the reprisal is a party to any tribunal proceeding[243] and has the right to make submissions accordingly.[244] In addition, to obtain an order from the tribunal disciplining the individual who reprised against the complainant, the tribunal must be satisfied that the reprisal was taken intentionally as retaliation because the complainant made a protected disclosure.[245]

Once a complaint is before the tribunal, the complainant bears the burden of proving, on the balance of probabilities, that they made a protected disclosure, that they were the subject of one of the measures listed in the definition of reprisal, and that the reprisal was taken against them because they made a disclosure, by which is meant a "nexus" between the disclosure and the reprisal.[246]

Finally, the commissioner has the power to authorize free access to legal advice for public sector and non–public sector employees who are considering making a disclosure of wrongdoing, serving as a witness,

---

237 *Agnaou v Canada (Attorney General)*, 2017 FC 338 at para 7.

238 *Ibid.*

239 *PSDPA*, s 20.7.

240 *Ibid*, s 21.7(1). Under the original Act, the Board had all of the same remedial powers, except for the $10,000 payment for pain and suffering.

241 *Ibid*, s 21.8.

242 *Ibid*, s 21.8(4).

243 *Ibid*, s 21.5(2)(d).

244 *Ibid*, s 21.6.

245 *Agnaou*, above note 193 at para 67.

246 *Dunn v Indigenous and Northern Affairs Canada and Lecompte*, 2017 PSDPT 3 at paras 66 and 86. This decision was upheld on appeal, without explicitly referring to these issues: *Dunn v Canada (Attorney General)*, 2018 FCA 210.

or alleging a reprisal.[247] The maximum payment under the Act for legal advice is $1,500, or $3,000 in exceptional circumstances.[248]

This statutory whistle-blowing regime has been heavily criticized during its existence for not going far enough to protect employees who disclose wrongdoing. For example:

- The commissioner's ability to refuse to deal with a complaint because of the availability of other procedures to address the issue may be problematic because allegations of wrongdoing are often tied to a number of other issues, including staffing, harassment, and poisoned work environments. The commissioner's ability to refuse to deal with complaints on this ground means that employees in the federal public service may be faced (as is often the case) with a multiplicity of jurisdictions for possible redress.
- The requirement that complaints and disclosure be made in good faith is problematic. For example, if an employee has filed a harassment complaint against a person and then makes a disclosure of wrongdoing, is that second disclosure made in good faith? There is no requirement that a complainant prove that they are acting in good faith when complaining about violations of the *FPSLRA*, for example, and it is unclear why such a requirement is necessary in this Act.[249]
- The report of the Commission of Inquiry into the Sponsorship Program and Advertising Activities (the Gomery Report) recommended that in the event that a whistle-blower makes a formal complaint alleging a reprisal, the burden of proof should be on the employer to show that the actions taken were not a reprisal.[250] Similarly, the House of Commons Standing Committee on Government Operations and Estimates repeated this recommendation in 2017.[251]

---

247 *PSDPA*, s 25.1.

248 *Ibid*, s 25.1(5)–(6).

249 Jacquie de Aguayo, "A Union Perspective on the Adequacy of Bill C-11: *The Public Servants Disclosure Protection Act*" (Ottawa: Canadian Institute, 28 November 2005).

250 Commission of Inquiry into the Sponsorship Program and Advertising Activities, *Restoring Accountability: Recommendations* (2005) at 186, online: https://publications.gc.ca/site/eng/287355/publication.html [Gomery Report].

251 Report of the Standing Committee on Government Operations and Estimates, above note 198.

- The Gomery Report also recommended that the list of wrongdoings and reprisals should be "an open list" so that actions similar to those listed would also be covered.[252]
- The Public Service Alliance of Canada[253] criticized the provision (not discussed above) that amended the *Access to Information Act*, creating a five-year ban on the release of information collected in the course of an investigation into a wrongdoing. The *Federal Accountability Act* then extended that ban indefinitely.[254]

These criticisms aside, the most important question is whether the Act will create a climate where the exposure of wrongdoing is not punished, but instead celebrated, in the federal public service. Whistle-blowers can be punished in subtle ways as they find that promotional prospects dry up and, years after their disclosure, they still have not progressed in their career in the same manner as their co-workers who kept silent. So far, the indications are not good. The 2019 Public Service Employee Survey found that only half of public servants felt safe to initiate a formal recourse process without fear of reprisal.[255] It is also noteworthy that there have been over 300 reprisal complaints filed with the commissioner. Of those, only two made it to a hearing—and both complaints were dismissed at the hearing stage.

Whether this new Act is sufficient to change the culture of the federal public service from one of silence to one of openness and frank disclosure of perceived wrongdoing can only be tested over time.

E. TERMS AND CONDITIONS CONCERNING PAY

For employees represented by bargaining agents, their pay is determined by their respective collective agreement. Some separate employers have their own methods of determining pay; however, this section

---

252 *Ibid.*

253 Editorial, *Toronto Star* (7 November 2005).

254 *Access to Information Act*, RSC 1985, c A-1, ss 16.4–6.5.

255 Fifty percent agreed or strongly agreed that they could initiate a formal recourse process without fear of reprisal. Twenty-nine percent disagreed or strongly disagreed. The remaining responses were either neutral or did not know. Treasury Board of Canada Secretariat, "2019 Public Service Employee Survey, Question 43," online: www.tbs-sct.canada.ca/pses-saff/2019/results-resultats/bd-pm/00/org-eng.aspx#i4-s12.

will provide an overview of the rules governing pay in the core public administration.[256]

1) Public Service Terms and Conditions of Employment Regulations

Most of the rules governing pay in the core public administration are set out in the *Directive on Terms and Conditions of Employment* (*T&C Directive*).[257] This directive used to be referred to as the *Public Service Terms and Conditions of Employment Regulations* (*PSTCER*). As the Federal Court has pointed out, "Despite its name, the 'Regulations' are not enacted subordinate legislation. Rather these 'Regulations' are simply another Treasury Board policy."[258] However, most collective agreements governing employees in the core public administration contain a clause providing that "[e]xcept as provided in this Article, the terms and conditions governing the application of pay to employees are not affected by this Agreement" or some similar clause.[259] Collective agreements containing such a provision or a similar provision incorporate, by reference, the *PSTCER* (now the *T&C Directive*).[260] Therefore, represented employees may grieve breaches of the *T&C Directive* and then refer those grievances to adjudication. Furthermore, the Treasury Board has a number of other policies and directives concerning pay. In the event of a contradiction between the *T&C Directive* and those other policies, the *T&C Directive* governs.[261]

---

256 The Canada Revenue Agency (CRA), for example, technically has its own method of calculating pay; the CRA's staffing program states that the rate of pay for external employees from the core federal public service will be determined in accordance with the terms and conditions applicable to the core federal public service. Therefore, the *Public Service Terms and Conditions of Employment Regulations*, discussed below, apply to employees moving to the CRA. See *Harris v Canada Revenue Agency*, 2006 PSLRB 106.

257 Treasury Board of Canada Secretariat, *Directive on Terms and Conditions of Employment* (1 April 2014), online: www.tbs-sct.gc.ca/pol/doc-eng.aspx?id=15772 [*T&C Directive*].

258 *Glowinski*, above note 37.

259 See, for example, art 64.01 of the Public Service Alliance of Canada collective agreement for the Program and Administrative Services (PA) group, online: www.tbs-sct.canada.ca/agreements-conventions/view-visualiser-eng.aspx?id=15.

260 *Canada (AG) v Jones*, [1978] 2 FC 39 at para 42.

261 *Broekaert v Treasury Board (Correctional Service of Canada)*, [2005] CPSLRB No 78 at para 38.

Pay rates in federal public service collective agreements are set out using a grid for each classification level. For example, the pay grid for the PM-1 classification from 2013–17 was as follows:

PM-1				
$) 21 June 2013	48,796	50,652	52,576	54,575
A) 21 June 2014	49,406	51,285	53,233	55,257
B) 21 June 2015	50,024	51,926	53,898	55,948
X) Restructure effective 21 June 2016	50,274	52,186	54,167	56,228
C) 21 June 2016	50,902	52,838	54,844	56,931
D) 21 June 2017	51,538	53,498	55,530	57,643

The letters indicate dates: for example, the row for "A" is effective on 21 June 2014, the row for "B" is effective on 21 June 2015, and so on. Each column is called a pay "increment." Employees move up one increment every twelve months, unless their collective agreement provides otherwise.[262] Pay increments are calculated on the date of a public servant's appointment, with some exceptions for employees who are deployed to a new position.[263] A "pay increment" is referred to as a "quasi-automatic progression"[264] up the wage grid—so called because they may only be withheld in prescribed circumstances (e.g., in the case of excluded and unrepresented employees, pay increments may be withheld by the deputy head due to unsatisfactory performance);[265] however, most represented employees have negotiated guarantees that progression through the salary grid is automatic. Employees continue to move up increments while on leave with pay[266] and on leave without pay unless their collective agreement prevents it.[267] Finally, if an employee is laid off and then reappointed within one year because of a layoff priority under the *PSEA*, then the period from the last pay

262 *T&C Directive*, above note 257, para 2.5.3. This applies to full-time, part-time, and casual employees: *Broekaert*, *ibid* at para 39.

263 *T&C Directive*, above note 257, para 2.5.4.

264 *Association of Justice Counsel v Treasury Board*, 2012 PSLRB 32 at para 37.

265 *T&C Directive*, above note 257, para 2.5.6. The *T&C Directive* does not expressly state that this rule only applies to unrepresented or excluded employees; however, collective agreements routinely state that pay increments "shall" be granted, and these provisions supersede the discretion in the *T&C Directive* to deny a pay increment due to unsatisfactory performance: *Professional Institute of the Public Service of Canada v Treasury Board*, 2019 FPSLREB 7 at paras 100–15.

266 *T&C Directive*, above note 257, para 2.5.8.

267 *Ibid*, para 2.5.9.

increment until the time of the layoff is counted when determining the new increment date—in other words, you get to bank your increment time for one year if you are laid off.[268]

Some occupational groups have wage grids that are not based on pay increments but, instead, based on wage ranges whereby employees move up the wage scale based on their performance rating for the previous fiscal year.

2) Rate of Pay on Appointment

The *PSEA* gives the Treasury Board the exclusive right to determine the rate of pay on appointment to a position;[269] therefore, this is one facet of public servants' pay that cannot be negotiated in a collective agreement.[270] The *T&C Directive* provides that the rate of pay on appointment will be established in accordance with the rules that are established for promotions, deployment, or demotion.

a) Appointment from Outside the Public Service

If a person is appointed to the public service for the first time (i.e., not on promotion, deployment, transfer, or demotion), then they are presumptively placed on the lowest increment level, subject to any other Treasury Board enactment.[271] The *T&C Directive* permits a deputy head (or their delegate) to set an initial rate of pay above the minimum in one of three circumstances:

- There is a shortage of skilled labour in the field involved, as evidenced by local or regional labour market surveys from recognized institutions.
- There are unusual difficulties in filling the position with properly qualified candidates.
- Operational conditions require the presence of a highly skilled or experienced employee who can assume the full duties of the position immediately upon taking employment.

---

268 *Ibid*, para 2.5.10.

269 *PSEA*, s 60.

270 See *Mark and Treasury Board (Transport Canada)*, [1992] CPSSRB No 36; *Raphael and Treasury Board (Transport Canada)*, [1996] CPSSRB No 5.

271 *T&C Directive*, above note 257, para 2.2.1.1.

There is no effective legal mechanism to require an employer to pay a new employee more than the minimum required as a refusal to pay above the minimum cannot be judicially reviewed,[272] nor can it be the subject of a grievance referred to adjudication.[273]

b) Promotion

An appointment constitutes a promotion when the maximum rate of pay for a position to which the employee is being appointed is greater than the maximum rate of pay of the employee's old position by an amount equal to the lowest pay increment of the position to which they are being promoted or an amount equal to at least 4 percent of the maximum rate of pay for the position held before the promotion.[274] When an employee is promoted, they are placed at the pay increment level nearest to their old rate of pay that gives the employee a raise of the lowest pay increment applicable to the new position (or, if there are no increments in the new position, at least 4 percent of the maximum rate of pay in the new position).[275] For example, the pay implement grids for the PM-1 and PM-2 positions as of 21 June 2020 are listed below. An employee who is at the third increment level of the PM-1 position and is then promoted to a PM-2 position would receive a rate of pay at the second increment level. The lowest increment level of the PM-2 position is $2,087, so the employee is entitled to a raise of at least that amount. Since that amount plus the employee's old rate of pay is greater than the lowest increment level of the PM-2 position ($59,129 + $2,087 = $61,216), they will be paid at the next highest increment level ($63,474).

PM-1:	54,878	56,965	59,129	61,379
PM-2:	61,152	63,474	65,887	

When assessing whether an appointment is a promotion, the employer must compare the new position and the employee's substantive position, not an acting position.[276] However, when an employee continues in an assignment without any change in duties and the position

272 *Glowinski*, above note 37.

273 *Glowinski v Treasury Board (Department of Industry)*, 2007 PSLRB 91.

274 *T&C Directive*, above note 257, para 2.2.2.3. See also *Definition of Promotion Regulations*, SOR/2005-376, s 3.

275 *T&C Directive*, above note 257, para 2.2.2.4.

276 *Sinclair v Canada (Treasury Board)*, [1991 FCJ No 1266.

to which they have been assigned is reclassified, this is not a promotion (as there has been no change in duties).[277] In other words, a change to classification because of a conversion (i.e., a new classification standard, as described in Chapter 12) is not a promotion.[278]

c) Demotion

A person is demoted if they are appointed to a position that has a lower maximum rate of pay than the maximum rate applicable to the employee's former substantive level.[279] When an employee is demoted, they will be paid the rate of pay that is nearest to but not more than the rate of pay the employee was entitled to in their substantive level immediately before the demotion.[280]

d) Deployment

A deployment occurs when the appointment is neither a promotion nor a demotion.[281] When the appointment is a deployment or a transfer, the employee is paid the rate of pay that is nearest but not less than the rate of pay the employee was entitled to in their old position or, if there is no such rate, at the maximum rate of pay for the new position.[282]

e) Acting Pay

When an employee is required to perform the duties of a higher level, they are entitled to acting pay at that level, provided that the acting assignment is of a duration of at least the qualifying period for that position.[283] Acting pay is calculated using the promotion or transfer rules listed above.

---

277 *Bearss v Treasury Board (Department of Foreign Affairs and International Trade)*, 2009 PSLRB 51, aff'd *Canada (Attorney General) v Bearss*, 2010 FC 299.

278 *Professional Association of Foreign Service Officers v Treasury Board*, 2010 PSLRB 53.

279 *T&C Directive*, above note 257, para 2.2.2.7.

280 *Ibid*, para 2.2.2.8.

281 *Ibid*, para 2.2.2.5. See also *PSEA*, s 51(5)(a)—a deployment may not constitute a promotion.

282 *T&C Directive*, above note 257, para 2.2.2.6.

283 *Ibid*, para 2.6 and following. The qualifying period is typically set out in a collective agreement. See Chapter 12 for a discussion of the difference between an acting pay claim and a classification grievance.

f) Appointments During Retroactive Periods of Collective Agreements

One of the features of collective bargaining in the public service is that new collective agreements are almost never negotiated prior to old collective agreements expiring. As a result, those new collective agreements often contain retroactive pay increases for employees. For example, the Public Service Alliance of Canada agreement governing the Program and Administration Services bargaining unit was signed on 23 October 2020 but contained retroactive pay increases dating back to 21 June 2018. Since the rate of pay in a new position is determined based on the wage grid in both the new and the old position, the Federal Court and adjudicators have had to decide whether these retroactive pay changes mean that the employer should recalculate which pay increment level an employee should be placed at if they were promoted, demoted, or transferred during a retroactive period.

In *Canada (Attorney General) v Lajoie*,[284] an employee was promoted from a PM-3 position to an AU-2 position after the expiry of the AU group collective agreement. After the AU collective agreement was finally negotiated, employees received a retroactive wage increase. The employer recalculated the employee's rate of pay, deciding that "the whole matter had to be reopened, first to determine whether the respondent's appointment dated July 29, 1987 was still a promotion, and second to recalculate the increments to which he was entitled at the time of the appointment."[285] The adjudicator and Federal Court of Appeal disagreed with the employer, instead concluding that the appropriate increment level should not be changed because of a retroactive pay increase. The Court of Appeal stated:

> I find it hard to read ss. 65 and 66 of the Regulations [now article 2.2.2 of the *T&C Directive*] as allowing retroactive revision of all the consequences of an appointment every time a collective agreement gives employees retroactive salary increases. In my opinion, s. 65 should be read as enabling both employer and employees to know at once whether a new appointment is a promotion (s. 65(1)), a demotion (s. 65(2)) or simply a transfer (s. 65(3)). It seems to me that any other conclusion would lead to utter confusion: an employer who believed he had disciplined an employee for incompetence by demoting him would realize two years later that as the result of retroactive

284 *Canada (Attorney General) v Lajoie*, [1992] FCJ No 1019 (CA).

285 *Ibid* at 6.

> pay he had actually given the employee a transfer or even a promotion; on the other hand, an employee who enthusiastically accepted what seemed to him to be a promotion would two years later, to his great disappointment, find it was actually a demotion.[286]

Treasury Board staffing experts refer to this approach as the "straight down" approach.

The Federal Court of Appeal decision did not deal with a situation where the employee's *old* position underwent a retroactive pay increase. In such a situation, the appropriate increment level in the new position will be recalculated. In *Buchmann v Treasury Board (Canada Customs and Revenue Agency)*,[287] the employee was promoted from a PM-2 position to an AU-1 position after the PM bargaining unit's collective agreement had expired. When the PM collective agreement was finally negotiated, it included retroactive pay increases. Mr. Buchmann argued that his increment level in his AU-1 position should be recalculated as a result. The adjudicator agreed and ordered Mr. Buchmann's pay in his new position to be recalculated to reflect the retroactive increase in pay in his old position.

Similarly, adjudicators have ordered recalculation of pay when an employee is in an acting position and their substantive position receives a retroactive pay increase.[288]

When there has been a retroactive adjustment of pay in both the old and new positions, an adjudicator has ordered that an employee's pay increment be recalculated only using the retroactive adjustment to their old position (i.e., only using the retroactive adjustment that helps the employee). In *Grant v Treasury Board (Agriculture and Agri-Food Canada)*,[289] an employee was promoted from a CR-04 position to an FI-01 position during the retroactive period of the FI collective agreement (which received a retroactive pay increase after she was appointed). After she was promoted, her previous CR-04 position was reclassified to the CR-05 level retroactive to a date prior to her promotion. The employer refused to adjust her pay increment level for any of these events. The

286 *Ibid* at 6.

287 *Buchmann v Treasury Board (Canada Customs and Revenue Agency)*, [2002] CPSSRB No 8.

288 *Tyrrell v Treasury Board*, [2003] CPSSRB No 11; *Copeland v Treasury Board (Solicitor General Canada—Correctional Service)*, [2003] CPSSRB No 19.

289 *Grant v Treasury Board (Agriculture and Agri-Food Canada)*, [2004] CPSSRB No 97.

adjudicator disagreed and adjusted her pay increment level in her new FI-01 position to take into account the retroactive reclassification of her old position, but not taking into account the retroactive increase in pay to the FI-01 (i.e., only taking into account the retroactive adjustment that increased her increment level and not the subsequent adjustment that could have decreased her increment level).

3) Allowances and Increments

Many positions in the federal public service receive allowances in addition to their base pay, either to encourage candidates with higher levels of education (by an educational allowance)[290] or to encourage employees to remain in the public service in positions that are in demand in the private sector (typically referred to as a "terminable allowance"). When an employee is the incumbent of a position classified in those bargaining units, they are entitled to the allowance, even where an employee's position is retroactively reclassified into that bargaining unit.[291]

On occasion, issues have arisen about how to treat those amounts when calculating the correct increment level for an employee upon an appointment. In *Billett v Treasury Board (Department of Veterans Affairs)*,[292] an employee was promoted from a WP-03 position to an NU-CHN-3 position. Nurses in the NU-CHN-3 position received an education allowance. The issue in that case was whether the educational allowance should be incorporated into the pay rates before the employer calculated the incremental step, or should the incremental step be calculated first and then the education allowance added after? If the education allowance was added first, that would result in an employee being placed at a lower increment level than if the allowance was added after the appropriate level had been calculated. The adjudicator accepted the grievor's position and decided that the education allowance should be added only after the increment level had been determined.

---

290 Such as for nurses in the collective agreement with the Professional Institute of the Public Service of Canada (Appendix B).

291 *Parker v Treasury Board (National Archives of Canada)*, [2004] CPSSRB No 6, where some employees were retroactively reclassified into a CS-1 position and the adjudicator ordered that they receive a terminable allowance dating back to the effective date of their reclassification (1 October 1998).

292 *Billett v Treasury Board (Department of Veterans Affairs)*, [2006] CPSLRB No 27.

Similar reasoning prevailed in *Larose v Treasury Board (Department of Public Works and Government Services)*,[293] this time to the detriment of the grievor. In that case, the grievor used to work for the Library of Parliament and took a new job with the Department of Public Works and Government Services. While employed at the Library of Parliament, the grievor received a terminable allowance (which was designed to make up the difference between the rate of pay at the Library of Parliament and the rate of pay of the equivalent position in the Treasury Board). When the grievor took a new job with the Department of Public Works and Government Services, the employer did not include the Library of Parliament's terminable allowance when calculating the grievor's new rate of pay with the employer (which decreased her rate of pay). The adjudicator agreed with the employer that the terminable allowance was distinct from the grievor's salary and therefore could not be used to calculate the appropriate increment step on the pay scale.

Therefore, both of these decisions stand for the proposition that allowances are not included when calculating the rate of pay according to the *T&C Directive*.

F. NATIONAL JOINT COUNCIL DIRECTIVES

The National Joint Council is a council composed of the bargaining agents representing employees in the federal public service on the one hand and the Treasury Board and four other separate employers (Canadian Food Inspection Agency, Communications Security Establishment Canada, the National Research Council, and the Office of the Auditor General of Canada) on the other. One of the roles of the National Joint Council is to allow bargaining agents and employers to "co-develop" directives and policies governing employees in the federal public service. Once a National Joint Council Directive has been co-developed, it often becomes part of collective agreements between the bargaining agents and employers.

As discussed in Chapter 2 concerning the historical development of labour and employment law in the federal public service, the National Joint Council was established by an order in council in 1944. Its purpose was to promote the efficiency of the public service and the well-being of

---

293 *Larose v Treasury Board (Department of Public Works and Government Services)*, 2006 PSLRB 114.

public servants by providing for regular consultation between the government and employee organizations. Before the advent of collective bargaining, the National Joint Council was the major vehicle for discussions between the employer and staff associations. With the introduction of collective bargaining in 1967, the scope of the National Joint Council's activities was narrowed. However, the National Joint Council remained in existence and has developed into a forum for the co-development of service-wide issues. The National Joint Council Directives are therefore designed to address service-wide issues by way of co-development instead of the more adversarial approach in collective bargaining.[294]

Disagreements about National Joint Council Directives may be grieved and then, if incorporated into the collective agreement, referred to adjudication. The National Joint Council has a separate grievance procedure for its directives, with three levels: the employer's representative, a departmental liaison officer, and the Executive Committee of the National Joint Council (composed of three employer–side members and three bargaining agent–side members).[295] Grievances are decided on the basis of the intent of the directive or policy concerned and are not decided by strict consideration of the wording of the directive or policy.[296] The grievance would then proceed to the Board for a final resolution by adjudication, if necessary. The Board's decisions are not clear about whether it interprets the National Joint Council Directives using the normal approach to collective agreement interpretation or, alternatively, on the basis of the intent of the directive as prescribed in article 15.1.2 of the National Joint Council bylaws. In one case, the Board stated clearly that it was required "as a quasi-judicial decision maker to follow generally accepted rules of the legal interpretation of collective agreements" and therefore could not apply the "intent of the parties" approach;[297] however, in a later case, the Board stated that it "must be attentive to the unique process of co-development used to develop the *Directive*, and the unique grievance process followed prior to the referral

294 Second Report of the Advisory Committee on Labour-Management Relations in the Federal Public Service, *Working Together in the Public Interest* (Ottawa: Treasury Board, 2001).

295 National Joint Council By-Laws (1 October 2018), art 15.1.5, online: www.njc-cnm.gc.ca/s18/s97/en.

296 *Ibid*, art 15.1.2.

297 *Daigneault v Treasury Board (Correctional Service of Canada)*, 2017 PSLREB 38 at para 28.

to adjudication"[298]—implying, at least, that the "intent of the parties" approach should be followed (although the Board went on to assess the case in light of the plain wording of the directive at issue in that case).

While a detailed description or discussion of the National Joint Council Directives is beyond the scope of this book,[299] we will discuss one of the most important (or most frequently litigated) directives—the *Work Force Adjustment Directive*.

1) *Work Force Adjustment Directive*

The *Work Force Adjustment Directive* is the directive protecting job security and providing compensation for employees impacted by layoffs in the federal public service. While the two largest employee organizations (the Public Service Alliance of Canada and the Professional Institute of the Public Service of Canada) have opted out of the directive, they have both incorporated similar provisions into their collective agreements with the Treasury Board. Therefore, all employees of the Treasury Board are covered by the *Work Force Adjustment Directive*, or a similar set of rules, in one way or another.

The *Work Force Adjustment Directive* came into force in November 1991, replacing an earlier Work Force Adjustment Policy. The original form of the *Work Force Adjustment Directive* promised "essentially lifetime job security for federal public servants."[300] In the mid-1990s, the *Work Force Adjustment Directive* was suspended in many departments (the departments most affected by the downsizing of the federal public service in the 1990s), and its protection in the remaining departments was also decreased. After the large-scale downsizing was completed, the *Work Force Adjustment Directive* has not been restored to a guarantee of lifetime job security, but some additional protections have been negotiated. What follows is a description of the main features of the *Work Force Adjustment Directive* as of the date of publication.

The *Work Force Adjustment Directive* is triggered by a "work force adjustment," defined as follows:

---

298 *Nowlan v Treasury Board (Department of Foreign Affairs, Trade and Development)*, 2021 FPSLREB 34 at para 43.

299 The *Foreign Service Directive*, for example, is over 300 pages long.

300 Gene Swimmer & Sandra Bach, "Restructuring Federal Public-Sector Human Resources" in Gene Swimmer, ed, *Public Sector Labour Relations in an Era of Restraint and Restructuring* (Toronto: Oxford University Press, 2001) at 187.

> **Work force adjustment** is a situation that occurs when a deputy head decides that the services of one or more indeterminate employees will no longer be required beyond a specified date because of a lack of work, the discontinuance of a function, a relocation in which the employee does not wish to relocate or an alternative delivery initiative.[301]

There have been disputes concerning whether a particular staffing decision has constituted a workforce adjustment under the directive. In *Public Service Alliance of Canada v Canada Customs and Revenue Agency*,[302] the agency decided to automate the processing of certain tax forms and, as a result, eliminate some jobs. It argued that this was a "work force change" as opposed to a "work force adjustment." The Board refused to accept the employer's own characterization of the technological change and concluded that the elimination of those jobs was a "work force adjustment."[303]

In *Moore v Treasury Board (Canadian Grain Commission)*,[304] on the other hand, an adjudicator concluded that a cessation of employment was not a workforce adjustment because the cessation was not certain, and it was not permanent, on the date alleged. Ms. Moore was an indeterminate seasonal employee working for the Canadian Grain Commission in Thunder Bay. Seasonal workers typically worked from April until January each year. As a result of a decrease in grain shipments in 2002, Ms. Moore was not recalled to her job that year. Ms. Moore argued that a workforce adjustment had occurred on 1 April 2002 and that the employer did not comply with its obligations triggered by a workforce adjustment. The Board disagreed, stating:

---

301 *Work Force Adjustment Directive*, "Definitions." This definition is common across collective agreements: see, for example, Public Service Alliance of Canada collective agreement for "PA" group, Appendix D, "Definitions." See online: www.njc-cnm.gc.ca/directive/d12/en.

302 *Public Service Alliance of Canada v Canada Customs and Revenue Agency*, [2002] CPSSRB No 14. The Canada Customs and Revenue Agency was a separate employer at the time and therefore was not subject to the *Work Force Adjustment Directive*. However, the union had negotiated a Work Force Adjustment Policy into its collective agreement with the agency, and that policy was triggered by a "work force adjustment" with the same definition as in the directive.

303 *Ibid* at para 68. In actual fact, the agency complied with most of the requirements of its collective agreement, and the affected employees were assured of continued employment.

304 *Moore v Treasury Board (Canadian Grain Commission)*, [2006] CPSLRB No 33.

> It seems to me that this involves a presumption that, in a [Work Force Adjustment (WFA)] situation, the employee's existing position is in fact disappearing, is likely to disappear or is at some significant risk of disappearing. The determination made by the employer to trigger a WFA situation is, after all, one which can eventually result in an action to sever the employment relationship permanently. Ms. Moore has not shown that the employer was contemplating scenarios on April 1, 2002 that would permanently eliminate Ms. Moore's position or permanently lay Ms. Moore off.[305]

The addition of duties to a position does not trigger a workforce adjustment, even if an employee is laid off as a result of failing to become trained for those positions.[306] It is, however, triggered when the employer contracts out work: the fact that the work is being done by outside employees does not mean that there is no "lack of work" or the "discontinuance of a function."[307]

A workforce adjustment occurs once the deputy head knows that a substantial number of employees would no longer be required, even if they have not yet identified the specific employees whose jobs will be affected.[308]

A block transfer under section 132 of the *PSEA*—that is, the transfer of a large number of employees between departments or between a separate agency and the core public administration—does not constitute a workforce adjustment. Thus, for example, transferring computer workers from the Canada Revenue Agency to Shared Services Canada was not a workforce adjustment,[309] and a transfer of various inspectors from the Canada Food Inspection Agency to the Canada Border Services Agency was likewise not a workforce adjustment (or the equivalent term in the collective agreement applying to that unit).[310]

---

305 *Ibid* at para 107.

306 *Jamieson v Treasury Board (National Defence)*, [2002] CPSSRB No 79, aff'd [2005] FCJ No 531.

307 *Canada (Attorney General) v Public Service Alliance of Canada*, [1991] 1 FC 428 (CA), aff'd [1993] 1 SCR 941.

308 *Public Service Alliance of Canada v Treasury Board (Department of Employment and Social Development)*, 2014 PSLRB 27.

309 *Public Service Alliance of Canada v Canada Revenue Agency*, 2013 PSLRB 2.

310 *Public Service Alliance of Canada v Canadian Food Inspection Agency*, 2004 PSSRB 155, aff'd *Public Service Alliance of Canada v Canada (Canadian Food Inspection Agency)*, 2005 FCA 366.

A workforce adjustment triggers the obligations in the directive. The first obligation is to advise and consult with the affected bargaining agents "as completely as possible" and to make available to the bargaining agent the name and work location of the affected employees.[311]

The predominant obligation of the *Work Force Adjustment Directive*, however, is the promise of a "reasonable job offer." A "reasonable job offer" is defined as follows:

> Reasonable job offer is an offer of indeterminate employment within the core public administration, normally at an equivalent level. Surplus employees must be both trainable and mobile. Where practicable, a reasonable job offer shall be within the employee's headquarters as defined in the Travel Directive. In alternative delivery situations, a reasonable offer is one that meets the criteria set out in Type 1 and Type 2 of Part VII of this Directive. A reasonable job offer is also an offer from a *FAA* Schedule V employer, providing that:
>
> a. The appointment is at a rate of pay and an attainable salary maximum not less than the employee's current salary and attainable maximum that would be in effect on the date of offer;
> b. It is a seamless transfer of all employee benefits including recognition of years of service for the definition of continuous employment and accrual of benefits, including the transfer of sick leave credits, severance pay and accumulated vacation leave credits.[312]

Deputy heads are expected to provide a guarantee of a reasonable job offer for employees affected by a workforce adjustment. If a deputy head is not going to provide such a guarantee, they must provide reasons if requested.[313] Prior to providing a reasonable job offer, the employer must engage in effective human resource planning to minimize the impact of the workforce adjustment. This is an enforceable obligation against the employer, as stated by an adjudicator as follows:

> The employer must find such employment opportunities by carrying out effective human resource planning, and, in so doing, reduce as much as possible the impact of the adjustment upon those affected employees, and all the while by ensuring that the affected employees are treated equitably and that they be given every opportunity to

---

311 *Work Force Adjustment Directive*, art 1.1.12.

312 *Ibid*, "Definitions."

313 *Ibid*, art 6.1.1.

> continue their career in the public service. To find alternative employment without the qualifiers or conditions precedent stated here would achieve nothing, and that is why those conditions precedent are so important and they make sense in labour relations matters.[314]

Nevertheless, the burden of proof rests with the grievor to show that the employer did not meet its obligation to provide a reasonable job offer.[315]

The definition of a reasonable job offer contains four core elements: it must be an offer of indeterminate employment; the offer is normally at an equivalent level but may include lower levels; the surplus employee must be mobile and trainable; and, to the extent possible, the employment is found within the employee's headquarters area (currently within 40 kilometres of their current workplace).[316]

The second element above does not permit the employer to only consider positions at an equivalent level. The employer must consider positions at lower levels—and not just one or two levels lower than the employee's current level.[317] It is, however, a last resort to consider lower-level positions, and an employer must exhaust all other options first before considering a reasonable job offer at a lower level.[318] The term "equivalent" is not defined in the *Work Force Adjustment Directive*, but the term is defined in the Public Service Alliance of Canada collective agreements for the purposes of alternation as "when the maximum rate of pay for the higher-paid position is no more than six-per-cent (6%) higher than the maximum rate of pay for the lower-paid position"—and an adjudicator concluded that this definition of "equivalent" should also apply to the assessment of a reasonable job offer (as well as alternation). Therefore, a reasonable job offer could constitute a promotion or demotion, within limits.[319]

---

314 *Bonia v Treasury Board (Royal Canadian Mounted Police)*, [2002] CPSSRB No 71 at para 84.

315 *Thomas v Treasury Board (Department of Human Resources and Skills Development)*, 2012 PSLRB 49 at para 58.

316 *Lainey v Treasury Board (Correctional Service of Canada)*, 2019 FPSLREB 63 at para 162 [*Lainey*].

317 *Nesic v Treasury Board (Health Canada)*, 2016 PSLREB 117; *Public Service Alliance of Canada v Treasury Board (Correctional Service of Canada)*, 2015 PSLREB 10 at para 54.

318 *Ibid* at para 59; *Choinière v Treasury Board (Department of Fisheries and Oceans)*, 2018 FPSLREB 36 at para 161.

319 *Kreway v Canada (Customs and Revenue Agency)*, 2004 PSSRB 172 at para 67.

The third element requires that an employee be mobile and trainable. A job offer does not become unreasonable because the employee thinks they do not have the necessary skills to perform the duties of the position.[320] A reasonable job offer could be a job offer conditional on successfully completing retraining for the position,[321] but an employer is not required to make a job offer that is conditional on retraining and can instead insist that the employee have the relevant qualifications already.[322]

The fourth element above does not require the employer to make a reasonable job offer within any particular geographic limit. An employer must endeavour to respect an employee's location preferences, but "nothing precludes them from offering relocated positions to employees in receipt of GRJOs [guaranteed reasonable job offers] from their deputy heads, after spending as much time as operations permit looking for a GRJO in their preferred locations."[323] Therefore, it is difficult to argue that a job is not a reasonable job offer on geographic grounds. An employee cannot restrict their mobility for deployment purposes to the point that it becomes impossible to guarantee a reasonable job offer.[324]

In conclusion, a reasonable job offer must be reasonable, not perfect. As the Federal Court has stated:

> There is nothing in the definition that implies that a job offer is not reasonable because the employee does not want it. Nothing in the definition implies that the employer is bound to work out a working relationship "fully acceptable to both parties."[325]

Employees who do not receive a reasonable job offer may still try to use a process called "alternation." Essentially, if an affected employee can convince another employee to resign and they are qualified to

320 *Lainey*, above note 316 at para 171.

321 *Carby-Samuels and Treasury Board (Energy, Mines and Resources Canada)*, [1993] CPSSRB No 37, application for judicial review dismissed [1994] FCJ No 1284.

322 *Boucher v Treasury Board (Canada Border Services Agency)*, 2021 FPSLREB 69 at para 163 [*Boucher*].

323 *Obreja v Treasury Board (Department of the Environment)*, 2021 FPSLREB 131 at para 153.

324 *Sampson and Treasury Board (Indian and Northern Affairs Canada)*, [1996] CPSSRB No 34.

325 *Attorney General of Canada v Edwards* (18 January 1999), T-105-98 (unreported), aff'd [2000] FCJ No 645 (CA).

occupy that employee's position,[326] then they may exchange jobs.[327] The "alternate" employee must irrevocably resign from the public service effective within five days of the alternation.[328] Even though this "alternation" procedure has elements similar to an appointment process, the responsibility to implement the alternation process rests with the employer—that is, the Treasury Board. This means that the Treasury Board must ensure that departments facilitate opting employees to switch positions with alternates and respond to alternation requests within the 120-day window for employees to select their option when they do not receive a reasonable job offer.[329]

Employees who do not receive a reasonable job offer have three options. First, they may go on surplus status for twelve months in an effort to find a reasonable job. If the employee chooses to resign during the twelve-month period, they may receive a lump sum payment of up to six months' pay, compensating them for the duration of their surplus period remaining.[330] Second, they may be paid a transition support measure: a cash payment based on the employee's years of service (ranging from four to fifty-two weeks).[331] Third, the employee may receive a transition support measure plus a payment of up to $17,000 for education purposes. Employees can exercise this option in one of two ways: resign immediately or go on a two-year unpaid leave of absence (thus preserving their health and pension benefits).[332]

The *Work Force Adjustment Directive* is a residual directive—meaning that it applies where no other directive governs that employee's entitlements in the event of a workforce adjustment. These other replacement directives must clearly and transparently provide for alternative entitlements. In *Appleby-Ostroff v Canada (Attorney General)*, the employer attempted to rely on an older executive employment transition policy that expired roughly a year before the employee's position was abolished. The employer alleged that the Treasury Board

326 This includes holding any required security clearances and other qualifications for the position: *Boucher*, above note 322 at paras 156–58 and 164.

327 *Work Force Adjustment Directive*, art 6.3.

328 *Appointment or Deployment of Alternates Regulations*, SOR/2012-83, s 3.

329 *Public Service Alliance of Canada and Professional Institute of the Public Service of Canada v Treasury Board of Canada*, 2013 PSLRB 37 at paras 21, 24–25, and 30; aff'd *Canada (Attorney General) v PSAC*, 2014 FC 688.

330 *Work Force Adjustment Directive*, art 6.4.1(a).

331 *Ibid*, art 6.4.1(b).

332 *Ibid*, art 6.4.1(c).

decided to extend that policy to certain employees, but the Treasury Board's decision to do so was secret and could not be revealed because of Cabinet confidence. The Federal Court of Appeal concluded that the employer could not "claim 'secret' undisclosed exceptions to publicly available policies and rules affecting individual rights in the absence of clear statutory authority to do so" and therefore the *Work Force Adjustment Directive* applied to that employee.[333]

Therefore, executives, including certain other managers, are excluded from the *Work Force Adjustment Directive* because their entitlements in the event of a workforce adjustment are set out in the *Directive on Terms and Conditions of Employment for Executives* (formerly called the *Directive on Career Transition for Executives*).[334] Executives are not entitled to a reasonable job offer. Instead, they are given two options: to leave the core public administration after reaching a "career transition agreement" (typically a lump sum payment of between twenty-six and thirty-two weeks' salary plus other benefits—although payments of up to or, rarely, in excess of fifty-two weeks are permitted), or go on surplus status for a period of time while they look for an alternative position within the public service (and then be laid off at the end of that surplus period if they are unsuccessful). The old *Directive on Career Transition for Executives* required the career transition agreement to be approved by the deputy head so that it was not an enforceable agreement until the deputy head approved it;[335] the new *Directive on Terms and Conditions of Employment* has changed that to the head of human resources so that career transition agreements are now enforceable without being signed or approved by the deputy head.

G. BILINGUALISM

1) Constitutional and Legislative Foundations of Bilingualism in the Federal Public Service

One of the defining features of the federal public service is that it is a bilingual public service. Bilingualism has both constitutional and

333 *Appleby-Ostroff*, above note 14 at para 38.

334 Treasury Board of Canada Secretariat, *Directive on Terms and Conditions of Employment for Executives*, online: www.tbs-sct.canada.ca/pol/doc-eng.aspx?id=32625&section=html.

335 *McEwan*, above note 181 at para 134.

legislative foundations. The constitutional foundations can be found explicitly in the *Charter*. Section 16(1) of the *Charter* states: "English and French are the official languages of Canada and have equality of status and equal rights and privileges as to their use in all institutions of the Parliament and government of Canada." Section 20 of the *Charter* then specifies the right of Canadians to receive service from the federal government in the language of their choice:

> 20(1) Any member of the public in Canada has the right to communicate with, and to receive available services from, any head or central office of an institution of the Parliament or government of Canada in English or French, and has the same right with respect to any other office of any such institution where
> a) there is a significant demand for communications with and services from that office in such language; or
> b) due to the nature of the office, it is reasonable that communications with and services from that office be available in both English and French.

Aside from these specific written guarantees to preserve bilingualism in Canada, Canada's constitutional structure was designed to protect linguistic minority rights. The protection of minority rights (including linguistic minorities) is an unwritten principle of the Canadian Constitution, in part because "the protection of minority rights was clearly an essential consideration in the design of our constitutional structure even at the time of Confederation."[336] The unwritten constitutional principle of federalism also supports linguistic minorities: "the principle of federalism facilitates the pursuit of collective goals by cultural and linguistic minorities which form the majority within a particular province."[337] Therefore, both Canada's written and unwritten Constitution require the protection of linguistic minorities throughout Canada by providing Canadians with access to federal government services in both English and French.

Legislatively, bilingualism in Canada is guaranteed by the *Official Languages Act*.[338] The *Official Languages Act* was first enacted in 1969, and it "serves as a special tool for the recognition, affirmation and

---

336 *Reference re Secession of Quebec*, [1998] 2 SCR 217 at para 81.
337 *Ibid* at para 59.
338 *Official Languages Act*, RSC 1985, c 31 (4th Supp).

extension of the linguistic rights recognized by the *Canadian Charter of Rights and Freedoms*."[339] The preamble to the *Official Languages Act* specifically refers to bilingualism in the federal public service as follows:

> AND WHEREAS officers and employees of institutions of the Parliament or government of Canada should have equal opportunities to use the official language of their choice while working together in pursuing the goals of those institutions;
>
> AND WHEREAS English-speaking Canadians and French-speaking Canadians should, without regard to their ethnic origin or first language learned, have equal opportunities to obtain employment in the institutions of the Parliament or government of Canada;
>
> AND WHEREAS the Government of Canada is committed to achieving, with due regard to the principle of selection of personnel according to merit, full participation of English-speaking Canadians and French-speaking Canadians in its institutions;

The *Official Languages Act* applies to Crown corporations as well as the federal public service; however, for the purposes of this book, it will be sufficient to describe its impact on the federal public service.

Part IV of the *Official Languages Act* affirms the right of the public to communicate with federal institutions (including the federal public service) in the official language of their choice, subject to certain geographic constraints. This right extends to government services in all offices in the National Capital Region[340] and to other offices where there is a significant demand for service in that official language.[341] Institutions that provide services to the travelling public must be able to provide those services in either official language,[342] and offices providing some other services must be able to provide services in both languages.[343]

Since the federal government is required to provide services in both English and French, this requires it to employ people who can provide these services. Therefore, without anything else, the requirement to serve the public in English and French would require a bilingual

339 *Canada (Commissioner of Official Languages) v Air Canada*, [1999] FCJ No 738 (CA) at para 16.

340 *Official Languages Act*, s 22(a).

341 *Ibid*, s 22(b). Those areas are determined according to the *Official Languages (Communications with and Services to the Public) Regulations*, SOR/92-48, s 5.

342 *Official Languages Act*, s 23.

343 *Ibid*, s 24 (e.g., health and safety).

workforce. However, the *Official Languages Act* goes further and also creates language of work rights within federal institutions. Part V of the *Official Languages Act* provides that "officers and employees of all federal institutions have the right to use either official language" in accordance with that part.[344] That right extends to all federal institutions located in the National Capital Region[345] and to the regions of Canada set out in Annex B of the part of the Treasury Board and PSC Circular No 1977-46 of 30 September 1977, entitled "Official Languages in the Public Service of Canada: A Statement of Policies."[346] In those regions, the federal government must ensure that it is "conducive to the effective use of both official languages and accommodate[s] the use of either official language by its officers and employees."[347] In particular, this means that the federal public service must offer its employees any service normally provided to employees in both official languages;[348] offer employees work instruments[349] and automated data systems[350] in both official languages; ensure that managers responsible for the direction of the particular federal institution are able to communicate in both official languages;[351] and, where necessary, ensure that supervisors are able to communicate in both official languages.[352]

These rights apply whenever an employee works in a designated area, regardless of whether they are dealing with an office in a non-designated area. For example, in *Lavigne v Canada (Human Resources Development)*,[353] an employee in Montreal had frequent dealings with the Quebec Regional Office. The commissioner of official languages concluded that the employee's rights to use the English language were violated when the Quebec Regional Office did not accommodate him in the

---

344 *Ibid*, s 34.

345 *Ibid*, s 35(1)(a). The National Capital Region is described in Schedule 2 to the *National Capital Act*, RSC 1985, c N-4.

346 *Official Languages Act*, ss 35(1)(a) and 35(2)—essentially, parts of Northern and Eastern Ontario, the Montreal region, parts of the Eastern Townships, the Gaspé and West Quebec, and New Brunswick.

347 *Ibid*, s 35(1)(a).

348 *Ibid*, s 36(1)(a)(i).

349 *Ibid*, s 36(1)(a)(ii).

350 *Ibid*, s 36(1)(b).

351 *Ibid*, s 36(1)(c)(ii).

352 *Ibid*, s 36(1)(c)(i).

353 *Lavigne v Canada (Human Resources Development)*, [1997] 1 FC 305.

use of the English language, despite the fact that the Quebec Regional Office was not a designated area.

The obligation to provide a "service" to employees in both official languages does not extend to interactions between public servants in the course of their shared duties. Section 36(1)(a)(i) requires that a federal institution make available to employees "services that are provided to them as individuals and services that are centrally provided by the institution to support them in the performance of their duties." These services that are centrally provided are those that

> A. [S]erve a common function and are provided in an organized manner within an administrative body by the federal institution in a prescribed bilingual region;
> B. Are made available to the majority of employees by the federal institution;
> C. Are provided by employees to provide auxiliary support to other employees of the institution in the performance of their duties;
> D. Do not include all forms of assistance required to enable employees to perform the duties associated with their positions—employees must exercise their right to use the official language of their choice in a reasonable manner; and
> E. Exclude occasional interactions or exchanges of information among employees on the same work team. Rather, those interactions are examples of interregional communications as provided for in the aforementioned language of work policy.[354]

Thus, for example, a specialist who contributes to a file is not providing a "service" to a generalist who is applying that specialized advice to the outcome of that file.[355]

Additionally, in the prescribed regions, each federal institution must take measures "as can reasonably be taken to establish and maintain work environments that are conducive to the effective use of both official languages and accommodate the use of either official language by its officers and employees."[356] Whether the measures taken by a federal institution to satisfy this requirement are reasonable depends on three

354 *Canada (Commissioner of Official Languages) v Office of the Superintendent of Financial Institutions*, 2021 FCA 159 at para 87 [*Canada (Commissioner of Official Languages)*].

355 *Ibid* at para 89.

356 *Official Languages Act*, s 36(2).

non-exhaustive factors: the significant or serious operational difficulties (above the level of inconvenience or administrative burden) that the measures may create, a demonstrable conflict with the duty to provide services to the public in their official language, and any conflict with the institution's mandate.[357] These factors do not include the bilingual nature of the position. The Federal Court has stated that "a federal institution cannot circumvent its language of work duties under Part V of the [*Official Languages Act*] simply by resorting to bilingual employees."[358] The Federal Court of Appeal was even more blunt that "the burden of translation should never rest entirely on bilingual employees":

> Therefore, an example of possible measures for establishing and maintaining a work environment that is conducive to the effective use of both official languages would be to provide a robust translation service. By applying the approach in *Tailleur* to the facts of this case, while incorporating the concept of substantive equality, it would follow that a unilingual English employee would be entitled to an effective translation service that meets the needs of the public if the employee's duties involved, for example, the preparation of reports in English using documents written in French or information that is partially in French. Consequently, in my view, regardless of the ability to communicate in both official languages, employees who hold a bilingual position in a prescribed bilingual region whose work involves preparing reports for the public in French, using documents written in English or information that is partially in English, would be entitled to receive an effective translation service from their employer. The institution is therefore responsible for providing an effective translation service to support and equip bilingual employees in the performance of their duties.[359]

Everywhere else in Canada, the federal public service must ensure that "the treatment of both official languages in the work environments of the institution in parts or regions of Canada where one official language predominates is reasonably comparable to the treatment of both

---

357 *Tailleur v Canada (Attorney General)*, 2015 FCA 1230 at para 75 [*Tailleur*]. This test was affirmed by the Federal Court of Appeal in *Canada (Commissioner of Official Languages)*, above note 354.

358 *Tailleur*, above note 357 at para 82.

359 *Canada (Commissioner of Official Languages)*, above note 354 at paras 108–9.

official languages in the work environments of the institution in parts or regions of Canada where the other official language predominates."[360]

2) Specific Measures to Ensure Bilingualism

To meet the requirements of the *Official Languages Act*, the federal public service needs to have a sufficient number of employees capable of working in both official languages. The most efficient way to meet this objective is to hire (or promote) employees capable of working in both official languages—hence the requirement that candidates for some positions be bilingual.

The *PSEA* grants the employer (the Treasury Board) the power to establish qualification standards in relation to language that the employer considers necessary or desirable when considering the nature of the work and the present and future needs of the public service.[361] Other employers have similar powers.

The Treasury Board has enacted directives on the linguistic requirements of positions.[362] The institution must first determine its obligations under the *Official Languages Act* (its obligations to both the public and employees). After determining those obligations, institutions must "objectively" determine whether a position requires the use of one or both official languages and, if so, "objectively" establish the required level of proficiency in the second official language. There are four categories of linguistic requirements:

- bilingual, when the functions must be carried out in English and in French
- English essential, when the functions must be carried out in English
- French essential, when the functions must be carried out in French
- either/or, when the functions may be carried out in English or in French, in accordance with the employee's choice

The institution must also determine the level of proficiency required in each official language. Language proficiency is a measure of skill

---

360 *Official Languages Act*, s 35(1)(b).

361 *PSEA*, s 31(1).

362 In particular, Treasury Board of Canada Secretariat, *Directive on Official Languages for People Management* (15 October 2012), online: www.tbs-sct.canada.ca/pol/doc-eng.aspx?id=26168.

in three areas: reading, writing, and oral interaction. There are three levels of proficiency: A (beginner), B (intermediate), and C (advanced). There are two other levels of proficiency: P (a special level of proficiency required for translators) and E (an advanced level of proficiency that exempts an employee from having to demonstrate their proficiency in that language skill ever again). While the level of proficiency for most positions is set on a case-by-case basis, some executive positions must have a superior level of second-language proficiency (i.e., "CBC," meaning level C in reading and oral interaction and level B in writing).

The linguistic profile of a position may change from time to time. Incumbents used to have the right to remain in their position whether or not they could meet the new bilingualism requirement.[363] However, in 2005, the *Public Service Official Languages Exclusion Approval Order*[364] was amended to remove this right. Instead, there are only three exclusions from the requirement that certain positions be bilingual: medical grounds (if the employee has a disability making them unable to be trained in the other official language); if the employee is within two years of being able to take an immediate annuity under the *Public Service Superannuation Act* and also agrees to retire no later than the end of that two-year period; and if the employee has entered into an agreement to become bilingual to be appointed on a non-imperative basis to a bilingual position.

Positions may be either bilingual imperative (i.e., only applicants who meet the required language proficiency at the time of appointment may be appointed) or bilingual non-imperative. Imperative staffing is the standard position. There are also three circumstances when imperative staffing is absolutely required: when a bilingual position is for a specified period (term); when a bilingual position requires technical or specialized language skills; and when the position or function is indispensable for providing services to the public or employees in both

363 *R v Kelso*, [1981] 1 SCR 199 [*Kelso*]. See, however, *Schrieber v Canada*, [1999] FCJ No 1576, aff'd [2000] FCJ No 2053 (CA), where the Federal Court questioned whether the rule in *Kelso* remained valid in light of the addition of linguistic rights to the *Charter* and various changes to the *Official Languages Act*. The Court in that case concluded that the exclusion order that created the exception in *Kelso* violated the *Charter* and the *Official Languages Act* in the circumstances of that case only.

364 *Public Service Official Languages Exclusion Approval Order*, SI/2005-118, 14 December 2005.

official languages. In other circumstances, managers may use non-imperative staffing to fill positions that are not covered by the obligation to use imperative staffing. Managers need to justify non-imperative staffing and show that the bilingual requirements of the position will be carried out while the incumbent is taking language training. The institution will then provide language training to allow the incumbent to meet the language requirements of the position.[365] The incumbent must agree to acquire the necessary language skills within a certain period of time and also to be deployed to another position if they do not acquire the necessary language skills.[366]

Acting appointments in the core public administration need not always meet the linguistic requirements of the position. The *Public Service Employment Regulations* list two exceptions to the general rule that a candidate for an acting appointment needs to meet the language requirements of a position: if the acting appointment is between four and twelve months and cannot be filled with an acting appointment of a person who meets the language proficiency qualification or if the acting appointment is between four and eighteen months to fill a bilingual position, while the incumbent is on language training, that cannot be filled with an acting appointment of a person who meets the language proficiency qualification.[367]

When candidates apply for a position, they are entitled to be interviewed in their choice of English or French (except, obviously, interviews conducted for the purpose of language testing).[368] The old *Public Service Employment Regulations* used to require a certain level of language proficiency on the part of selection board members; if the selection board members did not have sufficient language proficiency, then the competition violated the merit principle.[369] To attempt to get around that requirement, the employer began to create selection boards with "passive"

365 There is a maximum of two years to complete the training that can be extended in exceptional circumstances: *Public Service Official Languages Appointment Regulations*, ss 4 and 7.

366 Treasury Board of Canada Secretariat, *Directive on the Staffing of Bilingual Positions* (25 April 2006), online: www.tbs-sct.canada.ca/pol/doc-eng.aspx?id=12525.

367 *Public Service Employment Regulations*, SOR/2005-334, ss 15–16 [*PSER*].

368 *PSEA*, s 37.

369 *McKinnon v Canada (Public Service Commission Appeal Board)*, [1990] FCJ No 455. In that case, the selection board member had only level "A," which the Court concluded was insufficient. The Court refused to decide whether level "B" would be sufficient, but that was the conclusion of the appeal board in that case.

members who did not have the required level of language proficiency or to change the membership of the selection board to rotate in people who could understand English or French as the need arose. The Federal Court criticized both of these practices in *Ali v Canada (Attorney General)*,[370] concluding that changing the composition of the selection board was problematic unless significant steps were taken to eliminate any subjectivity on the part of the different board members and that using a "passive" member was also problematic. A selection board is not a service to the public under Part IV of the *Official Languages Act*, so candidates cannot rely on that part of the *Official Languages Act* to ensure that selection boards assess them in their language of choice[371]—any right rests within the *PSEA*.

In addition to these staffing rules, the Bilingualism Bonus Directive of the National Joint Council requires the employers to whom the directive applies[372] to pay a bonus of $800 to employees who occupy positions that are designated as bilingual. The bonus is not payable to employees in the translation group, Governor-in-Council appointments, temporary employees (appointed for three months or less), employees locally engaged outside of Canada, and some executive employees. Employees who are temporarily assigned to a unilingual position continue to receive the bonus only if the basic monthly salary of their new position is less than or equal to the basic salary of their regular position plus the bonus.[373] Finally, employees must be actively performing their duties to receive the bilingualism bonus; they need not be paid the bonus, for example, while employees are on maternity or parental leave.[374]

H. RELIABILITY STATUS AND SECURITY CLEARANCES

All employers in the federal public administration require their employees to pass an assessment of their honesty and whether they can be trusted to protect the employer's interests. The result of this assessment

370 *Ali v Canada (Attorney General)*, [2004] FCJ No 725.

371 *Ayangma v Canada*, [2003] FCJ No 457 at para 31.

372 The National Research Council, the Canadian Institutes of Health Research, and all departments, agencies, and Crown corporations listed in schedules I and IV of the *Financial Administration Act*.

373 National Joint Council, *Bilingualism Bonus Directive*, art 1.4.2, online: www.njc-cnm.gc.ca/directive/d1/en.

374 *Lavoie v Treasury Board of Canada*, 2008 CHRT 27 at para 139.

is called a reliability status or a security clearance. The basic architecture of this assessment is set out in the Treasury Board's *Standard on Security Screening*.[375] This policy applies to the core public administration and may be adopted by separate agencies and Crown corporations. Separate agencies that have not adopted the *Standard on Security Screening* have their own security policy that generally works the same way.

In essence, the *Standard on Security Screening* divides this topic into two items: a reliability status and a security clearance. Reliability status is the minimum standard of security screening for employees. Within this category there is standard reliability status and enhanced reliability status. All employees are required to undergo a standard reliability status screening; enhanced reliability status screening is required for all positions that perform security and intelligence functions. A reliability status screening provides a verification of the employee's identity and background, their educational and professional credentials, a criminal record check, and personal references. More controversially, the *Standard on Security Screening* was amended in 2014 to add a credit check to the standard reliability status screening. The Federal Court of Appeal, on hearing a challenge to that amendment, concluded that a credit check is appropriate even for positions that do not handle money and that the credit check component violates neither section 8 of the *Charter* nor section 3 of the *Privacy Act*.[376] A reliability status is valid for ten years and then must be renewed; it may also be reconsidered whenever the relevant department or agency obtains adverse information about an employee that casts doubt on their reliability.

Security clearances are likewise divided into two categories: a secret level security clearance and a top secret level security clearance. A top secret security clearance also has two levels: top secret and enhanced top secret. Security clearances require a reliability status assessment plus a security assessment of increasing intensity for top secret level and enhanced top secret (including a polygraph examination for the enhanced top secret level). The *Standard on Security Screening* sets out several factors used to assess whether a security clearance is required for a particular position and, if so, what level. The enhanced top secret level clearance, for example, is reserved for positions that perform security

---

375 Online: www.tbs-sct.canada.ca/pol/doc-eng.aspx?id=28115&section=html.

376 *Canada (Union of Correctional Officers) v Canada (Attorney General)*, 2019 FCA 212.

and intelligence functions or that have unsupervised access to secret law enforcement information. Security clearances are granted after a security assessment by the Canadian Security Intelligence Service (CSIS). CSIS's authority to conduct these assessments is also set out in statute.[377] CSIS is only providing an assessment, though; the actual decision is made by the deputy head or a delegate.

The process for challenging decisions made about reliability status and security clearances is different for current employees and applicants for positions. Employees who lose their employment as a result of the revocation of a reliability status may grieve and refer that grievance to adjudication with the Board. For years, there was some dispute over whether an employee who was dismissed as a result of losing their reliability status could refer any grievance about that revocation to adjudication. The employer took the position that the decision to revoke a reliability status was an administrative action and that the dismissal of the employee that flowed from that decision was therefore not a "termination of employment" (and certainly not disciplinary) but, rather, a purely administrative act. In two decisions in 2017, the Federal Court of Appeal rejected that argument and concluded instead that the Board has jurisdiction to inquire into the employer's reasons for revoking a security clearance without needing to assess whether the decision constituted "disguised discipline."[378] Thus, when an employee is dismissed because they lost their reliability status or security clearance by, for example, a conviction for impaired driving[379] or because other criminal charges were laid,[380] or for a border officer not reporting that they had been mailed a

---

377 *Canadian Security Intelligence Service Act*, RSC 1985, c C-23, s 13.

378 *Canada (Attorney General) v Féthière*, 2017 FCA 66 [*Féthière*], and *Canada (Attorney General) v Heyser*, 2017 FCA 113 [*Heyser*].

379 This description understates the actual facts of the case, which the Board summarized as "aggressive and dangerous driving, road racing, road rage, impaired driving, failing to remain at an accident scene, serious alcohol abuse, repeatedly failing to have proper licensing or vehicle documentation, neglecting to pay numerous provincial offence tickets, repeatedly driving with a suspended licence, failing to properly identify himself to police by impersonating his twin brother, threatening and intimidating other drivers, and repeatedly engaging in aggressive and belligerent interactions with police officers." *Grievor X v Canada Revenue Agency*, 2020 FPSLREB 74 at para 90.

380 *Jassar v Canada Revenue Agency*, 2019 FPSLREB 54. The Board set aside the dismissal in that case as there were in fact no charges laid and the employer could not substantiate its other concerns about the grievor's reliability.

package of hashish by their sometimes-romantic partner, the employee may grieve their dismissal and refer that grievance to adjudication.[381]

Prior to those Federal Court of Appeal decisions, challenges to the revocation of a reliability status were made by way of judicial review. The Federal Court concluded that the employer owed a duty of procedural fairness prior to revoking a reliability status and that, at the very least, an employee is entitled to know the information upon which the decision is being made and to be given an opportunity to explain any adverse information.[382] After *Féthière* and *Heyser*, even complaints of procedural fairness must be grieved and referred to adjudication[383]—although since an adjudication process is conducted *de novo*, any procedural defects in the investigation or grievance process will be cured by the adjudication hearing in any event.[384]

The process for employees who lose their security clearance but are not terminated and applicants for reliability status or security clearance is different. For a decision not to grant a reliability status, the only avenue is an application for judicial review to Federal Court.[385] A person who is denied a security clearance, though, may complain to the National Security and Intelligence Review Agency (NSIRA).[386] The NSIRA has the jurisdiction to review any denial of a security clearance when the denial means that a person has been refused employment or results in a decision to "dismiss, demote or transfer an individual or to deny a promotion or transfer to an individual."[387] The NSIRA may also review a complaint from a contractor who is denied a security clearance and has been denied a contract as a result.[388] The NSIRA investigates these complaints and then makes a recommendation to the minister of public safety and emergency preparedness, the director of CSIS, and the

381 *Campeau v Deputy Head (Canada Border Services Agency)*, 2019 FPSLREB 123. The Board set aside the dismissal in that case and substituted a two-year suspension without pay.

382 *Myers*, above note 33, and *Koulatchenko v Financial Transactions and Reports Analysis Centre of Canada*, 2014 FC 206.

383 *Breau v Canada (Attorney General)*, 2022 FC 98.

384 *Ibid*, citing *Tipple v Canada (Treasury Board)*, [1985] FCJ No 818, and *Philps v Canada Revenue Agency*, 2016 PSLREB 110.

385 See, for example, *Alakozai v Canada (Attorney General)*, 2019 FC 550.

386 *National Security and Intelligence Review Agency Act*, SC 2019, c 13, ss 2, 18(1).

387 *Ibid*.

388 *Ibid*, s 18(3).

deputy head (with a copy to the complainant).[389] The NSIRA's recommendations are not binding on the deputy head, who is permitted to reject a recommendation to restore or grant a security clearance.[390] The NSIRA has no jurisdiction over reliability status decisions.

I. SUPERANNUATION

1) History of Superannuation in the Federal Public Service

The federal government has been providing superannuation to federal public servants in one form or another since 1870.[391] The first federal government wanted to encourage the retirement of a significant number of civil servants who had been taken over as part of the transfer of certain services from the provinces to the new post-Confederation federal government. Therefore, in 1869, the federal government appointed a commission of senior civil servants (the Langton Committee, named for its chair, John Langton) to examine the problem. At that time, the common method of running superannuation plans was to provide retiring allowances based on length of service. Those retiring allowances were sometimes financed through employee contributions (of up to 10 percent of a civil servant's salary) and sometimes financed entirely through the government. Governments at that time did not maintain separate interest-earning funds to finance superannuation plans: if employee contributions could not pay for that year's retirement benefits, then the government would simply make up the difference. The British government, for example, abolished employee contributions in 1859 and did not reinstate them until after 1931.

The Langton Committee, on the other hand, recommended a compulsory contribution scheme whereby employees would bear half the cost and the public would bear the other half of the cost. The government rejected that recommendation and decided that employees should bear a greater proportion of the costs. Therefore, when it enacted the

389 *Ibid*, s 29(3).

390 *Thomson v Canada (Deputy Minister of Agriculture)*, [1992] 1 SCR 385.

391 See *Margolis v Canada*, [2001] FCJ No 402 [*Margolis v Canada*]. Superannuation plans have always been established by legislation. The terms of those plans are not subject to collective bargaining: *FPSLRA*, s 113(2). The public service superannuation plan is monitored by a Pension Advisory Committee, which has the mandate to review the operation, design, and funding of benefits provided: *Public Service Superannuation Act*, RSC 1985, c P-36, s 41.

Civil Service Superannuation Act in 1870,[392] it set out contribution rates that were designed to cover the full cost for new employees: employee contributions were 4 percent on salaries of $600 and above and 2.5 percent on lower salaries. These contributions would not cover the full cost of pension benefits in the short term, but the superannuation plan was meant to be self-supporting in the long run. The basic benefit formula in 1870 was 2 percent of the average salary over the last three years of service for each year of service with a 70 percent maximum. Contributions therefore ceased after thirty-five years. The Act contained special provisions for gratuities or pensions in the case of compulsory retirement before age sixty with service of less than ten years or on abolition of office. There was no return of contribution in the case of death or termination of service that did not qualify for a pension or gratuity. One of the stated purposes of the superannuation plan was to encourage people to join the civil service: by refusing to return their superannuation contributions, the Act also discouraged people from leaving the civil service.

By 1873, employee contributions were no longer sufficient to fund pension payments, and the government was effectively paying for half the cost of the superannuation plan (as suggested by the Langton Committee). By 1880, the total contributions by employees were $44,996, and the total pension payments were $147,362—so much for the "pay as you go plan." In 1893, the federal government closed the old superannuation plan to new employees and started a new plan with a contribution rate of 3 percent on salaries under $600 and 3.5 percent for salaries over $600. Employee contributions were put in a fund (the Superannuation Fund No 2), and their benefits were to be charged to this fund. Unlike the original superannuation plan, this fund earned interest at the rate of 6 percent per annum. The government was required to make good the full amount of any deficiency in the fund based on an actuarial valuation of the prospective annuities payable from that fund. In effect, the government had to make good any unfunded liabilities in the fund each year. This useful change to the law was quickly overturned when the Liberals won election in 1896, and in 1898 the government closed the Act to new entrants completely. Civil servants at the time did not all protest this decision. Civil servants were dissatisfied with the superannuation plan at the time, especially concerning the strict conditions for eligibility, the lack of survivor pension benefits, and the

392 *Civil Service Superannuation Act*, 33 Vict, c 4 (1870).

non-return of contributions for those who did not qualify for pensions. Moreover, the plan was confined to "permanent" employees, leaving "temporary" employees with no retirement income for their work. The 1898 "reforms" did address the concern about return of contributions at least. The new superannuation plan required employees to contribute 5 percent of their salary each year to the plan, and the plan earned interest at the rate of 4 percent per annum, compounded biannually. Employees who died in service or who retired without being eligible for a pension had their contributions returned with interest.

In 1924, the federal government enacted a new *Civil Service Superannuation Act*.[393] This Act contained a defined benefit for retirees based on their average salary in their last ten years of service and required employee contributions of 5 percent of salary. The government contribution rate was set out in regulation as equal to the employee contributions until such time as the government could complete an actuarial valuation.[394] The 1924 Act contemplated a return of contributions without interest in certain circumstances (including those employees subject to mandatory retirement on marriage); otherwise, the employee received nothing. The 1924 Act did not end the earlier superannuation schemes: instead, employees could elect to come under the new plan. If they so elected, then their pension was calculated using the last five years of service instead of the last ten.[395] Under the 1924 Act, only those employees who were in or appointed to a permanent position were subject to the plan.[396] Employees could be in a temporary position for years before being made permanent. Benefits were granted on separation for age, disability, or abolition of position and for resignation or dismissal if the contributor had ten or more years of service.

The next significant statutory reform occurred in 1954 with the enactment of the *Public Service Superannuation Act*.[397] That Act made the following changes to public service superannuation:

---

393 *Civil Service Superannuation Act*, RSC 1927, c 24.

394 When the government finally completed an actuarial valuation in 1931, it reported a liability of $53 million as of 31 March 1933. The government did nothing about this liability until after World War II except raise the contribution rate for new male contributors to 5.5 percent for those with salaries between $1,200 and $1,500 and 6 percent for those with salaries over $1,500.

395 *Civil Service Superannuation Act*, s 16. See *Martindale v Canada*, [1956–60] Ex CR 153 [*Martindale*], for a discussion of that election right.

396 *Civil Service Superannuation Act*, s 2. See *Martindale*, above note 395.

397 *Public Service Superannuation Act*, SC 1952–53, c 47.

- Pension benefits were provided as of right, instead of a grant by the Governor in Council.
- Temporary employees were eligible to participate after twelve months of continuous employment.
- Pension benefits were based on an employee's best ten years of earnings instead of the last ten.[398]
- The government had the power to enter into reciprocal pension transfer agreements with other employers, so public servants could carry their pension contributions to other employers who entered into these transfer agreements.

In 1955, the government introduced the Statutory Death Benefit. Prior to 1955, public servants were eligible to receive a gratuity of two months' salary under the *Civil Service Act* if they died after completing two years of service. In addition, life insurance coverage was available under the *Civil Service Insurance Act*, but only to permanent employees. The Langton Committee recommended that life insurance be provided as part of a general superannuation scheme; however, the *Civil Service Insurance Act* was not introduced until 1893, and it only provided permanent employees with the opportunity to purchase individual life insurance policies on favourable premium rates. The Statutory Death Benefit was enacted in 1955 after consultation with the National Joint Council, which endorsed the broad outlines of the plan as a whole. Employees' dependants received the employee's annual salary (up to $5,000) upon the employee's death; retirees could continue to participate up to age seventy, but with a one-tenth reduction of the nominal full amount for each year that the participant's age exceeded sixty. The plan was called a Statutory Death Benefit (and not life insurance) to placate the life insurance industry: the statutory death benefit has characteristics of both life insurance and a payment to provide for the costs of death.[399]

The next major change to public service superannuation occurred upon the introduction of the Canada and Quebec pension plans. Those plans provided virtually all Canadian workers and their families with a degree of earnings-replacement protection in the event of the retirement,

398 This was changed to the best six years in 1960.

399 See *Margolis v Canada*, above note 391, Appendix "Report on Supplementary Death Benefits and Survivor Income Insurance" by H.D. Clark (June 1982). See also *Withler et al v Canada (Attorney General)*, [2006] BCJ No 101 at paras 113–27, summarizing the affidavit evidence of H.D. Clark, which included the same report appended to the *Margolis* decision.

disability, or death of the wage earner. When the Canada Pension Plan (CPP) was introduced, employers and employees were required to contribute 1.8 percent of earnings to the CPP. Private sector pension plans had to decide how to react to the CPP—namely, whether to ignore the CPP and stack its plan on top of the CPP, or to integrate its plan with the CPP to recognize the contributions and coverage of the CPP. The federal government decided to integrate the public service superannuation plan with the CPP. Therefore, the superannuation contribution rates were reduced by the amount that both sides contributed to the CPP. A similar rule was in place for the Quebec Pension Plan.

The federal government began to index pensions in 1969. The 1969 legislation[400] provided for maximum indexing of 2 percent (the same level of indexing that was in place for the CPP at the time). In 1974, future pensions were granted full indexing to match the consumer price index.[401]

In 1975, the federal government amended the *Public Service Superannuation Act* to require that male and female employees be treated equally.[402] Prior to 1975, female employees contributed less to the superannuation than did male employees. Widowers also received less than widows. There were other incidental amendments in 1975, including full payment of benefit entitlement during re-employment in a non-contributory position; an extension of the election period for transferring service of former retired RCMP and Armed Forces members employed in the public service; a change in the reduction formula on early retirements; removal of Treasury Board approval for payment of an annual allowance in cases with less than twenty years of pensionable service; and the introduction of the five-year minimum benefit entitlement.

From 1975 until 1999, there were no comprehensive changes to the public service superannuation plan but merely some changes to the details. For example, in 1993, the federal government removed two age-based restrictions on contributing to the public service superannuation plan: it permitted contributions by employees under the age of eighteen and employees over the age of sixty-five and in receipt of CPP benefits.[403]

---

400 *Supplementary Retirement Benefits Act*, RSC 1970, c 43 (1st Supp).

401 *Statute Law (Supplementary Retirement Benefits) Amendment Act*, 1973, SC 1973-74, c 36, s 2(1).

402 *Statute Law (Superannuation) Amendment Act*, 1975, SC 1974–75–76, c 81.

403 *Act to amend certain Acts in relation to pensions and to enact the Special Retirement Arrangements Act and the Pension Benefits Act*, SC 1992, c 46, s 2.

Employees and pensioners who had been prevented from accruing service under the *Public Service Superannuation Act* because they were over the age of sixty-five were given an opportunity to purchase the service, and individuals who were still employed and who elected for the past service recommenced their contributions. Amendments effective in 1981 and 1994 created early retirement options for air traffic controllers employed in "operational services"[404] and correctional service employees, respectively.[405] Finally, amendments in 1996 shortened the period required to qualify for a pension from five years to two; locked in an employee's pension contributions after two years of pensionable service; and introduced the transfer value benefit (the right to transfer the lump sum actuarial value of an employee's pension to a locked-in registered retirement savings plan (RRSP) or other investment vehicle if the employee terminates employment prior to the age of fifty).[406]

In 1999, the federal government introduced more significant and controversial amendments to the public service superannuation plan. Prior to the 1999 statute, the federal government and employees both contributed to the public service superannuation plan: the employer was required to match employees' contributions and also to make up any actuarial deficiency in payments. The contributions were placed in a Superannuation Account (a separate account in the Consolidated Revenue Fund). According to most estimates, the Superannuation Account had an actuarial surplus of approximately $30 billion in 1999 for all three superannuation plans that used that account (the public service, RCMP, and Armed Forces plans). The federal government changed the contribution and accounting rules for the public service superannuation plan effective 1 April 2000, in the *Public Sector Pension Investment Board Act*.[407] That Act closed contributions to the Superannuation Account and created two new funds: the Public Service Superannuation Investment Fund and the Public Service Pension Fund. Effectively, the Public Service Superannuation Investment Fund comprises some funds transferred from the Superannuation Account to invest those funds in

404 That term is defined by s 50 of the *Public Service Superannuation Regulations* as, essentially, service that requires an air traffic controller licence or a data systems coordinator (or in training for those positions).

405 *Superannuation Amendment Act, 1981*, SC 1980–81–82–83, c 64, s 3 and SC 1992, c 46, s 12.

406 *Budget Implementation Act, 1996*, SC 1996, c 18, s 25.

407 *Public Sector Pension Investment Board Act*, SC 1999, c 34 (sometimes also referred to as Bill C-78).

the market. The Superannuation Account is liable to pay out benefits payable under the *Public Service Superannuation Act* that were earned by contributors before 1 April 2000. The Public Service Pension Fund contains the superannuation contributions made after 1 April 2000. Those funds are also invested in the market, in the manner described later in this chapter, and are used to pay for benefits earned after 1 April 2000.

The more controversial steps taken in the 1999 amendments were to end the requirement that the federal government contribute at least an equal share to the public service superannuation plan, to end the linkage between CPP contributions and superannuation contributions, and to effectively permit the federal government to withdraw the $30 billion surplus. First, prior to 1999, the federal government was required by the *Public Service Superannuation Act* to contribute an amount that was at least equal to the employees' contributions to the Superannuation Account. That provision of the Act was repealed. Instead, the federal government is only required to deposit in the Public Service Pension Fund the amount, based on actuarial advice, that is required to provide for the cost of benefits that have accrued.[408] In determining that amount, the federal government may take into account any surplus in the Public Service Pension Fund.[409] Therefore, if the employee contributions are sufficient to cover the accrued benefits for a particular month, then the federal government is not required to contribute anything to the Public Service Pension Fund. Furthermore, as of 1 January 2004, the Treasury Board may unilaterally determine the rate of employee contributions, so long as the contributions do not "result in a total amount of contributions that would exceed forty per cent of the current service cost for the portion of the period in respect of the benefits payable under Parts I and III of this Act."[410] The concern expressed by employee organizations is that, effectively, the federal government would decrease its funding of the public service superannuation plan to ensure that there is no actuarial surplus in the Public Service Pension Fund and then increase employee contributions the next year to ensure that it could still contribute lower amounts to the Public Service Pension Fund.

Second, the contribution rate for 1 January 2000 to 1 January 2004 was frozen at 4 percent of salary below an employee's year's maximum pensionable earnings (YMPE) and 7.5 percent of the salary above an

408 *Public Service Superannuation Act*, s 44.2(3).
409 *Ibid*, s 44.2(4).
410 *Ibid*, s 5(1.4)(b)

employee's YMPE.[411] As described above, the contribution rates for the public service superannuation plan used to be fully integrated with the contribution rates for the CPP. However, an employee's CPP contribution rate has increased significantly. From 1986 to 1996, the CPP contribution rate increased by 0.1 percent each year (from 1.8 percent in 1986 to 2.8 percent in 1996). Then the CPP contribution rate increased substantially from 2.8 percent in 1996 to 4.95 percent in 2003. Employee contributions to the public service superannuation plan would have been reduced accordingly. However, the 1999 Act ended the full integration between CPP contribution rates and the public service superannuation plan contribution rates, which effectively resulted in employees paying more in contributions.

Third, the 1999 amendments effectively permitted the federal government to "scoop the surplus" out of the Superannuation Account. Sections 44(10) and (13) of the *Public Service Superannuation Act* now permit the federal government to debit the Superannuation Account and Public Service Superannuation Investment Fund by an amount that would ensure that the amount of money in the account and fund does not exceed 110 percent of the amount that is estimated to be required to meet the costs of the benefits payable for service prior to 1 April 2000. In other words, the federal government has the right to debit the $30 billion surplus (for all three plans)—and is in fact obligated to debit most of the surplus.[412] This withdrawal must take place over fifteen years.[413]

Finally, in 2012, Parliament enacted two other important changes to the *Public Service Superannuation Act*.[414] First, Parliament changed the share of contributions paid by public servants to 50 percent, up from contribution rates that were not more than 40 percent of the cost of pension benefits. Second, the pensionable age was increased from sixty to sixty-five for all persons who became contributors on or after 1 January 2013. All other ages for "early" retirement were also increased by five years.

411 *Public Service Superannuation Act*, s 5(1.1). The CPP sets a maximum amount of earnings on which you can contribute to the CPP, called the YMPE. In 2004, for example, the YMPE was $40,500.

412 Several employee organizations and pensioner organizations have challenged these changes in Ontario Superior Court. This litigation is still ongoing at the time of publication.

413 *Public Service Superannuation Act*, s 44(11).

414 *Jobs and Growth Act, 2012*, SC 2012, c 31, division 23.

2) Pension Benefits and Contributions Under the *Public Service Superannuation Act*

The formula for calculating a basic pension (referred to in the Act as an "immediate annuity") is 2 percent for each year of pensionable service credit (to a maximum of thirty-five years) multiplied by the retiree's average annual salary over the best five consecutive years of service.[415] For example, the pension of a person who retired at age sixty with twenty-five years of pensionable service and an average salary over the best five consecutive years of service of $35,000 would be

$$\frac{2\% \times 25 \text{ years} \times \$35{,}000}{12 \text{ months}} = \$1{,}500 \text{ per month}$$

The limit of thirty-five years of service effectively means that the highest pension an employee could receive is equal to 70 percent of their average salary over the best five consecutive years of service.

This basic pension formula applies to employees who have reached their retirement age, which varies according to whether they joined before or after 1 January 2013, or who were disabled.[416]

An employee's pension benefits "vest" after two years of service. If an employee has less than two years of service, then they are entitled to a return of contributions.[417]

An employee who ceases employment after two years of service, but before they are entitled to a full pension, has four options:

1) **A deferred annuity.** A deferred annuity is a pension that is payable at age sixty, calculated in the same manner as an immediate annuity.[418]
2) **A pension transfer.** If an employee leaves the federal public service to work for another employer who has a pension transfer agreement with the federal government, the employee can transfer their pension credits and have them recognized by the new employer's pension plan.[419]

---

415 *Public Service Superannuation Act*, s 11.

416 *Ibid*, ss 13(1)(a)–(c) and 13.001(1)(a)–(c).

417 *Ibid*, s 12(3). There are some exceptions to this rule set out in s 12(2), including counting pre-1954 service and service with the RCMP or Canadian military.

418 *Ibid*, s 13(1)(c)(ii)(A) and s 10(1), "deferred annuity."

419 *Pension Plan Transfer Agreements Regulations*, SOR/98-445.

3) **A transfer value.** This is similar to a pension transfer, except it is a lump sum amount that is transferred to a locked-in RRSP, a registered pension plan, or a financial institution to buy a life annuity. A transfer value is equal to the actuarial value (in current dollars) of the pension to which the employee would have been entitled at age sixty. This is available only to employees who leave the federal public service more than ten years younger than pensionable age (i.e., before they turn fifty).[420]
4) **An annual allowance.** An annual allowance is a permanently reduced pension. It is payable to plan members who are between fifty and sixty years of age. For employees with less than twenty-five years of service, the annual allowance is the same as an immediate annuity, but with a reduction of 5 percent for every year the employee is under age sixty. For employees between fifty-five and sixty years of age, the lesser of the following two percentages will be used: a reduction of 5 percent for every year the employee is younger than age sixty or a reduction of 5 percent for every year the employee's pensionable service is less than thirty years. For employees between fifty and fifty-four years of age, the higher of the following two percentages will be used: a reduction of 5 percent for every year the employee is younger than age fifty-five or a reduction of 5 percent for every year the employee's pensionable service is less than thirty years.[421]

Pension eligibility differs for air traffic controllers and employees of the correctional service. Air traffic controllers in operational service who voluntarily cease to be employed are entitled to an immediate annuity if they have reached age fifty and have twenty-five or more years of service. If they are age forty-five or over and have at least twenty years of service, they are entitled to an annual allowance. The annual allowance is the value of the deferred annuity based on the employee's operational service reduced by the *greater* of 5 percent for each year to the nearest one-tenth of a year that their age is less than fifty at the time of exercising their operation, or 5 percent for each year to the nearest one-tenth of a year that the employee's pensionable operational service

420 *Public Service Superannuation Act*, s 13.01, and *Public Service Superannuation Regulations*, s 84.

421 *Public Service Superannuation Act*, s 13(1)(c)(ii)(B) and (D).

is less than twenty-five years.[422] If the air traffic controller does not leave voluntarily and has twenty years of service, they are entitled to an immediate annuity. If the air traffic controller does not leave voluntarily and has between ten and twenty years of service, they are entitled to an annual allowance equal to the value of the deferred annuity based on the operational service reduced by the *lesser* of 5 percent for each year to the nearest one-tenth of a year that their service in operational service is less than twenty, or 30 percent.[423] If the air traffic controller is less than forty-five years of age or has less than twenty years of service, then their options are the same as those of other employees.

Correctional service employees in operational service[424] also have early retirement options. Operational service employees who are age fifty or more and have at least twenty-five years of service are entitled to an immediate annuity. Operational service employees who are at least age forty-five and have at least twenty years of service are entitled to an annual allowance, which is equal to a deferred annuity reduced by the greater of 5 percent for each year of service less than twenty-five years or 5 percent for each year of age less than fifty.[425]

Employees in operational service as air traffic controllers or employed in correctional services must pay higher contributions in exchange for their early retirement options.

An employee who becomes disabled prior to the age of sixty is entitled to an immediate annuity—essentially, they are treated as if they are retiring at age sixty. A person is "disabled" if they are suffering from a physical or mental impairment that prevents them from engaging in any employment for which they are reasonably suited by virtue of the contributor's education, training, or experience and can reasonably be expected to last for the remainder of their lifetime.[426] An employee claiming a disability pension must undergo a medical assessment by Health Canada.[427]

---

422 *Ibid*, s 16.

423 *Ibid*, s 17.

424 That term is defined in the *Public Service Superannuation Regulations*, s 53. Essentially, if you work in a jail instead of an office, then you are in operational service.

425 *Public Service Superannuation Act*, s 24.2, and *Public Service Superannuation Regulations*, s 58.

426 *Ibid*, s 42.1.

427 *Ibid*, s 43.2.

3) Death Benefits

Employees are entitled to a statutory death benefit of twice their salary upon their death.[428] If the employee has retired, then they may elect to continue to participate in the statutory death benefit scheme by paying contributions toward the death benefit after their retirement.[429]

The Act reduces the basic benefit available to employees or retirees who die between the ages of sixty-five and seventy-five.[430] The death benefit is subject to a reduction of 10 percent for every year of age in excess of sixty-five attained by the participant—effectively reducing the benefit to zero for participants over the age of seventy-five.[431] The constitutionality of this reduction has been challenged on two occasions, with conflicting results. In *Margolis v The Queen*,[432] a widow whose husband died at age sixty-nine challenged this reduction and was successful before the Federal Court. The Federal Court concluded that this reduction in the statutory death benefit violated section 15 of the *Charter* because it was discriminatory on the basis of age.

In *Withler v Canada (Attorney General)*,[433] the Supreme Court of Canada came to the opposite conclusion. *Withler* was a class action challenging the constitutionality of the reduction in both the *Public Service Superannuation Act* and the identical reduction (effective from age sixty to seventy) in the *Canadian Forces Superannuation Act*.[434] The BC Supreme Court at trial explicitly decided not to follow *Margolis v The Queen*[435]

428 *Public Service Superannuation Act*, s 47(1).

429 *Ibid*, s 51. The contributions for every participant (elective or not) are 15 cents per month for every thousand dollars in the amount of the participant's basic benefit, with a reduction for employees over the age of sixty-five: *ibid*, s 53.

430 The reduction used to be between the ages of sixty and seventy, but that was changed to sixty-five and seventy-five in 1999: *Public Sector Pension Investment Board Act*, s 98(1).

431 *Public Service Superannuation Act*, s 47(1).

432 *Margolis v The Queen*, 2001 FCT 85 [*Margolis v The Queen*].

433 *Withler v Canada (Attorney General)*, 2011 SCC 12 [*Withler*].

434 *Canadian Forces Superannuation Act*, RSC 1985, c C-17.

435 The judge in that case decided not to follow *Margolis v Canada*, above note 391, because the *Margolis* case did not involve the same oral evidence as in *Withler*, stating:

> The *Margolis* case was heard in one day. I do not believe the court heard any viva voce testimony. In contrast, this court heard evidence and submissions for fourteen days. From [paragraph] 14 of the reasons in *Margolis*, I infer that the court had the benefit of at least some of the historical documents that are in evidence before me. I do not believe Campbell J. had the benefit

and then concluded that the reduction was not discriminatory because it did not harm the essential human dignity of the surviving spouses who were the plaintiffs in that case. In so doing, the BC Supreme Court also chose to disregard a 1980 report by the Canadian Human Rights Commission stating that the reduction provisions were discriminatory.[436] The Supreme Court of Canada upheld the trial decision, concluding that the age-based rules were, overall, effective in meeting the actual needs of the claimants. The Supreme Court of Canada stated that a pension plan needs to be reviewed as a whole because each benefit is "integrated with other benefits and balanced against the public interest."[437]

In addition to death benefits, an employee's survivor receives a survivor's benefit. Broadly speaking, if the employee dies while still working and has more than two years of service, then their survivor is entitled to an immediate annual allowance equal to 1 percent × the contributor's pensionable service × the average salary for the best five consecutive years. Surviving children under the age of eighteen (or between eighteen and twenty-five and still in school) receive one-fifth of a survivor's pension up to a maximum of four-fifths for all children. If the employee had retired at the time of their death and was entitled to an immediate annuity, to a deferred annuity, or to an annual allowance, the survivor and children are entitled to an immediate allowance. The formula for calculating the survivor's allowance in cases of death after retirement is the same as for a death in the service (1 percent × the contributor's pensionable service × the average salary for the best five consecutive years). Each eligible child (i.e., under eighteen or between eighteen and twenty-five and attending school) is entitled to receive one-fifth of the survivor's allowance up to a maximum of four-fifths. If the employee

---

> of the expert evidence and evidence from numerous plaintiffs, as well as civil servant administrators of the [Supplementary Death Benefit] Plan. It is not clear to me if the standing argument was made. Mrs. Margolis and the estate of Dr. Margolis, the plan participant, were both plaintiffs. In *Margolis* the *Charter* infringement seems to have been argued on the basis that the Reduction Provisions violated the *Charter* rights of the deceased participant and the surviving spouse. In the case before me the plaintiffs do acknowledge that an estate cannot maintain an action for breach of the *Charter*. For these reasons, as well as those set out in my earlier ruling on this matter, I conclude that I ought to consider this matter afresh.

(*Withler et al v Attorney General of Canada*, above note 399 at para 63).

436 *Ibid* at para 127.

437 *Withler* (SCC), above note 433 at para 76.

had less than two years of service when they died, then the survivor receives a return of contributions plus interest.[438]

An employee's survivor is either a person who was married to the contributor at the time of the contributor's death or a person with whom the employee was cohabiting in a relationship of a conjugal nature for at least one year immediately before the death of the employee.[439] This definition leaves open the possibility that there are two survivors: a spouse from whom the employee separated and a second person with whom the employee lived and had conjugal relations. In such a case, the survivor's benefit is apportioned proportionally in accordance with the length of time that each survivor was married to or cohabited with the employee.[440] The question of whether a particular person is a spouse is a question of fact determined by the Treasury Board. This finding of fact can be reviewed by the Federal Court but will only be overturned if it is patently unreasonable.[441]

Finally, if the survivor is criminally responsible for the employee's death, then the survivor is not entitled to a survivor's benefit.[442] In any event, the general legal rule (under both common law and civil law) that a person convicted of making an attempt on the life of the deceased is unworthy of inheriting prohibits a survivor who killed their spouse from receiving a survivor's benefit or death benefit.[443]

4) Scope of Public Service Superannuation: Who Is Covered?

The *Public Service Superannuation Act* covers a larger number of employees than the *FPSLRA*.[444] All employees of the core public administration, and the separate employers covered by the *FPSLRA*, are participants in the public service superannuation plan. The public service superannuation plan also includes employees of the House of Commons, Senate, Library of Parliament, and Office of the Ethics

---

438 *Public Service Superannuation Act*, s 12.

439 *Ibid*, ss 3(1), "survivor," and 25(4).

440 *Ibid*, s 25(10).

441 *Belanger v Canada (Attorney General)*, [2003] FCJ No 1322.

442 *Public Service Superannuation Act*, s 25(8).

443 *St-Hilaire v Canada (Attorney General)*, [2001] FCJ No 444 (CA). In that case, the widow was convicted of manslaughter in the death of her late husband and was denied benefits as a result.

444 *Public Service Superannuation Act*, s 3(1), "public service," and Schedule I.

Commissioner—essentially, the employees covered by the *Parliamentary Employment and Staff Relations Act*. Then the Act goes further and covers employees of several Crown corporations that are otherwise governed by the *Canada Labour Code*, including Atomic Energy of Canada Limited and the Canadian Museum of Civilization. The *Public Service Superannuation Act* applies for some limited purposes to employees of corporations governed by the *Government Corporations Operation Act*.[445] The corporations governed by the *Government Corporations Operation Act* are those corporations that are entirely owned by the Crown and that have been made subject to that Act by a proclamation of the Governor in Council.[446] Employees of those corporations are not covered by the *Public Service Superannuation Act*; however, if a person who, immediately prior to their employment by a corporation, was a contributor under the *Public Service Superannuation Act*, then for the purposes of that Act that person's service with the corporation shall be counted as pensionable service under the Act.[447] Finally, the *Public Service Superannuation Act* also governs employees of the governments of Yukon, Northwest Territories, and Nunavut.

The *Public Service Superannuation Act* does not cover members of the Canadian Armed Forces or members of the RCMP.[448] Both of those forces have their own superannuation regimes that are similar to the public service regimes.[449]

The *Public Service Superannuation Act* states that it applies to people who are "employed in the public service." However, as discussed in Chapter 3, recently the Federal Court has interpreted that phrase broadly so that it includes persons who are not appointed under

---

445 *Government Corporations Operation Act*, RSC 1985, c G-4.

446 See the *Proclamation declaring that the Government Corporations Operation Act is applicable to The Federal Bridge Corporation Limited beginning on December 1, 1998*, SOR/98-578; *Proclamation Declaring that the Government Corporations Operation Act is Applicable to Canada Lands Company Limited beginning on September 16, 2003*, SOR/2003-312; *Proclamation Declaring that the Government Corporations Operation Act is Applicable to Parc Downsview Park Inc beginning on September 16, 2003*, SOR/2003-313; and *Proclamation Declaring that the Government Corporations Operation Act is Applicable to BDC Capital Inc*, SOR/2006-43.

447 *Government Corporations Operation Act*, s 5(2).

448 *Young v Canada*, [1988] FCJ No 162 (CA).

449 *Royal Canadian Mounted Police Superannuation Act*, RSC 1985, c R-11, and *Canadian Forces Superannuation Act*, RSC 1985, c C-17.

the *PSEA* or similar statute for a separate agency but, instead, includes those workers characterized as "contractors" for the purposes of the *FPSLRA* and *PSEA* but who would meet the definition of an "employee" for tax or employment law purposes.[450]

5) Investment of the Superannuation Funds

Both the Public Service Superannuation Investment Fund and the Public Service Pension Fund are invested in the market. The investments are made by the Public Sector Pension Investment Board, a Crown corporation established by the *Public Sector Pension Investment Board Act*. The directors of the Public Sector Investment Board may not be employees of His Majesty or who are in receipt of a pension invested by the Board; however, the directors are appointed after being nominated by a committee who has a representative of both staff associations and pensioners.[451] The *Public Sector Pension Investment Board Regulations* impose the following restrictions on the investments the Public Sector Pension Investment Board is permitted to make:

1. The board may only hold or invest in derivatives if the purpose is either to offset or reduce the risk associated with an existing investment or group of investments or to hold or invest in the derivative as an alternative to holding or investing in the underlying asset itself. Investments in derivatives are limited to a market exposure covered by cash or other assets designated for that purpose.
2. The board may not invest in the securities of a corporation to which are attached more than 30 percent of the votes that may be cast to elect the directors of a corporation.
3. The board may not invest more than 10 percent of the assets (at book value) in any one person or two or more associated persons or two or more affiliated corporations.
4. The board cannot invest in real or immovable property if:
   (a) the book value of the investment in any one parcel of real or immovable property or Canadian resource property exceeds 5 percent of the book value of the Board's assets;

450 See, for example, *Céré v Canada (Attorney General)*, 2019 FC 221, discussed in greater detail in Chapter 3.

451 *Public Sector Pension Investment Board Act*, s 10(1).

(b) the aggregate book value of all investments in Canadian resource properties exceeds 15 percent of the book value of the Board's assets; or
(c) the aggregate book value of all investments in real or immovable property and Canadian resource properties exceeds 25 percent of the book value of the Board's assets.[452]

The Public Service Pension Investment Board reported a rate of return in fiscal year 2006 of 19.1 percent and a rate of return since its inception of 5.5 percent.[453] The Board also reported net assets of almost $20 billion: these assets include the money invested for the public service superannuation plan, as well as the RCMP and military plans.[454]

6) Definition of Salary

An employee's benefit entitlements are determined as a proportion of their "salary." The term "salary," for remuneration received in the federal public service (as opposed to in the Armed Forces or RCMP when the pension is transferred), is defined as

> the basic pay received by the person in respect of whom the expression is being applied for the performance of the regular duties of a position or office exclusive of any amount received as allowances, special remuneration, payment for overtime or other compensation or as a gratuity unless that amount is deemed to be or to have been included in that person's basic pay pursuant to any regulation made under paragraph 42(1)(*e*).[455]

However, the Act defines the term "salary" differently for the purposes of calculating the statutory death benefit. The definition of "salary" for that purpose is as follows:

> "salary" means
> (a) in the case of a participant employed in the public service, the salary as defined for purposes of Part I, expressed in terms of an

---

452 *Public Sector Pension Investment Board Regulations*, SOR/2000-77, ss 11–14.

453 Public Sector Pension Investment Board, *2006 Annual Report* at 11, online (pdf): https://publications.gc.ca/collections/collection_2012/investpsp/CC511-2006-eng.pdf.

454 *Ibid* at 26.

455 *Public Service Superannuation Act*, s 3(1), "salary."

annual rate, except that where a retroactive increase is authorized in the salary of that participant, the increase shall be deemed to have commenced to have been received by him on such day as the regulations prescribe,

(b) in the case of an elective participant, his salary in the public service at the time he ceased to be employed in the public service, expressed in terms of an annual rate, and

(c) in the case of a participant who is required to contribute to the Retirement Compensation Arrangements Account by section 8 or 9 of the *Retirement Compensation Arrangements Regulations, No. 1*, the salary referred to in subsections 8(3) or 9(1) of those Regulations.[456]

Furthermore, the *Supplementary Death Benefit Regulations* also prescribe, in certain situations, the date of the deemed receipt of a retroactive salary increase, stating that a retroactive increase is effective the month following the month in which the increase is approved.[457] These differences between the definitions of "salary" for the basic pension benefit and the supplementary death benefit mean that retroactive salary increases are treated differently depending on the type of benefit being claimed. In *Reid v Canada*,[458] the Federal Court of Appeal concluded that a retroactive salary increase is part of "salary" when calculating the basic pension benefit, but not necessarily part of "salary" for the purposes of calculating the statutory death benefit. In that case, Mr. Reid retired from the public service and elected to continue to contribute to the statutory death benefit, but then died two years after retiring. The collective agreement governing his employment expired before he retired, and a new collective agreement was not concluded until after he retired. That collective agreement included a retroactive pay increase. Therefore, Mr. Reid's salary for the purposes of calculating his basic pension benefit was increased. However, the Federal Court of Appeal concluded that the retroactive increase did not apply to the death benefit because it did not comprise part of his salary when "he ceased to be employed in the public service."

456 *Public Service Superannuation Act*, s 47(1), "salary."

457 *Supplementary Death Benefit Regulations*, CRC 1360, s 23.

458 *Reid v Canada*, [2006] FCJ No 276 (CA).

Concerning the breadth of remuneration that comprises "salary," the Federal Court of Appeal concluded in a 1975 decision[459] that two bonuses (a "settlement bonus" and a "lump sum" bonus) comprised part of the employee's salary under the *Public Service Superannuation Act* because they were remuneration for services performed. However, the definition of "salary" at that stage referred to "compensation received" by an employee, not "basic pay" as in the current version of the *Public Service Superannuation Act*. The Federal Court has stated, therefore, that *Gruber v Canada (Treasury Board)* is no longer good law and that "Parliament's intention is quite clear in the post-*Gruber* era. 'Basic pay' is part of salary without more."[460] In that case, therefore, shift and weekend premiums of $2.00 per hour were not considered to be part of "salary" for superannuation purposes.

7) Transfer of Pension to Third Parties

There are two situations in which an employee of the federal public service may wish to transfer the actuarial value of their pension to a third party. The first situation, a transfer of pension funds to an approved employer, was discussed briefly above as one of the options upon departure from the federal public service; this situation is generally uncontentious.[461] The second situation is a pension division as part of a divorce or separation settlement.

The *Public Service Superannuation Act* provides that pension benefits and death benefits cannot be assigned and are exempt from attachment, seizure, and execution, either at law or in equity.[462] Therefore, it was not possible under the *Public Service Superannuation Act* to divide an employee's pension upon a divorce. However, in 1992, the federal government introduced the *Pension Benefits Division Act*[463] to remedy this defect. The *Pension Benefits Division Act* provides that members

459 *Gruber v Canada (Treasury Board)*, [1975] FCJ No 77 (CA).

460 *National Automobile, Aerospace, Transportation and General Workers Union of Canada (Caw-Canada, Local 2182) v Canada (Attorney General)*, 2007 FC 449 at para 124.

461 With the exception of *Ault v Canada (Attorney General)*, [2003] FCJ No 1461, where an employee wanted to revoke her consent to a transfer to an "employer" whom the government considered to be acting fraudulently.

462 *Public Service Superannuation Act*, ss 10(10) and 58.

463 *Pension Benefits Division Act*, SC 1992, c 46.

or spouses can apply to the minister to approve the division of pension benefits between them in the event of divorce or separation.[464] The division must be made pursuant to a separation agreement or a court order.[465] The other spouse may object to the division on the grounds that the court order or spousal agreement has been varied, that the terms of the order or agreement are being satisfied by other means, or that the order or agreement is currently being challenged in court.[466] The minister shall refuse to divide the pension where it would not be just to approve the division.[467] This means that the minister must consider evidence from the objector concerning whether the division would be just.[468]

The purpose of the *Pension Benefits Division Act* is to provide a mechanism for making payments out of pension funds, not to fix the value of the pension between spouses in property settlements made upon the breakdown of their relationship.[469] The "value" of the pension is fixed by the provisions of applicable provincial legislation. However, the *Pension Benefits Division Act* and associated regulations contain provisions setting out rules of the actuarial valuation of pensions that vary considerably from those provincial rules.[470] Furthermore, the *Pension Benefits Division Act* only permits a transfer of 50 percent of the value of the pension on the valuation day, and not some other value, unless the terms of the court order or agreement specify the payment of a particular lump sum amount.[471]

8) Erroneous Advice

If this chapter has done nothing else, it should make it clear that the pension rules in the federal public service are confusing and difficult for employees—let alone the supposed "experts"—to understand.

464 *Ibid*, s 4(1).
465 *Ibid*, s 4(2).
466 *Ibid*, s 6(2).
467 *Ibid*, s 7(5).
468 *Dube v Canada (Superannuation Division)*, [1996] FCJ No 341.
469 *Smith v Canada (Attorney General)* (1999), 179 FTR 134.
470 *Eddie v Canada (Attorney General)*, [2003] FCJ No 749 at para 25 [*Eddie*], and *Shafer v Shafer* (1996), RFL (4th) 410 (Ont Gen Div), aff'd (1998), 37 RFL (4th) 104 (Ont CA). The rules are set out in ss 13–16 of the *Pension Benefits Division Regulations*, SOR/94-612. The rules applied under provincial law are different and are set out in *Best v Best*, [1999] 2 SCR 868.
471 *Pension Benefits Division Act*, s 8(1) and (4). See also *Eddie*, above note 470.

Employees in the federal public service usually rely on the employer's pension experts to explain the pension scheme, including the pension benefits an employee would receive upon retirement on different dates and advice about their ability to "buy back" pensionable service acquired for a different employer. The federal government has been held liable when the advice it gave was incorrect.

The leading decision concerning erroneous advice is *Spinks v Canada*.[472] Mr. Spinks worked for about twenty years as a nuclear engineer for the Australian Atomic Energy Commission. In 1967, he came to Canada on a two-year secondment and then returned to Australia. However, shortly after his return, Australia decided not to pursue a nuclear power program. Mr. Spinks applied for work to Atomic Energy of Canada Limited and was hired and emigrated to Canada in 1972. Upon arriving for his first day of work, Mr. Spinks was presented with some information about his pension rights. He was not told, and did not know, that he could elect to count prior employment service with the Australian government for the purposes of his Canadian superannuation benefits, provided that he paid a fairly small amount of money. Mr. Spinks eventually discovered in 1986 that he could "buy back" his Australian service. When he asked his employer about this option, he was told that the buyback would cost $201,697.48. Mr. Spinks eventually brought an action against his employer as a result of their failure to inform him of his pension rights back in 1972.

The Federal Court of Appeal allowed the action on two grounds. First, section 42(10) of the *Public Service Superannuation Act* contains a provision for "erroneous advice" concerning the ability to buy back pension time.

Essentially, the *Public Service Superannuation Regulations* enacted pursuant to section 42(10) state that the minister may permit an employee who received erroneous advice to "buy back" his previous service at the price that it would have cost had the employee not received erroneous advice. In Mr. Spinks's case, this would have meant that he could buy back his pension at the 1972 cost, not the (much higher) 1986 cost. However, the minister refused Mr. Spinks's application, stating that he had not received "erroneous advice": he had simply received no advice at all. The Federal Court of Appeal disagreed with this narrow definition of "erroneous advice" and concluded that

472 *Spinks v Canada*, [1996] FCJ No 352 (CA).

"the failure to divulge material information" is also erroneous advice.[473] Therefore, the minister should have allowed Mr. Spinks to buy back his Australian pensionable service at the 1972 rate.

Second, the Federal Court of Appeal concluded that the employer was liable in tort for negligent misrepresentation. The tort of negligent misrepresentation has five elements: (1) there must be a duty of care based on a "special relationship" between the representor and the representee; (2) the representation in question must be untrue, inaccurate, or misleading; (3) the representor must have acted negligently in making said representation; (4) the representee must have relied, in a reasonable manner, on said negligent misrepresentation; and (5) the reliance must have been detrimental to the representee in the sense that damages resulted.[474] The Federal Court of Appeal concluded that all five elements were present in this case. Mr. Spinks was in a position of complete reliance on his employer for the pension information he needed, so there was a duty of care. Mr. Spinks was misled by the missing information about his ability to buy back his Australian service, which amounted to a misleading representation. The employer was negligent and should have recognized Mr. Spinks's unique needs and the necessity of informing him of his right to buy back his Australian service. Mr. Spinks reasonably relied on the employer for pension information and suffered damages as a result of his reliance (in that he now had a lower pension). Therefore, the Court of Appeal ordered that either the minister allow Mr. Spinks to buy back his Australian service at the 1972 rate or that the employer pay Mr. Spinks damages to compensate him for the increase in the cost of buying back his Australian service.

In *Gauthier v Canada (Attorney General)*,[475] Mr. Gauthier was a member of the RCMP. Mr. Gauthier's case did not involve advice about the counting of service, and in any event the *Royal Canadian Mounted Police Superannuation Act* does not contain a provision respecting "erroneous advice"; therefore, Mr. Gauthier's claim was decided purely on the basis of negligent misrepresentation. Mr. Gauthier had worked for the Canadian military and then the RCMP for a number of years. In 1988, he became interested in a job with Canada Customs. The job involved a reduction in pay, so Mr. Gauthier wanted to know his

473 *Ibid* at para 14.

474 *Queen v Cognos Inc*, [1993] 1 SCR 87.

475 *Gauthier v Canada (Attorney General)*, [2000] NBJ No 143 (CA).

pension benefits if he retired from his position with the RCMP — essentially, to make sure that his income did not drop too precipitously. He consulted the Compensation Branch of the RCMP, which calculated his pension benefit without considering the penalty for retirement prior to twenty-five years of service. He was told that his annual pension would be $20,157.94; in actual fact, that pension was overstated by about $3,000 a year. Mr. Gauthier retired from the RCMP and took the job with Canada Customs. The RCMP paid him the higher pension benefit for approximately eight years, at which point they discovered their "administrative" error. They stopped paying Mr. Gauthier the higher pension and demanded that he repay $32,033.93 to them.

Mr. Gauthier successfully claimed damages for negligent misrepresentation. The New Brunswick Court of Appeal concluded that the Compensation Branch was required to exercise "reasonable care and diligence to ensure that their representations to Mr. Gauthier were accurate." It was no excuse that the miscalculation was made honestly. However, Mr. Gauthier was not entitled to a pension at the $20,157.94 rate. Instead, the Court of Appeal measured the damages by putting Mr. Gauthier back into the situation he would have been in but for the negligent advice — that is, if he would have continued working for the RCMP (rather than Canada Customs) until he retired in 1991. The damages amounted to $78,386.60, reflecting the higher pay he would have received at the RCMP and his higher pension upon retirement, less the amount of "extra" pension he received in error.[476]

476 On this topic, see also *Bresson v Canada (Chambre des communes)*, (2003) 42 CCPB 33 (Ont SCJ).

CHAPTER TEN

Resolution of Rights Disputes

A. INTRODUCTION

One of the eccentricities of federal public service labour law is the method of resolution of rights disputes. Under most labour relations statutes, almost every possible subject of dispute may be grieved and then referred to binding third-party arbitration. The *Canada Labour Code*, for example, requires the parties to a collective agreement to refer "all differences between the parties . . . concerning [the collective agreement's] interpretation, application, administration or alleged contravention."[1] This provision — coupled with a long line of jurisprudence indicating that almost all workplace disputes arise under the collective agreement[2] — means that arbitrators have jurisdiction over just about every dispute that arises in the workplace.

In the federal public service, however, this is not the case. The *Federal Public Sector Labour Relations Act* (*FPSLRA*) limits the matters that are capable of being grieved and then places further limits on what grievances can be referred to adjudication. This chapter largely concerns those limits.

1 *Canada Labour Code*, RSC 1985, c L-2, s 57(1).

2 See, for example, *Weber v Ontario Hydro*, [1995] 2 SCR 929 [*Weber*], and *Northern Regional Health Authority v Horrocks*, 2021 SCC 42 [*Horrocks*].

B. INFORMAL CONFLICT MANAGEMENT SYSTEM

Section 207 of the *FPSLRA* requires any deputy head in the core public administration, subject to any policies or directives issued by the employer, to establish an informal conflict management system. Deputy heads must establish this system in consultation with bargaining agents representing employees in the portion of the public service for which they are the deputy head. Separate employers are not required to establish informal conflict management systems.

The *FPSLRA* does not define what an "informal conflict management system" is supposed to be. However, the Treasury Board's policy describing the informal conflict management system describes it as "a systematic approach to preventing conflict escalation by managing and resolving conflicts in the workplace quickly and constructively."[3]

An internal conflict management system is supposed to be more than just an alternative dispute resolution mechanism, however. As one commentator has put it:

> At first blush, most readers will assume that [section 207] simply means that departments must introduce "Alternative Dispute Resolution" ("ADR") at the front door of grievance and workplace complaint processes, and will conclude that their departments already meet the requirements.
>
> In fact, s. 207 goes well beyond ADR. The terminology "conflict management system" was chosen advisedly, because only a conflict management *system* approach will result in the desired new culture. Systems involve the development, support and use of *behaviours that prevent* unnecessarily destructive conflict ("conflict competence") and the proactive *management of the causes* of conflict. By specifying a systems approach in s. 207—and the involvement of employee representatives in its development—Canada has taken world leadership in the evolution of organizational conflict management.[4]

---

3 Government of Canada, "Getting to Know Informal Conflict Management System (ICMS)" (12 August 2008), online: www.canada.ca/en/government/publicservice/wellness-inclusion-diversity-public-service/harassment-violence/informal-conflict-management-system/getting-to-know-informal-conflict-management-systems-better.html.

4 Jennifer Lynch, "The Federal Public Service Modernization Act—State of the Art Innovations in Conflict Management," *Canadian Government Executive* (February 2004) at 27.

Departments and separate agencies in the federal government have all introduced informal conflict management systems. Their efficacy remains a matter of some debate, although early reports prepared by some departments indicated that employees were moderately satisfied with the results of informal conflict management.[5] Finally, most collective agreements in the federal public administration contain a provision stating that when an employee and an employer agree to use the informal conflict management system, this suspends the time limits for filing a grievance or taking some further step within the grievance process.

C. GRIEVANCES

The *FPSLRA* provides that almost all disputes between employees and employers within the federal public administration must be resolved using the grievance procedure. However, only a subset of grievances is capable of being referred to adjudication. The bulk of this chapter will explore these questions: what can be grieved, what need not be grieved (i.e., which disputes can be addressed in other forums), and what grievances can be adjudicated.

1) Matters That May Be Grieved

The right of an employee to grieve a particular issue or dispute is set out in section 208 of the *FPSLRA*. Section 208(1) of the *FPSLRA* sets out the broad subject matters of a grievance as follows:

> 208(1) Subject to subsections (2) to (7), an employee is entitled to present an individual grievance if he or she feels aggrieved
>
> (*a*) by the interpretation or application, in respect of the employee, of
>
> (i) a provision of a statute or regulation, or of a direction or other instrument made or issued by the employer, that deals with terms and conditions of employment, or
>
> (ii) a provision of a collective agreement or an arbitral award; or

---

5 See, for example, Department of Justice, "Informal Conflict Management System Evaluation Final Report" (May 2010), online (pdf): www.justice.gc.ca/eng/rp-pr/cp-pm/eval/rep-rap/11/icms-sgice/icms-sgice.pdf, and Agriculture and Agri-Food Canada, "Evaluation of Informal Conflict Management Services Offered by AAFC's Office of Conflict Resolution" (9 June 2009), online (pdf): https://publications.gc.ca/collections/collection_2010/agr/A22-497-2009-eng.pdf.

> (*b*) as a result of any occurrence or matter affecting his or her terms and conditions of employment.

In essence, section 208(1) begins with the proposition that an employee may grieve anything concerning their terms and conditions of employment. As discussed in Chapter 6, the *FPSLRA* does not define the term "term and condition of employment." The Supreme Court of Canada, in addressing different labour relations statutes, has stated that a provision may be "characterized as a condition of employment on the basis that it had a real connection with the contract of employment."[6] Thus, this particular requirement is not a significant barrier to filing a grievance. Decisions involving section 208(1) of the *FPSLRA* have taken a similarly broad view of what constitutes a "term and condition of employment." For example, it includes the terms of a memorandum of understanding between a bargaining agent and an employer about the processing of other, earlier grievances;[7] a revocation of an employee's reliability status;[8] findings of wrongdoing under the values and ethics code or conflict of interest policies;[9] an allegation that the employer has violated those same policies;[10] and allegations of discrimination or psychological harassment in the workplace.[11]

Sections 208(2) through (6) of the *FPSLRA* then go on to list five exceptions to the general rule that all disputes concerning terms and conditions of employment may be grieved. Those exceptions, in order, are as follows:

> 208 (2) An employee may not present an individual grievance in respect of which an administrative procedure for redress is provided under any Act of Parliament, other than the *Canadian Human Rights Act*.
>
> (3) Despite subsection (2), an employee may not present an individual grievance in respect of the right to equal pay for work of equal value.
>
> (4) An employee may not present an individual grievance relating to the interpretation or application, in respect of the employee, of a provision of a collective agreement or an arbitral award unless the employee has the approval of and is represented by the bargaining

6 *Isidore Garon Ltee v Tremblay*, [2006] SCJ No 3 at para 26.

7 *Public Service Alliance of Canada v Canada (Attorney General)*, 2020 FC 481.

8 *Varin v Canada (Public Works and Government Services Canada)*, 2016 FC 213.

9 *McCarthy v Canada (Attorney General)*, 2020 FC 930.

10 *Burlacu v Canada (Attorney General)*, 2021 FC 610.

11 *Chamberlain v Canada (Attorney General)*, 2012 FC 1027 [*Chamberlain*].

> agent for the bargaining unit to which the collective agreement or arbitral award applies.
>
> (5) An employee who, in respect of any matter, avails himself or herself of a complaint procedure established by a policy of the employer may not present an individual grievance in respect of that matter if the policy expressly provides that an employee who avails himself or herself of the complaint procedure is precluded from presenting an individual grievance under this Act.
>
> (6) An employee may not present an individual grievance relating to any action taken under any instruction, direction or regulation given or made by or on behalf of the Government of Canada in the interest of the safety or security of Canada or any state allied or associated with Canada.

These limitations will be addressed below, followed by a discussion of other limitations found outside of section 208 and other rules relating to the grievance process.

2) Limitations on the Grievance Process

a) Alternative Procedure for Redress Provided Under an Act of Parliament (208(2)) and Policy for Redress (208(5))

Section 208(2) of the *FPSLRA* prevents employees from blocking an individual grievance "in respect of which an administrative procedure for redress is provided under any Act of Parliament, other than the *Canadian Human Rights Act*." The Federal Court of Appeal has explained the purpose behind this limitation as follows:

> This Court and the Trial Division of this Court has consistently taken the view that Parliament, by the language used in the section, intended to remove from the normal grievance procedures under the *PSSRA* certain specialized areas which it was thought should be dealt with under the administrative process set out in the legislation governing those particular areas.[12]

Under section 208(2), a grievance may not be presented if it relates to a matter where an administrative procedure for redress is provided under any Act of Parliament. Where a procedure is so provided under which an employee's grievance may be redressed, the aggrieved

12 *Canada (Treasury Board) v Boutilier*, [1999] FCJ No 1867 (CA) at para 3 [*Boutilier*].

employee cannot resort to the grievance procedure under section 208 of the *FPSLRA* but must instead submit their complaint to the authority that has, under the appropriate statute, the power to deal with it. An employee who is dissatisfied with the decision of that authority may not file a grievance in respect of that decision.

By limiting access to the grievance procedure in this way, Parliament has sought to ensure that disputes are resolved by the specialists in those particular areas. While decision-making by specialists is a worthy policy objective, it has led to difficulties in the federal public service. As noted by the Fryer Report, "In the public service today, there is a bewildering array of mechanisms for resolving disputes between individuals and the employer.... The existing system is inefficient.... The system is also complex."[13] There were (when that report was written) at least six different mechanisms for recourse by Treasury Board employees, and the chart attempting to summarize and explain those methods of recourse spanned seven pages.[14] This bewildering array of recourse procedures lead to delays as employees attempt to determine which avenue of recourse to pursue and can also lead to a game of "jurisdictional roulette" as claimants try to find some administrative agency that will take jurisdiction over their complaint.

The administrative recourse need not provide the same remedies or procedure as the grievance procedure, but it does need to result in a "real" remedy[15] or in "some redress" for the employee.[16] The alternative recourse needs to offer "real and beneficial redress" to the grievor.[17] There is some dispute over whether this means that when the grievance makes a claim for damages, the alternative administrative recourse must also be capable of paying damages or some other form of financial redress. In *Galarneau v Treasury Board (Correctional Service of Canada)*, the Board concluded that the alternative redress must be capable of paying damages when the substance of the grievance includes a

13 Final Report of the Advisory Committee on Labour Management Relations in the Federal Public Service, *Working Together in the Public Interest* (Ottawa: Treasury Board, 2001), s 5.1, online (pdf): https://publications.gc.ca/collections/collection_2011/sct-tbs/BT22-70-1-2001-eng.pdf [Fryer Report].

14 Public Service Commission, "Recourse and Redress in the Public Service" (June 2000), online: http://pscac-cccfp.gc.ca/publications/rpt_redress_e.php.

15 *Ibid.*

16 *Byers Transport Ltd v Kosanovich*, [1995] 3 FC 354 (CA).

17 *Galarneau v Treasury Board (Correctional Service of Canada)*, 2009 PSLRB 70 at para 58 [*Galarneau*].

claim for damages;[18] however, the Federal Court of Appeal, in a decision decided shortly after *Galarneau*, required only that the alternative forum provide real redress that was of personal benefit to the grievor, without stating specifically whether this real redress had to include damages.[19] The Board also concluded that *Galarneau* only applied where the claim for damages was an essential component of the grievance; where the essence of the grievance concerned a health and safety issue and the damages were merely incidental, the alternative redress was adequate, and the issue was outside the scope of the grievance procedure.[20]

A similar provision existed in the 1967 version of the *Public Service Staff Relations Act* (*PSSRA*). In his testimony before the Special Joint Committee of the Senate and the House of Commons on employer–employee relations in the Public Service of Canada, Dr. Davidson (then president of the Treasury Board) only mentioned the *Public Service Employment Act* (*PSEA*)[21] when discussing the scope of that provision. Thus, there is little controversy that complaints about appointments that violate the merit principle may not be addressed through the grievance procedure, but must be addressed through the mechanism set up in the *PSEA*.[22] The Board has also concluded that this principle applies to the staffing process more generally—for example, the decision to use a performance evaluation in a staffing process was not grievable, even though the performance evaluation at issue may have violated the collective agreement.[23] The Board in that case characterized the issue as about ensuring the division between "two self-contained and mutually exclusive spheres of labour relations and staffing."[24] The Board in later cases made it clear that the dividing line between these mutually

18 *Ibid* at para 60.

19 *Johal v Canada Revenue Agency*, 2009 FCA 276 at para 35.

20 *Public Service Alliance of Canada v Treasury Board (Department of Human Resources and Skills Development)*, 2012 PSLRB 84 [*PSAC v Treasury Board (HRSD)*].

21 *Public Service Employment Act*, SC 2003, c 22, ss 12, 13, s 61(1) [*PSEA*].

22 See, for example, *Brown v Canada (Attorney General)*, 2011 FC 1205. This also means that an adjudicator or a grievance officer does not have the jurisdiction to make appointments to the public service as a remedy in a grievance. However, it is within an adjudicator's jurisdiction to order the employer to offer a grievor suitable employment as a remedy in a complaint that the employer has failed to accommodate the grievor's disability to the point of undue hardship: see *Witherspoon v Treasury Board (Department of National Defence)*, 2006 PSLRB 102.

23 *Pelletier et al v Treasury Board (Department of Human Resources and Skills Development)*, 2011 PSLRB 117.

24 *Ibid* at para 43.

exclusive spheres was not as clear as that quotation makes it appear. For example, an employee may grieve the failure to offer an acting position (quintessentially a staffing issue) when the pith and substance of the grievance violate the no-discrimination clause in the collective agreement—although, in that case, the acting position was less than the four-month minimum that would have allowed the complainant to file a complaint under the *PSEA*.[25] Similarly, an employee may file a grievance alleging a breach of the *Work Force Adjustment Directive* (about processes and entitlements upon layoff) even when the alleged breaches of that directive also touch upon staffing issues.[26]

Subsequent court and board decisions have clearly stated that section 208(2) extends beyond the *PSEA*.

This book has already discussed this provision (in Chapter 7) and explained that "any Act of Parliament" includes the *FPSLRA* itself. Thus, if a matter may be presented as an unfair labour practice complaint to the Board, it may not be presented by way of grievance.[27]

Prior to 2005, the *FPSLRA* (more accurately the *PSSRA*, as it then was) contained a similar provision that did not explicitly exempt the *Canadian Human Rights Act* from its ambit. The Federal Court of Appeal has also concluded that "any Act of Parliament" included the *Canadian Human Rights Act*.[28] Therefore, if a purported grievance involves a complaint of discriminatory practice, even in the context of the interpretation of a collective agreement, the matter must be referred to the Canadian Human Rights Commission. The 2005 amendments to the Act specifically overturned this decision so that human rights issues may be grieved.

Whether the processes set out under the *Canada Occupational Health and Safety Regulations* (*OHS Regs*)[29] and the *Work Place Harassment and Violence Prevention Regulations*[30] are an alternative procedure for redress remains to be conclusively determined. In *Chickoski v Canada (Attorney General)*,[31] the department dismissed a grievance alleging that

---

25 *Haynes v Treasury Board (Canada Border Services Agency)*, 2013 PSLRB 85 at para 30.

26 *Santawirya v Deputy Head (Canada Border Services Agency)*, 2017 FPSLREB 10, set aside on other grounds in *Canada (Attorney General) v Santawirya*, 2019 FCA 248 [*Santawirya*].

27 *Ryan v Canada (Attorney General)*, [2005] FCJ No 110.

28 *Boutilier*, above note 12.

29 *Canada Occupational Health and Safety Regulations*, SOR/86-304 [*OHS Regs*].

30 *Work Place Harassment and Violence Prevention Regulations*, SOR/2020-130.

31 *Chickoski v Canada (Attorney General)*, 2017 FC 772.

the grievor had been the subject of workplace harassment and violence in the form of psychological bullying on the basis that this complaint could (and therefore must) be addressed using the *OHS Regs*, which, at the time, included workplace harassment within their ambit. The Federal Court quashed that decision because the final-level grievance decision failed to adequately explain whether the *OHS Regs* provided a personal remedy to the complainant. While the Federal Court stated that it had "serious doubts that the remedies available under the *OHS Regs* are capable of producing some real redress,"[32] it did not definitely make that conclusion and, instead, set aside the grievance decision because the decision did not adequately address this point. Two of the cases about the availability of damages discussed above[33] were *OHS Regs* cases that did not dispositively address this issue either.[34]

The procedure for redress under the *Government Employees Compensation Act*[35] is excluded by section 208(2) of the *FPSLRA*. This means that claims based solely on work-related illnesses and accidents are outside the jurisdiction of the grievance procedure and, instead, fall to be determined using the normal workers' compensation regime available for public servants.[36] This does not preclude claims alleging that the employer failed to accommodate a disability sustained at the workplace, but an employee may not grieve (and claim redress) for the injury itself.

The Board has also concluded in one case that the complaint procedure under the *Access to Information Act*[37] is not a forum for redress that bars a grievance. In that case, a professor at the Royal Military College of Canada grieved to obtain an order that his personal course notes were not "a record under the control of [the] institution" under the *Access to Information Act* and, therefore, he did not have to provide copies of those course notes in response to a request made under that Act. The employer argued that the procedure under the *Access to Information Act*—which allows the information commissioner to receive and investigate complaints—barred the grievance. The Board disagreed, stating

32 *Ibid* at para 89.

33 *Galarneau*, above note 17, and *PSAC v Treasury Board (HRSD)*, above note 20.

34 The Federal Court also mentioned this issue while refusing to provide an answer in *Karn v Canada (Attorney General)*, 2017 FC 123.

35 *Government Employees Compensation Act*, RSC 1985, c G-5.

36 *Cyr v Treasury Board (Department of Human Resources and Skills Development)*, 2011 PSLRB 35 at para 58; *Miller v Treasury Board (Correctional Service of Canada)*, 2013 PSLRB 164 at para 86.

37 *Access to Information Act*, RSC 1985, c A-1.

that the grievor's entire case was predicated on the position that his course notes were exempt from the *Access to Information Act*; therefore, the complaint procedure under that Act was not an administrative process as contemplated by section 208(2) of the *FPSLRA*.[38]

Adjudicators have also had to determine their jurisdiction over a separate agency's internal recourse mechanisms concerning staffing issues (issues dealt with under the *PSEA* for Treasury Board employees). Both the Canada Revenue Agency (CRA) and the Canadian Food Inspection Agency (CFIA) have enacted staffing policies under the powers over staffing granted to them in their enabling statutes. However, those policies do not automatically mean that employees may not grieve staffing matters.

The *Canada Revenue Agency Act* (*CRA Act*) requires the employer to develop a staffing program: "The Agency must develop a program governing staffing, including the appointment of, and recourse for, employees."[39] An adjudicator in *Dhudwal v Canada Customs and Revenue Agency* concluded that the employer "has established a staffing program with staffing recourse under section 54 of the *CRA Act*. The evidence is also that this staffing recourse does provide an administrative procedure for redress."[40] In *Dhudwal*, employees dissatisfied with the recourse available under this policy filed a grievance; however, the adjudicator concluded that he did not have jurisdiction to hear the grievance because the CRA's method of recourse was an alternative procedure for redress under an Act of Parliament.[41]

The CRA's internal recourse mechanism does not foreclose grievances on all topics. That recourse mechanism also deals with recourse for employees rejected on probation. The CRA's jurisdiction to reject employees on probation is governed by section 51(1)(e) of the *CRA Act*, not section 54. Therefore, the adjudicator in *Lundin v Canada Customs and Revenue Agency*[42] concluded that the recourse mechanism was not established "under" the *CRA Act* when it dealt with rejection

---

38 *Lukits v Treasury Board (Department of National Defence)*, 2017 PSLREB 6.

39 *Canada Revenue Agency Act*, SC 1999, c 17, s 54(1) [*CRA Act*]. For a discussion of this staffing recourse procedure, see Chapter 11.

40 *Dhudwal v Canada Customs and Revenue Agency*, [2003] CPSSRB No 96 at para 23 [*Dhudwal*].

41 See also *Sherman v Canada (Customs and Revenue Agency)*, [2005] FCJ No 209 at para 24.

42 *Lundin v Canada Customs and Revenue Agency*, [2004] CPSSRB No 151.

on probation (as opposed to staffing matters). The adjudicator also concluded that the CRA's recourse mechanism did not provide a real method of recourse because it did not include the possibility of reinstatement after a rejection on probation and did not result in recourse to an independent third party.[43]

In *Melnichouk v Canadian Food Inspection Agency*,[44] an adjudicator concluded that the CFIA's internal staffing recourse mechanism did not bar grievances. Section 13 of the *Canadian Food Inspection Agency Act* (*CFIA Act*) states that "[t]he President may set the terms and conditions of employment for employees of the Agency and assign duties to them."[45] The employer argued that its policy was enacted "pursuant to" the *CFIA Act* and thereby triggered the statutory exception. The adjudicator rejected that argument, recognizing that all executive acts are done "pursuant to" some statutory authority. The *FPSLRA* requires more: it requires that the recourse be "provided under an Act of Parliament." Since there is no express authority under the *CFIA Act* to establish a recourse procedure, the CFIA's recourse policy does not constitute an administrative procedure for redress "provided under" an Act of Parliament.

Melnichouk was decided under the *PSSRA*, which did not have the equivalent to section 208(5). That provision, as quoted above, states that an employee may not present a grievance after first presenting a complaint using an internal employer policy where the policy expressly provided that a complainant may not also grieve. Therefore, if an internal recourse procedure explicitly stated that the process ousts the grievance procedure, then an employee who begins using that procedure may not later file a grievance. Section 208(5) of the *FPSLRA* does not prevent an employee from filing a grievance at the outset, however, instead of using the internal policy in question.

b) Bargaining Agent Approval and Representation for Grievances Alleging a Breach of the Collective Agreement (208(4))

The parties to a collective agreement are the bargaining agent and the employer; individual employees are not a party to a collective agreement. In most unionized workplaces, this means that individual employees

43 *Ibid* at paras 82–86. The Board later affirmed this decision in a similar case in *Lavoie v Canada Revenue Agency*, 2011 PSLRB 91.

44 *Melnichouk v Canadian Food Inspection Agency*, [2004] CPSSRB No 167.

45 *Canadian Food Inspection Agency Act*, SC 1997, c 6, s 13(2) [*CFIA Act*].

do not have the right to file grievances against their employer or refer grievances to arbitration; that right is reserved exclusively for the bargaining agent.

The regime set out in section 208(4) of the *FPSLRA* is different because it states that the individual employee—not the bargaining agent—is the party who commences the grievance. This means that the parties to the grievance are the individual grievors and the employer; the bargaining agent is not a party.[46] However, the bargaining agent is still responsible for interpreting and enforcing the collective agreement. Section 208(4) of the *FPSLRA*—and a similar provision in section 209(2) of the Act requiring union approval and representation to refer collective agreement grievances to adjudication—is designed to ensure that bargaining agents retain control over the interpretation and application of the collective agreement.[47]

The Board has also interpreted sections 208(5) and 209(2) to mean not only that the bargaining agent has to approve the grievance and be the employee's representative in the sense of their certified bargaining agent, but also that the bargaining agent has to actively represent the grievor at each stage of the grievance process, including adjudication. The bargaining agent cannot simply approve of the grievance at the point it is filed or at the point it is referred to adjudication; it must continue to represent the grievor throughout.[48] This requirement of representation does not, however, extend to judicial review of an adjudication award, and an individual grievor has standing to judicially review the Board's decision dismissing their grievance without the participation of their bargaining agent.[49]

c) Security Issues (208(6))

The *FPSLRA* prohibits employees from filing grievances relating to any action taken under any instruction, direction, or regulation given or made by or on behalf of the Government of Canada in the interest of the safety or security of Canada or any state allied or associated with Canada.[50] For the purposes of that exclusion, an order made by

---

46 *Insch v Canada (Attorney General)*, 2019 FCA 211 at para 31 [*Insch*].

47 *Sousa-Dias v Public Service Alliance of Canada*, 2018 FPSLREB 46 at para 71; *Cavanagh v Canada Revenue Agency*, 2014 PSLRB 21 at para 24.

48 *Cavanagh*, *ibid*.

49 *Insch*, above note 46.

50 *FPSLRA*, s 208(6).

the Governor in Council is conclusive proof of the matters stated in the order in relation to those security concerns.[51] In other words, an employee cannot use the grievance procedure to challenge the factual content or conclusions in an order of the Governor in Council concerning safety and security issues. The proper interpretation of section 208(6) of the *FPSLRA* has not yet been litigated.[52]

3) Timeliness of the Grievance

The procedure for filing a grievance—including any time limits—may be set out in a collective agreement; if it is not, then the *Federal Public Sector Labour Relations Regulations* (*FPSLR Regulations*)[53] stipulate the grievance procedure to be followed.[54] The *FPSLR Regulations* require a grievance to be filed at first level within thirty-five days after the earlier of the day on which the grievor received notification and the day on which the grievor had knowledge of the alleged violation or misinterpretation or any occurrence or matter affecting the grievor's terms and conditions of employment.[55] Many collective agreements stipulate twenty-five-day deadlines to file a grievance; however, those agreements also define "day" to mean a working day so that the deadlines are almost always five weeks whether under the collective agreement or the *FPSLR Regulations*. The grievor then has fifteen days to refer the grievance up to the next level after receiving a decision at the lower level, or forty days from the date that they should have received a decision at that particular level.[56] After the final-level grievance decision, the

51 *FPSLRA*, s 208(7).

52 In *Bergey v Canada (Attorney General)*, 2017 FCA 30 [*Bergey*], the Federal Court of Appeal suggested that s 208(6) would have the effect that employees could not grieve the denial or removal of a security clearance, although that statement was clearly made in *obiter* and was not expanded on in a meaningful way.

53 *Federal Public Sector Labour Relations Regulations*, SOR/2005-79 [*FPSLR Regulations*].

54 *FPSLRA*, s 237(2). See also *Pannu v Treasury Board (Correctional Service of Canada)*, 2020 FPSLREB 4 at para 27: "The grievance procedure in the federal public service is governed by the Act, the *Regulations*, and any group-specific collective agreement that may be entered into between an authorized bargaining agent and the employer with respect to employees in a particular bargaining unit."

55 *FPSLR Regulations*, s 68(1).

56 *Ibid*, s 68(2). The employer has twenty days to respond to a grievance, unless it is a classification grievance, in which case it has eighty days: *FPSLR Regulations*, s 72.

grievor has another forty days to refer the matter to adjudication.[57] The timelines under the *FPSLR Regulations* are the same for group grievances and policy grievances.[58]

These time limits to file grievances (and refer the grievances to the next level) are mandatory and not directory, meaning that non-compliance with the time limit results in the dismissal of the grievance.[59]

The deadline to file a grievance occurs when the matter being grieved has crystallized. This date occurs when the employer announces its decision, not when the employer acts on its decision. Thus, an "unequivocal and clearly communicated decision by the employer to take action" triggers the right to grieve and also triggers the time limit for a grievance.[60]

If a grievor or bargaining agent misses a time limit for filing a grievance, there are certain avenues of recourse. First, they can ask the employer to voluntarily extend the time limit for filing a grievance.[61] If the employer refuses, then the grievor or bargaining agent may apply to the Board for an extension of time to file the grievance "in the interests of fairness."[62] While these requests are technically a separate filing, in practice they are typically filed at the same time as a referral to adjudication, and the Board assigns the same member to hear the grievance (as an adjudicator) and the request for an extension of time (as a member of the Board). The request for an extension of time is also typically heard simultaneously with the grievance.

The Board's jurisprudence concerning extensions of time establishes five criteria for granting an extension of time:

- the presence of a clear, cogent, and compelling reason for the delay
- the length of the delay
- the due diligence of the grievor
- balancing the injustice to the grievor against the prejudice to the employer in granting an extension
- the chance of success of the grievance

---

57 *Ibid*, s 90.

58 *Ibid*, ss 78 and 85.

59 *Trenholm v Staff of the Non-Public Funds, Canadian Forces*, 2005 PSLRB 65; *Duncan v National Research Council of Canada*, 2016 PSLREB 75.

60 *Prévost v Office of the Superintendent of Financial Institutions*, 2011 PSLRB 119 at para 87.

61 *FPSLR Regulations*, s 61(a).

62 *Ibid*, s 61(b).

These criteria are not necessarily of equal importance in every case and are weighted differently depending on the circumstances. In some cases, the Board will not consider certain factors when the remaining factors weigh heavily for or against the extension of time. The underlying purpose behind these factors is to act in the interests of fairness.[63]

The Board considers attempts to resolve matters informally as an insufficient reason to extend the time limits of the grievance procedure.[64] The Board expects that parties will file a grievance, and then attempt to resolve it informally, while still respecting all of the time limits set in the *FPSLR Regulations* or collective agreement. The *FPSLR Regulations* provide some relief against this view by stating that the time limits are suspended if the parties avail themselves of an informal conflict management system established pursuant to section 207 of the *FPSLRA*.[65] The Board has accepted health-related concerns as a compelling explanation for a delay when there is a link between the grievor's health and their ability to meet the grievance deadline.[66] The Board has also accepted poor advice from a bargaining agent or legal counsel as a sufficient explanation for delay.[67] Finally, grievors have applied for an extension of time on the basis that they needed more time to obtain the documents required to properly prepare or argue their grievance. The Board will review this explanation by assessing whether the documents are or were truly necessary to prepare and argue their grievance.[68]

In examining the final factor, the Board used to consider whether there was a "serious" chance of success of a grievance but now prefers to determine whether there is "no chance" of the grievance succeeding.[69]

---

63 *Apenteng v Treasury Board (Canada Border Services Agency)*, 2014 PSLRB 19 at para 88.

64 *Pomerleau v Treasury Board (Canadian International Development Agency)*, [2005] CPSLRB No 130; *Popov v Canadian Space Agency*, 2018 FPSLREB 49 at para 67 [*Popov*]; *Slivinski v Treasury Board (Statistics Canada)*, 2021 FPSLREB 35 at para 210.

65 *FPSLR Regulations*, s 62.

66 *Riche v Treasury Board*, 2009 PSLRB 157 (extension granted); *Popov*, above note 64 (extension not granted).

67 *Cowman v Treasury Board (Department of Transport)*, 2021 FPSLREB 36.

68 *Gagnon v Treasury Board (Department of Public Works and Government Services)*, 2021 FPSLREB 83.

69 *Schenkman v Treasury Board (Public Works and Government Services Canada)*, [2004] CPSSRB No 1 [*Schenkman*]; *Chow v Treasury Board (Public Health Agency of Canada)*, 2015 PSLREB 81 at para 36.

If an employer wishes to object to the timeliness of a grievance, it must do so immediately at the first level of the grievance process and also at each subsequent level.[70] If the employer fails to object to the timeliness of a grievance at the first level and at each subsequent level, it has waived its right to object later to the timeliness of the grievance.

A grievance that is untimely on its face may be timely if it involves a continuing breach of the collective agreement. This occurs most often in grievances involving pay calculations: each paycheque that is wrong is a new breach of the collective agreement and therefore may give rise to a new grievance. When this occurs, the grievance is still processed; however, any remedy is only retroactive to thirty-five days (or such other time period set out in the collective agreement) prior to the date the grievance was filed.[71]

Finally, the employer also has deadlines to follow to respond to grievances: twenty days in most cases, but eighty days for classification grievances.[72] If the employer does not comply with those deadlines, the grievor has a thirty-day window of time in which to refer their grievance to the next level[73] or to adjudication if the grievance is at the final level.[74] The employer's failure to respond to a grievance in a timely fashion does not prevent the employer from defending the grievance at adjudication,[75] nor is there any other real penalty or consequence if the employer does not respond to a grievance in a timely fashion. On the other hand, if the employer does not respond to the grievance, then the Board may still be seized with that grievance if the grievor has referred it to the Board; the requirement is that a grievor "present" the grievance, not that the grievor wait for the employer to make its decision.[76]

---

70 *FPSLR Regulations*, s 63; *LeFebvre v Treasury Board (Correctional Service of Canada)*, 2020 FPSLREB 87.

71 *Canada (National Film Board) v Coallier*, [1983] FCJ No 813 (CA); *Camilleri v Canada Customs and Revenue Agency*, [2003] CPSSRB No 74; *Moyes and Treasury Board (Revenue Canada—Customs and Excise)*, [1994] CPSSRB No 18.

72 *FPSLR Regulations*, s 72.

73 *Ibid*, s 73(1)(b).

74 *Ibid*, s 76(1).

75 *Elliot v Deputy Head (Correctional Service of Canada)*, 2019 FPSLREB 4 [*Elliot*].

76 *Union of Canadian Correctional Officers—Syndicat des agents correctionnels du Canada—CSN v Treasury Board (Correctional Service of Canada)*, 2022 FPSLREB 38.

4) The Wording of the Grievance

Arbitrators generally will refuse to address issues that were not first raised in the grievance procedure; the Board is no different in this regard. Decisions in the federal public service, though, have a difficult time balancing two competing principles.

First, there is a broader principle that adjudicators should not insist upon specific language in a grievance but, instead, should hear the grievance so long as the real dispute between the parties is captured in the grievance. The Ontario Court of Appeal (in a passage adopted by the Supreme Court of Canada) has stated:

> Certainly, the Board is bound by the grievance before it but the grievance should be liberally construed so that the real complaint is dealt with and the appropriate remedy provided to give effect to the agreement provisions and this whether by way of declaration of rights or duties, in order to provide benefits or performance of obligations or a monetary award required to restore one to the proper position he would have been in had the agreement been performed.[77]

Second, not every grievance is capable of being referred to adjudication (as discussed below). A grievor cannot clothe an adjudicator with jurisdiction by fundamentally changing the nature of their grievance at adjudication. This principle was articulated by the Federal Court of Appeal in *Burchill v Canada (Attorney General)*. In that case, the grievor did not specify in his grievance that he considered his dismissal to be disguised discipline. The grievor attempted to refer his grievance to adjudication, but the adjudicator rejected it because the grievance did not refer to the allegation of disguised discipline. The Court agreed with that rejection, stating:

> [I]t was not open to the applicant, after losing at the final level of the grievance procedure the only grievance presented, either to refer to a new or different grievance to adjudication or to turn the grievance so presented into a grievance complaining of disciplinary action leading to discharge within the meaning of subsection 91(1).... In our view, the applicant having failed to set out in his grievance the complaint

77 *Re Blouin Drywall Contractors Ltd. and United Brotherhood of Carpenters and Joiners of America, Local 2486* (1975), 8 OR (2d) 103 (CA) at 108, cited in *Parry Sound (District) Social Services Administration Board v OPSEU, Local 324*, 2003 SCC 42 at para 68 [*Parry Sound*].

> upon which he sought to rely before the Adjudicator, namely, that his being laid off was really a camouflaged disciplinary action, the foundation for clothing the Adjudicator with jurisdiction under subsection 91(1) was not laid. Consequently, he had no such jurisdiction.[78]

In another similar case, the Federal Court confirmed that if the grievance did not specifically use the phrase "financial penalty," the adjudicator did not have jurisdiction to hear the grievance regardless of whether there was in fact a financial penalty.[79]

These two principles conflict from time to time in various cases. The Federal Court has attempted to reconcile these two principles as follows:

> The Court notes that the arbitral decisions referred to by the Supreme Court in *Parry Sound* ... establish that "the grievance should be liberally construed so that the real complaint is dealt with" (*Re Blouin Drywall Contractors Ltd. and United Brotherhood of Carpenters and Jeiners* [*sic*] *of America, Local 2486*, (1975) 1975 CanLII 707 (ON CA), 8 OR (2d) 103 (CA) at page 108) and, as stated by the Supreme Court of Canada in *Parry Sound*, ... at para 69, reflect the view that procedural requirements should not be stringently enforced in those instances in which the employer suffers no prejudice. The Court sees no inconsistencies with these principles and what the Federal Court of Appeal has decided in *Burchill* ... as long as the referral to adjudication under section 209 of the Act does not change the nature of the grievance originally filed by an employee or the bargaining agent under section 208 of the Act or the collective agreement.[80]

Despite the Court's effort to say that these two principles are not inconsistent, they act that way in practice, and employers frequently file "*Burchill* objections" to grievances, alleging that the grievor is improperly expanding the scope of the grievance at adjudication by asking for different remedies, advancing different arguments, or relying on different sections of the collective agreement. The Board often attempts to examine this issue in a common sense fashion by examining whether the employer knew what the grievance was about and whether it had the opportunity to address the issue during the grievance process in light of the wording of the grievance, the evidence of what was said

78 *Burchill v Canada (Attorney General)*, [1981] 1 FC 109 (CA) at para 5.
79 *Schofield v Canada (Attorney General)*, [2004] FCJ No 784.
80 *Boudreau v Canada (Attorney General)*, 2011 FC 868 at para 18.

during the grievance hearings, and a review of the employer's responses to the grievance.[81]

The *FPSLR Regulations* require the employer to prepare an individual grievance form for employees, setting out the information that must be provided by the grievor.[82] The employer may not reject a grievance simply because it does not use the grievance form, and a failure to use the form does not nullify the grievance.[83] The letter or other correspondence commencing the grievance must express an intention to grieve: a letter requesting an investigation is not sufficient to constitute a grievance.[84]

5) Response to the Grievance

While the *FPSLR Regulations* do not specify who is responsible for hearing grievances at each level, a collective agreement may do so. Collective agreements typically require the deputy head (or chief executive) or their delegate to respond to grievances at the final level; however, unless the agreement specifies the use of a delegate, the deputy head must personally confer with the grievor or representatives. This does not necessarily mean that the deputy head must sign the grievance, but they must "personally direct his attention to each grievance which reaches the final level [and] accept responsibility for the reply that is made regardless of whether he is the actual author."[85] Furthermore, where the collective agreement gives the bargaining agent or grievor the right to "consult" with the employer, this includes the right to meet directly (and communicate orally)[86] with the person responsible for giving the response at that particular level—even including the deputy head.[87] In other cases, though, where the collective agreement only sets out a right to "present" a grievance (or for all unrepresented employees), the actual decision-maker does not need to attend the grievance meeting

81 *Hurley v Treasury Board (Department of National Defence)*, 2018 FPSLREB 35 at para 264.

82 *FPSLR Regulations*, s 66.

83 *Perron v Treasury Board (Canada Border Services Agency)*, 2013 PSLRB 109 at para 18.

84 *Tuquabo v Canada (Revenue Agency)*, 2006 PSLRB 128, aff'd *Tuquabo v Canada (Attorney General)*, 2008 FCA 387.

85 *Public Service Alliance of Canada and Canada (Treasury Board)*, [1974] CPSSRB No 4 at para 37.

86 *Public Service Alliance of Canada and Treasury Board*, [1982] CPSSRB No 129.

87 *Ibid* at paras 30–31.

and can, instead, send a delegate to hear the grievance presentation and report back to them.[88]

6) Rights of Former Employees to File Grievances

The *FPSLRA* specifically addresses the standing of former employees. Section 206(2) of the *FPSLRA* states that the definition of "employee" for the purpose of standing to file a grievance includes a former employee for grievances with respect to disciplinary action resulting in a suspension or termination of employment. Notwithstanding section 206(2) of the Act, a former employee still has standing to file a grievance when the grievance concerns a rejection on probation or is related to matters that arose while the grievor was still employed in the federal public service.[89]

D. MATTERS THAT MAY BE REFERRED TO ADJUDICATION

Having restricted the matters that may be grieved, the *FPSLRA* then further restricts the matters that may be referred to adjudication. The relevant parts of sections 209 and 211 of the *FPSLRA* read as follows:

> 209(1) An employee who is not a member as defined in subsection 2(1) of the *Royal Canadian Mounted Police Act* may refer to adjudication an individual grievance that has been presented up to and including the final level in the grievance process and that has not been dealt with to the employee's satisfaction if the grievance is related to
> (a) the interpretation or application in respect of the employee of a provision of a collective agreement or an arbitral award;
> (b) a disciplinary action resulting in termination, demotion, suspension or financial penalty;
> (c) in the case of an employee in the core public administration,
> (i) demotion or termination under paragraph 12(1)(d) of the *Financial Administration Act* for unsatisfactory performance

88 *Association of Justice Counsel v Treasury Board*, 2016 PSLREB 48 (attendance by the decision-maker is not required when the collective agreement uses the word "present"), and *Hagel v Canada (Attorney General)*, 2009 FC 329, aff'd *Hagel v Canada (Attorney General)*, 2009 FCA 364, for the proposition that the rules of procedural fairness do not require the decision-maker to attend an oral grievance meeting.

89 *Salie v Canada (Attorney General)*, 2013 FC 122 at paras 58–68; *Santawirya*, above note 26 at para 11.

or under paragraph 12(1)(e) of that Act for any other reason that does not relate to a breach of discipline or misconduct, or

(ii) deployment under the *Public Service Employment Act* without the employee's consent where consent is required; or

(d) in the case of an employee of a separate agency designated under subsection (3), demotion or termination for any reason that does not relate to a breach of discipline or misconduct.

211 Nothing in section 209 or 209.1 is to be construed or applied as permitting the referral to adjudication of an individual grievance with respect to

(a) any termination of employment under the *Public Service Employment Act*; or

(b) any deployment under the *Public Service Employment Act*, other than the deployment of the employee who presented the grievance.

Section 209.1 of the *FPSLRA* also permits adjudications of claims by non-managerial employees under the *Accessible Canada Act*,[90] but the provision was only added in 2019, and, as of publication, no such grievances have been adjudicated.

The scope of matters that may be referred to adjudication under the *FPSLRA* is broader than under the old *PSSRA*. The original 1967 version of the *PSSRA* only permitted adjudication on the interpretation of a collective agreement or an arbitral award and disciplinary action resulting in discharge, suspension, or a financial penalty. After the 1992 *Public Service Reform Act*, employees of the Treasury Board could also refer termination of employment or demotion pursuant to then paragraph 11(2)(f) or (g) of the *Financial Administration Act* to adjudication.[91] Employees of separate employers still could only adjudicate collective agreement breaches and discipline resulting in termination, suspension, or a financial penalty. Section 211(a) of the *FPSLRA* was also added in the *Public Service Reform Act* (as section 92(3) of the *PSSRA*).

Unlike in the private sector, an adjudicator cannot assume jurisdiction over a grievance simply by consent of the parties alone.[92] The griev-

90 *Accessible Canada Act*, SC 2019, c 10.

91 *Financial Administration Act*, RSC 1985, c F-11.

92 See, for example, *Fok and Granger v Treasury Board (Department of Transport)*, 2006 PSLRB 93. In that case, the adjudicator refused to hear two grievances because the grievances were "prospective in nature" and "premature." The grievances involved a management order for the two grievors to use their annual leave

ance must be a matter that is capable of being grieved and referred to adjudication. Some of the common areas of dispute over the jurisdiction of an adjudicator have already been addressed above when discussing bargaining agent approval for grievances and the wording of grievances. This chapter will go through the other main areas of dispute over the jurisdiction of adjudicators as set out in those two sections.

1) Disciplinary Versus Administrative Actions

A threshold requirement for the Board's jurisdiction to hear a grievance under section 209(1)(b) of the *FPSLRA* is that the grievance must be related to a "disciplinary action." Not all actions on the part of an employer that have a negative impact on an employee are necessarily disciplinary in nature: some of those actions are simply administrative instead.[93] That said, the fact that many non-disciplinary matters fall outside the jurisdiction of the Board creates an incentive for an employer to characterize those actions as administrative instead of disciplinary in nature. These circumstances are commonly referred to as "disguised discipline"—namely, some action that is characterized as administrative but, in reality, is disciplinary in nature.

The concept of disguised discipline is easy to state but often difficult to apply in practice. In some cases, the employer has terminated an employee's employment or taken some other action without characterizing its decision as disciplinary. Instead, the employer will often characterize its decision as administrative in nature and not related to discipline. The employer will therefore argue that the grievance cannot be adjudicated. The concept of "disguised discipline" means simply that the employer's characterization of the reasons for the so-called "administrative" action is not binding and conclusive for the purposes of determining the jurisdiction of an adjudicator. An adjudicator has the

---

credits in excess of twenty-five days prior to the end of the fiscal year. Management eventually agreed to pay out annual leave credits in excess of the maximum twenty-five-day carryover, but the parties still wanted an adjudicator to rule on whether management could require employees to take annual leave to reduce their leave credits to twenty-five days or fewer. The adjudicator refused to hear the grievances because they were both prospective (management ordered them to do something in the future, and the grievors had not yet obeyed that order) and moot (because management paid out the annual leave credits in any event).

93 *William Porter v Treasury Board (Department of Energy, Mines and Resources)* (1973), 166-2-752 (PSLRB).

jurisdiction to look behind the employer's characterization and determine whether it is a form of "disguised discipline." The Federal Court has summarized this jurisdiction as follows:

> Since *Penner*, ... it has been established that an adjudicator does not have jurisdiction to hear a grievance relating to termination of employment but, when an employee maintains that the termination is actually the result of a disguised disciplinary action, he or she has jurisdiction to determine whether this actually was a termination of employment under the *Public Service Employment Act* or was in fact a disguised disciplinary action. In the former case, the adjudicator must dismiss the grievance forthwith for lack of jurisdiction. In the latter case, he has jurisdiction to decide it.[94]

Whether a particular action is disciplinary or purely administrative is predominantly a question of fact. The resolution of that issue will depend on several factors, including the impact of the action of the employee's career, the nature of the employee's conduct that gave rise to the action, the nature of the employer's response, the employer's stated intent, whether the employee's behaviour was culpable, and whether the employer's intent (whether real or disguised) was to correct or punish misconduct.[95]

This is simply the application of the more general principle of law that form cannot take precedence over substance:

> That would be an application of the principle that form should not take precedence over substance. A camouflage to deprive a person of a protection given by statute is hardly tolerable. In fact, we [then] approach the most fundamental legal requirement for any form of activity to be defended at law, which is good faith.[96]

To be referred to adjudication, a grievance must have resulted from actual discipline, not potential discipline. In *Canada (Attorney General) v Assh*,[97] the grievor was a lawyer employed as a pensions advocate with Veterans Affairs Canada. Acting as such, he had, between 1993 and 1996, assisted Mrs. Maria Orn (the widow of a veteran) to obtain certain benefits. He had no further contact from her. In 2001, Mr. Assh

94 *Fortin v Canada (Attorney General)*, [2003] FCJ No 1490 (CA) at para 6.
95 *Bergey*, above note 52 at para 37; *Chamberlain*, above note 11 at para 56.
96 *Canada (Attorney General) v Penner*, [1989] 3 FC 429 (CA) at 440.
97 *Canada (Attorney General) v Assh*, [2005] FCJ No 923.

learned, much to his surprise, that he was the beneficiary of a $5,000 bequest in Ms. Orn's will (which she had revised a few weeks before her death). Mr. Assh reported the bequest to his superiors, who ordered him to return the bequest. Mr. Assh obeyed that order and then grieved the decision unsuccessfully. He then attempted to refer his grievance to adjudication. The adjudicator accepted jurisdiction over the grievance on the grounds that had Mr. Assh disobeyed the order he would have been disciplined and suffered some financial penalty as a result of that discipline. The Federal Court quashed the adjudicator's decision, stating:

> Many rules, if disobeyed, could lead to disciplinary action. But by section 92 it is clear that in respect of the interpretation and application of such instruments adjudication is only provided in respect of a limited field of grievances, namely those involving disciplinary actions resulting in suspension or a financial penalty or termination of employment or demotion. While counsel could provide me with no judicial authority on this subject in relation to the scheme of the *PSSRA*, I believe that is the obvious intent of subsections 91(1) and 92(1) [now 208 and 209]. For this reason I think that one must take subparagraph 92(1)(b)(i) [now 209(1)(b)] to mean what it says, namely to refer to actual disciplinary action resulting in suspension or a financial penalty and not possible disciplinary action of this sort.[98]

There is little question that the decision of the adjudicator makes better labour relations sense: employees should not be denied the right to have their grievances determined by a third-party decision-maker simply because they followed the "obey now, grieve later" rule. However, the *FPSLRA* requires "disciplinary action," not possible or even probable disciplinary action; therefore, an employee may not adjudicate an order that they obeyed (unless that order contravened the collective agreement in some fashion).[99]

The Board has had to determine many cases about whether a suspension pending an investigation into alleged wrongdoing was

98 *Ibid* at para 11.

99 The story did not have a happy ending for Mr. Assh. He applied for judicial review of the final-level grievance decision and was successful at first as the Federal Court agreed with him that there was no conflict of interest in accepting a bequest from a former client. However, the Federal Court of Appeal overturned that decision. See the discussion on conflict of interest in Chapter 9.

disciplinary or administrative. As with other "disguised discipline" cases, these cases are factually driven. The Board has decided not to follow the approach laid out by the Supreme Court of Canada[100] for non-unionized employees in the private sector to the effect that a suspension without pay is unreasonable, concluding that the "different statutory context" in the federal public administration requires a different approach.[101] In a case of an allegedly administrative suspension, the employer bears the burden of proving, on a balance of probabilities, that its intent was non-disciplinary at the time that it imposed the suspension.[102] The employer also has a burden to show that its intent remained non-disciplinary throughout the suspension. For example, if an employer holds a disciplinary meeting and decides that some form of discipline is warranted but is uncertain of the level of discipline and continues the employee's suspension, the suspension has become disciplinary at that point.[103] Additionally, an investigation can be so dilatory that it changes from administrative to disciplinary through the simple passage of time.[104]

When an employer suspends an employee without pay because of criminal charges against the employee, the Board applies what it refers to as the *Larson*[105] criteria (which are paraphrased below):

1) Does the employee's presence present a reasonably serious and immediate risk to the employer's legitimate concerns?
2) The employer must establish that the nature of the charge will create a risk to its reputation, will render the employee unable to perform their duties, or will have a harmful effect on the employer's employees or clients.
3) The employer must show that in fact it investigated the criminal charge to assess the risk of keeping the grievor in their functions.

---

100 *Cabiakman v Industrial Alliance Life Insurance Co*, 2004 SCC 55 at para 60.

101 *King v Deputy Head (Correctional Service of Canada)*, 2011 PSLRB 45 at para 64.

102 *Ibid* at para 62; see also *Basra v Deputy Head (Correctional Service of Canada)*, 2014 PSLRB 28 at para 128 [*Basra*].

103 See, for example, *Campeau v Deputy Head (Canada Border Services Agency)*, 2019 FPSLREB 123 at para 156, and *Lemieux v Deputy Head (Correctional Service of Canada)*, 2021 FPSLREB 20 at para 170 [*Lemieux*].

104 *Basra v Deputy Head (Correctional Service of Canada)*, 2007 PSLRB 70 at para 137, and *Basra*, above note 102 at para 161.

105 From *Larson v Treasury Board (Solicitor General Canada—Correctional Service)*, 2002 PSSRB 9.

The burden is lower if police investigated the matter and laid the charge.

4) The employer must show that it looked at whether it was possible to mitigate the risk by assigning the grievor to another position.
5) The employer remains responsible for regularly considering the possibility of reinstating the grievor in a position.[106]

If the employer has evidence that the grievor has engaged in misconduct and refers to or relies on that evidence in suspending the grievor without pay, then the suspension is considered disciplinary.[107]

An indefinite suspension is sometimes followed by a decision to terminate the grievor's employment after the employer concludes its investigation. In these circumstances, the first day of the suspension becomes the effective date of the termination[108]—or, as the Board has put it in other cases, the grievance against the suspension becomes moot.[109] This in turn means that if the employer cannot demonstrate just cause for the termination of employment, the suspension is also set aside, and any remedy will be backdated to the start of the suspension.[110] In other circumstances, though, an employer may not purport to act on an administrative basis and then, after the Board concludes that the action was in fact disguised discipline, attempt to argue that there was just cause for that discipline.[111]

Finally, while many of these cases were decided under the pre-2005 *PSSRA*, the principles they describe are equally valid under the current *FPSLRA*.[112]

---

106 *Lemieux*, above note 103 at para 52.

107 *Basra*, above note 102 at para 128.

108 *Canada (Attorney General) v Bétournay*, 2018 FCA 230.

109 *Apenteng v Deputy Head (Canada Border Services Agency)*, 2017 PSLREB 58 at para 99, and *Gravelle v Deputy Head (Department of Justice)*, 2014 PSLRB 61 at para 101. While one board member has questioned this approach (*Girard v Canada Revenue Agency*, 2019 FPSLREB 37), the predominant and better approach by the board has been to treat the suspension and termination as one in the same: see, for example, *Viner v Deputy Head (Department of Health)*, 2022 FPSLREB 74.

110 *Weinstein v Deputy Head (Correctional Service of Canada)*, 2021 FPSLREB 100 at paras 306–7.

111 *Jassar v Canada Revenue Agency*, 2019 FPSLREB 54 [*Jassar*].

112 *Gariépy v Deputy Head (Department of National Defence)*, 2020 FPSLREB 103 at para 391.

2) Disciplinary Action and Section 211 of the *FPSLRA*

Section 211(a) of the *FPSLRA* states that an adjudicator has no jurisdiction over a termination of employment under the *PSEA*. As pointed out immediately above, however, section 211(a) does not bar an employee from arguing that their dismissal was, in fact, a form of disguised discipline. That section only bars a referral to adjudication where there was in fact a termination of employment under the *PSEA*: if an employer "disguises an unlawful dismissal under cover of the abolishment of a position through a contrived reliance on that Act," then this action falls within the jurisdiction of an adjudicator.[113]

Section 211(a) of the *FPSLRA* refers to a termination of employment under the *PSEA*. That Act in turn contemplates two types of terminations: a rejection on probation and a layoff. This chapter will address those two types of terminations in turn.

a) Rejection on Probation

For employees of the core public administration, a person appointed from outside the public service is on probation for a period set out by regulation.[114] Most employees have a twelve-month probationary period, while research scientists and university teachers have longer probationary periods of twenty-four and thirty-six months, respectively. The probationary period does not include any period of leave without pay, leave with pay of more than thirty consecutive days, full-time language training, and off-season periods for seasonal employees.[115] This means that when an employee has taken thirty consecutive working (not calendar) days of leave with pay, any leave with pay in excess of thirty days is added to the probationary period.[116] An employee on probation may be terminated from their employment at the end of a notice period prescribed by the regulations (either two weeks or one month, depending on the type of employee).[117] An employee may be paid their salary during their notice period instead of receiving working notice.[118]

---

113 *Canada (Attorney General) v Rinaldi*, [1997] FCJ No 225 at para 17.

114 *PSEA*, s 61(1), and *Regulations Establishing Periods of Probation and Periods of Notice of Termination Employment During Probation*, SOR/2005-375, Schedule [*Regulations Establishing Probation*].

115 *Ibid*, s 2(2).

116 *Gill v Deputy Head (Correctional Service of Canada)*, 2018 FPSLREB 55.

117 *PSEA*, s 62(1)(a), and *Regulations Establishing Probation*, Schedule.

118 *PSEA*, s 62(2).

Separate agencies may also establish probationary periods and notice periods in accordance with their own constituting statutes.

While it is common practice for employers to set out the probationary period in the initial offer of employment, this practice is not required by the legislation. When the probationary period is established by statute or regulation (i.e., under the *PSEA*), that probationary period exists notwithstanding an employer mistakenly not including the period in the initial letter of appointment.[119]

The Supreme Court of Canada addressed the situation of an employee of the public service being rejected on probation in *Jacmain v Canada (Attorney General)* and concluded that "[t]he employer's right to reject an employee during a probationary period is very broad."[120] However, the Court explicitly refused to address the issue of when an adjudicator has jurisdiction to hear a case involving a rejection on probation. That issue was left to adjudicators and the Federal Court to resolve in subsequent years.

The two controlling issues in challenges to a rejection during the probationary period are whether the employer has an employment-related reason for the rejection during the probationary period and whether the rejection on probation was a sham or otherwise in bad faith. Initially, the Board and the Court required the employer to prove that it had an employment-related reason for the rejection on probation, and then the burden shifted to the grievor to prove that this employment-related reason was a sham or camouflage. In *Tello v Deputy Head (Correctional Service of Canada)*, however, the Board concluded that this traditional practice was incompatible with the new wording of the *PSEA* in force as of 2005. The older version of the *PSEA* required that a deputy head give notice to an employee that they intended to reject the employee "for cause" at the end of the notice period; the current *PSEA* does not contain the phrase "for cause." The Board reasoned that this did not change the substance of its approach to probationary employees, but it did change the burden of proof. The Board concluded that the deputy head's burden is limited to establishing that the employee was on probation, that the probationary period was still in effect at the time of termination, and that notice or pay in lieu of notice has been

119 *Kot v Deputy Head (Royal Canadian Mounted Police)*, 2020 FPSLREB 29 [*Kot*].
120 *Jacmain v Canada (Attorney General)*, [1978] 2 SCR 15 at 37.

provided.[121] The deputy head may meet this burden by tendering the letter of termination. The burden then shifts to the grievor to show that the termination of employment was in bad faith, a sham, or a camouflage for some other reason for termination. The grievor may meet this burden by showing that there were no legitimate employment-related reasons for termination—in other words, by showing that the rejection on probation was not based on a bona fide dissatisfaction with job performance or other suitability for employment.[122]

The Board's reasoning in *Tello* was based on the change in the wording of the *PSEA*. It is therefore unclear whether this new approach applies to separate agencies or whether the old approach—in which the employer bore the burden of proof to establish an employment-related reason for the rejection on probation—remains in place. The Board has cited and purported to rely on *Tello* in cases involving separate agencies, but then dismissed a grievance because "the employer has established a clear employment-related reason for the decision to reject the grievor before the end of her probationary period"[123] or, in another case, stated that the onus was on the employer to show that the rejection on probation was related to employment issues.[124] Part of the confusion over this issue may arise because of a 2014 Federal Court decision in which the Court did not cite or address *Tello* but, instead, only cited pre-*Tello* jurisprudence to the effect that the employer bears the burden of demonstrating an employment-related reason for the rejection on probation. The Federal Court of Appeal has since cited *Tello*, although it did not weigh in on the burden of proof controversy directly.[125]

An employment-related reason requires that the employer have a bona fide dissatisfaction with the employee's suitability or ability to perform their duties.[126] This is a lower standard than showing just cause for discipline or a dismissal and can be met by showing inadequacies in

121 The failure to provide pay in lieu of notice immediately does not invalidate the rejection on probation, so long as it is ultimately corrected: *Kagimbi v Canada (Attorney General)*, 2014 FC 400.

122 *Tello v Deputy Head (Correctional Service of Canada)*, 2010 PSLRB 134 at paras 110–11 [*Tello*].

123 *Le Page v Canada Revenue Agency*, 2015 PSLREB 13 at para 21.

124 *Bell v Staff of the Non-Public Funds, Canadian Forces*, 2020 FPSLREB 14 at para 109. See also *Ebada v Canada Revenue Agency*, 2021 FPSLREB 94 at para 153 [*Ebada*].

125 *Canada (Attorney General) v Alexis*, 2021 FCA 216 [*Alexis*].

126 *Ebada*, above note 124 at para 153.

the quality of work[127] regardless of whether the employee was informed of those inadequacies.[128] To be an employment-related reason, the reason must be something within the control of the grievor and not an involuntary reaction.[129] This standard can also be met by relying on misconduct that could form the basis for discipline: an employer is not required to follow the disciplinary process for probationary employees but can, instead, simply reject them on probation.[130] While an employer may not discipline an employee for misconduct and then rely on that same misconduct as the employment-related reason for dismissal,[131] an employer may consider a disciplinary record when assessing whether other employment-related concerns justify rejecting the employee on probation.[132] The employer is free to choose whether to impose disciplinary measures or to reject an employee on probation as long as it is acting in good faith.[133] In other words, "the fact that the conduct is subject to disciplinary measures alone does not constitute evidence that the termination of employment is in fact a disciplinary measure."[134]

The issue of other forms of bad faith are heavily fact driven, so there are no firm rules about what constitutes bad faith,[135] although the burden rests on the grievor to demonstrate bad faith—or, to put it another way, the Board presumes that the deputy head acted in good faith.[136] For example, failing to provide a grievor with a performance assessment is not automatically bad faith[137]—although it could

---

127 *Premakanthan v Deputy Head (Treasury Board)*, 2012 PSLRB 67.

128 *Kagimbi v Deputy Head (Correctional Service of Canada)*, 2013 PSLRB 19 at para 74, aff'd *Kagimbi v Canada (Attorney General)*, 2014 FCC 400 and 2015 FCA 74.

129 *Dalen and Deputy Head (Correctional Service of Canada)*, 2006 PSLRB 73.

130 *McMath v Deputy Head (Correctional Service of Canada)*, 2011 PSLRB 42 at para 14; *D'Aoust v Deputy Head (Department of Public Works and Government Services)*, 2015 PSLREB 94 at para 133, and *Kot*, above note 119 at para 216 (in that case, off-duty misconduct and using the employer's computer and email system to engage in a dispute with private citizens).

131 *Tello*, above note 122 at para 116.

132 *Smith v Deputy Head (Correctional Service of Canada)*, 2012 PSLRB 126 at para 30 [*Smith*].

133 *Canada (Attorney General) v Penner*, [1989] FCJ No 461 (CA).

134 *Morin v Treasury Board (Department of Fisheries and Oceans)*, 2006 PSLRB 35 at para 94.

135 *Alexis*, above note 125 at para 22.

136 *Ebada*, above note 124 at para 159.

137 *Smith*, above note 132 at para 31.

constitute bad faith in the right circumstances.[138] Similarly, a letter rejecting an employee on probation does not need to identify the names of the people who assessed the employee or the assessment date,[139] but it is bad faith for a responsible manager to fail to follow up and verify whether performance concerns expressed by certain employees were justified.[140] The Board has also found that rejecting an employee on probation because of an unfounded suspicion that they were abusing sick leave was in bad faith,[141] and an employer cannot reject an employee on probation for something that is "trivial."[142] This is not an exhaustive list of the types of behaviour that could constitute bad faith but merely some examples. Bad faith is inherently fact specific, and the Board will consider all of the surrounding circumstances before finding bad faith.

b) Layoffs

From time to time, the federal public service has laid off employees because of a lack of work. The term "layoff" is defined in the *PSEA* as when an employee ceases their employment "by reason of lack of work, the discontinuance of a function or the transfer of work or a function outside those portions of the federal public administration named in Schedule I, IV or V to the Financial Administration Act."[143] These layoffs cannot be referred to adjudication unless they are actually a form of disguised discipline.

As with the situation of rejection on probation, the employer cannot hide behind an administrative dismissal (because of a layoff) if the dismissal was in fact motivated by disciplinary concerns. An adjudicator's analysis when faced with a grievance alleging that a layoff was in fact disciplinary is thus twofold.

First, the adjudicator will examine whether the dismissal was actually a layoff under the particular legislation governing that employee (e.g., the *PSEA* for employees in the core public administration)—that is, that

138 *Alexis v Deputy Head (Royal Canadian Mounted Police)*, 2020 FPSLREB 9 at para 235, aff'd *Alexis*, above note 125; *Bergeron v Canadian Security Intelligence Service*, 2011 PSLRB 103 (in that case, a failure to provide a statement of shortcomings to the grievor before rejecting the grievor on probation).

139 *Rouet v Deputy Head (Department of Justice)*, 2021 FPSLREB 59 at para 321.

140 *Ebada*, above note 124 at para 169.

141 *Dyson v Deputy Head (Department of Fisheries and Oceans)*, 2015 PSLREB 58.

142 *Boyce v Treasury Board (Department of National Defence)*, [2004] CPSSRB No 34 at para 59.

143 *PSEA*, s 64.

there is a lack of work, the discontinuance of a function, or the transfer of work or a function outside the public service. Second, if the deputy head discharges that burden, the onus shifts to the grievor to demonstrate that the deputy head's actions were in bad faith, a sham, or camouflage.[144]

As an example of the inquiry at the first stage, in *Lo and Treasury Board (Treasury Board Secretariat)*,[145] the grievor was dismissed, and the employer argued that it was a layoff under the *PSEA*. In fact, the grievor was dismissed long after the "downsizing exercise" that occurred in that workplace had been completed. For that and other reasons, the adjudicator concluded that

> [t]he evidence is overwhelming and demonstrates clearly that placing the grievor on surplus status was not done in the normal course of surplus or lay-off, that this was not carried out in accordance with the Public Service Employment Act, PSER and WFA policies. I am of the opinion that this situation is disguised discipline and surely was done in bad faith.[146]

The term "lack of work" does not necessarily mean that the employee being laid off was not busy or fully occupied with their duties. When budget cuts require that a department, a branch, or some other work unit reduce its activities, the corresponding reduction in the number of employees is because of a lack of work.[147] The term "discontinuance of a function" also does not mean that the duties of a position are no longer being performed. A "function" is a bundle of duties; when that bundle of duties is no longer being performed by a single person but, instead, has been parcelled out among a number of people within an organization, that is a layoff. If the duties were given to a single person, or if there was simply a different job title, that would not be a layoff, but spreading the duties among a larger group of employees is a valid discontinuance of a function.[148]

---

144 *Tipple v Deputy Head (Department of Public Works and Government Services)*, 2010 PSLRB 83 at para 250 [*Tipple*]. A judicial review application against the remedy in that case was allowed in part, *Canada (Attorney General) v Tipple*, 2011 FC 762, and, in turn, that case was overturned in part in *Tipple v Canada (Attorney General)*, 2012 FCA 158.

145 *Lo and Treasury Board (Treasury Board Secretariat)*, [1998] CPSSRB No 39.

146 *Ibid* at para 44.

147 *Canada v Gonthier* (1986), 77 NR 386 (CA) at para 26.

148 *Flieger v New Brunswick*, [1993] 2 SCR 651.

As an example of the type of finding at the second stage, in *Matthews and Canadian Security Intelligence Service*,[149] the adjudicator concluded that the employer used a bona fide downsizing exercise as cover for a decision to terminate the grievor for disciplinary reasons:

> When the employer was faced with the prospect of downsizing some time later, it conducted what can only be characterized as a semblance of a ROM [reverse order of merit] exercise leading to what the employer characterized as a lay off. In fact, the choice to terminate the grievor had already been made. I find, based on the whole of the evidence that the employer acted in bad faith in arbitrarily ridding itself of the grievor under the guise of lay off. In effect, the grievor was terminated for disciplinary reasons.[150]

While that case involved a separate agency and, therefore, did not involve an employee governed by the *PSEA*, the logic of that decision applies to the core public administration.

Another example of a sham layoff is in *Tipple v Deputy Head (Department of Public Works and Government Services)*. In that case, a senior executive in what was then the Department of Public Works and Government Services was dismissed from his employment. While the department characterized the dismissal as a layoff and purportedly eliminated the position, the adjudicator found that the termination was actually a result of negative publicity about the senior executive (publicity that the adjudicator also concluded was both unjustified and contributed to by the department).[151]

On the other hand, the fact that an employee has had a "turbulent" relationship with their employer is not proof that the layoff was in bad faith. As one adjudicator put it, "[I]t would be neither objective nor fair for an employee to be sheltered from his position being cut because of 'turbulent' working relations with his employer."[152]

---

149 *Matthews and Canadian Security Intelligence Service*, [1997] CPSSRB No 22, decision on jurisdiction aff'd *Canada (Attorney General) v Matthews*, [1997] FCJ No 1692. The Federal Court quashed the adjudicator's remedy in a separate judicial review application, remitting the matter back to the adjudicator for redetermination.

150 *Ibid* (CPSSRB) at para 139.

151 *Tipple*, above note 144 at paras 285 and 330–49.

152 *Freve v Treasury Board (Agriculture and Agri-Food Canada)*, [1999] CPSSRB No 113 at para 107.

The *PSEA* has a separate method of recourse when some but not all employees are laid off and the employee alleges that their selection for layoff was an abuse of authority.[153]

Finally, one area of dispute that often arises is whether a particular grievance is about the layoff (in which case it may not be referred to adjudication) or whether it is about the interpretation or application of the Work Force Adjustment Directive incorporated into a particular collective agreement or the non-discrimination clause in a collective agreement. The Board's jurisdiction to hear the grievance will depend on the nature of the subject of the grievance: if the true subject matter of the grievance concerns some provision of the collective agreement, then the Board has jurisdiction; otherwise, it does not.[154]

3) Discipline Resulting in a Financial Penalty

A disciplinary action may be referred to adjudication if it resulted in a "financial penalty." To be adjudicable, both discipline and a financial penalty are required.[155]

There is a difference between a "financial penalty" and a financial loss. The Board has concluded that the term "financial penalty" must be read in the context in which it is found—that is, adjacent to the words "termination, demotion, and suspension." The term therefore must have some sort of disciplinary aspect to it, such as a fine imposed by the employer.[156] As the Board put it in one case:

> Actions can be taken in an employment relationship that are both foreseeable and that have a financial impact on an employee but that do not equate to a financial penalty. For example, due to a lack of work, an employer may cut back an employee's hours, which results in the employee earning less money. While that could be construed as a financial loss, it would not be a financial penalty. However, that same employer may decide that an employee has committed an infraction of some form at work and cut back his or her hours, which would have

---

153 *PSEA*, s 65(1).

154 See, for example, *Charette v Parks Canada Agency*, 2015 PSLREB 43 (no jurisdiction); *Santawirya*, above note 26 (Board had jurisdiction).

155 *Hanna v Deputy Head (Department of Indian Affairs and Northern Development)*, 2009 PSLRB 94 at para 19.

156 *Chafe v Treasury Board (Department of Fisheries and Oceans)*, 2010 PSLRB 112 at para 91.

a financial consequence in the form of a financial loss. Under those circumstances, it would equate to a financial penalty.[157]

Adjudicators and the Federal Court have distinguished between the loss of an opportunity to earn more money (which is not a financial penalty) and the actual loss of some premium or bonus pay (which can be a financial penalty). For example, the loss of a foreign service overseas premium because of a disciplinary transfer back to Canada is a "financial penalty" under the *FPSLRA*,[158] as is the loss of a bilingual bonus due to a disciplinary transfer.[159] On the other hand, an action that results in the loss of opportunity to earn as much overtime (or that results in overtime at a lower rate of pay) is not a financial penalty, unless the collective agreement contains some right to the overtime to which the employee was deprived.[160]

The fact that there may be financial consequences from a decision does not automatically mean that it involves a financial penalty. For example, a negative performance appraisal may have negative financial consequences in the future; however, it is not considered a "financial penalty" under the *FPSLRA*.[161] On the other hand, a loss of performance pay can be a "financial penalty." The real issue is whether the decision denying performance pay was disciplinary or simply administrative in nature.[162] In light of these decisions, grievances concerning performance pay are therefore better analyzed by examining whether there was a "disciplinary" decision instead of focusing the question of whether performance pay is a "financial penalty."[163]

A failure to reimburse an employee the wages owed to them is a financial penalty if the failure goes on for long enough to constitute negligence. In *Winn and Treasury Board (Public Service Commission*

---

157 *Green v Deputy Head (Department of Indian Affairs and Northern Development)*, 2017 PSLREB 17 at para 347 [*Green*].

158 *Massip v Canada (Treasury Board)*, [1985] FCJ No 12.

159 *Menard* (1980) (Board File No 166-2-5943).

160 *Cameron and Treasury Board (Transport Canada)*, [1991] CPSSRB No 22.

161 *Bratrud v Office of the Superintendent of Financial Institutions Canada*, [2004] CPSSRB No 17 at para 92 [*Bratrud*]; *Charest v Deputy Head (Department of Public Works and Government Services)*, 2017 FPSLREB 18 at para 73.

162 *McMullen v Canada Revenue Agency*, 2013 PSLRB 64 at paras 123–25 (the loss of performance pay in that case was tied up with the alleged misconduct and therefore disciplinary).

163 This was the approach taken by the board in *Green*, above note 157 at para 348.

of Canada),[164] the employer first suspended an employee for one day and then replaced that suspension with a written reprimand. However, six months later the employer still had not reimbursed the employee for that one day's pay. Therefore, the adjudicator took jurisdiction over the grievance concerning what was now a written reprimand:

> It seems to me that the delay of about six months to pay back the salary lost by the grievor is tantamount to a financial penalty. The grievor is being penalized, with or without intent on the part of the employer. There is also so far the loss of the interest and this, in itself, is a financial penalty. I understand that a delay of perhaps one month or two before an employee is reimbursed should be perhaps recognized as being normal, but surely a delay of six months is abnormal and there is somewhere negligence which is now causing a financial loss and in this case the continuation of a financial penalty which existed when the suspension was imposed.[165]

An employer's attempt to recover money from an employee (for example, because of an overpayment) is not a financial penalty because it is not a punishment but simply an amount owing, which the employer attempts to recover from an employee.[166]

4) Discipline Resulting in a Demotion

Canada (Attorney General) v Robitaille[167] establishes that a grievance against a demotion may be founded even if an employee's classification is not changed if the punitive nature of the reassignment is evident. In that case, the Federal Court held that a demotion had taken place once the employee at issue no longer supervised employees, performed none of the duties of his substantive position, was isolated from his workplace, was assigned duties of little value, had little to do, and was assigned to a junior office. In other words, a "demotion" may be about more than the grievor's rate of pay.

---

164 *Winn and Treasury Board (Public Service Commission of Canada)*, [1988] CPSSRB No 74.

165 *Ibid.*

166 *Andrews v Brent*, [1981] 1 FC 181 (CA).

167 *Canada (Attorney General) v Robitaille*, 2011 FC 1218 at para 33.

5) Non-disciplinary Terminations and Demotions

As quoted above, section 209(1)(c)(i) of the *FPSLRA* permits employees in the core public administration to refer a termination to adjudication when the termination was the result of unsatisfactory performance or any other reason aside from a breach of discipline or misconduct. Section 209(1)(d) then goes on to provide the same right to employees of separate agencies who have been designated by regulation. At the time of publication, the only agencies so designated happen to be the two largest separate agencies—the CRA and the CFIA.[168]

While this provision may appear straightforward, several issues have emerged about the Board's jurisdiction over certain types of terminations of employment. This chapter will go through some of those areas of dispute.

a) Reliability Status Cases

As discussed in the previous chapter, employees in the federal public administration are required to possess a "reliability status" to remain employed. Certain employees are also required to have higher levels of "security clearance" to remain in more sensitive positions. A department or separate agency can revoke an employee's reliability status in accordance with the relevant security policy in place at that time. Such an employee is then dismissed from the public service and is no longer an employee.

In almost all cases, the reasons for revoking an employee's reliability status would also be reasons to discipline that employee. Employers nevertheless took the position that the Board had no jurisdiction to review the merits of a decision to revoke an employee's reliability status. In three decisions in 2017, the Federal Court of Appeal rejected this position and stated clearly that the decision to revoke a reliability status can be grieved and referred to adjudication.

In the first of the three cases,[169] the Board had decided that it did not have jurisdiction over the revocation of a reliability status because that revocation was not an act of "disguised discipline." The Federal Court of Appeal set aside that finding, concluding that there was "disguised discipline" in that case and, therefore, the Board had jurisdiction over the

168 *Public Service Labour Relations Act Separate Agency Designation Order*, SOR/2005-59.

169 *Bergey*, above note 52.

grievance by virtue of section 209(1)(b) of the *FPSLRA*. In the course of its reasons, though, the Court hinted strongly that the Board would also have jurisdiction under section 209(1)(c)(i) of the *FPSLRA*—although it was not necessary to resolve that issue in that case.

In the next two cases,[170] though, the Federal Court of Appeal squarely addressed the Board's jurisdiction under section 209(1)(c)(i). In both cases, the Court concluded that "the Board has jurisdiction, pursuant to paragraph 209(1)(c) of the Act and paragraph 12(1)(e) and subsection 12(3) of the [*Financial Administration Act*], to hear and determine, on their merits, decisions made by an employer revoking an employee's reliability status."[171] Consequently, it is no longer necessary to rely on the concept of disguised discipline when hearing a case concerning the revocation of a reliability status. Instead, the Board has the jurisdiction to determine whether the revocation was justified on the basis of the relevant policies. If so, the employer has shown that the termination was for cause and lawful; if not, then the termination must be set aside. Importantly, the Court also stated that an employer may not terminate an employee as a result of revoking their reliability status and then "change its tack" at adjudication and argue that the termination was justified on disciplinary grounds as well: once the employer decides to use the reliability status process, it is bound by that decision and cannot justify the termination as disciplinary "in the alternative." In closing, the Federal Court of Appeal removed any doubt that the "disguised disciplinary" approach to reliability status cases was unnecessary:

> In my view, paragraphs 209(1)(*b*) and (*c*) of the Act are free-standing provisions which allow the Board to deal, on their merits, with both disciplinary and non-disciplinary terminations. As part of its mandate under these provisions, the Board has full jurisdiction to determine whether the termination at issue has been made for cause. Consequently, the concept of disguised discipline, used by the Board to assume jurisdiction over terminations resulting from revocations of reliability status, is no longer necessary. By that I mean that in regard to non-disciplinary terminations, the Board has full jurisdiction to inquire into the circumstances of the termination and into the revocation

170 *Canada (Attorney General) v Féthière*, 2017 FCA 66, and *Canada (Attorney General) v Heyser*, 2017 FCA 113.

171 *Ibid* at para 73.

> which led to the termination. Thus, if the Board determines that there was no cause for the termination (i.e. that the revocation was not made on legitimate grounds) it becomes irrelevant what the specific reason for the revocation was. In other words, whether the revocation is the result of disguised discipline or some other non-legitimate ground, the result is that the Board will set aside the termination and may order the reinstatement of the employee. In that sense, it is my view that in the current legislative context the concept of disguised discipline no longer has the importance that it had under the previous case law.[172]

Section 209(1)(c)(i) of the *FPSLRA* only applies to the core public administration. While the Federal Court of Appeal's reasons certainly apply to separate agencies who have been designated for the purposes of section 209(1)(d) of the Act, it does not apply to undesignated separate agencies.[173] The Board has also concluded that it has the jurisdiction to examine a decision to revoke a reliability status made after the employee was already terminated for disciplinary reasons as part of the Board's jurisdiction to ensure that it can reinstate an employee dismissed without cause.[174]

b) End of Term

A termination is a unilateral decision by the employer to terminate an employment contract that would otherwise have continued to exist.[175] Therefore, the termination of a term appointment does not constitute dismissal when the termination results from the expiry of that term.[176]

---

172 *Ibid* at para 79.

173 In *Jassar*, above note 111 at paras 46–50, the Board concluded that the decision to revoke the employee's reliability status was disguised disciplinary action without considering whether it had jurisdiction to consider the reliability status issue in the absence of disguised discipline. The Board, though, ended up applying the same non-disciplinary standard as in other reliability status cases—namely, "the employer must establish on a balance of probabilities that it had legitimate reasons to consider that he represented an unacceptable risk to its operations when it revoked his reliability status" (at para 484). By way of background, the CRA was not designated under s 209(1)(d) of the *FPSLRA* at the time the employee was terminated.

174 *Bétournay v Canada Revenue Agency*, 2017 FPSLREB 37 at para 140.

175 *Monteiro v Treasury Board (Canadian Space Agency)*, [2005] CPSLRB No 35.

176 *Dansereau v National Film Board*, [1979] 1 FC 100 (CA); *Foreman v Treasury Board (Indian and Northern Affairs Canada)*, [2003] CPSSRB No 63 at para 17. This principle is also codified in the *PSEA*, s 58(1).

Similarly, the failure to renew a term contract is not a termination for the purposes of section 209(1)(c)(i) of the *FPSLRA*.[177]

c) Resignations and Constructive Dismissals

Adjudicators have taken jurisdiction over cases where the grievor resigned where the resignation was involuntary and there was a disciplinary element to the decision-making of the employer. In a 1984 adjudication decision, the adjudicator put the requirement as follows:

> In order for such a grievance to be referable to adjudication pursuant to paragraph 91(1)(b) of the Act, two interrelated conditions must be satisfied. First, the grievor must establish that the employer's role in obtaining the resignation, or its refusal to allow the employee to withdraw his resignation was tainted by a disciplinary motive. Secondly, it is incumbent on the grievor to demonstrate that the act of resignation was to a significant degree involuntary—for example, that the resignation was extracted under duress, or that it was tendered on the spur of the moment in a charged, emotional atmosphere, or at a time when the employee was not capable of making a rational decision in his own interest. In other words, the existence of a "disciplinary taint" does not ipso facto transform a resignation into a disciplinary penalty within the meaning of section 91 of the Act; it is also necessary to demonstrate that the resignation was involuntary. Conversely, in the absence of the disciplinary element, an adjudicator is without jurisdiction to entertain a reference to adjudication simply on the grounds that it was involuntary.[178]

The reasoning in that decision has been followed in more recent decisions to the effect that an employer's refusal to accept the recission of an employee's resignation is capable of being referred to adjudication if the refusal was driven by disciplinary motives or the resignation was involuntary.[179] In order for a resignation to be involuntary, it needs to be truly coerced. Even where an employee is faced with the prospect of a disciplinary discharge and instead chooses to resign,

177 *Pieters v Treasury Board (Federal Court of Canada)*, 2001 PSSRB 100 at paras 45–46 [*Pieters*]; *Loiselle v Treasury Board (Service Canada)*, 2021 FPSLREB 101 at para 17.

178 *McNab v Treasury Board (Transport Canada)*, [1984] CPSSRB No 24 at para 39.

179 See *Rinke v Canadian Food Inspection Agency*, [2004] CPSSRB No 131; *Robertson v Deputy Head (Department of National Defence)*, 2014 PSLRB 63 at para 50.

that is not considered coercion sufficient to turn the resignation into a termination.[180]

Grievors have also alleged that they have been constructively dismissed. A constructive dismissal occurs when an employer's conduct evinces an intention no longer to be bound by the employment contract. In such cases, an employee has two choices: accept the conduct or treat the conduct as a repudiation of the contract and bring a claim against the employer. Since the employee has not been formally dismissed, the employer's act is referred to as a "constructive dismissal."[181] As the Supreme Court of Canada has put it, "the employee has the right to treat the imposition of those changes as termination."[182] To date, the Federal Court of Appeal[183] and the Board[184] have been careful not to rule on whether the Board has jurisdiction over a "constructive dismissal." The Ontario Court of Appeal, however, has concluded that a constructive dismissal is a form of "termination of employment for any reason" for the purposes of section 236(3) of the *FPSLRA*;[185] this conclusion likely also applies to the word "termination" in section 209(1)(c)(i) of the *FPSLRA*.

d) Unsatisfactory Performance

Section 209(c)(i) of the *FPSLRA* permits a grievor employed in the core public administration to submit a grievance to adjudication concerning demotion or termination for unsatisfactory performance. Section 230 of the *FPSLRA*, though, limits the power to review a decision to demote or terminate an employee because of unsatisfactory performance by stating that the Board "must determine the termination or demotion to

---

180 *Arsenault and Treasury Board (Solicitor General—Correctional Service Canada)*, [1993] CPSSRB No 135.

181 *Potter v New Brunswick Legal Aid Services Commission*, 2015 SCC 10 at para 30.

182 *Evans v Teamsters Local Union No 31*, 2008 SCC 20 at para 26.

183 *Nadeau v Canada (Attorney General)*, 2018 FCA 203 at para 9.

184 *Lemieux*, above note 103 at para 178; *Elliot*, above note 75 at para 7. The Board came close to recognizing the doctrine in *Holmes v Deputy Head (Office of the Director of Public Prosecutions)*, 2019 FPSLREB 67 at para 199, stating: "*Potter* sets out that the burden rested on the grievor to establish that she was constructively dismissed by establishing either that an express term of the employment contract was breached and that the breach was serious enough that it constituted dismissal or that the employer's conduct demonstrated that it would not be bound by the contract. The grievor did not meet that burden."

185 *Pearce v Canada (Staff of the Non-Public Funds, Canadian Forces)*, 2021 ONCA 65 [*Pearce*].

have been for cause if the opinion of the deputy head that the employee's performance was unsatisfactory is determined by the adjudicator or the Board to have been reasonable."

The Board has addressed section 230 of the *FPSLRA* by referring to four criteria (often referred to as the *Raymond* criteria) to assess whether a performance assessment process has been reasonable:

- the deputy head or the supervisors who assessed the employee's performance were involved in a bad faith exercise;
- the employee was not subject to appropriate standards of performance;
- the employer did not clearly communicate the standards of performance to the employee that they were required to meet; or
- the employee did not receive the tools, training, and mentoring required to meet the standards of performance in a reasonable period.[186]

There are some Board decisions stating that it may consider the reasonableness of the employer's judgment of the employee's performance.[187] This does not mean that the Board conducts its own independent evaluation of an employee's performance—in fact, doing so runs contrary to section 230 of the *FPSLRA*.[188] The best way to describe this approach is likely to state that the *Raymond* criteria are non-exhaustive and that, in an appropriate case, there may be other criteria that are relevant—although no such case has arisen yet.

This is a departure from the Board's jurisprudence prior to the introduction of section 230 of the *FPSLRA*, and cases decided under the earlier regime should be read with caution. For example, in a case decided under the old *PSSRA*, an adjudicator concluded that the employer was obliged to explore alternative solutions before an employee is terminated or demoted because the employer's staffing manual listed that criteria, reasoning that the employer should be required to adhere to its

186 *Raymond v Treasury Board*, 2010 PSLRB 23 at para 131. The Federal Court of Appeal recently adopted this same test in *Canada (Attorney General) v Yates*, 2021 FCA 74 at para 13. The Board restated these four criteria somewhat differently in *Dussah v Deputy Head (Office of the Chief Human Resources Officer)*, 2020 FPSLREB 18 at para 434, but the meaning of those criteria remained the same.

187 *Gagné v Canadian Food Inspection Agency*, 2016 PSLREB 3 at para 166.

188 *Forner v Canada (Attorney General)*, 2016 FCA 136 at paras 17–18; *Williams v Treasury Board (Correctional Service of Canada)*, 2017 FPSLREB 39 at para 111.

"self-imposed obligation."[189] In a post-section 230 decision, however, the Board stated that it "cannot decide . . . that the employer failed in its obligations by not helping the employee find another position"[190] because of section 230 of the *FPSLRA*. The Board later more clearly stated that its jurisprudence was a deliberate "departure from earlier approaches to non-disciplinary terminations for unsatisfactory work performance."[191]

Once the Board concludes that the employer's performance assessment is reasonable, the Board's jurisdiction is exhausted. This means that the Board cannot conclude whether an employee should have been demoted rather than terminated as a result of their unsatisfactory performance.[192]

6) Deployment

A "deployment" is a transfer of an employee from one position to another in accordance with Part 3 of the *PSEA*. Deployments are not promotions but are, essentially, lateral transfers.[193] A change of position from one geographic location to another is a deployment;[194] however, a change in the hours of work (even a significant change from part-time to full-time employment) is not a deployment.[195] Deployments can be made from a separate agency to the core public administration only if

---

189 *Nnagbo v Treasury Board (Public Works and Government Services Canada)*, 2001 PSSRB 1 at para 59.

190 *Plamondon v Deputy Head (Department of Foreign Affairs and International Trade)*, 2011 PSLRB 90 [*Plamondon*].

191 *Mazerolle v Deputy Head (Department of Citizenship and Immigration)*, 2012 PSLRB 6 at para 126.

192 *Raymond v Treasury Board*, above note 186 at para 124; *Plamondon*, above note 190 at para 48; *McLaren v Deputy Head (Statistics Canada)*, 2020 FPSLREB 58 at para 219.

193 *PSEA*, ss 2(1) "deployment" and 51(5)(a). A promotion is defined according to the *Definition of Promotion Regulations*, SOR/2005-376, as "the assignment to an employee of the duties of a position for which the maximum rate of pay is more than the maximum rate applicable to the employee's substantive level immediately before the assignment of the duties, by an amount equal to or greater than (*a*) the smallest increment on the pay scale for the new position, if it has more than one rate of pay; or (*b*) 4% of the maximum rate of pay for the previous position, if the new position has only one rate of pay."

194 *Pereverseff* (1993), 934-001-CAE (Lee).

195 *Onagi* (2002), 02-REH-028 (Stewart); *MacDonald* (1995), 956-016/017-HRD (Franklin).

the Public Service Commission has reviewed the staffing program of this separate agency, at the agency's request, and has approved the agency for deployment purposes.[196]

Deployments must be made on the consent of the employee with two exceptions: when the employee has agreed to deployments as a condition of their original appointment or when the deputy head has found that the employee has harassed another person.[197] For example, the Treasury Board's Directive on Terms and Conditions of Employment for Executives states that all executives appointed after 1 April 2020 (and all executives above the EX-3 level) agree to be deployed as a condition of employment upon appointment[198]—although the binding nature of this directive in the absence of a more specific agreement in the executive's letter of appointment has not been tested.

Prior to the *FPSLRA*, deployments were not subject to grievances. Instead, complaints about deployments were dealt with by an investigation under the *PSEA*. Under the *FPSLRA*, complaints about deployments are now dealt with through the grievance procedure. While all deployment issues may be grieved, only some may be referred to adjudication: only the employee being deployed may refer a deployment grievance to adjudication,[199] and only if they allege that the deployment was made without consent where consent is required.[200] A deployment is not considered an "appointment" and, therefore, cannot be the subject of a complaint under the *PSEA*.[201]

Grievors have, on occasion, argued that a particular action (an assignment, change in duties, or change in reporting relationship) constitutes a "disguised deployment" and may therefore be challenged at adjudication. The Board has rejected that argument, relying instead on the Federal Court decision in *Canada (Attorney General) v Dawidowski*[202] (decided prior to the amendments to both the *PSEA* and the *FPSLRA*) to the effect that a deployment requires an intention on the

---

196 *PSEA*, s 51(2).

197 *PSEA*, s 51(6).

198 Treasury Board of Canada Secretariat, *Directive on Terms and Conditions of Employment for Executives* (last modified 21 June 2022), art A.II.16.1, online: www.tbs-sct.gc.ca/pol/doc-eng.aspx?id=32625&section=html.

199 *FPSLRA*, s 211(b).

200 *Ibid*, s 209(1)(c)(ii).

201 *Lysak v Commissioner of the Royal Canadian Mounted Police*, 2020 FPSLREB 110.

202 *Canada (Attorney General) v Dawidowski*, [1994] FCJ No 1791.

part of the employer to deploy and compliance with the conditions set out in the *PSEA* and any Treasury Board directives.[203]

Other than consent, the other conditions of a deployment to or within the core public administration are that they "shall be made in the manner directed by the Treasury Board and in accordance with any regulations of the Treasury Board."[204] The Treasury Board used to have directives governing all deployments in the core public administration; however, it has rescinded its general policy and instead simply provided a template for each department to develop its own deployment policy. Whether section 51(4) of the *PSEA* permits the Treasury Board to adopt no regulations or policies concerning deployments has not yet been tested in Federal Court.

7) Pay Versus Classification

One of the common disputes over jurisdiction that arises at adjudication is whether a grievance concerns classification (which is not adjudicable) or is a grievance for acting pay (which is adjudicable). In a classification grievance, the grievor claims that the duties the employer requires on a continuing basis are undervalued and argues that an assessment of those duties against the relevant classification standard justifies upgrading the level of their substantive position within an occupational group (and/or changing the occupational group).[205] In an acting pay grievance, the grievor claims that the employer has assigned extra duties for a specified period of time over and above those of the employee's substantive position, as outlined in the job description. Those extra duties are associated with a higher-paying position; therefore, the grievor asserts that they are entitled to acting pay. Since "he who objects must prove," the onus is on the employer to prove that the grievance concerns classification; if the employer cannot meet that onus, then the burden shifts back to the grievor to show that the employer has breached the acting pay provisions of the collective agreement.[206]

---

203 *Yarney v Treasury Board (Department of Health)*, 2013 PSLRB 45, and *Taticek v Treasury Board (Canada Border Services Agency)*, 2015 PSLREB 12 at para 117.

204 *PSEA*, s 51(4).

205 For a discussion of classification grievances, see Chapter 12.

206 *Doiron v Treasury Board (Correctional Service of Canada)*, 2006 PSLRB 77.

The "common sense" way to distinguish between an acting pay and a classification grievance is that in an acting pay case, the grievor's position is presumed to be properly classified.[207] Adjudicators have set out some indications that a grievance is a classification grievance instead of an acting pay grievance as follows:

- The claim for acting pay is an ongoing claim (or for a period going forward indefinitely) and not for a specified period.
- The grievor has sought a reclassification, either informally or through a classification grievance.
- The grievor continues to perform the duties they have always performed, and only the classification levels in the workplace have changed.
- The acting pay grievance is based, in part, on a comparison with similar positions in other work areas.[208]

This list is not exhaustive, and there is no requirement that all of these factors be present to support a conclusion that classification comprises the real subject matter of the grievance.[209]

Acting pay grievances may also postdate a reclassification by the employer. For example, if the employer reclassifies a position as the result of duties added at a certain date, but does not make that reclassification effective until some time after the date the duties were added, then the employee in that position has a claim for acting pay from the date the duties were added until the date the position was reclassified.[210]

---

207 *Ibid* at para 97.

208 *Bungay v Treasury Board (Department of Public Works and Government Services)*, 2005 PSLRB 40; *Fong v Canada Revenue Agency*, 2017 PSLREB 45, aff'd *Insch*, above note 46.

209 *Lagueux et al v Treasury Board (Department of National Defence)*, 2012 PSLRB 80 at para 58.

210 *Stagg v Canada (Treasury Board)*, [1993] FCJ No 1393. Justice Muldoon in that case stated:

> The employer's posture herein leads only to the nefarious notion that after imposing more onerous duties upon employees and according the commensurate upgrade of classification of position—proper and exclusive employer's functions, the employer can then, by dragging its feet on remuneration, obtain the employees' extra services free for a time by just delaying the commensurate raise in remuneration. This is a notion philosophically akin to that of slavery or forced labour because it exploits employees' (increased) work without remuneration.

8) Human Rights

As stated above, section 208(2) of the *FPSLRA* states that an employee may not present an individual grievance in respect of which an administrative procedure for redress is provided under any Act of Parliament other than the *Canadian Human Rights Act*.[211] The *PSSRA* did not expressly list the *Canadian Human Rights Act* as an exception to the rule that grievances are not permitted when there is some other administrative procedure for redress. The Federal Court of Appeal in *Boutilier* confirmed that this rule applied to complaints of discrimination on grounds set out in the *Canadian Human Rights Act* even if a collective agreement contained a "no-discrimination" clause.[212] This ruling was inconsistent with the broader jurisprudence that human rights complaints in the unionized workplace can[213]—and in many cases, must[214]—be grieved instead of referred to human rights complaints processes. Parliament addressed that problem explicitly in section 208(2) of the *FPSLRA*.

Parliament did not, however, specifically address whether grievances based on human rights complaints can be referred to adjudication. For unionized employees, this typically does not raise an issue as collective agreements in the federal public administration all contain "no-discrimination" clauses, meaning that complaints about discriminatory treatment contrary to the *Canadian Human Rights Act* can be referred to adjudication in the same way as any other alleged collective agreement breach.[215] Non-unionized employees, though, cannot refer a grievance based solely on a breach of the *Canadian Human Rights Act* to adjudication.[216] Parliament enacted legislation that would have expressly granted jurisdiction to address all grievances related to a discriminatory practice prohibited by the *Canadian Human Rights Act*,[217] but that legislation was repealed before it ever came into force.[218]

---

211 *Canadian Human Rights Act*, RSC 1985, c H-6.

212 *Boutilier*, above note 12.

213 *Parry Sound*, above note 77.

214 *Horrocks*, above note 2.

215 *Souaker v Canadian Nuclear Safety Commission*, 2009 PSLRB 145 at paras 124–28.

216 *Chamberlain v Canada (Attorney General)*, 2015 FC 50.

217 *Economic Action Plan 2013 Act, No 2*, SC 2013, c 40, s 326.

218 *An Act to amend the Federal Public Sector Labour Relations Act and other Acts*, SC 2018, c 24, s 32.

When a grievance concerning human rights is referred to adjudication, the party referring the grievance must give notice of an issue involving the interpretation or application of the *Canadian Human Rights Act* to the Canadian Human Rights Commission, which then has standing to make submissions regarding those issues.[219]

Adjudicators under the *FPSLRA* have the explicit authority to award damages for "pain and suffering" if the employer has breached the *Canadian Human Rights Act*. The *FPSLRA* also gives adjudicators the authority to issue damages if it concludes that the employer has engaged in discriminatory conduct either recklessly or wilfully. The *FPSLRA* grants this jurisdiction by explicitly stating that adjudicators have the authority to give relief under section 53(2)(e) or 53(3) of the *Canadian Human Rights Act*. Damages for "pain and suffering" or "reckless or wilful" discrimination under the *Canadian Human Rights Act* are limited to $20,000 each.

9) Harassment

Similarly to human rights grievances, allegations of harassment may be grieved and may then be referred to adjudication if the harassment is also a breach of an employee's collective agreement.[220] If the collective agreement only prohibits harassment on certain prohibited grounds (e.g., the grounds listed in the *Canadian Human Rights Act*), then an allegation of personal harassment that is not based on one of those grounds may not be referred to adjudication.[221] Some bargaining agents have responded to this decision by negotiating broader anti-harassment clauses that preclude "personal harassment" and "abuse of authority."[222] In those bargaining units, employees may refer allegations of personal harassment to adjudication. Unrepresented employees have no ability to refer harassment grievances to adjudication because they are not covered by a collective agreement, unless the harassment happens to take the form of a disciplinary penalty that is capable of being adjudicated (because it results in dismissal, suspension, or a financial penalty).

---

219 *FPSLRA*, s 210.

220 *Bratrud*, above note 161.

221 *Rheaume and Treasury Board (Revenue Canada—Customs and Excise*, [1994] CPSSRB No 89; *Canada (Attorney General) v Lâm*, 2008 FC 874; *Hill v Treasury Board (Correctional Service of Canada)*, 2020 FPSLREB 61 at paras 173–75.

222 See *Bratrud*, above note 161, for such an example.

10) Settlement Agreements

Collaboration and compromise are the hallmarks of effective labour relations. While sometimes disputes are too important to compromise, the vast majority of disputes are resolved through voluntary settlements. For example, in the fiscal year 2020–21, the Board closed 1,050 files—of which 733 were closed because of a settlement.[223] Parliament has also codified the importance of settling grievances and other disputes. The preamble to the *FPSLRA* states that "effective labour-management relations represent a cornerstone of good human resource management and that collaborative efforts between the parties, through communication and sustained dialogue improve the ability of the public service to serve and protect the public interest";[224] the Board is required to provide mediation services for grievances and other disputes;[225] and the Board also has the general power to assist parties to resolve issues without a formal hearing.[226]

Sometimes, though, a settlement is not the final disposition of a case as the parties may sometimes dispute either the validity of the settlement or whether the other party has complied with its terms. Under the old *PSSRA*, the existence of a final settlement was a complete bar to an adjudicator's jurisdiction.[227] This rule does not apply to the *FPSLRA*, and an adjudicator has jurisdiction to (1) determine whether the parties' settlement agreement is final and binding, (2) hear an allegation that a party has not complied with a settlement agreement, and (3) make an order that the adjudicator considers appropriate in the circumstances as a result of non-compliance.[228] These propositions were established by the Board in the decision of *Amos v Deputy Head (Department of Public Works and Government Services)*.[229] In that case, the grievor had not withdrawn his grievance because the terms of the settlement were that the grievance would only be withdrawn after the settlement had been

223 Federal Public Sector Labour Relations and Employment Board, *2020–2021 Annual Report* (2021) at 18, online (pdf): www.fpslreb-crtespf.gc.ca/en/about-us/annual-reports/2020-2021/documents/fpslreb-20202021-en.pdf.

224 *FPSLRA*, preamble.

225 *Ibid*, s 14.

226 *Federal Public Sector Labour Relations and Employment Board Act*, SC 2013, c 40, s 365, s 23.

227 *Lindor v Canada (Treasury Board)*, 2003 PSSRB 10.

228 *Amos v Canada (Attorney General)*, 2011 FCA 38.

229 *Amos v Deputy Head (Department of Public Works and Government Services)*, 2008 PSLRB 74 [*Amos*], aff'd *ibid*.

implemented. When the Federal Court of Appeal ultimately upheld the Board's decision, it did so on the narrow question of whether an adjudicator had jurisdiction over a settlement when the grievance had not yet been withdrawn; however, neither the initial decision in *Amos* nor subsequent decisions applying *Amos* have applied the rule that narrowly. The Board has stated definitely that it has the power to decide the validity of a settlement agreement regardless of whether the grievance was withdrawn[230] and routinely refers to *Amos* to mean that "an adjudicator has jurisdiction to decide whether the parties have reached a binding agreement, whether a party has complied with the agreement and, if not, what order is appropriate in the circumstances."[231]

This jurisdiction means that the Board may determine whether the grievor had the capacity to enter into the agreement.[232] The Board has also confirmed that settlements do not need to be in writing and that it can determine the existence of a verbal agreement.[233]

The Board, though, does not have jurisdiction over settlement agreements reached in other proceedings, such as human rights complaints or staffing complaints—its power is limited to settlements of grievances that have been referred to adjudication.[234] Disputes over settlement agreements reached in other proceedings such as staffing complaints can be grieved (and, ultimately, judicially reviewed by the Federal Court) but not referred to adjudication.[235]

The Board has also concluded that it will not apply the doctrine of repudiation to settlement agreements. The common law doctrine of repudiation allows the innocent party, in response to a breach of contract by the other party, to repudiate the agreement and consider itself discharged from future obligations under the contract. The Board has concluded that the doctrine of repudiation would have a harmful impact on labour relations and be a waste of the resources the Board

---

230 *Palmer v Canadian Security Intelligence Service*, 2010 PSLRB 11.

231 *Godbout v Treasury Board (Office of the Co-ordinator, Status of Women)*, 2016 PSLREB 5 at para 48 [*Godbout*]. See also *Osman v Deputy Head (Department of Employment and Social Development)*, 2018 FPSLREB 15, where the Board assessed whether a settlement had been performed despite the grievance having been withdrawn.

232 *Reid v Deputy Head (Library and Archives of Canada)*, 2021 FPSLREB 104.

233 *Godbout*, above note 231.

234 *Abeysuriya v Treasury Board (Department of Public Works and Government Services)*, 2016 PSLREB 15.

235 *Taticek v Canada (Border Services Agency)*, 2014 FC 281.

has expended on mediating or otherwise assisting the parties in reaching their settlement.[236]

Finally, settlement agreements are supposed to be confidential. The terms of a settlement are subject to "settlement privilege" and may only be disclosed to a tribunal in limited circumstances. One of those circumstances is to enforce their terms. The Board has concluded that when disputes over settlement agreements are heard, it will not disclose the confidential content of the agreements and will grant a sealing order accordingly when asked.[237]

E. GROUP GRIEVANCES

Section 215 of the new *FPSLRA* allows a bargaining agent[238] to organize a "group grievance" on behalf of employees in a bargaining unit who feel aggrieved by the interpretation or application of a collective agreement or an arbitral award that affects them all in common. Group grievances are also subject to the same limitations as other grievances (e.g., there must not be an alternative means of administrative redress under an Act of Parliament).[239] The bargaining agent must seek the consent of all employees who are members of the "group."[240] The Board has a form for that purpose that need only be signed at the outset of the grievance—there is no requirement for fresh consent at each level of the grievance process or when the grievance is referred to adjudication; furthermore, when a bargaining agent does arrange fresh forms at each level, the initial form is still binding (such that, in one case, two grievors who signed the first form but not the second remained part of the group grievance).[241]

The group members must also be a part of a "single portion" of the federal public administration. The term "portion" is not defined in the *FPSLRA*; however, the *Financial Administration Act* defines the

236 *Jadwani v Treasury Board (Federal Economic Development Agency for Southern Ontario)*, 2015 PSLREB 22.

237 *Chaudhary v Deputy Head (Department of Health)*, 2013 PSLRB 160 at para 11.

238 There is nothing in the *FPSLRA* expressly permitting employees to bring a group grievance without a bargaining agent.

239 *FPSLRA*, ss 215(4)–(8).

240 *Ibid*, s 215(2).

241 *Public Service Alliance of Canada v Treasury Board*, 2018 FPSLREB 86 at paras 101–8.

term "core public administration" as "the departments named in Schedule I and the other portions of the federal public administration named in Schedule IV." Furthermore, the definition of "public service" reads as follows:

> "public service" means the several positions in or under
> (a) the departments named in Schedule I;
> (b) the other portions of the federal public administration named in Schedule IV;
> (c) the separate agencies named in Schedule V; and
> (d) any other portion of the federal public administration that may be designated by the Governor in Council for the purpose of this paragraph.[242]

Therefore, we know that the entities listed in Schedule IV to the *Financial Administration Act*[243] are "portions"; by referring to "departments . . . and the other portions of the federal public administration," it is likely that a department is also a "portion" of the federal public administration. The *Financial Administration Act* also does not say whether separate agencies are a "portion" of the federal public administration; however, by listing separate agencies in paragraph (c) of the definition of "public service" and then listing "any other portion of the federal public administration" in paragraph (d), separate agencies are likely "portions" of the federal public administration as well.

Therefore, a group grievance must relate to a single department, a separate agency, or other portion of the federal public administration listed in Schedule IV to the *Financial Administration Act* or designated by order in council. This contradicts section 215(1) of the *FPSLRA*, which allows a bargaining agent to present a group grievance "on behalf of employees in the bargaining unit." Since bargaining units in the core public administration span multiple departments, it is likely that matters that a bargaining agent would like to present a group grievance on will also span departments. Nevertheless, section 215(3) of the *FPSLRA*—read literally—prevents bargaining agents from presenting a group grievance on behalf of members in more than one department. This does make some sense since the final level of the grievance procedure is typically the deputy head of a department (or their designate).

---

242 *Financial Administration Act*, above note 91, s 11(1) "public service."
243 See Chapter 3 for more details.

However, it does make group grievances less effective in the core public administration. Group grievances should remain an effective tool in separate agencies because bargaining units do not span multiple separate agencies.

Group grievances are not the labour relations equivalent of a class action. The defining characteristic of a class action is that it binds non-participants to the result. Class actions in Canada are brought by a representative on behalf of a defined group of individuals who have common claims against one or more defendants. Class actions must be "certified" by the courts before they are allowed to proceed.[244] Once a class action has been certified, people caught by the definition of the class must affirmatively "opt out" of the class action; otherwise, they are included in its scope.[245]

Group grievances are different from class actions in two important respects. First, they do not require employees to "opt out" but rather require each employee to consent to being included in the group. Second, there is no third-party approval required prior to bringing a group grievance. Class actions, on the other hand, must be certified by a court before proceeding.

With respect to the subject matter of group grievances, they are limited to the interpretation of collective agreements or arbitral awards. Any group grievance may also proceed to adjudication if they are not resolved to the bargaining agent's satisfaction.

F. POLICY GRIEVANCES

Section 220 of the *FPSLRA* allows employers and bargaining units to bring a "policy grievance" on a matter that "relates to either of them or to the bargaining unit generally"[246] in respect of the interpretation or application of a collective agreement or an arbitral award. These grievances are subject to the usual criteria of individual grievances (e.g., they are prohibited if there is another administrative method of redress under an Act of Parliament) and may proceed to adjudication if either party is unsatisfied with the result (because they are about collective agreements).[247]

244 See *Class Proceedings Act*, SO 1992, c 6, ss 2(2) and 5(1).

245 *Ibid*, s 9.

246 *FPSLRA*, s 220(1).

247 *Ibid*, s 221.

The Board has explained that in addition to these other standard criteria a policy grievance must satisfy two conditions: it must relate to the interpretation or application of a collective agreement or an arbitral award, and it must relate either to the bargaining agent, the employer, or bargaining generally.[248]

Addressing the first condition, the Board has concluded that a bargaining agent may bring a policy grievance challenging an employer policy on the grounds that the policy violates the collective agreement—the policy does not need to be incorporated into the collective agreement to be an appropriate subject matter for a policy grievance.[249]

Addressing the second condition, the Board has concluded that the phrase "as it relates to . . . the bargaining unit generally" means subjects that are of general interest to the employees in the bargaining unit, without requiring that every employee in the bargaining unit be affected by the issue. It is not the number of members in the bargaining unit affected that matters but the nature of the grievance instead.[250] For example, a bargaining agent may file a policy grievance when the dispute concerns only one workplace or location.[251]

There is no bar against filing both policy and individual grievances on the same matter.[252] The procedure for policy grievances is virtually identical to group or individual grievances, the only significant difference being that a policy grievance process may only consist of one level; group and individual grievances may have up to three levels.[253] The provisions of the *FPSLRA* and *FPSLR Regulations* governing policy grievances permit employers as well as employees to file policy grievances.[254]

Section 232 of the *FPSLRA* states that if a policy grievance relates to a matter that was or could have been the subject of an individual or

---

248 *Public Service Alliance of Canada v Treasury Board (Canada Border Services Agency)*, 2008 PSLRB 84 at para 52 [*PSAC v Treasury Board (CBSA)*].

249 *Ibid*; see also *Professional Institute of the Public Service of Canada v Treasury Board*, 2019 FPSLREB 7 at paras 91–96 [*PIPSC v Treasury Board*].

250 *PSAC v Treasury Board (CBSA)*, above note 248 at para 58; *Professional Institute of the Public Service of Canada v Treasury Board (Correctional Service of Canada)*, 2008 PSLRB 95 at para 56.

251 *Union of Canadian Correctional Officers—Syndicat des agents correctionnels du Canada—CSN v Treasury Board (Correctional Service of Canada)*, 2021 FPSLREB 22 at para 92.

252 *Ibid* at para 97; *PIPSC v Treasury Board*, above note 249 at paras 92–93.

253 *FPSLR Regulations*, ss 64, 74, and 83.

254 *FPSLRA*, s 220(1).

a group grievance, the remedy is limited to declaring the correct interpretation, application, or administration of the collective agreement or arbitral award; declaring that the collective agreement or arbitral award has been contravened; and requiring the employer or bargaining agent to interpret, apply, or administer the collective agreement or arbitral award in a specified manner. The use of the word "requiring" in section 232(c) of the *FPSLRA* means that an adjudicator may require compliance with the collective agreement by requiring that the employer pay persons in accordance with the collective agreement—in other words, a policy grievance may be remedied by an award of compensation to affected employees.[255]

G. EXCLUSIVITY OF THE GRIEVANCE PROCESS

The final issue to address in this chapter on rights disputes concerns the exclusivity of the grievance procedure. By exclusivity, I mean whether the grievance procedure is the exclusive mechanism by which employees in the federal public service may enforce their rights or whether they may also do so by way of a court action. The grievance procedure is obviously not an exclusive mechanism for administrative redress: the requirement that employees use alternative administrative procedures for redress established under an Act of Parliament means, as discussed above, that the grievance procedure has limited jurisdiction. However, this does not address the issue of whether, once jurisdiction has been established, that jurisdiction is exclusive or whether employees still have recourse to court action.

The Supreme Court of Canada established in *Weber v Ontario Hydro* that rights arbitrators have exclusive jurisdiction over matters arising either expressly or inferentially from the collective agreement—in other words, where the "essential character" of the dispute arises out of the collective agreement.[256] Courts in Canada have taken a fairly broad view on what arises from the collective agreement, concluding that claims for defamation,[257] negligence,[258] negligent misrepresentation,[259]

255 *Canada (Attorney General) v Canadian Merchant Service Guild*, 2009 FC 344 at para 18; *Delios v Canada Revenue Agency*, 2016 PSLREB 77 at para 121.

256 *Weber*, above note 2 at para 67.

257 *Giorno v Pappas*, [1999] OJ No 168 (CA).

258 *New Brunswick v O'Leary*, [1995] 2 SCR 967.

259 *Guilbeault v Cornellier*, [2002] OJ No 4415 (SCJ).

and other torts have all arisen from the collective agreement. Therefore, if these types of claims could be presented as grievances capable of being referred to adjudication, then the courts have no jurisdiction to hear those claims.

As set out above, the dispute-resolution system in the federal public service is different from that in the rest of Canada in that not all grievances may be referred to adjudication. Even though alleged breaches of collective agreements may be referred to adjudication, the scope of bargaining in the federal public service is much narrower than in the private sector, so the sort of generic clauses that have been found to confer jurisdiction on private sector arbitrators to hear tort claims may not be present in federal public service collective agreements. For those or other reasons, adjudicators in the federal public service have not been presented with as many claims based on tort or other general laws as have their private sector counterparts, and adjudicators have been reluctant to accept jurisdiction over those types of claims in any event. For example, adjudicators have declined jurisdiction over a claim based on a breach of an agreement settling grievances that were adjudicable[260] and a claim that the failure to renew an employee's term contract was a breach of the *Charter of Rights and Freedoms*.[261]

Therefore, most of the claims based on negligence, defamation, or other torts that arise from the workplace are not referred to adjudication. Furthermore, there are a large number of federal public servants who are not represented in a bargaining unit because they are excluded from Part I of the *FPSLRA*. Those employees often wish to make claims based on their contract of employment.[262] However, as such claims often involve the interpretation of a regulation, a direction, or other instrument made or issued by the employer, or are the result of an occurrence or a matter affecting the employee's terms and conditions of employment, these claims may be referred to the grievance procedure under section 208 of the *FPSLRA*. For these claims that may be grieved but not referred to adjudication, do employees have access to the courts?

Parliament has enacted a provision of the *FPSLRA* that may bar employees from proceeding to the court, where they have the opportunity to grieve (but not adjudicate) their dispute. Section 236 of the

260 *Fox v Treasury Board (Immigration and Refugee Board)*, [2001] CPSSRB No 101.

261 *Pieters*, above note 177.

262 See Chapter 9 for a discussion of the terms and conditions of employment and the legal status of unrepresented employees.

FPSLRA reads as follows (and I have included the title and marginal notes deliberately):

No Right of Action

Disputes relating to employment 236. (1) The right of an employee to seek redress by way of grievance for any dispute relating to his or her terms or conditions of employment is in lieu of any right of action that the employee may have in relation to any act or omission giving rise to the dispute.

Application (2) Subsection (1) applies whether or not the employee avails himself or herself of the right to present a grievance in any particular case and whether or not the grievance could be referred to adjudication.

Exception (3) Subsection (1) does not apply in respect of an employee of a separate agency that has not been designated under subsection 209(3) if the dispute relates to his or her termination of employment for any reason that does not relate to a breach of discipline or misconduct.

On a plain and ordinary reading, section 236 bars employees from bringing an action concerning any matter that could be grieved.

In *Vaughan v Canada*, a former employee of the federal public service brought a civil action against his former employer concerning his eligibility for the Early Retirement Initiative (ERI). The government responded by arguing that the matter was within the exclusive jurisdiction of the grievance procedure, notwithstanding that the matter could not proceed to adjudication. The Supreme Court of Canada concluded that the grievance procedure in the *PSSRA* did not have exclusive jurisdiction over claims that could not be adjudicated. However, while courts retained a residual jurisdiction to hear claims that could be grieved, as a matter of discretion they should generally decline to hear such claims. The Supreme Court went on to say that courts may agree to hear claims where the facts of the case disclose a "particular and individualized conflict problem (as in the whistle-blower cases)."[263]

Section 236 of the *FPSLRA* does not contain any explicit "whistle-blower exception." Thus, the court no longer has any residual discretion to entertain a claim that is otherwise grievable under section 208

263 *Vaughan v Canada*, 2005 SCC 11 at para 37 [*Vaughan*].

of the *FPSLRA*.[264] There is one outlier case suggesting that "residual" discretion still exists, but only in cases where a plaintiff can prove that the grievance system is "corrupt,"[265] but that decision has never been applied (as there was no corruption in that case). Furthermore, even the Ontario Court of Appeal's decision in *Bron* suggests that there may be "residual discretion" where "the grievance process could not provide an appropriate remedy."[266] With respect, to the extent that those decisions state or imply some residual discretion on the part of the court, that residual discretion is inconsistent with the plain wording of section 236. Section 236 bars both civil actions and applications for judicial review[267] (with the exception of judicial review of harassment investigation findings[268]) concerning issues that may be grieved.

Section 236(3) provides an exception to this general rule when the subject matter of the dispute is a termination of employment from a separate agency that has not been designated under section 209(3) of the *FPSLRA*. Employees of separate agencies that have been so designated—which, at the time of publication, were only the CFIA and the CRA[269]—may refer all termination grievances to adjudication. Employees of other separate agencies who are terminated for a reason unrelated to a breach of discipline or misconduct are caught by the exception in section 236(3) and may therefore bring a civil claim for wrongful dismissal[270] or constructive dismissal[271] without having to go through the grievance procedure. Dismissals for poor performance, for example, are unrelated to a breach of discipline or misconduct; therefore, such employees of separate agencies may bring wrongful dismissal claims in the civil courts.[272] Section 236(3) therefore ensures that termination of employment, at least, may always be tested by an

---

264 *Bron v Canada (Attorney General)*, 2010 ONCA 71 at para 29 [*Bron*].

265 *Attorney General of Canada, on behalf of Correctional Service of Canada v Robichaud and MacKinnon*, 2013 NBCA 3 at para 10.

266 *Bron*, above note 264 at para 29.

267 *Gupta v Canada (Attorney General)*, 2021 FCA 202.

268 *Thomas v Canada (Attorney General)*, 2013 FC 292. An employee may still grieve the results of harassment investigations and judicially review the grievance decision instead: *Gagnon v Canada (Attorney General)*, 2017 FC 373.

269 *Public Service Labour Relations Act Separate Agency Designation Order*, SOR/2005-59.

270 *Haroun v Canada (National Research Council)*, 2015 FC 1168 [*Haroun*].

271 *Pearce*, above note 185.

272 *Haroun*, above note 270.

independent body—adjudication for most employees and a civil action for the remainder.

In the first edition of this book, I argued that the use of the term "dispute" in section 236(1) (which is a defined term in the *FPSLRA* to mean a difference that arises in connection with the entering into, renewal, or revision of a collective agreement) meant that section 236 should only apply to collective agreement grievances. I also suggested that the basis of the decision in *Vaughan* was flawed in that, in essence, the Supreme Court of Canada has concluded that when employees have had a civil wrong committed against them whose essential character affects their terms and conditions of employment, they must have their claim decided by—at the end of the day—the deputy head or their designate. The majority of the Supreme Court of Canada saw no unfairness in this result, stating:

> I do not agree with the appellant's broad suggestion, however obliquely made, that the departmental procedure reeks of conflict of interest. The appellant's own success with his 1995 grievance shows this not to be true in practice. The suggestion that departmental officials have an interest in denying ERI benefits to an employee who comes within the applicable policies so as to constitute some sort of institutional bias is simply not credible. If the facts in another case were to disclose a more particular and individualized conflict problem (as in the whistle-blower cases) other considerations will come into play.[273]

Yet why is the claim that departmental officials are institutionally predisposed to rejecting grievances not credible? The Federal Court of Appeal—in a passage adopted by the Supreme Court of Canada in a later case—has recognized that heads of government institutions are predisposed to rejecting access to information requests, stating:

> Heads of government institutions are not disinterested in the interpretation and application of the *Access to Information Act* and are likely to have an institutional predisposition towards restricting the public right of access and construing the exemptions broadly.[274]

273 *Vaughan*, above note 263 at para 37.

274 *3430901 Canada Inc v Canada (Minister of Industry)*, [2002] 1 FC 421 (CA) at para 30, cited in *Macdonell v Quebec (Commission d'accès a l'information)*, 2002 SCC 71 at para 8.

The Supreme Court of Canada did not explain why it is credible to presume that heads of government institutions are institutionally predisposed toward rejecting access to information requests but not credible to suggest that the same heads are institutionally predisposed toward rejecting claims for damages made as the result of negligence or other wrongdoing by managers.

While one decision referred to this point as "of some interest,"[275] to date the jurisprudence remains that section 236 applies to bar all disputes that can be grieved, subject of course to the exception in section 236(3).

The Federal Court of Appeal has addressed this concern about the impartiality (or absence thereof) of the grievance procedure by relying on the availability of judicial review to correct any injustices. The Federal Court of Appeal at one point recognized that the grievance procedure is "not independent of the employer" and that consequently decisions made at the final level of the grievance procedure are reviewed on the correctness standard unless the issue is "purely factual in nature."[276] More recent decisions, though, apply the reasonableness standard of review, as discussed in Chapter 15.

Even presuming that it is fair for an employee's claim for damages to be resolved by the head of the government department responsible for inflicting that damage in the first place, the decision in *Vaughan* has had a negative impact on labour relations in the federal public service. The grievance procedure is designed to facilitate informal discussion between management and employees (typically through their bargaining agent). The grievance procedure has been described in the following ways:

> [G]rievance procedures intend more to provide opportunity for the parties to resolve their differences in an informal fashion than they intend a procedure for the full disclosure of the information upon which a party will be relying to prove its case. Indeed, that the content of grievance settlement discussions are generally viewed as confidential for purposes of grievance arbitration, supports this view that such procedures are designed to facilitate complaint settlements.[277]

---

275 *Renaud v Canada (Attorney General)*, 2013 FC 18 at para 30.

276 *Canada (Attorney General) v Assh*, [2006] FCJ No 1656 (CA) at para 44.

277 *Re FW Fearman Co and UFCW, Local P1227* (1990), 15 LAC (4th) 294 (Marcotte).

> A grievance procedure is designed to encourage a dialogue between the employer and the employees or between the employer and members of the trade union representing the employees. Indeed, one does not expect that the meetings at a grievance procedure will be conducted with the decorum of a tea party—it is expected that complaints and grievances be thrashed out and it is hoped that problems will be mutually resolved to the reasonable satisfaction of all concerned. Often the meetings will generate more heat than light. But that too is intended. A grievance procedure may also serve a useful function by allowing the parties to ventilate. Often if they are unburdened it is helpful to the enterprise. The grievance procedure is designed both to enable the parties to reach reasonable solutions, but also to provide an outlet for festering discontent.[278]
>
> [T]he grievance procedure is intended as an informal mechanism for the review of a grievance for the purpose of determining whether or not a satisfactory resolution of the issues is possible. It may also serve as an opportunity for the disclosure of relevant documents and an exchange of views and perspectives on the grievance. In my opinion, the process is informal and the grievance hearings are at the lowest level of the collective agreement administrative process. The meetings contemplated clearly do not have any of the trappings of an adjudicative proceeding. In my view, only minimal procedural fairness is to be accorded at this stage of the grievance procedure.[279]

The grievance procedure is not meant to be a formal procedure to resolve disputes but instead a chance for management, employees, and bargaining agents to meet, air their differences, and attempt to resolve those differences in an informal way. For that reason, discussions during the grievance procedure are considered privileged and not admissible during adjudication.[280]

Requiring employees to grieve disputes that cannot be referred to adjudication has changed the nature of the grievance procedure. It is no longer an informal procedure for management, employees, and bargaining agents to air their differences; it has become a formal procedure to resolve complicated legal and factual claims that traditionally were

278 *Re Scarborough (Borough) and International Association of Fire Fighters, Loc 626* (1972), 24 LAC 78 (Schime).

279 *Windsor (City) and ONA* (1998), 77 LAC (4th) 218 (Brunner).

280 *Schenkman*, above note 69 at para 74.

the preserve of judges. Since the grievance procedure is the last resort for many employees (subject to judicial review), it has to be formal to protect the procedural rights of those employees.

In response to the grievance procedure becoming more formal, the *FPSLRA* now requires an internal conflict management system (at least in the core public administration) to do the job that the grievance procedure does in most workplaces: permit an informal resolution of employee concerns. Having formalized the grievance procedure by preventing independent third-party resolution of many grievances, Parliament has had to create a new level of dispute resolution to do the job that the grievance procedure was meant to do. Parliament has never explained why it could not have resolved this dilemma by simply permitting third-party adjudication of all grievances and thus permit the grievance procedure to do its job of informally resolving disputes.

This book is largely an explanation of the eccentricities of labour and employment law in the federal public service, and this is certainly one of the largest eccentricities: employees have no right to have all their complaints resolved by an independent third party but must instead file a grievance and plead with management to protect their fundamental rights and receive redress for any damage suffered as the result of the infringement of those rights. Putting aside any questions about the fairness of this approach, it has had an adverse effect on labour relations in the federal public service by formalizing what should otherwise be an informal opportunity to air differences through the grievance procedure.

PART IV

APPOINTMENTS AND STAFFING

CHAPTER ELEVEN

Appointments and the *Public Service Employment Act*

A. INTRODUCTION

This chapter aims to set out the rules governing "employment" or "staffing" of employees whose appointment and employment are governed by the *Public Service Employment Act* (*PSEA*).[1]

In most labour law texts, including texts dealing with public service labour law, there is no need to distinguish between "labour" and "employment" law. In the private sector, "labour law" refers to the laws governing unionized employees, and "employment law" refers to the laws governing all employees, regardless of whether they are members of a union. Hence, in Ontario, there is a *Labour Relations Act* for unionized employees, and an *Employment Standards Act* setting out minimum standards that govern unionized and non-unionized employees alike. In the federal public service, "employment" law refers largely to appointments to the core public administration. While the *PSEA* also governs political activities of public servants and layoffs, those powers have already been addressed in previous chapters. The core of "employment law" in the federal public service is about appointments — or, to use jargon common to the federal public service, "staffing."

There was nothing requiring the federal government to isolate staffing into a different statutory or legal regime from collective bargaining. In Ontario, for example, where there is no statutory "merit principle," allegations about promotions that are not made according to merit

1 *Public Service Employment Act*, SC 2003, c 22, ss 12 & 13 [*PSEA*].

(and seniority) are dealt with by way of grievance like any other complaint.[2] The Fryer Report recommended some level of integration of the "labour" and "staffing" areas, although not a full-scale integration, as is the case in Ontario. The *Federal Public Sector Labour Relations Act* (*FPSLRA*)[3] does go some way toward that integration by permitting grievances about deployments, a subject matter that (under the old Act) was dealt with exclusively by the Public Service Commission on the "staffing" side of the divide. However, for the most part, the federal government has decided to deal with appointments through a specific statutory regime rather than permit the parties to negotiate aspects of the promotional process.

The cornerstone of "employment law" in the federal public service is the "merit principle." This principle was first enshrined in the 1908 *Civil Service Act*[4] and then extended to employees outside of Ottawa in the 1918 version of the *Civil Service Act*.[5] As discussed in the historical overview in Chapter 2, the principle of appointment according to merit evolved throughout the latter half of the nineteenth century and the early part of the twentieth century due to an emerging consensus that appointments to the federal civil service should be based on merit instead of patronage. However, despite that consensus, the term "merit" was not defined by legislation. Instead, a rich body of jurisprudence developed (particularly after employees gained the right to appeal against promotions and transfers), defining and then refining the merit principle.

On 1 April 2005, the old *PSEA* was repealed and replaced by a new Act of the same name. The new *PSEA* made wholesale changes to the merit principle, including a statutory definition of "merit" and a more limited right of appeal against appointments that are alleged to be contrary to merit. However, as explained below, the old jurisprudence about the merit principle—now almost twenty years old—is still relevant to interpreting the new Act and should not be discarded out of hand.

Finally, it is worth examining why the *PSEA* and the merit principle were amended in 2005, and whether those amendments were truly

---

2 Timothy Hadwen & David Strang, *Ontario Public Service Employment & Labour Law*, 2e (Toronto: Irwin Law, 2024) at 18–21.

3 *Federal Public Sector Labour Relations Act*, SC 2003, c 22, s 2 [*FPSLRA*].

4 *The Civil Service Amendment Act, 1908*, 7-8 Edward VII, c 15 (1908).

5 *The Civil Service Act*, 8-9 George V, c 12 (1918).

necessary. The purpose behind the amendments to the merit principle and the appointments process was to permit greater flexibility in making appointments to and within the federal public service. The minister responsible for the Act testified before the Standing Committee on Government Operations and Estimates as follows:

> We have all heard the complaints about the current staffing system: it is too cumbersome, too slow and too focused on unnecessary red tape. It is an obstacle course. We need to fix this if we want to compete with more agile employers.
>
> The provisions of the bill are designed to promote increased flexibility in staffing. They will improve the way we achieve results for Canadians by ensuring our continued ability to put the right people in the right place at the right time.[6]

The federal public service was rife with anecdotal evidence about the glacial pace of the appointments process and the inevitable frustration this caused. Nowhere is this better demonstrated than in *Sampson v Canada (Attorney General)*.[7] Mr. Sampson had been employed on a term basis as an immigration counsellor with the Immigration Department since 1990. He won a competition for an indeterminate position in July 1993. Unfortunately for Mr. Sampson, one of the unsuccessful candidates in that competition appealed against his appointment. The Public Service Commission Appeal Board allowed that appeal in February 1994. The government applied for judicial review but lost that application at first instance in June 1995 before being successful in May 1997. The Federal Court of Appeal returned the matter to the appeal board for redetermination on the basis that the original appeal must be dismissed. However, when Mr. Sampson asked to be appointed to the position he had won, he was informed that due to anticipated staff reductions he would not be appointed to that position, and he was in fact released from the public service in March 1998 upon the expiration of his last term contract. Mr. Sampson applied to Federal Court to force the federal public service to appoint him, but, although expressing sympathy for him, the Court concluded that the government was not

---

6 House of Commons, Standing Committee on Government Operations and Estimates, *Evidence*, 37-2 (27 February 2003) at 9:15 (Hon Lucienne Robillard), online: https://www.ourcommons.ca/DocumentViewer/en/37-2/OGGO/meeting-12/evidence.

7 *Sampson v Canada (Attorney General)*, [1999] FCJ No 1030.

obligated to appoint him to a position. Therefore, Mr. Sampson was denied an indeterminate position in the federal public service (and the various rights to redeployment under the Work Force Adjustment Directive discussed in Chapter 10) only because another candidate launched an unsuccessful appeal, and the appeals process (which went all the way to the Federal Court of Appeal) took almost four years to run its course.

Anecdotal evidence, along with more concrete examples such as that of Mr. Sampson, indicates that the appointments process in the federal public service was problematic. Competitions were taking too long to complete because managers were worried about appeals, and the appeals themselves were causing disruptions to the staffing system. However, as with all anecdotal evidence, it is worthwhile to check these assumptions against the actual data. Below is a chart with the number of appointments to or within the federal public service, the number of appeals, and the number of successful appeals during the years leading up to the amendments to the *PSEA*.[8] The chart excludes appointments to casual positions and student positions as unlikely to generate many appeals (there were, in the years covered, between 22,000 and 30,000 casual and student appointments each year).

Year	Appointments	Selection Processes Appealed	No. of Completed Appeals Allowed	Percentage of Appointments Successfully Appealed
2000–1	68,532	1,343 (1.95%)	79 (9.3%)	0.12%
2001–2	80,558	1,432 (1.78%)	75 (6.5%)	0.09%
2002–3	77,401	1,604 (2.07%)	160 (9%)	0.21%
2003–4	66,796	1,111 (1.66%)	168 (15%)	0.25%
2004–5	58,605	1,223 (2.09%)	213 (17%)	0.36%

As the chart above shows, roughly 2 percent of appointments were appealed in each of those years, and of those small numbers of appeals, between 6.5 and 17 percent were eventually allowed. Therefore, between one-tenth and three-tenths of 1 percent of all appointments were overturned on appeal. Yet the government decided that a 0.3 percent chance of having an appointment overturned on appeal was enough to generate "unnecessary red tape" and create "an obstacle course."

8 The amendments were made by Parliament in 2003 and came into force in 2005.

Of course, the chance that a competition is overturned on appeal is only part of the "red tape": the other part involves the steps necessary to avoid a successful appeal in the first place. Therefore, the chart cannot judge whether the requirements of the merit principle made it more difficult for federal public service managers to make appointments. In 2004, the Public Service Commission could report that

> [o]ver the past year [2003–4], the speed of staffing for both internal and external sources remained comparatively stable. On average, it took 11 weeks to fill an executive position and 21 weeks to staff an indeterminate position below executive level with:
> - a competitive process taking 23.5 weeks; and
> - a non-competitive process taking 17 weeks.[9]

However, in 2002, the Public Service Commission reported that

> [i]f these "bulk" processes [large competitions designed to fill a number of positions] are excluded on the basis of the above, the overall elapsed time for staffing an indeterminate position through a competitive process is estimated to be on average 14 weeks, a number identical to the median, indicating a relatively normal distribution for these processes.[10]

The Public Service Commission did not say whether this was the time elapsed from the announcement of a competition or from the date a competition closed. Parliament concluded that this delay was sufficient to justify limiting the merit principle.

With the benefit of over fifteen years of experience with the "new" *PSEA*, did the experiment work? Looking first at the issue of delay, the data is not positive. The Public Service Commission's 2020–21 annual report states that from 2016–20, it took, on average, 176 days to staff an internal appointment process and 193 days to staff an external appointment process—or twenty-five weeks to staff an internal appointment process, longer than the twenty-one-week average under the "old" *PSEA*.

9 Public Service Commission, *2003–2004 Annual Report* (2004), ch 2.7, online (pdf): https://publications.gc.ca/collections/Collection/SC1-2004E.pdf.

10 Public Service Commission, *2001–2002 Annual Report: Protecting Merit and the Public Trust* (2002), ch 4.7.10, "speed of staffing," online (pdf): https://publications.gc.ca/collections/Collection/SC1-2002E.pdf.

Turning to the prospects of challenges to appointments, the data is more difficult to assess. As discussed below, complaints about appointments can be made to the Federal Public Sector Labour Relations and Employment Board (the FPSLREB)[11] or to the Public Service Commission depending on the nature of the appointment process and complaint, as discussed below. Between 2016 and 2020, the FPSLREB received between 463 and 727 complaints about appointments depending on the year.[12] During the same period, the Public Service Commission received between 191 and 280 complaints or requests for investigation each year that fell within its mandate about appointments.[13] A table going year by year, based off of each year's annual report, follows:

Year	FPSLREB Complaints	PSC Investigations	Total
2016–17	727	280	1,007
2017–18	614	191	805
2018–19	575	250	825
2019–20	463	228	691

The Public Service Commission no longer reports the total number of appointments it makes each year, so it is more difficult to compare the number of complaints against the number of appointments—but it is clear that the number of complaints has decreased under the new *PSEA*.

Therefore, in short, the changes to the *PSEA* were designed to make it easier and faster to appoint public servants in part by making it harder

11 Prior to amendments to the *PSEA* that came into force on 1 November 2014 (*Economic Action Plan 2013 Act, No 2*, SC 2013, c 40, s 414), complaints were heard by the Public Service Staffing Tribunal. In this chapter, references to the FPSLREB include the Public Service Staffing Tribunal for all cases heard prior to that date. Furthermore, earlier chapters refer to "the Board" instead of the FPSLREB. There are a number of different "boards" involved in selection processes: assessment boards, selection boards, and (prior to 2005) appeal boards. To avoid ambiguity, this chapter will use the acronym FPSLREB instead of the generic "the Board."

12 Federal Public Sector Labour Relations and Employment Board, *2020–2021 Annual Report* (2021) at 29, online (pdf): https://pslreb-crtefp.gc.ca/en/about-us/annual-reports/2020-2021/documents/fpslreb-20202021-en.pdf.

13 Public Service Commission of Canada, *2015–2016 Annual Report* (2016), online: www.canada.ca/en/public-service-commission/services/publications/public-service-commission-canada-2015-2016-annual-report.html, and Public Service Commission of Canada, *Annual Report 2020–2021* (2021), online: www.canada.ca/en/public-service-commission/services/publications/annual-reports/annual-report-2020-21.html. These exclude the Public Service Commission's investigations into improper political activities.

for unsuccessful candidates to complain. The changes have decreased the number of complaints, but somehow the appointment process takes longer today than it did before those changes.

B. SCOPE OF THE APPOINTMENT RULES IN THE *PUBLIC SERVICE EMPLOYMENT ACT*

The *PSEA* governs the appointment of employees to the federal public service subject to two exceptions: those appointments that are governed by another statute and exceptions set out in the *PSEA* itself.

Since most separate agencies are governed by statutes that grant them the power to appoint employees to positions, in practice the *PSEA* applies primarily to employees in the core public administration. Additionally, the constituting statutes of several separate agencies state that the *PSEA* applies to them;[14] therefore, that Act governs the appointment process in those agencies. Section 123 of the *PSEA* permits the Governor in Council to make regulations applying the terms of that Act to any other organization.

In terms of the exceptions set out in the Act, section 20 of the *PSEA* permits the Public Service Commission, with the approval of the Governor in Council, to exclude a given position or person, or class of positions or persons, from the operation of the Act.[15] The *PSEA* appointment rules do not apply to deputy heads, associate deputy heads, and special advisors to a minister;[16] high diplomatic personnel (ambassadors, high commissioners, and consuls-general);[17] and other listed senior officials.[18] These rules also do not apply to "ministerial staff," whose circumstances are described in Chapter 14.[19]

14 For example, the *PSEA* applied to the Office of the Superintendent of Financial Services (*Office of the Superintendent of Financial Institutions Act*, RSC 1985, c 18 (3rd Supp), Part I, s 13) and the Financial Consumer Agency of Canada (*Financial Consumer Agency of Canada Act*, SC 2001, c 9, s 10) at the time of publication of this edition.

15 *PSEA*, s 20(1). For example, certain positions within the Office of the Governor General's Secretary are excluded from the Act (*Office of the Governor General's Secretary Exclusion Approval Order*, SI/2017-25), and most students are also excluded from the Act (*Student Employment Programs Participants Exclusion Approval Order*, SI/2010-46).

16 *PSEA*, s 127.1.

17 *Ibid*, s 131.

18 *Ibid*, s 130.

19 *Ibid*, s 128.

C. LEGAL ARCHITECTURE OF THE APPOINTMENT AND RECOURSE PROCESS

The legal architecture of the appointment process can be divided into five parts:

1) The employer (i.e., the Treasury Board or separate agency) determines what positions are required.[20]
2) The employer classifies the positions.[21]
3) The employer determines qualification standards for the work to be performed by the positions.[22]
4) The deputy head establishes the specific qualifications for the position.[23]
5) The Public Service Commission appoints an employee to the position on the request of the deputy head.[24]

Each of these five steps is delegated to employees in the federal public administration. The *PSEA* states that one of its purposes is that "delegation of staffing authority should be to as low a level as possible within the public service."[25] Thus, the employer's powers are performed by a deputy head,[26] who in turn may subdelegate that power to other employees;[27] the Public Service Commission's appointment powers are delegated to a deputy head,[28] who may in turn subdelegate those powers;[29] and the deputy head may delegate its own powers.[30] In practice, all of these powers are delegated or subdelegated to employees within an organization.[31]

The Public Service Commission retains some control over the appointments process through its power to establish policies respecting

---

20 *Financial Administration Act*, RSC 1985, c F-11, s 11.1(1)(a).

21 *Ibid*, s 11.1(1)(b).

22 *PSEA*, s 31(1).

23 *Ibid*, s 30(2)(a).

24 *Ibid*, s 29. This approach is similar to that under the pre-2005 *PSEA* and was explained by the Supreme Court of Canada in *Canada (AG) v Brault*, [1987] 2 SCR 489 [*Brault*].

25 *PSEA*, preamble.

26 *Financial Administration Act*, s 11.2(1).

27 *Ibid*, s 11.2(2).

28 *PSEA*, s 15.

29 *Ibid*, s 24(2).

30 *Ibid*, s 24(1).

31 *Canada (Attorney General) v Shakov*, 2017 FCA 250 at para 22 [*Shakov*].

the manner of making appointments,[32] and those policies are binding on deputy heads and their subordinates to whom they have subdelegated the power of appointment.[33] However, the Public Service Commission's current appointments policies are long on platitudes and short on details, and the policies do not, on their face, significantly limit the discretion of government managers.

There is no recourse available concerning the first step of the appointment process. The classification of positions, and recourse therefrom, is addressed in Chapter 12. There is likewise no recourse available against the determination of the qualification standards for a position.

The situation for the determination of specific qualifications for a position is more complicated. A person may challenge the linguistic standards for a particular position by a complaint to the commissioner of official languages on the basis that the linguistic standards for the position are not objectively required to perform the functions for which the staffing action is undertaken.[34] Complainants bear a "fairly heavy burden" to establish this[35] and must demonstrate "that there is no evidentiary basis for the designation, that the designation is unreasonable, or that the language requirements are imposed frivolously or arbitrarily."[36]

For non-linguistic qualifications, the rule under the old version of the *PSEA* was that there was no recourse against the establishment of qualifications. However, the dividing line between establishing a qualification and assessing a qualification was not always easy to draw. In *Lee v Canada (Attorney General)*,[37] a candidate made it to the top of the eligibility list for a competition but was not appointed because he did not receive a security clearance from the RCMP. He appealed under the Act against this decision, alleging that the decision to refuse him a security clearance was unreasonable. The appeal board accepted jurisdiction over his appeal, but the Supreme Court of Canada overturned that decision. The Supreme Court adopted the decision of the Federal Court of Appeal, which read:

---

32 *PSEA*, s 29(3).

33 *Ibid*, s 16.

34 *Official Languages Act*, RSC 1985, c 31 (4th Supp), s 91.

35 *Professional Institute of the Public Service of Canada v Canada*, [1993] 2 FC 90 (TD) at 106.

36 *Rogers v Canada (Department of National Defence)*, 2001 FCT 90 at para 27.

37 *Lee v Canada (Attorney General)*, [1981] 2 SCR 90.

> The additional "qualification" or requirement of a security clearance was not, and could not be, evaluated or assessed by the selection boards and was not, for the reasons I have indicated, part of the selection process contemplated by s. 10. As such, it could not in my opinion be subject to review by an Appeal Board.[38]

The Supreme Court essentially concluded that the authority to require a security clearance as a condition of appointment and the authority to determine whether such clearance should be granted was part of the management authority that had not been assigned to the Public Service Commission.

The Federal Court has affirmed on many occasions that the department's jurisdiction to establish qualifications for a position under the old *PSEA* was absolute. In *Canada (Attorney General) v Viola*[39] and *Canada (Attorney General) v Asselin*,[40] for example, the Federal Court of Appeal stated that the appeal board did not have the jurisdiction to challenge the linguistic qualifications or conditions established by a department for obtaining a position. In *Chang v Canada (Attorney General)*,[41] the Federal Court also affirmed that Revenue Canada had the right to establish an educational requirement for the position. An appeal board did not have the jurisdiction to review the choice of qualifications and had "no say with respect to the qualifications which an employer-department considers necessary or desirable."[42] On the other hand, the Federal Court of Appeal in *Delanoy v Canada (Public Service Commission Appeal Board)*[43] decided that the qualifications for a position must have a "rational link" to "selection according to merit" and could be challenged on that basis.

Under the new *PSEA*, the Public Service Commission may investigate "any external appointment process" without limitation. On its face, this includes all aspects of the appointment process—including the establishment of a qualification.

38 *Ibid* at 5 (QL).

39 *Canada (Attorney General) v Viola*, [1991] 1 FC 373 (CA).

40 *Canada (Attorney General) v Asselin*, [1999] FCJ No 1572 (CA).

41 *Chang v Canada (Attorney General)*, [2000] FCJ No 767.

42 *Canada (Attorney General) v Perera*, [2000] FCJ No 829 (CA). See also *Davies v Canada (Attorney General)*, [2005] FCJ No 188 (CA).

43 *Delanoy v Canada (Public Service Commission Appeal Board)*, [1977] 1 FC 562 (CA).

Internal appointment processes are subject to a complaint to the FPSLREB on the grounds that the complainant has not been appointed by reason of "an abuse of authority by the Commission or the deputy head in the exercise of its or his or her authority under subsection 30(2)."[44] Section 30(2) states that an appointment is made on the basis of merit when "the Commission is satisfied that the person to be appointed meets the essential qualifications for the work to be performed, as established by the deputy head."[45] By way of context, most positions have two types of qualifications: essential qualifications (which are mandatory for the successful candidate) and asset qualifications (which are not mandatory but are still helpful). To be appointed, a candidate must meet the essential qualifications for the position, but not necessarily the asset qualifications. In other words, the delegated manager may consider asset qualifications but may also appoint a candidate who does not possess any of the asset qualifications for the position.[46]

The FPSLREB has interpreted section 30(2) of the *PSEA* as giving the deputy head and their delegates the authority to establish the essential qualifications for the position and, therefore, has taken jurisdiction over complaints about particular qualifications.[47] The FPSLREB, however, has also affirmed that it is not its role to establish qualifications or second-guess the establishment of qualifications by a department, stating that there is "broad discretion given to delegates to establish the necessary qualifications for the position they want to staff."[48] The delegate does not need to prove that the qualifications are necessary to perform the position, but must show that the qualifications do not exceed the qualification standards set by the employer.[49] Additionally, the department cannot change the qualifications after advertising the

---

44 *PSEA*, s 77(1)(a). This is an odd way to put this point as the actual appointment is made under s 29, and s 30(2) defines when an appointment has been made on the basis of merit.

45 *PSEA*, s 30(2).

46 *Jalal v Deputy Minister of Human Resources and Skills Development Canada*, 2011 PSST 38 at para 95.

47 *Rinn v Canada (Deputy Minister of Transport, Infrastructure and Communities)*, 2007 FPSLREB 44 at para 41 [*Rinn*].

48 *Trites v Deputy Minister of Public Works and Government Services Canada*, 2009 PSST 16 at para 54 [*Trites*].

49 *Rinn*, above note 46 at para 41; *Kilbray v Canada (Attorney General)*, 2009 FC 390, and *Payne v the Deputy Minister of National Defence*, 2013 FPSLREB 15 at para 84.

position (called an expression of interest). For example, in one case the department changed an educational qualification of two years of post-secondary education to add that this qualification may be met by an "acceptable combination of education, training and/or experience" after it had advertised the position and obtained applications. The FPSLREB concluded that changing qualifications after advertising the position was an abuse of authority.[50]

Another way to consider this issue is whether the qualification has been improperly amended by someone without the delegated authority to do so. In some cases, the qualifications are set by one official and the assessment of candidates is made by other officials (commonly referred to as a selection or assessment board). A selection board acts outside its authority by amending the definition of a qualification for a position.[51] For example, one appointment process had a qualification of "significant" experience defined as two periods of "approximately 12 months'" or a single period of "approximately 24 months'" experience. The assessment board abused its authority by creating a cut-off of a minimum acceptable two 11-month or one 22-month assignment, as this altered the qualification that was intended to provide discretion rather than create strict temporal limits.[52]

The fifth step—the actual appointment—is subject to two different avenues of recourse depending on the nature of the appointment and the particular ground of the complaint. External appointment processes (i.e., a process for appointment in which persons outside the public service are eligible[53]) are investigated by the Public Service Commission, which may investigate whether there has been an error, an omission, or improper conduct that affected the selection of the persons appointed or that the appointment was not made on the basis of merit.[54] The Public Service Commission is also responsible for investigating all allegations of fraud[55] and political influence[56] in an appointment. Finally, and most

50 *De Santis v Commissioner of the Correctional Service of Canada*, 2016 PSLREB 34 at para 39 [*De Santis*].

51 *Canada (Attorney General) v Blashford*, [1991] 2 FC 44 (CA).

52 *Bowman v Deputy Minister of Citizenship and Immigration Canada*, 2008 FPSLREB 12.

53 *PSEA*, s 2(1).

54 *Ibid*, s 66.

55 *Ibid*, s 69.

56 *Ibid*, s 68.

frequently, an unsuccessful candidate or a person in the area of selection for a non-advertised position may file a complaint with the FPSLREB that they were not appointed by reason of an abuse of authority or the failure to assess them in the official language of their choice.[57] These recourse mechanisms will be described in much greater detail below.

D. WHAT CONSTITUTES AN "APPOINTMENT"?

As discussed above, section 29 of the *PSEA* states that the Public Service Commission has the exclusive authority to make appointments to or from within the public service except as otherwise provided in that Act, and this power is delegated and subdelegated to deputy heads and lower-level employees.

The term "appointment" is not defined in the *PSEA*. Since only appointments may be subject to a challenge to the FPSLREB, courts have had to define what is and is not an appointment. The leading cases on this issue are two decisions of the Supreme Court of Canada released on the same day: *Canada (AG) v Brault*[58] and *Doré v Canada*.[59] In those cases, the Supreme Court concluded that substance is more important than form when determining whether a staffing action constitutes an "appointment"—in other words, whether a particular staffing action is an "appointment" does not depend on whether the government chooses to characterize it as such. Instead, courts should focus on the duration of the assignment, whether there has been a significant change in functions, or whether the assignment is an attempt to avoid the merit principle when deciding whether a particular assignment is an "appointment."

In *Brault*, the Department of National Revenue Customs and Excise authorized the establishment of a canine detection unit and posted a notice inviting customs inspectors to apply for assignment as a "dog handler." Two unsuccessful candidates for the position challenged the selection of the successful candidates by way of appeal under section 21 of the old *PSEA*. The department argued that the assignment was not an "appointment" under the Act, and therefore there was no right of appeal. The Supreme Court eventually concluded that this staffing action was an "appointment" under the Act, thus triggering both the

---

57 *Ibid*, s 77.

58 *Brault*, above note 24.

59 *Doré v Canada*, [1987] 2 SCR 503 [*Doré*].

right of appeal and the application of the merit principle. The Supreme Court focused on the new duties and functions of the "dog-handler" position. It stated:

> Obviously the administration must have reasonable flexibility to make minor changes in the functions of an existing position in the Public Service which the occupant of the position may be called on to perform, without thereby creating a new position for which an appointment based on selection according to merit must be made. Where, however, as in the present case, the change in functions is of such a significant or substantial nature as to call for additional or special qualifications requiring evaluation and therefore what amounts to a new selection for the position, a new position within the meaning of the Act is created.[60]

In *Doré*, an employee of a Canada Employment Centre was assigned the functions of a supervisor pending classification of a new position for such functions. When another employee appealed that assignment, the department argued that it was a temporary assignment and therefore not an "appointment" under the *PSEA*. Again, the Supreme Court disagreed. The Court stated that the functions of the supervisor were sufficiently different from the employee's old functions that there was a new position, just as in *Brault*. The issue in *Doré* really revolved around the duration of the assignment. The Supreme Court was willing to accept that temporary assignments were possible, but after a certain point in time those temporary assignments eventually became "appointments" under the Act. The Supreme Court stated:

> [W]hile it must be possible for the administration to assign a person in the Public Service to new functions on a temporary basis without giving rise to the application of the merit principle and the right of appeal, that reasonable flexibility should no longer be available where, as in the present case, the assignment is permitted to become one of such significant and indefinite duration as may be presumed to place the occupant of the position at a distinct advantage in any subsequent selection process.[61]

---

60 *Brault*, above note 24 at para 13.

61 *Doré*, above note 59 at para 9.

In *Doré*, the assignment had gone on for at least nine months, which the Supreme Court concluded was too long to remain a temporary assignment.

In both *Brault* and *Doré*, the Supreme Court of Canada emphasized that substance is more important than form when determining whether a staffing action constitutes an "appointment." As it stated in *Doré*:

> [T]he application of the merit principle and the right of appeal under section 21 of the *Public Service Employment Act* cannot depend on whether the Department chooses to regard what is done as the creation of a position and an appointment to it within the meaning of the Act. It is what the Department has objectively done as a matter of fact and not what it may have intended or understood it was doing as a matter of law that must determine the application of the merit principle and the right of appeal.[62]

The Federal Court has, on a number of occasions, interpreted and applied the principles established in *Brault* and *Doré*. In *Abercrombie v Canada (Attorney General)* for example, the Federal Court summarized the legal test as follows:

> (i) was the assignment of Ms. Wipp of such "significant and indefinite duration" to be presumed to place Ms. Wipp at a "distinct advantage" in any subsequent selection process?; (ii) was there such a significant or substantial change in functions requiring "additional or special qualifications" so that the assignment was tantamount to a new position?; and (iii) was the staffing action in fact an attempt by the Department to avoid observance of the merit principle?[63]

In *Abercrombie*, Ms. Wipp had been occupying her position from 5 June 1996 until 31 March 1999, through two term appointments (from 5 June 1996 to 31 March 1997) and then a number of temporary "assignments." The Federal Court did not conclusively decide that this three-year period was long enough to trigger an "appointment" (it instead referred the matter back to the appeal board to be decided in accordance with the proper legal test).

The three-part test in *Abercrombie* does not limit the circumstances where an assignment may constitute an appointment. In *Baur v Canada*

62 *Ibid* at para 7.

63 *Abercrombie v Canada (Attorney General)*, [2000] FCJ No 435 at para 16.

(Attorney General),[64] the appeal board concluded that the particular staffing action at issue did not fit within any of the three categories identified in *Abercrombie* and was therefore not an appointment. The Federal Court considered this decision to limit the review to the three *Abercrombie* circumstances to be a reviewable error and quashed the decision. In that case, the Canadian Coast Guard changed a large number of indeterminate full-time employees into indeterminate seasonal employees in 1997. In actual fact, the Coast Guard granted extensions to its seasonal employees so that they ended up working all year and then in 2001 converted the seasonal employees back into full-time employees. Three of the employees who refused seasonal work back in 1997 appealed, alleging that the conversion from seasonal to full-time status was an appointment. The Federal Court concluded that this conversion was an appointment in light of the context behind the conversion (in particular the switch to and from full-time status) and the financial benefits of the conversion for those employees. Therefore, a staffing action may constitute an "appointment" even if the circumstances do not concern the three factors listed in *Abercrombie*.

These cases were all decided prior to the 2005 amendments to the *PSEA*, but they remain valid today. For example, the FPSLREB concluded that an allegedly temporary assignment was in fact an acting appointment based on the intention of management, an assessment of the duties of the supposed assignment, and the fact that the employee was eventually retroactively appointed for a period corresponding to the beginning of the assignment.[65] This issue remains highly factually dependent. For example, in *Canada (Attorney General) v Smith*,[66] the Federal Court of Appeal addressed another dog-handler case that was almost identical to *Brault*. A dog-handler's dog was retired in 2009. The department decided to rotate dog-handling duties, and as a result, another employee was assigned to dog-handling duties. Despite the facial similarity to *Brault*, the result in *Smith* was different because the work description of the position held by both employees listed dog handling as a possible duty. The FPSLREB and Federal Court of Appeal both concluded that this case did not involve the creation of additional functions or duties. Despite acknowledging that relying on the work

64 *Baur v Canada (Attorney General)*, [2004] FCJ No 926.

65 *Beyak v Deputy Minister of Natural Resources Canada*, 2009 PSST 35 at para 95 [*Beyak*].

66 *Canada (Attorney General) v Smith*, 2012 FCA 326.

description "may appear to some to be too formalistic,"[67] the Federal Court of Appeal upheld the FPSLREB's decision that this was an assignment and not an appointment.

Appointments under the *PSEA* are presumptively indeterminate.[68] An appointment may be made for a fixed term. An extension of a term appointment by a deputy head (or their delegate) does not trigger a new right to complain about that appointment to the FPSLREB.[69] Also, the Act requires the employer to develop a policy whereby employees already appointed to term positions for a certain length of time convert to indeterminate employees.[70] This conversion does not constitute a new appointment.[71] Currently, the Treasury Board Directive on Term Employment states that term employees with a cumulative working period (i.e., without a break of longer than sixty days) within the same department of at least three years become indeterminate employees.[72]

An acting appointment is different from a term appointment. An acting appointment is the temporary performance of the duties of another position by an employee if the performance of those duties would have constituted a promotion[73] had they been appointed to the position.[74] Acting appointments are excluded from certain priority provisions of the *PSEA* (discussed below).[75] Acting appointments of a cumulative period of less than four months are also exempt from challenge to the FPSLREB,[76] and acting appointments of between four and twelve months are exempt from challenge to the FPSLREB on the basis of failure to meet the official language proficiency.[77] These four- and twelve-month periods apply to the position and not the individual given the acting appointment. For example, appointing one employee for just

67 *Ibid* at para 24.
68 *PSEA*, s 57.
69 *Ibid*, s 58(1).
70 *Ibid*, s 59(1).
71 *Ibid*, s 59(2).
72 Treasury Board of Canada Secretariat, *Directive on Term Employment* (1 April 2021), online: www.tbs-sct.canada.ca/pol/doc-eng.aspx?id=32629.
73 A "promotion" means the assignment to an employee of the duties of a position that involves an increase of salary of a defined amount: *Definition of Promotion Regulations*, SOR/2005-376, s 3(1).
74 *Public Service Employment Regulations*, SOR/2005-334, s 1 [*PSER*].
75 *Ibid*, s 12.
76 *Ibid*, s 14.
77 *Ibid*, s 15.

under four months and another employee for just under twelve months meant that the department exceeded the twelve-month threshold for the exception to the official language proficiency rule.[78]

Additionally, an acting appointment may exceed the time limits set out above when the acting appointment is part of a rotational system established by the Department of Citizenship and Immigration, the Department of Foreign Affairs and International Trade (now called Global Affairs Canada), and the Canada Border Services Agency.[79] This provision was adopted "to cover temporary postings to missions abroad when such a posting is above the person's substantive position. If the rotational posting is at-level, there is no appointment."[80] Rotational appointments are also exempt from challenge to the FPSLREB, even if the rotational position was filled after an advertised competitive process.[81]

A "deployment" is yet another type of appointment, being a consensual transfer from one position to another that is not a promotion. Not all temporary lateral transfers must be done by way of a deployment: an assignment is still available. In *Roberts v Canada (Attorney General)*,[82] two employees were temporarily assigned to other positions in the same department. The unsuccessful candidates for this temporary assignment attempted to appeal. They argued that any assignment is either a deployment or an appointment and that as this assignment was not a deployment, it must be an appointment and therefore subject to the merit principle and the right of appeal. The Federal Court of Appeal disagreed, stating that "a department may move an employee from one position to another, on a temporary basis, without having to deploy him."[83] The Federal Court of Appeal then fell back on the *Brault* and *Doré* tests and concluded that the assignments were not so long in duration, or so significant a change in functions, as to constitute an appointment.

Within the federal public service, staffing actions are sometimes referred to as either assignments or secondments. The term "assignment" describes a transfer to a position within the same department,

78 *Doucette v Deputy Minister of Veterans Affairs Canada*, 2021 FPSLREB 96.

79 *PSER*, s17.

80 *George v President of the Canada Border Services Agency*, 2017 PSLREB 28 at para 50.

81 *Ibid.*

82 *Roberts v Canada (Attorney General)*, [1999] FCJ No 323 (CA).

83 *Ibid* at para 5.

and the term "secondment" describes a transfer to a position in another department.[84] Either an assignment or a secondment may or may not be an appointment under the Act, depending on the application of the tests in *Brault* and *Doré*. In *Canada (Attorney General) v Canada (Public Service Commission)*,[85] the Department of National Revenue appointed an employee to a new position pursuant to a secondment agreement, promising to appoint the employee to an indeterminate position in Western Canada at the conclusion of his secondment. The Federal Court agreed with the appeal board that this was an appointment under the Act because of the significant change in duties at the end of the secondment.

The decision in *Doré* that an assignment becomes an appointment if the assignment is for a significant duration does not mean that occupants of temporary positions automatically become permanent or indeterminate employees with the passage of time. In *Langlois v Canada*,[86] an employee had a "temporary" assignment of several years at a higher salary level. Eventually, the higher position was reduced to a lower level. The employee claimed that, with the passage of time, his higher position became permanent and that he was entitled to the higher salary. The Federal Court disagreed, concluding that the passage of time did not have the effect of allowing an employee to acquire a permanent position.

An appointment does not take place immediately after the successful candidate is selected. There is instead a period of time to conduct an informal discussion with candidates who have been eliminated from consideration for an appointment.[87] The informal discussion is not mandatory, and a poorly conducted informal discussion is not itself an abuse of authority,[88] but the FPSLREB has stated that it is strongly encouraged.[89] The informal discussion is

> intended primarily to be a means of communication for a candidate to discuss the reasons for elimination from a process. If it is discovered an error has been made, for example, if the assessment board

84 *Keenan v Canada (Public Service Commission)*, [1989] 3 FC 643 (CA).

85 *Canada (Attorney General) v Canada (Public Service Commission)*, [1994] FCJ No 1788.

86 *Langlois v Canada*, [1991] ACF No 616.

87 *PSEA*, s 47.

88 *Lirette v Deputy Minister of National Defence*, 2011 PSST 42 at para 39 [*Lirette*].

89 *Laporte v Deputy Head (Shared Services Canada)*, 2022 FPSLREB 31; *Henry v Deputy Head of Service Canada*, 2008 PSST 10.

> did not consider some information listed on a candidate's application, this provides the opportunity for the manager to correct that mistake. However, informal discussion is not an opportunity to request that the assessment board reassess a candidate's qualifications.[90]

The *PSEA* also sets out a requirement for two notifications concerning appointments. After the assessment of all candidates has been completed, each person who participated in the process (in the case of an advertised internal appointment process) or each person in the area of selection (in the case of a non-advertised appointment process) receives notice that they are not being appointed.[91] There is then a waiting period before the appointment takes place to give time for informal discussion to occur.[92] After this waiting period, a second notice is issued informing those same people of the name of the successful candidate.[93] The notices are supposed to be published in a timely manner, but lateness in publishing the notice is not an abuse of authority.[94]

E. LIMITS TO THE CANDIDATES ELIGIBLE FOR SELECTION

The *PSEA* permits limits on who may apply in a selection process. These limitations are discussed below.

1) Internal and External Selection Processes

As mentioned above, an internal selection process is a selection process open only to employees of the public service; an external selection process is open to any member of the public. The definition of the "public service" in the *PSEA* includes separate employers, so employees of separate agencies may participate in an internal selection process. This is specifically set out in section 35 of the *PSEA*, which permits employees of separate agencies and certain designated organizations to participate in competitions unless the area of selection of that competition excludes them. Unsuccessful candidates who are employees of separate agencies

90 *Rozka et al v Deputy Minister of Citizenship and Immigration Canada*, 2007 PSST 46 at para 76.

91 *PSEA*, s 48(1).

92 *Ibid*, s 48(2). This purpose is described in *Richards v Deputy Minister of Fisheries and Oceans*, 2009 PSST 28 at para 73.

93 *PSEA*, s 48(3).

94 *Merkley v Deputy Minister of National Defence*, 2017 PSLREB 47 at para 32.

have the right to complain to the FPSLREB on the same grounds as employees who are governed by the *PSEA*. Similarly, members of the Canadian Armed Forces may participate in internal selection processes and also complain to the FPSLREB if they are unsuccessful,[95] as may former members of the Canadian Armed Forces who have been honourably released after at least three years' service,[96] ministers' staff,[97] staff of the Leader of the Opposition in the Senate or the House of Commons,[98] and employees of the Senate, House of Commons, Library of Parliament, Office of the Conflict of Interest and Ethics Commissioner, Parliamentary Protective Service, or office of the Parliamentary Budget Officer[99] to have the same rights as employees of separate agencies. Finally, casual employees are not eligible to participate in an internal selection process.[100]

Participants in an internal selection process have greater rights than participants in an external selection process. Those greater rights are

- the right to ask the commission (or deputy head or subdelegate) to informally discuss a decision to eliminate a candidate from consideration;[101]
- the right to know the name of the person being considered for each appointment after the assessment of candidates has been completed;[102] and
- the right to refer a complaint to the FPSLREB instead of the commission.[103]

The old *PSEA* used to contain a presumption that appointments would be made from within the public service except where, in the opinion of the Public Service Commission, it was not in the best interest of the public service to do so. If an employee wanted to complain that the commission should not have permitted an external selection process (then called an "open competition"), then the employee could

95 *PSEA*, s 35.1.
96 *Ibid*, s 35.11.
97 *Ibid*, s 35.2. This rule replaced the previous rule that ministers' staff had a priority for appointment over other employees.
98 *Ibid*.
99 *Ibid*, s 35.3.
100 *Ibid*, s 50(4).
101 *Ibid*, s 47.
102 *Ibid*, s 48(1).
103 *Ibid*, s 77.

file a complaint with the commission itself, which would investigate the decision to hold an open competition. The new *PSEA* does not contain this avenue of complaint. Therefore, complaints that a particular staffing action should have been completed by an internal rather than an external process must be brought by way of judicial review.

In *Ethier v Canada (Royal Canadian Mounted Police)*,[104] the Federal Court quashed a decision to hold an open instead of a closed competition because the decision was not made reasonably or in good faith. In that case, the Federal Court concluded that the decision to hold an open competition was made because the RCMP wanted to enable a previous occupant of the position to be eligible to compete for it again. The Court stated that "the respondent's discretion in deciding how to staff the position of canteen manager was not absolute, and was restricted to considerations within the purview of the Public Service Employment Act."[105] The Court was particularly concerned that the decision to hold an open competition immunized the competition from review by an appeal board. Similarly, a decision to hold an external selection process immunizes the competition from review by the FPSLREB. Therefore, *Ethier* is likely still binding law, and the decision to hold an external selection process must be made in good faith, reasonably, and be based on considerations within the purview of the *PSEA*.

2) Area of Selection

For the purposes of eligibility in any appointment process other than an incumbent-based process, the Public Service Commission may determine an area of selection by limiting the geographic, organizational, or occupational criteria or by establishing, as a criterion, belonging to a designated group under the *Employment Equity Act*.[106] The area of selection is an absolute bar to participating in a selection process, and if a candidate submits an application without being within the area of selection, then they do not have the right to complain to the FPSLREB about that selection process.[107]

---

104 *Ethier v Canada (Royal Canadian Mounted Police)*, [1995] FCJ No 691, aff'd *Canada (Royal Canadian Mounted Police) v Ethier*, [1996] FCJ No 1272 (CA).

105 *Ibid* (FC) at para 30.

106 *PSEA*, s 34(1).

107 *Ibid*, s 77(2)(a).

The Public Service Commission may not limit access to a competition by reference to the salary currently earned by candidates. In *Bullion v Canada (Deputy Minister of Indian Affairs and Northern Development)*,[108] an employee was excluded from a closed competition on the ground that he occupied a position in which the maximum rate of pay was less than $22,600 per annum. The commission argued that its restriction on the basis of salary was actually a restriction based on the "occupational nature and level of positions" (the phrase used in the old *PSEA* at that time). The Supreme Court disagreed, concluding instead that the commission did not direct its mind to the level of position as it relates to its occupational nature. A minimum salary level does not relate to the occupational nature of positions.

The choice of area of selection does not need to be made consistently with the merit principle. The merit principle "does not require that every available qualified person be considered for appointment"; therefore, the merit principle does not limit the choice of areas of selection.[109] However, if an area of selection is chosen specifically to favour one candidate or reject another candidate, this would likely be grounds for judicial review[110] of the choice of area of selection because the choice was arbitrary and an abuse of discretion.

3) Advertised and Non-advertised Appointment Process

In making an appointment, the Public Service Commission (or deputy head or subdelegate) may use an advertised or non-advertised appointment process.[111] The *PSEA* does not define what is meant by an advertised or non-advertised appointment process, nor are there any regulations specifying when a department may use an advertised or a non-advertised appointment process. During a non-advertised process, the deputy head or delegate only assesses the qualifications of the individual intended to be appointed.[112]

108 *Bullion v Canada (Deputy Minister of Indian Affairs and Northern Development)*, [1980] 2 SCR 578.

109 *Attorney General of Canada v Landriault*, [1983] 1 FC 636 (CA).

110 Decisions to delineate an area of selection used to be within the jurisdiction of the appeal board: *ibid* and *Gayef v Canada (Treasury Board)*, [1993] FCJ No 1006.

111 *PSEA*, s 33.

112 *Vaudrin v Deputy Minister of Human Resources and Skills Development Canada*, 2011 PSST 19 at para 52.

A person within the area of selection of an internal, non-advertised appointment process may file a complaint with the FPSLREB that the choice between an advertised and a non-advertised process was an "abuse of authority," as that term is discussed below.

The choice between an advertised and a non-advertised appointment process is not just important because a non-advertised process may not consider every available candidate. The statutory priorities for appointment for veterans[113] and Canadian citizens[114] depend on the use of an advertised appointment process.[115]

Either process may mean that only one person was considered for an appointment.[116]

F. THE MERIT PRINCIPLE

The cornerstone of the *PSEA* is that appointments to and from within the federal public service must be made according to merit. As the Federal Court of Appeal has put it, "Selection according to merit is the dominant objective and consideration of the *Public Service Employment Act* and the essential criterion by which the exercise of powers under the Act is to be judged."[117] The preamble to the *PSEA* states that

> Canada will continue to benefit from a public service that is based on merit and non-partisanship and in which these values are independently safeguarded.[118]

However, selection according to merit is simply a platitude without tribunals and courts breathing life into that concept. This section explains how those tribunals and courts breathed life into the merit principle under the old *PSEA* and the extent to which the merit principle under the new *PSEA* will extend that life.

---

113 *PSEA*, s 39(1).

114 *Ibid.*

115 See the discussion of the statutory priorities and preferences below.

116 *PSEA*, s 30(4). See *Labaie et al v Deputy Minister of National Defence et al*, 2009 PSST 30 at para 55.

117 *Bambrough v Canada (Public Service Commission Appeal Board)*, [1976] 2 FC 109 (CA) at para 10 [*Bambrough*].

118 *PSEA*, preamble.

1) What Was the "Merit Principle" Under the Old *Public Service Employment Act*?

The old *PSEA* did not contain any legislative definition of "merit." Section 10 of the old Act required appointments to be made on the basis of merit and read as follows:

> 10. (1) Appointments to or from within the public service shall be based on selection according to merit, as determined by the Commission, and shall be made by the Commission, at the request of the deputy head concerned, by competition or by such other process of personnel selection designed to establish the merit of candidates as the Commission considers is in the best interests of the public service.
>
> (2) For the purposes of subsection (1), selection according to merit may, in the circumstances prescribed by the regulations of the Commission, be based on the competence of a person being considered for appointment as measured by such standard of competence as the Commission may establish, rather than as measured against the competence of other persons.

Therefore, it fell to the courts to define "merit" under the Act. The Federal Court of Appeal said that selection "according to merit" meant that "the best persons possible will be found for the various positions in the Public Service"[119] or that the public service must "find the best qualified persons from among those who are available."[120]

In *Evans v Canada (Public Service Commission Appeal Board)*,[121] the Supreme Court of Canada took its turn at defining the term "merit." At issue in that case was whether a correctional officer's application for the position of senior correctional officer should be prejudiced by the report of a parliamentary subcommittee that named him as the instigator of a prison riot at Millhaven Penitentiary or whether considering this "external" attribute violated the merit principle. The Supreme Court defined the merit principle as follows:

> The process starts with s. 10 which I have already set out and which requires that the personnel selection system "establish the merit of candidates." The issue reduces itself to a determination as to the correct

119 *Nanda v Appeal Board Established by the Public Service Commission*, [1972] FC 277 (CA) at 297.

120 *Canada (Attorney General) v Greaves*, [1982] 1 FC 806 (CA) at 5.

121 *Evans v Canada (Public Service Commission Appeal Board)*, [1983] 1 SCR 582.

> meaning in the context of the statute of the word "merit." If the word be given its broadest interpretation, then the term will include not only inherent, internal elements of credit, meritorious characteristics, achievements of the candidate and so on, but also external characteristics which would include the suitability or usefulness of the candidate in the office or position in question. That is to say, merit might on the one hand embrace only inherent or intrinsic values as discerned in the nature, personality, character, training and experience of the candidate, or it might additionally include the extra-natural or man-made attributes such as usefulness, suitability or incapacities created in the community and not intrinsic in the candidate....
>
> In the context in which the word is employed in s. 10, and considering particularly the importance of s. 10 as enunciated in the fundamental principles of the pattern adopted by Parliament in the Act, I conclude that the word merit refers to the intrinsic, natural characteristics of the candidate. Conversely, this term, in my view, does not include any man-made restrictions or limitations which might, as in this case, be imposed upon a candidate and which limitations by themselves do not necessarily have any relationship to the inherent, meritorious qualities of the candidate.[122]

Therefore, candidates for positions in the federal public service had to be appointed on the basis of their intrinsic, natural characteristics. In the case of Mr. Evans, the mere fact that he was named by a parliamentary subcommittee was not an intrinsic, natural characteristic impacting his merit.

The merit principle did not mean that whenever a public servant is meritorious they acquire the right to be appointed. It meant, rather, that when there is an opportunity for an appointment, the most meritorious person should be promoted.[123]

Amendments to the *PSEA* in 1993 changed sections 10(1) and 10(2) to create two different versions of the merit principle, generally referred to as "relative" merit and "individual" merit. These were simply different applications of the merit principle, and "individual" merit was not

122 *Ibid* at 7.

123 *Leckie v Canada*, [1993] 2 FC 473 (CA) at para 11.

intended to be an exception to the merit principle.[124] Section 10(2), or individual merit, only applied in a limited number of circumstances.[125]

Whether merit was assessed using section 10(1) or 10(2), unsuccessful candidates had the right to appeal that appointment to the Public Service Commission Appeal Board and argue that the appointment violated the merit principle. The appeal was not meant to be a forum to complain about the selection process per se, but was against the appointment itself. As the Federal Court of Appeal stated:

> An appeal under section 21 of the *Public Service Employment Act* is not directed against a selection process but against one or more appointments or proposed appointments. The question to be determined by an Appeal Board under section 21 is not whether the selection process that culminated in the appointment under attack was, in all respects, regular and fair, but whether that appointment would contravene the merit principle. Once an Appeal Board is satisfied that the result of a competition has not been influenced by an irregularity, it may not rely on that irregularity to allow the appeal.[126]

Therefore, not every "irregularity" in a selection process meant that an appeal against the appointment would be successful. Instead, an unsuccessful candidate would have to demonstrate that the irregularity had a material effect on the result of the appointment.[127] Procedural irregularities were therefore not relevant unless they led to the conclusion that the selection process was not based on merit.[128] Furthermore, there was no closed list of categories with respect to when the merit principle had been violated.[129] That being said, there were a number of common categories of errors or allegations of breaches of the merit principle.

124 *Buttar v Canada (Attorney General)*, [2000] FCJ No 437 (CA) at para 4.
125 *Public Service Employment Regulations, 2000*, SOR/2000-80, s 5(2) [repealed].
126 *Caldwell v Canada (Public Service Commission)*, [1978] FCJ No 918 (CA) at para 4.
127 *Aplin v Canada (Attorney General)*, [2004] FCJ No 848 at para 24.
128 *Bambrough*, above note 117 at para 10.
129 *Baur v Canada (Attorney General)*, 2004 FC 725 at para 41(8).

2) The Merit Principle Under the New *Public Service Employment Act*

The new *PSEA* maintains the requirement that appointments to the federal public service shall be made on the basis of merit.[130] However, unlike its predecessors, the new Act defines the term "merit" as follows:

> 30(2) An appointment is made on the basis of merit when
> (*a*) the Commission is satisfied that the person to be appointed meets the essential qualifications for the work to be performed, as established by the deputy head, including official language proficiency; and
> (*b*) the Commission has regard to
> (i) any additional qualifications that the deputy head may consider to be an asset for the work to be performed, or for the organization, currently or in the future,
> (ii) any current or future operational requirements of the organization that may be identified by the deputy head, and
> (iii) any current or future needs of the organization that may be identified by the deputy head.

The new Act goes on to state that the current and future needs of the organization may include the current and future needs of the public service as a whole as identified by the employer and that the deputy head determines to be relevant to the organization.[131] Finally, the new Act confirms that the Public Service Commission (and by extension deputy heads and their subdelegates) is not required to consider more than one person for an appointment to be made on the basis of merit.[132]

The thrust of the merit principle under the old *PSEA* was that the "best" candidate should be appointed to each position in the federal public service. Now, on a very narrow reading of the new *PSEA*, it is sufficient if the successful candidate meets the minimum qualifications for the position.

The scope of the "merit principle" under the new *PSEA* can only be considered in light of the new redress procedure established under that Act. There are two redress procedures under the *PSEA*. First, a person may complain about an internal appointment process to the FPSLREB on three grounds: an abuse of authority in the appointment

130 *PSEA*, s 30(1).
131 *Ibid*, s 30(3).
132 *Ibid*, s 30(4).

of the successful candidate, an abuse of authority in choosing between an advertised and a non-advertised internal appointment process, or the failure to assess the complainant in the official language of their choice.[133] Second, a person may ask that the Public Service Commission investigate an external appointment process,[134] an internal appointment process where the commission has not delegated appointment power to a deputy head,[135] or any appointment process tainted by fraud[136] or political interference.[137]

3) Complaints to the FPSLREB

a) Standing to File a Complaint

As set out at the outset of this chapter, the majority of complaints are heard by the FPSLREB. The FPSLREB has jurisdiction over an appointment culminating from an internal appointment process, which is a process in which only persons employed in the public service may be considered.[138] The complainant must be in the area of selection for a selection process, which is a geographic, organizational, occupational, or employment equity criterion for an appointment.[139] For advertised appointment processes, a complainant must have applied for the appointment to file a complaint. A complainant cannot complain that some other candidate should have been promoted—to have standing, their complaint must be about their own treatment in the appointment process.[140] The key is whether the complainant was assessed against the essential qualifications for the position. If an employee did not formally apply for a position but was instead referred through a priority process to the position and assessed, the employee has standing to file

133 *Ibid*, s 77(1).
134 *Ibid*, s 66.
135 *Ibid*, s 67(1).
136 *Ibid*, s 69.
137 *Ibid*, s 68.
138 *Ibid*, s 2(1).
139 *Ibid*, s 34(1). The Board has no jurisdiction to assess whether the choice of an area of selection constitutes an abuse of authority: *Shafaie v Deputy Head (Department of Health)*, 2022 FPSLREB 15.
140 *Beyak*, above note 65; *Silke v Deputy Minister of National Defence*, 2010 PSST 9; *Soo-Markell v The Commissioner of the Correctional Service of Canada*, 2016 PSLREB 86.

a complaint.[141] By contrast, if the employee was considered as part of a duty to accommodate process and therefore not assessed using the essential criteria but using other criteria linked to the duty to accommodate instead, then the employee does not have standing to complain.[142]

b) Process of Filing a Complaint

Complaints to the FPSLREB must be made within fifteen days of the candidate receiving notice[143] of the appointment or proposed appointment to which the complaint relates,[144] although the FPSLREB has the power to extend this time limit "in the interest of fairness."[145] A complaint must be filed in writing and contain certain information specified in the *Public Service Staffing Complaints Regulations*.[146] The FPSLREB must schedule mediation unless the complainant or deputy head elects, within twenty-five days of the FPSLREB acknowledging receipt of the complaint, not to participate in mediation.[147]

The parties must "exchange information" (i.e., complete disclosure) within twenty-five days after the FPSLREB has written to acknowledge receipt of the complaint or such further time as ordered by the

141 *Agnew v Deputy Minister of Fisheries and Oceans*, 2018 FPSLREB 2 [*Agnew*].

142 *Casper v Deputy Minister of Citizenship and Immigration*, 2016 PSLREB 49.

143 The notification must be complete in that it informs employees of the right and grounds to make a complaint. If the notification is incomplete, then the time limit for making a complaint will be extended: *Sherif v Agriculture and Agri-Food Canada*, 2006 FPSLREB 3. If there is no notice published, it is not necessary to wait for a notice to be posted before filing a complaint: *Soccar v the Commissioner of the Royal Canadian Mounted Police*, 2013 FPSLREB 14.

144 *Public Service Staffing Complaints Regulations*, SOR/2006-6, s 10 [*Complaints Regulations*].

145 *Ibid*, s 5. In *MacDonald v Service Canada*, 2006 PSST 2, the complainant put her complaint in the mail within the fifteen-day limit, but it was not received until after the fifteen-day limit had expired. The complainant had a postage meter marking proving that she mailed her complaint within the time limit. The FPSLREB allowed the complaint to proceed, stating that "it is in the interests of fairness that the request for extension of time be granted when a complaint is mailed within the 15-day time limit and that the date of mailing can be easily proven. Complainants would be well advised when sending a complaint to the Tribunal by mail to not rely solely on postmarks or postage meter markings. If the complainants choose to send a complaint by mail, the Tribunal encourages them strongly to confirm by sending a copy by email or fax within the time limit for filing a complaint."

146 *Complaints Regulations*, s 11.

147 *Ibid*, s 15.

FPSLREB.[148] The purpose of this mutual disclosure is "to facilitate, very early on in the process, the resolution of the complaint by the principle parties to the dispute."[149] If a party refuses to provide information, the FPSLREB may order that the information be produced. The threshold test for a disclosure order is arguable relevance. This requires that the requesting party demonstrate "a nexus, or a clear link, between the information sought and the complaint."[150] The *Privacy Act* is not a sufficient reason to refuse disclosure of relevant information to the complainant.[151] However, the onus is on the complainant to show that the material sought is relevant.[152] This stage often happens through a face-to-face meeting where the parties discuss the complaint with a view to either correcting any problems identified by the complainant or explaining the appointment process to the complainant in a way that leads the complainant to withdraw the complaint.

If the complaint continues, then both parties provide more detailed explanation for the complaint and the defence, called "allegations"[153] for the complainant and a "reply"[154] for the deputy head or any other party (which includes the employee appointed or proposed for appointment to the position at issue in the complaint).[155]

The *FPSLREB Regulations* state that the Public Service Commission may refuse to disclose materials if providing that information might "affect the validity or continued use of a standardized test or parts of the test or affect the results of a standardized test by giving an unfair advantage to any individual." Under the old *PSEA*, there were similar provisions. The Federal Court concluded that the commission only needs to prove possible (and not probable) harm by the release of tests or other assessment material and that confidentiality of test materials is an important aspect of the merit principle. Therefore, the Federal Court developed three factors for weighing a request for disclosure: the material sought must be relevant to the underlying proceeding; whether

---

148 *Ibid*, s 16.

149 *Larose v Canadian Human Rights Commission*, 2006 PSST 1.

150 *Akhtar v Deputy Minister of Transport, Infrastructure and Communities*, 2007 PSST 26 at para 27.

151 *Ibid.*

152 *Jolin v Service Canada*, 2006 PSST 6.

153 *Complaints Regulations*, s 22.

154 *Ibid*, s 24.

155 *PSEA*, s 79.

access to the confidential materials might prejudice the continued use of the standardized test or offer an unfair advantage to any individual; and, finally, whether any resulting prejudice cannot be avoided through the imposition of conditions.[156] These same principles apply in the new *Complaints Regulations*.[157] The usual conditions for disclosure include that the complainant and representative view the information at the employer's premises, not be permitted to make copies of the information, and undertake not to disclose the information obtained except during the complaint hearing.[158]

c) Grounds of a Complaint: "Abuse of Authority"

The FPSLREB is required to determine whether an appointment was made by reason of an "abuse of authority."[159] Therefore, the impact of the merit principle depends on what is an abuse of authority. The term "abuse of authority" is not defined in the *PSEA*. The only reference to the term is in section 2(4) of the Act, which provides as follows:

> 2(4) For greater certainty, a reference in this Act to abuse of authority shall be construed as including bad faith and personal favouritism.

Therefore, the content or meaning of the merit principle depends in large part on what constitutes an abuse of authority. The FPSLREB has stated that section 2(4) of the *PSEA* must be interpreted broadly, meaning that "abuse of authority" is not limited to bad faith and personal favouritism.[160] Furthermore, the complainant bears the burden of proving that, on a balance of probabilities, the respondent abused its authority.[161] Under the old Act, the burden of proof was on the complainant to establish that there was a real possibility the merit principle was not applied; once the complainant has established a real possibility of a breach of the merit principle, the selection board that assessed the candidates must establish an evidentiary framework to show that merit

---

156 *Canada (Attorney General) v Gill*, [2001] FCJ No 1171.

157 *Aucoin v Canada Border Services Agency*, 2006 PSST 12.

158 *Ibid*.

159 *PSEA*, s 77(1)(a).

160 *Ross v Commissioner of the Correctional Service of Canada*, 2017 FPSLREB 48 at para 14; *Turner v Deputy Head (Royal Canadian Mounted Police)*, 2021 FPSLREB 52 at para 36 [*Turner*].

161 *Ibid*.

was respected.[162] Under the new process, the onus of proof remains on the complainant throughout the hearing. However,

> [w]hile it is open to the respondent, for its part, to simply deny the assertion, once the complainant has presented some evidence in support of his or her assertion that abuse of authority has occurred, then the respondent will likely wish to raise a positive defense to the assertion. Moreover, it is open to the Tribunal to draw reasonable inferences from uncontested facts and, thus, if the respondent does not present evidence to explain its reasons for a particular course of action or conduct, it risks being faced with an adverse finding by the Tribunal, namely, a substantiated complaint.[163]

The FPSLREB's leading decision outlining the concept of abuse of authority remains its 2006 decision in *Tibbs v National Defence*. In that case, the FPSLREB borrowed the definition of "abuse of authority" from the five generic types of abuses in the exercise of discretion cited by Jones and de Villars in their leading text:[164]

1. Exercising discretion with an improper intention in mind, which subsumes acting for an unauthorized purpose, in bad faith, or on irrelevant considerations.
2. Acting based on inadequate material, including where there is no evidence or without considering relevant matters.
3. Coming to an improper result, including unreasonable, discriminatory, or retroactive administrative actions.
4. Exercising discretion on an erroneous view of the law.
5. Refusing to exercise discretion by adopting a policy that fetters their ability to consider individual cases with an open mind.[165]

The FPSLREB pointed out that what these five categories of abuse have in common is that Parliament could not have intended to delegate the authority to act in such ways—in other words, the conduct must have been "unreasonable, unacceptable, or outrageous in some way such

---

162 *McGregor v Canada (Attorney General)*, [2006] FCJ No 1487 at paras 10–12.

163 *Tibbs v National Defence*, 2006 PSST 8 at para 54 [*Tibbs*].

164 David Jones & Anne de Villars, *Principles of Administrative Law*, 4th ed (Scarborough, ON: Thompson, 2004).

165 *Tibbs*, above note 163 at para 70. See also *Chiasson v Deputy Minister of Canadian Heritage*, 2008 PSST 27, quoted favourably in *Makoundi v Canada (Attorney General)*, 2014 FC 1177 at para 39 [*Makoundi*].

that Parliament could not have intended the person with the authority to exercise its discretion in this manner."[166]

The FPSLREB decided that intent was not a requirement for abuse of authority. Abuse of authority requires more than "simply errors or omissions,"[167] although this does not require carelessness or recklessness.[168]

I want to emphasize at this stage that the categories of "abuse of authority" discussed in FPSLREB and Federal Court decisions are not exhaustive. The Federal Court has clearly stated that "it would not be appropriate to try to limit the concept of abuse of authority to narrow and well-defined categories."[169] There is no set list of grounds for "abuse of authority."

There are, of course, certain types of complaints that arise more often than others. This chapter will describe the FPSLREB's approach to some of the more common issues that arise in staffing complaints. This list is not intended to be exhaustive—as there can be no exhaustive list of the categories of abuse of authority. Nevertheless, since these particular grounds arise most frequently, they will be set out below.

i) Choice of Non-advertised Process

Section 33 of the *PSEA* provides specifically that a deputy head or delegate has the discretion to use either an advertised or a non-advertised selection process. There are no set criteria for this decision, nor is there ever a requirement to use either an advertised or a non-advertised process.[170] This appears to be one of the more discretionary decisions available to a deputy head; therefore, the FPSLREB tends to require bad faith to allow a complaint on this ground.[171] In one case, the FPSLREB found bad faith when the deputy head's delegate chose a non-advertised process purportedly because the situation was urgent; in fact, the successful candidate was appointed for an initial period of less than four months (thus avoiding any possibility of a complaint) knowing that the appointment would be at least six to nine months, and then the

---

166 *Davidson v Canada (Attorney General)*, 2021 FCA 226 at para 25. See also *Agnew*, above note 141 at para 95.

167 *Ibid* at paras 72–73.

168 *Canada (Attorney General) v Lahlali*, 2012 FC 601 at para 38.

169 *Ibid* at paras 21 and 38.

170 *Canada (Attorney General) v Kane*, 2012 SCC 64.

171 *Beyak*, above note 65.

appointment was extended using a non-advertised process because of the supposed "urgency" in filling the position. The FPSLREB was also concerned that the complainant was not considered for the position purportedly because he lacked experience, but the employee appointed also had very little experience. The FPSLREB concluded that the delegate acted in bad faith in extending the initial four-month appointment by means of a non-advertised appointment process.[172]

ii) Use of References as a Selection Tool

Hiring managers almost always use references as a tool to select a candidate for a position. The Public Service Commission has published a fifty-four-page guide to conducting a "structured reference check"[173]—and at the risk of sounding cynical, the existence of or need for a fifty-four-page guide helps demonstrate that reference checks are an area of concern.

Assessment boards are permitted to contact referees not included on a list provided by the candidate;[174] however, they must first consult referees proposed by the candidate and try to obtain information from them before pursuing others.[175]

The role of a referee is to provide a candid assessment of a candidate. The fact that a candidate disagrees with the comments by the referee does not establish that the reference is unreliable.[176] Furthermore, "[t]he bias of a referee in itself does not necessarily show that an assessment board abused its authority; the board in question must

172 *Cameron and Maheux v Deputy Head of Service Canada*, 2008 PSST 16, aff'd *Canada (Attorney General) v Cameron*, 2009 FC 618 (although the FPSLREB's remedy was quashed, as discussed in the section on remedial authority).

173 Public Service Commission, *Structured Reference Checking: A User's Guide to Best Practices* (2009) online (pdf): www.canada.ca/content/dam/canada/public-service-commission/migration/plcy-pltq/guides/checking-verification/rpt-eng.pdf.

174 *Oddie v Deputy Minister of National Defence*, 2007 PSST 30. While the decision in this case relied on a Public Service Commission guide that it is permissible to contact a referee from within a "federal institution" and that consent is required to contact referees from outside the public service, there is no reason given for that instruction. It may be the result of privacy considerations and not abuse of authority; if so, the decision in *Pierre v President of the Canada Border Services Agency*, 2013 PSST 28 at para 34, aff'd *Pierre v Canada (Border Services Agency)*, 2016 FCA 124 [*Pierre*], points out that the collection of information in a reference check is permitted under s 8(2) of the *Privacy Act*, RSC 1985, c P-21.

175 *Ammirante v Deputy Minister of Citizenship and Immigration*, 2010 PSST 3 at para 129.

176 *Pellicore v President of the Canada Border Services Agency*, 2010 PSST 23.

be witness to an element that calls into question the reliability of the information provided by a referee."[177]

When a candidate informs the assessment board about some issue with the reference check, however, the assessment board or selection committee has an obligation to consider the issue by speaking with the referee about this new information and then assessing the quality of the reference. The failure to investigate or at least inquire into evidence that calls into question the reliability of the information provided by a referee is an abuse of authority. As one example, a complainant notified the assessment board of a conflict with his manager who provided the reference. The assessment board abused its authority by not speaking with the manager about the information it received from the complainant to assess the quality of the information it received.[178] To give another example, when a candidate receives a negative reference by the same person who provided them with a positive performance evaluation and then tells the selection committee about this contradiction, the selection committee must investigate further instead of simply ignoring the contradiction between the reference and the performance evaluation.[179]

The challenges of reconciling a reference check with other, more objective information has led one FPSLREB member to recommend that reference checks never be used to assess whether a candidate meets the essential qualifications for a position but, instead, reserve reference checks for the final "right fit" assessment of which qualified candidate to appoint. The FPSLREB pointed out that, particularly with written references, it is the referee who is actually being assessed, not the candidate, as a "referee may be loquacious, taciturn, well disposed, or malicious, which is all independent of the candidate."[180]

177 *Pierre* (PSST), above note 174 at para 37.

178 *Laviolette v Commissioner of the Correctional Service of Canada*, 2015 PSLREB 6.

179 *Bazinet v Deputy Minister of Employment and Social Development*, 2021 FPSLREB 82.

180 *Rizqy v Deputy Minister of Employment and Social Development*, 2021 FPSLREB 12 at para 64. The FPSLREB in that case also recommended that the "second look" of a reference after a complainant raises a bona fide concern be conducted by somebody who was not on the initial selection committee so that this second look is conducted objectively. These are non-binding recommendations but interesting nonetheless.

iii) Exercise of Discretionary Powers

An assessment board often has a significant degree of discretion—to select the appropriate selection tools or to require the use of particular forms, for example. Where an assessment board is left with discretion, it cannot exercise that discretion in a way that is inconsistent among candidates. For example, an assessment board cannot reject one candidate because they did not use the proper format for an application but allow other candidates to proceed despite not using that same format.[181]

A more difficult case arises when a selection board decides to rigidly follow some rule instead of exercising its discretion. This sometimes arises when the members of the selection board have personal knowledge that a candidate meets an essential qualification, but the candidate's application package omits that qualification. As a general rule, an assessment board is not required to consider their personal knowledge when assessing candidates, nor are they required to infer qualifications (particularly when the applicants are told in advance to clearly demonstrate their qualifications in their applications).[182] However, it must also not use a "rigid and inflexible approach" by constraining itself not to consider its personal knowledge when fairness requires a departure from the normal rule.[183] To put this another way, it is an abuse of authority for a selection board to fetter its discretion by refusing to consider exceptions to general rules. Additionally, each member of the assessment board must exercise their own judgment: it is an abuse of authority for one member of an assessment board to simply echo another member's assessment because they feel intimidated by them.[184]

iv) Personal Favouritism

Personal favouritism is expressly listed as included within the definition of "abuse of authority." The term, though, is *personal* favouritism, not simply favouritism—"it is personal favouritism, not other types

---

181 *Poirier v Deputy Minister of Veterans Affairs*, 2011 PSST 3 [*Poirier*].

182 *Lirette*, above note 88.

183 *Payne v the Deputy Minister of National Defence*, 2013 PSST 15 at para 51. In that case, there was also an element of unequal treatment. Two candidates were screened out because of a lack of technical expertise. For one candidate, the assessment board contacted his manager to find out whether he had the necessary expertise (he did not), but for the other candidate the assessment board screened him out despite their personal knowledge that he possessed the required expertise.

184 *Snelgrove v Deputy Minister of Fisheries and Oceans*, 2013 PSST 35 at para 30.

of favouritism, that constitutes abuse of authority."[185] Thus the FPSLREB examines whether there is a personal relationship between the hiring manager or someone on the committee responsible for assessing candidates. Where a personal friendship or family relationship exists, there is "such a strong presumption of there being personal favouritism that it creates an apprehension of bias with regard to the outcome regardless of the fact that the appointee might have been qualified and might otherwise have deserved the appointment on the basis of merit."[186] Committee members who are personal friends of a candidate must therefore recuse themselves from the appointment process entirely.

Personal favouritism can also be demonstrated in the absence of a pre-existing friendship or familial relationship with a candidate. Selection of a person as a personal favour, or to gain personal favour with someone else, is another example of personal favouritism.[187] Additionally, when a member of the assessment board gives one candidate information about an exam or assessment process prior to the candidate's interview, that is also a type of personal favouritism.[188] Simply getting along well with a colleague, though, is not the type of personal relationship contemplated by "personal favouritism."[189]

v) Bias

In addition to personal favouritism, complainants may also allege that an appointment constituted an abuse of authority because of other forms of bias. The FPSLREB has adapted the test for bias (the reasonable apprehension of bias test) from the judicial or quasi-judicial setting such that there is bias in an appointment process "[i]f a reasonably informed bystander could reasonably perceive bias on the part of one or more of the persons responsible for the assessment."[190] For example, when a member of the assessment board told a candidate that "the only way I would give you this job is if I am ordered to," the FPSLREB found

185 *Glasgow v Deputy Minister of Public Works and Government Services Canada*, 2008 PSST 7 at para 39 [*Glasgow*].

186 *Myskiw v Commissioner of the Correctional Service of Canada*, 2019 FPSLREB 107 at para 39 [*Myskiw*].

187 *Glasgow*, above note 185 at para 41.

188 *Martin v Deputy Minister of National Defence*, 2010 PSST 19.

189 *Charest v Deputy Minister of Human Resources and Social Development*, 2008 PSST 19 at para 59.

190 *Drozdowski v Deputy Head (Department of Public Works and Government Services Canada)*, 2016 PSLREB 33 at para 26 [*Drozdowski*].

this was actual bias as well as giving rise to a reasonable apprehension of bias.[191] By contrast, the FPSLREB concluded that a statement that "he could not trust anyone working in the Brampton office" did not give rise to a reasonable perception of bias because it was an isolated, emotionally charged response made at a moment of stress that had nothing to do with the complainant personally.[192]

The mere fact that the complainant has filed grievances or other complaints against a hiring manager does not meet the FPSLREB's test for bias: the FPSLREB will not infer bias simply because an employee has filed a grievance, complaint, or some other recourse.[193] A claim of bias must be supported by evidence that discloses bias that is "real, probable, or reasonably obvious"—suspicion and speculation are not enough.[194]

vi) Establishing Qualifications

The FPSLREB has been clear that its role is not to establish the qualifications for a position, and it will easily second-guess the decision to establish a particular qualification for a position.[195] This includes both essential and asset (or non-essential) qualifications and also permits a deputy head or delegate to establish a large number of essential qualifications.[196] Deference, though, does not mean that the choice of qualifications is beyond challenge. The FPSLREB could find that the choice of qualifications constitutes an abuse of authority if the qualifications were not related to the duties of the position.[197]

Once the qualifications for a position have been established, a selection board may not change those qualifications. This freeze on the qualifications begins as soon as the expression of interest for the position is posted.[198] The qualifications can be clarified,[199] but they cannot

191 *Ryan v Deputy Minister of National Defence*, 2014 PSST 9.

192 *Johnston v Director of Public Prosecutions*, 2018 FPSLREB 65 [*Johnston*].

193 *Gandhi v Canada (Canada Border Services Agency)*, 2015 FC 436 at para 53, aff'd *Pierre* (FCA), above note 174; *Hansen v Deputy Head (Department of Justice)*, 2022 FPSLREB 9 at para 61 [*Hansen*].

194 *Denny v Deputy Minister of National Defence*, 2009 PSST 29 at para 124; *Hansen*, above note 193 at para 63.

195 *Visca v Deputy Minister of Justice et al*, 2007 PSST 24 at para 42.

196 *Trites*, above note 48 at para 56.

197 *Makoundi*, above note 165.

198 *De Santis*, above note 50; *Burke v Deputy Minister of National Defence*, 2009 PSST 3.

199 *Jean-Pierre v Chairperson of the Immigration and Refugee Board*, 2016 PSLREB 62 at para 88.

be interpreted in a manner contrary to the plain and ordinary meaning of their words.[200] There is no obligation to define the merit criteria for candidates (in that case, the definition of "significant experience"),[201] nor is there a duty to tell candidates which asset qualifications will be used to select appointees.[202]

vii) Assessing Qualifications

A large number of complaints allege that a candidate's qualifications were not assessed properly. Such complaints are difficult to make out. As the FPSLREB has pointed out, "The assessment board must have some leeway in determining what constitutes satisfactory answers and to what extent the answers reflect the qualities sought."[203] Parties often disagree about the assessment board's answer ratings; this disagreement usually reflects the fact that the assessment board must make a judgment call when deciding the degree to which a candidate was successful.[204] The FPSLREB's role is not to reassess a candidate's qualifications.[205] Furthermore, unlike under the old *PSEA*, it is not necessary for an assessment board to rank the candidates and, in fact, the FPSLREB has discouraged ranking candidates.[206]

Despite that deferential approach, it is still an abuse of authority when an assessment board does not actually assess each qualification—it may not rely on the assessment of other qualifications as a proxy.[207] This rule also applies to the methods used to assess qualifications: "if the tool

---

200 *Renaud v Deputy Minister of National Defence*, 2013 PSST 26 at para 43.

201 *Neil v Deputy Minister of Environment Canada*, 2008 PSST 4 at para 51. The FPSLREB was still very critical of the decision not to clearly define what constituted "significant experience," but that decision by itself was not an abuse of authority. Note also *Kavanagh v President of Shared Services Canada*, 2017 FPSLREB 38 [*Kavanagh*]: there is no obligation to inform candidates in advance that private sector experience will be considered.

202 *Wall v Canada (Fisheries and Oceans)*, 2009 PSST 2 at para 61.

203 *Drozdowski*, above note 190 at para 36.

204 *Wilkinson v Deputy Minister of National Defence*, 2017 PSLREB 1 at para 70.

205 *Boutzouvis v the Director of Public Prosecution Service of Canada*, 2012 PSST 25 at para 27.

206 *Visca v Deputy Minister of Justice*, 2006 PSST 16 at para 44.

207 *Regier v Deputy Head of the Correctional Service of Canada*, 2021 FPSLREB 123; *Phelan v Deputy Minister of the Department of Fisheries and Oceans*, 2016 PSLREB 115 at para 27.

is flawed, then the outcome is unreliable."[208] It is an abuse of authority when the methods used to assess a qualification have no connection to the qualification or the tool is otherwise so flawed that the outcome cannot be considered reasonable or fair.[209] This does not prohibit something referred to as a "top-down" assessment method, where an assessment board starts by assessing some of the essential qualifications and then only the top candidates have their remaining qualifications assessed.[210] An assessment board may also use an aggregate scoring system (in that case, requiring a mark of 50 percent for each essential qualification and an aggregate score of 60 percent for each category of qualifications namely knowledge, abilities, and personal suitability).[211]

It is also an abuse of authority to make serious or even careless errors that resulted in the qualifications for a position not being assessed.[212] An assessment board may decide to use its personal knowledge of the candidates as an assessment tool,[213] but it is not required to do so[214] (subject to the discussion about the assessment board fettering its discretion). Finally, candidates must expect that their entire application will be used to assess them, such that it is not an abuse of authority to use a candidate's cover letter to assess their ability to communicate effectively in writing,[215] and it is up to the assessment board to decide whether there is sufficient information in an application package to assess a particular qualification.[216]

An assessment board must assess candidates consistently, so it is an abuse of authority to give one candidate a failing grade while giving the same answer by two others a passing grade.[217]

---

208 *Elazzouzi v Deputy Minister of Human Resources and Skills Development Canada*, 2011 PSST 11 at para 9.

209 *Rochon v Deputy Ministry of Fisheries and Oceans*, 2011 PSST 7 at para 72 [*Rochon*].

210 *King v Deputy Head of Service Canada*, 2008 PSST 6; *Anwar v Chief Public Health Officer of the Public Health Agency of Canada*, 2011 PSST 24.

211 *Jogarajah v Chief Public Health Officer of the Public Health Agency of Canada*, 2008 PSST 15 at paras 29 and 34.

212 *Goncalves v RCMP*, 2017 FPSLREB 2; *Rochon*, above note 209.

213 *Robertson v Deputy Minister of National Defence*, 2010 PSST 11 at para 63.

214 *Warford v Commissioner of the Royal Canadian Mounted Police*, 2016 PSLREB 56 at paras 39–41.

215 *Myskiw*, above note 186.

216 *Kavanagh*, above note 201.

217 *Hughes v Deputy Minister of Human Resources and Skills Development Canada*, 2011 PSST 16 at paras 96–97.

The assessment of candidates often uses something that human resources professionals call "right fit." As described by the FPSLREB, "[t]he term 'right fit' is not a term found in the PSEA. It is a term used in the human resources community to describe the basis for deciding who will be appointed from among qualified candidates in an appointment process."[218] The "right fit" rationale can be prepared after the candidates have been assessed and does not need to be set out in advance. For example, "the rationale may be different in situations where two candidates have the same performance on an essential qualification. In such a situation, the delegated manager might use an asset qualification to assist in making its selection. But if one candidate performs very well on an essential qualification and another one barely meets the qualification, the delegated manager might decide not to give much weight to the asset qualifications and prefer the candidate who performed very well on the essential qualification."[219] A delegated manager may therefore use any combination of essential and asset qualifications to determine the "right fit" for a position.[220]

viii) Ambiguity in Instructions to Candidates

Sometimes the instructions to candidates for an appointment process are ambiguous. Applicants therefore should have the opportunity to correct a mistaken impression during the informal discussion stage, and it is an abuse of authority to ignore those corrections during the informal discussion stage.[221] The FPSLREB has treated this type of concern as one way in which the assessment board has improperly fettered its discretion.

ix) Composition of the Assessment Board

There is no requirement that the individuals who are assessing candidates have certain qualifications. For example, it is not necessary to have

218 *Marcil v Deputy Minister of Transport, Infrastructure and Communities*, 2011 PSST 31 at para 48.

219 *Ibid.*

220 *Stamp v Commissioner of the Correctional Service of Canada*, 2014 PSST 4 at para 30.

221 *Poirier*, above note 181, and *Agnew*, above note 141.

a human resources specialist on an assessment board,[222] and it is not necessary to have subject matter specialists on the assessment board.[223]

x) *Unfair Advantage*

Under the old *PSEA*, a large number of complaints turned on whether the successful candidate had an unfair advantage in the competition—usually because they had received an acting appointment or assignment that gave them the necessary qualifications or some other form of advantage over other candidates. The Supreme Court of Canada decision in *Doré* stated that an assignment was an appointment when the assignment lasted so long as to give the employee a "distinct advantage" in subsequent competitions. Appeal boards and the Federal Court interpreted this passage as also indicating that appointing a candidate who had received an "unfair advantage" in the competition through a previous assignment or appointment was a breach of the merit principle.

For example, in *McAuliffe v Canada (Attorney General)*,[224] the Public Service Commission confirmed appointments made after a flawed selection process because the candidates appointed using the flawed process were performing satisfactorily. The Federal Court concluded that this reasoning violated the merit principle:

> Thus, the merit principle may be compromised where a candidate in a selection process receives an unfair advantage due to his assignment to the position in question prior to a valid selection being made. Familiarity with the actual duties of a position may provide the candidates in place with an unfair advantage with the risk that a selection process may not result in selection according to merit....
>
> Their actual performance only shows that they qualify for the job. It does not indicate that they are the best qualified in accordance with the merit principle.[225]

Therefore, when selecting a candidate for a position that was being filled by one of the candidates in the selection process, the Public Service Commission had to be careful to ensure that the qualification criteria

---

222 *Sampert et al v Deputy Minister of National Defence et al*, 2008 PSST 9 at para 53.

223 *Abi-Mansour v Chief Executive Officer of Passport Canada*, 2014 PSST 12 at para 48.

224 *McAuliffe v Canada (Attorney General)*, [1997] FCJ No 161, aff'd *McAuliffe v Canada (Attorney General)*, [1999] FCJ No 1466 (CA) because of mootness.

225 *Ibid* (FC) at paras 17–18.

for the position were not devised to "suit the incumbent."[226] In other words, "an assignment in combination with a selection process that gave an unfair advantage to the candidate assigned to the position could compromise application of the merit principle."[227] This did not mean that the selection process must ignore any knowledge gained during an assignment, but the candidate could not receive a "bonus" because of the quality of their work performed while on assignment.[228]

In applying the new *PSEA*, the FPSLREB has taken a more flexible approach to concerns about a candidate receiving an unfair advantage through acting assignment opportunities. The FPSLREB has focused on whether there is a reasonable justification for the particular workplace action that gave an advantage to a candidate, instead of the old approach of focusing on the existence of the advantage itself.[229] The question of whether an acting opportunity constituted an abuse of authority will therefore depend on the particular facts and circumstances of a given case.[230] Conversely, successfully occupying a position on an acting basis does not guarantee success in a subsequent appointment process, as the qualifications may be more stringent in the permanent selection process.[231]

d) Remedies and Redress After a Successful Complaint

If the FPSLREB finds that a complaint concerning an appointment under an internal process is substantiated, then the Board may order the Public Service Commission or the deputy head to revoke the appointment and "take any corrective action that the Board considers appropriate."[232]

The FPSLREB may not order the Public Service Commission or the deputy head to make an appointment or conduct a new appointment

226 *Berger v Canada (Attorney General)*, [2004] FCJ No 580 at para 42.

227 *Canada (Attorney General) v Pearce*, [1989] 3 FC 272 (CA) at para 16. See also *Ordines v Canada (Attorney General)*, [1998] FCJ No 1436.

228 *Levac v Canada (Attorney General)*, [1994] FCJ No 622 at para 10. In this case, both candidates received less than the minimum score of 168.8 points on the knowledge test. However, the employee temporarily occupying the position that was the subject of the competition was given 8.5 bonus points because of a "supplementary evaluation based on the work performed." The Federal Court agreed with the appeal board that this bonus was an unfair advantage for the incumbent.

229 *Johnston*, above note 192 at para 85.

230 *Ship v Deputy Minister of National Defence*, 2010 PSST 25 at para 46; *Jones v Deputy Minister of Fisheries and Oceans*, 2013 PSST 32 at para 96.

231 *Richard v Deputy Minister of National Defence*, 2013 PSST 24 at para 62.

232 *PSEA*, s 81(1).

process,[233] although it may order that a candidate's application be reassessed.[234] The FPSLREB also does not have the jurisdiction to award damages for lost opportunity in an appointment process.[235] Additionally, the FPSLREB's order must relate only to the appointment process at issue in the complaint. The FPSLREB may not, for example, order a review of other appointments made by a manager who abused their authority or order particular training after a finding of abuse of authority.[236] The FPSLREB may, however, make non-binding recommendations as a result of its decision.[237]

The most common remedy ordered by the FPSLREB is a declaration that an abuse of authority occurred in the application of merit in a particular appointment. One FPSLREB decision states that it will only revoke an appointment "under rare circumstances," but the member deciding that case cited no authority for that proposition.[238] The FPSLREB has declined to revoke an appointment when, despite the abuse of authority, the successful candidate was qualified for the position and has occupied the position for a significant period of time (in that case, more than three years).[239] The FPSLREB has also revoked acting appointments even though the acting term had expired years before the FPSLREB's decision and has revoked the appointment of employees who have since left the department or even the public service.[240] The FPSLREB cites an earlier decision from the Federal Court of Appeal that such orders are not moot because otherwise it "would be too easy for a department or an appointee to avoid the appeal process and prevent an inquiry as to whether the merit principle has been respected in the selection process by simply moving to another position."[241]

The FPSLREB has the authority to make awards under sections 53(2)(e) and 53(3) of the *Canadian Human Rights Act* and section 102

233 *PSEA*, s 82.

234 *Gomy v Deputy Minister of Health*, 2019 FPSLREB 84 at para 147 [*Gomy*].

235 *De Santis*, above note 50 at para 53.

236 *Canada (Attorney General) v Cameron and Maheux*, 2009 FC 618.

237 *Canada (Attorney General) v Beyak*, 2011 FC 629.

238 *Turner*, above note 160 at para 79.

239 *Gomy*, above note 234 at para 142.

240 *Spirak v the Deputy Minister of Public Works and Government Services Canada*, 2012 PSST 20 at para 81; *Beyak*, above note 65; *De Santis*, above note 50 at para 54.

241 *Lo v Canada (Public Service Commission Appeal Board)*, [1997] FCJ 1784 (CA) at para 12.

of the *Accessible Canada Act* in allowing a complaint about an internal selection process.[242] The FPSLREB may not order lost wages flowing from a breach of the *Canadian Human Rights Act* as a remedy in a staffing complaint, as that is tantamount to an order appointing the complainant to the position they sought, contrary to a prohibition against that remedy in the *PSEA*.[243]

Where the Public Service Commission has made or proposed an appointment as the result of the implementation of a FPSLREB corrective order, then the person whose appointment was affected by the original complaint, the person who brought the original complaint, or any other person directly affected may complain to the FPSLREB that they were not appointed to the position as the result of an abuse of authority by the commission or deputy head in the implementation of the corrective action.[244] The FPSLREB may order the commission to revoke the appointment and also give any appropriate directions with respect to the implementation of the corrective action.[245]

If the commission has revoked an appointment as the result of its own investigation, then the person whose appointment was revoked may file a complaint with the FPSLREB that the revocation was "unreasonable."[246] Where the FPSLREB upholds such a complaint, it may order the commission or deputy head to set aside the revocation.[247]

Under the old *PSEA*, the appeal board could also hear appeals about corrective action taken by the commission after a successful appeal. The Federal Court made it clear that appellants could only raise issues concerning the corrective measures taken after the appeal and that appellants could not raise further concerns that the original staffing action violated the merit principle. As the Federal Court put it: "On the second appeal, the corrective measures are assessed for their conformity

---

242 *PSEA*, s 81(2) & 81(3). See also *Canadian Human Rights Act*, RSC 1985, c H-6, and *Accessible Canada Act*, SC 2019, c 10.

243 *Spruin v Deputy Minister of Employment and Social Development*, 2019 FPSLREB 33 at para 117. In that case, the FPSLREB ordered $2,000 under s 53(2)(e) of the *Canadian Human Rights Act* and another $2,000 in special compensation under s 53(3) of that Act. The Canadian Human Rights Tribunal, though, may order a promotion as a remedy to a human rights complaint, notwithstanding the provisions of the *PSEA*: *Canada (Attorney General) v Uzoaba*, [1995] 2 FC 569.

244 *PSEA*, s 83.

245 *Ibid*, s 84.

246 *Ibid*, s 74.

247 *Ibid*, s 76.

with the merit principle but all other matters, whether or not they might have been raised on the first appeal, are a closed book."[248] The FPSLREB's jurisdiction in complaints about corrective measures is also likely limited to the events comprising the implementation of prior decisions, not new complaints about the original staffing action.

4) Investigations by the Public Service Commission or Deputy Head

As discussed above, the Public Service Commission has the jurisdiction to investigate external appointment processes, internal appointment processes that were not made by a deputy head or delegate, and any appointment process for political influence or fraud. This jurisdiction does not require a complaint or request for investigation; the commission may investigate on its own initiative.[249] Additionally, a deputy head may investigate its own appointments and may also revoke an appointment if it is satisfied that there was an error, an omission, or improper conduct that affected the selection of the person for appointment. This chapter will explore those grounds of investigation in turn.

a) External Appointment Processes and Limited Internal Appointment Processes

The Public Service Commission may investigate an external appointment process or an internal appointment process conducted otherwise than by a deputy head or delegate. If the commission is satisfied that an appointment "was not made or proposed to be made on the basis of merit, or that there was an error, an omission or improper conduct that affected the selection of the person appointed or proposed for appointment," then the commission may revoke the appointment or take any other corrective action it deems appropriate.[250] The commission, in other words, is not limited to examining whether there has been an abuse of authority—a mere error is sufficient to trigger the commission's jurisdiction. The Federal Court has referred to this as a

248 *Johnson v Canada (Attorney General)*, [1998] FCJ No 191 at para 14, aff'd [1999] FCJ No 1638 (CA). See also *Adams v Canada (Attorney General)*, [2003] FCJ No 135.

249 *Cadostin v Canada (Attorney General)*, 2020 FC 183 at para 48, aff'd 2021 FCA 21 [*Cadostin*].

250 *PSEA*, ss 66 & 67.

"broad supervisory jurisdiction over internal and external appointments within the public service."[251]

Intent is not required for there to be "improper conduct" under section 66 or 67 of the *PSEA*, but there must be some conduct that undermines the values enshrined in the Act.[252] The Public Service Commission has defined "improper conduct" broadly as "unsuitable behaviour," including personal favouritism.[253]

b) Political Influence

The Public Service Commission may also investigate an appointment if it was "not free from political influence."[254] The commission has, internally, defined political influence as follows: "To conclude that an appointment was not free from political influence, the evidence must show, on the balance of probabilities that the appointment process was not without effect of actions from individuals such as those from the office of a minister or a member of Parliament."[255] This definition has never been tested by the Federal Court, and the Public Service Commission has not published a summary of any investigation concluding that the appointment process was tainted by political influence.

c) Fraud

The Public Service Commission may investigate fraud in an appointment process. Unlike the other provisions of the *PSEA* already discussed, it is not necessary that the appointment itself be the result of fraud or that any appointment have been made at all: the purpose is to protect the integrity of the appointment process.[256] The term "fraud" in this context has two essential elements: "(1) dishonesty, which can include non-disclosure of important facts; and (2) deprivation or risk of deprivation."[257] This test is adopted from the criminal law, the only distinction being the standard of proof that is the balance of probabilities

251 *Samatar v Canada (Attorney General)*, 2012 FC 1263 at para 2.

252 *Shakov*, above note 31 at para 66.

253 *MacAdam v Canada (Attorney General)*, 2014 FC 443 at para 68 [*MacAdam*]. The Federal Court upheld the commission's decision in that case.

254 *PSEA*, s 68.

255 Public Service Commission, "Appointment Process Investigations" (last modified 10 March 2021), online: www.canada.ca/en/public-service-commission/services/oversight-activities/investigations/appointment-process-investigations.html.

256 *Cadostin*, above note 249 at para 47.

257 *Seck v Canada (Attorney General)*, 2012 FCA 314 at para 39 [*Seck*].

instead of the criminal standard of beyond a reasonable doubt.[258] The first element is established where an individual knowingly undertakes a dishonest act; factual findings of deceit, lies, or other fraudulent means are required to meet the threshold for dishonesty.[259] This is a subjective test, as a finding of fraud may also have criminal consequences for the person being investigated.[260] The second element focuses on whether the appointment process could have been compromised: there is no requirement for the Public Service Commission to establish actual compromise or injury to the process.[261]

Investigations into fraud typically concern falsifying credentials or accessing unauthorized sources (such as sharing or obtaining a copy of an exam). The commission has also stated that plagiarism is automatically fraudulent, but the Federal Court disagreed, stating that plagiarism is not automatically fraudulent and that whether it amounts to fraud "is often a question of degree rather than kind."[262] Thus, copying the answer guide to an exam is fraudulent,[263] but cutting and pasting information from the internet is not automatically fraudulent depending on the instructions given to candidates (which did not prohibit the use of the internet or any other external sources in any way).[264]

d) Remedies

The Public Service Commission has a wide array of remedies available to it. It may revoke an appointment or take any corrective action that it considers appropriate. This has included revoking a manager's delegated staffing authority, a requirement that a person seek permission from the commission before applying for public service positions, and certain managers completing training courses relevant to their conduct. The decision to revoke an appointment is not a disciplinary measure but, instead, an administrative measure taken to "ensure the integrity of the

---

258 *Egbers v Canada (Attorney General)*, 2015 FC 1342 at para 40 [*Egbers*].

259 *Blair v Canada (Attorney General)*, 2019 FC 1295 at para 17. The Federal Court has commented that this may include recklessness but declined to determine that issue conclusively: *Dayfallah v Canada (Attorney General)*, 2018 FC 1120 at para 97 [*Dayfallah*].

260 *Egbers*, above note 258 at para 56. Section 133 of the *PSEA* also states that fraud in an appointment process is an offence punishable on summary conviction.

261 *Seck*, above note 257 at para 41; *Cadostin*, above note 249 at para 64.

262 *Egbers*, above note 258 at para 57.

263 *Challal v Canada (Attorney General)*, 2009 FC 1251.

264 *Egbers*, above note 258.

appointment process in the federal public service."[265] This means that traditional disciplinary principles such as proportionality or progressive discipline do not apply to the corrective action.[266]

The decision to revoke an appointment appears especially harsh in circumstances when the employee was blameless (e.g., when there was improper conduct by a hiring manager that the candidate played no part in). The Federal Court of Appeal was concerned by the fairness of this remedy in *Canada (Attorney General) v Shakov* and quashed a revocation because the commission failed to consider that the employee was not complicit in the impugned decisions and the harshness of the result to him.[267] Additionally, section 73 of the *PSEA* grants the commission the power to appoint a person to another position after their appointment was revoked if they meet the essential qualifications of that new position.[268] This power is, though, discretionary, and there is no right to another position. The Federal Court has also suggested that an employee must apply for an appointment under section 73 of the Act because they are in the best position to set out their qualifications,[269] although this is not always going to be the case, and the Court's decision on this point is best seen as non-binding *obiter dicta*.

An employee whose appointment has been revoked may file a complaint with the FPSLREB to set aside the revocation on the grounds that the revocation was unreasonable.[270] The FPSLREB has concluded that such a revocation is unreasonable when it is tainted by procedural unfairness—in that case, the failure to provide the employee with the anonymous note that triggered the deputy head's investigation. The FPSLREB was also concerned in that case that the investigators were instructed only to meet with current employees instead of engaging in a full investigation.[271] The FPSLREB has also stated that it is not acting akin to a court on judicial review: it is entitled to hear new evidence

265 *Seck*, above note 257 at para 48 (for fraud); see also *MacAdam*, above note 253 at para 109 (applying the same rule in a s 66 "improper conduct" case).

266 *Seck*, above note 257 at para 51; *MacAdam*, *ibid* at para 112.

267 *Shakov*, above note 30 at para 80.

268 A deputy head has the same power under s 15(6) if they revoke an appointment after their own investigation.

269 *Dayfallah*, above note 259 at para 52.

270 *PSEA*, s 74.

271 *McMillan v Deputy Minister of Indian and Northern Affairs Canada*, 2011 PSST 20.

beyond that turned up in the investigation process and make its own decisions about the facts of the case.[272]

On substantive grounds, though, the FPSLREB has treated the term "unreasonableness" in the same way as courts on judicial review. In a 2010 decision, therefore, the FPSLREB borrowed from existing administrative law norms to state that it "must therefore determine whether the decision to revoke the appointment is one that does not fall within a range of possible acceptable outcomes which are defensible or that is one that cannot be supported by a somewhat probing examination."[273] Since that time, the Supreme Court of Canada has reformulated the concept of reasonableness to emphasize the intelligibility and justification of the reasons for a decision, rather than whether the result falls within a range of possible outcomes.[274] It remains to be seen whether the FPSLREB modifies its approach to section 74 of the *PSEA* accordingly. The FPSLREB in that same case also considered the extent to which the employee contributed to the error and the length of time it took to revoke the position.

G. STAFFING PRIORITIES

The *Public Service Employment Act* and the *Public Service Employment Regulations* (*PSER*) set out a number of people who have priority in any staffing action. This means that so long as that person with a particular characteristic meets the essential qualifications of a position, they must be appointed in preference to any person who does not share that characteristic. This is more than a "tiebreaker": a candidate with a staffing priority must be appointed if they are qualified for the position, regardless of where they would rank in a list based on merit. There are staffing priorities set out in statute that are ranked, so some people have a greater priority than others. There are then priorities listed in regulations; these regulatory priorities are not ranked and have no relative order. Finally, there are two final priorities in the statute that are subordinate to all others. The staffing priorities do not apply to term employees.[275] Also, if

272 *Goldsmith v Deputy Minister of Human Resources and Skills Development*, 2010 PSST 20.

273 *Ibid* at para 57.

274 *Canada (Minister of Citizenship and Immigration) v Vavilov*, 2019 SCC 65 [*Vavilov*].

275 *PSEA*, s 45, and *Public Service Employment Regulations*, SOR/2005-334 s 4(2) [*PSER*].

the Public Service Commission concludes that the appointment of a person using a priority would generate a priority right for another employee, then the commission may decide not to apply the priority in that case.[276]

When a candidate is unsuccessful in a competition because the successful candidate was appointed pursuant to a statutory or regulatory priority, then they do not have the right to file a complaint with the FPSLREB.[277]

A number of the priorities are time limited. Those time limits are mandatory, and the *PSEA* does not provide for any extension of the period of time during which the priority is valid. That said, when the Public Service Commission finds that there has been an error in an appointment process that affected a priority employee, the commission's remedy must meaningfully respond to that error and not simply require training for those who made the error.[278] Additionally, the FPSLREB has ordered that a grievor be deemed to be laid off (and therefore placed on a priority list) as a remedy for the employer's failure to accommodate the grievor during a staffing process in which the grievor had priority status.[279]

The staffing priorities, in their proper order, are set out below.

1) Statutory Priorities

a) Superordinate Priority: Priority for Employment Equity

A member of a designated group, within the meaning of section 3 of the *Employment Equity Act*, may be appointed, in accordance with an employment equity program, without regard to any entitlement to appointment in any other priority, unless the person who is entitled to appointment in priority in accordance with the other provisions of the *PSEA* is also a member of a designated group within the meaning of section 3 of the *Employment Equity Act* to which the employment equity program applies.[280] In other words, employment equity criteria may trump the other priorities, but those other priorities are used to rank two or more candidates who meet the requirements of an employment equity program.

---

276 *PSEA*, s 43.

277 *Ibid*, s 87.

278 *Agnaou v Canada (Attorney General)*, 2015 FC 523.

279 *Santawirya v Treasury Board (Canada Border Services Agency)*, 2018 FPSLREB 85.

280 *PSER*, s 3.

b) Priority for Disabled Veterans

Members of the Canadian Forces who were released for medical reasons attributable to their service have the next-highest priority for appointment.[281]

c) Priority for Surplus Employees Prior to Layoff

After a deputy head informs an employee that they are going to be laid off, but before the layoff becomes effective, that employee has a priority over all other candidates for positions within that deputy head's organization.[282] Essentially, this means that any employee who has been declared surplus but not yet laid off has a priority in any position within their department. This is commonly referred to as "surplus priority."

d) Priority for Persons on Leave of Absence

When an employee on a leave of absence's substantive position is filled by another person appointed for an indeterminate period (something commonly referred to as "backfilling"), then the employee on leave has priority for the period of their leave and one year thereafter.[283] If the employee on leave returns to their original position, then the employee who replaced that employee has a priority of appointment for a period of one year.[284]

e) Priority for Persons Laid Off

A person who is laid off has a priority of appointment over other candidates.[285] The period of that priority ends on the earliest of three events:

- the day that is one year after the day on which the person is laid off,
- the day on which the person is appointed to a position in the public service for an indeterminate period, or
- the day on which the person declines an appointment to a position in the public service for an indeterminate period without good and sufficient reason.[286]

---

281 *Ibid*, s 39.1.
282 *Ibid*, s 40.
283 *Ibid*, s 41(1)(a).
284 *Ibid*, s 41(1)(b).
285 *Ibid*, s 41(4).
286 *PSER*, s 11.

2) Regulatory Priorities

a) Priority for Surplus Employees, Prior to Layoff, Who Are Candidates for Positions in Other Departments

The priority for employees who have been informed of their layoff, but not yet laid off, extends to any position, but this priority is lower in rank than their priority to positions within their own department.[287] This priority does not extend to acting appointments or incumbent-based appointments.[288] This particular priority expires when the employee is appointed or deployed to another indeterminate position, refuses a reasonable job offer, or is laid off.[289] The term "reasonable job offer" is not defined in the *PSER*, but presumably the definition is the same as in the Work Force Adjustment Directive.[290]

b) Priority for Employees with Disabilities

An employee who becomes disabled and is unable to perform the duties of their position has a priority of appointment to another position.[291] An employee is "disabled" if they are eligible for disability compensation under the Canada Pension Plan, the Quebec Pension Plan, the *Public Service Superannuation Act*, the *Government Employees Compensation Act*, or a public service group disability insurance plan.[292] The priority period is triggered whenever a "competent authority" declares the employee to be disabled (so long as that declaration is within five years from the date they become disabled) and lasts for two years or until the employee is appointed or deployed to an indeterminate period position or refuses an indeterminate position without "good and sufficient reason."[293] The term "competent authority" is not defined in the *PSER*; however, in *Tench v Canada (Attorney General)*, the Federal Court indicated (in *obiter*) that a disability insurance company may be a "competent authority."[294]

---

287 *Ibid*, s 5(1).

288 *Ibid*, s 4.

289 *Ibid*, s 5(2).

290 See the discussion of this directive, and the interpretation of the term "reasonable job offer," in Chapter 9.

291 *PSER*, s 7(1). If there is an employment equity plan in place for people with disabilities, they may be entitled to a higher priority for employment equity reasons.

292 *Ibid*, s 7(4).

293 *Ibid*, s 7(2).

294 *Tench v Canada (Attorney General)*, [1999] FCJ No 1716 at para 22.

c) Priority for Members of the Canadian Forces and the RCMP Discharged for Medical Reasons

Members of the RCMP have a priority if they are released or discharged from service for medical reasons.[295] Members of the Canadian Forces who are released for medical reasons unrelated to their service also have a priority.[296] The member of the force must request the priority within five years, and it is good for two years or until they accept an indeterminate position or turn down an indeterminate position without good and sufficient reason.[297]

d) Priority for Spousal Relocation

An employee who is on a leave of absence because their spouse has relocated, but whose position has not been backfilled, is entitled to the same type of priority as an employee on leave whose position has been backfilled, except the priority without backfilling has a lower rank.[298]

e) Priority for Demoted Employees

An employee who had a priority and who was appointed or deployed to a lower-level position is entitled to a priority in any position that is not higher than the position they held immediately before being appointed or deployed to the lower-level position.[299] In other words, priority employees who accept a demotion have a second priority to be appointed to a position back to the level they started at.

3) Final Statutory Priorities (External Appointment Process)

a) Priority for Military Veterans

A person who is in receipt of a pension by reason of service in World War I or World War II is given a priority over other candidates.[300] Veterans of World War I or World War II and their survivors (if they died while in service during those wars)[301] and members of the Canadian Forces with at least three years' service who have been honourably

---

295 *PSER*, s 7.1.
296 *Ibid*, s 8.
297 *Ibid*, s 8(2).
298 *Ibid*, s 9.
299 *Ibid*, s 10.
300 *Ibid*, s 39(1)(a) and Schedule, s 1.
301 *Ibid*, s 39(1)(b) and Schedule, s 1 ("veteran" paragraphs a–e).

released[302] are given a priority of a lower rank than veterans in receipt of a war pension.

b) Priority for Canadian Citizens and Permanent Residents

Finally, Canadian citizens and permanent residents have a priority over non-citizens who are not permanent residents. Canadian citizens have enjoyed preferential access to the federal public service since 1908.[303] Until 1961, citizenship was a prerequisite for civil service appointment, but in that year the requirement was changed to a preference.[304] This priority is meant to further Canada's citizenship policy by granting citizens certain privileges not enjoyed by immigrants. This in turn enhances the meaning of citizenship as a unifying symbol for Canadians and encourages permanent residents to naturalize.[305]

In *Lavoie v Canada*,[306] three non-citizens challenged the constitutionality of the citizenship preference on the grounds that it discriminated against them on the basis of citizenship. The majority of the Supreme Court of Canada upheld the constitutionality of the citizenship preference. A human rights complaint about the Canada Revenue Agency's priority for Canadian citizens was also dismissed on the grounds that the *Canadian Human Rights Act* does not prohibit discrimination on the grounds of citizenship.[307]

H. LAYOFFS UNDER THE *PUBLIC SERVICE EMPLOYMENT ACT*

Section 64 of the *PSEA* gives deputy heads the power to lay off an employee whose services are "no longer required by reason of lack of work, the discontinuance of a function or the transfer of work or a function outside" the core public administration. The term "layoff" is not defined in the *PSEA* or the *PSER*. However, the Act specifically states that an employee ceases to be an employee when they are laid off.[308]

---

302 *PSEA*, s 39(1)(b) and Schedule, s 1 ("veteran" paragraph f).

303 *The Civil Service Amendment Act, 1908*. More accurately, since there was no Canadian citizenship at that time, natural-born or naturalized British subjects had a priority.

304 *Civil Service Act*, SC 1960–61, c 57, s 40(1)(c).

305 *Lavoie v Canada*, 2002 SCC 23 at para 54.

306 *Ibid*.

307 *Ozcevik v Canada (Revenue Agency)*, 2021 FC 13.

308 *PSEA*, s 64(4).

Therefore, unlike the situation in the private sector when a layoff does not necessarily mean that the employee has been dismissed, "a public servant cannot be said to be laid off if his employment has not been terminated."[309] When an employee is placed on "off-duty status" (similar to what in the private sector might be considered a temporary layoff), then this is not a "layoff" under the Act and does not trigger the various rights that flow from being laid off.[310]

Sections 64(2) and 65(1) of the Act provide two scenarios in which layoffs will occur. The first scenario is when all of the employees in the part of the organization identified by the deputy head will be laid off. The second scenario is when some but not all of the employees will be laid off. Section 65(2) of the Act states that no complaint can be made against the decision to lay off employees, the determination of the part of the organization from which employees will be laid off, or the number of employees to be laid off from that part. Therefore, in the first scenario, there is no recourse available.[311]

In the second scenario, though, the layoffs must be made in accordance with the regulations established by the Public Service Commission. The *PSER* require the deputy head to choose the employees to be laid off in accordance with merit. This method of selection for layoff, under the old *PSEA* and the *PSER*, used to be referred to as "reverse order of merit." The common parlance now refers to this as a selection of employees for retention and layoff, or "SERLO" process, and "[t]he purpose of a SERLO process is to select on the basis of merit those employees who are to be retained to carry on the continuing work of an affected part of an organization and those employees who are to be laid off."[312]

Section 65(1) of the Act permits an employee in the second scenario to complain to the FPSLREB if their selection for layoff constitutes an abuse of authority. The term "abuse of authority" in this section

---

309 *Brescia v Canada (Treasury Board)*, [2005] FCJ No 1086 (CA) at para 48.

310 *Ibid*.

311 *Pinard v Deputy Minister of Natural Resources*, 2016 PSLREB 65 at para 33 [*Pinard*]. See also *Landoulsi v Deputy Minister of Public Works and Government Services*, 2014 PSST 7: with the elimination of the management trainee program (which had its own unique classification), there was no need to conduct a SERLO process for the one employee who happened to remain in the program at the time it was finally eliminated.

312 *Hailu v Deputy Minister of Health Canada*, 2013 PSST 27 at para 34 [*Hailu*].

has the same meaning as in section 77 of the Act,[313] discussed in detail above. For example, the FPSLREB has assessed narrative assessments of employees in the SERLO process in the same way as it assessed reference checks in the appointment process[314] and has set aside a layoff because of a rule that prevented the assessment board from seeking information in circumstances where "if this had been a 'normal' appointment process, she would certainly have sought the answers to her questions. . . . If it would be appropriate to ask questions or seek clarification when choosing employees for appointment, it should be equally appropriate when deciding whom to retain in the context of a SERLO process."[315]

One difficult issue for the FPSLREB has been whether an employee has the right of recourse if they were the only employee considered for layoff. Despite an earlier decision to the contrary,[316] the FPSLREB has concluded that such an employee may file a complaint with the board and that "Parliament cannot have intended that recourse to the Tribunal should be denied because a deputy head's requirements can be met by eliminating only one position and laying-off only one employee."[317] Therefore, an employee has standing to complain to the board unless the deputy head has completely eliminated the part of the organization it has identified.[318]

Another issue concerns when the obligation to conduct a SERLO process is triggered—that is, when does section 21 of the *PSER* apply? That section requires the deputy head to "assess the merit of the employees employed in similar positions or performing similar duties in the

---

313 *Tran v the Commissioner of the Royal Canadian Mounted Police*, 2012 PSST 33 at para 13 [*Tran*]; *Raymond v Chief Statistician of Canada*, 2013 PSST 25 at para 13 [*Raymond*].

314 *Tran*, above note 313 at para 45: "[A] referee must be familiar with an employee's work and be able to provide sufficient information to the assessment board so it can conduct an adequate assessment of the employee's qualifications. A similar level of familiarity is required by those providing a narrative assessment in a SERLO process."

315 *Hailu*, above note 312 at para 37.

316 *Molander v Commissioner of the Royal Canadian Mounted Police et al*, 2007 PSST 42.

317 *Lishman v the Deputy Minister of Environment Canada*, 2013 PSST 12 at para 23 [*Lishman*]. The Public Service Commission and employer both argued against this *volte-face* in *Pinard*, above note 311, but the Board confirmed its earlier decision in *Lishman*.

318 *Lishman*, *ibid* at para 42.

same occupational group and level within that part of the organization."[319] The requirement of being in the same occupational group and level can be read two ways: as applying both to similar positions and similar duties or only applying to similar duties. The FPSLREB adopted the first interpretation, such that "a deputy head is required to conduct a merit-based assessment of employees who a) occupy positions that are classified at the same occupational group and level and are similar, or b) perform similar duties at the same occupational group and level."[320] Thus, when an employee occupying a particular classification (in that case, ENG-04) was laid off, the deputy head was not required to assess an employee occupying an ENG-03 position along with her.[321] Similarly, the deputy head was not required to conduct a SERLO process for employees in two separate classifications (in that case, GT-05 and AS-03) despite the similarities between their duties.[322]

The FPSLREB has not yet ruled on how similar positions need to be (within the same occupational group and level) to trigger section 21 of the *PSER*. However, the Federal Court did have to interpret an earlier version of the *PSER* that required a reverse order of merit exercise comparing the employees laid off to employees "of the same occupational nature and level." The Federal Court stated that concerning the determination of whether particular employees had the same occupational nature and level,

> it was impossible to say what degree of similarity must exist between positions so that they may be held to be of the same nature.... [I]t was a question of opinion, better left to the authorities of the department concerned.... [W]hen departmental authorities have answered the question, their judgment must be respected.[323]

The old *PSER* had a very narrow definition: the duties of the positions must be the same, and the positions must be "interchangeable" to be of the same nature.[324] In that case, the Court commented (in *obiter*) on the new wording of the *PSER* (which were replaced again in 2005) and stated that "Parliament has now provided a broader net to include

319 *PSER*, s 21.
320 *Lishman*, above note 317 at para 52.
321 *Ibid*.
322 *Pinard*, above note 311.
323 *Chandler v Canada*, [1987] FCJ No 11, aff'd [1988] FCJ No 407 (CA).
324 *Ibid*.

'similar positions'"[325]—implying at least that the positions do not need to be interchangeable to be similar.

Section 21 of the *PSER* also refers to "one or more employees of a part of an organization." The FPSLREB has not articulated a legal test for what constitutes an "organization" but, in the one case where the issue arose, considered the matter purely as a question of fact.[326]

A complainant must make a complaint within fifteen days of receiving the notice of layoff or, if it is a public notice, fifteen days after that public notice has been made.[327] The deadline to make a complaint begins to run when the selection for layoff process is complete and the employee has been notified—not at the end of the "surplus period" when their employment actually comes to an end.[328] As mentioned above, no complaint may be made against the decision to lay off employees, the determination of the part of the organization from which employees will be laid off, or the number of employees to be laid off from that part.[329] Finally, where the FPSLREB upholds the complaint, it may order the deputy head to set aside the decision to lay off the complainant and take any corrective action it considers appropriate other than the layoff of another employee,[330] including an award of damages under the *Canadian Human Rights Act* if the layoff was a violation of that Act.[331] The typical order is to set aside the layoff decision, effectively reinstating the employee.[332] Otherwise, an employee ceases to be an employee when they are laid off—meaning that they cannot grieve issues that arise after their layoff (such as their treatment while on a priority list).[333]

I. INCUMBENT-BASED STAFFING PROCESSES

The previous version of the *PSEA* required that appointments be made on the basis of relative merit. The concept of relative merit, though,

325 *Ibid.*

326 *Pinard*, above note 311.

327 *Complaints Regulations*, s 10.

328 *Tran*, above note 313. In that case, the FPSLREB found that the complaint was untimely but extended the deadline to file the complaint in large part because the department did not mention the complainant's right of recourse in its layoff notice.

329 *PSEA*, s 65(2).

330 *Ibid*, s 65(4).

331 *Ibid*, s 65(8).

332 This was the remedy in *Hailu*, above note 312, and *Raymond*, above note 313.

333 *Canada (Attorney General) v Santawirya*, 2019 FCA 248.

did not fit neatly within certain appointment or promotion processes. Therefore, in 1993, Parliament amended the Act to state that selection according to merit may, in certain circumstances, be based on the competence of the person being appointed rather than as measured against the competence of other persons[334]—something the Federal Court of Appeal referred to as "individual merit."[335] The identity of those appointment processes that would be made in accordance with individual merit was set out in regulation[336] and included promotions as part of apprenticeship programs, reclassifications, junior lawyers, and promotions within a classification group in which positions were classified according to the qualifications of incumbents. The latter category was mainly research scientists.

The current *PSEA* preserves this final category as an exception to the recourse process to challenge appointments. Section 34(1) of the Act permits the Public Service Commission (or a delegate) to determine the area of selection for any appointment process "other than an incumbent-based process." This exempts incumbent-based processes from the complaint procedure in the Act. The term "incumbent-based process" is defined in section 2 of the *PSER* to mean the internal appointment process within the research and university teaching groups. The *PSER* go on to say that this exception to the complaint procedure only applies "if there is a career progression framework established by the deputy head in consultation with the authorized bargaining agents that includes an independent recourse mechanism."[337] Thus, the combination of section 34(1) of the *PSEA* and section 2 of the *PSER* means two things: a department must establish an independent recourse mechanism for research scientists, and, provided that they do so, a research scientist must use that mechanism instead of filing a complaint with the FPSLREB.

Research scientists are promoted "when the work of the incumbent position holder reaches a certain quality."[338] In other words, research scientists "are promoted as their research work progresses."[339] The incumbent-based process operates similarly to the tenure system in

334 *Public Service Reform Act*, SC 1992, c 54.

335 *Canada (Attorney General) v Laidlaw*, 1998 CarswellNat 5463 (Fed CA) at para 1.

336 *Public Service Employment Regulations, 1993*, SOR/93/286, s 4.

337 *PSER*, s 2.

338 *Gladman v Canada (Attorney General)*, 2016 FC 917 at para 3, aff'd 2017 FCA 109.

339 *Rabbath v Canada (National Revenue)*, 2014 FC 999 at para 5 [*Rabbath*].

Canadian universities[340] as a way to attract research scientists who would otherwise end up in academia.

The independent recourse mechanism for research scientists is relatively consistent across different departments and different types of research. In essence, research scientists who apply for a promotion but are dissatisfied with not being promoted may apply for independent recourse. The department then appoints an independent reviewer, who is typically a senior scientist (or panel of scientists) from another department. The independent reviewer assesses the case on grounds specified in the review mechanism, which include whether there has been an "abuse of authority."[341] The reviewer then makes a recommendation to the deputy head, who is responsible for deciding the appropriate outcome of the request for review. The reviewer may not recommend that the research scientist be promoted[342] (thus mirroring the prohibition against the FPSLREB granting a complainant a promotion), but can recommend that the research scientist's case be re-examined to correct some flaw. The reviewer's role is thus broader than simply examining the process followed by the promotions committee (usually called a career progression committee); they are tasked with reviewing whether there has been an improper result or there was some issue that negatively affected the promotion's committee's decision.[343] For example, a promotion committee cannot add a new criteria when assessing candidates (e.g., requiring that the candidate's achievements be documented by externally recognized sources—such as peer-reviewed journals).[344] Finally, a deputy head must engage with and respond to the reviewer's recommendation and provide a meaningful remedy to the candidate that responds to their circumstances.[345]

---

340 John Smart, "Professional Historians in a National Union: The Collective Bargaining and Classification Experience of the Historians of the Federal Government of Canada, 1967–1984" (6 April 1984) at 19.

341 *Gladman* (FCA), above note 338 at para 11, described the five grounds of recourse available in that case.

342 *Gultepe v Canada (Attorney General)*, 2015 FC 645 at para 8.

343 *Ibid* at para 14.

344 *Ollevier v Canada (Attorney General)*, 2008 FC 199. The committee may, though, elaborate upon the existing standards: *Gultepe v Canada (Attorney General)*, 2016 FC 1404.

345 *Rabbath*, above note 339 at para 32.

J. STAFFING PROCESSES OUTSIDE THE *PUBLIC SERVICE EMPLOYMENT ACT*

As stated above, the appointment process in the *PSEA* applies unless another Act of Parliament grants some other entity the authority to make appointments. Therefore, when another Act of Parliament grants the authority to a person to make appointments to a particular agency or entity, then those appointments are no longer made by the Public Service Commission. This is typically the case for separate agencies. For example, the *Parks Canada Agency Act* gives the chief executive officer of Parks Canada the authority to make appointments and to "establish standards, procedures and processes governing staffing";[346] the *Canada Revenue Agency Act* (*CRA Act*) gives the commissioner of customs and revenue the authority to appoint any employees necessary for what is now called the Canada Revenue Agency;[347] and the *Canadian Food Inspection Agency Act* gives the president of that agency the authority to appoint employees.[348] By consequence, the *PSEA* also no longer governs appointments to or from within those agencies, as well as other separate agencies with similar legislation. The appointments need not be made in accordance with the merit principle unless required by the particular rules established by that agency for appointments and other staffing measures.

Each of those separate agencies has their own staffing recourse policies. Those staffing recourse policies themselves are not publicly available (although they are available internally to employees of those agencies). Those policies all, however, contemplate some method of review of staffing decisions (in particular decisions about appointments).

---

346 *Parks Canada Agency Act*, SC 1998, c 31, s 13(1).

347 *Canada Revenue Agency Act*, SC 1999, c 17, s 53 [*CRA Act*]. The Act refers to the "Canada Customs and Revenue Agency." However, on 12 December 2003, the parts of the Canada Customs and Revenue Agency dedicated to the administration of customs statutes were transferred to the minister of public security and emergency planning under the *Order Transferring Certain Portions of the Canada Customs and Revenue Agency to the Canada Border Services Agency*, SI/2003-216, pursuant to the *Public Service Rearrangement and Transfer of Duties Act*, RSC 1985, c P-34. The decision to separate customs and trade services from the agency and transfer these functions to the new Canada Border Services Agency was the result of the government's commitment to enhanced security through strong border protection. As a consequence, the agency is now known as the Canada Revenue Agency (CRA).

348 *Canadian Food Inspection Agency Act*, SC 1997, c 6, s 13(1).

1) Canada Revenue Agency

The Canada Revenue Agency (CRA) is by far the largest separate agency whose staffing decisions are not governed by the *PSEA*. The CRA was established on 1 November 1999. It was established as part of the federal government's experiment with "alternative service delivery," and the legislation gives the CRA considerable flexibility and latitude in the human resources, financial, and administrative areas.

As part of this "alternative service delivery," the *CRA Act* requires the CRA to set up its own staffing program. Section 54 of the Act states:

> 54 (1) The Agency must develop a program governing staffing, including the appointment of, and recourse for, employees.
>
> (2) No collective agreement may deal with matters governed by the staffing program.

Prior to the *CRA Act*, approximately 40 percent of staffing appeals heard by the Public Service Commission were filed by employees of Revenue Canada (the predecessor department to the CRA).[349] The number of staffing challenges, and consequently the delay in appointing employees, was of concern to the CRA. The CRA has stated:

> As a result of this new process, staffing recourse has been transformed from an adversarial and defensive process into one where openness and dispute resolution practices predominate. This has had a positive effect on the time spent on recourse within the Agency. Prior to 1999, the average time to complete an internal competitive process was 166 days excluding recourse. Recourse could frequently add anywhere from 3 to 12 months to the selection process due to the size of CRA's competitions, the number and complexity of selection processes being managed, and the scheduling of related appeal process activities.
>
> In the first year of the Agency, the time to staff a position through internal staffing (including recourse) was reduced by 33% and by 20% for external staffing. Since November 1, 1999, there have been only

349 Professional Institute of the Public Service of Canada, "Presentation to the House of Commons Standing Committee on Finance on the Five Year Review of the *Canada Revenue Agency Act*" (June 2006) at 6. See also, online: www.ourcommons.ca/DocumentViewer/en/39-1/FINA/report-9/page-105.

211 requests for independent third party review of Agency staffing decisions. This equates to 1.3% of placement decisions.[350]

The CRA staffing recourse system is predicated upon staffing "principles." The *CRA Act* requires the CRA to provide a statement of "staffing principles" in its corporate business plan,[351] and the *CRA Act* also permits the Public Service Commission to review and report on the consistency of the CRA's staffing program with the principles set out in its corporate business plan.[352] The Public Service Commission has confirmed that those principles are consistent with the values in the *PSEA* and that the CRA's staffing recourse system is also consistent with those principles.[353] The current iteration of the CRA's staffing process sets out eight principles: adaptability, efficiency, fairness, productiveness, transparency, competency, non-partisanship, and representativeness of employment equity designated groups.[354]

The CRA's staffing program (the Policy)[355] is established pursuant to statute. As a result, at least one judge of the Federal Court has characterized the Policy as "quasi-legislation limited only by the context and the meaning of the Act," or even as a "Regulation."[356] Despite this "quasi-legislation" status, the Policy has been amended on a number of occasions, without notice in the *Canada Gazette* or other formal instrument of amendment. This is, in fact, one of the major bargaining agent complaints about the Policy. As one bargaining agent representative put it: "When an [independent third-party reviewer] interprets a directive in a way that expands employees' rights, the employer amends the directive to limit that right once again."[357]

---

350 *The Canada Revenue Agency: The First Five Years* (25 April 2005), online: https://publications.gc.ca/Collection/Rv4-3-2005E.pdf at 35–36.

351 *CRA Act*, s 49(3).

352 *Ibid*, s 56.

353 Public Service Commission, *Annual Report 2000–2001* (2001) at 8, online (pdf): https://publications.gc.ca/collections/Collection/SC1-2001E.pdf, and Public Service Commission, above note 9, ch 3.4.

354 Canada Revenue Agency, *Summary of the Corporate Business Plan 2021–22 with Perspectives to 2023–24* (2021), online (pdf): www.canada.ca/content/dam/cra-arc/corp-info/aboutcra/corp-bsns-plan/smmry-cbp-2021-24-en.pdf at 44.

355 Also referred to as the Canada Revenue Agency Staffing Program or "the Program."

356 *Canada (Attorney General) v Gagnon*, [2006] FCJ No 270 at paras 18 and 21 [*Gagnon*].

357 House of Commons, Standing Committee on Finance, *Evidence*, 39-1, No 12 (14 June 2006) at 16:40 (Mrs. Betty Bannon).

Broadly speaking, the Policy splits job competitions into three stages: the prerequisite stage, the assessment stage, and the placement stage (i.e., the appointment stage).[358] The Policy also contains three levels of staffing recourse: individual feedback, decision review, and independent third-party review (ITPR). Individual feedback is available for candidates who are unsuccessful at any level of the selection process and must be completed before any other recourse is attempted.[359] It is also the final level of review for any decision at the prerequisite stage of the staffing process.[360] Decision review is available only if a candidate is screened out at the assessment or placement phase. ITPR is available only to those candidates who are screened out at the placement phase for permanent promotions, and only if they opt not to engage in decision review—in other words, a candidate must have completed informal feedback at the placement stage and not have requested decision review.[361] When there is a link between the assessment stage and the placement stage, then the ITPR has the jurisdiction to consider assessment issues. For example, in *Sargeant v Canada (Attorney General)*,[362] the CRA used the assessment criteria at the placement stage without first telling candidates that it may do so. On those facts, the Court concluded that there was a sufficient link between assessment and placement to grant jurisdiction to the ITPR. By contrast, in *Qui v Canada (Revenue Agency)*,[363] the candidates knew or should have known that their scores at the assessment stage could be used at the placement stage; therefore, the ITPR had no jurisdiction to address concerns about those scores, which should have been addressed through decision review after the assessment stage.

The sole ground of review under the Policy is that an employee was treated arbitrarily. The term "arbitrary" is defined in the Policy as follows:

358 *Qui v Canada (Revenue Agency)*, 2018 FC 392 at para 3 [*Qui*].

359 *Sutton v Canada (Attorney General)*, 2006 FC 848 at para 19: "a candidate who does not seek individual feedback from a manager cannot challenge the decision of that manager"; aff'd 2007 FCA 165.

360 *Tran v Canada (Attorney General)*, 2013 FC 455 at para 11.

361 *Professional Institute of the Public Service of Canada v Canada (Customs and Revenue Agency)*, [2004] FCJ No 649 at para 31; *Qui*, above note 358 at para 9.

362 *Sargeant v Canada (Attorney General)*, 2002 FCT 1043.

363 *Qui*, above note 358.

> In an unreasonable manner, done capriciously; not done or acting according to reason or judgment; not based on rationale or established policy; not the result of a reasoning applied to relevant considerations; discriminatory, i.e. as listed as the prohibited grounds of discrimination in the *Canadian Human Rights Act.*

The Federal Court's decision in *Canada (Customs and Revenue Agency) v Kapadia*[364] provides a fairly detailed examination of what is or is not arbitrary. In that case, the CRA posted a competition for positions of audit manager in the Hamilton and Toronto West Tax Services Offices. The CRA made a number of appointments based on this particular competition. Ms. Kapadia was placed into that position on an acting basis from 13 November 2001 until May 2003; however, on 22 April 2003, the CRA made final permanent appointments to those positions and did not appoint Ms. Kapadia. The notice of competition for those positions identified four placement criteria: employment equity, geographic location, experience, and qualifications/competencies. In turn, the placement criterion of "qualifications/ competencies" listed ten qualifications for the position. When the hiring manager made his final decision at the placement stage, he decided to use only two of the four placement criteria (geographic location and qualifications). Then, when he used the criterion of "qualifications," he chose to consider only six of the ten qualification factors. He also averaged the score for two of the qualifications (leadership and team building) and counted them as one combined qualification. The hiring manager then appointed the two candidates with the highest score using his unique calculation of the various test scores for the qualifications. Finally, other candidates for the same position had been appointed after considering the placement criterion of "employment equity," but the last placement did not use that criterion. In fact, Ms. Kapadia was appointed on an acting basis to that same position using "employment equity" as one of the criteria for placement.

Ms. Kapadia was successful in her appeal to an independent third-party reviewer. The reviewer concluded that the placement decision was arbitrary in the following ways:

1) the hiring manager erred in basing his placement decision on only six of ten qualifications factors considered at the assessment stage;

364 *Canada (Customs and Revenue Agency) v Kapadia*, [2005] FCJ No 2086.

2) the hiring manager improperly merged the team building and leadership qualification criteria, which decreased the weighting of both;
3) the hiring manager did not use the "employment equity" placement factor in all appointments and failed to explain why he did not use it in all cases;
4) there was an appearance of injustice by allowing the same hiring manager to chair the selection board at the assessment stage and make the final decisions about placement.

The CRA applied for judicial review of the reviewer's decision. The Federal Court upheld the reviewer's decision on the first two grounds but did not uphold the decision on the last two grounds.

Concerning the choice of which "qualifications" to consider at the placement stage, the Court stated:

> It is not fair or reasonable for the candidates found qualified by the Selection Board to allow the hiring manager at the placement stage to pick and choose amongst the ten qualifications for the position of audit manager in selecting the successful candidate for the position. This approach opens the door to favouritism, arbitrariness, and unfairness, and is contrary to the protection of fairness and objectivity ensured by the Selection Board stage.[365]

Similarly, it made "no sense" to combine two qualifications for the purpose of measuring the relative qualifications of the candidates.[366]

However, it was open to the hiring manager not to consider the placement criterion of "employment equity." There was evidence that the hiring manager did not use that criterion because there was no gap in the representation of women in 2003, whereas there was a gap in 2000. Thus, the decision to use the employment equity criterion for some appointments but not others was not arbitrary in this particular case.[367]

Finally, the Federal Court decided it was not arbitrary to have the same person chair the selection board and also make the placement decisions. Ms. Kapadia argued that, as chair of the selection board, the hiring manager knew the scores of the candidates on each of the four placement criteria. Therefore, the hiring manager could favour one candidate over another by simply deciding to use particular placement

365 *Ibid* at para 19(1).
366 *Ibid* at para 19(2).
367 *Ibid* at para 19(3).

criteria, knowing that by using those criteria they would be able to appoint the candidate they prefer. The Federal Court rejected that argument, stating:

> The decision of the ITPR that the applicant created an appearance of bias by allowing Mr. Webster to serve both as chair of the Selection Board, and as the hiring manager responsible for the placement decision is wrong in the view of the Court. The applicant has discretion to ensure that the persons most familiar with the requirements of the position be on the Selection Board, and be involved in the final hiring decision. There is no reasonable apprehension of bias in having Mr. Webster serve in both capacities.[368]

An independent third-party reviewer has criticized the CRA for three things: using a "localized" assessment tool when a "standard" assessment tool was available; not clearly communicating the assessment of one qualification (contrary to the staffing value of "transparency"); and being unclear about how often certain qualifications would be assessed.[369] It should be noted that ITPR decisions are "not precedent setting, they are case specific,"[370] such that each case must be considered on its own merits. The Federal Court did not elaborate further on this principle. It is likely similar to the rule in labour arbitrations in the private sector: arbitrators are not bound by *stare decisis*, but arbitrators are still required to adequately explain the basis for a departure from earlier decisions.[371] The rule in this case is likely that ITPR decisions are not *binding* precedent, but that inconsistent decisions are to be avoided and must be carefully explained and justified.

In a later case, the Federal Court focused on the phrase "not the result of a reasoning applied to relevant considerations" in the definition of "arbitrary." The Court focused on its inability to understand the results of the marking key used to assess each candidate. The Court stated that a "reasonable decision requires that one can see and

368 *Ibid* at para 19(4).

369 As cited in *Plato v Canada (Revenue Agency)*, 2013 FC 348 [*Plato*].

370 *Mitchell v Canada (National Revenue)*, 2012 FC 1508. This is also set out in art 4.4 of the Policy itself.

371 *Re United Steelworkers and Triangle Conduit & Cable Canada (1968) Ltd* (1970), 21 LAC 332 at 344, cited in *Communications, Energy and Paperworkers Union of Canada, Local 30 v Irving Pulp & Paper, Ltd*, 2013 SCC 34 at para 78 (in dissent, but not on this point).

understand the reasoning of the selection board and observe from a scoring key that the candidate passed or failed depending on objectively allocated points. When one cannot determine the value of the items to be scored or identify the minimum items required to obtain a pass mark, it becomes impossible to determine that the decision was reasonable."[372] The Court thus treated this aspect of arbitrary behaviour as akin to the reasonableness review on an application for judicial review, requiring that the assessment of a candidate be transparent and intelligible in a way that evokes the reasonableness standard of review required in *Canada (Minister of Citizenship and Immigration) v Vavilov*.[373]

The Federal Court has also stated that the term "arbitrary" does not require an improper motive or bad faith, instead taking the definition of "arbitrary" at face value to include any decision "not based on rationale or established policy."[374] In that case, an employee was appointed to a permanent position on 16 October 2008 and then had that appointment revoked on 7 November 2008 because of purported errors in the initial selection process. The Court concluded that the reviewer overstated the significance of the errors (namely, the failure to notify one employee about the position and failing to specify the term of employment as indeterminate in the notice provided to other employees); more importantly, the Court concluded that the CRA could only set aside its initial appointment if those errors rose to the threshold of "arbitrary" behaviour. In other words, the CRA does not have the same powers as the Public Service Commission or deputy heads in the core public administration to review appointments and revoke those appointments upon discovering errors: the CRA may only revoke an appointment if it concludes that the errors rise to the level of arbitrary conduct.

When the decision is subject to ITPR, the reviewer does not have the jurisdiction to order any particular remedy. Instead, the reviewer simply makes a finding of arbitrary conduct and orders that it be corrected. The reviewer may recommend[375] that another manager be involved in

372 *Mayrand v Canada (Revenue Agency)*, 2011 FC 159 at para 32.

373 *Vavilov*, above note 274 at para 95.

374 *McLaughlin v Canada (Attorney General)*, 2010 FC 399 at para 38.

375 An earlier version of the Policy required management to implement the reviewer's recommendations: *Burstyn v Canada (Canada Customs and Revenue Agency)*, 2006 FC 744 [*Burstyn*]. That rule was changed to the current version whereby the reviewer may order the correction of an error and only make recommendations otherwise: *Plato*, above note 369 at para 3.

correcting the error or the revocation of an appointment, but the final corrective action rests with the CRA. The ultimate remedy ordered by management must correspond with the reviewer's decision.[376] If, for example, the reviewer exceeds their jurisdiction and makes some positive order, the CRA must fulfill that order unless it applies for judicial review against that order—it cannot "use the back door to accomplish what it should have done through the front door."[377]

Management's decisions purporting to implement an order to correct the process may not be the subject of another complaint: disputes over corrective action therefore proceed directly to judicial review.[378] The Federal Court has been clear that a manager's corrective action must correspond with the reviewer's decision.[379] In that case, the reviewer found three separate breaches in the staffing process (listed above), but the manager's remedy only addressed two of those breaches: the Federal Court ordered that the CRA assign a new manager to issue corrective measures that responded to all three breaches. In another case, the Federal Court went further and concluded that the failure to order retroactive compensation (as a remedy for an arbitrary staffing process that delayed the complainants' promotion for two years) was unreasonable because "[r]etroactive compensation is central to the meaningfulness of the remedy in question because the principal harm suffered is a delay in appointment."[380]

---

376 *Ibid* at para 21.

377 *Burstyn*, above note 375 at para 49. See also *Sherman v Canada (Customs and Revenue Agency)*, [2005] FCJ No 209, granting an order of *mandamus* of a reviewer's decision despite it being outside the jurisdiction of the reviewer. Finally, see *Gagnon*, above note 356, as an example of the CRA successfully applying for judicial review of a reviewer's decision ordering that that the complainant be appointed to the position at issue.

378 The FPSLREB has found that the Policy is an "administrative procedure for redress provided under any Act of Parliament" for the purposes of s 208(2) of the *FPSLRA* and, therefore, issues about staffing at the CRA may not be grieved: *Dhudwal v Canada (Customs and Revenue Agency)*, 2003 PSSRB 116 (decided under the old *Public Service Staffing Relations Act*), *Malette v Canada Revenue Agency*, 2008 PSLRB 99, and *Swan and McDowell v Canada Revenue Agency*, 2009 PSLRB 73 (applying the *FPSLRA*).

379 *Plato*, above note 369.

380 *Haire v Canada Revenue Agency*, 2014 FC 165 at para 12.

CHAPTER TWELVE

Classification

A. INTRODUCTION

This book is the only legal text that would dedicate an entire chapter to job classifications. This reflects the importance of job classification to employees in the federal public service. The second-largest federal public service union—the Professional Institute of the Public Service of Canada—was founded in 1920 in response to concerns about classification reform, in particular the hostility of some civil servants to the American firms that had been hired to survey the organization and classification structure of the Canadian civil service. The larger bargaining agents in the federal public service have dedicated classification "experts" to assist their members in challenging the classification of their jobs. Management also has its own classification "experts" to review classification decisions and, when necessary, reclassify positions. Employees of the federal public service are very concerned about their job classification, hence the need for all of these experts.

Classification is important because the identity of an employee's bargaining agent, the level of pay for an employee, and their promotional prospects depend on their classification. As discussed in Chapter 5, bargaining units in the federal public service typically follow classification lines. Furthermore, the various collective agreements in the federal public service contain different levels of pay for each classification level. Finally, some positions in the federal public service require experience at a particular classification level for a candidate to be eligible for that position. Therefore, classification can have a significant impact on an employee's career.

Classification in the federal public service has also been subject to legislative control. The 1992 *Public Service Reform Act* required the federal government to prepare new occupational groups.[1] The impact of this Act on the bargaining unit structure in the federal public service has already been addressed;[2] however, creating new occupational groups required new job classifications as well. Thus began what seemed like an endless stream of classification reform.

While attempts to reform the public service classification system date back to the mid-1980s, the first attempt at major reform began in 1997 with the Universal Classification Standard (UCS) project. The goal of this project was ostensibly to make the classification system simpler and less burdensome and to reduce administrative costs. The original design was to reform the classification system on a universal basis applicable to all occupational groups, except the Executive Group. There were two reasons for this plan. First, it was hoped that a common approach to job measurement (one standard versus the seventy-two in place in 1997) would greatly simplify the system, reduce the administrative burden on managers, and lower the administrative overhead costs of maintaining the system. Second, a single classification standard would facilitate the creation of a single corresponding pay structure. Collapsing all of the occupational group pay structures into one structure also appeared to be the most promising way to ensure compliance with the requirements of the *Canadian Human Rights Act* for equal pay for work of equal value.

Despite these good intentions, the Treasury Board abandoned the UCS project in 2002.[3] It decided that a universal approach to classification would impair human resources. While the Public Service Human Resources Management Agency of Canada maintained that the UCS project provided a benefit to the public service, it is hard to escape the conclusion that the public service wasted millions of dollars on fruitless classification reform.

---

1 *Public Service Reform Act*, SC 1992, c 54, s 101.

2 Above in Chapter 6.

3 This was announced in a press release euphemistically called "Government Moves Ahead with Classification Reform" (8 May 2002).

Undeterred, the Treasury Board decided to try again. In 2010, the Treasury Board announced a classification program renewal initiative.[4] The goal was initially to work on two specific occupational groups (the Program and Administrative Services (PA) and Computer Systems (CS) groups) by 2012. In fact, the work on the CS Group was completed in 2021 (when it was formally renamed the Information Technology (IT) Group),[5] and the work on the PA Group continues. A 2018 evaluation of the classification program reported that the Treasury Board classification program "is not operating as efficiently as it could."[6]

These political or human resources initiatives have not changed the substantive law of classification in the federal public service, which is discussed below.

B. JOB DESCRIPTIONS

Employers in the federal public service have adopted a practice whereby, before they will hear a classification grievance, the grievor must agree that their job description is accurate.[7] Regardless of whether this practice is supported by the *Directive on Classification Grievances* or any other formal instrument,[8] an employee's classification is determined according to their work description. Therefore, a frequent preliminary step to a classification grievance is a grievance concerning the grievor's

4 Treasury Board of Canada Secretariat, "Evaluation of the Classification Program" (12 September 2018), online: www.canada.ca/en/treasury-board-secretariat/corporate/reports/evaluation-classification-program.html#toc12.

5 The change to this occupation group was published in the *Canada Gazette* on 2 June 2018, and the corresponding change to the bargaining unit definition was made on 1 February 2019: *Treasury Board v PIPSC*, 2019 FPSLREB 13. The change came into force on 9 December 2021: www.canada.ca/en/treasury-board-secretariat/services/collective-agreements/occupational-groups/information-technology.html.

6 "Evaluation of the Classification Program," above note 4.

7 *Currie v Canada (Customs and Revenue Agency)*, [2006] FCJ No 784 (CA) at para 11 [*Currie*]. To put this another way, a classification grievance committee does not have the jurisdiction to amend or modify the content of a job description: *Roopnauth v Canada (National Revenue)*, 2016 FC 1307 at para 31.

8 From the Federal Court's discussion in *Trepanier v Canada (Attorney General)*, [2004] FCJ No 1601, it would appear as if there is no such instrument. However, art A.2.10.3 of the appendix to the Treasury Board of Canada Secretariat's *Directive on Classification Grievances* (1 April 2020), online: www.tbs-sct.canada.ca/pol/doc-eng.aspx?id=28698, states that a classification grievance is put in abeyance if a job content grievance has also been presented, which amounts to the same thing.

job description. Most if not all collective agreements in the federal public service contain a provision permitting employees to demand a job description. For example, the collective agreement between the Public Service Alliance of Canada and the Treasury Board covering employees in the Program and Administrative bargaining unit contains the following provision:

> **56.01** Upon written request, an employee shall be provided with a complete and current statement of the duties and responsibilities of his or her position, including the classification level and, where applicable, the point rating allotted by factor to his or her position, and an organization chart depicting the position's place in the organization.[9]

These "job description grievances" are addressed through the normal grievance procedure and, because they concern a provision of the collective agreement, may also be referred to adjudication. This is the appropriate recourse if an employee is regularly doing work beyond the scope of the duties set out in their job description. In *Currie v Canada (Customs and Revenue Agency)*,[10] an adjudicator suggested that reclassification was the appropriate remedy for an employee regularly engaged in doing work beyond the scope of their job description. However, the Federal Court of Appeal quashed that decision because it was irrational in light of the fact that a reclassification grievance could not proceed unless there was agreement on the content of the job description.

As the Court pointed out in *Currie*, a job description is more than just a tool for classification. It is "the cornerstone of the employment relationship"[11] between employee and employer.[12] It is referred to with regard not only to classification but also to staffing, remuneration, discipline, performance evaluation, identification of language requirements, and career planning. However, the main purpose of a job description is to permit the appropriate classification of positions. Therefore,

9 Treasury Board of Canada Secretariat, *Agreement Between the Treasury Board and the Public Service Alliance of Canada, Group: Program and Administrative Services (All Employees)* (2020), online (pdf): https://psacunion.ca/sites/psac/files/pa_collective_agreement_-_en.pdf.

10 *Currie*, above note 7.

11 *Breckenridge and The Library of Parliament*, [1996] CPSSRB No 69 at para 70; *Jennings and Myers v Treasury Board (Department of Fisheries and Oceans)*, 2011 PSLRB 20 at para 51 [*Jennings and Myers*].

12 The Treasury Board has also stated that "classification is the cornerstone of human resources management" ("Evaluation of the Classification Program," above note 4).

the accuracy or completeness of a job description is typically viewed through that lens: "[I]f significant elements are omitted that preclude the classification committee from fairly evaluating the position, the work description must be amended."[13]

A job description does not, however, need to contain the same sections or titles as in a plan of classification. In *Hymander v Canada (National Parole Board)*,[14] the grievors argued that their job descriptions were incomplete because they did not contain a section titled "consequences of error," a category in the classification standard for the position. The adjudicator concluded that this did not mean that the job description was incomplete. The job description did contain a title for "Well Being of Individuals," under which there was no description of duties (what the adjudicator called a "narrative"). The adjudicator concluded that this absence of any description was an error: if a job description contains a heading, there must be a description of duties under that heading. Furthermore, a job description needs to contain a list of all of the duties that an employee performs, but it does not need to spell out the details of how each task is performed. This is particularly true in what are often referred to as "national" job descriptions. As an adjudicator has put it:

> [T]he statement may not be incomplete in the sense that it omits to make reference to a particular duty or responsibility which the employee is otherwise required to perform. It does not, however, mean that the statement must spell out in infinite detail every possible variation, combination or permutation of how a function is performed.[15]

A job description must, though, "contain enough information to accurately reflect what the employee does." It must not omit a particular duty or responsibility that the employee must perform. A job description does not need to contain a detailed listing of all activities that an employee performs, nor does it need to list the manner in which those activities are accomplished. Thus a broadly worded or "generic" job

---

13 *Public Service Alliance of Canada v Treasury Board (Correctional Service of Canada)*, 2020 FPSLREB 99 at para 154.

14 *Hymander v Canada (National Parole Board)*, 2002 PSSRB 71.

15 *Taylor v Treasury Board (Revenue Canada—Customs and Excise)*, [1990] CPSSRB No 223. See also *Fedun and Treasury Board (Revenue Canada—Taxation)*, [1998] CPSSRB No 49, and *Jaremy v Treasury Board (Revenue Canada—Customs, Excise & Taxation)*, [2000] CPSSRB No 35.

description can be acceptable so long as it contains a "complete and current statement of the duties and responsibilities" of the employee.[16]

Collective agreements commonly require a "complete and current" statement of duties. The term "current" takes its meaning from the context and can include tasks that are done seasonally even if the request for a job description was made off-season. The term "complete and current" also does not encompass tasks that employees are asked to carry out on an odd occasion—the "proverbial 'one-offs' are not covered by their work description" and do not have to be.[17] Additionally, the Board will not "wordsmith" a job description simply because there may be a better way to word the tasks performed.[18]

C. CLASSIFICATION

1) The Legal Basis of Classifications

The legal authority for classification of positions in the federal public service lies within the sole authority of the employer.[19] For employees in the core public administration, the ability to classify positions lies with the Treasury Board pursuant to section 11.1(1)(b) of the *Financial Administration Act*, which permits the Treasury Board to "provide for the classification of positions and persons employed in the public service."[20] For separate employers, their authority to classify positions arises from their constituting statutes. Some constituting statutes explicitly grant the employer the power to classify positions,[21] whereas others simply grant the separate employer the power to make appointments.[22] However, since a reclassification of a position is an appointment,[23] the power to appoint also includes the power to classify and reclassify positions. In any event, the *Federal Public Sector Labour*

16 *Jennings and Myers*, above note 11 at paras 52–54.

17 *Currie v Treasury Board (Correctional Service of Canada)*, 2021 FPSLREB 102 at paras 170–71.

18 *Ibid* at para 167.

19 *Fischer v Canada (Attorney General)*, 2012 FC 720 at para 4; *Lawlor v Canada (Attorney General)*, 2022 FC 821 at para 25 [*Lawlor*].

20 *Financial Administration Act*, RSC 1985, c F-11.

21 See, for example, *Canada Customs and Revenue Agency Act*, SC 1999, c 17, s 51(1)(c): "The Agency may . . . provide for the classification of Agency positions and employees."

22 See, for example, *Canadian Food Inspection Agency Act*, SC 1997, c 6, s 13(1).

23 *Canada (Attorney General) v Jones*, [1978] 2 FC 39 (CA) [*Jones*].

Relations Act (*FPSLRA*) specifically preserves for all employers the right to "determine the organization of those portions of the federal public administration for which it represents His Majesty in right of Canada as employer . . . and to classify positions and persons employed in those portions of the federal public administration."[24]

First, however, it is useful to attempt to define what is meant by "classification." The term "classification" is not defined by statute or regulation. However, the old *Public Service Employment Regulations, 2000*, defined "reclassified" as follows:

> "[R]eclassified" in respect of a position, means a change in either or both the occupational group and level of the position as the result of a classification decision other than a classification decision that affects an entire occupational group.[25]

This distinguished a "classification" from a "conversion" within the core public administration. A "conversion" is "a situation in which a new group and/or level is established or a new classification plan and/or pay structure is introduced for an established group"[26]—in other words, a reclassification that affects an entire occupational group.[27] The ability to conduct a "conversion" was first created by the *Conversion and Post Conversion Pay Regulations*[28] in 1967, now the *Directive on Terms and Conditions of Employment*.[29] Outside of the core public administration, there is no concept known as a "conversion": all decisions affecting classifications (whether affecting an entire occupational group or not) are reclassifications.[30]

This does not provide a complete definition of a "classification," nor is it possible to provide a definition by reference to statute or regulation.

---

24 *Federal Public Sector Labour Relations Act*, SC 2003, c 22, s 2 and 7 [*FPSLRA*].

25 *Public Service Employment Regulations, 2000*, SOR/2000-80 (repealed 31 December 2005).

26 Treasury Board of Canada Secretariat, "Reclassification/Conversion" (10 October 2004), online: www.canada.ca/en/treasury-board-secretariat/services/innovation/human-resources-statistics/demographic-snapshot-federal-public-service-glossary-key-terms.html.

27 *Hagel v Canada (Attorney General)*, 2009 FC 329 at para 43.

28 *Conversion and Post Conversion Pay Regulations*, TB 669255 (25 May 1967). See *Jones*, above note 23.

29 Treasury Board of Canada Secretariat, *Directive on Terms and Conditions of Employment* (1 April 2014), online: www.tbs-sct.canada.ca/pol/doc-eng.aspx?id=15772&section=html.

30 *Johnson v Canada (Customs and Revenue Agency)*, [2004] FCJ No 909.

However, a "classification" referred to below concerns a decision about the appropriate occupational group and level for a given position. A "reclassification" is a change in the occupational group or level assigned to a position. In the core public administration, these do not include the creation of a new occupational group or a classification decision that affects an entire occupational group—as noted above, those decisions are referred to as "conversions" in the core public administration.

The occupational group definitions for every position in the core public administration were set out in 1999 in the *Canada Gazette*[31] and have been amended from time to time.[32] These occupational group definitions are also the definitions of bargaining units in the core public administration.[33] There are thirty-one occupational groups in the core public administration. Several of those occupational groups have been further divided into occupational subgroups.[34] For example, the Ship Repair Chargehands & Production Supervisors occupational group has been divided into twenty different subgroups.

Each occupational group (or subgroup) has a job evaluation standard. The job evaluation standard lists the various factors and subfactors that go into classifying a position within that standard. To classify a position, a position's work description is assessed against each factor or subfactor and given a degree. The higher the degree, the more points will be assigned to the position. The total number of points determines a position's classification. Additionally, each job evaluation standard has benchmarks assigned to it—sample positions that have a particular rating for each factor and also an overall classification. If a position is similar to the benchmark position for a particular factor or subfactor, then it will be scored the same as the benchmark position.[35] Classification is not limited to a comparison between the position being classified and the benchmark positions. Instead, it also contemplates a comparison between non-benchmark positions and the position being classified. Therefore, the position being classified should also be compared to non-benchmark positions when relevant.[36]

---

31 *Canada Gazette Part I*, Vol 133, No 13—27 March 1999.

32 See, for example, *Canada Gazette Part I*, Vol 152, No 22—2 June 2018 (replacing the Computer Systems Group with the Information Technology Group).

33 See the discussion in Chapter 5.

34 *Canada Gazette Part I*, Vol 138, No 29—17 July 2004 at 1963–95.

35 *Séguin v Canada (Attorney General)*, 2021 FC 45 at paras 5–8.

36 See *Chong v Canada (Attorney General)*, [1995] FCJ No 1600 [*Chong*].

The person or committee classifying a position examines the position in question, assigns tentative degrees for each factor or subfactor, and then compares those degrees to the benchmark positions to ensure their accuracy.[37] This creates a total number of points that in turn generates a particular classification.[38]

The ultimate objective of job evaluation or classification is to determine the relative value of positions in each occupational group[39] so that employees in those positions may be paid at rates consistent with their duties. Positions that fall within a designated range of point values will be regarded as of equal difficulty and value and will be allocated to the same level. As the Federal Court has put it:

> The purpose of the Treasury Board policy on the classification system is to ensure that the classification system determines the relative value of all work performed in the Public Service in an equitable, uniform, efficient and effective manner, and provides the bases for the payment of public service employees. Another purpose of that policy is to authorize managers to classify positions in their respective Departments in accordance with the policy, the applicable classification standard and the guidelines prepared and issued by the Treasury Board Secretariat.[40]

2) Classification Grievances

Employees who are dissatisfied with the classification of their positions may file a "classification grievance." A classification grievance filed by an employee of the Treasury Board is governed in part by the *FPSLRA* and *FPSLR Regulations*,[41] and in part by the Treasury Board's *Directive on Classification Grievances*.[42] On one occasion, the Federal Court stated that "classification grievances cannot be dealt with under the *Public Service Staff Relations Act*";[43] however, since the Court cited section 92 of the old *Public Service Staff Relations Act* (which addressed the availability of adjudication) in support of that premise, the Court

37 *Lapointe v Canada (Treasury Board)*, [2006] FCJ No 921 at para 11 [*Lapointe II*].

38 *Adamidis v Canada (Treasury Board)*, 2006 FC 243 at paras 6–9.

39 *Chong*, above note 36.

40 *Laplante v Canada (Food Inspection Agency)*, 2004 FC 1345 at para 15.

41 *Federal Public Sector Labour Relations Regulations*, SOR/2005-79 [*FPSLR Regulations*].

42 *Directive on Classification Grievances*, above note 8.

43 *Maurice v Canada (Treasury Board)*, [2004] FCJ No 1165 at para 25 [*Maurice*].

was simply trying to state that classification grievances cannot be adjudicated. All other Federal Court decisions concerning classification state that classification grievances are governed by the grievance procedure established pursuant to the *FPSLRA*.[44]

Furthermore, the *FPSLR Regulations* specifically govern classification grievances. Section 71 of the regulations states that classification grievances (unlike most other grievances) may proceed directly to the final level of the grievance process — which is why the classification grievance procedure only has one level of decision-making. Additionally, section 72 of the regulations states that classification grievance decisions must be made eighty days after the grievance is filed, unlike twenty days for other grievances.[45]

Aside from those provisions, the *Directive on Classification Grievances* establishes the rest of the rules of a classification grievance. It stipulates that a classification grievance must be filed, in writing, no later than thirty-five days after the employee received notification of a classification or after "an action or circumstance affecting the classification of the position he or she occupies."[46] The action could be a new work description (which explains why the first step in a classification challenge is often to file a request for a new job description) or some other review that substantively analyzes the classification of the position.[47]

Once an employee has filed a valid and timely classification grievance, the grievance is referred to a classification grievance committee. The committee is composed of three members: a chair who is accredited in classification, a grievance officer from the Office of the Chief Human Resources Officer, and an individual from outside the organization who has knowledge of the job evaluation standard(s) being used. The committee is expected to bring expertise to the classification exercise.[48] The committee is entitled to rely on its own knowledge and expertise when assessing the grievance; it is not required to obtain submissions or evidence from an employer representative in an adversarial

---

44 See, for example, *McKenzie-Crowe v Canada*, [2003] FCJ No 702 at para 47, and *Hale v Canada (Treasury Board)*, [1996] FCJ No 685 at para 15 [*Hale*].

45 This deadline is honoured as much in the breach than in the observance. I am personally unaware of any classification grievances that have been decided within the eighty-day deadline, with the consent of both parties.

46 *Directive on Classification Grievances*, above note 8, art A.2.10.

47 *Adamidis v Canada (Attorney General)*, 2019 FC 331 at para 45.

48 *Wilkinson v Canada (Attorney General)*, 2020 FCA 223 at para 19 [*Wilkinson*].

sense,[49] although the directive permits them to contact a management representative to respond to questions "where necessary."

The committee may not seek management's advice or additional information without informing the grievors about the nature of that evidence and giving them the opportunity to respond where that information is fundamental to the outcome of the grievance. In *Lapointe v Canada (Treasury Board)*,[50] the committee sought information from management after the grievors made their submissions but did not disclose this information to the grievors. The Federal Court concluded that this constituted a breach of procedural fairness, stating:

> [A] grievor in the classification grievance process should have an adequate opportunity to respond to information or an issue which the Committee regards as fundamental to the disposition of the grievance, where the issue is one that the grievor did not realize or could not reasonably have been expected to anticipate would be in dispute.[51]

In *Hale v Canada (Treasury Board)*,[52] the committee relied on expert evidence to reduce the number of points for a particular criterion that the grievor did not know was at issue in his grievance and did not make any submissions about. The committee did not disclose this evidence to the grievor. The Federal Court quashed the committee's recommendation as a result. Similarly, in *Bulat v Canada (Treasury Board)*,[53] the Federal Court of Appeal concluded that the committee had violated the rules of procedural fairness by basing its decision on evidence provided to it by a representative of management without giving the grievor the opportunity to respond to that evidence. The Federal Court came to the same conclusion in *Majdan v Canada (Attorney General)*[54] when the committee relied on a manager's evidence describing the grievor's duties without giving the grievor the opportunity to respond; the Court was also critical of the committee's failure to warn the grievor that it could reject all three proposed comparators on fairly technical grounds.

49 *Canada (Attorney General) v Allard*, 2018 FCA 85 at paras 39–40.

50 *Lapointe v Canada (Treasury Board)*, [2004] FCJ No 283 [*Lapointe I*].

51 *Ibid* at para 54.

52 *Hale*, above note 44.

53 *Bulat v Canada (Treasury Board)*, [2000] FCJ No 148.

54 *Majdan v Canada (Attorney General)*, 2011 FC 1465.

This right to respond to management's evidence is not always automatic. In *Utovac v Canada (Treasury Board)*,[55] the Federal Court upheld a committee's recommendation despite the fact that the committee obtained evidence from management without disclosing it to the grievor or giving the grievor the opportunity to respond. In that case, however, the Court concluded that the evidence did not give rise to a new consideration central to the committee's decision. In any event, the Court concluded that the only evidence the grievor had to rebut management's evidence did not actually support the grievor's position. While the Court did state that "neither the grievor nor employer has a vested right to respond to the other's submissions to the Committee,"[56] the decision in *Utovac* turned on the fact that management's evidence was not central to the committee's decision, and the grievor's "rebuttal" evidence did not actually support the grievor's position. In short, the committee must disclose relevant information that it obtains from management or experts; if the information is not central to its decision, then it need not be disclosed. There is no automatic right of reply unless the information obtained from management has altered the committee's view.[57]

The committee must provide simultaneous translation services and teleconference or videoconference services when possible and necessary—all at the expense of the grievors.[58] Finally, the committee is obligated to provide the grievors with a reasonable period of time in which to present their grievance and must not hold the hearing in a "rushed manner."[59]

The committee hears the grievance and then prepares a report (with minority reports as necessary) that is submitted to the deputy head or their nominee. The onus of proof to convince the committee to recommend reclassification is on the grievor.[60] The deputy head or nominee is then the true final decision-maker. The deputy head or nominee is free to reject the committee's recommendation; however, if the decision is to reject the committee's recommendation (or accept a minority

---

55 *Utovac v Canada (Treasury Board)*, [2006] FCJ No 833 [*Utovac*].

56 *Ibid* at para 19.

57 *Julien v Canada (Attorney General)*, 2008 FC 115 at para 46, aff'd 2008 FCA 270 at paras 8–9 [*Julien*].

58 *Lapointe I*, above note 50.

59 *Ibid* at para 48.

60 *Chong*, above note 36 at para 40.

recommendation), then the decision must be personally approved by the deputy head.

While the deputy head or nominee "has the discretion to accept or reject a unanimous recommendation of the Grievance Committee,"[61] this discretion is not entirely unfettered. A deputy head "is not altogether free to substitute his decision for the Committee's," and their reasons for rejecting a recommendation must be "tied to the reasons given by the Committee."[62]

Notwithstanding that the deputy head or nominee is the final decision-maker, the committee must hear the grievance in accordance with the rules of procedural fairness.[63] The deputy head must also comply with the rules of procedural fairness, such that when the nominee or deputy head consults with officials or obtains any additional information not contained in the committee's recommendation, they are obliged to disclose those views to the grievors and give them an opportunity to respond.[64]

One common complaint is that a committee has failed to consider all relevant information before it, in particular the classification of positions that are not included as "benchmarks" in the classification standard. In *Chong v Canada (Attorney General)*, the grievors were employed as intelligence analysts with Immigration Canada in the BC/Yukon region. Their position was classified at the PM-03 group and level. The intelligence analyst position in the Ontario region was classified at the PM-04 group and level. The crux of the grievors' argument was that their position was the same as the Ontario position and should be classified at the same level. The committee did not address that issue in their reasons. On judicial review, the Court overturned the decision, stating:

> In my view the Classification Standard is not limited to comparing the grievors' positions with bench-mark positions. The Classification Standard states that the "ultimate objective of job evaluation is to determine the relative value of positions in each occupational group. The relation of the position being rated to positions above and below in the organization is also studied." The grievors submit

61 *Herzig v Canada (Industry)*, [2001] FCJ No 180 (TD) at para 16, aff'd [2002] FCJ No 127 (CA) [*Herzig*].

62 *Wilkinson*, above note 48 at para 20.

63 *Chong*, above note 36.

64 *Herzig* (CA), above note 61 at para 23.

> that the closest job description to the B.C./Yukon one is the one for the Ontario job description and, accordingly, although it was not a bench-mark position, the committee was bound to consider why a different classification should be assigned to the B.C./Yukon position. There may be very good reasons for the distinction between the two positions but there is nothing in the evidence upon which such a conclusion could be made.... The Treasury Board guidelines insist on equity and consistency and, without proper consideration of the Ontario position, it is difficult to determine whether those aims have been met in the instant grievance.[65]

Therefore, the committee erred by refusing to compare the BC/Yukon and Ontario positions.

The employer's next step after this application was to reclassify the Ontario position downwards to the PM-03 level. They did this without informing the grievors and then dismissed their grievance. The Federal Court of Appeal quashed that decision on the grounds that the employer should have informed the grievors that it had reclassified the Ontario position:

> To the extent that the downgrading of the Ontario Region position was triggered by the appellants' grievance procedures and resulted for all practical purposes in the dismissal of their grievance, they should have been informed that the basis of the comparison they were seeking to establish had been dramatically altered and they should have been offered the opportunity to pursue the other arguments available to them.[66]

Therefore, comparable positions are always relevant to a classification grievance, and it is a violation of procedural fairness to ignore comparable positions or to change those "comparison" positions without notice to the grievors.

Relevance, though, does not mean that the comparable positions are determinative. The Federal Court of Appeal in *Morrisey v Canada (Attorney General)*[67] set aside a committee decision because the committee did not adequately turn its mind to the internal relativity of positions—in that case, the argument that a similar position had been

---

65 *Chong*, above note 36 at para 46.

66 *Chong v Canada (Treasury Board)*, [1999] FCJ No 176 (CA) at para 14.

67 *Morrisey v Canada (Attorney General)*, 2018 FCA 26.

reclassified at the CS-02 level instead of the incumbents' CS-01 level. In doing so, though, the Federal Court of Appeal concluded that "the benchmark analysis should take precedence over relativity," although internal relativity remains "valuable."[68] This is consistent with an earlier decision of the Federal Court to the effect that the committee is entitled to give more weight to a benchmark position than to a comparable position and that it must examine benchmark positions and not just the comparable positions presented by the grievor.[69] The benchmarks, though, are to be applied factor by factor; the committee may not read the benchmark position in its entirety and compare it to the grievor's position in its entirety.[70]

Notwithstanding its right to assign different weight to different positions, the committee is not permitted to ignore a comparable position simply because it does not consider the description of duties of that position to be detailed enough. In *Maurice v Canada (Treasury Board)*,[71] the grievor wanted her position compared with a number of "surrounding" positions. The committee refused to compare her position with those surrounding positions and did not give reasons for doing so. On application for judicial review, one of the committee members explained in an affidavit that the committee did not assess one of those positions because the rationale for the classification of that position was not valid (in that it was not signed by a certified classification officer).[72] The Court quashed the grievance decision because the committee did not consider the comparable positions. The Court pointed out that there was no guideline on the form or content of the description of the duties of a comparable position that needs to be presented in evidence to the committee. Therefore, the committee should have informed the grievor that it considered her evidence about the comparable positions to be inadequate and provided her with a period of time to resolve those inadequacies.

68 *Ibid* at para 22.

69 *Argyracoupoulou v Canada (Treasury Board)*, [2003] FCJ No 1641 at para 15.

70 *Lawlor*, above note 19 at para 71.

71 *Maurice*, above note 43.

72 The Court was critical of this affidavit as violating the rule that a tribunal may not supplement its reasons on judicial review by having one of its members swear an affidavit.

Similarly, in *Lapointe v Canada (Treasury Board)*,[73] a committee refused to consider the comparable position of trademark opposition board member in a grievance by immigration adjudicators because the grievors did not provide a "classification rationale" for that position.

Another common issue that arises in classification grievances concerns the content of the job description. As discussed above, job description grievances are addressed before classification grievances. Once a classification grievance has been filed, the job description becomes fixed: the grievor may not challenge the job description in a classification grievance. The corollary of this rule, though, is that the committee must also take the work description as given and may not modify the work description.

The binding nature of the job description was the main issue in a ten-year dispute over classification of the regional programs manager position within the Canada Border Services Agency. In 2010, the occupants of that position were successful in a work description grievance that resulted in a generic job description. The occupants then proceeded with classification grievances based on the new job description. In 2012, the classification grievance committee recommended that the factor of decision-making warranted an increase from degree 5 to degree 6, which resulted in an overall points increase that moved the classification as a whole up from FB-06 to FB-07. In 2013, the deputy head rejected that recommendation. The Federal Court set aside that decision in 2014 because, among other things, the deputy head based their decision on the "organizational context" — in particular, that some managers were responsible for two or more programs while others were only responsible for one. The Federal Court concluded that this assessment was unreasonable because

> the Committee was confronted to a generic job description, approved in November 2010 by the employer after a grievance about job content. It is on that basis that the grievance was heard. The fact that job descriptions could have differentiated between positions does not change the reality with which the Committee had to contend: there was one job description to evaluate.[74]

---

73 *Lapointe II*, above note 37 at paras 19–20.

74 *Wilkinson v Canada (Attorney General)*, 2014 FC 741 at para 37.

The grievance was sent back to the deputy head, who again (in 2015) rejected the committee's recommendation. The Federal Court concluded that this second decision was unreasonable because the deputy head relied on a chart prepared by human resources officials that contained portions of the work description that omitted other relevant aspects of the work description. The Court this time stated more bluntly that "[i]n a classification exercise, the work description must be evaluated against the appropriate classification standard, and it is an error to modify the work description or refuse to consider the duties and activities in the work description."[75] The differences between the summary chart and the actual work description amounted to a modification of that work description, rendering the deputy head's decision unreasonable.

The matter went back to the deputy head, who this time hired a consultant to make a recommendation. The consultant disagreed with the committee and stated that decision-making should be rated at degree 5. The deputy head sided with the consultant over the committee and, in late 2017, rejected the committee's recommendation for a third time. Ultimately, the Federal Court of Appeal concluded that the deputy head acted unreasonably again. The consultant hired by the deputy head, in addition to reviewing the classification of the position, also reviewed the content of the work description. The Federal Court of Appeal stated that it was unreasonable to do so because "[t]he Work Description is what it is and must be taken as such. The consultant's report missed the point of the Court's direction which was that the Deputy Head's decision must be more inclusive of the elements of the Work Description, not less so."[76] The deputy head also concluded that degree 5 was more appropriate than degree 6 for decision-making because the positions only made recommendations about national policies (instead of "substantive recommendations"), but the Federal Court of Appeal also pointed out that making "substantive recommendations" was not a required element of decision-making at degree 6 and that the deputy head erred by relying on the fact that two of the three "examples of work activity" descriptions in the classification standard used the term "substantive recommendations"—examples are just examples, not a rule. This amounted to rewriting the classification standard, which the

75 *Wilkinson v Canada (Attorney General)*, 2016 FC 1062 at para 13.

76 *Wilkinson*, above note 48 at para 26.

deputy head could not do.[77] This time, the Federal Court of Appeal returned the matter to the deputy head with directions to accept the recommendations of the committee.

Similarly, when positions are compared for classification purposes, the position under review must be compared to the job descriptions of other positions, not the actual duties the incumbents of those positions are performing. In *Eksal v Canada (Attorney General)*,[78] the committee concluded that the grievors had to demonstrate that they managed multiple subordinate supervisors to achieve their desired degree of classification. The grievors argued that they did not need to meet this requirement, and they compared themselves to a position called MG 0305 (a regional manager). Although the job description for the MG 0305 position required multiple subordinate supervisors, the grievors relied on the fact that the incumbents in that position did not in fact perform that duty. The committee did not agree with the grievors' submissions. The Federal Court of Appeal upheld the committee's recommendation, stating:

> In the absence of evidence to the contrary, it must be assumed that at the time the MG 0305 positions were filled, the successful candidates met all the requirements specified in the job description. The fact that the incumbents may be called upon to fulfill only some of those requirements does not modify the job description or establish that the requirements which it embodies are no longer in effect. Indeed, it will be a rare case where an employee is called upon to fulfill all the requirements embodied in a job description all of the time.[79]

Employees also will sometimes perform duties that fall outside their work description. This does not entitle them to a higher classification.[80]

Just as the work description must be taken as a given, so too must the classification standard be taken as is. In *Peck v Parks Canada*,[81] for example, the employer's classification standard required that employees at the PM-06 level have a degree (in this case, an engineering degree); employees without such a degree were classified at the EG-07 level. The grievor stated that this was unfair as he was performing the same duties

---

77 *Ibid* at paras 42–43.

78 *Eksal v Canada (Attorney General)*, [2006] FCJ No 164 (CA).

79 *Ibid* at para 10.

80 *Julien*, above note 57.

81 *Peck v Parks Canada*, 2009 FC 686.

as a PM-06 position and had been doing so for many years. The Federal Court dismissed his application for judicial review, concluding that the employer had the undisputed authority to require an engineering degree for the PM-06 classification.

The classification exercise is not as simple as doing a "word match" between the work description and the classification standard; the entire work description and classification standard must be read together in context.[82] Nevertheless, the experience in the *Wilkinson* cases demonstrates that the work description must be taken as is in a classification grievance and cannot be modified by either the grievor or the deputy head in that process.

82 *Bourdeau v Canada (Attorney General)*, 2015 FC 1089 at para 50.

PART V

THE RCMP AND PARLIAMENTARY EMPLOYEES

CHAPTER THIRTEEN

Royal Canadian Mounted Police

A. INTRODUCTION

This chapter will address the specific legal rules that apply to members of the Royal Canadian Mounted Police (RCMP).

B. CATEGORIES OF WORKERS IN THE RCMP

There are three categories of workers in the RCMP: regular members, civilian members, and public service employees.

Regular members of the RCMP are persons who are appointed to a rank or who are a special constable with the RCMP.[1] Regular members are, in other words, police officers. The *Royal Canadian Mounted Police Regulations, 2014* (*RCMP Regulations, 2014*) lists the thirteen ranks of regular members in the RCMP.[2] The *Royal Canadian Mounted Police Act* (*RCMP Act*) divides these ranks between "officers" (i.e., the Commissioner, Deputy Commissioner, Assistant Commissioner, Chief Superintendent, Superintendent, and Inspector)[3] and the remaining ranks, often referred to as non-commissioned officers (Corps

1 *Royal Canadian Mounted Police Regulations, 2014*, SOR/2014-281, s 1 [*RCMP Regulations, 2014*].

2 *Ibid*, s 12(1).

3 *Royal Canadian Mounted Police Act*, RSC 1985, c R-10, ss 5(1) and 6(1) [*RCMP Act*].

Sergeant-Major, Sergeant-Major, Staff Sergeant-Major, Staff Sergeant, Sergeant, Corporal, and Constable).[4]

A civilian member is a member of the RCMP, appointed under the *RCMP Act* but who is appointed to a "level" in the RCMP instead of to a rank.[5]

Finally, public service employees (also referred to as "civilian employees" or "civilian staff")[6] are employees appointed under the *Public Service Employment Act* who happen to work in the portion of the federal public administration called the RCMP.

The RCMP is in this way similar to most police forces in that it provides for the use of workers other than sworn police officers to perform duties on behalf of the police force. This concept of using a combination of sworn police officers and "civilian" workers dates back to Sir Robert Peel's creation of a professional police service in London, England, in 1829.[7] More recently, the use of civilian workers in police forces has been referred to as "civilianization," defined as "the deployment of non-sworn personnel in police services to augment and support agency operations."[8]

The differentiation between "civilian members" and "civilian employees" is less common in police forces. In the RCMP, identical positions can be categorized as staffed by either a civilian member or a civilian employee. The confusion over the line between civilian members and civilian employees has led the RCMP to engage in a project that it has called the "category of employee" project or, sometimes, "deeming" since the early 2000s. In the *Enhancing Royal Canadian Mounted Police Accountability Act*,[9] Parliament permitted the Treasury Board to publish in the *Canada Gazette* a date on which every civilian member is deemed to be a person appointed under the *Public Service*

---

4 *RCMP Regulations, 2014*, s 12(1).

5 *Ibid*, s 1.

6 *RCMP Act*, s 10. The section itself uses the term "civilian employee," but the heading is "civilian staff."

7 John Kiedrowski et al, *The Civilianization of Police in Canada*, Research Report 2015-R024 (Ottawa: Public Safety Canada, 2017) at 1, online (pdf): www.publicsafety.gc.ca/cnt/rsrcs/pblctns/2015-r042/2015-r042-en.pdf.

8 John Kiedrowski, Rick Ruddell & Michael Petrunik, "Police Civilianization in Canada: A Mixed Methods Investigation" (2019) 29:2 Policing and Society 204. See also Christian Leuprecht, *Where to Draw the Blue Line* (Ottawa: Macdonald-Laurier Institute, 2019) at 13, online (pdf): https://macdonaldlaurier.ca/files/pdf/20191108_MLI_POLICING_Leuprecht_PAPER_FWeb.pdf.

9 *Enhancing Royal Canadian Mounted Police Accountability Act*, SC 2013, c 18.

Employment Act. The amendments to the *RCMP Act* also clarified that the Treasury Board has the power to determine the "categories of members" in the RCMP.[10] The Treasury Board initially set that "deeming" date on 26 April 2018;[11] however, it extended that end date and then revoked that order before it was implemented,[12] and, as of the date of publication, this "deeming" project remains indefinitely on hold, having run up against serious opposition from the remaining civilian members coupled with the practical difficulties of changing the pension rights of civilian members (who are entitled to a pension under the *Royal Canadian Mounted Police Superannuation Act* (*RCMP Superannuation Act*) instead of the *Public Service Superannuation Act*).

Finally, members of the RCMP are not treated as "employees" at common law. Courts have concluded that the "paramilitary" nature of the RCMP means that RCMP members are sufficiently different from other types of public servants that they are not considered "employees" at common law—in other words, *Wells v Newfoundland*[13] has no application to them. This means that RCMP members, even before they were permitted to unionize, could not advance a claim against the Crown based on breach of contract or other similar common law concepts, such as a constructive dismissal.[14]

Civilian members, though, fall under the definition of "employee" in the *Federal Public Sector Labour Relations Act* (*FPSLRA*).[15] This means that they fall within the bargaining unit most closely associated with the duties of their position. Thus, for example, civilian members whose primary role is data entry are included in the bargaining unit representing clerical workers in the core public administration.[16] The Federal Public Sector Labour Relations and Employment Board (FPSLREB) has considered this to be a "common sense" approach—in other words, not to wait for "deeming" to occur but, instead, including civilian members in the same bargaining unit as other employees performing similar or identical duties.[17] Civilian members still have some differences from other

---

10 *RCMP Act*, s 20.1(a).

11 *Canada Gazette, Part I*, Vol 151, No 6—11 February 2017.

12 *Canada Gazette, Part I*, Vol 154, No 18—2 May 2020.

13 *Wells v Newfoundland*, [1999] 3 SCR 199, discussed in Chapter 9.

14 *Flanagan v Canada (Attorney General)*, 2014 BCCA 487.

15 *Federal Public Sector Labour Relations Act*, SC 2003, c 22, s 2 [*FPSLRA*].

16 *Public Service Alliance of Canada v Treasury Board*, 2020 FPSLREB 109.

17 *Canadian Union of Public Employees v Treasury Board (Royal Canadian Mounted Police)*, 2017 FPSLREB 36 at para 92.

public servants — most importantly, they remain members of the RCMP Superannuation Plan instead of the Public Service Superannuation Plan; however, those terms and conditions that are contained in collective agreements apply equally to civilian members as to other employees.

C. LABOUR RELATIONS FOR MEMBERS OF THE RCMP

1) History of Labour Relations in the RCMP

For most of the history of the RCMP, members were not permitted to join an employee association or engage in collective bargaining. Section 2 of the *FPSLRA*, until its amendment in the circumstances discussed below, excluded RCMP members from the definition of "employee," which effectively prohibited RCMP members from joining unions and being represented by unions in collective bargaining.

This policy had existed for decades. Between 1918 and 1974, members of the Royal Northwest Mounted Police and subsequently of the RCMP were expressly prohibited by order in council from *any* union-related activity on pain of instant dismissal. The order in council stated:

> No member of the Royal Northwest Mounted Police or of the Dominion Police, whether officer, non-commissioned officer or man, shall become a member of or in any wise associated with any Trades Union Organization or any Society or Association connected or affiliated therewith; or with any union, Society or Association of employers or any Society or Association connected or affiliated therewith; or with any Union, Society or Association having for its object the rights or interest of employees or of labour, or of employers or of capital in competition with each other; and any contravention of this regulation shall be cause for instant dismissal.[18]

The policy underlying this order in council of 1918 was founded on the fear that the organization of RCMP members into an employee organization would result in members experiencing a "divided loyalty" or conflict of interest between their allegiance to their fellow workers and their required obedience to their superiors' orders. RCMP members might be unable or unwilling to obey commands if they felt that obedience would be inconsistent with allegiance to the cause of their fellow employees. This concern was particularly pronounced in relation to the

18 PC 1918-2213.

role of the RCMP in quelling labour unrest. The federal government felt that RCMP members might refuse to obey the command to subdue labour uprisings, or to fill in for a striking local police force, if their allegiance to their fellow employees came into conflict with such a command. Hence, the government sought to attack the perceived problem at its source by prohibiting even informal employment-related associations. The federal government expressed these particular concerns in the preamble to the order in council, which stated:

> Whereas attention has been called to the public importance of excluding the members of the regular police forces of the country from membership or association with Trade Union Organizations or affiliated Societies or unions or societies of employers or employees constituted for the purpose or with the object of regulating relations of employers and employees or as between capital and labour;
>
> And whereas unfortunately occasions arise when it is necessary to invoke the aid of the police for the maintenance of order in connection with strikes, lock-outs or labour disturbances;
>
> And whereas it is considered that the public might in a measure be deprived of the service which it is entitled to expect from the police or that the quality of that service might be prejudicially affected, if the police were in any manner permitted to identify themselves with one side or the other of a controversy resulting in breach of the peace.[19]

In 1945, the federal government confirmed this rule prohibiting RCMP members from membership in a trade union in certain regulations that read:

> 31. Towards the attainment of complete police efficiency it is essential that members of the Force cultivate and maintain the respect and esteem of the general public. This may be accomplished by pursuing a steady and impartial line of conduct in the discharge of duty and by a respectful bearing to all classes; also, by prompt obedience to all lawful commands, and by clean, sober and orderly habits.
>
> (a) Membership in any organization or union, which by its nature may influence or constrain the individual concerned against the impartial exercise of his duty, is prohibited to members of the Force.[20]

---

19 *Ibid.*

20 *Canada Gazette*, 1945 (1577) (*Rules and Regulations for the Government and Guidance of the Royal Canadian Mounted Police Force of Canada*).

Instead of proper employee organizations with no connection to management, RCMP members had two forms of employee representation. The first was the Division Staff Relations Representative Program (later called the Staff Relations Representative system), which the RCMP is required to establish.[21] The program, introduced in 1974, is supposed "to provide for representation of the interests of all members with respect to staff relations matters."[22] The *Commissioner's Standing Orders (Division Staff Relations Representative Program)*[23] make it clear that the program is meant to replace, not implement, free collective bargaining. Division staff representatives were forbidden from engaging in activities that "promote alternative programs in conflict with the non-union status of the Division Staff Relations Representative Program" or that "may undermine the credibility or effectiveness of the Division Staff Relations Representative Program."[24] Representatives under the program were elected by other members from each of the fourteen geographic divisions across the RCMP. Their primary duties involve representation of members at the local level within their respective divisions. However, the RCMP reserved the right to limit representatives' right to represent members in situations where that representation "could impair the efficiency, administration or good government of the Force."[25] The program does not include collective bargaining, although it did include a national pay committee that was involved in the RCMP's discussions with the Treasury Board about compensation of RCMP members.[26]

The second form of employee representation involves ad hoc and informal employee associations. RCMP members in Quebec founded the Association des membres de la Division "C" in 1985, and similar informal organizations were created in Ontario, British Columbia, and the Capital Region. These informal organizations had no formal legal status, and in most provinces there were no such informal organizations.

---

21 *Royal Canadian Mounted Police Regulations, 1988*, SOR/88-361, s 96(1).

22 *Ibid*, s 96(1).

23 *Commissioner's Standing Orders (Division Staff Relations Program)* (unpublished), signed by the Commissioner on 9 June 1993 and amended in subsequent *Standing Orders*.

24 *Ibid*, s 3(2).

25 *Commissioner's Standing Orders (Representation), 1997*, s 3(b).

26 *Commissioner's Standing Orders (Division Staff Relations Representative Program)*, above note 23, s 14.

In *Delisle v Canada (Deputy Attorney General)*,[27] some RCMP members challenged this prohibition on collective bargaining and unionization as a breach of the freedom of association guaranteed by the *Charter of Rights and Freedoms* (the *Charter*). A majority of the Supreme Court of Canada rejected their claim, in part because section 2(d) of the *Charter* does not guarantee the right to engage in collective bargaining and in part because the existence of the informal employee associations — in the opinion of the Supreme Court in that case — indicated that RCMP members were free to associate.

The Court's decision in *Delisle* predated the decision in *Health Services and Support — Facilities Subsector Bargaining Assn v British Columbia*[28] that section 2(d) of the *Charter* did in fact protect the right to engage in collective bargaining as an aspect of freedom of association. Therefore, the Court overturned its previous decision in *Delisle* in *Mounted Police Association of Ontario v Canada (Attorney General)*.[29] The Court concluded that the staff relations representative model of labour relations violated freedom of association and the right to collective bargaining because that model was not independent from the employer (in that it was part of the management structure of the RCMP and was prohibited from even trying to negotiate on members' behalf) and that RCMP members lacked a constitutionally required element of choice of their representative (in that members did not choose this system and could not meaningfully choose how the existing system would represent it). The Court initially suspended its declaration of invalidity for twelve months and then extended that suspension for another four months so that the existing system came to an end on 16 May 2016.

2) Provisions of the *FPSLRA* Specific to Members of the RCMP

Parliament eventually amended the *FPSLRA* to include RCMP members within its ambit on 19 June 2017.[30] These amendments contained

---

27 *Delisle v Canada (Deputy Attorney General)*, [1999] 2 SCR 989 [*Delisle*].

28 *Health Services and Support — Facilities Subsector Bargaining Assn v British Columbia*, 2007 SCC 27.

29 *Mounted Police Association of Ontario v Canada (Attorney General)*, 2015 SCC 1.

30 *An Act to amend the Public Service Labour Relations Act, the Public Service Labour Relations and Employment Board Act and other Acts and to provide for certain other measures*, SC 2017, c 9.

several special provisions unique to RCMP regular members[31] in Part 2.1 of the *FPSLRA*. In addition, one of these amendments required the FPSLREB to "take into account the unique role of the Royal Canadian Mounted Police as a police organization in protecting public safety and national security and its need to deploy its members and reservists as it sees fit" whenever exercising any of its duties or functions or when hearing a grievance.[32] This relatively new provision has never been cited or interpreted, so neither the FPSLREB nor a court has considered what it is supposed to mean. This chapter discusses the provisions of the *FPSLRA* that are unique to the RCMP; other than these provisions, the remainder of the *FPSLRA* applies to members of the RCMP.

First, Part 2.1 of the *FPSLRA* has several provisions to preserve the confidentiality of information that impacts law enforcement, public safety, or national security. The Commissioner of the RCMP may object to the disclosure of such information to the FPSLREB, at which time the minister must refer the issue to a former judge, who decides whether the information satisfies the requirements to be kept confidential.[33] Even if the information is disclosed to the FPSLREB or a party, the FPSLREB and any party who receives the information must in turn keep it confidential regardless of the outcome of the judge's deliberations about whether it is disclosed in the first place.[34]

Second, the *FPSLRA* specifies the bargaining unit structure for regular members of the RCMP, stipulating that there may only be a single, national bargaining unit for all regular members plus reservists.[35] In response to a challenge by an organization representing RCMP members in the province of Quebec, the FPSLREB concluded that this legislated single national bargaining unit was consistent with section 2(d) of the *Charter* and, alternatively, justified under section 1 of the *Charter*.[36]

Third, any employee organization applying to be the bargaining agent for regular members and reservists must have as its primary

31 The *FPSLRA*, confusingly, uses the term "RCMP member" instead of "regular member" but defines the term "RCMP member" as a member appointed to a rank. For consistency, this chapter will continue to use the term "regular member."

32 *FPSLRA*, ss 238.05 and 238.33.

33 *Ibid*, ss 238.07–238.08 and 238.27–238.29.

34 *Ibid*, ss 238.1 and 238.3.

35 *Ibid*, s 238.13(1).

36 *Association des membres de la Police Montée du Québec v Treasury Board*, 2019 FPSLREB 70.

mandate the representation of regular members[37] and may not be affiliated with any other association that does not have as its primary mandate the representation of police officers or be certified as the bargaining agent for any other group of employees.[38] This requirement that police unions only be affiliated with other police unions, and not the broader union movement, is common in Canada.[39]

Fourth, regular members and reservists may not engage in strike activity, and all bargaining disputes are resolved by arbitration.[40] The standard factors for an arbitral award apply to regular members, but the *FPSLRA* adds an additional factor whereby the arbitration board must consider the "operational effectiveness of the Royal Canadian Mounted Police" when making an award.[41] Finally, there are limits on the content of an arbitral award that are similar to the limits on awards for other public servants—namely, that the award may not require the amendment of legislation, set a term or condition that is provided for in certain statutes, affect the organization of the public service (including categories of members) and classification, or affect the right or authority of the Commissioner of the RCMP to "ensure that police operations are effective."[42] Oddly, the named statutes that cannot be impacted in an arbitral award include the *Public Service Employment Act* and the *Government Employees Compensation Act* even though RCMP members are not subject to any of the provisions of those Acts; one suspects that the legislative drafters were overzealous in their use of "cut and paste" from section 113(b) of the *FPSLRA*.

Fifth and finally, the grievance process under the *FPSLRA* for regular members is limited to grievances that concern a breach of the collective agreement or arbitral award.[43] Adjudication is similarly restricted to collective agreement issues.[44] Part 2.1 of the *FPSLRA* has no equivalent

---

37 *FPSLRA*, s 238.13(2)(a). This provision is particularly bizarre given that the term "RCMP member" in the *FPSLRA* does *not* include a reservist, but the bargaining unit *must* include reservists. In other words, RCMP reservists are represented by a bargaining agent that is required by law to have its primary mandate be to represent other employees.

38 *FPSLRA*, s 238.13(2)(b) & (c).

39 See, for example, *Police Services Act*, RSO 1990, c P-15, s 117.

40 *FPSLRA*, s 238.18.

41 *Ibid*, s 238.21.

42 *Ibid*, s 238.22(1).

43 *Ibid*, s 238.24.

44 *Ibid*, s 238.25(1).

to section 208 of that Act permitting grievances about anything concerning terms and conditions of employment.

3) Dispute Resolution for RCMP Members Outside of the *FPSLRA* and the Disciplinary Process

Instead of *FPSLRA* grievances, regular members have a myriad of different administrative processes available to them depending on the nature of their dispute. The "rules" for these disputes are referred to as the *Commissioner's Standing Orders* (CSOs).[45] The *RCMP Act* permits the Commissioner of the RCMP to make "rules" concerning thirteen aspects of the work of a regular member.[46] The *CSO (Grievances and Appeals)* then provides that an RCMP member (whether regular or civilian) may file an "appeal" of the following eight decisions.

a) Appeals Against Selection Process for a Promotion

First, an RCMP member may appeal a written decision made in the course of a selection process for a promotion or that is in respect of a job requirement established for a position, other than an official languages requirement.[47] The requirement of a "written decision" means that this type of appeal is rarely triggered; instead, challenges to the promotion process are more commonly addressed through the grievance process discussed below.[48]

---

45 *RCMP Act*, s 2(2).

46 *Ibid*, s 21(2), lists thirteen of them; additionally, ss 9.3, 9.4, 31(4.2), and 36 of the Act provide for other rules that touch on terms and conditions of employment. There are other "rule-making" powers in the Act, but they touch either upon disciplinary matters (which are discussed below) or public complaints against the RCMP.

47 *Commissioner's Standing Orders (Grievances and Appeals)*, SOR/2014-289, s 37(a) [*CSO (Grievances and Appeals)*].

48 See, for example, *Mitchell v Canada (Attorney General)*, 2022 FC 33 (whether a candidate included on the shortlist for a position was eligible for the position), and *Podmoroff v Canada (Attorney General)*, 2021 FC 421 (whether the successful candidate received assistance from someone involved in the selection process), both of which were decided using the grievance process.

b) Appeals Against Refusal to Permit Representation in a Disciplinary Proceeding

Second, an RCMP member may appeal a decision refusing permission for one member to represent another member in a disciplinary proceeding.[49] The *RCMP Act* contains a provision permitting a member to represent either another member or the conduct authority in a disciplinary matter[50] and also protects communications with that representative as if they were protected by solicitor-client privilege.[51] Members used to have access to a Member Representative Unit composed of lawyers employed by the RCMP for the sole purpose of representing members in the disciplinary process;[52] however, that unit was disbanded in light of the representation by members of their bargaining agent instead. The *CSO (General Administration)* also sets out limits on the ability to choose a representative.[53]

c) Appeals Against Decision to Revoke an Appointment

Third, an RCMP member may appeal a decision to revoke their appointment when there has been an error, an omission, or improper conduct that affected the member's selection for appointment.[54]

d) Appeals Against Probationary Discharges

Fourth, an RCMP member may appeal if they are discharged during their probationary period.[55] RCMP members have a probationary period of two years plus certain periods of time during which a member does not perform their duties.[56] Prior to the appeal mechanism, a probationary member who is at risk of being dismissed during their probationary period is provided with a Notice of Intention to Discharge a Probationary Member setting out the grounds on which the decision-maker

---

49 *CSO (Grievances and Appeals)*, s 37(b); *CSO (General Administration)*, SOR/2014-293, s 9(2); *RCMP Act*, s 47.1(3).

50 *RCMP Act*, s 47.1(1).

51 *Ibid*, s 47.1(2).

52 See *Vaillancourt v Canada (Attorney General)*, 2012 FC 70, for a description of that system.

53 *CSO (General Administration)*, s 9(1).

54 *Ibid*, s 37(c); *CSO (Employment Requirements)*, SOR/2014-292, s 20(1); *RCMP Act*, s 9.2.

55 *CSO (Grievances and Appeals)*, s 37(c); *CSO (Employment Requirements)*, s 20(1); *RCMP Act*, s 9.4.

56 *CSO (Employment Requirements)*, s 14.

intends to discharge the member.[57] The member then has fourteen days in which to provide a written response (or request an extension of time to do so). If new information comes to light after the notice of intent is served but before a final decision is made, the member is entitled to a copy of that information and seven days to provide a written response (or request an extension of time to do so).[58] Only then may a member be discharged during their probationary period, and then they can appeal that decision.[59] This lengthy process (involving written submissions plus an appeal) is necessary to comply with the legal requirement that probationary police officers may only be dismissed after being provided with procedural fairness.[60] As mentioned above, RCMP members are not "employees" at common law; therefore, the decision in *Dunsmuir v New Brunswick*[61] that procedural fairness is no longer necessary before dismissing a public servant does not apply to RCMP members.

e) Appeals Against Other Non-disciplinary Discharges

Fifth, an RCMP member may appeal a decision to discharge or demote them for unsatisfactory performance, reasons of economy and efficiency, or reasons "other" than disciplinary ones.[62] These "other" reasons are then listed as "including" six different circumstances set out in the *CSO (Employment Requirements)*.[63] In these cases, the decision-maker must serve the member with the recommendation to discharge them for one of these reasons. The member has fourteen days to provide a written response.[64] The decision-maker may also agree to meet with the member,

57 *CSO (Employment Requirements)*, s 16(3).

58 *Ibid*, ss 16(5)–16(6).

59 For a description of this process, see *Zak v Canada (Attorney General)*, 2019 FC 1503, aff'd 2021 FCA 80.

60 *Nicholson v Haldimand-Norfolk Regional Police Commissioners*, [1979] 1 SCR 311.

61 *Dunsmuir v New Brunswick*, 2008 SCC 9 [*Dunsmuir*].

62 *CSO (Grievances and Appeals)*, s 37(c); *CSO (Employment Requirements)*, 20(1)(c); *RCMP Act*, s 20.2(1).

63 *CSO (Employment Requirements)*, s 6. These circumstances are having a disability, being absent from duty without authorization or having left an assigned duty without authorization, being absent from duty as a result of being in custody or serving a term of imprisonment, being in a conflict of interest, no longer possessing a basic requirement for carrying out their duties, and being convicted of an offence that is punishable by indictment.

64 *CSO (Employment Requirements)*, ss 8–9.

but if they do have this meeting the member must provide a written summary of their oral submissions two days prior to the meeting.[65]

f) Appeals Against a Stoppage of Pay and Allowances

Sixth, an RCMP member may appeal a decision to stop their pay and allowances (referred to as a "stoppage of pay and allowances").[66] The Commissioner may direct that a member's pay and allowances be stopped if the member is unable to perform their duties as a result of the loss of a basic requirement (as set out in the *CSO (Employment Requirements)* as being legally authorized to possess a firearm, holding a motor vehicle licence, and having a reliability status or security clearance),[67] is absent from duty without authorization, has left an assigned duty without authorization, or has been suspended for disciplinary reasons.[68]

g) Appeals Against Medical Examinations

Seventh, an RCMP member may appeal an order that they undergo a medical examination.[69] The *RCMP Act* gives the Commissioner the authority to order a member to undergo a medical examination for the purposes of establishing their ability to perform their duties or participate in conduct-related proceedings.[70] The *CSO (Employment Requirements)* then further specifies that a member who receives such an order must present themselves when ordered and undergo any tests required by the medical practitioner.[71] Unlike in most labour relations regimes, the RCMP is not required to find a less intrusive option (such as examination by a "neutral" doctor) before making this order.[72]

h) Grievances Under the *RCMP Act*

In addition to these appeals, the *RCMP Act* contains a grievance process. An RCMP member may grieve any decision, act, or omission "in the administration of the affairs of the Force."[73] That term is broadly

---

65 *Ibid*, s 10.
66 *Ibid*, s 37(c); *CSO (Employment Requirements)*, s 20(1); *RCMP Act*, s 22(2).
67 *CSO (Employment Requirements)*, s 2(1).
68 *RCMP Act*, s 22(2).
69 *CSO (Grievances and Appeals)*, s 37(d); *CSO (Employment Requirements)*, s 20(2).
70 *RCMP Act*, s 20.2(1)(c).
71 *CSO (Employment Requirements)*, s 19.
72 *Gravelle v Canada (Attorney General)*, 2017 FC 742 at para 35.
73 *RCMP Act*, s 31(1).

interpreted to contemplate matters affecting the terms and conditions of members;[74] however, the term does not encompass decisions by the Treasury Board to actually set or determine those terms and conditions under section 22 of the *RCMP Act*.[75] The grievance process is a residual process in the sense that a member may not grieve if there is any other process for redress provided for in the *RCMP Act*, regulations, the Commissioner's standing orders, or any other Act of Parliament[76]—in other words, if a member may appeal an issue, they must use the appeal mechanism and not the grievance mechanism. The *RCMP Act* specifically states that any grievance that can be filed under the *FPSLRA* (i.e., a grievance alleging a breach of the collective agreement) must be filed under that process;[77] the *RCMP Act* also specifically states that human rights issues may be grieved.[78]

Members must file their grievance within thirty days from the date that they knew, or ought reasonably to have known, of the decision, act, or omission giving rise to the grievance.[79] This provision of the Act incorporates the "discoverability principle"[80] into the limitation period to file a grievance but still requires that the grievance be filed when the member could reasonably have expected the action being grieved. For example, when a member had been informed twice that they would not be paid overtime for the time spent participating in a promotional exam, the member was outside of the thirty-day limitation period when he waited to have his actual overtime claim denied.[81] This time limit can be extended,[82] and the RCMP typically applies the four factors set out in *Canada (Attorney General) v Pentney*[83]—namely, (1) a continuing intention to bring the grievance, (2) any prejudice to the parties

74 *Eddie v Canada (Attorney General)*, 2003 FCT 577.

75 *Poiron v Canada (Attorney General)*, 2021 FC 1175, and *Pasic v Canada (Attorney General)*, 2022 FC 1171; see also the External Review Committee's Grievance Case Summary G-335 (23 March 2015), online: www.canada.ca/en/rcmp-external-review-committee/services/case-summaries/grievance/g-335.html.

76 *RCMP Act*, ss 31(1) & 31(1.1).

77 *Ibid*, s 31(1.01).

78 *Ibid*, s 31(1.1).

79 *Ibid*, s 31(2).

80 *Horton v Canada (Attorney General)*, 2004 FC 793 at para 25.

81 *Beaulieu v Canada (Attorney General)*, 2010 FC 1149.

82 *RCMP Act*, s 47.4(1).

83 *Canada (Attorney General) v Pentney*, 2008 FC 96.

opposite, (3) a reasonable explanation for the delay, and (4) whether the grievance has merit.[84]

The RCMP grievance system has two levels. If a member is unsuccessful at the first level, they may refer their grievance to the second level within fourteen days of receiving the first-level decision.[85] The *RCMP Act* contemplates that the External Review Committee will review some grievances and provide a recommendation; however, amendments to the *RCMP Regulations, 2014* mean that no grievances are currently referred to the External Review Committee for a review. While the *RCMP Act* states that the second-level decision-maker is the Commissioner, that authority has been delegated to an official called an "adjudicator." Confusingly, the first-level decision-maker is also called an "adjudicator."[86] The *CSO (Grievances and Appeals)* sets out the other procedural rules for grievances, and I do not propose to reproduce those rules here. As with appeals, the final level of the grievance process does not conduct a *de novo* review of the grievance but, instead, only assesses whether the first-level decision was clearly unreasonable, based on an error of law, or violated the rules of procedural fairness.[87]

i) General Rules Governing Appeals

An RCMP member may appeal certain interim decisions during the disciplinary process.[88] Those appeals are discussed further below.

The appeals about the revocation of an appointment, discharge or demotion for unsatisfactory performance, disability, being absent from duty without authorization, a conflict of interest, and a stoppage of pay and allowances are referred to the External Review Committee before a final decision is rendered in that appeal.[89]

An appeal is commenced by filing a statement of appeal within fourteen days after the event being appealed.[90] Appeals are processed by the Office of Co-ordination of Grievances and Appeals—something akin to a registry office. Appeals are decided by an "adjudicator"—a

84 See *Sauve v Canada (Attorney General)*, 2017 FC 453, for the application of these factors to s 47.4(1) of the *RCMP Act*.

85 *RCMP Act*, s 31(2)(b).

86 *CSO (Grievances and Appeals)*, s 2.

87 *Ibid*, s 18(2).

88 *Ibid*, s 37(3); *CSO (Conduct)*, s 32(1).

89 *RCMP Regulations, 2014*, s 17.

90 *CSO (Grievances and Appeals)*, s 38.

senior member or employee in the RCMP.[91] The RCMP has internal manuals spelling out the process of an appeal. While the *CSO (Grievances and Appeals)* is silent on the method of appeal, it is in practice conducted entirely in writing on the basis of written submissions by the appellant member. Certain appeals are first referred to the RCMP External Review Committee for a review and recommendation[92] unless the appealing member requests otherwise.[93]

Finally, an appeal is decided on the basis of whether the initial decision contravened the principles of procedural fairness, is based on an error of law, or is clearly unreasonable.[94] The term "clearly unreasonable" means the same thing as "patent unreasonableness" in older administrative law decisions.[95]

These various dispute resolution forums use terms such as "appeal" and "adjudicator" that give the appearance of an independent tribunal system available to RCMP members. This system is not independent from the employer. The grievance system involves "a paper review of a paper decision" that is an "internal process that is overseen by those in the RCMP management structure including supervisors of the grievors."[96] The RCMP grievance system is simply management reviewing itself. This explains why courts have commonly been reluctant to apply the Supreme Court of Canada's decision in *Vaughan v Canada*[97] and have found that the grievance process does not oust the ability of RCMP members to file civil actions, particularly for claims based on harassment or similar behaviour.[98] The courts have also noted that grievance adjudicators consider themselves bound by internal RCMP policy[99] and have allowed court proceedings to continue in lieu of the grievance

91 *CSO (Grievances and Appeals)*, s 2.

92 *RCMP Act*, s 35(13), stipulates that the External Review Committee makes "findings and recommendations," not final decisions.

93 *RCMP Regulations, 2014*, s 17.

94 *CSO (Grievances and Appeals)*, s 47(3).

95 *Smith v Canada (Attorney General)*, 2021 FCA 73 at para 56 [*Smith*].

96 *The Attorney General of Canada et al v Smith*, 2007 NBCA 5 at paras 3 and 17.

97 *Vaughan v Canada*, 2005 SCC 11, discussed in Chapter 10.

98 See, for example, *Canada v Greenwood*, 2021 FCA 186; *Merrifield v Canada (Attorney General)*, 2009 ONCA 127 [*Merrifield*]; *Sulz v Minister of Public Safety and Solicitor General*, 2006 BCCA 582.

99 *CSO (Grievances and Appeals)* states (at s 16(2)) that an adjudicator "must consider whether the decision, act or omission that is the subject of the grievance is consistent with the relevant law, or the relevant Treasury Board or Force policy," which adjudicators have wrongly treated as if it reads "must *only* consider."

procedure because that procedure is just a "paper tiger."[100] Courts have also struggled with whether grievance adjudicators have the authority to award damages or financial compensation to grievors. Some decisions have stated, in passing, that adjudicators do not have the jurisdiction to award damages,[101] while one more recent decision has called that conclusion into question.[102]

The Federal Court has also struggled to address the precedential value of internal grievance decisions. In a normal workplace grievance system, there is no concept of "precedent" because every grievance is capable of being eventually referred to a third-party arbitrator for a binding decision. The RCMP grievance system, though, does not contain any third-party review. The Federal Court has therefore treated earlier grievance decisions as holding some precedential weight so that the RCMP may not render inconsistent grievance decisions on an identical set of facts without a good reason on the basis that inconsistent managerial decisions are inherently unreasonable,[103] and the Court has even implied that grievance adjudicators have a positive obligation to search for other grievance decisions (which are not a matter of public record) to ensure that their decision does not result in "two alike factual circumstances … not being treated similarly."[104]

In conclusion, the law around dispute resolution for members of the RCMP cries out for clarity. There is no principled reason to differentiate between appeals and grievances, nor a principled basis on which cases are divided into those that are referred to the External Review Committee and those that are not. The artificial distinctions between items in the "administration of the Force" and those that are reserved for the Treasury Board should be avoided—after all, there is only one Crown and one employer for RCMP members, like all public servants. The fact that RCMP members are expected to cross-reference four different instruments (the *RCMP Act*, the *CSO (Grievances and Appeals)*, the *CSO (Employment Requirements)*, and the *RCMP Regulations, 2014*) to figure out how to challenge different sorts of decisions is simply unnecessary and begs for reform.

---

100 *Atwood v Canada (Attorney General)*, 2022 FC 1202 at para 12.
101 *Merrifield*, above note 98 at para 10.
102 *Lachance v Canada (Attorney General)*, 2022 FC 1080.
103 *McBride v Canada (Attorney General)*, 2018 FC 118 at paras 28–29.
104 *Dhaliwal v Canada (Attorney General)*, 2021 FC 1480 at para 38.

D. DISCIPLINE OF RCMP MEMBERS

1) The RCMP Code of Conduct

Similar to most other police organizations in Canada, there is a distinction between discipline and other terms and conditions of employment.[105] Unlike most labour relations regimes (including the *FPSLRA*), where grievances about discipline and other issues are both dealt with using the same procedure,[106] in the police sector discipline is typically dealt with using a distinct dispute-resolution system.

The RCMP has had a distinct discipline regime since the early days of the organization (when it was called the Northwest Mounted Police). The RCMP was modelled on the Royal Irish Constabulary, which in turn modelled its own disciplinary regime on the process for discipline in place in the Armed Forces.[107] While the current RCMP disciplinary process is different from that in place when the force was founded in 1873, that disciplinary process continues to evolve separately from normal "employee" discipline in a standard labour relations regime.

The more modern justification or explanation for this different disciplinary regime is the public interest in ensuring a high standard of conduct for police officers and public confidence in the police.[108] Even those

---

105 See *Regina Police Assn Inc v Regina (City) Board of Police Commissioners*, 2000 SCC 14.

106 Although, in the *FPSLRA*, not all disputes end up at the same place (some go to adjudication, others to the final level of the grievance procedure).

107 *Report of the Commission of Inquiry Relating to Public Complaints, Internal Discipline and Grievance Procedure Within the Royal Canadian Mounted Police* (Ottawa: Information Canada, 1976) at 22, online (pdf): https://publications.gc.ca/collections/collection_2014/sp-ps/JS22-34-1976-eng.pdf.

108 Paul Ceyssens & W. Scott Childs, *"Phase 1" Final Report Concerning Conduct Measures, and the Application of Conduct Measures to Sex-Related Misconduct Under Part IV of the Royal Canadian Mounted Police Act* (24 February 2022), online: www.rcmp-grc.gc.ca/wam/media/6145/original/787edb1f00955240ae4502c22871ca80.pdf [Ceyssens Report]. See also *Coady* v *Ryan* (1992), 103 Nfld & PEIR 155 at 160 (NL TD) (in which the court referred to the "broad public purpose" served by the police discipline process: "to ensure high standards of conduct within the Royal Newfoundland Constabulary"); *White v Dartmouth (City)* (1991), 106 NSR (2d) 45 at 51 (TD) (the purposes of the Nova Scotia *Police Act* include "public protection from abuse of police power"); *Halifax Regional Police Service* v *Wilms* (1999), 177 NSR (2d) 320 at 320 (SC) (one of the purposes of the Nova Scotia *Police Act* is "to maintain public confidence in the police force and its reputation through a disciplinary process that imposes sanctions against those members of the police force who engage in discreditable conduct"; and the

cases that refer to the interests of the police force as an employer couple the employer's interest with the public interest in maintaining respect for and confidence in police officers.[109] This purpose is reflected in the *RCMP Act*, which lists the purposes of the disciplinary regime as follows:

> 36.2 The purposes of this Part are
> (a) to establish the responsibilities of members;
> (b) to provide for the establishment of a Code of Conduct that emphasizes the importance of maintaining the public trust and reinforces the high standard of conduct expected of members;
> (c) to ensure that members are responsible and accountable for the promotion and maintenance of good conduct in the Force;
> (d) to establish a framework for dealing with contraventions of provisions of the Code of Conduct, in a fair and consistent manner, at the most appropriate level of the Force; and
> (e) to provide, in relation to the contravention of any provision of the Code of Conduct, for the imposition of conduct measures that are proportionate to the nature and circumstances of the contravention and, where appropriate, that are educative and remedial rather than punitive.

The "public interest" explains why the discipline regime in place for RCMP members is different than for public servants. As for "how" the regime is different, the regime is different procedurally and substantively. This chapter will now explain both the substance and the process of the discipline regime in the RCMP.

2) Substance of the Code of Conduct

The *RCMP Act* sets out eight broad responsibilities of each member of the RCMP.[110] The crux of the substance of the disciplinary regime,

judgment of the England and Wales High Court in *R (ex parte Williams) v Police Appeals Tribunal*, [2016] EWHC 2708 at para 66 (the purpose of police discipline is to "maintain public confidence in and respect for the police service").

109 *Lévis (City) v Fraternité des policiers de Lévis Inc*, 2007 SCC 14 at para 24.

110 *RCMP Act*, s 37. These are (a) to respect the rights of all persons; (b) to maintain the integrity of the law, law enforcement, and the administration of justice; (c) to perform the member's duties promptly, impartially, and diligently, in accordance with the law and without abusing the member's authority; (d) to avoid any actual, apparent, or potential conflict of interests; (e) to ensure that any improper or unlawful conduct of any member is not concealed or permitted to continue; (f) to

though, is the Code of Conduct. The *RCMP Act* permits the enactment of a Code of Conduct in regulation,[111] and the *RCMP Regulations* therefore contain this Code of Conduct.[112] The *RCMP Act* then states that every member of the RCMP who has violated the Code of Conduct may be dealt with using the process set out in that statute and the associated "rules" (i.e., the various *CSOs*).[113] This orientation around the Code of Conduct means that the entire process is typically referred to as a "conduct process" or the "conduct regime," and this chapter will begin referring to it in that way instead of the more generic "disciplinary regime."

The Code of Conduct spells out nine subjects or areas and then lists an obligation (or, for four subjects, a series of obligations) under each of those subjects. The broad subjects set out in the Code of Conduct are respect and courtesy, respect for the law and the administration of justice, duties and responsibilities, use of force, conflict of interest, discreditable conduct, reporting, confidentiality and public statement, and political activity. These broad areas are similar to those provided for in police discipline regimes across Canada, and a complete discussion of each of those areas is beyond the scope of this book.[114] This book will mention two areas of the Code of Conduct because they are the subject of recent authority and because their meaning is not obvious from the wording of the Code of Conduct: discreditable conduct and the use of force.

The Code of Conduct requires that "[m]embers behave in a manner that is not likely to discredit the Force."[115] This offence of discreditable conduct is fairly broad on its face and, therefore, has been sharpened in the caselaw with the following four-step test:

A. The Conduct Authority must prove the identity of the member;
B. The acts constituting the alleged conduct must be established on the balance of probabilities;

---

be incorruptible, never accepting or seeking special privilege in the performance of the member's duties or otherwise placing the member under any obligation that may prejudice the proper performance of the member's duties; (g) to act at all times in a courteous, respectful, and honourable manner; and (h) to maintain the honour of the Force and its principles and purposes.

111 *RCMP Act*, s 38.

112 *RCMP Regulations, 2014*, Schedule.

113 *RCMP Act*, s 39.

114 For a more complete discussion, see Paul Ceyssens, *Legal Aspects of Policing* (Salt Spring Island, BC: Earlscourt, 1994) (loose-leaf), chs 5 & 6.

115 *RCMP Regulations, 2014*, Schedule, art 7.1

C. The Conduct Authority must determine if a reasonable person in society, informed of all the pertinent circumstances, and understanding the realities of police work in general and of the RCMP in particular, would be of the opinion that the conduct of the member casts discredit on the RCMP; and
D. The Conduct Authority must conclude that the conduct is sufficiently linked to the duties and functions of the member to give the RCMP a legitimate interest in disciplining the member.[116]

In respect of the third element, the requirement is not for actual discredit to the organization. A potential damage for reputation is sufficient to meet the requirements of this offence. In other words, discreditable conduct is measured against the extent of the potential damage to the reputation and image of the RCMP should the action become public knowledge. In conducting this assessment, the misconduct must be considered against the reasonable expectations of the community.[117] Finally, the conduct authority or conduct board may rely on a finding by a court in Canada that a member is guilty of an offence under an Act of Parliament or the legislature of a province to decide that the member has contravened the Code of Conduct—in other words, a conviction is *prima facie* evidence of discreditable conduct.[118]

The Code of Conduct requires RCMP members to "use only as much force as is reasonably necessary in the circumstances."[119] This phrase has been interpreted in a way that is synonymous with section 25(1) of the *Criminal Code*, which authorizes a police officer to use "as much force as is necessary" for the enforcement of the law.[120] In other words, an RCMP member accused of inappropriate use of force may rely upon section 25 of the *Criminal Code* to justify their actions—that is, they may justify their actions using the principles of proportionality, necessity, and reasonableness.[121]

---

116 *Laporte v Canada (Attorney General)*, 2021 FC 118 at para 22.
117 *Commanding Officer "D" Division v Corporal Prettie*, 2017 RCAD 4 at paras 34–35.
118 *CSO (Conduct)*, s 23(2).
119 *RCMP Regulations, 2014*, Schedule, art 5.1.
120 *Criminal Code*, RSC 1985, c C-46, s 25(1).
121 *Commanding Officer "K" Division v Constable Bigras*, 2020 RCAD 02. These principles derive from the Supreme Court of Canada's interpretation of s 25 of the *Criminal Code* in *R v Nasogaluak*, 2010 SCC 6.

3) Remedial Measures for Breach of the Code of Conduct

RCMP members who breach the Code of Conduct are then subject to a series of "conduct measures." The *RCMP Act* states that the Commissioner shall make rules establishing the conduct measures available for a breach of the Code of Conduct "other than dismissal or recommendation for dismissal"—as the power to dismiss a member (or recommend a deputy Commissioner for dismissal)[122] is set out expressly in the statute.[123] There is a long list of "conduct measures" in the *CSO (Conduct)*, ranging from an admonishment to a demotion and financial penalty deducted from the member's pay.[124]

The purpose of conduct measures is "educative and remedial rather than punitive."[125] This has been an ongoing evolution of discipline within the RCMP. Originally, discipline within the RCMP was treated as punitive in nature and even included the possibility of imprisonment for up to one year.[126] The *RCMP Act* was amended in 1988 to remove the possibility of imprisonment and to add new sanctions "aimed more at correction than punishment."[127] The 1988 version of the Act, though, did not mandate the use of corrective rather than punitive principles. The most recent version was the result of amendments in 2014 designed specifically to shift the discipline system away from punishment and toward correction.

Unlike most other police services, the RCMP has published a *Conduct Measures Guide* to assist decision-makers in determining the

---

122 The Deputy Commissioner, like the Commissioner, is a Governor in Council appointment and, therefore, can only be dismissed by order from that body: *RCMP Act*, s 6(3).

123 *Ibid*, s 45(4).

124 *CSO (Conduct)*, ss 3–5, lists the available conduct measures. The conduct measures include both an "admonishment" and a "reprimand." There is no decision explaining the difference between an admonishment and a reprimand or why they constitute two separate conduct measures.

125 *RCMP Act*, s 36.2(e).

126 See the discussion of this point in *R v Wigglesworth*, [1987] 2 SCR 541, in which the Supreme Court of Canada ruled that the *Charter* does not apply to the RCMP discipline process except to the extent that it could lead to a true penal consequence (imprisonment in that case). With the elimination of imprisonment as a penalty, the *Charter* no longer applies to the conduct process in the RCMP.

127 Royal Canadian Mounted Police External Review Committee, *Sanctioning Police Misconduct—General Principles*, Discussion Paper #8 (Ottawa: RCMP External Review Committee, 1991) at 3, online (pdf): https://publications.gc.ca/collections/collection_2013/cee-erc/JS74-3-8-1991-eng.pdf.

appropriate conduct measure in any given case. The guide provides examples of different ways an RCMP member can breach each provision in the Code of Conduct and gives examples of the appropriate measure for cases in the "mitigated," "normal," or "aggravated" range for each of those examples.[128] The *Conduct Measures Guide* is just a policy and therefore not binding on decision-makers,[129] although in practice most decisions rely upon the *Conduct Measures Guide* to ensure consistent practices for conduct measures. As one conduct board put it:

> The *Conduct Measures Guide*, while not prescriptive, is intended to promote parity of sanctions. It has its limitations, as examined below. What is clear is that the *Conduct Measures Guide* must be read in the context of evolving societal standards, as established by the jurisprudence or applicable policies and legislation.[130]

The Federal Court has been even more blunt in stating that parity of sanctions is relevant but "cannot be applied in such a manner as to fetter the discretion" of a decision-maker.[131]

In hearings before a conduct board, the conduct authority and the member will sometimes make a joint submission as to the appropriate conduct measure for that particular case. Conduct boards treat these joint submissions in the same way as judges treat joint submissions on criminal sanctions: the conduct board is not bound by the joint submission but will only reject a joint proposal if the proposal is contrary to the public interest—a high threshold to meet.[132]

When a conduct authority or conduct board imposes a conduct measure, they go through a three-part test: (1) consider the appropriate range of conduct measures applicable to the misconduct at issue; (2) consider the aggravating and mitigating factors; and (3) impose the conduct measures that accurately and fairly reflect the gravity of the misconduct at issue, keeping in mind the parity principle of sanctions.[133] This is slightly different from how other police discipline regimes assess

---

128 See description in Ceyssens Report, above note 108 at 11.

129 *Commanding Officer "K" Division v Constable Bigras*, above note 121 at para 20.

130 *Commanding Officer "K" Division v Constable Deroche*, 2022 CAD 13 at para 84.

131 *Rendell v Canada (Attorney General)*, 2001 FCT 710 at para 13; see also *Elhatton v Canada (Attorney General)*, 2014 FC 67 at paras 70–71.

132 *Commanding Officer "C" Division v Constable Noel*, 2019 RCAD 11 at paras 28–29.

133 *Commanding Officer "K" Division v Constable Martin*, 2021 CAD 23 at para 90.

the appropriate measure: those regimes begin by identifying the relevant considerations; assess whether each consideration is aggravating, mitigating, or neutral; and then balance or weigh those considerations in each case.[134] As the Ceyssens Report identifies, the weakness with the RCMP's current approach is that it does not contemplate the possibility that certain factors are "neutral" in the sense of being neither aggravating nor mitigating.[135]

The *Conduct Measures Guide* lists a series of mitigating and aggravating factors based on previous decisions of conduct boards. A complete discussion of every mitigating and aggravating factor is beyond the scope of this chapter. One more recent issue, though, has been the application of *R v McNeil*[136] as a factor in assessing the appropriate conduct measure. *McNeil* requires that the Crown disclose findings of serious misconduct made against the investigating police officer when the misconduct is either related to the investigation or the finding of misconduct could reasonably impact on the case against the accused.[137] This decision means, in practice, that RCMP members with serious misconduct on their record are unlikely to be assigned to positions where the eventual disclosure of their disciplinary record may harm the chances of a conviction. Conduct boards have considered the *McNeil* reporting obligation as an aggravating factor in assessing the appropriate conduct measure, but one that can be minimized depending on the evidence brought forward about the actual impact of a member being "*McNeil*-positive."[138]

In closing, the substance of the conduct regime in place for RCMP members is different from a standard employee disciplinary system. The conduct regime, simply put, imposes higher standards on RCMP members than public service employees or other members of the public.[139]

---

134 *Reeves v London Police Service*, 2021 ONCPC 3 at para 11.

135 Ceyssens Report, above note 107 at 25.

136 *R v McNeil*, 2009 SCC 3 [*McNeil*].

137 *Ibid* at para 15.

138 *Commanding Officer "E" Division v Constable Vellani*, 2017 RCAD 3, aff'd on appeal 2021 CAD 11, aff'd on judicial review *Vellani v Canada (Attorney General)*, 2023 FC 37 at para 102 [*Vellani*].

139 *Canada (Attorney General) v Muller*, 2022 FCA 99 at para 15. On police officers more generally, see *Montreal (City) v Quebec (Commission des droits de la personne et des droits de la jeunesse)*, 2008 SCC 48 at para 33 ("exemplary probity" is required of police officers), and *Lévis (City)*, above note 109 at para 42 (in the treatment of off-duty misconduct).

4) The Conduct Process

The disciplinary process for members of the RCMP (more commonly referred to as the "conduct process") is the product of two contradictory purposes. The first purpose is to ensure that the process followed "provides for a high degree of procedural fairness."[140] As described above about the discharge of probationary RCMP members, the Supreme Court of Canada's decision in *Dunsmuir* that public servants are not owed procedural fairness in their dismissal has not been extended to RCMP members. Therefore, all of the pre-*Dunsmuir* admonitions about procedural fairness for public servants still apply to RCMP members. Additionally, RCMP members (like other police officers) frequently testify in criminal proceedings. Their experience of the high level of procedural fairness required in criminal trials has led them to expect similar levels of procedural fairness for disciplinary matters.

The second purpose is to have the disciplinary process proceed as quickly as possible and have decisions made by the lowest-level RCMP member possible.[141] As mentioned briefly above, Parliament comprehensively amended the *RCMP Act* in 2014.[142] The government's stated purpose behind the amendments to the conduct process was to speed up the decision-making process and to delegate those decisions to the lowest possible level of authority. As a result of those comprehensive amendments, decisions emanating from the pre-2014 version of the *RCMP Act* should be read with caution as the conduct process is very different now from what it was prior to those amendments. These two purposes—procedural fairness and efficiency—are often in tension or even in conflict in the *RCMP Act*, *CSOs*, and even in the decisions about the conduct process.

The conduct process begins when a "conduct authority" becomes aware that an RCMP member may have breached the Code of Conduct. A "conduct authority" is a person designated as such by the Commissioner of the RCMP.[143] The *CSO (Conduct)* then sets out that three types of persons are conduct authorities. Individuals are designated as

140 *Vellani*, above note 138 at para 71.

141 *Lewis v Canada (Attorney General)*, 2021 FC 1385 at para 82, aff'd 2023 FCA 15 [*Lewis*].

142 *Enhancing Royal Canadian Mounted Police Accountability Act* (which came into force on 28 November 2014).

143 *RCMP Act*, s 2(3).

a conduct authority by virtue of the position they occupy and not their personal identity.[144] A conduct authority may also be the person who investigates a particular conduct matter,[145] and they are permitted to consult with internal advisors (known as a "conduct advisor") at any stage of the conduct process.[146]

The three types of conduct authorities are referred to internally within the RCMP as Level 1, 2, and 3 conduct authorities. A Level 1 conduct authority is a member who is in command of a detachment and persons who report directly to an officer or to a person who holds an equivalent managerial position.[147] A Level 1 conduct authority has the power to impose "remedial" conduct measures, ranging from an admonishment to a financial penalty of not more than eight hours' pay.[148] A Level 1 conduct authority and a subject member may also agree on the imposition of "any other conduct measure, other than a financial penalty or a corrective or serious conduct measure."[149]

A Level 2 conduct authority is an officer or person who holds an equivalent managerial position.[150] That conduct authority may impose either a remedial or a "corrective" conduct measure, which ranges from ineligibility for promotion of up to a year to a financial penalty (or forfeiture of annual leave) of not more than eighty hours' pay.[151]

A Level 3 conduct authority is an officer in command of a division.[152] They may impose a "serious" conduct measure (in addition to a remedial or corrective conduct measure) ranging from a modification of duties for up to three years, to a demotion, to a suspension from duty, to a financial penalty (without limitation on the length or amount of the penalty—although, strangely, a forfeiture of annual leave is capped at 160 hours).[153]

If the conduct authority concludes that the conduct measures set out in the *CSO (Conduct)* are insufficient in light of the gravity of the

---

144 *Firsov v Canada (Attorney General)*, 2022 FCA 191 at para 47.

145 *RCMP Act*, s 40(1). See also *Smith v Canada (Attorney General)*, 2019 FC 770 at para 52, aff'd on other grounds above note 95.

146 *Firsov v Canada (Attorney General)*, 2021 FC 877 at para 95, aff'd above note 144.

147 *CSO (Conduct)*, s 2(1)(a).

148 *Ibid*, s 3(1).

149 *Ibid*, s 3(2).

150 *Ibid*, s 2(1)(b).

151 *Ibid*, s 4.

152 *Ibid*, s 2(1)(c).

153 *Ibid*, s 5(1).

contravention and the surrounding circumstances, the conduct authority notifies the officer designated by the Commissioner to appoint a conduct board.[154] In addition to the remedial, corrective, and serious conduct measures, a conduct board has the power to dismiss a member or direct that the member resign within fourteen days of having been directed to do so.[155]

The conduct authority begins by investigating the member accused of misconduct, either personally or (more commonly) by having someone else investigate the member. During this investigation, the investigator may ask the member to provide a statement. The investigator may also order the member accused of misconduct (or any other member) to make a statement; this statement cannot be used against the member in any other criminal, civil, or administrative proceeding.[156] The *RCMP Act* also contains provisions about warrants for searches during the conduct investigation[157] and production orders,[158] but those provisions are rarely used.

The investigation culminates in an investigation report that is prepared for the conduct authority. It is typically at this stage that the conduct authority decides whether to ask for a conduct board; additionally, the conduct authority may decide to pass the matter on to a different-level conduct authority where appropriate. When the matter is proceeding to a conduct board, the *CSO (Conduct)* requires that the investigation report be produced to the member;[159] the member may also request a further investigation,[160] although the conduct authority may not make any further investigation without the approval of the conduct board once the investigation report has been provided to the accused member.[161] The member is provided with a notice of conduct hearing setting out the allegations against them, and the conduct board

154 *RCMP Act*, ss 41(1) and 43(1).

155 *Ibid*, s 45(4). The "direction to resign" exists so that an RCMP member may resign but protect their pension: *Girard v Canada (Attorney General)*, 2022 FC 578 at para 52.

156 *RCMP Act*, ss 40(2) & (3).

157 *Ibid* s 40.2.

158 *Ibid*, ss 40.3–40.8.

159 *CSO (Conduct)*, s 15(2).

160 *Ibid*, s 15(4).

161 *Commanding Officer "H" Division v Constable Pulsifer*, 2019 RCAD 9, aff'd on appeal but without addressing this point, 2022 CAD 6 [*Pulsifer*].

then conducts a hearing.[162] The *CSO (Conduct)* sets out the rules of procedure for a conduct board hearing; in short, though, a conduct board hearing is like any other quasi-judicial proceeding, with the exception that the hearing must be recorded and a transcript produced if a party appeals.[163] The conduct board hearing is also open to the public.[164]

The *RCMP Act* and *CSO (Conduct)* are silent about the process followed for a conduct matter other than before a conduct board. In practice, the RCMP has internal policies for these matters. The member accused of wrongdoing is provided with a copy of the investigation report along with a "notice of conduct meeting" that spells out the allegations against them. The member is given an opportunity to provide a written statement, followed by a "conduct meeting" with the conduct authority, at which time the member may also make oral submissions. The conduct authority may then consult with their conduct advisor (but not with any witnesses or subject matter experts) and finally render a decision.[165]

Any finding of misconduct by either a conduct board or conduct authority must be restricted to the matters raised in the allegations and particulars set out in the notice of conduct meeting or the notice of conduct hearing.[166] As the Commissioner put it in one appeal, a conduct board cannot "stray outside the particulars"[167] in a notice of conduct hearing.

The *RCMP Act* contains a one-year prescription period to conduct a hearing before a conduct board or for a conduct authority to impose a lesser conduct measure.[168] The period begins to run when the "contravention and the identity of that member became known to the conduct authority that investigated the contravention or caused it to be investigated."[169] This does not require any formal complaint to be filed

---

162 *RCMP Act*, ss 43(2) & (3).

163 *CSO (Conduct)*, s 22.

164 The old *RCMP Act* stated that conduct hearings were conducted in private, but that provision was struck down as violating s 2(b) of the *Charter* in *Southam Inc v Canada (Attorney General)* (1997), 36 OR (3d) 721.

165 For a summary of this process and the rule against the conduct authority consulting with anyone other than a conduct advisor, see *Carola v Canada (Attorney General)*, 2021 FC 1347.

166 *Gill v Canada (Attorney General)*, 2006 FC 1106 at para 67, aff'd *Canada (Attorney General) v Gill*, 2007 FCA 305.

167 *Pulsifer*, above note 161 (appeal decision) at para 88.

168 *RCMP Act*, ss 41(2) and 42(2).

169 *Ibid*, ss 41(2) and 42(2).

against an RCMP member, but it does not begin to run until the conduct authority has sufficient information to understand the possibility of a breach of the Code of Conduct.[170] The conduct authority also does not need evidence beyond all reasonable doubt or for its existence to have been confirmed by proof or verification for the prescription period to begin to run.[171]

The one-year prescription period in section 42(2) of the *RCMP Act* is only against the imposition of conduct measures: a conduct authority may still hold a conduct meeting outside of that prescription period for the purposes of making findings against an RCMP member.[172] The Commissioner can also extend that time limit[173] and has in practice delegated that authority to other officers in the RCMP. The delegated officers apply the usual factors for granting an extension of time: a continuing intention to proceed, prejudice to the other side, a reasonable explanation for the delay, and that the case has some merit.[174] More controversially, this extension of time may be granted retroactively after the one-year period has expired.[175] In cases heard by a conduct board, the board may overturn the extension of time;[176] when the case is decided by a conduct authority, a member may appeal that decision using the appeal process described below.[177]

The *RCMP Act* prescribes an appeal process for conduct decisions. Either the accused member or the conduct authority may appeal a conduct board's decision to the Commissioner, and a member may also appeal the decisions made by a conduct authority (both the finding and the conduct measures imposed).[178] While the *RCMP Act* states that an appeal lies on "any ground of appeal," the *CSO (Grievances and Appeals)* stipulates that the appeal only lies on three bases: a clearly unreasonable finding (which is equivalent to the patent unreasonableness standard of review), an error of law, or a breach of procedural

170 *Lewis*, above note 141.

171 *Thériault v Royal Canadian Mounted Police*, 2006 FCA 61 at para 47. While this decision was made under the pre-2014 regime, it remains good law under the new regime.

172 *Lewis*, above note 141.

173 *RCMP Act*, s 47.4(1).

174 *Calandrini v Canada (Attorney General)*, 2018 FC 52 at para 89, aff'd 2019 FCA 73.

175 *Ibid* at paras 81–82.

176 *Keddy v Assistant Commissioner MacLatchy*, 2020 CAD 20, aff'd 2021 CAD 14.

177 *Quibell v Canada (Attorney General)*, 2021 FC 1208.

178 *RCMP Act*, s 45.11.

fairness.[179] Appeals that relate to conduct cases that involve a financial penalty of more than one day's pay or some greater penalty are referred to the External Review Committee unless a member requests otherwise and the Commissioner agrees.[180] The Commissioner of the RCMP is not obligated to follow the recommendation of the External Review Committee (and often does not),[181] but when the Commissioner declines to follow the committee's recommendation, they are obligated to provide written reasons why.[182]

The Commissioner (or a delegate, referred to as a "conduct adjudicator") may dismiss the appeal or allow the appeal and either order a new conduct board hearing or make the finding that the conduct authority or conduct board should have made.[183] A member dissatisfied with a conduct proceeding must appeal and may not proceed directly to judicial review in Federal Court.[184]

E. RCMP SUPERANNUATION

As mentioned above, the RCMP has its own superannuation statute. It is substantially similar to the *Public Service Superannuation Act*; however, there are three differences that are worth noting.

First, the *RCMP Superannuation Act* permits earlier retirement than the *Public Service Superannuation Act*. The *Public Service Superannuation Act* contemplates retirement at age sixty or at age fifty-five if the employee has thirty years of service. The *RCMP Superannuation Act* contemplates retirement at the "retirement age," which is set out in the *RCMP Superannuation Regulations*.[185] The "retirement age" is currently

179 *CSO (Grievances and Appeals)*, s 33(1); see also *Smith*, above note 95, affirming the validity of this regime.

180 *RCMP Act*, s 45.15.

181 Interestingly, in *Millard v Canada (Attorney General)*, [2000] FCJ No 279 (CA), the Federal Court of Appeal stated that a Commissioner who relies on the decision of an External Review Committee "should be subject to minimal judicial scrutiny." The Federal Court has yet to state specifically whether the converse is true—namely, whether a Commissioner who overturns the committee's recommendation is subject to judicial review on a less deferential standard of review.

182 *RCMP Act*, s 45.16(8). See *Jaworski v Canada (Attorney General)* (2000), 25 Admin LR (3d) 142 (Fed CA), for a discussion of this obligation.

183 *RCMP Act*, s 45.16.

184 *Dhillon v Canada (Attorney General)*, 2020 FC 1167.

185 *Royal Canadian Mounted Police Superannuation Regulations*, CRC c 1393 [*RCMP Superannuation Regulations*].

- age fifty-eight for a corps sergeant-major, staff sergeant-major, sergeant-major, or staff sergeant;
- age fifty-seven for a sergeant;
- age fifty-six for a corporal, constable, or special constable; and
- age sixty for all others (including officers).[186]

Additionally, RCMP regular members may retire without penalty after twenty-five years of service (or with a reduced pension at twenty years of service); civilian members may retire without penalty at age fifty plus thirty years of service or with a reduced pension at age fifty plus twenty-five years of service.[187] There are also special early retirement rules for RCMP members who are dismissed "to promote economy or efficiency" (i.e., an economic layoff).[188] The calculation of the full pension is similar to that in the *Public Service Superannuation Act* (2 percent of the average of the best five years of pay multiplied by the years of service), except that the *RCMP Superannuation Act* and *RCMP Superannuation Regulations* set limits on the rate of pay for pension purposes.[189]

Second, the *RCMP Superannuation Act* contains special provisions for disabilities that occur during service. RCMP members who become disabled in connection with their service with the RCMP are entitled to a pension under the *Pension Act*.[190] The *Pension Act*[191] provides disability pensions for military personnel. There are two situations that attract pensions under the *Pension Act*: disabilities that occur during "peace time" and disabilities that occur during wartime or "special duty service." The *RCMP Superannuation Act* contains a definition of "special duty service" for RCMP members who are on duty outside of Canada in, for example, rescue, peacekeeping, or counterterrorism operations.[192] The difference between normal duty and "special duty service" is that—for RCMP members injured on special duty service—the disability pension will not be reduced because of a pre-existing disability[193] and the

186 *RCMP Superannuation Regulations*, s 26(3).

187 *RCMP Superannuation Act*, ss 11(5) and (9); *RCMP Superannuation Regulations*, ss 53–54.

188 *RCMP Superannuation Act*, s 11(3).

189 *Ibid*, s 10(1)(b), and *RCMP Superannuation Regulations*, s 8.1.

190 *RCMP Superannuation Act*, s 32.

191 *Pension Act*, RSC 1985, c P-6.

192 *RCMP Superannuation Act*, ss 32.1–32.15.

193 *Pension Act*, s 21(1)(c).

pension shall not be refused solely on the grounds that no substantial disability or disabling condition is considered to have existed at the time of discharge of that member.[194] For disabilities that occur outside of special duty service, an RCMP member is eligible for compensation under the *Pension Act* for injuries or diseases (or the aggravation thereof) that arose out of or were directly connected with their service with the RCMP.[195] This can include disabilities arising from medical treatment for a service-based injury depending on whether the treatment had a significant relationship to the member's service with the RCMP.[196]

Applications for these disability pensions are made to the minister of veterans affairs. If the RCMP member is dissatisfied with the decision of the minister, they may apply to the Veterans Review and Appeal Board (VRAB) for a review of the decision. The *Veterans Review and Appeal Board Act*[197] contains an interesting provision concerning how the board shall evaluate evidence in any given case:

> **39.** In all proceedings under this Act, the Board shall
> (a) draw from all the circumstances of the case and all the evidence presented to it every reasonable inference in favour of the applicant or appellant;
> (b) accept any uncontradicted evidence presented to it by the applicant or appellant that it considers to be credible in the circumstances; and
> (c) resolve in favour of the applicant or appellant any doubt, in the weighing of evidence, as to whether the applicant or appellant has established a case.

This provision does not mean that the VRAB must accept whatever submission is made by a veteran, but the evidence must be accepted if it is credible, reasonable, and uncontradicted. This test is conjunctive, in the sense that the VRAB does not need to accept all evidence presented by an appellant if it finds that evidence not credible, even if it is not contradicted.[198] The onus is also on an applicant to demonstrate a causal

194 *Pension Act*, s 21(1)(d).
195 *RCMP Superannuation Act*, s 32.
196 *Re Interpretation Decision I-3*, 2021 CanLII 43088 (CA VRAB).
197 *Veterans Review and Appeal Board Act*, SC 1995, c 18.
198 *MacDonald v Canada (Attorney General)*, [1999] FCJ No 346 at para 23 [*MacDonald*]; *Canada (Attorney General) v Wannamaker*, 2007 FCA 126 at para 29.

link between the disability and their years of service with the RCMP.[199] However, "evidence is not 'contradicted' unless there is inconsistent physical evidence or a conflicting opinion which is properly assessed in accordance with the requirements of the Act to be clearly more credible."[200] If the board is going to rely on its right to reject evidence as not credible, as contemplated by section 39(b), then it must specifically state that it finds the evidence lacking in credibility and its reasons for so finding.[201]

Third, and finally, members of the RCMP are entitled to a "supplementary retirement benefit" when they turn sixty, or as young as fifty-five if they retire with an "85 factor" (a combined age and service of eighty-five).[202] The amount of the supplementary retirement benefit is calculated according to the *Supplementary Retirement Benefits Act*.[203]

199 *Nisbet v Canada (Attorney General)*, [2004] FCJ No 1340 at para 18.
200 *Bremner v Canada (Attorney General)*, [2006] FCJ No 122 at para 23.
201 *Ibid*, and *MacDonald*, above note 198.
202 *RCMP Superannuation Act*, s 35 "recipient."
203 *Supplementary Retirement Benefits Act*, RSC 1985, c S-24.

CHAPTER FOURTEEN

Parliamentary Employees

A. INTRODUCTION

As stated in Chapter 3, employees of the House of Commons, Senate, Library of Parliament, Parliamentary Service, and the Office of the Parliamentary Budget Officer are not covered by the *Federal Public Sector Labour Relations Act* (*FPSLRA*) or the *Public Service Employment Act*, nor are they covered by the *Canada Labour Code*.[1] Instead, they are covered by the *Parliamentary Employment and Staff Relations Act* (*PESRA*).[2] When *PESRA* was first enacted in 1986, it was designed to be very similar to the *Public Service Staff Relations Act* then in force. As discussed in previous chapters, the *Public Service Staff Relations Act* underwent some significant revisions in 1992 and then again in 2005 when it became the *FPSLRA*. *PESRA*, on the other hand, has not undergone all of those same revisions. Therefore, some of *PESRA* is different from the current *FPSLRA* because of changes to the *FPSLRA*, and some of *PESRA* is different from the *FPSLRA* because of differences deliberately made when *PESRA* was enacted. However, for the most part, *PESRA* is very similar to the *FPSLRA*. It is administered by the Federal Public Sector Labour Relations and Employment Board, and the Board follows precedent from the *FPSLRA* in deciding *PESRA*

1 *House of Commons v Canada (Labour Relations Board)*, [1986] 2 FC 372 (CA); *Mélanie Bellemare v Communications, Energy and Paperworkers Union of Canada, Local 232*, 2013 CIRB 798.

2 *Parliamentary Employment and Staff Relations Act*, RSC 1985, c 33 (2nd Supp) [*PESRA*].

cases. This chapter, therefore, will concern itself with the differences between those two statutory regimes.

Parliamentary employers have occasionally argued that parliamentary privilege immunizes them from certain obligations as an employer. In *Canada (House of Commons) v Vaid*,[3] the speaker of the House of Commons argued that it was immune from the *Canadian Human Rights Act* because of parliamentary privilege concerning the management of employees. The Supreme Court of Canada stated that the speaker "can show that historically both the House of Commons in Britain and in Canada had the power to hire and fire employees, but this is not proof of the necessity that such hiring and firing be immunized from judicial review by the doctrine of parliamentary privilege."[4] Similarly, in *Sabourin v House of Commons*, an adjudicator concluded that House of Commons employees were protected by the *Canadian Charter of Rights and Freedoms* (the *Charter*).[5]

B. *PARLIAMENTARY EMPLOYMENT AND STAFF RELATIONS ACT*

1) Scope of Coverage of *PESRA*

PESRA applies in respect to people employed by the Senate, House of Commons, Library of Parliament, Office of the Senate Ethics Officer, Office of the Conflict of Interest and Ethics Commissioner, Parliamentary Protective Service, Office of the Parliamentary Budget Officer, and employees of members of Parliament who provide research or associated services to the caucus members of a political party represented in Parliament.[6] The Parliamentary Protective Service (PPS) was created in 2015[7] after an incident on 22 October 2014 in which an armed man entered the Centre Block of Parliament. That incident crystallized a series of proposed reforms to integrate the different security components

---

3 *Canada (House of Commons) v Vaid*, 2005 SCC 30 [*Vaid*].

4 *Ibid* at para 56.

5 *Sabourin v House of Commons*, [2006] CPSLRB No 35 at para 91. In that case, the *Charter* right at issue was the right to privacy (s 8): specifically, whether the grievor had a reasonable expectation of privacy that prevented the employer from conducting video surveillance while he was off duty. The adjudicator concluded that the video surveillance was unreasonable and therefore a breach of the grievor's privacy interests.

6 *PESRA*, s 2.

7 *Economic Action Plan 2015 Act, No 1*, SC 2015, c 36, ss 98–122.

that have as their mission the protection of Parliament. The aim was to "combine the diverse components into a single service, the PPS, under the direction of RCMP officers."[8] The parliamentary budget officer was added to *PESRA* in 2017 as part of broader reforms to make the parliamentary budget officer an independent officer of Parliament.[9]

Part one of *PESRA* (which governs collective representation of employees) excludes Governor-in-Council appointees, employees who work less than 700 hours in a calendar year or one-third of the normal period for people doing similar work, casual or temporary employees (unless they are employed for a period of six months or more),[10] and managerial employees.[11] Managerial employees include similar categories to the definition of the same in the *FPSLRA*, such as confidential employees (in this case, confidential to certain named positions, including the speaker of the Senate and House of Commons and the Usher of the Black Rod), employees who address grievances,[12] and parliamentary counsel or legal counsel to either House.[13] Section 4 of *PESRA* then excludes employees of certain officials from the right to engage in collective representation and to file grievances:

- the staff of any member of the King's Privy Council for Canada holding the office of a minister of the Crown;
- the staff of the leader of government, leader of the Opposition, government whip, or opposition whip in the Senate;
- the staff of the leader of the Opposition, government whip, and chief Opposition whip in the House of Commons;

---

8 *Parliamentary Protective Service v Public Service Alliance of Canada*, 2020 FPSLREB 7 at para 12.

9 *Budget Implementation Act, 2017, No 1*, SC 2017, c 20, ss 174–77.

10 The Board applies the same jurisprudence under both statutes: if an employee is hired on a continuing series of six-month contracts with an "artificial" break in service between each contract, then they are considered permanent employees: see *House of Commons Security Services Employees Assn and House of Commons of Canada*, [1996] CPSSRB No 55. There is therefore no implied probationary period, and the only issue is the number of consecutive months of employment: see *Markovic v Parliamentary Protective Service*, 2021 FPSLREB 128.

11 *PESRA*, s 3, "employee."

12 The Board applies the same test under both the *FPSLRA* and *PESRA*: see *Professional Institute of the Public Service of Canada v Library of Parliament*, [2003] CPSSRB No 90.

13 *PESRA*, s 3, "person employed in a managerial or confidential capacity."

- the staff of a leader or whip of a party in the House of Commons with twelve or more persons in the House of Commons;
- the staff of an individual member of Parliament;
- staff hired to provide research to caucus members of a political party in Parliament; or
- people employed on a temporary basis by a committee of one or both Houses of Parliament.[14]

The "employer" under *PESRA* is not the Treasury Board. Instead, the "employer" is one of seven entities:

- the Senate, as represented by the Standing Senate Committee on Internal Economy, Budgets and Administration;[15]
- the House of Commons, as represented by the Board of Internal Economy;[16]
- the Library of Parliament, as represented by the parliamentary librarian;[17]
- the Office of the Senate Ethics Commissioner, as represented by the ethics officer;[18]
- the Office of the Conflict of Interest and Ethics Commissioner, as represented by the conflict of interest ethics commissioner;[19]
- the Parliamentary Protective Service, as represented by the director of the Parliamentary Protective Service on behalf of the speakers of the two Houses of Parliament;[20] and
- the Office of the Parliamentary Budget Officer, as represented by the parliamentary budget officer.[21]

There are some differences in the internal organization or status of these different employers. The Standing Senate Committee on Internal Economy, Budgets and Administration is a standing committee subject to the control of the Senate.[22] It is composed of fifteen members, appointed in accordance with the rules of the Senate (meaning that its

---

14 *PESRA*, s 4(2).
15 *Ibid*, s 3, "employer," and *Parliament of Canada Act*, RSC 1985, c P-1, s 19.3(a).
16 *PESRA*, s 3, "employer," and *Parliament of Canada Act*, s 52.3(a).
17 *PESRA*, s 3, "employer."
18 *Ibid.*
19 *Ibid.*
20 *Ibid.*
21 *Ibid.*
22 *Parliament of Canada Act*, s 19.1(4).

membership is proportional to the party standings in the Senate) and the leader of the government and leader of the Opposition as *ex officio* members.[23] The House of Commons Board of Internal Economy, on the other hand, operates more as a management board: it is not subject to Parliament, and only its budget is referred to Parliament. It is composed of the speaker of the House of Commons, two members of the King's Privy Council for Canada, an appointee of the leader of the Opposition, one member from each non-governing party, and members of the governing party equal to one fewer than the total number of members of non-governing parties.[24] This means that the governing party has an equal number of members as the non-governing parties, excluding the speaker of the House of Commons. The parliamentary librarian is appointed by the Governor in Council and is akin to a deputy head of a government department.[25] The Parliamentary Protective Service is ultimately the responsibility of the speaker of the Senate and of the House of Commons.[26] The actual managerial control is exercised by the director of the Parliamentary Protective Service, who is selected according to an arrangement reached between the two speakers and the minister of public safety but who must be a member of the RCMP.[27]

Part 1 of *PESRA* states that employees (who are not excluded) have the right to join employee organizations and participate in their activities, including collective bargaining.[28] *PESRA* then sets out a mechanism for certifying employee organizations as the bargaining agents for bargaining units in a manner that is almost identical to the *FPSLRA*. The appropriate bargaining unit, for example, must take into account the plan of classification as in the *FPSLRA*.[29] One difference between the *FPSLRA* and *PESRA* is that *PESRA* prohibits bargaining agents

---

23 *Rules of the Senate of Canada* (updated July 2022), s 12-3, online: https://sencanada.ca/media/0ondtze4/cs_rules_sept2017-repostedjuly312022_b_-pdf-final.pdf.

24 *Parliament of Canada Act*, s 50(2).

25 *Ibid*, s 75.

26 *Ibid*, s 79.52(2).

27 *Ibid*, ss 79.54–79.56.

28 *PESRA*, s 5(2).

29 *Ibid*, s 23(2). The Board also uses the same test for deciding which bargaining units employees belong to: the "best fit" test comparing their job description to the bargaining unit description (as set out in the occupational group definition). See *Communications, Energy and Paperworkers Union of Canada v House of Commons*, [2000] CPSSRB No 71.

from contributing any money toward political parties.[30] *PESRA* also permits union mergers and creates successor rights when unions merge; however, there are no other successor rights.[31]

There are thirteen bargaining units certified under *PESRA*. They are represented by the three largest federal public service unions (the Public Service Alliance of Canada, the Professional Institute of the Public Service of Canada, and the Canadian Association of Professional Employees); the Communications, Energy and Paperworkers Union of Canada; and two unions unique to parliamentary employees: the House of Commons Security Services Employees Association and the Senate Protective Service Employees Association.

2) Collective Bargaining Under *PESRA*

The outset of collective bargaining is almost identical under *PESRA* and the *FPSLRA*. A party may serve a notice to bargain when no collective agreement is in place or two months before a collective agreement expires.[32] Both the bargaining agent and the employer are obliged to bargain in good faith and make every reasonable effort to enter into a collective agreement,[33] and a statutory freeze is in place after the notice to bargain has been given.[34]

The scope of bargaining is limited, just as in the *FPSLRA*. Collective agreements may not involve the alteration of an Act of Parliament and may not involve pension or workers' compensation arrangements.[35]

However, the process for dispute resolution if the parties cannot agree on a collective agreement is different. The parties may request conciliation, but there is no provision for "binding" conciliation and no additional limits on the topics that may be addressed in conciliation.[36]

---

30 *PESRA*, s 27(2).

31 *PESRA*, s 49(1). See *Canadian Association of Professional Employees v Library of Parliament*, [2003] CPSSRB No 86, for a union merger resulting in the Canadian Association of Professional Employees, and *House of Commons Security Services Employees Association v Parliamentary Protective Service*, 2020 FPSLREB 46, for a merger between the two associations representing protective employees at the House of Commons and Senate, respectively.

32 *PESRA*, s 37(2).

33 *Ibid*, s 38.

34 *Ibid*, s 39.

35 *Ibid*, s 43(2).

36 *Ibid*, s 40.

Then, if the parties still have not entered into a collective agreement, either of them may apply for binding interest arbitration. Employees may not strike,[37] and employee organizations may not call for a strike.[38] Employees who go on strike may be fined $100, officers of employee organizations who call for strikes may be liable to pay a fine of up to $300, and employee organizations may be fined up to $150 for each day that they declare or authorize a strike.[39]

Interest arbitration is conducted by a three-person board. Prior to any particular request for arbitration, the Board appoints two panels of at least three representatives of employers and employees, respectively.[40] When faced with a request for interest arbitration, the Board then appoints one member from each panel and then a neutral chair of the arbitration board who is also a member of the Board or an "outside" arbitrator.[41] The arbitration board then considers five factors in making its decision:

- the needs of the employer for qualified employees;
- the need to maintain appropriate relationships in the conditions of employment between different grade levels within an occupation and as between occupations of employees;
- the need to establish terms and conditions of employment that are fair and reasonable in relation to the qualifications required, work performed, responsibility assumed, and nature of the services rendered by an employee;
- the comparability of conditions of employment with those that are applicable to persons in similar employment in the federal public administration; and
- any other relevant factors.[42]

Like under the *FPSLRA*, *PESRA* limits the scope of topics that may be referred to binding interest arbitration. *PESRA* states that no arbitral award may deal with the standards, procedures, or processes dealing with appointment, appraisal, promotion, demotion, transfer, layoff, or release of employees—in other words, matters that would be covered

37 *Ibid*, s 73.
38 *Ibid*, s 74.
39 *Ibid*, s 75.
40 *Ibid*, s 47.
41 *Ibid*, ss 45–49.
42 *Ibid*, s 53.

by the *Public Service Employment Act* for employees of the Treasury Board.[43]

The fourth factor—comparability of pay with the federal public administration—reveals an important general policy: that parliamentary employees be treated similarly to their counterparts in the federal public service. Parliamentary employees often seek to be treated the same as their counterparts in the federal public service. For example, there was a memorandum of understanding between the Library of Parliament and the Public Service Alliance of Canada (PSAC) that the library would match payments "based on Equal Pay" to certain groups of its own employees with payments made by the Treasury Board to equivalent groups of employees. Therefore, when the PSAC won its large pay equity award in 1998, the Library of Parliament had to give its employees a "pay equity" adjustment as well.[44]

3) Grievances Under *PESRA*

Like the *FPSLRA*, *PESRA* sets out an employee's right to file a grievance and then refer the grievance to adjudication under some circumstances. Employees have the right to file a grievance concerning collective agreement violations, breaches of statutes or other instruments dealing with terms and conditions of employment, and any other occurrence that affects an employee's terms and conditions of employment.[45] However, the right to refer a grievance to adjudication is broader under *PESRA* than under the *FPSLRA*. Employees may refer grievances about the following topics to adjudication:

- the interpretation of a collective agreement
- disciplinary action resulting in a suspension or financial penalty
- termination of employment, other than rejection on probation
- a demotion

---

43 *Ibid*, s 55(2). See *Public Service Alliance of Canada v Senate of Canada*, 2011 FCA 214, concluding that a proposal to post bargaining unit vacancies was outside the scope of arbitration because of the prohibition in s 55(2).

44 *Auclair v Library of Parliament*, [2002] FCJ No 1054. The employer argued that the special pay adjustments negotiated between the Treasury Board and bargaining agents representing those employees impacted by the 1998 award was not a payment based on equal pay.

45 *PESRA*, s 62(1).

- where the employee has been denied an appointment, the employer's evaluation of the skill, fitness, and ability of the employee with respect to the employee's qualification for the appointment
- the employer's classification of the employee
- a breach of the *Accessible Canada Act*[46]

The fifth ground for referring a grievance to adjudication was referred to as "the merit question" when the legislation was first introduced.[47] This provision reflects the fact that there is no equivalent to the *Public Service Employment Act* for parliamentary employees. Like under the *FPSLRA*, adjudications are typically conducted by members of the Board. However, when an employee refers a grievance concerning a demotion, denial of appointment, or classification, the adjudication is conducted by an outside arbitrator (appointed by both the employee and the employer). If an arbitrator cannot be agreed upon, the chair of the Board must hear the adjudication.[48]

Adjudicators under *PESRA* have much greater jurisdiction than under the *FPSLRA*. For example, the fifth ground for adjudication is similar to the grounds for complaint under the *Public Service Employment Act*. However, adjudicators under *PESRA* are not limited to deciding whether a particular action was an abuse of authority, and they need not follow any of the more restrictive rules adopted by the Public Service Commission. Additionally, adjudicators under *PESRA* have jurisdiction to hear all termination cases, regardless of whether those terminations are disciplinary. Adjudicators also are not limited to the approaches adopted to termination cases under the *FPSLRA* or *Public Service Employment Act* and, instead, have adopted a wider scope of review more common under private sector arbitral jurisprudence.[49]

PESRA also contains provisions for policy grievances brought by the bargaining agent or employer when the subject of the grievance involves the interpretation of the collective agreement and may also not

---

46 *PESRA*, s 63(1).

47 *Minutes of Proceedings and Evidence of the Legislative Committee on Bill C-45*, Issue No 7 (5 June 1986) at 7:9 & 7:10, (Hon Ray Hnatyshyn, President of the Queen's Privy Council for Canada).

48 *PESRA*, s 66.

49 *Groulx and Senate of Canada (Gentleman Usher of the Black Rod)*, [1991] CPSSRB No 77 at 9.

be the subject of an individual grievance.[50] This is similar to the old provision for policy grievances under the *Public Service Staff Relations Act.*

The grievance procedure is also the exclusive forum for disputes concerning terms and conditions of employment—in other words, the *Vaughan v Canada (Attorney General)*[51] decision applies to *PESRA* as well as the *FPSLRA*. In *Vaid*,[52] the Supreme Court of Canada dismissed a human rights complaint filed by a former driver of the speaker of the House of Commons on the grounds that he should have grieved and then referred the matter to adjudication under *PESRA*.[53] Subsequent decisions have also concluded that employees governed by *PESRA* must grieve workplace disputes and may not proceed to other forums.[54]

4) Statutory Minimum Terms and Conditions of Employment Under *PESRA*

Part 2 of *PESRA* states that Part 3 of the *Canada Labour Code* applies to all employees of the Senate, House of Commons, Library of Parliament, the Office of the Ethics Commissioner, and employees of a member of Parliament who provide research or associated services to caucus members of a political party represented in Parliament. Part 3 of the *Canada Labour Code* governs minimum employment standards such as maximum hours of work, minimum wages, vacation time, maternity leave, severance pay, sick leave, and unjust dismissal.[55]

Part 2 of *PESRA*, however, has never been declared in force. It has remained on the statute books, but there is no indication that it ever will be declared in force.

C. MINISTERIAL STAFF AND STAFF OF MEMBERS OF PARLIAMENT

The term "ministerial staff" refers to staff members of any member of the King's Privy Council holding the office of minister of the Crown,

---

50 *PESRA*, s 70.

51 *Vaughan v Canada (Attorney General)*, 2005 SCC 11. See the discussion in Chapter 10.

52 *Vaid*, above note 3.

53 *Ibid* at para 83.

54 *Canada (House of Commons) v Dupéré*, 2007 FCA 180.

55 *Canada Labour Code*, RSC 1985, c L-2, Part 3.

along with the staff employed by certain leadership positions within the House of Commons or Senate.[56] There is not a lot to say about the legal position of ministerial staff.[57] Ministerial staff fall outside the scope of *PESRA*. They are, in a sense, "statutory orphans":[58] they are not covered by *PESRA* and cannot organize under the *FPSLRA* because they occupy positions confidential to a minister of the Crown. In terms of their role in the federal public service, they have been referred to as

> an intermediate class of persons in the Minister's Office, who are political rather than bureaucratic in their functions, appointed rather than elected, and who operate in an area which strict constitutional theory does not recognize as existing.[59]

The only statutory provision governing ministers' exempt staff is section 128 of the *Public Service Employment Act*, which reads as follows:

> 128. (1) A minister, or a person holding the recognized position of Leader of the Opposition in the House of Commons or Leader of the Opposition in the Senate, may appoint an executive assistant and other persons required in his or her office.
>
> (2) A person who is employed in an office referred to in subsection (1) ceases to be so employed thirty days after the person holding a position referred to in subsection (1) ceases to hold that position.

The *Public Service Employment Act* also states that ministers' exempt staff with three or more years' service may participate in internal advertised appointment processes as if they were an employee in the public service for a period of one year after they cease to be a minister's exempt staff.[60] Employees under *PESRA* have the same right.[61]

---

56 *PESRA*, ss 4(2)(a)–(d).

57 Although there is a lot to say about ministerial staff generally: see L. Benoit, "Ministerial Staff: The Life and Times of Parliament's Statutory Orphans" in *Restoring Accountability: Research Studies, Vol 1* (Ottawa: Commission of Inquiry into the Sponsorship Program and Advertising Activities, 2005), and the numerous articles and studies on the institutional role played by ministerial staff.

58 *Ibid*.

59 J.R. Mallory, "The Minister's Office Staff: An Unreformed Part of the Public Service" (1967) 10:1 Can Pub Admin at 25.

60 *Public Service Employment Act*, SC 2003, c 22, ss 12, 13, s 35.2.

61 *Ibid*, s 35.3.

The Treasury Board has published *Policies for Ministers' Offices*,[62] which set out the classification plan and salary scale for exempt staff as well as other rules concerning the employment of exempt staff. Ministers' exempt staff are dismissed thirty days after their minister is replaced (either through a Cabinet shuffle or a general election). If they do not find employment with another minister within thirty calendar days, then they are entitled to severance pay and "separation pay" at the discretion of the minister.

Individual members of Parliament also employ their own staff, who are also exempt from *PESRA*.[63] Staff members of caucuses of a political party represented in Parliament are also exempt,[64] as are staff members hired by individual senators.[65] Individual members of Parliament are the legal employer of their own staff, and the House of Commons is not a common employer to these staff members.[66] Any recourse for these staff members lies in the superior court of a province against the member of Parliament personally.

62 Treasury Board of Canada Secretariat, "Policies for Ministers' Officers—January 2011," online: www.canada.ca/en/treasury-board-secretariat/services/policies-ministers-offices-january-2011.html.

63 *PESRA*, s 4(2)(e).

64 *PESRA*, s 4(2)(f).

65 *Routliffe v Senate of Canada*, 2009 PSLRB 46.

66 *Vandon Alex Gene v The Honourable Deepak Obhrai*, unreported Action No 1801-12717, Alberta Court of King's Bench, 30 September 2020; *A et Caucus A*, 2015 QCCLP 3110.

PART VI

THE ROLE OF COURTS

CHAPTER FIFTEEN

Court Proceedings for Federal Public Servants

A. INTRODUCTION

This chapter is designed to provide a brief overview of the interaction between the court system and labour and employment law of the federal public service. That interaction takes place in two ways. The first, and more common way is when a party applies for judicial review of the decision of one of the tribunals discussed in previous chapters or of a decision that cannot be referred to one of those tribunals. These applications for judicial review are typically made either based on the merits of the decision or alleged procedural unfairness by the tribunal in question. The second less common way is when an employee of the federal public service brings an action in civil court against the federal Crown for events arising out of their employment. This chapter briefly describes the rules applicable to both types of court proceeding.

B. JUDICIAL REVIEW

Decisions of the Federal Public Sector Labour Relations and Employment Board, the Commissioner of the RCMP, a deputy head or designate acting as the final level of the grievance procedure responding to a grievance that cannot be referred to adjudication, and the various other decision-makers described in this book may be judicially reviewed by the Federal Courts. Applications for judicial review are governed by sections 18, 18.1, and 28 of the *Federal Courts Act*.[1] Section 28 of the *Federal Courts Act* sets out a list of federal boards whose decisions are judicially reviewed at first instance by the Federal Court of Appeal instead of the Federal Court. Applications for judicial review from the Board are referred directly to the Federal Court of Appeal. Prior to amendments to the *Federal Public Sector Labour Relations Act* (*FPSLRA*) in 2013[2] stating that the Board is seized of the grievance (instead of a Board member being appointed as an adjudicator), adjudication cases were judicially reviewed by the Federal Court; with that 2013 amendment, though, both grievance decisions by the Board and other Board decisions are judicially reviewed directly by the Federal Court of Appeal. Any other decision (such as a final-level grievance decision that cannot be referred to adjudication or any of the various decisions made under the *Royal Canadian Mounted Police Act*[3]) proceeds to the Federal Court instead.

Judicial review is only available against the decision-maker's final decision. Where the decision is merely interim, or where an alternative ground of administrative redress is available, then the applicant must exhaust the statutory procedure before applying for judicial review of the Board's final decision.[4] For example, an employee cannot apply for judicial review of a decision that may be grieved regardless of whether it may be referred to adjudication.[5]

Applications for judicial review are commenced by a notice of application.[6] A person who wishes to challenge a decision by judicial review must file their notice of application within thirty days of receiving the decision or such further time as a judge of the Federal Court may fix or allow after the expiration of thirty days.[7]

There is a wealth of jurisprudence from the Federal Court and Federal Court of Appeal about whether the Court should defer to the decision being reviewed—known as the issue of the appropriate "standard of review." Since the Supreme Court of Canada's decision in *Canada (Minister of Citizenship and Immigration) v Vavilov*,[8] however, the

1 *Federal Courts Act*, RSC 1985, c F-7.
2 *Economic Action Plan 2013 Act, No 2*, SC 2013, c 40, s 374.
3 *Royal Canadian Mounted Police Act*, RSC 1985, c R-10.
4 *Harlekin v University of Regina*, [1979] 2 SCR 561.
5 *Gupta v Canada (Attorney General)*, 2021 FCA 202.
6 *Federal Courts Rules*, SOR/98-106, Rule 301.
7 *Federal Courts Act*, RSC 1985, c F-7, s 18.1(2).
8 *Canada (Minister of Citizenship and Immigration) v Vavilov*, 2019 SCC 65 [*Vavilov*].

Federal Courts have consistently applied the rule set out in that case that "reasonableness" is the presumptive standard of review. While the Federal Court of Appeal had earlier applied the correctness standard of review to questions of law decided at the final level of the grievance process on the grounds that the decision was not made by an independent adjudicator,[9] that result has not been followed in later cases and is now inconsistent with the Supreme Court of Canada's decision in *Vavilov* that the reasonableness standard of review applies to all administrative decision-makers, whether they are tribunals, independent regulators, or just "front-line decision makers."[10] There are few exceptions to the reasonableness standard of review, and the correctness standard is used sparingly.[11]

Judicial review may also be sought on the grounds that the decision-maker violated the rules of procedural fairness (where there is no alternative administrative avenue for redress). Decisions involving a significant right, a privilege, or an interest of a person are subject to a duty of procedural fairness.[12] In the federal public service, the rules of procedural fairness have been applied to, for example, decisions of classification grievance committees,[13] deputy ministers denying security clearance[14] or a reliability status,[15] the Public Service Commission[16] or the Public Sector Integrity Commissioner[17] deciding not to commence an investigation, and deputy ministers under the old Code of Conduct.[18] The rules of procedural fairness have two components: *audi alteram*

9 *Appleby-Ostroff v Canada (Attorney General)*, 2011 FCA 84.

10 *Vavilov*, above note 8 at para 88.

11 One of those exceptions is for general questions of law that are of importance to the legal system as a whole. There are few such questions in the federal public sector. Two examples, though, are solicitor-client privilege (*Canada (Attorney General) v Quadrini*, 2011 FCA 115 at para 45) and the calculation of a statutory limitation period for an attempt by the Crown to recover an alleged overpayment (*Gardner v Canada (Border Services Agency)*, 2009 FC 1156).

12 *Knight v Indian Head School Division No 19*, [1990] 1 SCR 653.

13 *Chong v Canada (Treasury Board)*, [1999] FCJ No 176 (CA).

14 *Thomson v Canada (Deputy Minister of Agriculture)*, [1992] 1 SCR 385.

15 *Myers v Canada (Attorney General)*, 2007 FC 946, although as discussed in Chapter 10, these issues now should be grieved instead of proceeding directly to judicial review.

16 *Baragar v Canada (Attorney General)*, 2008 FC 841, and *Badmus v Canada (Attorney General)*, 2020 FC 892.

17 *Gupta v Canada (Attorney General)*, 2016 FCA 50, and *Gordillo v Canada (Attorney General)*, 2022 FCA 23.

18 *Peet v Canada (Attorney General)*, [1994] 3 FC 128.

partem (the right to be heard) and *nemo judex in sua (propria) causa (debet esse)* (no one may be a judge in their own cause—or the rule against bias). The *audi alteram partem* rule may require, for example, disclosure of the case against a person[19] and an oral hearing under rare circumstances.[20] It may also require written reasons for a decision,[21] and such reasons must set out a clear and coherent explanation for the conclusion.[22] The requirements of both elements of procedural fairness are set out in a large number of cases and also vary depending on the nature of the decision being made, the nature of the statutory scheme under which the decision is made, the importance of the decision to the individual affected, the legitimate expectations of the person affected, and the choice of procedures of the agency making the decision.[23] Thus, the rules of procedural fairness vary from case to case and must be determined by examining the context of the particular decision being made. As such, it is impossible to provide an exhaustive or a comprehensive list of the procedural rules that apply in the federal public service.

C. COURT ACTION

As described in Chapter 10, the Supreme Court of Canada's decision in *Vaughan v Canada*[24] and section 236 of the *FPSLRA* effectively prevent employees of the federal public service from bringing court actions against their employer for workplace-related events where those employees could grieve the subject matter of their dispute.[25]

---

19 *Hale v Canada (Treasury Board)*, [1996] 3 FC 3, where the Court required disclosure of an expert report prior to a classification committee decision.

20 The Federal Public Sector Labour Relations and Employment Board, as discussed in Chapter 4, is not required to hold an oral hearing: *Professional Institute of the Public Service of Canada v Canada (Treasury Board)*, [2006] FCJ 806 (CA).

21 *Vennat v Canada (Attorney General)*, [2006] FCJ No 1251.

22 *Chowdhury v Canada (Attorney General)*, [2004] FCJ No 679.

23 *Baker v Canada (Minister of Citizenship and Immigration)*, [1999] 2 SCR 817.

24 *Vaughan v Canada*, 2005 SCC 11 [*Vaughan*].

25 There are still some instances where a grievance procedure will not bar an employee from bringing a court action: see *Sulz v Canada (Attorney General)*, [2006] BCJ No 121 [*Sulz*], where the RCMP dealt with Ms. Sulz's complaint about systemic harassment but without providing her with any redress for her complaint. Thus, "there was nothing to grieve," and a court action could proceed. Furthermore, the Supreme Court in *Vaughan* recognized a possible exception when there is an individualized conflict between the employee and the grievance officer responsible for deciding the grievance (such as in a whistle-blower situation).

Even if an employee manages to overcome *Vaughan* and a court takes jurisdiction over their claim, then the employee may be faced with additional difficulties spelled out in the *Crown Liability and Proceedings Act*.[26] The Crown used to be immune from suit; that changed with the enactment of the *Crown Liability and Proceedings Act*. Also, claims against the federal Crown used to be within the exclusive jurisdiction of the Federal Court: that rule was amended in 1992, and the Federal Court now has concurrent jurisdiction with provincial courts to hear claims against the federal Crown.[27]

Even without those two exclusionary rules, section 9 of the *Crown Liability and Proceedings Act* states that no proceedings lie against the Crown "if a pension or compensation has been paid or is payable out of the consolidated revenue fund or out of any funds administered by an agency of the Crown in respect of the death, injury, damage or loss in respect of which the claim is made."[28] This section prevents "double recovery" as the result of a particular event:

> In my view, the language in s. 9 of the *Crown Liability and Proceedings Act*, though broad, nonetheless requires that such a pension or compensation paid or payable as will bar an action against the Crown be made on the same factual basis as the action thereby barred. In other words, s. 9 reflects the sensible desire of Parliament to prevent double recovery for the same claim where the government is liable for misconduct but has already made a payment in respect thereof. That is to say, the section does not require that the pension or payment be in consideration or settlement of the relevant event, only that it be on the specific basis of the occurrence of that event that the payment is made.[29]

Therefore, if a former employee is receiving a disability pension from the federal government as a result of some workplace incident or incidents (including harassment leading to a mental disability), then that former employee may not bring a tort claim against the Crown based on those incidents.[30]

---

26 *Crown Liability and Proceedings Act*, RSC 1985, c C-50, s 3.
27 *Federal Courts Act*, s 17(1).
28 *Crown Liability and Proceedings Act*, s 9.
29 *Sarvanis v Canada*, 2002 SCC 28 at para 28.
30 *Sulz*, above note 25.

Finally, a party can still seek interim relief or an interim injunction from the Federal Court,[31] particularly as the Board has no jurisdiction to grant interim relief.[32] The Federal Court applies the standard three-part test for an injunction: the party seeking an injunction must demonstrate a serious issue to be tried, irreparable harm, and that the balance of convenience supports an injunction.[33] A complete discussion of interim injunctions is beyond the scope of this text. Of particular relevance to the federal public administration, though, is that the Federal Court has also stated that "the loss of employment, while a significant and important consequence, is something that can be compensated in monetary damages,"[34] which effectively prevents a public servant from obtaining an interim injunction against a termination of employment.

---

31 *Brotherhood of Maintenance of Way Employees, Canadian Pacific System Federation v Canadian Pacific Ltd*, [1996] 2 SCR 495 (on the right to obtain an injunction from a court where a labour board has no jurisdiction to grant an injunction), and *Canada (Human Rights Commission) v Canadian Liberty Net*, [1998] 1 SCR 626 (the Federal Court has the jurisdiction to grant this injunction).

32 *Marchand v Deputy Head (Canada School of Public Service)*, 2015 PSLREB 63, among others.

33 *Google Inc v Equustek Solutions Inc*, 2017 SCC 34.

34 *Wojdan v Canada (Attorney General)*, 2021 FC 1341 at para 37.

Secondary Sources

ADELL, BERNARD, MICHEL GRANT & ALLEN PONAK. *Strikes in Essential Services* (Kingston, ON: IRC Press, 2001).

ADVISORY COMMITTEE ON LABOUR MANAGEMENT RELATIONS IN THE FEDERAL PUBLIC SERVICE. *Identifying the Issues* (May 2000).

———. *Working Together in the Public Interest* (Ottawa: Treasury Board, 2001), online: https://publications.gc.ca/collections/collection_2011/sct-tbs/BT22-70-1-2001-eng.pdf.

AGRICULTURE AND AGRI-FOOD CANADA. *Evaluation of Informal Conflict Management Services Offered by AAFC's Office of Conflict Resolution* (9 June 2009), online: https://publications.gc.ca/collections/collection_2010/agr/A22-497-2009-eng.pdf.

AYLMER, G.E. *The King's Servants: The Civil Service of Charles I*, 2d ed (London, UK: Routledge & Kegan Paul, 1971).

BENOIT, L. "Ministerial Staff: The Life and Times of Parliament's Statutory Orphans" in *Restoring Accountability: Research Studies, Vol 1* (Ottawa: Commission of Inquiry into the Sponsorship Program and Advertising Activities, 2005).

BHUPSINGH, TREVOR & P. EDWARDS. *Tracking the Role of the PSC in the Governance System of the Federal Public Service* (Ottawa: Public Service Commission of Canada, 1997).

BLAIR, LEO. "The Civil Servant—Political Reality and Legal Myth" (1958) Pub L 32.

BORDOGNA, LORENZO & DAVID WINCHESTER. "Collective Bargaining in Western Europe" in Carl Dell'Aringa, Giuseppe Della Rocca & Berndt Keller, eds, *Strategic Choices in Reforming Public Service Employment: An International Handbook* (New York: Palgrave, 2001).

CALLAHAN, E.S., T.M. DWORKIN & D. LEWIS. "Whistleblowing: Australian, U.K., and U.S. Approaches to Disclosure in the Public Interest" (2004) 44 Va J Intl L 879.

CANADA REVENUE AGENCY. *Summary of the Corporate Business Plan 2021–22 with Perspectives to 2023–24* (2021), online: www.canada.ca/content/dam/cra-arc/corp-info/aboutcra/corp-bsns-plan/smmry-cbp-2021-24-en.pdf.

CANADIAN UNION OF PUBLIC EMPLOYEES. *Battle of the Wages: Who Gets Paid More, Public or Private Sector Workers?* (December 2011), online: https://cupe.ca/battle-wages-who-gets-paid-more-public-or-private-sector-workers.

CARTER, DONALD. "Legal Regulation of Collective Bargaining in the Ontario Public Sector" (1974) 29 RI 776.

CEYSSENS, PAUL. *Legal Aspects of Policing* (Salt Spring Island, BC: Earlscourt, 1994) (loose-leaf).

CEYSSENS, PAUL & W. SCOTT CHILDS. *"Phase 1" Final Report Concerning Conduct Measures, and the Application of Conduct Measures to Sex-Related Misconduct Under Part IV of the Royal Canadian Mounted Police Act* (24 February 2022), online: www.rcmp-grc.gc.ca/wam/media/6145/original/787edb1f00955240ae4502c22871ca80.pdf.

CHAYKOWSKI, RICHARD P. "Advancing Public-Sector Labor-Management Relations Through Consultation: The Role of the National Joint Council of the Public Service of Canada" in Bruce Kaufman & Daphne Gottleib Taras, eds, *Nonunion Employee Representation* (New York: M.E. Sharpe, 2000).

———. *Time to Tweak or Re-boot? Assessing the Interest Arbitration Process in Canadian Industrial Relations* (4 April 2019), C.D. Howe Institute, Commentary No 539, online: www.cdhowe.org/sites/default/files/2021-11/Commentary_539.pdf

COHEN, EMMELINE W. *The Growth of the British Civil Service 1780–1939*, 2d ed (London, UK: Frank Cass & Co, 1965).

COMMISSION OF INQUIRY INTO EMPLOYER-EMPLOYEE RELATIONS IN THE PUBLIC SERVICE OF BRITISH COLUMBIA. *Making Bargaining Work in the British Columbia Public Service*. 1972.

COOKE, WILLIAM N. "Product Quality Improvement Through Employee Participation: The Effects of Union-Management Administration" (1992) 46 Indus & Lab Rel Rev 119.

CURRAN, BRUCE. "Event History Analysis of Grievance Arbitration in Ontario: Labour Justice Delayed?" (2017) 72:4 RI 621.

DAINTITH, TERENCE & ALAN PAGE. *The Executive in the Constitution* (Toronto: Oxford University Press, 1999).

DAU-SCHMIDT, K. & M. KHAN. "Undermining or Promoting Democratic Government? An Economic and Empirical Analysis of the Two Views of Public Sector Collective Bargaining in American Law" (2014) 14 Nevada LJ 414.

DAVIES, P. & M. FREEDLAND. *Kahn-Freund's Labour and the Law*, 3d ed. (London, UK: Stevens and Sons, 1983).

DAVIS, RONALD. *The OLRB Policy on Bargaining Units for Part-Time Workers* (Kingston, ON: IRC Press, 1991).

DAWSON, ROBERT MACGREGOR. *The Civil Service of Canada* (London, UK: Oxford University Press, 1929).

DE AGUAYO, JACQUIRE. "A Union Perspective on the Adequacy of Bill C-11: *The Public Servants Disclosure Protection Act*" (Ottawa: Canadian Institute, 28 November 2005).

DEPARTMENT OF JUSTICE. *Informal Conflict Management System Evaluation Final Report*" (May 2010), online: www.justice.gc.ca/eng/rp-pr/cp-pm/eval/rep-rap/11/icms-sgice/icms-sgice.pdf.

DOUCOULIAGOS, C. & P. LAROCHE. "What Do Unions Do to Productivity? A Meta-Analysis" (2003) 42:4 Indus Rel 650.

FEDERAL PUBLIC SECTOR LABOUR RELATIONS AND EMPLOYMENT BOARD. *2020–2021 Annual Report* (2021), online: www.fpslreb-crtespf.gc.ca/en/about-us/annual-reports/2020-2021/ar-202021.html.

———. "Policy on Postponements of Hearings" online: https://pslreb-crtefp.gc.ca/en/resources/policies/postponements-of-hearings.html.

FINKELMAN, JACOB. *The Rationale in Establishing Bargaining Units in the Federal Public Service of Canada* (Kingston, ON: Industrial Relations Centre, 1974).

———. "When Bargaining Fails" in *Collective Bargaining in the Public Service: Theory and Practice* (Chicago: Public Personnel Association, 1967).

FINKELMAN, JACOB & SHIRLEY GOLDENBERG. *Collective Bargaining in the Public Service: The Federal Experience in Canada* (Ottawa: Institute for Research on Public Policy, 1983).

FRANKEL, SAUL J. *Staff Relations in the Civil Service: The Canadian Experience* (Montreal: McGill University Press, 1962).

FREEMAN, R. & MEDOFF, J. *What Do Unions Do?* (New York: Basic Books, 1984).

GILL, CAROL. "Union Impact on the Effective Adoption of High Performance Work Practices" (2009) 19 Hum Resource Mgmt Rev 39

GILROY, T.P. & A.C. RUSSO. *Bargaining Unit Issues: Problems, Criteria, Tactics* (Chicago: International Personnel Management Association, 1973).

GOVERNMENT OF CANADA. "Getting to Know Informal Conflict Management System (ICMS)" (12 August 2008), online: www.canada.ca/en/government/publicservice/wellness-inclusion-diversity-public-service/harassment-violence/informal-conflict-management-system/getting-to-know-informal-conflict-management-systems-better.html.

HADWEN, T. *Ontario Public Service Employment & Labour Law*, 2d ed (Toronto: Irwin Law, 2023).

HODGETTS, J.E. et al. *The Biography of an Institution: The Civil Service Commission of Canada 1908–1967* (Ottawa: Public Service Commission of Canada, 1972).

HOGG, P.W. & P.J. MONAHAN. *Liability of the Crown*, 3d ed (Toronto: Carswell, 2000).

ILLINGWORTH, J. "Collective Bargaining, Dispute Resolution and Strike Action: New Procedures, New Challenges" (Paper presented in "Public Service Modernization Act," Canadian Institute, 31 May 2004).

INTERNATIONAL LABOUR OFFICE. *Freedom of Association and Collective Bargaining*, International Labour Conference, Eighty-First Session 1994 Report 3 (Part 4B) (Geneva: ILO, 1994).

JONES, DAVID & DE VILLARS, ANNE. *Principles of Administrative Law*, 4th ed (Scarborough, ON: Thompson, 2004).

KERNAGHAN, KENNETH. "East Block and Westminster Conventions, Values, and Public Service" in *The Handbook of Canadian Public Administration*, 3d ed (Toronto: Oxford University Press, 2018).

———. "Power, Politics, and Bureaucracy" in R.S. Blair & J.T. McLeod, eds, *The Canadian Political Tradition: Basic Readings*, 2d ed (Scarborough, ON: Nelson Canada, 1993).

KIEDROWSKI, JOHN et al. *The Civilianization of Police in Canada*, Research Report 2015-R024 (Ottawa: Public Safety Canada, 2017), online: www.publicsafety.gc.ca/cnt/rsrcs/pblctns/2015-r042/2015-r042-en.pdf.

KIEDROWSKI, JOHN, RUDDELL, RICK & PETRUNIK, MICHAEL. "Police Civilianization in Canada: A Mixed Methods Investigation" (2019) 29:2 Policing and Society 204.

LABOUR LAW CASEBOOK GROUP. *Labour and Employment Law: Cases, Materials and Commentary*, 9th ed (Toronto: Irwin Law, 2018).

LAMMAM, CHARLES et al. "Comparing Government and Private Sector Compensation in Canada" (2015), online: www.fraserinstitute.org/sites/default/files/comparing-government-and-private-sector-compensation-in-canada.pdf.

LEMELIN, MAURICE. *Public Service Alliance of Canada* (Los Angeles: Institute of Industrial Relations, 1978).

LEROY, M., J. SCHWARZ & K. KOZIARA. "The Law and Economics of Collective Bargaining for Hospitals: An Empirical Public Policy Analysis of Bargaining Unit Determinations" (1992) 9 Yale J of Regulation 1.

LEUPRECHT, CHRISTIAN. *Where to Draw the Blue Line* (Ottawa: Macdonald-Laurier Institute, 2019), online: https://macdonaldlaurier.ca/files/pdf/20191108_MLI_POLICING_Leuprecht_PAPER_FWeb.pdf.

LYNCH, JENNIFER. "The Federal Public Service Modernization Act—State of the Art Innovations in Conflict Management," *Canadian Government Executive* (February 2004).

LYSYK, K., L. SOSSIN & J. HOSKINS. *Barristers & Solicitors in Practice* (Markham, ON: LexisNexis Canada, 2006) (loose-leaf).

MALIN, M. "Public Sector Labor Law Doctrine and Labor-Management Cooperation" in J. Brock & D. Lipsky, eds, *Going Public: The Role of Labor-Management Relations in Delivering Quality Government Services* (Champaign, IL: Industrial Relations Research Association, 2003).

MALIN, M. "The Motive Power in Public Sector Collective Bargaining" (2018) 36 Hofstra Lab & Empl LJ 123.

———. "The Paradox of Public Sector Labor Law" (2009) 84 Ind LJ 1369.

MALLORY, J.R. "The Minister's Office Staff: An Unreformed Part of the Public Service" (1967) 10:1 Can Pub Admin.

MCLEAN, JANET. "Between Sovereign and Subject: The Constitutional Position of the Official" (2020) 70 UTLJ 167.

MOYSER, MELISSA. *Women and Paid Work* (Ottawa: Statistics Canada, 2017).

OECD. "Fostering Diversity in the Public Service" (2009), online: www.oecd.org/gov/pem/paper-fostering-diversity-public-service.pdf.

OFFICE OF THE PARLIAMENTARY BUDGET OFFICER. *Federal Personnel Spending: Past and Future Trends* (20 March 2018), online: www.pbo-dpb.gc.ca/web/default/files/Documents/Reports/2018/Fed%20Personnel%20Spending/Fed_Personnel_Spending_EN.pdf.

OFFICE OF THE PUBLIC SECTOR INTEGRITY COMMISSIONER OF CANADA. "Gross Mismanagement," online: www.psic-ispc.gc.ca/sites/default/files/2019-03/gross_mismanagement2.pdf.

———. "Misuse of Public Funds or a Public Asset," online: www.psic-ispc.gc.ca/sites/default/files/media/misuse_of_public_funds.pdf.

———. "Serious Breach of a Code of Conduct," online: www.psic-ispc.gc.ca/sites/default/files/2019-03/seriousbreach2.pdf.

ONTARIO LABOUR RELATIONS BOARD. *Annual Report, 2018–2019* (2019), online: www.olrb.gov.on.ca/Publications/AnnualReports/OLRB-Annual-Report-2018-19-EN.pdf.

ONTARIO LAW REFORM COMMISSION. *Report on Political Activity, Public Comment and Disclosure by Crown Employees* (Toronto: Ministry of the Attorney General, 1986).

PARK, SANGHEE & JIAQI LIANG. "Merit, Diversity, and Performance: Does Diversity Management Moderate the Effect of Merit Principles on Government Performance?" (2020) 49:1 Pub Personnel Mgmt 83.

PARKS, DEBRA. *Employment Standards That Work for Women*. Submission to the Manitoba Employment Standards Review.

PEGNETTER, R. *Multiemployer Bargaining in the Public Sector: Purposes and Experiences* (Chicago: International Personnel Management Association, 1975).

PINK, RONALD & DAVID WALLBRIDGE. "The Future of Labour Arbitration" (Paper delivered at the 2010 Administrative, Labour and Employment and Privacy and Access Law Conference, Ottawa, 26–27 November 2010), online: Canadian Bar Association www.cba.org/cba/cle/PDF/adm10_pink_paper.pdf.

PRIME MINISTER OF CANADA. News Release, "Prime Minister Announces New Governor in Council Appointment Process" (25 February 2016), online: https://pm.gc.ca/en/news/news-releases/2016/02/25/prime-minister-announces-new-governor-council-appointment-process.

PRIVES, M.Z. *Unionism and the Merit System in Municipal Labour Relations in Canada* (Montreal: 1958).

PRIVY COUNCIL OFFICE. "Terms and Conditions of Employment for Full-Time Governor in Council Employees," online: www.canada.ca/en/privy-council/programs/appointments/governor-council-appointments/compensation-terms-conditions-employment/terms-conditions.html.

PROFESSIONAL INSTITUTE OF THE PUBLIC SERVICE OF CANADA. "Presentation to the House of Commons Standing Committee on Finance on the Five Year Review of the *Canada Revenue Agency Act*" (June 2006).

Public Service 2000: The Renewal of the Public Service of Canada (Ottawa: Minister of Supply and Services, 1990).

PUBLIC SERVICE COMMISSION. "Appointment Process Investigations" (10 March 2021), online: www.canada.ca/en/public-service-commission/services/oversight-activities/investigations/appointment-process-investigations.html.

———. "History of Employment Equity in the Public Service and the Public Service Commission of Canada" (October 2011), online: https://publications.gc.ca/collections/collection_2012/cfp-psc/SC3-159-2011-eng.pdf.

———. "Recourse and Redress in the Public Service" (June 2000), online: http://pscac-cccfp.gc.ca/publications/rpt_redress_e.php.

———. *Structured Reference Checking: A User's Guide to Best Practices* (2009), online: www.canada.ca/content/dam/canada/public-service-commission/migration/plcy-pltq/guides/checking-verification/rpt-eng.pdf.

PUBLIC SERVICE HUMAN RESOURCES MANAGEMENT AGENCY. "Classification Modernization, FAQ Manager" (23 November 2006), online: www.hrma-agrh.gc.ca/Classification/FAQ/Manager_e.asp.

———. "Report of the Working Group on Disclosure of Wrongdoing" (2003), online: www.hrma-agrh.gc.ca/reports-rapports/wgdw-gtdaf-PR_e.asp?printable=True

PUBLIC SERVICE STAFF RELATIONS BOARD. *33rd Annual Report 1999–2000* (Hull, QC: Minister of Supply and Services, 2000).

Report of the Commission of Inquiry Relating to Public Complaints, Internal Discipline and Grievance Procedure Within the Royal Canadian Mounted Police (Ottawa: Information Canada, 1976), online: https://publications.gc.ca/collections/collection_2014/sp-ps/JS22-34-1976-eng.pdf.

Report of the Preparatory Committee on Collective Bargaining in the Public Service (Ottawa: Queen's Printer, 1965).

ROHR, JOHN. *Civil Servants and Their Constitutions* (Lawrence, KS: University Press of Kansas, 2002).

———. *Public Service, Ethics, & Constitutional Practice* (Lawrence, KS: University Press of Kansas, 1998).

ROOTHAM, CHRISTOPHER. "Bargaining Unit Structure in the Federal Civil Service" (2002) 9 CLELJ 361.

ROSE, JOSEPH B. "Constraints on Public Sector Bargaining in Canada" (2016) 58:1 J Indus Rel 93.

———. "Public Sector Bargaining: From Retrenchment to Consolidation" (2004) 59:2 RI 271.

ROSE, JOSEPH. "The Leech, the Tortoise and the Owl: The World of Interest Arbitration in Ontario" (1994–95) Labour Arbitration Yearkbook 387.

ROSENTHAL, D. "Public Sector Collective Bargaining, Majoritarianism and Reform" (2013) 91 Or L Rev 673.

ROYAL CANADIAN MOUNTED POLICE EXTERNAL REVIEW COMMITTEE. *Sanctioning Police Misconduct—General Principles*, Discussion Paper #8 (Ottawa: RCMP External Review Committee, 1991), online: https://publications.gc.ca/collections/collection_2013/cee-erc/JS74-3-8-1991-eng.pdf.

SACK, JEFFREY, MICHAEL MITCHELL & SANDY PRICE. *Ontario Labour Relations Board Law and Practice*, 3d ed (Toronto: LexisNexis, 1997).

SANES, MILLA & JOHN SCHMITT. *Regulation of Public Sector Collective Bargaining in the States* (Washington, DC: Center for Economic and Policy Research, 2014), online: https://cepr.net/documents/state-public-cb-2014-03.pdf.

SAVOIE, DONALD J. *Breaking the Bargain: Public Servants, Ministers, and Parliament* (Toronto: University of Toronto Press, 2003).

SHEEHY, BENEDICT & DONALD FEAVER. "Re-thinking Executive Control of and Accountability for the Agency" (2016) 54:1 Osgoode Hall LJ 175.

SIMMONS, G. & K. SWAN. *Labour Relations Law in the Public Sector* (Kingston, ON: IRC Press, 1982).

SLATER, JOSEPH E. "Public-Sector Labor in the Age of Obama" (2012) 87 Ind LJ 189.

SMART, JOHN. "Professional Historians in a National Union: The Collective Bargaining and Classification Experience of the Historians of the Federal Government of Canada, 1967–1984" (6 April 1984).

SOSSIN, LORNE. *Defining Boundaries: The Constitutional Argument for Bureaucratic Independence and Its Implication for the Accountability of the Public Service* (2006), online (pdf): https://publications.gc.ca/collections/Collection/GomeryII/ResearchStudies2/CISPAA_Vol2_2.pdf.

———. "Speaking Truth to Power? The Search for Bureaucratic Independence in Canada" (2005) 55 UTLJ 1.

STANDING COMMITTEE ON GOVERNMENT OPERATIONS AND ESTIMATES. *Strengthening the Protection of the Public Interest within the Public Servants Disclosure Protection Act*, 42-1 (June 2017) (Chair: Tom Lukiwski), online: www.ourcommons.ca/Content/Committee/421/OGGO/Reports/RP9055222/oggorp09/oggorp09-e.pdf.

STATISTICS CANADA. "Union Status by Industry," online: www150.statcan.gc.ca/t1/tbl1/en/tv.action?pid=1410013201.

———. *Women in Canada, 2000: A Gender-Based Statistical Report* (Ottawa: Department of Canadian Heritage, 2000).

STILBORN, JACK. *Federal Public Service Renewal—The La Relève Initiative* (Ottawa: Library of Parliament, 1998).

SWIMMER, GENE. "Collective Bargaining in the Federal Public Service of Canada: The Last Twenty Years" in Gene Swimmer & Mark Thompson, eds, *Public Sector Collective Bargaining in Canada: Beginning of the End or End of the Beginning?* (Kingston, ON: IRC Press, 1995).

———. "Public-Sector Labour Relations in an Era of Restraint and Restructuring: An Overview" in Gene Swimmer, ed, *Public-Sector Labour Relations in an Era of Restraint and Restructuring* (Toronto: Oxford University Press, 2001).

SWIMMER, GENE & SANDRA BACH. "Restructuring Federal Public-Sector Human Resources" in Gene Swimmer, ed, *Public-Sector Labour Relations in an Era of Restraint and Restructuring* (Toronto: Oxford University Press, 2001).

TASK FORCE ON CANADA LABOUR CODE. *Seeking A Balance: Review of Part I of the Canada Labour Code* (13 February 1996).

TEPLITSKY, M. Speech to the Ontario Bar Association—Ontario Labour Law Section, 30 January 1996.

"The Civil Service of Canada," Special Issue, *The Civilian* (Ottawa: 1914)

THOMPSON, MARK & SARA SLINN. "Public Sector Industrial Relations in Canada: Does It Threaten or Sustain Democracy?" (2013) 34:2 Comp Lab L & Pol'y J 393.

TREASURY BOARD OF CANADA SECRETARIAT. "2019 Public Service Employee Survey, Question 43," online: www.tbs-sct.canada.ca/pses-saff/2019/results-resultats/bd-pm/00/org-eng.aspx#i4-s12.

———. *Directive on Classification Grievances* (1 April 2020), online: www.tbs-sct.canada.ca/pol/doc-eng.aspx?id=28698.

———. *Directive on Conflict of Interest* (1 April 2020), online: www.tbs-sct.gc.ca/pol/doc-eng.aspx?id=32627.

———. *Directive on Official Languages for People Management* (15 October 2012), online: www.tbs-sct.canada.ca/pol/doc-eng.aspx?id=26168.

———. *Directive on Term Employment* (1 April 2021), online: www.tbs-sct.canada.ca/pol/doc-eng.aspx?id=32629.

———. *Directive on Terms and Conditions of Employment* (1 April 2014), online: www.tbs-sct.gc.ca/pol/doc-eng.aspx?id=15772.

———. *Directive on Terms and Conditions of Employment for Executives* (1 September 2021), online: www.tbs-sct.canada.ca/pol/doc-eng.aspx?id=32625&section=html.

———. *Directive on the Staffing of Bilingual Positions* (25 April 2006), online: www.tbs-sct.canada.ca/pol/doc-eng.aspx?id=12525.

———. "Evaluation of the Classification Program" (12 September 2018), online: www.canada.ca/en/treasury-board-secretariat/corporate/reports/evaluation-classification-program.html#toc12.

———. "Policies for Ministers' Officers—January 2011," online: www.canada.ca/en/treasury-board-secretariat/services/policies-ministers-offices-january-2011.html.

———. "Population of the Federal Public Service," online: www.canada.ca/en/treasury-board-secretariat/services/innovation/human-resources-statistics/population-federal-public-service.html.

———. "Reclassification/Conversion" (10 October 2004), online: www.canada.ca/en/treasury-board-secretariat/services/innovation/human-resources-statistics/demographic-snapshot-federal-public-service-glossary-key-terms.html.

VAISON, ROBERT A. "Collective Bargaining in the Federal Public Service: The Achievement of a Milestone in Personal Relations" in Barbara Carroll, David Siegel & Mark Sproule-Jones, eds, *Classic Readings in Canadian Public Administration* (Toronto: Oxford University Press, 2005).

WALLACE, JOAN. *Part-Time Work in Canada: Report of the Commission of Inquiry into Part-Time Work* (Ottawa: Supply and Services Canada, 1983).

WALSH, PAT, RAYMOND HARTBRIDGE & AARON CRAWFORD. "Public Sector Industrial Relations in New Zealand" in *Strategic Choices in Reforming Public Service Employment: An International Handbook* (New York: Palgrave, 2001).

WATT, ROBERT. "The Crown and Its Employees" in Maurice Sunkin & Sebastian Payne, eds, *The Nature of the Crown: A Legal and Political Analysis* (Oxford: Oxford University Press, 1999).

Table of Cases

Index

Note: References in *italic* and **bold** refer to figures and tables, respectively.

About the Author

Christopher Rootham has a Bachelor of Law from Queen's University and a Master of Labour Law from the London School of Economics. He practised law for over twenty years at the firm of Nelligan Law in Ottawa, Ontario. He also taught on a part-time basis at Queen's University Faculty of Law in 2008 and at the University of Ottawa Faculty of Law from 2008 to 2022. On April 3, 2023, he was appointed as a member of the Federal Public Sector Labour Relations and Employment Board. This book, of course, represents his personal views and does not represent the views of that Board.

Printed and bound by CPI Group (UK) Ltd, Croydon, CR0 4YY

15/09/2026

14962403-0005